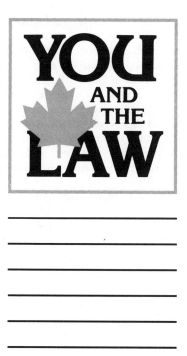

YOU
AND
THE
LAW

A practical family guide
to Canadian law

THIRD EDITION
REVISED AND UPDATED

To the reader—a *caveat*

The laws described herein are those in effect in Canada at the time this book was being revised. Laws are constantly under revision and therefore no action should be based solely on the statements made. Any legal consultant will advise on the current state of the law.

In preparing the book, the editors were faced with a task of some difficulty. Although the Criminal Code applies equally to every part of the country, there are two different systems of civil law in Canada. Nine of the ten provinces have legal systems based essentially on common law, inherited from England and adapted to Canadian requirements. Quebec, however, has a system of civil law derived from that of France, whose famous *Code Napoléon* formed the basis of civil law in Quebec.

As a result, in matters that fall within provincial rather than federal jurisdiction, the solution to a legal problem may be different in Quebec from that in another province. Often, even where the results are the same, the process of arriving at a decision differs.

This book deals basically with legal situations from the point of view of the common law system. While many of the major differences on matters of civil law between the English-speaking provinces and Quebec are noted throughout the text, a book of this kind cannot pinpoint them all. This should be borne in mind by the reader when a question of Quebec law arises.

The acknowledgments and credits that appear on page 912 are herewith made a part of this copyright page.

© 1984 The Reader's Digest Association (Canada) Ltd.
215 Redfern, Westmount (Qué.) H3Z 2V9

THIRD EDITION

Second printing, December 1985

ISBN 0-88850-122-6

Printed in Canada

Table of Contents

You and Your Rights

You and Your Property

You and Your Money

You and Your Family

At Factory and Office

You and Your Leisure

You, Crime and the Law

How to use this book

You and the Law is divided into seven parts and 20 chapters. Each chapter is divided into sections which discuss various aspects of the law as it affects you and your family. Chapters and sections are listed in the Table of Contents. To help you further, each chapter opens with an expanded listing of its sections and the principal topics discussed in them. There are more than a thousand such topic headings in the book.

Using the Table of Contents

The Table of Contents, beginning on page 5, is a good place to start looking when you want information. Suppose you want to know what to do if you are involved in an automobile accident. The Table of Contents shows that Chapter 5 is called "You and Your Car" and that it contains a section called "Traffic accidents." Turning to pages 194 and 195 for the expanded listing of topics for Chapter 5, you find that "Traffic accidents" covers six topics including the one you want—"In case of accident" on page 222. Also in the section are such related topics as "The reluctant witness" and "Liability for passengers."

Using the Index

Detailed subject matter is listed alphabetically in the index beginning on page 900. Taking the same example, both "Accident(s)" with its sublisting "automobile", and "Automobile(s)" with its sublisting "accidents" refer you to pages 222–25. In each case the additional sublisting "What to do" refers you to more specific information on pages 220–21.

Using cross-references

Throughout the text are cross-references to other sections that give more information on the same topic or deal with related subjects. For example, on page 218 under the topic heading "The manufacturer's warranty" there is a reference to a section in Chapter 6 called "Guarantees and standards." This section provides information about the different types of warranty.

Using the glossary

More than 700 legal and related terms are explained in the glossary beginning on page 867.

The law is a protection, not a pitfall

T HE LAW UNDER WHICH WE LIVE was molded by men who wanted a wide range of individual freedom. But they knew that there must be rules indicating where the freedom of the individual ends and the freedom of others begins. For everybody to be free to use the highway, there must be rules of the road that everybody obeys; without them, the highway becomes a graveyard. The same considerations apply with equal force in many other avenues of life. Seen in this light, law is an instrument of liberation. It is not a series of booby traps cunningly concealed. It is, in large measure, a guide through the maze of human relationships that surround us, many of them strange until we have explored them.

The law is an instrument of liberation

You would not think of taking a journey through a strange country without a map and a guidebook. No one should expect to get through life without trouble unless he has some awareness of what the law permits and requires, and of the ways to conduct himself in the presence of the law. *You and the Law* is intended to be such a guidebook, including some easy-to-understand "maps."

Although the research for this book about the law in Canada was done by a team of lawyers, it is not a book for lawyers. It does not deal with academic points in technical language, or with the fine distinctions lawyers often have to make in difficult cases. It deals rather with many aspects of everyday life where, without realizing it, you may find yourself rubbing up against the law. It tells you how to avoid legal tangles as well as suggests how to disentangle yourself once you are in legal difficulty. It tries to do this in everyday language to reassure you that the law has in it more common sense than forbidding mystery. The law is a protection rather than a pitfall.

Those who wish may read the book from cover to cover; but that is not the best way to use it. It is basically a reference book to which you turn when you have a problem in relation to your family or your work, your house, your neighbor, your holidays or your investments. Because our guidebook covers such a wide range in relatively small space, it cannot provide closely detailed maps to the

11

reader. One volume of this size could not explain *all* the law on any one of the many topics dealt with.

Despite the exhaustive precautions taken in preparing it, there are no doubt some errors in this book. In addition, many parts of the law are always undergoing changes, to correct defects and to meet new situations and emerging abuses. A look at the bulk of the annual lawmaking by the federal parliament, and any one of the provincial legislatures, would astonish the average citizen. And there is always at least an equal annual output of new, and amended, rules and regulations coming from government departments, boards and commissions. Most of these have the force of law because parliament or a legislature has authorized these bodies to make them. No amount of precaution by the editors could predict, year by year, what such changes in the law would be, or when they would be made.

For these and other reasons, there could not be any intention to try to instruct the average person on how to be his own lawyer: it has been well said that a person who tries to be his own lawyer has a fool for a client. In mountainous country, you need more than maps and guidebooks: you need a guide. In water dotted with rocks or shoals, you need a pilot. The trained and conscientious lawyer is that guide, that pilot.

The advocacy of law

The practicing lawyer is always the spokesman for a cause

YOUR CHOICE OF A LAWYER is an important decision. Lawyers differ greatly in experience, ability, persistence, and conscientious attention to a client's affairs. Some are sleuthhounds in running the facts to earth, yet not so sharp on questions of law. Others are the reverse. The best choice is likely to come from consulting the experience of friends and relatives about the lawyers who have given them satisfactory service.

As you make your choice, you can take some comfort from the fact that lawyers, as a profession, are much better than the popular view of them. Distrust and suspicion of lawyers have a long history; revolutions often put lawyers at the top of the list for liquidation. In earlier times, when the gap between rich and poor was wide, most lawyers had to serve the rich in order to make a living. In those harsh days, the poor had dealings with lawyers as agents of the rich, and often came to regard lawyers as the authors of their misfortunes.

These are the roots of the endless stories showing suspicion of, and hostility to, the lawyer. A visitor to a town was being shown through the cemetery. He came upon a gravestone with the inscription: "Here lies a lawyer and an honest man." He remarked, "Land must be very scarce around here when you have to bury two men in one grave."

Whatever may have been true in the distant past, lawyers do not now deserve the mistrust many people have of them. The gap between rich and poor has narrowed. Most people can afford a lawyer when they really need one and lawyers do not need to serve only the rich. This is a more compassionate age. Lawyers have more sympathy for the underprivileged, as the growth of Legal Aid agencies in recent years shows.

Much of the distrust is spread by those who got hurt in their brushes with the law. When a lawyer fails to get what his client thinks he should have got, the client more often concludes that he had a bad lawyer rather than that he had a bad case. It is always hard for us to believe that we are in the wrong. Some of the distrust arises from a misunderstanding of the function of the lawyer in society. When a lawyer defends an accused person who is widely believed to be guilty (even the lawyer himself may believe this), it is difficult to escape the notion that the counselor may be obstructing justice. In other cases the lawyer is seen arguing with great earnestness for unpopular persons or unpopular causes, and again may be thought by many to be obstructing justice.

Many have doubts about lawyers, thinking them to be actors, playing any role with conviction, rather than men of integrity. They overlook the simple explanation: the practicing lawyer is always an advocate, the spokesman for a cause. And why shouldn't unpopular causes have someone to say whatever can be said for them? Many unpopular causes of the past are now among our most cherished beliefs and institutions.

THE PRACTICING LAWYER is not called upon to judge between the parties to a conflict in the courts, or to decide the justice of a particular cause. That is the function of the judge and the jury. The lawyer's professional duty is to protect his client in every way he can, subject only to two limitations: he must not falsify a fact and he must not deliberately mislead the judge in a court. *An accused person is presumed innocent until proven guilty.* The client is entitled to have the advantage of everything that can be said in his or her favor. Even after being found

"The whole truth and nothing but..." *You must place complete trust in your lawyer and never withhold information from him*

guilty, a client is entitled to have everything possible said in mitigation of sentence.

The fact that the lawyer is an advocate has many advantages. When you are in real trouble, you want an advocate who will say everything that can be said for you. Your lawyer wants to protect you in a dispute, wants you to win in the lawsuit. Except when you have made a disastrous choice of a lawyer, you will get the best advocacy he can give you. But you must not withhold information from him. You must trust him. You must tell him the whole truth about everything that has any bearing on the matter in hand, and you must answer all his questions truthfully. Lawyers do make mistakes, like everybody else. A frequent cause is that, in the middle of the negotiations or the trial, he learns from the other side an important fact that had been withheld from him. Taken by surprise, he is not prepared to meet or handle it.

This can be bad enough in private negotiations for a settlement; if it happens at a trial in the courts, it may be disastrous. First, it is likely to hamper your lawyer in his examination of witnesses and in his efforts to explain away an awkward fact. Second, how the law bears on your case depends on *all* the facts. A surprise fact may worsen or better your case. Your lawyer should know about it in advance so that he can think about how to argue it.

All lawyers have seen cases in which small differences in the facts have led to different results. That is to say, it often is not clear how the law will be applied to the facts of a particular case. This may be a sad truth, but it does make a number of things clear. It explains many of the lawsuits that go to the courts. If the law was really clear in all its applications to every case, most of them would be settled outside the courts. If you stop to think about it, you can quickly see that nearly all the arguments, contentions and disputes that arise every day could be settled without going near the courts, just because the law was so clear in relation to them that it would be lunacy to take them to the courts. The disputes we hear about are precisely the ones to which the application of the law is not clear. These are the "trouble cases," as the lawyers call them—meaning legal trouble. They are numerous enough, but they are only a minor fraction of the total contentions in society.

The "trouble cases" also explain why sometimes Mr. X wins in the first court (the trial court) and then loses on appeal to a higher court. It is not unknown for Mr. X to take a further appeal to the Supreme Court of Canada at great expense, and to get the judgment of the trial court in his favor restored. "Trouble cases" are risky ventures and, even if you win in the end, it may not be worth the trouble. Voltaire said he had only been ruined twice—once when he lost a lawsuit, and another time when he won.

Instances of this kind do happen and the publicity they get exaggerates them, raising distrust of the law as well as of lawyers. Why, it is asked, are the laws not clear in every instance? When a person runs foul of the law, he finds that ignorance of the law is not an excuse. Is that fair if, in this instance, the law is obscure and uncertain? Thus suspicions arise that there is a conspiracy to keep the law obscure and thus make lawyers busier and richer.

The charge of conspiracy is unfair and groundless. Lawyers do thrive on contentious people: in pioneer Canada, they drank frequent toasts to "the old line-fence dispute." But insofar as they have influence on the wording of the law, whether as members of legislatures or as judges in the courts, they try to make it as clear as they can. In recent years, both federal and provincial governments, pushed by associations of lawyers, have set up permanent law-reform commissions. These are staffed by lawyers who keep reviewing the law, not only to reform it when clearly it does not serve justice but also to clarify it where it is obscure. Efforts are being made to make the law as clear as can be. Some obscurities are always being cleared up.

THESE EFFORTS always get caught on the horns of a dilemma. On the one hand, it is important to get the substance of the law on any subject expressed in terms of a general principle. Then the principle can be applied to a host of cases in which there are always similar facts (facts with common features) and always some very unusual and different facts. The different combinations of facts that come up are almost endless. What are the common features that call for the application of this principle, and how much difference in the facts does it take to call for the application of some other principle? This is where the uncertainties arise.

The horns of a dilemma *If there were special laws for every situation, the law would become hopelessly complicated*

Often, an attempt is made to abolish the uncertainty by making special and detailed rules for every conceivable factual situation. This hooks us on the other horn of the dilemma. It is quite impossible to foresee all the combinations of facts that will arise. Then, when the situation which was unforeseen and unprovided for does arise, it is found that there is no law covering it at all—unless we go back to a general principle, which is what we were trying to escape. If we were to go on making a special law for every new situation that arises, we would have so many specific rules for special situations, multiplying every year, that not even a computer could keep track of them.

Attempts are made to state much of the law in terms of general principles, and with some success. An example of a broad general principle is that anyone who negligently causes harm to another is liable for the damage. What is negligence? It is the failure to use the degree of care which a reasonably prudent person would have exercised in the circumstances. This principle, or standard, should be imprinted on the consciousness of every adult, and it can be applied to a vast range of unintentional damage to person or property. Whether a person's conduct measures up to this standard is a question of fact in each new situation, and not a question of law.

However, as everything gets more complex, urban crowding gets denser, and mechanical gadgets put great power into the hands of young and old, the simple standard of reasonable care comes to be thought of as inadequate. To take the example of motor traffic, we have established a detailed code of specific rules such as limiting speeds, stopping at railroad crossings, observing traffic signals. There is a list of specific traffic offenses as long as your arm. The need for rules is not open to question. But some of them are always producing "trouble cases."

A magistrate who had sat on the Bench for ten years thought there was nothing new under the sun. One morning, however, a man was brought before him charged with an offense against a traffic regulation. The regulation made it an offense "to operate a motor vehicle without a windshield wiper. The accused admitted that he did not have a windshield wiper, but pleaded not guilty because his vehicle did not have a *windshield* on it at the time of the alleged offense. The traffic code did not make it an offense to drive without a windshield. Nevertheless, he was caught by the literal wording of the regulation.

It would have been easier to handle this case in a sensible way if the traffic code had simply made it an offense to drive negligently on the highway. This would then have raised the question of the circumstances and conditions in which he was driving. Was he driving into the evening sun, was it raining or sleeting, was there a fierce dust storm blowing in his face? There would only have been questions of fact. Was it negligent of him to be driving without a windshield in the circumstances? Or without a windshield wiper? Making precise rules for each specific set of facts causes trouble because no one can foresee all the combinations of facts that are likely to arise.

Going back to the first horn of the dilemma again: the general principle, or standard, does not apply automatically to every situation that comes up. So it is necessary to see how the courts have applied it in a succession of cases. This gives clues of how they will apply it in the future. But it takes skilled lawyers to assess these clues. So, to sum up, refinements in the law do not make it any easier to get rid of the lawyers than the miracles of medical science enable us to get rid of the doctors. In a complex society, we are likely to become more dependent on both.

THE MAIN REASON for wanting the law to be certain and clear is not so much to get us out of troubles we are already in, as to enable us to find out beforehand what we can safely do to keep out of trouble altogether. If the law is so uncertain that not even a lawyer can tell us the legal consequences of doing this or that, we are nearly helpless. In a free country, where individuals have wide freedom to do what they see fit (and then have to take the consequences of what they have done), it is important for the law to be clear and certain. This freedom is not as great as it was 60 years ago, but it is still true that the broadest principle of law we have is that what is not forbidden (and therefore subject to penalty) is permitted.

"Our rights and their rights"
We are free to do that which is not forbidden, but in exercising such freedom we tread a fine line

Such freedom and responsibility is painful at times, and we yearn for more security. But we would not want to live in countries where the law or the government, or both, tell us exactly what we must do and must not do. Our resistance to wage and price controls shows how the nation feels at heart. Ask anyone who has escaped from a secure but unfree country where he or she prefers to live.

We are free to do what is not forbidden. We are forbidden to encroach on the rights of others. A man appearing in court on a charge of assault was making much of his right to wage his fists in the air. The judge told him that his freedom to raise his fists ended where the other man's nose began. To exercise our freedom vigorously in a society where millions of others are trying to do the same thing, we must know the fine line between our rights and their rights. That depends on the law, and on a large measure of certainty and clarity in the law, including a reasonable certainty of redress against wrongdoers in the courts.

Nearly all our economic life—our way of making a living and of satisfying our needs for goods and services—rests on the law about property and contract. The law of property protects us in the enjoyment of our property and tells how to get, or to give, a good title to land or goods. The law of contract tells us how to make deals in which one or both parties bind themselves to do, or refrain from doing, something in the future. These two bodies of law provide what is called "the security of transactions." The law is also very precise about how to make a valid will disposing of your property upon your death. These laws, above all, must be clear and certain; otherwise we would never know what we could count on.

Someone eager to have his own home exactly as he wants it decides to build a house. He must first get a piece of land and be sure he has good title to it before he builds on it. He must explore the municipal bylaws which provide him with services, laws to which he must conform because they are part of the obligation attaching to property. After the plans have been prepared (perhaps under a contract with an architect) he must make a contract with a builder. The contractor must be sure that the owner is legally bound to pay him, and the owner must be sure that the contractor cannot quit with impunity in the middle of the job. The contractor must have assurances beforehand that he can get the materials and labor he will need (more contracts). Equally, he must have contracts with subcontractors for plumbing and electrical work, perhaps also for masonry and painting. Unless the owner has a lot of ready cash, he will need to arrange for a contract of loan and mortgage on the property so that he can pay the contractor. And prudence requires that he have an insurance policy (another contract) on the house in case it burns down in the course of construction—or after it is completed.

Everywhere there is contract! And there has to be if we are to exercise our freedom and try to look after ourselves. We work at what our circumstances require, or at what we know best, and contract for all the other goods and services. In fact, the law of contract so fills our lives that the editors decided to let it surface naturally in nearly every chapter rather than try to restrict it to a chapter of its own.

Anyone who has built a house knows that there are still a dozen uncertainties on which the owner has to take the risks. But these are nothing compared to a situation which lacked "security of transactions" on all the matters enumerated above. These are secured for us because property must be respected and contracts kept in accordance with clear reliable laws, or compensation paid for the failure to do so.

Without such assurance in this, and in other enterprises, our freedom would lose its meaning. We would have to look for some other protector, a strong man (as in the feudal system), or an omnipotent government (many of which we have seen elsewhere in our time), which would promise us security at the price of our freedom.

THESE ARE THE REASONS the law relating to everyday life should be as certain as can be. It used to be said, and widely believed, that it is more important for the law to be certain than exactly just in all its terms and in all its applications.

In the eyes of the law
The argument has gone on for 2,000 years as man yearns ceaselessly for equality of justice

At the same time, we also believed that a just society is one in which everybody is equal before the law, and everybody is free within the law to make what he can of himself. That is to say, each is justly entitled to what his talents and energies enable him to achieve.

We don't believe this with wholehearted conviction anymore. We have seen that persons differ in health, energy and intelligence. We have seen that some have amazing good luck, others are dogged by misfortune. We have been stirred by consciousness of injustice and we have lost some of our confidence at finding our own way in a complex society. We have developed the welfare system to cushion various forms of misfortune. We still believe in equality before the law, but we don't believe in equality of incomes. We do believe, however, in reducing large inequalities of income by taxing higher incomes at higher rates and using much of the proceeds to provide welfare services to lower-income groups. At any rate, this has been the persistent trend in income tax for 60 years.

Today, many more people are concerned about laws that will guarantee justice. This is a much harder demand to meet. We know a lot about how to give a fair measure of certainty to the law; we do not agree on how to make the law, in its wording and countless applications, equally just to everybody.

This is a big order! For more than 2,000 years, there have been endless discussions about what would be equal justice. Preachers, prophets, philosophers and politicians have argued about it, and hundreds of books have been written on its hundred different aspects. This shows that there is a ceaseless yearning for justice. Everybody wants it for himself, and many persons want it passionately for those who are lost and bewildered. A community that does not strive for justice will not hold the loyalty of its people. So something must be said about it, even though what is said will deal more with difficulties than with solutions.

We will understand the problem of getting an exact justice if we examine the difficulties in the way. The first is that we do not agree about what would be justice for all kinds of people in all kinds of circumstances. Perhaps an all-wise lawgiver would know. But mankind has never been able to find such a lawgiver. In the course of history, we have tried kings, aristocracies and dictators. Out of these diverse experiences, we decided we wanted a lawgiver who would listen to our complaints and grievances, yet be one we could control. We settled for a democratically elected legislature, and we have not found any good reason to change our minds.

This brings us to the second difficulty. If the people who elect the legislature do not agree about justice, how can they expect their elected representatives to agree about it? Even if the majority party in the legislature gets a vision of justice it would like to pursue, it has to be cautious about going farther than the electorate is willing to go. If it goes too far, it is likely to be defeated in the next election. Over the long run, a democratically elected legislature cannot go further in the pursuit of justice than the electorate is willing to go.

As illustration of this truth, it may be recalled that, in the 1968 federal election, Pierre Elliott Trudeau boldly proclaimed his allegiance to the "Just Society". Was the sharp decline in his popular support in the 1972 election due to his failure to advance justice in a way that appealed to the electorate, or was it that many disliked what he did in the name of justice? Nobody has decided the answer with certainty. But it seems clear that he lost the votes of some because they thought he was not doing justice to the plight of the unemployed, and lost the votes of others because they thought he was doing too much for the unemployed and thus doing an injustice to the taxpayer. How many votes he lost on these counts doesn't matter. But I shall say here what does matter: the 1972 election illustrates clearly the different views of justice among the electorate when we get down from pious statements to real issues. The arguments over the death penalty for murder, over the conditions under which abortion should be permitted, also show an electorate seriously divided in its views. In any event, Trudeau has never in any subsequent election made the achieving of the "Just Society" a specific plank in his platform.

There is more to it than this. Given the distrust of politicians and the fallibility of legislatures, how many of us would give the legislature a mandate to do justice to everybody, taking care to see that nobody got more than his or her deserts? As individuals, we tend to exaggerate our deserts. Some of us would be just as upset to see the law giving some rascal more than is deserved as to get less than our fair share ourselves.

It therefore seems that the notion of getting a truly equal justice through changes in the law depends on human nature undergoing a drastic change. While this may seem unlikely, we should not despair. We can at least go on trying to eliminate gross injustices. We should always be exploring how much approximate justice we can achieve by legal change. In a society that is changing as rapidly as ours, there is always a lot of that to be done by trial and error, which will tax legislatures to the limit.

I S IT MORE IMPORTANT for the law to be certain than for it to be just? Is it more important to have food than to have drink? We must try to have some of both. If the law is so uncertain that we cannot find out what we must do to stay within it—or what we count on it doing to protect us from others—it fails us. We lose our confidence in action, our freedom as individuals becomes meaningless, and the law, such as it is, falls into contempt. On the other hand, if the law protects, or permits, what a large part of the community thinks is grossly unjust, our faith in our society crumbles and its law comes under contempt. In anger, we say we must wipe the slate clean and start over again. In either case, public order on which we all depend is threatened. The law needs elements of both certainty and justice.

Some societies have become so corrupt, and the law so much a servant of greedy and selfish interests, that the

Certainty and justice
The law can neither serve the interests of the individual over society nor vice versa

21

demand to wipe the slate clean becomes irresistible. That is what happened under absolute monarchy in France before the French Revolution, and under the Czarist regime before the Russian Revolution. Whatever the causes of the growing contempt of law and of the rising violence and disorder of the recent years in our own country, we are still far from the desperation that calls for revolution. We need only look at the conditions of life for ordinary folk in France and Russia before the revolutions, or at almost any earlier time and place in history, to be satisfied with that conclusion.

This is the century of the common man, not because he always gets a full measure of justice but because he is protected in his freedom to agitate about grievances and to organize for their redress—far beyond what he has ever had before. Indeed, some who agitate about grievances, often genuine and distressing grievances, have been emboldened to think that there are no limits to how far they can go in threatening public order in an effort to get their claims recognized. In this, they are wrong. If they destroy the orderly system of airing grievances and of working out tolerable solutions by discussion, they defeat themselves and the rest of us as well.

We have not come anywhere near the point at which our society is beyond rescue. But we have not reacted as firmly against violent disruptions as we should have. The average person seldom considers what public order does for us, or realizes how easily a few determined and violent men can put it in deadly peril—the tragedies of Northern Ireland and the Lebanon through recent years provide prime examples. Only people who have seen public order dissolve into anarchy and violence have a quick grasp of the terrible consequences. We have lived so long in Canada without serious challenges to public order that the possibility of its destruction has almost faded from our consciousness. We take public order for granted, as if it were part of the order of nature.

But it is not part of the order of nature. It exists first, because of a body of law that is reasonably certain in its terms and reasonably certain of enforcement. It exists second, because the bulk of the people are determined to uphold it and will support the police and the courts in doing so. Public order deserves this support because it is the most precious thing the law gives us. The claims of justice in whose name public order is scorned, challenged, and broken, more and more often in our day, cannot be established in this way.

When public order has been destroyed, it is not the compassionate, the rational and the civilized who can restore it: they are too sensitive. Rather, it is the tough, ruthless and insensitive who do it by the brutal means needed to restore it. And the evidence of history is that people who have looked anarchy in the face will gladly pay the price of hard masters in the hope of restoring public order when they can see no other way.

LAWS THAT ARE REASONABLY CERTAIN and seem reasonably just to most people in the community are the first requisite for maintaining public order. But that is not the whole story. There are always some people who cannot be convinced that what they have, or want, is contrary to law; they will fight for their desires to the bitter end. There are always some who cannot live with the restraints of civilized life, people who are reckless of the rights of others, and will bow only to superior force.

There must be an orderly means of making the laws effective and of bringing the organized force of the community to bear on those who will not play the game according to the rules. We can't have lynch law as the way of enforcing the criminal law, or leave the redress of private wrongs and the settlement of bitter disputes to self-help—which is as bad as no help at all.

This is the reason the courts are agents of the community, and sheriffs, police and jails are there to carry out the judgments of the courts. Judges who are fair-minded and incorruptible will, within the limits of human frailty, administer justice according to the law. But judges cannot carry the duties we impose on them unless there is a fair, firm and fixed procedure in the courts which they can compel the parties to a lawsuit to observe.

Disputes that are too stubborn to be settled outside the courtroom usually rouse strong passions. If these passions are not contained, the courtroom threatens to become a battlefield. In fact, the majesty of the law is at its best in the courtroom where the calm firmness of an impartial judge subdues the passions and compels the parties to abide by the orderly procedure already fixed in advance.

But the greatest importance of upright judges and the firm, fair procedure is not the way they handle disputes in the courtroom. It lies rather in the number and kinds of

Maintaining public order
The law seeks to protect all against the malicious vengeance-seeker

23

disputes they keep out of the courtroom. There are always vindictive people looking for ways to harass and destroy their enemies. Wherever judges and judicial procedure have been open to manipulation, they have been manipulated with gross abuse of justice.

On the other hand, where the judges cannot be bribed or intimidated, and the procedure gives ample opportunity for the truth to be told, few really phony cases come to the courts, and they get sharp rebuke when they do. There is a crime called malicious prosecution: pursuing trumped-up claims with malice. Without knowing about it, or ever thinking about it, we enjoy in this way a very precious aspect of justice.

Due process
Both the accuser and the accused are entitled to tell their sides of the story

WE DO NOT KNOW HOW to make laws that will give exact justice to everybody. But over a long period, we have learned a lot about, and have come to full agreement on, what is a just procedure. For more than 300 years we have been steadily improving on what is called "due process of law." Due process requires that the judge in a case be free of interest or bias on either side of the case. It requires that the party being complained about have notice of the specific charge or complaint against him, and that a long enough time be given him to prepare his defense. It also requires a fair hearing where he has every chance to tell his side of the story, to confront those who started the lawsuit, to disprove what they are alleging, and to argue that the law is on his side. Of course, a fair hearing has to hear all parties to the lawsuit fairly, plaintiff as well as defendant.

The law applicable to a dispute is often clear enough. The real dispute arises out of an honest difference about the facts, differences about what was said, what was done, and in what circumstances. Who is the judge, or jury, to believe? The real hazards in many trials arise from uncertainties as to who, if anyone, is telling the whole truth. Innocent persons from time to time have been convicted of crime because some witnesses don't tell the truth, or because the persons who do know what actually happened don't come forward, or haven't been discovered.

Such injustices are not the fault of the law. In most instances of this kind, the injustices are not the fault of judge, jury or procedure. They are due to defects of human nature or to weakness of the powers of observation of witnesses. We know there are people who do not tell the truth, or who are honestly mistaken about what, precisely, they saw or heard. Judges or juries may be misled, or may draw the wrong conclusions from circumstantial evidence, that is, reach a verdict of guilty because the accused had a motive, had threatened the victim, or was the only person seen near the scene of the crime just before it was committed. Who of us has not believed things that were untrue because we did not closely pay attention to what we heard or saw, because we were misled by someone, or jumped to conclusions on circumstantial evidence?

Judicial procedure, particularly the "adversary system" aspect of it, puts up nearly every conceivable safeguard against miscarriages of justice of this particular kind. The basic assumption of the adversary system is that there are always two (or, perhaps, more) sides to a story, and it is vital to hear all sides. Both sides are entitled to have skilled lawyers to represent them; someone who will draw out the evidence on both sides. All the witnesses, including the main parties, are put under oath and required to confine their evidence to what they heard or saw that is relevant to the case. Every witness on each side is subject to cross-examination by the lawyers on the other side.

Cross-examination has been described as the most effective means ever devised for the extraction of truth. It is a lie-detector of a high order. The right—and the burden—of cross-examination became a regular feature of judicial procedure in England about 1700. This came about partly because of a growing distaste for torture as a means of trying to extract the truth and partly because torture could be used by those in power to persuade witnesses to say what they wanted them to say. We know many governments use it for that purpose today.

Hectoring cross-examination may lead witnesses into falsehoods through confusion, but the lawyer is there to protest if his witness is being badgered. More than that, the secret of effective cross-examination is not to examine crossly. When cross-examination is patiently, quietly and skillfully developed, every witness learns at least that there is no such thing as a simple lie. To make his lie seem credible, he nearly always has to support it by other fabrications. In the course of cross-examination, his hesitations, minor inconsistencies and sudden failures of memory weaken or even destroy his credibility.

To put it at its simplest, the prospect of cross-examination underlines the wisdom of telling your lawyer the whole truth before the trial begins. To put it at its highest, the adversary system, under the safeguards of due process and cross-examination, reveals truth that might never have been discovered in any other civilized way.

". . . open to everyone"
The adversary system assumes roughly equal expertise on both sides of a case

IF YOU ARE DETERMINED to have your day in court, or are compelled to it by the outrageous demands put upon you, you can face it with some confidence of getting justice according to law subject to one condition: the services of a lawyer competent to carry your side of the story. All praise of the adversary system assumes roughly equal legal expertness on both sides.

People who haven't the means to hire a lawyer and/or the experience needed to select the best lawyer for their particular case, often find this the biggest hazard of getting involved in a lawsuit. To appear in court, in a matter of difficulty or large consequence, without a lawyer or with one who is not a match for the lawyer on the other side, is a serious disadvantage of the adversary system.

About 60 years ago an English judge, irritated by assertions that everybody was equal before the courts, said "Yes, the courts are open to everybody—just like the Ritz Hotel." However, it is reassuring to know that there have been considerable reductions in these inequalities in the last 40 years. Crippling poverty, while still a serious problem, is not as widespread as it was: a much larger proportion of the Canadian population can now afford a lawyer if they genuinely need one.

Another difference has come through changes in attitudes, both of governments and of the legal profession. The welfare system which aims to cushion people against mishaps and misfortunes beyond their means has recognized involvement in legal troubles as one of these mishaps or misfortunes. Some welfare experts are now saying that the case for "justicare" is as valid as the case for medicare.

In cautious response to these welfare considerations, all provincial governments now provide financial aid of varying amounts to help the poverty-stricken get the assistance of counsel. The federal government is giving financial aid to provincial systems of Legal Aid. Legal Aid centers are now established in most of the larger cities to give advice on matters not yet in litigation.

There is evidence of a significant change in the attitude of lawyers toward the problem of legal assistance to the poor. For a long time, the law was an individualistic profession. Lawyers shared the widespread view that everybody should look after himself and be content with the goods and services he could pay for. Particular lawyers, of course, always took cases for which they could not expect any adequate pay. Some of these followed a mild Robin Hood policy of charging well-to-do clients rather more to compensate for the poor who could pay little or nothing. But the generous were never enough—and never could give enough time—to come close to meeting the need.

As public attention has come to focus strongly on the plight of the poor, lawyers have become much more fully aware of the legal needs of the poor—and more sensitive to the jibe about the Ritz Hotel. Increasing numbers of lawyers are now prepared to cooperate with Legal Aid plans and to provide the services only they can provide.

Leadership and heartening example has been given by the Canadian law schools. In all or nearly all of them, law students maintain Legal Aid agencies in the cities where the law schools are located, and their professors help them with organization and advice. The law school participation may not make much of a dent in the legal needs of the destitute, but it does promise well for the future. Young lawyers graduate and go out into legal practice with a firsthand acquaintance of the nature and scale of the need, and some skill and sympathy for meeting it.

The total of Legal Aid may still fall short of even conservative estimates of what total "justicare" would require. The future is not too promising because, in the present stringent economic circumstances, some governments have been cutting back on Legal Aid expenditures.

As we know from sensational disclosures about unemployment insurance and medicare, in this country and elsewhere, all schemes for using public funds to cushion the misfortunes of large numbers of individuals always involve some abuses. That has to be accepted as part of the price for doing rough justice. Such schemes will involve large abuses unless their limits are clearly defined and they are effectively organized. Like so many other things, litigation can be fun if it is free.

"Justicare" is another instance where the law will need to be certain as well as just. And it will have to be fairly and firmly administered if it is to be just between those who make claims on it and those who have to pay for it.

Kingston, Ont. J. A. Corry

You and

Your Rights

1/The Origin of Law and Order

The British ascendancy   51

Under Canadian writ   58

From earliest times

HOWEVER the term may be derided and the concept attacked, law and order remains the bedrock of civilization. Without it, human society must degenerate first into anarchy, then into totalitarianism and ultimately into the darkness of barbarism. The unrestricted practice of individual freedom leads inevitably back to the jungle. This truth is not always clearly understood in the democracies—some think freedom means you can do as you like. Under dictatorships, the leaders understand it well, and impose law and order grimly.

All around the world, the subtle balances and pressures of international law and order restrain the would-be agressor, and many argue that another "world" war is now unlikely.

More than 5,000 years of recorded history show man making laws and punishing those who break them. Even our caveman ancestor had to obey some tribal orders and long-established customs concerning the hunt or the possession of women. The penalty would have been a cracked skull or, worse, banishment from the tribal community. Laws can be described simply as the rules that men agree to live by for the good of the community. Bad law may thrive temporarily, like weed, but eventually it is rooted out.

From ancient Egypt to our own times, there has always been recognition of a dictation of conduct from "above"—once, literally, rooted in the interpreted will of God, and now in the relentless might of the state. Of course, in earliest times, there were many gods and even more interpreters—priests who wielded almost absolute power. Even the ancient princes were wary of opposing the mystic author-ity of their high priest. When only a handful could read the sacred scrolls and tablets, the people could be held in fear of the most elementary of natural phenomena. For instance, the exact Egyptian prediction of the earth's wheeling around the sun was evidence enough to the masses of the Pharaoh's kinship with the heavens.

It would require a separate book to tell the full story of the evolution of "divine law" into a written form. The first set of broad moral principles (the Mosaic laws) laid the groundwork. Step by step the "customary" or "natural" law—you could call it simple justice—based on man's developing reason and conscience took shape and finally led, through the centuries, to the English law on which our Canadian statutes and codes are principally based. The law slowly lost its spiritual basis as the jurists of each succeeding age had to change and refine it to deal with the onrushing complexity of industrial life. As the law became more rigid and more mechanical, some legal philosophers began to recall Cicero's statement that the foundation of justice was the natural inclination to love one's fellow-man—not to condemn him for his error or to label him as forever "outside the law." The Hon. James C. McRuer, former chief justice of Ontario, once wrote that although justice is a term that could be no more precisely defined than love or hate or charity, it is clearly something that the human heart acknowledges.

The reforms in penalties, the experiments in parole, more flexible bail provisions, the extension of free legal aid, the unselfish work of "poverty lawyers" in many cities, and the willingness of the legal profession and the judiciary both to initiate and accept change—all these give strong evidence that a humane justice is alive in Canadian law today.

Canada is a comparatively young country, and the Canadian seeking an understanding of the laws that rule his life should first glance at the past. He will discover that our everyday laws are rooted in the most ancient lands of history.

A rock of Babylon

King Hammurabi (who died in 1750 B.C.) reunited the Babylonian empire by defeating the Elamites and his other enemies on the Persian Gulf and in the valleys of the Tigris and Euphrates. He may have been the man who built the Tower of Babel. He is thought by some to be the Amraphel, King of Shinar, mentioned in *Genesis 14:1*. In cementing his dynasty, Hammurabi had to create a workable harmony between a mixed Sumerian and Semitic population. After editing and refining laws already ancient, Hammurabi ordered them cut into a two-metre-high column of green diorite rock. The work required 3,600 lines of cuneiform (the wedged-shaped Sumerian writing). It was topped by a carving showing Hammurabi being ordered by Shamach, the Sun God, to inscribe the law in permanent form.

The Code of Hammurabi, unearthed at Susa, Persia (Iran), in 1902, and now in the Louvre in Paris, is a marvelously detailed summary of later Babylonian law. It follows the sternest line of justice based on revenge, setting out penalties for such offenders as the crooked contractor and the incompetent doctor. While the papyrus archives of the ancient Egyptians crumbled through the years and were lost, this Babylonian stele (or cylinder) remains as our oldest written code of law.

The Sumerians also left the first documented record of common contracts such as we know them today. From baked clay tablets, archaeologists have deciphered bills of sale, wills, marriage contracts and mortgages. The rate of interest was 20 percent, payable monthly. The Sumerian number system, base on 60, can still be traced in our division of the minute into 60 seconds, the hour into 60 minutes and the circle into 360 degrees. The schoolboys of the time had tablet libraries covering geometry and arithmetic, medicine and business practices.

The Ten Commandments

The entire story of civilization is in the inheritance of knowledge, its adaptation to changing conditions and its expansion by progressive man. The Babylonians were conquered by the Hittites and the Assyrians, but many of their laws can be seen enshrined in the next major surviving code—the Ten Commandments, According to the Old Testament, Moses received these laws directly from the Hebrew god, Jehovah—sometimes written Yahweh—on Mt. Sinai. The date accepted by most biblical scholars is about 1300 B.C.

This Hebrew law was also notably stern—its philosohy was "eye for eye, tooth for tooth" (*Exodus 21:12*). For instance, a son who cursed his father "shall surely be put to death" (*Exodus 21:15*). At the same time, the Commandments introduced the protection of the weak, honorable dealing and selfless devotion to others—moral principles lacking in the Babylonian legacy. They also set down the beginning of a labor code—a Hebrew slave, for instance, had to be freed after six years' service—and of civil law under which, for example, if corn was accidentally burned, the man who kindled the flame had to repay the loss. Taking the advice of his father-in-law, Jethro, and possibly following the Egyptian example, Moses set up a judicial system to interpret and enforce the laws. He chose "able men out of all Israel" to judge the people.

You can read in the Bible (*Deuteronomy 16*) that the judges were ordered to be strictly neutral, not showing favor to the strong over the weak and never taking bribes—"that which is altogether just shalt thou follow." It is not difficult to trace the descent of these principles to our legal bodies today.

The laws of Manu

Eastern systems of law, their beginnings lost in legend, were also being collected and permanently recorded in India and China. Around 200 B.C. the name of the

Hindu lawgiver Manu became attached to a summary of Sanskrit texts that had existed in various forms among the people of the Ganges River from earliest times. Again, these laws are founded upon what was claimed as divine revelation, in this case from Brahma, the greatest of the Hindu gods. Manu (meaning "man" in Sanskrit) was himself considered "born of the sun." This code laid down detailed regulations for daily life among the high-caste Brahmans and also for governmental practice.

Warren Hastings, appointed as the first governor-general of British India in 1774, leaned heavily on the Laws of Manu when formulating a legal code for the conquered subcontinent. He did not, however, incorporate the Indian "trial by ordeal," the lingering susperstition that concluded that a man was innocent "whom the blazing fire burns not."

Reforms of Solon

The debt we owe to ancient Greece is incalculable: Hellenic scientists, architects, artists, doctors, playwrights and philosophers laid the foundations of much of our western civilization. So too, obviously, did the men of law, called jurists, who, by the fourth century B.C., had established that while every citizen of Athens had to obey the law he also had full and equal access to it if he thought himself wronged. The oldest law court, standing on the Areopagus close to the Acropolis, offered the same law to rich and poor and the same treatment under it. In an age of tyrant kings and abject slavery, the Greeks had formulated the remarkable concept that every man was free and was equal to any other man. They established the principle that the true aim of law was to achieve a harmonious society.

In 594 B.C. the Athenians elected the statesman Solon, a former poet-philosopher, as supreme *archon* (a sort of chief magistrate), giving him the powers such as are wielded by one of our premiers. This bearded sage halted the process by which all land and power was being concentrated in the hands of the nobles. At a stroke, he canceled all contracts under which one man's liberty could be pledged

to another; he outlawed serfdom in Attica (the city state of Athens); he dissolved oppressive mortgages; and he reformed the constitution. Under the law of "ostracism" passed later, the people could vote to banish a dangerous dissenter—someone who was a threat to the state.

In the previous century, Athenians had been under the harsh law put together by Draco. (We still refer to severe legislation or punishment as being "Draconian.") Under Draco's regime, even trivial offenses drew the death penalty. Draco did, at least, establish that murder was to be punished by the state and not through a vendetta, or blood feud, by the aggrieved family. Solon's reforms represented a more humane approach and, at the same time, raised the law above human frailty so that rulers could not interpret the code as it happened to suit them.

The Greek jury system

It is among the ancient Greeks that we find the beginning of our jury system, the judgment of a man by his fellow citizens. In the Athenian democracy, any citizen (there were only 40,000 who could be called citizens) could take a case to court. He had to present it himself as there were no lawyers; nor was there cross-examination or a formal bench of judges. Six thousand men were chosen by lot to serve as jurymen for a set period of time and up to a thousand could pack the "court" on the Areopagus to hear the arguments.

Each juryman held two metal disks: one with a solid center, the other pierced. The jury did not "retire" to consider a verdict but immediately cast one of their disks in a voting box. The solid disk was a vote for innocence; the other for guilt. There was no appeal.

The Code of Justinian

When Roman power superseded that of the Greeks, the Romans adopted (or adapted) Greek mythology, philosophy, coinage, alphabet and art. While the Roman may have lacked the imagination and the spirituality of the Greek, he was superior as a politician, administrator, developer, diplomat and legal organizer. Profiting from the Greeks' experience, the Romans showed a remarkable ability to apply enlightened practical common sense to every problem they encountered.

In 450 B.C. the patricians, or ruling class, widened the Republic of Rome and allowed the plebs, or less privileged, to elect their own spokesmen. The Roman law, developed over the centuries from tribal custom, was revised and partly reduced to writing. This was inscribed on the famed Twelve Tablets. These bronze columns, which stood in the meeting place, the Forum, are now lost. But it is believed they included the rules by which Rome was to be governed: who had voting rights, who had to pay taxes, as well as other mainly constitutional regulations.

The written law made giant strides forward as the conquering legions brought home foreign problems—sometimes old problems with fresh solutions—for the jurists of Rome to argue and interpret. Transformed by Greek Stoic philosophy,

Hammurabi's Stone

THIS ENDURING RECORD in cuneiform, carved in greenstone, preserves the Laws of Babylon, 3,700 years ago. Two metres high, the elaborate column is one of the treasures of the Louvre, in Paris. Since the laws of the earlier Egyptians were inscribed on papyrus parchment that fell to dust, this Babylonian column remains as the world's oldest surviving statement of written law. Cuneiform writing, developed by the Sumerians from Egyptian pictographs, was deciphered by Sir Henry Rawlinson and Georg Grotefend in the mid-nineteenth century. It had fallen into disuse before the birth of Christ.

The column was ordered carved by King Hammurabi of Babylon after he had established his ascendancy all through the "cradle of civilization" of Mesopotamia. He sifted the laws going back to earliest times, edited and improved them, and reduced them to 3,600 lines inscribed around the shaft's circumference.

Justice was ensured for the orphan and the widow—in fact, "women's lib" was accepted, with females practicing as scribes and women in business on their own account. If a house roof fell, killing the son of the buyer, then the son of the builder was condemned to die also. The stone was erected in the Temple of Marduk in Babylon, and was buried in the sands of time after the Assyrian horde "came down like the wolf on the fold." It was not recovered until 1902.

The stone that started it all...

the law became a cosmopolitan system suited to the ruling of a great empire. Constantine the Great laid the foundation for impartial justice by forbidding judges to accept even the most trifling gift.

During the reign of the Emperor Justinian (A.D. 527–564), the vast body of Roman law was collected, sorted and simplified. This Code of Justinian—the *Corpus Juris Civilis*, the body of law dealing with the relationships between citizens—is better remembered today than all the battles Justinian fought to hold the Roman Empire against the barbarian hordes from the north. Justinian didn't win those battles but he did leave us these principles: Live honorably, respect others, give every man his due.

In the eleventh century, law students in Spain "rediscovered" the Justinian civil code. They were impressed with its simplicity: the fact that a few general principles could deal adequately with a multitude of complex and different sets of circumstances. They championed the ideas that underlay the code: (1) that formal rules of law could be tempered by *equity* (a term, used to describe "fairness," that would become a cornerstone of law) and (2) that all men are by nature equal and should be equal before the law. As Europe moved toward the Renaissance of reason and classical revival, the code spread from country to country. With strong backing from the Roman Catholic Church, the code became the strongest rival of the fast-developing Common Law of England.

Strong echoes of the *Corpus Juris Civilis* can still be heard today—in the Civil Code of Quebec.

Talmud and Koran

While the Greek and Roman empires waxed and waned, and throughout the 500 years of the Dark Ages, the laws of Moses (the Torah) were continually being studied, reinterpreted and adapted to changing conditions. Despite the many assaults on Jerusalem by the Romans, the Turks and the Crusaders, the Hebrew priests and scholars persisted with the writing and expansion of the commentary called the Talmud ("study") until this group of books contained all the thousands of laws and rules that regulate Jewish life. The legal sections of the Talmud, explaining and interpreting some of the earliest of all recognized laws, have had a profound influence on the evolution of law the world over.

Second only to the Bible, the Koran remains the world's most influential book; it is the most recent of all the great religious works that contribute to the basic substance of law. Orthodox Moslems believe the Koran contains the literal word of God as revealed to the Prophet Mohammed by the Angel Gabriel. Orphaned at the age of six in Mecca, Mohammed never attended school. He was in turn a stable boy, caravan guide and Arab merchant. When he was 40 years old, he began to have visions, both in Mecca and Medina. In these visions, he received the laws and advice of Allah— most of them similar to earlier Jewish and Christian examples—from which he created the religion of Islam.

Nothing was put to paper until after Mohammed's death at the age of 62, in 632 A.D., when the scribe Abu Bakr collected his master's sermons and statements into the 144 *suras* (sections) of the Koran. With its curious (at least to Europeans) combination of sword and sacred writ, the religion of Islam swept much of the Mediterranean and Asian lands. The insistence that all men, whatever their material fortune, were equal in the eyes of God and that religious counselors were not needed, gave the creed strong appeal among peasants in Asia and Africa.

Under Islam, limited polygamy (not more than four wives to a man at one time) was permitted, but intoxicating drink forbidden. Equality, it must be noted, was not extended to women or slaves.

Many present-day laws can be traced to the Koran. For example, in the sixth *sura*, the law ensures the property rights of minors and demands that merchants give "full measure and a just balance." The Koran further insists that justice be observed "even in the affairs of a kinsman"; that there be kindness to animals and charity to beggars; and that the truth be stated in all circumstances.

The growth of canon law

The Holy Roman Empire was founded by Charlemagne in 800 A.D., but canon (or church) law dates back to the beginnings of the spread of Christianity.

When Europe was swept by the barbarians into the chaos we now know as the Dark Ages, Roman law almost perished. The one institution that kept the flame of justice alive was the Church. Although they were on the wrong side of the law at the time, the early Chistians had learned Roman law. They used the Roman example to fashion the strong code of canon law by which medieval Europe came to be governed.

Alaric, a chieftain of the Visigoths (in the part of Europe that is now West Germany), combined Roman principles and his own tribal traditions into a code. This law, in the form of a breviary, or prayer book, he proclaimed throughout the Spanish peninsula. The breviary of Alaric was an important development in the law of the times. And out of all this the Roman Church emerged with a set of supranational laws, laws that stood above those of individual nations and tended to draw them together. These were then systematized into a code in the eleventh century and with revisions through the centuries produced the 2,414-canon code of 1917—binding on all Roman Catholics. In January 1983, Pope John Paul II approved a new 1,752-canon code that replaced the 1917 code and incorporated many of the reforms made by the Second Vatican Council of 1964–65. The new code came into force almost a year later, to enable Roman Catholics to become familiar with the revisions.

Although it lost much of its influence in England when Henry VIII broke with the Church of Rome, canon law is still apparent, for example, in the Canadian laws governing succession to property, inheritance, marriage and incest.

Sabbath observance laws are still with us today—and though they are not rigidly enforced they are, nevertheless, widely obeyed. It may surprise you to know that Canada's Lord's Day Alliance Act forbids work on a Sunday—though provincial legislations allow many exceptions.

The saint who wrote law

WHEN THOMAS, the son of the Count of Aquino, was a student at the famed abbey of Monte Cassino in central Italy, his fellow students referred to him as the "dumb ox." But, when he was still in his early twenties (in 1248 A.D.), he had degrees from the universities of Paris, Cologne and Naples, and he went on to become the "Prince of Scholastics" of the Roman Catholic Church.

Thomas Aquinas probably did more than any other person to revive and define the rule of law—canon, or church, law—in the confusion as Europe emerged from the Dark Ages. In his renowned *Summa Theologica*, he worked out a persuasive interrelationship between the laws of God ("eternal law") and the laws of man ("natural law" as revealed by man's reason).

Aquinas wrote that law was "nothing else than an ordinance of reason for the common good, made by him who has the care of the community." His style of reasoning is still known today as the Thomist system, combining Greek philosophy, Roman law, Christian dogma and pragmatic realism.

The law, to Thomas Aquinas, was basically "the reason of divine wisdom." Although he upheld the authority of the Church, he taught that law was the common possession of all people. Therefore, he helped prepare the way for the acceptance of the equality of all before the law.

Thomas visited London in 1263 to assist the establishment of the Dominican Order. He died eleven years later at the age of 48. When writing *The Divine Comedy*, the author Dante Alighieri suggested that Aquinas was poisoned. Pope John XXII raised Aquinas to sainthood in 1323.

The rise of English law

Trial by ordeal

Juryman as witness

The great charter

Divine Right

Parliament is paramount

Reform bills

NINE HUNDRED years ago in the sparsely populated British Isles there was little evidence that a semi-feudal system held the seeds of a legal system that would eventually order life across half the world.

It is often said that English law had its informal beginnings in 1066 with the invasion by William, Duke of Normandy—known to most as "William the Conqueror." But Celts, Romans, Germans and Vikings had each made earlier contributions, and under the Wessex kings a tradition of district "shire" courts developed in which the noble landowners dispensed a rough-and-ready justice to their vassals and serfs. These landowners had to answer to the shire-reeve (sheriff), a royal official who looked after the king's business in the shire.

Even at this time, the guiding principle was *precedent*—the use of a legal decision made in a previous situation that was similar. The local earl or baron would attempt to follow the local long-standing custom, both in the manner of judging and in the penalties or punishment imposed. His verdict would stand unless it was changed or quashed by a higher authority—by the witenagemot (a group of earls, bishops and other leaders of the community) or by direct royal intervention. This would in turn establish a fresh precedent, or standard.

Through the centuries of political and social change to our own times, the principle of precedent has remained central to our law. Since the circumstances of any two cases can never be exactly the same, trying to follow precedent may appear difficult at times. But it is much more reassuring that the accepted law be known than that each individual judge be free to interpret a situation as he might choose.

Trial by ordeal

William I interfered little with the established Anglo-Saxon law in his new kingdom, supplementing it with Norman rulings only where necessary. The feudal system was general across Christian Europe, and William's disciplined and sometimes educated barons merely replaced those of the defeated Harold.

In a simple case, the judge would give his decision immediately; but in a complicated issue, where guilt and innocence were hotly contested, he could seek the assistance of divine wisdom. It was assumed that when a person thought to be guilty was put to the test—a test beyond normal human powers—God would step in to help the innocent. This system was known as "trial by ordeal." It was based on biblical judgments by fire and water, the *judicium Dei*, and was, in effect, the highest court of appeal.

When Emma, mother of Edward the Confessor, was accused of fornicating with Alwin, the Bishop of Winchester, she "proved" her innocence by walking barefoot over red-hot plowshares. In another test, an accused person was tried by the "hot iron." A glowing brazier was set up in church and a path nine feet long marked off in the nave. There were three irons ranging in weight from one to three pounds, the use of each depending on the seriousness of the offense. The accused person had to pick up the red-hot iron in one hand, walk the nine feet and throw it down. He then walked to the altar where a priest bound up the hand. After three days, the bandage was removed. If the wound was clean, the person was innocent; if the burn had festered, guilty.

Water was traditionally the symbol of purity and thus it was used a lot for "trials by ordeal." In one water test, the accused person had to plunge his arm into a pot of boiling water and pick out a ring; if his skin became badly blistered, he was considered guilty. A "friend at court" would have been useful in those days, especially if he was in charge of heating the water. In another case, an accused thief was bound and tossed into a pond; if the water rejected him (that is, if he floated), he was convicted. Presumably, someone fished out the innocents who sank to the bottom before they drowned. This was also a favorite test for witches. Trial by ordeal was abolished by the Plantagenet king Henry III after the church, in 1215, withdrew its support of this type of "legal test." Gradually, trial by jury took its place, a major triumph in the struggle of human reason over superstition.

Trial by combat

Almost as old and perhaps just as chancy was the tradition, popular among the Norman knights, of settling disputes by combat (armed duel). This was the last resort open to an accused murderer—in effect, a final appeal. The alleged murderer could challenge his accuser to a duel; the underlying principle was that God would give an extra edge to the sword of the truly innocent. If the accuser was a woman, or someone elderly and/or infirm, or in the priesthood, a "champion" could be hired to do the fighting.

If the accused was beaten but not slain, he was immediately hanged; if he killed his opponent, he was set free. If this sounds like some fanciful echo from ancient times, it may surprise you to learn that in the century only just past, a man named Abraham Thornton, found not guilty of murder and rape by a jury, was challenged to "trial by combat" by the deceased girl's brother. This "appeal" was heard in London before Lord Chief Justice Ellenborough. The fact that the law of trial by combat had fallen into disuse did not mean that it could no longer be exercised. Thornton declined to duel, but the brother was not satisfied. Lord Ellenborough's verdict has become famous for the following statement: "It is our duty to

Magna Carta

ALTHOUGH HE WAS the brother of Richard the Lion Heart, King John (1199–1216) depended more on diplomacy for his successes. To head off a revolt by his barons he agreed to sign a charter of rights for his "freemen," having craftily obtained in advance a promise from the Pope that no pledges extracted from him by duress would be held valid.

The terms were mostly drawn up by Stephen Langton, the French-educated Archbishop of Canterbury, whom John had at first refused to acknowledge. The signing took place at Runnymede, on the Thames between Staines and Windsor, in 1215. The 63 clauses included:

• To no man will we sell or delay right of justice.

• No freeman shall be seized or imprisoned save by the law of the land.

• No scutage [tax] shall be imposed save by consent of the common council of the realm.

• The rights and liberties of the Church shall not be interfered with.

Although these items originally applied to the barons and knights alone, as serfdom died out they came to apply generally to all free Englishmen. John's son, Henry III, was required to sign the Great Charter, and this practice was demanded of succeeding kings.

It was established henceforth that custom and law must stand even above the king. Thus, Magna Carta became recognized as the foundation of British liberty.

pronounce the law as it is, and not as we may wish it to be." He turned down the would-be duelist and granted Thornton his freedom.

The King's Bench

When William conquered England in the eleventh century, he set to work consolidating a strong central authority so that he could control the local landowners. He replaced the witenagemot with the *Curia Regis*, or "court of the king."

Committees were appointed under the Curia Regis to carry on the daily work of the kingdom and to settle disputes. As these committees developed rules of procedure and established records of their activity, they slowly adopted the form of courts, called the King's Bench and the Exchequer Court. As the king centralized the administration of justice, they ousted the shire courts (still largely under the sway of the lords) and other courts by being more efficient and fairer. For one thing, they replaced trial by ordeal and trial by combat with trial by jury.

Prominent in the work of organizing these courts was the chief justiciar, an official of the Curia Regis, whose title can be recognized today in that of our chief justice. The judges who were appointed by the chief justiciar traveled throughout the country, holding regular court sessions, *assizes*, in county towns. In this manner, they were able to curb and break the power of the local despots, apply a more nearly equal justice and increase the power of the king.

Some minor magistrates were authorized to visit towns and "make trial of all the wine and beer" to ensure its quality. Poor stuff was to be poured into the gutter. They could also fix a fair price for oxen, sheep and chickens. The later Plantagenets introduced the custom whereby only men of high character and honesty were appointed as judges, another precedent happily followed today by civilized countries.

The compurgation

One of the Anglo-Saxon legal traditions that dies hard was that of the "compurgator," literally an "oath taker." This was a person who would swear that the accused person was not guilty. A solemn oath before God was considered valid evidence— the more important the person doing the swearing, the more weighty his oath.

If an accused man could raise 11 oath takers (he himself was the twelfth, thus, the 12-man jury of today) he stood a fair chance of being freed—unless, of course, his accuser could raise a greater number of equally important compurgators. In effect, the man who fielded the biggest team would win. Compurgators could be hired outside Westminster Palace ready to "swear to order," although at the risk of perjury. Such men advertised by displaying a straw sticking out of one of their boots. This later gave rise to the derisive label, "man of straw."

The juryman as witness

As developed from its separate Grecian and Teutonic beginnings, the jury system in Britain was not a last line of defense but a method of official inquisition. Jurymen were originally authorized to pry from an accused person those facts proving the guilt he was supposedly concealing. The jury system was used particularly in cases of suspected tax evasion. The jury's specific job was to advise the court whether charges should be made and, if so, what they should be—not unlike the task of our grand juries today. If its findings did not satisfy the royal establishment, the jury itself could be fined and even imprisoned.

Evolution of the jury to its present form of juridical power was a slow process, beginning with the appointment of the traveling justices to the King's Bench. Without counsel to present cases, these judges had no way of knowing the details of local disputes. But the local jurymen did, and presumably they were capable of weighing the issues. However, their final opinion would not necessarily sway the presiding judge. Later, the role of the jury was reversed. It came to court ignorant of the case to be settled, having to be informed of the facts by the parties concerned and then by the legal counsel. In this change, the laws and rules of evidence were born. It was not until Tudor times, however, that the principle was established of juries bringing in verdicts based solely on the evidence presented. The right of an accused to "trial by jury" in criminal cases was not formally accepted until the Bill of Rights in 1689.

Cementing the common law

As the clerks serving the justices of the King's Bench started to compare and logically put together the jumble of legal customs that were "common" across the country, a system of common law began to take shape in England. The term "common law" is used to describe all the law built up by custom and precedent, from the days of Roman influence forward. For centuries, the law varied widely as exercised in the manorial courts of, say, Northumberland compared with those of Sussex and as applied in the "shire courts" of the shires. Yet it proved to be sturdy, resisting the advance of civil law as that system took over much of Europe. Then an attempt was made to form a national standard that we can speak accurately of as the English Common Law, a system that was widely exported and is found in

such countries as Canada, the United States and Australia.

Common law is based on decisions by judges (case law), as opposed to decisions laid down in parliamentary legislation (statute law). It must be emphasized that the common law has never actually been set down in a formal system in England. Although there are literally thousands of weighty tomes containing cases and judgments. It can still be referred to as the "unwritten law."

Bound to the tradition of precedent, common law quickly became inflexible and unwieldy, as early as A.D. 1300 when international trading and industrialism began to change the life of England. It got to the point that judges would refuse to hear certain cases unless they fell into a known pattern with a specified range of penalties. Obvious wrongs and hardship brought to the king a flood of petitions for fair treatment, since it was he who was always regarded as the fountain of justice. He began to delegate the authority to hear such appeals to the chancellor, the head of the royal offices. The rulings of the king's chancellor (mostly dictated by

The Inns of Court

THE INNS OF COURT, off Fleet Street in central London, are not—as tourists might think—pubs for thirsty judges and lawyers. On lands once owned by the crusading Knights Templar, professors of law took up residence and gathered their students about them. Circuit judges of the King's Bench came to dine and debate when in London. Here, the laws of England—the foundation of future Commonwealth and Canadian law—were hammered out over coffee and good brandy.

Today, four inns survive—Gray's Inn, Lincoln's Inn, Middle and Inner Temple—constituting a legal university where all members of the English Bar must first be admitted. The "benchers" of the inns can disbar a barrister for professional or other misconduct. Dining at the "inns" is still a

tradition for jurists and lawyers, in an atmosphere of fine food, fine wines and fine argument.

The Middle Temple Hall, dating from 1570, saw the first performance of Shakespeare's *Twelfth Night*, and a table built from timbers out of Sir Francis Drake's *Golden Hind* is still in use.

The Elizabethan dramatist Ben Jonson described the "Inns of Court" as the "noblest nurseries of humanity and liberty in the Kingdome." A rather more cynical (but anonymous) poet expressed his views in the well-known jingle:

"The Inner for a rich man,
The Middle for a poor,
Lincoln's for a parchmenter,
And Gray's for the law."

41

his own conscience) can be called the first pronouncements of the "Court of Equity." In this fashion, the third great element of English law came into being.

Equity has long since been fused into the general body of law and is interpreted and applied by the ordinary judges. The attorney-general in Britain, and the minister of justice in Canada—in each instance a member of cabinet—if convinced of some unfairness in the law, can exert strong influence in the introduction of new legislation which his political party, usually holding a majority in Parliament, can ensure will become law. It also falls to the minister of justice in Canada to appoint judges of our higher courts.

The great charter

The schoolboy's drilled-in identification of the Magna Carta as the basic document of civil liberties in the English-speaking world is founded not upon original fact, but upon the significance of the charter in the evolution of the written law.

When the barons pressured King John to put his seal on that roll of parchment at Runnymede one June morning in 1215, they were concerned only with ensuring that the despotic sovereign would respect *their* rights. Yet, at the same time, the charter also put a permanent dent in the absolute power of the monarch.

Apart from the items of value to the selfish nobles, mainly concerning the security of their feudal holdings, the Magna Carta insisted upon strict and fair administration of justice; the establishment of a permanent home at Westminster for the Court of Common Pleas (one of the courts that split off from the Curia Regis), to which the common people could bring cases; regular sittings in the county towns of the Assize Courts, or the King's Bench; and the introduction of standard weights and measures.

With some alterations and additions but little basic change in its essential character, the charter was formally reaffirmed several times as a means of curbing some of the more despotic Plantagenet kings. Three hundred years later the Stuarts aroused parliamentary fury by their audacious assumption of quasi-divine powers. Once again, Magna Carta was taken out of the archives of legal history, to become the rallying standard of free men.

Divine right of kings

Like their Bourbon cousins in France, the Stuarts of Scotland were convinced that they were ordained by God to rule and, consequently, that their every word was the law of the land. The 75-year reign of the Stuart dynasty in England interrupted the forward march of democracy yet, at the same time, hastened its total adoption.

When James VI of Scotland became also James I of England—following the death of Elizabeth I—a head-on collision with the ever-developing House of Commons became only a matter of time. The historian G. M. Trevelyan recorded that the diminutive James was so ignorant of English justice that, when a purse snatcher was caught in the act just as the king passed in the street, he ordered the wretch to be hanged immediately "without a trial, at a word from his royal mouth." The actual blowup didn't occur until the reign of James's son Charles, when the Parliamentarians soundly beat the Royalists in civil war and claimed the king's head as trophy.

Oliver Cromwell's rule was too dour and puritanical to convince the public of the benefits of republicanism and Charles II resumed the Stuart rule. In an excess of cynicism, Charles appointed his mistress Nell Gwyn, a former orange seller from Drury Lane, as registrar of court. He appointed as chief justice George Jeffreys, who proceeded to earn himself another title, the "Hanging Judge."

After the Monmouth Rebellion in 1685, Jeffreys ordered 233 persons hanged, drawn and quartered in Somerset, and had another 800 sent into exile. He sentenced Lady Lisle to burn at the stake for having sheltered two Protestant dissenters (a punishment later commuted to beheading). In summing up a case, the Roman Catholic Jeffreys said: "Gentlemen of the jury . . . how can one help abhorring both these men and their religion? . . . Show me a Presbyterian and I will show you a lying knave." The Marquis of Halifax risked royal vengeance by stating, "Obedience shall be looked upon as a better qualification in a judge than skill or severity." James II showed his appreciation for Jeffreys by appointing him lord chancellor. In the fate often reserved for tyrants, he died in the Tower of London at age 44.

The "Glorious Revolution"
The debasement of justice under the Stuart kings was one of the major forces that led to the bloodless uprising of 1688, known today as the Glorious Revolution. After only three years under the would-be absolutist James II, the Whigs (Liberals) and the Tories (Conservatives) of the parliament, along with the bishops of the Church of England, joined forces to ask William of Orange and his consort Mary (Protestant daughter of James) to assume the throne of England. King James threw the Great Seal into the Thames and fled to France. The Bill of Rights, proclaimed in 1689, redefined the relationship between sovereign and subject—an updated Magna Carta with guarantees for free assembly, free elections and free speech. Parliament established its solid supremacy. By changing the succession to the throne, it gave the deathblow to the so-called divine right of kings.

The indestructible civil and political rights of Englishmen, and of those whom they came to govern in other lands, were further buttressed by the Act of Settlement, 1701. The leading Canadian scholar of law, James McRuer, hails this statute as the greatest milestone in the development of "an incorrupt and free judicial process." Although its basic purpose was to prevent any future Catholic succession to the throne, the act also reaffirmed that the law was above the Crown. It also decreed that judges were to be appointed for life, not—as had previously been the case—dependent upon the favor of the Establishment for their tenure. Thus, British (and, in turn, Canadian) judges had to answer only to their own consciences in administering and applying the law they have sworn to uphold. Our judges can only be removed by the governor general following a motion from both houses of the Canadian Parliament. (*See* Chapter 3, "Judges and courts.")

Parliament is paramount
While we take it for granted today that the elected representatives of the people as a whole should choose the laws under

A calendar of legal power

H OW THE RIGHT to make laws evolved in Canada from colonial times to the sovereignty of the present day:

1583 — English sea power brings intermittent authority to the Atlantic shores.

1608 — French trading companies exercise arbitrary rule on the St. Lawrence.

1663 — Control by French Crown through governor, intendant and bishop.

1760 — British martial law imposed following conquest; customary French civil law retained.

1763 — Governor, directed from London, rules with assistance of appointed Executive Council.

1791 — Assemblies elected by popular vote in all Canadian colonies but power remains with Crown.

1848 — Responsible government follows armed uprising; recommended after survey by Lord Durham.

1867 — Confederation. B.N.A. Act divides power between the provincial and federal parliaments.

1931 — Canada's total sovereignty is recognized in the declaration of the Statute of Westminister.

1982 — Patriation of the Canadian Constitution. Its provisions include an amending procedure for constitutional change and a charter of rights and freedoms.

which we all live, it took several centuries to achieve that right. Yet today the democratic birthright is still denied to the great majority of the world's peoples—including those of some of the newest countries of Africa and Asia. These people are ruled in most cases by military dictatorships or one-party political systems.

The 19th-century economist and political theorist, Walter Bagehot, authority on the English constitution, traces the steps in comparatively modern times by which "the slavish parliament of Henry VIII grew to the murmuring parliament of Queen Elizabeth, the mutinous parliament of James II and the rebellious parliament of Charles I." In analyzing the forces that led to the eventual assumption of supreme power by the House of Commons, Bagehot concluded: "The steps were many, but the energy was one—the growth of the English middle class and its animation under the influence of Protestantism."

The laws passed in parliament were presented in the form of petitions to the king so that he might put his seal on them, thus formally making them law. Since the monarch could not tax without the consent of the people, and since he couldn't get that consent from parliament until he put his seal on the legislation (drafted by the representatives of the people), a most effective squeeze play existed.

Parliamentary "privilege"—freedom to debate without fear of arrest or penalty—was another significant step. By the time of the Reformation, both houses of parliament had developed into something close to their present form. The Commons demonstrated its power when it formally established the Church of England.

Under the Tudors and Stuarts, there were setbacks to parliament's judicial progress as sovereigns tried to resume an authority beyond the law through Star Chamber and Privy Council. But the arrival of William and Mary signaled an end to those attempts. After their successor, Anne, employed the royal veto over legislation in 1707, it was never attempted again and became obsolete. In the eighteenth century, the principle was established that the prime minister had to hold the confidence of the Commons, thereby ending the tradition of the Crown's appointing a ministry of its own choice.

The Reform Bills

The Reform Bills completed the development of democracy in the British House of Commons, ultimately bringing about universal suffrage in the present century. Until the Industrial Revolution, parliament was dominated by the propertied, or landowning, classes, with only 400,000 voters from a population of 24,000,000 in 1831. The Reform Bill of 1832 gave the voting right to a further 450,000, and this was extended again in the statutes of 1867, 1884 and 1918 at which time all adult males had the vote. The process was not completed until the Representation of the People Act was passed in 1928, giving women full voting equality with men.

The law merchant

One other part of English law that the Canadian legal system has inherited is commercial law, known since the late Middle Ages as the *law merchant*. At that time, it covered matters of shipping, buying and selling, banking, insurance, and disputes between traders. The first scenes of action of commercial law were in the amusingly named Courts of Pie Powder, the name derived from *pied poudré*, French for "dusty foot." Traveling merchants, in their haste to get top prices for their goods brought from distant countries, did not pause to clean "the dust of travel" off their boots. A "court" of senior traders decided on rates of exchange and settled any arguments. The decisions were widely adopted to create stability and were scrupulously observed by the traders of practically all nations.

These special international customs and rules were first written down in England in 1285. The first insurance act is dated 1601. During Lord Mansfield's 30-year tenure as lord chief justice in the eighteenth century, the law merchant was brought within the body of the English Common Law and applied to everyone, merchant or not. It was thus prepared for its export to Canada and the rest of the expanding British Empire.

Justice in New France

BEGINNING with the founding of Quebec in 1608, the first justice in what is now Canada was that meted out by the senior officer of the trading company currently holding the Canadian fur monopoly. He didn't hesitate to order the harshest of punishment—for instance, flogging with a tarred rope was only for misdemeanors. His power was based on the total authority granted the merchant companies by successive French kings. For example, one man, the Sieur de Monts, was appointed by Henri of Navarre as lieutenant general and vice admiral of Canada, Hochelaga, Saguenay, Labrador and all other points then known on the sketchy maps. He was given complete power to make laws, and even wars if necessary.

In 1627, when Cardinal Richelieu organized the Company of New France—commonly called the Company of One Hundred Associates—its 12 directors (resident in France) exercised full authority through appointed governors over the known mainland of Canada and all its inhabitants; the monopoly excluded only the fishing and slave trades. Both the English and the Iroquois took a hand in obstructing this authority which, in reality, ran only fitfully along a slender strip of the St. Lawrence River between Tadoussac and Montreal.

Several times the company was in such financial difficulties that it leased its trading rights to other groups. Nevertheless, for its 30 years of rule, aided both spiritually and materially by the Roman Catholic Church, the company could point to a population of 2,500 as well as a framework of justice, education, health care and administration for that population. Within this system of laws, or jurisprudence, could be found the bones of Roman law that had survived in feudalist France.

In 1663, Louis XIV abolished all trading charters and New France came under the direct rule of the royal cabinet—in effect, the personal rule of the sovereign. When Louis said *"l'état, c'est moi,"* ("I am the state") he really meant it—although he was skilled enough as a politician to avoid confrontations. Thus, for the century that preceded the British conquest, Canada lived under the edicts of Bourbon royal despots. During that period, the boundaries of French influence and claims were thrust north and west, and south to the shore of the Gulf of Mexico.

Company rule at Quebec

Samuel de Champlain, the true Father of Canada, left his mark on this land as a discoverer, explorer, administrator and even as a judge. In the autumn of 1608, the first year at Quebec, while the walls of the famous *Habitation* were still being raised below Cap Diamant, a locksmith named Jean Duval tried to stir a revolt among the band of 28 settlers. The scheme was possibly hatched by some Basque traders hovering at the Saguenay River who wanted to seize Champlain's supplies. When the plot was discovered, Champlain got the conspirators drunk and then arrested them. He convened the first criminal trial held in Canada, as his journal attests:

After Pontgravé and I, along with the captain of the ship, the surgeon, master, mate and other seamen had heard their stories, and cross-examined them, we decided it would be sufficient to execute Duval as the

45

ringleader, and to serve as an example to those who remained to conduct themselves properly in future.... We decided the three others should be condemned to be hanged but meanwhile should be taken back to France and handed over to the Sieur de Monts to receive fuller justice, according as he might decide.... Duval was hanged and strangled at Quebec and his head placed on the end of a pike and set up in the highest place in our fort.

Champlain had earlier given a glimpse of his reading of justice. When four Europeans were killed by Indian arrows on a Cape Cod beach, the French enticed six unsuspecting Indians to their boat at another beach and had them "hacked and hewed in pieces." Champlain wrote that his party departed feeling that "God had not left unpunished the misdeeds of these barbarians."

Although his formal education could not have extended beyond his village school in Brouage, Champlain became sufficiently skilled as an advocate to argue with Richelieu and to appear before the Prince de Condé at Fountainbleau to plead (successfully) for support for the frail colony at Quebec. He eventually became governor at Fort St. Louis—the direct representative of Richelieu.

Conseil and Syndics

The despotic powers vested in the Company of One Hundred Associates—most of them living in France—began to irk those immigrant families which had adopted Canada as a homeland. A group of them took over the fur trade under the name of the *Compagnie des Habitants*. In 1647, they appointed a *conseil*, a people's council, to advise Governor Montmagny—or, more plainly, to try to curb his arbitrary actions. The council was led by the Superior of the Jesuits and the town governors of Quebec and Montreal; the governors were supported by two elected members, called *syndics*. By the next decade, there were four syndics, two from Quebec and one each from Trois Rivières and Montreal.

Much of the early legal system in New France was developed along feudal lines. As the country was parceled into large estates *(seigneuries)*, the new landed gentry began to hold regular court sessions at their isolated farmhouses in the feudal manner of their homeland. Major offenses and damage suits had to be heard at Quebec. The *seigneur* had the right to impose a charge for all land transfers and for the use of his mill as well as to collect the customary *cens et rentes*, small fees paid by the tenant farmer.

When the *habitants'* trading company fell into difficulties, Chief Minister Jean-Baptiste Colbert advised the young Louis XIV that Canada should be brought completely into the French family group; it should be just another province of France. Three thousand miles of ocean was no barrier to the man whom history has labeled the Sun King.

Under the "Sun King"

Although the idea of a set judicial system arose earlier in France than in Britan, it had not resulted in an independent legal body. The early kings had sent travelling magistrates through the provinces to conduct trials, but royal power diminished greatly in the rise of feudalism. Under the feudal system, the regional nobles and the Church were in effective control, although there is some evidence that the citizens of large towns agitated for rudimentary freedom charters, including terms not unlike those of Magna Carta.

Beginning with the reign of Henri IV, the Bourbons began to reassert their royal might, and Cardinal Richelieu broke the power of the barons for Henri's son, Louis XIII. When Louis XIV, at 22, dismissed his counselors and assumed absolute authority, there was nothing to prevent his slightest whim, although the pragmatic Colbert kept him in check for the first half of his long reign.

Louis set up a Sovereign Council to govern New France, headed by a governor, a bishop and an intendant. The Sovereign Council also included five appointed councilors, an attorney general and a clerk. The council heard criminal and civil cases, as well as appeals from lower courts at the three population centers on the St. Lawrence. The king, of course, retained the right to change or annul any decision of the council as he saw fit. He changed the name of the council from "Sovereign" to "Superior" when he became suspicious of its pretentions.

The council's first act, on September 28, 1663, was to forbid the trading of brandy or rum with the Indians, on pain of severe penalties. This was a victory for Bishop Laval, who had quarreled bitterly on this issue with previous governors and had tried to punish liquor traders himself by excommunicating them. It would not be the last time that canon and civil law would collide in Canada.

Although the governor represented the person of the king, it was the intendant who represented the royal will. Justice, civic security, finance and commerce were all concerns of the intendant, who soon became head of the Sovereign Council. Colbert persuaded Jean Talon, Intendant of Hainaut, to accept the new post. This gifted and resolute executive was to leave an enduring mark on Canada.

Talon was the first official in Canada to be specifically given the responsibility for maintaining law and order and ensuring the *habitants* a swift and impartial justice. He heard all minor civil cases alone, although his decisions could be appealed to the full Sovereign Council. He could arbitrate commercial law decisions personal-

By order of the "Sun King"

IN 1663, Louis XIV took New France—as central Canada (pop. 3,215) was then known—under his personal rule. All laws from that date to the fall of Quebec nearly a century later were founded on royal edicts, carried across the sea by ship. Louis Gaudais, the Sieur du Pont, was sent to Quebec that autumn to investigate the state of the colony. He carried the following detailed orders under the signature of the King:

"First, the Sieur Gaudais must obtain accurate information on the country: how many degrees is it from the Pole. The length of the days and nights; the good or bad qualities of the air. The regularity or irregularity of the seasons and the general lay of the land. After these first considerations, he should carefully inform himself of the fertility of the land.

"It would be well to describe the three habitations of Québec, Montréal, and Trois Rivières; the number of souls of both sexes; to what, in particular, do the inhabitants apply themselves? In what consists their commerce and the means of sustenance available? How do they bring up their children?

"The Sieur Gaudais will note if the country lacks women or girls so that provisions may be made for sending some in the coming years.

"The principal menace to the inhabitants of the country being the Iroquois, who at all moments attack the French, the King has resolved, if it is necessary, to send next year some regular troops to the country. Examine with great care the number of men required, munitions and food needed, and the supplies and help that may be expected from within the country itself.

"As the main source of revenue consists of the fur trade, which has been found to be damaging to the interests of the country, because the inhabitants apply themselves to the trade rather than, as in the past, to the development of agriculture, the King wishes the Sieur Gaudais to inform himself by what means His Majesty may derive the profit from the said trade and to inform the inhabitants that it is their welfare he wishes and that he would contribute substantial sums every year to their maintenance.

"The Sieur Gaudais will inform himself if, in the country, there are iron deposits; what they would produce should they be developed by the King or by some individuals to whom a concession might be granted. What must be even more clearly verified is if there are prodigious quantities of trees of great height of which masts could be made."

ly and, if the parties were willing, sit in judgment on major cases. He could decide which tribunals would hear a case, or he could decide to hear it alone. When he walked the streets of Quebec, he was preceded by two archers and, when in official processions, he walked beside the governor. *Les Canadiens* were never in doubt of the intendant's power.

Outside the courtroom, the intendant created and enforced the maze of regulations that deal with the routine problems of everyday life—such as those controlling building standards, traffic, hours of work, weights and measures. Talon supervised a population-growth plan in which 1,000 single girls were sent out from France to provide wives for the farmers' sons; he allowed annulments by the notary if the parties decided a mistake had been made in the rush.

The Custom of Paris

Voltaire once remarked that a man traveling through France changed laws as often as he changed horses. Yet most of the central and northern provinces followed *la coutume de Paris*—that is to say, the customary (or common) law as built up by precedent through the centuries which had significant elements of Roman law in it. William of Normandy had brought some of this law to England when he conquered it 500 years earlier. In 1663, in a revised form consisting of 362 sections, it was declared to be the law of Canada.

La coutume de Paris was, in some ways, a more moderate legal system than that ruling in England and in the American colonies in the seventeenth century; in other ways, it was notably harsher. The *Canadien* could not be put in jail for debt, nor could his livestock or farm tools be seized. On the other hand—for instance, if he was stubborn under questioning—he could be tortured at the hands of *le maître des hautes oeuvres*. Also, it was only when the evidence had been gathered that the accused was informed of the charge against him. He had to build his own defense as there were no lawyers in New France. Records were kept by notaries.

Sentences of execution or banishment could be appealed to the Sovereign Coun-

cil. But generally a hanging ordered by the court in the morning was carried out in the afternoon. A doomed man was marched barefoot through the streets of Quebec, a rope around his neck, a lighted torch in his hand. He was permitted to halt at the door of the church to beg forgiveness of God. When pronounced dead, his head was cut off and propped on a post as a warning to others to keep the king's peace.

The law included many rulings peculiar to Canada, some of them handed down from the days of Champlain. In the interest of increasing the population in the countryside, stiff fines were imposed on *habitant* fathers who failed to marry off their daughters by age 16 and their sons by age 20. A townsman was hauled into court in Montreal if he rented a room to a farmer—a rather effective method of stopping the population drift to the cities. The rigid moral code of the Jesuit fathers was reflected in the banning of women from the streets after 9 P.M. A man who was caught for the second time using profane language had his lips seared with a red-hot iron. At one time, even the independent trapper, the famed *coureur-de-bois*, risked the gallows if he ventured into the forest for furs—furs on which the trading companies wanted to keep a monopoly.

Under the *coutume de Paris*, someone sentenced to death could make a final appeal to the king (or his ministers). When a considerable number of *Canadiens* took advantage of this right, Colbert lost patience and sent all the appeals back to Quebec. The facts were known in Canada, he said, not in France. The Sovereign Council of New France thus became the highest court of appeal.

Flirting with democracy

During his first term as governor (1672–82), the Comte de Frontenac attempted to establish a Canadian version of the States General, the ancient consultative body that had once aired public grievances to the Bourbon kings of France. To the traditional three *estates* ("classes") of noblemen, priests and commoners, Frontenac added the local judiciary. The group met for the first time in Quebec City in late October 1672. It seemed that a democracy was taking shape in the far-flung domain of the Sun King—although critics of Frontenac suggested he was merely trying to surround himself with a petty court.

Word came back from Versailles the following spring and the experiment came to an abrupt end. Colbert was afraid that the idea might grow to threaten the royal authority. Colbert also ordered the governor "quietly to abolish the syndic which presents requests in the name of all the *habitants*, it being a good thing that

each man speaks for himself and that no one speaks for all." In this way, even the token popular representation of 30 years' standing was dissolved. Intendant de Meulles wrote at the time that, "It is of very great consequence that the people should not be at liberty to speak their minds." The king was the fount of justice and, while the French regime lasted, the *Canadiens* had to be satisfied with that.

The Code Napoléon
Until the bloody upheaval of the Revolution there was no unified system of laws in France. Although the proclamation of a

The intendant: man of power in New France

NO PUBLIC OFFICIAL in Canada, before or since, wielded the power of the intendants of New France. From 1663 to the British Conquest, 12 men served in this unique position, virtually controlling the administration of justice, the police, and business life of the Crown colony.

The job had been created in France to provide comptrollers for conquered territories, and men capable of the heavy and difficult duties were hard to find.

While officially ranking only third behind the governor and the bishop, the intendant was, in fact, No. 1 in some administrations. He received 12,000 *livres*, the same basic salary as the governor. He presided over the Sovereign Council and, since he was usually the only member with legal experience, it was his will that carried.

He sat in solitary judgment on civil cases, judging infractions or evasions of regulations that he had himself drawn up and proclaimed. These covered consumer protection, building regulations, currency, traffic, and liquor laws.

All military supply was the intendant's sole responsibility and some, alas, waxed rich on kickbacks from contractors.

The greatest of the intendants was, by popular agreement, the first of them—Jean Baptiste Talon, a brilliant bureaucrat from

Champagne. Talon would brook no disobedience of his ordinances and, since he served under soldier-governor Courcelle, his word was virtually law.

Talon was responsible for increasing the population by immigration; he also imported the "King's girls" to provide wives for the lonely settlers. He started three satellite towns near Quebec City and settled the soldiers of the Carignan-Salières Regiment on the land. Talon built a brewery and founded a shipbuilding industry.

If Talon was the first and best intendant, François Bigot from Bordeaux was the last and worst.

Trained as a lawyer, Bigot served first in Canada at Louisbourg, where he was appointed Administrator of Ile Royale (Cape Breton) in 1739. He immediately began to enrich himself by corruption, particularly by selling for his own pocket stores and materials sent from France for the fortress.

In 1748, he went to Quebec as Intendant of New France. Now, his embezzlements began in earnest. As he both made the laws and occupied the seat of judgment, Bigot did as he pleased. Practically the whole civil administration was in his hands and all business done in the colony had to pass through his private company. His warehouse at Quebec was known locally as La Friponne ("the Cheat").

civil code was a major priority under the constitutions of 1791 and 1793, little was accomplished until Napoléon Bonaparte came to power. In 1800, he appointed five commissions to examine the main body of existing French law and to refine and categorize it under five headings: civil (or private) law, court systems, precedence (case law), commercial and penal.

Napoléon did not originate the idea of the civil code, or did he write it (as is sometimes stated), but he deserves to be named as its author. As first consul, then as emperor, Napoléon took a personal and prominent interest in drafting the code. It was due to his drive that the project was finally completed.

Completely self-taught in legal matters, this stocky Corsican had consumed the works of the liberal philosophers of the eighteenth-century enlightenment—men like Rousseau, Voltaire and Raynald; yet he had remained a practical and independent thinker. It was said of him that he learned to "despise monks, to hate kings and to disbelieve in the doctrines of the Christian religion"; yet the *Code Napoléon* is one of the world's great humanist documents, "founded upon the principles of tolerance and equity (or fairness)." Not only that: all of its original 2,281 articles could be read and understood by quite ordinary citizens in a day when only Latin scholars had been able to plumb the mysteries of the written Roman law. Stendhal later recommended the prose style of the code as a model for all writers.

The civil code, or *Code Napoléon*, was divided into three books: The first dealt with the individual and the family, the regulation of marriage and divorce, the authority of the father and the adoption and care of minors; the second book dealt with property; and the third, with contracts, mortgages, gifts and obligations. No code since that of Justinian, 1,300 years earlier, had more widespread authority or more lasting influence. It extended unchallenged from the north of Italy to the Low Countries and into some cantons of Switzerland, Luxembourg and those German territories then controlled by France. It deeply influenced law in Spain and, in turn, spread into all Latin America. With modern amendments, it is still the law of France and is noticeably present in the civil law of Puerto Rico, Louisiana and, of course, Quebec.

Civil Code of Lower Canada

The civil law of Quebec, founded on the "Custom of Paris" (as discussed earlier), apart from a tangle of special Canadian additions and modifications—such as the deadlines on marriage for sons and daughters of the *habitants*—had been left relatively undisturbed by the British conquerors. After the union of Upper and Lower Canada in 1841, it became increasingly obvious that an overhaul and clarification were needed. For one thing, the French law on which the Quebec code was originally based had itself been dramatically reshaped at the fall of the *Ancien Régime*.

In 1857, the one-time Kingston lawyer, John A. Macdonald, prime minister of the united Canadas, appointed commissioners to codify the civil laws of Lower Canada (then, officially, Canada East). The work went on for no fewer than nine years. There was one guiding principle: "That the Quebec laws be updated along the lines of the modern *Codes civil, de Commerce* and *de Procédure civile* of France."

This had the effect of bringing the *Code Napoléon* of 1804 into Canada. The main sections of the new Quebec code, officially proclaimed in 1866, followed the formal French draft closely, sometimes borrowing a little from the long-established Civil Code of Louisiana (founded by the Montreal family of Le Moyne). There are some traces of Swiss and Sardinian contributions. And the secretary of the commission once commented that, when the code was being translated, Scottish law terms were often adopted as being nearer the French intention.

Between 1870 and 1879, some sections of the civil code were modified to keep pace with changing conditions and, in 1954, the Rt. Hon. Mr. Justice Rinfret, former chief justice of Canada, accepted the task of a general revision of the entire code. At the time of this writing, the code was still under revision.

The British ascendancy

Martial law

The Quebec Act

"Representative but irresponsible"

Habeas corpus

Constitutional Act

"Double majority" problems

DESPITE ITS late entry into Confederation, Newfoundland has always been an important part of the Canadian sphere, and its earliest experience of European law deserves mention. Our British legal inheritance began there, in the seventeenth century. Following Sir Humphrey Gilbert's proclamation of sovereignty "200 leagues in every direction" from St. John's on behalf of Queen Elizabeth I, haphazard attempts were made to exert some control over the international cod-fishing fleets. After the defeat of the Spanish Armada, there were few to dispute the English anywhere on the seas.

Because shore stations were needed on Newfoundland by the English merchants to dry their catches, some ragged settlements sprang up where every man was basically a law unto himself. In the early 1600s, attempts were made to establish disciplined colonies around the Avalon Peninsula. Charles I brought a semblance of law and order to Newfoundland when, in 1634, he proclaimed the Charter of the Western Adventurers.

The charter put Newfoundland under the care of the wealthy fish companies of the west of England. It stipulated that the first, second and third captains arriving in each harbor from England each season be ranked as admiral, vice admiral and rear admiral. From March to September, these high-ranking seamen meted out a rudimentary justice to everyone, on land or water. This "justice" was based on the English Common Law but highly flavored with self-interest. The authority of the "fishing admirals" was strengthened by both Cromwell and Charles II. This unique form of law was organized into a code under William III in 1699, and re-

mained the basis of law in Newfoundland for a century and a half.

A Court of Justice with the authority to rule over both civil and criminal cases was established at St. John's in 1791, but it was another quarter-century before a governor who presided over the court first "wintered over" in Newfoundland. Responsible government—that is to say, self-government—came in 1855, although it was suspended for the 15 years immediately prior to the island's entry into the Canadian federation in 1949.

On mainland Canada, for the first 30 years following the surrender of Montreal to Gen. Jeffrey Amherst, British rule was almost as arbitrary as had been that of the Bourbons. Following the initial period of military control, the law was handed down by governor and advisory council, much as it had been since 1663.

Concessions were freely made to the great majority of the French who had remained in Quebec by choice; they were never really treated as a conquered people. The first British governor, Gen. James Murray, sent one of his own soldiers to the gallows for plundering a house, and he ordered his officers to raise their hats to religious processions. General Amherst previously instructed that the *habitants*—referring to them as "fellow subjects"—be permitted to settle differences among themselves according to their own laws and customs.

In the older colonies of British North America, the demand for some democratic participation was met by the granting of an elected assembly to Nova Scotia in 1758. New Brunswick won an assembly in 1784. Seven years later, this "representative but not responsible" system was extended to Upper and Lower Canada, provinces that were carved out of the old territory of New France. This was the system that had been established—and found lacking—in the 13 American colonies before 1776. As history showed, it was no more successful in the north.

As the wilderness of western Canada was opened, as dreams of a nation were born and as war and rebellion raged above and below the border, the "unwritten" book of British laws and institutions permitted and encouraged a step-by-step democratic advance.

Under martial law

The British Army ruled in Canada from 1760 to 1763 when, following the signing of the Treaty of Paris, civil government was established. By "Canada" at this time, we are speaking of the former territory of New France—the villages, towns and countryside flanking the St. Lawrence River and the chain of forts and settlements bordering the Great Lakes. As noted before, the citizens of Nova Scotia had won an assembly five years earlier.

General Murray, a mercurial little Scotsman who had been a brigadier with Wolfe at Louisbourg and on the Plains of Abraham, remained in Canada as military commander-in-chief and governor. Murray stationed military commanders at Trois Rivières and Montreal and set up a Superior Court at Quebec. He followed General Amherst's policy in delegating the authority to settle all civil disputes to the *Canadien* captains of militia, who acted as justices of the peace. Appeals could be made to the Quebec City court, but seldom were. Murray commissioned a *Canadien* as senior judge to assist him in civil cases. Day-to-day justice was left in the hands of the remaining *seigneurs* and the local militia captains, much as it had been for a century or more.

Under the British military regime, the law was as strict on the soldier as it was on the civilian. A garrison soldier got 20 lashes for drunkenness and the gallows for theft. Stiff penalties were imposed to stop officers galloping their horses in the narrow streets of the capital. Murray brought in price-control regulations to curb profiteering. It was not until the period of martial law ended that Murray learned from London that his courts had no power to impose capital punishment— too late for those who had been hanged.

Governor and council

The royal proclamation of October 7, 1763, defined the boundaries of the new Quebec, reserving the western territories for the Indians, giving the Gulf of St. Lawrence to Newfoundland, and what was later to become Prince Edward Island was given to Nova Scotia. The following year, Murray changed hats and became the first civilian governor, with an appointed council consisting mostly of retired officers and prominent (and malleable) senior citizens.

French was recognized as "the language of the countryside," much to the displeasure of the traders and contractors who had swarmed in from New England and New York. The idea of assimilating *les Canadiens* by allowing French to wither away would long retain its appeal to *les Anglais*, but the legal history of this earliest period is notable for the governor's protection of the French from the influx of "carpetbaggers" (or profiteers). Murray was particularly hated for his seizure of ships suspected of smuggling. In Montreal, a masked gang cut an ear off one of his magistrates as a warning.

The proclamation gave to the governor the authority to call an assembly, but Murray never did so. He knew that anyone elected to that assembly would have to be both Protestant and a landowner. He realized that this would place his 60,000 *Canadien* charges—the vast majority of them *habitant* tenants—under the rule of a few hundred comparative newcomers. He ruled instead with the advice of a council which held full executive powers but only limited legislative powers. Thus, Murray invented what came to be known as "Crown Colony Government." His most trusted colleague was Hector Cramahé, born in England to French parents.

The judicial system now consisted of the King's Bench for major cases and appeals; the Court of Common Pleas which heard run-of-the-mine cases of medium importance; and the justices of the peace. Murray appointed Capt. John Fraser of Montreal as judge of Common Pleas; through his marriage into the Deschambault family, Fraser had acquired an insight into *Canadien* customs. To some extent this offset the ignorance of Chief Justice William Gregory who knew neither the French language nor any French law. The Court of Common Pleas, which heard cases involving more than £10, came to be known as "the Canadian Court." Murray ordered that *Canadiens* could practice there as lawyers and that Roman Catholics could serve on juries. The power of final appeal was designated to the Privy Council in London.

The Quebec Act, 1774

Gen. Guy Carleton was governor of Canada for a total of 22 years. During his first term of office, 1766–78, he was responsi-ble for the introduction in the British parliament of the Quebec Act. Under this act, French civil law, as customarily practiced in New France, was officially accepted in the place of English civil law, and British criminal law was officially confirmed. Land-transfer documents give clear evidence that the old Paris *coutume* was followed scrupulously in property deals, even when the purchaser was English. Also, eight *Canadiens* were appointed to the Executive Council in Quebec. During his second term, Carleton—now titled Baron Dorchester—fathered the Constitutional Act of 1791 which introduced representative government to the Canadas. In the march to democratic rule, these were legislative milestones.

The Quebec Act extended the Canadian boundary west and south, staking claim to the heartland of the continent. This move infuriated the American colonies, which had claimed the Ohio Valley under

What kind of law for Canada?

TWO OF THE GREATEST political orators of the eighteenth century rose in the British House of Commons in the spring of 1774 as the Quebec Act, deciding the style of law and government for Canada, was being debated. The bill reflected Governor Sir Guy Carleton's view that Quebec should be governed by an appointed Legislative Council (of the leading *seigneurs* and officials) rather than through an elected Assembly like Britain's House of Commons.

Charles James Fox, brilliant 25-year-old Liberal, fought for the beginnings of Canadian democracy with this speech:

"I cannot conceive why we should not give them the law of this country. If we gave them that law, it would be easy to alter it in many respects, so as to make it agreeable to them. To establish a perfectly despotic government, contrary to the genius and spirit of the British constitution, carries with it the appearance of a love of despotism, and a settled design to enslave the people of America. My idea is that America is not to be governed by force, but by affection and interest."

Edmund Burke, Fox's mentor at 45, believed passionately in individual liberty but was also convinced that without a settled state of law and order there would be no real liberty. Burke argued:

"The learned gentleman observes that it is a tyranny to place over a whole people a law they do not understand. But is it not less a tyranny to place a law over them which we do not understand ourselves? Does this House know what that law and custom is which they are going to impose upon their fellow subjects?

"If you are prepared to give them [the Canadians] a free constitution, I should be in haste to go on; but necessity—'necessity, the tyrant's plea'—is urged for proceeding immediately. Let us have evidence, then, of that necessity."

When the dust settled, Parliament passed the Quebec Act as Carleton wanted it. But Fox and Burke won in the long run.

their original charters. Something *had* to be done as there had been no effective system of law at Detroit, Mackinac and on the Illinois River for a decade. An unofficial "judge," Philip Dejean, was sitting at Detroit, trying even capital cases.

Under the Quebec Act, rule from Quebec by governor and an appointed council (of 23 members) was confirmed, with legislative powers somewhat expanded. The Roman Catholic Church was restored to recognized status, and the clergy and *seigneurs* were won over to the Union Jack; New France had definitely become French Canada.

Carleton, like Murray before him, ran afoul of the merchant community which pressed hard for an assembly, and he treated them with all the contempt the "gentleman officer" is said to hold for those "in trade." When the governor showed sympathy for small debtors, the traders raised a petition seeking more rigid application of the law. Carleton told them loftily that if he was to be swayed "by dint of numbers only," then the laws of the country would be made by "the lowest dregs of the people, and the most ignorant among them."

"Representative but irresponsible"

The type of government existing in the various parts of Canada for most of the century before Confederation was a legislative "odd couple." Although part of the lawmaking body in each Crown colony was "representative" (that is, elected by the people), the whole was "irresponsible" because the real responsibility and authority lay in the Colonial Office in London. The British executive power was exercised through an appointed governor or lieutenant-governor assisted by an appointed executive council of prominent men. The legislature consisted of an appointed upper house (the Legislative Council) and an elected lower house (the Legislative Assembly).

Any new laws, or amendments to existing statutes, that were proposed in the assembly had to win the support first of the Legislative Council, then of the Executive Council and finally the lieutenant-governor. Although the bulk of everyday business was conducted quite efficiently through this system, any matter arising in the assembly that hinted at reforms for the people could be easily blocked. In a time of strict social stratification, it was only to be expected that a governor—invariably drawn from Britain's upper classes, traditionally of a conservative bent—would surround himself with like-minded councilors. One governor noted sadly that, "most of the assemblymen eat with their servants." The frustrated and sometimes unruly assemblymen did, however, find ways and means to keep up the struggle toward a wider democracy.

Nova Scotia led the way. In 1758, the year before Wolfe captured Quebec, the Maritimes colony won the first elected assembly in the future Dominion of Canada. Col. Edward Cornwallis, who founded Halifax in 1749, was instructed to summon "a general assembly of the people, with two representatives from each township of 50 or more families." Jonathan Belcher was sent out from London as chief justice with orders to hurry things along. Arriving in Halifax, he appeared in the full wig and robes of Westminster, bedazzling the citizens of the rough naval depot. He went home and informed his superiors there were no persons in Halifax fit to be elected to a legislature.

The British eventually ordered Charles Lawrence, governor of the Maritimes colony, to call an election. An assembly of 20 members took office in the autumn of 1758. Of course, the governor and his appointed council still effectively controlled the colony but, for the first time, ordinary Canadians were taking a hand in drafting the laws under which they lived. Fifteen years passed before Prince Edward Island reached the same dignity, followed in 1784 by the new Loyalist colony of New Brunswick.

Habeas corpus

One of the most vital guarantees of individual liberty, the right of habeas corpus, was introduced into Canada in 1784 by an ordinance of Sir Frederick Haldimand, then the governor. The Latin words *habeas corpus* "You produce the body"), came to be used for a writ—that is, a written order symbolizing the power of the issuer—demanding that a prisoner be brought before a judge and publicly informed of the reason for his detention.

This protection was granted in England in 1679 to guard against the arbitrary actions of the king. It can be suspended only in cases of treason or in times of war or rebellion. The right of habeas corpus was last suspended in Canada during the Gouzenko spy scare of World War II.

The Constitutional Act

Lord Dorchester was nearing the end of his long service to Canada when Colonial Secretary William Grenville, a cousin of the great commoner William Pitt, decided that representative government should be introduced in the swiftly developing lands of the St. Lawrence. The governor and the landowning *seigneurs* were notably unenthusiastic.

In the Constitutional Act of 1791, the great sprawl of Quebec was divided into two provinces: Lower Canada, with its great preponderance of Roman Catholic French Canadians: and Upper Canada, with its Protestant Loyalist English-speaking population. Each was granted a legislature on the model of Nova Scotia's,

with the governor appointing a house speaker or chairman.

Grenville warmly advocated the creation of a Canadian peerage to supply the aristocratic influence and wisdom that had been missing among the "rabble" of the 13 American colonies. Lord Dorchester squashed that idea on the grounds that Canadian society was not sufficiently stable or sophisticated to provide its own lords and ladies.

The British had just dearly learned (in the revolt of the American colonies) the lesson of "no taxation without representation" when they decided to tax the two Canadas £100,000 a year to pay for their own civil government. Laws now flowed from the colonial legislatures, but Lower Canada's civil code remained unchanged except that, for the first time, Crown lands could be granted to all Canadians in freehold tenure.

The first legislature of Upper Canada passed a law to draft every man between 16 and 50 into the militia, it issued regulations for the practice of law and medicine, and put a bounty on bears. Chief Justice William Osgoode set up a judicial system ranging from Quarter Sessions to King's Bench. (*See* Chapter 20, "The lawyer in society.")

When slavery was legal

CANADIANS are usually surprised to learn that human beings were bought and sold openly in this country until the beginning of the nineteenth century. The first antislavery law, passed by the Legislature of Upper Canada, prohibited importing of slaves and required slaves already in the country to be freed at age 25.

The explorers and fur traders of the French regime found slavery rampant among the Indian tribes of Canada and they, in turn, bought slaves for their own use (often Pawnees captured by the raiding Iroquois and Hurons armed with their European guns).

Louis XIV authorized the transportation

of black slaves from the West Indies in 1689, and when the British took over Quebec 70 years later the terms of capitulation allowed the French residents to keep their black and Indian slaves.

The British who settled Halifax, and the American Loyalists who joined them after 1776, brought black slaves with them.

The move toward freedom began when the courts of New Brunswick and Nova Scotia in 1780 denied the rights of slaveowners to regain possession of their "lost property (runaway slaves)." The same technique was used in Quebec.

The British Parliament did not formally abolish slavery until 1833.

Before he retired in 1796, Lord Dorchester's ability to regulate the course of the new country was put to severe test when the French Revolution threatened the very foundations of rational and orderly government. The New York-born Chief Justice William Smith proposed a radical plan for a federal government which would bring together all the "petty assemblies" of what remained of British North America. Smith's proposal was ignored.

The "Family Compacts"

There never was any significant family connection among the elite groups that rose to such great political influence in all of the Canadian provinces in the late eighteenth and early nineteenth centuries. Since the members of the upper houses of the legislatures were appointed by the executive and not elected by the people, it was hardly surprising that the governor would select men from the rather limited supply of respectable, wealthy persons with some education in the pioneer capitals. This provision of the Constitutional Act of 1791 proved to be a major weakness in the new governments.

With similar interests and a common distaste (if not a horror) for the republican style of government, these archconservative cliques were able to ensure that the lawmaking of the legislatures did not imperil their local supremacy, both in social and in financial spheres. They also controlled and influenced the dispensing of all government patronage. Colorful names were attached to these groups by the reformers. In Nova Scotia, the group was called the Council of Twelve; in Lower Canada, the Chateau Clique; in Upper Canada, the Family Compact.

Although opposition to these provincial oligarchies was visible before 1812, the American Revolution temporarily eclipsed it. The explosion came in 1837 when, through a storm of rhetoric and minor rebellion, the message blazed out that the common man of Canada was determined to make the laws under which he was to live. Furthermore, he was determined that these laws would be applied equally to all men.

An insight into the harshness of Canadian law at this period was provided by former Prime Minister John Diefenbaker, himself a lawyer. When the House of

"Let the majority govern"

JOURNALIST-TURNED-POLITICIAN Joseph Howe was the dominant figure in the struggle for representative government in the Maritimes in the mid-nineteenth century. He used the columns of his newspaper, *Nova Scotian*, to attack the arbitrary rule of the appointed Legislative Council known as the Council of Twelve.

When Lord Durham was sent to check out Canada after the minor uprisings of 1837, Howe welcomed the subsequent "Durham Report" in glowing terms:

"The people of Nova Scotia should study it as the best exposition that has yet been given of the causes of the dissensions in the Canadas, and containing the best suggestion for the avoidance of kindred troubles in all the Provinces, that has yet appeared.

"The remedy for the state of conflict between the people and the local executives, which prevails or has prevailed in all the colonies, has two prime recommendations, being perfectly simple and eminently British. It is to let the majority and not the minority govern, and compel every Governor to select his advisers from those who enjoy the confidence of the people, and can command a majority in the popular branch."

Nova Scotia won responsible government in January 1848—a first in the Canadian colonies. Howe later bitterly opposed his province's entry into Confederation— he called it "the Botheration Scheme"— but he eventually accepted a cabinet post at Ottawa.

Commons was discussing law reform in 1972, he informed the members that his great-grandfather in the Upper Canada of 1837 had attended the public hanging of a 17-year-old boy caught picking pockets. Two leaders of the abortive rebellion that flared in that same year, 1837, were publicly executed in Toronto and others were exiled to penal colonies. Every jail was full of rebels.

Lord Durham's Report

The following year, 1838, a shocked British administration sent the Earl of Durham to investigate the situation. His appointment made him in effect Canada's first governor general and his authority covered the entire territory of British North America, including Newfoundland.

Durham's nickname "Radical Jack" was appropriate. On arrival at Quebec he dismissed the Executive Council and replaced it with one representing all parties and factions. After a month in Canada, he freed all but a few ringleaders of the rebellion of 1837.

After eight months, Lord Durham resigned and returned to England. His *Report on the Affairs of British North America*, laid before the British parliament on January 31, 1839, became the keystone of the new Canadian democracy. It led to the union of Upper and Lower Canada in 1841, to the introduction of responsible government, and to the beginning of municipal government. Durham added his voice to the growing number of persons who strongly advocated an eventual union of all the British colonies of Canada.

"Responsible" in this context meant, of course, that executive power over domestic affairs passed into the hands of a premier and his cabinet, all of them elected by the people and required to answer to their actions in the open forum of the elected assembly. It meant that laws could no longer be imposed or rejected by a governor and his clique. Nova Scotia again took the lead by proclaiming responsible government on January 25, 1848. The new Province of Canada (formerly Upper and Lower Canada) followed on March 11 of the same year; then

came Prince Edward Island in 1851, New Brunswick in 1854, and Newfoundland in 1855.

"Double majority" problems

Canada's constitutional history bristles with such awkward and baffling terms as "responsible but not representative." This term explains the situation that arose following the granting of equal representation to Lower Canada and Upper Canada (despite the difference in population) in the joint legislature provided for by the Act of Union, 1841. Lord Durham had expressly warned against this idea, the purpose of which originally was to prevent true-blue Upper Canada from being outvoted by a more populous and French-speaking Quebec. Within a decade, this situation was reversed, as British immigrants swarmed into Ontario. The census of 1851 reported 952,000 people in Canada West (Ontario) and 890,000 in Canada East (Quebec). As this trend grew stronger, so did the Upper Canadian demand for "rep by pop" (representation by population) under the vociferous leadership of George Brown, editor of the Toronto *Globe*.

The clumsy device of the "double majority" was invented in an attempt to soothe suspicions and jealousies. If a new bill before the legislature affected, say, only some part of Canada West, then it had to win majority approval not only of the joint legislature but also of the members from Canada West. The legislature finally reached the state where votes were usually cast solidly in two blocs, thus stalemating the most important lawmaking and reform. Four governments were formed within four years, but no party was able to gain a working majority.

Out of this deadlock, two of the coolest heads representing the founding nations—John A. Macdonald and George-Etienne Cartier, both lawyers—stepped forward. They pledged to work together to bring about the long-sought confederation of British North America. Through their steadfast effort, they proved that honest differences could be submerged in the greater union, with constitutional safeguards for the rights of all.

Under Canadian writ

DESPITE the political deadlock in United Canada—as the capital shifted between Kingston, Montreal, Toronto, Quebec City and Ottawa—much of the framework of the workaday judicial system which would regulate and condition the future federation was laid down. The expansion of canals, the coming of the railway, the export of grain and timber to Britain, the free-trade agreements with the United States—all of these combined to generate a roaring boom in the 1850s. Each new development demanded its own set of legislation. The lawmakers leaned on both British and American experience. The insatiable demand for Canadian sawn lumber south of the border led quite naturally to American investment in timberlands and sawmills along the Ottawa River, a pattern of economic development that would mean gray hairs for Canadian legislators of the future. Trade unionism began in the "benevolent societies" of the times, also owing much to American examples and fraternal associations.

The Reciprocity Treaty, which had taken a full decade to debate and organize, was signed by the United States and representatives for British North America in 1854. It had to be "ratified," or confirmed, by the colonial legislatures—a significant indication of the advance of their powers. Under its terms, most natural products flowed across the border duty free. The result was that Canada's exports more than doubled in volume and, in a single year, hourly wages doubled. The United States canceled the treaty after the American Civil War a decade later; subsequent attempts by Canada to revive it were rejected by the United States Senate. This experience served as a source of much of Canada's early economic legislation.

Canada, a land of vast distances, was affected more than most countries by the railway fever of the Victorian age. Eager politicians pushed through a veritable mountain of railway charters, often recklessly incurring debt far beyond the public purse of the infant colonies, and handed out huge concessions in Crown lands to prospective builders. Many of the latter proved to be mere speculators who never laid a yard of track. Even municipalities were funding lines to nowhere. By 1860, more than 2,000 miles of rail were laid and the "Grand Trunk" was operating from Sarnia, Ont., to Rivière du Loup, Que. Strong pressure was being applied to extend this line to the Maritimes where the first steam engine, known affectionately as Puffing Billy, had been operating as early as 1839.

Following the Baldwin-Lafontaine election victory in the Province of Canada in 1848, lawyers, judges and legislators struggled to keep up with the social and industrial revolution swirling around them. Railways were the first major invention in land travel for centuries, and all movement of goods and people—the very pace of life itself—was suddenly accelerated. Those first years of responsible government saw the introduction of the daily newspaper, the telegraph and the steamship. New Brunswick and Prince Edward Island were connected by cable in 1852. Steamboats chugged along the Red River to the site of modern Winnipeg and, in 1857, the first moves were made toward bringing the fur kingdom of the west into the Canadas.

In 1858, the colony of British Columbia

was founded, with an assembly sitting at New Westminster. Discovery of gold on the Fraser River brought a rush of rowdy miners to the west, but Governor James Douglas, a former fur trader, was determined to block the lawlessness that had plagued the earlier California gold camps. With the aid of his chief justice. Matthew Begbie, as well as 150 officers and men of the Royal Engineers, he tamed the miners and gambling men, achieving that remarkable acceptance of fair-minded law and order that would continue to characterize the Canadian scene.

To raise money for the construction of railways and the development of resources, the provincial legislators had to widen and increase customs and excise duties—those duties imposed on foreign and domestic manufactured goods, respectively. (There was no income tax in the nineteeth century.) Thus, the link was forged between government and transportation that was to become a seemingly fixed element of Canadian public policy, even into the jet age.

Banking and currency were brought under regulation, with decimal money introduced by the Currency Acts of 1853 and 1857. The first shipment of Canadian silver and copper coinage was delivered by the Royal Mint in 1858. The Bank of Montreal had been organized in 1817 on the model of the first Bank of the United States, and was chartered in 1822. The Bank of Upper Canada followed, with 25 percent of its capital supplied by the provincial government. The Bank of New Brunswick was the first to be chartered in the Maritimes (1820); the Bank of Nova Scotia followed in 1832. In the boom of the 1850s, a dozen new banks were chartered in a two-year span; insurance companies and savings societies matched their pace.

As Confederation approached, no fewer than 78 banks had been chartered by the colonial legislatures. Failures and mergers cut down this number and eventually resulted in the modern Canadian banking system. Today, there are 11 Canadian chartered banks, with hundreds of country-wide branches, and about 60 foreign banks. Under the Bank Act 1980, foreign banks obtained chartered status. All banks in Canada are supervised by the Bank of Canada, the Inspector General of Banks, and the Canada Deposit Insurance Corporation. The Bank of Canada issues all currency, manages the public debt— that is to say, it is responsible for money that Canada borrows as a nation—and acts as banker to the government. (*See* Chapter 7, "The role of the bank.")

In the fields of transportation, communication, business, mining, agriculture, banking, labor, urban development, religious observance and education, the provincial legislators and jurists more than a century ago laid down a firm outline of the law to govern a Canada which was only then beginning to develop.

Path to Confederation

To fully understand the special character of law and order in Canada, one must realize that, of all the countries of the Americas, only Canada rose to nationhood without revolution. Throughout the early nineteenth century, following the example of the republicans in the 13 colonies of the United States, a series of rebellions in South and Central America broke the colonial hold of Spain and Portugal. The Canadian colonies grew up within an empire, enjoying the protection and the guidance of the British motherland; even when independence was achieved, they chose to retain the old connections within a commonwealth. It was, in fact, the Canadian example that created the British Commonwealth. It was this steady step-by-step approach to self-government that instilled in the Dominion much of its admired stability and calm demeanor.

Around the 1850s, the French Canadians began to support the principle of partnership, and their more practical politicians began to join the advocates of Confederation. Led by the aging Louis-Joseph Papineau, one group of French Canadians attempted to sabotage the Canadian union—they preferred annexation by the United States. But they failed to gain the support of their countrymen whose feelings had warmed toward the English following Lord Elgin's signing of the Rebellion Losses Bill—a piece of legislation that called for payment by the government for damage caused during the rebellion of 1837.

It was essential to throw off not only the shadows of conquest from a century earlier but also the remnants of the feudalism of old France. In 1854, "An Act for the Abolition of Feudal Rights and Duties in Lower Canada" was passed to bring the old seigneurial system to an end; thus, the *habitant* discarded the last vestige of vassal and became purely a tenant farmer, with every right to become a landowner. The old regime had played its part in nurturing and protecting a distinctive French Canadian society but *les Québécois* had less reason to fear its loss.

The Anglo-French partnership in the Crimean War made a deep impression in Québec. People began to see a better chance for French survival within a Canadian union than within the "godless" embrace of the republican giant below the border. The Sulpician Order of the Roman Catholic Church was a big investor in the railway that linked Montreal with the Atlantic through the Protestant lands of Vermont and Maine. While leaders such as Louis-Hippolyte Lafontaine, Etienne Parent, Joseph Masson and George-Etienne Cartier urged their people to take a more forceful place in Canadian national affairs, immigrant ships crowded at the ports and the population soared. The Canadian census of 1861 revealed a total population of 3,230,000.

Drama at Charlottetown

Once again it was the Maritime provinces that set the stage for the dramatic leap forward. The Atlantic governments had arranged to meet in Charlottetown in September 1864, to discuss a Maritime union. They were prompted by a real fear that the Northern armies in the American Civil War might turn on Canada after subduing the South, to fulfill what many Americans called the "manifest destiny" of the United States to control the entire continent. Also, they did not expect that Washington would renew the free-trade treaty. In the vulnerable Maritimes, these were pressing reasons to seek strength in

unity—even though regional differences still smoldered.

At this juncture, driven primarily by their hopeless deadlock, the statesmen of the Province of Canada suggested that the infant scheme be widened to a federal union of all British North America and they asked for invitations to the Charlottetown conference.

Conditions were ripe and the idea caught fire. A month later, 33 delegates met in Quebec City and, within two weeks, hammered out what are referred to as the Seventy-Two Resolutions. These proved to be the guidelines of a new nation, although it required another three years for the idea to become fact.

The British North America Act

Formerly referred to as the "Canadian Constitution," the British North America Act was passed by the British House of Commons on March 29, 1867, to be proclaimed on July 1 of that year. Today, the B.N.A. Act is still part of the Canadian Constitution but, after patriation in 1982, it was officially renamed the Constitution Act 1867.

The B.N.A. Act did not cover the Canada we know today; only four colonies were united in 1867 (Ontario, Québec, New Brunswick and Nova Scotia), while two decided to stay out (Prince Edward Island and Newfoundland). The other provinces then came into Confederation in the following years: Manitoba, 1870; British Columbia, 1871; Prince Edward Island, 1873; Alberta and Saskatchewan both in 1905; and Newfoundland, 1949. Canada's control over the Arctic islands was confirmed in 1880.

The preamble to the B.N.A. Act states that the colonies had "expressed their desire to be federally united into one Dominion under the Crown . . . with a constitution similar in principle to that of the United Kingdom." This meant, in effect, that Canada's "constitution," like Britain's, would be largely unwritten, following in parliamentary style the well-tried customs fashioned by centuries of British progress. John A. Macdonald had pressed for the name "Kingdom of Canada," but British Foreign Secretary Lord

Derby insisted on "Dominion" so as not to disturb the republicans to the south. The name Canada was selected from a list which also included Columbia, Cabotia, New Britain and Laurentia.

The 147 paragraphs that followed in the complex act gave Canada a federal parliament composed of an elected House of Commons, an appointed Senate and a governor general to represent the Crown. It provided each of the provinces with its own legislature, with a lieutenant-governor to represent the Crown.

Canada now had the full apparatus for making its own laws on internal matters and appointing its own legal administration. Authority to legislate was clearly divided between the federal and the provincial parliaments: the provinces ruled in 16 specified areas, while the federal parliament assumed authority in all others. The use of either the English or French language in the federal parliament and in any federal court was officially confirmed.

The British Parliament reserved the right to disallow measures passed by the Dominion parliament and to amend the B.N.A. Act if it thought it wise to do so. It was not until 1949 that Ottawa sought and gained the right to amend the constitution, as far as federal powers run.

The Fathers of Confederation had labored so well that the system of government they laid down remains essentially the same today—after more than a century that has witnessed rebellion, bloodshed and oppression in many other countries.

Federal and provincial law

"There is no other instance on record," George Brown, a notable Father of Confederation, once said, "of a colony peacefully remodeling its own constitution." It was, he said, an "example of a new and better state of things." The terms were actually written by Canadians; the British legislators contributed only advice, goodwill and formal approval.

It is satisfying to think that the art of world government took a solid forward step in the form of Canadian federation, but it is equally sensible to note that the provinces of British North America, while acknowledging the values of union, still kept a healthy regard for their own local interests. In this balance of interests lay the pattern of the Canadian compromise, another of the conditioning elements of our system of law and order.

It was Nova Scotia rather than French Quebec that had pressed hardest for the separate dignity of the provinces, which the B.N.A. Act provided for in designating 16 specified areas for exclusive provincial

The Fathers of Confederation

The creation of Canada was the result of three conferences held in Charlottetown, Quebec and London, England, between 1864 and 1866. The 36 delegates, now known as the Fathers of Confederation, who attended one or more of these meetings, were:

Canada: Etienne Paschal Taché, John A. Macdonald, George Etienne Cartier, William McDougall, William P. Howland, George Brown, Alexander Tilloch Galt, Alexander Campbell, Oliver Mowat, Hector L. Langevin, James Cockburn, Thomas D'Arcy McGee, Jean Charles Chapais.

Nova Scotia: Charles Tupper, William A. Henry, Robert B. Dickey, Jonathan McCully, Adams G. Archibald, John W. Ritchie.

New Brunswick: Samuel Leonard Tilley, John M. Johnson, Robert D. Wilmot, Peter Mitchell, Charles Fisher, Edward B. Chandler, William H. Steeves, John Hamilton Gray.

Newfoundland: Frederick B. T. Carter, Ambrose Shea.

Prince Edward Island: John Hamilton Gray, Edward Palmer, William H. Pope, George Coles, Thomas Heath Haviland, Edward Whelan, Andrew A. Macdonald.

authority. These areas include education, the administration of justice within provincial boundaries, civil and property rights, the appointment of provincial officers, operation of hospitals and prisons, licensing of businesses and the development of railways, roads and telegraph lines. Even these did not satisfy Nova Scotia and Joseph Howe went to London asking for release. John A. Macdonald, the great persuader, was able to make him change his mind.

It must be noted that while nearly all civil law remained within provincial jurisdictions, criminal law was reserved to the federal parliament. As a result the broad elements of British criminal law were applied to all provinces—with provisions for its extension to those other provinces which would, hopefully, join the federation in the future.

At Confederation, all existing customs and excise laws of the individual provinces remained in force until the federal parliament amended them. The B.N.A. Act established unrestricted trade across all interprovincial boundaries. Also, the government promised that the intercolonial railway "connecting the River St. Lawrence with the City of Halifax in Nova Scotia" would be under construction within six months of Dominion Day.

The Crown (in newly defined Canadian usage, the federal minister of justice) would appoint and pay the judges of all the higher courts, but the judges of the courts of Quebec were to be selected only from the Bar of that province. The federal body was granted authority to establish a general court of appeal and, most generously, "any additional courts for the better administration of the Laws of Canada." (*See* Chapter 3, "Judges and courts.")

The provinces could delegate lawmaking powers to municipalities and counties so that all the bylaws and ordinances—that is to say, municipal regulations—necessary for local government could be proclaimed within a strictly legal framework. Even incorporated companies could be empowered to pass their own bylaws, binding on their own members.

In short, the federal government held the power to make laws in matters of national interest, while the provinces ruled over the matters of local and private concern. What this amounts to in terms of the bulk of the written law is that the Revised Statutes of Canada run to more than 6,000 pages of small print, and the provincial statutes are not noticeably slimmer.

The Criminal Code

At Confederation, the criminal law—covering offenses from treason and murder down to theft and mischief—was placed under the legislative authority of the federal government to ensure uniformity in justice throughout the new country. It was fair that a Canadian should expect the same treatment from his courts, regardless of the province in which he was accused of a crime.

Before 1867, each of the provincial courts had applied its own justice. These courts all operated on legal systems deriving from the common law of England—even in Quebec following an ordinance issued by Governor Murray in 1764, criminal cases had been tried "agreeable to the laws of England." But wording and interpretation varied from province to province; the writing of a Canadian criminal code was essential.

The English criminal law had never been written down. When this task was undertaken in the 1870s, the result was rejected in London but approved, with modifications, in Ottawa. The Canadian Criminal Code came into force on July 1, 1893. It was substantially revised in 1953–54, and sweeping changes were proposed by the federal government in 1984.

Court of last resort

Every province of Canada has its own supreme court and appeal court, each consisting of a chief justice and a panel of other judges, all appointed by Ottawa. Further appeals may be heard by the Supreme Court of Canada. (*See* Chapter 3 "Judges and Courts.")

Even after the B.N.A. Act, which said nothing on the matter, decisions of the Supreme Court of Canada were still appealed in certain circumstances to the

Judicial Committee of the Privy Council of Great Britain. In 1949, such appeals were abolished and the Supreme Court of Canada became the court of last resort. This meant that, finally, Canadian law was completely in Canadian hands. Canadian citizenship, as distinct from British nationality, had been proclaimed in 1947.

International recognition

At the Versailles Peace Conference following World War I, Prime Minister Sir Robert Borden insisted that Canada's contribution to the victory had been such as to warrant Canada being represented separately on a basis equal to that of at least the smaller European allies.

The idea of a British Dominion speaking as an independent nation while still retaining close ties with the mother country was pretty hard for some governments to swallow, but the point was won. Canada signed the peace treaties in her own right and they were solemnly ratified by the Canadian Parliament.

Canada became one of the original members of the League of Nations (forerunner of the United Nations) and, in 1926, Senator Raoul Dandurand served as president of the League's Assembly. The following year, Canada was elected to the nine-member Council of the League. In this way, Canada had already achieved sovereign status in international law before the fact was documented in the Statute of Westminster.

Should B.C. join the rest?

VANCOUVER ISLAND had been a Crown colony since 1849 and British Columbia on the mainland was established nine years later when Fraser and Cariboo gold brought miners swarming up from Oregon and California. The two colonies were joined in 1866, with the older Victoria winning the laurel as capital city.

As the 1870s dawned, the British enclave on the western side of the Rockies, 3,000 miles from the capital of the new federation of Canada, was sorely divided over the benefits or penalties of joining the union.

Could British Columbia go it alone?

John Robson, editor of the Victoria *Colonist*, a pro-Confederation member of the legislature, poured scorn on the opposition on March 9, 1870.

"The Honourable Gentleman tells us that Confederation is unnecessary, that this Colony is one of the richest spots on the face of the earth, with a climate inferior to no part of the world . . . . Why should it not go on alone? And he tells us that his view of the question is held by the majority of the people of the Colony.

"Why, Sir, the Colony has had all this opportunity for fifteen years; and what is the fact? Ten years ago the Colony had a very much larger population than now, and very much larger commerce. Are we, then, under these circumstances, to ask the people to wait and work out their own salvation?

"But, Sir, in addition, we are told in a State paper that we are not to be allowed to hang on the skirts of Great Britain, like a mendicant's child. I can hardly reconcile the position of manly independence with the position of hanging on to unwilling Imperial skirts.

"Rather than that, I would ask for union with the Sandwich Islands [Hawaii, then still under British protection] or with Hindostan.

"British Columbia has tried long enough to get on by herself. After fifteen years' hard struggle, she finds herself worse off than she was at the beginning. Her progress has been like that of the crab— backward."

When Sir John A. Macdonald guaranteed that the Canadian Pacific Railway would indeed reach the Pacific, resistance crumbled.

On July 20, 1871, Canada became truly a Dominion from sea to sea.

Canada posted its first high commissioner (Sir Alexander Galt) to London in 1880 and, following World War I, stationed ambassadors in Washington, Paris and Tokyo. The official Canadian presence abroad became recognized and respected. Today, Canada is represented in more than 150 countries.

"International law" is that wide body of accepted customs by which nations agree to govern their interlocking actions. It is not strictly "law" because it lacks the machinery of ultimate enforcement—short of war. However, it wields a strong hand in many critical areas, including inshore ocean boundaries, fishing regulations, air travel, diplomatic representation, radio and television frequencies and the conduct of blockades and wars.

There is, today, an International Court of Justice at The Hague, Netherlands, whose judgments carry weight at least within the courtroom of international public opinion. The Security Council of the United Nations can invoke physical collective action against a country when war is threatened, but such a decision can be nullified due to the veto power held by the so-called "Big-Five" powers. Although intervention is now more a threat than a reality, this power has been exercised in actual practice: against North Korea, in the Congo and in the Middle East. Canada volunteered to supply troops in some of these limited conflicts.

The Statute of Westminster

Although the B.N.A. Act provided a foundation for Canadian law, it did not confer full sovereignty. This had to wait for the Imperial Conferences, in 1926 and 1930 at London, which declared that Canada had equal status with Great Britain. The legislative enactment of equality came in 1931, when the Statute of Westminster was passed by the British parliament. The Statute also recognized the full sovereignty of the other dominions (Australia, New Zealand, Newfoundland, and South Africa).

From this date forward, no legislation made in Canada could be voided by Britain and no law of Britain was enforceable in Canada except by the express consent of the federal parliament. All Canadian laws were now effective "extraterritorially"—in other words, Canadians now controlled their own external, as well as internal, affairs. This meant, for one lively example, that during the American Prohibition, Canada could prosecute rumrunners who entered our territorial waters, whether they touched land or not.

All of the original Dominions freely accepted the Monarchy as "the symbol of the free association of the members of the British Commonwealth of Nations." Queen Elizabeth II is in actual fact Queen of Canada and her heirs will reign over us for as long as can be seen into the future. It is in the Queen's name that all our laws are passed.

Prelude to patriation

The long struggle to patriate the basic constitutional law enshrined in the British North America Act of 1867 began at a federal-provincial conference held in Ottawa in 1927. (Canadians recently coined the word *patriate* to describe the business of bringing the constitution under Canadian control.) The B.N.A. Act had given Canada self-rule, established the parliamentary system and divided the powers between the federal and provincial governments. But the Act was a statute of the British Parliament and, as such, could only be amended in London. The 1927 conference was called to find a formula by which Canadians might make their own amendments to the Act, in Canada. Failure to reach agreement on the amending formula during this first attempt at constitutional reform appeared to set a pattern that was repeated at subsequent conferences until the early 1980s.

In 1931, the Statute of Westminster recognized Canada's equal status with Great Britain. Even before the Statute was passed by the British Parliament, a second federal-provincial conference had ended. Because the conference had disagreed on how to adapt the B.N.A. Act to Canadian circumstances, Canada asked Britain to retain the authority to amend the Act.

In 1949 the federal government was granted power to amend the provisions of the B.N.A. Act without further action by the British Parliament. That power was restricted, at Canada's request, only to those matters that related to the nation as a whole. In other words, it did not give the federal government the right to alter exclusive legislative powers such as rights and privileges granted to the provinces under the B.N.A. Act. This did not reflect a desire by Britain to control Canada's affairs, but rather the fears of the provinces that the federal government was intent on consolidating its power. These fears frustrated all attempts to patriate the constitution. The provincial premiers came close to an acceptable formula in 1971 at Victoria, but this effort failed when Québec refused to approve the plan.

The search for a workable constitutional settlement became more pressing when Prime Minister Pierre Trudeau made a commitment for "renewed federalism" during the campaign leading up to Québec's referendum on sovereignty-association in May 1980. Following the rejection of the referendum proposals by roughly 60 percent of Québec's voters, Trudeau met with provincial premiers in September 1980. After the failure of this confer-

ence, Prime Minister Trudeau announced that the federal government would act unilaterally (without provincial consent) on the patriation issue. To this end, a federal resolution asking the British Parliament to enact provisions for the patriation of the Canadian constitution was introduced in Ottawa in October 1980. The legality of the resolution was immediately challenged by three provincial governments. It was then agreed by the federal and provincial governments that the matter should go before the Supreme Court of Canada. In September 1981, the Court ruled that the federal government could act unilaterally but, by convention, "substantial provincial consent" was needed for changing the constitution.

The federal-provincial impasse was eventually broken on November 5, 1981, when Prime Minister Trudeau and the premiers of nine of the ten provinces came to a compromise on which they could agree. Only Quebec refused to sign this accord, but its attempts to block patriation failed. The agreement was drafted into the form of a patriation resolution, known as the Canada Bill, which was passed by the Canadian Parliament

Under international law

ONE OF THE FOUNDING MEMBERS of the ill-fated League of Nations in 1920, Canada also took a leading part in the creation of its successor, the United Nations, at San Francisco in 1945.

Under the terms of the U.N. Charter, Canada is expected to respond to any call from the Security Council when the Council decides that military intervention is necessary to enforce the peace anywhere in the world.

When Russia, itself a permanent member of the U.N. Security Council, openly supported a Communist *coup d'état* in Czechoslovakia in 1948, Canada's Louis St. Laurent was the first to advocate the formation of the North Atlantic Treaty Organization.

Canada has helped maintain N.A.T.O.'s standing army to warn off any further Communist aggression in Europe for the past quarter-century.

As it fulfills its voluntary role in international law, Canada is occasionally called "the policeman of the world"—not always in admiration. We sent forces to South Korea (a total of 21,940 Canadians served under the blue U.N. flag), and peacekeeping units were dispatched to tinder-dry areas in the Middle East, Southeast Asia, India and Africa.

As this book was being prepared, men of the Canadian armed forces were once again on international peacekeeping patrol—supervising ceasefires in the Middle East and Cyprus.

Guidelines for a new nation

SNOW HAD FALLEN unseasonably on Quebec City during Saturday, October 8, 1864. When the delegates, their wives and daughters arrived for the conference that would create Canada, they had to pick their way through slushy streets to the St. Louis Hotel. Although fully aware of the portentous occasion, the ladies from the capitals of Prince Edward Island. New Brunswick, Nova Scotia. Newfoundland and Canada (Quebec and Ontario) were determined to do some shopping in Canada's most glamorous city, then the rich timber capital of North America. At Spencerwood, the residence of Governor General Lord Monck, the jubilant lawyer-politician John Alexander Macdonald told his Lordship's pretty Irish niece, Frances Monck, that she would see the foundation of "a new empire."

At 11 o'clock on Monday, October 10, the Fathers of Confederation met in the reading room of the Legislative Council, where arched windows looked down on the St. Lawrence and the Ile D'Orléans. The railway barons of the Grand Trunk, the Great Northern and Great Western were in the lobbies; the railways were to play a large role in turning the dream of union into solid fact. The chairman was the 69-year-old Sir Etienne-Paschal Taché, descendent of the explorer Jolliet: the scheme for confederation was presented by the persuasive 49-year-old Macdonald.

The central Canadians had been actively planning for union since 1858. They had seized the opportunity of attending the Charlottetown conference the previous month—originally called to discuss union of the Maritimes only—to push the idea of the greater union of all that was left of British North America after the American breakaway. The Quebec conference had been agreed upon at a subsequent meeting in Halifax.

It is fascinating to realize, more than 100 years later, that all we know of what went on at the conference is what the delegates decided to tell the country when it was over. The rest is basically speculation. The press was excluded from all sessions and total secrecy maintained. None of the delegates ever published any notes made during the sessions.

The Canadian cabinet met daily, before and after the conference sessions, to orchestrate the whole affair. (The Quebec *Morning Chronicle* had carried a resumé of the proposed details of the union before it started.) After Macdonald proposed a new country from Atlantic to Pacific, there was a four-hour discussion, followed by unanimous acceptance of the resolution.

The second day, Toronto's George Brown proposed that "the system of government should be federal with local governments in each province" and with provision made for the later admittance of other territories. Difficulties arose over Maritimes' representation, Prince Edward Island objecting to being lumped in with New Brunswick and Nova Scotia as a single "Acadian" legislature.

When the famous Seventy-Two Resolutions—the core of the eventual British North America Act—were hammered out and agreed to by the majority, Macdonald's plan for a federal government with virtually overriding national powers had given way to the concept of distinct provincial sovereignty—the system we live with today.

Prince Edward Island and Newfoundland rejected the plan and decided, for the time being, to go it alone.

By the time the conference adjourned on October 27, the statesmen were, on the whole, satisfied. The pattern of the great Canadian compromise had been set. The ladies were more than happy. Their two and one-half weeks in Quebec had been crammed with tea parties, diplomatic receptions, vice-regal dinners and a glittering ball. The smart shops of the city had been looted for the latest fashions, and the wine cellars dug into rock of the city were noticeably empty.

and then sent to Britain. The Canada Bill, designed to bring about the patriation proposals, was presented in the British Parliament before the end of the year. It passed through the Commons on March 8, 1982, and the House of Lords, on March 25. Finally, it received Royal Assent on March 29, exactly 115 years to the day after the B.N.A. Act had become law.

On April 17, 1982, at a ceremony before the Parliament Buildings in Ottawa, Queen Elizabeth II signed the proclamation that put into effect the Constitution Act 1982. The Queen declared to a crowd of 32,000 people that the constitution was "truly Canadian at last." Prime Minister Trudeau, who had sought for years to obtain complete constitutional independence, also addressed the crowd, saying that Canada "at long last had acquired full and complete sovereignty."

The Canadian Constitution

The Constitution Act 1982 includes the B.N.A. Act—now officially renamed the Constitution Act 1867. Since Confederation, the B.N.A. Act had been popularly referred to as the Canadian constitution. The Act, its amendments, and the Statute of Westminster, made up the most important *written* parts of the old constitution. The rest of the old constitution was *unwritten*—a long heritage of the traditions of English common law, embodying Canada's most basic political institutions, legal practices and civil rights.

Under the Constitution Act 1982, the B.N.A. Act remains in force, but it has been revised to include an amending procedure—the power to change Canadian laws without the approval of the British Parliament—which had been the elusive goal of federal-provincial conferences since the 1920s. The amending procedure gives the provinces a greater role in making future constitutional changes. At least seven provinces, representing 50 percent of Canada's population, must consent to any constitutional amendment before the change can be implemented. Unanimous federal-provincial consent is required for any alterations to the status of the Monarchy in Canada or to language rights. The new Constitution also has an "opting out"

clause that enables a province to bar any proposed change, other than rights legislation, not approved by its legislature.

In addition to the amending formula, the Constitution Act 1982 includes these provisions: a 34-part Charter of Rights and Freedoms acknowledging "the supremacy of God and the rule of law"; an affirmation of the existing rights of native peoples; a provision for a future constitutional conference to review issues left unresolved before patriation; a commitment to the principle of equalization (the tradition of sharing wealth among the provinces through payments by the federal government to ensure that all Canadians will receive a reasonable standard of public service); and a strengthening of the provincial ownership of natural resources. The Constitution Act 1982 also lists all past constitutional laws and indicates whether they have been repealed, amended, or left unchanged. (The full text of the Act is printed at the end of this book.)

For many Canadians, the Charter of Rights and Freedoms is the major provision of the new Constitution. The Charter protects the basic human rights and fundamental freedoms that Canadians have traditionally enjoyed. But it goes beyond familiar protections to recognize some important new rights—for example, protection against discrimination is extended to the handicapped under the Charter's "equality rights" section.

The Charter applies to all levels of government—federal, provincial and territorial. Because the Charter is part of the Constitution, the rights of Canadians are *entrenched*—that is, they are elevated above the other laws of the land. This innovation in Canada's constitutional history limits the powers of the federal government or of any provincial legislature, acting alone, to change or abolish our liberties. Entrenchment makes the courts the final recourse for any individual or group whose rights have been violated. In future, the courts will play a key role in interpreting, clarifying and strengthening the provisions of the Charter of Rights and Freedoms, as well as the terms of the other parts of the new Constitution.

2/Civil Rights and Civil Duties

The duties of the citizen 95

How to become a Canadian citizen 100

The two faces of freedom

N O CIVIL RIGHT, liberty or individual freedom, no matter how hotly it might be demanded, can be absolute in a democracy such as Canada's. The reason is simple: if any right was made absolute, it would almost certainly infringe upon the equal right of another Canadian. Like free men the world over, Canadians just do not all think alike, nor do they want the same things. At the core of all our democratic freedoms is tolerance of the ideas and beliefs of our fellow citizens, even if we do not happen to like or agree with those beliefs.

Basically, freedom has two faces. On the one hand, as a Canadian citizen, you have solidly entrenched rights; on the other, you have clearly defined duties. You demand the maximum of personal liberty and look especially to the courts to protect you from any infringement of your rights, whether this may come from government at any level or from self-interest pressure groups like business combines or large labor unions. At the same time, as an intelligent reasonable citizen, you understand that you can only expect to take out of the system what you put into it.

Our elections are as honest as those held anywhere (in a world where democratic political systems are in a clear minority), and our justice is as fair as men are likely to make it. Once we have exercised our rights to speak, assemble and vote freely, and once a government has been selected that truly represents a majority among us, it is our duty to obey the laws which that government makes in our collective name and which the government has a duty to enforce. If we don't obey, we will soon discover just how real that duty is!

This obligation does not, of course, mean that any group among us has to pretend to agree with every law and regulation that may be passed, or with every judgment handed down by the courts. Dissent is the seed of progress. Every legislature has its "opposition." But it does mean that we must all respect the law as it stands, even while we are working and arguing for changes in it. The law of Canada clearly permits us to attempt by peaceful methods to tighten or slacken or even repeal any law. "Peaceful" is the key word in that sentence. You can rent a hall tomorrow night and criticize the prime minister as harshly as you like, but if you suggest in any way that someone should go to Ottawa and shoot him, you will likely be arrested and charged under the Criminal Code.

It would be far from the facts of democratic life to interpret "peaceful" to mean that dissent is restricted to writing a stiff Letter to the Editor. Urban dwellers everywhere have become used to noisy demonstrations in which they see placards bearing slogans that are often impolite if not insulting, and we all hear fiery speeches of denunciation. Generally, few arrests arise from these protests, even when the police encounter some jostling. But there is a line that, if crossed with impunity, would lead inevitably to a breakdown of public order. If Canada did fall to mob rule, one end result would almost certainly be severe repression of exactly the minority groups most given to protest. All the violent revolutions of modern times—with perhaps the sole exception of the American Revolution—have led to some form of dictatorship, the extinguishing or curtailment of individ-

70

ual freedoms and, often, the liquidation of the original protesters.

The courts of Canada have the often thankless task of upholding the inalienable ("untouchable") rights of the arch-conservative, the middle-of-the-roader and the flaming radical—all at the same time. While each one's rights may indeed be equal before the law, each sees the world through glasses of different tint. And to add to the difficulty, the radical who was chanting in the street yesterday is probably the young married suburbanite of tomorrow, with opinions of quite another tone. Age and experience change us all, and we should be grateful that the democratic system allows for this change.

You might say that the law simply cannot win. In the highly subjective field of civil rights, it certainly cannot satisfy everyone. And it does not really ever hope to. But it is undeniable that, especially since World War II, the range of Canadian rights and freedoms has widened dramatically. Or, to put it another way, many rights that have been there all the time, as our major inheritance from Western civilization, have been brought forward in a liberal climate and, for the first time, been given the weight of statute law. These rights, and the duties that accompany them, are outlined in the sections that follow.

Legacies from other lands

The modern concept of *constitutional rights* had its origins in seventeeth-century England, and spread from there to America and France. It was associated with the decline of an aristocratic society based on land ownership and its replacement by the rising commercial society. The absolute power of the monarch was slowly whittled away and replaced with the concept that sovereignty rested with the people. The people agreed to confer part of their personal sovereignty on the government (their alienable rights) and to reserve the remainder to themselves (their inalienable rights).

Following the abdication of the last Stuart king in 1688, certain inviolable civil and political freedoms were guaranteed to Englishmen in their Bill of Rights but were never listed in detail in any legislative document. Colonial Canada received this inheritance from 1760 onward, embodied in the English Common Law that remains the main foundation and bulwark of Canadian law.

The world's best known and perhaps most eloquent statement of the individual rights of the common citizenry is embodied in the stirring words of the American Declaration of Independence, written by Thomas Jefferson and adopted by the Continental Congress at Philadelphia on July 4, 1776. Even allowing for the separate and different development of Canadian law and tradition, the echoes of Jefferson's oratory can still be heard throughout North America:

"We hold these truths to be self-evident, that all men are created equal, that they are endowed by their Creator with certain inalienable Rights, that among these are Life, Liberty and the Pursuit of Happiness—That to secure these rights, Governments are instituted among men, deriving their just powers from the consent of the governed. . . ."

The American example deeply influenced the French revolutionaries who, not long after the loss of Canada to the British, rose against the ruling *ancien régime* of the Bourbon kings. The Declaration of the Rights of Man and Citizen, written by the Abbé Sieyès in 1789, and adopted as the preamble to the first French Constitution, stated that every man had certain "inalienable rights," including the rights to liberty, property, security, freedom of speech and of the press and resistance to oppression. Although there was scant interest shown by France in the lost colony in Canada, its declaration had great influence on progressive thought generally in the nineteenth century, particularly among the Whigs (Liberals) of England.

While it can be said that the concept and development of civil liberties owe a great deal to English thinking and example, the British never pushed the formal constitutional guarantees of individual liberty as far as did the French or the Americans. According to the strict letter of the law, the British Parliament could abolish the Bill of Rights of 1689 at any time. But traditionally, it has always upheld the common-law rights of Britons. This tradition was passed on to colonial Canada. Because of its strong ties with Britain, Canada built its constitutional and political institutions after the model of Westminster.

Although the influence of liberal legacies from other lands runs deep in Canadian history, it was not formally apparent in our constitutional documents. For Canadians, the lack of constitutional guarantees was an abiding concern until our

rights were set down in that part of the Constitution Act 1982 known as the Charter of Rights and Freedoms. Furthermore, this omission bequeathed modern Canada with another as yet unresolved question. Which legislative body (federal or provincial) has the power to modify or extend our civil rights, and provide a final judgment in cases where changes are contested?

Rights, liberties, freedoms

The terms "civil rights," "civil liberties," "constitutional rights" and "individual

The rights of man, *en français*

ON AUGUST 26, 1789—six weeks after the Paris mob stormed the Bastille—the Constituent Assembly of France adopted the Declaration of the Rights of Man, drawing heavily on the U.S. Bill of Rights. This declaration was reaffirmed in the written French constitutions of 1946 and 1958. Its articles state:

● Men are born and remain free and equal.

● The natural rights of man are liberty, property and resistance to oppression.

● The nation is the source of sovereignty and no body of men or any individual shall exercise authority that is not expressly derived from the people.

● Liberty consists of the power of doing whatever does not injure another; these limits are determinable only by the law.

● What is not prohibited by the law should be permitted; no one should be compelled to do what the law does not require.

● All citizens have the right to concur, either personally or by representation, in the formation of the law, which is to be the expression of the common will.

● No one shall be arrested, accused or imprisoned, except in cases determined under the law; all citizens summoned or apprehended by virtue of the law must obey immediately.

● The law should impose only those pen-

alties as are absolutely and evidently necessary, promulgated before the offense.

● Every man is to be counted as innocent until convicted.

● All honors, employment and appointments must be open to all citizens equally, without any other distinction except that of their virtues and talents.

● No man is to be interfered with because of his opinions—not even because of his religious opinions—provided his avowal of them does not disturb public order.

● Every citizen may speak, write and publish freely, provided he be responsible for the abuse of this liberty.

● A public force being necessary to give security to the rights of men and of citizens, that force must be used for the benefit of the community and not for the benefit of the person to whom control of the force is entrusted.

● The right to property being inviolable, no one shall be deprived of it, except in cases of evident public necessity and on condition of a just indemnity.

● The citizens have the right to demand from all their agents an account of their conduct.

● A common contribution being necessary for defraying the expenses of government, it should be divided equally among all members of the community according to their abilities.

freedoms" take on different meanings according to the context in which they appear, but all mean much the same thing. Briefly, our civil liberties embrace the rights to freedom of speech, movement, assembly, association, enterprise and property, worship, voting, and the protection from discrimination on grounds of sex, color, race or religion.

Civil rights and liberties are what the law is about, and they are the basis on which a free society rests. They govern the relationship between the individual and the state and the relationship and interaction between individuals. Governments are temporary, and even dictators must someday fall. Civil liberties must be, in outline at least, enshrined in law, and backed by some guarantees beyond the government. They also must be enforceable *against* the government.

It is because the courts of Canada exert a power separate and distinct from that of government that we can call Canada a free country. (The courts can uphold our civil rights against a government—and they have done so on more than one occasion.) To be secure in these freedoms, we have to be sure that the courts will uphold them when they are being threatened or undermined. Luckily, the unbroken tradition of the highest Canadian courts—inherited from the centuries-old development of British justice—gives us that security.

Charter of Rights and Freedoms

The first advance in setting out civil rights came in 1960, when the federal parliament adopted the Canadian Bill of Rights. The passage of this historic declaration through parliament was a personal triumph for John Diefenbaker, who had been its main architect. (The full text is printed at the end of this book.)

Although the Bill of Rights had the power to override laws inconsistent with its terms, it was applicable only at the federal and not the provincial level of government. Furthermore, it could be amended or repealed by the government.

More than 20 years were to pass before Canadians would see their civil rights formally entrenched—that is, raised above

the laws of the land—in the Charter of Rights and Freedoms, part of the Constitution Act 1982. The entrenchment of civil rights has finally secured them against capricious alteration by the government. (The Bill of Rights is not abolished by the Charter, but will co-exist with it.)

The rights enshrined in the Charter can be divided into the following categories:

FUNDAMENTAL RIGHTS The Charter guarantees protection for the freedom of conscience, religion, thought, belief, expression, assembly, and for the freedom of the press and other media.

DEMOCRATIC RIGHTS The Charter protects the right to vote and run for office, and guarantees regular elections.

MOBILITY RIGHTS Under the Charter, Canadians have the right to live and work in any part of the country.

LEGAL RIGHTS These rights include the right to life, liberty and security of the person according to the "principles of fundamental justice." This section upholds the right to be secure against unreasonable search and seizure, and the right not to be detained or imprisoned arbitrarily. If you are arrested, you are guaranteed the right to be informed why, the right to retain counsel, and the right to challenge detainment. The rules of fair trial are also listed under this section of the Charter.

EQUALITY RIGHTS The Charter bans discrimination on grounds of race, national or ethnic origin, color, religion, sex, age or mental or physical disability.

LANGUAGE RIGHTS The Charter guarantees the use of English and French in all federal institutions. It recognizes the use of both official languages in New Brunswick. It affirms the continuation of bilingual provisions already in force in Quebec and Manitoba. The Charter also guarantees minority language education "where numbers warrant."

The Charter represents a progressive approach to rights legislation that is widely regarded as one of the best in the world. But, some of its provisions pose problems. Under the federal-provincial compromise reached before the agreement on patriation, both levels of government have been allowed to retain limited power to pass laws that may cancel some protections in the Charter. Either the federal government or a provincial legislature can pass laws concerning fundamental freedoms, legal rights and equality rights. If they do so, however, they must insert a clause in the law declaring that it is being passed *notwithstanding*—that is, despite the specific provisions in the Charter. Under the Charter, such laws must be renewed every five years. The *notwithstanding* clause is unlike the "opting out" provision included with the constitutional amending formula, because no province can opt out of the Charter.

The *notwithstanding* clause does not apply to language rights. At the time of this writing, Quebec was seeking to protect Bill 101—its provincial charter of the French language—by another means available in the Charter of Rights and Freedoms. In defense of its language legislation, the province cited a qualifying phrase which states that rights are subject to ". . . reasonable limits . . . as can be demonstrably justified in a free and democratic society." Defining this phrase is only one of the many challenges the courts will have to face when called upon to interpret the Charter.

Division of authority

From Confederation, Canada followed the "unwritten" tradition of Britain. The British North America Act (now the Constitution Act 1867) contained no declaration of our rights, as found in France and the United States, and now included in the Charter of Rights and Freedoms part of the Constitution.

The B.N.A. Act gave Canada's provinces exclusive authority to make laws in relation to "property and civil rights." But, the rights over which the provincial legislatures were given control pertained to contracts, wills, inheritance, marriage, and so on, and *not* what we now call civil liberties. The B.N.A. Act did not clarify which legislative body—federal or provincial—had the power to modify or extend our civil rights. As a result, this ambiguity led to the intergovernmental wrangling that has been part of the Canadian political scene for so long. At this

writing, some cases before the courts were still being tried over this point.

The only palliative offered to this debate in the B.N.A. Act was a statement that matters not expressly the responsibility of the provinces fell within the sphere of the federal government. Now that the B.N.A. Act has been incorporated into the Constitution Act 1982, the power to legislate on civil liberties follows the same distribution of legislative powers as set out in 1867. As a result, the uncertainty over many jurisdictional divisions remains to be resolved through continuing federal-provincial debate. The Constitution Act 1982 went some way toward clarifying these divisions. For example, it reaffirms the provincial ownership of natural resources and gives the provinces greater powers over their production, export and taxation.

Some of the problems in clarifying the debate over civil rights legislation may have been removed by the Constitution Act 1982. A most significant development is the power to amend vague or unacceptable parts of the Constitution within Canada. In the past, some legal scholars argued that neither the federal parliament nor the provincial legislatures were empowered to make *any* laws that infringe on our civil liberties. They cited the preamble to the B.N.A. Act which provided Canada with a constitution "similar in principle to that of the United Kingdom." This was taken to mean that all of the civil liberties which are part of the British constitution (even though unwritten) were also considered part of the Canadian "constitution." Since, in theory, Canadians started out with those rights at Confederation in 1867, no legislature could make laws altering those liberties without first amending the B.N.A. Act. And such an amendment was extremely difficult to achieve. Under the Constitution Act 1982, the power to make amendments is placed firmly in the hands of Canadians.

It was also pointed out that in a political system dominated by the supremacy of parliament—such as we have in Canada—what parliament had done, parliament could undo. To illustrate this point, we can recall that while the federal government enacted the Canadian Bill of Rights in 1960, it could (as it did in 1970) suspend it with the War Measures Act. Even under the Constitution Act 1982, the federal government retains this overriding power. (*See* "When rights are suspended" in this chapter.)

In practice, the doctrine of parliamentary supremacy has been challenged by the Supreme Court of Canada. In an Alberta case (1937) involving freedom of the press, the court declared that since the B.N.A. Act contemplated a parliament working under the influence of public opinion and public discussion, no provincial legislature could, by muzzling the press, reduce the liberty to discuss public affairs freely. The precedent established in that case amounted to saying that there was in the B.N.A. Act an "implied bill of rights" covering the right to free political discussion. Under the Charter of Rights and Freedoms, our liberties are no longer "implied"; instead, they are *explicitly* set forth. The Charter guarantees "freedom of thought, belief, opinion and expression, including freedom of press and other media of communication."

Under the Constitution Act 1982, it appears that, if the federal government or any provincial legislature should move in peacetime to curtail any fundamental freedom of the citizen, the Supreme Court would rule that the freedom concerned was protected by the Charter of Rights and Freedoms.

The court as guardian

Judicial review is the procedure by which courts may be called upon to examine the validity of acts passed by a legislature. In the United States, the Supreme Court has power under the constitution, in any case

The rights of man, Chinese version

IT IS MORE difficult for Westerners to assess the state of civil liberties in Red China than in most dictatorships because of a long generation of tight censorship and the rigid application of ideological programs. When selected tourists began to be admitted to certain designated areas of mainland China in the 1970s, one asked a bright young interpreter about his individual freedoms. "Of course there is freedom in the People's Republic of China," he smiled. "I am totally free to follow the teachings of Chairman Mao." Nevertheless, in 1949, in the first constitution proclaimed by Mao Tse-tung and his victorious Communist supporters, one chapter spelled out the "Fundamental Rights and Duties of Citizens." These have not been abrogated in any official document known in the West. Some excerpts follow:

● Citizens of the People's Republic of China are equal before the law.

● Citizens who have reached 18 have the right to vote and stand for election, irrespective of their nationality, race, sex, occupation, social origin, religious belief, education, property status, or length of residence—except the insane and persons deprived by law of these rights.

● Citizens have freedom of speech, press, religion, assembly, association, procession, and demonstration.

● The homes of citizens are inviolable and the privacy of correspondence is protected by law.

● Citizens have the right and the duty to work, and the right to rest and leisure. Workers have the right to material assistance in old age, illness and disability.

● Citizens must abide by the constitution and the law, uphold discipline at work, keep public order and respect social ethics.

● The public property of the republic is sacred and inviolable. It is the duty of every citizen to respect and protect public property.

● It is the sacred duty of every citizen to defend the homeland, and the honorable duty of citizens to perform military service.

where the validity of any piece of legislation is in question, to examine it and declare it *ultra vires* (beyond the jurisdiction of the legislature) if it infringes the American Bill of Rights or any other article of the constitution. This declaration effectively quashes the law concerned.

Until the Charter of Rights and Freedoms, Canadian courts exercised similar review powers mainly to declare laws *ultra vires* if they were found to stray outside the jurisdictional area specified for the legislature in the B.N.A. Act (now the Constitution Act 1867). In other words, judicial review was used to maintain the division of authority between the federal and provincial lawmaking bodies.

It may be too early to say, but it appears that the Charter of Rights and Freedoms increases the power of Canada's courts, particularly that of the Supreme Court. The role that the courts will play will be defined as judges hand down their rulings. At this writing, no one could do more than to speculate on the future of judicial review. Possibly, Canadian judges will profit from the experiences of their American counterparts.

For the moment, Canadian courts are working to clarify the definition of our rights as they have been stated in the Charter. Opponents of the Charter claim that the entrenchment of rights and the powers of judicial review amount to a transfer of authority from the federal parliament and the provincial legislatures.

Judicial review has friends and critics. It is argued that it tends to whittle away the legislative power of the lawmaking body which, in a democracy, represents the will of the people. It appears to create the situation of an appointed body—the court—being able to interfere with the authority of an elected body—the legislature—becoming, in effect, a lawmaking body itself. This appears to conflict with the basic concept that sovereignty—that is, the power to rule the country—rests with the people who exercise it through their elected representatives.

While logical, this supposition is not really as serious as it may sound. The tradition of nearly a thousand years reveals our law as the servant, and not the master, of the people. In the few cases where the Supreme Court of Canada has "struck down" (ruled invalid) a provincial law, the act in question has clearly run against the grain of the national interest. Following the example of the British judiciary, Canadian judges can also work more subtly, changing the impact or effect of the law through their interpretation of it in cases before the Bench. When our senior judges are ill at ease about a certain statute, and this is illustrated by judgments swinging this way and that, the government of the day will, at least, seriously consider amending the law.

With 11 legislative bodies in Canada—plus two territorial councils with considerable powers—it makes good sense to have an ever-vigilant, impartial watchdog. At the same time, one must not forget that the courts by themselves cannot totally protect or advance civil liberties. It is the citizens who have sovereignty in a democratic nation and it is up to the citizens to protect the rights and liberties which sovereignty implies. John Philpot Curran, the 18th-century Irish orator and lawyer, said it well: "The condition upon which God had given liberty to man is eternal vigilance." Curran's proverb is usually rendered today as: "The price of liberty (or freedom) is eternal vigilance."

When rights conflict

When one set of civil rights collides with another set, which has the right-of-way?

To assert your rights often involves infringing on another person's rights. For example, your right to freedom of speech might conflict with another person's right to be protected against slander. And it is generally agreed that justice requires the vindication of the person slandered.

How about the man accused of a crime? Should he have the right to remain silent? If he didn't, the rate of convictions would probably be higher. Should this right stand above the right of the community at large to be protected against criminals? Many think it should not: a law-reform commission in Britain has advocated that this freedom be curtailed. On the other hand, civil-liberties associations and some lawyers urge that it be maintained.

We speak boldly of the right of a newspaper or magazine to publish without governmental interference, but it is much more difficult to define the citizen's "right to know" or his right to truth in advertising. In a period notable for subjective reporting in the media, the exercising of these "rights" can easily cause collision with other rights equally strongly held. It has been well said that "truth often suffers from the heat of its defenders."

Let us explore this problem more thoroughly. The right of a given person to enjoy his private property frequently conflicts with the right of other people to enjoy *their* private property. Consider the case of the person who owns a lot in a residential area and wishes to build a factory on it: should his right have priority over the rights of other nearby owners who firmly believe that the noise of the factory will limit the enjoyment of their properties? Should the right of a person who owns a suburban lot and wants to build a high-rise apartment on it have priority over the rights of nearby property owners who feel that such a building will reduce the serenity, privacy and attractiveness of the neighborhood?

What about the prospective tenants of that high-rise: should the landlord be at liberty to charge whatever he pleases for rent, or should the right of a tenant to adequate shelter, and at a price that he can afford to pay, have priority?

These thorny questions of conflicting rights sometimes have to be resolved by the courts giving some rights priority over others. Although the court decision perhaps satisfies one set of interests, the losing party is left feeling that he has been robbed of his rights. In recent years, many laws have been introduced (zoning bylaws, landlord-and-tenant regulations, curbs on misleading advertising) in an attempt to provide ready-made solutions. But even if our present mountain of printed law were doubled, trebled or quadrupled, it still could not anticipate half of the variants in our human squabbles.

Arrival of the ombudsman

Since World War II, Canada has seen a tremendous expansion of bureaucracy in the government. Decisions of administrators—faceless heads of departments or even quite lowly officials—were suddenly affecting the lives of millions of citizens. There was no effective machinery for dealing with the complaints which inevitably arose. The rights of the citizen could easily be crushed by the juggernaut of the government's administrative machine.

The Scandinavians answered this problem by creating the office of *ombudsman*, a civil servant appointed to investigate complaints against public servants. Sweden led the way early in the nineteenth century, followed by Finland, Denmark and Norway. New Zealand appointed an ombudsman in 1962, and Britain took up this idea in 1966. In Canada, Alberta was first to take this step, followed cautiously by other provinces. In 1973, the Public Service Commission appointed an official to act as an ombudsman to hear complaints of federal employes.

Although ombudsmen are basically watchdogs guarding against the abuse or misuse of administrative power, their powers and terms of reference vary widely. None of them has actually been granted power to overrule any administrative decision or to compel any administrator to do or to abstain from doing anything. The ombudsman must work through persuasion and publicity, and can only come down heavily on delay, insolence, abuse of authority or out-and-out neglect.

Critics of the institution argue that the ombudsman is ineffective because he has no punitive power of enforcement and that basically he is repeating a function that is, or should be, performed by the members of the legislature. And, again, if the ombudsman's office is given wider powers and a larger staff to deal more efficiently with the "juggernaut" of bureaucracy, it could easily become enmeshed in the coils of bureaucracy itself.

Advocates of the institution reply that scrutiny, persuasion and publicity can indeed have a powerful effect on bad or lax administrators. They go on to argue that members of the legislature cannot devote the time, energy or expertise required to adequately investigate the various complaints, real or fancied, of the citizenry.

77

Our conditional rights

Freedom of speech

Freedom of worship

Freedom of association

The right to vote

The right to a fair trial

Freedom from discrimination

IT SEEMS TO BE HUMAN NATURE that we loudly claim our rights as citizens when we are curbed in some activity close to our own hearts (or wallets), but we are somewhat less energetic in defending the rights of others, particularly those who think differently. Not many of us would state, as Voltaire did: "I disapprove of what you say, but I will defend to the death your right to say it." Even so, most of us accept that in everyday life our precious freedoms—including those guaranteed under the Charter of Rights and Freedoms—cannot ever be total. In times of war or national emergency, just about all our civil rights can be suspended.

Even in a Western democracy, individual rights must be conditional. Under the Charter, the federal parliament and the provincial legislatures retain powers to override certain of its provisions. (*See* "The two faces of freedom" in this chapter.) But, if a government proposes a law limiting some of our liberties, it would have to explain its action clearly and accept responsibility for the political consequences.

The sure result of absolute and unqualified civil liberty would be chaos or anarchy. It is noted elsewhere in this book that your right to wave your fists about ends where the other fellow's nose begins. It is a fine and inspiring thing that our inalienable rights be proudly proclaimed and extended to cover all citizens without regard to racial origin, skin color or religion. Yet it must be noted soberly at the same time that almost all the laws ever made curb our freedom as individuals to some degree. Many are made for that express purpose: for example, your right

to freedom of speech does not permit you to shout "Fire!" in the supermarket if there is no fire or to interrupt a play or other public performance with a string of obscenities.

The civilized person does his best to welcome and obey such laws, perhaps not always with Voltairean fervor and perhaps even while trying peacefully to get one of them rescinded or changed.

He can see only too clearly in some other countries of the world that the alternative to the rule of law is the implacable authority of the dictator.

Freedom of speech

One of the pillars of democracy is the right of the individual citizen to speak his mind, in praise or in criticism, and to attempt peaceably to persuade others to his point of view. As we point out elsewhere, freedom of speech is so highly valued that our lawmakers, as well as certain other carefully defined groups, have the privilege of completely unfettered expression at certain times. (*See* Chapter 18, "What is a tort?")

The freedom of the Canadian press to publish what it pleases without censorship is, in effect, a form of freedom of speech, but it is separately documented in the Charter of Rights and Freedoms. These two freedoms are part of our inheritance of English Common Law and individual liberty. The Constitution Act 1982 formally acknowledges this legacy. Despite their being documented, these freedoms are not absolute.

Sir Lyman Poore Duff, chief justice of Canada from 1933 to 1944, once stated: "Democracy cannot be maintained without its foundation: free public opinion and free discussion throughout the nation of all matters affecting the state, within the limits set by the Criminal Code and the common law."

The legal limits mentioned by Chief Justice Duff restrict both freedom of speech and freedom of the press in the interests of the community as a whole. For instance, common law makes it an actionable wrong to falsely smear another person's character (*See* Chapter 18, "Defamation of character.") Actions that injure the rights of the general public are crimes. The Criminal Code contains sections against the crimes of *sedition* (advocating the use of force to overthrow the government), *blasphemous libel* (publishing attacks on religion that would offend believers), *defamatory libel, obscenity* and *public mischief* (publishing false reports intentionally designed to mislead the law-enforcement authorities). It is also a crime to deliberately mislead the public with false advertising. (*See* Chapter 6, "Guarantees and standards.")

Anyone who advocates or promotes genocide ("annihilation of a race of people") or who incites hatred against any identifiable group by statements in a public place is committing a crime which carries a penalty of five years' imprisonment. This offense was added to the Criminal Code in response to rallies held by the Canadian Nazi Party in Toronto at which speakers preached anti-Semitism (hatred of Jews). In this case, the Canadian parliament decided that it was necessary to limit freedom of speech (and the right of assembly) to protect Jewish and other minority groups from abuse of their civil liberties.

In a time of swiftly changing values, in which part of the population enjoys the publication of material that shocks and offends another part, it it often difficult to determine where freedom of speech ends and an offense against society begins. For example, the publication of obscene matter (that is, selling it or making it available to others) is a crime. But what is *obscenity*? In 1959, a revision in the British law stated that an article was obscene if its effect was to deprave and corrupt anyone likely to read, see or hear

the material. But no one in Britain, the United States, Canada or elsewhere can offer acceptable or convincing standards on what is likely to deprave. And, deprave whom: the clergyman or the man-about-town, the student or the senator?

How to deal with blatant commercial obscenity and *pornography* (the depiction of erotic behavior in pictures or writing intended to cause sexual excitement) while preserving the vital freedom of the press is one of the most difficult problems facing the courts today. The printing of erotic photographs in magazines no doubt causes grave offense in certain circles; it has led to police confiscation of some issues of some publications following complaint from a citizen. On the other hand, it can be argued that reasonably intelligent people should be fully aware of the stock-in-trade of such publications and they buy or read them at their own risk. But the problem comes into sharper focus when it concerns a general-interest daily newspaper. The Toronto *Globe and Mail* published a picture of a Hollywood actor with a girl half his age, both nude, limbs entwined, in a "still" shot from a notorious movie. This newspaper entered thousands of unsuspecting homes, being opened by immature children who would not be permitted, by the widely adopted regulations of cinema censorship, to see the film itself.

The argument of censorship in literature, movies, television and on the stage has been running hot for a decade. Every city has its cinema specializing in explicit ("hard core") sex movies. Lavishly illustrated pornography is usually available openly at your local news-agent, and even in some food chain stores. One of Canada's best-known publishers issued a novel in which a woman makes love, in unblushing detail, with a bear in the Ontario woods.

The Canadian courts have yet to offer a concerned public any consistent lead in this controversial matter. Nevertheless, there is some evidence of a backlash to these excesses. In one of the most extreme public reactions, a militant women's group in Vancouver recently claimed responsibility for an incendiary attack on three pornographic outlets that destroyed one store completely. The attackers stated that they had taken the law into their own hands because the authorities had made no attempt to close the outlets, which were selling pornographic tapes showing scenes of violence and degradation, in contravention of the Criminal Code and the British Columbia guidelines on pornography.

Freedom of worship

Under the Charter of Rights and Freedoms, every citizen of Canada has the right to *freedom of conscience and religion.* This means that he can belong to any religion that suits him and openly follow its teachings—except where they might clash with the law. Certain rites of fringe sects can fall under censure.

As a federalized state, Canada has never had an *established church* (an official state religion, similar to the Church of England in the United Kingdom, or the Roman Catholic Church in Italy). The presence of so many ethnic and religious groups from pioneer times has made this impossible in Canada, although the Anglicans in Ontario and Nova Scotia and the Roman Catholics in Quebec at times enjoyed something coming close to official status.

Before the charter, freedom of religion was guaranteed under the 1960 Bill of Rights and confirmed in provincial codes of human rights. In the past, however, Canada had seen a great deal of court action concerning religious freedom—perhaps more than about any other freedom. When provincial authorities prosecuted minority religions (the Jehovah's Witnesses were perennial sufferers), the Supreme Court of Canada would quash the convictions and "strike down" (rule invalid) the provincial laws under which the charges had been laid. The court had insisted that legislation oppressive of religion, as with freedom of the press, is solely within the jurisdiction of the federal government.

A Quebec act permitting municipal bylaws to order shops to close on church holy days was disallowed, even though the federal Lord's Day Act (forbidding

most business activity on Sunday) may be modified or amended by the provinces. The Criminal Code sets out as offenses the obstructing of clergymen in the performance of their duties, interrupting religious worship and publishing blasphemous libel.

Sometimes none of these clauses or precedents seems to fit, especially in cases where the courts must decide just what can be construed as a part of religious observance and what is strictly illegal. For example, a bitter dispute arose between the Doukhobor sect and the government of British Columbia over whether the Doukhobors were required to send their children to school. The child-welfare authorities insisted, and the Doukhobors refused, on religious grounds.

The case eventually came before Mr. Justice Smith who, in the course of ruling in favor of the province, stated:

"This clearly to my mind involves the claim that a religious sect may make rules for the conduct of any part of human activity and that these rules thereby become for all the world a part of the sect's religion. This cannot be so."

The gist of his judgment was that, however precious the principle of freedom of worship might be, the individual does not have an absolute right to make final decisions unassailable by the state on everything he will or will not do. In short, religious faith does not absolve the citizen from his responsibility to obey the law.

A further illustration arises from the well-known refusal of Jehovah's Witnesses to take blood transfusions. Their objection is based on religious principles. Sincere convictions can, of course, be respected, and no responsible adult can be forced to accept any medical treatment. But the issue becomes complicated when a Witness parent refuses to permit a blood transfusion to be given to his child even though the doctor insists that a transfusion is necessary for the welfare of the child. The law will not accept the parents' objection as a valid right under the provisions for the freedom of conscience and religion. The Criminal Code imposes the duty to provide for the "necessaries of life" for a child under the age of 16, and failure to do so without a lawful excuse is an offense. "Necessaries" covers medical attention, blood transfusions, medicines or surgery.

Freedom of association

The Charter of Rights and Freedoms reaffirms the historic right of freedom of association and assembly in Canada. In essence, these rights derive from the right of the individual person to move freely where he wishes. "Association" is, as a famous law dictionary states, a "word of vague meaning used to indicate a collection of persons who have joined together for a certain object." It also means "an unincorporated society; a body of persons united and acting together . . . in some common enterprise." Basically, the term covers just about every type of group from a Boy Scout troop to the biggest trade union in the country, from a local citizen's committee to a national political party. These associations have the right of assembly—to hold meetings at which any views or opinions may be expressed, except ones that might stir up racial hatred or lead to a breach of the peace. Association and assembly are permitted (and encouraged) in the interests of community life and, in the political sphere, in the hope of ensuring the widest discussion of public affairs and the presentation of all points of view.

The authorities are generally reluctant to interfere with these rights and usually will do so only if the "assemblers" become disorderly or violent, or there is incitement to commit crime. Occasionally in Canada, as elsewhere among Western countries, citizens become irritated, even infuriated, at seeing the police intervene at meetings to ensure the physical safety of radicals who are advocating actions or policies that are anathema to the majority. They liken such activity to handing matches to a firebug so that he can burn down your house. Yet perhaps the greatest strength of democracy is the fact that it can allow dissent, and even attack on its basic tenets, and grow stronger itself from the exercise.

There have been cases where provincial governments have moved against certain trade unions (legally, "associations") dominated by Communist leaders. In one well-known case, the Labor Relations Board of Nova Scotia refused to certify a union because its secretary, who had a dominant influence in the union, was a Communist. On appeal, the Supreme Court of Canada ruled that since it was not an offense in Canada to be a Communist, the Nova Scotia L.R.B. could not discriminate against Communists in this way; it ordered that the union be certified. In his judgment, Mr. Justice Rand observed that "the danger from the propagation of the Communist dogma lies essentially in the receptivity of the environment." (The Communist Party has, in fact, been declared an illegal organization in Canada several times since its beginnings in Canada in 1921 in Guelph, Ontario. It would probably be outlawed again should its leaders revert to openly advocating the violent overthrow of the government.)

The right of assembly is challenged most frequently today in connection with street demonstrations. (*See* "When rights are suspended," in this chapter.)

The right to vote

The traditional rights of Canadian citizens to vote or seek election are guaranteed, although the Charter imposes "reasonable limits" on the voting rights of minors and the mentally incompetent. The Charter's section on democratic rights states that no federal parliament or provincial legislature may continue for more than five years, except in the cases of war or invasion. Even under these circumstances, two-thirds of the members must vote in favor of continuation. The Charter also states that parliament and the provincial legislatures must sit at least once every 12 months. Formerly this requirement applied only to the federal government, but it now pertains to the provinces as well.

There are few requirements for individuals wishing to run for office. The candidate must be a Canadian citizen, either native-born or naturalized. British immigrants have been elected prime minister of Canada (for example, Sir John A. Macdonald), just as a Canadian immigrant has been elected prime minister of Britain (Andrew Bonar Law). The second requirement is that of age; in federal elections, the qualifying age is 18 and this is now generally followed across the country.

No qualifying tests—intelligence or other—are imposed on Canadians seeking office; thus, theoretically, someone who can neither read nor write could in fact be elected to sit in parliament or to fill other lesser posts.

Certain persons are disqualified from holding office, and from voting. These include judges (Citizenship court judges are allowed to vote in federal elections), inmates of penal institutions, persons judged mentally incompetent, and persons disqualified under the various provincial election acts for corrupt practices. The paid servants of any city council or similar municipal body cannot stand for office; presumably, this exclusion is meant to forestall a conflict of interests—for instance, they might be tempted, if elected, to boost the wages of civic employes unreasonably.

Equality rights in the Charter of Rights and Freedoms ensure that religion, race, color or sex can have no bearing on candidature. At the time of this writing, Canada had a Roman Catholic prime minister, Indian and black members of parliament and a female ministers of the Crown; members of the Jewish faith and other minority religions had seats in the House of Commons and in provincial legislatures.

In municipal and rural council elections, there are still various property qualifications. In Ontario, for example, a person has a vote in each ward where he owns real estate, and persons who own no real estate cannot vote in any referendum involving a money bill. In Saskatchewan, to cite another example, a person running for a seat on a city council must live in the city and pay taxes there. Furthermore, he cannot be a businessman with contracts to supply goods or services to the city.

Under constitutional arrangements in force since Confederation, those appointed to the Canadian Senate must be at least 30 years old, must own real estate valued at $4,000 or more, and must not be in a state of bankruptcy.

Mobility rights

Under the Charter of Rights and Freedoms, Canadians are free to enter, to leave or to remain in Canada, and to seek employment anywhere in the country. Although these mobility rights are taken for granted by most Canadians, this is the first time such rights have been guaranteed. Before the Charter, mobility rights were, on occasion, withheld. Some provinces denied employment to workers from other provinces. The Charter still provides that, in a province where the employment rate is below the national level, the provincial legislature has the right to institute programs that favor disadvantaged local workers. For example, Newfoundland has introduced a program that gives its residents first opportunity to apply for jobs on offshore drilling rigs.

The right to a fair trial

We take so many of our freedoms and rights for granted that it is genuinely difficult for us (and particularly for young native-born Canadians) to realize just how rare these rights are in the rest of the world. The right of every citizen to a fair trial, to the *principles of fundamental justice*, is a dramatic case in point. In the age of space travel, roughly 40 years after the United Nations Charter, citizens of some member countries of the U.N. are still being tortured, tried by closed military-style courts and executed by firing squads in public. Others in this modern age of so-called civilization are exiled, or shut up in mental asylums, for nothing more than holding and expressing political or social views contrary to those of the Establishment. This seems almost unbelievable to Canadians who, with almost no riot or bloodshed, inherited a system of equitable justice that reaches back seven and one-half centuries to the foundation of civil rights in England based on the Magna Carta. (*See* Chapter 1, "The rise of English law.")

Chapter 3 of this book deals with the Canadian courts in everyday action. This section will concentrate on outlining the basic rights that protect the citizen from arbitrary or unjust treatment.

Under the Charter of Rights and Freedoms, individuals have the right to know the nature of the charges that have been brought against them and, in civil cases, the evidence upon which the charges are based. A person who is being prosecuted on a criminal charge has the right to be informed of the details of the complaint against him well before the case is due to come to court, so that there is plenty of time to prepare a defense. This principle had its roots in an earlier period of history when it was not uncommon for a person to be tried and sentenced without having any knowledge of it.

This rule is still enforced at times. Back in 1969, a racehorse owner invoked it in successfully challenging a decision of the Ontario Racing Commission which had suspended his license. The owner was under the impression that the commission was merely conducting a general investigation and only realized that he was on trial when he reached the hearing. The Ontario High Court, in setting aside the decision of the commission, declared:

"The commission was acting in a judicial or quasi-judicial capacity; it is required therefore to observe the rules of natural justice, those basic principles of fair procedure which are an indispensable concept and the basis of the safeguards of individual rights."

The press and the law

CANADIAN publishers, editors and newsmen may find themselves in the dock if they break any of the laws that curb the freedom of the press. The Charter of Rights and Freedoms might categorically guarantee this right but, in fact, the freedom is far from absolute.

Writings that injure the reputation of a person ("libel") without bestowing some obvious public benefit can be punished with up to five years' jail.

Most newspapers with a taste for the sensational may find themselves risking criminal contempt of court. This charge will likely be brought if a paper comments on a person, or a case, currently before the courts in such a way as to prejudice the chances of a fair trial, or if the comment reflects in a derogatory way upon the dignity or impartiality of the Bench. Our courts are always on guard against any hint of "trial by newspaper."

In 1954, British Columbia journalist Eric Nicol (an opponent of capital punishment) wrote a column after sentence of death was passed on a man for murder. Nicol pictured himself being tried by God in the hereafter for the hanging of the convicted murder. He referred to the jury as "the 12 people who planned the murder" and to the judge as "causing the victim to suffer the exquisite torture of anticipation." His newspaper was found guilty of contempt of court.

No matter how zealously a journalist guards the sources of any "leaks" and "tip-offs," the law may not allow him to refuse to divulge the sources of his reports when ordered to do so in court. The late well-known Ottawa pundit Blair Fraser was found guilty of contempt of court in these circumstances in a celebrated case.

In the 1970s, the law reached out to curb the "new journalism," as represented by subjective comment in a Vancouver "underground" paper. A decision by a local judge apparently infuriated the editors and they printed an article awarding him "the Pontius Pilate Certificate of Justice ... By closing his mind to justice, his eyes to fairness and his ears to equality (he) has encouraged the belief that the law is not only blind, but also deaf, dumb and stupid." The owner of the paper and the writer of the article were subsequently found guilty of defamatory libel. The court would not accept their defense that the article represented "fair comment."

In civil cases, each party has the right before the trial to be informed of the main points of evidence and rebuttal (this is known as the *examination for discovery*).

Everyone has the right to be represented by counsel, not only when on trial but as soon as he or she is arrested. If a person arrested on a criminal charge is not allowed to contact a lawyer when necessary, any information given while in custody could be rejected as evidence at the trial. Too often, persons in trouble with the criminal law cannot afford a lawyer. As Legal Aid becomes more widely available, the situation improves.

The principles of fundamental justice safeguard the right of the citizen to a fair trial. The first of these rules is that the burden of proof is always on the accuser (except in cases of treason and sedition). In other words, the accused is presumed innocent until proven guilty. Similarly, the plaintiff in a civil action must prove that the defendant actually did the deed which forms the basis of the complaint.

The defendant always has the right not only to cross-examine any witnesses called by the accusers, but also to call his or her own witnesses.

A person on trial for a grave criminal offense must be tried before a jury. For most other indictable offenses (those crimes carrying a maximum penalty of five years' imprisonment or more), the accused can choose trial by either judge alone or judge and jury. The jury panel, consisting of ordinary citizens chosen from the local voting lists, determines the guilt of the accused on the strength of the evidence presented to it during the trial.

Exercising another right under principles of fundamental justice, the accused may question individual jury members before trial in order to exclude anyone who might have grounds for hostility or prejudice. As a legal proverb says, "A fox should not be on the jury at a goose's trial."

Every person has the right to have any charges against him or her heard publicly—that is, not behind closed doors. As the saying goes: it is not enough that justice be done, it must be seen to be done.

This rule involves not only the right to have the trial conducted in public but also the right to have a record, known as *minutes*, of the trial kept.

In certain situations, the judge may order some or all of the spectators from the courtroom—perhaps if the spectators are interrupting the proceedings, or in the interest of public morals. However, he has no power to prevent a record being kept of the proceedings.

The exception to this rule involves children and the law. All social welfare and juvenile courts are closed to the public: one reason for this is to protect the young offender from exposure in the press, although court records are maintained.

Because the onus is on the prosecution to prove its case in a criminal trial, the accused person has the right to remain silent. He cannot be compelled to testify against himself, nor can his wife be compelled to give evidence without his consent. The reason for this is that husband and wife should be able to confide in each other in their married life without fear that they will ever be forced to divulge any secrets. There are actual cases on record in which the person accused of a crime has married the key witness for the Crown for the sole purpose of excluding her testimony.

When a witness gives evidence that incriminates himself, such evidence cannot be used against him in a subsequent trial where he is the defendant; but he must have claimed his legal rights to the protection of the Canada Evidence Act beforehand.

The laws of evidence state that evidence illegally obtained is generally admissible at a trial, but confessions obtained illegally are not always admissible. As the Crown attorney and the defense lawyer thrust and parry in the time-honored *adversary proceeding*, the judge will sit as impartial referee to make sure that the right of the accused to the fairest possible trial is scrupulously observed.

Some legal questions

The Charter of Rights and Freedoms protects your right against unreasonable search and seizure, arbitrary detention, and cruel and unusual punishment. The legal rights section of the Charter begins with a statement that guarantees your right to life, liberty and security of person. Under its provisions, you are presumed innocent until proven guilty and you must be tried within a reasonable time. Bail cannot be denied without just cause, and the accused has the right to an interpreter.

This section of the Charter raises some questions for the future because its terms still have to be legally defined. The courts will have to decide, for example, what punishments are "cruel and unusual." Another question arises from the statement guaranteeing your right to life, liberty and security of person. At the time of this writing, the abortion issue was before the courts, which would have to decide, among other matters, when a fetus begins to live and when it obtains legal rights.

Under the Charter, you may not be detained in an arbitrary manner, which implies that an officer must show "reasonable" cause for arresting an individual. This clause protects you, but the term "reasonable" is likely to come under the legal microscope. It will be up to the courts to ensure that law enforcement agencies do not become too powerful. Another phrase in this section of the Charter—"to be tried within reasonable time"—may cause legal headaches. In future, the courts might have to start setting deadlines for trials.

Freedom from discrimination

Under the Charter of Rights and Freedoms, equality guidelines come into force in April 1985. The Charter states your right to protection against discrimination on the grounds of race, national or ethnic origin, color, religion, sex, age or mental or physical disability. The three-year delay in implementing equality rights was designed to let the federal and provincial governments alter laws that might conflict with this section of the Charter.

Canadian law—both provincial and federal—was not always so liberal. In the late nineteenth century and the early part of the twentieth, the British Columbia government passed legislation forbidding Chinese from residing in the province and from working at certain jobs. These laws were struck down as being unconstitutional by the Supreme Court of Canada. It ruled that these acts related to naturalization and citizenship which are within the exclusive power of the federal government. In spite of the fact that a great many Chinese and Japanese living in British Columbia were naturalized citizens, they were not allowed to vote—and that law, incidentally, was upheld by the British Privy Council in the days when it was Canada's highest court of appeal. In 1949, British Columbia repealed the law and, in fact, became the first province in Canada to allow native Indians to vote.

The most notorious case of racial discrimination in Canadian history was the wholesale roundup and relocation by the federal government of persons of Japanese descent during World War II. Regardless of the fact that they were Canadian citizens, they were removed forcibly from all areas close to the Pacific coast and their property was expropriated and sold at fire-sale prices.

Until the 1950s, the law still tolerated practices that prevented the sale of land to certain races. In a famous case, the Supreme Court of Ontario and that province's Court of Appeal had both upheld the right of a property owner to dispose of his property as he wished. A Jewish man wanted to purchase a residential property that was for sale, but the owner had acquired it under a "restrictive covenant" in his deed which forbade him to sell to Jews or blacks. The case was taken to the Supreme Court of Canada which reversed the decisions and ruled that such *restrictive covenants* were unenforceable.

The Charter's antidiscrimination listing has broken new ground by adding the categories of sex, age and disability. The Charter makes clear that, for women, legal equality is an existing state and not a right to be acquired. Its provisions will allow special assistance for the creation of equal opportunity programs for women.

Some of these new rights may raise legal questions. The rights of the aged, for example, may be delayed until legislators have grappled with such problems as mandatory retirement. Under the Charter, there are provisions for the establishment of programs for the disabled and for laws ensuring that these programs will be upheld. But, in this instance, the courts have yet to decide whether inaccessibility to public buildings and services is unduly discrimatory, and whether governments are financially responsible for correcting these problems.

The right to hold property
Although this freedom is not enshrined in the Charter of Rights and Freedoms, no right is more strongly defended in Canadian law than the right to hold and enjoy private property. (*See* Chapter 14, "Rights and obligations.") Even a convict serving life imprisonment in Canada is allowed to own property. As a general rule, where property rights have come into conflict with some other civil rights, it is the other rights that have given way. Here is one basic point of division between our way of life, our political and economic system, and that of Communist countries. Nevertheless, the many regulations which control our economic system are always limiting some aspects of our property rights.

The word "property" means anything to which ownership can be attached: a department store, the suburban house or condominium, your car or the book you are now holding. It also includes such things as money, stock in a company, copyrights, patents or future royalties. Ownership can be outright (total), partial (shared with others) or conditional (such as some condition being satisfied before eventual inheritance). It can also consist of an interest in someone else's property—such as the right to take gravel from another's land.

The 1960 Bill of Rights, although a federal document, still provides a legally acceptable summary of the law of property in all of the provinces. It states that there exists the "right of the individual to . . . enjoyment of property and the right not to be deprived thereof except by due process of law." Some 100 sections of the Criminal Code deal with "Offenses

Against Rights of Property"; these include such crimes as theft and breaking and entering. In addition, the property owner has many civil remedies against those who deprive him of his property, or damage it, in any way. (*See* Chapter 18, "Trespassing prohibited.")

Your right to privacy ensures that no one is allowed to enter your land unless he has your permission or has lawful authority. That "no one" includes your chief of police and your prime minister.

Nevertheless, even the right to hold and enjoy private property is restricted by the law. You cannot drive your automobile exactly as you please—you must obey the rules of the road and keep your vehicle in a safe condition. You may own a house but your "enjoyment" of it will be restricted by zoning bylaws, pollution laws, wiring and plumbing standards and fire regulations, and your lot is always subject to *expropriation*—being taken over by the state for some public purpose, such as a highway, a school or an airport. However, property cannot be expropriated until the owner has been given the opportunity of a fair hearing, and the owner will be compensated for its loss (the amount will usually be somewhat higher than the property's true market value in order to compensate "for hardship").

Your right to own weapons is strictly controlled. You need a firearms acquisition certificate to own a firearm. (The definition of firearms is so broad that it may even encompass target pistols.) You can own a set of golf clubs, but you are advised not to play chip shots into your neighbor's rosebed. Possession of certain drugs and explosives is forbidden to the citizen unless he can demonstrate a legal need for that property.

The right to welfare
Canada is an affluent country—compared to most of its fellow members of the United Nations—and upholds the principle that everyone has a right to a reasonable standard of living. If a family cannot keep itself at that standard from its own resources, the state steps in. This is not a traditional right (like, for example, free-

dom of speech), or is it enshrined in the Charter of Rights and Freedoms; nevertheless, it is comfortingly real all the same.

If a wage earner becomes ill, or loses his or her job, and unemployment-insurance benefits run out, he or his family can be left without money for basic necessities, like food or rent. Caught in such straits, he can apply for assistance to the welfare department of the municipality where he lives. (*See* Chapter 14, "The welfare system.") Welfare assistance is based on need; the amount granted depends on the income (if any) of the family, size of the family and ages of any children.

Federal funds are made available through the Canada Assistance Plan to any province that has passed welfare-assistance legislation directed to aid "persons in need." A "person in need" is one "who by reason of inability to obtain employment, loss of the principal family provider, illness, disability, age, or other cause of any kind acceptable to the provincial authority is found to be unable to provide adequately for himself, or his dependants." It is a wide and generous definition. Provinces are not prevented, however, from setting residency requirements for certain social and welfare benefits.

Some provincial acts entrench the rights to welfare in written law. For example, the Ontario Family Benefits Act states that "an allowance *shall* . . . be provided," and the General Welfare Assistance Act states "a municipality *shall* provide assistance." The municipalities, which usually handle the actual payments, cannot decide to turn off the welfare tap without proper reason. On a much wider stage, but bringing some moral weight to bear everywhere, the Universal Declaration of Human Rights of the United Nations provides, in Article 22:

"Everyone, as a member of a society, has the right to social security and is entitled to realization through national effort and international cooperation . . . to the economic, social and cultural rights indispensable for his dignity and the free development of his personality."

These idealistic views contrast sharply with the popular notion that just about everyone who cannot provide for himself is lazy or prefers drinking beer to caring for himself or his family. No doubt this is true enough for a fraction of welfare cases, but the majority do not abuse this right to social security. The Manitoba Department of Community Services and Corrections summed up the situation in the following words:

"What concerns society is that a large group of the people are drawing public aid because they are improvident, lazy, dishonest, or irresponsible. It is easy to accept the fact that the death of a breadwinner, or his disability, or his age, or even his incarceration in jail is a justifiable reason for providing support for the dependents involved. It is much more difficult for the public to accept the need for support when the dependency is caused because of the desertion, alcoholism, irregular employment or lack of initiative in job seeking, job holding and other apparently irresponsible behavior."

Everyone who meets the qualifications has the right to call upon the extensive range of tax-supported benefits that constitute social security. These include: medical and hospital insurance, unemployment insurance, family allowances, pensions at age 65, old-age assistance, pensions at 18 years of age for the blind or disabled, child welfare and protection, mothers' allowances, medical and dental care for the needy, subsidized housing for low-income families and for the aged, plus nursing homes and convalescent hospitals for the aged and infirm.

No one has a statutory right to the many private welfare services that supplement the government-sponsored ones; however, these are almost all available on the basis of need—although some are designed to serve only persons of a particular religious, age or ethnic group. They include: care and rehabilitation of the physically handicapped, health clinics and home nursing, family counseling, foster care and adoption of children, youth clubs and camps, rehabilitation of prisoners, housing for the homeless, disaster relief, and emergency supplies of food, clothing and furniture.

When rights are suspended

OST OF THIS CHAPTER, and much of this book, is concerned with the rights and duties of the Canadian citizen under the laws as they exist in normal peaceful times. But when violence stalks the streets or the security of the nation is threatened, these laws may be replaced by a completely different set of edicts. Even the threat of such a crisis, as seen by reasonable men, can be enough to sweep aside temporarily many of the individual freedoms we have discussed. Canada saw this happen in 1970 when the federal government moved dramatically against a suspected conspiracy among Quebec "separatists" to take over that province by violent means.

The imposition of any draconian laws that shackle civil liberties will always arouse indignation among those particularly sensitive to the rights of the individual, as well as bitter opposition from those who are directly affected by the measures. It can be said confidently that most Canadians regard all repressive regulation with distaste, if not abhorrence, and are distressed when those in authority find it necessary to put it to use. But it must also be said that in the example mentioned above, a substantial majority in the nation approved the federal action; support for this legal, if arbitrary, action was particularly strong in Quebec itself, where the voters in the following federal election returned an overwhelming number of government candidates.

Democracy often appears to sleep, but it is armed with ample powers to strike down those who would take the law into their own hands, irrespective of their political, sectarian or class labels. These powers range from the imposition of cur-

few (an order that certain persons stay off the streets during certain times, usually the hours of darkness), to prosecution for creating a disturbance, unlawful assembly, unlawful picketing in labor strife, to laying criminal charges of riot, treason and sedition, and to the proclamation of the War Measures Act.

Lawlessness during strikes

The right of workers to strike and to picket when not bound by a collective agreement (a contract between the employer and the union, the certified bargaining agent of the employes) is discussed later in this book. (*See* Chapter 12, "Strikes and lockouts.") However, these rights can be suspended if violent or illegal means are adopted by the strikers in their attempts to "persuade" others from entering the business premises, or in their efforts to cause economic loss to the uncooperative employer. In a strike that is itself illegal, there can be no legal right to picket.

The instrument used against unlawful picketing is normally the injunction, granted to the employer by a judge until the issue can be resolved within the regular machinery of labor legislation. Refusal to obey an injunction (which can be seen as a temporary law) will usually earn the transgressor a "vacation" behind bars. In the summer of 1976, a judge of the Supreme Court of British Columbia granted the school trustees of Nanaimo an injunction forbidding the parents of some pupils to picket schools where nonteaching staff had been on strike, legally, for several months.

At stake are the economic interests of the contesting parties. On a broader scale the issue is, how far can the right of one individual or group be extended before it comes into conflict with the rights of others? Should the right of a group of workers to strike have priority over the right of the employer and the shareholders of the company to make use of their property as they see fit, and—in some instances—the right of the public at large not to be deprived of goods and services that may be essential? When a strike continues for a long time and no compromise is in sight, and the general public is being deprived of vital goods and services, the government will probably intervene and enact back-to-work legislation; the federal government has taken this action, for example, in strikes by railway employes and by air-traffic controllers. The question of intervention always is how to balance the often opposing interests and rights of the employer, the public and the worker.

Workers in some essential services in certain provinces do not have the right to strike; these include members of police forces and fire departments, and hospital workers in some jurisdictions.

In picketing, the line must be drawn between the kind of action that amounts to a blockade and that which involves only the peaceful persuasion of persons not to do business or work for the establishment concerned. Clearly, the right to picket does not include preventing access to someone's property, either through the use of large numbers of pickets or by any other means; nor does it include the right to molest anyone.

Until 1951 in Canada, anyone who participated in a picket line (even peaceful "informational" picketing) could be charged with the crime of *watching and besetting*. (*See* Chapter 19, "Offenses against the person.") This was overturned by the Supreme Court of Canada in a landmark decision known as the "Aristocratic Restaurants case." A company operated five restaurants in Vancouver, but only one had a union certified as bargaining agent for its employes. The other restaurants were not unionized. In the course of a legal strike, the workers from the unionized establishment picketed three of the five restaurants and the owner brought an action against the union based on the tort of nuisance. (*See* Chapter 18, "Trespassing prohibited.")

The case went all the way to the Supreme Court of Canada where it was decided that the union had committed no tort ("civil wrong") merely by picketing the restaurants. Even though the strikers had not been charged with the crime of watching and besetting, the court took it upon itself to issue a statement on that offense. It ruled that anyone who attempted to justify a charge of watching and besetting in those circumstances would first have to prove that some wrongful act had been committed in the course of the picketing. This ruling generally put an end to the prosecution of picketers for watching and besetting.

Many weapons still remain, however, to curb illegal action during strikes. The owner of property being picketed can usually obtain an injunction if he can show that a wrongful act has been or is being committed in the course of the picketing. Such wrongful acts have included: the inducement of a breach of contract by the presence of the picket line; the furtherance of a conspiracy to commit a wrongful act; picketing in conjunction with an illegal strike; mass picketing; the commission of a criminal offense by a picketer; and blockade picketing.

The injunction, of course, imposes no penalty of itself, but anyone who disobeys it can be charged with contempt of court. The whole array of the law, both criminal and civil, is ready to clobber anyone who resorts to violence or other illegality during labor strife.

Causing a disturbance

The individual's rights of freedom of speech and of assembly can be swiftly cut off if the police consider they have reasonable grounds to lay a charge of *causing a disturbance*. This offense can be committed by one or any number of persons. In formal definition, it is committed whenever anyone who, not being in a dwelling house, causes a disturbance in or near a public place by fighting, screaming, shouting, swearing, singing, using insulting or obscene language, or impeding or molesting other persons.

A conviction will usually follow if the magistrate agrees that the act was likely to disturb the public at large. In other words, it is not necessary for the police to prove that any persons in particular were disturbed, but only to show that the conduct in question could reasonably have caused a disturbance. A very surprised young man was convicted on this charge for shouting "Traitor Trudeau" at a Liberal Party picnic.

Disturbing the peace is a summary conviction offense under the Criminal Code, meaning that it can be dealt with by a magistrate (or provincial judge) alone with minimum formality. A grave disturbance, or repeated disturbances, can bring a fine of $500, six months' impris-

onment in a provincial jail, or both. If the disturber was merely "sounding off" while intoxicated, he would probably be charged with the less serious offense of being *drunk in public*, for which he might be either "bound over" (set free with a warning), or given the option of paying a $25 fine or spending 30 days in jail.

Unlawful assembly

Whereas one or more persons can cause a disturbance, in legal terminology, the offense of *unlawful assembly* requires three or more persons. Three individuals are courting arrest if they cause persons nearby to fear, on reasonable grounds, that they will disturb the peace "tumultuously." The offense also applies to three

Blue pencil and scissors

CENSORSHIP, to some, is a suspension of the right of free speech, no matter how lurid the material. To others, it is a last-ditch defense against general depravity. In a serious study, *Pornography and Obscenity*, D. H. Lawrence wrote, "What is pornography to one man is the laughter of genius to another."

Lawrence, author of *Lady Chatterley's Lover*, was no stranger to the edicts of the censor and he died (1930) long before the general public read his earthy works in uncut editions. He probably would not have believed that the *cinéma vérité* of the 1970s would include a production of his *Women in Love* in which famous actresses and actors appeared together in the nude.

The 50-year span between tight censorship and "anything goes" was marked by some remarkable official decisions:

In 1935, Britain's Attorney General, Sir Thomas Inskip, stated about a novel: "This book deals with what everybody will recognize as an unsavory subject—the gratification of sexual appetite."

In 1939, before any film shown in the United States was approved for general exhibition, it had to be free of the following words: broad, chippie, fairy, hot (applied

to a woman), pansy, tart, tomcat (applied to a man) and whore. That same year, the Ontario censor cut the following line of dialogue from a movie: "You can't trust them English."

In 1957, in an obscenity action against a magazine in Australia, the prosecutor complained that actress Jayne Mansfield was depicted on the cover with dyed hair. It was a common thing among prostitutes, he averred, to dye their hair.

Also in 1957, an official of the British Customs Department (responsible for some aspects of censorship) gave evidence that photographs of the nude body would not be officially obscene unless they were "in the common phrase, portrayed 'warts and all.'" The body photographed from the rear was not obscene; from the front it was definitely so.

In 1966, the British stage censor ordered that female members of a cast must at no time "appear in any costume which consists of less than briefs and an effectively controlling brassiere."

By the 1980s, things had got to the point where films including nude love scenes were being piped into hotel bedrooms across the land.

or more persons who provoke others to disturb the peace tumultuously. (The law does not define the term "tumultuously," but the dictionary defines a "tumult" as a violent disturbance, outburst or disorder.) The law is written in vague terms—no doubt deliberately so—and it catches a variety of activities in its net. Dissenters argue that the charge of unlawful assembly is used to break up protest demonstrations; others may wish it was used more often for that purpose.

According to the legal definition of unlawful assembly, there must be "three or more persons engaged in carrying out a common purpose." On a noisy occasion, this phrase might catch an innocent bystander who had just stopped off to watch the fun. The police attempting to break up an assembly cannot always tell the bystander from the participant. If you don't want to risk becoming involved in an unlawful assembly, you should not hang around a gathering that looks as though it's going to become one.

If, on the other hand, you do become seriously involved and if you believe the police acted without justification, remember that damage suits or criminal charges can be brought against a policeman in the same way as they can against any other citizen. Charges could include assault and battery, false arrest and false imprisonment.

Reading the "Riot Act"

The main difference between unlawful assembly and *riot* is that the first only raises the threat of tumult, whereas the riot has graduated from the unlawful-assembly stage into the stage of tumult ("violent disorder"). The police are probably already on the scene and, as they move in to restore the peace, they will not be fretting a great deal about the civil rights of the rioters. "First things first" will be the order of the moment, and that means stopping the riot.

When 12 or more persons are rioting, the sheriff, mayor or a justice of the peace may go to the place where the riot is occurring and order the crowd to disperse. He will do this by reading what has come to be known as the "Riot Act." In reality, there is no such act. What is read is the following proclamation from the Criminal Code:

"Her Majesty the Queen charges and commands all persons being assembled immediately to disperse and peaceably to depart to their habitations or to their lawful business upon the pain of being guilty of an offense for which, upon conviction, they may be sentenced to imprisonment for life."

Yes, *imprisonment for life!* And the same goes for anyone who hinders, opposes or attacks the official trying to read the proclamation. Thirty minutes is the maximum time permitted for dispersal after the "Riot Act" has been read.

A mob running wild is an awesome, never-to-be-forgotten sight, with enormous potential for damage and danger. Officialdom must always move relentlessly to halt it.

The street demonstration

The criminal offenses of unlawful assembly, rioting and sedition are aimed at the suppression either of a violent demonstration, or of a demonstration that is likely to end in violence. These laws place limits on the liberty to assemble freely and speak freely when the likely result is a disturbance of the peace, whether it be the peace of the immediate neighborhood or the peace of the whole nation. These laws were drafted, of course, before the street demonstrations and confrontations the late 1960s and which are still, in smaller measure, with us today.

Organizing and holding a peaceful demonstration in a public place is a perfectly valid way to exercise your basic freedoms of assembly and speech. However, you may not exercise this freedom to the extent that you are infringing on the rights of others who wish to go about their normal business unimpeded and in safety. Protest rallies and marches almost always bring police into close contact with demonstrators. Even trivial incidents can lead to riotous behavior when emotions are aroused.

Municipal bylaws will usually have something to say about how the streets must be used. We have the right to walk and travel on the highways but not necessarily to "assemble"—to hold a meeting—on them. In almost every municipality in Canada, as elsewhere, the police commission or chief of police has the power to determine the time and the route of marches. These bylaws exist to prevent traffic tie-ups, but some protest organizers argue they are aimed at robbing demonstrations of their potency. Most rallies, they say, are conducted for the purpose of communication and persuasion and, if a march is shunted into the back streets, its aim is largely defeated. In London, England, the cradle of our liberty, no leaflets may be distributed within six miles of Charing Cross without police permission, and government permission is required to make a speech in Trafalgar Square.

It is not difficult to make out a case that an assembly of hundreds, or even thousands, of demonstrators, no matter how peaceful at any given moment, contains potential for violence. And there are usually enough hotheads in such a crowd that police can lay charges of disturbing the peace against individual demonstrators. With the hotheads sparking the crowd, the threat of violence rises.

No one has the right to participate in a demonstration that involves violence, or that is likely to become violent. Yet everyone has the legal right to engage in peaceful, public demonstrations. Democracy must be served and civil liberties respected; but the rule of law must be upheld, public order must prevail. This conflict of interests had not been clearly resolved by the mid-1970s. In 1976, protesting farmers threw milk and butter over a cabinet minister outside the House of Commons, then set fire to benches and trees. Some of the protesters were later charged.

Sedition

A major curb on freedom of expression in Canada—as in every country with a legacy of English law—is contained in the offense known as *sedition*. It is a crime for anyone to teach or advocate, or publish or circulate any writing that advocates the use of force as a means of

---

Ladies on the judgment seat

STATUS OF WOMEN CANADA, established in 1971, reported that over half the women in Canada were active in the labor force, but only about four percent were in managerial positions. Women in Canada were far from getting a fair deal when top appointments were being handed out.

Prime Minister Trudeau gave moral support. "It can be said with certainty that our society would not now be as it is if, in the course of the last half century, women had occupied a larger number of positions in government and industry."

Trudeau's administration made a start by elevating several women to the Bench. Bertha Wilson was appointed to the Supreme Court of Canada; Réjane Laberge-Colas and Claire Barrette-Joncas were named to the Superior Court of Quebec; Mabel van Camp and, later, Janet Boland were appointed to the Supreme Court of

Ontario; and Constance Glube was appointed Chief Justice of the Supreme Court of Nova Scotia. Mme Pierre Laporte, widow of the assassinated Quebec labor minister, became a judge of the Citizenship Court.

Other important appointments have included: Monique Bégin, Minister of Health and Welfare; Judy Erola, Minister of State (Mines) and Minister responsible for the Status of Women; Dr. Sylvia Ostry, Head of the Economics and Statistics Department of the Organization of Economic Cooperation and Development in Paris; and Mme Jeanne Sauvé, Governor General of Canada.

If Canadian women still feel they get a raw deal, they can take heart from the examples of the prime ministers of India, Sri Lanka (Ceylon), Iceland, and Great Britain: they all are women.

accomplishing governmental change. What this means, in effect, is that no person can preach the overthrow of parliament or any legislature by violence.

This crime carries a maximum penalty of imprisonment for 14 years. The same penalty applies not only to those who preach, or advocate, the use of force to change a government, but also to persons (two or more) who conspire (that is, plan, agree, or attempt) to do so. This was the crime that cost Guy Fawkes and his fellow conspirators their lives when they were caught trying to blow up the British Houses of Parliament in 1605.

You will not be held guilty of sedition if you argue publicly that the whole caboodle of politicians should be run out of Ottawa on a rail, or even if you were overheard saying that Canada should be a republic. Sedition requires the actual commission of the offense as the Criminal Code defines it. However, once the seditious words have been used, the intention to achieve their seditious purpose (to overthrow the government) is presumed. This places the onus on the accused to prove that the crime was not committed.

It will be noted that not only does the law prohibit an act of force aimed at overthrowing a government in Canada, but it also prohibits speech in support of such an act. It seems to draw no distinction between those who might actually constitute a threat to the existing order and reckless crackpots who obviously do not. It can be assumed that the definition of sedition is vague so that the state will have wide latitude in deciding whom it should prosecute.

The War Measures Act

By a simple order-in-council (a decision of the federal cabinet), the civil liberties of Canadians can be suspended at a stroke, even under the Charter of Rights and Freedoms. This action can be taken under the War Measures Act, 1914, an act so designed that it must be freshly proclaimed before it can be invoked. Although it gives the government powers to do just about anything, it does not create an authoritarian state; it is an act of parliament that can be amended or repealed

by parliament at any time before, during or after its proclamation.

The purpose of the act is to protect the national security, and the safety of Canadians as a whole, in a time of dire emergency. The opening paragraph reads:

"The issue of a proclamation by Her Majesty, or under the authority of the Governor-in-Council, shall be conclusive evidence that war, invasion or insurrection, real or apprehended, exists and has existed for any period of time therein stated, and of its continuance, until by issue of a further proclamation it is declared that the war, invasion, or insurrection no longer exists."

The War Measures Act has been proclaimed in force on only three occasions: during World Wars I and II, and during the crisis of October 1970, which followed the murder of the Quebec Minister of Labor, Pierre Laporte, by members of the Front de Libération du Québec (F.L.Q.).

Having proclaimed the act to be in force, the cabinet must lay the proclamation before parliament immediately or, if the House of Commons is not sitting, within 15 days after parliament reconvenes. If ten or more members insist, the War Measures Act will be debated.

The act gives the cabinet authority to do anything it considers necessary for the security, defense, peace, order and welfare of Canada. Included is the power to censor or forbid any communications at all in any media and to order any person arrested and held for any length of time *incommunicado* (that is, without any right to contact members of his family, legal counsel or anyone else outside the prison walls). The right of *habeas corpus* is also suspended. (*See* Chapter 1, "The British ascendancy.")

Another aspect of the all-powerful War Measures Act is that the powers it gives to the cabinet include the authority to make retroactive laws. One of the principles of Canadian law is that a law does not apply to actions done before its enactment, unless the law expressly rules otherwise. This means that a person cannot ordinarily be punished for an act done before a law was passed making that act a crime. This principle is suspended under the

War Measures Act. When the law was proclaimed in force in 1970, an order was made that outlawed the F.L.Q., making it an offense not only to belong to the organization but to have been a member of it in the past.

The penalties for breaking any regulation or order made under the War Measures Act are fines of up to $5,000 or imprisonment for up to five years. However, once the crisis was past and the act revoked, the appeal courts would, by past examples, agree to hear cases alleging injustices suffered during an emergency.

Fighting for Canada

In the event of war, the federal parliament has power to pass legislation ordering the conscription (forced enrollment) of any citizen into the armed forces. It is generally accepted that conscription provides the fairest method of distributing equally the risks and burdens of defending one's country from its enemies, either at home or abroad.

The Canadian government introduced conscription in World War I in 1917, less than a year before that war ended. The measure encountered opposition among several groups in Canada and brought Quebec to a state of near-rebellion. In 1944, toward the end of World War II, conscription for active duty overseas was again introduced; it had been in force prior to that time, but only for service within Canada. Fewer than 2,500 conscripts actually reached the front lines in Europe and of that number, 69 were killed. A grand total of 1,086,771 Canadians served in World War II.

Victoria was not amused

THE LEGAL CONCEPT of privacy as an individual right (it is sometimes called "the right to be let alone") is more clearly defined and defended in our day of highly sophisticated photography and electronic eavesdropping than it was a century or more ago. Then, even the august Queen Victoria and consort Prince Albert had to go to court to prevent a London publisher from issuing for sale a pirated collection of their amateur art dabblings.

Victoria and Albert, married in 1840, took up the then-popular craft of etching—a method of engraving on metal plates. For their own amusement, they did mostly portraits of members of the royal family and other personal friends, and copied some favorite pictures in the royal collections. In some mysterious way, about 60 prints from the engraved plates filtered through to publisher William Strange.

Strange issued a descriptive catalogue of "the Royal Victoria and Albert Gallery of Etchings," and seemed all set to reap a small fortune from the Queen's loyal subjects in Britain's golden age. It did not bother Strange that he had no permission to publish but, at least, he had left a set of the prints at Buckhingham Palace with a note stating his intention.

Prince Albert sued through the courts, asking that all prints of the etchings be returned to him and that all copies of the catalogue so far printed be destroyed.

Strange's lawyer argued that there had been no violation of any law, and that publication of the catalogue was protected under the doctrine of the freedom of opinion and of the press. What was being considered was not privacy as we know it today but the rights of property. Strange's case rested fundamentally on the argument that there was "no such property as the exclusive rights of seeing and talking about property."

In a complex pioneering decision (still quoted in the courts today) the judge ruled that, in this case, the rights of property and privacy were one. But a separate concept of personal privacy as an individual right was emerging. It might be okay for a cat to look at the Queen, but neither cat nor citizen could look at the Queen's private etchings without permission.

The duties of the citizen

The duty to pay taxes
Assisting the police
Jury duty
At the ballot box

THE CITIZEN is entitled to enjoy without qualification the rights conferred by Canadian law but is subject to all the obligations, duties and responsibilities the law imposes. There are also certain moral duties that society expects from a citizen, although in that area the law largely leaves each one free to face his or her own conscience. The willing acceptance of responsibility by the individual is central to the survival of democracy. As Victorian philosopher John Stuart Mill wrote: "A people may prefer a free government but if, from indolence, or carelessness, or cowardice, or want of public spirit, they are unequal to the exertions necessary for preserving it . . . they are unlikely long to enjoy it."

Almost all criminal laws impose a legal duty on citizens to abstain from certain actions. But rarely does the law impose upon a citizen the duty to *do* a particular act. One obvious duty that citizens have is to pay taxes; failure to do so—or to report income correctly—can result in heavy fines and even prison sentences. Another duty, met less frequently but no less real, is to assist a policeman in the execution of his duties if he so requests. (*See* Chapter 3, "The policeman's lot.") The citizen also has a legal duty to serve on a jury. (*See* Chapter 3, "How a case is tried.")

High on the citizen's list of moral duties is to participate in the political process and, particularly, to vote in elections.

There is no legal requirement that you must vote (as there is in Australia, for example) but anyone who does not exercise his franchise may find he is permitting some minority faction to rule the country.

Reformers for centuries have raised a troubling question: are we morally bound to accept laws we feel are unjust? But it must also be asked whether the rule of law can survive if we each make personal judgments on laws enacted under our open democratic system. Do we really respect that democratic process? And are we serving that process by ignoring what we consider to be unjust laws? On the issue of crime and punishment, for instance, do we agree with the dictum of Sir Edward Coke that "he threatens the innocent who spares the guilty"? And if we feel morally bound to obey *all* laws, how do we distinguish ourselves from the surviving Nazi leaders who claimed at the Nuremberg trials following World War II that they were "only following orders." The example of Nuremberg gives a lot of strength to the argument that citizens at some point are morally obliged to resist bad laws.

The civil rights enumerated and discussed in this chapter are the product of the slow evolution of civilized throught, historic outbursts of civil disobedience, and even insurrection. We do not adopt principles merely for the luxury of enjoying their possession; to give them meaning, we must try to act in accordance with them, even if we should risk offending the law or current public opinion.

Perhaps the best guarantee of continuing the development of civil rights lies in steady, reasoned, open discussion, striving to move forward at the maximum rate the majority of the adult population will accept without reaction. The danger was emphasized in early 1973 by Mr. Justice Haines of the Ontario Supreme Court. In the course of a speech to an audience of psychiatrists, he said the public was getting fed up with what it considered to be a "civil rights binge," with laws that protected the criminal and not the public. "Bless those concerned with civil rights," he said, "but they can go so far that everything will boomerang."

The duty to pay taxes

There is a bill to pay for the rule of law and order and for government services. Since earliest times, it has been paid by means of *taxation*; it was the necessity of paying the tax levied by the Roman emperor Caesar Augustus on "all the world" that took Joseph and Mary to Bethlehem where Jesus was born. Today, we pay taxes on our income (above a certain amount), on the value of our real estate and on our capital gains. We also pay sales and other taxes on a wide range of goods and services. Corporations pay a tax based on their business profits.

Each year, all governments—federal, provincial and municipal—present *budgets* which estimate the expected public expenditures for the year ahead, and announce the taxes to be imposed on the citizenry to provide the funds to pay the public bill. Thus, since taxes change yearly, it is impractical to provide details of taxation levels in a book of this kind. Current information is readily obtainable from any district tax office.

The duty to pay taxes—particularly income tax—brings the average citizen most keenly into contact with his obligations to Canada. If you have any income,

---

The pig that walked like a man

IF IT WAS Thomas Jefferson who wrote the most stirring exhortation on the freedom of the individual ("all men are created equal"), then it was Eric Blair who wrote the most devastating satire on egalitarian beliefs ("all animals are equal—but some animals are more equal than others"). If Blair's name doesn't ring a bell, perhaps you know him better as George Orwell, British author of the 1945 bestseller *Animal Farm*, and its chilling successor, *1984*.

An India-born, Eton-educated soldier and schoolteacher, Orwell dies in 1950. But his story of how Napoleon, the pig who walked on his hind legs, took over the people's (animals') republic of Manor Farm is unlikely to be forgotten as long as men can read.

With his lieutenant Squealer, the boar Napoleon led the rebels who decided that Farmer Jones was getting rich on their labors and that it would be like heaven-on-earth if the animals ran the farm themselves. They chased the drunken Jones off the place, and repelled counterattack from the neighboring squires. On the end of the barn, a literary pig painted the Seven Commandments of the new regime:

Whatever goes upon two legs is an enemy.
Whatever goes upon four legs, or has wings, is a friend.

No animal shall wear clothes.
No animal shall sleep in a bed.
No animal shall drink alcohol.
No animal shall kill any other animal.
All animals are equal.

Being the cleverest of the animals, the pigs did not actually do any physical work; they directed their comrades in the necessary chores of the farm. Since the pigs labored with their brains, they naturally needed the best food. Soon all the milk and apples were reserved for the pigs, while the others worked 60 hours a week and grew thin. The pigs moved into the farmhouse and ate from the best china. The dogs became their bodyguards.

One by one the Seven Commandments were broken (or amended by the brilliant Squealer) while the pigs entrenched themselves as a nonproductive bureaucracy. Eventually, a truce was reached with the human neighbors who admired the way the pigs made even more money than they could by dropping holidays, lengthening the workday and cutting rations.

As Napoleon struts around dressed in riding breeches, carrying a whip, smoking a pipe and guzzling whisky, Benjamin the donkey reads out the newly painted addition to the seventh commandment:—

"—but some animals are more equal than others."

you have probably felt that contact. By April 30 of every year, you have figured what your income was for the previous year, filled in the tax forms and paid your income-tax bill to the national treasury. Some persons have to send the receiver general a cheque for more than half of what they make. Others experience the pleasant sensation of getting some money back because of overpayment through payroll deductions or other causes.

Failure to pay by April 30 brings interest charges; any false declaration can bring fines and imprisonment. Deliberate evasion of due tax is regarded in the light of theft; where large amounts are concerned, severe penalties are almost routinely imposed. The person who dodges paying his proper share of tax is not really cheating the government; rather, he is forcing his fellow citizens to pay more than their fair share. On the other hand, the law requires that you pay only the true amount due; if you are asked for more than what you believe you should pay, you can argue about the bill and, if still not satisfied, you can file an objection with the Tax Review Board. There is an avenue for such an appeal to go clear up to the Supreme Court of Canada.

At the same time as you have a duty to pay your taxes, you have a second—if unwritten—duty to ensure that your hard-earned money is well spent. The vote-hungry politician is ever-ready to promise large sums of public money for a host of "worthy causes." The citizen has a right to question when it is *his* money that is being spent, say, to build an opera house in some city that obviously prefers sing-alongs around the Legion Hall piano, or to send libraries of Canadiana to Outer Mongolia. Extravagant government seldom makes for good government.

On the other hand, the virtuous citizen might consider making some inquiries to ensure that he is being taxed enough! To attract persons of principle and skill into the public service, the salaries offered must be commensurate with the required talents. Remember that the public payroll must keep pace with expanding national services and endeavors. If, for instance, you want Canada to play a role on the world stage by acting as international policeman in Cyprus or by hosting a U.N. conference at Vancouver, you must expect to pay for it. Of course, inflation provides its own addition to the tax bill. Like extravagance at the opposite extreme, penny-pinching seldom makes for good government either.

Assisting the police

The citizen has a duty to obey the law and, in one of its many clauses, the law demands that you must come to the aid of a policeman (also to a properly appointed fire ranger) when directly requested to do so. The Criminal Code (Section 118) provides for up to two years' imprisonment for anyone who "omits, without reasonable excuse, to assist a public officer or peace officer in the execution of his duty in arresting a person or in preserving the peace, after having reasonable notice that he is required to do so."

This is a pointed reminder that the police act as our agents; they enforce the laws that we have collectively made. (*See* Chapter 3, "The policeman's lot.") Remember that some police work in ordinary ("plain") clothes rather than in uniform; but all peace officers carry an identification badge or card.

As a good citizen you should inform the police if you see a crime committed, or know that a crime has been committed. The great majority of Canadians willingly assist and appreciate their police, recognizing that, by comparison with certain countries abroad, we are fortunate indeed to be served by a virtually incorruptible force. In Toronto, during the 1970's, despite bitter weather conditions, more than 12,000 people—most of them young —took part in a "Cops are Tops" rally to show their appreciation of that city's police force.

If you have been called to assist a peace officer in the execution of his duty and are injured while performing that duty, you will be automatically compensated by the government of the province where the incident occurred. Some provinces will compensate any person who is injured even if he volunteered his assistance.

Jury duty

In all provinces, the *jury list* is drawn from either tax-assessment or electoral rolls. All adult citizens have a duty to report when summoned by the sheriff to serve on a jury, unless they belong to certain occupations and professions. Most provinces exempt judges, magistrates, surgeons, newspapermen and lawyers. Serving on a jury brings the citizen into intimate contact with the law at work, and it is one of the most important services that he can provide to his community.

The ordinary citizen may be called to serve on any one of three types of jury. THE TRIAL (OR PETIT) JURY is the panel of citizens, usually 12, familiar to the fan of television whodunits. It is assembled to determine issues of fact from the evidence presented in serious criminal cases where trial by jury is mandatory, and in other cases (both civil and criminal) where all or one of the parties concerned are given the chance to choose trial by judge and jury.

Elaborate precautions are taken to ensure that the members of a trial jury are not biased either for or against any of the parties to a case. Once the judge has delivered his charge to the jury (that is, in short, summarized the evidence and sent them out to the jury room), the members will be kept in seclusion until they have reached their verdict.

Either the defense or the prosecution can ask the judge for an order forbidding any publication of news (or comment) about a trial still in progress.

While it is the jury that finds the defendant innocent or guilty, it is the judge who decides upon the sentence that is pronounced. (*See* Chapter 3 "How a case is tried.")

THE GRAND JURY has a different function, where it still exists. It may act on information from its own knowledge and investigation or at the request of the prosecuting attorney or a judge following an inquest. Under a provision of the Criminal Code, this jury can even influence a judge of the criminal court to dismiss a charge—thus protecting the citizen against unwarranted prosecution. In most instances, when a person is charged with an *indictable offense,* a serious charge that carries a maximum penalty of at least five years, imprisonment, a provincial judge or magistrate will first hold a preliminary hearing to weigh the evidence put forward by the police; if he thinks there is enough evidence to warrant the Crown bringing the case to court, he will commit the accused for trial. However, as a second check, the prosecution's case will be reviewed at the next sitting of the grand jury.

This jury is a remnant of the jury system that prevailed in England during the Middle Ages. For civil cases, it is used now in only four provinces and its membership varies. It consists of six members in Ontario; 7 in Prince Edward Island; and 9 in Newfoundland. In Nova Scotia, a judge can pick as many jurors as may be deemed sufficient for trying the case. After the members have investigated and reviewed the evidence, they come to a majority decision.

As required by the provisions of the Criminal Code, the grand jury is called in serious criminal cases in all provinces, and is always composed of 12 members. In the Yukon and the Northwest Territories, there are only six jurors for criminal cases. If a grand jury decides the accused should go on to trial, it will return what is called a *true bill.*

A grand jury may also be called upon to review any recommendation arising from an inquest. If you are called for this kind of jury duty, you may find yourself on an inspection tour of prisons or mental institutions.

THE CORONER'S JURY is selected in the same way as are the others. Usually, it consists of five persons, and its verdicts can be determined by a simple majority vote. (*See* Chapter 3, "Judges and courts.") It serves at a coroner's inquest, called by the local coroner when it is believed a death has occurred in the district from other than natural causes or when public opinion advises that the circumstances leading to accidental death—perhaps a traffic accident involving a school bus in which several children died—should be investigated.

At the ballot box

Canada allows the citizen to choose whether he or she will vote or not, as desired, with the result that in some elections there is not always a fully representative turnout of eligible voters. A few elitist-minded commentators do not consider that sheer numbers are important: it is better, they argue, that 50 well-informed persons vote than that 100 votes are cast by people who haven't studied the candidates or the issues. There is, however, a considerable moral pressure to vote, exerted by the news media, as well as community and national leaders.

Every citizen should be eager to exercise the *franchise*—this democratic right to vote. The voter has plenty of opportunities to help choose legislators, mayors, aldermen, reeves and councillors.

It took centuries of sometimes bloody struggle for the ordinary people to win the right to be governed by representatives of their own choosing. (*See* Chapter 1, "The rise of English law.") If no one voted, there would be no election, no people's choice and, hence, no democracy; if only a limited number cast their ballots, the government may fall into the hands of second-rate politicians or those with selfish or even dangerous views. It has been said, with some truth, that the citizens of any country get the government they deserve.

The citizen, whether native or naturalized, can vote in all government elections for which he or she is qualified by residence; the only exceptions are those persons who happen to be in prison or a mental hospital at the time (and any others judged by the court to be mentally incompetent), those who are too young, or those who are involved in the machinery or the administration of an election. (Quebec allows prisoners serving less than two years the right to vote.) Citizenship court judges can vote in federal elections but otherwise, judges may not vote.

No beer for Mr. Christie

RACIAL DISCRIMINATION is properly outlawed in Canada today, being seen—along with its blood-brother, ultranationalism—as one of the most insidious obstacles to social harmony and world peace. Perhaps we still have a distance to go to the perfect state, but a look at the recent record will show just how far we've come in a hurry.

In 1939, as World War II began, a black man named Christie was refused a beer by a Quebec tavern keeper. He sued for damages on account of his humiliation, and the case went all the way to the Supreme Court of Canada. The learned judges in that high place confirmed the hotelier's right to refuse to serve blacks. Any merchant, they said, was free to deal as he chose with an individual member of the public.

When a black man was refused an orchestra seat at Loew's theater, in Montreal, he sued and lost. The court then held that "the management has the right to assign particular seats to different races and classes of men and women as it sees fit." In 1924, a black was refused service in a London, Ontario, restaurant; his civil action for damages was dismissed.

In British Columbia, in 1940, a black refused service in a beer parlor took his case eventually to the B.C. Court of Appeal. He lost.

The experiences of World War II, with men of all races, religions and shades of skin fighting together in common cause, is thought by jurists to have had much to do with today's enlightenment. Wide-spread air travel by tourists in the last 30 years has brought an unheralded bonus. Argument can still be found that "you can't legislate morals" and that only education can truly cut the roots of racial discrimination. But it's obvious that the general public attitude to minorities has improved—in the courts, as in the taverns. The civil rights legislators can surely take some credit for that.

How to become a Canadian citizen

By birth or by naturalization

Residence qualification

The oath of allegiance

The points system

Entry of dependents

How to apply for citizenship

CITIZENSHIP, or nationality, is the greatest privilege that Canada can bestow on anyone. Although it is possible to reside in Canada under the protection of our laws without being a citizen, full enjoyment of all our rights is reserved for those who are citizens either by birth or by naturalization.

It has been steady federal government policy to encourage the growth of the population by immigration. In the ten-year period before the outbreak of World War I, nearly 2,700,000 immigrants streamed into Canada, a rate equaled in 1957 when 282,164 arrived. Canada also provided a haven for a great number of refugees fleeing from religious or political persecution—including notably the Doukhobors of Russia and some 8,000 Czechs who fled their homeland after the Russian invasion of 1968. More recently, Asians expelled from Uganda, Chilean and Vietnamese refugees were received.

Traditionally, the *landed immigrant* tends to regard his citizenship certificate with a special pride: he exhibits something of the zeal of the convert. Those Canadians-by-birth who take their citizenship for granted would be well advised to attend a sitting of the Court of Canadian Citizenship when new citizens swear the *oath of allegiance* and receive their prized certificates. ("Landed immigrant" is the term used by Employment and Immigration Canada to denote the status of the newcomer who is granted permanent residence and the opportunity to apply for citizenship after living in Canada for the required period.)

January 1, 1947, is an important date in this story. Before that day there was, strictly speaking, no such person as a Canadian citizen. Until the Canadian Citizenship Act came into force, the labels "Canadian national" and "British subject" were used to describe all those who were non-alien in the population. October 1, 1967, is another important date: on that day, immigration regulations such as we know them today came into effect; these included entry standards based on 100 "assessment units," or points. If the newcomer wants to become a landed immigrant, he must score at least 50 points. Points are based on the person's age, education and training, personal qualities and job classification.

One provision in the 1967 regulations represented a dramatic switch; it had the effect of making Canada about the easiest country in the world to enter at that time. Persons arriving in Canada ostensibly as visitors—for the most part without any previous contact with Canadian immigration officers abroad—were permitted to apply to stay permanently. Many thousands—a majority of them unskilled workers—walked off planes in Montreal, Toronto and Vancouver, or streamed over the United States border, and then proceeded to apply for status as landed immigrants. Of the 121,900 persons granted landed-immigrant status in 1971, nearly 40,000 came in a "visitors." In 1974, total immigration was up to tidal proportions at 218,465.

Prompted by strong public reaction to the flood of visitor applications, the government altered the law. At the end of 1975, the number of immigrants had fallen to 187,881—a drop of 14 percent. This downward trend continued until 1978, when 86,313 immigrants arrived, and then rose again to 142,435 in 1980.

Further changes in Canadian immigration policy resulted in the Immigration Act of 1976 (proclaimed in 1978). The Act states the principles underlying Canadian policy—nondiscrimination, family reunification, and humanitarian concern for refugees. It requires immigrant visas, as well as student and employment authorizations, to be acquired at Canadian immigration offices abroad. The Act links immigration to the needs of the Canadian labor market. Skilled workers can enter only when there are insufficient numbers of Canadians to fill particular jobs. The Act requires annual forecasts of the number of immigrants the country can comfortably absorb. For example, as Canada began to recover from an economic slump in 1983, the government limited immigration to 110,000 arrivals—roughly 25 percent less than the previous year.

Within Canada, up-to-date information can be obtained from any office of Employment and Immigration Canada, or from Citizenship Registration, Department of the Secretary of State, Ottawa, Ont., K1A 0M5

A Canadian by birth
There are only two ways in which one can acquire Canadian citizenship: by birth or by naturalization (but see also "A Canadian by active service," on page 105).

Anyone who was born in Canada, or on a Canadian ship or aircraft, before January 1, 1947, and who had not assumed another nationality, automatically became a Canadian citizen on that date. This also applied in most cases to someone who was born outside of Canada but whose father was a Canadian. Again, in most cases, if the father was a British subject but had Canadian domicile at the time of the person's birth, citizenship was granted to the child automatically. The same privilege was also granted to a person born out of wedlock to a Canadian woman in the period described.

Under the Citizens Act, Canadians born or living abroad cease to be citizens at the age of 21, unless they make an application to retain citizenship and register as citizens. Applicants must have lived in Canada at least one year immediately preceding the date of application. They must also establish a substantial connection with Canada.

All Indians and Inuit are Canadian citizens if born in Canada, or if they were born abroad, had Canadian domicile at January 1, 1947, and had lived ten years in Canada prior to January 1, 1956.

All foundlings discovered in Canada are regarded in law as having been born in Canada and are citizens.

Being born in Canada does not mean automatic citizenship for someone whose parent was an alien at his birth, had not been admitted to Canada for permanent residence and was employed as a representative of a foreign government.

A Canadian by naturalization
Naturalization is the term universally used to describe the process by which a person becomes a citizen, or national, of a country other than the one in which he was born. The basic requirememts to qualify for naturalization in Canada are:

(1) To gain admission legally to Canada for permanent residence (that is, be a landed immigrant).

(2) To be at least 18 years old or to reside in Canada with a Canadian spouse.

(3) To have resided in Canada for at least three years.

(4) To have adequate knowledge of either the French or English language.

(5) To have some knowledge of the rights and duties of the Canadian citizen.

(6) To be willing to swear allegiance to the Queen of Canada.

(7) To intend to have your place of domicile permanently in Canada.

With the exception of United States, Mexican and certain West Indian nationals, all foreigners require a passport to enter Canada—this applies, for instance, equally to citizens from France and from all countries (including Britain) of the British Commonwealth. (*See* Chapter 15, "Rights of the traveler.") For the exceptions mentioned, other evidence of nationality is usually acceptable. A visa is also required for persons coming from many countries; this takes the form of a seal stamped in the person's passport by a Canadian consular official abroad.

There are different visas for the student, the visitor and the intending immigrant. Visitor's visas are valid only for limited periods and do not grant permission for the holder to work in Canada without obtaining a separate work permit.

Passport and visa are inspected by uniformed immigration officials at Canadian ports of entry; this inspection serves as a screening process by which known drug addicts, criminals and other undesirables can be stopped from entering the country. Immigration officers are specially trained to spot forged documents.

The residence qualification

To apply for Canadian citizenship, landed immigrants must meet certain qualifications. Among other things, immigrants must be 18 years of age or older, and must show proof of legal entry into Canada. They must also have lived in Canada for

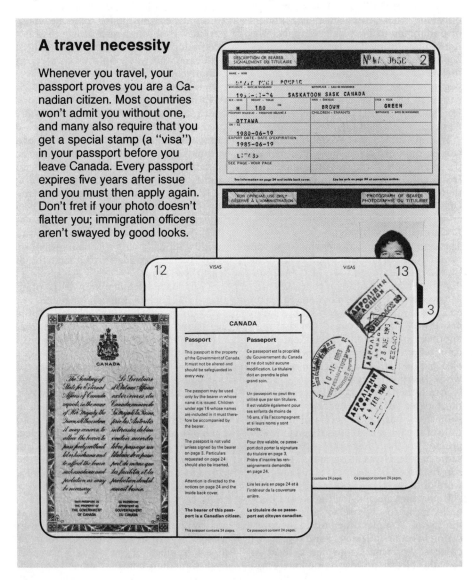

A travel necessity

Whenever you travel, your passport proves you are a Canadian citizen. Most countries won't admit you without one, and many also require that you get a special stamp (a "visa") in your passport before you leave Canada. Every passport expires five years after issue and you must then apply again. Don't fret if your photo doesn't flatter you; immigration officers aren't swayed by good looks.

three years prior to making an application for citizenship. If individuals have resided in Canada as students or visitors before becoming landed immigrants, they are allowed to count half of each full year spent in the country as part of the qualification.

Time spent in a Canadian prison does not count for residence qualification. Landed immigrants must also be free from legal prohibitions—that is, they should not be security risks, be under deportation orders, be on probation or parole, or be convicted of an indictable offence.

The language qualification

To become a citizen, you must have an adequate knowledge of one of Canada's two official languages. No one insists that you be fluent, but you should be able to get by in your trade or social group. Language-improvement classes are sponsored by provincial education authorities.

In the past, exceptions were made for three distinct groups of immigrants. The spouse, widow or widower of a Canadian citizen was not refused citizenship because she, or he, could not fulfill the language requirement. The same applied to anyone younger than 40 at the time of admission to Canada who had lived here continuously for more than 20 years, or to anyone older than 40 at the time of admission who had lived here for more than 10 years. Although these exceptions no longer apply, a judge may still exercise discretion in such cases.

Character reference

Although a "good character" qualification no longer appears in the Citizenship Act, this requirement is inherent in its regulations. Members of the community may testify on your behalf by giving you letters of reference or appearing before the court to support your application. Your employer, your bank manager, religious and community leaders—indeed, any reputable citizen is suitable.

The assessment of character would naturally include examination of any criminal convictions against the applicant. A criminal conviction is not an absolute bar. The citizenship court would take into consideration the seriousness of the offense, the length of time since it was committed and the possibility of continued criminal activity.

The qualification of knowledge

The would-be citizen is expected to have a reasonable knowledge of Canada, its political, judicial and economic systems, as well as a grasp of the basic rights and responsibilities of the Canadian citizen.

Booklets containing simplified histories and social commentaries are provided for newcomers by the federal departments concerned and by some provinces; orientation courses are offered in evening classes run by the Department of Employment and Immigration. The Citizenship Registration Branch of the Office of the Secretary of State has designed social programs to help the alien immigrant adjust to ordinary Canadian society.

The oath of allegiance

The monarchy holds an important position in Canadian life. To become a citizen, the applicant must swear an oath of allegiance, or make an affirmation, of his loyalty to the monarch in the following terms:

"I, John Doe, swear that I will be faithful and bear true allegiance to Her Majesty Queen Elizabeth the Second, Her Heirs and Successors according to law ... "

An "affirmation" is a solemn and formal declaration acceptable from those persons who, for religious or other reasons, have scruples about swearing an oath which refers to God.

The points system

Applicants for the status of landed immigrant—the essential stepping-stone to citizenship through naturalization—are graded and selected by an assessment system. Under this system, the landed immigrant must have 50 out of a possible maximum of 100 points.

Ten points are awarded if the new arrival is 35 years of age or younger. One point is deducted for every year beyond that age—up to a maximum of ten points. It is assumed that the younger the immigrant, the easier will be the adjustment to the Canadian way of life. For an immigrant arriving fresh from a remote village in Spain or Korea, the pace of Canadian urban life can be an unnerving experience.

There is no maximum number of points awarded for professional skills. Standards in this category, however, are regularly reviewed and updated by the Department of Employment and Immigration. In general, up to eight points may be awarded for professional skills, and another eight, for job experience. (At the time of this writing, virtually all immigrants were being rated at zero because of the high unemployment situation in Canada.) The assessment system awards ten points to an immigrant who is coming to a job approved by Employment and Immigration Canada. If this is not the case, ten points are deducted.

A maximum of 12 points are awarded for educational background. One point is allotted for each year of schooling completed. For a knowledge of English and/or French, a maximum of five points for each language is awarded, depending on the degree of fluency.

Ten points is the maximum allotted for the personal qualities of an immigrant, as assessed by the immigration officer. He may look for such traits as motivation, adaptability and initiative.

Before totaling applicants' scores, immigration officials are permitted to add up to a maximum of 30 supplementary points at their discretion.

In recent years, about 43 percent of Canada's immigrants have opted to live in Ontario, British Columbia, and Quebec.

Entry of dependents

Canadian citizens or landed immigrants are entitled to bring their dependents to Canada. The regulations outline technical differences between dependents who will be supported by the new or prospective citizen, and other relatives who will enter the work force.

There are two classes of "dependent" immigrants: sponsored dependents and "assisted" relatives. A "dependent" is defined for immigration purposes as: husband or wife, fiancé or fiancée; unmarried son or daughter younger than 21; parent or grandparent over 60, or younger if widowed or unable to work; an orphaned brother, sister, nephew, niece or grandchild younger than 18. Provision is also made for an adopted child and, where the only official dependent is a husband or wife, for the closest living relative. A dependent will be admitted to Canada provided he or she is in good health and of good character.

The "assisted" relative category includes: son or daughter 21 or older; married son or daughter younger than 21; brother or sister; parent or grandparent younger than 60; nephew, niece, uncle, aunt or grandchild. The citizen or landed immigrant who wants to bring these dependents to Canada must be willing and able to provide accommodation, care and maintenance for the person being brought in, to generally assist that person getting started, and must promise to provide help for at least five years. Because of the assistance that the nominator has promised to provide the immigrant, the "assisted" relative is assessed on only some of the selection factors—education, personal qualities, occupational demand, age and occupational skill.

On the general assumption that the immigrant who has already become a Canadian citizen usually will be better established in Canada than one who has only recently arrived—and thus in a better position to help relatives—a slightly higher preference is given to a relation nominated by a Canadian citizen than to one nominated by a permanent resident who has not yet graduated from landed-immigrant status.

Marriage and citizenship

A woman neither gains nor loses her Canadian citizenship by marriage. To acquire citizenship, she must go through the same steps as a man.

Children as citizens

The minor children of immigrant British subjects or aliens do not automatically become Canadians when their parents take up citizenship. After one parent has become a Canadian, the responsible parent who has custody and maintains the child may apply for citizenship on the child's behalf. A legal guardian (*tutor* in Quebec) may also apply on a child's behalf. The Secretary of State of Canada is empowered to grant citizenship to a minor under special circumstances that do not comply with the regulations.

How you become a British subject
A Canadian citizen is automatically a citizen of the British Commonwealth. Citizens of Commonwealth countries (naturally including the United Kingdom) or of the Republic of Ireland are also British subjects in the eyes of Canadian law. Among these are citizens of Australia, New Zealand, India, Pakistan, and such nations as Bangladesh, Barbados, Bermuda, Jamaica and Sri Lanka. South Africans and former Rhodesians are classed as British Subjects.

The non-Canadian British subject who has landed-immigrant status may file his application for citizenship directly with the Registrar of Canadian Citizenship.

How to apply for citizenship
The alien-born landed immigrant may apply for a certificate of citizenship—using the special form provided—at the courthouse in his district or, in most major cities, at a Court of Canadian Citizenship. Each prospective adult citizen must apply personally on his own behalf; in other words, a husband may not apply for his wife. As explained above, the responsible parent will apply on behalf of any minor children.

The Courts of Canadian Citizenship are located at: Vancouver (1075 Georgia Street West); Calgary (220 4th Avenue S.E.); Edmonton (9828 104th Avenue); Regina (2101 Scarth Street); Winnipeg (303 Main Street); Sudbury (19 Lisgar Street South); London (451 Talbot Street); Hamilton (150 Main Street West); Toronto (55 St. Clair Avenue East); Ottawa (150 Kent Street); Montreal (1080 Beaver Hall Hill); Moncton (860 Main Street); Halifax (5281 Duke Street).

If his application is approved, the landed immigrant receives his certificate of citizenship at a public gathering in the nearest Court of Canadian Citizenship. At the court presentations, important local personages attend and the new citizen is warmly welcomed into his new home and nation.

He will learn that, as a citizen, he is liable for conscription for military service in time of war, for jury duty at all times, and that he must go to the aid of the police or fire rangers when called upon.

A Canadian by active service
The law provides that citizenship may be granted, without satisfying the residence requirement, to a person who has been on active service in the Canadian Armed Forces in a war in which Canada was engaged. This also applies in connection with any action taken by Canada under the United Nations Charter, under our obligations through the North Atlantic Treaty Organization or other similar instrument for collective defense.

How to lose your citizenship
There are four ways in which a Canadian can lose his citizenship. The first is by formal renunciation. This applies to a person who has another nationality acquired by marriage or while a minor. The second is by not claiming Canadian rights by age 21 (see "A Canadian by birth," in this chapter). The third is by voluntarily and formally becoming (while outside of Canada and other than by marriage) a citizen of another country. The fourth is by having your certificate of citizenship revoked on grounds that it was obtained through fraud or misrepresentation.

A Canadian citizen who is also a citizen of another country and who serves in the armed forces of that country when it is at war with Canada ceases to be a Canadian. (This does not apply to a Canadian who became a citizen of another country when it was at war with Canada, although the minister has the option of revoking citizenship in such cases.)

Any noncitizen resident of Canada can be deported for any one of a long list of reasons. Conviction on any criminal charge or violation of the drug laws can be enough.

3/How Our Legal System Works

When the law is broken   108

The policeman's lot   113

Judges and courts   121

How a case is tried 130

Decisions from the Bench 139

The penal system 145

When the law is broken

L ET US IMAGINE that just as you and your family drive into your car-port, an intruder bursts through the kitchen door of your home carrying the portable TV and your teen-age son's digital clock radio. Broken glass from a window is scattered about. You jam on the brakes and shout "Stop!" Your son tries to grab the thief who drops the television set and lashes out with a fist. Your son is knocked down and in falling cuts his hand deeply on the glass. The thief runs off, still clutching the radio.

It all happened in less than a minute; yet in those frightening seconds you have been involved in a crime, and the elements of a civil lawsuit have been created. As you move automatically to call the police, you are setting in motion the intricate machinery of law enforcement. Then, as the thief is sought and, one hopes, caught and sentenced, your family will have a front-row seat at a demonstration of how the Canadian legal system works.

When you rush your son to the hospital's emergency department to get his cuts patched up, producing your provincial medical card; when your insurance adjuster calls with forms for you to fill in concerning the stolen radio, the ruined television set and the damage to your house; when you decide to borrow money from the bank to make your home harder to rob in future—in all of these associated actions you will be involving yourself further with the network of law and regulation that plays a vital part in the life of every citizen.

Until something such as was described above actually happens to you, or to your neighbor, the law often seems remote. You read about sensational crimes—bank robberies, murders, rapes—in the newspapers, but they always seem to happen in other places and to other people. You might go through most of your life without bumping into the law. But suddenly, the police car that you have only seen shrieking along the highway is stopping at your own door. You discover that the uniformed men inside it are not the hard-bitten heroes of movieland but quite ordinary guys doing a difficult, and sometimes unpleasant, job. The picture that some people draw of the police as "a bunch of Hitlers" intent on "pushing you around" quickly fades.

If you get involved in laying charges and court appearances, you will be taking part in procedures that are literally centuries old. However, you will find that some of the ancient principles, such as the "vengeance motive" in the punishment of criminals—the old biblical "eye for an eye"—have given way to more humanitarian principles, always aiming at the possible rehabilitation of a wrongdoer. You will see an impartial police force bring the suspect to the bar of justice, and see a highly qualified judge weigh the facts of the case and carefully make his decision, based on the mass of previous experience with similar cases and on the permitted penalties written into the legislation passed by federal parliament or provincial legislature. You can ponder the subsequent sobering experience of the convicted thief if he is fined or deprived of his liberty for a time in one of Her Majesty's prisons.

In the Introduction to this book, a well-known legal scholar and writer versed in the ways of law and government has described the spirit of Canadian justice and explained how it continues to shape itself as the protective shield and not the flail of the public. Chapter 1 recounts the history of law as we know it. It outlines steps by which a code of principles and rules was set down to guide the sparsely settled colony to its present state of flourishing nationhood. The chapter you now are reading is devoted to practical matter, describing the Canadian law-enforcement agencies, the judiciary, the establishment and working procedure of the courts, and the changing nature of the penal system.

Arrest by a citizen

The individual citizen does not have to wait for the police to make an arrest. By the time the police arrive on the scene, the criminal could be a mile or more away. In the case described at the beginning of this chapter, the son of the family attempted to make what is called a *citizen's arrest*.

Any citizen has the right, without a warrant, to arrest a person he sees committing an *indictable* offense or a person fleeing from the police. The term "indictable offense" refers to the more serious kind of offenses—like robbery. (*See* Chapter 19, "Threat to the community.")

A property owner (or someone authorized by him) may arrest a person he finds committing an offense on or in relation to that property.

Although the police naturally applaud any citizen who assists them with their work (special commendations are issued), they are quick to warn of the physical danger that might arise and of the necessity that only reasonable force be used against the person concerned. There is a good reason why Canadian policemen are armed with pistols while on duty and they are trained in unarmed combat methods.

Even if your nerve is strong enough for this kind of initiative, make sure you have the right person before making an arrest. If the court accepted the accused's story and acquitted him, you might find yourself being sued for wrongful arrest and perhaps for assault. (*See* Chapter 18, "The intentional tort.")

It is always wise, if circumstances permit, to telephone the police—or have someone call them—before trying to make a citizen's arrest.

If you should ever arrest someone, don't beat him up. Remember it is not for you to punish him. That is the job of the penal authorities, if the courts find him guilty.

Most citizen's arrests are made by store detectives or retail-shop personnel when they suspect someone of shoplifting—that is, stealing property from the owners of the business. (*See* Chapter 6, "In the supermarket.")

The citizens' hot line

WHEN THE LAW has been broken, chances are that some citizens—apart from the criminal and his victim—are well aware of the fact. If they did not see the crime committed, perhaps they were talking to someone who did. Maybe they heard someone boasting in a bar, or accidentally saw stolen goods, prohibited drugs or illegal firearms.

If all persons who pick up information about a crime would immediately get in touch with police, there's no doubt the law enforcement success rate would soar.

The police are hired by the citizenry: why not help them all the way? This was the reasoning behind the television program, Police Code, which recounted a recent crime, then asked viewers to phone any clues or comments either to the TV station or to the police.

When a Police Code show was televised over CFAC in Calgary, more than 100 calls were received by the police. The Chief of Police said he was highly impressed by the accuracy of the information volunteered by the general public.

Enter the police

The police are your most common link with the law. They work for you and will see to it that the law protects you when it should—and prosecutes you when it should. Canada has three police systems: federal, provincial and municipal.

When the police arrive at your home (as in the case described at the beginning of this chapter), they will take into custody any suspect you have arrested. If you are not holding anyone, they will launch a search for him themselves. In either case, they will start to investigate the incident and will ask you for a full statement of the occurrence.

The investigating officer will want all the factual details you can remember—but no guesses. Your statements and those of any other witnesses can play an important part in determining the guilt or innocence of the suspect when the case goes to court.

It is not always necessary for those giving evidence to appear in court; their signed statements being read to the court may be enough. The courts will always try to cut out any unnecessary formalities, especially if the case is clear-cut. As it is, it can take weeks, and even months, for some cases to be called. The police will not lay a charge until they are convinced they have sufficient evidence.

Be careful about giving positive identification of a lawbreaker. If you are sure who it was, then speak out; but keep your imagination in check. It is fatally easy to smear an innocent party.

Town and city forces

In most dealings with the police, you are in touch with officers of municipal police forces. These are your local cops. Incidentally, too many crime serials have flowed out of the TV tube for policemen to seriously object to "cop." But say it with a smile.

There are more than 40,000 policemen working for the municipal forces of Canadian cities, towns, villages and townships. Montreal alone has more than 4,400, while some villages only have a single constable. You should regard them as your neighbors, important and essential members of society. (*See* "The policeman's lot" in this chapter.)

Provincial laws require that cities and towns maintain adequate policing at the local level to ensure that law and order prevails in the communities. These forces are administered by municipal police commissions. If villages and townships are sufficiently large and their tax revenues can support a police force, the provincial minister of justice can order them to establish police departments.

There are no municipal forces in either the Yukon or the Northwest Territories. Instead, the Royal Canadian Mounted Police handles enforcement, even in urban centers like Yellowknife, Dawson and Whitehorse. Under special arrangements with the provinces, the R.C.M.P. handles all police work in a total of 190 municipalities across Canada.

The provincial police

Two provinces—Ontario and Quebec—maintain their own provincial police forces. These operate outside those municipalities which maintain their own systems, and can be seen mostly on the highways of the provinces concerned. They fill part of the role that the R.C.M.P. plays totally in the other eight provinces and the two northern territories: that of enforcing, outside the cities, the Criminal Code and the provincial statutes.

The Quebec force (the *Sûreté du Québec*), known to Anglophones as the Q.P.F. (Quebec Police Force), is charged with maintaining "the peace, order and public safety" of the province. The main headquarters is in Montreal with eight regional headquarters in Quebec City, Rimouski, Baie Comeau, Chicoutimi, Sherbrooke, Trois Rivières, Hull and Noranda. The force is over 4,500 strong, spread through 107 detachments.

The Ontario Provincial Police, known to most residents as the O.P.P., numbers about 4,100 in the uniform branch backed up by a support force of about 1,100 radio operators, clerks, and so on. Its headquarters is in Toronto, with specialized branches dealing with rackets, gambling, automobile theft, intelligence and security. Regional HQs are at Belleville, Chatham, Peterborough, London, Perth, North Bay, Sudbury, Sault Ste. Marie, Thunder Bay, Kenora, South Porcupine, Barrie, Mount Forest, Downsview, Burlington and Long Sault. The O.P.P. handles the job of law enforcement in 10 municipalities under special contract.

The private radio network of the O.P.P. is world renowned among enforcement agencies. It includes 158 fixed stations and more than 1,200 mobile units (including motorcycles and aircraft). There is a 24-hour service on criminal records and fingerprint identification, missing persons, laundry-mark identification and stolen property lists.

The Mounties

The Royal Canadian Mounted Police—the world-famous "Mounties"—are responsible for enforcing all federal laws across Canada, as well as all provincial laws in eight provinces and the two territories.

The R.C.M.P. has a 110-year history that has ranged from horses to computers. It is probably the best known symbol of Canada abroad, along with its proud, if unofficial, motto: "They always get their man." The official motto is in French and some-

what easier to live up to: *Maintiens le droit* ("Uphold the right").

The R.C.M.P. is responsible to the solicitor general of Canada and is headed by a commissioner who holds the rank of a deputy minister. In enforcing the Criminal Code and provincial law, the Mounties deal with the attorney general of each province where the force operates.

Operations of the R.C.M.P.—there are 15,000 men in this "arm of the law"—are directed from Ottawa through 13 operational divisions across the country. These divisions are split into 48 subdivisions and 709 detachment areas. All officers are commissioned by the Crown and are drawn exclusively from the ranks; their position entitles them to be saluted in military fashion.

The force was formed in 1873 as the North West Mounted Police. Its first task was to promote an orderly movement of settlers to the northwest (most of Canada west of Ontario) without conflict with the Indians. It also checked the booming illicit whisky trade from the United States into the territories now known as southern Saskatchewan and Alberta. The Mounties played a vital role in the Northwest

Insignia and oath

Badge of the "Mounties". The buffalo head recalls the beginnings of the force on the prairies during the late nineteenth century.

The following oath must be sworn by every recruit joining the ranks of the R.C.M.P.:
I .... do solemnly swear that I will faithfully, diligently and impartially execute and perform the duties required of me as a member of the Royal Canadian Mounted Police, and will well and truly obey and perform all lawful orders and instructions which I shall receive as such, without fear, favor or affection of or towards any person. So help me God.

Rebellion of 1885, and won the prefix "Royal" for distinguished service.

Through the years of peacekeeping in the northwest, the R.N.W.M.P. was joined by another force in the field of federal law enforcement—the Dominion Police. In 1920, the Dominion Police and the Royal North West Mounted Police were merged to form the Royal Canadian Mounted Police. The R.C.M.P. then took charge of the enforcement of all federal law from coast to coast and from the icy wastes of the Arctic to the U.S. border.

In 1928, the R.C.M.P. was empowered to administer provincial law in Saskatchewan. Four years later, Manitoba, Alberta, Prince Edward Island, New Brunswick and Nova Scotia added their names to its list of provincial responsibilities. In 1950, both Newfoundland and British Columbia also passed over provincial law enforcement to the R.C.M.P.

Today, the Mounties have the help of the latest technology in attempting to "always get their man." Foremost among the facilities at their disposal is the Canadian Police Information Center, staffed by 500 men, which serves as a central storehouse of information on crime for the entire country. This computer center serves more than 2,500 police agencies that are connected to it by terminals.

The Mounties' equipment includes 5,000 vehicles, 350 vessels and 29 aircraft—not to mention 142 horses.

Special forces
The Canadian Pacific and the Canadian National railways, plus Ports Canada, each maintains its own police force, mainly to patrol the extensive real estate involved. These officers—about 900 in all—have all the powers of arrest and investigation granted to the other better-known forces.

Private security
Since World War II, there has been a large growth of uniformed private security forces, operated by nongovernmental organizations that sell a protection service to companies and individuals. The oldest and most famous of these is the Pinkerton agency, founded by a Scottish immigrant who became the first detective on the Chicago police force. Also well known is Brink's, which makes a specialty of guarding money transfers. Wells Fargo is another notable force.

Many large corporations—and even some government departments and agencies— hire these forces to guard factories and offices with specially trained private security officers. Some work with trained attack dogs for protection.

These guards make citizen's arrests and carry out the lawful instructions of their employers; but they do not have the powers of municipal, provincial or federal police. Like the average citizen who has made a citizen's arrest, they must hand over their prisoner to the regular police force as soon as possible.

To help cut down the chances of international aircraft hijackings, airlines have hired private guards to screen passengers. Pinkerton's, for example, are active in this new specialty. In the 1970s, some foreign airlines carried armed guards on certain flights and several in-flight gunfights occurred. Improved security has lessened this threat.

Worldwide Interpol
Crime knows no borders, but neither does law enforcement. The major police forces of the world (including Canada's) combine their crime-fighting activities and expertise in the form of the International Criminal Police Organization—known better as Interpol.

Once centered in Vienna but now in Paris, Interpol keeps tabs on the international activities and travel of known criminals. If a criminal leaves a country that is a member of this international police force, the Interpol communication network alerts police in other countries who will then be on the watch for him. It has had great success in breaking up international rings in counterfeiting, art and jewelry theft, smuggling and narcotics.

A suspect arrested in Canada for a crime committed in another country would most likely be returned to the country concerned, if Canada had an extradition treaty with that country.

The policeman's lot

When constabulary duty's to be done,
to be done,
The policeman's lot is not a happy one!

SO THEY SANG in Gilbert and Sullivan's witty operetta, *The Pirates of Penzance*, when Good Queen Victoria was on the throne. And so it has been ever since Sir Robert Peel organized the first force of permanent police in London in 1829, bequeathing the British constable for all time with the nickname, "Bobby." And so they might sing today—if one accepted the cliché of the heavy-handed cop at odds with the citizenry. But like so many stereotypes, this is a wild distortion. Canada's more than 60,000 policemen provide, in fact, a true mirror of our society. They may well be somewhat fitter physically than the rest of us; otherwise, they run the gamut of society's faults and virtues. They are no better, and no worse, than the people on your street. Yet they must set an example to us in public: the R.C.M.P., for example, will not permit a man in uniform to smoke on duty. They must be efficient since there is only about one policeman or policewoman to every 350 persons in the country to keep us on the rails—and that includes those with desk jobs. In an average year, this small army handles more than one million breaches of the Criminal Code, as well as other federal and provincial penal laws and municipal bylaws. The most serious crimes are treason, first-degree (premeditated) and second-degree (unpremeditated) murder (some 600 cases a year), attempted murder (400), manslaughter (44), rape and other sexual offenses (13,300), wounding and assault (120,000). Traffic violations are charted separately, totaling nearly half a million charges, excluding parking tickets.

Before permanent paid police forces were set up in Canada, citizens had to organize their own protection. They set up "night watches," with volunteers taking turns to patrol the streets. There was no protection after dawn. Six years after Sir Robert Peel's "Bobbies" appeared in London, England, Toronto formed the first regular police force in Canada.

By establishing a police force, the citizens were merely hiring specialists to do the job in their stead. There is a significance to this that bears remembering: in our democratic way, power has never passed from the people to a police or army force. The policeman does not make the laws, nor has he the authority to punish anyone. His job is simply to enforce the laws that are made by our elected legislators. He apprehends suspected lawbreakers and brings them to the courts to be tried by our carefully selected judges according to those laws.

Joining the police
If you think you would enjoy a career in law enforcement, you should make a start as early as possible—perhaps while you are still in high school. You can get application forms from your local police headquarters or, if your ambitions are wider, from R.C.M.P. Headquarters, Recruiting Section, 1200 Alta Vista Drive, Ottawa, Ontario, K1A 0R2.

The first advice you should take is to stay at school until you pass your matriculation exams; most forces today set a minimum requirement of a Grade 12 education. (The Police Act in your province may specify Grade 10, but the hiring officer might have his own thoughts about that.) Today's peace officer has a lot of technology to master; the more groundwork you have laid, the better chance you will have of being accepted.

The day of the six-foot "limb of the law" has passed; brawn is not the basic requirement of today's policeman. But average size is essential (172 cm minimum, 195 cm maximum) and physical fitness must be such that you can tackle outdoor duties and, at times, go for long hours without rest. Perfect natural vision is not necessary but, with glasses, you are expected to have the equivalent of near-perfect vision. You will also be given a medical examination.

As an applicant, you will be asked searching questions designed to reveal your aptitude for law-enforcement work. Your character and habits, even the clubs and associations you belong to, will be probed. The reason is simple enough: the police don't want any bullies or extremists "protecting" the public. You must also have a clean police record, with no criminal offenses in your background. A traffic violation would probably not rule you out, taken on its own.

Fluency in an extra language is a considerable asset for a policeman in this multi-tongued land. Ability in sketching, photography, painting, drafting, typing or shorthand is valuable. Skill in scuba diving, judo, karate, boxing, swimming, or with firearms, are also assets.

Intelligence and psychological tests are often given to candidates to determine whether they have good learning ability, sound general knowledge and the right attitudes for the job.

For a municipal police force, candidates who know the community well often have an advantage over outsiders; yet, in the smaller town, being well known is sometimes a handicap since it may mean that a rookie will be called upon to deal with his buddies.

College for cops

There is growing emphasis on brains in the Canadian police. The increasing sophistication of crime prevention and law-enforcement techniques calls for an ever

higher level of mental skills. Although the police are not eager to explain in detail just how they keep tabs on known criminals or track down violaters, you can safely assume that they possess and make full use of every electronic and other scientific aid available.

Some applicants who have graduated from high school are asked to go on to a chosen university, with the sponsoring force assisting with costs. The Royal Canadian Mounted Police maintains a recruit-training academy, the Depot Division, at Regina, and the Ontario and Quebec provincial police forces both have their own academies to train cadets. Some of the larger city forces have their own schools as well. For instance, the Montreal police force sends recruits to its police academy; it also runs a police college where specialized courses are given—for example, courses in child psychology for men who are going to work in the youth section.

Police chiefs want to ensure that the cadet they are sending to college is worth the expense. The average recruit faces at least 12 weeks of basic training, with courses including traffic law, liquor control, the Criminal Code, first aid and the powers of arrest. The R.C.M.P. puts its recruits through a six-month course that covers 60 subjects.

As his career advances, the policeman may be required to take additional courses geared to specializing him for specific work—such as criminal investigation or counterespionage. The R.C.M.P. selects potential pilots from its Air Services Directorate or air division and from among commercial pilots. Cadets are also selected to maintain a patrol service in Canadian waters. Ten patrol vessels (each more than nine metres in length) operate on the Atlantic and Pacific coasts, while over 350 smaller vessels are used for inland water transport.

Lectures in law and in courtroom procedure are given to all police whose line of work involves their spending a lot of time giving evidence before the Bench. In smaller centers, police officers may also act as public prosecutors, presenting evidence to the magistrate in court.

The lawyer and the liquor

FACTS

During prohibition days in Ontario, two police officers went into a hotel to search for liquor, kept contrary to the law. They found eight men in one room with two bottles of liquor. When the police were about to take the names of the men, the defendant (who apparently was a lawyer) pushed his way in the room and said "Don't give your names to these skunks: give them 'Smith,' 'Jones' or any old thing." The Ontario Temperance Act specifically authorized the police in such circumstances to "demand the name . . . of any person found therein." The defendant was arrested and charged with the crime of "obstructing constables in the execution of their duty."

ARGUMENT

Among the submissions made on behalf of the defendant was that while the Temperance Act authorized a police officer to demand names, it did not make it an offense "for somebody to advise somebody else not to give his name." It was also argued that when the act used the words "may demand," this did not place an obligatory duty upon the police officers, and, in any event, the conduct of the defendant was neither willful nor had it, in fact, amounted to an obstruction. It was argued on behalf of the Crown that while the word "may" was perhaps permissive, it did indicate an obligatory duty on the part of the police, and, in any event, the defendant's conduct amounted in law to obstructing a constable, notwithstanding that the obstruction was neither physical nor effective.

JUDGMENT

The court ruled that the conduct of the defendant not only amounted to obstructing, but also amounted to "counseling to commit an offense." The judge also said: "It is elementary that it is the moral duty of every citizen to do his part in having the law obeyed; no one has any moral right to oppose the operation of any law, however much he may disapprove of it. There is a constitutional method of repealing noxious law. But, as long as the law is on the statute book, it must be obeyed by every law-abiding man . . . . There are many moral duties of which the law takes no cognizance and many acts to be deplored which cannot be punished."

Commenting on the fact that the accused person before the court was said to be a lawyer, the Bench remarked: "There is no legal evidence here that the defendant is a lawyer; but, if we assume that such is the fact, he is not advantaged; nor would he profit if the persons to whom he gave the advice were his clients. A lawyer has no more right to advise his clients to break the law than a layman so to advise another layman."*

*Based on an actual case (1922).

115

What police can do

Police in Canada depend a great deal on the assistance of the citizenry they serve. It follows, then, that our police are only as effective as we allow them to be.

The peace officer's powers of interrogation, search and arrest are limited by law. He or she must be free to perform effectively; yet at the same time the public must not suffer any unnecessary interference with *its* freedom. Police have the right to ask—even demand—any citizen to assist in arresting a lawbreaker. In making the arrest, the law authorizes the use of such force as is necessary.

If you are driving, a policeman may stop you and ask to see your driver's license and automobile insurance papers. If you don't comply, he has the authority to arrest you. You may be asked to justify your presence in a place, if you are wandering, trespassing or have no apparent means of supporting yourself financially.

A peace officer has the power to search your person or vehicle when there are "reasonable grounds" to justify this action. To search your house or apartment without your permission requires a search warrant or similar document called a writ of assistance. (The issue and use of the writ of assistance has been challenged in Ontario courts on the grounds that it violates provisions against unreasonable search and seizure in the Charter of Rights and Freedoms.) Police are not free to enter unless they have documents giving them authority, or they have the occupier's permission or they have reasonable grounds to believe a crime is being, or has just been, committed there.

Police can arrest without a warrant only under specific circumstances—such as when they find someone committing an offense or suspect a person of having committed an indictable offense—one that carries a penalty of at least two years' imprisonment. Neither do they need a warrant to arrest someone they have reasonable grounds to believe is *about* to commit an indictable offense. For instance, a policeman would be justified in arresting a person found in a shop doorway carrying burglary tools.

The police are given these powers of arrest without warrant to prevent a person from carrying out an offense and also from committing other offenses; to hold a suspect for questioning pending further investigation; and to ensure that a suspect will be available to appear in court.

Under the Charter of Rights and Freedoms, an individual has the right to be informed promptly about the reasons for his or her arrest or detention. Suspects must also be informed that they are under no compulsion to make a statement and that, if a statement is made, it may be used as evidence. While this may seem to load the dice in favor of the lawbreaker, it serves to make doubly sure that a person is not incriminated by hasty or ill-considered remarks. A statement made by an arrested person who was not "cautioned" could, however, still be admitted as evidence.

Apart from having the power to arrest, the police officer may ask a justice of the peace to issue a *summons*, ordering a specifically named person to appear in court. The officer may himself issue an *appearance notice*, which he will ask the suspect to sign; this commits the suspect to appear in court and sidesteps the mechanics of a formal arrest, thus saving the courts valuable time.

The officer who has issued an appearance notice must provide the courts with a statement, known as an *information*, before the date named on the appearance notice for the suspect to come to court. In the information, the police must give an outline of the alleged offense. If a judge in reviewing the information does not think that an offense has actually been committed, he or she may cancel the appearance, releasing the suspect from commitment in the appearance notice.

What police cannot do

As a citizen, it is your duty to cooperate with the police; furthermore, common sense should prompt you to work with them in the job of protecting society's majority from the minority of lawbreakers. Children can be told in truth that if we all obeyed the law it would not be necessary to have police.

But police are human first and law en-

How to recognize "the brass"

Established in 1909 to combat lawlessness in northern mining camps, the Ontario Provincial Police is now the third largest police force in North America. All the officers from the rank of inspector up to the commissioner receive a written commission directly stemming from the Queen, in the same way as is traditional in the armed forces. The rank insignia in the force is as follows:

COMMISSIONED RANKS

Commissioner

Deputy
Commissioner

Assistant
Commissioner

Chief
Superintendent

Staff
Superintendent

Superintendent

Chief
Inspector

Inspector

NONCOMMISSIONED RANKS

Sergeant
Major

Staff
Sergeant

Traffic
Sergeant

Identification
Sergeant

Sergeant

Corporal

forcement officers second; they are sub-ject to most human failings. For this reason, the law carefully limits their authority and range of action.

The police officer cannot get away with breaking the law any more than you can. An officer cannot on a whim stop you on the street and demand your name, age or address (but you can be asked why you are in a particular place if you have no business being there).

Except when you are driving a car or truck, the police officer cannot demand that you show any identification, your wallet or its contents, or any other item in your possession. (We do not yet have to carry ID cards in Canada, although this has been discussed at both federal and provincial levels.)

Police cannot insist that you answer questions in conversation, and your silence cannot be used as evidence against you if you appear in court. (People often live to regret foolish statements they have made when flustered. You need only say: "I am innocent but will say nothing further until I have seen my lawyer.")

The officer cannot take you to a police station "just to answer a few questions." Of course, if there are reasonable grounds to make an arrest,—for instance, if the officer thinks you are about to commit an indictable offense—the situation is as described above ("What police can do").

Although these restrictions merit being spelled out, it should also be emphasized that by replying politely and respectfully to a police officer's questions, you may easily be able to end the incident right there. It is more often the person who has "a chip on the shoulder" and refuses to cooperate who finds himself inside a police station. Telling lies to the police is a sure ticket to trouble; giving false information can be a crime in itself.

Arrest and charge

Although fewer arrests are made today than was routine in the recent past, this does not mean that lawbreaking is on the decline—unhappily, the contrary is true. But for most charges of a minor nature, the suspect will now receive a *summons* (a notice to appear in court on a given date) and will not be required to go to the police station at all.

If you are arrested, the policeman concerned must inform you of that fact and you must be told why if you ask.

Under no circumstances should you resist arrest physically. Keep your temper in check, even if you sincerely believe a mistake is being made. Remember that the officer concerned can call for as many reinforcements as may be necessary to subdue an unruly suspect.

If you believe you are being falsely arrested, calmly state your belief that you are innocent and try to get the names of any witnesses to the incident that led to the arrest. Then "go along quietly."

The peace officer who arrests you must make out a report stating the charge or charges against you and outlining the incident that led to the arrest. If you choose, you can still refuse to make any statement until you have spoken with a lawyer. This might ensure you a night's free lodging since few lawyers are in a position to drop everything and rush to your side. If you do not know a lawyer—or cannot afford one—you could ask for Legal Aid (*See* Chapter 20, "How the lawyer is paid").

Suing for false arrest

The policeman who arrests without a warrant is protected from being charged with a criminal offense; however, he can be accused of a civil offense (false arrest) if the arrested person can satisfy a court that the officer acted without "reasonable and probable grounds."

If the suspected person had resisted arrest physically, then that in itself could be sufficient grounds for arrest. "Resisting an officer" is a crime. Thus it is never wise to attempt any active confrontation with a peace officer. If you think a mistake is being made, you'll get plenty of opportunity to say so later.

In a manual issued as a guide to police officers in arrest procedure, the following example is included:

"A policeman on the beat receives a report that a short distance away an unidentified male is committing an indecent act in a public place within the sight of people living in an apartment block. The officer goes to the place and sees a man who matches exactly the description given. The man at this point is not misbehaving himself in any way but is simply standing on the sidewalk. The officer arrests him for the offense of willfully doing an indecent act in a public place in the presence of one or more persons, and tells the man his reason for arresting him.

"Without admitting or denying the offense, the man resists by pushing, struggling and fighting with the officer. The officer subdues the man and takes him to the police station where he charges him with the indecency offense and also with the offense of obstructing a peace officer in the execution of his duty.

"Irrespective of whether the man is or is not guilty of the offense of doing an indecent act, he has a civil right of action against the officer for unlawful arrest and he is not guilty of the obstruction charge. The reason for this is that in the circumstances the officer had no power to arrest without warrant. The offense for which he arrested the man is a summary-conviction offense and a peace officer has the power to arrest without warrant in such a case only if he actually finds the person committing the offense. As the officer was not therefore in the execution of his duty, the man was entitled with impunity to resist arrest."

Freedom on bail

Bail is an assurance a suspect gives that he or she will appear in the courtroom on the date the case is scheduled to be heard. It may require the payment of money, the deposit of a property bond or simply a personal pledge. Having given this assurance, or "recognizance," the suspect is allowed to leave the police station. A person can also be released on the recognizance of a friend or relative.

Bail can be seen as a vehicle that gets you out of custody after you have been arrested and charged. Since you probably won't be arrested for minor offenses, bail won't be involved; you will probably simply receive a summons (appearance notice) to appear in court on a specified date. Even in more serious cases, bail may not be required unless police feel it is needed. At one time, the onus was on the accused—the suspect who was charged with an offense—to prove that bail was deserved. At present, the accused will be released unconditionally—with bail payment—unless the prosecution can justify detention. Anyone charged with an offense punishable by life imprisonment must show why he should not be detained, before bail will be granted.

Bail arrangements of up to $500, for offenses punishable by five years' imprisonment or less, may be made by the ser-

Diplomacy in the streets

SURELY ONE of the most satisfying "perks" in being a diplomat in a foreign country is that you can leave your automobile in the no-parking zone and tear up your parking tickets with a laugh. While the ordinary Canadian taxpayer grits his teeth and drives around Ottawa for miles looking for a parking space, the man with the red-and-white CDA license plates can just stop, switch off and walk away. He will likely get a summons all right, but under the doctrine of diplomatic immunity he cannot be prosecuted.

In 1982, Ottawa's parking police (known as "Green Hornets") ticketed 4,982 diplomatic autos from the capital's 103 foreign embassies. Ottawa keeps the names secret for reasons of "international courtesy."

The value of the uncollected fines has been estimated at about $50,000.

A very few embassies do insist that their staffs obey the city parking regulations. One hundred sixty-nine (169) parking fines were paid in a recent year.

Foreign consular officials in cities outside Ottawa have the same immunity. Their cars have special plates bearing the letters CC.

geant at the police station. An actual deposit of money is not required unless the suspect ordinarily lives outside the province where he or she was arrested. Should the case call for a higher bail figure, a justice of the peace will be called in to decide the type and amount of bail required. Bail figures are determined on the basis of the offense and the record or background of the alleged offender.

If the police feel that a suspect should be kept in custody, the Crown must be able to convince the justice of the peace at a bail hearing that it has reasonable and probable grounds to believe that the accused might flee, and is a threat to society, or may interfere with the administration of justice (perhaps by approaching or threatening witnesses).

The accused must be taken before a justice of the peace who will usually proceed within 24 hours after the arrest, except in special cases. However, the hearing date may be adjourned for three days by the court—this happens on weekends.

If a person granted bail does not show up in court on the appointed day, a warrant is immediately issued for arrest, and the bail (if in money or property) is likely to be forfeited to the Crown. Make sure that your friend is trustworthy before you agree to provide bail.

Diplomatic immunity

Canadian police are not permitted under any circumstances to search foreign embassies and consulates. Similarly, Canadian embassies abroad are exempt from invasion by police or other security forces of the foreign country.

By international convention—under the doctrine of *extraterritoriality*—these foreign embassies in Canada are considered to be foreign soil and Canadian law cannot be enforced there: nor can the laws of other nations be enforced on our missions abroad. These privileges do not extend to foreign commercial concerns.

Government foreign-service staff are protected from police prosecution by the wide privileges of *diplomatic immunity*. Ordinary travelers are, of course, subject to all the laws of the land. It is the usual practice, when a diplomat (with immuni-

ty) has a serious brush with the law, that he is ordered by the government in question to leave the country; he can be asked to leave even if that government only suspects that he is committing an offense (such as spying). Icy politeness is observed: the diplomat concerned is not kicked out; he is declared *persona non grata* (*i.e.* he is "not welcome").

If this sort of situation should arise in Canada, the government will act on advice from the Royal Canadian Mounted Police; the police themselves do not give such marching orders to a diplomat.

Extradition treaties

Many criminals have learned that by fleeing the country, they are not escaping the law. Through treaties the Canadian government has negotiated with many foreign nations, suspected criminals may be sent back to face trial in Canada. By the same agreement, the Canadian authorities will normally return criminals, and suspects, to the countries where they have broken, or allegedly broken, the law. This arrangement is known as *extradition*.

An extradition treaty will list all the offenses for which a person may be returned to Canada and, similarly, from Canada to another country. Generally, political offenses are excluded, and this can lead to international tensions. For instance, during the American intervention in the Vietnam civil war, Canada refused to return to the United States offenders against that country's Universal Military Training and Service Act (these offenders were known as "draft dodgers"). Canada seemed to feel that the unwillingness of these young men to obey their country's law was not covered by the extradition treaty. If Canada should ever be faced with a similar internal situation, the United States would presumably be free by established precedent to offer a haven to any Canadian draft dodgers.

Before being extradited, an individual is granted a hearing before our courts. The country that wants him back must then give its reasons for requesting extradition and the fugitive may present arguments as to why he should be allowed to stay in Canada.

Judges and courts

WITH RESPONSIBILITY under the Constitution for "the constitution, maintenance and organization of provincial courts, both of civil and of criminal jurisdiction," the provinces provide a multilevel system of courts that are authorized to handle every offense from illegal parking to murder and treason. Only the Federal Court (formerly Exchequer Court) and the Supreme Court of Canada are outside provincial authority. Nevertheless, under the Judges Act, 1952, the federal government appoints and pays all judges, except for the magistrates and justices of the peace who try only cases of lesser importance.

Following the British pattern, Canadian courts fall into three main categories: the trial courts, the intermediate courts of appeal, and—the final arbiter—the Supreme Court of Canada. Following the Canadian pattern, the actual courts differ in name and work load from province to province. The basic setup for the trial courts is as follows: a lower tier consisting of the magistrates's court (also called police courts and provincial courts); a middle tier represented by a county (or district) court; and a top tier including a superior court which handles the graver cases and hears appeals from the lower provincial courts.

There is also a small group of miscellaneous courts which seldom involve members of the general public. These include a Courts-Martial Appeal Court, which handles only cases under the National Defense Act; a Tax Review Board for matters concerning the Income Tax Act and Estate Tax Act; and the Canadian Transport Commission which acts as a court in matters concerning transportation. The Canadian Radio-Television and Telecommunications Commission deals with matters related to telephone and telegraph service.

About 90 percent of all cases are heard in the lowest courts by a magistrate sitting alone, with a minimum of formality. Aided by the skilled and experienced clerk of the court, justice is sometimes handed out so rapidly in a kind of judicial shorthand that the casual onlooker can have difficulty in following the action in detail. With the exception of the juvenile and family courts, all courts in Canada are normally open to the public.

The structure of the judicial system varies from province to province, and the names of the civil and criminal courts in each province are numerous. In Ontario alone, the trial courts dealing only with civil matters include the High Court of Justice (with its branches for bankruptcy and divorce cases), the County and District Courts, the Surrogate Courts, the Small Claims Courts, and many others. In the following sections, you will find the judicial establishment described in broad outline with only some of the most striking variations noted. But the picture given is sufficiently detailed to establish a roughly accurate pattern.

How a judge is appointed

Judges are appointed by the lieutenant-governors of the provinces on the advice of the provincial governments, or by the governor general on the advice of the federal government. Likely candidates are distinguished lawyers with years of service in the courts.

All Quebec judges must be drawn from the Bar of that province, and at least three

121

justices of the Supreme Court of Canada must come from Quebec.

In communities where there is no full-time judge, or when pressure of work demands it, experienced men and women are appointed as justices of the peace. They can issue warrants and summonses. They may also hear cases involving offenses against municipal statutes. Two justices sitting together may try minor *summary-conviction* offenses and hold preliminary hearings; however, they cannot try indictable offenses. Most justices are not lawyers. While most are paid a salary, some work on a fee basis.

County and district court judges, as well as provincial superior court judges, are appointed by the governor general in council (really by the federal cabinet). Justices of the Supreme Court of Canada and judges in other federal courts are appointed by the governor general on the advice of the federal cabinet—in effect, the advice of the minister of justice who normally consults the Canadian Bar Association for its opinions. Traditionally, the Chief Justice of the Supreme Court of Canada is appointed on the advice and recommendation of the prime minister.

Although a judge is traditionally appointed "for life," retirement age is 75 in superior courts, 70 in county courts. A superior court judge can be unseated if the Canadian Judicial Council so recommends to the federal minister of justice after a formal inquiry. The grounds include conduct incompatible with the high standards demanded.

As befits the responsibility and importance of the job (and, one hopes, to place them above any financial temptation), judges are highly paid. Yet most of them could undoubtedly make larger incomes in private law practice. The Chief Justice of the Supreme Court of Canada is paid $106,600 a year and the chief justices of the highest provincial courts get $98,100. Various allowances and expenses raise these figures. On retiring, judges receive a pension of two-thirds of the salary they were receiving at retirement. Retirement can begin at 70 or even earlier, under certain conditions (such as permanent disability or infirmity).

The widow of a judge who died while still on the Bench can get a life pension amounting to one-third of her late husband's salary; when death comes to a judge who has retired on pension, his widow will continue to receive one-half of the pension.

Magistrate's courts

The busiest of all courts, the magistrate's courts, handle about 90 percent of all cases. New Brunswick, Ontario and British Columbia call theirs Provincial Courts; the names Police Court and Recorder's Court are also used. Here, violations of municipal bylaws, parking and traffic regulations, as well as criminal charges of all kinds (except the most serious) can be tried by the magistrate without jury. In general, the magistrate's courts deal with most cases except those involving serious offenses and large financial claims.

Before a graver offense comes to trial, the magistrate (or provincial judge) of this court will hold a preliminary hearing to determine whether the Crown has sufficient evidence to justify putting the alleged offender on trial. If the answer is "yes," the Crown attorney (the prosecutor) files an indictment (a formal written charge) against the accused. (*See* Chapter 19, "Trial and sentence.")

Anyone accused of an indictable offense can choose to be tried by jury; if he does, the magistrate would commit the accused for trial before a higher court. However, with the consent of the accused, the magistrate may try him for the offense—if the crime involved is one which falls within his jurisdiction.

At the close of the trial, the magistrate delivers his sentence, which can be appealed to higher provincial courts.

Juvenile and family courts

The provinces provide specially constituted and staffed courts to handle cases that involve family domestic troubles and youthful offenders.

In many provinces, there are juvenile courts operated under both provincial legislation and the federal Juvenile Delinquents Act (*See* Chapter 11, "Children in trouble"). Juvenile offenders in Quebec, for example, appear in the Youth Court, which also handles adoption cases. Actions under the Mental Patients Protection Act are heard in the Superior Court, and those that fall under the Quebec Charities Act are heard in the Provincial Court. Ontario's juveniles are channeled into the Provincial Court (Family Division) and appear before a provincial judge.

The public is not admitted to trials in juvenile courts, nor does the law allow newspapers, radio or television to publish or broadcast a juvenile's name when reporting the case.

If a child is found guilty of a *juvenile delinquency*, the offense will not be written into a criminal record and, if restrained, he may be sent to a house of detention or training school rather than to prison. If parents are judged to have neglected their children, they may be handed stiff fines. Contributing to juvenile delinquency (by bad examples or by helping or encouraging criminal activity) carries a penalty of up to two years behind bars.

Juvenile and family courts handle a variety of other domestic problems, such as hearing the grievances of deserted wives and their claims for support payments. The family court is also responsible for trying to settle domestic disputes, including assaults; but it does not hear divorce cases.

The actual powers of the juvenile and family courts are limited, and their effectiveness is often closely related to the quality of community social resources available to them. For instance, solving a domestic problem might require qualified marriage and psychiatric counseling services or, perhaps, finding suitable homes for the children. Welfare agencies that grant aid to families which the father has deserted often stipulate that the mother must take legal action against the runaway in a family court.

All the provinces have a Reciprocal Enforcement of Maintenance Orders Act. This ensures that a maintenance order granted in one province will be enforced in any other.

Small claims courts

Ranking lowest among the civil courts is the small claims court, sometimes known as the division court, or as the justice's court or magistrate's civil court. A small claims court does what its name indicates; it hears actions for modest sums of money and minor personal actions, including breaches of contract. The maximum amount that can be claimed varies from province to province. In British Columbia, Nova Scotia, and Prince Edward Island, for example, the maximum claim is $2,000. In Ontario, the upper limit is $1,000; and, in Quebec, $800.

These courts are not empowered to deal with many varieties of action—such as libel or slander—nor can they deal with land titles or wills.

Appeals from decisions of this court may be made within the time limits and according to the procedures specified by the regulations of the particular province where the claim was made. In Ontario, for example, appeals may be made within 15 days. But, in Saskatchewan, an appeal may be brought within 30 days. No appeal from the decision of the Small Claims Court can be made in Quebec.

Cases before the small claims courts are always heard in summary (that is, informal) fashion. Every effort is made to simplify action; this is one court in our legal system where you do not need the services of a lawyer.

Coroner's courts

A coroner, who is a medical doctor with a general practice appointed to the post by the provincial cabinet, may call a coroner's court into session. The essential question to be answered by this court is how a person met his or her death when there was no attending physician to issue a death certificate. This session is called a coroner's *inquest*.

Often, the coroner is able to determine the cause of death at the scene of an accident without having to call for an inquest. However, if he is uncertain about the cause of death, particularly when the case arouses public interest, he will call a coroner's court into session. (*See* Chapter 14, "When death occurs.")

The Canadian court system

The three levels of the Canadian court system are the trial courts, the appeal courts, and the Supreme Court of Canada, which is the court of final appeal in the country. The relationship of the three levels of courts with jurisdiction over civil matters, and the ranking of some of the courts within its trial division, are shown below. The ranking reflects the seriousness of the cases these courts handle. The arrows show the route of an appeal from court to court when this is granted. (The criminal court system has a similar organization.) Although the diagram below gives the basic structure of the civil court system, there are wide variations in name, jurisdiction and work load from province to province. In Alberta, for example, appeals from all trial courts may be taken directly to the appeal division; but, in Ontario, appeals from the lowest ranking courts must first pass through the Divisional Court. The Federal Court, which also has trial and appeal levels, handles only suits brought by or against the federal government.

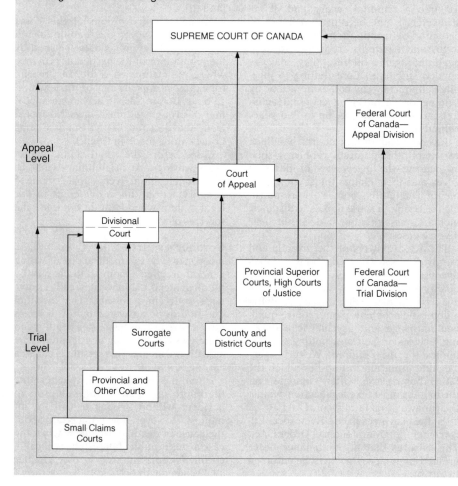

At the inquest, a jury of five persons will hear evidence from witnesses before presenting its finding as to the cause of death. A typical roster of witnesses will include medical specialists, the police officer who investigated the death and those persons who knew the deceased or saw him about the time of his death. Generally, they will decide that death occurred in one of four ways: natural, accidental, suicide or by unknown causes.

While the coroner's verdict itself does not have automatic legal consequences, it can lead to legal action. The coroner can issue an arrest warrant if the jury's verdict indicates that a particular person may be responsible for the murder or manslaughter of the deceased.

The coroner's jury is free to make recommendations as to how similar deaths might be avoided in the future. For example, a fatal accident at a railway crossing might prompt the jury to suggest that the warning signals at the particular crossing be improved.

In a suicide, the jury will probably be asked to state whether, in its opinion, the act was committed while the person concerned was of sound, or unsound, mind (the distinction can be important for insurance claims).

Surrogate or Probate Court

Six of the provinces (Nova Scotia, New Brunswick, Ontario, Manitoba, Saskatchewan and Alberta) maintain a separate court, called either surrogate or probate court, for the sole purpose of dealing with the estates of deceased persons. In the other provinces, this work is usually performed at either the county or superior court level. Thus, when a will is found to be authentic by such a court, it is said to be granted *probate*. (*See* Chapter 9, "The parties to a will.")

One of the primary responsibilities of this court is to appoint administrators for estates of persons who die *intestate*— that is, without leaving wills. The surrogate court also deals with disputes concerning the division of assets under a will and with wills that do not include all of a deceased person's property; in Ontario, the interpretation of wills may be referred to a provincial Supreme Court judge. The Ontario Surrogate Court supervises the work of executors and administrators of estates. Should any interested party have a grievance, he can appeal.

Bankruptcy court

A creditor or group of creditors may force a debtor into bankruptcy by filing a petition for bankruptcy in the superior court of the province where the debtor resides. If the debtor has a debt of at least $1,000 and has committed an *act of bankruptcy* within the preceding six-month period, the court will issue what is called a *receiving order*, officially decreeing him bankrupt, ("Acts of bankruptcy" include fraudulent practices, general inability to meet bills and deliberately avoiding payment.)

Once the receiving order has been issued, a trustee appointed to look after the interests of the creditors begins to assemble the assets of the bankrupt estate for division among its creditors. The trustee has the power to call for questioning anyone who may provide information about the bankrupt estate.

The debtor has the right to oppose these actions in court; similarly, any creditor can appeal a decision of the trustee within 30 days. Of course, in the average case, it is the debtor who seeks the relief of bankruptcy.

The responsibility for the administration of bankruptcies is handled by the Bankruptcy Branch of the federal Department of Consumer and Corporate Affairs (*See* Chapter 13, "If the business fails"). The superintendent of bankruptcy heads this branch and licenses all trustees in bankruptcy. Trustees are "officers of the court"; thus, even though appointed by the creditors, trustees are subject to the court's direction.

County or district court

In the middle tier of the Canadian judiciary is the county (or district) court with wide civil and criminal jurisdiction. Logically, these courts are located in county towns or regional "capitals" and are presided over by judges appointed by the federal government.

Their powers to hear criminal cases are limited in different ways from one province to another. For example, in Ontario (where the criminal division is known as the Court of General Sessions), the County Court tries some cases, and hears cases appealed from the decisions of justices of the peace and provincial judges (magistrates). In no province do these courts have the authority to try the most serious crimes—including murder and treason—but they can hear manslaughter cases.

The accused person has the choice of trial either by a judge and jury, or by a judge alone, depending on the laws of the province.

County and district courts have the authority to try civil cases—notably contract and personal property actions—up to certain limits. The amount of damages in such cases varies from province to province. Newfoundland, for example, has no upper limit. But in Nova Scotia, the upper limit is $50,000, while in Ontario, it is $15,000.

Provincial Superior Court

The highest-ranking court in each province is known variously as the superior court, supreme court, or high court. The justices of the superior court try the gravest criminal and civil cases, and, in some instances, they hear appeals from the rulings of the lower courts.

In Prince Edward Island, both trials and appeals are heard by a single Supreme Court. Quebec operates a Superior Court for trials and a Court of Appeal. In British Columbia, there is a Supreme Court for trials and an appeal court. The Supreme Courts of Ontario, Newfoundland, and Nova Scotia have two separate divisions, one with the power to hear appeals and the other to conduct trials. Each division is headed by a chief justice.

Ontario's High Court Division, the senior trial court in the province, has headquarters in Toronto, but it also sends a judge to hold sessions (*assizes*) on a regular basis in regional centers throughout the province. If there are no criminal cases requiring the attention of the *circuit* (traveling) justice, he is traditionally presented with a pair of white gloves.

In the Alberta trial division, the accused may elect to be tried by judge alone or by judge and jury; however, in all other provinces a jury is required for those offenses falling under Section 427 of the Criminal Code (murder, rape and treason).

For criminal cases, Quebec, Manitoba, Saskatchewan, British Columbia, New Brunswick and Alberta maintain two separate high courts to exercise their trial and appeal authority at the supreme court level—not just one court for the two divisions.

The trial divisions of the superior courts in the provinces have authority over civil cases no matter how large the claims involved. Such cases are heard either by a judge and jury or by a judge sitting alone.

Juries, traditionally comprising 12 persons "good and true," have recently been cut down in number for trials involving civil suits. In Newfoundland, the number has been pared to nine; in British Columbia, to eight; in Prince Edward Island and New Brunswick, to seven; and, in Ontario, Manitoba and Alberta, to six. In Nova Scotia, the number of jurors may be any number "sufficient for the civil matter." There are no jurors for civil cases held in Quebec. Only Saskatchewan keeps to the original dozen.

Appeals from decisions of the provincial appeal courts may be heard by the Supreme Court of Canada.

Federal Court of Canada

A relatively new court (established in 1970), the Federal Court of Canada has the powers formerly held by the Exchequer Court of Canada. Housed in the massive Supreme Court Building in Ottawa, it has original (as distinct from appellate) jurisdiction over all suits in which claims are made by or against the Crown—that is, the Government of Canada, or its agencies (including Crown corporations, such as the CBC).

Although the Federal Court is located in Ottawa and its judges must live in or near the national capital, the trial and appeal divisions can and do try cases at locations from coast to coast. The Federal Court plays a vital role in federal-provincial relations, handling legal disputes between one or more provinces and Ottawa, and between the provinces themselves.

Claims resulting from allegedly dangerous conditions on federal properties or alleged negligence on the part of government employes are dealt with in this court, along with certain income tax disputes and cases dealing with trademark, copyright and patent legislation.

The Federal Court inherited admiralty jurisdiction—authority over maritime affairs—from the Exchequer Court. This jurisdiction derived from the colonial courts set up originally under the authority of the Admiralty Act of 1890. Maritime disputes can be brought directly to the court, or indirectly through appeals from decisions of judges in Admiralty situated in the coastal provinces.

Among the new functions exercised by the Federal Court is power to hear appeals from the decisions of federal boards, commissions and tribunals.

The members of the Federal Court are a chief justice in both the trial and the appeal divisions, plus ten other justices. They have somewhat the same standing as justices of the Supreme Court.

At one time, appeals could go from the Appeal Division of the Federal Court to the Supreme Court of Canada only if the value of the matter was more than $10,000. There now is no monetary limit. Anyone wishing to appeal a case before the Supreme Court must ask permission. If the Supreme Court feels the case is worthwhile, it will hear it.

Territorial Court

Under federal laws concerning the administration of the Yukon and the Northwest Territories, one or more judges of Superior Court status may be appointed to form a Territorial Court.

The commissioners of the territories (appointed by the federal government and responsible to the minister of Indian Affairs and Northern Development) have authority to appoint magistrates, justices of the peace and court officials.

The attorney general of Canada supervises the commissioner in his role as attorney general of the territories.

Appeals from the Territorial Courts will be heard by justices from the Courts of Appeal of British Columbia and Alberta, sitting with judges from the territories.

Court of arbitration

Although there is no formal court of arbitration, the ruling of a properly appointed *arbitrator* carries considerable judicial weight. Arbitration is a recognized method of settling disputes; it often saves the costs of a court action and is usually much faster. Another big attraction is that arbitration is private: there is no "washing of dirty linen" in public.

Employment contracts often include a clause stipulating that any dispute between the parties will go to arbitration. The arbitrator selected must be satisfactory to both sides in the argument because they have previously agreed to accept whatever decision he brings in. Sometimes, each party will appoint an arbitrator. These two arbitrators will then choose a third by mutual agreement; when this method is followed, a majority decision is acceptable.

Persons chosen as arbitrators are usually familiar with the subject matter of the case but not involved in it directly. Lawyers are often likely candidates, but any adult may be appointed.

The terms of a contract usually state that there can be no appeal from arbitration. The courts will normally refuse to adjudicate a suit until the period of arbitration specified in the contract has been completed with no settlement having been reached. On the other hand, if both parties decide to skip arbitration and go directly to court, they may do so. A judge would not normally upset an arbitrator's decision unless it was contrary to law.

Several countries have tried establishing formal courts of arbitration, usually for the compulsory settlement of labor-management disputes. However, these have mostly been abandoned in favor of conciliation procedures (*See* Chapter 14, "Strikes and lockouts"). Since arbitration often ends in compromise—the "saw-off" principle—this system tended to result in trade unions making excessive wage claims in the first place.

127

Special courts and tribunals

To cope with the complexities of government business at both the federal and provincial levels, many special courts and tribunals have been set up, each having responsibility over certain areas of activity. Some serve for a short term, dealing with an unusual situation or emergency. Others are designed to handle a continuous work load.

In Ontario alone there are more than 100 boards, commissions and licensing bodies to handle matters ranging from prices of commodities to the location of development projects. Security practices, illegal strikes, discriminatory actions, and environment protection all fall under the responsibility of different tribunals. Many of these have some of the powers of formal courts—for instance, the power to call witnesses and to impose penalties.

Civil rights legislation in some provinces now fully provides for the protection of anyone whose rights are at stake in hearings before boards and tribunals. He is assured of reasonable notice of a hearing in public, and entitled to be represented by a lawyer. He is entitled to examine and cross-examine witnesses, and to be given a written copy of the decision, including the reasons for decision—if he requests it. He is entitled to have the decision of the tribunal reviewed by a regular court for errors in law and for failure to follow a fair procedure.

Three of the Atlantic provinces—Nova Scotia, New Brunswick and Prince Edward Island—have specialized Courts of Divorce and Matrimonial Causes, which were established before Confederation. However, only Nova Scotia's court still operates as such; the federal Divorce Act

The gun-totin' Johnny Canuck

CANADIANS generally like to believe that, in comparison with certain other nations, they live in a basically peaceable country.

But it is possibly a long time since they looked closely at national crime statistics. The hard-edged facts tell a somewhat different story.

Our courts are dealing with an increasing number of crimes involving the use of guns. In a five-year period, a total of 1,110 murders were committed with either handgun, rifle, sawed-off shotgun or other type of gun. This is considerably more than the rate in England which has considerably more population than Canada.

During the period 1957–1982, Criminal Code offenses in Toronto zoomed an incredible 525 percent. In 1982, 1,003 persons were charged with assaulting Toronto police. In the 1970s, within one 12-month period, four policemen were killed by gunfire while on duty. Calgary, Montreal and Moncton have recorded similar tragedies.

Fearing that the police cannot protect them adequately, more and more citizens now possess firearms—registered or not. You must have a police permit in Canada to possess a pistol or revolver, and more than half a million Canadians have been issued with such permits.

How many unregistered firearms are in Canadian homes—left over from the four wars Canadians have served in this century, or bought clandestinely—is anybody's guess. In one recent year, 33,878 guns were reported stolen, misplaced or lost, and 1,648 were reported recovered or found.

Trying to appease a citizenry angered by the rise in violent crime, the federal government has tabled tougher firearm controls. But international experience shows that there seems to be no way to stop criminals from getting guns. Should, therefore, only their law-abiding potential victims be penalized? As one participant in this hot argument points out: "Guns are inanimate objects. It's people who are the problem. We don't need more law. What we need is more respect for the law we've got." Our judges say *amen* to that.

transferred jurisdiction over these matters to the provincial superior courts.

Apart from the better-known federal tribunals—such as the Canadian Transport Commission, the Public Service Commission and the Tax Review Board—there are many that cover a wide range of activity. The Anti-Dumping Tribunal formally investigates any seemingly unfair threat to Canadian production; the commissioner of the Official Languages Tribunal can launch inquiries into alleged breaches of the "spirit and intent" of the Official Languages Act; and the National Energy Board regulates the construction and operation of oil and gas pipelines, as well as the import and export of gas and electric power.

Rights of appeal

To ensure that the process of law is fair, as well as seen to be fair, both provincial and federal court systems provide that many decisions of the lower courts may be appealed.

In criminal matters, decisions of a magistrate's (or provincial) court may be appealed to the provincial, county, or district court. Decisions from county or district courts, or the high court of justice, may be taken to the provincial court of appeal. In civil matters, appeals from the county and district courts, as well as the superior court level, may go to the court of appeal. For example, rulings of juvenile or family courts may be heard by a county court judge and, if the issue is taken farther, by a superior court of appeal. In Ontario, decisions from the lower provincial courts may be taken to the Divisional, rather than the County or District, Court.

The decisions of the provincial appeal courts can, with permission, be appealed to the Supreme Court of Canada. (In some instances, however, a person convicted of an indictable offense, such as murder, may have an automatic right of appeal to the Supreme Court of Canada.) Even if permission to appeal is refused at the provincial level, the Supreme Court may decide to hear a case.

The Supreme Court may also decide to hear appeals from decisions made by the Federal Court. It will always accept such appeals when the case asks questions regarding the validity of a provincial or federal statute.

Supreme Court of Canada

The Supreme Court of Canada, situated in Ottawa, is the highest court of appeal in the land for both civil and criminal cases; thus it is sometimes called "the court of last resort." Until 1935 in criminal cases and 1949 in all other matters, its authority ranked below that of the Judicial Committee of Britain's Privy Council. (*See* Chapter 1, "Under Canadian writ.")

The leading figure is the chief justice of Canada; he is supported by eight *puisne*, or associate, justices.

No court case begins in the Supreme Court. All cases are referred to it by provincial courts of appeal or the Federal Court of Canada. Even the trials of such crimes against the state as treason are originally conducted at the provincial superior court level. The Supreme Court of Canada has the final word in any disputes between federal and provincial governments and their agencies.

Permission to appeal to the Supreme Court in civil cases is granted only if the importance of the principle involved merits it. At one time, only cases involving more than $10,000 were heard by the Supreme Court, although cases involving lesser amounts were sometime allowed by special leave of the court. There is no monetary minimum now, but the great expense in bringing a case to this judicial level is a massive deterrent.

Apart from appeals, the Supreme Court can be required to advise the governor general (in effect, the Cabinet) on any questions that may be referred to it. These questions would probably be of a constitutional nature. The Senate or the House of Commons may also seek the court's advice on issues raised in private bills.

In each and every case, the judgment of the Supreme Court of Canada is final, being subject only to a pardon that could, theoretically, be granted by the minister of justice (with Cabinet approval) in the name of the Queen (*See* "The penal system" in this chapter).

How a case is tried

"SILENCE IN THE COURT!" "Will the accused rise and face the Bench." "Order! Order in the court!" "Gentlemen of the jury—have you reached your verdict?" All these familiar courtroom phrases have one thing in common: they are seldom heard in the Canadian courts. Thanks to thousands of crime novels, movies and television dramas, the average person has an almost entirely phony picture of what actually goes on in court.

In real life, it's a pretty dull affair. Few ringing speeches and even fewer impassioned appeals to principle and the higher ideals of man. Lawsuits are seldom dramatic and criminal trials are often heart-wrenching and sordid. It is basically the sober and unfortunate business of human beings in dispute and trouble, with highly skilled (if somewhat world-weary) professionals following well-beaten paths as they attempt to sort fact from fiction, apportion responsibility, and decide which of the penalties the law provides would best suit the case.

We pay the police to maintain law and order; but we look to the barrister, solicitor and the judge to uphold the law and apply it even-handedly and with as much compassion as the law allows. Through time and tradition, formulas have been developed and procedural rules codified to allow this work to be done fairly and efficiently. Although the layman might get the idea that the courts are hog-tied with out-of-date formality and ceremony, he would find it difficult, even after closely examining an everyday court action, to decide where corners could be cut without causing some reduction in the protection of either the individual or the public.

Before you can understand Canada's legal system, you must realize that there are two kinds of law: private and public or, more specifically, *civil* and *criminal*. Civil law concerns property, financial transactions, contracts, torts (private wrongs) and civil rights—essentially private troubles between citizen and citizen; criminal law concerns itself with such offenses as murder, assault, theft, and, by extension, traffic violations. Civil actions, called *suits*, are brought by individuals, while criminal actions are usually brought by the state: a crime committed against an individual is considered an attack upon the whole community.

Unless you are simply trying to recover a minor debt in the Small Claims Court, you will most likely need the advice and assistance of a lawyer in any legal action. Therefore, there is no need for you to try to become an expert (*See* Chapter 20, "When you need a Lawyer"). But you will be better equipped to advance your interests if you have at least a rudimentary grasp of how cases are tried, what your options are, what is likely to happen and what jobs are done by all the officials you will perhaps meet for the first time.

For one thing, you should understand some of the terms and titles that are involved. The person who brings a suit is called the *plaintiff* and the other party is the *defendant*; this case would be listed on the *docket* or court agenda, as "Jones vs. Smith." If the state is bringing the charge, as in a criminal case, it will be listed as "*R*. vs Smith." (*R*. stands for *Regina*, Latin for "Queen"; in this case Elizabeth II, Queen of Canada, in whose name all state prosecutions are launched and in whose name all justice is dispensed.)

Magistrates are formally addressed as

"Your Worship," judges as "Your Honor" and justices at the Superior Court level as "Your Lordship" or "My Lord"; a more simple "Sir" is acceptable, indicating respect for the law (which outranks prime ministers, presidents and kings).

The court that hears your case will, in a sense, be preselected by the nature and gravity of the issue involved. If the accused, the defendant, has the right to choose a jury trial, that choice will also have a bearing on the selection of the court. The great majority of all legal action takes place before the magistrate (or provincial judge) where, in the interest of efficiency, formality is at a minimum. Generally speaking, the higher up the court ladder your case ranks, the more complex will the procedure become—and the tougher the struggle, the heavier the penalties.

The decision to sue
The decision to take legal action for a civil wrong (say, a slander or a breach of contract) should never be taken hurriedly—especially not in the heat of anger. Are you certain, for instance, that you in no way contributed to the occurrence? Better discuss the whole matter with a lawyer. He will do his best to help you settle the matter out of court.

Civil wrongs to the person are called *torts*, like the injury suffered by the young man in the case quoted at the beginning of this chapter. They include willful or negligent damage to person or property, slander, deceit and trespass. The fact that some of these acts are also treated as crimes against the general public does not excuse the wrongdoer from liability to the individual harmed by his action. That individual can claim damages from the wrongdoer in a separate court action. (*See* Chapter 18, "What is a tort?")

Sometimes injured parties will seek only nominal (known in courtroom slang as "peppercorn") damages. They are usually trying to defend their reputations, or a principle, and are not primarily interested in financial redress.

Again in contrast to the public's image of legal disputes, civil suits can actually be brought quite amicably. For example,

two parties (or their lawyers) who simply cannot come to agreement in a business dispute may, in effect, ask the court to decide the issue.

The civil action
If it is human to err—as Alexander Pope maintained—it is just as human to differ. Undoubtedly, many thousands of disagreements, injuries to persons and property and other breaches of civil law occur every week in Canada. The entire machine of the law would grind to a shuddering halt if even one-tenth of these causes of action resulted in court cases. Of the fraction that have legal reactions, only a comparative handful actually go to trial. It has been estimated that in the average major city, perhaps one or two percent of the legitimate claims that could be pursued are actually taken to court; the others are settled out of court.

The first step in launching proceedings is always the drafting of *a writ of summons*. This is issued by either the County Court or the provincial Superior Court on behalf of the plaintiff and delivered to (*served* on) the defendant; in special cases it may be sent by registered mail.

There are several types of writs; we will first deal with the most common form, known as the "generally endorsed" writ, which is commonly used to collect a debt. This writ details the claim made against the defendant by the plaintiff and commands that the defendant enter a defense within 15 days. If the defendant intends to contest the claim or allegation made against him, he takes the step known as *entering an appearance*.

If the plaintiff had issued a "specially endorsed" writ, the defendant would then enter an appearance and file a document called an *affidavit of merits*, outlining his side of the story in detail.

Incidentally, in the Small Claims Court, where formality is kept to a minimum, these writs are not required. The plaintiff merely fills out a printed form known as a *claim* and the defendant can choose to reply on a form called a *dispute*.

In a regular suit, if the defendant does not file his appearance within 15 days, the plaintiff signs a document called the *affi-*

davit of nonappearance which will lead to a judgment against the defendant in his absence. (In Quebec, the delay for filing an appearance is ten days.)

If the defendant does file his appearance papers, the plaintiff must then supply him with a full *statement of claim*, further detailing the claim and outlining the basis on which the amount sought in compensation (if any) was determined.

The defendant replies to this with a *statement of defense*, setting out his position on the claim made against him. He may, if he has grounds, even launch a *counterclaim* against the plaintiff.

With these documents revealing most of the strengths and weaknesses on both sides of the dispute, the party who sees his case to be weaker usually gives in and agrees to settle the claim in some way. Experienced lawyers know exactly how to work out these compromises. If a payment is made privately, the winning side usually signs a *release*, by which he formally forgives the wrong and releases the other party from further liability.

If a court case seems inevitable, each party is entitled to an even more thorough preview of the documentary evidence that will be presented by the other; extensive probing questions will be permitted. This pre-court session is known as the *examination for discovery*. The total file of all papers, both of accusation and defense, is known as the *pleadings*. The obvious purpose of all these preliminaries is to define the issues as sharply as possible in order to save the time of the courts; litigants, as the opposing sides in a court case are called, are seldom permitted to introduce surprise evidence in the manner beloved by writers for television.

When the parties, having been unable to settle on their own, are ready to bring the dispute to trial, the plaintiff (or the defendant) will have the case listed on the *docket* for a future sitting of the court.

The criminal trial
Most minor crimes are tried in the magistrate's (or provincial) court, with more serious charges going on to the criminal

What actually happens in court

PUT PERRY MASON'S SHENANIGANS out of your mind. In real life, the due process of law unfolds in the Canadian courtroom in unfailingly routine fashion as the sorry line-up of mostly petty criminals—many of them just like the guy next door—enter the dock and face the duty magistrate.

In an average case, the clerk of the court rises and drones:

John Doe, you stand charged that on or about the 16th day of November, 1983, in the City of Lancaster, in the County of St. John, you did unlawfully have in your possession one Sony color television set of a value exceeding two hundred dollars, knowing it to have been obtained by the commission in Canada of an indictable offense contrary to Section 312 (1) (a) of the Criminal Code

of Canada. How do you plead to this charge?
Accused: Not guilty [*or* guilty].
Clerk of the court: John Doe, you have the option to elect to be tried by a magistrate without a jury; or you may elect to be tried by a judge without a jury; or you may elect to be tried by a court composed of a judge and jury. How do you elect to be tried?
Accused: By magistrate [*or* other].

The case then proceeds with the Crown outlining the case for the prosecution. If John Doe confirms the police evidence, and admits the offense, then the magistrate may proceed to sentencing, although he may first call for the report of a probation officer or for other specialized advice.

Pleas of guilty are entered in about 80 percent of all Canadian criminal cases.

division of the county court; the gravest of all (murder, rape, treason) will be heard only in the provincial superior courts. Court procedure is essentially the same across the country.

A conviction in a criminal trial hinges on the Crown being able to convince the judge and jury (or perhaps a judge alone) that the defendant is beyond a reasonable doubt guilty of the offense. It is up to the lawyer retained by the defendant to show that his client is innocent of the charge, that flaws exist in the case presented by the Crown or that reasonable doubt of guilt exists. Under Canadian legal system, the defendant is assumed to be innocent until the Crown proves he is not. (*See* Chapter 1, "The rise of English law.")

The prosecuting attorney opens proceedings in court by giving an outline of the case as he sees it. Then he presents witnesses and questions them. He expects the evidence given by his witnesses to back up the Crown's allegation that the defendant committed the crime in question. Each witness must also submit to questions by the defendant's lawyer who will attempt to test the evidence given; this is known as the *cross-examination.*

In turn, the defense lawyer may call witnesses to support his client's innocence; he may call the defendant himself, if the defendant chooses to give evidence on his own behalf. The defense witnesses are also subject to cross-examination, this time by the Crown attorney. If the accused had been "caught red-handed", then his lawyer would try to present evidence that would lessen the severity of sentence.

The questions asked of witnesses by either prosecution or defense must be relevant and fair, or the judge will not allow them. Scrupulous attention is paid to the laws of evidence: there is in Canadian courts an absence of the theatricals and browbeating that are so much a part of the fictional courtroom.

Each side makes a concluding argument to the court, following which the judge sums up the evidence heard during the trial, instructs the jury on the law (if there is a jury) and advises it on the verdicts it may return. When a verdict of guilty is delivered by the *foreman* of the jury, the judge will then determine the sentence to be imposed.

Most criminal cases are tried by a magistrate (in Ontario and British Columbia, by a provincial judge). He has the authority to deal *summarily* ("at once," "without ceremony") with all charges for which the maximum penalty is a $500 fine or six month's imprisonment—although, in fact, he can hand down a life sentence. The summary-conviction procedure covers the widest range of offenses, from traffic violations and petty vice charges to minor thefts and damage to property, and even extends to rape and manslaughter.

If the alleged crime carries a heavier penalty—for instance, two years or more in federal penitentiary, making it what is called an indictable offense—the magistrate can still try it summarily, if the accused consents. Otherwise, the accused will be committed for trial at a higher court. All sentences in the lower courts can, of course, be appealed. (*See* Chapter 19, "Trial and sentence.")

Officers of the court

There are many other courtroom workers who help carry out the functions of the law. If you were to become involved in the average court case, you would probably enter the following scene and see the principal actors as described below.

A typical magistrate's (or provincial) court will be situated in the local courthouse, or in an office at your city hall. (In fact, a court can "sit" anywhere.) Furnishings are simple: a high desk for the presiding magistrate underneath a photograph of Elizabeth II (to remind you that all justice stems from the Queen of Canada). There will be several tables and chairs for officials and lawyers. On one side is the *witness box*, possibly just a small raised platform where anyone giving information on oath to the court will stand (it is raised so that everyone can clearly see who is testifying). Directly in front of the judge is a similar place for the accused to stand. This is often close to an adjacent room where prisoners can be kept until required. Chairs or benches are provided for the public, because all Canadian trials (except those of juveniles) must be open to the public; a judge can order a court to be cleared of the public in order to maintain order or to protect someone's feelings while sordid evidence is being given, but this happens only rarely.

Action begins, usually, at 10 A.M. when the *clerk of the court* walks in to herald the arrival of the magistrate. The officers of the court will have read the *docket*, or agenda, to find out what cases are to be tried and in which order. Police witnesses are ready to present their evidence. At the entry of the magistrate, everyone stands and remains standing until he is seated.

The clerk is at the hub of the court. He is also responsible for the administration aspect of claims, pleadings and money received by the court. He is also responsible for the availability of juries and to ensure that the court's business follows the schedule. He usually reads the charge to the accused and asks how he chooses to be tried. Experienced in the emotions of trials, he quietly advises the newer magistrates or justices of the peace.

Bailiffs and sheriffs assist by carrying out the decisions of the court and acting as agents for court business.

The magistrate, or judge, ranks as the foremost officer of the court, receiving the respectful attention of all parties. He is neither a god nor an ogre. His duty is strictly to justice, not to the government or the Crown, and he will see to it that the accused, particularly, understands exactly what is going on. Sometimes, a judge will personally read the charge to the accused. He will ask simply: "How do you plead to this charge?" Even if the accused answers "Guilty," the judge may decide *not* to accept the plea. He may decide instead to have the Crown actually prove its case.

If the judge has any doubts about the ability of the accused to understand the charge, or the proceedings generally, he may set aside the plea and order a psychiatric examination of the accused. He must order a translator, if he feels this is required. Or, if the accused has appeared without a lawyer, the judge will likely refer him to the always-available duty lawyer. On the other hand, the judge's

word is quite literally the law—unless upset by a higher court or other level of authority. If a judge sentences a person to imprisonment, the term begins at that moment and the defendant is taken into custody immediately.

The Crown attorney is a lawyer given the responsibility of presenting the case for the prosecution, in accordance with the rules of courtroom procedure.

The defense lawyer, while naturally serving his client, also has a responsibility to the court. He must not knowingly permit his client to give false testimony, nor is he allowed to use trickery or deceit to forward his client's cause.

Everything of significance said during the hearing will be recorded by the court reporter, or stenographer, so that it can be repeated word-for-word if required for study later. The reporter records the decision of the Bench.

Adjournment

Neither the defense nor the prosecution is forced to bring its case to trial before it is ready to do so. With his duty to ensure the fairest possible trial, the judge will normally accept a variety of good reasons for postponing a case. By this procedure, termed an *adjournment*, a case may be kept out of court for weeks and even months. However, an adjournment cannot be sought by either the Crown attorney or the defense lawyer simply to delay the process of law.

The judge may grant an adjournment because more time is needed to prepare arguments or because witnesses may be unavailable until a later date.

A judge may postpone sentencing until he has received reports from probation officers. These can assist the judge in determining what the most appropriate sentence might be. For instance, a study into the offender's background and present family situation might influence the judge to release the prisoner on probation rather than send him to jail. In a difficult case, especially where fine points of law have been argued by counsel, the judge may simply require extra time to consult legal authorities or just to think the matter over.

Long delays at the Bar

Long, exhaustive and expensive delays in the judgment of an action are caused also by the sheer volume of cases before the courts.

Increasingly, individuals have to wait in line for their day in court. While this problem is not as great in Canada as it is in the United States, it can take many months for cases to be tried, even though both sides are prepared to go ahead.

The longest delays occur in the higher courts, particularly in the provincial superior courts and in the Supreme Court of Canada. Even at the best of times, a trial before a high court can be delayed because these courts sit for only limited periods during the year.

Long delays at the Bar can, of course, have an effect on the cases themselves. The defense may sometimes succeed in having a case dropped for want of prosecution—for instance, if a key witness dies or moves abroad.

Further delay in the final settlement of a case can arise from the right of appeal which a convicted person may exercise, even though justice appeared to have been done in the lower court. Some people might argue that the law is not even-handed in this instance: an individual with enough money to pay for a string of appeals can extend his freedom over a long period while further argument is heard; yet another individual, in the same circumstances but without the same resources, might have no choice but to accept the verdict given by a lower court and go to jail, if that is his sentence. Legal Aid lawyers have, of course, full opportunity to appeal any decisions of the lower court they may consider to be unjust; however, their time, their skill and their experience are sometimes limited.

A choice of courts

For most serious offenses—those that can bring a fine of more than $500 or more

---

"Horse-trading" on sentences

THE PRESS calls it "plea bargaining," the lawyers call it "plea negotiation," and to the ordinary observer it looks something like an old-fashioned horse trade. Under any name, it's the widespread but little-publicized system by which the Crown prosecutor and the defense lawyer often get together to work out a deal.

Let us assume there is little room for doubt that the accused John Doe is guilty of the alleged crime. There may be several charges outstanding. If Doe pleads guilty, the trial is over and he will likely draw a penitentiary sentence. If he pleads not guilty, there must be a full-scale trial, costly in terms of money and court time.

Doe's lawyer and the Crown attorney go into a private huddle. Defense counsel suggests that his client would possibly plead guilty to a lesser charge, one that did not put him in risk of the penitentiary. The prosecutor decides that—considering the clogged state of the courts and the particular facts of the case at hand—justice will be adequately served by a compromise. The charge is reduced, Doe pleads guilty, and the judge imposes a sentence within the range related to that class of offense.

While some jurists seek abolition of this legal wheeler-dealing, Winnipeg lawyer Harry Walsh, at a meeting of the Canadian Bar Association, stated that the administration of justice would be seriously hampered without the system. He pointed out that more than 80 percent of all criminal cases were disposed of quickly by pleas of guilty, many of these resulting from deals between counsel. He suggested that the chief justice of each province publish guidelines for acceptable plea negotiation to remove "the aura of surreptitiousness."

Plea bargaining doesn't necessarily result in a softer touch for the criminal. As in all horse-trading, the seller (in this case, the Crown prosecutor) tends to begin bargaining with maximum expectation.

than six months' imprisonment—the accused has a choice of court procedures.

He may elect to be tried in one of three ways:

(1) A magistrate, or provincial court judge, without a jury.

(2) A county, or district, court judge, with a jury.

(3) A county, or district, court judge, without a jury.

Most lawyers will advise their clients to choose a trial in the magistrate's court, for sentences are apt to be lighter there. However, if the local magistrate was known to have strong feelings about the type of offense involved, the lawyer might suggest trial in the county court—provided his client's alleged offense was serious enough that he had the option.

Before appearance in the county court, the defense would have had the advantage of a preliminary hearing where the prosecution must outline its case. In a preliminary hearing, the onus is totally on the Crown to convince the magistrate that its case is strong enough to warrant a trial; the defense does not have to reveal its case at all. This hearing allows defense counsel to get a better idea of how strong his client's position is.

Summary-conviction cases are tried in the magistrate's court without a jury, as are minor crimes outlined in Section 483 of the Criminal Code (break, enter and theft, etc.). (*See* Chapter 19, "Threat to the community.")

The gravest crimes, as specified in Section 427 of the Criminal Code (treason, mutiny, bribery of public officials, and murder), must be tried before the provincial superior court with a jury.

The role of each court in the Canadian judicial structure is more completely detailed earlier in this chapter in the section titled, "Judges and courts."

The jury: trial by citizens

Most people know what a jury is: a panel of ordinary citizens called to determine a case and render a verdict in a court of law. The idea of being judged by one's *peers* ("equals") arose in England in post-Norman times (*See* Chapter 1, "The rise of English law"). In modern times, however, the tendency seems to be for a defendant to choose trial by judge alone where permitted—reflecting the general belief that the Bench is likely to be much more liberal than the general citizenry.

Each province has its own legislation regarding the selection of juries. Minimum age to qualify as a juror varies from 18 to 21, and the maximum age from 60 to 65. Sometimes, owning property is one of the qualifications.

Certain individuals are exempt from jury service: these include members of federal and provincial governments, judges, police, the clergy, lawyers, doctors, members of the press, the Canadian Armed Forces and those employed in some essential services.

Jurors are drawn from either tax-assessment rolls or voters' lists and are paid a fee for each day they serve the court; in addition, they are sometimes granted traveling expenses.

Both prosecution and defense have the right to challenge jurors for partiality or to complain that the jury was not properly and fairly selected. Anyone who is seen to be biased or prejudiced against or for the accused will not be allowed to serve.

In Quebec courts, the accused has the right to be tried by a jury composed entirely of either French- or English-speaking citizens.

In a civil action in Ontario, either the plaintiff or the defendant (or both) can insist that a prospective juror stand aside. No reasons whatever have to be given. Each side has the right to four of these peremptory rejections.

In all provinces except Alberta, a jury in criminal proceedings is composed of 12 members. In Alberta, as well as in the Yukon and the Northwest Territories, the law calls for six jurors.

A jury must base its verdict only on the evidence presented to it, taking into consideration the rules of admissibility and relevancy of evidence, as explained by the presiding judge.

The verdict in criminal cases must be unanimous. If the jury cannot reach a verdict, the judge will adjourn the trial; a decision to have the case retried is up to the Crown. Recently there has been strong pressure in some quarters for a two-thirds jury majority to be sufficient for conviction. It is pointed out that a bare majority vote in Parliament is enough to get the law passed in the first place.

In civil actions, other than in Quebec, a jury is mandatory only to try cases involving libel and slander. For these, only Saskatchewan insists on 12 jurors; elsewhere the number ranges from six to nine. The decision here does not have to be unanimous.

Laws of evidence

For both criminal and civil proceedings, there are laws that govern the giving of evidence in the courtroom. These have evolved over one thousand years, for the ultimate protection of all parties. (*See* Chapter 1, "The rise of English law.")

Under the terms of the Canada Evidence Act, which sets the rules for evidence in criminal cases everywhere, both the accused and the husband (or wife) of the accused are allowed to give evidence for both the prosecution and the defense. However, neither spouse can be *compelled* to give evidence against the other, except in cases of incest, indecency, rape and similar offenses. Neither spouse can be forced by law to disclose any "communication" made between them during the marriage.

Although these rules allow witnesses with professional status (such as doctors

Twelve good men—and true?

THE IDEA of the ordinary citizen, pulled from office chair, workbench or kitchen stove to weigh the highly complex matters often put before juries for decision has always stirred the fancy of novelists and playwrights.

However sound and just, the situation is rich in ironies. One day a man's biggest problem may be whether to buy new tires for the family car, the next he can be on a jury finding a fellow citizen guilty of murder and thus ensuring the imposition of a life sentence.

It is precisely the ordinary, average citizen who is usually selected for this ancient judicial duty.

Counsel for both prosecution and defense are traditionally leery of the intellectual person.

In **Pickwick Papers**, Charles Dickens introduced a novel thought:

"I wonder what the foreman of the jury has got for breakfast," said Mr. Snodgrass.

"Ah!" said Perker, "I hope he's got a good one."

"Why so?" inquired Mr. Pickwick.

"Highly important, my dear Sir," replied Perker. "A good, well-contented, well-breakfasted juryman is a capital thing to get hold

of. Discontented or hungry jurymen, my dear Sir, always find for the plaintiff."

Lewis Carroll wrote in **Alice in Wonderland**:

"Write that down," the King said to the jury, and the jury eagerly wrote down all three dates on their slates, and then added them up, and reduced the answer to shillings and pence.

John Bunyan **(Pilgrim's Progress)** was scornful:

Then went the jury out, whose names were Mr. Blind-man, Mr. No-good, Mr. Malice, Mr. Love-lust, Mr. Live-loose, Mr. Heady, Mr. High-mind, Mr. Enmity, Mr. Lyar, Mr. Cruelty, Mr. Hate-light, and Mr. Implacable, who unanimously concluded to bring him in guilty before the Judge.

Mark Twain offered this typical observation on the jury system:

The most ingenious and infallible agency for defeating justice that human wisdom could contrive.

But when you are called for jury duty, you can take comfort in Sir William Blackstone's differing (and decisive) view:

The trial by jury ever has been, and I trust ever will be, looked upon as the glory of the English law.

or accountants) to give opinions as evidence, no more than five such witnesses are allowed by either side without special permission from the court.

Children may be called to give evidence in criminal cases if the judge decides that they are sufficiently intelligent. However, most cases are not conclusively decided by testimony from children; their statements usually have to be backed up by other sworn evidence.

Under the basic rules of the *adversary proceeding* (where each lawyer fights for his client and the judge acts as referee), all witnesses may be cross-examined by counsel for the opposing party.

Provincial legislation covers the rules of giving courtroom evidence in civil-law cases. Both the defendant and his (or her) spouse may be called to give evidence. However, in cases relating to adultery, neither may give testimony to the effect that the other is guilty of adultery. As in criminal trials, neither spouse is required to reveal "communications" made by the other.

At no time are you forced to testify against yourself in criminal proceedings. However, you will not enjoy the same privilege in a civil case.

Voluntary confessions are acceptable as evidence in the courts because they are likely to be true. On the other hand, "induced" confessions are not admissible. As a rule, the judge will decide whether a confession was voluntary and therefore admissible as evidence. If the judge should believe that unfair influence by police, or anyone else, led to the confession (for example, the police may have indicated to the accused there was advantage for him in making a confession), he will not allow it to be used as evidence in the court.

Items of what is called circumstantial evidence are considered as valid evidence if they give some support to the prosecution's case that the accused performed the criminal act. While such testimony will usually be *corroborated* ("backed up") by independent evidence, this is not essential for a conviction. As a general rule, hearsay will not be permitted as evidence, because the original speaker is not in the witness box under oath. In a murder case, an exception is sometimes made for remarks attributed to the deceased before his death.

If the accused is testifying, the judge is allowed to be informed of any past criminal record he might have. The reasoning here is that the previous behavior of the defendant gives the court some measure of the credibility of his evidence in the case being tried. The defendant's past record is not to be used to establish his personal character.

The laws of evidence provide that deliberately avoiding knowledge of criminal activity does not rank as ignorance, but rather as *willful blindness*. In other words, if you do not want to know where cut-rate merchandise came from, the court might assume that, in a sense, you know it to be illicit, even though you do not know the specific details of its history. By your "not wanting to know" where it comes from, you are being willfully blind, which is no evidence of your innocence before the courts.

The summing-up

At the close of the trial, when all evidence has been introduced and all witnesses have been examined and cross-examined, the judge will call on both the prosecuting attorney and the defense lawyer to sum up their positions. They will each deliver, in effect, a capsule version of their respective arguments.

If the defense has put forward evidence during the trial, the lawyer for the defense will be called upon first to give his summary. If the defense has not offered evidence, the prosecution will make the first summation.

Neither side is permitted to introduce new evidence or fresh information during the summation.

The summation takes on a greater importance in borderline cases, particularly those being tried before a jury. Where there is a jury, the prosecuting attorney and defense lawyer address their summations directly to it. The judge will give his own summation of the main arguments by both sides as he advises the jury on the types of verdict that it may bring in.

Decisions from the Bench

WHEN ALL ARGUMENTS have been presented, all evidence produced and probed, all witnesses (and perhaps outside experts) heard, the spotlight turns on the judge who must decide the case. If the case was heard before a jury, the question of guilt or innocence will have been answered for him; he alone, however, must decide the penalty. If the case was before a judge alone—as are the vast majority—he must pass judgment, then sentence.

For some crimes the exact or minimum punishment is laid down in the law enacted by parliament or the legislatures. (First-degree murder carries a minimum sentence of life imprisonment.) For other crimes only the maximum terms or fines are stated. For many offenses, the judge can impose either imprisonment or fines, or both.

In actual practice, the Bench has wide powers of discretion and thus a grave responsibility. It must consider not only the protection of the community but also the future of the convicted person. In a society that celebrates freedom, depriving someone of his liberty is second only to depriving him of his life.

When a definite penalty is not provided in the legislation, a judge will in most cases be guided by *precedent*: what punishments have other judges meted out in the past for similar violations? But he is also guided by local circumstances. Let's say the offender was found guilty of rape and recently there had been a dangerous rise in cases of women being molested in the local streets. Wanting to deter other would-be offenders, he might impose a much harsher sentence than he normally would for this crime. Variations in sentences for similar offenses will almost certainly continue in Canada because the administration of justice remains within the hands of the several provinces. Local conditions and even attitudes have their impact on the interpretation of the law as well. Once in a while, you will read of a judge sentencing someone to ordinary workaday chores in community service instead of fining or imprisoning him. Such an example was set when two Ontario youths convicted of vandalism were ordered to work Saturdays in clearing rubbish from a town creek. And in another recent case, a judge sentenced a youth, convicted of turning in a false fire alarm, to answer *every* fire alarm in his town for a six-month period.

Theoretically, there are few restrictions on a judge's powers; however, as he formulates sentence, he is aware that his decisions can be overturned in higher courts. Any vindictiveness or personal preference would soon be revealed. If a case contained some novel features, outside recent legal experience, a judge might quite deliberately impose an extra stiff (or extra mild) sentence, expecting his decision to be appealed to the Supreme Court. In effect, he is calling on the extra experience and wisdom of his more elevated colleagues to be brought to bear on the special problem of the case.

In minor cases, the magistrate or provincial judge will give his decision orally, immediately following the summing-up by the counsel—or perhaps after a short recess. In complicated or especially important cases, he will probably *reserve* judgment; this means that he wants time to check his notes thoroughly and to examine case law for guidance on how to handle the particular circumstances before him. Reserved judgments are usually given in writing and then published in the *Law Reports* of the province if they involve interesting points of law. Thus, in legal paradox, more and more of the "unwritten law" is written down.

Acquittal

When a court finds a person not guilty of a crime, he is acquitted. The acquittal, applying only to criminal trials, automatically follows when the Crown fails to prove the charges against the accused.

A jury itself does not acquit a defendant. The acquittal is a decision from the Bench; it is the legal and formal certifica-

tion that the person is not guilty of the charge for which he was brought before the court. It is worth noting that the court does not issue any statement that a person is innocent, but rather that he is not guilty. The acquittal carries the authority of the state for his immediate release from custody and from any further obligation to the court.

In civil actions, if the *plaintiff* fails to win his case against the *defendant*, the case will be *dismissed* by the court.

Although acquitted of the charges against him, a person might still suffer indirectly: the publicity surrounding a trial can be damaging to his personal or business reputation—for instance, the

Justice in the North

I N THE CENTENNIAL YEAR OF 1967, Justice William Morrow, the sole judge of the Superior Court of the Northwest Territories, caused a legal storm when he allowed Joseph Drybones, an Indian convicted of being drunk while off a reserve, to appeal his case. Judge Morrow later found Drybones not guilty and ruled that the Indian Act, under which the case was tried, infringed upon equality rights set out in the 1960 Bill of Rights.

Justice Morrow's next crusade concerned Indian land ownership in the North. Through skilled lawyers, the natives complained that they never ceded some one million square kilometres in the Mackenzie Delta and Valley to the Crown.

Justice Morrow travelled 80,000 kilometres in seven years dispensing justice to Canada's native peoples, many of whom still struggle to understand the white man's law, a far cry from their traditional "eye for an eye" justice. Native peoples are under the supervision of the federal Department of Justice in this regard, and the department has published a booklet (*Justice in the North*) aimed directly at Canada's citizens above the 60th parallel.

Phrased in simplest language, the booklet describes civil law this way:

"Legal rights as between one person and another are called 'civil law.' For example, if you are run over and hurt by someone driving a skidoo carelessly or if you have serious trouble with your wife or husband, or an argument over who owns a boat, you call this 'civil law.'"

Illustrating the different and more serious status of criminal law, this explanation:

"In a general way, if you do something that the Government of Canada or the Government of the Northwest Territories says you shall not do, then you are breaking the criminal law. You must not hit a person or steal his money, or abandon game you have killed. These are examples of the criminal law."

The Royal Canadian Mounted Police supervise law enforcement in the Northwest Territories. The booklet describes their role as follows:

"The police are there to protect the people and their homes and property from wrongdoers. In doing their job they sometimes have to arrest people and bring them to court to answer for the wrongdoing that they are accused of doing. It is not for the police to decide who is right or who has done wrong—it is for the court to make the decision."

public may feel he was found not guilty only because of a technicality in the law. Faulty logic might lead people to conclude that he wouldn't have been accused in the first place if he hadn't done something wrong—the sort of reasoning that is backed up by such sayings as, "Where there's smoke, there's fire." This stigma factor is taken into consideration by the magistrate in the preliminary hearing when he must decide whether to commit a person to stand trial.

A person can be acquitted on one charge but then immediately re-arrested and charged with a second but different offense related to the same unlawful incident. For example, separate charges of murder and kidnapping were brought against Jacques Rose, a political agitator involved in the killing of Quebec politician Pierre Laporte. It is important to remember, though, that a man who is acquitted on a murder charge cannot be later charged with, say, manslaughter—even if apparently conclusive evidence of his guilt is unearthed. If you were to be accused of a second crime for the same offense, you would be in a position of "double jeopardy." Your lawyer could plead of *autrefois acquit* ("formerly acquitted") and most likely win.

Receiving an acquittal does not give a citizen any right to sue the Crown for damages, nor does it relieve him of the costs of his defense. If he had been convicted in error (perhaps on false evidence?), imprisoned, then acquitted and released, he might receive a modest sum of money from the Crown in apology and compensation for his inconvenience and suffering; however, there is no law which says he must be compensated.

Damages

Damages in legal language is an amount of money that the court decides should be paid by one party to compensate another for injury or damage to his person or his property. In a legal dictionary, the definitions of "damages" fill several pages, many of them extremely specific—such as "damage feasant": when one man's cattle trample down another man's standing crops. But the editors of this book are more concerned with damage to the person, to reputation or to property.

In civil actions, as when someone is injured on someone else's land or in an automobile accident, the court often rules that the defendant must pay the plaintiff, the victim, a sum to compensate him for injury. If the injury directly resulted in a sustained loss of income or permanent disability, the damages could be substantial. Insurance companies pick up the damages bill, of course, where the defendant has a covering policy in force.

Except in cases of libel, slander and some assaults, actual damage will have to be proved before financial compensation will be awarded.

Damages are classified as *compensatory, punitive* or *nominal*. The first type, as is obvious, compensates the victim for his loss. Punitive damages, sometimes *exemplary* damages, involve larger sums of money to punish wrongdoers. Nominal damages are merely a token (perhaps 10¢ or $10) to mark the victory without granting any real financial compensation. Nominal damages are often all that is asked in certain cases where a principle of some kind is at stake. People who take up the court's time with technically valid but basically frivolous suits (some people enjoy suing) may get only nominal damages and they may find the judge unwilling to allow them costs against the loser.

If you are injured, or "damaged," you must still act reasonably to keep the financial loss as low as possible. The courts are on the lookout for any attempt to make money out of an accident.

Courts may compel a defendant to give back, or make restitution for, lost money or property if he is responsible for the loss. This has an interesting application to property bought by installments.

Compensation can seldom be extracted from criminals. At this writing, however, three provinces (Alberta, Quebec and Ontario) had special commissions which hear requests for cash damages by victims of criminals. Through these compensation boards, the injured party (or his dependents if he died) could receive damages up to a maximum of $15,000 out of provincial funds in Ontario. In Quebec, compensation is calculated on a percentage of the victim's average earnings.

There is also a separate commission in Quebec to compensate victims of hit-and-run traffic accidents.

Fines

Canadian courts and some tribunals have the power to punish an individual (or a company) for infractions of municipal, provincial or federal legislation by imposing a fine. Although fines are a form of punitive damages, they differ from financial penalties in that they are not awarded to any injured party but are paid to the federal, provincial or municipal government.

They can be levied for just about any offense, from parking violations to theft, and for breaches of the anti-pollution laws. They can run from $2 up to many thousands of dollars.

In a judgment, the court may impose a fine alone, or a fine together with other forms of punishment. Since nearly everyone is vulnerable in the wallet, many lawmakers feel that taking money away from lawbreakers acts as a useful deterrent. They go on to argue that not only do fines help cover the costs of law enforcement, but they also provide an alternative to costly imprisonment (estimated recently at nearly $600 a week per inmate).

Some observers, however, argue that only prison terms are truly democratic. They maintain that every day of every man's life is of equal value, but the rich man can afford fines while the poor man cannot; thus, the poor man will more often go to prison because he cannot raise the money for the fine. Allowing convicted persons to pay their fines by installments helps to bridge the gap a little.

Probation

If a judge believes—or is advised—there is a good chance that a convicted person can rehabilitate or reform himself, he may place him, or her, *on probation*. Probation differs from the two types of penalty discussed earlier in that the emphasis is on correction rather than on punishment. Instead of going to jail for a term, the offender can retain his freedom if he agrees to abide by rules set down for him to follow for a certain length of time.

The rules are laid down in what is known as the *probation order*. This may state that the individual concerned must not stay out at night after a specified time, or drink alcoholic beverages, or leave the area of the court's jurisdiction without permission of a probation officer. The offender may be ordered to maintain his wife and children, to seek employment, to repair anything he damaged, as well as to comply with any other conditions for his good conduct that the judge may feel are required for his rehabilitation.

A major condition of his freedom on probation is that the individual not break any other provincial or federal laws during the probation period. If he is convicted of another offense during that period, he may face a term of imprisonment for the original offense, as well as for the new one. Under the Criminal Code, anyone breaking a condition of probation is guilty of a separate offense which carries a penalty of up to six months' imprisonment.

Before deciding to put someone on probation, the judge will ask the local probation officer (a provincial civil servant, not a policeman) to prepare a pre-sentence report on the background and character of the person concerned. If the officer feels that the convicted person is not a danger to society and could benefit from probation, he is likely to recommend that the judge suspend sentence and issue a probation order.

Probation is granted in Canada for periods of up to three years. It is usually reserved for young or first offenders, or for those with only limited criminal backgrounds. If the probation period passes without the offender getting into trouble with the law again, he is theoretically reformed and there will be no prison record to dog him in the future.

Suspended sentence

The prisoner at the Bar has been judged guilty and the magistrate ponders his decision. He may feel the case is too serious for probation, yet a prison term could well be harmful to the convicted party and his family. For example, the magistrate may feel that a first offender who has been holding down a decent job and supporting a family should not go to jail because it would pose undue hardship on his dependents and perhaps harm the man's chances of future employment.

The circumstances appear to call for a second chance for the offender. The magistrate decides upon the *suspended sentence*. The man is thus found guilty but the court does not proclaim sentence, placing the offender on probation. If the individual abuses the sympathy of the court during the period of the probation, he will be returned to court and then sentenced for the original offense, plus perhaps an extra penalty for any other violation.

Under changes made in the Criminal Code in 1972, someone who pleads guilty, or is found guilty, may be conditionally or absolutely discharged at the judge's discretion without being given a criminal record or penalty. The judge may, however, impose conditions on the discharge or place the guilty party on probation.

Imprisonment

Irrespective of the law of the land, or of the extent or savagery of the crime, no one has been hanged in Canada since 1962. Under the 1976 legislation, this anomaly has been swept away and *life imprisonment* is now the ultimate punishment that will be imposed for any civilian offense.

But the new law, contested so bitterly by abolitionists and retentionists, does not in fact mean exactly what it says—as any police chief or prison warden will explain to you. A bank robber, for example, who kills a policeman while escaping, would almost certainly be found guilty of *first-degree murder* and thus be given the mandatory sentence of life imprison-

The most difficult decision of all

THE JUDGE has an awful responsibility. If in Canada he no longer holds (in effect) the power of life and death, he can at least put a man or woman behind bars, depriving that person of a liberty almost as dear as life itself. Some idealists have, in the very shadow of the gallows, preferred death to captivity.

The judge has a second responsibility that can be equally awesome: deciding to set free a person found guilty of an offense in the hope that he will have learned his lesson and will keep to the straight and narrow in future. He has all the resources of complete discharge, probation, suspended sentencing and the imposition of fines (rather than jail terms) at hand to achieve this. He must attempt to strike a balance between the need to protect the public from the criminal, and the need to attempt rehabilitation of the criminal.

Lurid cases of men committing serious crimes while free on bail, suspended sentences, on parole or on temporary-absence passes from prison, keep public opinion aflame against reform. Quebec was shocked, for instance, to read that a man serving a life sentence for the murder of an eight-year-old girl had stabbed and raped a nurse while he was out of prison on a 12-hour pass.

While press sensationalism focuses attention on spectacular failures, Canadian penal authorities issue statistics claiming that the temporary-absence program is over 99 percent successful. Former commissioner of penitentiaries Paul Faguy told a Senate committee that a man who had killed his mother was working at an outside job and paying for his room and board at the penitentiary. A murderer was employed as a cleaner in a federal office building. Another was taking university courses, hoping to become a parole officer.

In 1980–81, Correctional Service Canada issued 45,373 temporary-absence permits. Only 168, or less than one percent, failed to return on time.

ment. However, a judge and jury could consider the prisoner eligible for parole after 25 years. Until recently, the parole board had the power to consider the criminal's release into the community after only seven years.

With something like 70 to 80 percent of the general population indicating in opinion polls that it favors the death penalty (not withstanding the views of their Ottawa M.P.s), it must remain to be seen how the mandatory life imprisonment alternative to "the rope" for the cop killer or premeditated murderer will work out in practice.

Prison terms can be for a few days only—imposed as an alternative to a modest fine, as sharp incentive to the culprit to pay up or, possibly, because the offender would hardly feel the "punishment" of the fine. "Thirty days" is a customary term for a wide range of minor offenses where the judge may be convinced that a fine or the alternatives of probation or suspended sentence are inappropriate.

Magistrates will often be heard handing out sentences of "two years less one day" for lesser offenses. This is a device for keeping the convict out of the federal penitentiary, where about 30 percent of inmates are "repeaters", or "recidivists." Sentences of up to two years are served in provincial jails or reformatories; longer sentences must be served in "the pen."

Prison sentences of more than a few days' duration are often accompanied by the added penalty of *hard labor*. This archaic term no longer means such work as breaking rocks with a sledgehammer, but it does require the inmate to perform reasonably useful work while "inside." Some prisons teach the inmate a trade while working in the machine shop.

When an individual has been convicted of a serious personal-injury offense, and continues to pose a threat to the life, safety, physical and mental well-being of other people, he or she may be considered a *dangerous offender* by the Court and sentenced to a penitentiary for an indeterminate period.

A person who is acquitted—that is, found not guilty—of a crime because of insanity will normally be kept in a spe-

cially designated sanatorium, or other institution, for an indefinite period. The time is described as lasting "until the pleasure of the lieutenant-governor is known." This is another way of saying that the sick person will remain confined until the authorities are convinced he has been cured. (*See* Chapter 19, "Threat to the community.")

Contempt of court

Immediate imprisonment is usually the reward of anyone who willfully challenges the dignity or authority of the court. This is known as *contempt* (*See* Chapter 19, "Offenses against authority"). The judge can impose a term that he thinks fits the gravity of the incident.

Award of costs

In criminal proceedings, even when you win your case you will still have to pay your lawyer's fees—that is, unless you qualify for Legal Aid. (*See* Chapter 20, "The lawyer in society.") If you lose, the Crown has power (seldom exercised, except in unsuccessful appeals) to bill you for its costs of administering justice, including the expense of calling witnesses.

(Although the idea that you have to pay for the Crown's work of finding you guilty may seem unjust, the policy sometimes discourages persons from pleading innocent who know they are guilty. The courts are crowded enough without having to contend with such cases.)

Although court costs may be levied against the guilty party in addition to a fine (perhaps in a traffic case), the judge will often take the size of the cost claim into consideration in setting the fine.

In civil actions, both the plaintiff and defendant take the risk of being found liable for the costs of the other party. Civil courts almost invariably rule that the losing party pay the reasonable legal costs of the winner. (*See* Chapter 18, "The question of damages.") Your lawyer might regard the case you want to take to court as risky and advise you to drop it.

Even if you won your case in court, if the Bench thought it vindictive, it might levy the costs against you, causing you to lose heavily in the long run.

The penal system

IN AN AVERAGE YEAR, there are about 23,000 prisoners in federal penitentiaries and provincial jails in Canada, with another 7,500 still under sentence but on parole or conditional release.

Apart from these well-known places of detention ("correctional institutions," in officialese), sentences of imprisonment can be served in training schools, guidance centers, reformatories, certain hospitals, prison farms, unguarded camps and numerous other specialized institutions. Several are exclusively for females; all female criminals in Canada sentenced to two years' imprisonment (or more) are in the stone-walled Kingston Prison for Women.

Prison life is changing rapidly, and for the better. Today, every inmate is classified at the start of his sentence and a serious attempt is made to launch him on a program of rehabilitation. Young and first offenders are usually kept away from hardened criminals.

While keeping in mind the twin needs for punishment and for the protection of law-abiding society, prison wardens direct their efforts toward helping the prisoner prepare himself to cope successfully with the world he will face after release. Except for those who may die while still in prison, all inmates must someday return to society. All penal experts argue that punishment alone merely brutalizes and embitters; unless well-directed and sincere efforts are made to teach prisoners how to conform tolerably to acceptable behavior patterns—which includes being willing and able to make an honest living—their return to crime is all too likely. The record of rehabilitation is not encouraging: three-quarters of all penitentiary inmates are repeaters, some of them having spent as much of their lives behind bars as beyond them.

In a recent year, about 8,000 Canadian prisoners participated in adult education and vocational training programs. The penitentiaries now provide full-time vocational-training courses in numerous trades and other practical occupations, including computer science.

Graduates of these courses may obtain their certificates as qualified tradesmen or at least earn credits toward fulfillment of apprenticeships. (*See* Chapter 13, "The licensed trades.") The correctional service coordinates its industrial-training courses with the Department of Employment and Immigration to ensure that inmates are developing skills and talents that will give them a chance of getting good jobs when they return to society.

To humanize old institutions, walls and wire have come down, cells have been decorated and numbered uniforms have given way to "civvies"—or informal dress. Prisoners may now send letters out without having them censored; entertainment has been stepped up; and men willing and able to work on certain construction projects are being paid a normal wage, which they can save for their release.

All jails now allow some inmates temporary leave to visit family and friends. A recent summary available from the penitentiary service showed that 45 inmate students were attending university, high school or community college; others on temporary-absence passes were working outside the walls. In one year (1982) there were more than 6,500 inmates who had been granted passes under the supervision of the correctional service. Although

145

a number of prisoners have abused these privileges, this new approach is considered largely successful.

The local lockup

Many cities and the larger county towns maintain a local *lockup*—a minijail—where offenders may be held temporarily. Most offenders are held for no more than 24 hours, usually only until bail arrangements can be made, or until their case comes up in court.

Serving a full sentence in a local jail is uncommon today because the facilities do not permit the kind of corrective detention that has become routine penal practice across Canada in recent years. Yet, in an isolated region, the court may not think it worthwhile to send a convicted person perhaps several hundred miles to the nearest regular provincial jail or other institution to serve only a short term. The lockup might be chosen so as not to isolate an offender unnecessarily from his family and community.

A drawback of the lockup (often just a cell or two at the rear of the police station) is that an arrested youth, or minor offender, can find himself lodged temporarily with an apprehended bank bandit or unbalanced murderer.

The reformatory

All the provinces operate *reformatories* and *training schools* for offenders serving shorter sentences—up to two years' duration. Adult offenders who should benefit from instructional programs and counseling are often sent to a reformatory, while the training school is for youthful offenders ("juvenile delinquents") with similar needs. In a recent year (1982), more than 2,100 juvenile offenders (almost 200 of them female) were committed to these institutions across the country. There is a strong emphasis on rehabilitation, and security is kept to a minimum. Not trying to escape from a reformatory—which may not even have locks on the doors—is often regarded as the first indication of a lawbreaker's rehabilitation.

Within the provincial jurisdictions, there are many variations in these institutions—in name and policy, in range of facilities, as well as in skill and training of staff. Alberta, for example, places the care of offenders under the age of 12 in the hands of provincial social services and community health departments. Lawbreakers between the ages of 12 and 17 are the responsibility of the provincial solicitor-general. They are looked after in a variety of institutions—ranging from group homes and wilderness camps to secure detention centers—throughout the province.

Manitoba maintains the Agassiz Centre for Youth for boys in the 12–18 age group (at Portage la Prairie) and a similar home for girls, the Doncaster Centre, in Winnipeg. There is the Marymound School (also in Winnipeg), a private school run by a Roman Catholic order of nuns (Sisters of the Good Shepherd). All the provincial jails for adults are referred to as *correctional institutions*.

Under Quebec's Youth Protection Law, a young offender who has had several encounters with the law is referred by the police and social workers to the director of the local social services center. If necessary, the young offender will appear before the juvenile court with an attorney. The court may suggest a corrective procedure. It is the director, however, using all the means open by law to the social services, who decides where to send the youth. Quebec has several institutions for young offenders. Some such as St-Vallier and Berthelet are security or protection homes; others such as Ste-Hélène in Pierrefonds, Mont St-Antoine and Boscoville are called re-education centers *(centres de rééducation)*, where children between the ages of 13 and 18 are cared for, educated and taught vocational skills.

Some provincial facilities are shared. For example, the Nova Scotia School for Girls in Truro accepts young offenders from New Brunswick and Prince Edward Island, as well as Nova Scotia.

The provincial jail

In the middle ground between the training schools and the reformatories on the one hand, and the federal penitentiaries on the other, stand the provincial jails which—in most provinces—receive those sentenced by the courts to terms of less than two years.

As a rule, persons sent to these provincial institutions have had more than one conviction, but have not been sentenced to serve a full two-year term. It will be noted that judges often make the sentence "two years less one day" so that the person concerned will not be sent to a federal penitentiary.

Security and the general regime in the provincial jails are more strict than at the reformatory level and there may be less emphasis on rehabilitation. Since some provinces—especially the smaller ones—make use of the city lockups, conditions can vary widely across Canada.

With the idea of improving and standardizing detention and correctional facilities across the country, a Royal Commission on the Penal System was set up in 1938. Out of this came the Archambault Report, which proposed that all penal institutions be brought together under the authority of a federal penitentiaries commission. Like other suggested reforms, this proposal was snagged on the rocks of provincial-federal rights. In the interim there has been no sign of progress in putting this idea into action.

John Howard's great idea

IN THE YEAR 1755 an earthquake leveled much of the Portuguese capital, Lisbon, killing more than 30,000 people. Many more thousands were homeless and starving. A wealthy young English philanthropist named John Howard set out with a mercy mission but was captured by the French, with whom Britain was then at war. He won his freedom by organizing an exchange of prisoners, but not before he had sampled the rough penal treatment of those times.

When he was 47, Howard was appointed High Sheriff of Bedfordshire. He renewed his personal knowledge of jails and the treatment of felons in the reign of George III by touring prisons throughout Britain and the Continent. His experiences convinced him that he should devote his energies to penal reform, particularly to easing the in-prison handling of convicts and assisting them to re-enter society after sentence was served. The reports he tabled in the House of Commons led to the first major reforms since medieval times. He died in 1790, while touring Russia.

Howard's name has been immortalized by the societies around the civilized world which carry on his work in prisoner-aid, crime prevention and penal reform. Canada has John Howard Societies in at least 26 cities, from Victoria to St. John's.

The movement began in Canada as the Prisoners' Aid Society in Toronto, a century ago. The Salvation Army, always concerned with prisoner welfare, opened a prison-gate home in 1890, and pioneered a program of taking released convicts into its homes for a period of rehabilitation.

The first John Howard Society was titled as such in Vancouver in 1931, and the name is now synonymous with the after-care of prisoners. Most of the self-governing societies maintain permanent offices, staffed with qualified social workers. They are supported in large part by state grants.

A voluntary welfare organization for women prisoners is named for Elizabeth Fry, the British Quaker of the early nineteenth century who campaigned against the atrocious conditions in London's Newgate Prison. Public executions were held outside Newgate until 1868, to the sadistic delight of large crowds.

John Howard had died when Elizabeth Fry was a girl of 10, but no champion had come forward to help female prisoners. When Elizabeth was 37, she set up the first society for this purpose. Women were being shipped out to Australia for even trifling offenses and she visited every convict ship to try to ease their lot and to arrange useful instruction for their new lives as colonial pioneers.

The penitentiary

The Correctional Service of Canada, under the control of the solicitor general, maintains and operates 59 penal institutions across Canada. In these centers, lawbreakers, 30 percent of them recidivists, serve terms ranging from two years to life imprisonment. It is the formal responsibility of the service to "care for and train" all those committed to it.

The federal prison system consists of 14 maximum-security, 15 medium-security, 30 minimum-security and other specialized institutions. In Newfoundland, where there are no federal penitentiaries, those receiving sentences of two years or more usually serve their time in the provincial jail at St. John's.

All of the medium- and minimum-security institutions offer their inmates vocational training: some are specifically designed to deal with young criminals and the emphasis is on rehabilitation.

The maximum-security prisons are situated at Dorchester, New Brunswick; Ste-Anne-des-Plaines and Laval, Quebec; Kingston and Bath, Ontario; Stony Mountain, Manitoba; Prince Albert, Saskatchewan; Edmonton, Alberta; Abbotsford and Agassiz, British Columbia. Some 30 percent of the total penitentiary population of approximately 11,300 is at these locations. Many of these inmates are considered unlikely to respond to progressive methods; others are considered to be dangers to society.

When a newly sentenced man enters one of these prisons, he is examined by doctors—including psychologists and psychiatrists—and interviewed by social workers. Young and first offenders are separated from repeaters; across Canada, generally, about 38 to 39 percent of all serious robberies and crimes against the person are committed by individuals who have previously served one or more terms of imprisonment. Those considered suitable for training in a trade or in farming (or in such sophisticated skills as computer programming) are normally transferred at once to medium-security institutions.

The policy of the service is officially described as being directed primarily at assisting the inmate to prepare himself to take up a proper place in society on his release; the staff tries to balance its attitude between permissiveness and strict discipline. The medium-security penitentiaries are at Springhill, Nova Scotia; Laval, Cowansville and L'Annonciation, Quebec; Kingston, Joyceville and Campbellford, Ontario; Winnipeg, Manitoba; Drumheller and Innisfail, Alberta; Agassiz, Abbotsford, Victoria and Mission City, British Columbia. One of the Quebec institutions (known as the Federal Training Centre) is specially designed for the rehabilitation of young offenders.

The 30 minimum-security facilities include community correctional centers, correctional camps and farming annexes to other institutions. There are specialized units for hostile inmates, elderly prisoners, as well as for drug addicts.

The Correctional Service of Canada is directed by the Commissioner of Corrections from the headquarters in Ottawa. There are regional administrative centers at Abbotsford, Kingston, Laval, Saskatoon and Moncton, where the service also maintains facilities for training staff.

Remission and parole

Under the Criminal Code, *remission* refers to the reduction, in whole or in part, of fines and forfeitures imposed by the courts on an offender.

Parole is the early release (on certain conditions) from prison of a person convicted of a violation of any federal law—if he has given definite indication that he intends to live a law-abiding life in future.

The National Parole Board, formed in 1959, is totally responsible for selecting those inmates who will be granted parole. Its 26 members travel the country, interviewing every applicant for parole. Even if a prisoner does not apply, the board will generally review his case every two years anyway.

The purpose of parole, as described by the board, is to protect society through the rehabilitation of the criminal; by releasing the prisoner, the board is showing confidence in the offender's ability to serve the remainder of his sentence in society. The idea is that the offender will respond to this show of confidence by doing his best to "stay clean"; the board keeps him under supervision until his sentence expires. The board is constantly trying to balance the welfare of the individual offender against the overriding need to protect society—an unenviable task.

A prisoner serving a sentence of less than two years is eligible for parole after one-third of the time has passed. If he is serving more than a two-year term, he is eligible after one-third of the sentence is served or after seven years, whichever is less; however, he must serve at least eight months of a sentence that is more than two years.

Under 1976 legislation, the eligibility of "lifers" for full parole rests on whether the inmate was convicted for first- or second-degree murder. For first-degree murder, eligibility for full parole is possible after 25 years; for second-degree murder, eligibility becomes possible after inmates have served between 10 and 25 years of their sentence.

Parole boards also grant "day paroles" so that prisoners can leave jail during the day (to work or attend college), returning to their cells at night. Further concessions may be granted at Christmas, and "temporary absences" are allowed "in exceptional circumstances."

Under "mandatory supervision," an inmate who has earned time off for good behavior is entitled by law to serve the last third of his sentence in the community, subject to the release conditions of parole. The board is not involved in granting mandatory supervision.

If a prisoner wants to serve the full term handed to him, he must advise the board in writing that he does not wish to be considered for early release.

The Parole Board does not consider itself concerned with either the validity of the original conviction or the length of sentence imposed. It is solely concerned with the possibilities of reformation.

This philosophy has earned the board some sharp criticism, both from some members of the judiciary and from the public. In one celebrated example, a group of young men convicted of kidnapping a wealthy Toronto woman was released on parole after having served as little as 20 months. In another case, a Quebec man convicted of strangling his wife was given "temporary absence" to marry his mistress; although his pass was only good for 50 hours, it was months later when he was picked up in Europe.

A person on parole is placed under the care of a supervisor who, in turn, reports to one of 17 district directors. The parolee must report to the supervisor once a week and to the police once a month. If he commits another offense or misbehaves, the board may suspend his parole and return him to prison.

During its first 15 years (1959–1973), when the Parole Board granted 43,847 full paroles, 8,968 were revoked or forfeited. In 1982, the board granted 1,667 full paroles, and 4,593 "day paroles."

The Queen's pardon

Although any majority decision of the Supreme Court of Canada is final, to all intents and purposes, there is still one ultimate appeal against the judgments of our courts. This takes the form of the *Queen's pardon.*

All Canadians are *subjects* of the Queen of Canada—convicted criminals included—and therefore have the right to appeal to Her Majesty, requesting that she exercises her power of *clemency*, or mercy. This "royal prerogative of mercy" exists more in theory than in fact. For the Queen acts only through her representative to the elected government, the governor general, and he acts only with the advice of the federal cabinet. In practice, therefore, the power of Queen's pardon is exercised by the federal cabinet through the solicitor general.

Usually about 5,000 Canadians are on parole; the board considers 12,000 applications a year. Former chairman T. George Street expressed the board's overall point of view in these words: "There are far too many persons sentenced to prison in Canada who could be better dealt with in the community. The true purpose of corrections should be the reformation of the offender and not merely vengeance or retribution."

You and

Your Property

4/Renting or Buying a Home

Closing the deal   176

Building your own home   184

Arranging the mortgage   188

Finding a place to live

SOME 300 YEARS ago a famous British jurist, Sir Edward Coke, rephrased a segment of Roman civil law from the sixth century into the enduring phrase: "A man's house is his castle." Today it is a philosophy which applies to the average Canadian. His lifetime ambition is to own a house, a detached or semi-detached single-family dwelling in which he and his family can enjoy privacy and independence.

Not everyone, however, is able to realize this ambition. The reasons are often financial: not enough savings for a down payment or not enough income to meet mortgage installments and taxes. Sometimes circumstances dictate: a man who is frequently transferred from city to city would probably decide that it does not make much sense for him to buy a fixed abode. Married couples without children often prefer smaller quarters, especially when both partners work.

The alternative for an increasing number of Canadians in recent years has been to rent an apartment or house. By this arrangement, the occupier (the *tenant*) pays the owner an agreed amount of money (the *rent*) on regular dates in exchange for the right to exclusive use of the property for a specified length of time.

Both owning and renting involve legal obligations and have certain advantages and disadvantages. In this chapter we will examine and discuss these rights and limitations which affect just about everyone in Canada at some stage of life.

If you buy a home you can, within the limit of your pocketbook, obtain exactly the kind of accommodation you require. If nothing suitable exists, there are plenty of contractors who will build what you want. When renting, however, you have to take what is available within your price range. And, inevitably, your rights as a tenant will not be as wide as they would be if you owned the property. Your rights and your obligations are usually spelled out in a written agreement (the *lease*).

The leasing and renting of property is controlled in nine of the provinces by what is called "the law of landlord and tenant." There are certain provincial variations, but the law is essentially the same everywhere. In Quebec the Civil Code prevails.

Quebec has a rent control act, passed in 1979, which provides tenants with a tribunal to hear appeals against rent increases. In the prevailing mood of economic restraint, all provinces now have some form of rent control legislation, limiting rent increases subject to appeal by tenant or landlord.

Apartment renting represents the greatest proportion of residential leasing everywhere in Canada. About 15 percent of all Canadians now live in apartments, the accommodation ranging from modest to elegant—and even regal. Apartments are the most popular of all rental housing for economic reasons: the cost of land and other factors make for higher rental charges for a similar amount of living space in detached homes.

In recent times, few houses have been built especially for rental. In the late 1960s, a swing began toward the construction of town houses (or row housing), and the subdivision of existing larger homes—often for rental purposes. Nevertheless, the rate of high-rise apartment construction still far exceeds the town-house trend on a unit basis.

A nation of nomads

The ease with which a family can move due to improved long-distance truck haulage is one of the main reasons for renting, rather than buying, living quarters. Canadians have become more nomadic, moving house more frequently, either for business or personal reasons; thus, many people are reluctant to undertake the long-term financial burdens of home ownership. However, there are drawbacks to renting. For one thing, the lease can be as restricting in some ways as private ownership. If you own your own home, and the necessity arises, you can sell it at any time, probably at suitable terms. It could be more difficult and costly to get out of a formal lease.

The desire for security, of each man to have his "castle," prompts most Canadians to seek to buy a home, instead of renting. In any rental agreement, there is always the prospect of having to move when the lease expires. Even the most respectable tenants can be evicted when their lease is up. Long-term leases—three years or more—can provide at least a partial solution to that problem.

Another big plus for the homeowner is the likely growth in the value of his investment. In spite of rising interest rates, maintenance costs and property taxes, the owner derives a sense of satisfaction in knowing that at least a portion of his monthly mortgage payment represents accumulating equity—that is, a step toward complete ownership. A tenant, on the other hand, builds up no ownership throughout the term of his lease.

The snobbery factor

The tenancy versus ownership question can also have social overtones, however irrational that may be. Some renters feel a certain inferiority to those who own homes. For years, tenants' associations have argued that our laws, while paying attention to the rights and problems of landowners, have tended to ignore tenants as a group. While this situation is changing, an example of the benefits given homeowners can be seen in tax legislation, specifically the capital-gains tax. In most cases when you buy something and sell it later at a profit, you have to pay capital-gains tax on that profit. However, if you sell your house for a profit, that money is not taxed as a capital gain.

Taking an apartment

Before you decide to rent an apartment you should ask yourself several questions. Can you afford the monthly rent? Will your children be happy without a yard of their own? Will you enjoy living "on top of" your neighbors? Although these are largely emotional questions, they could affect your contentment and your family life. The best view in town will not necessarily compensate for a sense of disharmony with your surroundings. Several books have been written on the social aspect of apartment living, especially in the high-rise blocks. Look them up in your public library.

Two of the most important questions you should ask yourself before signing: Are the terms of the lease clear—and fair? Make sure that the building in which you will be living and the facilities it provides are described in enough detail that there will be no question in your mind about your rights. If you have the right to use a swimming pool, gymnasium, sauna or laundry room, the lease should spell it out. Extra charges are sometimes levied, particularly for parking.

One of the most debatable elements of rental agreements has been that of the *security deposit*. Usually in the form of one month's rent (most often stipulated as the final month's rent), this deposit must be paid before you move in. Make sure that the security-deposit clause is clearly defined in your lease; check whether your deposit money earns interest. In Ontario, the landlord must pay the tenant 6 percent per year on any money held during the period of the lease.

Can you sublet?

Since subletting can raise serious complications for the tenant, you should pay close attention to any sublet clause in the lease. Most "standard" lease forms in Canada contain a clause prohibiting you from subletting without the landlord's consent. This means that the onus is on you to find an acceptable tenant to take on the remainder of your lease period.

What makes a tenant "acceptable"? Generally, the landlord—and it is his decision—will accept someone whom he is convinced will take good care of his property and who can show that he is able to afford the rent.

You cannot force a landlord to rent to someone of your choice, but he cannot withhold his consent unreasonably or arbitrarily. Disputes over subletting can be taken before the District (or County) Court.

Renewal provisions in the lease should always be studied. Many leases contain renewal options of some kind, which give you the chance to rent the apartment for another term on certain conditions. Make sure that if an option is available, you are informed of the date on which you must give formal notice of your wish to renew the lease.

Rules of the landlord

Many leases also contain what are called "landlord's rules and regulations," which outline a code of behavior within the

Living on wheels

HOME, THEY SAY, is where you hang your hat. And for more and more Canadians these days, this means a mobile home that can be moved without fuss just about anywhere the owner wishes. Don't be confused by memories of jolting "trailers": the new homes on wheels range in cost from $20,000 to $40,000 and some of them are equipped with wall-to-wall broadloom, built-in hi-fi, saunas and showers, dishwashers and garbage disposals, and either electric or gas heating. Some have a kennel for the family pup.

Do we really have a hidden gypsy wish? Maybe. But there's no doubt that what the manufacturers call "the mobile home and recreational vehicle industry" is definitely mushrooming in Canada. Apart from the lure of the open road, the cost of bricks-and-mortar housing is now running ahead of the buying power of lower-income groups (and some middle-income groups) and many are turning to a modification of the Romany life.

According to the industry, 90 percent of all single-family homes now sold for less than $20,000 are on wheels—or, at least, can be jacked up and put on wheels at an hour's notice. The idea particularly appeals to some retired couples who find that they can sell the old family bungalow, buy a mobile home and have a sizable chunk of cash to add to pensions. Often, they will get

towed to a park (a permanent, commercially operated "community") in a warm climate, and settle there. Sometimes, close friends and neighbors from the same suburban street back home will each buy a mobile home, move to the same "community" in California or Florida, and resume living in happy neighborliness, side by side.

The first crude house-trailers appeared in the 1920s, providing cheap homes for many wanderers in the Depression years that followed. In World War II, governments bought a great many house-trailers as temporary accommodations for workers in war plants. Trailer parks sprang up on the outskirts of cities, providing power points, communal washing and toilet facilities. Thousands became accustomed to a life on wheels.

In the 1960s and 70s, the ugly-duckling trailers began to turn into swans as luxury mobile homes. Models are offered with dining space, living room, kitchen, one or two bedrooms and bathroom. There are even two-story models. You have many choices of decor: traditional, contemporary, French provincial, early American, Oriental or Mediterranean. Most are still built to be towed (or trucked), but some now come equipped with their own motive power. Father can drive the house from his favorite chair.

apartment building. These rules can forbid pets, noise after certain hours, or the use of certain types of wall fasteners or perhaps awnings. The lease will usually contain a clause requiring that you abide by these regulations. Once you sign the lease, you have contracted legally to obey all its conditions.

It is generally only the landlord who can enforce these rules. Let's say you are a tenant and your neighbor is holding an excessively noisy party. If the landlord refuses to ask the co-tenant to tone it down, it's unlikely you can force him to take action. (In Quebec you have recourse against the landlord and the co-tenant.) You could complain to police that your neighbor committed a public nuisance.

In reading an apartment lease, check any restrictions as to what use can be made of the premises. If you intend conducting a business, even on a part-time basis, make sure that the lease permits it. Some leases contain a provision covering the subletting of rooms within your apartment. If it is your intention to rent rooms, check that the lease permits this.

The anonymous landlord

In this era of high-rise complexes, it is becoming increasingly rare for a tenant to come in direct contact with his actual landlord. More often than not, you will find yourself dealing with resident property managers or real estate agents who have management control.

Reputable property companies do not put up smokescreens, but tenants sometimes get that impression. If you want an amendment to a lease or rental agreement and can't get in touch with "the proper authority," don't give up. Press your point. Ask the landlord's representative to telephone the owner, in your presence, and to ask whether the requested change or changes can be made in the lease. If you still can't get satisfaction, get the owner's business address and write to him about the problem.

The legal name and address of your landlord is probably posted somewhere around the building entrance or lobby; in Ontario it is compulsory that this information be posted in a conspicuous place.

Do not forget that the agent acting for the landlord is, in effect, a salesman selling you a leasehold interest in the premises. He would soon be out of a job if he failed to sell enough space in the building. Like any other salesman, he can be expected to use a certain amount of exaggeration. In other words he can "puff." Check what he says against the actual wording of the lease.

If you move to a new city, it is a good idea to check with the local better business bureau or real-estate board about the reputation and reliability of your prospective landlord.

Room and board

A great many Canadians begin their college days, or their working lives, living in a rooming house or boardinghouse. In some cases, they will be provided with meals at a common table with other roomers, or with the resident family. Maybe they will be permitted to prepare light meals on a hot plate, but in many cases this is either forbidden, or frowned upon, for reasons of fire safety—not to mention the cooking odors.

Roomers seldom have the rights of tenants. The law establishes them not as lessees, such as apartment tenants, but as licensees—paying guests, so to speak— who are subject to "house rules." An exception to the licensee status occurs when a boarder is given a key to his room and can exclude others from it. He is then considered to be a lessee, or tenant.

Whether you're a licensee or lessee, you have certain basic rights. The operator of a rooming house cannot discriminate among tenants on the grounds of race or religion. You cannot be prevented from entertaining as long as you or your guests do not disturb others in the house.

If you are an owner planning to operate a rooming house, you should check provincial landlord-and-tenant legislation and the municipal bylaws for the area in which the house is located. For instance, zoning regulations might call for single-family dwellings only. You should also make sure the municipal government isn't planning to impose such a regulation if there isn't one at the moment.

Examining the lease

LIKE ANY OTHER CONTRACT a lease, once signed, is legally binding. If the legal language in which it is written seems to defy easy reading and raises questions in your mind, consult a lawyer before signing anything. This will entail an expense, of course, but in the long run it could save you a great deal of money and a lot of trouble.

Lease forms used in the routine apartment rental are standardized. They are available at most office supply or stationery stores. (In Quebec, there is a standard form of lease prescribed by law.) You should get one, if only to give yourself a "dry run" before the real thing. Most big landlords have their own printed forms but, while these may be presented to you as "standard" leases, they can vary widely in terms and language. The lease is sometimes called a *demise*.

Since the landlord writes the lease, his interests are sure to be well protected. His "standard" lease form may contain some clauses that no court would make you obey. On the other hand, the lease might omit some of the legal obligations of the owner. In any case, the major responsibility will fall on you as the tenant (the *lessee*) and the courts cannot help much if you sign first and ask questions later.

If you are dealing with a realty company or commercial developer, it's unlikely you will be able to have any significant changes made in any lease you are offered. But if there are clauses you feel should be amended, discuss them frankly with the owner. If an agent is the spokesman, ask that he talk the matter over with the landlord. You might win a concession or two, particularly if the apartment is not filling very rapidly.

In the final analysis, a lease is actually a hodgepodge of rights and responsibilities, mixed with your own terms of agreement. Since it is a contract, it should be in writing; however, if the period covered by the lease is less than three years, a verbal agreement may be sufficient.

In keeping with the minimum requirements for any contract, regardless of form, the rental contract, or lease, must identify the parties involved, describe the premises being rented in enough detail so that there can be no mistake about them, state the rent to be paid and define the length of time the lease is to be in force.

Don't sign hurriedly

If you decide you don't need legal advice, at least take the lease home with you before signing it so that you can read it calmly, away from the subtle excitements and promises of the agent's office. You will find a glossary of legal terms at the end of this book ("An A.B.C. of Canadian law") helpful in translating the legalistic language in which the lease is written.

In most provinces, a lease becomes effective when you sign the contract. The landlord can enforce its provisions, even if you do not take possession of the property. When a tenant takes possession, he is protected by the provincial landlord and tenant laws; until then, he has only contractual rights which could be subject to argument and which he would likely have to go to court to enforce.

Tenancy for a fixed term

The most common type of rental agreement, used almost exclusively for apartments, is the "tenancy for a term certain," or "tenancy for a fixed term." These phrases simply convey the fact that the lease expires automatically on the date stated without further action by either landlord or tenant.

Let's say your lease for a two-bedroom apartment runs from September 1 to August 31. If "tenancy for a fixed term" is stated, you are required to vacate on the expiry date written into the lease. It all depends, though, on whether formal notice to vacate is given; if not, the old lease does indeed expire but you can usually continue in occupation on a "month-to-month" basis.

In Quebec, tenancy rules are substantially different in that notice has to be given three months before the expiry of a lease that runs for at least a year. If the original term was for less than a year, notice must be one month. Unless the lease provides differently, it is renewed for a year or for the original term, whichever is less.

The lease can be renegotiated and renewed. If it isn't and if the tenant refuses to vacate, he is considered under the law to be a "holdover tenant," subject to eviction by court order upon request by the landlord. However, if the holdover tenant continues to pay rent which the landlord accepts, he becomes a "periodic tenant."

The periodic tenancy

Periodic tenancy means what it implies: tenancy for a period—be it a week, a month or a year—according to terms agreed upon by tenant and landlord.

In most cases, periodic tenancies arise when a tenant stays on after expiry without negotiating a new lease. He becomes a "periodic tenant" when the landlord continues to accept regular payments.

Periodic leases may also be arranged on a weekly, monthly or yearly basis by verbal or written agreement, or by implication—that is, by the fact of the landlord accepting regular rent. Such leases differ from fixed-term leases chiefly with respect to termination. The fixed-term lease expires automatically. Under a periodic lease, the landlord must be given notice of termination. If rent is paid weekly, the landlord must be advised one clear week before the day of termination; on a monthly tenancy, one clear month's notice is required. Three months' notice is required on a quarterly or half-yearly tenancy, while six months' notice is to be given on a year-to-year tenancy.

Tenancy at will

A "tenancy at will" is not a true rental agreement and is recommended only as a stop-gap measure. Let's say your fixed-term lease has expired but your new accommodation is not yet available. You may be able to persuade your former landlord to let you stay on from day to day until you can move to your new home.

It is by no means a secure arrangement. The landlord can at any time and without notice ("at will") ask for possession, and you will have to move out, whether you have somewhere to go or not. Should this happen to you, your local welfare office, or any social services agency, will offer advice and most probably assistance. (*See* Chapter 3, "Our conditional rights.")

Tenancies at will can also be arranged in cases where it is necessary for a home purchaser to move in before the deal has been closed and the house legally belongs to him. This does not affect the sale-purchase transaction or the legal rights of the buyer and seller. It is a temporary agreement and the prospective owner can be evicted if the vendor wants it that way.

Another application covers such persons given free accommodation by landlords in return for services as, for instance, building superintendents or janitors.

Tenancy at sufferance

The term "tenancy at sufferance" covers the situation in which a tenant whose lease has expired retains possession without his landlord's consent and without paying rent. The term also applies to trespassers: persons who enter and remain in premises without permission.

In either case, the offender can be speedily (even forcibly) evicted and charged a reasonable amount to cover "use and occupation rent." The amount would be set by the courts upon the application of the owner.

159

The oral lease

Oral or verbal leases—with nothing committed to paper—are obviously not the most secure contracts, but they do have a distinct legal standing. They are often convenient if you only want to rent on a short-term or monthly basis. A sizeable percentage of the total rental agreements in Canada take the form of verbal leases on a short-term basis.

The lease form

This lease form (legally, it's called an "indenture"—a "deed between two or more parties with mutual covenants") is typical of those used today for the leasing of apartments or houses. It almost always includes a "schedule"—an appendix containing details—that lists the landlord's rules and regulations controlling the keeping of pets, the hanging of laundry, the decoration of walls. The rules often state that "pianos, pianolas, organs, violins and other musical instruments shall not be played after 11 P.M. or before 9 A.M." If you sign, all these clauses are legally binding.

Lease

Gouvernement du Québec
Régie du logement

LEASE

Between the landlord: and the tenant:

(Name)   (Name)
(Address)   (Address)
                    (Telephone number)   (Telephone number)
"The landlord"   "The tenant"

Description of premises
By this lease the landlord rents to the tenant the premises located at ____

Use of premises
The premises will be leased as a dwelling.

Term
The term of the lease will be of ____ months, from the ____ day of ____ 19 ____,
to the ____ day of ____ 19 ____

Rent
The total amount of the rent will be ____ dollars
($ ____) which the tenant will pay the landlord in equal ____
                                                            (monthly, weekly or other)
and consecutive payments of ____ dollars ($ ____),
each of which will be paid on the ____ day of each ____
                                                            (month, week or other)

Signing of the lease

Additional clauses

Building rules
• Before making the lease, the landlord must give the tenant a copy of the building rules, if there are any. These rules, covering the use of services or common areas, for instance, then form part of the lease.

Copy of the lease
• The landlord must give his tenant a signed copy of the lease within **ten days** after its making.
• In the case of a **verbal agreement**, the landlord must also give the tenant a written document in which the compulsory provisions of the lease and his name and address are indicated.

Language of the lease
• The lease and accompanying documents must be written in **French** unless the parties agree that they are to be written in another language.

Notices
• Upon making the lease, the landlord must give his new tenant certain notices; these can be found on page 4.
• All **notices** must be given **in writing** in the same language as the lease, except the notice of a visit to the dwelling, which may be given verbally.
• It is assumed that the notice has been **sent** and **received** the same day as the postmark, if it is sent by mail.

(Include here any additional clause which may be agreed upon by the parties: for instance, repairs, maintenance, painting, snow removal, janitor service, heating, description of the premises and of the furniture, etc.)

____
____
____
____
____
____
____
____
____
____

☐ The parties agree that the lease should be drawn up in English.
To signify our agreement, we have signed at ____
this ____ day of ____ 19 ____

Landlord ____

Tenant ____

The nature of the oral lease might lead you to believe that there are no rights or obligations involved. Don't be misled. Many rights and obligations arise out of landlord-tenant relationships under both the common law and, in Quebec, the Civil Code. Others are written into provincial statutes. No one in Canada is outside the reach—or the protection—of the law.

Paying the rent

For most people, payment of the rent is the crucial part of any lease. By approving the contract (signing the lease), you have committed yourself not only to paying the full agreed sum but also to making sure that the landlord receives the rent on time. Merely mailing the payment by cheque or money order on the date it is due is not good enough; strictly speaking, the tenant should make the payment in person by the due date if there is any doubt about a mailed payment reaching its destination on time.

The landlord has absolutely no right to increase the rent once a figure has been agreed, unless you consent to the change.

In most provinces, strange as it may sound, the tenant is obliged to keep on paying rent even if the house he has rented has burned down. This law applies to apartment dwellers as well, but would be impossible to enforce in the case of highrise complexes where tenants on upper floors would be unable to reach their apartments. You might think that access is also denied to those renting burned-out houses, but the law holds that these tenants would still have use of the land itself, theoretically for temporary shelter (like a tent); thus the obligation to pay rent stands. Make sure your insurance covers this possibility.

A good example of the landlord's protection regarding payment of rent is the fact that any dispute over a breach of the lease must be settled in court by civil action. Tenants are not advised to deduct any amount from their regular rental payments. When tenants arbitrarily decide to hold back some or all of their rent money in the form of a "rent strike," they are doomed before they start. The only legally acceptable exception is when an apartment tenant has had to vacate because of damages over which he had no control (fire, flood, etc.)

Most leases stipulate that the rent must be paid in advance on the first of each month, or other agreed time period. Actually, the law says that unless the lease makes a special provision as to payment in advance, the rent is not due until the end of each period. One advantage to paying in advance is that when the lease is up, your last month is already paid for. This leaves cash to cover moving costs.

Rent control

Canadians first experienced rent controls at the beginning of World War II. The influx of people into industrial centers created a congested accommodations market where excessive rents were charged. To remedy this situation, the federal government introduced legislation that froze rents across the country. Although federal rent control was abandoned in 1951, the Quebec government set up its own control system and established *la Régie des loyers* to enforce rental regulations. The power of this agency, renamed *la Régie du logement* in 1980, was eventually extended to cover mediation between landlords and tenants.

Throughout the rest of Canada, rental control boards were created in the 1970s to meet the concerns of city dwellers who were faced with soaring costs of accommodation. Today, many provincial boards oversee laws relating to rent increases. Some agencies also rule on claims made by landlord or tenant, without cost to either party. In Ontario, the Residential Tenancy Commission's power is limited to rent review, but it does inform the public about rental rights and ways of making claims. In Alberta, the Landlord and Tenant Advisory Board, a nonlegal body, has information and mediation services only.

In most provinces, anyone seeking to appeal a rent increase will find a nearby agency listed in the telephone book. In Quebec, *la Régie du logement* has more than 30 offices in major centers, as well as mobile units for outlying towns. Ontario has 20 offices throughout the province.

161

Rights and obligations

Landlord's right of entry

The right to assign

Responsibility for repairs

Insurance and taxes

Keeping pets

Termination and eviction

YOUR RIGHTS as a tenant are three-fold: first, your rights as stated in the lease itself; second, the rights given you by statutory laws (acts of the federal parliament and the provincial legislature); third, the rights granted according to common or civil law.

The most important single right has the most undramatic label: the right to "quiet enjoyment." This means that the landlord is not allowed to interfere with your physical possession of the premises. You are the master within the area you have leased. You may welcome whomever you wish into your home and may conduct yourself as you wish in that home, provided you do not break the terms of the lease or the law at large.

If the landlord should violate your right of quiet enjoyment (by turning off your water supply, for instance), he may be found to have broken the lease; as a result you could be freed of your obligations under the contract. Of course, such a breach has to be substantial; a temporary inconvenience, such as a plumbing leak, or a crack in the plaster, would not be considered sufficient.

There is a matching obligation on the part of the tenant not to "commit waste" on the premises; for example, you may not knock out walls or cut down trees on the property without the landlord's permission. If you were judged guilty of such conduct, the landlord could have you evicted and could probably sue you for damages as well. (*See* Chapter 18, "The question of damages.")

The tenant, under most leases, agrees not to use the premises in an "unreasonable" way. This is a wide generalization, but common sense should tell you what it entails. For instance, the owner of a rented house could possibly evict you or make you pay damages if you failed to heat the premises adequately during cold weather, allowing the pipes to freeze. You can't practice the drums at 3 A.M. in a high rise without the risk of drumming up trouble—the other tenants have a right to their quiet enjoyment as well.

Landlord's right of entry

Your legal right of quiet enjoyment should be cherished. As long as you intend to abide by the terms (the *covenants*) of your lease, you should also understand and insist upon your rights to privacy. For the period of the lease, that piece of rented space is, in effect, your "castle."

As the owner, the landlord does have the right, under common law, to enter his property; but this right is always curtailed in some measure by the terms of the lease. You will probably have to agree that he may enter to make repairs or to enforce some particular clause in the lease. This permission should be spelled out clearly in the lease. And make sure you are prepared to live with such terms before you sign the lease.

In most of the provinces, even if an eviction order has been served because the rent remains unpaid, the landlord cannot enter his rented premises without giving a 24-hour written notice to the tenant. However, the landlord has the right to enter, without written notification, to show the premises to prospective tenants during reasonable hours, if there are provisions in the lease that permit such an entry.

Should the landlord enter your premises without permission, forcibly or otherwise, to snoop or to harass you, you could probably terminate your lease on grounds that he violated your right to quiet enjoyment. You might also have grounds for damages in a civil suit.

The right to assign

As long as you, the lessee, remain personally responsible for paying the rent and satisfying other basic terms (including repairs), you have the right to *assign* your lease for the balance of your term. In other words, you can hand the place over to your brother, or to anyone else. But the situation immediately becomes very different if you want someone else to take over the financial burden as well.

The laws dealing with subletting in most provinces have gone through a series of changes. At one time, you could freely assign your lease along with the obligation of paying the rent in a sublet, unless there was a clause in the lease to the contrary. Later, "standard" contracts stipulated that a lease could not be assigned or sublet without the landlord's consent. As this seemed to be loaded too much against the tenant, the various landlord and tenant laws were again amended. Today, the average, or standard, contract states that the tenant may not assign or sublet without the landlord's consent but adds that "such consent may not be unreasonably withheld." This phrase is intended to restrict arbitrary action by the owner.

You may still have to deal with a landlord who refuses to include that phrase in the sublet clause of his otherwise "standard" lease. If you are faced with such a landlord, you should make sure that personal circumstances are not likely to force you into a move before the lease period is up. The cost of paying out the full term of your lease might be such that you could not afford to accept a career advancement which would require you to move to another town.

The right to "clean, warm shelter"

WHILE JUST ABOUT every urban center in Canada now boasts its blocks of gleaming high-rise apartments, or rows of integrated town houses, there is still an obstinate shortage of adequate housing for the really poor. Ever since World War II, successive governments (both federal and provincial) have tried to provide low-cost housing for the disadvantaged. Much has been done, with rent-subsidized apartments and modestly priced condominiums, but the problem is far from solved.

The subject was examined at the U.N. Habitat Conference in Vancouver in 1976. National housing conferences have been held in Ottawa and task forces tour the country. The federal Task Force on Housing insisted "every Canadian should be entitled to clean, warm shelter as a matter of basic human right." But the 1981 census revealed that about 500,000 of Canada's 8,000,000 homes remain substandard, and perhaps 1,000,000 Canadians are not enjoying that "basic human right." Many of these citizens are totally supported by welfare and social-security funds.

By the end of the century, statisticians predict Canada will require twice as many homes as it possesses now. Sociologists warn that building "ghettoes" of public housing—large concentrations of the poor—creates as many problems as it solves. Yet property owners everywhere object to government housing corporations seeding subsidized housing into their trim and respectable suburbs. The renovation of old housing ("urban renewal") is now popular. But such schemes appear to benefit the affluent rather than the needy.

The Senate Committee on Poverty reported that it knew of no realistic alternative to the expansion of public housing programs. "They are obviously not ideal," the report concluded, "but no better solution has been found to the housing problems of the poor."

Responsibility for repairs

Who is responsible for repairs to rented houses and apartments? Many tenants assume that they are obliged to look after "reasonable wear and tear," and the landlord is responsible for major or structural repairs. This assumption is wrong.

In all provinces, the landlord is responsible (especially in apartment blocks) for such minor matters as drain stoppages, heating or lighting malfunctions, appliance failures—in short, for 'reasonable wear and tear." The landlord is also responsible for major repairs required to maintain premises in a state fit for habitation.

The tenant's responsibility is limited mainly to repairing damage caused to the premises by his own negligence, "reasonable wear and tear" excepted. Keeping the premises clean is an obligation of the tenant.

Most landlords are naturally eager to protect their investment and will voluntarily make any important repairs. However, you can easily meet a landlord who doesn't care a whit, in which case you could get stuck with the job if you want it done.

Read the lease carefully and, if it contains a clause putting the major burden on the tenant, try to have it changed. Failing this, check the condition of the premises carefully before signing or, better still, have a registered builder do it. Make a list of the items you feel are in poor shape and ask the landlord, or his agent, to sign it. This list is sometimes called a *schedule of dilapidations.*

Press the owner to make all repairs before you move in. If this cannot be done, at least get his agreement in writing that you can return the premises to him in the same state of disrepair as existed when you moved in. You should take the precaution of having the landlord put in writing, before you take possession, any promises he makes about improvements.

If you decide to lease an unfurnished house, unless the owner clearly agrees to make repairs, you have to take it "as is." After you take possession, you cannot force him to fix anything, even if rain is pouring through the roof. The situation is quite different if you lease a furnished house. The law here says that there is an "implied warranty" that the house is fit to live in; the owner must ensure that it is.

Responsibility for major repairs has long been a subject of debate and reform in landlord-tenant relations. All provinces have taken important steps to improve matters in favor of the tenant. In Ontario, for example, the Landlord and Tenant Act has been amended so that in residential tenancies a landlord must not only offer, but also maintain, the rented premises in a good state of repair. The premises must be fit for habitation and must comply with all health, safety and housing standards. The amended act also prevents the landlord from adapting a lease by inserting a clause under which the tenant waives—that is, agrees to forfeit—his legal rights.

The duties of a tenant in Ontario are now more in the nature of good housekeeping: making sure the premises are clean, changing light fuses, unblocking minor stoppages in sinks and toilets. If the landlord fails to live up to his responsibilities, the tenant can apply to the courts for an order obliging the landlord to perform repairs. If he still refuses, the court might permit the tenant to have the repairs carried out and then deduct the cost from the rent due. If a court should find proof of disrepair, the tenant could break his lease without penalty.

The new interpretations are not entirely one-sided, however. The tenant must live up to official standards as well. He must not only maintain a reasonable standard of housekeeping but he is also responsible for property damage caused by what is termed "willful or negligent conduct"—such as allowing his children to deface walls or ride bicycles in the halls of an apartment building.

The tenant is also required by law to notify the owner promptly about any small problem that, if neglected, could become a big and expensive matter—for example, a leak in the roof or plumbing which, if neglected, could lead to serious structural damage.

In Quebec, the interpretation of the lease contract under the Civil Code places the responsibility on the owner to inspect his own property and to determine whatever repairs may be necessary to keep the premises in a fit and proper condition for habitation.

The landlord must carry out all major repairs, as well as any improvements, such as the repainting of the walls and the ceiling of a rented apartment, arising from normal "wear and tear." The tenant is responsible for any minor repairs resulting from the use of the premises—for example, the patching of holes made by picture-hanging nails.

Insurance and taxes

Although not bound by law to do so, an owner will usually insure his property to protect his investment. Even if the property is insured, however, the policy would not cover your personal possessions as a tenant. You should arrange your own insurance—such as a personal property floater—to cover your chattels and personal effects.

Insurance is meant to cover the possibility of total or partial damage to a property through fire, severe storms, explosions, floods and so on. While nor-

mal coverage has probably been taken out by your landlord, you should always check your lease carefully to establish your position as tenant in any of these emergency conditions. (*See* Chapter 13, "Insurance at home.")

Generally, the landlord is under no obligation either to repair or to replace the premises should they burn to the ground. Not only that, a tenant may be obliged by the terms of his lease to continue paying rent. As discussed earlier, this would not likely apply in the case of an apartment building, but might happen in the case of a detached home.

Usually, with apartments or town houses, the landlord is responsible for all taxes on the property. But you should examine the lease carefully on this point. For instance, a lease for a detached home will often state that the tenant must pay the taxes.

Keeping pets

If you own a dog, cat, monkey, ocelot, or even just a budgie, your chance of renting an apartment in one of today's highrise complexes may be slim. Not many apartment blocks, old or new, roll out the red

Looking after *les locataires*

QUEBEC TAKES SPECIAL CARE of its *locataires* (tenants). Under the terms of the Civil Code, the landlord has to maintain the dwelling in habitable condition, and to make all repairs legally required of him. If the landlord does not take corrective action, the tenant can, in urgent cases, have the repairs done and then sue the owner for the cost. The tenant can also apply to the court to withhold rent in order to proceed with repairs that the landlord neglected to take.

Montreal leads most Canadian cities by proclaiming its own housing code (with particular reference to rented property) and by providing for enforcement through municipal bylaw. Some excerpts:

• The kitchen sink, washbasin, bathtub or

shower shall be supplied with hot and cold water. The hot water shall be delivered at a minimum temperature of 49°C.

• Foundation walls shall always be kept in condition to prevent the entry of vermin or rodents.

• Roofs shall at all times be kept free of any accumulation of snow or ice liable to be a hazard to persons or property.

• Walls and ceilings shall be kept in good repair and shall at all times be free of holes and cracks.

If this sounds like Shangri-la to some Montrealers, they can get a copy of the code from city hall and check it out. If you decide to present a marked copy to your landlord, point out that these standards are merely minimums.

carpet for pets. It is not the landlord who always objects, but rather the other tenants who complain. One man's mutt can be another man's poison.

In most cases the lease will forbid pets of any kind; so it is pointless to move in and try to hide the fact that you are keeping one. Sooner or later you will be found out—even white mice squeak—and it will be a case of you getting rid of the pet or the landlord getting rid of you.

Termination and eviction

On the date your lease expires, you are obliged to move out unless you have renegotiated your contract or come to some other agreement to extend your tenancy on a periodic basis—perhaps on a weekly or monthly basis.

If you have been properly served with notice of the expiry and you still do not vacate, the landlord can go to court (County, District or Provincial, depending on the province) and obtain an eviction order. He cannot secure that order, however, if he accepts regular payments after the expiry date. If he does, you are automatically recognized under the law as a periodic tenant (*See* "Examining the lease" in this chapter).

Provincial laws vary considerably in this field. If your lease is for a fixed term (the normal type) it may automatically assume periodic (say, month-to-month) status on expiry, unless the landlord has given you written notice to leave. In Ontario, for example, the conditions upon which the owner can enforce that notice are strictly limited by law.

With a periodic tenancy, your obligation is more specific. For example, if you have paid rent each month, you are a tenant on a monthly basis; thus, you are required by law to give the landlord notice of your departure at least one clear month ahead of the date you wish to go. A period of notice is not absolutely necessary, of course. With the consent of both parties, a tenancy can be terminated at any time.

The death of either the landlord or the tenant does not terminate a lease, unless the lease specifically says so.

To the average person, "eviction" usual-ly means the forcible removal of a tenant by his landlord. In the legal sense, it is much more complicated. The term can, for example, include reference to conditions imposed by a landlord with the intention of depriving the tenant of his right of quiet enjoyment of the premises, thus causing him to move.

Even if the lease still has considerable time to go, the owner has the right to obtain possession from a tenant who has violated any substantial term of the lease. The most common breach is failure to pay the rent. Others are: causing damage, overcrowding, operating a bawdy house or remaining on the premises after the expiry date.

Varying provincial laws govern proceedings by which a landlord is able to repossess his property. A tenant must be given notice as to how he has breached the lease and he must be given a chance to remedy that breach. If you are behind in your rent, you could put your lease back in good standing by paying into court the amount you owe, plus a small amount for costs.

If your landlord threatens legal action to evict you, don't panic or start barricading your apartment door. If there is some matter in dispute, consult a lawyer to make sure of your position.

On the other hand, the tenant's right to break the lease is generally limited to one area: the owner's violation of his covenant to provide for your quiet enjoyment. Such a violation must be substantial. If you decide to try to break your lease—by moving out before the end of your term and refusing to pay the rent for the whole period—you may have to prove in court that the landlord has failed seriously in his obligations. For instance, if an apartment building had been allowed to deteriorate into a filthy condition, with broken windows and infestation of vermin, a judge might consider that you had justification in breaking the contract. In law, this is known as *constructive eviction*. On the other hand, if your complaint is that someone practices the clarinet for an hour every evening along the hall, the judge might suggest that you take a course in music appreciation.

The halfway house

STEEP INTEREST rates on mortgages, soaring property taxes, high prices of houses "in their own grounds" in the suburbs—these are harsh realities that have made it difficult for many Canadians to realize their ambition of owning their "dream house." This applies particularly to young married couples who are starting a family while earning small to average incomes. Others, because of their jobs, must live in central city areas where house prices can be astronomical.

Until recently, people had no alternative but to rent the required accommodation. But in city centres, where the demand for housing is greatest and where taxes are highest, the single-family detached dwelling has become too expensive for the average family to rent or buy. The increase in high-rise apartment and town-house living has been one result.

Logical and efficient as these units are, they have not satisfied the urge of the individual to be king in his own castle. He still yearns for the psychological security and social status which seems to be a vital part of home ownership. This problem has been met by the evolution of the condominium and of cooperative ownership (the British term "co-ownership" is sometimes seen). Real estate law is still being adapted and new legislation proclaimed to regulate this style of ownership.

Although built in the form of an apartment or town house (the row-housing system), individual units can be bought instead of rented, thus providing that psychological lift of becoming an owner rather than a tenant, and the prospect also of increasing the family's assets. Private ownership is complete indoors at a condominium; an elected board of directors controls the hallways, public rooms, common services and the grounds surrounding the building.

How the condominium works

"Condominium" may be an awkward word but it exactly describes this concept in housing—"joint government, joint sovereignty, over property." The basic features are:

(1) The property is divided into units which are owned by individuals.

(2) The common elements (services, play areas, etc.) are owned jointly.

(3) There is an administrative framework to manage the common areas and to set out the rights and obligations of individual owners.

The main financial advantage of a condominium derives from the common use of land and services. Because of this, the unit cost to the individual is in most cases much less than that of an equal living area in a detached home. Taxes per unit are lower and swimming pools, tennis courts, playground equipment and sauna baths are often provided at no extra cost.

Group responsibility might have drawbacks for some and "closing costs" on the deal can be surprisingly high because so many items have to be prepaid (such things as your contribution to the maintenance fund for common utilities, and the sales tax on appliances). But you will get your individual property title (the "deed") when the new condominium corporation is registered and, within the limits of the group's operational bylaws, your property title makes you independent from other owners and from the management corporation.

As an owner, having arranged your own financing, you have what is legally termed a *fee simple* property interest (*See* "Before you buy" in this chapter), complete with an ownership deed. If the value of the property should increase over the years, any profit made in a sale would come to you.

A condominium corporation elects a board of directors to manage the property and its common assets. Expenses for maintenance of driveways and lawns, for snow removal and swimming pools are paid by unit owners, in proportion to each one's share of the whole.

The corporation bylaws will probably

The condominium concept

This type of advertisement illustrates how "the condominium concept" attempts to shed any vestige of tenement or slum image. Many large blocks similar to that described below are being built for modest-income families with the help of provincial housing corporations. Mortgages guaranteed by the province can provide up to 95 percent of value in approved projects, thus bringing home ownership within financial range for the widest possible group of buyers. The individual homeowners together own the entire building and its lands, just as shareholders own a business company.

Management is usually passed to a professional management company, employed by the condominium.

authorize property managers to take certain routine actions without the consent of the owners. But on serious matters, the bylaws of a condominium normally stipulate that unit owners must decide any course of action by a majority vote. These decisions would most likely be upheld in the courts because the co-owners commit themselves to obey the bylaws when they enter the scheme. The unit owners essentially sign a joint contract and are thus bound by the laws of contract.

Money-back guarantees

By the 1980s, the building and marketing of condominiums had become a highly competitive business in the major urban areas of Montreal, Toronto, Vancouver, Edmonton, Winnipeg and Hamilton. Prospective owners were being offered a wide variety of options for interior fittings and decor. These items can include sunken baths and fireplaces.

"Buyer protection plans" are offered in writing, giving them the force of warranties. (*See* Chapter 6, "Guarantees and standards.") When the economy slows down, some of the condominium developers offer very easy terms. For example, some guarantee that you can resell your town-house to the developer without loss within 18 months after purchase if you are not satisfied with your buy. In other cases, incoming purchasers are offered cash loans to assist them in buying appliances or carpeting.

The cooperative plan

Cooperatives are another comparatively new alternative in home ownership. The principle is much the same as applies to condominiums: the units are part of an apartment block or town-house complex. However, you do not individually own your private area. Instead, all participants are shareholders in the company which owns and operates the whole.

Another difference is that you cannot finance your unit as you wish. You can't, for instance, arrange your own mortgage since there is an over-all mortgage arranged by the company. You have to make regular payments according to the size and position of the unit you occupy.

Under a cooperative agreement, you will usually share in the increased value of your home unit if it is sold after you have paid your installments for an agreed period of years.

Some co-ops demand that you stay at least a year. If you plan to move, the period of notice you have to give can vary from one to three months. A deposit is normally required on joining a scheme. If you move out, the deposit money may be used to repair or to redecorate the vacated premises.

Getting along with the neighbors

Condominium implies "communal" to a certain extent; thus, the key to your enjoyment can lie in your tolerance and willingness to get along with fellow owners and management. Success of the mini-community requires the cooperation of everyone so that a healthy form of self-government is achieved.

Long-term management contracts are usually worked out with a division of the developer's organization when condominium projects get under way. It is important that the individual unit owners get to know the system of managing the property and get to know each other so that, in later years when the developer has sold all the units and no longer holds a majority position on the board of directors, the owners will be capable of administering their own affairs.

Before buying into a condominium, carefully study the bylaws regarding elections and removal of directors, meetings and voting provisions. You will own your own home all right, but your over-all "quiet enjoyment" can be marred by disputes over policy controlling the areas of common rights. If you don't think children should ride bicycles on the tennis courts, the time to check out the regulations on such things is before you sign.

Whether you are considering an apartment, a house, a condominium or a cooperative, your lawyer should be consulted. He will get you answers to any questions, and advise you of your rights and obligations. His expertise and insight can help you make a wise decision for yourself and your family.

Before you buy

BUYING a house will quite likely be the largest and most important financial move you will ever make. To the average Canadian, a home represents his greatest asset. Although you may "own" it the day you and your family move in, you will probably be paying for it for 20 years, and maybe much longer than that.

Your choice of house and district will have an effect on the way you will live, and will certainly have an influence on your growing children.

Because of this—and for other reasons discussed in this chapter—think long and coolly before you decide to purchase *that* house, even if your heart is set on it. Real-estate brokers say that some people buy their lifetime home with less care than they lavish on a new car. The law is there to protect you but, to get under its cover, you must understand what you are doing.

Quite apart from looking hard at the financial facts, you should walk around the entire neighborhood and examine the other houses. Do the other residents cut their grass? Do your prospective neighbors believe in such things as fresh paint?

It is a good idea to go back on different days of the week. Take your spouse with you. What is the traffic like? A dream of a suburb seen on a Wednesday can look quite different on a Saturday. You will want to check on how far the children will have to walk to school. Where is the bus stop, or the subway? How about the bank and the shops?

Appraisal by experts
The neighborhood looks good and the financial setup checks out; but what about the house itself? What do you know, really, about foundations, furnaces or rafters? Don't be shy about asking your buddy Fred, the one who is a building foreman, to look the dream house over for you. If you don't happen to know an expert, you can hire a professional appraiser. The next question is, are you getting your money's worth? Again, you can pay for an expert valuation of the house, but there's a cheaper way: buy the local paper on Saturdays and compare asking prices.

If some summer day you are thinking of buying out in the countryside, consider for a moment what that long drive out to the highway will look like with three feet of snow on it. If you will have to be a commuter, are you sure you can survive a full hour going and coming each working day? And that pretty little creek near the house might flood in the spring and turn your basement into a swimming pool. The working farmer thinks first of the land, but his wife thinks in terms of extra cupboard space, a roomy kitchen and probably a large rec room for the family fun that adds pleasure to country life.

The questions may seem endless, but it is better to ask and to get them all answered before you are hooked. Since it is almost certain you will be calling in a lawyer later to process the deal, you should consider getting in touch with one at the outset.

The lawyer is well versed in the pitfalls of home ownership and his experience will probably raise a few questions you would never think of. His advice on how much to offer could save you real money. And his guidance the whole way through may not cost you a dollar more than the regular fee you will have to pay anyway.

The ultimate owner

No. Despite all you've heard and read about "freehold," no one owns any part of Canada absolutely. The basis of land law in Canada is that all land is owned by the Crown. This means that when you buy a parcel of land, the Crown is granting you the right to use it, but retains ultimate ownership of it; you become a tenant holding rights directly from the Crown. If municipal or provincial authorities ever decide to expropriate all or part of your house lot, you will discover that this is no mere technicality. It is also a fact that you do not have the right to dispose of your property entirely as you may wish.

This system, which is called "freehold tenure," dates back to the invading Norman, William I, who regarded all English soil as his by right of conquest. When he parceled lands out to his barons, he did not make outright gifts: the lands were to be held "of him" as overlord. Thus, no land in England was *allodial* (without a lord). In terms of the law, a land grant was a conditional gift, subject to certain obligations.

As land was the major source of wealth, the Crown, or overlord, insisted that tenants provide services in return for their acreage. One tenant might have to supply armed horsemen to fight for the King; another might be required to provide fat hogs for food.

The relationship was known as *tenure,* and the type of tenure varied acccording to services rendered.

This was the semifeudal structure: a pyramid starting at the top with the King granting large tracts of land to his barons. The barons, in turn, subdivided their holdings among their vassals, who were tenants "of their lord" for certain services. And so it went down the line to the broad base of peasants who actually worked the soil. A variation of this land-holding system existed in Quebec under the French regime and persisted, in fact, until 1854. (*See* Chapter 21, "Justice in New France.")

Tenure merely referred to the conditions upon which land was held. It did not specify the length of time involved, which was (and still is) called the *estate.* A man might, for example, be granted tenure for his own lifetime (a "life estate"), or for as long as he or any of his heirs were alive (a "fee simple estate"). The term *tenant in fee simple* is still used today as the legal label for the owner of a routine freehold. "Fee" is derived from "fief," the feudal term for a landholding.

The various types of tenure have been swept away by land-law reform statutes, and all tenures converted into free and common agreements. With this change, the "fee simple estate"—the firmest title you can hold to land—has come to resemble total ownership.

The tenure relationship may no longer exist, but the basic idea of the system lives on. As landowners, we still technically hold land "of the Crown" only as tenants. The taxes we pay can be compared with services originally paid to the lord. Also, if a property owner dies leaving no will and if no heirs can be found, his land reverts to the Crown. This occurrence is known as *escheat,* a term derived from the French and originally from two Latin words meaning "fall from," and it applies everywhere in Canada. (In Alberta, the annual income derived from property that has reverted to the Crown is paid to the Universities Commission.)

What is referred to as Crown land, is land that has not been granted for private occupation or use.

Five-point checklist

Consumer-protection agencies, newspaper economists and homemaker magazines will give you plenty of sound advice on the type of home that is probably best for your family. Houses come in dozens of shapes and sizes: old and new, conventional and avant-garde. Whatever type you fancy, there are certain elements common to all home purchases that you should consider. These are not necessarily of immediate legal character but, if ignored, they could involve you in serious difficulties within a short time.

MORTGAGE RENEWAL. Many starry-eyed young buyers stretch themselves to the limit in meeting mortgage payments, getting into 20- or 25-year mortgages at fixed interest rates. They may be able to handle the interest, principal and taxes at first,

171

but many overlook the fact that while they are counting on long-term amortization (paying off the mortgage) at fixed monthly payments, there is generally a short-term renewal clause (usually five years). At this point, the mortgage must be renegotiated, quite possibly at a higher rate of interest. Before you sign anything, analyze what your finances will probably be like in five years' time and figure out whether you would be able to meet higher payments.

TAX RATES. Check the prevailing taxes for the neighborhood you want to move into and try to find out from city hall whether there are expensive local improvements (new parks, new sewers) on the drawing board which could skyrocket your tax bill. If the taxes have stayed the same for years, watch out! They are probably due for a jump.

ZONING BYLAWS. City hall or the township office should be able to supply you with a copy of the planning bylaws for the area in which you want to buy. Municipal officials can tell you how your chosen location is zoned and explain the various zoning descriptions used. Also, try to find out from the township planners whether or not your area could be changed from a strictly residential to a residential-commercial zone in the foreseeable future. Otherwise, a factory or gas station might some day locate in your immediate neighborhood—perhaps next door—and, as a result, sharply reduce the value of your property.

PUBLIC SERVICES. Don't wait until after you have moved in to find that police, fire and sanitation services are not up to standard in your district. This could bring about an increase in your insurance premiums. You could also be forced, with unexpected but compulsory costs, to link up with a new municipal sewage line.

Investigate your water supply thor-

Ten traps for the unwary

HERE'S A CHECKLIST prepared by impartial government experts to warn you of common pitfalls when buying a house. It could save you time, money—and perhaps even heartache.

Whether a house is new or used, part of a terrace or row (the town house), condominium or standing in its own grounds, the principles of good design and construction apply. Remember, too, that a home should give you more than just shelter from the rain and frost; on the right lot, it can be a joy to live in and—as a bonus—it will almost certainly grow in value while you are enjoying it.

• Deal only with reputable real estate agents. Beware of the man who is "operating on his own."

• Before you sign anything—including any offers—see your lawyer. His services are virtually essential later anyway.

• Multiply your annual income by three. If the price is greater than that you should probably look elsewhere.

• Have the property checked by a professional appraiser for structural defects. The charge may run to $300, but you'll probably have to pay this in any case before you get a mortgage.

• Are you certain that all the relevant details have been clearly stated in the "Agreement of Purchase and Sale?"

• Is the neighborhood really the place you want to bring your kids up in? What about shops and schools?

• Older houses will almost certainly be costlier to maintain. How's the plumbing? Flush the toilets to find out for yourself.

• Allow money for moving costs, land-transfer tax, and for such things as insurance, telephone connection, TV cable hook up.

• Remember that your lawyer will be presenting his bill. Ask in advance what he will charge.

• Don't necessarily accept the first mortgage financing you are offered. Shop around a bit . . . it's a competitive business.

oughly. If you are buying a rural property, for example, you may have to drill a well. Check with the local public health authorities, particularly if there are a number of lots near you being developed for new housing. If the lots are smallish and if each one will require a septic tank, your drilling plans might be frustrated.

When buying a house with an existing well, always have a sample of the water analyzed, particularly if the house is serviced by a septic tank. The tank itself should be checked by an engineer to make sure it is functioning properly.

NEW ROAD WORK. Find out from the engineers at city hall, township or county office if new roads are planned for the area, and determine how they might affect the property you have chosen. That quiet street could become a speedway in a proposed new pattern of traffic flow.

If it is rumored that the highway is to be widened to four lanes in front of your land, remember that the extra ground has to come from somewhere. Will some unknown draftsman carve five metres off your front garden in the years ahead? With more and more traffic, this is happening to someone's cherished property every day of the week.

Brokers and agents

A private sale notice ("No Agents") in the classified section of the local newspaper may lead you to your dream home, and the seller might share with you some of the broker's fee he would otherwise pay (normally about six percent of the price). But it is more likely you will be dealing with one of the real estate agents whose ads make such tempting reading in the weekend newspapers.

The biggest agency is not necessarily the best, but a firm that has a good reputation has no doubt earned it. Some people prefer a smaller office, offering a more individualized service. It is a matter of personal preference.

Real estate companies (or brokers) are the focal point of the residential housing market. They are familiar with property and financing and they have a specialized knowledge of the local market. They will know which houses are for sale—or

might be for sale—in the areas in which you are most interested. And they can usually suggest where you might apply successfully for your mortgage money.

Some city real estate boards maintain multiple listings of properties. Brokers who are members of such a board receive detailed information and photographs on each property placed "on multiple"—that is, made available to all agents—so that they can provide information not only about their own listed homes but about homes listed by other companies. When a property is "on multiple," it does not mean any more expense for the purchaser. It is the seller who pays—usually a percentage point more on whatever is the commission rate paid to the broker who actually finds the buyer.

For each listing, whether exclusive or multiple, a broker should have details on the type of construction of the house, its age and condition; the area of the house and the lot; present financing, taxes and any extras—for example, a television antenna or drapery tracks.

The real estate broker is almost everywhere a licensed professional. He must take specialized courses in real estate financing, land regulations and property law, and must pass qualifying examinations. His sales staff is also required to take certain courses.

The real estate boards are professional associations, setting out standards of conduct for their members and making sure that these standards are maintained. A real estate board will investigate for you the reliability of any firm within its area. The local better business bureau, or your banker, would also be able to provide information. There are certain regulations which must be followed by these professionals. In Ontario, for example, brokers must comply with the terms of the Real Estate and Business Brokers Act.

It is essential for the buyer to remember in dealing with a real estate firm that the agent is representing the seller—known formally as the *vendor*.

He is not a neutral party. His main concern is to obtain the best deal for the vendor, mindful of the fact that the higher the price, the greater his commission.

The real estate agent, however professionally dedicated, is still basically a salesman and, as such, is entitled by law to a certain amount of exaggeration. You can imagine how many sales he would make if he dwelt on the defects of his houses. He (or she) is allowed to paint a rosy picture, but exaggeration must not go to the extent of false representation.

If a vendor's agent deliberately misrepresents a material fact and the purchaser relies on its being a fact, the agent could be charged with fraud. For instance, if the agent said the house in question had solid oak floors, you might believe him, and sign up. If the "oak" turned out to be plywood, you could possibly withdraw from the deal without penalty; the situation might turn on whether you had the opportunity to make a thorough examination of the house before buying.

The prospective buyer should bear in mind that the vendor, or seller, is not responsible for *all* acts of the agent. In the case of fraudulent misrepresentation, you would not necessarily have grounds for taking action against the vendor personally; the agent may have acted outside the scope of his authority. Your action would then be limited to the agent, or broker.

If you really want to buy a certain house but have doubts about claims being made in its favor, you would be wise to have experts from specific trades—such as a plumber and electrician—check the house for you.

Inspecting the house

Steady house hunting can produce a numbing effect. A continuous round of visiting other people's homes, occupied or empty, can dull your sensibilities, causing you to overlook deficiencies. When you have actually found a house you like, it is advisable not to say very much on the first visit. Go back with a neutral expert who can inspect the premises thoroughly and point out actual or possible drawbacks you might have missed. A hard-nosed friend can sometimes fill this role. The suggestion applies to new houses as well as old.

Once your offer to purchase has been accepted and the deal closed, it is unlikely that you could come back on the vendor for any undetected deficiencies. The legal process known as *rescission of contract* (canceling the deal, returning the house and getting your money back) is seldom possible in the field of real estate. You

What do you know about design?

MANY PEOPLE APPEAR to buy houses for price alone. Others fall in love with the view. Some are snobs, wanting to rub close to the town's social set. But comparatively few seem to consider the paramount factor of design. If the house simply does not do its job, it's a bad buy at any price.

When you enter a house you should be able to go straight from the entrance foyer to any room, certainly without traversing the living room.

Kids with muddy feet should have space (a mud room) by the back door to drop their rubbers in. This should connect with the kitchen for the delivery of groceries.

Direct access to bathrooms and bedrooms is essential. Remember that if the master bedroom has an interior private bath, your guests will have to take their chances in the children's bathroom.

The kitchen shouldn't be away out in left field. Modern housewives spend most of their working day there and long hikes to the front door are tiresome. Kitchen windows should face southeast.

The single-story house should allow for a "work zone" (kitchen, laundry, workshop) and a "sleep zone" (bedrooms and bath). A solid wall to absorb noise should separate the zones.

That wall-to-wall picture window offers a great view of the street. From the street, of course, if offers anyone passing by your house a great view of you.

would not have a chance in a court action unless you could prove conclusively that the seller or his agent had cheated you.

Role of the lawyer

There are individuals who have successfully completed real estate transactions on their own, negotiating the price, signing the offer to purchase, closing the deal and registering the necessary documents. But few of us have the business aptitude that is required, nor the time to attend special courses to acquire it. For most people, a lawyer's services are essential.

Costly mistakes can be made right from the outset. Unfortunately, the buyer seldom engages a lawyer until his "offer to purchase" has been accepted and signed. Yet this is the most important piece of paper in the whole transaction. If the vendor accepts your offer, that seals the deal. It is extremely important that you hire a lawyer early enough for him to study your offer, to correct any mistakes you might have made and to guide you during the actual negotiations.

Presuming your lawyer starts working for you at the offer-to-purchase stage, he will pay particular attention to the financial aspects (for instance, how much less than the asking price you should offer), the timing, the conditions contained in the offer and your commitments under the offer. He also will advise on how to go about "taking title," and will explain the procedure you should follow.

The lawyer then contacts the vendor's solicitor, starts to prepare the documents, searches the title to ensure that the house and land are truly as described and checks the registry office for possible liens—that is, financial claims—against the vendor or his property. All this accomplished, he works with the other party on formally closing the sale: he exchanges documents, transfers funds, obtains the keys to your new house and conveys possession to you.

In the vital area of mortgaging, a lawyer is almost indispensable. The institutions that lend money on house mortgages (banks, trusts, insurance and loan companies) insist that a solicitor handle the transaction and provide them with a certificate proving that ownership of the property is clear and uncontested. (*See* Chapter 12, "The role of the bank.")

The cost of drawing up the mortgage and searching the title normally is deducted from moneys advanced on the mortgage. Thus, in most cases, even the purchaser who does not want a lawyer pays for one in the long run, by deduction. At the time of this writing, one large law society in Ontario was suggesting the following fee schedule for arranging a house purchase or drawing up a mortgage: $500 for the first $50,000 of the house price, plus ¼ to ½ of 1 percent of the next $50,000 to $200,000. If the lawyer arranges both the purchase and the mortgage, he will charge more than this, but not twice as much.

When you decide to engage a lawyer, you might care to find out who is representing the firm or individual lending you the mortgage money. If the same lawyer is representing both parties regarding the same piece of property, he might provide double certification at a reduced rate.

Inescapable extra costs

Don't forget that a buyer has to pay the provincial land-transfer tax on top of those expenses incurred by his lawyer in carrying out the transaction. In Ontario, for example, the tax stood recently at ⅖ of one percent of the first $45,000 of the purchase price, plus ⅘ of one percent on the remainder. In almost all sales of existing houses, the purchaser takes over existing insurance policies. (*See* Chapter 13, "Insurance at home.")

If you are taking a brand-new house, allow for the unavoidable costs of stove, refrigerator, storm and screen windows, floor coverings and window drapes. And you may have to pay for a television tower to get good broadcast reception. Then there are pathways, sodding, and perhaps fences. But don't forget your moving bill. An older house will probably soon require expensive repairs (or perhaps replacement) of heating equipment, plumbing and roofing. If it needs a paint job, get an estimate from a contractor and add that to your list of expenses in advance.

Closing the deal

ACONTRACT for the sale of real estate is governed by the same laws that control any other contract: essentially, there must be an offer and an acceptance of the offer, both of these to be in writing and signed by the parties. It could be a simple two- or three-line paragraph, as long as it contained the indispensable terms; however, it is much more likely to be a lengthy document loaded with legalistic jargon, negotiated between solicitors. These are not simplistic times.

The most common form of contract between the purchaser and the seller (called the *vendor*) is a standardized printed form called an "offer to purchase," or "agreement of purchase and sale." In the routine case, after you have decided to buy, the real-estate agent who represents the vendor completes the form and gets you to sign it. He asks you for a deposit, a sizeable sum of money (perhaps $1,000) by certified cheque, as evidence of your sincerity and financial ability. He takes the offer to the vendor who, if he accepts your terms and conditions, adds his own signature.

Technically, the contract is an "offer to purchase" only until it is signed by the vendor. At that point it becomes an "agreement of purchase and sale." In most regions today, the original two papers have become merged. The wording of the forms is pretty much the same all across Canada.

If you are the buyer, it is vital to remember that the printed offer form is prepared by the agent acting for the vendor and, as such, it could be slanted in that direction. For this and other reasons, as stressed already in this chapter, you would be wise to have a lawyer check the offer before you sign. If the vendor accepts, then—barring some illegality—the property is yours. You have much at stake, so find out what you are getting into before you sign.

You can make your offer conditional, for example, upon your success in getting a mortgage. You can also work out certain terms with the vendor or his agent, for example, to delay the possession date to suit you. But remember that any such conditions must be written into the contract. If this is not done before you sign the agreement, you would stand a poor chance of success later, should any dispute arise over these conditions. The contract is regarded as the *sum* of your agreement, and the courts would be unlikely to interpret it otherwise.

Spell out the "extras"

Disputes often arise over "extras"—such as light fixtures, drapes, appliances or garden equipment. Make sure the agent spells out exactly what is to be included in the purchase price. It is not enough to write in "broadloom and draperies" in a general way. The offer should specify whether it is *all* broadloom and *all* draperies, and should state in which rooms of the house these items are to remain (for example, "broadloom in the living and dining room area, draperies in the master bedroom").

It is unethical—but quite possible—that a broker might hold your offer, using it to try to nudge another interested party into offering a higher price. In Britain, this practice is referred to by the curious label, *gazumping*. You can prevent this from happening by laying down a deadline—perhaps 48 hours—for acceptance of your offer by the vendor. In what is known as a buyer's market—that is, a situation in which there are more houses available than there are potential buyers, thus driving prices down—you might cut the time to 24 hours.

Searching the title

Whenever you obtain an interest in property, whether it is the purchase of a house or a lot, a mortgage or an easement (the right to make limited use of another's property), the transaction must be recorded officially. In case of dispute, your claim to the property will be governed by the date of registration.

In Canada, there are two basic methods of recording interests in land: the land-titles system and the older registry office system. The registry system rules in Newfoundland, Nova Scotia, New Brunswick, Prince Edward Island, Quebec and in the greater part of Ontario and Manitoba. The land titles system (sometimes called the Torrens, or "new," system) operates in British Columbia, Alberta, Saskatchewan, the Northwest Territories, and in some parts of Ontario and Manitoba. All Crown land in Canada is now held under the Land Titles Act, and this simplified system is becoming more widely accepted as time passes. At the time of this writing, for example, the land titles system had been adopted by New Brunswick and Prince Edward Island, but it was not yet in force in either province.

Under the land titles method, the various interests on a specific piece of property are recorded. If there is no clash with a previously recorded interest, the Crown will guarantee title to the property. The parcel of land itself is recorded as a unit of property in the land titles office. Upon request, the office will provide a short statement describing all preceding transactions affecting that particular registered property. Thus, when you are dealing with a registered proprietor, you don't have to look beyond the certificate of title.

The registry system is more complicated. Its core is the central registry office where individuals interested in property are recorded in what are called "books"

of entry." However, the system provides only listings of owners or part owners individually, without necessarily grouping them in relation to one particular piece of property. The registry, unlike the land titles office, does not list the property itself with the names of all interested parties included. Consequently, if your lawyer sets out to search a title through the registry system, he faces the possibility of having to find and examine a series of entry books before he is able to determine the true status of the property at that moment. He will have to prepare what is called an "abstract of title"—a record of all documents and previous transactions concerning the property.

The "abstract" should cover a preceding period of between 40 and 60 years (the period varies in different provinces). The lawyer then checks the abstract to make sure all previous interests in the land have been properly nullified or *conveyed*—that is to say, the title has been duly transferred—so that you, the purchaser, will be receiving the property free from any of those previous interests—in other words, with no strings attached from the past.

In contrast, under the land titles system, the solicitor's clerk merely goes to the appropriate office and obtains a certificate of title showing the registered proprietor, along with a simple statement regarding any other interested parties.

On the basis of this title search, your lawyer may ask the vendor's lawyer to clear up certain problems appearing on the title. If the request is valid and the vendor's solicitor is unable to comply, you could then back out of the deal and ask for the return of your deposit.

If problems are cleared up satisfactorily, your solicitor will then give you his personal certificate of title. In most cases, he will give you a warranty that you have a good and marketable title to the property, ensuring that any future buyer of your property would find no defects.

It could be counted as a flaw in the registry office system, as far as titles to land is concerned, that your title could possibly be marred by carelessness on the part of your solicitor during his search of the various entry books. If you discovered that there was some defect and that your title was not "good and marketable," you could sue the lawyer. However, in most provinces, you would have to act within six years of his issuing the certificate of title. After six years, the lawyer would be protected under the Statute of Limitations—and of course, such a defect might not come to the surface until you attempted to sell the property many years later. It is always possible that a defect is minor, not really affecting the enjoyment of full ownership; in this case, any future owner would probably accept the title, including the defect, as you had done before him.

Completion of contract

"Closing"—the popular way of saying "concluding a real estate transaction"—is, in theory anyway, the most important phase of the whole procedure.

The solicitors for both parties set the stage. They meet, exchange documents,

---

Agreement of purchase and sale

Once called the "Offer to Purchase," now mostly known as the "Agreement of Purchase and Sale," this form—when signed by both buyer and seller—virtually closes the deal. When your offer is accepted, naturally enough, you can figure that (barring accidents) you've bought your dream house. The deal can be upset only by nonfulfillment of any conditions written into the contract, or by some illegality.

The form below is widely used in Ontario, and the printed forms used in other provinces are basically similar. But remember that it is the agent for the vendor (the seller) who fills in the blank spaces. Make sure that you understand and agree with every word. Better still: show the document to your lawyer before you sign.

ONTARIO REAL ESTATE ASSOCIATION
AGREEMENT OF PURCHASE AND SALE

PURCHASER, ..., offers to buy from
VENDOR, ..., through Vendor's
AGENT, ..., the following
PROPERTY: fronting on the .... side of .... known municipally as ....
in the .... of ....
and having a frontage of .... more or less by a depth of .... more or less and described as

....

....

.... at the PURCHASE PRICE of

.... Canadian Dollars ($Can. ....)

on the following terms:

1. Purchaser submits with this offer .... Dollars ($

   cash/cheque payable to Vendor's Agent as a deposit to be held .... be
   and to be credited towards the Purch .... their respective solicitors who are hereby expressly

   .... ney hereunder may be made upon Vendor or Purchaser or their respective solicitors on the day for completion
   of this Agreement. Money may be tendered by bank draft or cheque certified by a chartered bank, trust company or Province of Ontario
   Savings Office.

19. This Agreement shall constitute the entire agreement between Purchaser and Vendor and there is no representation, warranty, collateral
    agreement or condition affecting this Agreement or the property or supported hereby other than as expressed herein in writing. This Agreement
    shall be read with all changes of gender or number required by the context.

DATED at..this..................day of..19..........

SIGNED, SEALED AND DELIVERED
in the presence of: IN WITNESS whereof I have hereunto set my hand and seal:

....   Date..........................
                                                   (Purchaser)

....   Date..........................
                                                   (Purchaser)

The undersigned ac..ts the above Offer and agrees with the Agent a.......... in conside....

transfer funds and make all necessary last-minute checks on details of the transfer. When both are satisfied, the keys to the property are handed over and the deal is finally closed. From that moment, all expenses relative to ownership of the property are the responsibility of the new owner. The vendor pays the real estate taxes only up to that day. If the property is mortgaged, the interest charges start immediately.

The procedures of closing are vital to the purchaser. Your lawyer must make sure that all expenses and taxes have been paid up to the date of closing. If you are paying for a full oil tank, check that it is full. Find out whether all other promises or conditions contained in the "offer to purchase" have been met. For example, if the vendor had agreed to paint the interior, make sure this has been done before the closing. If you accept the house in unpainted condition, you will have no grounds for claiming from the vendor on this score at a later date.

The standard offer-to-purchase form says "time is of the essence," meaning that the closing date is of utmost importance. If the parties concerned allow the given closing date to pass without completing the contract or without agreeing to an extension, they may lose all rights under the contract in a subsequent dispute.

Agreement for sale

The *agreement for sale* should not be confused with the "agreement of purchase and sale," which was discussed in the introduction to this section. The "agreement for sale" is a contract containing all of the essential terms for a real estate sale, but which calls for further steps to be taken and provides for further conditions and rights to be added before the deal is completed.

The agreement-for-sale document is drawn up between the vendor and the buyer; it includes descriptions and affidavits that are required under provincial law. It is registered on the title records of the property and is regarded as evidence of title or ownership. It can be viewed as both a conveyance (transfer of title) to the purchaser and a simultaneous mortgage back to the vendor. (*See* "Arranging the mortgage" in this chapter.)

This kind of agreement is sometimes used instead of the usual deed and mortgage arrangement. One case could be where the purchase price is not all paid on closing, but where there is a down payment and the balance of the price is to be paid in installments. The same effect can be obtained by the deed being given to the purchaser and a separate mortgage being taken back by the vendor. In some areas, the agreement for sale is used in all installment contracts.

The agreement for sale might be used where the property being sold is tied up with existing mortgages which cannot be paid off, or assumed. In this case, the vendor agrees to pay off the outstanding mortgage and the purchaser agrees to reimburse the vendor.

This agreement could be used again in the case where the down payment is very small. The vendor is concerned about giving the purchaser all the rights of an owner when the new owner has such a small financial stake in the property. He is reluctant to follow the usual procedure of giving a deed and taking back a mortgage; the agreement for sale gives him better protection.

The rights given to the purchaser under an agreement for sale can be quite restricted. However, when the balance owing under the agreement is paid in full, the vendor gives the purchaser a normal freehold deed "in fee simple," confirming the legal equivalent of full ownership.

Restrictions on freehold

It is natural for the new owner to rejoice in the feeling that he is now, at last, absolute master as far as that piece of property is concerned. He may believe that he is free to do *anything* he wants on it, under it or over it. Not so. While he can use his property in any way that does not interfere with the rights of his neighbors or the public, he will find that the law can restrict his freedom in several basic ways.

Provincial planning acts may prevent the subdivision of a property into parcels to suit the wishes of the owner. You must always ask for permission to subdivide,

Stony acres in Toronto

FACTS

George Lewis had leased a small plot of land which is today in the center of Toronto. At the time of the lease, the property was in "a state of nature" and there was a quantity of stones on the land.

In order to cultivate the land and eventually use it as a market garden, Lewis cleared the stones off the land and piled them in a heap. When the stones were all collected, the landlord stepped in and sold them to a third party who came onto the land and removed them. For this trespass, Lewis went to court, claiming the stones as his property.

ARGUMENT

For the plaintiff, Lewis, it was argued that the stones became his absolute property and he had the right to sell them as he could not have used the land for which he was paying rent without preparing for cultivation by clearing and removing the stones from it. Having the right to clear the land and to remove the stones from it, he had the right to do as he pleased with the stones.

For the defendant, it was alleged that while Lewis was certainly within his rights in removing the stones from the land for the purpose of cultivating it, the stones belonged to the owner of the property and could not be sold by the tenant.

JUDGMENT

The court held for Lewis. It ruled that a tenant who, for the purpose of clearing his land and making it more fit for cultivation, collects the stones therefrom, is the owner of the stones. The landlord has no interest in them and is liable for their value if he decides to dispose of them. Judgment was given to Lewis for the value of the stones, with full costs.*

*Based on an actual case (1888).

and your reasons will probably be thoroughly investigated by planning authorities. There are often local bylaws demanding that house lots be of a certain minimum frontage and overall area.

The zoning laws of municipalities govern the use of land and the types of construction permitted on residential property. Any kind of business activity may be prohibited. Bylaws may also dictate how many persons are permitted to occupy a property, thus restricting your rights to take in tenants or roomers. Tents or caravan trailers may be forbidden. In summer cottage areas, local ordinances may prohibit year-round living.

While you do have the right to exclude people (trespassers) from your property, there are many exceptions. The police may enter without permission in carrying out their duties. Several other officials—such as those involved with tax assessment, fire protection, the environment and public health—are also empowered by law to enter private property for spe-

cific purposes without the consent of the owner. The mortgagee (the lender of purchase money) may enter the property if the mortgage contract allows it. Should the mortgator (the owner) fail to make his mortgage payments, the mortgagee then has a right to enter the property.

The right to "quiet enjoyment" exists for your neighbor, too. He may complain to the municipal authorities or take an action against you (there might be local bylaws to back him up) if you bring on your property things which could constitute a danger or hazard to him—for example, dynamite or a vicious animal. The same sort of civil action could be taken to stop you from creating regular loud noises to the distress of your neighbors. (*See* Chapter 18, "Trespassing prohibited.")

Your right to excavate on your property is limited. For instance, you cannot remove earth if it would physically affect your neighbor's buildings; nor can you alter drainage in the area if it will mean flooding your neighbor's land.

Watch out for the tempting "lemon"!

IT'S NOT TOO DIFFICULT anywhere in Canada to make a fair estimate of the going market price for houses. If you have need of three bedrooms for a growing family, then the newspaper advertisements and the agents' listings will soon inform you of about what you'll have to pay. Age of house, size of lot, type of neighborhood—all these will cause variations, of course, but they can be averaged out.

If the high prices of today's housing—a worldwide problem—shock you, there's danger of falling for that "bargain" the agent digs up for you. If a house has all you want, yet is priced a couple of thousand dollars below other comparable houses, then you should proceed only with utmost caution. Your lucky find may turn out to be a lemon.

A larger, graceful house from an earlier era, still sound but needing some renovation, may seem like a great buy. But note

the encircling ring of new bungalows. If you want to sell in a few years, will you get your price (plus improvements)? You can easily make the mistake of over-improving a house for its location.

A Toronto couple bought an older house with a big dry basement, suitable for conversion to a family "rec" room. It was dry, all right. No water could get in—or out. The drains were all blocked.

Another starry-eyed pair fell for a large stone fireplace. In the first rainstorm after they moved in, it sluiced water across their living room.

There was a rambling gem of a house on a quiet rolling hillside just outside the city. The agent took his clients to see it on a day with a strong westerly wind. They bought. After they moved in, the jets turning for landings at the nearby airport just about drove them frantic. They were on the main easterly flight path.

Although you hold a valid deed for your land, it may contain restrictions preventing you from mining your property, sinking an oil well, digging a well for water or removing timber from it.

Riparian rights

An owner whose property is in actual contact with water is called a *riparian* owner. If his land borders a river, he does not own the flowing water (the Crown owns that) but he does own the bank and perhaps half of the riverbed; however, he also has the right, although it is restricted, to make use of the water.

He is legally entitled to have the water flow through, or past, his land in its natural state, without the flow being unnaturally increased or decreased. Similarly, movement of native fish must not be prevented. The fact that a riparian owner makes no use of the water does not affect his rights.

If your property is on a river or a lake, you can take as much water as you need for all ordinary or domestic uses. You can take it for manufacturing and other purposes as long as you do not interfere with the water rights of those owners above or below you on the stream. In Saskatchewan, you must get permission from the provincial government before you divert the course of any surface water.

You may build a dam as long as the backed-up water does not harm properties on the upper stream. Some provinces demand that you apply for permission before constructing any dam and they hold the right to order improvements to existing dams on private property. If the government views your dam as an "obstruction," it may decide in the public interest to have it removed, paying you reasonable compensation in some cases.

Easements

One of the major limitations of the rights of ownership is the *easement*. (In Quebec, this is known as a *servitude*.) As it frequently figures in property disputes, it is important to have at least a general understanding of what it is and what it does.

In law, an easement is a right attached to one piece of land (referred to legally as the *dominant tenement*) giving the owner of that land the right to do a specific thing on an adjoining parcel of land (the *servient tenement*) owned by someone else, or perhaps by the city, county, province or Crown. Common examples are easements for services—mutual driveways and rights-of-way to cottage property.

Your property deed may include one or more easements, either in your favor or in a neighbor's favor. Perhaps you get your water from a spring on the next-door neighbor's land? Perhaps the neighbor drives across one corner of your lot? Any easement must be clearly and concisely defined and easily identifiable. A vaguely worded easement may not be valid.

When you need an easement for, say, a right-of-way across another man's land, you should obtain what is called a deed of grant with a carefully drafted description. Remember that an easement does not give possession; it merely conveys the "right to use." Thus, an easement for a right-of-way across your neighbor's lot for your automobile would not entitle you to park there. You would only be allowed to drive back and forth.

Easements can be established in any of three ways. Usually, they are created by what is called "express grant," a properly drafted and registrable document with a full description both of the easement's location and of the rights being given. Under the registration statutes of several Canadian provinces, easements have to be recorded on the title deed of the property, granting the right. Unless they are registered, they are not binding on any person later buying the particular property that is the servient tenement.

Easements can also be established "by implication." This usually applies only in rather special cases, such as landlocked property. If an owner sells you a piece of land lying in the middle of his own parcel without access, the court may "imply" an easement "by necessity" to give you the required access.

A third form is an easement "by prescription," which boils down to mean, "by custom." If you drive across your neighbor's lot for more than 20 years without him ever once objecting, then you have, in effect, established an easement. Any objection after that stretch of years is not likely to be recognized by the courts. After 20 years, you could establish the easement officially by depositing a formal declaration against the "servient" owner's land title, setting out all details. This registration would serve as notice to prospective purchasers that the right-of-way was now guaranteed. (In Quebec, a servitude cannot be established by prescription.)

An easement may be eliminated if the purpose for which it was granted ceases to exist. It also can be revoked if the right is no longer being exercised by the benefited party. The most practical way is for the owner of the servient tenement, the land that is affected by the easement, to get a release, or *quit claim*, from the other party and register it on the title.

Profit à prendre
Something like an easement in practice, but quite different in law, is the *profit à prendre*, the right granted to enter property belonging to another person to earn profit from the land. This right has to be granted in written form and is transferred by deed. Such a grant might confer the right to extract minerals, to harvest trees, or to take fish or game.

Squatter's rights
The term squatter's rights conjures up visions of Wild West days with penniless settlers fanning out onto the open plains. However, these rights are still present in Canadian law today. They are now referred to more formally as *title by possession*, sometimes as *adverse possession*.

In case you feel like venturing into Canada's still wide-open spaces, here's how it works: if you find some unoccupied land, you merely "take possession" of it, treat it as your own, occupy it continuously and pay taxes on it. Of course, it is not as simple as it may sound. You would probably have to argue convincingly that you did not know that anyone owned the land. The owner can order you off or have you put off. But if he takes no action to assert his title for a period of years, then the place could finally be legally yours.

The squatter must actually put the land to some use—such as farming it. It is not enough to merely fence in a lot and claim it; the law considers this trespassing.

The period of time that must pass without challenge from the true owner varies across the country: in Saskatchewan, Alberta and Ontario, it is 10 years; in the Yukon and the Northwest Territories, 10 years; and in Newfoundland, New Brunswick, Nova Scotia and Prince Edward Island, 20 years. Quebec protects the absent owner with a 30-year requirement. In British Columbia, Manitoba and parts of Ontario, a squatter has no chance at all once a certificate of title has been issued under the land titles system.

What's in a name? Plenty!

IN A SOCIETY saturated with advertising slogans, it is perhaps not surprising that developers reach for the heights (literally) in naming their housing subdivisions. A browse through the weekend papers will show you that "Heights" is a magical selling word. "Come and live in lovely Appledene Heights!" the ads say. Never, you'll notice, Appledene "Flats." The great bulk of Canada is, of course, as flat as most of Russia or Australia.

Very popular tags are "park," "dale," "mill," "oaks," "wood," "grove," and, strangely enough, "ravine." They can even sell a hole in the ground.

Snob appeal pays off—judging by the abundance of "royal family" names. See the Kingsways and Queensways, the Princetons, Gloucesters and Windsors. The postwar Churchill fad has faded.

In the summer of 1976, a new townhouse development blossomed forth on the plains north of Toronto. Its name: Piccadilly Corner. Good show, chaps!

Building your own home

IN ONE OF THE ROSIEST of all housing dreams, you fall in love with a softly curving hillside overlooking some tree-lined stream and decide that here you will build your dream house. You call in an architect and together you design the house that is exactly right for you and your family. As the weeks pass, the walls rise and the landscape gardeners subtly carve and style the grounds. Then you wake up.

The expense and problems associated with the custom-built house in Canada today will turn away all except those with almost unlimited funds. We are speaking of the true custom project—a house specifically designed for you by the architect of your choice and erected on land separately purchased (or previously owned) by you. We will discuss later the quite different case of the house in the new development that the contractor will "customize" for you.

If you are determined to be exclusive, you will probably have to pay at least double what the same area of living accommodation would cost if you settled for a home in the "Sunny Acres" or "Harmony Hill" type of development. And remember, there are many ways in which the law today restricts the freedom of the rugged individualist. If it is wise to have your lawyer check the documentation of the standard real estate purchase, it is doubly wise when you are planning to build your own dream house.

Zoning and building laws

There was a time when, as long as you owned the land, you could put up any kind of house anywhere you liked on that land. That time has passed. Today, the zoning bylaws of your municipality or township usually include firm rules about what you can and cannot do on your own property. How you may use the buildings may be restricted to, say, residential use only, with no horses permitted. Thus, you would be effectively prevented from building your own stable.

The size and number of buildings you want to erect may be controlled, as well as their position on your property. Most authorities declare height limits, particularly if the intended site of your house would bring it close to existing neighbors' houses. You may be required to build at least a certain stated distance back from the public roadway.

Once you and your architect are sure your plans do not violate the zoning rules, you must then consider the local building code. This will set certain standards of construction methods and materials, and of acceptable workmanship from all trades concerned, such as plumbers and electricians. Your local code will most probably be based on the National Building Code.

Essentially, the purpose of both zoning and building regulations is to allow for the orderly and intelligent planning of housing—to avoid the slums and other detrimental forms of urban development of earlier times—and to protect the health, safety and "quiet enjoyment" of those residents who have previously built in the area.

Unless your private plans satisfy both zoning restrictions and the local building code, you will not receive a permit to build. You would be foolish to go ahead without a permit—as some people in Hull, Quebec, can assure you. In that city, some years ago, a partially completed large apartment block was ordered demolished when local house owners protested that it violated the zoning bylaws of the area.

What the architect will do

That highly trained artistic professional, the architect, will be the key man for you to see if you insist on having a home that is different. (*See* Chapter 10, "Professions and trades.") He will listen to your ideas and study your land—and he will probably ask point-blank how much you can afford to spend. Then he will work with a sketchbook and at the drawing board to bring your dreams to reality.

Don't be surprised if he gives you a hard time on some points. Any architect worth hiring will have ideas of his own—ideas that might just be superior to yours. Some wealthy home builders carefully check out their chosen architect (mainly by looking at the houses he has built for friends) and then give him a free hand within certain spending limits.

The architect will design the house, choose the materials, select a contractor and make sure that blueprints are followed precisely. He will also check all bills for the work as they are presented for payment. When the work is done, he will inspect the whole property and authorize final payment to the main contractor. Together with your lawyer, the architect can relieve you of any worry about possible mechanics' liens on the job—in other words, claims on the property to cover unpaid bills to tradesmen or subcontractors.

The law considers an architect you have retained to serve you as your agent, and consequently considers you to be personally responsible for any arrangements that he might make with the contractor, or anyone else concerned with the project. You might escape this responsibility, however, if the architect's actions were so obviously wrong that he could be found guilty of professional malpractice.

If you are operating in this league, costs may not be your greatest concern; nevertheless, you should at least inquire in advance about the fee your architect is going to expect. Fifteen percent of the total expenditure is often mentioned, but

The National Building Code

Drafted in the form of a bylaw so that it can be adopted easily by any municipality, the National Building Code is divided into the following parts: definitions; general requirements; use and occupancy; design; wind, water and vapor protection; heating, ventilating and air-conditioning; plumbing services; construction safety measures; and housing and small buildings.

Inquiries concerning the code (a section of which is shown here) should be sent to The Secretary, The Associate Committee on the National Building Code, National Research Council of Canada, Ottawa, Ont., K1A 0R6

(3) The headroom clearance for doorways shall be at least 2 030 mm.

(4) No device such as a door closer shall be installed so as to reduce the headroom clearance of a doorway to less than 1 980 mm.

SUBSECTION 3.4.4. FLAME-SPREAD RATING FOR EXITS

3.4.4.1.(1) Except as permitted in Sentences (2) and (3), the *flame-spread rating* of a wall or ceiling in an *exit* shall not exceed 25.

(2) The *flame-spread rating* of interior finish for doors, door frames and trim in *exits* may exceed 25 provided such finish has a *flame-spread rating* of not more than 150 and does not exceed 10 per cent of the wall or ceiling areas.

(3) The *flame-spread rating* of the wall finish of a lobby used as an *exit* as permitted in Sentence 3.4.5.1.(5) may exceed 25 provided such finish has a *flame-spread rating* of not more than 150 and does not exceed 25 per cent of the wall area.

SUBSECTION 3.4.5. REQUIRED FIRE SEPARATION FOR EXITS

Grade of fire separations

3.4.5.1.(1) Except as provided in Sentences (5) and (6) and in Sentence 3.3.7.7.(3), every *exit* shall be separated from the remainder of the *building* it serves by a *fire separation* having a *fire-resistance rating* at least equal to the *fire-resistance rating* required for the floor assemblies of the *storeys* through which it penetrates or which it serves, but in no case shall the *fire-resistance rating* be less than ¾ h.

Exposure protection

(2) Except as required in Sentence (3), where an *exit* enclosure has exterior walls that may be exposed to fire from openings in the exterior walls of a *fire compartment* in the same *building*, the openings in either the exterior wall of the *exit* or the exterior wall of the *floor area* shall be protected with wired glass in fixed steel frames or glass block conforming to Article 3.1.6.8. when the openings in the exterior wall of the *floor area* are within 3 m horizontally and are
(a) less than 3 *storeys* or 10 m below, or
(b) less than 2 m above any openings in the exterior wall of the *exit*.

(3) Where an exterior *exit* door may be exposed to the hazards of a fire from openings in a separated *fire compartment* located within 3 m horizontally of the *exit*, such openings shall be protected with wired glass in fixed steel frames or glass block conforming to Article 3.1.6.8.

Exits through lobbies

(4) Except as provided in Sentence (5) an *exit* from any *floor area* may lead through a lobby, provided the *first storey* shall not lead through a lobby, including the foyer or entrance hall of another *floor area* at ground level.

(5) Not more than 1 required *exit* from a *floor area* may lead through a lobby, and where the *exit* leads through the lobby
(a) the lobby floor shall be not more than 4.5 m above *grade*;
(b) the path of travel through the lobby shall not exceed 15 m,
(c) the adjacent rooms or premises having direct access to the lobby shall not contain a Group C or Group F occupancy,
(d) the *building* shall not contain a Group B. Division 2 *major occupancy*,
(e) the lobby shall not be located within an *interconnected floor space* other than as described in Sentence 3.2.9.1.(8), and
(f) the lobby shall conform in all respects with the requirements for *exits*, except that
(i) rooms other than garbage rooms, furnace rooms, boiler rooms, incinerator rooms and storage rooms may open on to the lobby.

many will serve you well for considerably less. Of course, if you have chosen a famous architect, you get that extra intangible pleasure of being able to drop his well-known name at cocktail parties.

Moving into "Sunny Acres"

By far the most common decision today for families who want to own their own home is to buy a new house in a "development" or "subdivision." Nothing new about a subdivision, except the name. Their ancestors were those terraces built in brick by large employers in nineteenth-century England. After the Industrial Revolution, but before the introduction of cheap public transportation, it was necessary to supply economical accommodation for factory hands close to their work. Row after row of identical houses were quickly built around the plant gates. The housing blocks were often given imaginative, if somewhat misleading, names—like Mulberry Gardens or Oaktree Grove, the forerunners of today's Sunny Acres.

The developments still tend to be created by major companies and they still attract mostly working families, but the air of paternalism has gone. Once Canada caught up on the housing shortage created fundamentally by the fact that almost no houses were built during World War II, the keen edge of competition prompted the large builders to offer attractive, soundly constructed homes at prices within the reach of average incomes. Big-city newspaper advertisements in the early 1980s offered detached houses in new developments in the suburbs ("two-car garage," "R-20 insulation") at prices of $40,980–$97,000 with down payments starting at about $5,500. In smaller centers, you could do better.

The prices reflect the savings made possible by factory production of standardized components, and by an uninterrupted use of labour and heavy mechanical equipment. Design variations within a certain range alleviate the monotony that once marked the "instant suburbs." However much the construction is standardized, the materials used must conform in quality to the municipal building code, and the completed house must pass inspection by the building inspector. The law lays its hand evenly on mansion and bungalow.

Check construction progress

If you agree to take a unit as yet unbuilt in a development, you still have the basic protection that the law of contracts provides. But take the precaution of having your lawyer look through all the papers.

If you go to a lawyer at the outset, before you sign anything, he will first check that your developer is reputable. Most developers are, but some small-time builders trying to make a killing with low-cost houses get overextended financially and file for bankruptcy—leaving the sorrowing customer with just a hole in the ground for his down payment. The lawyer will find out if your builder is involved in civil suits based on client dissatisfaction. Local consumer-protection agencies can help you make inquiries about any developer.

If you do handle things yourself—with the assistance of the agent or developer—check particularly that the house described in the contract is indeed the same as the model you were shown when you agreed to buy. To the untrained eye, dimensions and technical descriptions tend to blur. Visit the site frequently during the building and, to be on the safe side, take along an expert in house construction.

Builders will seldom allow themselves to be tied down legally to an exact completion date, and rightly so when you consider the things over which they have no control—a week's rain, for example, can stop all truck movement on the site and a labor union might call a strike over some grievance. Even if you are given a date for possession, say, "about September 1st," it's unlikely a court would award you any damages if you were still cooling your heels in October. It would be wise to arrange for your present accommodation to remain available to you until you know exactly when you can move in.

Taking possession

Whatever route you take toward your dream house, obey the cardinal rule: never be in a hurry to take possession.

If your lawyer is not satisfied that the vendor has met all promised conditions of the offer to purchase, accept his advice to postpone your moving date—even if you are sick of living with your mother-in-law. After you take possession, the vendor may no longer be responsible for any unsatisfied promises. If you move in before everything is completed to your satisfaction, the courts might decide that, by this action, you dropped any complaints you had about the original contract.

This holds particularly true in the case of a home which has been built for you. If you close a deal for an uncompleted house and take possession of it immediately, you may find that you have lost your right to complain about inferior work, or about errors in construction.

As a possible solution to the problem of taking possession before the deal is finally closed, your lawyer might be able to arrange a "tenancy at will," giving you the right to move in without waiving any of your other rights. (*See* "Examining the lease" in this chapter.) This agreement would have to be carefully negotiated and signed by both parties.

The do-it-yourself builder

Do-it-yourself home building is not uncommon in Canada, especially in small towns and rural areas. For many people, it is the only way they can afford a home of their own. Others look on it as a challenge. These competent types act as their own contractors and labor force, handling everything from basement excavation to the final brick and paint work.

Some private housebuilders settle for acting as their own general contractors, hiring most of the subtrades and restricting their own efforts to laboring or semiskilled tasks. Both of these methods should prove more economical than the conventional ways, and there is also a deep satisfaction in living in a home you have built with your own hands. But there are some yawning pitfalls.

Through ignorance, amateur contractors often run afoul of zoning laws, building restrictions, mechanic's liens and other similar problems that abound in the building field. Rosy dreams have often had tragic awakenings; a lawyer's fee in this situation can be a good investment.

The do-it-yourself builder will find a mortgage very hard to get. Even if his credit is good, the main lending institutions will insist that he build in conformity with their own specifications. This might increase the builder's costs much more than he had anticipated. A mortgage inspector would approve financial advances as the work progressed but, if construction bogged down, the advances would be withheld and the builder might be stuck with a half-finished home.

The mechanic's lien

Anyone who builds his own house, or contracts to have it built by another, should become familiar with the mechanic's lien act in his province. To be ignorant of this law is to risk serious trouble.

Basically, the law is designed to protect creditors who have done work at, or provided materials for, a construction or other project. They may not necessarily be owed money by the principal contractor, but by one of the subcontractors. If they have not been paid to their satisfaction, they can register a lien (a claim) against the property title involved. They must file within a certain number of days (usually 30) after the work is done.

At this point, the principal contractor becomes involved. The law requires that he withhold a stipulated percentage (perhaps 15 or 20 percent) from each payment he makes to subcontractors or suppliers. Before handing over the accumulated percentage at the end of the job, after the 30-day period, he must check with the land titles office to make sure no liens have been registered against the property by anybody claiming against subcontractors or suppliers.

If a lien has been filed, the main contractor will then hold up the final payment to the individual or firm in question and refer the matter to his lawyer.

To be fully protected, the main contractor must not only hold back the proper amount as required by the mechanic's lien act, but he must also maintain careful records as to the completion dates of each phase of work.

Arranging the mortgage

How much do you need?

Who will lend the money?

First and second mortgages

The existing mortgage

If you are "in default"

Early repayment privilege

NOT MANY OF US are lucky enough to be able to pay the total price for a house in cash, especially when it is the first home for a young family. The need for a house and the piece of land usually coincides with the arrival of children when the family income is often already stretched. There is some irony in the fact that we generally need houses during the early family years when our earnings have not yet reached their peak. By the time we own the property completely, the children have left home and all that room is no longer needed.

The universal answer to the financial problem is the mortgage. Derived from two medieval words meaning, literally, "dead pledge," the mortgage is basically an agreement (a contract) by which the purchaser puts the property itself on the line as security for a loan that helps him to buy it. The mortgage is registered officially as a charge against the property, and the buyer does not have a clear title of ownership until the debt is discharged, or paid off. Mortgages are available for buying new and older homes, for the purchase of rental housing and for financing major repairs or additions.

If the mortgagor (the borrower) fails at any stage to pay the installments of interest or principal on the loan, the mortgagee (the lender) has the legal right, after going through certain preliminaries, to put the property on the market in order to get his money back. If the house sells for more than enough money to pay off the mortgage, the balance goes to the mortgagor. If the sale does not cover the debt, the mortgagee can then sue the mortgagor for anything still owing.

It should be obvious that even a routine mortgage is a most important document—the deal of a lifetime for most people—and, therefore, the guidance and advice of a lawyer is strongly recommended. Even experienced businessmen can stumble over the special legal language used in such documents to ensure very precise meanings.

How much do you need?

The amount of the mortgage will naturally be dictated by the price asked for the house, the amount of cash the buyer has on hand for the down payment and by the percentage of the total appraised value that the mortgagee is willing to lend. For ordinary commercial mortgages, the amount of the loan ranges up to between 75 and 90 percent of the property value; under mortgages guaranteed by the federal government to assist lower-income groups, it can rise to 98 percent.

You can shop around for mortgage money, as conditions and rates definitely vary, but you will probably find that few lenders will be willing to do business if the price of the house you want to buy is more than three times your annual income—which includes anything your spouse may bring in as well. Economists warn that you will be on shaky ground financially if you try to pay more than one-third of your net income for all housing costs, including mortgage payments, taxes, heating and repairs.

You can ensure that your family would not be burdened with the mortgage if you died unexpectedly by taking out mortgage insurance. The cost is reasonable, particularly if you are young; for example, a man of 33 could insure a mortgage of $60,000 for only $19 per month.

If you still can't swing the purchase with the mortgage you have been promised, you can usually arrange a second mortgage. Since you now have only the already-mortgaged property to put up as security, the second mortgage takes second position and thus represents a greater risk. For this reason, the second lender, or mortgagee, will demand a considerably higher rate of interest.

In Quebec, there are no mortgages such as they are known in the other nine provinces. Instead, there is what is called the *hypothec*, a contract loan which, though different in format, is generally similar in effect. Under the *hypothec*, the lender has the right to have the property sold to satisfy the debt if the borrower fails to make his payments. The *hypothec* document must be sworn before a notary, then sealed and recorded at the registry office. (*See* "Closing the deal" in this chapter.)

Who will lend the money?

There are a half-dozen recognized sources of mortgage money in Canada: conventional mortgage loans from trust and insurance companies and banks; loans guaranteed under the National Housing Act (N.H.A.); purchase-money mortgages (supplied by vendors); and finance companies that specialize in second mortgages and other types of loans.

Conventional mortgages account for two-thirds of the housing loans granted in Canada. They are supplied mostly by the large financial institutions. Chartered banks can lend up to 75 percent of the appraised value of a house under a conventional mortgage, but this percentage can be increased for a new house if the borrower will agree to take out mortgage insurance.

N.H.A. mortgages can cover 90 percent of the house's appraised market value for the first $80,000 and 80 percent of the balance. These funds are supplied (or guaranteed) by the federal treasury through the Canada Mortgage and Housing Corporation (C.M.H.C.) at an interest rate lower than that for commercial mortgages. Also, the period allowed for repayment is longer—up to 40 years.

You can apply for an N.H.A. mortgage at any chartered bank. If successful, you are required to pay a mortgage insurance fee of approximately one or one and a half percent, plus a fee to the C.M.H.C. The latter fee ($100 at the time of writing) covers the cost of examining your building plans and inspecting the site during construction of the house.

Both conventional and N.H.A. mortgages can be sought not only to finance the construction of new homes and the purchase of land, but also for improving property or refinancing existing mortgages. To obtain an N.H.A. loan on an existing house, the house must meet the minimum housing standards, or at least be improved to meet those standards. The C.M.H.C. also provides mortgages for approved low-rental housing projects and for student and senior-citizen residences.

Mortgages "taken back" by the vendor (called *purchase money mortgages*) are often granted for investment purposes, especially where the seller is looking for a steady source of retirement income. The mortgage will yield higher interest than he would get from a bank or trust company on a comparable investment. Sometimes the vendor will take back a mortgage for the full amount over and above the down payment.

If you are the seller, you should thoroughly check the credit standing of any would-be borrower and then, if you decide to provide him with a mortgage loan, make sure that he meets the monthly payments promptly. Be sure that he has taken out adequate insurance on the property and that he is paying the taxes regularly. Some vendors pass all problems on to a mortgage-management company on a fee basis. If you decide you want your cash in a hurry, you can usually sell the mortgage—but at a discount.

The first mortgage

The major financial institutions will lend only on a first mortgage. In other words, they insist that their claim on the property have top priority.

Before committing a large sum to finance your purchase, the prospective lender, or mortgagee, is going to examine your personal credit position closely. He

189

The mortgage application

When you go looking for mortgage money to buy your dream house, you are going to have to provide a case history of youself that demands blunt answers. The application forms can vary, but this trust company form is typical. They'll probably want to know the state of your bank account, how much your car is worth, and whether you and your spouse have any outstanding debts. You will have to agree to pay any costs the mortgage company incurs because of your application, and authorize the company to obtain credit information on you.

VG **VICTORIA AND GREY TRUST**
Since 1844

APPLICATION FOR A MORTGAGE LOAN
RESIDENTIAL

Agent: _____
Address: _____
Tel. No.: _____
V&G Branch: _____
Date: _____ 19 ___

Applicant: _____
Name of Spouse: _____
Applicant's Present Address: _____
Spouse's Address _____
Name of Guarantor: _____ Address: _____
Loan Request $ _____ Interest Rate _____ % Term _____
Amortization _____ Monthly Payment _____
Applicant now: Owns ☐ Rents ☐ How long has applicant resided at present address? ___ years
If under 3 years, state previous address: _____
Credit Reference (2) _____ Acct. No. _____
_____ Acct. No. _____
Name of Bank _____ Br. _____ Acct. No. _____
or Trust Co. _____ Br. _____ Acct. No. _____
Solicitor's Name _____
Address and Phone No. _____
Have you ever declared bankruptcy? Yes ☐ No. ☐

Tel. No. Home: _____
Bus.: _____
Postal Code: _____
Marital Status _____

PURPOSE

Purpose of Loan: Purchase ☐ Construction ☐ Refinance ☐

PURCHASE: Price $ _____ 1st Mortgage $ _____ Cash $ _____
2nd Mortgage $ _____ Term _____ Payment $ _____
Closing Date _____
Do you intend to occupy property: Yes ☐ No ☐
Present Occupant _____

CONSTRUCTION: Building Cost $ _____ Lot Cost $ _____ Total $ _____
2nd Mortgage $ _____ Term _____ Payment $ _____
Completion Date _____ Sale Price $ _____
REFINANCE: Purchase Price $ _____ Date Purchased _____
Present Mortgage $ _____ Rate ___ % Mortgagee: _____
Second Mortgage $ _____ Rate ___ % Mortgagee: _____
Total Mortgages $ _____

PROPERTY OFFERED AS SECURITY

LOCATION: Address: _____
Lot(s): _____ Block _____ Plan _____ Conc. _____ Twp. _____
Lot Size: _____ x _____ Taxes $ _____
BUILDINGS: Detached ☐ Semi Detached ☐ Duplex ☐ Condo. ☐ Other ☐
Construction _____ Age _____ No. Rooms _____
Rented ☐ Building Income $ _____
Insulation Type _____
SERVICES: Hydro ☐ Mun. Water ☐ Well ☐ Sewers ☐ Septic ☐ Paved Road ☐

PERSONAL

APPLICANT: Name: _____ Date of Birth: Mo. ___ Day ___ Yr. ___
Spouse: _____ Date of Birth: Mo. ___ Day ___ Yr. ___
Age of Dependants: _____
Employer: _____ Address: _____
Type of Business: _____ Position _____ No. Yrs. _____
Salary: $ _____ Commission: $ _____ Overtime: _____
Other Income (Specify) _____ $ _____
Previous Employer: _____ No. Yrs. _____ Salary $ _____
Previous Occupation _____
CO-APPLICANT Name: _____ Date of Birth: Mo. ___ Day ___ Yr. ___
OR Employer: _____ Address: _____
GUARANTOR: Type of Business: _____ Position _____ No. Yrs. _____
Salary: $ _____ Commission: $ _____ Overtime: _____
Other Income (Specify): _____ $ _____
Previous Employer: _____ No. Yrs. _____ Salary $ _____
Previous Occupation: _____

Form 26 (6/82)

—Courtesy of Victoria and Grey Trust Company

will try to balance your income against the future mortgage and any other payments you plan to make. Normally, he will not agree to an arrangement whereby you would be paying much over 30 percent of your income for housing.

The lending corporation will have the property appraised by its own men to ensure that, in their view, it warrants the amount of the requested loan. Don't be surprised if they report a value figure significantly lower than the one you had been prepared to pay.

You can apply for a first mortgage under the N.H.A. at all chartered banks in Canada. Normally, by C.M.H.C. rules, you will not be granted a loan if your total debt for the principal, interest, taxes and heating costs for the house exceed 32 percent of your income, or 42 percent if you're buying a duplex.

Most mortgages today require equal monthly payments, covering principal and interest, for the duration of the loan. This repayment procedure is referred to as the *amortization* of the loan. Sometimes, a sum will be added to the installments to cover municipal taxes and fire-insurance premiums.

The second mortgage

The second-mortgage lender operates in a different market from that of the first mortgagee. He will be interested in your equity—that is, how much of the property you actually own—rather than in your other financial commitments. As long as you have enough equity, he will be protected in the event you get into serious trouble. However, in a forced sale, he will get nothing until the first mortgage is taken care of.

You should shop for a second mortgage with particular care. The interest rates are much higher than they are for first mortgages because the security you offer is limited, and the terms are always for much shorter periods. Don't be too eager to accept the first deal you are offered. It is a competitive field and some of the offers might have dangers lurking in the fine print.

Second mortgages are usually taken out to make up the difference between the total amount of a purchaser's down payment plus the first mortgage money and the price of the house. But they can also be applied to existing properties that may have increased in value, thus enabling the owner to raise a cash loan. The amount of the mortgage would normally match the increase of the current valuation over the original purchase price.

Purchase-money loans quite often take the form of second mortgages. For example, Smith is buying a house from Jones for $60,000. Smith has $10,000 in cash and has arranged a mortgage loan from his bank of $40,000. He is still $10,000 short. Jones offers to take back a second mortgage for $10,000. It probably has to be repaid within five years. Since he is now paying off two mortgages, Smith might not be able to accumulate the $10,000 within that time. Therefore, he might have to seek a renewal after five years, possibly at a higher interest rate if credit is tight.

Anyone who buys a more expensive house than he can afford without continual strain is said to be "house poor." Perhaps you should not plunge into a purchase until you have saved enough down-payment cash to swing the deal with only one mortgage.

The existing mortgage

When you buy a lived-in house (you could call it a "used house"), it is likely that there is already a mortgage on the property. If the mortgage was taken out in an earlier time of lower interest rates, it could be to your advantage to take it over. But before you do, get the advice of a lawyer skilled in real estate procedures.

You can buy mortgaged property in two ways: either subject to the mortgage, or by assuming the mortgage. The distinction is quite technical, the main difference being that the assumption of the mortgage involves a formal assumption agreement. In either case, you pick up the mortgage payments where the vendor has left off and continue making them monthly. And you have to agree to abide by all the conditions of the existing mortgage.

As discussed earlier, a mortgage loan involves a promise by the mortgagor to repay, plus the giving of security in the form of the property.

Therefore, if the existing mortgage (the one that you have taken over) happened to be in default, the original mortgagee could always take over the property. Moreover, the original mortgagor (the first borrower) would remain responsible for the repayment of the loan even though he had long since sold the property—unless he had a written agreement with the new mortgagee that released him from that responsibility.

It follows that when you buy a property subject to a mortgage, or agree to assume the mortgage, your contract with the vendor-mortgagor (the original borrower) does not affect the rights of the mortgagee (the original lender). In fact, in some provinces, the mortgagee may sue either the original mortgagor (who has just sold his property) or the present holder of the equity (the new buyer) when the mortgage is in default.

If you are "in default"

"Default" is a word that everyone with a mortgage should understand and respect. Failure to make your monthly payments is the most common form of default, but there are several other ways by which you could be in danger of losing your home.

All mortgages include strict conditions designed to protect the lender who is, after all, risking his money (or the money that others have entrusted to him). One such condition will require monthly payment: a lawyer will explain to you that the mortgage deed is so worded that, if you skip a payment, not only is the missed payment due, but your default also allows the mortgagee to demand immediate payment of the entire loan.

Of course, if you are having some temporary financial difficulty, the mortgagee (be it bank, trust or individual) would probably agree to postpone a payment or two. The key point is that you are bound by law to the contract—that is, the mortgage agreement—you signed, and you cannot count on any leniency, or even any understanding, from the other party. If you do receive permission to withhold a payment, get that permission in writing. Mortgages usually stipulate a *period of grace* (15 days is common) during which, unless you have some special agreement, you must square your account—or else!

Paying the mortgage

How big a mortgage do you need? How much a month can you afford?
This chart does the arithmetic for you

Loan	25-Year Mortgage			
	11%	12%	13%	14%
$25,000	240.75	258.00	275.60	293.47
$30,000	288.90	309.60	330.72	352.16
$35,000	337.05	361.20	385.84	410.86
$40,000	385.20	412.80	440.96	469.55
$45,000	433.35	464.40	496.08	528.24
$50,000	481.50	516.00	551.20	586.94
$55,000	529.65	567.60	606.32	645.63
$60,000	577.80	619.20	661.44	704.33
$65,000	625.95	670.80	716.56	763.02
$70,000	674.10	722.40	771.69	821.71
$75,000	722.25	774.00	826.80	880.41

One standard mortgage form allows the mortgagee, when you are 15 days in default of payment, to sell the property after giving you 35 days' notice. This notice can be given to "a grown-up person on the said lands," by publishing it once in the local newspaper or by sending it by registered mail to you at your last known address. Statutory notice requirements differ in the various provinces.

You can also be in default by allowing the fire insurance on your house to lapse, if having such insurance was stipulated in your mortgage. (It usually is.)

The mortgagee will normally reserve the right in the mortgage contract to come onto the land himself—or to send his agent—to inspect the state of the buildings and property generally. You will probably have promised, in signing the mortgage, to keep things "in good condition and repair" and not to "commit or permit any act of waste" on the land. This may be loosely interpreted and hard to define, but the gist of it is that you must not do anything that will reduce the value of the property. It was on the original appraisal of the value that you were loaned the money.

Again, if the mortgagee decides that you have let the property run down unreasonably, he can claim that you are in default and demand full payment of the principal sum of the mortgage. If you cannot pay, or refuse to, he has the right to sell the property from under you. Not only that, he can first make any repairs deemed necessary and add the cost of that to your indebtedness. Of course, you could have your day in court to argue that you had obeyed the conditions.

Remember that it is the lawyer of the mortgagee who writes the mortgage document: you will find he holds all the best cards. Here are the options open to the mortgagee in the event of a default:

(1) He can sue the mortgagor according to provisions of the mortgage itself, in the same way as he would in the case of anyone else owing him money.

(2) He can issue a writ for possession of the premises, removing the purchaser who is in default and moving in himself as the tenant.

(3) He can take action to foreclose (seize the property).

(4) Upon foreclosure, he can still take legal action against the mortgagor for outstanding payments.

The term "foreclosure" may remind you of some sinister cloaked figure in a Victorian melodrama, but the possibility of it happening should not be taken lightly. Foreclosures happen every day, so make your payments promptly and keep to the terms of the mortgage.

If you want to tear down any buildings on mortgaged land, check with your mortgagee to make sure you have permission; otherwise, you might be held in default.

Early repayment privilege

Let us take the optimistic view that your financial status will improve a great deal in the years following the purchase of your home. Perhaps a rich uncle will leave you his fortune in bubble gum stock. You might win a lottery.

If anything like this should happen, you would be glad of the fact that your lawyer had arranged for your first mortgage to be "open." In an open mortgage, you may increase the amount of your principal payments or even pay off the full amount at any time before it is due, without notice or bonus.

More often than not, you will find that your mortgage is "closed," meaning that it cannot be paid off, except over a certain number of years. To pay off your mortgage before the due date, you would have to give the mortgagee notice of your intentions and pay him a penalty—usually three months' principal and interest, or the difference between the mortgage interest rate and the current rate until maturity. The imposition of penalty is intended to compensate the mortgage company for the expense and trouble of rearranging its investment and for the interest that it will have lost through your premature payment.

While you would be lucky to arrange an open first mortgage, you wouldn't have the same problem with a second mortgage. Most of them contain an open provision.

193

5/You and Your Car

Traffic accidents — 222

Driving offenses — 226

Using a car on holiday — 231

Getting ready for the road

Learning to drive
Getting a driver's license
Fitness requirements
Registration and plates
A safe car
Insurance

D RIVING A MOTOR VEHICLE is a privilege, not a right. As a driver you are involved with a lot of people on the public thoroughfares—other drivers, passengers, cyclists and pedestrians, for example. Error or negligence by you could seriously affect the life and safety of innocent persons.

In granting a driver's license, therefore, all provinces and both territories stress that it can be withdrawn if it is abused. This can be done at the discretion of the registrar of motor vehicles, without a court order. An example of this in practice is the demerit system, where a license is automatically suspended if a motorist exceeds the number of points allowed.

You guard your privilege as a driver by conforming to a lot of laws. Some of them, such as those in the Criminal Code, apply everywhere in Canada but most originate with provinces and municipalities. Like many other civil laws, they vary in different parts of the country. You should check provincial or local laws for precise information on a specific case.

Every province and territory issues a free driver's handbook. Whether you are a beginner or an experienced driver you should have a copy to be up on the latest regulations. Here is where you can write for a handbook and for other information:

Newfoundland
The Registrar
Motor Registration Division
Department of Transportation
  and Communication
Viking Building
Crosbie Road,
St. John's, Nfld.
A1C 5T4

Prince Edward Island
The Registrar of Motor Vehicles
Highway Safety Division
P.O. Box 2000
Charlottetown, P.E.I.
C1A 7N8

Nova Scotia
The Registrar
Motor Vehicle Registration Branch
Department of Transportation
6061 Young Street
Halifax, N.S.
B3K 2A3

New Brunswick
The Registrar
Motor Vehicle Division
York Tower, King's Place
P.O. Box 6000
Frederiction, N.B.
E3B 5H1

Quebec
Le Directeur
La Régie de l'assurance automobile
  du Québec
880, Chemin Ste-Foy
Québec, Qué.
G1S 2K8

Ontario
The Registrar of Motor Vehicles
Ministry of Transportation
  and Communications
1201 Wilson Avenue
East Building
Downsview, Ont.
M3M 1J8

Manitoba
The Registrar of Motor Vehicles
Motor Vehicles Branch
Department of Highways
  and Transportation

1075 Portage Avenue
Winnipeg, Man.
R3G 0S1

Saskatchewan
The Chairman
Highway Traffic Board
2260 11th Avenue
Regina, Sask.
S4P 3V7

Alberta
Alberta Solicitor General
Motor Vehicles Division
7th Floor, Melton Building
10310 Jasper Avenue
Edmonton, Alta.
T5J 2W4

British Columbia
The Superintendent of Motor Vehicles
Motor Vehicle Department, Ministry of
   Transportation and Highways
Parliament Buildings
Victoria, B.C.
V8T 5A3

Northwest Territories
Motor Vehicle Branch
Department of Government Services
Government of the Northwest Territories
P.O. Box 1320
Yellowknife, N.W.T.
X1A 2L9

Yukon
The Registrar of Motor Vehicles
Government of the Yukon
P.O. Box 2703
Whitehorse, Y.T.
Y1A 2C6

Provincial and territorial licensing authorities generally consider a motor vehicle to be any self-propelled road vehicle—car, motorcycle, truck, bus, fire engine—but not a rail vehicle, snowmobile or piece of farm machinery. The Criminal Code is broader in its definition and includes any self-propelled vehicle except one on rails. In practical terms, however, when we think of a motor vehicle we think of an automobile.

The first commercially built cars in Canada were electrics, produced by the Canadian Motor Syndicate in Toronto in the late 1890s. Practical commercial production of gasoline cars got under way in 1902 with introduction of the LeRoy in Kitchener, Ont.

A few years later, giants such as the McLaughlin Motor Car Co. of Oshawa, Ont., Canada Cycle & Motor Co. (CCM) of Toronto, and Ford of Canada in Windsor, Ont., were producing cars by the thousands. At the outbreak of World War I Canadians were proudly bouncing around in 50,678 passenger cars.

After a half-century love affair with the automobile, a negative reaction set in and ecologists pressed arguments against a burgeoning highway network. It seems certain the motorist of the future will need more intensive driving instruction, and he or she may have to face greater legislative control of the automobile.

New laws pour steadily from provincial legislatures and from Parliament—laws about safety and antipollution, speed and noise, licenses and permits, equipment, manufacturing standards and insurance requirements. Getting ready for the road now usually involves instruction at a driving school, stringent practical and theoretical examinations and a careful check on physical fitness. Elderly drivers, for example, must undergo retesting almost everywhere; some provinces demand a medical test every year after age 75.

To a large extent, though, every motorist is "on his own". Stirling Moss, one of the world's best-known motoring personalities, says the only good and safe driver is the person who knows his or her limitations and drives within them. Moss says he is wary of every driver he meets. He practices *defensive driving*, as recommended by traffic authorities, motor clubs and safety councils. The "defensive" driver protects himself and his passengers; he is on constant guard against error or stupidity by the other fellow. More than that, he even tries to "defend" the other motorist from his own bad driving by allowing more than the minimum road courtesies—by giving more than the letter of the law actually requires.

Learning to drive
Would-be drivers are strongly urged to go to a driving school for instruction. Profes-

197

sional instructors, who are regulated and licensed to ensure competence, can be coolly objective with pupils. Friends or family members might be less objective—or pass along bad habits.

Trained high school teachers in every province teach students how to drive. This program is supported by provincial governments and other interested organizations, including automobile clubs. Ei-

Speaking up for the motorist

THE FIRST CARS IN CANADA set horses rearing and neighing in fright, seemed to fill the countryside with dust and noise, and left trails of dead and maimed chickens and dogs. Outraged farmers sought to curb the newfangled intruders. This hostility was among the things that drew motorists together into clubs that today form the Canadian Automobile Association.

Motorists started clubs as early as 1903, to fight for the right to drive and for better roads, and to enjoy one another's company and support. The legislators of the day were hard to convince. In 1908 an amendment to the Criminal Code was proposed that would have jailed for two years any motorist who caused a horse to run away. Prince Edward Island banned cars entirely. One Ontario rural paper advised readers to use barbed wire and shotguns against this "curse to the country."

Farmers dug mud pits on the rudimentary roads, then waited nearby with horses, ready to pull out the mired autos for a fat fee. A. C. "Ace" Emmett, a pioneer prairie motorist, used to recall how Manitoba Motor League members once caught a farmer preparing such a trap. The group included a judge and two barristers, so court was set up on the spot. The farmer was convicted and dunked in his own rain barrel.

Winnipeg motorist C. F. Grundy got in trouble in 1904 for parking his car so that it was "an obstruction to the safety of travel." The Winnipeg Automobile Club (predecessor of the MML) sent a committee to the mayor on his behalf and backed him in court. The judge agreed that Grundy's machine had as much right on the street as a horse and buggy—but fined him $1 because the white tarpaulin covering it had frightened a horse.

Clubs dealt effectively with members who got out of hand. The New Brunswick Automobile Association, for example, had its own courts for imposing fines on members who broke the speed limit. Evidence was presented and sentences were handed down as in a regular trial.

The first provincial speed limits were geared to horse and buggy traffic. The average was 10 m.p.h. (15 km/h) in towns and 15–20 m.p.h. (25–30 km/h) in the country. Nova Scotia set its limits in minutes per mile instead of miles per hour, resulting in a limit of exactly 7.5 m.p.h. (10 km/h) in town. Quebec's limit was 4 m.p.h. (5 km/h) over the top of a hill or around a blind curve.

When the Ontario government wanted to impose an 8 m.p.h. (10 km/h) limit, every MLA was taken for a ride to see for himself that even 10 m.p.h. (15 km/h) wasn't "scorching"—and the bill was changed. The rides were arranged by Dr. Perry Doolittle, another famous pioneer motorist, who was instrumental in forming the Ontario Motor League and later became the "Father of the Trans-Canada Highway."

In 1913 the leading motor clubs decided to form the Canadian Automobile Association to give the motorist a national voice and permanent influence in Ottawa. Dr. Doolittle became president in 1920 and launched the crusade for a trans-Canada highway.

In 1925 Dr. Doolittle managed to drive across the country in 40 days, though for part of the trip his car ran on the Canadian Pacific tracks with flanged wheels. It was not until 1946 that the first automobile was driven coast to coast entirely on Canadian roads, and the Trans-Canada Highway as we know it was not completed until 1962.

ther individually or through the Canadian Automobile Association, clubs also conduct regular driver training courses and refresher courses. Drivers under 25 make up only 21 percent of all Canadian drivers but are involved in nearly 47 percent of all fatal road accidents. Effective traffic and driving education courses at the high school level can help ensure increasingly disciplined and safe driving.

As highways become more crowded, motorists get into more potentially dangerous situations. Accidents happen very quickly even at permitted speeds—much faster than the reaction time of even an alert 18-year-old. An accident at 90 km/h —say, a car swerving into a ditch—is all over in seven tenths of a second. Only intelligent preparation can hope to prevent a mounting death toll.

Studies strongly indicate that students who take high school driving courses have fewer accidents than those who do not. Several insurance companies reduce premiums (as much as 27 percent) to graduates of courses sponsored by, or approved by, provincial authorities.

The economic loss from road accidents in Canada runs at over $2 billion a year, and the cost to the taxpayer of driver education in high schools should be assessed against this huge bill. It is estimated that for every $1 the classes cost, $3 is saved in accidents avoided.

Getting a driver's license
In all provinces and both territories you must have a driver's license to operate a motor vehicle on a road or other public property.

Your driver's license must be carried at all times and produced on demand. Some provinces also require a driver to carry a vehicle's registration permit, although in most cases authorities will allow you a reasonable time to produce both it and proof of minimum required insurance or financial responsibility.

The age for obtaining a license for a motor vehicle is generally 16—with the consent of a parent or guardian. New Brunswick, Nova Scotia and Prince Edward Island may grant tractor licenses to 14-year-olds. In New Brunswick, a 14-year-old can obtain a license to operate a motorcycle. In the Yukon and Northwest Territories, a learner's permit may be obtained at the age of 15, a license at the age of 16. Alberta may grant a "Class 7" license (a learner's permit, in fact) to a person of 14, for a moped or a car.

The license may allow operation of a vehicle for personal use only or it may allow operation for profit or for hire. The license holder may be restricted to a certain type of vehicle with special equipment (as in the case of an amputee), or he may be obliged to meet certain conditions, such as wearing prescription glasses when driving.

It is a serious offense to drive on a highway if you are not qualified for a license. If your license has been suspended or revoked, you could be jailed or barred from renewing a license. For serious or repeated offenses, your license could be revoked permanently.

To apply for a license, you must go to an office of the provincial licensing authority. After correctly answering questions on the laws and regulations applying to the operation of a motor vehicle, and passing eyesight and sign-recognition tests, you are usually issued a temporary permit allowing you to drive while a fully licensed operator is in the front seat beside you, for instruction purposes. You must also pay a small fee. Once you have sufficient practical experience you return to the licensing office to prove your driving ability to an examiner. If you are successful a driver's license will be issued.

Commercial drivers
Until recently, it was an offense to operate a motor vehicle for pay when not licensed as a chauffeur or not specially licensed, and it was also against the law for an employer to permit such operation. Truckers, school bus drivers and taxi drivers needed such licenses. So did traveling salesmen who received travel allowances as part of their pay. Traditionally they were issued a chauffeur's license. It was applied for in the usual way but the standards were higher.

A new system, however, adopted first by Alberta, British Columbia and the

Yukon, sets out roughly seven classes of driver's licenses ranging from the top-rated commercial driver down to the learner. This classification system, with certain variations, is now in force in all provinces except Ontario. It covers every driver and abolishes the chauffeur's license, as such. Endorsements permitting extra privileges or spelling out conditions can be added in each class. In the Yukon, for example, even a Class I driver needs an endorsement to operate a vehicle with air brakes, and persons who need glasses to drive must have their licenses so endorsed. A driver in a higher class is usually permitted to operate vehicles covered in lower classes. Here is roughly what the classifications cover:

Class 1 – Semi-trailer and tractor-trailer combinations exceeding 11,000 kilograms gross vehicle weight.

Class 2 – School and passenger buses with a seating capacity for more than 24 passengers.

Class 3 – Single trucks and truck-trailer combinations exceeding 11,000 kilograms of gross vehicle weight.

Class 4 – Buses with a seating capacity of 24 passengers or fewer, taxis and ambulances.

Class 5 – All single motor vehicles not exceeding 11,000 kilograms, and motor vehicle-trailer combinations not exceeding 11,000 kilograms where the trailer does not exceed 4,500 kilograms.

Class 6 – Motorcycles.

Class 7 – Learning.

License suspension

A driver's license can be suspended by a provincial or territorial registrar of motor vehicles. In practice the most common reason is a bad driving record. All provinces have systems whereby various infractions earn a driver demerit points—the worse the infraction the higher the number of points.

Points are entered on a driver's record after conviction or payment of a fine out of court for an offense in which his or her vehicle was moving. Parking offenses, for example, are not included. In Ontario failing to signal costs a driver two points, following too closely behind another vehicle costs four points, and failing to remain at the scene of an accident costs seven points. The points stay on the record for two years.

In Ontario, if you get nine points, you must appear for an interview and you may be required to take a driving test; if you get 15 points, your license is suspended for 30 days. As soon as your license is suspended, your points are reduced to seven. If you reach 15 points again after you resume driving, your license is suspended for six months.

Ontario has a probationary system for newly licensed drivers. Under this system, a new driver must complete two years of suspension-free driving before a permanent license is issued. If the driver is suspended during this time, the probation period may be either extended or begun again. After accumulating five demerits or less, the new driver is sent a warning. A 30-day suspension period follows the accumulation of six demerits or more.

Prince Edward Island has a two-year probationary period for new drivers, and Manitoba, a one-year period. In Alberta, all new drivers are on probation until age 18.

Conviction for a driving offense under the Criminal Code usually means an automatic license suspension. You can appeal a suspension, and in rare cases a restricted license if driving is essential to your livelihood. This license will permit you to operate a vehicle for work—and in some cases to commute as well.

Fitness requirements

Physical fitness is important if a person is to drive properly and safely. Thus, if you were partially or completely color-blind your license might allow you to drive only if accompanied by somebody who could identify colors like those in traffic lights. If you had only one leg your license would probably restrict you to a car with an automatic transmission.

Some physical handicaps do not prevent a person from getting a license provided he or she drives under certain conditions—in the daytime, for example.

In some cases applicants have to take a special course of instruction before a license is issued. On the other hand, there are some physical disabilities, such as a history of heart attacks or fainting spells, which might prevent the issuance of a license altogether. Even if your driver's license was issued without restrictions, you should inform the authorities if you become physically disabled in any way. The license would then be subject to restriction or cancellation.

Some temporary physical disabilities are covered by specific legislation. It is a criminal offense to operate or be in the care and control of a motor vehicle while you are impaired by alcohol or drugs. The highway traffic acts insist that you drive with due care and attention, and with reasonable consideration of other persons using the highway. Careless driving—even if due to anxiety—is an offense.

It is your responsibility as a driver to be in full control of your vehicle and to be fully aware of all other persons and things in the immediate vicinity of the road. If you don't feel well, perhaps you should not drive.

A driver's license expires and has to be renewed from time to time. Normally, a renewal application will be sent through the mail by the issuing department. But if you don't receive your application, it is your responsibility to apply for the renewal. It is also your responsibility to notify the licensing authority within a prescribed time if you change your address. Similarly, if you misplace your driver's license, it is up to you to apply for another immediately and, if necessary, to obtain a temporary permit to tide you over until the new license arrives.

Registration and plates

Motor vehicles operated on a public road must be registered with the licensing authority. A permit is issued to the owner; so are a set of license plates, which must be attached to the vehicle. These plates must be clearly visible and be kept clean. The rear one must be illuminated by a white light at night. It is an offense to alter or deface these plates, except to add a yearly updating sticker which some provinces issue to cut costs. The plates cannot be switched onto an unauthorized vehicle.

The operator should be able to produce the registration permit on demand. When a vehicle changes hands, the registration must be transferred to the new owner.

Form good pre-driving habits

EVERY DRIVER should learn good pre-driving habits, and practice them until they are automatic. The Canadian Automobile Association recommends the following steps:

• Before entering the car check for obstacles in its path; make sure children aren't playing behind the car.

• Sit in a comfortable, erect position squarely behind the steering wheel so your hands grip it at the 3 and 9 o'clock positions. Have lots of leg room.

• Lock all doors to reduce the chances of being thrown out in an accident.

• Secure loose objects such as books and luggage so they don't become flying objects in an accident.

• Make sure head restraints, which reduce the risk of whiplash if you are hit from the rear, are adjusted correctly.

• Adjust mirrors so you get maximum sight without moving your head. Remember mirrors don't eliminate blind spots.

• Fasten your seat belts and remind your passengers to do the same.

• Note the location of gauges and indicator lights on the instrument panel so you can glance at them while driving.

• Note the location of switches and other controls, and learn to use them without looking or fumbling.

• Make sure your transmission is in neutral, or your automatic transmission in neutral or park, before you start the car.

A registration permit is not, strictly speaking, an ownership permit since it does not necessarily show who owns a vehicle. A vehicle's owner should always keep the bill of sale, though it is possible in some provinces to get an official ownership certificate from the government.

When you move
If you move permanently to another province or territory, you must get a new driver's license and vehicle registration permit. It is not necessary to pass a complete new driving test. You simply hand in your old driver's license and a new one will be issued to you after you have passed an eye test. A vehicle must meet the safety standards of the area where you have moved, and may have to undergo a safety inspection.

A safe car
A law officer can stop a motor vehicle and inspect it for safety. If he deems the vehicle unsafe, the owner can be obliged to make the necessary repairs within a certain period. Items checked include tires, brakes (including the parking brake), steering and wheel alignment, lights and turn signals, horn, windshield wipers and washers, mirrors and defroster. A badly rusted body can make a car unacceptable. Some provinces order yearly checks.

Most provinces also require inspection of new and used cars before they can be registered. In Ontario, for example, a certificate of mechanical fitness, signed by a licensed mechanic, should be filed at the same time as a transfer of ownership. A transfer of ownership can be made without the certificate but the licensing authority will keep the vehicle's license plates until the certificate is produced.

Insurance
No matter how safe your car, no matter how skillfully and carefully you drive, you need insurance. Your car might be stolen, damaged in a collision or destroyed by some disaster. You might be involved in an accident resulting in property damage, bodily injury or death. All such losses can be costly and you may need insurance to meet such expenses.

Three main types of insurance are available. Liability coverage protects you against claims made by other persons for property damage, injury or death in an accident in which you as the driver and/or owner could be declared at fault. Accident benefits coverage pays medical or funeral expenses and an indemnity for you, passengers in your vehicle and pedestrians (and can pay benefits for you and your family if you are victims of an accident while in someone else's vehicle). Collision coverage and comprehensive coverage pay respectively for damage to your vehicle in a collision, and damage from almost any other cause such as fire, theft, earthquake, flood, or vandalism.

Policy costs vary widely, depending on the type of vehicle, who drives it (and for what purpose), and the part of the country in which it is driven.

Some provinces have compulsory no-fault insurance whereby victims are compensated according to a fixed scale. A victim gets financial relief without waiting for possibly long litigation, but is not permitted to sue for extra damages.

Unsatisfied judgment funds
All provinces compensate victims of uninsured or hit-and-run drivers. In Quebec, the provincial government compensates for personal injury while the insurance company settles property claims. In other provinces, compensation from an "unsatisfied judgment" can reach $200,000. Injury claims in the same accident are limited to $5,000–$10,000. Most Ontario claims are paid by victims' insurance companies; the fund compensates only uninsured victims, such as pedestrians. In all provinces, hit-and-run property claims are paid only if the driver is identified.

In all provinces except Quebec, if there is a claim against a driver, he must pay the amount of the claim back into the fund or to the insurance company. Generally, the guilty driver loses his license until he has made the appropriate payment. He is also obligated to pay the injured party any difference between the amount of the court award and that paid by the fund or insurance company.

Buying your car

IF YOU PLAN TO BUY a motor vehicle, remember the Latin adage *caveat emptor* (let the buyer beware). When you purchase a car it becomes your property and your responsibility. You have a claim against the dealer or manufacturer only in matters covered specifically by warranties or service agreements, or for defective parts affecting safe operation. (*See* Chapter 6, "Guarantees and standards.")

If you pay any sum by cash or cheque without receiving delivery of the vehicle, insist on a written agreement concerning any further payments and delivery of the vehicle. It is important to know and have confidence in the seller since any written agreement or contract is, in the final analysis, only as good as the parties involved. You should also understand and be satisfied with the financing arrangements. Study the dealer's terms for repairs and inspection prior to delivery, get a firm delivery date and understand any penalty or other provision that will apply if the date is not met.

If you are trading in and cannot obtain immediate delivery of your new car, make sure you understand (it should be part of the contract) who owns the trade-in car until the new one is delivered. That owner is responsible for insurance coverage in the meantime. (*See* Chapter 8, "Insurance at home.")

Be alert for extra pitfalls if you are buying a used car. Don't let style dictate your choice; reliability should matter much more. Have a mechanic you trust look at your choice before you sign any purchase agreement. Although it is an offense for a salesman to turn back the odometer on a car, you should still study the reading skeptically; the balance of a

warranty or the word of the previous owner can verify the figure.

Whether buying new or used, decide what you can afford *before* you go to the dealer. Apart from the price on the windshield, consider interest on any loan you need, sales tax, insurance, registration and license fees, plus an annual sum for fuel and oil, tires and maintenance.

Don't be shy about haggling; the dealer's profit on a new car is 10–12 percent of the windshield sticker price.

What type of car?

The law has a lot to say about automobile safety standards and about the sales contract you sign, but it can't help much in your choice of vehicle. When Ford of Canada was turning out its famous Model T there were many years when buyers could have any color they wanted as long as it was black. Today there is a confusing array of colors and models. The buyer is faced with two-door and four-door sedans, hardtops, hatchbacks, station wagons, limousines, sports models, four-wheel drives, and camper trucks.

What is the best vehicle for your family? *First,* establish your price range and stay within it. Let no salesman lure you upward with remarks such as "After all, it's only $10 a month more." *Second,* within your price range, choose the vehicle that will best perform the job at hand. Keep in mind, if you need space and power, that you can often buy a basic standard-size car for about the same price as a smaller car loaded with extras.

Choice of vehicle is often dictated by simple statistics. If it's to be the family car it must be able to carry everybody comfortably. Will you use it for camping and for hauling a lot of gear? A station wagon might be best. Do you live in hilly country? Will you ask your vehicle to pull a trailer? You'll need lots of power. Are you a salesman clocking 3,200 kilometres a month on the freeways? Are you in the market for a "shopper's special," a commuter job, or a first car for a teenager? Requirements vary widely and you'd be wise to choose a car that fits your needs.

Options can be costly

Optional extra equipment can range from superior tires to flashy body decals. In recent years, manufacturers have tended to group their options into "packages" and the purchaser can find that to add a single desired option can be pretty expensive. There's a subtle temptation to add the whole package—the "toys" as they are irreverently known in the salesroom.

HORSEPOWER Option decisions usually begin with the number of cylinders: four, six or eight? Each engine type may come in different sizes. If you make no heavy demands on your car, the standard size is powerful enough. If you add options such as an automatic transmission or air conditioning, or if you pull trailers or carry capacity loads, you'll want a bigger engine.

TIRES Choosing tires is complex and confusing. Generally, however, an inexpensive bias tire should be adequate for a second car used on errands near home; a high-quality bias tire or a bias-belted tire would be better for a family car used for getting to work and on the highway; a high-quality bias-belted or radial tire would be best for frequent high-speed highway driving.

DO-IT-YOURSELF GEARS Manual gear shifting is still offered on most cars although automatics are usual on bigger models. Manual gears are less costly and, enthusiasts believe, keep the driver more "in touch" with his vehicle and the road.

REAR-END RATIO If you haul heavy loads, particularly in hilly country, you should consider a lower rear axle gear ratio.

POWER EQUIPMENT There is no doubt that power options make driving less physically demanding, but any healthy person should be able to handle any automobile that has standard equipment.

There are some disadvantages to power assists. For example, if a heavy car's power steering system fails, steering could tax the strength of some persons. If brakes lose their power assist, much heavier pedal pressure is suddenly required. Power windows can be accidentally shut on passengers—including small children.

If several persons of different shapes and sizes drive the same car, a power seat may be justifiable.

DISC BRAKES Many models have front-wheel disc brakes as standard equipment, with conventional drum-type brakes at the rear. Some cars can be ordered with disc brakes on all four wheels. They are considered useful for surer braking.

ENTERTAINMENT AS YOU DRIVE Radios, both AM and FM, with or without tape players, are available for just about all car models, factory-installed. Citizen-band radios and car phones are by no means uncommon today, and rear-seat TV can be custom-ordered. Dual rear speakers give greater listening pleasure.

Ten-point checklist

The more than 3,700 new-car dealers in Canada employ more than 100,000 persons. They are not all saints. The Canadian Automobile Association warns the prospective buyer against the blandishments of the few unscrupulous dealers and offers these ten tips:

1. Don't borrow to make up the down payment, or you'll find yourself trying to pay off two loans at once.

2. Demand a test drive. Refuse to sign *anything* before that trial, even if the salesman tells you the paper is merely for "insurance" or some vague legal purpose.

3. Read any contract with great care before signing. Are all the blanks filled in with the word "none" or figures or words you understand? An x can easily be turned into a figure later. Inspect all copies of any document, and make sure all are filled in the same. (*See* Chapter 6, "Safeguards when shopping.")

4. Never place your trust in a verbal promise. Remember that even a formal written warranty is only as good as the company or individual giving it. Pay not one cent without a receipt.

5. Don't sign up for insurance without shopping around. You might do better with your own company or another in the open market. When you do get insurance, particularly if it's through the dealer, make sure it has full liability coverage. (*See* Chapter 8, "The role of the agent.")

6. Check that the price and the monthly payments in the contract are those quoted by the salesman.

7. The contract and the warranty will list the car's engine and body plate numbers. Check them against the registration.

8. Demand an exact copy of the sales agreement (bill of sale) before you leave a used-car lot. Accept no excuses about the copy being mislaid or assurances that it will be mailed to you later.

9. Have an adult witness present during all negotiations. Don't permit the dealer, on any pretext, to exclude your witness from the room. If you were cheated and wanted to sue the dealer it would be your unsupported word against his written and signed contract. (*See* Chapter 6, "The arts of selling.")

10. Be sure you have the complete financial picture before you hand over the down payment—even if the salesman whispers urgently that someone else is about to buy the car you want. For how long will you be paying? What will be your total outlay in principal and interest? What is the rate of interest expressed as a yearly percentage?

The test drive

A reputable dealer will let you test-drive a car you are considering buying. If it's a new car, you'll probably be offered a "demonstrator" similar in major detail to the model you like; if the deal is for a used car, insist on driving the actual vehicle.

Try to take your test run over a course that includes hills, some bumps, a fast flat highway and stop-and-go traffic. Do some backing up and parking.

You should be assessing the vehicle for safety, performance, comfort and convenience—and for condition if it's a used car. Test every piece of equipment you can reach, including the door locks and the parking brake.

Is it smooth and reasonably quiet, or is there a clatter as the car accelerates? Does the automatic transmission whine or hum? Close all windows and listen to the engine idling. Open a window at high

Trade in your horse

BUYING A CAR wasn't always a simple case of visiting some showrooms and signing a contract. Shortly after the turn of the century, before most manufacturers had their own dealers, a customer often bought a car by mail. The instruction book for the Orillia-built Tudhope started off by informing an owner how to unload his car from the box car in which it arrived.

Most buyers didn't know how to drive, so it was part of the salesman's job to provide driving lessons after delivery. Servicing was usually done by the local blacksmith although sometimes the factory would send a trained mechanic by train to look into a problem.

Dealers would often take a horse as part payment on a new car. Sometimes so many horses were taken in on trade that a dealer started a profitable sideline selling them.

A typical deal in a rural area (where no horse was involved) might go like this: A farmer would give the dealer a note for spring delivery, and the note would be discounted at the bank for cash so the dealer could buy more cars. The farmer would make one payment at milk time in the spring and another at harvest time in the fall. This cycle continued until the car was paid for.

A powerful car was important for geting through mud and sand. One Toronto salesman used to show a hole his car had made hitting a three-inch plank wall. "She couldn't have done that if she wasn't strong," he would say admiringly.

speed to find out what kind of wind roar you can expect.

If the automobile is second-hand, check particularly for play in the steering (five centimetres at the steering wheel is normal), and be warned if the transmission slips. Look under the car for leaks before you leave the dealer's lot and after you bring it back. Tap the exhaust pipe and muffler for evidence of rot. A side sag could indicate damaged springs or faulty shock absorbers. Examine the tires.

During the test drive take the car to a mechanic you trust and get his opinion. Have him or somebody else drive behind the car, noting the efficiency of tail and stop lights, whether the car "tracks" properly and whether there's excessive smoke from the exhaust. One practiced glance can sometimes diagnose serious ills.

Try to contact the former owner. He may give you an objective opinion of the vehicle and his reasons for selling it.

In Ontario, the Motor Vehicle Dealer's Act has established a registrar of dealers with wide powers to regulate the business. Every used-car salesman has to be registered and his past conduct is considered before registration is approved. Advertising is scrutinized for misleading or deceptive statements.

How to finance your purchase

If it is necessary to finance the purchase, even partially, you will probably make arrangements with your bank or enter into a financing agreement with the dealer. The dealer, in turn, will probably take such an agreement to a finance company. The finance company will pay the dealer for the vehicle and then collect all of your payments, including interest. (By a recent change in law, if you have a complaint against the dealer and have stopped payments, you can raise this complaint as grounds for defense should the finance company take you to court for failure to pay under the financing agreement).

In studying the cost of financing you should look not only at interest rates but also at the methods of calculating the interest. For example, interest calculated monthly will be more expensive than interest calculated half-yearly.

You are under no obligation whatever to use the finance company with whom the dealer may be associated. (*See* Chapter 7, "When you borrow.")

Remember that your vehicle can be more easily seized or repossessed under terms of a conditional sales contract with the dealer than under a chattel mortgage given to a bank as security for a loan.

Usually, in any form of financing where the vehicle itself is the security, it must be substantially insured, particularly for collision. Before arranging financing, therefore, you should find out about collision insurance rates available to you with your driving record. You could find your financing costs sharply increased by an extremely expensive premium.

Dealing with individuals

If you buy a used car from an individual, you usually pay less than you would to a dealer. On the other hand you get no company-backed warranty. Usually the vehicle should be inspected and tested. Make sure there is no lien on the vehicle—that no third party has a claim on it. If it is not fully paid for, if it represents security for a loan, or if there are unpaid repair bills, the vehicle could be seized from you after you bought it.

A dealer's car also might have a lien on it, though in Quebec at least you are protected if you buy from a government-licensed dealer.

There is no absolutely foolproof way to find out about a lien but you can:

1. Make a lien search at the court office of the county where the seller lives (except in Quebec, which has no lien registration).

2. Get the date the seller bought the vehicle and the name of the previous owner from the provincial or territorial licensing authority. (The date might indicate the likelihood of a lien and the previous owner will likely tell you whether the car is paid for.)

3. Have the seller give you a receipt stating there are no liens on the vehicle. It might still be seized by the authorities, but the seller would be open to a fraud charge and could be sued.

When you do buy a vehicle privately its

registration must be transferred at the appropriate government office.

You may decide to sell your old car to an individual—it's more trouble than trading it in but you'll probably get more money. The impressive allowance a dealer offers for your trade usually includes a substantial discount on the new purchase, which you should get even without a trade.

Don't spend a lot on mechanical or body repairs before offering your car for sale but do give it a thorough cleaning.

Inform the buyer of any lien on the vehicle. Insist on cash, and advise the buyer to arrange financing if he doesn't have cash. Keep a copy of the bill of sale, signed by buyer and seller. Notify your insurance company when the deal is complete.

Don't forget that you are legally responsible for the vehicle until the registration has been transferred. So make sure this happens immediately; accompany the buyer personally to the licensing authority office if this seems wise. If the buyer is going to scrap your vehicle and doesn't want to pay for a transfer, mail the old registration and plates to your provincial or territorial licensing authority with a registered letter explaining this.

Purchasing abroad

If a motoring vacation in Europe—or perhaps Japan—appeals to you, and if you happen to be thinking of a new automobile, you might consider getting a car on arrival abroad, using it for your holiday, then bringing it back to Canada.

The law permits you to import an automobile on payment of the assessed customs duty as long as it is not more than a year old and complies with the Canadian Motor Vehicle Safety Act. There are some exceptions to this rule. (*See* Chapter 15, "Going through Customs.") Any provincial sales taxes and registration fees have to be paid at dockside.

It's advisable for the traveler to order his car and pay for it before departure. This avoids currency exchange headaches and may earn a discount.

If you pick up your purchase at the factory gates, you'll save delivery costs.

Plan to end your vacation at a shipping port. The local representative of the motoring organization affiliated with the Canadian Automobile Association will gladly help members with shipping arrangements and marine insurance. Canadian dealers will honor the manufacturer's warranty.

A motorcycle may be purchased abroad under the same terms.

Leasing a car

Individuals and companies often lease motor vehicles, sometimes for convenience and sometimes to save money.

For an individual who drives only occasionally, or who briefly needs a second or a specialized vehicle, short-term leasing can make good sense. It can also be useful for an individual whose own vehicle is temporarily out of commission.

Leasing a car during a business trip may well be cheaper and handier than relying on taxis.

Long-term leasing, with contracts for a year or more, can also be advantageous for businessmen. There are tax savings to consider, the certainty of fixed costs, and the advantage of having capital free for other uses.

Another advantage to leasing is that the lessee doesn't run any risk of being stuck with a "lemon." The leasing firm must ensure satisfactory performance and, in its own interests, keep up maintenance.

Insurance is important in leasing. You can be held responsible by the vehicle's owner for damages arising from your negligence. Many leasing contracts, however, are for the minimum amount of insurance allowed in that province. This is not adequate protection and in such cases you should increase the limits. You should also list in the contract the names and ages of all drivers who will use the vehicle. (*See* Chapter 8, "Insurance at home.")

The advertised monthly payment can make a lease look very attractive. However, the advertised figure will probably be for a net lease and will not include insurance, maintenance and other services. Make sure you get the whole story before signing.

On the road

To TAKE THE WHEEL of an automobile and turn the ignition key is to enter a new world of freedom, mobility and excitement. You can drive to the edges of the continent. Your car adds efficiency and zest to life; it brings independence; it makes travel convenient and comfortable.

But these benefits are matched by responsibilities. The conscientious driver automatically accepts a measure of responsibility for the safety and well-being of others—not only his or her passengers for but all members of the public. In the hands of the careless, neurotic or impaired driver, the auto can be as lethal as a gun.

It is not enough to drive with skill and knowledge. A motorist needs foresight, self-control, sportsmanship and a good attitude toward law and law enforcement. The Canadian Automobile Association, in its handbook for teachers, sums up these qualities as "the driving conscience." You are obliged morally to do more than merely obey the law.

There is no end to learning from experience, as this story shows:

A driver in a line of slow-moving vehicles was caught on a railway track as a train approached. Cars ahead and behind were unable to move until just as she jumped for safety. Her new station wagon was struck by the train, dragged along the track and demolished. The driver not only lost her car but also had to pay to have the wreck removed. Weeks later she received a bill for repairs to the locomotive. The law is clear: You should not enter a railway crossing until you know you can clear it. To do otherwise is to drive without due care and attention.

Rules of the road

Rules of the road are laws from various highway traffic acts that govern the movement of motor vehicles and pedestrians on all roads. They derive basically from common sense and have been continually revised through court decisions to meet changing facts and conditions. Rules of the road apply on all types of roads in most of Canada and the United States.

THE BASIC RULE Driving with due care and attention, and with reasonable consideration for other people, is the fundamental obligation. The motorist should not proceed unless the road ahead is clear, and should steer clear and/or stop whenever necessary to avoid a collision. This basic rule stands above all others, to be followed at all times.

If a car pulls out from a stop sign, you cannot simply "stand on your rights" and insist that the other driver stop and yield to you. Your obligation is to avoid a collision—by applying your brakes, turning to the left if there is no oncoming traffic, turning to the right if there is a good shoulder, sounding your horn, and so on.

You are entitled to assume—to a reasonable extent—that other drivers will observe the rules of the road, but you cannot rely on it. Nor should you, for example, rely on another person giving you sufficient warning of the intention to stop if you are following too closely. Everyone makes mistakes and the law says it is the responsibility of the *last* person who could avoid an accident to do so.

PEDESTRIANS The motorist must always give the right-of-way to a pedestrian. A driver is legally and morally responsible for taking all necessary precautions to avoid hitting a pedestrian.

POLICE DIRECTIONS You must obey all police directions that you have had a reasonable opportunity to become aware of. This includes instructions from a traffic officer and an order to pull over and stop.

TRAFFIC LIGHTS You may proceed through an intersection on a green light or turn left or right unless otherwise prohibited. If turning, you must yield to oncoming traffic and pedestrians, unless the light is flashing green, which indicates that oncoming traffic is facing a red light.

When approaching a yellow light you may proceed cautiously through the intersection—but only if you have insufficient time to stop safely before entering it. The yellow light is to clear the intersection, not to warn of an impending red light so you can rush through.

A red light means you must stop until it changes to green. In some provinces, unless a sign indicates otherwise, you can turn right on a red light after first coming to a full stop and yielding the right-of-way to all traffic (pedestrians included).

A red light and another light with a green arrow mean you can turn in the direction of the arrow. You need not come to a full stop but you must yield to pedestrians and other traffic.

A flashing yellow light means you should slow down and proceed with caution; it indicates a potential traffic hazard. Never shrug off the warning of this light even if you already know it marks a spot where other traffic must stop.

A flashing red light is like a stop sign. You must come to a full stop, yield to oncoming traffic, then proceed cautiously into the intersection.

Traffic lights sometimes have "walk" or "don't walk" signals for pedestrians. Where a green light and a "walk" signal are on together the pedestrian has the right-of-way.

STOP SIGNS A stop sign means you must come to a full stop before entering an intersection, although the location of the sign does not necessarily indicate *where* you must stop. You are required to halt before reaching the painted stop line or crosswalk.

If nothing is marked, the crosswalk is considered to be the hypothetical extension of a sidewalk. You must yield to any pedestrian or vehicle close enough to constitute an immediate hazard; only when the coast is clear may you proceed, and then only with caution.

If a driver at a stop sign finds his view obscured by a building or a hedge he must take extra care before proceeding. Many a driver has argued that he fulfilled his obligation by stopping at the stop sign and that the obstruction of his view (and a resulting accident) was the fault of whoever put the stop line where it was: that argument is not accepted.

In case of four-way stop signs, the first vehicle to arrive has the right-of-way. If two vehicles arrive at the same time the driver on the right generally has the right-of-way—but must, of course, exercise the basic rule of "due care."

CAUTION SIGNS On approaching a yield sign, you must slow to whatever speed "due care" demands in the circumstances —or stop—and yield to any traffic that would constitute an immediate hazard. The obligation is similar to that at a stop sign, except that you don't *have* to stop. "Slow" signs, warnings of turns, hidden intersections or other things requiring extra caution, should be treated in the same way as flashing yellow lights.

UNMARKED INTERSECTIONS Intersections without traffic signs are treated much like intersections with four-way stop signs. You must yield to a vehicle or pedestrian already entering or about to enter the intersection, and if two vehicles arrive at the same time the driver on the right has the right-of-way. Even though one driver may be on a bigger "through" road, "due care" should slow him down.

PEDESTRIAN CROSSINGS A motorist must drive defensively at a crosswalk (whether it is totally unmarked or merely the hypothetical extension of a sidewalk) because the law protects a pedestrian who is using it. At intersections where there are traffic signals, a pedestrian must obey the signals, but, once lawfully in the intersection, has the right-of-way.

Some provinces have crosswalks at which all traffic in both directions must yield to pedestrians who indicate in good time their intention to cross. In some areas pedestrians who cross in the middle of a block can be found guilty of jaywalking.

RAILWAY CROSSINGS Where flashers or other signals are operating, or a flagman is giving warning of a train, you must come to a stop more than five metres from the tracks. It is an offense to proceed before the signals cease. A school bus or other public vehicle with ten or more persons must stop at every crossing. The operator of such a vehicle must open the door to listen for an oncoming train, and when crossing the tracks must not shift gears.

PRIVATE DRIVEWAYS Before entering or crossing a road from a driveway, shopping center, parking lot or private lane, you must yield the right-of-way to all approaching vehicles near enough to constitute an immediate hazard. A stop is not mandatory but you must be prepared to stop if necessary.

CHANGING LANES You should indicate your intention to change lanes well in advance and move only when there is room. It is important to make sure the other lane is clear not only immediately beside you but also to your rear and ahead. It is best to use your vehicle's flashing turn signals, but hand signals are better than nothing in an emergency. Your left hand held straight out indicates a left turn. Held up

Signaling

The law requires you to signal other drivers of your intention to stop or suddenly decrease the speed of your vehicle . . . to turn to the left or the right . . . to change from one traffic lane to another . . . to leave the roadway . . . to set your vehicle in motion from a parked position. Signals shall be given by turn signals, stoplight or hand and arm.

Turn signals must not be used for any purpose other than turning, changing lanes, or pulling away from a parked position. They must not be used to indicate a stationary vehicle.

Signal in time Give correct signals well in advance and in such a way as to make them plainly visible to other drivers. Check your signaling devices frequently to ensure they are working properly.

To change lanes Never move from one traffic lane to another until you make certain that you can do so safely. This means you must have safe clearance beside, ahead of, and behind your vehicle in addition to giving the proper signal.

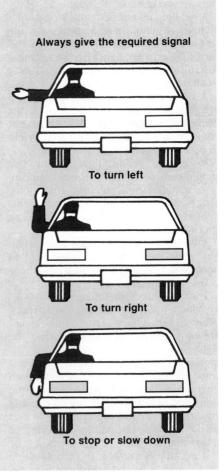

Always give the required signal

To turn left

To turn right

To stop or slow down

it indicates a right turn. Held down it indicates you are slowing or coming to a stop.

Collisions frequently occur when a driver who has been parked at the curb pulls into a traffic lane, or when a driver parked facing an intersection moves ahead into the path of another vehicle coming from behind and turning right. In such cases the driver who was parked should have ensured that the traffic lane was clear not only ahead of his vehicle but also behind it.

PASSING Normally you should overtake another vehicle on its left, after making sure that the road is clear in both directions and signaling your intention. Passing on the right is permitted only when the driver ahead is making or signaling the intention to make a left turn on one-way streets, or on streets and highways marked for multilanes. You may pass on the right only when it is safe to do so, but you are not permitted to do so by driving onto the shoulder unless that shoulder has been especially paved to permit the maneuver.

Passing is forbidden when a solid white or yellow line is on your side of the center line. It is also usually illegal on a curve, when approaching the crest of a hill, at an intersection or railway crossing and on a bridge or in a tunnel.

TURNING Your signal well in advance of any intended turn gives other drivers an opportunity to adjust course and speed. Having signaled, move cautiously as far left or right as possible in preparation for your turn. If making a left turn, you must yield to oncoming traffic. Whether turning left or right, you must yield the right-of-way to any pedestrian using the intersection lawfully.

U-turns are generally permitted where there are no traffic hazards and where the driver has a long, unobstructed view, though regulations vary widely. When making a U-turn avoid hillcrests, curves and intersections with traffic signals, as well as areas where there are other vehicles or pedestrians or children are playing. Some municipalities prohibit U-turns on busy streets, and they are almost universally ruled out on freeways.

EMERGENCY VEHICLES As soon as you hear a siren or see the flashing light of a police car, fire engine, ambulance or other emergency vehicle you must pull to the right and stop, making sure you are clear of any intersection. Emergency vehicles are not exempt from the rules of the road but in emergencies they acquire the right-of-way over other vehicles. In Prince Edward Island, Nova Scotia, New Brunswick, Ontario, British Columbia and the Yukon, it is an offense to follow a fire engine at less than 150 metres when the vehicle is answering an alarm. In other areas, there is no specific distance stated, although drivers are advised to follow a fire engine at a reasonable distance.

SCHOOL BUSES A motorist coming from either direction must stop when a school bus has its lights flashing and is taking on or letting off children. The only exception is if the bus is on the other side of a divided highway.

FUNERAL PROCESSIONS Vehicles in a funeral procession are not exempt from the rules of the road and must obey all traffic signals unless given police clearance.

STREETCARS You must not pass a stopped streetcar when passengers are getting on or off. When the doors are closed, you may proceed with caution. It is not necessary to stop when there is a safety island for the streetcar passengers. It is an offense to pass a streetcar on the left, whether it is stopped or not.

TAILGATING It is an offense to follow another vehicle too closely and if you hit one from the rear—even in bumper-to-bumper traffic—you are usually "guilty until proven innocent." A driver you hit in the rear might be held partly responsible if his brake lights weren't working properly or if he cut in front of you and then applied the brakes without giving you a chance to fall a reasonable distance behind. A safe distance is about one car length for each 15 km/h of speed.

TOWING RIDERS It is an offense for anybody on a bicycle, toboggan, sled, skis or such to take a tow from a motor vehicle, whether the driver consents or not.

OVERLOADING There is a limit to the number of persons you can carry in your vehicle. The driver must not be crowded

Regulatory signs

Stop signs

Yield sign

Keep right

Maximum speed

Trucks maximum

Night speed

Minimum speed

Maximum speed ahead

No right turn

Turn left

No turns

No U-turns

Do not enter

Signs which prohibit urban parking use red; those which only restrict it use green

Overhead signs like these are used where the desired movement counters normal rules

School, pedestrian and playground crosswalks

Passing instructions

School zone

Pedestrian crossing

Playground

Trucks permitted

Trucks prohibited

212

Warning signs

 Sharp turn

 Turn

 Curve

 Reverse curve

 Winding road

 Road ends

 Stop ahead

 Signal ahead

 Hill

 Bump

 Pavement narrows

 Narrow structure

 Divided highway begins

 Divided highway ends

 Pavement ends

 Railway warning

 Railway crossing

 Low clearance

 Slippery when wet

 Men working

Guide signs

 Trans-Canada Highway

 Directions

 Distances

 Junction

 Hospital

 Fuel

 Trailer camp

 Tenting site

 Picnic table

 Telephone

213

and his vision must not be hindered. Common sense and the manufacturer's recommendations should be your guidelines when loading your vehicle with baggage or goods. A police officer can stop any vehicle he considers overloaded.

On the highway

More than 46 percent of all driving in Canada is done on highways, under conditions far different from those in cities and towns. Expert drivers remember extra rules of the road for highway travel.

CAUTION SIGNS Highways have a greater variety of caution signs than city streets do and the motorist must be alert for all of them. A simple "slow" sign may indicate a hidden intersection, a dangerous curve or road repairs. Other signs warn of narrow pavement or bridges, bumps, animal crossings, rock falls, slippery surfaces and built-up areas. A flashing yellow light indicates a very dangerous hazard: you should be prepared to stop until sure that the highway is clear.

PARKING If you have to stop along the highway, you must at least pull completely off the traveled portion of the highway onto the shoulder, if there is one—although the safest course is to get into a driveway or parking area.

If your car won't run and you can't move it off the highway, you probably have a good excuse for illegal parking. However, if an accident resulted, you might be found liable if you had failed to adequately warn oncoming traffic, or if it could be proved that you knew, or should have known before starting out, that the car might break down.

Special freeway regulations

The differences between highway and city driving are even more pronounced on freeways (limited-access highways). U-turns, for example, are forbidden, and parking on the shoulder is particularly risky because of traffic speed.

Planned for the fast, uninterrupted flow of a lot of traffic, freeways have an accident rate less than half that of ordinary highways in terms of miles traveled. Yet they are often the site of apparently inexplicable crashes.

Accident analysts say that the constant high speed of the freeway, the continuous hum of wind and tires, and a certain monotony that arises from the unbroken ribbon of bitumen streaming beneath you, produce a "highway hypnosis." It can, for example, cause a sober driver to steer off the pavement into the rear of a parked vehicle at mid-afternoon on a sunny day. On an open straight stretch, a driver may veer across the median strip and cause a head-on collision.

To help stay alert keep your eyes roving from the road to your dashboard to the rearview mirror to the horizon. Chewing gum, singing loudly, sucking a lemon and taking a whiff of smelling salts (a tip from long-distance truckers) help. Stop at times to stretch and break the monotony.

Since the opening in 1939 of Canada's first freeway—the Queen Elizabeth Way between Toronto and Fort Erie, Ont.— extra rules of the road have been adopted for freeway motoring. The main points:

ENTERING THE FREEWAY Most entrances have a special "acceleration" lane beside the right-hand traffic lane. This is to enable the motorist to reach a speed close to that of the flowing traffic and thus blend smoothly with it. A driver should not normally slow down or stop in the acceleration lane but must yield to an approaching driver on the freeway.

CHANGING LANES After entering a freeway you should remain in the right-hand lane until certain of your position and speed. You should drive as close to the speed of the general traffic as possible, keeping to the right as much as possible. The far right-hand lane is normally for the slowest traffic and for vehicles entering or exiting. The far left-hand lane is for fast traffic. Lanes between are for through traffic moving at the average speed.

The normal rules about checking traffic to the rear, sides and ahead, and signaling your intention, apply to lane-changing on the freeway. Bear in mind, however, that freeway traffic moves faster, and check for other drivers who may be seeking the same lane as you are. Move gradually, stay in your passing lane until you can see the vehicle you passed in your mirror, then return carefully to the right-hand lane and make sure your turn signal is off. Avoid changing lanes frequently.

PASSING The normal rule about passing on the left usually applies since the slower driver on a freeway should be in the right-hand lane. Passing on the right is normally permitted if a driver on the left is exiting or preparing to exit on the left. Anyone on a busy freeway will soon learn that if a driver "hugs" the left-hand lane—or any middle lane—he or she will be passed on the right. In some provinces, this has legal sanction as long as the maneuver conforms to all other legal requirements.

DAWDLING A vehicle traveling much below average speed can be a hazard. It is constantly being overtaken, causing a cluster of vehicles in the left, or passing, lane. This can lead to multiple collisions. Some freeways have a minimum speed limit.

LEAVING THE FREEWAY Signboards, maps and experience will all help you know when you are approaching your exit. Signal your intention early and take advantage of the "deceleration" lane, which is usually beside the right-hand traffic lane. Check your speedometer; you have been traveling fast and will probably need to brake to meet the sharply reduced speed limit on the exit ramp.

If you find yourself overshooting the exit, do not attempt to swerve into it. Do not, under any circumstances, stop on the freeway, and try to back up to the exit ramp. It's best to run on to the next exit—and keep a better lookout in future.

Seat belts

Seat belts do reduce death and injuries in car accidents but there is disagreement (even among MPs) as to whether we should be compelled to wear them.

Carmakers have been obliged since January 1, 1971, to install government-approved belts in new cars. In a front-end collision, a lap belt holds against the strong bone of the pelvis to keep the body

Two, Twelve, and Adjust

FOLLOWING TOO CLOSELY behind another vehicle, or failing to look far enough ahead down the road, can get you into trouble because you don't have time to react safely to sudden hazards.

Learning and applying the simple formula of "Two, Twelve, and Adjust" will enable you to avoid most situations where you are "trapped" in traffic without an adequate safety time cushion.

Two seconds is the minimum time it should take you to cover the distance between you and the car in front. As it passes a fixed mark such as a sign or pole, start counting. If you take less than two seconds to reach the mark you are following too closely. This "two-second" rule adjusts to any speed. If driving conditions are bad, add a second or two.

Twelve seconds is the minimum time it should take you to cover the distance between you and the point down the road where your attention should be concentrated. Again, pick a point such as a curve or the crest of a hill at the distance where you normally concentrate your attention. A freeway is a good place to practice this technique. If it only takes you six or eight seconds to reach the point don't worry—that's average for the untrained driver. Push your sight and you will be able to exceed the "12-second" goal. Again, this rule adjusts to all speeds although obviously you can't see 12 seconds ahead around a corner or in heavy city traffic.

Adjust your position within the traffic pattern. When you are two seconds behind another vehicle and 12 seconds from your focal point down the road you are in a good position to see hazards or potential hazards, and to adjust your lane position, speed and following distance accordingly.

"Two, Twelve, and Adjust" makes an entertaining and useful game for children during a long trip, and gives them a head start on learning driving safety.

from thrusting forward, while a shoulder belt keeps the torso from hinging forward. The combination of lap and shoulder belts gives by far the best protection when properly adjusted. This is particularly true for children, whose vital organs are not as well protected by strong bone and muscle. A small child is also somewhat top-heavy; the head is proportionately larger, which can put great strain on the spine in a collision. Children up to five should be in approved car beds or seats.

Many motorists object to "buckling up." Some argue that belts create a false sense of security. But several recent court rulings have established that a person not wearing a seat belt and involved in a collision has contributed to his own injuries through negligence.

Many foreign countries, including Australia and France, where the law requires the use of seat belts, report dramatic reductions in deaths and injuries. In Canada, at this writing, mandatory seat-belt laws were in force in Newfoundland, New Brunswick, Quebec, Ontario, Manitoba, Saskatchewan and British Columbia. Nova Scotia had yet to proclaim its seat-belt legislation.

Speed limits

Whether you see speed limit signs or not you are obliged to drive at a reasonable and prudent speed. Even where signs are posted you must drive at a speed safe for existing conditions. Snow, rain, fog, darkness, heavy traffic and fatigue must be considered. Signs posting maximum speeds are sometimes supplemented by others setting minimum speeds or warning of restricted speed zones ahead.

Speeds above 100 km/h are prohibited on all public roads in Canada. In some provinces, heavy commercial vehicles are restricted to 90 km/h. The permissible speed in built-up areas is normally 40 km/h. Some provinces have reduced speed limits as an energy conservation method, with early reports indicating a reduction in highway deaths and injuries.

Assuming you have a normal reaction time in applying your brakes, your minimum stopping distance depends largely on your speed; it is usually greater than most people guess. Minimum stopping distances with good tires on dry pavement are shown in the box below.

Worn tires and slippery pavement increase the distance, and safety authorities warn that poor visibility, fatigue, eyestrain, age, alcohol and drugs, carbon monoxide, and distractions within the automobile, can lengthen a driver's reaction time before he even touches the brake.

Safety guards

At intersections close to schools you will encounter juvenile safety patrols or adult crossing guards. The basic rules of the road oblige you to obey the direction of these patrols which are ensuring the safety of school children.

Flagmen warn of danger at highway construction sites. You can expect a flagman when you see an advance sign warning of construction ahead. When the flagman holds his sign or flag horizontally and raises his other palm toward you, you must stop. When the signal is held lower and vehicles are waved on with the other hand you may proceed.

Minimum stopping distances

Speed	Reaction distance	Braking distance	Total stopping distance
15 km/h	3 metres	2.7 metres	6 metres
50 km/h	10 metres	15 metres	25 metres
80 km/h	17 metres	40 metres	58 metres
115 km/h	24 metres	93 metres	115 metres

When trouble comes

ANY CAR, no matter how new or expensive, may break down—if only because so many things can go wrong. A car contains some 15,000 parts, most of them vital to its safe, efficient operation, and as much electrical wiring as a house.

Canadian Automobile Association records show that battery failure is the biggest single cause of car breakdowns, accounting for 30 percent of all calls. Other troubles (in descending order of frequency) are: tires; ignition; starter; carburetor; running out of gasoline; locks and keys; gas line; brakes; and lights.

Trouble signals

Regular maintenance is the best insurance against mechanical problems. As a general rule, the average motorist doing roughly 20,000 kilometres per year should have the vehicle tuned up in the spring and fall. Be sure to have your exhaust system fully checked in the fall.

Approaching trouble may be signaled by the instruments or warning lights on your dashboard; get in the habit of glancing at all your dash indicators, not only the speedometer. The odometer, which records the distance a vehicle has traveled, can indicate when an oil change or a tune-up may be necessary. Some cars have separate trip odometers for measuring distances traveled on specific journeys. The oil pressure indicator shows if the engine's oil pump is maintaining enough pressure.

Engine temperature is very important. A broken fan belt, a clogged cooling system, perished hoses or lack of oil can all raise the engine temperature quickly to a level where serious damage might result.

The ammeter or charge light tells if your battery is charging or discharging. When the car is running, the alternator should be charging the battery, restoring power needed for the electrical system.

Other dashboard instruments are available—the tachometer, for example, which shows engine revolutions per minute—but they are mostly for the specialist.

The alert driver can read another equally important set of signals—those recorded by his own hands, feet and ears. Too much play in the steering wheel denotes trouble, as does front-wheel "shimmy." If brakes "grab" or pull the vehicle to one side, or if the pedal continues to sink when pushed, you should drive slowly to the nearest garage. Strange noises and vibrations all require investigation.

The emergency stop

If, while driving, you suddenly realize something is wrong with your vehicle, don't jam on your brakes. First check in your rearview mirrors, then ease to the right, using your turn-signal lights or arm signals; you can flash your stoplights as an extra warning. Stop on the shoulder— or completely off the road if possible.

If you are stopped on the shoulder it is safer to get everybody out of the car in case of fire or a rear-end collision. This is particularly true at night: an approaching driver will sometimes steer right at shining taillights, mesmerized into thinking they are on a moving car. Using your four-way flashers will reduce the hazard. You should be prepared for a night emergency by carrying a reflective warning triangle, distress flares or a battery-operated flashing light. Set one or more of them out about a hundred metres behind your car.

217

Remember that stopping by the side of a highway is always dangerous.

You should also show some distress signal in the daytime. Raise the hood of your car and tie a white handkerchief or cloth to a roadside door handle or to the extended radio antenna.

Don't try to flag down cars or walk for help, particularly on a freeway, unless there is a service station fairly close. A police patrol or highway maintenance crew will come by before long. Especially since the popularity of CB radios, another motorist (or trucker) may report your breakdown.

The problem is aggravated in winter. Never venture on a highway in winter without a good battery, a full tank of gas and an emergency kit consisting of a shovel, blankets, candles and quick-energy rations such as chocolate and raisins. If you get stuck, stretch your gas supply by running the engine and heater intermittently. Always be alert for exhaust fumes; in winter, make sure the area around the tail pipe is clear of snow. When the fuel does run out, a candle not only provides cheer but a surprising amount of warmth and light. Don't walk for help unless you know where you are going and the distance is short. In a storm, you are safer right where you are: keep active, and wait for expert help.

When you need repairs

Your best protection against having a dispute over repairs with a garage is a written estimate of the repairs required and their cost. (The Canadian Automobile Association recommends garages which will prepare estimates for its members.) Get an explanation of the charges and make sure you aren't paying for work that is covered by your vehicle's warranty.

If a dispute does arise the estimate is seldom airtight but it is still your best protection. You can also ask for replaced parts if you doubt work was done.

You may have to pay your bill and argue later because garages have the right to hold a vehicle under a mechanic's lien if a bill is not paid.

A consumer protection service might help in a dispute or you could take your case to a small claims court. The Canadian Automobile Association intervenes in disputes between its members and the association's approved garages.

The manufacturer's warranty

Motor vehicle manufacturers "warrant" that their vehicles are in good condition and agree to repair defects. (*See* Chapter 6, "Guarantees and standards.") They do not guarantee a vehicle or your satisfaction with a money-back offer. When you receive your warranty, make sure that it documents all essential details, including the delivery date and the serial number of your vehicule.

Most warranties are for the repair or replacement of parts which normally wouldn't need early replacement, thus excluding items such as ignition points and spark plugs. Some items such as tires and batteries are usually covered by warranties from their own makers.

The manufacturer normally pays for parts and labor on items covered, and the usual warranty is for 12 months or 20,000 kilometres, whichever comes first. If you need to use your warranty far from home it will be honored by any dealer for your make of vehicle. The manufacturer may refuse to honor the warranty if it can be shown that you have driven or cared for the vehicle improperly or have neglected servicing.

Manufacturers are obliged by law to recall and replace at their own expense any defective parts which affect the safe operation of a vehicle.

Contact with the maker

Dealer servicing under warranty is the source of most customer complaints with new cars. If you cannot get satisfaction from your dealer you have other options.

One is to write to the manufacturer or importer. The Canadian Automobile Association advises addressing the letter to the president of the company and sending copies to the managers of the sales, service and customer relations departments.

You should include, in addition to your full name, address and phone numbers, the following information: make of vehicle, model, year, serial number, date of purchase, actual odometer reading, your dealer's name, and the place where you normally get service. You must also describe your complaint fully. Ensure that you have sufficient documentation, such as copies of work orders and invoices.

Here are some addresses:

American Motors (Canada) Inc.
350 Kennedy Road South
Brampton, Ont.
K6V 2M3

Automobiles Renault Canada Ltée
1305, boulevard Marie-Victorin
St. Bruno de Montarville, Qué.
J3V 4P7

Chrysler Canada Ltd.
2450 Chrysler Center
Windsor, Ont.
N9A 4H6

Fiat Auto Canada
5240 Finch Avenue East
Scarborough, Ont.
M1S 4P2

Ford Motor Company of Canada Ltd.
The Canadian Road
Oakville, Ont.
L6J 5E4

General Motors of Canada Ltd.
215 William Street East
Oshawa, Ont.
L1G 1K7

Lada Cars of Canada Inc.
405 Fairall Street
Ajax, Ont.
L1S 1R8

Mazda Canada Inc.
821 Brock Road South
Pickering, Ont.
L1W 3L6

Nissan Automobile Company (Canada) Ltd.
P.O. Box 2600
Streetsville Postal Station
Mississauga, Ont.
L5M 2L5

Toyota Canada Inc.
1291 Bellamy Road North
Scarborough, Ont.
M1H 1H9

Volkswagen Canada Inc.
1940 Eglinton Avenue East
Scarborough, Ont.
M1L 2M2

Volvo Canada Ltd.
175 Gordon Baker Road
Willowdale, Ont.
M2H 2N7

If the response from the company is unsatisfactory, you should contact the federal government.

For safety related defects write to:

Vehicle Safety Operations Branch Transport Canada
Tower "C", Place de Ville
Ottawa, Ont.
K1A 0N5

For all other defects, you should write to your provincial or territorial consumer services department.

Used car warranties

The usual used car warranty is for a 50/50 split on the cost of parts and labor between the buyer and the dealer, for either 30 or 60 days. You should get the warranty in writing and be vigilant if you have to use it. An unscrupulous dealer might inflate repair bills so you are really paying more than half.

When repairs are necessary get comparison estimates before the dealer has the work done. Be sure that the work is done as specified, with all new parts if called for.

If the work is already done and you think the bill is too high get comparison estimates anyway and confront the dealer with them. Used car warranty repair disputes can be handled like other disputes with garages: you can contact a consumer protection agency or take your case to small claims court.

Under Quebec's Consumer Protection Act, the provisions of the used car warranty vary according to the time the car has been on the market and the distance traveled. A Class "A" vehicle—a car less than two years old that has under 40,000 kilometres—carries a minimum warranty that the vehicle will remain in good working order for six months, or 10,000 kilometres, whichever comes first.

Beware of thieves

If it isn't practical for you to remove valuables from your parked car you should lock them in the trunk. If the trunk is full, conceal the valuables in the locked passenger compartment.

Your householder's insurance covers your property if it is stolen from your locked car or from a borrowed or rented car. Property stolen from an unlocked car is covered only if the insured has a personal property floater policy.

Things on a rack, such as skis or bicycles, are not normally covered by either type of policy even if the rack has a lock. Some insurers will, however, pay such a claim anyway, possibly adding special coverage to an existing policy.

Somebody whose property is stolen from your vehicle will have to claim under his or her own insurance policy.

What to do in an emergency

ANY DRIVER may suddenly be confronted with an emergency situation due to mechanical failure, a road hazard, a natural disaster or unpredictable behavior by another driver.

There is little or no time for decision making; the correct response must have been learned in advance so that it is automatic. You should rehearse mentally the procedure to be followed in various emergencies. This will reduce the emotional impact of the emergency and increase the chances of your responding correctly.

If your brakes fail try pumping the pedal rapidly to build up enough braking power to get off the road. If this doesn't work apply the hand brake steadily but not so hard as to lock the rear wheels. Shift the transmission into a lower gear to get the braking effect of the engine's compression. Watch for an escape route off the road, and signal your emergency to others with your horn and flashing lights. In an extreme case you may have to slow your car by scraping it along an embankment or wall, or driving it into a hedge or snowbank. Most brake failures result from poor maintenance; they can be avoided.

If you have a blowout keep a firm grip on the steering wheel and keep going straight. A front tire blowout will pull the car to one side; a rear tire failure can cause fishtailing or weaving. Do not slam on the brakes—this will only make the car harder to control. Take your foot off the accelerator; once the car is under control, apply the brakes slowly and steadily. Keep going until you can pull off the road completely; the blown tire is probably ruined anyway and is certainly not worth the risk of changing it close to fast traffic.

If you run off the pavement while traveling fast on the highway, keep a firm grip on the steering wheel. Keep the car going straight, straddling the pavement edge. Resist its tendency to pull to the right, and do not try to get it back onto the pavement immediately. Take your foot off the gas; if you must brake, do so gradually. When your speed is greatly reduced, and no other vehicles are coming in either direction, turn the wheel sharply so your car can climb the pavement edge. Under no circumstances allow the wheel to rub along the edge of the pavement.

If your car catches fire under the hood stop immediately, turn off the ignition and all switches, and use a fire extinguisher if available. The cause is probably a short circuit: rip out burning wires with a jack handle or some such tool. If the fire is out of control move at least 30 metres away from the vehicle because the gas tank may explode.

If your car is stolen, the police need immediate, accurate information. Keep your license plate number and vehicle serial number jotted down in a couple of handy places for quick reference, especially if you keep your registration permit and proof of insurance in the glove compartment.

Recent federal statistics show that more than 90,000 motor vehicles are stolen yearly and about 80 percent of them are recovered.

The normal automobile insurance policy (*See* Chapter 8, "Insurance at home") covers you against theft of your vehicle, usually for its replacement cost.

At the parking lot

Parking operators usually have signs on the lot and wording on their tickets disclaiming responsibility for theft or damage. Their liability is, in fact, fairly restricted. Your own insurance would cover your property stolen from your vehicle in a parking lot. If you didn't have insurance, or if your insurance company tried to collect from the parking lot operator, the success of a claim might depend on the wording on the lot's signs and tickets, and on whether the operator or an employe could be proven negligent.

If your vehicle was damaged on a lot your collision insurance would apply (if the claim was over the deductible minimum), and it would be possible to collect from the operator only if he or an employe could be proved negligent. This would also apply if your vehicle was damaged at a car wash.

The wording on signs and tickets can be crucial if your car is stolen from a parking lot. Two decisions by the Ontario Court of Appeal bear this out:

A Toronto operator was found responsible after a car was stolen from his lot because his ticket simply stated. "Parking conditions: we are not responsible for theft or damage of car or contents, however caused." An Ottawa operator was absolved in a similar case because his ticket read, "Charges are for use of parking space only. The company assumes no responsibility whatever for loss or damage due to fire, theft, collision or otherwise, to the vehicle or its contents, however caused." The difference was in the Ottawa ticket's phrase, "Charges are for use of parking space only." These words excluded any notion of safeguarding; they limited the arrangement to rental of a parking space. The Toronto ticket didn't make the distinction.

Pollution by automobiles

Environment Canada revealed in 1970 that light-duty motor vehicles (cars, pickups and vans) produced ten million metric tonnes of air pollutants—roughly 35 percent of all synthetic pollution in the country. The main emissions were carbon dioxide, hydrocarbons and oxides of nitrogen, although car tires shed about seven kilograms of particles per vehicle per year.

Canadian standards for automobile emissions were first established under the Motor Vehicle Safety Act in 1971, and control regulations were made more stringent in 1975. Attempting to meet the new regulations, carmakers concentrated on modifying conventional engines and adding hardware to purify exhaust fumes. Special crankcase valves were installed, engines were redesigned for lead-free gas, and catalytic converters were developed to convert carbon monoxide to water. An improvement of about 25 percent in fuel consumption resulted from the carmakers' modifications.

By the early 1980s, federal controls had cut the amount of airborne pollution from exhaust emissions in half, to five million tonnes. Today, about 25 percent of all non-natural pollution comes from this source.

Only Ontario forbids the altering or bypassing of antipollution equipment: owners are obliged to maintain it to meet the manufacturer's standards. On-the-road spot checks of the models affected may result in an order to repair the equipment, or in charges being laid. At the time of this writing, Quebec was considering legislation similar to that of Ontario.

Environment Canada announced in 1982 that more stringent controls of motor vehicle exhaust emissions were under consideration for 1986.

Traffic accidents

THREE PERSONS die for every 100 million vehicle kilometres traveled in Canada, and about 260,000 people a year are injured in traffic accidents.

Constantly seeking ways to reduce the toll of death, injury and financial loss, governments and private organizations press research on driver education and driver health, motor vehicle construction standards, highway design and computerized traffic control.

The motor vehicle industry has developed self-regulation and improvement programs with the Society of Automotive Engineers. The Road Safety and Motor Vehicle Regulation Directorate has worked on safety standards. Other concerned organizations are the Canada Safety Council, the Traffic Injury Research Foundation, the Roads and Transportation Association of Canada, the Canadian Standards Association and the Canadian Automobile Association. There is close cooperation with similar organizations in the United States, Australia, and many European countries. Developments from this research include safety glass, the energy-absorbing steering wheel, reinforced doors, child-proof locks, shoulder-and-lap belts and improved brakes.

Research has demonstrated these facts:
• Although seat belts can prevent traffic deaths, only about 46 percent of Canadians use them voluntarily.
• Fifty percent of fatally injured drivers have been drinking, most to excess.
• Twice as many fatal accidents occur on two-lane roads as on four-lane roads.
• Less than half the cars on the road are more than four years old, and roughly two thirds of all car accidents involve these older models.

The motorist can help avoid accidents by knowing and practicing the rules of the road (*See* "On the road" in this chapter). He can protect himself financially by having adequate insurance (*See* Chapter 8, "Insurance at home"). All motorists should practice defensive driving and seek to develop a "driving conscience."

In case of accident

If you are directly or indirectly involved in an accident resulting in property damage, bodily injury or death, you must (1) remain at the scene, (2) help any injured persons, (3) help prevent further accidents, (4) notify police [unless there are no injuries and damage is minor], (5) give appropriate information to other drivers, witnesses and police. If you fail to do these things the law will presume the neglect was intentional.

Failure to remain at the scene of an accident, commonly known as hit-and-run, is a criminal offense and is punishable with a substantial fine or imprisonment. Never drive away after an accident on the assumption that no damage resulted. A Toronto woman who bumped a taxi from the rear was convicted of leaving the scene of an accident in a case that went to the Supreme Court—even though fixing the taxi cost a mere $60.

Failure to give all possible help to anyone hurt is also a criminal offense. But unless you have medical knowledge you should probably restrict your help to sending immediately for an ambulance or a doctor. Except in an emergency, as when a vehicle is burning, it is unwise to move a seriously injured person and risk complications. You could be sued for negligence when you were trying to help.

"Wanton and furious driving"

FACTS

The defendant was arrested in Toronto in his automobile after he had been involved in an accident with a streetcar. He was charged with the wanton and furious driving of a carriage or vehicle. The streetcar motorman said that the defendant was going at least 30 km/h—a very fast pace in 1909.

A passenger on the streetcar said that the road was clear and the automobile could have got by if the driver had wanted to do so. There was also evidence that the car's engine was in bad working order.

ARGUMENT

The pioneer motorist maintained that an automobile was neither a carriage nor a vehicle, and that a speed of 30 km/h could not be considered wanton and furious driving. Moreover, since the automobile was in bad working condition it could not have been driven at the speed alleged.

JUDGMENT

The court held that a speed of 30 km/h was indeed excessive and that an automobile was, in fact, a carriage or vehicle. If the engine was in bad working order, then that could only be considered as an aggravation of the offense.

The court stated that the defendant must have known how improper it was to drive at the high rate of speed of 30 km/h in such circumstances, and because of this his act was wanton as well as furious.

As a consequence of this decision, the Criminal Code was amended the following year. The section under which the defendant in our case was charged was altered to read "carriage *or motor vehicle, automobile* or other vehicle."*

*Based on an actual case (1909).

You must attempt to prevent further accidents. If possible, station somebody to warn approaching traffic.

The local law enforcement agency must be notified if there is damage (over an amount fixed by the province or territory) or if there is bodily injury or death. Even if there is no apparent injury and damage seems slight, a police report may prove helpful later if a claim is made.

You must give other drivers your name and address, your driver's license and registration numbers, and the name of your insurance company. Get the same information from them. You should also get the names and addresses of as many witnesses as possible, showing them your driver's license and registration permit if requested. Ask in nearby homes or shops if anyone saw the accident. You must give a police officer routine information needed for his report; you have the right to consult a lawyer before giving information to be used in any other manner. Be brief and give only facts. Never argue, accuse anybody or admit fault. Make no threats or apologies. Such statements could later be used against you. If a driver is badly enough injured to require hospital treatment, somebody else must stay at the scene to give information.

Make your own notes and a sketch of the scene. If you have a camera, photograph anything relevant such as skid marks or road signs. Make a written note of new damage on the other vehicle and ask a bystander to confirm it, adding his name and address. This could protect you if your insurance company tries to raise your premium after paying for damage from previous accidents.

Call your insurance company, or independent agent, as soon as possible; you will be advised how to proceed.

If you collide with an unattended vehicle you should leave your name, address and phone number secured to it. Copy the vehicle's license number in case you have to trace the owner, and notify police in order to protect yourself.

If you come upon an accident where help is needed, you must give it. But, otherwise, don't stop to gawk. Your vehicle may create an additional hazard.

To move or not to move

Experts disagree on whether vehicles should be moved before police arrive after a minor collision.

Moving vehicles to a safe position nearby can avert further collisions and possible criminal charges arising from them. This is particularly true on freeways. But police may have trouble pinpointing the accident site if vehicles are moved. Skid marks may become obscured and debris may be gathered up. The choice of what to do rests pretty much with the judgment of the drivers.

A person involved in an accident who moves about at the scene directing traffic or shoving vehicles may have difficulty later proving that he or she suffered pain or anguish in the crash.

The reluctant witness

If other motorists, potential witnesses, refuse to give their names and addresses, note their vehicle license numbers; they can be traced by your provincial or territorial licensing authority. Many persons do not want to get involved in legal actions. They might doubt the validity of their evidence or fear that attending court will be time-consuming or inconvenient. Yet your chance to win damages in a civil suit, or to establish innocence of a criminal charge, could depend on the testimony of an independent witness.

A witness may be persuaded to testify if you point out that he could himself be a victim someday. The court can order witnesses to appear if you have their names and addresses. Don't overlook a child witness; the presiding judge decides if a youngster's testimony is valid.

The danger of fire

Spilled gasoline can turn an accident scene into an inferno; gas fumes are highly explosive. Beware if there is smoke after an accident; turn off the ignition and disconnect batteries so no spark ignites the gas. Try to get a fire extinguisher; trucks and buses carry them. Forbid smoking near damaged vehicles until you are sure there's no fire hazard. Don't light a distress flare until you are a safe distance from a damaged vehicle.

The borrowed car

As the owner of a motor vehicle, you can be held responsible for its negligent use by another driver, although normally your insurance will cover you in the case of any licensed driver who meets the terms of your policy.

A driver under 25, however, might not be covered even if living at your address. Or your insurance company might sue you to recover damages resulting from an accident involving a driver you knew was reckless and was thus likely to breach the terms of your policy.

If someone is driving your car without your consent you are not liable for damages that may result. But you may be liable for damages caused by family or friends who don't have specific consent if they have borrowed your car often in the past. General access to the car's keys would be considered implied consent.

Liability for passengers

The liability of a vehicle's owner or driver extends to his or her passengers.

In most provinces, where passengers are carried free, liability arises only in cases of gross negligence. If a passenger consented to the driver's behavior, as in urging him to speed, the passenger cannot claim gross negligence.

An owner or driver of a commercial vehicle who is paid by a passenger can be liable for any kind of negligence.

A private driver who is reimbursed in any way for carrying passengers—in a car pool for example—should notify his or her insurance company. The driver will probably have to pay a higher premium but the company will assume responsibility for passengers.

A driver's liability to a hitchhiker he picks up is the same as to any other non-paying passenger. But playing the Good Samaritan to transients can be dangerous: a sudden stop to pick him (or her) up can disrupt traffic, and there is a long list of assaults, thefts and other crimes by hitchhikers. Hitchhikers can also be victimized by persons who pick them up.

It is illegal in some provinces for a hitchhiker to solicit a ride while on the traveled portion of a road, and pedestrians are prohibited entirely from being on some freeways.

Young and old victims

THE VERY YOUNG and very old seem particularly prone to traffic accidents. More school-age children die from road mishaps than from all other accidents combined. Despite classroom lectures and school safety patrols about 5,000 children aged 5–14 are injured in vehicle-pedestrian accidents every year.

A study in 151 cities, published by the Canadian Automobile Association, found that one in five child pedestrians killed in traffic was walking to or from school; "playing in the roadway" was the key action leading to the fatality. Friday was generally the most dangerous day.

Children have greater exposure to traffic than any other pedestrians. Their daily routines of going to and from school and outdoor play make them most vulnerable.

The C.A.A. studied traffic accidents in representative cities involving persons aged 65 and over. Although they then made up only 7.8 percent of Canada's population, these senior citizens accounted for 22.6 percent of pedestrian fatalities.

Almost two thirds of the accidents were in fine daytime weather; Fridays and Saturdays were most hazardous. About two thirds of the victims had no apparent handicap or infirmity, although lack of agility and failing sight or hearing may have played a part.

Thirty-one percent of the victims struck at intersections were crossing under the "protection" of a signal. The C.A.A., like all safety advisers, warns pedestrians and motorists against placing total confidence in traffic control devices.

Driving offenses

Powers of the police

Police as troubleshooters

Speeding

Reckless driving

Driving, drinking and drugs

When charges are laid

THE PROVINCES have the biggest role in regulating drivers, vehicles, roads and traffic. Although three levels of government are involved, the Canadian Constitution makes the provinces responsible for all aspects not specifically delegated to other governments.

The federal government, through the Criminal Code, establishes penalties for impaired driving, dangerous driving, failing to remain at the scene of an accident, and criminal negligence. Ottawa also sets safety standards for new cars, trucks, buses and snowmobiles.

Municipal governments are responsible for local road and traffic engineering, subject to provincial approval. They erect traffic signs and signals (which must comply with provincial regulations) and they are responsible for local parking.

Traffic laws work best when motorists and pedestrians obey willingly. Police step in only when persons do not voluntarily obey. Then, depending on the violation, police issue warnings or traffic tickets, lay charges or make arrests. A driver may have to pay a fine, may lose his or her license, or may go to prison.

Powers of the police

You are driving, minding your business. Suddenly a policeman signals you to pull over. You stop, wondering what you've done wrong. It turns out the officer is making a safety check. All vehicles must operate safely and be properly equipped, and an officer may stop you at any time to see if yours conforms to the law. You must produce your license and possibly the vehicle's registration permit, plus proof of insurance or financial responsibility.

If you are on private property or there is some unusual circumstance an officer may ask you to get out of your car and explain what you are doing. He could be under orders to stop certain vehicles in the hope of catching a criminal but he need not explain his actions to you.

You can refuse to give additional information until you talk to your lawyer. This would probably result in a trip to the police station and might get you involved in arrest and interrogation procedures. (*See* Chapter 3, "The policeman's lot.")

Police as troubleshooters

Most of a highway patrol officer's time is spent keeping the road open and safe for traffic, and much of his work is preventive.

When on patrol he acts as a troubleshooter. He watches for anything that might lead to an accident, and acts quickly to divert traffic or otherwise reduce a hazard. On freeways he checks every parked vehicle; if he is on an emergency call he notes the vehicle's location and returns later, or notifies another officer by radio. He keeps a lookout for negligent driving and for speeding, and watches all vehicles for infractions of safety and equipment laws or signs of unsafe loading.

Speeding

All provinces and both territories have maximum speed limits and regulations for placing speed limit signs. All levels of government must meet the regulations.

A speeding charge against a driver is usually the result of a police radar check. Such evidence is generally accepted by the courts; it is harder to challenge than evidence obtained by observation or by following in another vehicle.

You won't have much luck fighting radar evidence but if a speed limit sign didn't meet the regulations (on lettering or location, for example) you might get off. Even if you have not exceeded the posted limit you can be charged with careless driving if roads are hazardous from freezing rain or some other factor and you have been driving at a speed that does not show due care and attention.

If you are stopped for speeding and act surprised when the officer mentions the speed at which you were traveling, you could be harming your case. The responsible driver *knows* his speed at all times.

The penalties for speeding may range from $1 to $5 per kilometre, depending on how far over the speed limit the offender was driving. Repeated offenses lead to increased fines, the accumulation of demerit points, and possibly suspension of a driver's license.

There are laws against driving too slowly. Generally, a "reasonable" rate of speed must be maintained; it is an offense to drive so slowly that you impede traffic.

Reckless driving

The phrase "reckless driving" is a popular catchall which describes three offenses:

1. Careless driving, which comes under provincial law, applies to inadvertent negligence. It involves driving without due care and attention or without reasonable regard for others. It is more serious than breaching the rules of the road, and can be punishable by a sizable fine.

2. Dangerous driving, a criminal offense, applies to conduct more dangerous than simple carelessness. Dangerous driving has been described as "advertent negligence" or "wanton and reckless dis-

Natural laws are powerful

WHEN YOU DRIVE, you are subject to natural laws—the laws of centrifugal force, friction, kinetic energy, gravity and impact—that can affect your safety.

Centrifugal force makes your car want to swing wide when you take a curve. It tries to keep you traveling in a straight line and you can weaken it by slowing down. Only *friction*, expressed through the contact of your tires with the road, permits you to make the turn. If the pavement is slippery friction can be reduced to the point where it will not master the centrifugal force and you will slide off the road.

Kinetic energy, the energy of motion, is what keeps your car moving after you shut off the engine. To stop quickly you must apply your brakes, converting the kinetic energy into heat.

Gravity, which holds you where you are on the ground, is what the motor vehicle is designed to overcome by carrying you somewhere else. Gravity also pulls your car downhill and helps bring it to an eventual stop if the engine is turned off.

Impact is familiar to almost anyone who has had a collision. If vehicle weight doubles, impact doubles; if speed doubles, impact quadruples.

The likelihood of sliding or skidding off the road is less if you control your speed, keep your tires and brakes in good condition, and recognize hazards well in advance. If you must brake on a slippery surface pump the pedal carefully so the wheels don't lock.

If your car does start to skid, do not apply the brakes because this may lock the wheels: locked front wheels cannot be steered. Let up on the gas, and steer in the direction in which the rear of the car is skidding. Straighten out when you feel the rear of the car straightening, but be prepared for it to swing around and skid in the opposite direction. Now you must steer this way, and be ready for additional countersteering until the car is under control. Do not remove your foot from the accelerator too suddenly or you may create an effect that is similar to applying the brakes.

regard for others." It involves a crime against the public as opposed to a mere failure to be careful, and is punishable by up to two years' imprisonment.

3. Criminal negligence applies to the same kind of offense as dangerous driving but usually in cases involving serious collision. Criminal negligence is punishable by up to five years' imprisonment.

Driving, drinking and drugs

Records indicate that half of all fatal accidents involve drinking and the campaign against driving after drinking reflects this.

It is an offense under the Criminal Code to drive or have care and control of a motor vehicle if the blood alcohol level is over 0.08 percent. Any driver may be required to take a breath test when so asked by police—and that includes at the side of the road. If the blood alcohol level tests over 0.08 percent, the driver is considered "under the influence of alcohol," is liable to a heavy fine and/or imprisonment (in 1976, an Ontario provincial judge achieved national publicity when he began handing down ten-day sentences for first offenses of impairment), and will probably have his or her driver's license suspended. Repeated convictions result in more severe penalties.

Refusing to take a breath test leads to serious penalties, and if the physical evidence of impairment is present you can face simultaneous charges of refusing to take a test and of impaired driving.

Even if your blood alcohol level should register under 0.08 percent you can be charged with impaired driving if the physical evidence is present.

In some jurisdictions you may have to surrender your driver's license for 24 hours if an officer suspects you have been drinking, even though your blood alcohol level is under 0.08 percent and the physical evidence is not present.

The amount of alcohol that can be consumed before the blood alcohol level reached 0.08 percent varies from person to person. The breathalyzer apparatus, which measures the alcohol in the bloodstream, has been gradually accepted as a reasonably accurate indicator of the degree of impairment.

You can also be charged with impaired driving after taking a drug, and the drug need not be illegal. Prescription drugs taken on a doctor's orders can affect your driving ability, as can common nonprescription drugs for colds and other minor illnesses. If you are taking drugs and have to drive, check with your doctor

The battle over breathalyzers

SINCE DECEMBER 1, 1969, federal law has made it imperative for the motorist suspected of drinking to blow into a breathalyzer. This instrument contains a chemical solution which changes color depending upon the amount of alcohol in the driver's breath. The break-even point is at 80 mg of alcohol in 100 mL of blood, expressed as a percentage figure on the breathalyzer meter.

A man weighing about 77 kilograms can usually drink four bottles of beer or four "singles" (40 mL each) of liquor in an hour and still pass a breathalyzer test. He can then drink another two-thirds of a bottle of beer, or two-thirds of a shot of liquor in

the next hour—and every hour after that—and still probably pass the test.

The most important factors are undoubtedly the amount of alcohol consumed, related to (a) the length of time since the drinking started and the length of time since the last drink, (b) the drinker's body weight, and (c) the amount and kind of food in the person's stomach at the time of drinking. Food only delays the transfer of alcohol into the bloodstream, it does not soak it up. Black coffee, cold showers and brisk walking may make you more alert, but they don't do anything to rid your system of alcohol. It's strictly a matter of time.

How the breathalyzer works

The breathalyzer widely used in Canada at present is the one shown here. The suspect blows through the mouthpiece and his breath raises the piston in the metal tube. When the blowing stops the piston drops, forcing the breath into a chemical solution. Within two minutes a chemical reaction takes place which is "read" by a photocell. The more alcohol there is in the blood, the clearer the solution becomes. Simultaneously, a photocell "reads" the normal solution on the other side of the machine. The nullmeter shows the difference between the amount of electricity flowing from the two photocells. A light between the photocells is moved closer to the normal solution until the nullmeter indicates that both photocells are receiving the same amount of light. The motion of the light activates the needle which gives the breathalyzer reading—the closer the bulb is to the normal solution, the higher the reading.

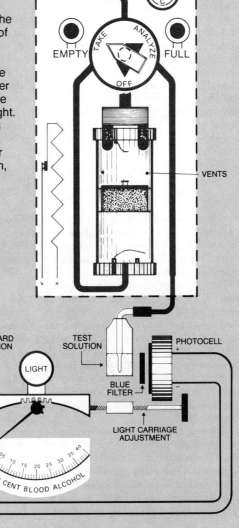

or pharmacist and read the label on the package.

Marijuana affects your driving ability, particularly at night, and users under its influence are classed as dangerous drivers. They tend to be vulnerable to glare from oncoming headlights, have slower reaction times, and experience difficulties with complex driving tasks.

You don't have to be driving to face impairment charges. You may be sitting in a parked car with the keys or you may be asleep behind the wheel; even though you have no intention of driving you are still considered to have care and control of the vehicle.

Carrying alcoholic beverages in your car is illegal unless you are proceeding home from the liquor store—although you are allowed to take drink to another person's home as a gift. You may not open bottles when taking drink home, nor may you take a partly finished bottle from a restaurant.

When charges are laid

Statistics prove that nearly every traffic accident involves at least one violation of the law. If the evidence is present charges will be laid.

Your legal responsibilities can be very serious. If you are to blame for the accident through a violation of the traffic laws, you may face a heavy fine, revocation of your driver's license and perhaps imprisonment. If there has been bodily injury or property damage, you may be sued for damages. You may be liable for injuries suffered by passengers in your car. If the car you were driving when the accident occurred belonged to somebody else, both you and the owner might be held responsible for damages.

When any charge is laid against you due to accident your first step should be to contact your lawyer. If you don't have one, or if you feel you can't afford one, you should follow the advice given in Chapter 20, "When you need a lawyer."

The first licenses

FOR A FEW YEARS after the turn of the century anybody brave enough to drive a motor car could do it anywhere he wanted to, with no thought to license plates. They hadn't been invented yet.

Ontario, in 1903, became the first province to license motor vehicles. The rate was a flat $2, in return for which the motorist got a permit and a little patent leather plaque with aluminum numbers and a metal crest of the province. This plaque was hung on the rear of the car. Provincial law also required the front numbers to be illuminated, so most motorists painted them on the lenses of their large kerosene parking lamps.

The first Canadian to actually license a car was Montreal alderman and promotor U. H. Dandurand. In March 1899 an alert city council had asked city officials to prepare regulations for automobiles. Nothing was done, however, and when the publicity-conscious Dandurand decided to seek a license for his Waltham Steamer later that year officials were stymied. The dilemma was finally resolved by selling Dandurand a bicycle license for the sum of $1.

Other provinces followed Ontario's lead in registering cars but none actually issued plates at first. The owner simply got a number. He was expected to make his own plate or have it made. Most motorists painted up bits of wood, metal or leather, or painted the numbers right on the vehicle. Not Joe Morris of Edmonton.

After the Alberta government passed its new Automobile Act in 1906 Morris was first in line to register his 1903 Ford, so he got license No. 1. But Morris scorned the effete conformity of painting his number on a board; what he did was stick a broom handle on the rear of his car. When he was taken to court for failing to show his registration number he argued that the broom handle obviously formed the number "1." The court agreed.

Using a car on holiday

A DRIVER GOING ON VACATION should get digests of traffic laws for areas he or she plans to visit. Digests are available from provincial and territorial licensing authorities, from state governments in the United States and from embassies or consulates of other countries. Helpful information is also available from your automobile club and the touring offices of major oil companies.

If you are convicted in another province or territory, or in one of the American states, for an offense in which your vehicle was moving, your provincial or territorial licensing authority may be told. The offense may go on your driving record and may earn you demerit points.

If you drive outside Canada, particularly overseas, you should study the customs regulations of the countries you will visit. Apart from your passport, you may need special international documents for yourself and your vehicle. You must have a good grasp of each country's rules of the road even if you already know the international traffic signs. In some parts of France, for example, cars can join a main highway from the right without conceding the right-of-way to through traffic.

Remember that driving hazards are increased when an automobile is heavily loaded, when bored children become fractious and when fatigue creeps up on drivers accustomed to shorter trips.

Before you leave home

Try not to announce your departure to would-be thieves. Cancel your daily newspaper so copies don't pile up at your door; arrange for your mail to be taken in by neighbors, and for the lawn to be mowed. You can get an electric timer to turn some house lights on and off at set times or to play a radio for a few hours a day.

In some areas you are invited to inform police that you're going away, leaving a vacation address and phone number. Patrolmen will try to keep an eye on your home. In any case you can leave your door key with a neighbor who agrees to drop in occasionally; when his holiday comes, you can do the same for him. Insurance companies require that an unoccupied house be checked regularly, particularly in winter when the furnace is on.

An easy trip

When you are rested and relaxed you are less likely to get in trouble with other traffic or the law. You can drive with more peace of mind if you check your car, pack it properly and drive sensibly.

Here's a last-minute checklist for the car that is already in good, safe running order: tire pressure, windshield wiper blades, and fluid levels of engine, battery, brakes and radiator. These items should be checked every morning during the trip. Make sure your jack and flashlight are working; stow some rags, chain for towing, and a strong square of lumber for jacking on soft ground. Clean your windows and fill your gas tank.

Here's a checklist for packing: clothing for all likely occasions; toys and games for small children; a trash bag; your driver's license and other documents; hotel reservations and maps. Try to load your vehicle so weight is distributed evenly; a lopsided car or one that's down at the rear is harder to steer. Don't forget money!

Driving sensibly includes remembering that long-distance touring is different from stop-and-go driving around home.

If you make early starts you'll have less traffic for the first few hours and more time to relax when you reach each day's destination. Don't try to go too far in a day: there are too many variables to set rules, but 500–600 kilometres is a good average. At the end of your trip don't try to reach home a day early: strain or fatigue make an accident more likely.

Children love trips but hate being cooped up in cars. Adults can help them pass the time but children should obey some basic rules: everybody in seat belts; no rough-housing in the car; nothing protruding from windows. Each small child should have a bag with toys, books, puzzles, crayons and paper. Everybody can join in games such as "I spy" or spotting different cars, license plates or gas stations. Stop frequently at rest areas or parks where the children can run, tussle or play ball to let off steam.

The overnight stay
When you walk into a hotel or a motel as a guest you walk into a legal maze. Generally, you must be accepted as a guest if there is room and you are sober, orderly, clean and able to pay. The operator can give you any room he wishes, within reason, and can ask you to switch to another room after you have settled in.

Your goods are handled by the establishment's staff at your risk, although you would have a case for damages if you could prove dishonesty or negligence. Valuable items such as jewelry should be put in the establishment's safe.

The hotel or motel operator is responsible for the safety of your vehicle when it is put in his care unless it is damaged by a vehicle driven by somebody other than an employe. He is not responsible for your vehicle's contents if you keep the keys, since you are then expected to leave the vehicle locked.

If you fail to pay, you can be evicted, have your luggage seized, and face a suit for the money owing. If you feel you have been overcharged, your best plan is to pay up, get your itemized receipt, then try to recoup later.

Across the border
A Canadian citizen or landed immigrant can normally enter the United States on vacation with little formality. Even a citizen, however, should carry some identification: a valid passport is best or a birth certificate, but a driver's license is usually acceptable and even that may not be required. A landed immigrant needs only proof of Canadian residence and, possibly, immigrant status. A noncitizen requires a passport and usually a visa.

Rules of the road are generally similar or identical to those in Canada but speed limits may vary; the top national limit in the United States since 1976 has been 90 km/h. "Tailgating," although generally forbidden, is more common because roads are more crowded.

Traffic laws—enacted by states, counties, townships and municipalities—may change along the same road as you pass from one jurisdiction into another. In

Percy Gomery and the Fort Garry speed trap

THE SPEED TRAP has been with us a long time. It was not new, apparently, when Percy Gomery was trail-blazing a route for a trans-Canada highway between Montreal and Vancouver back in 1920. Gomery found himself facing a magistrate in the Winnipeg suburb of Fort Garry.

Gomery's shameless flattery of the arresting constable, and his convincing point that Fort Garry would become a national laughing stock by fining a pioneer transcontinental motorist got him off. ("They beat my pride but I beat their pocket book," he told his wife.) The consensus among Winnipeg motorists next day was that to drive from Montreal was no great feat, but to beat the Fort Garry speed trap—ah, that was something!

some notorious locations, laws can vary within a few kilometres and can be affected by the time of day or the day of the week. Automobile clubs can give the locations of some known speed traps but tourists must pay if they are caught exceeding a posted limit.

If you are involved in an accident, follow the procedure outlined earlier in this chapter. Your pink slip showing proof of minimum required insurance is valid in the U.S. and you are covered for all stated risks. If you get in serious trouble you should contact the Canadian embassy in Washington one of our consulates situated in some major cities. (*See* Chapter 15, "Trouble while traveling.")

Taking your car overseas

If you travel outside North America with your motor vehicle (or pleasure boat) you may need: a Canadian nationality plate, with the letters CDN, fixed to your vehicle near the regular license plate; your regular Canadian registration permit; the *carnet de passages en douane* (carnet); and an international driving permit (IDP). Application forms for the carnet and IDP are available from the Canadian Automobile Association or member clubs.

The carnet

Motor vehicles are extremely expensive in some countries and visitors may be offered high black market prices for them. The carnet assures local customs officials that you will take your vehicle with you when you leave.

You do not need a carnet in Mexico, Central America or Europe. Some countries such as France permit entry without a carnet, but only for a certain number of months, and other countries impose other conditions. You will need a carnet in most of South America, Africa and Asia, and in Australia and New Zealand.

Carnets originate with the Alliance Internationale de Tourisme in Geneva and are usually good for a year. They are issued in Canada only by the Canadian Automobile Association, which is affiliated with the A.I.T. Carnets should be treated with the same care as passports.

The carnet is really a promise by the C.A.A. that if your vehicle is left behind, the country in question will be compensated. This promise is backed by a bank letter of credit from you to the C.A.A. The amount of the letter depends largely on the vehicle and countries involved; it often works out to about 300 percent of the vehicle's value. You must deposit $100 ($125 if outside Canada) to guarantee return of the carnet, and pay a service fee (currently from $50 to $60).

If the carnet is not stamped by customs to prove exit from all the countries where it was used, or if it has been lost or stolen, the C.A.A. will provide a "certificate of location" which must be taken, with the vehicle, to the nearest customs office. The vehicle can then be certified as having left any country in question, and your letter of credit and deposit will be returned.

International driving permit

Although your regular driver's license is valid in Mexico, Britain, France and some other countries, you should get an international driving permit if you plan to drive outside Canada, the United States or Mexico. You will need it to rent a car in such countries as Greece and Turkey.

Any Canadian aged 18 or over with a valid provincial or territorial driver's license can get an IDP at nominal cost. This useful document (it's the size of a passport) is valid for one year. Printed in ten languages, it allows you to drive in any country without undergoing any test.

Insurance overseas

You should carry plenty of insurance—and perhaps a bit more—when driving abroad because of widely differing traffic laws and driving conditions. Your Canadian policy will not normally cover you outside Canada and the United States.

Insurance is compulsory in most of Europe although it is not in many other countries. Many drivers pick up temporary policies after they arrive in a country but this can be risky and expensive. Your automobile club can arrange an all-risks policy that will protect you in almost every country where you can take your vehicle. Your insurance agent may also be able to arrange such a policy.

6/The Consumer and the Law

The arts of selling   255

Guarantees and standards   266

To protect the consumer   275

Safeguards when shopping

Food and Drugs Act

Common names of foods

Use of additives

Accurate labeling

"Miracle cosmetics"

Two-way protection

DESPITE the seemingly ponderous pace of our massive law machine, it can move with surprising speed at times. The best example of this can be seen in the tremendous increase recently in legislation and regulation aimed at protecting the consumer—the average citizen—in his dealings with the business world, and also at protecting the environment—the earth itself—from the bad and wasteful habits of us all.

Consumer law is one of the current glamour girls of the world of lawmaking. As the world economy settled down after World War II into relatively steady prosperity—at least, as far as the Western democracies are concerned—the centuries-old rule of *caveat emptor* ("let the buyer beware") came under fire. Reformers asked pointedly why it should be at his own peril that a householder buys a product—why the housewife has to run the risk of loss or harm in her weekly shopping. Is it right that an unsuspecting citizen, tempted by a misleading advertisement, should part with his or her hard-earned money for a "bargain" that turns out to be a fraud? The rule that the buyer should check carefully before paying is still sound; but it hardly covers the situation where a fault in manufacture, or bad workmanship, is hidden from normal scrutiny. A crack in the metal of the differential of a car is a good example.

The buyer could turn to the courts to bring an action for damages, fraud, or possibly for breach of warranty, but the cost and red tape of such a move usually put him off. And it might be months before the case would be heard—small comfort to the man who needs his balky car to get to work, or to the family whose wall-paper and furniture have been damaged by rain coming through a leaking roof. Warranties (guarantees) sometimes have actually *reduced* the buyer's protection under the law.

In the mid-1960s, legislators began in earnest to shift more responsibility on to the merchant supplying the goods, or the company providing the service. The lawmakers reasoned that since the merchants were supposedly offering sound and safe merchandise, or reliable services (such as wiring or paperhanging), then they should live up to their promises. If the refrigerator door won't stay shut after only six months of normal use, then the supplier should fix it, replace it or refund your money, whether a warranty has been issued or not. The dealer, after all, had promised in his sales pitch, or at least implied, that the product would remain serviceable for a reasonable time. He could hardly argue, after only a few months of use, that your expensive refrigerator had served you for "a reasonable time."

In many cases, the responsibility is passed through the dealer to the manufacturer, although recent legislation and the courts seek to place responsibility on both. The shopkeeper can argue (with some justice) that he, in turn, bought the faulty refrigerator from the maker in good faith. Where a brand-name product is concerned, the ultimate responsibility seems to rest with the manufacturer. Reputable firms have for years usually accepted this responsibility without the prod of legislation, but now all are under pressure to do so.

Many large stores and dealers go further; they will take back for refund *any* merchandise you find unsatisfactory, with little or no argument, however trivial your complaint. "Satisfaction or money refunded" has become a widespread slogan in Canadian shopping. It must be pointed out, however, that "satisfaction" is difficult to define in terms of the law. To ensure total customer goodwill, some department stores have been known to take back clothing which they strongly suspect was "bought" just for one wearing at a special function, and then returned.

Consumer protection laws can involve more than just refunds or replacement of goods. There is the question of damages for physical injury, pain or suffering when a product—a cosmetic, perhaps, or a flammable toy—causes harm to the unsuspecting buyer or to his family. Using newspaper notices, automobile manufacturers sometimes appeal to car owners to take certain models to dealers for adjustment. The car makers are prompted to do this, of course, by the knowledge that they might be sued if some hidden defect in an automobile results in injury to the driver or the passengers.

During 1967 the federal cabinet, aware that consumers were spending upward of $8 billion a year, decided to set up a separate Department of Consumer and Corporate Affairs. This federal body, backed by provincial and sometimes municipal organizations, now provides a cross-country army of watchdogs to guard the interests of consumers.

The federal department has four bureaus: Consumer Affairs, Corporate Affairs, Competition Policy, and Policy Coordination. The first of these, and the most active, breaks down into four more branches: Consumer Products, Product Safety, Consumer Services, and Legal Metrology. All elements of buying and selling—safety of contents, labeling, packaging, measures, retail inspection and enforcement, advertising, credit terms—are under constant scrutiny. Sales practices like "double ticketing" (putting a higher-price sticker over another) and "bait and switch" selling (advertising bargains not stocked in reasonable quantities) are already controlled through statutes and regulations. Fines for these offenses run up to $25,000 and a year's jail can also be imposed.

As yet, only a relatively few Canadians seem aware of these protective laws. To encourage wider public participation, the Bureau of Consumer Affairs invites citizens to write in with complaints about products or services anywhere in Canada. The complaint may be sent to the following address:

Bureau of Consumer Affairs
Department of Consumer and
   Corporate Affairs
Ottawa K1A 0C9

Does the buyer really want to know?

FEDERAL AND PROVINCIAL consumer-protection agencies spend long hours drafting regulations to ensure that innocent shoppers are not hoodwinked by rascally merchants. Advertising must not deceive, ingredients must be exactly stated, weights and measures must be scrupulously accurate. That's fine—but what if the buyer doesn't really want to know? The smart young matron in her Alaska sable won't rush to thank the bureaucrat who insists she's wearing dyed skunk. Don't tell her that her vicrina fox is sheep-skin, or that her Californian mink is ringtail cat.

Look at all the slinky fur jackets in the theater lobby or the smart restaurant: Russian leopard, electric seal, French chinchilla, Baltic tiger, Mendoza and Belgian beaver—every one of them the humble rabbit. In fact, under the National Trade Mark and True Labeling Act, a furrier can legally call rabbit fur by 38 different names.

If the furrier puts any label in a coat or jacket, the law states that the true fur name must be given along with the phony. But, who really wants to know?

Food and Drugs Act

Canada was a trailblazer in grading foods (beef, flour, fruits) for quality, and in the controlled labeling of canned goods. As early as 1790, Nova Scotia was demanding that either "prime," "second," or "third" be branded on each barrel of butter. Similarly, Canada was one of the first countries in the world to pass a national law forbidding the adulteration of food and drugs. That was in 1874.

The establishment and wide acceptance of standards of purity took more than a century. It was not until 1920 that the first really comprehensive Food and Drugs Act became law. Foods, household chemicals, cosmetics, medicines, and even contraceptives, came within the scope of the law.

The problem of ensuring accurate labeling and fair advertising was also tackled. Through the years the regulations have become tighter, but today the Canadian consumer can purchase almost any food or drug product with confidence.

Before a new drug is placed on the market, the manufacturer must supply detailed information about its safety and efficacy to Health and Welfare Canada. After the drug has been marketed, the manufacturer monitors its use by the public and reports back to the Drugs Directorate. Careful watch is kept over the drug for any unexpected side-effects— that is, symptoms that were not anticipated. At any time, a suspect product can be speedily removed from the drugstores.

It is illegal under all public health legislation to add any "foreign material" to food substances or to substitute one accepted ingredient for another. The penalty as set out under the Food and Drugs Act for the "presence of any rotten, filthy, putrid, decomposed or diseased animal or vegetable substance" in a food or drug product can be as much as a fine of $5,000 and/or three years in prison.

Separate parliamentary acts set out national standards for the quality and packaging of fish and related products, grains, eggs, honey, cheese and maple sugar products prepared for the interprovincial and export markets. Most provinces have matching legislation to ensure country-wide standards of quality.

Inspectors, with power to remove goods and impose penalties, fan out from regional offices to check both manufacturing plants and retail stores.

The various laws are administered by the Health Protection Branch of the Department of National Health and Welfare, the Departments of Agriculture and Fisheries. All of these departments work in cooperation with the Bureau of Consumer Affairs at the Department of Consumer and Corporate Affairs.

Common names of foods

Food manufacturers are under a legal obligation to "call a spade a spade." Consumers must not be misled concerning the exact nature of the food they buy. For example, margarine must be called by its own name, and the label cannot depict dairy symbols (such as a drawing of a cow) that suggest the product is butter.

If some of the butterfat content has been removed from milk, the resulting fluid must be labeled, for example, as "2% butterfat content." If all the butterfat is removed, the milk will be labeled "Skim."

If a food contains added coloring, then the manufacturer is required to specify on the package the presence of such a substance with the declaration of "food coloring" in the list of ingredients.

Use of additives

Food laws insist that the consumer be informed of all artificial substances in a product. All ingredients, including additives from either man-made or natural sources, must be declared on the label.

Certain potentially dangerous substances added to flavor, color or increase volume are prohibited. A recent example is saccharine which was banned for use in foods. Diabetics and others with special dietary needs, however, can purchase it in pharmacies as a tabletop sweetener. The sale of beef from animals injected with the growth hormone DES (Diethylstilbesterol) is prohibited in Canada.

In foods such as breakfast cereals and breads, manufacturers often volunteer a breakdown of the "nutritional" additives present. These sound impressive: "Iron 4.0 mg per 28 g (1 oz.) serving", but few customers realize that these elements are usually present in the natural substances. At this writing, Canada was developing stricter nutritional labeling regulations to provide consumers with detailed breakdowns of nutrients in packaged foods. The new system will give the recommended daily intake for any nutrient in one serving of a food product.

Accurate labeling

The law considers misleading, false or incorrect labeling, an offense. The buyer must not be misled by words or symbols about the "character, strength, quality or quantity of an article." With packaged foods, the label must state the name and address of the manufacturer, the names of all the ingredients (in descending order of quantity), the net weight of the contents, and the presence of any additive.

Under the Food and Drugs Act, if the shelf life of a product is 90 days or less, the label must have a "durable-life date," as well as instructions for preservation. For all products, the packaging date and the term "best before" must also appear on the label.

No cure-alls permitted

The first two trademarks registered in Canada (1861) were for Good Samaritan Balm ("for asthma, quinsy, frosted feet and toothache") and for Indian Root Pills ("for biliousness, indigestion, the stomach and bowels"). Today, under the strictures of the Food and Drugs Act, no one can advertise "cures" for any of the following conditions:

Schedule		Food and Drugs		Chap. F-27
	SCHEDULE A		ANNEXE A	
	(Section 3)		(Article 3)	

Alcoholism	Alcoolisme
Alopecia	Alopécie
Anxiety state	Appendicite
Appendicitis	Artériosclérose
Arteriosclerosis	Arthrite
Arthritis	Cancer
Bladder disease	Coeur (maladies)
Cancer	Convulsions
Convulsions	Dépression
Depression	Diabète
Diabetes	Dysenterie
Disease of the prostate	Epilepsie
Disorder of menstrual flow	Etats d'angoisse
Dysentery	Foie (maladies)
Edematous state	Gale
Epilepsy	Gangrène
Gall bladder disease	Glande thyroïdienne (affections)
Gangrene	Glaucome
Glaucoma	Goutte
Gout	Hernie
Heart disease	Hypertension
Hernia	Hypotension
Hypertension	Impétigo
Hypotension	Impuissance sexuelle
Impetigo	Influenza
Influenza	Leucémie
Kidney disease	Maladies thrombotiques et embolies
Leukemia	Maladies vénériennes
Liver disease	Nausées et vomissements de la grossesse
Nausea and vomiting of pregnancy	Obésité
Obesity	Oedème
Pleurisy	Pleurésie
Pneumonia	Pneumonie
Poliomyelitis	Poliomyélite
Rheumatic fever	Prostate (maladies)
Rheumatoid arthritis	Reins (maladies)
Scabies	Rhumatisme articulaire aigu
Septicemia	Septicémie
Sexual impotence	Tétanos
Tetanus	Troubles du flot menstruel
Thrombotic and Embolic disorders	Tuberculose
Thyroid disease	Tumeurs
Tuberculosis	Ulcères des voies intestinales
Tumor	Vaginite
Ulcer of the gastro-intestinal tract	Vésicule biliaire (maladies)
Vaginitis	Vessie (maladies)
Venereal disease	

SOR/67-259; SOR/77-824; SOR/81-195   DORS/67-259; DORS/77-824; DORS/81-195

In the case of proprietary medicines (brand-name drugs available without a doctor's prescription) the labels must reveal the presence, as well as the quantity, of all chemical compounds. This permits you to compare the strengths of the various pharmaceutical ingredients. For example, the important part of headache tablets, acetylsalicylic acid (which is sold as A.S.A. and often called "aspirin"), is measured in grains per tablet. You may find that you have been paying more for a brand-name tablet than for a "discount" one, although the labels show both have comparable strengths.

If you are allergic to various chemical compounds, you should pay even closer attention to the fine print on a label. Many cough medicines, for example, contain codeine, a drug that may cause unpleasant side-effects. Many antibiotic capsules prescribed under a brand name contain penicillin which could prove dangerous if you are allergic to it.

Federal labeling regulations indirectly prevent a drug manufacturer from trying to foist a "cure-all" drug on the public. If you suffer from arthritis, for instance, you are not likely to buy a bottle of a white mixture, however praised it may be, if you read on the label that it contains nothing more than water and cornstarch.

Labeling regulations require accurate descriptions of fur garments, the jewels in watch movements, and the fiber content of textiles. There are national standards for the sizes of children's clothes and shoes. Although not required by law, labels bearing one of five symbols now appear on textiles to indicate how the garment should be cleaned and pressed.

"Miracle" cosmetics

Some consumers pay good money for products which promise miracles: creams that remove wrinkles, lotions that banish acne, and shampoos that cure dandruff. Anyone who buys cosmetics which fail to meet the advertised claims can sue the maker for damages—either for breach of warranty or for misrepresentation. It is difficult, however, for consumers to prove that they believed in the promised miracles when the product was bought.

The consumer is more directly protected by the federal Combines Investigation Act which makes misleading advertising a criminal offense. There are also regulations under the Food and Drugs Act aimed at controlling the highly lucrative cosmetics business. When you closely examine the advertising and labeling of these "sucker" products, you will usually find that the manufacturer has avoided any outright claim for cures, however suggestive the advertising or label might be.

Drugs under prescription

Certain drugs are so dangerous that the consumer can only obtain them through a doctor's prescription. As a further protection, only licensed pharmacists are permitted to prepare and sell such drugs.

All provinces have laws that require the work of filling any drug prescription be done by a member of a recognized college of pharmacy, someone holding a degree in pharmacology. In Ontario, for example, the druggist behind the prescription counter must hold the degree of B.Sc. in pharmacy.

Drug products can be sold without prescription only if they are registered under the federal Proprietary and Patent Medicine Act. This includes such common drug products as A.S.A., cough syrups and stomach powders. Their manufacture is strictly controlled under federal law.

Control of narcotics

Those drugs that dull the senses and induce sleep are called narcotics. Canadian law recognizes two kinds of narcotics: those considered addictive—that is, habit-forming—and thus especially harmful; and a wider range of others that can be dangerous if used wrongly or to excess. Heroin and opium fall into the first group; such drugs as L.S.D., mescaline and the amphetamines, into the second. Both types are controlled by federal law—the first by the Narcotics Control Act, and the second by the Food and Drugs Act. There were recently 106 narcotics recognized in Canadian law.

Possession of narcotics for personal use and for trafficking (selling or distributing), as well as their cultivation, are considered criminal offenses. Offenders are vigorously prosecuted; the maximum penalty for trafficking—seldom if ever imposed—is life imprisonment. Some citizens seek milder penalties—or none at all—for the possession of small quantities of marijuana. The Narcotics Control Act, however, still provides for a maximum sentence of up to seven years' imprisonment for possession of marijuana.

Some narcotics are beneficially used in medicine; an example is morphine, the famous painkiller that is a cousin to the notorious heroin. When morphine and other narcotics are used medically, the possession restrictions under the Narcotics Control Act do not, of course, apply.

A special federal license is required to import, manufacture and sell narcotics of any type; and accurate records must be kept of all such transactions. The cultivation of *Cannabis sativa*, the marijuana plant, or of opium poppies is rigidly controlled.

Two-way protection

In the realm of buying and selling, the law tries its best to keep danger out of your way, as well as to protect you should you be wronged. In a country that prides itself on free competition and free choice, however, the law cannot regulate everything—nor can it foresee what you, the consumer, will choose to do. You are expected to use common sense and a certain amount of caution in making your purchases as well as in making use of them.

If you are hoodwinked in a deal, it might be your own fault. But, if you have been deliberately misled or if a deal does not work out as you were promised—and it means financial loss or damage—you can probably sue for breach of contract.

If you have suffered personal injury, you can look to the law of torts in preparing your claim for damages. (*See* Chapter 18, "What is a tort?")

There are specific statutes, discussed throughout this chapter, that regulate certain products and areas of activity. Under the authority of these laws, inspectors and government agencies may penalize anyone who disobeys the regulations. In some fields, responsibility is shared. For example, the federal government is concerned with the safety and quality of the food itself. The provincial and municipal governments ensure that foods do not become the source of the transmission of diseases. Under provincial public health legislation, inspectors check food in restaurants, packaging plants and slaughterhouses.

Beauty and the law

THESE DAYS Canadians spend more than $600,000,000 a year on cosmetics—including lipstick, eye shadow, rouge, powders, deodorants, perfumes, lotions, mouthwash, shampoos and hair dyes. Health and Welfare Canada does its best to ensure that, at the least, these products will not do you any actual harm.

The cosmetic section of the Food and Drugs Act states that no one shall sell a product which contains an ingredient that may cause injury to health when used as directed. The regulations demand that the name and address of the manufacturer or distributor must be printed on the label.

Other regulations limit the manufacturer's choice of package to standard sizes and require the net amount of the contents to be declared on the label. Some hair dyes contain a chemical that can cause skin irritations, and this should not be used on the eyelashes or eyebrows. The dyes should not be used near a skin cut or abrasion. Cosmetic labels should carry cautionary statements about possible risks.

Manufacturers are not permitted to publish claims of "facial rejuvenation" or "cell regeneration." Creams may keep facial skin moist but nothing will "smooth away" wrinkles. They're there for keeps.

In the home

Hazards in the home

Poison control centers

Warnings to children

The perilous pot

Hearing aids

Is the dry cleaner liable?

THE FRUSTRATION of trying to open a package—be it a bag of sugar, a carton of milk or a box of biscuits—and nearly demolishing it in the process, is something that most people have experienced. They look in dismay at the battered container—then they notice the caption: "Open at other end." The situation would be amusing except that labels often also include warnings, as well as special instructions for the use of the product. The point is that most people never read such labels.

Products are not dangerous if they are used and handled as directed—the law sees to that. Some, however, if used carelessly, can be dangerous and even lethal. To protect the consumer, the lawmakers of Canada have banned certain products. They have also forbidden certain materials to be used and have set up standards for the manufacture of many products.

You should read and heed all warnings and instructions that are printed on the label or included in a package. Parents should make sure that they inspect everything they give children, whether the children are old enough to read or not.

Hazards in the home
Poisonous or hazardous substances for use in the home must carry adequate, clearly understandable warnings, both in words and in pictures—such as the skull and crossbones or other symbol.

A stronger deterrent on the manufacturers of such products is the fear of a damage suit by an injured consumer who suffers because he did not know that the product was potentially dangerous. A housewife who mixes a cake for her family after she has used a toilet-bowl cleanser and who somehow manages to get this caustic substance into the food, could probably sue the maker of the cleanser for a large sum if a member of her family suffered injury or death, because she was not advised of the dangerous ingredients in the cleanser. In 1981, there were more than 26,500 reported (nondrug) household poisonings in Canada.

As of 1971, under the Hazardous Products Act, the container of every potentially dangerous household product (bleaches, cleansers, hair sprays, antifreeze) must be labeled, in English and French, to inform you not only of the danger of the contents but also of the first-aid treatment to employ should an accident occur.

Poison control centers
The Department of National Health and Welfare has provided for the establishment of poison control centers at hospitals, or other convenient locations, for the treatment of accidents caused by any form of poisoning. Today, the centers are funded by provincial governments. The statistics gathered by the Department of National Health and Welfare from the centers provide guidelines for new legislation to control the sale, storage, accessibility and use of dangerous substances.

If you don't already know where to find a center nearby, you should immediately check your phone book or ask your doctor, the police or a hospital. If someone has been poisoned at your house, make sure you track down the container concerned and then telephone the poison control center or your doctor. If you use a baby-sitter, she should know where the required phone numbers are.

Warnings to children

About 74 percent of all reported (non-drug) household poisonings involve children under the age of five. Manufacturers of drugs and hazardous products are required to include on their bottles and packages warnings to parents to keep certain substances out of the reach of children, or instructions to give certain medicines to children only in limited doses.

Of course, it is the parents' duty to take reasonable care of their children. Beneficial medicines, or useful products, cannot be barred simply because a child *might* get hold of them, with possible tragic results. However, if a manufacturer does not comply with regulations calling for warnings to children, the federal government can demand the relabeling of the product, remove the product from the shelves, or initiate a court action against the manufacturer. Should a mother give a drug to a baby, not knowing its effects because the necessary warning was not on the label, she could sue the manufacturer for damages if anything serious should happen to the baby.

Children in danger

Federal authorities are involved in a massive campaign to test toys, equipment, clothing and foods, in order to create and enforce national standards of safety for young children. In a recent year, 17 Canadian children under the age of five died in their cribs from suffocation. Regulations issued from time to time under the Hazardous Products Act are rigorously enforced.

Any toy which contains any poisonous or corrosive substance or is decorated with a lead-base paint is banned. Crayons and modeling clays must be nontoxic. Plush toys must have securely wired eyes and no internal sharp points. The use of glass, metal fasteners, elastic, exposed nails, screws and bolts is closely regulated. All plastic bags containing toys must have a notice warning parents to take off the bag before handing the toy to a child.

Straight pins are not allowed in dolls' clothing, and all projectile toys (like arrows and darts) must have protective tips. The shafts of push-pull toys must be built in such a way as to minimize the danger if a child should fall. The stuffing in toy animals must be clean and free of harmful materials.

Electrically operated toys must meet the safety levels set by the Canadian Standards Association. Wet cell batteries must remain leakproof, even when treated roughly. Toy steam engines and chemistry sets offer obvious dangers and are subject to special rules. Sulfuric acid, for instance, is banned in chemistry sets lest young "scientists" should harm themselves or their playmates.

Teething rings and pacifiers came under close inspection when analysts at Consumer and Corporate Affairs discovered that certain colored jelly used as attractive packing in teethers contained harmful microorganisms. Two brands manufactured in Montreal were taken off the market because they contained bacteria which could have caused eye infections. Medical experts are constantly checking all crib and playpen equipment.

Any hair or fur used on dolls or toy animals, or in funny beards or wigs for Halloween, must not be dangerously flammable. The same fire hazard standards that apply to fabrics in general also apply to materials used in dolls' clothing. If you are buying lights to brighten your family's Christmas tree, you should follow the expert safety advice offered by government researchers. For example, don't use indoor lights for outdoor display; you need heavier wiring and waterproof sockets.

A bubble gum wrapper that gave kids an idea for a potentially dangerous poolside game, and a magic trick with matches that was shown on a cereal box were both removed by the makers under pressure from the Bureau of Consumer Affairs.

Car seats for children too small for seat belts are evaluated for safety and controlled. Seventy percent of the seats originally on the market did not meet the department's standards; the strength of the webbing, the depth of the padding and the design of head-restraints are regulated. The simple type of infant's seat that was merely hooked over the back of the car's seat is banned.

The perilous pot

The Hazardous Products (Glazed Ceramics) Regulations are among the least known consumer protection laws. Even the hobbyist with his small basement kiln seldom realizes the serious health risk that is involved in working with lead glazes common in ceramic production.

The same lead that is recognized as a health hazard when it is given off by an automobile running on leaded gasoline can be released from the lead glaze on a pottery storage jar or bowl into acidic foods (like fruit juices). As a soluble compound this contamination can be dangerous, especially to young children. There are minute traces of lead in all foods, and the healthy body can take care of it. But if too much lead builds up in the bones, it can produce tragic results.

The current federal regulations state that glazed ceramic tableware or kitchenware must not release more than seven parts per million of lead in an 18-hour period when permitted to stand filled with a four percent acetic-acid solution at room temperature. This solution, by the way, is merely the strength of common vinegar. Since the law was passed, some items of Italian and English pottery have been withdrawn from Canadian stores.

Because glazed ceramics are durable, a lot of suspect pottery sold before the regulations were issued is probably still being used. It is quite safe to keep on using it— *except* to contain acidic foods like tomatoes, oranges, lemons, grapefruit (and their juices), cranberries, pickles, salads, vinegars and soft drinks. These should be kept in glass jars or plastic containers.

Storage of flammables

Regulations are imposed on manufacturers to give directions for the proper sale, use and storage of flammable products. But, if the homeowner is negligent with

Torture tests for toys

MORE THAN ANYTHING ELSE PERHAPS, a toy is a token of simple love—all the more reason why extra care should be taken to ensure that the gift cannot hurt or maim the child.

In a government laboratory in Ottawa, qualified engineers submit hundreds of toys to torture tests trying to eradicate health hazards from the toy counters. Dolls are torn limb from limb and their beady eyes pulled out; toy guns and bow-and-arrow sets are tested in a variety of ways. Chemistry sets get a special scrutiny. Rattles, teething rings—anything that a baby can suck—are tested for sharp edges and other faults.

All too frequently, indulgent uncles and grandfathers, somewhat out of touch with modern materials, choose gift toys for children without being aware of potential harm to the recipient. The suitability of a toy for the age and ability of the child is not always considered. A wood-etching set that is fine for a smart ten-year-old could be hazardous in the hands of his seven-year-old sister. Novelty toys that make use of the jequirity bean from Mexico are banned: these glossy scarlet beans with a black tip (sometimes used as eyes in toys) can be fatal if chewed and swallowed.

The testers look for hidden dangers, hazards the hurrying shopper wouldn't think about. If a cuddly toy has eyes that are fastened to the ends of pins, the small child may pull the eye out of the toy and try to poke it in his own eye. Anything that can possibly be inhaled or swallowed is double-checked; in a recent year, 31 Canadian babies died of suffocation (choking).

There are thousands of variations of toys reaching the shops every year and the testers cannot check them all. Most manufacturers collaborate willingly, sending new toys in to be tested before putting them on sale. The government tries to guide rather than direct, but any suspect toy can be seized under the regulations of the Hazardous Products Act.

such storage and a fire results, he will be blamed. Such negligence might lead to the cancellation of his home insurance. The wise man will not keep gasoline or other flammables in his house or garage.

The sale of some flammables or similar substances in any quantity is controlled by law. For example, Ontario's Gasoline Handling Act requires you to get a license before you can sell gasoline or an associated product to the public. The other provinces have similar legislation. The regulations set down specifications for tanks holding gasoline, kerosene, naphtha, and so on. Depending on their size and contents, the tanks must be a set distance apart, and a set distance from property boundaries.

The federal Explosives Act regulates the manufacture, sale, storage and importation into Canada of explosive substances. Licenses must be obtained from the federal Department of Energy, Mines and Resources. Violating the act is a criminal offense, and the department's officers have the power to confiscate and destroy unauthorized explosives.

Hearing aids

Slightly more than a million Canadians suffer from some form of hearing loss, but only four percent of this group use hearing aids. This represents a potential market for roughly 40,000 hearing aids, costing up to $600 apiece. And there are a few unscrupulous companies which seek to exploit that market. Markups have been reported as high as 230 percent.

At present there are no specific federal regulations for hearing aid selling and fitting. However, a Hearing Aid Enquiry in 1970 recommended that the provincial governments pass uniform legislation to license dealers and to enforce minimum training standards on the salespeople (they are often called "consultants"). In Quebec, there are regulations requiring dealers to have a certificate to sell and adjust hearing aids.

The Department of Consumer and Corporate Affairs is planning to formulate and publish a code of "acceptable trade practices" for the hearing aid industry. The government stands ready to enforce the provisions of the Consumer Packaging and Labeling Act (1974) and the Combines Investigation Act against any misleading advertising or misrepresentation in any sales promotions (which sometimes include door-to-door campaigns and referral schemes).

You should see a doctor before you buy a hearing aid—the equipment is a boon to some but of little use to others. Get detailed brochures from several manufacturers and compare the performance promises, *not* the aesthetic appeal.

Is the dry cleaner liable?

When you leave your dress or suit to be dry-cleaned, either at the service center of the department store or at a separate establishment, the cleaner is legally responsible for any damage done by his carelessness. He is also responsible if he loses your clothes, unless when you leave the articles he tells you that he will not be responsible for loss or damage, and unless he is doing the dry cleaning free of charge, in which case he is under a somewhat lesser duty to take care. Carelessness on his part still makes him liable, however, even if he is not charging a cent.

Even if the cleaner did not clear himself of responsibility, and even if you are paying for his services, he is still not responsible for your ruined clothing unless he or his employes had been careless. Since he is in the business, the law expects that he is an expert and demands from him a reasonably high standard of care. Again, what is "reasonable" is hard to pin down.

If the article to be cleaned is made of unusual or exotic material which a cleaner does not see in the normal course of business, and if he has not been warned by the customer to take special precautions, he would probably not be held responsible for any damage. Another situation would be if you brought to the cleaner a dress which had a label stating, "Do not dry-clean." Even if the label had been removed, or had fallen off, the cleaner would still be in the clear. The label was on the dress when you bought it, and it was up to you to see it, take notice of it, and therefore not attempt to have the dress dry-cleaned.

In the supermarket

Self-service selling

Liability for accidents

Accused of shoplifting

Headroom and cellophane

Control of perishables

Restaurants and imports

As DEPARTMENT stores and supermarkets began to dominate Canadian shopping, both in redeveloped downtown centers and in suburban plazas, customer and merchant alike were faced with new angles on old laws, and some situations that were entirely new. Customs developed from generations of "over-the-counter" trading—with an attentive salesclerk showing the goods and advising on qualities of wear or taste—are now so old-fashioned that they would mystify most customers.

Self-serve is the magic term that has changed the shopping scene at every level—except perhaps in expensive high-class shops. It was born of two elements: the ever-rising cost of labor, and the matching rise in public sophistication. Young girls now try on a whole rack of dresses in the same salon where their mothers would have hesitated to ask the saleslady for permission to slip into *one*. The new sales technique, through an open store design, also allows for a lavish and varied display of goods. Hundreds of items are placed right at the buyer's hand, to be picked up and closely examined.

While self-serve has made shopping easier and more fun, it has also brought problems. What happens, for instance, when the customer picks up an article from the shelf and accidentally breaks it? Does he have to pay for it? It could be an expensive porcelain figure. Must the store bear the risk of such breakage? Again, at what point is the shopper said to have "bought" the goods: when he first picks them up, or when he pays for them? Is it up to the buyer, left so much on his own, to make sure that he is not injured in falls, or while examining, say, plugged-in electrical appliances? The most troublesome problem may be that of shoplifting (by intent or through forgetfulness), so much easier when clerks are so few.

Self-service selling

All sales, however conducted, are in essence "contracts"—that is, binding agreements—under the law. And there is no absolute requirement for anything to be written down.

The law states that for a contract of sale to be valid (*i.e.* legal), a valid offer and a valid acceptance of that offer must first take place. When a store puts price-tagged goods on shelves, it is *not necessarily* making an offer to the public. This price tagging is viewed legally as a mere invitation to the potential customer to "treat," or negotiate, saying in effect, "I'm willing to offer you this article for a certain price." The *valid offer* does not occur in a self-serve shop until the customer presents the item to the cashier. The cashier then has the choice of accepting or rejecting the offer. It is a store's legal right to refuse to sell you something (for any reason), no matter how willing you are to pay for it.

The point at which the sale contract is completed is most important in considering the issues of responsibility for accidents and for theft. Thus, when a store operates on the self-serve principle it is important to define the point in time when the contract with the seller is considered closed—that is, when the offer is accepted.

The risk of loss belongs to the owner. This means that from the moment the cashier in a self-serve store accepts your money (your "offer," in legal terms) and puts the goods in your hands, it is up to you to protect the property. If you are buying from a store that offers home delivery, you are wise to have your purchases delivered. In the case of home delivery, the store is responsible until the goods arrive at your house or apartment.

Liability for accidents

If you drop a bottle of ketchup after lifting it from a supermarket shelf, you need not feel compelled to pay for it. Many large stores accept such breakage, without considering the legal position, purely as a matter of public relations policy. In a big operation, some mishaps are inevitable. Anyway, if the store tried to make you pay, you could argue that the sale contract had not been completed and thus the item was still the property of the store.

However, the storekeeper could maintain that you, the customer, had not exercised reasonable and proper care in handling property that was not yours, and therefore, you should pay for the ketchup. On the other hand, you could reply that it was the seller who did not exercise reasonable care; the bottle possibly had been precariously balanced on the edge of the shelf, or was dirty and hence slippery.

If someone dropped a dozen eggs and you happened to slip in the goo, twisting your ankle, you would not necessarily be able to sue unless you could prove that the store had had ample time to clean up the mess, or that it habitually left the floor in a dirty condition. You could have avoided the spill, or asked for help to cross it.

Supermarkets and department stores are subject to all the normal regulations concerning cleanliness, ventilation and sanitation that apply to retail premises. In general, they do more than the law requires in order to outdo their competitors.

The customer is (nearly) always right

Almost all of Canada's major department stores, and the great majority of the food supermarkets, now promise full customer satisfaction or, upon return of the merchandise, a complete refund of the purchase price. There are a few exceptions: certain goods "on sale," or perishables, or some lines of clothing and shoes. Some supermarkets will even give refunds on spoiled fruits and vegetables if they are returned the next day.

By law the buyer may cancel a sales contract if a definite promise made by the seller at the time of purchase is broken. Thus, if a store advertises "Satisfaction or money refunded," it has to stand by what it says. Of course, the definition of "satisfaction" is a bit tricky. Does it mean "reasonable satisfaction," or does it mean "complete and unquestionable satisfaction"? There have been cases where a buyer has sued on this point and won a refund, arguing that the seller should be prepared to honor the condition of satisfaction if it was dangled before the customer's eye to attract his business.

It is more than likely that a court would not stand behind a consumer who gave a ridiculous reason for his dissatisfaction. The consumer would likely have to prove that an average person buying the same product would be equally dissatisfied.

Accused of shoplifting

"Shoplifting" is really just another way of saying "stealing." (*See* Chapter 19, "The crime—society at bay.") However, since the introduction of self-serve shopping, the problem has become so prevalent that it should be discussed here as well.

Some social workers argue that the merchant contributes to the crime of shoplifting—in a sense, shares the blame—because he tempts people unfairly by placing expensive goods where they can be more easily stolen. This carries no weight in law. Theft is theft. It is like saying that the farmer is an accomplice of the thief because his apple trees laden with fruit are near the highway.

Several myths exist concerning shoplifting. One is that all the shoplifter has to do, when caught, is pay for the goods. Don't count on it! The management may accept your offer to pay and accept your excuse that the whole thing was a mistake or an oversight, or it may not.

Big stores lose so much money a year to shoplifters (some are professionals with a string of glib excuses) that managers are sometimes of necessity hardheaded.

Another misconception is that a person cannot be arrested for shoplifting until he has stepped from the shop into the street. Not true! A store and its contents are private property and a person suspected of stealing can be arrested in the shop, in the street, in the shop next door, or at home. Any member of the staff can ask a suspected shoplifter to accompany him to the manager's office and, furthermore, if the suspect refuses, he can make a "citizen's arrest." This is a serious action to take and can lead to a charge of false arrest against the store if the suspect is eventually acquitted.

It must be proved "beyond reasonable doubt" that the accused person intended to, and actually did, take the goods. In other words, the "taking" has to have been deliberate theft. The apprehended shoplifter can, and very often does, argue that

he merely forgot to pay for the goods; or that he was distracted, perhaps; or even sick and under medication. The judge would have to decide if the accused was telling the truth. In a self-service store, merely putting goods in your pockets is not necessarily theft. To be convicted in such a situation it would normally have to be proved that you were given the opportunity of paying but did not do so. Until a person has passed a cash register, there is no proof that he has actually committed theft. Nothing but the clearest intention to steal would satisfy the court. But you should note that in criminal law someone who has been accused is presumed to have intended the outcome of his actions. This means that if you are found to have a bottle of perfume under your raincoat,

The label that tells all

Thanks to government consumer laws, anyone with the time to spare and good eyesight can find out from packaged food labels just what he is eating. That is, assuming he knows what things like thiamine and niacinamide are when they are on his plate. The label illustrated is typical of many on the supermarket shelf today:

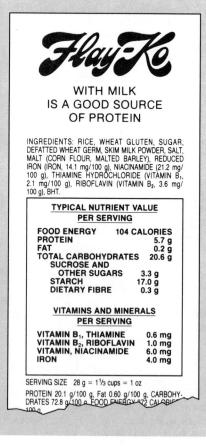

**WITH MILK
IS A GOOD SOURCE
OF PROTEIN**

INGREDIENTS: RICE, WHEAT GLUTEN, SUGAR, DEFATTED WHEAT GERM, SKIM MILK POWDER, SALT, MALT (CORN FLOUR, MALTED BARLEY), REDUCED IRON (IRON, 14.1 mg/100 g), NIACINAMIDE (21.2 mg/100 g), THIAMINE HYDROCHLORIDE (VITAMIN B$_1$, 2.1 mg/100 g), RIBOFLAVIN (VITAMIN B$_2$, 3.6 mg/100 g), BHT.

TYPICAL NUTRIENT VALUE PER SERVING	
FOOD ENERGY	104 CALORIES
PROTEIN	5.7 g
FAT	0.2 g
TOTAL CARBOHYDRATES	20.6 g
SUCROSE AND OTHER SUGARS	3.3 g
STARCH	17.0 g
DIETARY FIBRE	0.3 g

VITAMINS AND MINERALS PER SERVING	
VITAMIN B$_1$, THIAMINE	0.6 mg
VITAMIN B$_2$, RIBOFLAVIN	1.0 mg
VITAMIN, NIACINAMIDE	6.0 mg
IRON	4.0 mg

SERVING SIZE   28 g = 1⅓ cups = 1 oz

PROTEIN 20.1 g/100 g, Fat 0.60 g/100 g, CARBOHYDRATES 72.8 g/100 g, FOOD ENERGY 372 CALORIES/100 g.

the prosecution assumes that you intended to steal it. They don't have to produce a witness who can say, "Mary told me she was going to steal it." The action speaks for itself.

The bigger stores usually have some kind of surveillance system. It may be a set of mirrors, or floorwalkers who look just like ordinary customers themselves. Some stores have had such great losses to shoplifters that they are using uniformed guards to try to prevent thefts. Expensive items sometimes carry a magnetic sticker which rings a bell as the goods pass the cash desk. Closed-circuit television systems, which are coming into wider use, are monitored by a security officer in an interior office. Where these TV systems are in use, the management usually posts signs to warn the public. Store detectives have no more legal power than any other private citizen. If they make a citizen's arrest they must hand the person over to the police without delay.

If it happens that you are falsely accused of shoplifting, it is better not to start a riot on the spot. Remember, everyone makes mistakes. You will probably be asked politely to go to the manager's office. There, you will have the choice of either explaining or speaking to your lawyer by telephone. The manager does not *want* to charge you with a crime. First of all, he knows that the court will have to be convinced *beyond reasonable doubt* of your intention to steal. Secondly, he knows that any court action is considered bad for his store's "image." He may accept your honest explanation and your payment for any goods you might have in your possession. Or he might not.

If you were arrested by the store detective, roughly forced to go to the manager's office, then acquitted in court, you would possibly be able to charge the store with assault and false arrest (if you had no "stolen goods" in your possession).

If you were charged with shoplifting and found guilty, you could be fined or given two years in prison (for a theft of up to $200). First offenders are sometimes treated leniently in the hope that the sharp experience of arrest and trial will be enough to teach them a lesson.

Headroom in packages

Self-serve selling has greatly changed the packaging industry. Market analysts, advertisers and artists rack their brains to come up with the most attractive and tempting "dress" for their product. When all table salt is the same quality and price, the choice depends on the package. As the shopper reaches for the salt in the supermarket, which package will be chosen?

One result of the hot competition is that packages of cereal and detergents, among other products, are often somewhat larger than the contents require. The empty space in the package or jar is known in the trade as "headroom." Ecologists worrying about the mountains of refuse we create every day, and economy-minded shoppers seeking price reductions have asked the government to stop the practice of allowing headroom. Since 1974, this practice has been restrained by the federal Consumer Packaging and Labeling Act.

Fraudulent misrepresentation, or deceiving the customer, is against the law. When headroom is noticeable, the maker will cover himself by stating on the package, "As a result of handling, settling of the contents may result," or words to that effect. You will find also that the weight and/or volume of the contents will be clearly stated on any package (especially if it is not of the see-through variety). You do better to consider price by unit—that is, by the gram or kilogram—rather than by the package. (*See* "Guarantees and standards" in this chapter.)

If you paid a high price for a big package on the assumption that it contained a large quantity of the desired product, and then found that it was half empty, and the label did not state the volume of contents or warn of settling, you could accuse the manufacturer of "fraudulent misrepresentation." You would need to prove only that the actual quantity of product inside the package was not worth the price paid, presumably, by quoting as evidence the usual price of the commodity elsewhere.

Goods under cellophane

The consumer watchdogs have been alert to ensure that the widespread use of cellophane or other plastic wrapping does not create its own kind of misrepresentation in food packaging.

Although the transparency of the wrapping certainly allows housewives selecting the family's meat to "see what they are getting" with most prepackaged cuts, a few over-eager (or sometimes unscrupulous) packers arrange the slices to conceal fat, giving the impression that the cellophane-wrapped package is "all meat." There are cases, too, of chops being stacked to emphasize the lean. The fattier hamburger meat can possibly be passed off as "ground round steak" when the package looks so fresh and appealing.

There is no specific regulation forbidding this practice in Canada, although the federal packaging regulations state that prepackaged foods must not be "filled" in such a way as to mislead the shopper. In the United States, a regulation requires that 80 percent of the meat be visible in a cellophane package.

Our public health statutes of cleanliness exercise strict control wherever meat, or other raw foods, are prepared. Canadians visiting Europe are often shocked to see meat hanging inside and outside butcher shops, attracting flies and gathering street dust and fumes. Our laws forbid all displays of meat that fail to respect the standards set for sanitation and refrigeration. In this endeavor, cellophane and other wraps are important in keeping foods free from impurities and from early spoiling.

Another point: If you are tempted by the fresh red color of that slab of sirloin in the supermarket cool shelf, go ahead and buy it. It is possible that a chemical may have been used to enhance the color of the meat. In Canada, there are no restrictions on the use of chemical additives for this purpose, as long as the additive has not been prohibited. While there is no specific regulation about using them —there are lamps, for instance, which produce a red glow—a possible charge of fraudulent misrepresentation discourages stores from tricks of that sort.

"Whiter than white"

Phrases such as "whiter than white" (once used in a detergent sales campaign) are typical examples of "puffing" in advertising—that is, exaggeration intended to be harmless and made with the assumption that the consumer really knows there can be no such thing as "whiter than white." In the world of advertising, this is the aggressive manufacturer's way of saying, "We think this is the best product on the market today." It is legally impossible for you to complain that your clothes did not come out "whiter than white" after using the detergent, since there simply is no such condition.

However, if some detergent caused substantial damage to your clothing, unless the package stated that you use the washing powder or liquid at your own risk, you could probably sue the manufacturer for the value of the damaged clothes. You would have to prove, however, that you had used the cleansing product exactly as directed by the instructions on the package. It is the manufacturer's legal duty to the consumer to see that the product is reasonably fit and safe for the purpose for which it is intended. In legal terms, this means that the goods must be of "merchantable quality."

Control of perishables

Provincial laws demand the proper care of perishable foods when they are in storage or for sale in shop premises. Persons who handle food must also be specially careful of cleanliness and health. Inspectors check commercial premises where food is kept and can order the premises closed, and the food confiscated, until conditions are corrected. They can take legal action which can result in tough fines.

The building or place where food is sold is also subject to government specifications which call for proper ventilation, separate construction of washrooms, provision of hot water and towels.

Employes in food industries can also be subjected to periodic inspection for contagious diseases, such as tuberculosis.

Inspectors from various government departments—about six separate federal departments as well as provincial officials are involved—can descend on slaughterhouses, grading stations and retail outlets to check the quality and wholesomeness of food offered for sale. If you are dissatisfied with the quality of any food you buy, the provincial branches of the Consumers' Association of Canada, your provincial consumer agency (or Public Health authority), or the federal Bureau of Consumer Affairs would like to hear from you.

Checking on the farm

Provincial inspectors can descend on any farm to check that all livestock raised for food, either dead or alive, is fit for human consumption.

Some animals are more susceptible to germs than others. Hogs, for instance, can carry harmful microorganisms and may be destroyed if they are found to be eating rotting material. Farm slaughterhouses are inspected periodically for cleanliness and to ensure that only humane killing is practiced. Most slaughtering for the urban market is done at a few central slaughterhouses, and these are thoroughly and constantly inspected by officials of Agriculture Canada.

In recent years, livestock production in Canada has stabilized. This development reflects a change in Canadian eating habits. Since 1970, the per capita consumption of beef has fallen from 45 kilograms annually to 36 kilograms. Pork consumption, in the same period, has increased from 25 to 29 kilograms a year. The supply of poultry is strictly controlled by the Canadian Chicken Marketing Agency to meet our domestic needs. In general, Ca-

nadians eat what they produce. The exception is pork, of which 20 to 25 percent is exported.

Food animals—mostly cattle—imported from Europe are checked and processed at maximum security quarantine stations, the largest of which is situated at Grosse Isle, Quebec. France also cooperates in managing a separate livestock quarantine station on the island of Saint Pierre, southeast of Newfoundland in the Gulf of St. Lawrence. All food animals coming from the United States are screened and graded, although most of the cross-border traffic in food animals flows in the other direction.

Spraying of crops

Pollution was big news in the early 1970s and many housewives worried if the fruit and vegetables they brought home from the corner grocery or the supermarket had been sprayed with some dangerous chemical. Several sprays essential in pest control are dangerous (in major doses). Harassed officials in the federal and provincial departments of agriculture try to strike a sensible and safe balance.

Both federal and provincial governments have passed legislation controlling the manufacture and use of certain pesticides. The poisons used must all be approved under the Pest Control Products Act. As knowledge and experience expand, the use of some poisons has been limited and, in some cases, banned. A good example is D.D.T.: until 1969, it was still approved for use on a total of 62 food

Seeking the comfortable shoe

WHEN YOU REALIZE that you will walk about 400,000 kilometres—that's ten times around the world—in your lifetime, the care that you should take in choosing shoes is obvious. A pinching shoe is a curse, and can deform the foot of a growing child. Consumer advisors suggest that, because shoe sizes vary from one maker to another, you should always have your feet

measured before buying. *Both* feet. Most people have one foot larger than the other; if this is pronounced, then fit your larger foot and have the other shoe adjusted.

Feet expand in hot weather and when you put your weight on them. So always walk around in a new pair before paying. Never buy shoes thinking you'll "break them in." They'll break you, more likely.

Check these fire safety points on your farm

1 Clean up. Get rid of trash and rubbish, cast-off clothing, mattresses, old furniture, papers and dirty rags. Keep weathered surfaces painted and remove or replace old, rotting wood and fencing.

2 Have electric wiring and fuses checked by government inspectors. Replace worn wiring and use only 15-ampere fuses unless a circuit is specifically designed for a larger one.

3 Keep ordinary wiring and lighting away from wet areas—guard against breakage and contact with any combustible materials.

All electrical equipment must be CSA approved.

4 Be sure your pump is on a separate, dependable electrical circuit and located away from other buildings to safeguard the pressure of the water supply for fire fighting.

5 Put up "No Smoking" signs in hazardous areas.

6 Have the right extinguishers in the right places. Inspect them frequently and recharge when necessary.

7 Petroleum products should be stored at least 12 metres from any other building—underground

storage is best. If aboveground, tank should be on noncombustible support.

8 Always refuel equipment outdoors, away from open flames and sparks—be sure motor is shut off and cool before refueling.

9 Always keep cistern (and stock pond) safely full for fire fighting. Make sure it's accessible to fire apparatus at all times of the year.

10 Check lightning protection and grounding—check TV antenna stability and grounding (don't put it on the chimney).

11 "Bottled" gas cylinders should be securely fastened to a firm support and resting on a solid foundation, and located away from windows and basement openings.

12 Your fire-fighting tools should be accessible in an emergency.

13 Chimneys must be kept in good repair—especially in attic areas. Bracket supports are not approved. Rusty or pitted smoke pipes must be replaced and must be supported by approved metal thimbles when passing through walls and ceilings. Stoves and heaters must be kept away from walls, furniture and other combustible material.

crops. Now, the weed killer 2,4,5-T is not sold to the public and can only be used to control brush growth on rights-of-way and certain open rangelands.

The consumer himself must be careful in preparing food. The government cannot be in the nation's kitchens, and the consumer is expected to know that fruits and vegetables are often treated in order to control pests and plant diseases. You should wash these foods as a normal part of preparing them for the table.

Inspection of restaurants

The federal Food and Drugs Act forbids the sale of food that is unfit for human consumption or was manufactured or prepared under unsanitary conditions. This act gives government inspectors the authority to enter any slaughterhouse or packing plant at any reasonable time and remove any food they think is bad. They also have the power to close any establishment that doesn't meet acceptable standards. Provincial laws directly control standards in restaurants, hotel dining rooms and cafeterias.

Although some "greasy spoon" cafés make it seem otherwise, it is difficult to obtain a license for a restaurant. There are standards for the construction of the building which houses the restaurant, cleanliness of the employes, sanitary conditions where the food is being prepared, amount of ventilation, provision of washrooms and equipment for disinfecting utensils. If any of these requirements is not met, the province concerned can refuse a license to serve food, or it can cancel an existing license.

If you see a cook or waiter smoking a cigarette while preparing or serving food, you have grounds to complain to your local public health office.

Inspection of factories

It doesn't seem to bother most housewives that Blodgett's Homemade Chocolates or LeBlanque's Homemade Onion Soup are actually produced in huge factories with the ingredients brought in by the truckload. In some factories, no human hand touches the product from the unloading chute to the canning line. That motherly looking person shown smiling on the label is probably just a satisfied shareholder or more likely a professional model. The products may not be truly "homemade," but chances are they are safer to eat than if Aunt Mabel had made them in her own kitchen—the government inspectors see to that.

Provincial public health inspectors check food-producing factories, dairies, bakeries and restaurants. Everything must be clean and sanitary, the work force included. The inspectors scrutinize facilities for refrigeration, sterilization and storage. Penalties are severe, and firms can be warned, fined and even closed.

Working conditions in factories are inspected by officers of the provincial departments of labor. Apart from the basic purpose of making sure that factories are following the safety codes, the inspectors also see that the washroom facilities meet cleanliness standards—an important factor in consumer protection where food production is concerned.

Inspection of imports

The Customs and Excise branch of the Department of National Revenue controls the flow of goods imported from abroad and imposes duties (*See* Chapter 15, "Going through Customs"). All goods entering Canada must be brought in at a port of entry—any place with a customs house. The importer must declare the quality, type and value of the goods.

Goods intended for sale are inspected to ensure they are of "merchantable quality"—that is, reasonably fit and safe for the purpose for which they are intended. Departmental responsibility for checking imports varies according to the type of goods. Health and Welfare Canada, for example, examines food products. Officers from Consumer and Corporate Affairs inspect manufactured goods.

Labels must bear "a true and correct description of the contents." Officers check foodstuffs with particular care.

The customs officer is an expert at ferreting out illegal imports—such as marijuana and other illegal drugs—and severe penalties await anyone foolish enough to test his efficiency.

The arts of selling

WHEN THE well-dressed, well-spoken salesman assures you with warm sincerity that the piece of furniture you are looking at is "exclusive," "superior," "built to last," "an excellent value," remember that the law permits him to "puff" his product. You are expected to take his words with a grain of salt.

These days no one expects a salesman to announce that he is selling low-quality merchandise, or that the item you want to buy is not really worth the price asked for it. The law expects you to make reasonable inquiries before you buy and not to believe everything you are told. However, this does not mean that the shopper is a helpless target for outright misrepresentation or glib lies.

You, as a customer, especially if you buy the goods on the basis of actual promises made by the salesman, are entitled to sue the salesman, or the company, for misrepresentation if the statements made were clearly false or if you were deliberately misled. Although the "puffing" terms mentioned above couldn't be called a guarantee, the provincial Sale of Goods or Unfair Trade Practices Acts apply an effective brake on the salesman.

Let's say you need a bed strong enough for your teenaged son. You explain to the salesman the kind of bed you want and let him know through your explanation that you are willing to rely on his skill and judgment. If he sells you a bed, he does so with what is called an implied guarantee that the bed will reasonably fit the purpose you described. In other words, it should stand up under reasonable use by your son. This means that if the bed were to break when your son flopped on it you could hold the seller liable. In terms of the law, you could sue for breach of contract. Moreover, if your son had been hurt when the bed broke, you could possibly also sue for damages. (*See* Chapter 18, "The accidental tort.")

The store would certainly be liable if you were told a piece of furniture was upholstered in leather and the covering turned out to be a vinyl substitute.

Be warned, though, that the law also states that if you buy an article under its trade name, there is no condition implied in the name that it is fit for any particular purpose. Thus if you decided to buy, solely on the basis of its name, Landy's Handy-Dandy Hyde-a-Bed, without any further investigation on your part as to its usability and value, you could run into problems over a refund if the bed turned out to be unsuitable for your purpose.

If you personally examine an article before buying it, the salesman after that point is technically responsible only for latent defects—defects that wouldn't show up in the average once-over inspection. The buyer cannot later expect a refund for any defects which he should have noticed when he examined the article. For instance, in your examination of a sofa bed on the shop floor, you should notice if the covering is ripped. However, you are not expected to have noticed, say, a weakness in the bracing of the frame.

If the salesman tells you frankly that the bargain he is offering you is marked down because the item is old or defective, he cannot—under the law—be held to any promises about the "merchantable quality" of the bargain in question. If you are looking for a bargain, ask him in what way the article is defective.

A label stating that items are being offered "as is" or as "seconds" would possibly have the same effect. Such a statement or label has the effect of implying there is no guarantee that the particular product is "standard quality."

Breaking the contract

The law protects you from the salesman who shows you a sample on the shop floor, gets your order, and then delivers a different product without any attempt to get your approval of the switch. By doing this, the seller effectively breaks the sales contract made between you and the store, and you don't have to pay. (That "contract," which is a legally binding agreement, exists every time you buy something, even if nothing was written.)

If the purchase is a major one intended for later delivery (perhaps a new car), your offer to buy should always be in writing and you should, of course, check the descriptions and terms carefully before signing any sales agreement. Do not leave it to the salesman to "look after all the details," and *never* sign a blank form.

Although all contract law is somewhat complicated and outwardly simple sales and purchases are no exception—it can be said that, everywhere in Canada, the rosy promises of the salesman must stop short of misleading you about the quality or serviceability of the goods offered.

He can "puff" his product, but he cannot tell lies about it. In British Columbia, Alberta, Ontario and Prince Edward Island, intentional misrepresentation or undue pressure in selling will cancel a sales contract and may provide grounds for the award of damages heavier than those once levied under the Common Law.

Installment buying

For millions of consumers, installment buying has become routine for the purchase of expensive items: automobiles, furniture, television sets, carpets, and even airline tickets to far-off places.

The seller will accept a percentage of the price as a down payment (or deposit) and will allow you to have possession and use of the article you are buying provided that you sign an agreement to pay him the rest of the money, plus interest, in regular amounts and at regular intervals. If you have a general credit card or one from a department store, airline or gasoline company, you can usually assume that installments will be acceptable for larger purchases. (These are considered "running accounts.") The credit arrangement is spelled out in the contract you accepted when you signed your credit card.

Textiles must be sold "true to label"

THERE ARE more than 50 different brand names in man-made fibers on the Canadian market, but they can all be identified within a relatively small "family" of substances. Each family of fabrics has its own characteristics in washing, bleaching, drying and ironing. To reduce confusion, in home care of these fabrics, Ottawa passed the Textile Labeling Act and introduced a system of voluntary "care labeling."

The textile legislation requires the manufacturer to state on the label the fiber content by family ("generic") name and to give the percentages of any mixed fibers—*e.g.* 60% polyester and 40% cotton. The home-care symbols are not mandatory but many textile manufacturers are now incorporating them in the labels. There are five care symbols, each representing a method of textile care: A circle means dry cleaning; a triangle, bleaching; a square represents drying. The "pot" indicates water temperature or hand washing, and the iron means it can be pressed or ironed. If the symbol is red, it means "Don't do it." Amber means that caution is necessary. Green means that no special precautions are necessary.

The chart on the following page guides the consumer in both purchasing and care of seven of the best-known artificial fibers.

Fiber & Uses	Care Symbols	Care
Acetate Apparel, household textiles, *e.g.* printed blouse.	*no chlorine bleach*	Hand washable in lukewarm water, do not bleach, hang to dry, iron low, dry clean.
Acrylic Sweaters, blankets, pile fabrics; *e.g.* colored knit.		Machine washable in lukewarm water, do not bleach, tumble dry low, do not iron, dry clean low.
Metallic Decorative fabrics for glitter, *e.g.* evening dress.		Dry clean low.
Nylon Hosiery, rope, apparel, *e.g.* colored robe.		Machine washable in warm water, do not bleach, tumble dry low, iron medium, dry clean.
Polyester Apparel, sewing thread, *e.g.* knit dress.		Machine washable in warm water, do not bleach, tumble dry low, iron medium, dry clean.
Rayon Household textiles, linings, *e.g.* woven dress.		Machine washable in lukewarm water, do not bleach, tumble dry low, iron medium, dry clean.
Spandex Swimsuits, stretch fabrics, *e.g.* girdle.		Hand washable in lukewarm water, do not bleach, hang to dry, do not iron, dry clean low.

257

The system may be called installment buying or time payment, but the law calls it a contract of *conditional sale*. A nearly identical method of financing is by means of a *chattel mortgage*.

CONDITIONAL SALES: The chief characteristic of the conditional sale is that, even though the buyer is usually in possession of the object bought (let's call it a color TV set), the legal ownership of the set remains with the seller (vendor) until the total price (that is, the original purchase price plus interest) has been paid. If the buyer doesn't pay the installments, the seller can either take back the set but make no further claim on the buyer, or sue the buyer for the outstanding amount. In some provinces, the seller is permitted to take back a purchased object if the buyer has paid two-thirds of the amount due, but only after repossession has been authorized by a judge. Only in Nova Scotia, Prince Edward Island and New Brunswick, can the seller sue the buyer for any money lost on a resale.

Sometimes, a store or merchant assigns the seller's rights in the conditional sales contract to another person or company, usually to a finance company (although it could be to any individual), at a discounted price. The buyer is notified that he has to make the payments to the finance company. The finance company now has the rights of the seller already noted above.

There is nothing sinister in this. The TV dealer must sell sets in order to live and he must pay his supplier, his staff and other overhead costs. Since he is not in the consumer credit business, he cannot wait months for payment. The finance company, for a portion of the price, takes over the contract (the debt, in effect), providing the dealer with ready cash.

CHATTEL MORTGAGES: The chattel mortgage system of installment buying has a different legal makeup but, as far as the consumer is concerned, the effect is the same as other forms of such buying. Here, in the normal case, an independent institution lends the buyer enough money to add to his down payment so that the buyer can cover the full price of the goods. The legal ownership of the property is in the hands of the buyer, but he mortgages it

back to the lender who holds it as security for the loan. When the loan is paid off, the mortgage is automatically canceled and the buyer's title is clear.

If the buyer went himself to his bank to raise a loan with which to buy the goods, he would again probably get the loan by making a chattel mortgage on the goods he wished to buy. Many people follow this practice when buying a car.

Registering the contract

One important fact for the seller to remember about both conditional sales and chattel mortgages is that, to be effective, they must be registered with the clerk of the County Court in the county of the province where the goods are situated. This is done by depositing a copy of the contract. This is the only way that the seller (who still has money owing to him) can be protected if the buyer in turn sells to a third party pretending that he—the original buyer—has full ownership. (In Quebec, no such registration system exists.)

If a contract is registered at the courthouse and the original buyer sells to another party without mentioning that the goods are not yet legally his to sell, the new purchaser is deemed to have notice that a previous conditional sales contract or chattel mortgage exists. Thus, the new purchaser may find his purchase repossessed by the original seller—unless he is willing to pay any amount still owing under the original contract. The innocent third party could, of course, sue the original buyer. But, because it was registered at the County Court, he would stand little chance against the original vendor.

Ontario has introduced the Personal Property Security Act system which provides a province-wide computer record system—much better than the old one which is good only within a county.

The law insists that all interest charges —the cost of the credit arrangement—be spelled out in full for the consumer. It is not enough to state that the interest is, for example, 1½ percent a month—which doesn't sound too bad. It must be explained that this is the equivalent of 18 percent a year—which is a costly way to borrow money.

Buying stolen goods

In all provinces, a buyer cannot get a better title of ownership than the seller has to give. Thus, if you buy from a thief, you get no real title at all. In such a case, you would have to return the goods to the rightful owner, without necessarily being paid back in any way. After a certain period, however, the original owner loses the right to make a claim against the possessor of an object that once may have been his. In Quebec, for example, your title to a stolen object becomes lawful after three years of possession, and the original owner has no right to reclaim it. In most other provinces, the same principle applies after six years of possession.

The Criminal Code rules that when a thief is convicted, the stolen property (if recovered) has to be returned to the lawful owner, even though some innocent third party has paid good money for it. The man who bought the stolen goods can be paid back from any money found in the possession of the thief at the time of his arrest, except where there may also be some dispute as to the ownership of the money. If the money recovered is not enough to repay the innocent purchaser, the court may order the thief to repay him after serving his sentence.

If a person obtains something by fraud, he has either no title of ownership at all, or his ownership can be voided in court.

Door-to-door selling

Almost every Canadian has at one time or another found at the front door a smiling salesman who has launched into his pitch with oily ease. Of course, he is not really *selling*. No, he is simply telling you that you have already drawn a lucky number—with a chance to win the first prize: a Cadillac, or a trip around the world for two. Or he merely wants to leave a 14-volume set of books with you—just to get your opinion as an "intelligent consumer." If you have read this far, you are probably a potential victim of the door-to-door sales team.

In pioneer days, the traveling tinker with his pots and pans, piece goods and German clocks, was a useful part of our society. Today, every house in the country is either close to stores or served by reputable mail-order houses. Yet the doorstep peddler is still around and his routine is right up to the times. Almost invariably he starts off by assuring you he is not selling anything; this is your certain clue that he *is* selling something. From that point on, you can either listen at your own risk as the tale is spun (some are quite imaginative), or firmly ask the visitor to leave.

If you post a "No Canvassing" sign, he is technically trespassing, but a judge would probably rule him to be a *licensee*. This legal term covers people who enter your property without invitation but either with your express permission or as a matter of general routine—the milkman, for instance. You can get a large noisy dog, but there's no absolutely foolproof way to prevent the hardened door-to-door man from ringing your bell. The best advice is to say "good day" and then "goodby." He has no alternative but to leave your property immediately at your request.

Until recently, you might have been asking for trouble had you bought, say, an electric food mixer from a door-to-door salesman and accepted his "easy credit terms." Assuming the goods weren't stolen (and how could you be sure they weren't?), the price you paid was undoubtedly considerably higher than you could have found with careful shopping elsewhere. You signed a piece of paper promising to pay the balance owing, plus a steep interest. This was a "promissory note"—literally, your signed promise to pay. It was a legal contract, even if you did not fully understand the fine print at the time you signed it.

After a month or so, you found the mixer no longer worked. Next you learned that a loan company you had never heard of had taken over your note and expected payment on the dot each month. Seeking an exchange or refund, you tried to contact the salesman but—surprise!—your letters were returned: *Addressee Unknown*. He had skipped.

You wrote to the loan company. The polite reply was that they were sorry about your useless mixer but it was none of their business. Their interest was money, your money. They had the legal right to collect from you and were not responsible for your purchase.

That could have happened in every detail until quite recently, and with the facts altered somewhat, it could happen tomorrow. The federal Department of Consumer Affairs made it more difficult for high-pressure salesmen by introducing a new law that alters the conditions of promissory notes. Now if the note, or signed promise to pay, covers a consumer purchase, it must be marked CONSUMER PURCHASE. When one of these marked notes is sold routinely to a finance company, the company can no longer collect from the consumer if it can be proved that the seller has not met the conditions of the contract. This makes the finance companies very careful about the notes they buy and, in turn, holds the sales sharks in check. However, the department cannot cover every pitfall.

This law—a section of the Bills of Exchange Act—covers only promissory notes and cheques postdated more than 30 days. It removes from the consumer only the unconditional responsibility of paying no matter how he may have been cheated. If you stop the payments to the finance company, that company is likely to sue you. Then it's up to you to *prove* in court that you were cheated by the salesman. That can be a time-consuming, embarrassing and difficult business.

All provinces have a "cooling-off" period during which a customer can cancel a contract. Ontario has a two-day period after the purchaser has received a copy of the contract. In Alberta and Saskatch-

ewan, the period is four days. Manitoba allows four days, if the contract is not in writing; and 30 days after the delivery of the product, if the contract is written. New Brunswick has five days; British Columbia and Prince Edward Island, seven days; and Quebec and Newfoundland, ten days. Nova Scotia allows ten days after the purchaser has signed a contract without recision (cancellation) rights. If the contract includes these rights, the cooling-off period is 30 days. The value of contracts with "cooling-off" periods varies from province to province. Newfoundland, Nova Scotia, Prince Edward Island and Saskatchewan set no limit on the amount stated in the contract. But, in Alberta, Quebec and New Brunswick, the limit is $25. The limit in British Columbia is $20; and, in Ontario, $50.

To protect the naive customer, Ontario in 1975 legislated to make the seller check that there is "reasonable probability" that the buyer will be able to pay in full. If a salesman tempts an illiterate immigrant with an expensive automatic dishwasher, he could have trouble getting his money.

Referrals and pyramids
Federal consumer lawyers warn that if you are offered something for a song, check the accompaniment. You get very little for nothing in this workaday world, however tempting a prospect the salesman dangles before you. Two new systems of selling particularly deserve this warning: referral selling and pyramid plans. Charges of fraud and misrepresentation have been laid against some salesmen in such schemes. In Quebec, the

Goods that you can't import

GENERALLY SPEAKING, Canadians can roam the world to buy what they fancy and ship it home. Of course, if they exceed the value of exemptions permitted bona fide travelers (*See* Chapter 15, "Going through Customs"), they will have to pay customs duties at various levels on their purchases. There are, however, certain items that are prohibited—such as second-hand automobiles or airplanes, starlings and the snake-killing mongoose. The full list is printed in Schedule C of the Customs Act, an excerpt of which is shown on the facing page.

Schedule C   *Customs Tariff*   Chap. C-41

SCHEDULE C
PROHIBITED GOODS

99201-1   Books, printed paper, drawings, paintings, prints, photographs or representations of any kind of a treason-able or seditious, or of an immoral or indecent character.

99202-1   Reprints of Canadian copyrighted works, and reprints of British copyrighted works which have been co-pyrighted in Canada.

99203-1   Coin, base or counterfeit.

99204-1   Oleomargarine, butterine or other similar substitutes for butter, and process butter or renovated butter, unless in any particular case or class of cases exempted from the provisions of this item by a regulation of the Governor in Council.

99206-1   Goods manufactured or produced wholly or in part by prison labour, *unless in any particular case or class of cases exempted from the provisions of this item by a regulation of the Governor in Council.*

99208-1   Metallic trading checks in circular form, *unless in any particular case or class of cases exempted from the provisions of this item by a regulation of the Governor in Council.*

99209-1   Any goods
           (a) in association with which there is used any description that is false in a material respect as to the geographical origin of the goods, or
           (b) the importation of which is prohibited by an order under section 52 of the *Trade Marks Act.*

99210-1   Posters and handbills depicting scenes of crime or violence.

99212-1   Aigrettes, egret plumes or so-called osprey plumes, and the feathers, quills, heads, wings, tails, skins, or parts of skins of wild birds either raw or manufactured; but this provision shall not apply to:
           (a) the feathers or plumes of ostriches;
           (b) the plumage of the English pheasant and the Indian peacock; the plumage of wild birds of groups recognized as game birds in any Canadian game law, and for which an open season is provided thereunder;
           (c) the plumage of birds imported alive; nor to
           (d) specimens imported under regulations of the Minister for any Natural History or other museum or for scientific or educational purposes.

99213-1   White Phosphorous matches.

99214-1   (1) Common mongoose *(Herpestes griseus)* or mongoose of any kind;
           (2) Any bird of the Starling family *(Sturnidae)*, except the European Starling *(Sturnus vulgaris)*;
           (3) Any other non-game bird, except any of the following:
           (a) a domestic bird of a kind kept for food purposes;
           (b) a bird intended solely for exhibition in a public zoological park;
           (c) a bird intended solely to be kept in confinement in a cage or to be used for purposes of public entertainment.

99215-1   Used or second-hand automobiles and motor vehicles of all kinds, manufactured prior to the calendar year in which importation into Canada is sought to be made:
           This item does not affect in any manner automobiles and motor vehicles,
           (a) imported under tariff items 70200-1, 70505-1, 70600-1, 70700-1 and 70800-1, or under tourists' or travellers' vehicle permits;
           (b) imported by a *bona fide* settler on a first arrival but not entitled to entry free of duty under tariff item 70505-1;
           (c) bona fide purchased on or before June 1st, 1931 by consumers for their own use and not for resale;
           (d) forfeited or confiscated for any offence under the customs laws, or the laws of any province of Canada;
           (e) left by bequest;
           (f) exempted from the provisions of this item by a regulation of the Governor in Council in any particular case or class of cases.

99216-1   Used or second-hand aeroplanes and aircraft of all kinds:
           This item does not affect in any manner aeroplanes and aircraft,
           (a) imported under tariff item 70700-1 or 70800-1, or engaged solely in international traffic, or brought in by non-resident tourists for temporary use under permit issued by the Department of National Revenue;
           (b) bona fide purchased on or before March 22nd, 1933 by consumers for their own use and not for resale;
           (c) forfeited or confiscated for any offence under the customs laws, the Air Regulations or the laws of any province of Canada;
           (d) imported by the Department of National Defence for military purposes;
           (e) exempted from the provisions of this item by a regulation of the Governor in Council in any particular case or class of cases.

99217-1   Smoke screen apparatus, for use on motor vehicles or on water-borne crafts of all kinds.

99218-1   Used or second-hand periodical publications:
           This item does not affect in any manner periodical publications:
           (a) sent, gratis, to Canada for charitable purposes;
           (b) sent to persons in Canada as casual donations by friends abroad;
           (c) imported for personal of for institutional use, and not for resale;
           (d) imported by or for paper mills for use as stock in the manufacture of paper.

Consumer Protection Act, 1978, specifically outlaws pyramid selling.

In referral selling, the usual pitch is that you can get an expensive product (perhaps a vacuum cleaner with all the gadgets) at a fraction of the cost simply by giving the salesman the names and addresses of friends who might also be interested in buying such a machine. The idea, he will explain, is that as each of your friends buys a cleaner, you will get a further discount on the price of your own machine. You are required at the outset to pay a small deposit and to sign a form (in effect, a promissory note) committing you to pay the full purchase price. Of course, both you and the salesman are confident that enough of your friends will buy so that you will, perhaps, never need to make another payment.

In practice, as many Canadians have found to their chagrin, it works out quite differently. The salesman has not lied to you; you might say that he has just played on your marketing ignorance. In the first place, his company does not really care if your friends buy or not—*you* are already committed to the full price of *your* machine. And the price you will pay, with maximum interest, will in all probability turn out to be much higher than you would have paid at your neighborhood appliance outlet. The friends whose names you have supplied might not be too pleased to be bothered by door-to-door salesmen, and the thought that they would be helping to pay for your machine may not exactly thrill them.

An actual example can be found in a survey of a referral-sales scheme in the

Selling "wonder foods"

THERE HAS BEEN an upswing in the demand for "wonder foods" in recent years; some say it's part of a longing for the "good old days." The so-called health foods—blackstrap molasses, rose hips, sunflower seeds, brewer's yeast and others—are again being endorsed with almost magical properties for curing or preventing disease.

Under the Food and Drugs Act, it is illegal to sell or advertise any food as a treatment or cure for serious health conditions, including obesity. The truth is that there are no "wonder foods" and, in the interests of sound nutrition, Health and Welfare Canada offers these comments:

Blackstrap molasses, a by-product of sugar refining, is a source of iron but offers little else. Other sources of iron—such as meat, eggs and green vegetables—are just as good and are superior sources of other nutrients. There is no truth in claims that blackstrap molasses can cure ulcers, cancer, varicose veins or arthritis.

Rose hips, the seed pods of roses, are a rich source of vitamin C. But you may prefer such cheaper sources as tomatoes, oranges, grapefruit, broccoli, cantaloupe, strawberries or green peppers.

Brewers' yeast and *wheat germ* are sources of protein and the B vitamins, but eating wheat germ or yeast is neither the most appetizing nor the most economical way to obtain these nutrients. Protein and B vitamins are more readily available from such foods as bread and cereal products.

Garlic may give foods a zing but it will not cure intestinal disorders, nor will it prevent cancer, pneumonia or aging.

Honey, sometimes called the nectar of the gods, is a good source of energy, but is powerless to cure arthritis. Some persons claim it can be used without restraint by diabetics but nothing could be further from the truth.

To help counter food faddism and the exaggerated claims in today's "health food" movement, the federal government has prepared a series of pamphlets entitled *Food Hang-ups*. Presented in cartoon fashion, it provides answers to questions about food additives, "wonder foods" and fad diets, as well as information about federal protective legislation in the food field.

United States. The consumer was charged $282 for a vacuum cleaner which sold for $60 wholesale. Only ten percent of the customers received more than $75 in discount. When you consider how many people must have paid the full price, you can see who wins in the referral-sales system.

Have you ever been invited to become part of a "multi-level distributorship plan"? This is really just the pyramid system, a close relative of referral selling. Here, after the usual sales talk, you are offered the chance to become a "chief representative" of the company (which usually sells household items) by making a certain investment of cash. You are allowed to enroll other "assistant representatives," who also make an investment. They, in turn, appoint salesmen who must, of course, buy their stock of goods from the company. When a given number of salesmen are enrolled, the territory is broken up into divisions and your position, as No. 1 of your pyramid, automatically becomes more valuable. Both the "chief" and the "assistant representatives"—the executives, as it were—get slices of the commissions earned by their salesmen.

Sounds great? Yes—for the selling company. It reaps your cash investment and that of your appointees, plus the profit on the goods supplied to the salesmen (all sales are final). The flaw that tumbles the pyramid is simply that a given area can absorb only so much toilet soap or bathroom cleanser, and other merchants are in the same field with more expertise and capital strength than you can muster. Many would-be tycoons have ended up with a basement full of bubble bath.

Federal and provincial agencies have combined forces to put a fairly effective brake on referral and pyramid selling, but it is a complex problem. Some companies that sell cosmetics and kitchenware in the home are entirely reputable, giving a gift to a cooperating housewife whether her friends decide to buy a frypan or not. And their quality goods are offered at competitive market prices.

So far legal protection consists mostly of the normal obligations of the seller, as described in this chapter, plus the special conditions applying to promissory notes for consumer purchases and the "cooling-off" periods now allowed by several provinces during which you can have second thoughts about the deal. Pyramid sales are illegal except in British Columbia, Alberta and Saskatchewan, which have laws controlling these schemes.

Under 1975 amendments to the federal Combines Investigation Act, no one may "induce or invite" another person to participate in pyramid selling. This law does not apply in those provinces that have their own pyramid (or sales referral) laws.

Selling by telephone

You may suddenly be offered goods from strangers on the telephone. Usually this is because you have come to be regarded as a likely sales prospect. You may have bought something sizable on credit, you may be listed as a company director in the provincial records, or your name may appear on some other likely list. Many companies sell lists of names.

Always be on your guard with the telephone salesman. You can't see what you are buying and it is difficult to determine over the phone how trustworthy the seller is. The law tries to protect you by insisting that sizable contracts of sale (the amounts vary from province to province) are valid only if they are in writing and under seal, or if "consideration" (something of value like a down payment) has been given by one party to the other to confirm the contract. Since neither of these things can be done over the phone, you can back out of a telephone deal involving such a value before you hand over your money. But the seller can back out just as easily, and legally.

If the deal does go through, the consumer is relying on an oral description of the goods. When he receives them through the mail (probably c.o.d.—cash on delivery), if the goods do not fit the description or the promises made over the telephone, the buyer has the legal right to cancel the contract on the grounds that he did not get what he bargained for.

If you accept the goods c.o.d. and then find that you have been swindled, you can, of course, sue for damages—a difficult and chancy venture. The best advice is not to negotiate sales contracts over the telephone. However, you are reasonably well protected if you can reserve the right of rejection if the goods are not satisfactory on arrival.

Buying by mail

If you're thinking of buying by mail, remember the maxim, *caveat emptor* ("let the buyer beware"). Although many companies which sell their wares by mail order are completely reputable and will exchange goods or give refunds, they don't have to, unless these terms are clearly offered as a condition of the sale.

Mail-order catalogues and press advertisements offering goods by mail are prepared by experts. A fur coat or a power

mower can often look better than the real thing. Before you order, be sure you know exactly what you are buying and, furthermore, that the terms of payment are clear— and within your budget.

If things bought by mail order are unsatisfactory, and you have no stated return privilege, the only way that you can force the company to take them back is if the goods do not match the description under which they were ordered. At this point you can claim that these are not the things you contracted to buy—because of some either innocent or deceitful misrepresentation. The seller (vendor) could be obliged to refund your money or exchange the goods for ones matching the description in the original advertisement. In practical terms, however, if you have

---

Stop! Look! Take Care!

How can you tell if a household product is dangerous? The federal Department of Consumer and Corporate Affairs has the power to ban hazardous products and to regulate their sale, advertising and labeling. To protect the consumer, a system of symbols was evolved which certain products (bleaches, glues, sprays, cleansers, polishes) must carry on their labels. They denote the presence of one of the four main hazards—poison, explosive, corrosive, flammable—and indicate the degree of the danger in three ways: danger, warning and caution.

DANGER POISON

WARNING POISON

CAUTION POISON

DANGER FLAMMABLE

WARNING FLAMMABLE

CAUTION FLAMMABLE

DANGER EXPLOSIVE

WARNING EXPLOSIVE

CAUTION EXPLOSIVE

DANGER CORROSIVE

WARNING CORROSIVE

CAUTION CORROSIVE

An eight-sided figure always means *"Danger."* A diamond-shaped figure means *"Warning,"* and a triangle means *"Caution."*

fallen for "an incredible bargain" from some unknown or distant mail-order house, you might not even be able to find the seller. These operators have been known to make a swift killing, then fold their tents and vanish into the night.

Can a buyer cancel his order after he has put it in the mail? Generally speaking, the moment that you drop the order into the mailbox you have accepted a valid contract of sale. The law is still unclear as to whether you may cancel the purchase, by personal visit or by telephone, before the order is delivered to you by mail.

Unsolicited mail

One of the most popular sales gimmicks of recent times has been the pitch made through the letter box in the form of unsolicited mail. Almost everyone with a good credit rating is familiar with the important-looking envelopes containing offers of everything from steak knives to greeting cards. Although this business is legitimate, the law watches for attempts to victimize or deceive consumers.

The Canada Post Corporation Act prevents merchants from sending sales offers to you in envelopes that appear to be bills, unless printing on the front announces the true contents.

Although most direct-mail vendors are honest, there are others who try to profit from the normal forgetfulness of busy people. For instance, goods are sent unsolicited on a "free trial" basis and you, the recipient, are asked merely to fill in and return a pre-stamped card if you do *not* want further items to arrive. Let's say you don't want the goods, but you either lose the vital card or forget to fill it in; so next month's mail brings you another package—and a bill. "Do I have to pay?" you ask. If you were away all during the key period, you could come back to find a stack of unwanted, unordered stuff on your doorstep. The law answers that anyone receiving unsolicited merchandise (or credit cards) does not have to either return the stuff or pay for it. In British Columbia, Quebec, Nova Scotia and Newfoundland, the law states that the direct-mail vendor cannot take action to collect money for unsolicited goods.

Prince Edward Island prohibits the delivery of unsolicited merchandise.

Under the Canada Post Corporation Act, it is illegal to send unsolicited goods (goods no one has ordered) C.O.D. A particularly shady trick practiced before this law came into effect was to send some expensive item C.O.D. to a person who had just died. Relatives would often pay for the goods assuming that they had been ordered by the deceased before his death.

When unsolicited packages of greeting cards are sent out in the mail—in the hope that you'll keep them and send in the money—the Post Office Department requires that a notice be included stating that you do not have to pay any return postage if you reject the cards, nor are you under any legal obligation. In other words, you don't have to send the cards back, nor pay for them if you use them.

The post office is not allowed to handle anything "obscene, indecent or immoral"—but, like the rest of society, it is struggling to find acceptable standards by which to rule in these questions of individual taste. Pornography is freely sold and mailed today which only a few years ago would have brought publishers and news agents charges of "disseminating obscene matter" (as the offense is still known in the Criminal Code).

Other matter that is banned from the mails includes betting slips, wagering odds sheets or any material that attempts to deceive or defraud the public or to obtain money under false pretenses. The federal customs authorities have the right to open and inspect mail other than letter mail if it comes from outside Canada. The post office is prohibited from opening any first-class (letter) mail without the addressee's consent.

If you are irritated or bored with unwanted mail-order offers, you can simply write REFUSED on the envelope, sign it and return it to your nearest post office. If there is a return address, it is sent back. If not, the post office opens it. If there is anything of value inside, it goes to the receiver-general. If you are offended by unsolicited pornographic mail, or have any complaint at all about the mails, you should write to the postmaster-general.

265

Guarantees and standards

ONCE THE fact is clear that all sales are legally *contracts*, it is easy for the consumer to understand that the *terms*, or conditions, of a contract can vary in many ways. These depend on the goods sold, the way they are sold, and the responsibilities and obligations of both buyer and seller. In other sections of this chapter your attention has been drawn to the things that can affect your legal position when you buy something. In this section, we will look closely at the promises the merchant makes, either in his come-on advertising or his in-store promotion, as well as in the "guarantee" that he offers to assure you that the particular item will serve the required purpose.

Although the popular term "guarantee" is generally used, what is really being talked about is the "warranty." When a shopkeeper says, "We guarantee this clock will keep good time," he is offering you an oral, or verbal, warranty. In terms of the law, a "guarantee" is a promise made by one person to pay the debt of another person if the debtor—the person who owes money—fails to do so.

The seller's warranty—his promise to "stand behind" the goods he sells—can be of two kinds: "implied" or "express."

An IMPLIED WARRANTY exists to some extent in everything that is sold, even when there is nothing in writing between the buyer and the seller (the vendor). Arising from the Common Law and codified in sale-of-goods acts, it ensures that the dealer has the right to sell the item, that the goods measure up to the description given, that they are in good condition and are basically suitable for the purpose stated. Every consumer is protected against the out-and-out crook. Un-

der no circumstances can a back-street dealer represent a used sports car with a seized engine as being of top quality and hope to make the deal stick. Incredible as it may seem, some people will actually sign a sales agreement (contract) for a used car that they have not even driven.

An EXPRESS WARRANTY is the merchant's definite and specific promise concerning performance and quality of the goods. The express warranty is usually printed or written—although it doesn't have to be—and it usually includes all the "ifs" and "buts." While you should always try to get a written guarantee for large purchases, you should remember that by accepting that document you will normally be cutting yourself off from the protection of the implied warranty. The express warranty usually states that it is "the sole and only" warranty offered by the dealer. Make sure that it doesn't actually reduce the automatic protection you get in the implied warranty.

When the seller makes a promise that must be kept for the contract to be valid, it is not a warranty, but a *condition*. Delivery of the goods identical to the description given or sample shown to you would, for instance, obviously be a vital condition of the deal. If such a condition is not met by the merchant, you can cancel the deal for "breach of contract." A breach of warranty is *not* by itself grounds for breach of contract; your remedy is to seek damages in a civil action.

An ORAL WARRANTY can sometimes be as valuable as a written, or express, warranty—for instance, in a court action between yourself and the seller, if you can convince the judge that the promise was made as an inducement to get you to sign on the dotted line. The important thing to know about verbal warranties is what makes them "warranties" in the legal sense of the word. It is a lot more difficult to make a dealer honor as a warranty a statement such as "This is a good car" than a statement such as "I guarantee this car will cause you absolutely no problem for 20,000 kilometres." Even if "his word is his bond," you are wiser to have the seller put it in writing.

The language is very important in a written warranty. You should make sure that you understand every term and that, if in doubt, you get a complete explanation from the seller. You can't argue later that you did not understand. The courts assume that you have read, and understood, the agreement before you signed it. Do you think, for instance, that a "lifetime warranty" runs for your lifetime? Wrong. It usually means the lifetime either of the particular article or of the company that sells it, and those can be surprisingly short. But there are variations: a "lifetime" battery, for example, is warranted for the life of the car while owned by the person who purchased the battery.

A **PARTS WARRANTY** covers only certain parts of an article—perhaps all of a television set except the expensive picture tube. You may find, for instance, that it excludes parts not made by the brand-name manufacturer in his own plant, which could amount to quite a number of the components. You should also check whether the parts warranty covers service charges to repair or replace the faulty part. These charges, plus shipping costs, could add up to a lot of money.

An **UNCONDITIONAL WARRANTY** is obviously your best protection of all. Under this flat guarantee, the dealer is saying, perhaps, "This dishwasher will work to your satisfaction for one year." If it doesn't, you can choose to have him either replace it with a matching article or give you back your money. No "ifs" or "buts." This type of guarantee is now being offered as routine policy by several of Canada's largest department stores and food chains. Unless there is a credit arrangement (installment purchase), a written warranty may not even be offered. If

the company advertises widely that its policy is "Satisfaction or money refunded" and prints this slogan on its sales slips, that is commitment enough.

It is possible that the company might attach some special conditions to the sale of some individual article. But in that case, the company would have to draw to your attention those conditions. This is sometimes done by stamping the sales ticket and the customer's receipt: "Final sale—No refund."

Automobiles have earned special attention in the form of a warranty of their own. Generally, all manufacturers (including foreign producers) offer to Canadians buying new cars what is called a complete parts warranty, either for one year from the date of purchase or for 20,000 kilometres' travel. There are usually service and maintenance conditions. Used-car dealers sometimes offer a "fifty-fifty" warranty. Under this guarantee, the seller and buyer share repair costs during a stated period of time from the date of purchase. This subject is discussed fully in Chapter 5.

Misleading advertising

The advertising of goods and services in Canada began in Halifax in 1752. Some economists claim that the tremendous development of advertising in our society through two centuries has been a major factor contributing to the high standard of living for the "average man." The great majority of advertisements directed at the public through the communications media are fair and honest—allowing for the saleman's traditional right to "puff" his product. Trade associations of publishers, broadcasters and advertising men make genuine and continued efforts to raise standards. But it is a field that still has its share of shady characters.

While Canadians enjoy freedom of expression, which includes freedom of the press, it is unlikely that any government agency will attempt to censor or regulate the content of advertisements in any overall fashion. But there are many specific controls: (1) over the advertising of certain classes of food and drug products; (2) over political appeals; and (3) over

Rules for ethical advertisements

ADVERTISING is always open to attack because it is not only a work of fact but of the imagination. The major Canadian advertising agencies are well aware of the existence of a "credibility gap" with the consumer and, through the Advertising Advisory Board, they have proclaimed the Code of Advertising Standards. Its main points are:

- Advertisements may not contain inaccurate or deceptive claims or statements, either direct or implied, with regard to price, availability or performance of a product or service. Advertisers and advertising agencies must be prepared to substantiate their claims.
- No advertisement shall be presented in a format which conceals its commercial intent. Advertising content, for example, should be clearly distinguished from editorial or program content. Similarly advertisements are not acceptable if they attempt to use images or sounds of very brief duration or physically weak visual or oral techniques to convey messages below the threshold of normal human awareness. (Such messages are sometimes referred to as subliminal.)
- No advertisement shall include deceptive price claims, unrealistic price comparisons or exaggerated claims as to worth or value. "List price," "suggested retail price," "manufacturer's list price," and "fair market value" are misleading terms when used to imply a savings unless they represent prices at which a reasonable number of the items were actually sold within the preceding six months in the market area where the advertisement appears.
- Testimonials must reflect the genuine, reasonably current opinion of the endorser and should be based upon adequate information about or experience with the product or service advertised. This is not meant to preclude, however, an actor or actress presenting the true experience of an actual number of users or presenting technical information about the manufacture or testing of the product.
- The consumer must be given a fair opportunity to purchase the goods or services offered at the terms presented. If supply of the sale item is limited, this should be mentioned in the advertisement. Refusal to show or demonstrate the product, disparagement of the advertised product by sales personnel, or demonstration of a product of superior quality are all illustrations of the "bait and switch" technique which is a contravention of the Code.
- Advertisements must not discredit or attack unfairly other products, services or advertisements, or exaggerate the nature or importance of competitive differences. When comparisons are made with competing products or services, the advertiser must make substantiation available promptly upon the request from the Council.
- Advertisements must not distort the true meaning of statements made by professionals or scientific authorities. Advertising claims must not imply they have a scientific basis they do not truly possess. Scientific terms, technical terms, etc., should be used in general advertising only with a full sense of responsibility to the lay public.
- Advertisements shall not state or imply that foods, food substitutes, appetite depressants or special devices will enable a person to lose weight or girth except in conjunction with a balanced, calorie-controlled diet; and the part played by such a diet shall be given due prominence in the advertisement.
- No advertisement shall offer a guarantee or warranty, unless the guarantee or warranty is fully explained as to conditions and limits and the name of guarantor or warrantor, or it is indicated where such information may be obtained.
- No advertiser shall deliberately imitate the copy, slogans, or illustrations of another advertiser in such a manner as to mislead the consumer. The accidental or unintentional use of similar or like general slogans or themes shall not be considered a contravention of this Code, but advertisers, media, and advertising agencies should be alert to the confusion that can result from such coincidences and should seek to eliminate them when discovered.
- Advertisements shall not display a disregard for public safety or depict situations which might encourage inappropriate, unsafe or dangerous practices.
- Advertisements may not hold out false hope in the form of a cure or relief for the mentally or physically handicapped, either on a temporary or permanent basis.
- Advertisements must not exploit the superstitious, or play upon fears to mislead the consumer into purchasing the advertised product or service.
- Advertisements to children impose a special responsibility upon the advertiser and the media. Such advertisements should not exploit their credulity, lack of experience, or their sense of loyalty, and should not present information or illustrations which might result in their physical, mental or moral harm.
- As a public communication process, advertising should not present demeaning or derogatory portrayals of individuals or groups and should not contain anything likely, in the light of generally prevailing standards, to cause deep or widespread offence. It is recognized, of course, that standards of taste are subjective and vary widely from person to person and community to community, and are, indeed, subject to constant change.

certain types of broadcasting material. For example, no advertiser is allowed to say that his tablets will "cure" the common cold; nor can he beam obscene pictures into your living room via TV.

Since 1969, any advertiser attempting to mislead the Canadian consumer has run head-on into hard-hitting sections of the federal Combines Investigation Act. The law comes right to the point and its meaning is crystal clear.

The act states that it is an offense for someone, in order to promote the sale or use of an article, to mislead the public concerning its regular or ordinary selling price. This will make a merchant think twice before, say, increasing the regular price of an article, then lowering it and advertising it as a bargain. (*See* "Safeguards when shopping" in this chapter.)

Section 36 of the act states that it is illegal to publish an advertisement which contains a false, deceptive or misleading statement, or is intentionally worded so that it deceives or misleads the public.

The penalty for this offense can be as much as five years' imprisonment. It applies especially to the sale of real estate and to the promotion of any "business or commercial interest." Newspapers, magazines, television stations and other "publishers" are not held responsible if they have accepted and published the offending advertisement "in good faith"—that is to say, in the ordinary course of their business. Nor is an advertising company penalized if it receives information "in good faith" from the manufacturer.

Under section 36 it is also illegal for a manufacturer to publish a statement about the performance, effectiveness or long-lasting qualities of a product unless he has made "adequate and proper" tests of the item. In other words, it is up to the manufacturer to back up his statements.

The federal Department of Consumer and Corporate Affairs has a separate misleading advertising division, with investigators stationed at five regional offices in Vancouver, Winnipeg, Toronto, Montreal and Halifax. They keep busy. In a two-year period, the division received 4,500 complaints and laid 180 charges. The department cannot intervene on your behalf, but if it prosecutes an advertiser successfully, you could then perhaps sue the offending company for any damages suffered, with good chance of success.

Is it truly "on sale"?

Although a well-known law dictionary lists 26 different kinds of sale, almost everyone knows exactly what a sale is. And most cannot wait to get downtown to snap up some of those tempting bargains. Every newspaper, magazine, handbill, radio and television station informs the avid consumer that there is a sale on *"now!*—NOW!—NOW!" With January clearance sales, white sales, spring sales, summer bargain days, back-to-school specials and, the biggest of all, the six-week Christmas sales, it almost looks as though *everything* is on sale *all* the time. And that was sometimes the case until the law stepped in.

When the Combines Investigation Act set curbs on misleading advertising, marketing managers had to re-examine their pricing policies. Now when they reduce a price for a sale, a government inspector may suddenly appear and demand proof that the price is in fact, lower than before.

If a sales ticket reads, "Regular $9.95—now $8.75," the item must have been normally available in that particular district at the higher price—that is, in the same store before the sale or in other competing stores. Even if the ticket simply states "Reduced!" or "Special!" the seller can be called upon to justify it.

In terms of the law, "on sale" means that the price of an item is lower than it ordinarily is. "Ordinarily" is the key word here. Not long ago a big Canadian department store was convicted of advertising certain goods "on sale" for more than half of the business days of the year. In fact, the "on sale" price had become the price at which the goods were "ordinarily" sold. A manufacturer of shampoo was fined for displaying a label that read "Special $1.49" for two years.

A well-known Ontario camera dealer was prosecuted for advertising that a camera was on sale at a substantially lower figure than the "list price." The government inspector argued that the words "list

The bargain that wasn't

FACTS

The accused was a truck dealer. He ran an advertisement in a local newspaper announcing a ten-day sale of various models of trucks. The advertisement compared the "was" price of particular models with the "now" price, and listed a "save" figure which represented the difference between the two previous prices.

A careful investigation revealed that the saving was no greater than any other price reduction made by the dealer on transactions before or after the sale. The accused was subsequently charged under the Combines Investigation Act which provides: "No person shall, for the purpose of promoting, directly or indirectly, the supply or use of a product or for the purpose of promoting, directly or indirectly, any business interest, by any means whatever, make a representation to the public that is false or misleading in a material respect."

ARGUMENT

The Crown prosecutor stated that the "was" price represented the manufacturer's suggested retail price. The evidence showed that neither before nor after the sale had the dealer sold trucks at the suggested retail price.

Moreover, the Crown prosecutor disclosed that for similar vehicles, the average pre-sale price charged by the truck dealer was actually lower than the average price charged during the ten-day sale.

JUDGMENT

The court found the accused guilty. The fact that the accused had never sold similar vehicles at the manufacturer's suggested retail price at any time before or after the sale period was considered to be particularly significant.

The judge also pointed out that the sales practice of the accused, particularly with regard to the savings to the customer, was no different during the ten-day sale from any other period. In summing up, the judge said that "any reasonable person reading the advertisement would conclude that he could make a better bargain with the defendant during the sale than he could at other times during the year." As this was certainly not true, the dealer's advertisement was misleading.*

*Based on an actual case (1980).

price" suggested that the camera was being offered at less than the "regular" price—which was not so. Consider the phrase, "Manufacturer's suggested retail price 79¢—our price 59¢." This may not be wrong in strictly legal terms but it sounds pretty hollow if not a single retailer is selling at the "suggested retail price."

"Cents-off" promotions can mean real savings, as every supermarket shopper knows. But if the reduction goes on too long, the "cents-off" price will be regarded as the regular price, and the merchant will run up against consumer protection law. A maker of instant coffee was fined for running a "30 cents off" label for seven consecutive months. Other "on sale" items that have attracted prosecution range from jewelry and television sets to guns and mattresses.

The federal Consumer Affairs Bureau maintains a brisk prosecution campaign and is planning to tighten "on sale" regulations even more. It acts on complaints received directly from consumers and on those (30 percent of the total) that are lodged by competing retailers.

Accurate measure
Whenever you buy corn flakes or cabbages, sausages or steak, pantyhose or pajamas, stereo equipment or hearing aids—even when you order a shot of your favorite rye—the law stands silently beside you to make sure you get the quantity and quality you are paying for. The same is true whether you buy a single package of cake flour or a thousand bushels of wheat.

In the relatively new and very complex field of consumer protection, the law is still evolving and there are still many areas yet to be covered. It is impossible to keep a fool from his folly, and equally impossible to hold down the born salesman. The law-makers are just trying to give the consumer a better break.

The Weights and Measures Act (first proclaimed in 1872) has been updated in recent years to suit new packaging and labeling problems. Ottawa introduced the Consumer Packaging and Labeling Act (1974) to make retailers (as well as manufacturers) legally responsible for the product sold. This federal law also covers truth in quantity and quality, label descriptions, storage periods, types of container. Fines can run up to $10,000.

Government at all levels supports the research and decisions of the Standards Council, which is devoted to the establishment and acceptance of voluntary standardization of measurements and grading in all branches of industry and manufacturing not specifically regulated by law.

Accurate weights
The federal Weights and Measures Act sets down legal standards so that the consumer is protected from deliberate short weight or short measures in his purchases, as well as from a proliferation of measuring units in the marketplace. The types of commercial weighing machines (such as scales) and measuring devices (such as gasoline pumps) that can be used are controlled, and inspectors routinely do spot checks. It is basically up to you to check whether the butcher has his thumb on the scales.

The Weights and Measures Act insists that the net weight (that is, the actual weight of the food not counting the weight of the package) is clearly stated on the sales ticket or label of all prepackaged goods that are displayed for sale by weight or measure. Furthermore, it forbids a seller to use any weight, measure or machine that is "false or unjust."

From the beginning of the 1970s, Canada has been converting from the imperial system of weights and measures to metric units. The conversion was completed by the end of 1983. In the normal run of business and private affairs between Canada and many other countries, there has often been confusion in measures but this, it is hoped, will be ended by metrication.

Moving to metric
In January 1970, the federal government declared Canada's intention to join the decimal world of weights and measures. The benefits were obvious, particularly in the export trade, as the world becomes more and more what Marshall McLuhan

has described as the "global village." Ninety percent of the world's population already works in terms of tens.

In 1977, federal amendments to the Weights and Measures Act and eight other related statutes set the cut-off dates for metric conversion in such sectors of the economy as the retail sale of gasoline, home furnishings and food sold by weight. In conjunction with the Metric Commission, other industries—104 sectors in all, ranging from medicines to agricultural equipment—drew up their own voluntary conversion schedules. By the end of 1983, conversion in most sectors had been substantially completed.

Under the metric system, the basic units for measuring mass, length and capacity have become the kilogram (kg), the metre (m) and the litre (l). Canadians are becoming accustomed to using grams (g) instead of ounces, kilograms (kg) instead of pounds; the centimetre (cm) instead of the inch, the millimetre (mm) instead of fractions of inches, and the kilometre (km) instead of the mile. Dress fabrics, for example, are measured by the metre and a beauty queen might have the ample measurements of 91-61-91—in centimetres that is!

Many other governments have taken the lead in implementing the metric system by revising all relevant road signs. Great Britain and most Commonwealth countries are in the process of conversion. Sixty percent of the leading industries in the United States are now producing goods in metric format. Some U.S. states are further along than others in converting the measurements of products sold within their jurisdiction. In the United Kingdom, metric units have been legal for trade since 1864. The most recent revision of the British Weights and Measures Act gives metric equivalents for the yard, pound and gallon as follows:

1 metre = 1.093 yards
1 kilogram = 2.204 pounds
1 litre = .220 gallons

As everyone who listens to the weather forecasts knows, Canada has been referring to temperatures in degrees Celsius (°C) since 1975, instead of in the long-familiar degrees Fahrenheit. On the Celsius—or centigrade—scale, water freezes at zero degrees and boils at 100°. To convert Fahrenheit to Celsius, you subtract 32 and multiply by ⁵⁄₉ ths. Easy?

Unit pricing

Many consumers across Canada are now able to buy products ticketed in a "price per unit" weight or volume system. The basic idea of this system, called unit pricing, is that the consumer will be told the cost of the product by gram or kilo rather than by the package, tube or jar.

Meat counters in many supermarkets are marking unit prices on sales tickets. By stating both the price of the meat by the kilo and the price for the portion offered, the manager is helping customers to make informed and economical choices. Consumer advice columns usually quotes current prices in unit terms.

Regulations of the Consumer and Labeling Act have standardized packaging for a dozen products, ranging from toothpaste to peanut butter. As a result, consumers are better placed to calculate unit prices and to make money-saving comparisons when shopping. Manufacturers have also taken advantage of metric conversion to reduce the number of different sizes for their products. However, packaging is a complex matter, and at present, the position is that the government can step in to control container sizes for prepackaged items when inspectors are convinced the packages could "confuse or mislead" the shopper. The size of cans for fruits and vegetables has been controlled for years under the Agricultural Products Standards Act (there are 41 legal sizes).

Grading of foods

In the early 1800s, the Province of Upper Canada introduced grading regulations for food stuffs—for example, bread had to be "sound, good and well made" and had to include the correct amount of stated ingredients (no sawdust allowed). Before Confederation in 1867, all the five existing Canadian provinces had sketchy laws governing the grading, packing and inspection of food. These early protective laws encouraged farmers to bring high-

All you should need to know about metrication

The metric system is based on decimals

Some units of the metric system need never be learned by most persons. What must be known—only 10 units in everyday life—is easily learned, once you have familiarized yourself with the Celsius (centigrade) scale. (Some metric units are not at all unfamiliar; those for time and electricity—seconds and amps—have long been used in Canada.)

Basic measures

Metre: a little longer than a yard (about 1.1 yards)
Litre: a little smaller than a quart (about .96 of a quart)
Gram: about the weight of a paper clip

(Comparative sizes)

1 METRE

1 YARD

Common prefixes (to be used with basic units)
Milli: one-thousandth (0.001)
Centi: one-hundredth (0.01)
Kilo: one-thousand times (1000)

For example:
1000 millimetres = 1 metre
100 centimetres = 1 metre
1000 metres = 1 kilometre

Other commonly used units

Millimetre: 0.001 metre—thickness of paper clip wire
Centimetre: 0.01 metre—width of a paper clip (about 0.4 inch)
Kilometre: 1000 metres—somewhat more than ½ mile (about 0.6 mile)
Kilogram: 1000 grams—a little more than 2 pounds (about 2.2 pounds)
Millilitre: 0.001 litre—five of them make a teaspoon

Other useful units

Hectare: about 2½ acres
Tonne: about one ton

Temperature is shown on a centigrade scale in degrees Celsius (°C)—compared below with Fahrenheit (°F)

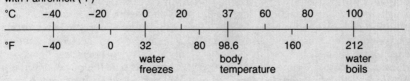

°C	−40	−20	0	20	37	60	80	100
°F	−40	0	32	80	98.6	160		212
			water freezes		body temperature			water boils

273

quality produce to market, because the higher grades fetched more money.

The consumer everywhere in Canada now shops with confidence as national acceptance of grading levels gives a reasonable assurance of buying quality, even if the contents (like beans and corn) are sold in cans. There are Canadian standard grades for meat and meat products, fish and shellfish, poultry and eggs, grains, dairy products, fruits, vegetables, honey and canned goods. Individual provinces require grading on regional products (such as fiddleheads in the Maritimes).

Egg grading provides a typical example. All eggs sold in Canada are graded according to the standards laid down by the federal Department of Agriculture. There are four grades; Canada A-1, A, B and C. Canada A-1 and grade A eggs are divided into four categories at the grading stations: extra large, large, medium and small. The grade Canada A-1 and A eggs must be fresh. The freshness is determined by the size of the air space at the blunt end of the egg; the bigger the air space, the older the egg. The yoke must be centered and not discolored. The shell must be clean and smooth.

The requirements for Canada A-1 (only available in selected markets) are even more stringent than for grade A. The eggs must be produced from flocks no older than 12 months. The egg whites must be firmer than grade A. The cartons must bear an expiry date of no more than nine days from the day of grading.

The grade B eggs must be no smaller than the A mediums, but the yolks can be darker and off-center in the shell. The shells don't have to be satin-smooth. The C eggs must be the same size as the A smalls, although they can be bigger if not so fresh. Cracked eggs can be sold quickly at a discount but they must be edible.

In the case of cheddar cheese, grading is compulsory only for the export trade—although it is widely practiced for the distribution of bulk cheddar on a voluntary basis for sale within Canada. On the average, more than 99 percent of export cheddar, such as the famous Black Diamond made around Belleville, Ont., is classified as Canada 1.

Since 1923, Canadian export butter has been compulsory graded. Grading for domestic use started in British Columbia and Alberta and now is common practice throughout the country. Butter grades, printed on each wrapper, are as follows: Canada 1; Canada 2 and Canada 3. Of all the pre-packaged butter graded by federal officials in a recent year, 93.4 percent rated Canada 1.

Canada Standards

Since 1970, the Standards Council of Canada has encouraged and coordinated the work of all organizations interested in establishing and improving voluntary standardization. Only 16 of the 57 council members are federal and provincial government representatives; the majority come from business, industry and manufacturing, trade associations, professional and consumer associations, and university faculties. This reflects the government's conviction that, however many laws are passed to protect consumers, the users, producers, researchers and regulatory agencies must in the long run be prepared to help themselves.

The Standards Council concerns itself with the construction, manufacture, production, safety, quality and performance of buildings, manufactured articles and other goods. It serves a double purpose: first, to benefit the health, safety and welfare of the public, and to assist and protect consumers; second, to help make the national business machine more efficient and profitable. If you wonder what this all adds up to, consider how convenient it is that you can so easily buy lamp bulbs that fit all the electric light sockets in your house. In a free enterprise society, these things don't just happen.

Since 1919, the aim of the Canadian Standards Association has been wider standardization and higher quality in everything, from pins and pajamas to pottery and paint. The association will put its C.S.A. seal of approval on a product—for example, an electrical appliance—only after independent testing has proved it safe. This tells the buyer that the product meets the minimum standards set by a government-approved laboratory.

To protect the consumer

The environmental agencies

The consumer watchdogs

The independent bodies

Consumer information

Better Business Bureaus

The provincial agencies

NO ASPECT of consumer protection has attracted more attention in recent years than environmental pollution. "Environment" in this sense can be described as "the sum of all social, biological, physical and chemical factors that make up man's surroundings"—in short, our world. "Pollution" can be described as anything "impure, foul or filthy." Lawmakers are struggling with the task of trying to legislate our land back to health while, at the same time, constructing more essential highways, high schools and houses, and encouraging industry to create more jobs. Nevertheless, a lot is being done to improve "the ecology"—or the living arrangement between man and his environment—particularly where public health is at stake.

The environmental agencies

Federal action is channeled through the Environmental Health Directorate of the Department of National Health and Welfare. Research and enforcement is distributed across four divisions: Bureau of Chemical Hazards, Bureau of Medical Devices, Radiation Protection Bureau and Laboratory Center for Disease Control.

The federal Department of Transport keeps an eagle eye on oil spills that not only wreak havoc among fish and seabirds, but also deny beach recreation to the public. Generally, the federal authorities act in cases of pollution that are larger than local; thus, offshore pollution and pollution of navigable waters come under Ottawa's control.

The department is also grappling with the problem of "noise pollution" by jet aircraft at major airports. Flight paths are already being controlled to regulate landing and takeoff noise. In the broader sphere of international air traffic, Canada is watching closely the introduction of supersonic planes because of the unsettling sonic boom, and other hazards.

All provinces have created agencies—for example, the Ontario Ministry of the Environment and, in Prince Edward Island, the Environmental and Technical Services Unit of the Department—to combat water, air and soil pollution, as well as to regulate sewerage systems (including the discharge of industrial wastes), smoke from factory chimneys, the use of bonfires and the dumping and destruction of garbage. Recycling of waste materials (glass, paper, metals) is being encouraged but is not as yet enforced anywhere.

As the most heavily industrialized province, Ontario has taken the lead in passing the strictest laws on pollution control. For example, if an industrial plant fails to meet the standards set down in the Air Pollution Control Act, the Ontario government can have the plant shut down until the problem is corrected. Ontario also stipulates technical standards for automobile exhaust emissions.

Virtually every province has environmental legislation already in place, or is about to bring into force a wide range of new laws. Ontario, for example, has the Environmental Protection Act and the Dangerous Goods Transportation Act, still awaiting proclamation at the time of this writing, which will extend and reinforce existing legislation. In Newfoundland, there is what is called the Clean Air, Water and Soil Authority Act; in Nova Scotia and Prince Edward Island, the Environmental Protection Acts; in New Brunswick, the Clean Environment Act and the Water Quality Regulations; in Quebec, the Environment Quality Act; in Manitoba, the Clean Environment Act; in Saskatchewan, the Department of the Environment Act and the Environmental Spill Controls Regulation; and, in British Columbia, the Environmental Management Act.

The consumer watchdogs

A small army of public servants, goaded and aided by private organizations, now stands ready to process complaints by Canadian consumers, to feed them information and to protect their rights. Associations and federations of manufacturers, professional societies, service clubs, labor unions, "pollution probe" groups, newspaper "action line" and radio "hot line" commentators, all are ready to intervene on behalf of the consumer. There are even press councils to investigate readers' complaints against newspapers.

Around the beginning of the century, the Women's Institute and the National Council of Women began to gain influence. They devoted much of their effort to consumer affairs, particularly to seeking stronger laws relating to food, textiles and home equipment. Early cooperative

movements, especially in farm areas, also encouraged housewives to press for legislative action.

A Consumers' League was organized in Ottawa during the Depression of the early 1930s, and regional councils demanded parliamentary action to lower prices. The Canadian Home Economics Association launched a campaign for more informative and accurate labeling of clothing and textiles.

It was the success during World War II of the Consumer Branch of the Wartime Prices and Trade Board that led to the growth of consumer influence. As price controls and rationing were slapped on a fighting nation, regulations poured out of Ottawa. The leaders of 18 national women's organizations had pledged support, and the Consumer Branch was set up to provide an open channel between government and people. Volunteers staffed 13 regional branches; every town and village had a liaison officer.

Consumer legislation was introduced and several times amended on the basis of information and research material provided by the volunteers. They published a paper, *Consumer News*. Their energy in seeking answers to consumer problems

Children's clothes that actually fit

UNTIL RECENTLY, shopping mothers had to try to find ready-made clothes to fit their children based on the age of the child. But age and size are only roughly related; three ten-year-olds can each require a different size. To solve this problem, the Canadian General Standards Board arranged to measure 100,000 children and from the resultant statistics developed Canada Standard Sizes (C.S.S.) for 80 children's garments.

Now the mother's shopping problem is sharply reduced. She first measures the child (over lightweight underwear) and compares the figures with those given on the charts on the next page to ascertain the nearest Canada Standard Size. Then she

looks on the store racks for clothes that bear the distinctive C.S.S. label (a coiled tape measure). It's a voluntary system, but the label can only be used by manufacturers licensed by the federal Department of Consumer and Corporate Affairs.

Remember, though, that the C.S.S. label is a statement of size only; it does not guarantee quality—that's still up to the individual shopper.

Look for this Label

led to the creation of a special Consumer Problem Division in Ottawa. Women had learned how to work together in the national interest and had demonstrated the need for the consumer to maintain a strong voice in the making of laws relating to the economy.

The independent bodies

The Consumers' Association of Canada (C.A.C.) has played a major role in the development of consumer protection law.

It was formed in 1947 to carry on the work of the Consumer Branch of the Wartime Prices and Trade Board. Since its establishment, the C.A.C. has remained a vital national force, and politicians listen carefully to its opinions.

The C.A.C. gets a grant of $200,000 a year from the federal government, but it depends primarily on membership fees and private donations. Nine provincial associations send representatives to sit on the board of directors in Ottawa. Other

Canada standard sizes for children's wear

BOYS' SIZES (MEASUREMENTS IN CENTIMETRES)

REGULAR SIZE	2	3	4	5	6	6X	7	8	10	12	14	16	18	20
CHEST	56	58	60	62	64	65	66	68	72	76	80	84	88	92
WAIST	51	52	53	54	55	56	57	58	60.5	63	65.5	68	70.5	73
HIP	50	52.5	55	57.5	60	62	62.5	65	70	75	80	85	90	95
CROTCH HEIGHT	—	—	—	—	—	—	54.5	57	64	70.5	73.5	75.5	77.5	79
WAIST HEIGHT	48.5	53.5	58.5	63.5	68.5	71.5	—	—	—	—	—	—	—	—

SLIM SIZE	2	3	4	5	6	6X	7	8	10	12	14	16	18	20
CHEST	51	53	55	57	59	60	61	63	67	71	75	79	83	87
WAIST	46	47	48	49	50	51	52	53	55.5	58	60.5	63	65.5	68
HIP	50	52.5	55	57.5	60	62	62.5	65	70	75	80	85	90	95
CROTCH HEIGHT	—	—	—	—	—	—	54.5	57	64	70.5	73.5	75.5	77.5	79
WAIST HEIGHT	48.5	53.5	58.5	63.5	68.5	71.5	—	—	—	—	—	—	—	—

HUSKY SIZE	2	3	4	5	6	6X	7	8	10	12	14	16	18	20
CHEST	—	—	—	—	—	—	—	—	77	81	85	89	93	97
WAIST	—	—	—	—	—	—	—	—	65.5	68	70.5	73	75.5	78
HIP	—	—	—	—	—	—	—	—	70	75	80	85	90	95
CROTCH HEIGHT	—	—	—	—	—	—	—	—	64	70.5	73.5	75.5	77.5	79

GIRLS' SIZES (MEASUREMENTS IN CENTIMETRES)

REGULAR SIZE	2	3	4	5	6	6X	7	8	10	12	14	16	18	20
CHEST	54	56	58	60	62	63	64	66	70	74	78	82	—	—
WAIST	49	50	51	52	53	54	54.5	55.5	58	60.5	63	65.5	—	—
HIP	50	52.5	55	57.5	60	62	62.5	65	70	75	80	85	—	—
WAIST HEIGHT	48.5	53.5	58.5	63.5	68.5	71.0	74	77	86	92	94.5	96	—	—

CHUBBY SIZE	6½	8½	10½	12½	14½
CHEST	75	79	83	87	91
WAIST	63	65.5	68	70.5	73
HIP	70	75	80	85	90
WAIST HEIGHT	86	92	94.5	96	97

board members are elected from among the C.A.C.'s membership. About 68 local C.A.C. associations across the country are staffed by volunteers. *Canadian Consumer*, the C.A.C.'s monthly magazine, publishes product test reports, consumer advice and information about local association activities.

The aims of the C.A.C. are: (1) to unite consumers in working for improved standards of living in Canadian homes: (2) to study consumer problems and to make recommendations for their solution; (3) to bring the views of consumers to the attention of government, trade and industry, and to provide a channel from them to consumers; (4) to obtain and provide information and counsel on consumer goods and services, and to conduct research and tests that will enable the association to accomplish its objectives better.

The C.A.C. has been successful in guiding (and forcing) the hand of government, and its doors are open to any Canadian genuinely concerned with consumer protection.

The Federation of Cooperative Family Economics Associations is active in Quebec in the field of consumer education and research. It has received sizeable grants from the federal government to carry on its work of counseling individuals with credit difficulties in particular.

The Canadian Toy Testing Council is typical of several private nonprofit bodies engaged in research and consumer education in specific fields. With government encouragement, the council tests toys for safety and age suitability. Every year it publishes a list of evaluations as a guide for shoppers. Its recommendations will continue to be embodied in forthcoming legislation for the protection of infants and young children.

Consumer information

Since a great many of the products available in Canadian stores are also on sale in the United States (usually under the same brand names), many Canadians study the independent assessments issued by the nonprofit Consumers' Union of the United States. For almost 50 years, the union's monthly magazine, *Consumer Reports*, has published down-to-earth critiques of just about everything from automobiles to zithers. Ralph Nader, the world's best-known crusader for consumer rights, was formerly on the union's board of directors.

Better Business Bureaus

All Canadian cities, and many sizeable towns, have a Better Business Bureau where the consumer can get specific information about the reliability and integrity of companies, agencies and tradesmen in the locality. Since their beginning in Montreal in 1918, the bureaus have dissolved the idea that all merchants are wicked money grubbers. Their motto is: "Before you invest—investigate," not *caveat emptor* (let the buyer beware).

The bureaus are supported by subscriptions from member firms, and the directors are local businessmen who volunteer their services. They make a point of collecting information on business frauds, bankruptcies, credit and service shortcomings. The Better Business Bureaus also publish such booklets as *Fact*, *Tip* and *About* that contain warnings and advice about misleading advertising, health "cures," legal and credit problems.

There are more than 750 Chambers of Commerce (C. of C.) in Canada, all dedicated to improving relations between the businessman and the consumer. The idea took shape in France in the late sixteenth century and spread to Canada in 1750. The main office of the Canadian Chamber of Commerce is in Ottawa.

The C. of C. usually includes the leading executives of the most important industries and trades and it has a great influence on consumer legislation. Although business is their main concern, the chambers have recently been playing a much wider role in community affairs. Determined to shoulder responsibility for the customers' satisfaction, and also to earn their goodwill, the C. of C. will respond to inquiry and complaint promptly.

Younger businessmen, aged 18 to 35, may enlist in the Junior Chambers of Commerce, usually referred to as the "Jaycees."

The provincial agencies

All provinces, as well as the Northwest Territories and the Yukon, have established their own consumer protection bureaus. These bureaus operate in collaboration with the federal departments of Consumer and Corporate Affairs; Environment and Fisheries; Health and Welfare; Industry, Trade and Commerce; Energy, Mines and Resources; and the Office of the Solicitor General.

Several provincial agencies are similarly active. In Ontario, for example, the Ministry of Consumer and Commercial Relations maintains a Consumer Services Bureau as part of its Business Practices Division. The Ministry also has a Property Rights Division, a Financial Institutions Division and a Technical Standards Division, which even includes an Upholstered and Stuffed Articles Branch. Ontario also has a Securities Commission to safeguard the rights of the investor—the small investor in particular. The Provincial Superintendent of Insurance looks into any complaints from policyholders, while the Registrar for loan and trust companies protects the interests of the shareholders and depositors in these companies. The other provinces provide similar consumer-protection services.

You can turn for help with consumer problems to the following provincial offices:

Newfoundland
Consumer Affairs Division
Department of Justice
P.O. Box 999
St. John's, Nfld.
A1C 5T7

Prince Edward Island
Consumer Services
Department of Community Affairs
P.O. Box 2000
Charlottetown, P.E.I.
C1A 7N8

Nova Scotia
Department of Consumer Affairs
P.O. Box 998
Halifax, N.S.
B3J 2X3

New Brunswick
Consumer and Corporate Affairs
Department of Justice
P.O. Box 6000
Fredericton, N.B.
E3B 5H1

Quebec
Office de la protection du consommateur
800 Place d'Youville
Quebec, Que.
G1R 4Y5

Ontario
Consumer Advisory Services Branch
Ministry of Consumer and Commercial Relations
555 Yonge Street—8th Floor
Toronto, Ont.
M7A 2H6

Manitoba
Consumers' Bureau
Department of Consumer and Corporate Affairs
307 Kennedy Street
Winnipeg, Man.
R3C 0V8

Saskatchewan
Consumer Information Centre
1871 Smith Street
Regina, Sask.
S4P 3V7

Alberta
Consumer Relations
Alberta Department of Consumer and Corporate Affairs
9945 50th Street
3rd Floor
Capilano Centre
Edmonton, Alta.
T6A 0L4

British Columbia
Ministry of Consumer and Corporate Affairs
865 Hornby Street, 6th Floor
Vancouver, B.C.
V6Z 2H4

Northwest Territories
Chief
Consumer Services
Department of Justice and Public Services
Government of the Northwest Territories
Yellowknife, N.W.T.
X1A 2L9

Yukon
Consumer Services
Department of Consumer and Corporate Affairs
P.O. Box 2703
Whitehorse, Y.T.
Y1A 2C6

You and

Your Money

7/Cheques, Cash and Credit

Writing a cheque 310

Using credit cards 316

When you borrow 320

If you can't pay 325

All about money

Coinage and counterfeiters
Paper money
The magic of credit
Livre and écu
Adopting the dollar
The Royal Canadian Mint

ALTHOUGH SHELLS, cattle, tea, tobacco—and even women—have been used as mediums of exchange through the centuries, man quickly focused on gold and silver. These rare and malleable metals soon came to have a widely recognized and acknowledged value and, from the start, lawmakers strove to control their use in the marketplace.

The system known as *barter*, the simple exchange of one commodity for another—perhaps a bag of corn for a clay jug—eventually proved itself too awkward to cope with the increasingly complex commerce that developed as trading spread around the ancient world bordering the Mediterranean. Where corn was plentiful, it would bring practically nothing in barter, but where it was scarce, it was many times more valuable. Transport was severely limited, making barter of large quantities of any commodity difficult. Something portable and permanent, something of easily reckoned value, was urgently required as a medium of trade.

The introduction of money—originally, crudely cut and stamped pieces of gold or free silver—is credited to the Lydians of Asia Minor in the seventh century B.C. Coins were almost always round, making them easier to handle and count and to prevent the edges or corners from being clipped off. Some had holes in the center so that the coins could be stacked on rods. Symbols and characters were stamped into the metal to state the value or indicate the authority issuing and guaranteeing them. The oldest known silver coins bear the figures of the turtle, owl and the legendary winged horse, Pegasus.

By 500 B.C. *mints* (official coin manufacturers) were operating in several Greek city-states with coinage based originally on the weight of the copper *talent* (the limit a man could carry), scaled down to handy equivalents in silver, *drachma*, of various weights. Greece and Imperial Rome spread the use of money wherever their armies marched and their merchants traded.

Gold and silver have never lost their underlying importance in the finances of the world. For instance, the monetary systems of nearly all modern countries can be traced back to be weight of a pound of pure silver—the British pound sterling (£) is perhaps the best-known example. Although the last gold coin in our commerce (the British sovereign) ceased to be issued after World War I, all currencies are still based, in theory at least, on their equivalent of gold bullion.

The expansion of trade, turning the whole world into one marketplace, would have been impossible without money. Money is at once a measure of value, a means of credit and an instantly convertible asset. The sage Publilius Syrus, who lived in the first century B.C., gave us the maxim: "Money alone sets all the world in motion." The money changers whom Jesus chased from the temple court in Jerusalem were merely operating the forerunner of today's foreign-exchange market—it was their choice of premises that was questionable.

When the movement of gold and silver itself became cumbersome or hazardous—as when the English sea pirates sacked the galleons of Spain—the use of such money substitutes as *bills of exchange*, already a long-established medium of land-based trade, grew rapidly. From these developed the various *nego-*

tiable *instruments* of finance that we know today, the best-known examples being the bank draft, money order, promissory note and cheque. (*See* "Negotiable instruments" in this chapter.)

From the beginning, kings, emperors and governments controlled the minting and issuing of money, attempting to keep its value steady within the surrounding trading area. During the Middle Ages, as international trade widened, the long-established mercantile customs (which included roughly agreed exchange rates for currencies) were set down to form the *lex mercatoria*—the law merchant. The law has continued to keep a close grip on money; even the humble cent in your pocket is regulated as to its exact design, weight and use as *legal tender*—the official description of our currency.

Coinage and counterfeiters

For many years, governments struggled to make sure their coinage actually contained precious metals equal to the face value of each coin. With coins being issued by so many small states—even by cities, large companies and, in a few cases, by families—suspicion was widespread that baser metals were being mixed with the precious; money changers were forced to use acid and other tests to establish authenticity.

While gold is one of the heaviest of metals, it is also one of the softest. Therefore, for use in practical coinage, copper or silver came to be added in a ratio of 1:12 to make it harder. Since one grain of gold can be beaten into a sheet that will cover 56 square inches, counterfeiters produced gold coins with lead centers!

As the intrinsic value of gold and silver continued to soar, coins of bronze, copper and nickel were introduced; the value of the coin came to be guaranteed by banks or by the state from their reserves and revenues instead of existing in the coin itself. Technically, all coins in common usage today in Western countries are known as *token* coinage. In an age of imitation, we had best take the advice of the Yukon poet Robert W. Service:

> *Give your gold no acid test:*
> *Try not how your silver rings*

Since the value of all coinage was based on the weight of the metals used, the lawmakers of the past had to struggle with varying standards. England, for example, has recognized four different "pounds" in its history: tower, troy, mercantile and avoirdupois. They varied in weight from 5,400 to 7,200 grains. There was a time when the English penny weighed one pennyweight *(dwt)* of a tower pound (12 ounces) of sterling silver. The present standard British pound (16 ounces: 7,000 grains avoirdupois) is represented by a platinum bar prepared in 1845; in metric terms, it is written as 453.59237 grams.

Since the days of Alexander the Great, coins have traditionally been stamped with a picture of the head of the ruler in power at the time of the minting. That's why we usually call that side of a coin the "face"; in official language, that's the obverse side (the "back" is known as the reverse). In all Moslem lands strict religious dogma prohibits the representation of any part of the human figure on coins.

Paper money

When Oliver Cromwell led his plebeian Roundheads against the Cavaliers of Charles I, wealthy families in England feared for their private hoards of gold and deposited them for safety with goldsmiths. The receipts they got from the goldsmiths soon became a form of currency in themselves. It was in this way that paper money is believed to have been brought into the English-speaking world. Of course, now it is the principal *currency* everywhere.

The goldsmiths were acting generally as bankers and discounters of loans, with large sums in gold coins, jewelry and ornaments in their vaults. Their receipts—in effect, *promissory notes*—were in wide circulation among the rich, so much so that the goldsmiths in 1694 strongly opposed the establishment of the Bank of England with its power to issue bank notes—again, basically, promises to pay. (The bank owed its beginnings to the overriding need to fund the wars against France.)

By 1709, the Bank of England had a monopoly within 65 miles of London to issue bank notes payable to the bearer. A little more than a century later, it was given complete monopoly in England. Scottish and Ulster banks retained their right to put out their own currency, and they still do today. The Bank of England was nationalized in 1946 becoming, in effect, the fiscal handmaiden of the government's treasury department. By regulating the amount of money in circulation and the interest rate at which it makes funds available to the commercial banks, it effectively controls the financial life of Britain. The example of the Bank of England profoundly affected the development and policies of the Bank of Canada which has, since 1934, regulated the supply and value of Canadian currency.

The criminal has always followed just one pace behind the latest development in the use of printed money—sometimes, briefly, he has been half a step ahead. The early printing processes offered only moderate difficulty to the forger, as notes were run off from crudely engraved flat steel plates on a hand press not much different from a mangle on a washtub. Today, the licensed bank-note companies take the most elaborate precautions in their engraving processes and in the selection of inks and paper, so that perfect forgeries are virtually impossible. A most intricate lathe is used for engraving the patterns on bank-note plates and its cutting is controlled by a secret preset combination of patterns and gears.

In recent times, counterfeiters have turned to the camera and photo-mechanical processes for printing their own money, but with only passing success.

Inflation has proved to be a bigger threat to paper money than forgery. When the idea of printing money was first discussed in the seventeenth century, people worried that kings or strong governments could not resist the temptation to simply run off what they needed for war or other purposes, irrespective of the state

When inflation ran wild

WHEN WE LOOK in the shop windows and note ruefully how prices have soared, we tend to think of inflation as a modern problem. And, in fact, the expression "inflation" in the realm of economics did not pass into general use until World War I. However, as a trend, it can be traced far back into economic history.

Whenever an influx of money creates a relatively sudden demand for goods—either apples, axes or automobiles—prices rise and we have inflation. In Shakespeare's day, the shiploads of gold and silver looted by the Spaniards from South America brought inflation to Europe. In the nineteenth century, the discovery of gold in South Africa, California, Australia and Canada did somewhat the same to those countries that based their currency on gold.

War is usually a major cause of inflation as governments borrow desperately and print bales of money to meet emergencies.

Economists claim that slight inflation is beneficial to prosperity (if people think prices are going to rise, they'll dash out and buy today) but when inflation runs riot, it quickly brings near-total ruin to the economy. Germany's deutsch mark is one of the world's strongest currencies today but immediately after World War I it was literally not worth the paper it was printed on. A housewife needed a shoebox full of money to buy a pair of shoes, a handful of bank notes to purchase a cabbage.

Eventually, in 1923, all paper money was called in and replaced with a new bank note at the ratio of one billion old marks for *one* new mark.

Will we ever really lick inflation? Not likely, if only because politicians who have to woo electors can't afford to relentlessly oppose claims (however justifiable) for more wages, salaries and other compensation. And private business must take its cue from government, like it or not.

of the national treasury. They knew it would mean that each extra piece of paper money would have less value, for there would be less gold and silver to back it up. When the supply of money exceeds the amount of goods and services available, we have inflation.

The magic of credit

Without the institution of *credit* we would certainly not enjoy the wide-ranging and generally prosperous life that is available to the great majority of the people of North America. While most people know what it is, credit is extremely hard to define. You probably know what it is like to borrow ten bucks from a friend—or out of the housekeeping money—but when you realize that our federal, provincial and municipal governments are run almost without exception on borrowed money and that Canada in turn lends huge sums of money to other countries—for instance to the U.S.S.R. to finance a wheat deal—you begin to wonder whether you understand the subject after all.

Essentially, though, credit is the same in all its guises, whether we are speaking of ten dollars or ten million dollars. It hinges basically upon confidence. The man (or bank) with the money, *the lender*, must feel reasonably certain that the person (or company) asking for the money, the *borrower*, will be able to pay the charge set for the service, the *interest*, and return the sum borrowed, the *principal*, when he promises he will. If that confidence does not exist, credit cannot exist either.

Credit can also be based on *collateral*. This involves the borrower being willing to transfer to the lender ownership or physical control of some property at least equal in value to the amount of the loan so that, should he fail to repay the lender as arranged, the lender is protected. When the loan is repaid, ownership is restored to the borrower. Loans will often be granted against partial collateral, but a high-risk borrower might be required to provide surplus collateral.

The granting and acceptance of credit always involves a contract, even if the whole thing is settled with just a hand-shake. In this field, the law stands on guard to protect both the lender and the borrower. Most consumer lending (including charges on overdue bills) is subject to government regulation under banking and consumer-protection laws. The law also insists that the lender tell the borrower both the total amount of interest to be paid on a loan, or debt, and the actual rate, stated in annual terms of interest, being charged. While permitted rates of interest cannot be set down comprehensively in legislation (because circumstances of loans differ so widely), several provinces prohibit the charging of more than a *fair rate* of interest. What's more, the responsibility of proving what is "fair" can be placed upon the lender.

Other federal and provincial laws regulate borrowing from pawnbrokers and from finance and loan companies that offer easy credit to the householder. These laws are discussed later in this chapter.

Livre and écu

Although the prime beaver skin used in barter was, perhaps, the original "money" used by Europeans on Canadian soil, the first coins that can be considered at least partly Canadian were the five-sou and 15-sou silver pieces struck by the order of Louis XIV in 1670 for use in his colonies in the Americas. Another colonial coin of copper worth nine deniers appeared in the early eighteenth century.

Of course, the ordinary run of French coinage of the time was in circulation, if sparingly, in New France for a century and a half, together with the silver dollar of Spain which was introduced through commerce with the West Indies and by the Atlantic cod trade. The French coinage, in descending order of value, included: the louis d'or, écu, livre, sou and denier. The livre (forerunner of the modern franc) was the common unit, filling a position in the currency table similar to that occupied by a quarter today. The louis d'or was worth about 25 livres. It must be noted, however, that in the eighteenth century the purchasing power of the livre was far greater than that of the quarter (25¢) today.

Intendant Jacques de Meulles of New

287

France (1682–86) added a novelty to the world history of currency when, short of money to pay troops, he created his own by simply writing the denomination across the face of a playing card and signing it. He had a law passed, guranteeing that these "bills" would be redeemed at full face value when the next ship arrived from France with cash of the realm. Several succeeding intendants followed his lead, and "card money" came to fill a useful role in bridging the gap of credit emergencies.

Government promissory notes, known as *ordonnances*, were also issued, more recklessly as the French regime grew more unstable. It was estimated that at one time paper money of a face value of 80 million livres was in circulation. The French abandoned their financial responsibilities when the British took over New France in 1760. The paper was eventually redeemed at 25 percent of its face value.

Adopting the dollar

The spanish silver dollar—the famous "piece of eight"(eight reales) was prized in Canada and throughout the rest of British North America from earliest days. The word "dollar" derived from the English pronunciation of the thaler, a silver coin minted in Bohemia (in central Europe) from the early sixteenth century.

When the British took over in Canada (1760), the currency situation was chaotic. Merchants were issuing their own printed notes (called *bons*), redeemable for goods at their shops—in much the same fashion as many department stores offer gift certificates today. These were exchanged hand to hand among the citizenry. Later, to pay for garrison supplies and military works, the colonial government authorized the issue of so-called army bills—in effect, printed paper money in convenient standard amounts that were guaranteed by the British treasury. Because of a chronic shortage of small change, larger coins were being sliced into smaller pieces.

In its private commercial empire in the vast Northwest—and throughout the fur-trading industry—the brass token money issued by the Hudson's Bay Company was standard. The largest coin—known as one made-beaver—was equal in value to a first-grade beaver skin.

In an attempt at standardization, Governor James Murray in 1764 had set the value of the Spanish dollar at six shillings and laid down English equivalent values for the multinational mixture of moneys circulating. The dollar became further entrenched when the United States adopted a decimal monetary system, and began operating its own mint in 1792. Although Britain made determined and repeated efforts in the nineteenth century to keep Canada to the pound-shilling-pence system, the dollar had become the general medium of business. Chartered banks were by then issuing their own paper money, in dollars.

Serious efforts were launched from 1841 to give Canada (then comprising just the central provinces) its own decimal currency; legislation to that effect was passed in 1851 and amended in 1853. A further act was proclaimed on January 1, 1858, requiring that all government accounts must in future be kept in dollars and cents. The official adoption of the dollar in Canada is dated from that act.

The Royal Canadian Mint

At Confederation, the jurisdiction over money and banking was given to the federal government. The Uniform Currency Act (1871) extented the decimal system to the Maritimes, and paved the way for its further extension to British Columbia and other provinces as they joined the union. The British gold sovereign (reckoned at $5) remained the standard in Canada until 1910 and silver coins continued to be imported from England. (The colonies of British Columbia and Newfoundland had gold pieces of their own until they joined Confederation.)

A branch of the Royal Mint was established at Ottawa in 1908. It remained under British control until 1931 when it was taken over by the federal Department of Finance. The mint now has the status of a Crown corporation. Renamed the Royal Canadian Mint, it manufactures all Canadian coins and official medals. It also operates a busy gold refinery. Between

1910 and 1914, the mint issued gold coins of $5 and $10 values, and British gold sovereigns (bearing a "C") were produced until 1919. Canada has never had a gold coinage of its own in general circulation, however.

Our present 25¢ and 10¢ pieces are made of pure nickel; silver dollars are only minted to commemorate special occasions of national or provincial importance. The 5¢ coin is made of copper and nickel, and the 1¢ "penny" of bronze. There are normally more than ten billion pennies in circulation.

Until 1945, paper currency issued by the privately owned chartered banks was circulating side by side with bank notes of the Dominion of Canada; however, from that date, this currency was gradually withdrawn and redeemed. All Canadian bank notes now are manufactured and issued by the state-owned Bank of Canada, which acts as banker to the federal government, reserve banker to the trading banks and administrator of the public debt. (*See* Chapter 1, "Under Canadian writ.")

Bills are issued in denominations of $1, $2, $5, $10, $20, $50, $100 and $1,000. Each note tells you that the Bank of Canada "will pay the bearer on demand . . ." whatever amount is designated as its face value. But don't turn up in Ottawa and ask for gold. The Bank of Canada is not required to maintain gold or foreign-exchange reserves to back up the bills' promises. In any case, each mint bar of the gold reserve weighs 400 ounces troy (which is 33.3 pounds in troy weight), and are worth about $200,000 a piece.

The playing-card money of New France

A shortage of coin aggravated by wartime blockades forced the authorities of New France to adopt novel solutions. There was no shortage of playing cards and, once given a denomination and signed by the governor and the intendant on the reverse side, the cards became legal tender. They are treasured today by collectors as Canada's first paper money.

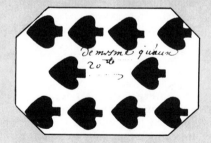

—courtesy Public Archives of Canada

Long after the fall of New France, the Spanish dollar and the British sovereign were the main coins in Canadian trade but fractional money was a problem. Some merchants solved this by issuing their own in the form of paper certificates, known as *bons.*

—courtesy Bank of Canada

When you pay cash

Cash-and-carry and C.O.D.

Discount for cash

Legal tender

Obsolete and torn currency

ANADA has not had a bank failure since 1923 when the Home Bank collapsed in Ontario. Although such an event appears unthinkable today, there are a surprising number of people around who still prefer to keep sizable funds on hand in ready cash.

In an imperfect world, some of them probably want to avoid giving taxation inspectors any more records of income than they have to. Others are prepared to risk being robbed for the simple satisfaction of "flashing a roll." Some are genuinely uneasy—mostly because of ignorance or language difficulties—about putting their hard-earned money into the hands of a stranger behind a bank wicket. Every year, police and firemen report finding treasure troves of bank notes and coins, often large amounts, hidden in walls, stashed in milk cans and cookie jars and even stuffed in the traditional mattress.

Although the law will attempt to protect your property—and that goes for your money as well as for anything else you own—the wise man does not tempt fate. Nothing is easier to steal and harder to trace than money.

Although at least 80 percent of all transactions involving money are carried out by cheque or credit card today, it is still true that the man with cash is assured of a warm welcome anywhere in the marketplace—and in most other places too.

They say a dollar bill has no conscience; nor has it a memory. The man who can lay his cash "on the barrelhead" is in a position to take immediate advantage of any bargain that comes his way.

The law states that cash has to be accepted in payment of any debt, subject to the regulation on legal tender.

For 2,000 years *cash* was the popular name of the copper coinage of China:

round coins with a distinctive square hole in the center. The word came to be used in the West to mean all ready money, not only "folding money" and coins in the pocket but anything immediately convertible, such as cheques, money orders, bearer bonds and eventually even deposits in a bank on *current account*. We use it as the opposite of *credit*. And we have made a verb of it: as in "cashing" a cheque.

Cash-and-carry and C.O.D.

Cash is at the core of the supermarket takeover in Canadian shopping. Where the family grocer, butcher, hardware merchant and draper since pioneer times had allowed the householder to run up a monthly bill, the chain supermarket operator sells his wares for cash only. Since the modern merchant does not have to incur interest charges at the bank to carry any customer *accounts receivable*, he can, theoretically, pass on the saving to the shopper.

In 1922, as mail-order selling mushroomed, the Canadian Post Office extended its facilities by providing cash-on-delivery (C.O.D.) service to the public. For a modest fee based on the amount collected, the post office will accept goods in the mail that must be paid for by the addressee before delivery is completed by the postman.

Some large department stores also offer a cash-on-delivery shopping service within their own delivery areas. You pay the deliveryman when he hands you what you have ordered.

When you are dealing C.O.D. with a well-known company, you are probably safe enough if you discover that the goods turn out to be damaged or otherwise unsatisfactory after you have opened the package. The store is almost certain to offer a broad guarantee of customer satisfaction (*See* Chapter 6, "Guarantees and standards"). But if you order goods C.O.D. from small or unknown companies—especially those using a post office box as an address—you could be defrauded. After you have paid the mailman and accepted the package, you cannot expect the post office to return your money or undertake to get unsatisfactory goods exchanged or repaired for you.

If you feel you have been treated unfairly in a cash-on-delivery deal, complain to the company concerned. If you have no luck there, take your story to the consumer-protection agency nearest you. If you don't live in an urban area, write to Bureau of Consumer Services, Consumer and Corporate Affairs, 240 Bank Street, 2nd floor, Ottawa, Ontario, K2P 1X4.

No matter what form of payment you use—cash, credit or cheque—every purchase is essentially a contract; and the laws of contract are there to protect your interests.

Discount for cash

Since Victorian times, to reward prompt payers, certain merchants offered a small discount on accounts that were paid within a short time (usually ten days) after the date of billing. But as consumer credit became more widespread after World War II, even payment at 30 days came to be considered prompt. In fact, 30 days' credit has become practically standard and is regarded by many merchants as "cash." This had led, especially in keenly competitive smaller businesses, to a revival of a discount being given for cash payment at the time of purchase—perhaps 1% or 2% for payment within ten days.

You don't have to be an economist to realize that the cost of credit (even 30 days' credit) must be included in the price of any article or service. Thus, where a period of supposedly interest-free credit is allowed in the normal run of business, you may want some recognition for paying cash over the counter. You could argue that the price should be reduced by

Payment C.O.D./Envoi C.R.

When goods are sent to you by mail "Cash on Delivery" (C.O.D.) they should arrive bearing this portion of the Canada Post Office docket. The mailman can't hand over the parcel until you pay him cash for the sum marked. The other sections provide a receipt for the sender, file copies for the Post Office and a delivery record.

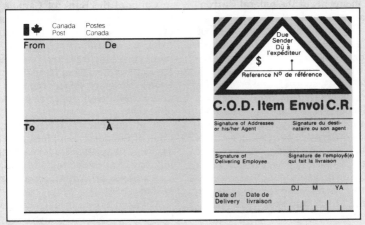

a percentage that would represent the store's saving in bank interest and in administrative costs resulting from sending out customer accounts. Since a retail company probably itself gets 30 days' credit, or more, from its wholesale supplier, it can, in turn, actually make more money from buyers who are prepared to pay cash for goods.

Where a merchant accepts credit cards, he is obliged to pay a fee to the card company for acting as his collection agency. Also, he often has to wait up to 60 days to get his money. Since his advertised prices are usually the same whether the customer uses a credit card or pays cash, he appears to be asking the cash customer to help cover the cost of the credit system and subsidize the card user. Some persons who buy for cash are asking, with growing emphasis and considerable logic, that they be charged a lower price in consideration of their saving the merchant both collection and interest charges. One recent development is the spread of discount stores where everything is sold on a cash-only basis.

Legal tender

Although the law provides that a creditor must accept cash in full discharge of a debt it also places some restrictions on the form in which the money is to be given. The creditor has the right to insist that he be paid in *legal tender*.

Under the terms of the federal Currency Exchange Act of 1970, legal tender consists of the bank notes of the Bank of Canada, gold currency coins minted in Canada, or subsidiary coins to the following limits: silver coins up to the value of $10; nickel coins, up to $5; and bronze, up to 25 cents. Strictly speaking, then, you have no legal right to insist on paying for a ride on a subway in pennies. Cheques and money orders can be refused by merchants—although it's highly unlikely they would be.

You cannot insist on paying for something with a bank note larger than the price of the article and then demand the difference in change. Under the law of contract, you are required to offer the exact amount due. Of course, it would be

rare for a shopkeeper to refuse to make change for you.

On the other hand, if you offer in legal tender the exact amount due on a debt and it is refused, then the debt or financial obligation can be considered discharged.

Obsolete and torn currency

When the Bank of Canada began operation on March 11, 1935, it was named the sole issuer of Canadian paper money. Up to that time, the chartered, or commercial, banks had each printed and issued their own paper money (up to an authorized level based on their assets and deposits) and the federal government had issued its Dominion of Canada notes. The government's currency was called in and replaced with Bank of Canada bills and the commercial banks were allowed ten years to reduce their currency to a maximum amount not exceeding 25 percent of their paid-up-capital.

At the end of World War II, the right of the commercial banks to issue currency was canceled and they were given five years to withdraw and redeem all issues outstanding. In January 1950, the commercial banks' responsibility for these obsolete notes was taken over by the Bank of Canada.

If you should find any of these old bills in a trunk in the attic (or any earlier currency issued by any legal government in Canada) the Bank of Canada will no doubt exchange them for modern currency, but you will probably get a better offer from a *numismatist* (collector of old money). A single penny token issued by the Bank of Montreal in 1838 is worth at least $150 today; depending on its condition, a 1948 silver dollar might be valued at $1,000.

As all currency is the property of the Bank of Canada, it is a criminal offense to deface it. If you have a torn or mutilated bill, any chartered bank will replace it as long as both serial numbers on the bill are visible.

Worn-out currency is continually collected and replaced by the Bank of Canada. Approximately $4.5 billion in worn or torn bank notes are burned every year.

Negotiable instruments

THE WORLD of commerce has its own special jargon—which you can study at your leisure in the business pages of any large daily newspaper, or in such specialized publications as *The Financial Post.* The vocabulary will include such terms as bills of exchange, sight drafts, promissory notes, installment notes, documentary drafts and letters of credit. These are all *negotiable instruments.* (The everyday cheques you write also fall into this category but they will be discussed later in this chapter.)

Negotiable instruments are, in effect, another form of money—a sort of super-cheque. Their history goes back perhaps 3,000 years and they are still in wide and general use in business today. They are woven into the fabric of international commercial law and it would require several volumes to explain in detail all their forms and usages. All that can be attempted in this space is to provide you with a general grasp of the main forms and indicate how they play an important role in the country's economic life and, indeed, in your own affairs.

The essential points about a negotiable instrument are (1) it is a written promise or request for the payment of a stated sum of money; (2) it is transferable to another party, either by endorsement or simply by delivery; (3) if it is properly drawn up and signed, it is enforceable at law—that is, the paper itself is accepted as valid proof of a contract that was the cause of its having been issued. The legal holder of a negotiable instrument can sue the original issuer to collect payment of the amount owing even if he has never met him or if no business has ever actually passed between them.

Custom becomes law

Although commerce may seem an unlikely source of romance, the negotiable instrument has a fascinating history, going back to the Greek and Roman merchants of pre-Christian times. By the Middle Ages, what we know as the *bill of exchange* was in use to facilitate trade between nations.

If a merchant in Bristol imported a cargo of wine from Lisbon, it was not necessary for the Portuguese captain to take back with him a chest full of *specie* (coin or other forms of precious metal with the official stamp on it attesting to its fineness). He would have been too easy a target for pirates, especially if he was calling at several ports on a journey lasting many months.

Instead of paying cash at the docks, the English buyer would arrange to pay the price of the wine to a banking house in England which would, in turn, issue a bill of exchange for the amount, payable in Lisbon in Portuguese currency. The vintner could by this arrangement have his money paid directly to him in his home town without risk.

With trade flowing both ways, the banking houses (in reality, international money changers) built up credits in one country and debts in another. The transactions would not, of course, always cancel out evenly and so lawyers were brought into the picture to work out ways to adjust the balances. At the annual fairs in the large trade capitals (similar to the business conventions of today), the bankers met to match up and exchange their "paper." When the swapping was done, those still holding favorable balances would be paid in coin.

It was only one logical step from there to having the bill of exchange made out in the first place to the favor of the original creditor or to his *order*. Now, the Portuguese wine merchant could use the same bill to pay someone to whom he owed money, possibly in another country. He could *endorse* the bill (by signing his name on the back) and order in writing that the amount be paid to a third party— maybe to a creditor who had stipulated payment in England as part of a contract. If the man in Lisbon merely endorsed the bill, without naming a new *payee*, then it could be presented for payment by the *bearer*—any person who had legal possession of the document. Thus, the bill originally drawn up by the English wine merchant could eventually be cashed by an exporter of timber from the Baltic, or by a spice merchant in the Levant.

To work efficiently, this system required that the bill of exchange was honored when presented by any bona fide holder to whom it had been assigned (called the *transferee*). The original issuer could not refuse to pay because, perhaps, his barrels of wine had turned out to be vinegary. He might well have a case for breach of contract against his supplier, but that would have no effect on the validity of the bill of exchange, which remained valid as money.

Although all this may sound clumsy in this era of instant telecommunications, it worked surprisingly well in the marketplace of the time. The first negotiable instruments provided a way for trade to flow across borders and seas when the seller could not effectively check up on the reliability of his buyer. Everybody gained by sticking to the rules. As discovery and exploration multiplied overseas trading in the sixteenth and seventeenth centuries, the ancient code of conduct known as the law merchant, which set out the basic obligations and rights of the parties to a trading deal, was brought within the English Common Law.

The nature of negotiability
In simplest terms, for the bill, draft or other "instrument" to be negotiable, the person (or company) to whom it is made out (the *payee*) must be able to transfer his right of payment to another without having to notify the original debtor (the *drawee)*. The instrument must, of course, be in writing and the wording of the promise to pay must be clear enough that it will be acceptable to an outsider quite ignorant of any of the terms of the contract between the original parties.

The instrument must be for an exact payment of money; it cannot be a promise to send goods or to provide services. It must be unconditional and it must be payable either at a fixed or determinable time in the future, or on demand.

If the paper does not include the words "to the order of" or "bearer," then it is not considered negotiable; such a bill could only be cashed by the person or company named as payee in the first place.

Bills of Exchange Act
The great British jurists, Sir John Holt (1642–1710) and William Murray, 1st Earl of Mansfield (1705–93), were mainly responsible for the Herculean effort of reducing the old customs and ready-made justice of the market courts to legal terms and incorporating them within the normal body of law, available not only to merchants in their guilds but to all citizens. A large body of case law was built up which proved flexible enough for most commercial disputes but became increasingly unwieldy as British overseas trade mushroomed with the growth of the British Empire. At that time, the Bills of Exchange Act, the Bank Act and the Personal Property Security Act were passed. These formed part of the law that was imported into the Canadian colonies.

Under the British North America Act (now the Constitution Act 1867), control over commerce was split between the federal and provincial governments. Power over bills of exchange, interest, banking, bankruptcy, shipping and patents was put in federal hands; the provinces were given authority over justice, civil and property rights, contract law, sale of goods, and partnerships.

Both levels of government shared company and insurance law. This mixed responsibility in the world of business caused some legal headaches. However, a considerable measure of uniformity was reached since all Canadian jurisdictions (including the legislature of Quebec) largely followed the British example.

In the late nineteenth century, the British lawmakers set to work sorting through the largely obsolete *lex mercatoria* and redefining the essential precedents, or standards, built up over centuries of case law. They issued a series of major statutes, including the Sale of Goods Act, the Factors Act and the Partnership Act. These statutes have been copied in practically every Western country.

Another pioneer work was the Bills of Exchange Act which Canada's federal politicians moved quickly to adopt in 1890. The Canadian statute is a copy of the British legislation with only minor modifications. This act clearly defines such commercial terms as *promissory notes* and *cheques*.

The draft

The draft is one of the most common bills of exchange used in credit transactions. A typical example would involve a small retailer who buys goods from a manufacturer or wholesaler. The buyer-retailer orders the goods and agrees with the supplier on the payment—how much for the goods, plus when and how payment will be made. Once the period of agreed credit is up—sometimes before the goods are dispatched—the supplier draws a draft through his bank on the merchant and sends it to the branch of the bank nearest to him.

When the bank receives the draft, it presents it to the buyer-merchant for payment. If the merchant chooses to honor the draft (*i.e.* acknowledge the debt he owes), which is likely if he has settled with the supplier beforehand, he must certify his *acceptance* by signing his name on the face of the draft.

Remember the three parties involved in this transaction: the person who writes the draft is the *drawer;* the person to whom it is addressed is the *drawee;* and the person to whom the money is to be paid is the *payee.* The drawer can name himself as payee, or he can direct that the

Speeding world trade

There was a time when Canadian businessmen—exporters and importers—had to depend on travelers arriving by sailing ship for accurate knowledge of the value of foreign money in Canadian terms. International deals were understandably slow and negotiations infinitely cautious. Today, with the blessing of telecommunications, a businessman just about anywhere in Canada can decide if he can close a profitable deal in Austria or Australia, Netherlands or Norway simply by glancing at the foreign exchange rates in his morning newspaper. These tables will usually be found in the financial section, in a form similar to this:

FOREIGN EXCHANGE

MID-MARKET RATES IN CANADIAN FUNDS, NOV. 17, 1983.
Prepared by the Bank of Nova Scotia.

Country	Currency	Noon
United States	Dollar	$1.2374
Britain	Pound	1.8295
Australia	Dollar	1.1358
Austria	Schilling	.0654
Bahamas	Dollar	1.2374
Belgium	Franc	.02261
Bermuda	Dollar	1.2374
Denmark	Krone	.1276
France	Franc	.1510
Greece	Drachma	.0130
Hong Kong	Dollar	.1584
Italy	Lira	.000758
Japan	Yen	.005240
Lebanon	Pound	.2597
Mexico	Peso	.00798
Netherlands	Guilder	.4095
Norway	Krone	.1655
Portugal	Escudo	.00973
South Africa	Rand	1.0283
Spain	Peseta	.00802
Sweden	Krona	.1560
Switzerland	Franc	.5671
West Germany	Mark	.4587
Antigua, Grenada, St. Lucia	E.C. Dollar	.4622

Prepared by the Royal Bank of Canada
The U.S. dollar was unchanged at $1.2371 in terms of Canadian dollars in Toronto Thursday. Pound sterling closed at $1.8321, down $0.0007.
In New York, the Canadian dollar was unchanged at $0.8083 in terms of U.S. funds. The pound was down $0.0005 at $1.4810.
The ECU exchange rate for the Canadian dollar was $1.04158.

Banking forms in common use

SAVINGS PASSBOOK

CANADIAN IMPERIAL BANK OF COMMERCE
SAVINGS ACCOUNT

DATE	PARTICULARS	WITHDRAWAL	DEPOSIT	BALANCE
JAN 10	DEP		****200.00	*****594.75
JAN 12	WD	*****30.00		*****564.75
JAN 17	DEP		*****150.00	*****714.75
JAN 20	WD	*****100.00		*****614.75
JAN 21	WD	*****35.00		*****579.75
JAN 24	DEP		****345.00	*****924.75
JAN 26	DEP		*****100.00	****1024.75
JAN 28	WD	*****300.00		*****724.75
JAN 31	DEP		****200.00	*****924.75
FEB 4	WD	****195.50		*****729.25
FEB 7	DEP		*****150.00	*****879.25
FEB 9	DEP		*****500.00	****1379.25
FEB 11	WD	*****50.00		****1329.25
FEB 14	WD	***1000.00		*****329.25

• A few cents a day will rent a Safety Deposit Box •

CHEQUING-SAVINGS ACCOUNT PASSBOOK

CANADIAN IMPERIAL BANK OF COMMERCE
CHEQUING SAVINGS ACCOUNT

DATE	PARTICULARS	WITHDRAWAL	DEPOSIT	BALANCE
NOV 7	DEP		****386.72	****792.66
NOV 11	CHQ	*****47.00		****745.66
NOV 14	CHQ	****295.00		****450.66
NOV 15	CHQ	******9.82		****440.84
NOV 18	DEP		****216.54	****657.38
NOV 25	CHQ	****115.00		****542.38
NOV 26	CHQ	*****12.67		****529.71
NOV 29	CHQ	*****18.92		****510.79
NOV 29	CM		****145.00	****655.79
DEC 2	CHQ	*****10.00		****645.79
DEC 3	CHQ	*****35.87		****609.92
DEC 3	DEP		****216.54	****826.46
DEC 9	CHQ	*****85.00		****741.46
DEC 10	DEP		****119.64	****861.10

• A few cents a day will rent a Safety Deposit Box •

PERSONAL CHEQUING ACCOUNT STATEMENT

CANADIAN IMPERIAL BANK OF COMMERCE
PAGE

140 Main Street West
Centreville, Sask.

RAYMOND L. CARTER
678 GROSSEILLERS BLVD. S.
CENTREVILLE, SASK. W3M2F6

ACCOUNT NO	TRANSIT NO		BALANCE FORWARD
12-21833	3512	23/07/76	572.37

DEBITS	CREDITS	DATE	BALANCE
	100.00	17 09	
26.17			
285.70			
	236.42	20 09	360.50
116.27			
56.30			424.35

PERSONAL CHEQUING ACCOUNT

CHEQUING-SAVINGS ACCOUNT CHEQUE

CANADIAN IMPERIAL BANK OF COMMERCE

HASTINGS AND RICHARDS
VANCOUVER, B.C.
19

PAY TO THE
ORDER OF $

DOLLARS

CHEQUING SAVINGS
ACCOUNT NUMBER

⑈00 200⑈0 ⑉0⑈ 00⑈00 ⑉6 7⑈

WITHDRAWAL SLIP

FORM 21-78

NOT FOR USE
OUTSIDE THIS OFFICE

DATE

CANADIAN IMPERIAL
BANK OF COMMERCE

ACCOUNT NUMBER

BRANCH

RECEIVED FROM CANADIAN IMPERIAL BANK OF COMMERCE $

DOLLARS

WITHDRAWAL
ALL ACCOUNTS

SIGNATURE

THIS FORM MAY BE USED TO TRANSFER FUNDS WITHIN THE BRANCH TO ANY OTHER ACCOUNT.

PERSONAL MONEY ORDER

PERSONAL CHEQUING ACCOUNT RECORD BOOK

DEPOSIT SLIP

PERSONAL CHEQUING ACCOUNT CHEQUE

SIGHT OR TERM DRAFT

297

BANKING FORMS IN COMMON USE (CONTINUED)

TRAVELER'S CHEQUE

BANK DRAFT

INTERNATIONAL BANK DRAFT

PROMISSORY NOTE

—Documents courtesy
Canadian Imperial
Bank of Commerce

debt be settled with the bank, thus naming the bank as payee. By naming the bank as payee, he is taking advantage of another of the draft's features: the drawee is likely to pay the draft right on time to the bank rather than chance becoming known as a poor credit risk. It is a technique that is quite often adopted with those companies or individuals known to put off settling their accounts.

Three types of drafts can be arranged, depending on the time allowed for payment:

A *demand draft* must be paid at once, as soon as it is presented.

A *sight draft*, stating literally that the bill must be paid "at sight" of the paper, actually allows the drawee three days (and perhaps more) to find the money. (*See* "Days of grace" in this section.)

A *time draft* allows a specified number of days, weeks or perhaps even months "after date" (that is, after the date when the draft was made out for payment). Sometimes a time draft will state that it must be paid a certain number of days "after sight," or after it is presented.

Some businesses needing immediate cash take their outstanding time drafts to a bank, or finance company, and assign them—in effect, sell them at a small discount, or use them as *collateral* for a loan. Of course, they could only do this with drafts that had already been accepted by the drawee, as described above.

If a supplier wants to make sure that a buyer will accept the debt obligation of his purchase before the goods are handed over, he can attach a draft to the *bill of lading* that is issued by the common carrier. The customer can inspect the goods at the carrier's warehouse but the carrier is not authorized to give him possession until he signs the draft as *acceptor*. Once the draft is accepted, the bill of lading is given to the customer and the carrier releases the shipment.

Even before a draft has been formally accepted by the debtor, it will sometimes be endorsed and may perhaps be used in several transactions. The fact that the drawer is a person (or a company) of reputation offers a strong guarantee that the draft will eventually be paid. The general reasoning is that it would not have been made in the first place if it did not cover a valid and enforceable contract.

Once the supplier and customer have confidence in each other, they usually dispense with using drafts. Goods are then dispatched upon receipt of orders, the customer paying his account by cheque within the agreed-upon credit period (normally 30 days).

The promissory note

The promissory note is perhaps the best-known and most widely used of all forms of "commercial paper" governed by the Bills of Exchange Act. It represents an unconditional promise in writing by one person, the *maker*, to pay another. The signed note records the maker's promise to pay, either at a fixed date or upon demand, an exact sum of money to (or to the order of) a specific person, the *payee* or the bearer.

The promissory note usually has to be repaid with interest added.

The main difference between a promissory note and a draft is the absence of a "third party" to the transaction. The promissory note usually involves two persons: one pledges to pay to another, or to that other person's order, a certain sum of money. In contrast, the draft (as explained earlier) calls upon the *drawee* to pay the sum of money involved. Another difference is that the draft is made out by the person to whom the money is owed, while the note is made out by the person who owes the money. Once the note is signed by the person to whom the money is owed, it can be used by him in other financial transactions without the agreement, or even the knowledge, of the *promisor* (the maker).

In order to be valid, a promissory note must include the date that it is issued, the date that the money is due, and a statement that there has been *value received* by the promisor. The note must, of course, be signed by the promisor and the unconditional nature of the promise to pay a certain sum must be stressed. This means that if the note is used as payment in a financial deal with some other person, the original promisor must still pay the debt. Be warned, however, that when the payee endorses the note in order to make payment to some other person, he in effect "backs" the note and (unless he endorses with the words "without recourse") he will be held responsible if the original promisor fails to pay the note when it is due.

A promissory note can be made out in foreign currency, as long as the actual payment is to be made in Canadian *legal tender*. The foreign-exchange rates are easy to obtain from any bank or from the financial pages of your newspaper.

Even if a note is written "payable on demand," it must be presented for payment at a reasonable time—not, for example, at midnight. It would only be after the payee had made a reasonable demand and been unable to collect that he could sue for overdue payment.

The simple I O U (these initials representing "I owe you" have been in use since the seventeenth century) is an acknowledgment of debt, not a promissory note; however, it becomes a legally enforceable note if it is signed and if it carries the date of repayment. So try not to scribble them too freely at all-night poker parties —that, in effect, is real money you are manufacturing.

Every Canadian bank note is really a promissory note since the Bank of Canada, in effect, "promises" to give value to the bearer for the denomination printed on the note. It is the least complicated of all negotiable instruments.

Letters of credit

The letter of credit serves two particular purposes. Sometimes a supplier who is not certain of getting his money from a new customer will ask the buyer to send him a *letter of credit* in advance. This negotiable instrument, issued by a bank, flatly promises to honor any order of payment (such as a draft) drawn against its account holder up to the amount set down in the letter of credit. Thus covered against the risk of nonpayment, the supplier ships off the goods ordered and probably draws a draft against his new customer; once the debtor has accepted it, that draft becomes negotiable—the sup-

plier can get his money immediately, although at a small discount. The supplier armed with the letter of credit could, of course, draw the draft on his debtor's bank and in that way probably avoid any loss in discounting. This might not encourage repeat orders, however.

Another kind of letter of credit is used by travelers. Instead of paying for traveler's cheques (*See* "The role of the bank" in this chapter), the man who is frequently on business abroad will get a letter from his bank authorizing withdrawals up to a set amount from any overseas agency or correspondent affiliated with his bank. (Most domestic chartered banks have branches, or correspondents, in almost every country around the world.) The charge for this service is small since the bank simply takes the required sum from the depositor's account.

As the traveler moves around on his business trip, he takes his letter into the designated foreign bank and gets the cash he needs. The teller will write into the letter the sum withdrawn. When the traveler has drawn cash up to the figure stated in the letter, the paper is worthless. If the traveler has some of his credit unused at the end of the trip, the bank will redeem the unspent portion, letting the residue of the money flow back into the client's regular bank account.

Days of grace

Section 42 of the Bills of Exchange Act provides for a three-day period of grace in the case of a draft or note which is not payable on demand or which states that the *days of grace* shall not apply.

Thus a draft payable "at sight" or a draft with a specified due date is not overdue until after the third day of grace.

It can happen, of course, that the third day of grace—known as the *maturity date*—is a Sunday, or a statutory holiday (in Quebec, also certain religious festival days), when most businesses are closed. On these so-called *nonjuridical days* the date of maturity can be postponed until the next normal business day. As you can see, the grace period can be spun out to four and, because of certain long weekends, five days.

The role of the bank

IT WAS ENTIRELY natural in colonial days that Canada should adopt British banking ideas, principles and practices, and that Canadian banking law should flow from British precedents in the same manner. In the Maritimes before Confederation, and in the national sphere after 1867, some techniques hammered out by trial and sometimes costly error in the United States were grafted on to our banking system. Nevertheless, the traditions and influences of London's Lombard and Threadneedle Streets have continued to dominate.

Evidence of the British legacy runs strongly through the economic life of Canada and can be studied in a number of specialized books on the subject. But there are two obvious ways in which this legacy has affected the economic life of just about everybody:

(1) Canadian banks have always been conservative; slow to take risks, they are equally cautious in safeguarding the deposits entrusted to their care and in maintaining the financial stability of the country as a whole.

(2) Charters to establish banks have been very difficult to obtain in Canada. For more than a century the government has enforced stiff standards of capital requirement and has strictly supervised the few banks it has chartered. Although privately owned, Canadian banks are really quasi-public institutions.

Some critics of Canada's conservatism in banking argue that commercial development has been hindered by the banks' unwillingness to provide capital for admittedly high-risk but potentially high-earning ventures. Yet this argument must be weighed against the great strength and stability of our financial machine. For more than 60 years, no Canadian who has deposited a dollar in a chartered bank has lost his money due to a breach of trust or bank incompetence. There are few countries in the world that can match Canada's record in this field.

The careful granting of bank charters has resulted in there being 13 Canadian chartered banks in existence today; they have more than 7,000 branches all across the country and some 300 branches abroad. Of these, ten have assets of a billion dollars or more. Several are regional institutions (for example, the Bank of British Columbia which recently was operating only 51 branches) or banks specializing in commercial business. The Canadian scheme of *branch banking* with strong centralized head-office control contrasts vividly with the system of *unit banking*, in the United States, with literally thousands of independent banks licensed by both state and federal authorities. A measure of stability was brought to the United States banking system when banks insured the deposits in their accounts with the Federal Deposit Insurance Corporation or with state authorities.

The chartered banks

The Bank of Montreal, chartered in 1822, holds the distinction of being the oldest bank in Canada. Several banks were, in fact, chartered earlier but they all failed or merged with other organizations. The Montreal bank's charter follows closely the terms of the charter of the first Bank of the United States, founded by Alexander Hamilton in 1791, but both were modeled on the Bank of England.

301

Started with a capital of only $150,000, the Bank of Montreal was limited by law to liabilities (loans) totaling three times its paid-up capital—that is, the amount of money represented in authorized shares it had issued—plus the amount of its deposits from the public. The bank's assets now total more than 63 billion dollars. Like all Canadian chartered banks today, it must maintain a stipulated minimum amount of cash reserves in the form of deposits at the Bank of Canada and in holdings of Bank of Canada notes.

The other Canadian chartered banks active today are the Royal Bank of Canada (the largest in terms of assets), the Canadian Imperial Bank of Commerce, the Bank of Nova Scotia, the Toronto-Dominion Bank, the Mercantile Bank of Canada, the National Bank of Canada, the Continental Bank of Canada, the Canadian Commercial Bank, the Bank of British Columbia, the Morguard Bank of Canada, the Northland Bank and the Western and Pacific Bank of Canada.

The bank is at the core of our financial life. It accepts deposits from the public and from corporations and repays them either on demand or with interest after a stated time. It offers three major kinds of accounts: a savings account; a checking account; and one that combines the two features. It makes loans for a wide range of business or private purposes—including mortgages on residential property.

The bank will sell and buy foreign exchange, issue letters of credit, provide guidance and arrange credit for business deals abroad. It will act as a broker in the buying and selling of bonds and will underwrite high-grade securities, mostly those issued at provincial or municipal levels.

The board of directors of the chartered bank has a duty to earn profits for the shareholders. You can become part owner of a bank simply by having a stockbroker buy shares for you on the stock market. It's a safe buy: the Bank of Montreal, for example, has never failed to make a profit and pay a dividend to its shareholders. But the banks are definitely not as free to run their own affairs as other businesses are. The Bank Act (re-viewed "in theory" every ten years) regulates their relationship with the public, the Bank of Canada and the federal government. The auditing of accounts, establishment of reserves, issuing of stock, type of loans permitted, and other matters, are supervised by law.

No individual or group of individuals may exercise the voting power of more than ten percent of the shares of a chartered bank. Except in the case of a Canadian subsidiary of a foreign bank, nonresidents of Canada are prohibited from owning more than 25 percent of a bank's shares. No bank may own more than ten percent of the voting stock of any Canadian corporation not involved in banking.

The word "bank" is restricted by law to apply to commercial banks operating under the Bank Act and to the City and District Savings Bank in Quebec.

Rights of depositors

The legal position of a depositor with respect to funds he has placed in a chartered bank varies from normal contracts of *bailment*. The basic standing of a bank deposit is that it is a loan from the client to the bank. The bank has to return the money you deposited (with or without interest, depending on the type of account). Obviously it will not give you back the actual bills that you originally deposited. Repayment means a return of an equivalent amount of currency.

When funds are deposited, they become the property of the bank to manage as it sees fit, within the scope of its legal powers. The bank does not have to account to the client for the way it uses his money or for any profits it may make on it. The implied contract of loan—created by the offer and acceptance of a deposit—goes beyond the simple relationship of debtor and creditor; unless the parties specifically agree otherwise, it includes the following terms:

(1) Deposits will be repaid only after a demand by the client and within the time specified in the contract (with a savings account this can be as long as 30 days, although banks do not normally enforce the rule).

(2) The bank is under an obligation to repay only at the branch where the account is kept, and during banking hours only.

(3) The bank will honor a cheque if there are sufficient funds in the client's account (and, usually, only if the cheque is presented at the branch where the account is kept).

(4) The client's banking affairs will be treated by the bank as confidential.

Established clients with large accounts will be offered a bank "courtesy card," enabling them to cash cheques at branches other than where they have their account.

Failure to honor a cheque when the client has sufficient funds on deposit can lead to trouble for the bank. Since a person's credit reputation is regarded as an important part of his character, the law considers that he is justified in suing the bank for damages if such an event occurs. Most depositors who sue a bank for damages for not honoring a cheque are awarded only nominal damages; however, a professional or executive, for whom a good credit rating is an important ingredient in his business reputation, can be awarded a substantial amount as compensatory damages, even if he couldn't prove a direct loss. (*See* Chapter 3, "Decisions from the Bench.")

The "near banks"

In the last decade or so, trust companies and mortgage loan societies—both venerable institutions in Canada—have entered the general banking field much more aggressively. Today, they provide most of the facilities that are offered by chartered banks—including checking accounts—but they are not subject to the same kind of supervision as banks.

These "near banks" can be incorporated under either federal or provincial laws. In Canada, only trust companies are permitted to conduct *fiduciary* business (to hold and manage assets in trust for someone else). Trust companies act as executors, trustees and administrators of wills, as agents in the management of

Banking in the Wild West

MAYBE BANKING IN CANADA is now pretty much a conservative pin-striped business, but it has had its rootin' tootin' times. There is nobody alive today who can personally recall the days when lean, grim-faced men with carbines rode shotgun on jolting stagecoaches as the upcountry bank managers sent heavy cases of gold bullion down to the cities—but it happened, nonetheless. Uneasy clerks, with loaded pistols on their desks, once took turns all night to guard bank safes stuffed with nuggets and miners' pokes of gleaming gold dust.

It happened mostly in British Columbia in the 1860s, when a wild and polyglot army of miners and assorted cutthroats swarmed up the Fraser, panning every sandbar in the river. More than $50 million in gold was eventually won, most of it from the rugged Cariboo country. Governor James Douglas struggled to maintain law and order with a handful of British soldiers.

The Bank of British Columbia was set up in 1862, with headquarters in Victoria and branches in just about every shacktown up the Fraser Valley. These were the days when in towns like Barkerville, saloons roared day and night and bordellos flourished on the main street, as some prospectors flung their new wealth to the winds. Others deposited their gold at the bank.

Governor Douglas had ordered the construction of the Cariboo Road to open the hinterland; a 640-kilometre metaled highway that cost more than $1 million—a gigantic sum in the infant colony. From its terminus at Barkerville down to Yale (at the head of river navigation), this twisting hazardous road around the canyons carried the bullion coaches of the Wild West days of banking.

estates and trusts, as guardians of minors or incapable persons, and as financial agents for individuals and corporations.

All the provinces have trustee acts which regulate the kind of investments trust companies may make; these investments are usually restricted to Government of Canada bonds, provincial and municipal bonds, corporate securities and mortgages.

The federal superintendent of insurance checks up on those companies that have federal registration (and, by special arrangement, on some provincial institutions). But these "near banks" are not required by law to hold specified cash reserves with the Bank of Canada (like the chartered banks); the bulk of their holdings consists of mortgages.

At the end of the 1982 financial year, the trust and mortgage-loan companies had total assets of more than $161 billion.

Trust and mortgage-loan companies are empowered to make personal loans to their customers; but some will only lend money on the strength of something other than the personal guarantee of the borrower—such as a chattel mortgage. (*See* Chapter 6, "The arts of selling.") Most of them operate as general lenders in the money market by issuing *guaranteed investment certificates* (for terms as short as 30 days) at attractive interest rates. They also manage registered retirement and home ownership savings plans, and provide financial and estate planning services. When these companies moved into the traditional banking field by accepting deposits—both chequing and non-chequing—the conventional banks responded briskly. One effect of the competition was that interest paid by the chartered banks on savings accounts increased. Traditionally sedate banks now advertise for new accounts on television with all the tempting techniques of the supersalesman.

Giveaways—such as free records and desk lamps and other merchandise—for opening an account also have resulted from the sharper competition.

The "near bank" operations of credit unions and consumer-finance companies are discussed later in this chapter in the section titled, "When you borrow."

Banking hours

Chartered banks are open a minimum of five hours per business day. Although it is not a legal requirement, banks generally do not remain closed for more than 72 hours at a stretch.

The Bank Act does not set maximum limits on banking hours. Although the official "banking day" begins at 10 A.M. and ends at 3 P.M., it is now common for banks in large cities to remain open until 6 P.M.—and even to 8 P.M. and 9 P.M. in some suburban shopping plazas. Some are experimenting with regular Saturday hours, particularly at branches in plazas. You should bear in mind, though, that if you deposit funds, let's say on a Friday evening, they might not be processed and credited to your account until the next business day (*i.e.*, the following Monday). This could have results unforeseen by a depositor not aware of the practice.

Money-dispensing machines are becoming common. Set into the outer wall of a bank, they operate at all hours. The client needing cash inserts a special card bearing a number code and then pushes buttons to "ask" the bank computer if he may withdraw a specific sum. The computer instantly "reads" the client's balance and, if the withdrawal is approved, a package of bills is ejected by the machine. The money-dispensing machine also lets clients make cash deposits, transfer funds between accounts, and pay bills.

The clearing house

Since 1890, the chartered banks have operated a clearing system for cheques so that each bank will quickly receive notice of all debits and credits to a client's account and adjust the balance accordingly. When all work was done by hand, clearing took three or four days. At that time, some people would risk "kiting" of cheques—that is, they would issue a cheque that would put their bank account "into the red" (in the days of pen and ink, red was traditionally used for debit entries) and then try to reach the bank with an adequate deposit before the cheque could be presented for collection.

Today, kiting is as risky as Russian roulette because all clearing is done by computers. The automated system has become essential to process the four to nine million cheques Canadians write on their bank accounts every business day.

The clearing system also handles cheques written on the "near banks," or negotiated by them on behalf of their clients. The trust and other companies offering some banking facilities pay an annual fee to the chartered banks for this essential service.

The safety deposit box

While the safety deposit box is one of the most convenient services offered by a bank to its clients, the public has several misconceptions about it. For one thing, the bank does not guarantee the safekeeping of the valuables you have placed in a box. The fine print of your box contract with the bank includes the warning that the bank is not liable for the contents of your box. And the banks have been backed up by the courts on this point.

Since the service given by the bank is basically one of bailment for reward, the regular law of *bailment* applies. (*See* Chapter 15, "Goods in transit.") This means that as long as the bank can show that it took the same prudent care of your box as it would take of its own property, the law will not hold it liable should something unfortunate happen to the box and its contents. Of course, the banks do take the utmost care of their safety deposit boxes but you are advised to carry insurance on what you put into them. (*See* Chapter 8, "Insurance at home.")

You should never leave cash in a safety deposit box. This violates the bank's contract with the client and even the most benevolent bank will not compensate you for stolen cash, regardless of whether it can be shown that the bank was negligent.

The banker makes a budget

AUDITOR-GENERAL Maxwell Henderson noted, upon his retirement in 1973, that Canadian taxes were comparatively high for "a young country." While this condition remains, and while inflation keeps prices soaring, there are few citizens indeed who don't have to plan their personal spending carefully. To assist the average depositor in keeping his family finances on an even keel, several of the biggest banks offer personal counseling services to their clients.

The banker will usually propose that you first strike a balance sheet of your assets and liabilities—what you own and what you owe. He will likely offer you a printed form that makes this relatively simple.

Then, in one typical budget plan, it's suggested to follow four clear steps.

(1) *Income:* Estimate all sources of earnings, such as take-home pay (for both husband and wife), commissions, bonuses, family allowances and pensions, investment dividends or annuity payments, rents (if you, perhaps, keep a boarder).

(2) *Regular expenses:* Start with an estimate of family food costs (Canadians spend more than 20 percent of income on food), then check rent or mortgage payments, household utilities (heat, power, telephone), clothing, transportation, medical and dental, extras (haircuts, children's pocket money, etc.), loan repayments, allocation for savings (five to ten percent of income is advised).

(3) *Irregular expense:* Property taxes, life insurance and other premiums, automobile license, home repairs (when was the house painted last?), furniture replacement, recreation (annual holidays and long weekends), charitable donations, and income tax (if not deducted at source).

(4) With the above items totaled, you can proceed to draw up a statement of income and expenditure. If the total of your estimated outgoings is higher than your earnings, then you've got to either earn a bit more, or pull in your horns. When the two sides balance (give or take a few bucks) then you have a realistic budget.

Special regulations control the opening of a safety deposit box after the death of the holder (*See* Chapter 9, "The parties to the will"). This is not the place to store the only copy of your will, your life insurance policies or the deed to a burial plot—it can take some time to get through the legal formalities before the box can be opened. Any currency found in the box would be considered the property of the deceased and thus part of his estate; it could not be immediately taken or used by the widow or family. And the taxation authorities would be interested in knowing the source of any substantial sum.

Two different keys are required to open your safety deposit box—yours and the bank's. If you lose your key, the box must be drilled open, because the bank does not hold a duplicate of your key.

Current and chequing accounts

Current accounts are similar to chequing accounts, but the account holders are usually different. Current accounts are generally designed for the larger depositor (such as a corporation); chequing accounts are for the average person.

Both types of account allow the holder to write as many cheques as his current balance will absorb. All cheques written on the account during the month are returned to the holder of the account at the end of each month. In this way canceled cheques serve as receipts of payment. Neither type of account pays interest for the money on deposit.

A fee of 25 cents is charged for each cheque written on a personal chequing account. Some banks offer free chequing with a certain minimum monthly balance. For about $5 a month, the bank offers a package deal of services, including unlimited free chequing, overdraft protection, preferred loan rates, traveler's cheques and a discount on a safety deposit box. Clients aged 60 and over receive these services without charge.

Daily interest chequing accounts pay interest on each day's closing balance, but the rate is lower than for savings accounts. A higher rate is paid by some banks when the minimum monthly balance is one or two thousand dollars. Most

banks charge 25 cents per cheque. Free chequing is available with a balance of at least several hundred dollars. This account also provides a monthly statement, but your cheques are not returned.

The combination chequing-and-savings account pays only three percent interest, calculated on the minimum half-yearly balance. There is a charge for each cheque, but a number of free cheques are allowed, depending on the minimum three-month balance. You receive a passbook as your account record, and the bank keeps your canceled cheques. Consumers often find their banking needs are better served with separate chequing and savings accounts.

The savings account

In competition for the excess cash of the average citizen, the banks offer various forms of savings accounts, each with different privileges and obligations. On some, you may write cheques and on others you may not.

Basically, the savings account is designed for someone who intends to accumulate savings and not withdraw them frequently.

When savings accounts became widely used as chequing accounts, the banks introduced what they called the "true" savings account. You cannot write cheques against "true" savings; you have to use a passbook and withdraw funds in person.

These accounts pay high interest, calculated on the minimum monthly balance and credited twice a year. Clients aged 60 or over can earn even higher interest.

A daily interest savings account pays interest on the closing balance of each day, but at a rate one-quarter to three-quarters of one percent lower than that paid on "true" savings accounts. The interest is credited monthly. A daily interest account is particularly useful if your savings balance fluctuates each month.

The term deposit

One of the more recent developments in the savings field is what is called the *term deposit*—in effect, a long-term loan to the bank by the client. The depositor lends the bank his excess money for as long as a five-year term at a rate of interest usually well in excess of the going rate on savings accounts.

Banks encourage these deposits because they can then commit funds themselves with fixed interest rates for longer periods, thus attracting more loan business. The bank will not usually hold its client to the strict terms of the note; however if the receipt is redeemed before it becomes due, there is a substantial drop in the interest paid.

Many individuals who are too cautious to invest their money in the stock market find the deposit receipt almost the perfect spot for safe and rewarding storage of surplus funds.

The joint account

Any type of account (savings, current and chequing) can be set up as a joint account, thus permitting more than one person to draw on it. Although most joint accounts are held between husband and wife, theoretically one can be set up by as many persons as want to draw on it.

Depending upon the arrangement made with the bank, it may require one or more signatures to withdraw funds from the joint account. Normally, in a husband-and-wife joint account, cheques may be signed by either the husband or the wife.

It is stating the obvious to advise that you should be more than well acquainted with the person with whom you are entering into a joint account in which either may sign cheques. Be *sure* you can trust him. He will be in a position, without your consent, to withdraw all of the funds in the account; furthermore, through his negligent operation of the account, you could find yourself liable for any overdraft the account may run up with the bank. Note that the bank reserves the right to recover the debt solely from one of the parties and is not obliged to go after the person who actually caused the overdraft.

The joint account has the right of survivorship built into it. In all provinces, except Quebec, if one of the partners in a joint account should die, then all the funds in the account go to the survivor, with no part of it being put into the estate of the deceased. In Quebec, it must be established first who has the right to the money in the joint account. (*See* Chapter 9, "Changing your will.")

Transferring funds abroad

There are several ways of transferring funds to a foreign country—including by bank money order, bank draft, postal money order, by cabling money or by personally mailing an ordinary cheque

A package of services

IF YOU WRITE a great number of cheques and, occasionally, find yourself short of funds, you can eliminate separate charges for these services by consulting your bank or trust company. Customers who make heavy use of banking facilities may wish to take advantage of the "packages" these institutions offer.

For a monthly fee of $5, you can have unlimited chequing privileges, personalized cheques, and overdraft protection. There is no charge for bank drafts, money orders, and payments of utility bills, and no commission on traveler's cheques. You are entitled to a preferred interest rate on general purpose personal loans and can arrange to have the bank transfer funds between your accounts automatically. The cost of renting a safety deposit box or other safekeeping service is reduced. A credit card and bank client card are usually included, enabling you to bank at other branches and at automated tellers.

Those aged 60 and over can obtain these service packages at no charge. As a further bonus, they earn higher interest on their savings accounts—as much as one-half of one percent above the regular rate.

(or a certified cheque). All these ways work, but some are more effective than others and the cost varies considerably.

The most effective and cheapest methods of transferring money are by bank order or draft and by postal money order. The bank draft, which is the best of all, causes the needed money to be available from a particular bank, the closest affiliated bank (a branch or correspondent) in the city to which the money is sent. The payee needs only reasonable identification to get his cash. But you, the drawer, have to purchase the draft from your bank and mail it yourself. The money order works the same way, basically, except that it is not drawn on a specific foreign bank; this could make it more difficult for the recipient to cash it.

The quickest but most expensive way to send money to the United States is to cable it. You can turn over a money order, bank draft or cash to any telegraph office and a cable authorizing that sum will be sent to a telegraph office at the destination, permitting the money to be paid to the individual or firm you have named in the cable. Your bank can also arrange to wire funds to any branch in any affiliated bank both at home or abroad.

If you want to send funds to someone abroad—perhaps to pay a debt—in the form of a personal or business cheque, you can expect a considerable delay before the cycle is complete. Banks outside North America are generally much more suspicious about extending credit than are those in Canada or the United States. You can assume that they will not commit the funds until your cheque has cleared, which may take several weeks or longer. If you are in a hurry, don't use cheques to send money abroad. And, incidentally, it is not wise to send cash (*i.e.,* dollar bills or coins or any "negotiable instrument" payable to the bearer) through the mails.

Foreign currency, traveler's cheques
When traveling abroad there are few experiences worse than arriving in a strange city only to find that the banks are closed (the hours are often vastly different to those of Canadian banks) and may remain closed for an extended period. You will most likely find a foreign-exchange counter at the airport, but you will probably also find that the exchange rate offered is less than a commercial bank would give you.

Canadian banks in larger centers normally carry reasonable supplies of foreign currency which they will sell to you at whatever the exchange rate is for the day on which you are buying. You should always take enough of the local currency to see you through the first day in a foreign country. Don't buy more foreign currency than you need because you will find that when you sell any excess back to the bank (or to the exchange bureau at the airport) you will not get the same rate that you paid. Apart from the overhead charges the bank must apply, the official exchange rate could fall in the interim.

Except for the seasoned business traveler requiring substantial sums (he will probably take a *letter of credit* from his bank), the best and safest method of taking money abroad is in the form of traveler's cheques. While they may seem to be expensive (they usually cost one percent of the total sum), they are a good buy when you consider that if you carry cash, you risk losing *all* your money to the professional pickpockets and hotel thieves who thrive on careless tourists.

Traveler's cheques can be bought at major travel agencies or chartered banks and can usually be converted into cash at your hotel if the banks should be closed. Remember, though, that you will get a better exchange rate at a bank, and the best rate of all at a foreign branch of a Canadian or American bank.

Unless you are going to the United States, you are better off to purchase your traveler's cheques in Canadian rather than American currency; otherwise, you will have to pay two exchange rates: the first when you convert your Canadian dollars into U.S. funds; the second time when you convert the U.S. funds into another currency when you cash your cheques. The Canadian dollar is stable compared with many other currencies and is welcome almost everywhere abroad.

Follow the advice that you make a list in a notebook of the serial numbers printed on your cheques, and carry this list separate from the cheques themselves. By doing this, if the cheques are lost or stolen, you can report the loss promptly and accurately. You will have signed the cheques once in the presence of the bank clerk or other agent who sold them to you; do not sign them the second time until you are in the presence of the person who is to cash them, or accept them in trade—and then sign only those cheques you are using at the moment.

If you do lose your traveler's cheques, they will be replaced, just as the advertisements promise; but they will not necessarily be replaced *immediately*. Before you are finally issued new ones, you must formally exempt the issuing agency or bank from all responsibility to honor the original cheques.

When the bank is in error

Despite their image of machine-like efficiency, bankers are as human as the rest of us and, being human, they make mistakes. Banks generally ask their clients to sign an agreement to the effect that they will report to the bank any error they find in their monthly bank statement within a specified number of days after receiving the statement. The agreement states that if the error is not reported, the bank is entitled to assume that the client has accepted the statement as reflecting the correct condition of the account. Whether this agreement is binding on the individual had not been determined by the courts at this writing.

Of course, all banks take great pains to be accurate, and mistakes are rare today thanks to computers. However, there is no harm in keeping your own record—just in case. Always make a written notation of each cheque you write, recording the payee and the date upon which the cheque was sent. The record book accompanying your cheque book is provided especially for this purpose and to help you keep track of your balance.

If your bank sends canceled cheques to you at the end of the month, always compare the number of cheques appearing on the statement to the number of cheques which your own record shows you have

written. If you find any error, or if you cannot figure out why the balance that appears in your records is different from the figure reported on the statement, notify the bank immediately. In this way, you will always protect yourself and will also have the added advantage of knowing exactly where you stand financially.

If there has been an error, the bank will adjust your account. In this event you should ask the bank for a corrected statement to confirm that the situation has been cleared up.

If someone forges cheques on your account and the bank pays them, the bank will normally absorb the loss. When payment is made in error under such circumstances, it is labeled a mistake of law.

The law does not provide a definite ruling on the bank's responsibility where payments are made by mistake of fact, rather than by mistake of law. However, it is the usual case that where the bank makes a payment on your behalf under a mistake of fact made by you—some clerical error, for instance—it will not be liable for that payment. However, where it makes the payment under a mistake of law—in effect, where it cashes an invalid cheque—the courts have ordered that the bank repay that sum.

Your right to secrecy

It has been established through the years that banks have an obligation to treat their clients' affairs in strict confidence. A depositor is entitled to have his affairs kept secret unless:

(1) He consents to the bank revealing information;

(2) The courts decide there is "public duty" on the bank to disclose the client's affairs;

(3) The interests of the bank require disclosure of the client's affairs.

If the courts compel the bank to disclose a depositor's affairs, the bank cannot be held guilty of a breach of the implied contract.

The third situation described in the above list could occur if the bank were suing a client to recover a debt. It would have to give details of the debt as evidence in court.

Writing a cheque

IF YOU THINK of a cheque as being merely a written instruction to your bank to pay out part of your own money, some of the air of mystery that still clings to banking may be thankfully cleared away. On the other hand, the "turned on" image that some banks try doggedly to portray often doesn't spread far beyond the advertising office. Too many branch managers, still responding unconsciously to the traditional association of money with social class, confuse their roles in today's business world; some appear to see themselves as stern father figures, almost as watchdogs over the treasury. In England, you may still be asked for a reference when you seek to open an account.

It should be obvious that it is the depositor who is "the boss"; it is his willingness to lend his excess money to the bank that makes it possible for the world of finance to turn. The cheque is the method you, as a depositor, use to give your orders to the bank. And it is an order, not a request. To make the position even clearer: If your bank failed to honor your cheque when there was enough money in your account to cover it, you could sue the bank for damages with good prospects of winning.

The cheque is classified as a *negotiable instrument*. (*See* "Negotiable instruments" in this chapter.) It is a bill of exchange drawn against a bank and payable on demand. The cheque appears to be steadily replacing all other methods of payment—particularly the draft—in financial transactions, except those in international business. Although the printed form supplied by banks and some trust companies is no doubt the most convenient and common style of cheque, the cheque can take the form of a simple letter or, indeed, can be scratched on a piece of birch bark. (Cheques written on eggshells and shirts have been cashed.)

The essentials of the cheque—spelled "check" by many—are that it must state an exact sum, it must be dated and it must be signed. The cheque is an unconditional written order to immediately pay the amount indicated to the bearer, to the named person or company or other party or to the order of the named party.

The body and the figure

Although the cheque is basically a simple document, you should take scrupulous care every time you write one. Remember, that's your hard-earned money you are signing away. Write legibly so that the busy bank clerk can read the name of the payee clearly, and can easily compare it with the signature of the person endorsing it. Don't make the mistake known as the "bodies and figures" difference.

Always make sure that the figures you write on the first line of the cheque agree with the sum in words spelled out on the second line—known as the "body" of the cheque. If these figures do disagree, the letter of the law states that the written sum takes precedence over the numerical sum; in practice, however, the cheque will be returned to you (at your expense).

You should get into the habit of writing cheques in such a fashion that they cannot be altered in any way. Otherwise, you run the risk of someone changing your cheque to make it payable to a person other than the one you made it out to, or to alter the amount. The key precaution is to leave no spaces before or after your figures or letters. A line should always be drawn after the amount so that nothing can be added by anyone else. The bank will instantly reject any cheque that has been altered, unless you have separately initialed the change. Cheque-writing machines are virtually foolproof and are used by most big businesses.

Look at each cheque carefully after you have written it. People often write cheques in a hurry, for instance, while standing in a supermarket or garage. Make sure the date is current, that the name of the payee is correctly spelled and is spelled out in full and that there is no "body and figures" difference. Lastly, make sure you have signed the cheque in the same style as you signed the card held in the files of your bank.

Computer coding
All banks provide their clients with personalized cheques. Each cheque is coded with magnetic ink. When it reaches the clearing house, a computer scans the code and it instantly sorts the cheque. You will find your personalized code printed at the bottom of your cheques.

Banks will also arrange for your name to be printed on your cheques. This may help the tellers and ledger clerks if you happen to have an illegible signature; apart from that, it has no bearing on the validity of the cheque. Because a non-coded cheque has to be sorted by hand at a higher cost in labor, banks are actively discouraging their use.

Think twice before you lend anyone one of your personally coded cheque forms on which to write a cheque of their own. If you do oblige, you should carefully cross out the code at the bottom of the cheque. If you don't, the cheque will automatically be sorted to your branch and may well be posted to your account in error. If you do obliterate the code, the computer will reject the cheque, which will then have to be sorted by hand—and will be posted to the correct person's account.

Not sufficient funds
It is an offense under the Criminal Code to knowingly write a cheque without having sufficient funds, either in your ac-count, or within your credit arrangement with the bank, to cover it. The emphasis is on the word "knowingly"; there must always be evidence of *intent* before a crime is committed.

If you inadvertently overspend, and thus overdraw your account, your bank has a choice of action. It can simply refuse to honor your cheque (in short, "bounce it") or, more usually, it can hold it temporarily and give you a fair chance to increase your balance sufficiently to cover it. If your banker knows you well and your record as a depositor is good, he may save you from embarrassment by honoring your order anyway—in effect, granting you an *overdraft*. The overdraft is, technically, a personal loan, at interest. Unless you are in a position to deposit money quickly enough to bring your cash balance back into line, the banker will probably ask you to sign a *promissory note*, formalizing the loan. (*See* "Negotiable instruments" in this chapter.)

If you maintain a savings account in the same branch as your chequing account, you can arrange to have your bank transfer funds from your savings account to cover your cheques. If you take a businesslike attitude to your personal finances, keeping careful track of your deposits and your payments, you will probably never have a cheque come back to you with initials N S F ("Not Sufficient Funds") stamped on it. Those initials put a black mark on your credit record. If you make an honest mistake in your figuring, or if you think the margin between plus and minus in your account is too narrow for comfort, better discuss the situation with your banker. A short-term personal loan might be the solution to this problem.

Order and bearer cheques
When you look at a standard cheque form, you will see the words "Pay to the order of" followed by a blank space for you to fill in the name of the payee. The words printed here between quotation marks create a specific legal situation. They make the cheque negotiable, meaning that the payee named may transfer to some other person (or company) the right

to collect on that cheque. If those words are printed on your pay cheque, for instance, you may endorse the cheque over to some other person to whom you owe money. (This is discussed later in this section.) If those words do not appear on the cheque, you do not have this privilege and the bank is authorized to pay you, and only you, the amount specified.

If a cheque is payable to "Bearer," it can be cashed at the bank by whoever brings it in and signs his name on the back. He might be asked for identification, if he is unknown at that branch of the bank. The same applies to a cheque made payable to "Cash" or to any similarly unspecified payee. Bearer cheques are seldom used in business because a thief may cash them without having to resort to forgery and you, not the bank, will bear the loss.

The bearer cheque can be converted into an order cheque by someone endorsing it to some named person's order. On the other hand, the order cheque becomes a bearer cheque as soon as the payee endorses it by signing his name on the back of it.

The crossed cheque

The Bills of Exchange Act allows you to "cross" a cheque as a further protection against theft or forgery. You do this by drawing two parallel lines across the face of a cheque; these lines signify that the

Making it easy for the forger

THE PICKPOCKET who takes your wallet and chequebook is almost certain to obtain several examples of your signature. It is on your driving license, your medical insurance card, and on your Visa and some other credit cards. If he copies your signature on to a blank cheque, he's not only a thief but a forger—and he can get up to 14 years' imprisonment for that.

Your local bank is probably pretty familiar with your signature style, and your banking habits. A large cheque written to "Cash," for example, might raise some suspicions, even if the signature looks reasonably accurate.

Many people make life easy for the forger. They give him all the opportunity he needs to rob them, using perfectly legitimate cheques that have been properly signed. By writing a cheque carelessly, you leave the clever penman dozens of ways of altering the name of the payee, the money amount, or both. With a few strokes, the dishonest store cashier or door-to-door salesman can change "five" into "fifty" in a way a teller could scarcely detect.

| Pay to the order of | _Gérard Coté_ | $ _100.00_ |
| _One hundred only_ | | /100 Dollars |

The forger merely has to add two letters to the abbreviation "Co." and endorse the cheque as "Coté" to collect the hundred dollars.

| Pay to the order of | _Federal Enterprises Ltd_ | $ _67.50_ |
| _Sixty Seven and 50/100_ | | /100 Dollars |

The only way to be certain your handwritten cheques are safe from alteration is to ensure that all spaces are filled or scored through. The empty spaces are an open invitation to the forger to write his own ticket.

cheque is no longer a negotiable instrument except when paid into the bank account of the original payee. The words "Bank," "A/c Payee Only" or "Not Negotiable" can be written between the lines.

To "uncross," that is, to reopen, a crossed cheque, the words "Pay Cash" must be written between the lines and initialed by the person who wrote the cheque. It is an offense for anyone but the drawer to obliterate, add to or alter the crossing which appears on a cheque. Cheque crossing is quite popular in Britain, but it is seldom practiced in Canada.

The certified cheque

Either the drawer or the payee can have the bank "certify" a cheque. This has the effect of guaranteeing that the cheque will be cashed when presented for payment. It is sometimes used as an alternative to withdrawing a large sum of cash, or as a means of assuring a nervous payee that the drawer's personal cheque will indeed be honored.

When you present a cheque for certification, the sum of money indicated on the cheque you have drawn is removed from your account and lodged in a special account in the bank. The bank then places its stamp on the face of your cheque certifying that the money is available to meet payment on that cheque.

The bank can also perform this service to the payee. In effect, the bank thus contracts to pay the amount of the cheque to the payee. Even if this cheque is dishonored at a later date—for instance, if the drawer goes bankrupt or dies—the bank still has to pay; otherwise the payee could sue the bank for the amount involved.

A certified cheque is often required when someone is paying a deposit to close a real estate deal.

Endorsing a cheque

Every cheque, unless it is deposited to the credit of the payee, must be endorsed by the payee in order to turn it into cash. *Endorsement*, in its simplest form, involves the payee signing his name on the back of the cheque. Once this has been done, the cheque becomes as good as cash in the hands of any third party and can be

negotiated ("cashed") by any holder ("bearer") of that cheque.

It is important to remember that if you are the payee, you should not endorse a cheque until you arrive at the bank with it or until you present it to some other person to be cashed—perhaps for payment of a debt. If you endorse a cheque and then lose it, you have no claim against the drawer for the loss. Once properly endorsed, a cheque can be cashed by any finder, or thief, with relative ease—it's a case of finders keepers, losers weepers.

You can endorse a cheque in such a way as to make it payable to another person. For example, if a payee (let's call him Jones) wrote on the back of a cheque "Pay to the order of Fred Smith," and signed it, then Jones would have given up all his rights to the amount of the cheque. The cheque would then be payable to Smith. Since the words "to the order of" were used, Smith would then have the right to pass the cheque along by further endorsing it over to another party. Theoretically, this could go on forever, with an extra piece of paper being attached to carry the fresh instructions. Each new endorser would, in turn, be assuming responsibility for the payment of the sum on the face of the cheque. If it bounced because there was not enough money in the original drawer's account, the last person to endorse it over to the new payee would have to pay.

We have mentioned only two types of endorsement, namely the *blank endorsement* (just the payee's signature on the back of the cheque) and the *special endorsement* (Jones signing it to the order of Smith). Other variations are:

RESTRICTIVE ENDORSEMENT. This effectively stops the further trading of a cheque by instructing that it be cashed only by the person to whom it has been endorsed. The endorsement would read, "Pay Fred Smith only" plus the signature of the last payee.

QUALIFIED ENDORSEMENT. This permits the current payee to pass along his rights in the instrument (the cheque) without personally guaranteeing that the cheque is good. The drawer could, after all, have issued a *stop-payment order* on the cheque since it was first issued. This kind of endorsement would read, "Pay Fred Smith without recourse."

ANOMALOUS ENDORSEMENT. This is really a guarantee by an outside party (usually someone with a high credit rating), backing up the original drawer's promise to pay the cheque. The endorser simply adds his signature on the back of the cheque. It does not mean that the cheque can be presented for payment at the bank of the endorser, but merely guarantees the named payee that the cheque is good.

IDENTIFICATION ENDORSEMENT. Since the bank has to absorb the loss if it pays a forged cheque (unless the client himself was negligent), it may ask for an identification endorsement when a cheque is presented by someone it doesn't know. This endorser would normally write: "Fred Smith is hereby identified" and sign his own name. In this way, the endorser would not be liable (like most other endorsers) for full payment of the cheque, but only for any loss that might arise from his identification being proved false.

The bank is insured against the chance of honoring forged cheques. It will usually also reimburse the legal holder of a cheque that it might cash for a thief, but it is not obliged to do so unless the thief forged the endorsement of the payee.

The postdated cheque

If you expect to be on a cruise, or otherwise unavailable, when a debt becomes due and you don't want to pay in advance, you can write a cheque in the normal way except that you write a forward date on it. Although a cheque by nature is an instrument payable "on demand," the demand is not effective until the date given is reached. The postdated cheque is rather like a *time draft*. (*See* "Negotiable instruments" in this chapter.)

Postdated cheques are becoming more common as more and more people turn to payment by cheque to meet their financial obligations. Some apartment landlords ask that you send them a series of postdated cheques to cover a year's rent before they will let you move into an apartment. Certain banks require that

mortgage payments be made by depositing a series of postdated cheques. The system works fine as long as the person writing the cheques has the funds in his account on the date on which the postdated cheque becomes valid. The drawer of a postdated cheque has been known to forget and not have sufficient funds on hand to meet such an obligation, having written other cheques in the meantime. If you have issued postdated cheques, leave yourself a reminder at the end of every month that they are still outstanding.

If you change your mind after issuing a postdated cheque, you can arrange for the bank not to honor it—although you will have to provide the bank with an adequate reason.

Period of negotiability

The best rule to follow is to negotiate a cheque as soon as you receive it, provided it has not been postdated by the drawer.

The normal "life" of a cheque is 180 days; banks make a practice of not cashing a cheque that is more than six months old. After this time, a cheque is considered to be "stale dated"—in short, valueless—and must be renewed by the drawer. Some companies warn that their cheques must be cashed within 30 or 60 days. It is difficult for companies to balance their accounts if cheques remain outstanding for long periods.

The banks usually get a flock of stale-dated cheques written in error at the beginning of January, before people have adjusted to the date of the new year. It is not unknown for a person in possession of a stale-dated cheque to wait until the new year and then attempt to pass his void cheque off as an error. Banks customarily allow cheques bearing the old year's date to go through for the first week or so of January but, strictly speaking, they should not do so. If you receive such a cheque, you would be surer of getting your cash if you asked the drawer to take it back and write a new one.

Stopping payment

You may decide, after you have written a cheque, that you do not wish to honor it. If the cheque has not yet been cashed, you can issue what is known as a "stop-payment order" on it at your bank.

Banks do not like to accept stop-payment orders over the telephone, and some of them flatly refuse. You must go to the branch of the bank where you have your account and sign a special form before the bank will agree to stop payment. You will be asked the reason for your action—perhaps a bearer cheque has been lost, or you have just discovered that you have been defrauded in a deal. Since the bank must legally honor your instruction to pay from your account, it must take care to ensure that you cancel that obligation legally.

Once the bank has been properly instructed to stop payment, it will return the cheque concerned to the person who endorsed and deposited it. The cheque will be charged back to him, or to the person who negotiated it for him.

Speed is essential if you wish to stop payment on a cheque. If you have been cheated, the cheque may well have been presented and cashed before you have had time to reach the bank. The crook may have quickly negotiated it with a shopkeeper, who would be allowed to keep the money even though the cheque was invalid—he would be considered a bona fide purchaser without notice of the fraud. Rather than find out the hard way, it is best not to pay anyone—either by cash or by cheque—until you are completely satisfied with the work done or the goods received.

Playing bank

Don't pretend to be a bank. If anyone whom you don't personally know asks you to cash a cheque, give him the address of the nearest branch of a bank, and, if you feel charitable, perhaps enough money for his busfare to get there.

Remember that thousands of identification cards and driver's licenses, as well as credit cards, are stolen every year—and that the people who most successfully pass dud cheques don't dress like bums.

If you still want to take a chance, then at least consider the following advice offered by bankers.

(1) Never cash a cheque that shows signs of alteration.

(2) Assure yourself that the cheque is drawn by a real company or individual on an actual bank. (The telephone book is a handy reference.)

(3) Insist that a cheque be endorsed in your presence: if it has already been endorsed, make the endorser sign again, then compare the signatures.

(4) Remember that a certified cheque can be stolen just as easily as any other kind.

(5) Shopkeepers should always be wary of any unknown customer who wants to cash a cheque for more than the amount of the purchase.

(6) If a savings passbook is offered as identification, phone the bank named to check the state of the account.

(7) Don't cash cheques for anyone who is younger than 18.

Never on Sunday?

IT REMAINS as a stubborn legacy from a stricter past that just about everybody still thinks that a cheque—or any "negotiable instrument"—dated on the Sabbath is not valid. Where money is concerned, Sunday is just another day.

The only exception could arise when the Sunday-dated cheque covered a transaction that was itself illegal on the Sabbath. The Lord's Day Act, a federal statute passed in 1906, prohibits buying or selling, and most other business, on Sunday—except for acts of "necessity or mercy." But the provinces have the right to modify the strictures of the act and, very obviously, they do so.

Hundreds of real-estate deals are closed every fine Sunday but, to be on the safe side, the salesman will probably move the date on your offer forward to the Monday.

Using credit cards

Under laws of contract
Terms and conditions
How the system works
Instant cash
Visa and MasterCard
If you lose your card

OUR GRANDFATHERS believed that there was something almost immoral, and certainly unwise, about going into debt for anything that was nonessential. They would have agreed with Polonius' stern advice to his son Laertes in Shakespeare's *Hamlet:*

Neither a borrower, nor a lender be;
For loan oft loses both itself and
Friend, and borrowing dulls the edge
of husbandry.

But attitudes regarding debt have changed dramatically in recent years; today's chartered banks blithely suggest that you borrow money to fly south for a winter holiday. The use of *credit* in commerce is as old as money itself, but its entry into our everyday lives, and its familiarity to the average person everywhere in the industrialized world, is still a comparatively recent phenomenon. The simplest and most innocent-looking agent of this change is the *credit card;* it is perhaps the most powerful as well.

Introduced as a simple method for identifying the credit-worthy customers of large department stores, or businesses with several branches, credit card use spread with amazing speed. If a person was considered a safe risk for, say, $500 worth of goods by a well-known retailer (such as Eaton's, Simpsons or the Bay), he or she was rated as a reliable bill payer by other stores and service industries. These smaller merchants would allow persons holding recognized credit cards to buy on credit from them too. Gasoline and hotel chains began issuing their own credit cards, valid for purchases at affiliated stations and hotels throughout North America. A similar, if more cautious, expansion of credit cards occurred in Britain and elsewhere.

The scope of the credit card was widened dramatically when specialized agencies entered the field in 1950, offering to good credit risks all-purpose cards (for an annual membership fee) that would be honored as a guarantee for payment just about everywhere in the world outside the Communist bloc. These companies (Diners Club and American Express are prime examples) concentrated on the traveler, providing him with what amounted to a universal banker's reference in towns and countries where he had never before set foot, and where he might stay for a mere 24 hours. The agency took over from the merchant the task of collecting payment on the card-user's bills. With a billing that was counted in mounting millions, the credit-card companies were soon able to convince many other businessmen that their cards were the next best thing to cash. Soon, airlines, restaurants, rent-a-car firms, florists and other businesses were accepting the powerful little cards with a smile.

Commercial banking houses looked in horror for a time at the little plastic oblongs. However, once the trend to easier credit was unmistakable, and the earnings of the card companies soared, the major banks in Canada, the United States and Europe jumped on the bandwagon. They introduced card schemes such as Visa, MasterCard, and Barclaycard.

Using their vast financial strength, the chartered-bank systems seem to be curbing the growth of the specialist card agencies, turning this tremendous new tributary of the credit stream back into traditional channels.

Under laws of contract

There has been, as yet, no broad legislation written specifically to regulate the use of the credit card, although all provinces have enacted legislation to discourage agencies from sending out unsolicited cards to local residents. If you suddenly receive (without having asked for one) a credit card through the mail, you may simply destroy it—cutting it in halves with scissors is recommended. If you should receive such an unwanted card and you happen to lose it, you cannot be held responsible for any charges that may subsequently be incurred with it.

Credit cards fall within the general law of contract. If it can be proved that you were aware of the terms and conditions attached to the card at the time it was issued to you, you will be bound by them. The contract document sent to the card carrier states that, by accepting the card, he agrees to be bound by the numerous terms and conditions of that credit-card system. As soon as you make use of a card, you are confirming your acceptance of the contract.

Since a number of the credit-card companies, often those associated with travel agencies, will arrange hotel accommodation, issue air, rail and bus tickets, promote mail-order purchasing, offer insurance and cash withdrawals, and provide other services, they come within the reach of commercial and consumer law.

The credit-card companies function fundamentally as lenders and must obey the regulations of the federal Interest Act. Any interest (usually termed "finance charges") added to overdue unpaid balances must be made known in advance to the client in annual-rate terms.

Terms and conditions

When you are granted a credit card by a retail or service business for use within that business only, the conditions of the contract you must accept are relatively simple. The card is nontransferable, it must be produced whenever you wish to make a credit purchase and, in addition, you may be asked to sign the sales slip. Some stores offer separate or joint cards for husband and wife.

In the more sophisticated stores, the sales clerk will insert your card in an electronic scanner before completing the sale. In a matter of seconds, this device will tell her whether your credit position is currently good enough to cover the proposed purchase. There is a figure marked on your account record which tells the sales clerk how much credit you may be allowed. The clerk may also ask you to show some extra identification. Assuming the clerk gets the green light from the computer, the purchase will be finalized and you will soon be on your way with the goods.

When your application for an all-purpose credit card—such as that issued by American Express or Diners Club—is accepted, you will find that the contract you have to sign before receiving your card is considerably more detailed. The company has to frame its terms and conditions to cover a greater variety of circumstances than those associated with a department store. The main features are:

(1) Although the card cannot be used by anyone but you, it remains the property of the issuing company.

(2) The credit privileges granted may be withdrawn at any time, and you must surrender the card when asked.

(3) If the card is lost or stolen, it is your responsibility as the holder to advise the company; if you are slow to do so, you run the risk of a forger charging goods and services to your account. Some provinces impose a limit on liability in such circumstances.

(4) The card company will not be responsible if your card is not honored somewhere, or if goods you buy with it are not satisfactory.

(5) All charges and business transacted by card are subject to all municipal, provincial and federal laws that might apply wherever the card is used.

(6) If the total balance due at billing date is not paid by the date specified (usually about 30 days), the company may suspend your privileges and impose a late-payment fee, or threaten cancellation of the card; after 60 days, the card may be canceled. You may also have to pay, up to a reasonable amount, any costs of collec-

tion that the company may incur because of your nonpayment.

(7) Where joint cards are issued to an individual card holder and to a company (or to other members of a card holder's family), all the joint holders are equally liable for payment of all purchases.

How the system works
The crux of the agency's service is that it takes over from the merchant or the hotel concerned the job of collecting from you, their member, the amount owing. The supplier is assured of his money and, for that assurance, he pays a fee to the agency—the fee ranges from 2 percent to 6 percent of the value of the goods or services involved. The agency has already collected and banked your membership fee (usually about $35 a year). Its third source of income arises from "late payment fees," which are a form of interest.

Although there are some variations, the chartered bank credit-card schemes in Canada currently charge a minimum of 1½ percent interest per month on all overdue accounts. This works out to at least 18 percent a year. In addition, most banks have introduced a user fee for their credit cards. The consumer now pays a modest annual fee or a small charge for each transaction. The companies operating the nonbank credit cards charge interest rates up to 30 percent a year.

Since the card companies can borrow or raise money at much lower rates, paying their card holders' bills and having the card holders pay interest on the debt can be seen as a very profitable business. There would, of course, be a number of bad debts—but Canadians are notoriously reliable payers.

Instant cash
Some credit-card systems allow you to obtain cash instantly with your card. An American Express office will cash your personal cheque for amounts up to $200, as long as it is satisfied that you are in fact the person who has the contract for the card with the company.

Many of the large hotel chains, which handle a lot of credit-card business, will also allow a client to cash a personal cheque, subject to cash availability, on the basis of his credit card—of course, their confidence is reasonably well founded if it is one of the major cards. If you have the privilege of virtually unlimited credit in the hotel dining room or bar, why shouldn't your credit extend to a modest personal cheque?

If you have a Visa card, for instance, you can draw cash (usually up to your

Credit and privacy

IT MIGHT seem innocuous but the basic credit application form which you fill out puts a large amount of data about you on record with national and international credit agencies.

Before a department store, say, will give you credit for an expensive suite of furniture, it has an obvious right to check on your ability to pay.

Government lawyers in most Western countries are currently struggling with the problem of drafting laws that will permit proper enquiry, but which will prevent wholesale invasion of your right to privacy. By the 1980s, all provinces, except Alberta and New Brunswick, had legislation dealing with consumer credit reporting. Some provincial laws forbid the disclosure of certain information—for example, reports of personal bankruptcies that may have occurred many years before—and allow consumers some right of access to the data contained in their files.

The typical application form is also a contract by which the customer, if granted credit, agrees to pay any "service charges" (that is, interest on outstanding debt) that may be incurred and also to surrender upon request any charge card that may be issued.

credit limit) from any branch of any of the banks participating in that credit system, even if you do not have an account with any of them. You also have access to foreign banks which participate in the Visa system. However, interest is charged immediately on such cash advances. Your Visa card also serves as identification for cashing personal cheques in other branches of your own bank.

Again, many hotels and some major merchants may accept such cards as confirmation of a person's financial substance and therefore be willing to provide them with some cash in an emergency.

Visa and MasterCard

The Visa system with its affiliates is one of the most widely accepted of all the credit-card systems. It was organized in Canada by the Canadian Imperial Bank of Commerce, the Royal Bank, the Bank of Nova Scotia, the Toronto-Dominion Bank and the Banque Nationale. These five chartered banks formulated a plan under which, in return for a percentage of the amount being billed, they guaranteed payment to the merchant. The basic principles of the system were taken from the United States model, the BankAmericard.

Under the plan, certain formalities must be observed at the time the sale is made, including a routine credit check when the goods purchased exceed certain price limitations. Once goods or services have been properly charged on a Visa card, the supplier is guaranteed payment, with Visa promising to absorb any loss that might occur. Although this was much the same as the card systems available elsewhere, Visa had the advantage of having the best individual depositors of all five banks as potential card holders. Furthermore, no membership fee was asked and an installment plan for payment was offered. The resources the banks had at their disposal with which to pay suppliers speeded the expansion of Visa.

By affiliating with Barclaycard (operated by Barclays Bank in Britain) and BankAmericard (by the Bank of America), Visa gained acceptance all through the Americas, the Orient and Europe.

When the Visa customer receives his

bill, he has 21 days from the statement date in which to pay it. He has the option of paying the full amount or a portion of the balance. But he must pay a minimum of $10 or five percent of the balance, whichever is greater. If he chooses to pay by installments—in effect, he is being granted a personal loan—he will have to pay interest (about 18 percent).

If you want to become a Visa card holder, you must complete a detailed application form and submit it to any one of the participating chartered banks. The application will be scrutinized and checked out from the point of view of your annual earnings, private income, property holdings, employment and so on. As with most of the credit-card systems referred to in this chapter, if you have been holding down a good job for a reasonable period and if you have a good record of paying your bills promptly, you are likely to be given a hearty welcome.

MasterCard was inaugurated in Canada in 1973 by the Bank of Montreal and the Banque Provinciale du Canada joining forces with many U.S. banks led by the First National City Bank of New York (now Citibank).

If you lose your card

Keep the number of your credit card written down in a notebook, the same as you are advised to do with the numbers of your traveler's cheques—not on a slip of paper in the same wallet where you keep your card! The number of your account is embossed on your card.

The contract you have accepted with the credit-card organization contains a clause stating that the company will not be responsible for purchases made on a lost or stolen card until it is notified in writing of the loss or theft. And this condition is legally binding. Fortunately, with most cards, your liability for unauthorized use is limited to $50. If you can't find your card, notify the company by telephone, cable or telegraph immediately and then follow up with a letter.

Your insurance agent can arrange full financial protection against any loss you might suffer from someone getting hold of and using your credit cards.

319

When you borrow

SOMETIMES there is no alternative to borrowing a sum of money—perhaps to tide you over an emergency, to get some pressing creditor off your back or to buy something you need when reasonable credit terms are not available from the seller.

In Chapter 4, you can read about the ways to raise money to buy a house. In Chapter 6, we discuss ways to finance the purchase of items like refrigerators. In Chapters 5 and 16, how to buy automobiles and snowmobiles is discussed. The role of the chartered banks and credit-card agencies in providing personal loans has already been outlined in this chapter. If you want to raise substantial sums for commercial enterprises, you should consider contacting the Federal Business Development Bank, operating under the auspices of the federal Department of Industry, Trade and Commerce. This section deals with those sources of cash loans open to the average person.

The cash loan is usually granted on the basis of your signature and character or by your pledging some valuable household goods or other personal property as *collateral*, or security. Generally speaking, you'll get your loan if you can demonstrate your ability to repay it. The cost of the loan, the interest, will normally reflect the amount of risk the lender considers he is taking.

In this century, the law has made a great effort to protect the unknowing and unsophisticated (and the desperate) from unfair terms and exorbitant interest rates (*usury*). Under a new section of the Criminal Code, charging a *criminal interest rate* on a personal loan is an offense. (The criminal rate is fixed at 60 percent.) This offense is punishable by either five years' imprisonment or a fine of up to $25,000 and/or six months' imprisonment.

Under the Bank Act 1980, the cost of borrowing must be disclosed up to a ceiling of $50,000 and, if the loan has been secured by a mortgage on a property, up to $150,000. The Interest Act stipulates that the interest must be expressed in terms of the annual rate being charged. The Bills of Exchange Act sets out the rights of both the maker and the holder of a *promissory note*. Provincial laws confirm and extend some of this protection. But the individual must still be cautious and depend, to a large extent, on his own judgment for general protection.

While it is a simple matter to quote excerpts from the relevant laws, it can also be misleading—the variety of human experience makes it virtually impossible to describe "average cases." For instance, you could find yourself paying 48 percent a year for a cash loan, and possibly more, if you had little or no security to offer the lender. On the other hand, if a contract stated that interest was to be paid but failed to state exactly the rate of the interest, you could hold the loan and pay only five percent a year on the unpaid balance over the full term.

Before you sign anything

Government economists who have made a special study of the consumer-loan field advise that the first step a would-be borrower should take is to ask himself seriously: Is the loan really necessary? How badly do I need the money? If you want to buy something and no one seems eager to offer you credit, perhaps the reason is that you can't sensibly afford it at that time. If you can possibly wait until you have saved up the cash yourself, do so! Remember that borrowed money is not income—you have to pay back every penny, and more. Thus, before you borrow, you must be sure your income is going to improve in the short-term future so that you will be able to make repayment and still have enough left over for your normal obligations.

The idea of taking a fresh loan to "consolidate" a lot of other financial commitments, of making just one payment a month instead of several, may be attractive—but it is also expensive. A statistical study has shown that such borrowers remain under obligation for such "refinancing" loans an average of seven years. Most problems in the consumer-loan field arise when people of modest means make unwise purchases; the inevitable interest payments mock them for their folly.

Borrow only the sum you actually need, and shop around for the best terms. You don't need a gilt-edged invitation these days to call on a banker—even if some banks still tend to look like temples. Read every word of the contract form and ask questions about any terms you don't understand. Under no circumstances should you ever sign a blank form of any kind.

Be sure that the cost you are quoted includes *all* charges that will be made. Sometimes insurance, various "service charges" and other fees are extra. The total interest on a loan granted over a fixed term is sometimes deducted at once; this means that, if you needed $250, you would have to borrow more than that amount in order to actually get the sum you require.

A loan from Uncle Albert

If you have a rich uncle, borrow from him by all means (he may be sympathetic on the matter of interest). But remember that you will still be entering into a contract recognizable at law. Contracts do not have to be written down and blood is not necessarily thicker than water when it comes to money.

A handshake is binding between gentlemen and, to a large degree, at law as well. If Uncle Albert should sue you, claiming

that he lent you $500 in cash on a verbal promise of repayment (with or without interest), the court may well support him unless you can convince the judge it's all a tissue of lies. Even if you had signed nothing, there would probably be some circumstantial evidence that you received some money.

There is a lot to be said for keeping your business affairs and your family affairs distinctly separate—whether you are going to lend or borrow. When emotion of any kind enters a financial deal, it will often cloud normal critical judgment. If Uncle Albert comes through with a loan, you should formalize the matter by giving him a *promissory note* to cover it.

Banks are best

As a general rule, the prospective individual borrower is advised to visit the local branch of one of the Canadian domestic chartered banks. These banks occupy a special place in our financial structure— quite different from, say, the position of even the largest American banks—and are responsive to their privileged status. In a competitive situation, they are willing to make a personal cash loan to anyone (white collar or blue collar) who they believe can repay it.

Some banks offer what are called "revolving credit" schemes by which the depositor can borrow cash in much the same way as he might extend his purchasing power under a department-store credit plan. He would be allowed a cash advance based on his recent financial history as recorded in his savings-account passbook.

The 13 domestic chartered banks are the main source of credit in Canada, and their interest rates (based on the *bank rate* established by the central Bank of Canada) generally tend to be lower than those charged by any other organizations in the commercial arena.

The credit unions

To their nine and a half million members, the credit unions—known in Quebec as *caisses populaires*—can offer a cash loan on comparatively attractive terms. (The general function of these "people's banks"

Solving the interest puzzle

IT'S THE LAW in Canada that the full cost of borrowing money, or buying on credit, must be made known to the customer. Under the Bank Act, the cost of borrowing must be disclosed up to a ceiling of $50,000. The interest must be expressed in terms of the annual rate being charged. In many instances, you will see this interest shown as a monthly rate. For example, a finance company can charge you a maximum of two percent per month up to $300. Doesn't sound too bad? But when that rate of interest is expressed as being 24 percent per annum, the borrower might think twice!

The real rate of interest is calculated on the amount of the loan outstanding. Those readers with a desire to work things out for themselves can use the chart below to figure the rate of interest they are being charged when paying off a consumer loan (either to a finance company or directly to a department store) in monthly installments. Simply divide the total amount owed by the monthly payment. Take that figure and look in that column of the chart with the appropriate number of repayment months; find the figure closest to the answer. The real interest rate is on the same line in the left-hand column.

For example, if you owed $500 and were paying $25 a month for two years, you divide the amount owed ($500) by the monthly repayment ($25), giving an answer of 20. The figure in the table under 24 months closest to 20 is 20-030. Follow that line to the left and the real interest rate is shown—18 percent.

REPAYMENT PERIOD in months

*	6	9	12	18	21	24	27	30	48
5	5-913	8-815	11-681	17-307	20-067	22-794	25-487	28-146	43-423
6	5-896	8-779	11-619	17-173	19-888	22-563	25-198	27-794	42-580
7	5-879	8-743	11-557	17-040	19-710	22-235	24-914	27-448	41-760
8	5-862	8-707	11-496	16-909	19-536	22-111	24-635	27-109	40-962
8½	5-854	8-689	11-465	16-844	19-449	21-999	24-497	26-941	40-571
9	5-846	8-672	11-435	16-779	19-363	21-889	24-359	26-775	40-185
9½	5-837	8-654	11-405	16-715	19-277	21-780	24-224	26-610	39-804
10	5-829	8-636	11-375	16-651	19-192	21-671	24-089	26-447	39-428
10½	5-820	8-619	11-344	16-587	19-108	21-663	23-955	26-285	39-057
11	5-812	8-601	11-315	16-524	19-023	21-445	23-822	26-125	38-691
12	5-795	8-566	11-255	16-398	18-857	21-243	23-560	25-808	37-974
13½	5-771	8-514	11-167	16-212	18-611	20-931	23-174	25-342	36-933
15	5-746	8-462	11-079	16-030	18-370	20-624	22-796	24-889	35-931
16½	5-772	8-411	10-993	15-850	18-133	20-324	22-428	24-447	34-969
18	5-697	8-361	10-908	15-673	17-900	20-030	22-068	24-016	34-043

*The column of figures at the left of this table represents the interest rate

is described in Chapter 13, under the title "The cooperative idea.")

The credit unions—particularly strong in rural areas of the Canadian West—reserve a significant portion of their funds for loans to their members. The caisses populaires invest their funds in member loans and municipal and school-board bond issues in their communities.

Quite apart from his financial involvement in the credit union, the member has an extra point in his favor when seeking a loan: the committee members who rule on loans will probably know him personally and thus be able to feel an extra confidence in his ability to repay.

Credit-union loans were somewhat easier to negotiate when members were allowed to assign their wages as security for the loan. However, this practice has now been prohibited in some provinces. In Ontario and Saskatchewan, for example, it is forbidden to assign wages as security for a loan, unless the assignment is made under the act regulating the Credit Unions.

Borrowing against insurance

Many life-insurance policies contain provisions which permit the policyholder to borrow cash against a percentage of the paid-up value of the policy—that is, the amount he has already paid into the policy, plus earned interest. In effect, the premiums he has paid act as security. (*See* Chapter 8, "Insuring your life.")

Although the options open to a borrower vary with the type of policy he holds, in most cases the cost of the loan (the interest charged on the amount) will be offset to a large extent by the interest the company would normally pay him on the policy. However, the face value of the policy will be reduced by the amount of the loan until the total sum advanced has been repaid.

Even if the policy does not contain direct borrowing privileges, you may still be able to borrow against it. Most banks will accept a life-insurance policy as adequate collateral, or security, for a loan. But you will have to make a temporary change in the terms of the policy to name the bank as beneficiary. In some provinces, you are not allowed to drop the preferred beneficiary named in the policy without the consent of that beneficiary. If your beneficiary consents, then there will be no difficulty; if not, you are out of luck.

A formula for the mathematically minded

THE QUESTION of what the real annual interest rate is on a credit purchase or cash loan is one that concerns many dollar-conscious people.

For the mathematically inclined there is a formula that will calculate precisely the interest charge in repaying a loan or buying "on time," if you are going to make monthly payments.

By applying this formula, you can find the "best buy" when it comes to credit.

The formula is:

$$R = \frac{2\,PC}{A\,(N+1)}$$

It is not really difficult, and it can help you make a wise decision.

The letters mean:

R = annual rate of interest
P = number of payments a year
C = the finance charge (in dollars)
A = the principal
N = installments needed to pay off debt

If you bought something costing $300 (or borrowed that sum) agreeing to pay $28.50 a month for 12 months, the total cost is 12 x $28.50, or $342. Your credit costs $42.

As P = 12, C = $42, A = $300 and N = 12, thus

$$R = \frac{2 \times 12 \times 42}{300\,(12+1)} = \frac{1008}{300 \times 13} = \frac{1008}{3900}.$$

therefore 1008 ÷ 3900 = 25.8% (the real annual interest rate).

The bank would want to be assured that the premium payments under an assigned policy are kept up. Without that assurance, the bank's security would not exist. The bank will therefore insist that the insurance company notify it if you have not paid a premium by the date it is due. To guard against the possibility of your not paying off the actual loan, the bank will not lend you more than the "cash-surrender value" of the policy. Furthermore, it will insist that you pledge to the bank all the money that would come from your cashing in your policy—that is, from its cash surrender.

The finance companies

The consumer-finance companies specializing in personal loans "with few questions asked" are listed as licensed moneylenders in national statistics. They constitute a powerful financial force: in a recent year their assets totaled over $12.5 billion and their profit before taxes was over $270 million. They make about one and a half million loans a year to Canadians.

Getting a guarantor

If your credit is a bit shaky, getting a *guarantor* to "back your note" may mean the difference between an average interest rate and a high one, and perhaps between getting a loan and not getting one.

Consumer-finance companies and moneylenders will often insist that you have a guarantor before they will lend you money. Although they may gloss over the guarantee requirement by saying that it is "just a formality" or something similar, don't take it lightly. If you have to get someone to guarantee your loan, remember that if anything goes wrong, the debt will land on his shoulders and he will have to pay it off.

If a friend asks you to guarantee a loan for him, remember that the same rule will be applied to you. If at any time he does not pay the due installment, you can be forced to honor your guarantee and pay the loan in full. And the lender has the right to demand all of the money from you; he is not forced to go after the original debtor.

The chattel mortgage

The chattel mortgage is sometimes used for the installment-plan purchase of such items as cars and boats. (*See* Chapter 6, "The arts of selling.") It can also be offered as security for a cash loan. (This form of security does not exist in Quebec.)

After he has observed certain legal requirements (discussed in Chapter 6), the holder of a chattel mortgage who has not been repaid according to the terms of the loan can seize the item, the "chattel," on which he holds the mortgage and sell it to satisfy the debt. The legal effect of a chattel mortgage, properly drawn and registered, is that it gives the lender (the mortgage holder, or *mortgagee*) first right to the item until the debt has been satisfied. If the debt isn't paid, he is entitled to exercise that right, but only to the extent of the unpaid loan. In other words, the mortgagee is entitled to keep only that part of the money he makes from the sale of the chattel which represents the amount of the loan he made plus accumulated interest.

If you are lending on the security of a chattel mortgage, make sure that your mortgage is the only one against the item concerned. You can check at the county courthouse. (*See* Chapter 4, "Closing the deal.") If yours would be the second mortgage taken out on the one item, it might not bring enough money to satisfy both mortgages if it were sold.

Your friendly pawnbroker

If worst comes to worst and no one seems willing to lend you money, the pawnbroker may be your last hope. Pawnbrokers operate on a simple system. You take some item to their premises. They appraise it (usually naming a figure that is a fraction of its real value) and then they may offer to lend you a certain sum on the basis of that value. They keep your item—maybe a watch or a diamond ring —and you take the money. You have a given amount of time to redeem the article by paying back the sum of the loan, plus a heavy finance charge. If you don't redeem, the pawnbroker may sell the article for whatever he can get for it and keep all the money he makes.

If you can't pay

M ANY THINGS can plunge a person into financial difficulties: loss of job, a poor crop, a dishonest employe, a house fire, a long labor strike, an accident or illness. Then there is the constant temptation that exists in our materialist society to succumb to the offer of easy credit—to try to "keep up with the Joneses" by buying things that the family can't really afford. Few situations cause more anguish than being harassed by money problems; training and tradition tend to make the "man of the house" particularly sensitive in this regard, for his ability to support the family comes under attack.

Your legal obligation to pay your bills is clear: as an adult (*i.e.* not a minor, or infant), you are bound by the terms of any contract that you enter into of your own free will. In not paying your bill, you are breaking the terms of the purchase-contract. Of course, you may believe that the other party to the contract—your creditor—has breached the contract in some way; perhaps you are not satisfied with the goods or services he supplied and, for that reason, you have decided to stop the payments. Maybe you didn't commit yourself to buy the stuff at all or perhaps you sent it back and it was lost en route.

The circumstances surrounding the broken contract will obviously have a bearing on your obligation to pay (*See* Chapter 6, "The arts of selling"). On the other hand, even if the responsibility for paying is clearly on your shoulders, the law will still give you a chance to forestall *insolvency*, the state of owing more money than you can possibly pay at the time. The law consistently favors the struggling debtor (as long as he does struggle). If all else fails, it permits him finally to wipe the slate clean after declaring a *personal bankruptcy.*

Sizing up the situation

There is no more dishonor or shame in owing some money than there is honor or pride in lending it. If you should find yourself in financial difficulties, don't panic. Equally, don't try to pretend that the black cloud will just blow away.

The first thing to do is get a pencil and paper and draw up a brutally honest report on your current financial position. Take your sheaf of bills, promissory notes and other debt documents and add up your total indebtedness. List all available cash and all nonessential assets that you could sell. Then, with your family, work out a *budget* that covers the basic living expenses. Finally, figure out the total present family income. With these lists in hand, you can easily tell whether you are in real trouble.

If the figures tell you there's no way you can pay your overdue bills as things stand, then face it, you are going to have to do something about it. You will have to accept some sacrifices and display a firm determination. But as economists warn, don't just rush out and borrow money at any cost to relieve the immediate pressure. Such solutions—often called "bill-payer loans"—are available, but at a price. A moment's thought should inform you that if you can't pay your comparatively small creditors, you certainly won't find it any easier to pay one large creditor at an even higher rate of interest.

Take your balance sheet and call on the most urgent or the largest of your creditors. Swallow your pride and explain your predicament, emphasizing that although you have made some mistakes, you are willing to work your way out. You will probably be surprised at the courteous and helpful reception you will get. The credit manager is an expert in his field. If he is convinced of your sincerity and can see that there is a possibility of your succeeding, the chances are he will help you. He might propose some kind of installment payment and perhaps drop the "late payment fees" that you would normally be charged. After all, he knows that his company would probably get nothing if you simply declared yourself bankrupt. Similar frank meetings with your other creditors might ease the pressure and result in a debt-reduction plan that would bring you finally into the clear. By taking that route, you would also avoid any court action against you.

Credit counseling

If you need financial advice or help with budgeting, you could ask any banker, accountant, trade union leader, or even the director of your local social-welfare agency. Many communities have credit-counseling services, affiliated with the provincial consumer-affairs department, which give advice on debt problems.

Some agencies will go as far as to prepare a family budget and a repayment plan for you. If you are willing to cooperate fully, the agency may take your cash surplus, organize your creditors and, after gaining their agreement to postpone any further action against you, persuade them to accept the payment plan it has drawn up, under which they will receive your cash as it comes in.

Unless the situation is hopeless, the key element will always be the genuine and demonstrable will of the debtor to face up to his problems and begin a practical attack on them. You might also draw some comfort from the realization that companies seldom find it financially worthwhile to take a customer to court in an attempt to recover modest sums. As the old saying goes: "You can't get blood out of a stone." Even if successful, lawyer's fees and court costs could eat up even more than the funds recovered. And the publicity does not encourage credit sales generally. However, don't count on this. Large companies, often with a lawyer on their staff, will sometimes decide to prosecute all defaulters, however small the sum involved, to discourage credit swindlers.

The polite reminder

When you don't pay a bill at the due date, the company concerned normally sends out a polite letter reminding you that you have an outstanding account and asking you to kindly remit immediately. If you pay the bill at this point, or before the end of the month, there will probably be no further consequences from your late payment.

But if you decide not to pay the account, or if you are unable to pay it and do not notify the company or make some arrangement with it, you will get another letter—this one stern and intimidating.

The polite reminder turns into a series of not-so-polite letters containing such statements as "Your credit rating is your most valuable asset: protect it by paying this bill immediately." You will be notified that a late-payment fee is being added to your indebtedness (usually at a yearly interest rate of from 18 to 24 percent).

These dunning letters are composed by experts to prod, plead and press, but not to threaten. Although they may carry the implication of "or else," they cannot suggest that you will, for example, risk jail by not paying. After receiving a series of dunning letters, you will probably be informed that the matter has been placed in the hands of a collection agency or that a judgment summons is being sought against you.

The collection agency

If an account is not paid after several dunning letters have been sent, it will be turned over to a collection agency. These agencies, which are licensed by the government, either buy the delinquent account from the creditor at a low rate or negotiate to receive a high percentage of what they are able to collect on the debt.

The agencies are masters of the art of collecting overdue accounts. They assume at the outset that the time for courtesy is past and start right in with a campaign of blunt letters and telephone calls to the debtor. They may phone the debtor's spouse and employer, as well as his or her associates. Personal calls at the debtor's home or workplace are not ruled out (of course, you are not obliged to speak to a debt collector and you have every right to ask him, or her, to leave your property should he make a personal call).

Although perhaps little may seem to be achieved by harassment, the agencies obviously have a large measure of success. Perhaps their most potent weapon is the realization by the debtor that the loss of his credit rating on central registers will mean that he won't be able to buy most things, except for cash. Also, the debt collector, having taken over the debt, has no public-relations image to lose in taking the debtor to court.

Legal proceedings

Most debt-collection agencies will resort to court action only when they are unable to collect otherwise. Legal proceedings are far more costly than get-tough letters. If the debt is one which can be collected in small claims court (in most provinces, the debt has to be up to $1,000 to qualify), then the agency can prosecute its own case and save lawyer's fees. If the debt is greater, however, the action has to be heard in county or district court, where lawyers are normally used (*See* Chapter 3, "Judges and courts").

If a creditor takes action against you for debt, the summons issued will state the nature and the amount of his claim. If you are served with such a summons and it is incorrect, or if you feel you have a defense to it, then you should dispute it. If the case is to come before the small

Would a flashing red light cut the bankruptcy rate?

AUTHORITIES IN BANKRUPTCY unite in blaming too-easy credit for the steady increase in personal bankruptcies in Canada. The number of bankruptcies of all types increased by 50 percent between 1980 and the end of 1982.

Melvin C. Zwaig, a trustee in bankruptcy, believes that too many credit managers in stores are overruled by sales managers, thus permitting an individual's level of debt to rise beyond his apparent ability to pay. Goods continue to be shipped out, even if a customer's account is already seriously in arrears. Zwaig suggests there should be a central credit bureau that would "flash a red light" whenever a shopper tries to exceed his credit limit.

Many credit bureau listings are based fundamentally on a person's payment record in the past and take no account of current circumstances. A wage-earner recently fired from a high-paying job is probably still carried as an excellent risk until his failure to meet due bills filters through to the bureau. Thus, down on his luck, he can be tempted through easy credit plans to buy expensive goods (perhaps a refrigerator or color TV) with very small down payments and then sell them to raise ready money. When the bill collectors run him down, he files in bankruptcy.

Sometimes, creditors will push a debtor into bankruptcy, even if they know they won't get one cent on the dollar. The reason is that the creditor can then write off the business loss due to bad debts against his tax liability. Also, those companies deeply involved in credit selling usually protect themselves against bad debts as they fix the price of their goods or services.

Incidentally, even after discharge as a bankrupt, the person concerned must still pay in full all debts incurred for the necessities of life—including rent, food, fuel, clothing and household furniture.

The most dangerous pitfall in consumer credit is the mistaken concept that credit is an increase of total income. Wages can become overcommitted by credit payments and any sudden reduction (perhaps by an extended illness) can be disastrous.

claims court, you simply go to the court office and write an explanation of why you do not think you owe the money. If the summons is to a higher court and you intend to dispute it or offer some defense, you should get a lawyer. No matter which court you are dealing with, do not delay in replying to the creditor's claim if you have a reasonable defense.

Many povinces allow their small claims court judges to make what is known as a *consolidation order.* The judge takes the debtor's bills that the creditors are claiming payment on (which are eating away at his income and giving him no chance to recover) and puts them all into one pile. He then sets a realistic amount for the debtor to pay into the court, weekly or monthly. All the creditors share this money according to their part of the total debt. While the order is in effect, the creditors may not take any other steps to recover their money. As you can see, the consolidation order can be a good way out of an apparently hopeless credit tangle.

The judgment summons
Most provinces have legislation that allows the creditor to have a *judgment summons* issued on the debtor. The creditor does this by taking your unpaid bill to court and asking the magistrate to summon you to appear. The summons compels you, the debtor, to appear before a magistrate and, under oath, answer searching questions about your income and assets. In this way, your ability to meet your debt obligations is formally established.

If you were ordered to pay your debtor after the hearing in court and you still refused to do so, you could be sent to jail—not for debt, but for *contempt* of the court's order to pay. (*See* Chapter 3, "Decisions from the Bench.")

If you are ever served with a summons, make sure you attend the hearing. Even if you have no defense, explain to the presiding magistrate just why you have not paid the bill. He will probably try to work out some compromise that will allow you to pay it off over a period of time. This could save you from going through the embarrassment and hardship of having your wages *garnisheed*—that is, seized in part—or it could forestall a *creditor's sale.*

In Quebec, the Voluntary Deposit of Salary and Wage Act permits the debtor to make a regular deposit five days after he receives a pay.

After judgment
Any defense or counterclaim you might have should be presented to the magistrate at the hearing. If you prove a partial defense, the creditor's claim might be reduced accordingly. At the end of the hearing, the creditor may then be granted a judgment against you. If you have not appeared, the judgment can be made anyway—by *default.* The creditor (or the collection agency) will now attempt to recover the money involved. If you still don't or can't pay, he can choose from three courses of action.

(1) He may seize any of your assets that are not considered necessities and therefore exempted.

(2) He may register a lien against any land that you own and arrange for the land to be sold if the judgment is not satisfied after a year.

(3) He may garnishee, or seize, your wages or any other payments due to you.

A seizure of assets is arranged under what is known in most provinces as the Executions Act. This law sets forth what goods and other assets may be seized to satisfy a judgment. Most provinces forbid the seizure of ordinary household items, clothing and other necessities, including work tools. Apart from these items, however, anything else of value may be seized by the sheriff and sold. Stocks and bonds may be seized and bank accounts frozen until the debt is satisfied. (*See* Chapter 13, "If the business fails.")

Where there are several judgments outstanding and assets are seized and sold, then all creditors share pro rata (according to the size of their claims) in the distribution of the proceeds. If the money made from the sale of the seized assets fails to pay off the creditors in full, a creditor is still entitled to collect the difference in the future. But, if more than enough money results from the forced sale, the debtor gets the balance.

A garnishee of wages is permissible in all Canadian provinces. This is a technique by which the creditor, having obtained a judgment, gets a *garnishee order* from the court on the debtor's employer. The employer must deduct, from any money due to the debtor, the sum directed by the court order and pay it into court. The creditor can continue to garnishee, or seize, until the debt is satisfied.

Most provinces have regulations that limit the percentage of wages that may be garnisheed (usually a maximum of 30 percent) so that the debtor will have some money to live on. If there are several garnishee orders outstanding, the first one served on the employer is the only one that will be acted upon for that pay period. Federal government employes were formerly not subject to garnishees. Under the Garnishment and Pension Diversion Act 1980–81, they are now subject to conditions set forth in provincial laws.

If the debtor happens to own real estate, the creditor will probably arrange to obtain a *lien* against it. The lien has the effect of charging the amount of the debt against the property, giving the creditor a claim to that much of the property's value. This claim can be renewed if the debt has not been paid. If you should buy land from any person who has a debt judgment against him in the form of a lien, you would be in danger of losing that property if you did not pay the judgment, despite the fact that it was not your debt. This is why it is imperative to have a *search of title* made when you are buying land.

The personal bankruptcy

If there is no hope that you will ever be able to meet your debts, the only way you can get them off your back is to declare a *personal bankruptcy*. In 1982, more than 30,000 Canadians declared bankruptcy. The law on bankruptcy applies to the individual as well as to the corporation. The application under the federal Bankruptcy Act must be made through a trustee in bankruptcy who will arrange all of the proceedings. There are two main conditions for declaring bankruptcy. You must have committed an act of bankruptcy— that is, you have shown that you cannot pay your debts—within a six-month period before filing a bankruptcy petition, and your liabilities must total $1,000. If your debts are $1,000 or more, your creditors may combine to force you into bankruptcy, whether you like it or not.

Bankruptcy is a serious step and should be taken only as a last resort. Once you have declared bankruptcy, your financial affairs will be administered by the court-appointed trustee, who may order that all of your assets be sold. All creditors who can prove their claims against you share in the proceeds of that sale, perhaps receiving only a few cents on the dollar.

While you are in a state of bankruptcy (before the court grants you a *discharge*) your financial affairs, as well as your personal life, will remain to a large extent under the scrutiny of the trustee, and will also be subject to review by the court. During this period, you may be ordered to pay off your creditors out of your earnings, if you are able to do so. Also, there are a number of things that you are ordered not to do: you may not be *bonded*— that is, sign a pledge which has a money-forfeit penalty; you may not engage in a trade or business without disclosing to everyone involved that you are in bankruptcy; you may not become a director of any limited-liability company; and you are not allowed to accept an appointment to the Canadian Senate!

When the court is convinced that, to the best of your ability, you have paid off your creditors, it will grant you a discharge from bankruptcy. Once discharged (unless your discharge is conditional), you are freed from your creditors —except where the debts were incurred for necessities of life. You will still have to pay any alimony or family maintenance you might owe.

Until recently, it was rightly said that the poor man couldn't afford to go bankrupt. The fees to the trustee, plus other inescapable expenses, can start at $500. When bankruptcy is the only solution for low-income earners, the Bankruptcy Branch of Consumer and Corporate Canada will refer them to certain private trustees who will accept such cases without the assurance of a fee.

8/Making Your Money Work

The role of the agent 360

Anatomy of the stock market 366

The beginning investor 375

Getting financial advice

Choosing your insurance agent
Choosing your stockbroker

MOST OF US work hard for our share of the good things of life, and we save and plan our finances in the hope that at some rosy time in the future we'll be able to take things a little easier. "When it comes to money," quipped Voltaire, "everyone is of the same religion." As family assets and responsibilities grow, we feel the need to protect our property against damage or theft, and to set up alternative income in case the breadwinner's capacity to earn is reduced, or even cut off in untimely fashion. True, the benevolent state stands ready with a whole raft of social-welfare legislation to succor those who falter— through bad luck or any other reason. However, it provides only minimal support at best. As savings slowly accumulate, or when we receive any sizable sums by gift or inheritance, good sense turns our thoughts toward putting this money to work. A few moments' reflection about the seemingly inevitable inflation that plagues us should convince anyone that money left lying idle decreases in value. If you put a dollar in the cookie jar today and take it out in a year's time, you'll find that its purchasing power has shrunk to about 93 cents—maybe less. Since 1971, inflation has reduced the value of our dollar by more than 60 percent.

You will find that there is no lack of suggestions about what you should do with your surplus money. Banks and trust companies vie for it through expensive television and press advertising, governments want to borrow it from you through Canada Savings Bonds, and new companies trying to get started—or established firms trying to expand—offer a tempting shopping list of stocks and bonds. Mutual funds beckon seductively. Stockbrokers and investment agencies of various kinds offer their services, and some lawyers and accountants will propose that you place extra funds in private loans or lucrative mortgages.

As you venture into the highly competitive and sometimes confusing world of investment, the law tries to guard you against potential dangers and to protect you from the unscrupulous who continue to prove the truth of the sixteenth-century adage that "a fool and his money are soon parted." You will be reassured to learn that Canadian law in the financial field is regarded by international opinion as being much stricter than most. There are critics, in fact, who feel that our business regulations (and taxation policies) are *too* strict: in seeking to protect the innocent general public, they say, the law puts too many obstacles in the path of the adventurous few, the risk takers, who are largely responsible for the creation and development of new ideas and job-producing industries. This may be part of the reason for the foreign ownership of a substantial percentage of Canadian business, and for stubbornly high unemployment.

Almost from pioneer days, Canadian business has been notably law-abiding, with comparatively few of the promoter scandals that have rocked the business communities of many other countries. Federal and provincial laws require the close supervision of all chartered banks, trust and loan companies and insurance companies; all incorporated companies, public or private, must lodge annual reports; and details of prospectuses (invitations to the public to invest) and of "insider trading" (share transactions by company directors and officers) are keenly scrutinized. (*See* Chapter 13, "The public corporation.") Any evidence of shady dealing can cause stock-exchange or security commission officials to freeze trading in that company's shares instantly, and stockbrokers who break the rigid (mostly self-imposed) rules of their business are certain to be refused stock-exchange privileges, a penalty similar to the disbarment of a lawyer.

Despite all its efforts, though, the law can provide a safe conduct for the novice only a short distance into the financial jungle. When profit is at stake, wits are at their sharpest. The newcomer with a modest sum of money at his disposal should avoid all "hot tips" or out-of-the-blue inspirations and begin by seeking professional advice.

A great deal of routine sound advice is available, free, from banks and trust companies and from insurance and large stockbroking firms. There are some impartial investment newsletters available at modest cost by mail subscription. Booklets providing basic rules on investment for the average man are published from time to time by the consumer agencies of government. The reference department of your nearest public library is sure to have a selection of books on the subject—although titles of the "How to make a million" variety are not recommended, except for a fun read. Most major daily newspapers carry financial news and comment that can help you form an objective picture, and at least one national weekly, *The Financial Post*, is devoted to an extensive coverage of business and financial matters.

Of course the experts will differ in their advice; that is only to be expected. If it were easy to make unearned income, then we would all be rich. But all the experts will tell you that if you feel inclined to venture beyond the safe confines of banks and government bonds, you should remember one fundamental principle: the higher the possible gain, the greater the risk. How safe do you have to play it? The cardinal rule is simple: never risk what you cannot afford to lose, if the worst should come to the worst (and once in a while it does).

The facilities offered by banks and some trust companies through savings accounts and longer term deposits have already been detailed (*See* Chapter 7, "The role of the bank"). While the chartered banks offer virtually total security, the money to be made through interest on savings is usually barely enough to keep pace with the shrinkage of the dollar through inflation.

In the sections that follow, attention turns to insurance and investment in securities—the two main avenues open to those of moderate income who seek financial security and a fair chance to build up their estates.

The confidence trick

No matter how certain you are of the integrity and expertise of your chosen stockbroker, there is another essential element that must always be present: confidence.

You can't really describe it; you have to feel it. Without it, you will never be at ease in the market, and you probably won't sleep nights.

To the average small investor, the broker is the man in touch with the arcane mysteries of the market; his office with its desktop computer seems like some downtown Aladdin's cave; his language is peppered with gilt-edged words like "profit-taking" and "stock splits." You must feel confident that, with the broker's advice (his firm's,

really), you will have every chance of backing investment winners.

He will work with a will to try to make you richer for the best of reasons: self-interest. Almost all brokers depend for most of their earnings on the commissions they bring into the firm. The younger stockbroker, who hopes to become a partner as soon as possible, will be eager to demonstrate his skill and judgment to his seniors by succeeding first with small accounts.

If he does so, he can expect to share in the bigger commissions that come his firm's way. He is also showing that he has the tact and personality to understand and win the confidence of clients.

Choosing your insurance agent

As any insurance *agent* or *broker* will inform you, a life insurance *policy* (it is, in fact, a contract) is usually the cornerstone on which a sound personal financial plan is developed. Canadians hold more life insurance *per capita* (an average of $22,100) than any other nation, except Japan and the United States. These policies are sold by more than 20,000 insurance agents—energetic and persuasive salesmen who normally will not hesitate to contact you. But if you want to buy a policy that will best fit your needs, which insurance agent or broker should you choose?

You should choose an agent as carefully as you would choose a lawyer or an accountant. You will probably be doing business with him for a long time and you want someone you can trust and who is also properly qualified to advise you.

The major insurers insist that their company agents take intensive training courses and each man or woman selling insurance must be licensed by the provincial government. The Institute of Chartered Life Underwriters of Canada administers a training program, in English and French, leading to the qualification C.L.U. (Chartered Life Underwriter). Because insurance advantages are affected by changes in taxation regulations, it is essential that the agent keep abreast of the frequent changes in this and other fields.

The *company agents*—who are in the great majority—naturally work for the insurance companies that employ them, not for you. They may be paid on a salary

You, too, can be an expert

EACH YEAR since 1964, the Canadian Securities Institute has conducted a tough qualifying course for those intending to enter the investment business, and for private students who want to know as much as the experts. The Securities Commission in each province requires enrolment in or completion of this course before granting the necessary registration to anyone selling securities to the public.

The non-profit institute is the national educational body created by the Investment Dealers Association of Canada and the stock exchanges of Toronto, Montreal, Calgary and Vancouver. Apart from its basic Canadian Securities Course, it supports simpler programs intended to increase the public's knowledge of the inner workings of the stock market. Evening lectures are given in the larger centers. The institute also conducts a course for those aiming at the highest rungs of investment counseling.

The Canadian Securities Course usually attracts a student body drawn 50 percent from the staffs of member firms of the C.S.I. and 50 percent from a varied group of the public. Study is done at home from supplied texts either on a six-month (October to May) term or on accelerated terms of three months. Since most of the "students" are in full-time employment, the course makes stiff demands on their leisure.

On completion of the course, an examination is set with a minimum pass mark of 60 percent demanded. A limited number of applicants—persons with high educational qualifications or considerable practical experience—are permitted to follow a course without assignments; for them, the pass mark is set at 70 percent.

The securities course covers a wide area of the investment business, with particular emphasis on Canadian stocks, bonds, and practices, including up-to-the-minute amendments to commercial and taxation law. The cost of the full course is $275 for private students and $160 for students in the investment business. It is available in English or French.

Applicants should write to 33 Yonge Street, Suite 360, Toronto, Ontario, M5E 1G4.

basis or, more probably, on a combination of salary plus commission on sales. Thus, the more insurance a salesman sells, the more he earns. The same is true, of course, of the *independent agent*, except that he is normally free to suggest a policy from any of the many insurance companies operating in Canada, or at least from a competing number of them. The *private broker* represents your interests, rather than those of any company; however, he sometimes handles only large accounts. (*See* "The role of the agent" in this chapter.)

Only some fly-by-night agent would try to sell you unsatisfactory coverage, or a policy requiring premium payments above your budget. Why? Because you would soon let the policy lapse, and the professional agent's success really depends on steady payment of premiums year after year. His success also depends, to some extent, on getting new business from people who seek him out on your recommendation.

Choosing your stockbroker

If you have decided on direct investment in the stock market, you will need a broker. He is the middleman, a professional who buys and sells stocks and bonds on behalf of you, his customer. He is, in fact, usually called a "customer's man." Probably the best way for the newcomer to the market to find a suitable broker is to be introduced by a friend who has similar investment objectives and has enough confidence in his broker to recommend him.

There is no reason, however, why you should not pick any established broker's office at random—see the classified section of your telephone book under "Stockbrokers"—and get an appointment with a customer's man. Just say you have some money you would like to invest (you will probably need, however, several thousand dollars to start) and you would like to talk to someone about it. You can walk in off the street, if you don't mind taking pot luck. Even the biggest brokerage houses welcome the business of the "little man"; there are thousands of small investors and only a few big ones.

All stockbrokers and their salesmen must be registered with the provincial Securities Commission. Most major firms are members of one or more of the five Canadian stock exchanges. They are probably also members of the Investment Dealers Association of Canada. These firms are best qualified to advise you and to carry out your investment orders. They will charge a brokerage fee, or commission, which is usually a small percentage of the value of the transaction. The Investment Dealers Association and the four largest stock exchanges maintain a national contingency fund to protect investors against the possible insolvency of any member firm.

If your town doesn't boast a full-time broker, it's probably worth your while to take a trip to the city; alternatively, your bank manager would act as intermediary with a distant qualified broker, charging you a small service fee above the usual brokerage commission.

If you have had little experience of investing so far, you will need practical advice; thus your relationship with your broker must be fairly intimate. You should tell him frankly the state of your financial affairs—your assets, your income and your financial responsibilities of the moment—as well as what you hope to achieve. He is a professional and will keep your private affairs strictly confidential. And don't feel obliged to give some business to the first broker you meet; seek out another if you don't feel any rapport with the first.

Whatever his other attributes, the broker must be a skilled analyst. He has to know the market thoroughly at present, to be able to estimate its future behavior to a certain extent, and be able to relate this information to your particular needs. It is important, therefore, that he is backed up by a strong investment research group. The written material published by this group will be made available to you. Summarizing the complex happenings in business and financial markets, these reports can save you many hours in your decision-making process, as well as help you to make intelligent investments.

335

Insuring your life

| Accepting risks in Canada |
| Achieving individual goals |
| Registered retirement savings plan |
| The appeal of the annuity |
| A personal consultation |
| Insuring your wife and children |

Accepting risks in Canada

A personal consultation

Registered retirement savings plan

The appeal of the annuity

Achieving individual goals

Insuring your wife and children

ALTHOUGH THE ROMANS started burial clubs that paid benefits to a member's survivors, the idea of life insurance as it is known today arose in the Middle Ages when shipowners began to insure their cargoes against loss on risky voyages. Pirates lay in wait around the Mediterranean to seize ship, cargo, captain and crew. Soon, the life and safe passage of the captain for the sailing season were being insured separately from the cargo, to provide ransom money if he were kidnapped. Passengers (or their creditors) began to demand insurance protection for the duration of the voyage, and bankers and trading companies were soon putting together the basically simple mathematical formula of life insurance.

Life can be seen to contain certain hazards (illnesses and accidents), but these perils each year claim only a small percentage of the population. If a large number of those exposed to the hazards pay a modest fee (known today as the *premium)* into a general fund, then a great pool of money is created, sufficient to provide benefits for the dependents or beneficiaries of the relatively few who meet untimely death. The loss that would financially crush an individual is easily borne when divided among many. All insurance is, fundamentally, risk sharing.

As census returns provided increasingly accurate information about the population, the relationship of the age of the insured to his probable span of life became a decisive factor in determining the premium necessary to carry the risk. The first mortality tables were drawn up in England in 1693 by Edmund Halley, the astronomer most famous for the discovery of Halley's comet.

All insurance archives acknowledge that the first specific life insurance on record was that issued to William Gybbons, "a citizen and salter of London," in 1583. Gybbons paid £32 for one year's insurance on his life. He died within the year and his beneficiary collected £140. Today, we call this kind of policy *term insurance.*

Life insurance developed quickly during the Industrial Revolution in England in the eighteenth century and soon spread to the British colonies in North America. The father of all North American life insurance companies was opened for business in 1759 in Philadelphia; the company was called "A Corporation for the Relief of Poor and Distressed Presbyterian Ministers and of the Poor and Distressed Widows and Children of Presbyterian Ministers" (it is still in business in the United States and Canada, mercifully under a shortened name).

Accepting risks in Canada

By the mid-nineteenth century, several British life insurance companies had opened branches in Canada (the earliest was started in Quebec in 1833) and U.S.-based companies were beginning to show interest in the prospering communities to the north.

The first truly Canadian company was organized in Hamilton, Ontario (then Canada West), in 1847 by Hugh C. Baker. To gain some first-hand experience, Baker had traveled to New York City by stagecoach, horseback and riverboat to take out a policy with an American company; he was charged one percent more than the going rate in New York because of the "climatic hazards of living in Canada."

When he organized the Canada Life Assurance Company in Hamilton, he also became its first policyholder, taking out coverage on his life for £500. That company, which later moved its head office to Toronto, is one of the world's largest.

Ten years after Confederation, 34 companies were operating in Canada; the federal government had appointed a permanent public servant, the superintendent of insurance, to supervise and regulate the business. Today, there are almost 200 life insurance companies and fraternal benefit societies (Canadian, American, British and foreign) registered under federal law, while some companies are registered only in the province where they do business.

Every life insurance company operating in Canada must each year obtain government certification of its right to continue to do business. At that time, it must provide the superintendent of insurance with proof of its ability to meet all outstanding obligations to policyholders. No approved Canadian life insurance company has ever defaulted on a single dollar owing to a policyholder at death or maturity.

Life insurance has become a fundamental part of the Canadian way of life (perhaps, more strictly, our way of death, since most policies pay off only on the death of the policyholder). Recent statistics reveal that Canadians own $547 billion in life insurance, and this figure has grown to more than four times the amount owned in 1970. It is estimated that the average amount of life insurance owned in each household in Canada is $66,200 a high figure compared with other nations.

Canada's international reputation for financial integrity is reflected in the remarkable sales of Canadian life insurance abroad. More than two million persons in more than 20 countries hold Canadian policies, worth a total of $155 billion. The flow of premium money to Canadian companies from these policies is reaching toward $3.1 billion a year.

Carrying risks on your behalf is obviously a profitable business. The total assets of life insurance companies in Canada (at the close of business in 1982) reached over $54 billion. This mountain of money is invested worldwide in mortgages, federal, provincial and municipal bonds, corporate stocks and bonds and real estate; it yields an average annual interest rate of approximately 10.7 percent.

A personal consultation

You will see it stated that a breadwinner should have four to five times his or her annual income covered by life insurance so that, in the case of sudden death, there will be an adequate "instant estate" to provide reasonable protection for dependents. But every case is different, and an integrated estate plan should be worked out in consultation with the agent or broker. There are too many variables—the client's current level of savings, the size of a house mortgage, any office or factory group insurance plan, inheritance prospects—for any single fixed plan to be universally suitable.

Before deciding on how much life insurance a client needs, as well as what type of policy, the experienced agent will normally explain the four main financial needs that life insurance can cover in the event that the family breadwinner dies:

(1) Cash to meet the final expenses—often called "the high cost of dying";

(2) Money to support the family while it readjusts to the new conditions;

(3) Income for the family while the children are being educated;

(4) Income for the widow after the children have left home.

It will be pointed out that if, happily, the breadwinner lives on beyond the time when protection for children is necessary, the insurance program can be adjusted to provide income for retirement.

How about current protection?

The "how much" factor cannot be accurately determined until the client's prospective benefits under any existing group insurance or pension plans are calculated. For instance, the Canada Pension Plan (*See* Chapter 14, "The pension network") provides benefits for retirement, for total and permanent disability and for the support of widows and orphans. The

Quebec resident has identical coverage under the separate Quebec Pension Plan. Your agent will be able to give you a pretty accurate rundown on the benefits which will be provided under those compulsory plans. The benefits provided by employers can include group life insurance, accidental death and dismemberment insurance, weekly indemnity, salary continuation and supplementary hospital benefits. The agent will make a thorough examination of any pension benefits provided for by your employer.

Most large industrial or administrative employers now make some contribution to group insurance plans under which the worker's life is covered. These plans are normally based on one-year renewable term insurance which usually requires no medical examination. The coverage provided under group life plans is either a flat sum or a multiple of the worker's salary—i.e., two or three times current salary.

A recent innovation in group life insurance policies is the provision of a lump-sum death benefit, together with a widow's and orphans' benefit, both based on a percentage of the worker's wage. The amount of this benefit is usually decided in relation to similar C.P.P. or Q.P.P. benefits.

Short-term disability payments are also taken into account. These will either be payable through Unemployment Insurance Commission benefits or weekly indemnity benefits provided by the employer in lieu of U.I.C. benefits. The latter arrangement is made possible by an optional clause in the Unemployment Insurance Act whereby indemnity can be paid by the employer's insurer. This results in the employer being charged a lower rate by the U.I.C. Long-term dis-

How long can you expect to live?

Since the first mortality tables were drawn up in the seventeenth century, life insurance premiums have been based on the probable death rate of those in the age group of the applicant. For example, the companies "know" that, based on past experience, 15 out of every 10,000 Canadian males aged 20 will die before reaching their next birthday. Premiums for that whole group must be adjusted to meet that number of policy claims. Instead of setting a new and higher premium as the policy holder gets older (and his life expectancy grows shorter), the companies have worked out the "level premium system." You pay more than is called for, actuarially, in the early years, somewhat less later on. The surpluses are invested by the companies, thus reducing the premiums over the average life of a policy. The table shows how long a Canadian male can expect to live. The figures are, based on the "average" person in the age group given.

Age and Expectancy	Age and Expectancy	Age and Expectancy	Age and Expectancy
0 74.22	19 56.23	38 38.32	57 22.49
1 73.33	20 55.32	39 37.40	58 21.79
2 72.39	21 54.41	40 36.48	59 21.11
3 71.43	22 53.49	41 35.57	60 20.45
4 70.47	23 52.56	42 34.67	61 19.80
5 69.50	24 51.61	43 33.77	62 19.18
6 68.53	25 50.67	44 32.89	63 18.57
7 67.56	26 49.72	45 32.02	64 17.99
8 66.58	27 48.76	46 31.15	65 17.43
9 65.61	28 47.81	47 30.30	66 16.89
10 64.64	29 46.85	48 29.46	67 16.36
11 63.67	30 45.90	49 28.63	68 15.86
12 62.71	31 44.94	50 27.81	69 15.37
13 61.75	32 43.99	51 27.01	70 14.84
14 60.79	33 43.03	52 26.22	71 19.62
15 59.85	34 42.08	53 25.44	72 19.23
16 58.92	35 41.14	54 24.68	73 18.97
17 58.02	36 40.20	55 23.93	74 18.10
18 57.12	37 39.26	56 23.20	75 15.26

Courtesy of Sun Life Assurance Company of Canada

ability benefits will usually provide between 50 and 60 percent of a worker's wage as it stood just prior to the onset of the disability.

Registered retirement savings plan

As your agent will point out to you as he helps you plan for adequate income on your retirement, the Income Tax Act provides a valuable tax concession for those who are prepared to store up reserves for their later years by paying regular amounts into a registered retirement savings plan—commonly known as R.R.S.P.

This scheme is available not only to those individuals who are self-employed, but also to those who contribute to a company pension plan. If you are self-employed, you may pay in as much as 20 percent of your earned income, to a maximum of $5,500 a year, and deduct the contribution from the total of your taxable income. Those who are covered by a company pension plan may contribute up to 20 percent of their salary, but no more than $3,500 a year less the amount of their contributions to the company plan.

If a policyholder so chooses, the agent will arrange for certain insurance contracts to be registered with the tax authorities as part of his R.R.S.P. Then, the part of the premium used to purchase the retirement benefit can be deducted from the person's taxable income. Of course, these benefits will be taxable as income when paid out later—but by then, in retirement, he will probably be in a much lower tax bracket.

The appeal of the annuity

Depending on your later income prospects, as well as your desire to keep your nose to the grindstone, the agent will explain the special appeal of purchasing an *annuity*. This term comes from the Latin word, *annuus*, meaning yearly; it has come to mean an amount of money to be paid yearly or at other regular intervals.

The agent will point out that while the ordinary life policy pays off at the death of the policyholder, and the endowment policy at some set date if the policyholder still lives, the annuity contract can provide a guaranteed monthly income after

the person reaches a certain age, for the rest of his life. Sometimes, a life insurance policy combined with an annuity is the best answer to a person's needs.

The annuity is based on the simple principle of risk sharing. The contracting company pools the money of a large number of people who are afraid that if they use their savings as income in their retirement years, they might outlive their capital. No doubt some of them will, but others will die earlier; this provides the balance that keeps the company in business. In simplest terms, the client turns all or part of his savings over to the insurance company in exchange for a promise that the company will pay him a steady fixed income as long as he lives. In 1982, Canadian insurance companies paid out over $2.7 billion to annuitants. Incidentally, payments from annuities can be arranged to begin at any age—at 60, if you like.

Since World War II, several systems of group annuities have developed, allowing people to bolster income after their retirement at 65. This remains a fast-growing sector, despite the introduction of the C.P.P. and Q.P.P. compulsory pension plans. Payments under group annuity systems amount to more than one billion dollars a year. Boss and worker usually share the cost, with the latter's portion being deducted from his weekly wage (such a contribution is currently tax free).

Under an option clause in most ordinary life insurance policies, the lump-sum payment to a beneficiary may be paid as an annuity—that is, as a series of guaranteed monthly payments as long as the beneficiary lives, or for a stated period of, say, ten or 15 years.

A reminder about taxation

Payments from an annuity are normally tax free because the income from which the original contribution was made had already been taxed. The portion of an annuity cheque that represents earned interest *is* taxable, but the average recipient is usually in retirement and in a tax bracket where his income tax is minimal.

The proceeds of a life insurance policy paid at the holder's death are not subject

339

to income tax, as long as they are paid in a lump sum. At the time of this writing, changes in the tax status of the proceeds from life insurance policies had been proposed under extensive revisions of the Income Tax Act. Under these circumstances, it is best to seek clarification of the rules from a qualified tax adviser.

When income tax began to be levied on one half of net capital gains in 1972, life insurance policies were exempted, but annuity contracts were not. Now, if you dispose of a life insurance policy or a life annuity, you are required to pay capital gains tax on a portion of the proceeds. At the time of this writing, it had been proposed to impose a capital gains tax on term-certain annuities—that is, annuities paid for specific periods of time.

Achieving individual goals

After evaluating your goals and your present coverage under group or government plans (and assuming that you hold no other life insurance), your agent will then be able to work out your short-, medium- and long-term needs for insurance.

Short-term needs can usually be covered best by term insurance, either level term or reducing term (these labels are explained below). Such needs could include repayment of a mortgage or bank loan. Medium-term goals, such as establishing a cash nest egg, can usually best be handled through ordinary life insurance. Retirement needs can be looked after with an endowment-type contract, a variable contract, or a combination of the two that best suits the individual case.

Par or nonpar

We are not switching to a discussion on golf when we mention par and nonpar. Insurance has its jargon, too. If you plan to invest in life insurance, your chosen agent or broker will no doubt explain the difference between participating contracts and nonparticipating contracts—hence "par" and "nonpar."

About half of Canadian individual life insurance policies are "par" contracts. A participating policy pays dividends—not in the sense of profits, but a refund of any portion of the premium not needed to cover the cost of the insurance. The non-participating policy's premium remains fixed for the life of the policy.

In the initial years, a "par" plan may be a little more expensive than a "nonpar" plan; but later on, it will likely be the cheaper. It depends to some extent on how efficiently the insurance company you have chosen manages its business.

The next question to be answered is: what policy best fits your needs? Although there are literally hundreds of variations, the choice boils down to three basic kinds of policy: term, ordinary (straight, or whole) life, and endowment. All three naturally provide payment at death, but the premiums vary widely because of the different savings, or investment, features in the ordinary and endowment policies.

Term life insurance

A term policy can be likened to a fire or automobile insurance policy in that it provides protection at lowest cost for a fixed period. However, if you outlive the expiry date of the policy, you get nothing back from your investment. As they say, you have to die to win.

Bluntly, it's a gamble between you and the insurance company. For so many dollars for every thousand dollars of insurance, based on your age and state of health, the company bets that you will stay alive until the next premium date. It's a popular policy with the younger husband and father who finds himself taking on big responsibilities while his income is still relatively small.

Although most term policies are dated for five years, they can usually be written to contain a renewal privilege for another five years (without a further medical examination) and, in some cases, this extension can go on until the buyer reaches 65 or even 70. However, for the buyer, the cost of term insurance rises steeply. The term rate for women is equivalent to the rate for men about three years younger.

Most term contracts can be converted to either ordinary life or endowment, prior to age 60, with no further medical examination required. In special cases, a term policy can be combined with the investment policies to good effect.

You can also buy a *decreasing term* policy. This type may be written to cover a long period, say, 25 years. It will give the young family maximum protection in the early years, then dwindle in value as time passes when, presumably, the financial demand on the breadwinner lessens. This kind of policy is often taken out especially to ensure payment of a house mortgage if the father should die; as the mortgage shrinks, so does the insurance coverage.

Ordinary life insurance

About 44 percent of individual life insurance in Canada is held under policies which are called variously "ordinary," "whole" or "straight." These can be written in several ways to meet individual needs. For instance, the premiums can be paid for the remainder of your life, for a stated number of years or until you reach a certain age. Premiums can even be paid in a lump sum if, perhaps, you happen to have just won a lottery.

The most popular type of policy sold today is the oldest of all: the contract providing insurance on your whole life. You pay a level premium forever and you go to sleep at night knowing that if you don't wake up, your insurance will take care of any financial responsibilities you may leave behind. Despite all other considerations, family protection remains the central purpose of life insurance.

Like all insurance except term contracts, *ordinary life* policies are also vehicles for saving money; as time goes on, your premiums accumulate to build up *nonforfeiture* value, more commonly referred to as *cash surrender value*. At one time, if a policyholder stopped paying his premiums—whether from necessity or design—he was considered to have forfeited any further rights under the contract. Today, as long as you have paid premiums for at least two years, if you wish to discontinue your insurance, you are entitled to a cash payment. The cash

Something for nothing

THE "TAX SHELTER" ADVANTAGES of the registered retirement savings plan (R.R.S.P.) are obvious, whether the plan is tied into an insurance package or not. You put aside tax-free money regularly while you are earning and take it back after your retirement, paying the tax when your rate will presumably be considerably lower. When the R.R.S.P. payments are invested in a life insurance contract, not all of the payment ("premium") is deductible but the long-term effect can be quite respectable.

The monthly payments under this combined R.R.S.P.-insurance annuity scheme would continue for life after 65 but, in any event, the payments would be guaranteed for a minimum of ten years. Combined with benefits from the compulsory Canada Pension Plan (or Quebec Pension Plan), they appear to provide an adequate retirement income for the average Canadian.

The following example, provided by the Life Underwriters Association of Canada, was drawn up for a fictitious man aged 35 who earns about $14,000 a year and who is willing to put aside $1,000 a year for his retirement at age 65.

You deposit each year..................	$ 1,000
You save in taxes approximately 40% or.............	$ 400
Your out-of-pocket cost...............	$ 600
In 30 years to age 65, your cost is 30 × $600	$ 18,000
At age 65 you receive a monthly life income of...........	$ 560
Assuming a life expectancy of 16 years, you will receive $560 × 16 × 12	$107,520
Assuming you are in a 30% tax bracket in retirement, you will pay taxes of 30% × $107,520	$ 32,256
Your net spendable after-tax income is....................	$ 75,264
Your out-of-pocket cost was........	$ 18,000
Net profit......................................	$ 57,264

surrender value of your policy year by year is now usually stated in a table included with your policy document.

All companies offer a choice of nonforfeiture values, apart from cash. For instance, if you can no longer pay your premiums (or if, for some reason, you don't care to) and you would still like to have some insurance protection, you can usually switch into a term policy. You can use the cash surrender value of your old ordinary life (or endowment) policy to buy protection up to the face value of the old policy which will continue for a limited period of time. The time factor will be set by the size of the policy's nonforfeiture value and your age at the time you make the switch.

Another option allows you to retain a reduced amount of protection as *paid-up insurance.* You pay premiums under the same conditions as in your original policy. But in this case, the cash-surrender value (in effect, something more than the premiums already paid in) of your old policy is applied to the purchase of a new paid-up policy, so that no further premiums are necessary.

If you simply stop paying your premiums under an ordinary life (or endowment) policy and do not opt for one of the stated surrender provisions, the policy will probably be kept in force automatically for a certain period. In policies written by most Canadian companies, this will be done by the company—after the 30-day grace period for late payment—making an *automatic premium loan* on your behalf against the cash value built up in your policy. When the loans made (at interest) to pay the premiums equal the cash value, the contract is terminated.

Provincial insurance regulations may require that if a policyholder withdraws for any reason, he must be reinstated into his policy if he changes his mind within 24 months; of course, he will have to pay all unpaid premiums, with interest, and also meet the qualifications as an acceptable risk under the terms of the policy.

Insurance companies commonly offer their policyholders cash loans at interest, using the accumulated cash value of any current policy as security. Any life insurance policy (except a term contract) of some years' standing is usually acceptable as collateral for a loan from a chartered bank or other commercial lender. (*See* Chapter 7, "When you borrow.")

Endowment life insurance

Endowment life insurance, the most expensive type on the market, is designed both for family protection and for disci-

Beware of "the twister"

THERE'S A BAD APPLE in just about every barrel. While the great majority of life insurance agents will try hard to sell you the best kind of protection for your individual needs, there are doubtless a few who think only of their own quick profit. Some will even offer, privately, to pay the first premium on a policy for you "to help you get started." This kind of approach contravenes provincial insurance laws. Be on your guard against the following:

The Pusher The commission the agent receives varies with the type of policy he sells you. The pusher will do his utmost to sign you to an endowment policy when straight life or term insurance is obviously more appropriate.

The Twister This is the agent who urges you to cash in your policy and reinvest in the one he is offering. Even if the suggestions made by the twister appear sound to you, you can be almost certain that your present company will match them.

The Pleader Remember that the good insurance agent is supposed to help you with *your* problems, not try to enlist your sympathy in *his.* Beware of the man who asks you to buy a policy because he is short "on his quota" and is afraid of being fired by his tough-minded company.

A test of nerve

FACTS

Visiting a large city on a business trip, two associates took a suite at a downtown hotel. One of them informed the other that he had just bought a racing car and intended to compete in races with it. His colleague attempted to dissuade him, pointing out the main reasons why, at his age and with his responsibilities, he should not enter such a hazardous sport. The first man apparently took this advice as an indication that his colleague thought he did not have sufficient nerve to race an automobile. Suddenly, he said, "I'll show you how much nerve I have," and then went out from the living room to a patio and balanced himself on a low coping. He lost his footing, slipped, and plunged 13 stories to his death in the street below.

The case came to court when the widow sued to recover on two accident insurance policies issued on her husband's life.

ARGUMENT

The widow based her case on the argument that her husband's death was caused by accidental means. The insurance company denied liability, stating—among other grounds—that her husband's death did not result directly and solely from accidental causes.

JUDGMENT

The court ruled that the man did not die by accidental means since it was clear that he knew the risk involved and courted the fall which, accordingly, could not be regarded as an unforeseen or unexpected incident associated with his actions, as could have been the case, if, for example, the coping had given way.

The widow's suit was dismissed and the insurance company did not have to pay.*

*Based on an actual case (1963).

plined saving toward a retirement income. The premiums are higher than in ordinary life insurance but, on the other hand, the cash surrender value is also higher. It is life insurance payable to the policyholder himself if he is still living on the maturity date stated in the policy, or to a beneficiary if he should die earlier.

Offering a combination of savings plan and life protection, endowment policies sometimes appeal to families that foresee the future need for a substantial sum—perhaps to put children through university. Such a policy could be taken out on the life of the child too, with the payoff date coinciding with his entry to college.

Under a *settlement option*, the payoff can be arranged in the form of a monthly lifetime income instead of the lump sum due at maturity. In the same way as the ordinary life policy—but faster—the endowment policy builds up a cash surrender value, against which the holder can borrow.

When all is said and done, endowment policies have little appeal over ordinary life contracts, except for the person who doubts his resolution at saving systematically by other means. In 1981, only two percent of life policies sold in Canada were of the endowment variety.

Insuring your wife and children

Most companies now offer a *family income policy*, combining the features of ordinary life with those of the term policy. Here, the life of the breadwinner is insured in the routine way while a geared-in term policy stands ready to provide extra funds over the 10- to 20-year period when demand upon family income is at its peak. If the breadwinner survives that period, the term policy has run out, but the family continues to be protected under the ordinary life insurance part of the policy. In other words, he or she has paid for the extra protection only for the period it was actually needed.

The *family-plan policy* (all of these labels can vary between the competing companies), also combines whole life and term policies. In this case, the ordinary life policy is taken out on the father, while specific term policies are taken on the mother's life (say, to age 60) and on the lives of the children (say, to completion of education).

It is perfectly legal to take out, and pay the premiums for, insurance on the life of another person—naming yourself as beneficiary. But there are certain conditions. You must have what is called an *insurable interest* in that person. If you do not have such an interest, you may still insure the person's life, but you must have his or her consent. In Manitoba, you have an insurable interest in any children of your marriage only until they reach 25. In all other provinces, there is no age limit. Children can also insure their parents' lives.

You can have an insurable interest in anyone whose death could mean financial loss to you; for example, a colleague essential to the success of your business. Such an employe could also insure you, his boss! If someone owed you a large sum of money and you thought there was some chance he might die before paying you back, you could probably get a term policy to cover the amount of the debt. Suspicion might be aroused if the amount applied for appeared excessive; most provinces set statutory maximum amounts for the insurance of minors.

The variable contract

You can also buy a life insurance policy in which the payment at death (or maturity) varies according to the state of the stock market. Called the *variable contract*, this policy places part of each premium in a segregated fund to be invested wholly or partly in common stocks (*i.e.*, the ownership shares of commercial corporations). The policyholder assumes the risks on this investment.

The part of the policy that is routine, guaranteed ordinary life insurance remains the same throughout; but this can be arranged on a decreasing scale to suit anyone who is certain that the stock market will go on rising forever. This policyholder, of course, hopes that in the long run his policy will yield higher benefits than would the normal policy in which the insurance company takes all investment risks.

Insurance at home

Fire, theft and accident

The No. 1 peril: fire

Insuring for "all risks"

Your personal liability

Package deals for the home

Protection on the road

DWARD LLOYD ran a coffeehouse in Abchurch Lane in seventeenth-century London. It was a time when business was beginning to boom in the surge of initiative and democratic energy that followed the declaration of the Bill of Rights in 1689. Most of his customers were shippers, warehousemen, traders and bankers. These men were vitally concerned about the loss of ships at sea, and in the over-all safety of their trade goods and other property. London was still being rebuilt after the great fire of 1666 which had burned out 400 streets and destroyed thousands of shops and warehouses. Lloyd's coffeehouse became the gathering place for the underwriters, those specialists who would accept some of the financial risks involved in just about any business on payment of a fee based on the average experience of loss in the field.

The principle of general insurance—the sharing of a small incidence of risk among a large number of persons—had been known since history was first written. The Code of Hammurabi of ancient Babylonia (_See_ Chapter 1, "From earliest times") records a type of insurance covering the camel caravans trudging across the deserts of the Middle East. The Phoenicians, Greeks and Romans were familiar with marine insurance and experimented with other types. The European guilds of medieval times formed syndicates to insure their buildings and goods from loss by fire, storm or acts of war. Fire insurance was available on a community basis in Germany before the end of the fifteenth century.

Edward Lloyd used to check London's dockyards personally for marine news, posting this in his coffeehouse for the information of his customers. This practice expanded to become Lloyd's Register of Shipping, the world authority on the safety and efficiency of seagoing merchant ships. The coffeehouse itself was taken over entirely to serve as the center of all British underwriting (except for life insurance, which developed separately). As the swelling trade of the eighteenth century brought more and more demand for insurance, operations were moved to the Royal Exchange, close to the already venerable Bank of England.

Incorporated as Lloyd's of London in 1871, the former coffeehouse now is the world center of general insurance. Lloyd's member firms (6,000 of them) will offer protection for a price against just about anything that can happen by accident. They will insure the largest tanker afloat or the principal assets of a strip-tease dancer. Companies all around the world share part of the risk of their obligations with Lloyd's through the system known as _reinsurance._

In the New World, the first fire insurance company was formed in 1735, in Charleston, South Carolina; by the time the republic of the United States was born, similar companies were flourishing in Boston, New York and Philadelphia. Disastrous fires in New York City (1835), Saint John, New Brunswick (1837), Quebec City (1845), St. John's, Newfoundland (1846), Toronto (1849), Montreal (1852), Chicago (1871), Vancouver (1886), among others, emphasized the need for large financial resources to meet the huge cost of fires occurring in closely settled urban areas. As the pioneer companies and branch operations expanded in Canada, they steadily widened the range of insurance protection available to both the businessman and the householder.

Fire, theft and accident

Marine insurance, the oldest of all types, is still essential to world trade, but it seldom comes to the attention of the layman. The average Canadian tenant or homeowner is much more concerned with protecting his property from fire, theft and other perils, and in making sure that he will not be beggared by a large damage claim against him if he should accidentally kill or injure someone or seriously damage another's property.

If you need more specialized protection, you will soon realize how flexible insurance has become. Policies invented to protect the lives of passengers in the early days of chancy coach and steam-train travel now cover travelers on buses or airplanes. Plate-glass insurance was first written in Ireland; burglary insurance was invented in the United States in 1885. Insurance of workmen against injury on the job was made mandatory in Britain in 1897 (*See* Chapter 14, "Accidents at work"). The federal superintendent of insurance in Ottawa recognizes 26 classes of insurance and each class is subdivided into several categories, many of them outside the scope of this book.

There are few among us who can regard with anything but horror the prospect of losing our homes, our furniture and furnishings, as well as other property, by fire or some other calamity. These principal assets often take half a lifetime to accumulate and pay for. The crime reports in any daily newspaper constantly remind us how vulnerable we are to thieves and vandals. The potential cost of a major car or boat accident (*See* Chapter 18, "The question of damages") could give anyone recurrent nightmares. With insurance, a substantial majority of Canadians gain financial protection from these perils at comparatively modest cost. The cost will obviously vary with the face value of the insurance policy and with its conditions and exclusions (risks that are not covered). But insurance is a buyer's market, so press your agent or broker for the best bargain available and the best arrangement to suit your needs.

As indicated, separate policies can be purchased to cover the main hazards that exist for the average consumer, while comprehensive "package" policies providing protection against a wide range of risks under the one contract are also popular. The choice of policy depends on the individual circumstances; the following sections briefly outline the options.

The No.1 peril: fire

About 75 percent of all reported fires in Canada occur in residences—houses, apartments or rented rooms—and the major villain in these conflagrations is the cigarette. Other important causes are defective or overloaded electrical wiring and defective heating appliances. Most people insure against the total destruction, or partial damage, of their home and its contents, and against the related damage that can be caused by heat, smoke or by the water used to put out the blaze.

Although the policies offered by various insurance companies differ in detail, they are similar in type. A "standard form" has been developed to cover most of the perils arising from the residential fire, while an *extended coverage endorsement*, or *rider*, can be added to the basic policy to protect you from just about any hazard except theft and nuclear war. Too many people make the mistake of not reading "the fine print" of the policy. Once you have applied for insurance and the risk has been accepted, an enforceable contract has been concluded. *All* its clauses are equally binding.

Your agent or broker will point out to you the importance of setting accurate figures for the value of the property you wish to insure and, in a time of spiraling inflation, of keeping the face value of your policies in line with the rising cost for replacement of the property covered by your insurance.

NEW FOR OLD. Under most dwelling-unit insurance policies available in North America, the formal basis of payment after a fire is the replacement value of the damaged property at the time that the loss occurs, with a certain amount deducted for depreciation. The intention here is that the householder should be completely covered against loss under the terms of his contract, but he should not profit from the loss. As an illustration: if a ten-year-old roof was damaged by fire, and if the roof had a normal life expectancy of 30 years, then the insurers would deduct approximately one-third of the cost of a new roof and pay the householder that reduced amount.

As this would not be satisfactory to most policyholders, an option called the "optional loss settlement clause" is included in dwelling policies. If this option is exercised, the settlement becomes one of full replacement cost. As a rare exception, the insurance company might opt to repair or even rebuild the house.

This type of settlement is made, then, on a "new-for-old" basis. In order to qualify for this option, the amount of insurance in force on the building at the time that the loss occurs must be close to the replacement cost of the structure. How

close? In most cases, the amount of insurance carried need only represent 80 percent of the replacement value of the property at the time of loss.

At the present rates of inflation in building costs, it is likely that a "cushion" will vanish over a policy term. Therefore, if you want to keep the new-for-old option open, you might be wise to increase the amount of your insurance on a regular basis so that it will keep pace with the rising replacement value of your home.

VALUE OF BUILDINGS. The true value of your house for insurance purposes cannot be arrived at simply by taking the current market value of the whole property, including land, and subtracting what would be the value of the empty lot. If a fire occurred in an older building, the cost to demolish, clear the site and rebuild a duplicate building—taking into consideration modern-day zoning bylaws—could be a lot more than the real estate market value of the entire property, including the land.

Lloyd's of London

From all around the world, including Canada, insurance premiums flow to Lloyd's of London. It is not a trading company but a central marketplace where risks are accepted competitively by individual member firms. The policy illustrated here covers every kind of travel peril, but Lloyd's will write virtually all kinds of insurance, except long-term life.

WORLD WIDE TRAVEL ACCIDENT INSURANCE

THE INSURER will pay subject to the exceptions, limitations shall commence at 12:01 a.m. on the departure date and application to which this insurance attaches.

BENEFITS

1) **Loss of Life, double dismemberment, loss of si dismemberment or loss of sight of one eye —** paid for injuries resulting from one accident but the Principal Sum. Dismemberment shall mean l ankle. With regard to the sight of an eye this s

AIR FLIGHT ACCIDENT INSURANCE

The Insurer in consideration of payment of premium show this insurance here-by insures the person named as the bodily injury sustained during the first one way or round t by a Scheduled Air Carrier between the point of departure before leaving said point of departure provided at the ti the whole of said airline trip issued to him for transporta aboard such aircraft after leaving the point of departure been issued before leaving the point of departure.

BENEFITS: The Insurer will pay the benefits as stated be

BAGGAGE INSURANCE

THE INSURER subject to the exceptions, limitations and o effects owned by and for the personal use, adornment or during any journey anywhere in the world, this insurance c and up to the insured limits as shown in the application

This insurance does not cover:—

1) Animals, self-propelled conveyance of any kin

TRIP CANCELLATION INSURANCE

THE INSURER will pay subject to the exceptions, limitations shall commence at 12:01 a.m. on the departure date and application to which this insurance attaches.
This Insurance is to pay either:

1) The round trip fare, and/or the cost of land arrange immediate family prevents the insured from undertaki of the round trip remains a charge to the Insured.

2) The extra cost of one way flight economy air fare by a

A three-story, six-bedroom Victorian brick home—not uncommon in the older urban districts of Canada—provides a good example. With such a residence, after total loss by fire, you would be involved in rebuilding something that was at least partly obsolete. If you were to start from scratch, however, it is unlikely you would want to duplicate such a structure. Yet most fires result in partial loss and, in order to meet the valuation requirement in the policy, it is necessary to insure that building as if you were indeed going to duplicate it today.

In addition to the inflation factor that affects the over-all cost of duplicating an existing structure, the homeowner should bear in mind the substantial capital investments that he has probably made in the house—for example, by modernizing or replacing bathrooms, finishing recreation areas, adding new heating or air-conditioning. All of these factors should be reflected in the amount of insurance he carries on the building.

A professional appraisal of the value of your home, both the dwelling itself and the land, can be arranged by your insurance agent or through any well-established real estate company. This can be of value in matters other than insurance as well.

INVENTORY OF CONTENTS. Both the householder and the apartment dweller equally require insurance protection against the risk of fire damage to the contents of their homes. Quite apart from the possibility of total destruction, furniture, rugs, draperies, appliances, books and clothing are highly vulnerable to damage by smoke and water.

If a fire occurred, for example, in the kitchen of a dwelling, or in the basement of an apartment building, the amount of structural damage to the building might be relatively slight; however, the damage done to the contents of your home could add up to a lot. Many expensive items might be damaged beyond repair due to smoke and water.

Most people accumulate over a period of time a much greater dollar value of goods in the home than at first glance they would believe that they have. The preparation and maintenance of a room-by-room inventory is an excellent idea; it requires little time and could prove invaluable if the occasion should arise to make an insurance claim. A realistic value should be placed against each item, with an allowance for depreciation or appreciation. Although such things as clothing and upholstered furniture, rugs, drapes and linens do depreciate, their value can remain almost constant as normal refurbishing is carried out. For instance, the man who owns four suits keeps the dollar value for his clothing constant as he replaces the oldest suit each year with a new one which has an increased replacement cost. There will probably be articles in most homes that are not subject to depreciation. Antique furniture, sterling silverware, tea services, crystal and fine china provide examples. These items become more and more valuable from an insurance standpoint as their replacement value increases. Periodic updating of your inventory will enable you to adjust your insurance so that your coverage remains adequate.

Certain items require special extra insurance, perhaps because they are of an unusual nature and especially vulnerable to damage, because of difficulty in establishing their dollar value at the time of a claim being made, or because of limitations in the "standard form" contracts. Among the items which should be considered for special insurance are jewelry (including costume jewelry, men's jewelry and watches), furs, paintings and other works of art, fine china, crystal, silverware, certain antiques, camera equipment, firearms, sporting goods, stamp and coin collections, other property that occurs in pairs or sets, rare tapestries, rare books, credit cards, valuable papers, professional or business property, freezer contents, boats, motors, all-terrain vehicles and other types of portable equipment. These items deserve a broader basis of insurance coverage. For example, the financial loss if an expensive camera is dropped from a boat, or if the canvas of a painting is marred or scratched, is every bit as real as the loss that would be sustained if those items were stolen or damaged by fire.

Unless he has an accurate appraised inventory, it is difficult for the layman to establish the value of unusually expensive items. If a ring is stolen or lost, the distraught owner, when asked about the value, will sometimes state that the ring had a platinum setting and a stone about as big as her small fingernail. Is that ring worth $300 or $3,000? Jewelry, fine arts and furs should be appraised by jewelers, art dealers and furriers. A diamond ring bought ten years ago for $1,000 might now have a replacement value of twice that amount, and it would therefore require that number of dollars in the insurance contract to duplicate the item and provide the owner with the kind of recovery she would expect under her policy.

Special items like those mentioned (including family heirlooms of indeterminate value) should be noted ("scheduled") in the policy on an "all-risks" basis.

Insuring for "all risks"

The traditional protection bought by most homeowners and apartment dwellers is known in the trade as *perils insurance*. It grew out of straight fire insurance—that is, from a contract which provided recovery in the event of property being damaged or destroyed by fire. As time passed (and insurance companies became more competitive), other "perils" were added: windstorm, lightning, explosion, theft, falling objects (most often a tree, or something of that sort), impact by aircraft and vehicles, damage by vandals, malicious damage, certain types of damage by water from leaking or bursting plumbing pipes, burglary, and so on. Remember that the insurance policy is a contract between competent adults (you and the company), and it is the responsibility of the insured to establish that any financial loss being claimed for actually resulted from one of the perils against which the policy provides protection.

A more recent concept, however, is the so-called *all-risk form*, where the insurer undertakes to cover all perils—still, however, with a substantial number of exclusions, some of which are war, nuclear contamination, earthquake, flood, damage by vermin, insects, as well as damage resulting from normal wear and tear. This policy is available as a *floater*—that is, it protects your property at home or wherever you may send or take it.

Under the all-risk policy, the contractual onus shifts to the insurance company. This means that if the householder claims payment for damage under his all-risk policy, the company has to honor the claim unless it can point out to the insured that an exclusion rules it out.

The premiums demanded reflect the different strengths of the protection, as well as such matters as the distance of your home from the nearest fire hydrant, whether the structure is of brick, masonry or wood, whether it is rural or urban. Ask your agent to explain the various coverages available. Study the list of exclusions carefully. Then you will be in a position to decide just how much real protection you are getting for your insurance dollar.

Your personal liability

Any well-thought-out program for financial security must include a substantial amount of protection through *comprehensive personal liability* insurance—known as C.P.L. This insurance provides you with an umbrella against damage you might cause. Consider, for example, the fact that you could be held responsible at law for an accident that was not actually your fault (*See* Chapter 18, "The accidental tort"). The natural sympathy of a jury for someone seriously injured, or crippled for life, can result in astronomical damages being awarded. Without adequate insurance you could be crushed financially.

The homeowner or tenant has a special liability arising out of ownership or tenancy in a building, as well as a potential general liability for his personal acts or those of his family. One thinks of the cartoon jokes about the tradesman tripping or sliding on an icy sidewalk, or stepping on a child's roller skate—and it's indeed true that the possibilities for serious injuries and damage around the home are limitless. C.P.L. insurance is designed to provide protection against injury or damage, whether at home or away, for which the insured can be held responsible; it will also cover the costs of defending any suit for damages brought against him. You would thus be equally protected whether someone broke a leg by tripping on your worn rug or if you dented someone's skull with a golf ball.

Within the framework of C.P.L. coverage, provision is often made to permit voluntary payments for medical expenses and property damage even where there may be no legal responsibility to do so. Let us say that a guest injures himself in your house and runs up a bill for X-rays or other medical attention, and perhaps for the replacement of damaged clothing. While you, as the building owner, may not be legally responsible in this particular case, you would probably feel a moral duty to compensate your guest. Most liability contracts contain a clause allowing you to make voluntary disbursements through the insurer, possibly up to a limit of $500 or more.

If you move

Property in the hands of a common carrier (See Chapter 15, "Goods in transit") for moving purposes is normally not covered by standard policies; thus special insurance is advisable.

Consult with your agent to make sure that the moving contract provides reasonable protection for your goods and that the mover is not allowed to "contract out" of some liabilities. If you are not satisfied, call another transport company, or take out a temporary policy with your own insurer. The cost is minor compared to the amount of damage that could be done to your household contents while they are outside the umbrella of insurance protection.

Sailboats and snowmobiles

Increased affluence and extra leisure time in recent years are reflected in some new concepts in insurance: there are policies relating to outboard motors, yachts, sailboats, all-terrain vehicles (of the dune-buggy type) and snowmobiles.

The methods of providing coverage for both direct damage and liability in this comparatively new field are quite varied,

and the range of premiums still reflects some uncertainties. For example, in many jurisdictions snowmobiles now are treated almost like other motor vehicles; they must be registered and insured very much as are cars. (See Chapter 16, "Your merry snowmobile.")

For yachts and boats, the scope of coverage is almost limitless. The amount of insurance agreed upon in the contract should be sufficient to provide for repair or replacement of the yacht or boat on a "new-for-old" basis without any deduction for depreciation.

The "floater" clause in a comprehensive personal liability policy will normally cover the weekend boating enthusiast as long as he restricts himself to an inboard of not more than 50 horsepower, an outboard of 16 horsepower, or a yacht no longer than 8 metres. You can easily extend your policy to cover a bigger craft, at slightly extra cost. Having proper C.P.L. coverage could save you from financial disaster if you were found responsible for a waterskiing accident.

Package deals for the home

Increasingly, homeowners and tenants are switching to insurance in the form of comprehensive package policies which offer protection in one simplified contract for most, if not all, of the hazards discussed in this chapter. Administration and other cost savings allow the companies to offer this insurance protection for about 20 percent less than the same coverage would cost through individual policies. A specimen homeowner's policy might take the following form:

Section A: Insurance against fire and other risks on the building.

Section B: Insurance against damage to any outbuildings; normally this is worked out as a percentage factor—perhaps ten percent of the amount of insurance on the principal building.

Section C: Insurance on contents and household effects, including property temporarily removed from the premises.

Section D: Insurance covering the homeowner's personal liability; however, to be protected at what are called "secondary locations"—that is, away from home, for example, while operating boats or riding horses—the policyholder must make special declarations.

Section E: Insurance providing additional living expenses—costs incurred in maintaining the household elsewhere while the dwelling is being repaired after a fire, or similar damage.

This specimen package policy would be duplicated for the apartment tenant, except that there would be no coverage as far as the building itself was concerned. The tenant is responsible, however, to the building owner—or perhaps, indirectly, to the building owner's insurer—for damage to the premises resulting from his negligence. This so-called tenant's liability would be covered on as broad a basis as possible in his package policy.

Both the homeowner's and the tenant's policy forms are relatively flexible and can usually be extended to cover any particular needs of the insurance buyer. Here is a sample of the special risks that can be added: liabilities from a stolen credit card; plate-glass coverage in homes; damage to TV antenna; coverage for earthquake, collapse from snow load, landslide, sewer backup, sump pump failure, and swimming pool overflow and rupture; coverage on trees and shrubs.

Package policies are usually issued for terms of six or twelve months, and the premiums paid fully in advance.

The man who made The Sun

AT AGE 22 Mathew Hamilton Gault was the head of a Montreal Irish immigrant family of seven, with a sick mother to provide for. For the next seven years, his efforts to keep the family together and educate his younger brothers and sisters seemed dogged by failure. He lost some money in a bank collapse and a farm he bought was far from profitable. He was suffering from a spinal injury caused by a fall from a horse.

Then, in 1851, young Gault, tall and handsome in his fashionable sideburns and muttonchop whiskers, obtained the Montreal agencies for two insurance companies—one British, one American. (The first Canadian insurance company, founded in Hamilton, was then only four years old.) In his office in St. James Street, Gault also housed the Montreal branch of the Royal Canadian Bank. As the Civil War raged in the United States, creating a boom in the Canadas, he launched his younger brothers into business careers.

A fervent believer in Confederation, Gault prepared for the birth of the new nation by founding his own Canadian insurance company. On March 18, 1865, Parliament granted a charter to The Sun Insurance Company of Montreal (it became Sun Life Assurance Company of Canada in 1882). One of the founding subscribers was George Stephen, the future Lord Mount Stephen of the C.P.R. The dislocation of trade that followed the repeal of the Reciprocity Treaty with the United States prevented action on the original charter for five years but, by 1871, the company was ready for business.

Policy No. 1, for $2,000, went to the founder, chief agent and managing director, M. H. Gault. In that first year, The Sun accepted 148 applications for life insurance (ten were turned down) and the total amount of insurance outstanding was $404,000. The Sun warned its policy holders that it would not pay off if they were killed while engaged in a duel.

When Mathew Gault died in 1887, the amount of Sun Life insurance in force was $10,873,777. The company had expanded through the Prairies to British Columbia and was flourishing in the West Indies.

Under other dynamic leadership, the company would forge ahead until it ranked as one of the greatest insurance concerns in the world. In 1982, Sun Life had assets of $10 billion, covering seven million policies and group certificates. It had paid out benefits totaling $1.5 billion.

351

Protection on the road

In recent years, almost 750,000 motor vehicle accidents a year have been reported in Canada. Of this number, more than 5,000 people a year have been killed and another 250,000 have been injured.

Transport Canada has estimated that the total cost of traffic accidents across the country amounts to more than two billion dollars a year. These appalling figures may come into closer focus when it is recalled that three years' involvement in the Korean War cost Canada only 294 lives—about one-fifth of the yearly highway death toll in Quebec alone.

An automobile owner is responsible for injury or damage caused by his own negligence or that of a person whom he permits to drive his car.

All but a small fraction of owners and operators cover themselves against the risks of road accidents with separate *automobile insurance* policies. In all provinces, it is compulsory to have liability insurance, at least, to cover people injured or property damaged by the vehicle. (*See* Chapter 5, "Buying your car" and "On the road.")

It is difficult to understand why anyone would take an automobile onto the highway without adequate insurance, but it does happen. Seeing a role here for state intervention, several provinces have moved—or are moving—into the automobile insurance field.

The policies are basically similar everywhere and the companies that issue them are strictly controlled by government regulations—as are all insurance companies. You can feel confident that any automobile insurance company trading in Canada will live up to the exact letter of its agreement. However, there can be no substitute for your own judgment; read every clause of your policy carefully and make sure you understand all the conditions of the agreement before you sign. Your contract, for instance, may offer only the amount of the province's compulsory level of liability coverage—perhaps $50,000; you would be wise to increase this sum.

The average automobile insurance policy consists of three sections; let's call them A, B and C.

Section A covers the liability of the owner and driver of the vehicle for injury or death to outside parties—persons other than the owner, driver and passengers of the vehicle—and for damage to the property of others. This is the most important section of the policy and the amount carried should be as large as you can afford.

Section B covers accident benefits to owners, drivers and passengers for injury or death, and usually allows medical expenses incurred within a year from the date of the accident. There is a growing tendency toward standardizing this coverage under various "no-fault" or "knock-

Making the unequal equal

IT WOULD BE DIFFICULT to find two men less alike than Calvin Coolidge, 30th President of the United States (1923–29), and Winston Churchill, twice prime minister of Great Britain (1940–45, 1951–55). But they shared one enthusiasm at least—insurance.

"Silent Cal" Coolidge saw insurance as an equalizer in economic life. "Insurance," he said, "is the modern method by which men make the uncertain certain, and the unequal equal . . . It is part charity and part business, but all common sense."

Churchill once gave these views on insurance:

"If I had my way, I would write the word 'insure' over the door of every cottage and on the blotting book of every public man; because I am convinced that for sacrifices inconceivably small, families can be secured against catastrophes which otherwise would smash them forever. It brings the magic of averages to the rescue of millions."

for-knock" schemes; where both parties involved in a collision are insured, the insurance companies agree not to take court action to establish responsibility. The theory is that they are likely to break even in the long run, while saving administrative costs and valuable court time.

Section C offers protection to the owner against theft or damage to his vehicle. Modern automobiles are expensive pieces of property and you stand to lose a lot if your vehicle is stolen or damaged in a collision or an upset (running off the road, etc.), or through fire, acts of malice or accidental windshield breakage.

Various combinations of damage coverage are available, the largest single variable being the "amount deductible." If insurance companies were to carry the cost of every single scratch or dent, the premiums required would be prohibitive. To get around this problem, insurance companies invented the deductible clause. A typical clause in the policy may state that if the vehicle is damaged by collision or upset, the first $50 or $100 or more of repair cost will be borne by the insured and the balance by the insurer. If the "other guy" takes the blame for the accident, or if he is found legally responsible, then it is likely that the entire cost of the repairs will be met.

Premium rates for automobile insurance are based on a number of factors: (1) the territory where the vehicle is being operated; (2) the type and value of the vehicle; (3) the age of the driver, and years of driving experience, plus his accident and conviction record.

Automobile insurance premiums fall hard on the wallet of the male driver who is younger than 25; he belongs to the driver category with the worst accident record. When he gets older and establishes a record of driving without accident, or without important traffic violations, he can expect a susbtantially reduced premium.

When licensed teenagers living at home drive a family car, they can be added as drivers under the parents' policy for an additional premium.

Whatever jokes may be made about women drivers, their accident record is better than men's, and insurance companies credit them for their record by setting lower premiums.

When there's no insurance

Most provinces have passed legislation setting up an *unsatisfied judgment fund.* The fund provides a minimum payment of damages in automobile accident claims for bodily injury where the person responsible for the accident carries no insurance, or the victim, such as a pedestrian, is not insured. In Quebec, the government automobile insurance board handles compensation for personal injury.

Depending on the province, the fund is maintained by insurance companies or subsidized by the fees from license or vehicle registration. In New Brunswick, a fee of $7 is added to the driver's license. In Nova Scotia, the fund has the authority to order a fee of at least $1 from every holder of a driver's license. Saskatchewan's fee is $20.

The funds sometimes allow for the payment of damages in hit-and-run accidents. If neither the owner nor the driver of the offending vehicle can be identified, the victim, or his family, may apply to the registrar of motor vehicles or the director of the fund; any damages won are paid out of the fund. All of these funds limit the amount that can be paid for one accident.

If an uninsured motorist is at fault in an accident and the victim subsequently receives payment from the unsatisfied judgment fund, the motorist at fault will generally be called upon to reimburse the fund for the amount paid. If he doesn't arrange to repay the fund, he will probably have his driver's license suspended.

In Ontario, an insured motorist involved in a collision with an uninsured driver may collect for his personal injuries under his own policy as if, in fact, the uninsured driver was specifically covered as a risk in his policy.

Under the Quebec Civil Code of Procedure, before a judgment is rendered, a plaintiff may seize the motor vehicle which caused him damage, regardless of the amount of property damage and whether the defendant is covered for third-party insurance or not.

Insurance in commerce

| How a business is protected |
| Loss-control engineering |
| Group insurance plans |
| Weather and crop insurance |
| Malpractice protection |
| The dishonest employe |

APART FROM the life, fire and liability insurance that just about every Canadian householder carries in some form or other, the manufacturer, the businessman, the shopkeeper and the professional find it essential to protect themselves from a much wider range of hazards. Depending on the business involved, they usually take out a large amount of *general liability insurance* as protection against any of the innumerable accidents that could happen: for example, in an auto plant with thousands of workers or in a crowded department store. There is a basic form of policy for those owning or operating theaters, shops, hotels and office buildings; another type is for the contractor or the manufacturer. Insurance designed for the professional man or the big farmer are other specialities.

Governments demand that businessmen cooperate in several schemes for the welfare and safety of their employes, or of the general public. For example, the employer, generally liable at law for the death or injury of any of his employes, must participate in the provincial Workmen's Compensation plans (*See* Chapter 14, "Accidents at work"); the employer is also required to contribute to the coffers of the Unemployment Insurance Commission (*See* Chapter 14, "Unemployment insurance"), and to pay special taxes to support other social security programs.

Commercial (or "casualty") insurance covers many billions of dollars of risk across thousands of businesses and industries; it is hard to imagine any hazard that has not been—or would not be—covered. No attempt can be made to list them all in this book. In our capitalist society, it is difficult to imagine how the economic system could exist and prosper without the pooling of risk that is the essence of insurance.

How a business is protected

While it is no doubt a gross oversimplification to say that commercial and corporate insurance planning is similar to household-insurance planning, there are definitely some areas of similarity. A company insures its buildings, equipment and stock in much the same way as the ordinary citizen insures his home and its contents. The loss of business that would inevitably follow a shop fire until the premises could be rebuilt has to be insured in the same way as the homeowner covers himself against possible additional living expenses under the fire policy on his dwelling. Some of the potential liabilities of the corporation are insured in much the same way as the homeowner insures his liability as owner of the premises.

The following simplified program illustrates the form that an insurance plan could take for a small importer, manufacturer or wholesaler:

Firstly, a value figure of insurance is placed on the fixed assets of the business—the building itself, stock, office or plant equipment, plate glass, signs, etc.—with special coverage for pressure boiler machinery, refrigeration and compressor units. The amount of insurance on stock might be varied in relation to seasonal importing schedules or stockpiling of finished goods. Incoming stock may need to be covered in transit.

Secondly, provision is made for business interruption to preserve the company's cash flow and profit if a loss occurs which causes a work stoppage.

Thirdly, adequate insurance is purchased to cover liability arising from the ownership of premises, operation of the business, acts of employes or the actual product sold by the insured. This class of insurance may be expanded to cover a host of different risks, including the cost of recalling products, liability assumed under contract, liability for the operation of aircraft, watercraft, automobiles and trucks, liability under the Workmen's Compensation Act and liability for all malpractice, errors and omissions.

These commercial insurance programs can also be expanded to include the risk of many crimes—for instance, fidelity risk, theft of cash, safe burglary, cheque or credit card forgery and misappropriation, conversion, damage to valuable papers, dies, patterns, etc.

The best way to find out how insurance can protect your business is to discuss your operation in detail with an experienced agent or broker. He can probably demonstrate how the new science of *loss-control engineering* may cut your losses—and, in the long run, your premium expenditure as well.

Loss-control engineering

Lawyers aren't the only professionals who invent trade jargon. When insurance consultants are called in to examine the risks inherent in a business, they do not restrict themselves to merely offering policies to meet an established peril position; they can also draw upon a wide and expanding research into new methods of reducing the perils themselves. This is referred to as *loss-control engineering.*

The essence of sound corporate insurance planning is for the agent or broker to spend considerable time with the prospective policyholder figuring out the company's potential hazards. When these hazards are established, it then remains for the agent to propose a plan of insurance that will guarantee the company adequate protection against the various hazards. Having worked out an overall protection plan for the company, the agent may suggest changes in plant. lay-

out, or business practices that would eliminate or minimize the hazards.

A simple illustration of loss-control engineering would involve an agent suggesting that the company install an automatic sprinkler system in an area of high fire risk. The cost could be related to potential premium savings. If the risk of fire damage drops, so usually does the cost of fire insurance. The agent might be in a position to point out, then, that the cost of sprinklering the building could be offset with about five years of premium savings.

As business becomes ever more sophisticated, as well as dependent upon highly expensive machinery and computers, loss-control engineering becomes an ever-more important concept in commercial insurance programming.

Group insurance plans

Group life insurance plans are usually organized to cover the employes of corporations, utilities or large administrative units; thus they are discussed in this section rather than in the section devoted to individual life insurance earlier in this chapter. More employers are introducing these plans—or acceding to them at the prodding of trade unions. The group plan has become the fastest growing class of insurance and now accounts for more than half of all life insurance in Canada: a total of about $318 billion.

In a simple group plan, a master contract is issued by the insurance company to the employer under which all of his workers are insured without the necessity of a medical examination. Sometimes the boss pays the entire premium; usually, however, he shares the cost with the worker through payroll deductions. Each worker gets a certificate stating the face value of his personal portion (usually the equivalent of a year's wages), listing the benefits and naming the beneficiary the worker has designated to receive payment on his death.

More elaborate group plans provide, for one example, a *conversion clause* so that an employe who quits his job can switch—without a qualifying medical—into a personal policy of the straight life or endowment type. In some provinces, benefits in private pension plans have been made "portable." This means that a worker can take his share of the group coverage with him when he changes jobs, assuming the new job is covered by a compatible plan. It is generally the case that the employer's share of the premiums becomes "vested" in the employe after he has completed a certain number of years' service.

In some provinces, an employe can convert his pension benefits into an annuity if he decides to leave his job. In general, the employe must be 45 or older and have worked for ten years with the company he is leaving. Payment from the annuity begins at retirement age. At this writing, this plan was in force in Nova Scotia, Quebec, Ontario, Manitoba, Saskatchewan and Alberta, but other provinces were considering similar legislation.

As a reward to workers retiring at age 65, some companies will continue to pay a part of the premium (or the whole premium) to continue the individual's coverage under the group plan.

Group insurance is usually founded on the *term insurance* principle—that is, providing protection year by year but not building any cash value. Thus it is the cheapest of all types of insurance and any employe given the option of acquiring coverage should take advantage it.

It is a particularly good deal for the older worker, because his premium rate "per thousand"—that is, for every $1,000 of life insurance—would be much higher under an individual term policy. Also, it may be the only way a worker in poor health can arrange a larger estate for his dependents in the event of his death.

Group annuity plans are also on the increase in Canada. Again, there is one master contract between the insurance company and the employer; again, boss and worker usually share the cost (deductible in income-tax returns). At a given retirement age, the insurance company begins sending along a monthly cheque which continues until the death of the *annuitant*.

In a further example of the advantages of the group-insurance principle, *credit insurance* is usually available through the lender as a low-cost option in time-payment plans covering large purchases. Under such a policy, the buyer is assured that if he dies before the account is paid, his family will not be saddled with debt.

Flight and other travel

As Canadian businessmen casually take off from Winnipeg to fly to Halifax or Vancouver for a day's work—or to cities abroad with equal ease—many corporations provide protection for these men's families as a matter of course under travel insurance plans (*See* Chapter 15, "Trouble while traveling").

Travel insurance can also be an element in what is known as *key man insurance*—the practice of a company protecting itself against the loss of a director or executive particularly valuable to the business. (Some companies will not permit more than two directors to travel in the same plane.)

Normally, flight or travel insurance provides for the payment of a large lump sum on the death by accident of the person insured, with lesser amounts for injuries and medical expenses. The policy may cover the period of the flight only, or it may provide 24-hour-a-day, 365-day-a-year protection against all forms of accidental death.

Is flight insurance really such a good buy? Some investment counselors point out that if you feel you need extra insurance just because you are flying, you should take a critical look at your workaday insurance protection. Why would your family need more money just because you died in a plane crash—in *any* kind of accident, for that matter—rather than in your own bed at home? Would those extra dollars splashed out on double-indemnity flight insurance at the airport be better spent on increasing your holding of term insurance or the value of your ordinary life policy? Your insurance agent can tell you where to use your insurance dollar most effectively.

Weather and crop insurance

Organizers of large public events—from race meetings to beauty contests—usually consider the advisability of insuring their box office receipts against a washout because of bad weather. Several insurance companies will accept such risks, based on the probabilities as revealed by long-term regional climate statistics.

Weather insurance can be purchased for a single event or on a continuing basis. The basic nature of the risk is that some financial loss would occur as a result of damage to the property through weather. For example, the officers of a Canadian regiment took out a policy to cover the risk of rain damage to their ceremonial uniforms at an outdoor military parade.

Crop insurance is a normal safeguard for farmers—especially grain, vegetable and fruit producers—whether the produce is still in the field or whether it is in storage. Under the terms of the Crop Insurance Act, 1959, the federal government is empowered to assist the provinces in providing direct contribu-

Insurance of your money

In the Canadian centennial year of 1967, spurred by serious losses suffered by the public in the collapse of a Toronto-based loan and investment company, the Canada Deposit Insurance Corporation was chartered by the federal government. Membership in the corporation is obligatory for all chartered banks and Quebec savings banks, and for all trust and loan companies that accept deposits from the public under federal charter. Provincial trust and loan companies are also eligible for membership if they first gain the consent of the province in which they are incorporated. In Quebec, deposits held in provincial trust and loan companies are guaranteed by the Quebec Deposit Insurance Board.

The main purpose of the C.D.I.C. is to guarantee the deposits of any member of the public with any member-company of the corporation up to a maximum of $60,000. Only C.D.I.C. members can display the special symbol printed here. In the C.D.I.C's bylaws, a deposit is defined as being money received by a member that is repayable in Canada in Canadian funds on demand, on notice or on a fixed date within five years. The insurance covers not only savings and checking accounts but also guaranteed investment certificates, deposit receipts, certain de-

bentures and other negotiable instruments. Contents of safety deposit boxes or securities placed in safekeeping are not insured against theft or fire.

A family can be covered for much more than $60,000, if separate deposit accounts are held in the names of individual members. Accounts can be held in trust for each of your children and each one of these accounts would be insured up to $60,000. If you have an account in your own name and a joint account with your spouse, both accounts are insured. The owner of an incorporated company can have his company account and his personal account in the same member institution with full coverage for each.

You do not have to apply for C.D.I.C. coverage; it is granted automatically to all clients of the member institutions with money on deposit. There is no premium to pay; that is taken care of by the member.

tions toward setting up crop-insurance schemes. Ottawa pays half of the administrative costs incurred by Quebec and Newfoundland in this regard and one-quarter of the premium payments necessary to make such a scheme financially sound. Elsewhere, Ottawa covers half of the premium payments, while the provinces bear all the administrative costs.

In the 1981–82 growing season, almost 120,000 Canadian farmers purchased crop insurance worth $2.7 billion. The payout on claims was $170 million. The main calamities of the season had been excessive rain that reduced vegetable and berry crops in British Columbia, hail and drought on the Prairies, wet harvesting conditions in Ontario and Quebec, and spring frosts in the Atlantic provinces.

Partnership "buy-sell"

The members of a business or professional partnership may purchase insurance on each other's lives as a means of providing an efficient and painless way to settle the estate of any one of them who should die while still a partner. The amount of each policy is related to each man's share in the partnership and the partnership itself can be named as the beneficiary.

The basic idea turns on the fact that each man's share in the partnership naturally forms part of his estate if he dies while still a partner.

The partnership contract will contain what is called a "buy-sell" clause under which the equity—that is, the share of ownership—of a deceased partner must be offered to the remaining partners. The insurance policy payoff is used to buy the equity from the deceased partner's heirs.

If this, or a similar arrangement, did not exist, a partnership could be in serious trouble if the unexpected death of a member, or members, found it short of liquid funds to pay off the deceased's heirs. (*See* Chapter 13, "Partnerships.")

Malpractice protection

The accountant, architect, dentist, doctor, engineer, lawyer or other professional through whose advice or action other persons may conceivably suffer physical or financial injury can protect himself against potentially crippling damages through *malpractice insurance.*

Essentially, this class of liability insurance protects the professional against someone bringing an action for financial loss, resulting from negligence in the operation of his business. A doctor might make a mistake during surgery resulting in the death or disability of his patient. A lawyer could allow a case to lapse through failing to file papers in court by a statutory date. A consulting engineer might specify wrong materials, causing the collapse of a bridge. Nobody is perfect. The newspapers often carry stories similar to these hypothetical examples.

There is a growing trend toward awarding larger damages in all areas of litigation—that is, legal dispute—but particularly in cases affecting the medical profession and certain engineering work. Consider what insurers call "the dollar-loss potential" of a skyscraper collapsing during construction: that enormous figure would likely be the amount claimed for in a malpractice suit.

Societies of engineers and doctors frequently purchase malpractice liability insurance on a group basis to obtain premium reductions and broader grounds of protection. The policies held by these societies sometimes provide an overall protection to the individual members, but every professional in the classes mentioned should check carefully to make sure that he is covered.

Facing a possible large "dollar-loss potential," it is not uncommon for a professional to invest in several levels of insurance; he might purchase an initial limit of liability insurance from one company and then an overriding limit of "umbrella liability" from another company. This practice of "layering" insurance will generally provide a greater overall protection.

"Umbrella" coverage means what it says: it covers everything, including risks that might already be covered by other policies. In other words, it will provide insurance beyond the limit provided by another policy. It is taken out by those who might be sued for enormous sums of money. A while ago, a movie star was suing a pornographic magazine for publishing a photograph of her partly nude. The amount of the claim: $2 million. Definitely a time to reach for the old umbrella.

The dishonest employe

A *fidelity bond* is a contract under which an insurance company agrees to make up any financial loss caused to the policyholder by the dishonesty of an employe ("servant") or agent. A large number of employes who handle cash or other valuables are bonded.

The main difference between fidelity bonding and ordinary insurance is that while an insurance policy is a two-party contract between the insured and the insurer, a fidelity bond is a three-party contract, involving the principal (in this case, the worker), the obligee (the insured) and the surety (the insurance company). What happens, in essence, is that the insurance company is prepared to guarantee to the employer the honesty of the employe. Thus, if the bookkeeper is caught misappropriating funds, the insurance company will make up the loss to the amount of the bond.

In large corporations, fidelity bonding is carried on a "blanket" basis, and the individual may be immediately and automatically covered under the bond when he takes a job with the firm. In most cases, the incoming worker must complete a bond application as a required part of the hiring procedure; while this seems somewhat intrusive, the theory is that anyone not willing to complete the application has something to hide.

The bonding company can choose to investigate the background of anyone who applies for a bond.

In the event of a loss, the insured employer must establish the amount stolen and show that the theft actually occurred through the dishonesty of one of his workers or, perhaps, a group of them.

Experienced insurance agents believe that large sums are embezzled each year from Canadian corporations by dishonest employes who are either not caught or not prosecuted. They think some important firms that deal with the public are loath to publicize the fact that they harbor

the occasional crook; this leads to a hesitation at the outset to insist on the fidelity bonding of all workers in positions of trust. A loss through *defalcation* ("misappropriation of property") can continue over many years. One elderly woman simply pocketed small cash receipts over a period of 20 years; the total amount of the theft was estimated at $100,000.

Fidelity bonding is frequently handled in conjunction with similar coverages, such as protection of money and securities in transit, cheque or securities forgery, and extortion. Large financial institutions generally carry a lot of insurance in this area with high limits of coverage. In other industries and businesses, however, where the directors or proprietors do not consider there is much likelihood of theft by the trusted employe, little use is made of fidelity bonding. But they are courting disaster.

Reinsurance of large risks

No one knows better than insurance companies that risk must be spread out as much as possible; when a company contracts to provide protection for a large amount—usually in the millions—it may well decide to "lay off" some of its liability. It does this through *reinsurance:* in essence, the insurance company is itself buying insurance from other insurers.

Most insurance companies have reinsurance agreements with others under which they are automatically guaranteed certain percentages of reinsurance for a specific risk. The usual procedure with a huge risk is that a number of companies subscribe to one policy in varying percentages as their capacity allows; this form of reinsurance is referred to as a *subcription policy*. Each of ten companies might take ten percent of $1 million risk so that if disaster struck, none of the insurers would stand to lose more than a tenth of the payoff value. The greater the odds of misfortune, the greater the appeal of reinsurance.

It is comforting for the average consumer to realize that the insurance companies which play such an important role in his financial plans are themselves firm believers in insurance.

The role of the agent

EACH PROVINCE has laws that regulate the insurance business within its own boundaries, and the legal position of the insurance agent, or broker, varies according to the licensing requirements of each jurisdiction. To sell insurance in some provinces, you must be a broker; in others, you may be either an agent or a broker. The role you play is determined, largely, by the contract you have with the insurance company.

Under the general *law of agency*, the *agent* is authorized to act for the *principal* (in this instance, the insurance company) and the principal is legally responsible for the actions or commitments made by the agent in the normal course of his work. In some offices (particularly in smaller towns), one salesman may act as agent for many insurers or he may be a so-called "captive" agent selling only the policies of his sponsoring company. On the other hand, the *broker* is generally considered the agent of the buyer; he sets up an insurance program for his client and then places it with an insurer.

Whatever his technical title or affiliation, the reputable agent can be trusted to advise and assist the average insurance buyer in setting up a suitable program of insurance at reasonable cost. With details of your family and possessions in his file, he will watch your interests as circumstances change, perhaps suggesting policy alterations as your family grows. He will indicate how you can get a loan using your policy as security and will guide you if you want to file a claim.

The insurance agent is much more than a salesman. Within his agent-principal relationship with his company, he is generally allowed to commit the company to a risk without the immediate consent of the company. This "binding" or "underwriting" authority enables the agent to issue a "binder" (in effect, a temporary policy), and then notify the company later. In an emergency, he can provide you with immediate protection over the phone, following it up with a written confirmation.

Strictly speaking, unless you have a written "binder," a policy is not legally enforceable until it has been signed by all parties and delivered to you. There is often a stipulation that the first premium be paid at signing. Simply agreeing to buy a policy, even if it is offered to you by an agent, does not constitute legal acceptance of the risk by the company.

The agent should point out clearly that a policy is a two-party contract and that certain definite responsibilities—apart from merely paying the premiums—rest with the insured party, the policyholder. For example, under most contracts there is no coverage for water damage if a house is left empty for a considerable period during the winter without provisions for the maintenance of heat. Nor will a policy cover you if you store certain explosive substances in or near your house. (*See* Chapter 6, "In the home.")

As the agent will explain, if you mortgage your house, the lender (the mortgagee) will almost certainly require you to take out fire insurance to safeguard his financial interest in your property. Under a clause in the policy, the insurance company will be instructed to pay the mortgage up to the amount owing on the mortgage if there is any loss from fire or other insured hazards.

In his role as adviser, the agent will explain that it is quite pointless to overinsure your house, or any property. In the event of a claim, the company will compensate you only for the actual amount of loss suffered—the replacement cost—irrespective of how much coverage you hold. If you underinsure, you may not recover the full cost of replacement.

You cannot legally make money from insurance, with perhaps one grim exception. Although attempting to commit suicide is technically a crime, and although it is illegal to benefit from any wrongdoing, provincial insurance laws require the companies to pay life-policy benefits to the stated beneficiary in the case of suicide of the policyholder two years or more after the issuance of the policy.

The truthful applicant

An insurance policy is classed in law as a *contract of the utmost good faith.* This means that the applicant for life insurance must not only answer all questions truthfully but must also disclose voluntarily any relevant information that might have a bearing on the insurance company's decision to accept the risk concerned. If your occupation is managing a village hardware store, the insurer would not consider that hazardous; but if you compete in stock-car races every Sunday, the picture obviously changes.

All policies contain a clause allowing the companies to pay only the amount that would have been due if the correct age of the applicant had been given. They have to be tough about this point because all life insurance premiums are based, primarily, on the exact age of the policyholder at signing.

Questions relating to the applicant's medical history must be answered as accurately as it is reasonable to expect. Doctors employed by insurance companies soon become expert in assessing vague or evasive answers of applicants; medical examinations are often required before ordinary life policies are issued.

Insurance companies are permitted two years to check up on the accuracy of information, medical and other, supplied to them by an applicant. Usually, they assure themselves that the person named in the policy actually exists, that his address and occupation are as stated and that his general reputation in the community is satisfactory. After two years, assuming the premiums are being paid, the company can only refuse to pay out benefits on the grounds that misstatements about age were made on the application form, or that a deliberate fraud was perpetrated. In Quebec, however, a misrepresentation about age would not lead to the cancellation of an insurance policy.

Payment of premiums

The premium is the price paid by the insured for the financial coverage specified in the policy contract. Depending on the class of insurance, the premium is paid once, twice or four times a year, and either directly to the insuring company or to the agent or broker.

A special kind of life policy offered to young people features premiums graded by age. The youngster pays a lower premium rate for several years before climbing to the normal *level premium* stage when his income, presumably, has risen.

If a premium on a life policy is not paid within the *period of grace* (usually 30 days) after the due date, the contract will lapse; however, there are exceptions (*See* "Insuring your life" in this chapter). When a general insurance contract approaches its expiry date, the agent customarily sends out a renewal notice with a bill for the premium. Until recently, the client would remain covered as long as the agent was prepared to extend him credit for the premium after the due date (the agent himself is usually allowed 30 days' credit by the company accepting the risk). In fact, if the agent—or the company—decided to cancel a policy, notice had to be given to the client.

The courts have now ruled, however, that unless the client notifies the agent that he wishes to continue the policy (by acknowledging the renewal notice and/or paying the due premium), then the policy will be deemed to have expired at midnight on the due date. Under this ruling, if you were too slow in paying your automobile insurance policy you could find yourself financially ruined following a serious highway accident. Procedures

361

vary, of course, according to the provisions of different insurance policies. In Quebec, for example, you must be advised of the impending expiry of your automobile insurance policy.

Where a life policy is bought on a "participating" basis, the true price paid by the policyholder is the sum of the premiums minus the dividends declared; if a policy is "nonparticipating," the premiums paid are the total cost for the full period covered.

All premiums are calculated on the statistically probable chance of an event occurring. In the case of life insurance, it is accepted that of every 1,000 men 65 years old, 22 will die in the current year.

What actually happens to the premiums you pay? Well, the total premium income of all life insurance companies in Canada in a recent year was $8,307 million, representing 62 percent of the companies' total income (the other 38 percent came from investments). Of that income 86 percent was either paid out as benefits to policyholders or added to reserves for the protection of future policyholders. This left 14 percent to be split among administrative expenses, taxes and profits for shareholders. In the year quoted, shareholders got about one-third of a cent out of the premium dollar. Four cents of every dollar went as commission to agents.

What you can't insure

No contract will be enforced by the courts if it is considered to be contrary to the public interest. In insurance, this blocks anyone from collecting on a policy if the loss was caused by his own design, or criminal act. As someone put it in an earlier era, you can't buy an insurance policy on your own life, murder someone and be hanged for it, and then expect the insurance company to pay your beneficiary. Nor can you collect fire insurance if you set the blaze yourself (or pay someone else to do it). You can, though, insure against your own carelessness; most car insurance is taken out with this in mind.

You can't take out insurance against the possibility of being fined in court; this would obviously defeat the purpose of legal punishment. Nor can you insure

against going bankrupt, losing at poker or having your marriage break up.

Insurance is distinguished from wagering, in a technical sense, by the fact that the policyholder must have an *insurable interest*. This means that you must have a direct and demonstrable interest in what you are insuring. The policy transfers that genuine risk of loss to the insurance company in exchange for the payment of the premium. This rules out that you might make a wager on, say, the life expectancy of Prince Philip or of Fidel Castro.

When insurance is void

The insurance policy sets out certain conditions which will act to void the policy; these vary from one classification to another, and from one company to another. In automobile insurance, for example, the policy may be voided by the operation of the vehicle while the insured is under the influence of drugs.

In a general insurance policy—for fire or some other peril—the company risk is understood to be of a certain stated kind, and it is the responsibility of the insured to advise the insurance company of any change that alters the nature of the risk. Obviously, a policy written to cover a dwelling unit is substantially altered when the owner turns it into a nightclub; failure to notify the insurer of such a change might void the contract.

Since a contract of insurance is drawn in "utmost good faith" between the two parties, the conditions relating to voidance (that serve to break the contract) are those which are necessary to maintain that good faith. To avoid technical problems, the insured and his agent should work together at the outset to establish broad terms of declaration so that the policy can tolerate a certain amount of change without the risk of breaking the contract terms and voiding the insurance.

All policies require the insured to notify the insurer promptly if a claim is to be made; if the insurance company is unable to investigate the claim, it may have grounds to refuse to pay. On the other hand, insurance companies are required by law to pay undisputed life insurance claims within a month and must pay all other undisputed claims within two months. The insurer will void a policy if it has proof of fraud, or concealment of material facts, by the policyholder.

Changing your beneficiary

Since a life insurance policy is often one of the major assets of a deceased person, it comes as a surprise to many heirs that its benefit is not included in the last will and testament (*See* Chapter 9, "Changing your will"). Of course, the answer is that a beneficiary is already named in the policy. The amount of the payment will only be added to the general sum of the estate if the estate itself is named as beneficiary.

The beneficiaries are, or course, usually dependents, relatives or close friends of the policyholder. But they don't have to be. An absolute stranger left Queen Victoria a fortune. It might be noted that a divorced spouse does not lose his or her rights as a beneficiary under a policy unless the policyholder actually writes that person out of it. The exception to this legal procedure is Quebec, where the court may order the deletion of the beneficiary from an insurance policy, if this is requested by one of the parties in the case of a separation or divorce.

An insured person can change his beneficiary at any time; simply by notifying the insurance company in writing. He may not do this, however, if a beneficiary was named permanently, or irrevocably—such a person might be a creditor who has a vested interest in the policy, having agreed to being paid off at the death of his debtor. However, if the irrevocable beneficiary consents, his or her name can be removed from the policy.

Since the spouses may have an equal interest in assets of the marriage, and assuming the premiums of the life policy were paid from community income, the consent of the partner might be necessary to change the beneficiary.

The policyholder, as owner, can normally make an *assignment* of his life policy to anyone he chooses; that party then

Life insurance league standing

When judged relative to the level of national income, cautious Canadians own more life insurance than any other nationals except the Japanese. We are obviously prepared to save and invest more of present income to ward off possible problems or disasters in the future. Coming fairly close behind Canada are the people of the United States and those of The Netherlands. Among the provinces, Alberta stood at the top of the league in the total amount of insurance owned at the end of 1982. The average per capita total for Alberta was $25,600; the overall Canadian per capita ownership was $22,100. Ontario was Alberta's nearest rival, as this chart shows:

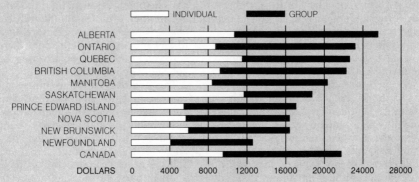

becomes the legal owner of the policy. A legal form has to be filled out and the guidance of a lawyer is advisable. The consent of the insurance company is not necessary for an assignment, although it is entitled to receive notice.

Lodging and paying claims

The routine for lodging a claim under an insurance policy is spelled out in the insurance contract itself. Generally, the policyholder is required to advise the insurance company—directly or through its agent—of any event that may give rise to a claim. This allows the company, or its adjuster, to investigate at the earliest possible moment and to minimize any further damage that might occur.

At the first practical moment after the claim occurrence, you should check your policy and follow the course of action it sets out. This might require, for example, that you notify the police in the event of a burglary. You should take steps to minimize further damage to your property, and then set about establishing the dollar value of the claim. The onus for establishing the size of the claim rests with you.

In some instances—such as in a "business interruption" loss—it is impossible to set the dollar value of a claim at an early stage. You should keep in mind the amount of time you are given to claim under the terms of the policy; if the final amount of claim cannot be established within that period, you should ask the insurance company for an extension.

Once you know the dollar value of the loss, you should submit the required claim forms and proof-of-loss forms to the insuring company. A properly documented loss is normally paid by the insurers without delay. If the company intends to contest a general claim, it will notify you within 60 days.

Many people do not seem to understand the difference between making a claim under their own insurance policy and making a demand against the insurer of another party, particularly in regard to liability payments after an accident. The injured pedestrian, for example, has no specific rights under any policy that may be held by a vehicle driver or owner involved in a collision. This means that he is not a party to the policy and thus cannot sue the insurance company. In order to recover damages, the pedestrian would have to sue the vehicle driver or owner. Although he may find himself dealing with an adjuster representing the driver's insurance company, that does not alter the legal position. An accident victim should discuss such a situation with his own insurance agent and, in a matter of any seriousness, should consult a lawyer.

The claims adjuster

An expert in the appraisal of property losses, the insurance adjuster is usually an independent professional who is hired by an insurance company to investigate claims by policyholders. Licensed by the province where he works, he is sometimes called an investigator, or examiner. He is called upon to verify three items:

(1) That the damage or loss did occur;

(2) That the risk was covered under the policy;

(3) That the dollar value claimed is accurate.

It is as well to remember that the adjuster is being paid by the insurance company; however, in the usual run of events, he will be fair-minded and helpful to the policyholder. Legally, the responsibility for establishing the dollar value of the claim rests with the claimant.

Where the claim is a minor one, the settlement can usually be made with a minimum of fuss—by your agent or broker without an adjuster getting involved at all. If the claim is large—perhaps involving physical injury to yourself or another—you might be advised to check with your lawyer before agreeing to any proposal for settlement. Be quite sure you know what you are doing before you sign any release form.

The adjuster can find himself, in a sense, acting for the claimant. This occurs when he represents an insurer whose policyholder is a "third party" claiming damages resulting from negligence, as in an accident of some kind.

If the insurance company wants to sue another party to recover money that it has paid to you under the terms of your policy, the adjuster will probably ask you to sign an authorization. This is known as a *subrogation*, or transfer of rights.

If a policy lapses

A policy is said to have lapsed when the premium has not been paid following a period of grace. Life insurance policies (except the term variety) usually include a provision that the premiums will be kept up for a time by making use of the cash value already accumulated in the policy. (*See* "Insuring your life" in this chapter.)

An important policy can lapse simply through forgetfulness, or carelessness with correspondence in the household. In general, there is no legal obligation on an insurance agent or company to renew a policy unless the contract contains some condition whereby the insurer or his agent must give the policyholder written notice that the policy is about to expire. In practice, however, the insured is usually notified by the agent who will ask for renewal instructions. If he does not receive instructions to renew, the insurer may then choose to let the policy lapse.

It is only common sense that you should keep a record of the expiry dates of your insurance policies, preferably where you keep other important data relating to your will, mortgage, credit cards, and so on. This record should be kept in a different place from the policy itself. And don't make the fundamental error of keeping your fire insurance policy in the house where it might be destroyed along with the property it is protecting.

The laws of insurance

The Canadian provinces fought with Ottawa for years to decide which level of government should have jurisdiction over insurance. Eventually, the decision went in favor of the provinces. However, the federal government controls the licensing and regulation of foreign insurance companies and companies doing business under a federal charter of incorporation.

Federal insurance law today is concerned almost exclusively with policing the financial reserves of foreign insurance companies and Canadian insurance companies operating under federal charters. (There are about 900 insurance companies and societies doing business in Canada, but only 460 are federally chartered—but each of them must also register in any province where it wishes to trade.) The federal superintendent of insurance requires the companies under his supervision to deposit certain reserve funds with him, to ensure that the legal claims of all policyholders will be met. He also limits the kind of securities in which the companies may invest; insurance companies hold large portfolios of government bonds and real estate mortgages.

Provincial laws govern the day-to-day operation of all insurance companies and the terms of their contracts, as well as the licensing and regulating of agents, brokers and adjusters. A provincial superintendent of insurance (each province has one) supervises those companies operating under provincial charters.

At one time, Canada had almost as many insurance laws as it had provinces; since 1925, however, the laws have become almost uniform across the country. Many of the main provisions of insurance policies must conform to these laws (known as "statutory conditions"), which set out the rights and duties of both the insurer and the insured.

Canada has two main types of insurance companies: stock companies which are owned by shareholders just like any other public corporations; and mutual companies which are technically owned by their policyholders and attempt to operate on a nonprofit basis (any "profits" are used for the benefit of the policyholders). The shareholders of the stock companies usually reap any profits earned from the nonparticipating life policies in force; by law, however, at least 90 percent of any profits derived from the participating policies must be paid to the policyholders as dividends, with the shareholders receiving the remainder.

The law also insists that one-third of the directors of a stock company that issues participating policies must be elected by the participating policyholders and no member of that group may hold shares.

Anatomy of the stock market

Oils, mines and industrials

Over-the-counter trading

Common and "preferred" stocks

Playing safe with bonds

The mutual funds

Disclosure and supervision

IT IS GENERALLY ACKNOWLEDGED that trading in the shares of Canadian companies began in the Exchange Coffee House on St-Paul Street, Montreal, in May 1832. The Champlain and St. Lawrence Railroad Company was offering stock to the public, and a small coterie of merchants met one morning to organize a trading group. The issue of shares was a success, providing the money (the *capital*) to build the first steam-run railway in Canada. It took another 30 years, however, before an organized stock exchange existed in Quebec.

Meanwhile, a group of Toronto businessmen began meeting every morning to buy, sell and exchange the few securities that were available toward the middle of last century. They formed the Toronto Stock Exchange in 1852; it consisted of 12 members, each of whom paid $5 to keep his own chair (or "seat") in the trading room. Today the T.S.E. dominates the Canadian stock market; in volume of shares traded, it is second in the world only to the New York Stock Exchange. The T.S.E. currently has 80 member firms and when a "seat" is up for sale the price reflects the buoyancy of the stock market. The high price in 1982 was $165,000; in 1981, the low price was $40,000; in 1980, the peak price was only $55,000.

Stock exchanges exist to provide common meeting places for those who wish to buy or sell shares in the well-established public commercial corporations (about 800 in number) whose securities have been *listed*—that is, accepted for trading —by the exchange authorities. When you decide that the time has come for you to share as a part owner in the wealth generated by Canadian industry, your purchase of shares in a public corporation will most likely be made through one of the nation's five stock exchanges. For Canadians, buying shares in the nation's corporations has an added attraction, because the dividends are eligible for federal tax credits.

If the stock exchange had not been invented, thousands of prospective buyers with money they wanted to put to work would be running around in endless confusion trying to find people who might be prepared to sell shares they already own. But centralizing the trading of shares was obviously not enough: the stock owners and the prospective buyers had their normal businesses to attend to and needed representatives to do the actual buying and selling for them. The representative, or agent, who filled that need is our present-day stockbroker.

The stock exchange is only part of the *money market*, that vast commercial arena housing the entire process of the flotation, evaluation, buying and selling of stocks, bonds, debentures, rights, warrants and other financial specialties. The market has been described as "not so much a market as a state of mind." It is international in scope; what happens "in the market" in New York, Paris or London quickly affects the trading scene in Canada. Yet the stock exchange is itself very much a market in the most traditional sense. It does not carry a supply of securities to sell to the public like a supermarket does groceries—but it is a place where the citizens come to trade, buy *and* sell, and where the prices are set by the principle of supply and demand. If there are more people wanting to buy the shares of Moon Charters Ltd., than want to sell, the price of the shares will rise; if sellers are plentiful, the price will fall. That's the heart of the matter—although it's true that certain regulators can be applied if stock zooms up or down too erratically.

The hours of business on the trading floor of the stock exchange are from 10 A.M. to 4 P.M. All trading is conducted in the open: not only that, it must be conducted at the top of the lungs. The would-be investor should visit the nearest stock exchange, especially as the clock ticks toward closing time. The place is in bedlam as men dash about shouting at each other around the "trading posts" (special areas where only shares of a certain class are traded). The rush is created by the floor men (called "attorneys") trying to keep up with the flow of telephoned orders from their offices, and the shouting is necessary because all *bids* to buy and all *asks* (offers to sell) must be conducted, according to exchange regulations, by "open outcry." The purpose of this is to prevent secret deals being clinched, to the detriment of the general public. Even the high-speed electronic quotations system—so mysterious at first-view—which keeps a running account of the shares being traded and their prices, can be understood after a few minutes' study.

Federal and provincial laws combine with the self-policing of such professional organizations as the five stock exchanges, the Investment Funds Institute of Canada and the Investment Dealers Association to provide a wide measure of protection to the investor; however, despite the polished courtesies and the pin-striped suits of the stockbrokers, theirs is a hardnosed world. Before you cross the threshold of the stock market, you should have a general understanding of the main kinds of securities you will be offered. They are discussed in the sections that follow.

Oils, mines and industrials

Canada boasts five stock exchanges, and these are linked by telephone, telex and computer terminals to the offices of brokers and investment dealers in all major cities and many towns across the country. When you place an order with a broker to buy some shares at the going market rate, the deal can usually be confirmed within five minutes, often within two. Some exchanges specialize in certain classes of stocks—familiarly known by such labels as "oils," "mines," "industrials"—of particular relevance to large industries or resources in their regions.

We have noted that the Toronto Exchange, recently installed in a three-storey pavilion in First Canadian Place (nationally known in financial jargon as T.S.E.), is the Canadian giant. Until recently, Montreal had two stock exchanges in downtown Place Victoria: the Montreal Stock Exchange (M.S.E.) and the Canadian Stock Exchange (C.S.E.). The M.S.E. was incorporated in 1874; among its most famous early "listings" was Bell Telephone in 1880 and Canadian Pacific in 1883.

In the 1920s, a group of brokers trading in stocks that were not listed on the Montreal Exchange—these included all the mining shares—organized the Montreal Curb Market (so named because this class of business trading had once been conducted literally at the street curb). In 1953, the 100 members of the Montreal Curb had the name changed to the Canadian Stock Exchange and formed a semi-merger with the Montreal Exchange; the two exchanges shared the same building and management; the amalgamation became total in 1975.

The Vancouver Stock Exchange was chartered in 1907 with 12 members, and its proudest boast is that it has been open every working day since then, come depression or war. It has provided an important market for lumber and mining shares, and the growth of secondary industry on the West Coast is clearly reflected in its current listings.

The Calgary Stock Exchange opened briefly during World War I when the first gas fields were discovered in the Turner Valley; then it closed for a decade until the pioneer petroleum wells blew in. Since 1980, the exchange, now called Alberta Stock Exchange, has been housed in a fine building on 5th Avenue, where a huge quotations board flashes with brisk trading action in oil and gas stocks, and "industrials." Even though the routine conservative policies of all stock exchanges are strictly observed, there is still a faint air of the gambling West about the big Calgary board. Maybe that's because you can occasionally glimpse a jaunty white Stetson turning in the front door.

In 1903, when Winnipeg was a city of about 56,000 people and had visions of becoming a second Chicago, a stock exchange was incorporated. It has survived through boom and bust and today concentrates on "industrials," and mining and oil securities, in a city that hums with strong growth as the central metropolis of Canada. Winnipeg is also the home of Canada's only commodity exchange, described later in this section.

Over-the-counter trading

Many of the securities bought and sold in Canada are not traded through the stock exchanges but in what is known as the *over-the-counter market* (reduced in financial language to O.T.C., and known in the trade as "the street"). The stock exchanges restrict their facilities, as stated above, to the trading of the common (or "ownership") shares in the largest and strongest of the public corporations. They do not handle corporation bonds or government debentures, the shares of privately owned companies, and new and smaller concerns not yet able to show the level of assets or meet other stipulations required by exchange regulations.

The stock exchange regulations vary across the country and (as with a large amount of other specialist financial data) fall outside the scope of this book. It must be mentioned, however, that some very valuable public companies of impeccable integrity, for a wide variety of reasons, do not seek listing on the stock exchanges. Conversely, there is nothing to prevent shares that are listed on the stock exchange from being sold "over the counter." In fact, it can be perfectly legal for two men to meet in a restaurant and conclude a deal.

The O.T.C. is a market without a marketplace; the transactions take place across a national network of the offices of brokers and investment dealers, who are connected by telephone, telex and computer.

The trades are negotiated by principals, rather than being consummated at auction by brokers acting as agents on the floor of a stock exchange. In O.T.C. trading, the dealer buys the securities from you, knowing that he can, in turn, sell them to another at a price that allows him a profit. The dealer's profit on unlisted stocks is generally comparable to the commission charged by stockbrokers.

The new investor should keep in mind that although many highly speculative "penny stocks" are traded "over the counter," so are the shares of several of Canada's life insurance companies. The name of the market refers basically to the method of trading and has no general significance beyond that.

Common stocks

The common stock of a corporation represents its ownership, divided into units which are called shares; the share itself is an engraved certificate, registered proof that the holder is part owner of the company concerned.

You are promised nothing when you buy a common share. In fact, you have taken on a personal liability for the debts of that corporation up to the value of the original purchase price of the share, or shares, you have bought. This does not mean you will have to pay more money if the company fails, but you will normally lose the money you had invested. (*See* Chapter 13, "The public corporation.")

If the company prospers, making a handsome profit, all its obligations to creditors and other classes of stockholder—such as persons holding preferred shares—will be met before any of that profit filters down to the owners— those who hold the common shares. And even then, the decision to pay a *dividend*—a portion of the earned profit— rests entirely with the board of directors. But the tempting lure of "the common" is that the profit remaining, even after sufficient reserves are put aside for expansion, can be sufficient to allow a substantial quarterly or annual dividend to the owners. Even more important: the successful company attracts buyer interest on the stock exchange and the value of the shares is almost certain to rise, thus providing the stockholder with an attractive *capital gain* if he decides to sell his shares.

Common shares mostly attract those people who are seeking *growth* in their estates, rather than maximum security and a fixed income.

The owners of the common stock of a corporation are entitled to participate in the management of the company—for instance, in the election of directors and by voting on other issues at annual meetings. Generally speaking, though, the influence of small shareholders on management is small, unless they band together.

Major corporations are largely controlled and administered by professional managers, who may also be directors sure of the support of large blocks of shareholders. In some cases, control of policy in a corporation by a certain group is ensured by the issuance of two kinds of common shares, only one of which carries voting rights.

The "preferred" stockholder

A *preferred share* of stock entitles its holder to a fixed dividend that is paid before the common shareholder gets anything; however, even the preferred shareholder gets no dividend until all other debts or obligations of the corporation have been met. And even if funds are available, the directors can choose not to pay a dividend. If the dividend is not paid within a specified period, the preferred shareholder is usually entitled to demand an increased say in the running of the corporation.

The investor should check whether the preferred share he plans to buy is *cumulative* or *noncumulative*. A "cumulative preferred" requires the corporation to make up all arrears of dividends before any dividend payments can be paid to common shareholders.

The fixed dividend on a preferred share is normally set at a fairly conservative level and the price of the share usually remains stable. However, a corporation seeking fresh capital may issue *convertible preferred stock;* the investor who buys shares of this type may convert his preferreds into ordinary commons at certain stated terms. Thus, if the company prospers and the value of the common shares rises, the price of the convertible preferreds will rise also, to some extent. If, on the other hand, the commons drop, the price of the convertible preferreds may not tumble so far because they still offer the attraction of the fixed dividend.

Playing safe with bonds

Bonds are usually issued in sums of $1,000 and run for periods of years—often five years, sometimes 15, 20 or even 30—at a fixed rate of interest. They are regarded as a safe and convenient investment, as they are, in effect, *promissory notes* (*See* Chapter 7, "Negotiable instruments") issued by a corporation or government in return for the loan of your money. In the case of the corporation, the bond is backed by some or all of the corporation's assets; in the case of the government, the security rests on the taxing powers granted by parliament. The term *debenture* is often more correctly used to describe a bond issued by the government, indicating that it is backed by the general credit of the state rather than by any specified asset.

The issuer of a bond contracts to pay a stated rate of interest on a regular basis (most often twice a year), over the term of the issue—in other words, over the period of the loan—and pledges to pay the face value at maturity. The price of the bond may be lower than the face value. A bond that is issued by any Canadian governmental body, or any major corporation, is almost certain to be honored. With its minimum-risk reputation, the bond is popular with life insurance companies, pension organizations and other groups with large sums of money to be put to work in the safest way possible. Also, these *institutional buyers* can be reasonably sure that they will not require their money until the given maturity date.

The individual investor may find that he needs his funds before the maturity date of a bond issue. He can sell his bonds in the over-the-counter market; however, by doing that, he may not receive face value for them. If interest rates on bonds go up, the dollar price for outstanding bond issues slides downward because a better return (the "yield") would be available on new issues.

There are several other guaranteed investments available—for instance, the federal government's 91 day *treasury bills* —but this "short-term paper," as it is known, is for professionals.

Canada Savings Bonds

Every fall since the end of World War II, the federal treasury has borrowed the savings of individual Canadians through the issuing of Canada Savings Bonds. Available in values ranging from $100 to $10,000, these bonds are undoubtedly the favorite investment of the average citizen. In 1983, over four million Canadians held roughly $32 billion in bonds.

There are several good reasons for this popularity. Here are two of them:

(1) The bonds are guaranteed by the federal government, and therefore are totally safe and liquid.

(2) They are *parity bonds*—that is, they can be cashed at any time at any bank for their full face value, plus any interest accrued up to that time.

Since these bonds can be turned into cash at any time without loss, the "little man" is protected in case interest rates should take an upward leap. He can cash in his old bonds and reinvest in the new issue to gain the higher return.

You can choose to buy a regular bond that will bring you an annual interest cheque from Ottawa, or a compound bond, which accumulates interest each year and pays it at maturity.

Canada Savings Bonds are heavily ad-

The lure of "penny" stocks

THE DISCOVERY of mineral deposits and the development of mines have played a remarkable role in Canadian history, and they remain vital to our economic life today. Gambling on the chances of finding fortune in a hole in the ground is, in some ways, a national mania in Canada. Taking a flier in "penny" mining stocks—in effect, providing risk capital for new ventures— has been likened to betting on the British football pools or the Irish sweepstakes. The chance of winning may be remote, but the reward for the lucky (or knowledgeable) can be riches.

Jacques Cartier and Jean de Roberval strove to find the source of the copper ornaments and utensils found in the Indian villages along the St. Lawrence Valley. Samuel de Champlain spent much of his energies looking for a nonexistent silver mine at the head of the Bay of Fundy (a search remembered today in the name of Minas Basin, Nova Scotia).

The earliest successful exploitation saw bog iron smelted near Trois-Rivières, and coal excavated on Cape Breton. The gold

rushes of the nineteenth century were followed by major discoveries in base metals, particularly in the vast area capped by the Precambrian Shield. By 1950, the value of Canada's total mineral production topped one billion dollars for the first time; it now exceeds 30 billion dollars a year.

Trying to hitch their wagons to this financial comet, thousands of beginning investors have fallen for the lure of the "penny" stocks (the price of new mining shares is kept low to tap this flow of funds). Nearly all, by the record, must lose their stake in this highly speculative market.

It's obvious that your stockbroker will be unlikely to recommend risky mining shares to the inexperienced.

"Our position is one of trust," says an investment counselor, "and no one can foretell with accuracy the extent and richness of the ore a new mining company may uncover when they begin to investigate a fresh claim. It could be another King Solomon's Mines, or just another hole in the ground. It's mainly a matter of faith or intuition."

vertised each year. The annual sale of the bonds is handled by the Bank of Canada. Any Canadian resident can buy them without any formality at any branch of any chartered bank or trust company, as well as from a stockbroker or investment dealer. They can be bought "on time" through payroll deductions by employers who offer to handle bond purchases for their employes, and through installment plans operated by some authorized bond dealers.

If you are wondering why any other kinds of bonds find buyers, remember that these bonds are nontransferable (meaning that they cannot be sold to another or traded in any way; they can only be cashed at a bank); secondly, the government sets a limit on the value of the bonds that one person can buy each year.

Convertible bonds
Although the security of bonds is universally appreciated—they are similar in many ways to first mortgages—the relatively low rate of return deters many buyers. The bogey of inflation is always there to spur the ambitious investor on in his quest for greater growth of his capital. To meet this demand, some large companies placing bond issues on the market will add a special condition to the offer known as a "conversion privilege."

If you buy a *convertible bond*, you have the right to exchange it, under certain conditions, for a fixed number of common shares in the corporation. It is similar to the privilege written into convertible preferred stock (which was explained earlier in this section). This bond gives you the normal full security—at least, as far as the assets of the corporation will stretch—of a regular bond, plus the steady income from the fixed rate of interest. At the same time, if the company expands its business and increases its dividends (thus forcing up the value of the common stock), our convertible bondholder can jump onto the gravy train by switching his bonds for common shares at the ratio that had been set earlier, and which is now advantageous. Even if he decides not to switch, the market price of his bond will have risen in these circumstances

since it is "tied" to the rising value of the common share.

It goes without saying that the purchaser of a convertible bond will pay a premium for these advantages. Only an expert analyst can decide confidently in the case of an individual bond if the privilege of convertibility is worth having in terms of the company's possible capital growth.

Warrants and rights
In the language of finance, a *warrant* is a certificate guaranteeing an option to buy common shares of a corporation at a specified price within a fixed period of time. Each warrant usually entitles the holder to buy one share of common stock. Warrants are sometimes attached to preferred stock or bond issues to make them more attractive to the investing public.

The only real difference between the warrant and the "conversion privilege" of a convertible bond is that the warrant can be detached from the corporation bond and traded separately—after a waiting period of, say, one year. There is a brisk market for the transferable warrants because they usually allow the investor (perhaps "speculator" is a better term here) to buy from two to four times as many common shares of a company as he could buy for an equal sum in the open market. To many investors, this advantage far outweighs the absence of current income from warrants.

A *right* is a specific type of warrant. When a company wishes to raise equity capital—in order, perhaps, to expand its business—it often feels that its present shareholders should be given the chance to buy more stock in proportion to their present holdings. The company will then issue a "right" for each outstanding, or currently owned, share of the corporation.

This right will contain certain favorable conditions. For example, the company may specify that if eight "rights" are presented to its transfer agent within, say, two months, the holder will be permitted to purchase a share of the company at a price which generally represents a discount of between ten and 15 percent off the current market value of the stock.

371

Gambling on the future

Although the Canadian Wheat Board sets wheat prices in Canada, there's not much else that falls outside the interest of specialist investors. The typical press reports below give the current market price—and the price for future delivery—of flax and rapeseed, Florida orange juice, plus cocoa, coffee, copper, cotton, gold, lumber, pork bellies and sugar.

Speculating in commodity futures—perhaps the most sophisticated gamble in the business world—is no game for the inexperienced investor.

Commodities

GRAIN

WINNIPEG (CP)—Grain quotes Friday in metric tons, basis Lakehead:

	Open	High	Low	Close	Thurs.
Flax					
Jly	293.10	293.10	291.30	291.60	293.60
Oct	302.60	302.60	301.00	301.20	303.00
Dec	—	—	—	303.60	308.20
Mar	—	—	—	315.50	315.00
Rapeseed (basis Vancouver)					
Jun	303.50	303.50	299.50	299.50	304.70
Spt	310.80	310.80	307.10	307.10	310.80
Nov	312.50	312.50	309.10	309.10	312.80
Jan	319.70	319.60	316.40	316.40	320.20
Mar	327.50	327.50	324.20	324.30	327.70

COFFEE

(NYCSCE)—37,500 lb.; ¢ per lb.

135.50	102.00	Jul	127.00	124.95	125.29	-1.88	33,801
131.75	101.00	Sep	127.15	125.60	126.19	-.85	3,954
130.00	98.00	Dec	126.30	125.00	125.97	-.48	2,446
127.65	110.50	Mar	125.25	123.25	124.48	-.05	232
126.00	108.00	May	122.75	122.75	123.25	-.40	110
124.00	104.51	Jul	122.00	120.50	120.01	-2.37	173
123.00	110.50	Sep			119.50		174

Est. sales 2,354. Prev. sales 2,691.

ORANGE JUICE

(NYCTN)—15,000 lb.; ¢ per lb.

142.20	104.70	Jul	116.80	116.50	116.50	-.45	1,327
139.00	106.10	Sep	115.60	115.30	115.40	-.40	1,435
131.95	105.50	Nov			113.10	-.40	959
132.50	100.15	Jan	108.10	108.00	108.00	-.35	1,044
132.20	100.00	Mar	106.80	106.60	106.60	-.20	1,167
130.50	100.90	May	106.30	106.30	106.30	-.40	350
111.00	101.00	Jul			106.00	-.40	126
104.50	103.80	Sep	107.00	106.90	105.70	-.40	18
		Nov			105.70	-.40	

Est. sales 300. Prev. sales 256.
Prev day's open int 6,426, up 1.

SUGAR

World (NYCSCE)—112,000 lb.; ¢ per lb.

13.47	6.40	Jul	12.08	11.54	11.61	-.15	15,985
14.08	6.80	Sep	12.30	11.82	11.91	-.25	5,623
14.05	7.05	Oct	12.60	12.10	12.14	-.24	42,901
14.23	7.65	Jan	13.00	12.79	12.79	-.11	172
14.48	8.08	Mar	13.40	12.93	13.04	-.18	26,282
14.70	8.35	May	13.55	13.20	13.24	-.18	6,904
14.95	8.65	Jul	13.75	13.35	13.45	-.13	1,985
14.93	9.65	Sep	13.86	13.70	13.70		388
15.30	7.86	Oct	14.30	14.10	13.90	+.05	446

Est. sales 18,478. Prev. sales 23,243.
Prev day's open int 100,686, up 3,164.

COCOA

(NYCSCE)—10 metric tons; $ per ton

2230	1475	Jul	2190	2153	2181	-6	7,561
2268	1527	Sep	2239	2203	2230	-7	10,437
2294	1560	Dec	2262	2223	2255	-3	1,664
2325	1650	Mar	2279	2250	2273	-9	2,977
2330	1809	May	2270	2270	2293	-9	345
2370	1835	Jul			2313	-9	66
		Sep			2318	-9	91

Est. sales 6,520. Prev. sales 6,841.
Prev day's open int 27,731, up 539.

COTTON

(NYCTN)—50,000 lb.; ¢ per lb.

78.90	66.60	Jul	78.30	77.35	77.38	-.99	5,806
79.80	65.65	Oct	79.40	78.57	78.90	-.52	1,554
80.89	65.50	Dec	80.50	79.75	79.81	-.62	24,325
82.00	67.10	Mar	81.30	80.70	80.75	-.35	2,873
82.00	67.00	May	81.49	80.90	81.25	-.26	465
81.90	70.50	Jul	81.55	81.40	81.45	-.04	322
79.00	68.80	Oct	77.99	77.90	77.45	-.45	55

Est. sales 6,000. Prev. sales 6,344.
Prev day's open int 35,400, up 733.

COPPER

(NYCX)—25,000 lb.; ¢ per lb.

80.55	74.50	Jun	75.20	75.15	74.70	-.65	28
103.00	63.10	Jul	76.15	74.90	75.15	-.65	34,817
76.25	76.25	Aug			75.90	-.65	1
93.60	64.50	Sep	77.65	76.40	76.65	-.65	31,762
93.00	66.30	Dec	79.70	78.40	78.65	-.65	16,396
89.50	66.90	Jan	80.20	80.20	79.25	-.65	736
90.40	68.00	Mar	81.50	80.50	80.50	-.65	7,848
88.60	69.00	May	82.80	81.90	81.75	-.65	2,536
89.80	70.70	Jul	83.85	83.00	83.00	-.65	2,575
90.80	73.20	Sep	85.30	84.00	84.25	-.65	3,056
92.70	82.10	Dec	86.85	86.70	86.10	-.65	1,092
92.00	82.90	Jan			86.70	-.65	294
93.00	86.90	Mar	88.90	87.90	87.90	-.65	345

Est. sales 13,000. Prev. sales 8,757.
Prev day's open int 101,486, up 755.

GOLD

(IMM)—100 troy oz.; $ per troy oz.

593.00	336.00	Jun	412.20	408.20	407.20	-5.80	145
584.00	380.10	Jul			410.00	-5.90	3
587.10	350.00	Sep	421.30	413.10	415.70	-6.00	3,214
453.40	416.50	Oct			419.20	-6.00	1
554.00	415.10	Dec	431.80	424.50	426.10	-6.20	864
563.50	433.50	Mar	443.00	435.00	436.90	-6.40	30
552.40	437.20	Apr			440.60	-6.50	2
573.00	444.40	Jun			448.10	-6.60	9

Est. sales 3,560. Prev. sales 3,393.
Prev day's open int 4,268, up 1,837.

LUMBER

(CME)—130,000 bd. ft.; $ per 1,000 bd. ft.

248.50	158.50	Jul	231.00	226.80	227.70	+.10	3,667
240.40	163.20	Sep	226.40	223.10	224.80	+2.40	2,319
229.90	170.00	Nov	222.10	218.00	218.80	+.40	2,085
234.00	179.00	Jan	225.80	223.40	225.10	+1.10	435
240.50	207.00	Mar	230.00	227.00	229.70	+1.70	247
245.50	221.00	May	230.50	229.00	229.00	+1.50	63
251.00	224.60	Jul			236.00	+1.50	29

Est. sales 3,047. Prev. sales 5,318.
Prev day's open int 8,845, up 73.

PORK BELLIES

(CME)—38,000 lb.; ¢ per lb.

84.10	58.40	Jul	62.85	62.00	62.57	+.85	8,761
81.20	56.55	Aug	59.90	59.20	59.77	+.67	6,972
70.00	58.30	Feb	59.22	58.30	58.47	-.13	1,732
69.00	58.80	Mar	58.90	58.90	58.70	-.10	214
68.00	59.00	May	59.55	59.50	59.70	-.10	106
68.00	56.95	Jul	57.50	57.05	57.05	+.10	51
63.80	54.60	Aug	55.00	54.50	54.50	+.03	60

Est. sales 8,028. Prev. sales 10,742.
Prev day's open int 17,896, up 433.

The Toronto Globe and Mail's *Report on Business*, June 11, 1983

This privilege naturally gives a real dollar value to the right itself. If the holder does not wish to invest further in the corporation by exercising his rights, he can sell them on the market. The purchaser can then proceed to pick up the shares at the discount price. You don't have to own shares in the corporation to buy up these rights.

The mutual funds

Someone with modest funds who is eager to make a beginning in investment but feels that he lacks confidence, time or aptitude to manage his own money may find what he wants in the investment corporation. These companies are far from new; they date back to the establishment in London, England, in 1868, of the Foreign and Colonial Trust which held a *portfolio* ("a collection of securities") that included the bonds of 15 different governments abroad. Investment corporations today sell their own shares (sometimes called "units") to the public in unlimited quantities, pooling the savings of many individuals which they then reinvest in selected securities. Active in Canada since 1932, they have come to be known as *mutual funds* (in Britain, they are called "unit trusts"). Some of them are now multimillion-dollar giants wielding considerable power in the financial life of the country.

The various funds (you'll find them listed in the financial pages of any city newspaper) have differing goals, and the prospective investor should check their aims before buying. Some strive for maximum regular income (concentrating on bonds); some aim for capital growth (through the purchase of common stocks); and others restrict their portfolios to certain classes of securities about which the management has particular expertise.

Most mutuals, however, try to achieve a relatively conservative mixture of considerable security plus some growth through capital gain. By spreading your money over many different securities in several fields of enterprise, the managers assume that gains will cover (hopefully, more than cover) losses, and that the fund will ride safely through most market fluctuations. Investors refer to this policy as *diversification.*

The most popular type of investment corporation today is described as the "open-end" fund. This means that the investment company constantly sells and buys back its own shares (or "units") at prices based on the net asset value of the shares. The selling price will always include a sales charge (of up to nine percent) to cover the salesman's commission. In stock market jargon, this surcharge is called the "front-end load." An annual management fee (generally one to two percent) is also charged against the assets of the fund.

Mutual fund shares can be bought or redeemed through the fund or through just about any stockbroker or investment dealer. They can be bought with lump-sum payments or under a contractual plan, which can start as low as $50.

Another type of investment corporation is the "closed-end fund," which is less popular because of the lack of liquidity. These companies sell a limited number of shares to the public, closing that fund when all are sold. As the capital increases by selected investment, dividends are paid to the shareholders. These types of mutual funds are also traded on the stock exchange.

The commodities market

Winnipeg has a *commodity exchange* that is known around the world. Here, since the late nineteenth century, wheat and other grains from the prairie provinces have been sold. The Winnipeg Commodity Exchange is a vital link in the chain of North American produce exchanges that operate in such centers as New York, Chicago and Kansas City.

Produce exchanges provide not only a trading market for those in the complex business of feeding the population but also an avenue of speculation for a special group of investors. In a general sense, a commodity exchange resembles a stock exchange in that quantities of beef, beans or barley are sold among brokers to the highest bidder, in much the same way as securities are traded. However, there is the added dimension of *trading in futures*. Futures trading is said to have begun when the warlords of seventeenth-century Japan raised money by selling rice that was still growing in the fields. In modern economics, it is obvious that while commodities (oats, for example) come onto the market seasonally, food processors must have access to a steady supply all year round. They cover their anticipated needs by buying now for delivery later.

It is a game of wits between the speculator and the genuine produce buyer, and each one plays a useful role in the market. The winner is the man who most correctly estimates the market price for the commodity at the time the delivery has to be made. If a speculator has sold oats that he does not actually own and has guaranteed delivery on a certain date, he must supply them exactly on schedule no matter how high the price may have risen in the interim; of course, if the price has slumped, he's sitting pretty.

Since the 1930s, the Canadian Wheat Board has set wheat prices; however, the Winnipeg Commodity Exchange still handles "futures" in oats, rye, barley, flax and other seeds.

Disclosure and supervision

In Canada, the investment business falls under provincial jurisdiction; each province has its own Securities Act, plus a permanent organization of trained public servants (the Securities Commission) to see that the act and regulations are followed. There is a large measure of uniformity across the country in the control of the business. The Ontario and Quebec commisions, not surprisingly, play a dominant role—these provinces initiate most of the action in the securities business.

Canadian securities legislation (like similar laws in the United States) has aimed at ensuring full disclosure of information by all public corporations, as well as registration and supervision of all major personnel who handle the investor's money on the market. The law also insists that all segments of society—from large conglomerates down to the private citi-zen—must have an equal opportunity to compete in the markets.

Under both federal and provincial legislation, all incorporated companies must publish annual reports, giving certain basic information. Public companies must also file quarterly reports with the Securities Commission and must take pains to ensure that important announcements are disseminated broadly to the shareholders and the public.

The securities acts also demand that a *prospectus*, an outline setting out certain information about the company's setup in a prescribed format, be filed with (and accepted by) the Securities Commission before a new issue of securities is offered to the public. The general purpose of the law is to ensure the full and frank disclosure of information, rather than to pass judgment on the investment merits of specific securities.

The commissions also exert their power over the stock market by demanding registration of all those who either sell securities or counsel in investment matters. This power extends to authority over the stock exchanges themselves as well as over the individual investment dealers. It is a black mark indeed for a broker or a firm to run afoul of the Securities Commission.

The novice investor can take comfort in the knowledge that tough measures have been introduced into securities legislation in recent years and that they are being vigorously administered. The professional associations are setting high standards of performance and integrity for their members. However, it would be a mistake to conclude that all unscrupulous elements in the securities business have been eliminated. They still exist, peddling the "fast buck" speculations that we all hear about from time to time.

The general consensus is, however, that the stock market now boasts a higher level of professional integrity than it has ever had before. This is due to the checks and balances discussed here, the rise of security analysis, the stricter organization of the market and intelligent but not oppressive government regulation and supervision.

The beginning investor

THE MOST COMMON PROBLEM for the beginning investor is not lawlessness in the marketplace but simply lack of capital. It is a problem he shares, to some degree, with most of struggling humanity. There is no guarantee that the apparent wealth of the family in the big house up the street will endure; "from rags to riches and back again" often describes the financial history of a family. Many a school dropout who started work in his early teens sits in the boardroom today, savoring that elusive pleasure of being "a millionaire." Lord Thomson of Fleet, the world's greatest newspaper tycoon, was still a penniless Canadian promoter in his late thirties.

Despite the siren songs of a hundred books promising that "Anybody can make a million," there is no certain, and certainly no easy, way to riches through the stock market. And, contrary to the tales of the gamblers, Lady Luck plays a very small role, if indeed she figures in the cast at all. However, one basic truth of the stock market is that you have to start out with a certain sum. It does not have to be a fortune. Stockbrokers who look as though they could light their cigars with sawbucks without singeing their bank balances say you can make a sensible beginning with several thousand dollars.

How do you get this money together these days that you don't need for something urgent? A similar question was asked years ago of a Scottish-born railway telegrapher who had become the world's richest man. "You want to know how to become rich?" asked Andrew Carnegie, rhetorically. "The answer is: Can you save money?" The same discipline that is required to pin together that all-important first stake will stand you in good stead as you advance gingerly into the heady world of high finance.

The person who succeeds in his investment program—that is, who succeeds in the goals he sets for himself—will require strong self-discipline. Firstly, he must not panic if the market falls and the newspaper quotations tell him his carefully selected common stocks are worth less than he paid for them; secondly, he must restrain himself from rushing in to sell if the market rises and his shares are quoted well above what they cost him. If there is any consensus among professionals, it is that money is made in the stock market by buying right and holding on. That takes knowledge and discipline; the steely ability not to follow the lemming-like crowds—you could also call it courage.

A novice in the market
Earlier in this chapter, we discussed the various ways in which you can put your money to work virtually without risk (in insurance policies and government bonds) and at partial risk (in corporation bonds and the mutual funds), and we have described the best-known among other types of securities. The advisability of seeking expert counsel—much of which is available free or for the price of a newspaper or magazine—has been stressed at every stage. The ways in which the law attempts to protect the public from the confidence trickster and the shady promoter have also been outlined. The experienced investor will now seek answers to his individual investment questions in other specialist media. In this final section, attention focuses exclusively on the problems the novice will

encounter as he approaches the speculative heart of the stock market.

Having your money make money is the name of the game. But you should reflect at the outset on the sobering fact that riches appear to have eluded the majority of those in the stockbroking business. Why is the investment counselor battering his brains on your behalf for a fee when he should be, in the romantic view, lolling on the beach at Monte Carlo? If it is not easy for the professionals to rope the golden calf, it must be difficult indeed for the novice.

The amateur is usually limited in the time he can devote to the study of the market. He is also competing with the "institutional investor" (say, a private pension fund) which can call upon market analysts trained to sift through the enormous amount of ever-changing corporate and other economic information to determine the best values in the marketplace. Securities legislation rules that key information be made available to all investors, large and small; however, in practice, it is almost impossible for the inexperienced individual to gather as much information as the institutional investor—let alone get to know the stock market as thoroughly.

After painting this cautionary picture, a veteran stockbroker would probably suggest that the novice investor do some research on his own. Try to determine whether the stock market is in the early stages of an economic recovery. That is the best time to enter it by purchasing some common shares in a selected company. Secondly, try to figure out whether the market is grossly over-valued in light of present business activity generally. Historically, in the latter stages of an expansive boom, speculative fever has a tendency to result in such an overpricing of stocks.

If time and price seem right, the next step is to decide which industry group appears to have the brightest outlook. Again, there is no substitute for research. Perhaps it's the year for containers, concrete or computers? Lastly, try to choose the company within the industry group which appears to be in the best position to take advantage of the expected growth. Happy endings do occur! The former financial editor of a New York newspaper who followed a similar routine to this concluded that the struggling Haloid company was a good bet. He bought in at $1 a share and held on, even when urged to sell; in fact, he bought more stock in the company. Haloid eventually became Xerox, and the price per share went up to $125. The one-time newspaperman became a multimillionaire as a result of that one well-researched, intelligent investment. Gambler's luck had nothing to do with it.

Government consumer agencies and stockbrokers alike warn bluntly that in no case should the beginner employ capital required for other purposes in his investment program. You should invest with savings, above and beyond all obligations. This is not just virtuous preaching. If you were forced to pull your money out of the market during a period of decline, you could well be sacrificing a sound investment.

The research factor

Investing on the basis of "hot tips" or grapevine rumors is courting disaster. It stands to reason that sound investments are based on solid research; however, where does the novice get information inexpensively to help him in the decision-making process?

Information on Canadian economic and business conditions is accurately reported and analyzed in the daily "Report on Business" section of *The Globe and Mail* and in national business newspapers such as *The Financial Post*, the *Financial Times of Canada*, and the *Northern Miner;* the foreign scene is covered in the American *Wall Street Journal* and the British *Financial Times.* It is as well to remember that the great majority of Canadian daily newspapermen have no special training in financial affairs; unless they are known to have professional qualifications, you should treat any comments they offer with caution.

If you want to examine the growth prospects of a given industry, you will most likely find that it is served by a trade journal. Although these specialist papers may appear enthusiastic in tone, be comforted by the fact that they must cover their territories accurately and knowledgeably in order to hold their expert subscribers. Statistics Canada will provide you with generalized performance information on major industrial groups (but not on individual firms).

The *prospectus* provides a basic source of information about any corporation. This legal document must be prepared and submitted to the provincial securities commission whenever a company offers shares or other securities to the public, or applies to a stock exchange to have its securities listed for trading. The prospectus must contain, among other things, a statement on the general aims of the company, the names of the directors and auditors, plus complete details of the share capital—the numbers and different kinds of shares—earnings, assets and liabilities.

You should also read the company's annual report; all incorporated companies must produce annual reports and file them with the government (*See* Chapter 13, "The public corporation"). *The Financial Post* of Toronto offers a corporation service to clients providing all the most recent data released by Canadian companies. Most of the larger corporations now issue half-yearly reports on profit-and-loss trading, and many make quarterly disclosures.

Some of the larger brokerage houses, and some of the chartered banks, issue periodic financial surveys of varying merit. You can normally arrange to receive these by mail simply by asking.

Keeping up with the Dow Joneses

INSISTENT REFERENCES to the Dow Jones "averages" are one of the first things that register on the newcomer approaching the stock market. And he could well spend a great deal of time trying to find out exactly what these "averages" are. For starters, they are not true averages at all, but adjusted indexes to the up or down movements of a selected group of securities on the New York Stock Exchange (the world's largest). They are, however, generally accepted everywhere as the most significant indicator of the condition of the North American stock market—and, really, of the state of business generally.

In 1900, Charles H. Dow began publishing his experiments in charting the movements of representative securities, hoping that the patterns that emerged would accurately predict the fluctuations of the whole market. Others joined and refined this study and three "averages" were established, based on the shares of 30 large industrial companies, 20 railroad corporations (including the Canadian Pacific), and 15 utilities (including power and gas companies).

As the prices of these shares advance or retreat on the New York Exchange, Dow Jones flashes half-hourly bulletins to other exchanges and to brokers' offices all over the continent, and abroad. The common answer to the question, "How's the market?" is to offer the current Dow quotation. A typical press report (spring 1983) reads: "The Dow Jones industrial average was up 7.11 points to 1,196.11. It held that gain throughout afternoon trading."

A warning note: the stock market is a very complex thing and the Dow figures are merely indicators. Experts disagree fundamentally over the significance of some of the major movements. When "the Dow" shows an advance, it may be merely signaling a "secondary" (temporary) reverse of a general (or "primary") decline.

As is often pointed out, if the indications were precise and unmistakable, everybody would be either buying or selling at the same time! Both the Toronto and Montreal exchanges, and other agencies, issue their own sets of averages or indexes which can also be used to judge the psychological moment to buy or sell to advantage.

The stock exchanges put out a daily sheet giving the prices of stocks traded during that business day plus a handy monthly summary of the market—you can usually pick up a free copy from the office of any broker.

If you are dealing through a sizable broker or investment dealer (or if your small-town broker has "a connection" with a major brokerage house in the city), you should arrange to pick up a package of the firm's research work that has been published over the previous few months. If you want to determine whether these papers meet your information needs, use the following check list:

(1) Does the material report on the outlook for the economy in general, on industry groups and on specific companies?

(2) Does the research comment on the quality of companies on which you have decided to fulfill your investment objectives?

(3) Do publications appear regularly, and does the firm continue the coverage of stocks over a long period?

Trying to beat inflation

If we accept that the Canadian dollar was worth 100 cents in 1971, in 1983 (when this was revised) it was worth only 36 cents. As prices and incomes race against each other, they create an economic pattern we call *inflation*. Every government would dearly love to pass a law that would prohibit inflation. However, the roots of the problem lie deep in the world's economic system. We will leave the experts to battle with their large-scale problems and concentrate on how the small investor can best prevent the erosion of his estate.

There are two broad approaches to countering the ravages of inflation. The first is to look for "an inflationary hedge;" the second is to seek a return from conventional securities that will compensate for the projected rate of inflation.

An inflationary hedge could consist of, for example, the shares of one or more companies in the space-travel business, bought not primarily for the dividends they may earn but because they seem certain to increase in value in the future.

For an investment to constitute an effective inflationary hedge, it will have to show a rate of value increase at least equal to the rate of decrease in the dollar value.

If your space-travel stock is not paying any dividends yet, the rate of anticipated increase must be high enough to compensate for the lack of current income—such as would be available, say, from bond interest—from the money you have tied up. And this is the rub. Gold was considered a fine inflationary hedge in the years immediately following World War II, but its value did not increase until the late '60s. The man who bought it as a hedge even as late as the early '60s would have great difficulty showing that he made money, even allowing for the subsequent upward revaluation of gold. A realistic accounting would show that he received no current income for a number of years and, in fact, had to pay storage costs while he held the commodity.

There is a theory in financial circles that investors should shoot for a rate of return of between three and four percent for long-term capital investment, excluding any consideration of inflation. The difference between this level of return and the current rate of yield for long-term government bonds is the amount of premium needed to compensate for inroads of inflation. Anyone following this system would be demanding a higher rate of return from his portfolio than can currently be found in many industrial bonds or "blue chip" preferred stocks. Even the investor who did manage to place his funds at the theoretically correct figure could still fail to meet his objective if his projection of the long-term rate of inflation was too low; however, he would probably at least be receiving a satisfactory rate of current income.

Is investing in common shares the best inflationary hedge? No matter what the circumstances, you get a higher rate of return from an equity investment (stocks) than from a long-term fixed-income investment (bonds, mortgages and loans) because the risks are greater.

The values of common stock have generally fared well during periods of moderate inflation because corporations are able to pass on cost-price increases quickly in the form of increased selling prices, thus adding the rate of inflation to their rate of profit growth. During periods of severe inflation, however, the average manufacturing or trading company is unable to pass on a large proportion of its cost increases and thus profits are squeezed, causing an overall decline in profits that leads, in turn, to a drop in the price of the stock.

The simple answer for the beginning investor is that while common stocks may be your best bet, they are only a hedge against inflation some of the time. The core reason for investing in equities is that, if chosen well, they should give you a superior long-term return combined with their dividend yield. Of course, this assumes that the company concerned will prosper and expand—if not in size, then at least in profitability. In the stock market, nothing is certain, except death, taxes and, it must be added, inflation.

Strange animals in the market

As in most other complex fields of human endeavor, the stock market has developed its own specialized language. Some of the terms commonly used in this jargon can frustrate the novice trying to penetrate the mysteries of the financial pages of the newspapers. Several of these are explained in the glossary of legal terms in the closing pages of this book, but they are so widely used that the conscientious beginner must make the effort to grasp

Woman in the market

MONEY HAS NO GENDER, and there's little sentiment in business (perhaps none at all). The gentler sex will be treated just as roughly as the other kind when they have invested savings or a legacy in the stock market. It's probable that the woman venturing into a broker's office will be steered resolutely into the safest of "blue chip" securities, but male courtesy (or chauvinism) stops about there.

There are, of course, female professionals in investment counseling and career women in other securities-related appointments who don't require any special treatment, thank you. But a majority of women still concern themselves with the important tasks of home and family, leaving most business matters to their husbands. It is often not until the arrival of widowhood, early or late, that they begin to look acquisitively at the stock market. Either they have inherited a portfolio of shares or bonds, or insurance benefits must be sensibly invested for income or growth.

Any woman who is determined to grasp the fundamentals of investing for profit can send for simplified brochures from any of Canada's six stock exchanges, or ask for beginners' publications at the offices of the large brokerage houses. Lectures by local investment counselors are often offered at community colleges or CEGEPs, or as university extension courses.

When Colleen Moore, one of the most famous of the early movie stars, married a partner of the Merrill Lynch securities firm he soon realized that, although she had earned more than a million dollars before age 25, she couldn't even balance her chequebook. He set out to give her a personal course in investment. More than 30 years later—and considerably richer— the one-time sweetheart of the silent screen wrote a book (*How Women Can Make Money in the Stock Market*) to report just how well she had learned her lessons. It is both shrewd and sensible, and often warmly witty.

Miss Moore believes that women approach the stock market—and most other things, too—in a different spirit than do men, but that anyone with fourth-grade arithmetic can do all the figuring necessary. And, as she says, nobody has ever made a fortune in the market solely because he (or she) was a whiz at math.

them at the outset if he is to safeguard his position.

BULLS AND BEARS. When the prices of shares of stock are generally in a strong upward trend, the market is described as being a "bull" market; conversely, when they are collapsing, it is described as being a "bear" market. A person who operates on the stock market in expectation of a rise, or in order to effect a rise, in share prices is said to be "bullish"; on the other hand, one who expects or wants a decline is said to be "bearish." He will be called a "bull" or a "bear" in each of these situations respectively. The origin of these expressions is unknown but they are the most broadly used and understood colloquialisms of the marketplace.

BOARD OR ODD LOTS. To help the investor gain a clear impression of the value of a given stock (because fractions require extra arithmetic), and to speed up trading, stock exchanges establish a quantitative category, normally called a *board lot*, for shares being traded. This generally represents the number of shares most frequently traded as a package—for instance, 100 shares is a common "lot." In some categories (mining stocks, for example), a board lot is frequently 500; while in others (high-priced industrials, for example), it may consist of only ten shares.

The *odd lot* is a block of shares that is not classified as a board lot; these lots are always traded in multiples of five shares.

The *broken lot* is a block of shares that is neither a board lot nor an odd lot; in other words, consisting of between one and four shares, six and nine shares, etc.

The stockbroker will charge a slightly increased commission for buying and selling odd or broken lots because they are more difficult to place on the market. For instance, he may have to combine the broken lots of several client-investors to form a standard board lot in order to attract a buyer.

THE POINT. You will frequently hear that this or that share is "up a point" or "down half a point." What a *point* is exactly depends on the price of the stock that is being traded. It usually means one dollar, except that if the price of a share is quoted in cents, it will mean one cent.

If bonds are under discussion, a point will mean $1 if the face value of the bond is $100; however, if the value of the bond is $1,000, the experts calculate a point as one percent of the bond, or $10.

PUT AND CALL. If you were to read *put* as "sell" and *call* as "buy," these terms that refer basically to options in the stock market would probably be less confusing. A *put* is an option to sell shares at a certain price; a *call* is the same thing on the buyer's side. These option contracts last for certain lengths of time—usually 30, 60 or 90 days. And the contract becomes void if the option is not exercised within the set time period. In this specialized form of trading, the speculator, hoping he can judge market fluctuations in advance, might get an option to buy or sell a large amount of stock at a favorable price.

Puts and calls are also used by large investors trying to hedge their "long" or "short" positions. More jargon. An investor can be described as *long* when he owns securities. For instance, if he said he was "long 1,000 in Moon Charters Ltd.," he would be announcing, in effect, that he had 1,000 shares of the company—and he would possibly consider an offer to purchase. An investor is said to be *short* if he has sold shares he doesn't own and will have to buy or borrow them by the deadline date to meet his commitment.

BUYING ON MARGIN. Not an avenue normally open to the novice, margin buying basically means purchasing stock partly on credit provided by your stockbroker. Before you can buy shares *on margin*, you must enter into a written agreement with your broker. The margin itself is the difference between the market value of the shares pledged as security for the loan and the amount of credit outstanding.

At least 50 percent margin (sometimes 60 percent or more, depending on the price of the shares and the credit standing of the client) is generally required by a broker to maintain a margin account. Stock Exchange authorities may also step in at any time and cancel, or alter, margin requirements.

If the level of margin is not maintained because of market fluctuations, the broker will usually make a "margin call," asking the client to put up more cash, pledge more securities or sell some or all of his currently pledged stock to remedy the situation. If the client cannot be contacted immediately, or does not comply with the request, the broker can exercise his right under the margin contract to sell out the client's account. If he cannot recover the amount of his loan through the sale, his client must make up the difference.

Rights of the stockholder

The beginning investor does not normally enter the market with the idea of altering the policies of the companies he invests in. He is basically interested in dividends or long-term capital gains. This is just as well, as the rights of the small stockholder are limited. Large corporations are administered by their directors and the professional management, and it is seldom indeed that any one block of stockholders is large enough to defeat management proposals. For one thing, management often owns a controlling percentage of the company's voting stock. (*See* Chapter 13, "The public corporation.")

The stockholder, large or small, has the right to receive an annual report, to see some of the company's financial statements and to attend annual meetings. He receives, of course, any dividends, rights or stock splits that may be declared by the board of directors and, if he is a bond holder, he has, in effect, a mortgage on the company's assets.

It might be said that the most important right of the stockholder is to liquidate his holding if he disapproves of the actions of the company's management. If enough stockholders sell their shares in anger, dissatisfaction or frustration, the price of the stock is sure to drop accordingly; and a change in direction by the board of directors is predictable. In fact, as they say in the trade, "heads will roll."

The annual meeting

All incorporated companies—large or small—are required by law to hold an annual meeting. It is at this meeting that the persons who own shares of stock in the company—the stockholders—get the opportunity to criticize or praise the past conduct of the business and seek information about future plans.

Each share of common stock entitles the stockholders to one vote in the election of directors for the ensuing year.

The larger public companies advertise their annual meetings widely in the financial press and the business pages of the larger daily newspapers.

Sometimes, when large public corporations have been experiencing problems in their daily operations, the annual meeting is scheduled at an out-of-the-way location, in the hope that not too many stockholders who might ask embarrassing questions would be able to attend.

The investment club

If after reading this chapter you are still eager to enter the stock market but are uncertain of your ability to prosper on your own, you should consider joining or starting an *investment club*.

Canada has several thousand investment clubs, mostly groups of friends or business acquaintances who meet once a month and contribute perhaps $10 or $20 each to an investment pool. This money is used to buy stock selected by a committee of the club. In taking part in the selection process—and in reading the monthly reports on progress or otherwise—the member gets a practical education in investing. He might make some money, too.

As a background text, the Canadian Securities Institute has published a study course called *How to Invest in Canadian Securities*. This includes booklets on how to read financial statements, how to manage your investments, how to understand federal taxation and Canadian investments, and how to interpret the whims of the stock market. The association can be reached at Suite 360, 33 Yonge Street, Toronto, Ontario, M5E 1G4.

For further information concerning investment clubs write:

Canadian Association of Investment
    Clubs
P.O. Box 122
First Canadian Place, Suite 3700
Toronto, Ontario
M5X 1E9

9/You Can't Take it with You

Changing your will   404

When there is no will   409

How to challenge a will   414

Giving your money away

I N 1937, the Hart-Kaufman playwriting team won the Pulitzer Prize with their comedy, *You Can't Take It With You*. And the inevitable stage and radio response ever since has been: "Well, in that case, I'm not going." It is, however, difficult for a family to exhibit a sense of humor when a departed one has left his or her affairs in such a tangle that the dependents may actually be suffering instead of benefiting.

Your will may well be the most important document you ever sign. Failure to make clear and legal disposition of money or property—or failure to make a will at all, despite all the prompting of lawyers, social agencies and family friends—is one of civilized mankind's commonest faults.

Making gifts before death, and making bequests by will and testament, can turn out to be much more complicated even in an average case than the "average man" might expect. It can, of course, also be very simple. "I leave everything to Jane Canuck" would probably stand up, even if scribbled on wrapping paper. But the point is that human affairs are seldom simple. Most of us live in a web of complications, even if we don't realize it.

The printed will form available at stationers can cause serious trouble if your real wishes deviate in the slightest shade of meaning from the supplied text. Amateur wills are often worse because the layman seldom understands that the legal meaning of a word can be quite different from the everyday meaning.

It is true that when a man thinks about leaving this earth he has the right to determine what is to happen to the possessions he leaves behind—but even in this, most provincial legislation insists that he allow "proper maintenance and support" for dependents and possibly even other close family members.

Although there is no such provision under Quebec law, proposed revisions of the province's civil code may allow the courts to award the family residence and household furniture to a surviving spouse.

Throughout Canada, the courts will disallow frivolous, humiliating or insulting bequests, or bequests "not in the public interest."

When the sums of money involved are substantial, consideration should be given to the setting up of trusts. In this way arrangements can be made for the wisest use of legacies.

Trusts may be used to minimize succession duties in Quebec. According to information available at this writing, Quebec was the only province where these duties, as well as gift taxes, were still being imposed. In all other provinces, succession duty and gift tax had been abolished completely.

The best course for you, sooner rather than later, is to call on a lawyer (or alternatively, in Quebec, a notary) and make a will—even if it should be the only occasion in a lifetime that you enter a legal office. Anyone—even the dashing young bachelor or swinging secretary—can die unexpectedly. Husband and wife often travel together in high-speed cars or planes and sometimes die together in accidents.

The cost of making a will is moderate in all provinces and the time required is normally brief. But the benefits can be tremendous, out of all proportion to the effort and expenditure. Thousands of sad stories have appeared in newspapers attesting to the truth of this.

Technique of beneficence

It is not as easy as you think to give away your money, your goods or your house, or even to be certain your gifts reach and benefit the people you intend to benefit. For instance, it makes a difference how, when and what you give.

Legally, there are two types of gifts: a gift given during the life of the giver (called the gift *inter vivos*—"between the living") and a gift of personal property by the person expecting to die within a short time after the gift is made (called a *donatio mortis causa*—"gift in expectation of death").

The first type of gift is a transfer of property with no strings attached from one person to another. The person making the gift, or donor, intends that the thing given shall not be returned; the person receiving the gift, or donee, has the same intention.

To be a valid gift *inter vivos*, the intention must be that the act of giving is final. There must be an actual transfer of the gift, or the handing over of a deed of ownership. The gift must take effect immediately and there must be acceptance by the recipient. If an unexpected gift is made, it can still be valid provided that when the donee is informed about the gift, he accepts it.

To be a valid gift *mortis causa*, it must be made by the donor at a time when he seriously believes he is near death. That is, he must be ill and must not expect to recover. There must be actual delivery, or symbolic delivery, although the gift will take effect legally only on the death of the donor. If the donor recovers, the gift is canceled.

If the donor hands over the gift to a person other than the donee, intending

Gift by living trust

ONE WAY TO DISPOSE of some of your property while you are still living is by creating what is called a "living trust." It is a legal and efficient method of providing, for example, an income for a dependent relative, or for taking care of the education and support of a child. There are many other applications.

A living trust is a written agreement under which the donor (the person making the gift) sets apart a certain portion of his estate, giving up his own income prospects from those assets. The trustee—either a trust company or an individual—is instructed to pay the income to others, as directed.

Living trusts can be both revocable or irrevocable. Under the revocable trust, the donor reserves the right to change the terms of the trust at his discretion; he may decide to play some part in the management of the trust assets or to leave that work entirely to others.

The irrevocable living trust provides a final method of disposing of portions of your estate during your lifetime. You can, however, arrange for only the income from the trust assets to go to the donee (the receiver of the gift), while you retain the capital for a different distribution under your will.

The living trust need not be canceled by your death; it can take the place of your will as far as the specified assets are concerned. In fact, it has attractive economical aspects in this role as no probate would be required, and no extra executor's fees or expenses. Also, the gift would remain concealed from the public gaze.

In a further variation of the living trust, a person whose health becomes impaired and who no longer wishes to continue the management of his property (either securities, royalties or real estate) can create a trust under which all the income is payable to himself for the rest of his lifetime, then upon his death is payable to stated beneficiaries.

that the other person should deliver the gift to the donee, and that "middle man" agrees, this is considered to be valid delivery. If it was the intention of the donor to make an outright gift, it cannot be considered *mortis causa*. A gift made by a person who is considering suicide is not valid under this law.

In most provinces, for both *inter vivos* and *mortis causa* gifts, it is essential that delivery be made. The problem with this is that "delivery" can be hard to define legally. Many cases have been contested in the courts as to what actually constitutes delivery.

With land, there is no difficulty because the property obviously changes hands with a deed. In the case of movable property where physical control has been handed over to the donee and the donee has accepted, there is no problem because there has been delivery. The gift is not invalidated if the recipient returns it to the donor for safekeeping.

A problem can arise where the gift is bulky and difficult to actually deliver. Objects such as a large trunk, a desk or a locked bureau have been ruled by some courts to have been "delivered" simply by the delivery of the key to the object. There is difficulty, for instance, in establishing that delivery has been made where a husband gives his wife all the furniture in the house.

In Quebec, an *inter vivos* gift is valid if both parties consent, and delivery is unnecessary. Deciding whether a bankbook, cheque, or promissory note is a gift depends on whether the donor has shown his intention of giving up ownership of the thing.

In other provinces, certain precedents dealing with particular gifts have been set in the courts. Certain types of bank books—the type that it is necessary to produce before money can be withdrawn—have been ruled to be gifts of money.

However, the giving of the ordinary chequing account passbook has been ruled not to be valid delivery. The giving of a cheque is not in itself a gift of the sum of money written on it because the cheque must be presented for payment before there can be considered legal delivery. An important point to remember is that uncashed cheques can be invalidated by the death of the signer. Neither is the giving of a promissory note a legal gift. The placing of money in a joint account where the person who shares the account is neither a child nor a spouse is not a gift but, in effect, a trust—although further evidence might show that it was "intended" to be a gift.

When a gift is not a gift

When land is purchased in the name of another, then the law does not presume it is a gift; this, the law says, smacks of making a trust. This interpretation would not stick, however, if you can provide satisfactory evidence that a gift was intended. When a wife makes a payment of money or goods to her husband, a gift is not presumed. Yet there is a presumption, in such a case, of a trust (which can be successfully rebutted by clear evidence that a gift was intended). On the other hand, in the common law provinces, a payment of money or the putting of land in the name of your spouse has long been presumed to be a gift. However, since 1975 in Ontario, the presumption of gift between husband and wife has been abolished. Now, if either spouse transfers money or land into the name of the other, the law presumes that a trust in favor of the donor was intended (which, of course, can be rebutted by evidence).

To this rule, there are two exceptions: (1) Money deposited in an account in the name of both spouses shall be deemed to be held by them as joint tenants; (2) Property transferred to both spouses jointly is presumed to be held by them as joint tenants—and when one of two joint tenants dies, the survivor becomes the sole owner.

Prince Edward Island has a Family Reform Law, which has provisions similar to those in the Ontario law. Other provinces are believed to be considering comparable legislation. Anyone involved in or contemplating such husband-and-wife property arrangements will be wise to consult a lawyer. Quebec has always had different rules about the property relations of husband and wife. (*See* Chapter 10, "Community of Property.")

A gift made by a minor can be reclaimed at the option of the minor. Once the minor becomes an adult he can still take back the gift, if he acts promptly.

A gift *inter vivos* is irrevocable and could only be overturned by the courts because of undue influence or duress. In such cases, a judge would first decide whether the donor intended to make the gift, or if the gift was really the result of pressure from the person to whom the gift was made. The relationships between people which could raise the possibility of undue influence include those between guardian and ward, solicitor and client, as well as doctor and patient.

In the case of pressure having been exerted, the court would set aside the gift unless it was proved that it was voluntarily given under circumstances which enabled the donor to exercise his own judgment.

A *donatio mortis causa* will always be reversed by law if (1) the donor requests the property back, (2) he recovers from his illness, or (3) the impending danger of death passes. In cases of undue influence, a judge would first have to decide whether the donor intended to make the gift, or if the gift was really the result of pressure from the person to whom the gift was made.

If they are requested, gifts made to a girl upon her engagement to be married must, usually, be returned if she breaks off the engagement. In some instances, this may include the engagement ring (*See* Chapter 10, "The engagement"). Even furniture bought with money given by the future bridegroom for a future house, or for a house which is already owned, is normally recoverable by him.

The whimsical will of Williston Fish

IN 1898, Harper's New Monthly Magazine—ancestor of today's Harper's—published the imaginary will of one Charles Lounsbury. It was written by Williston Fish and disposed of the testator's "interests in the world" in such an appealing fashion that it became a literary favorite. Brief excerpts follow:

"I leave to children exclusively all the dandelions and daisies of the field with the right to play among them freely, warning them at the same time against the thistles.

". . . I leave to children the yellow shores of creeks and the golden sands beneath the waters, with the dragonflies that skim the surface and the white clouds that float high over the giant trees. . . .

"I leave to boys all the fields and commons where ball may be played, and all snowclad hills where one may coast, and all streams and ponds where one may skate. . . . And all the woods with their squirrels and birds and echoes and strange noises. . . .

"To young men, I bequeath all boisterous, inspiring sports of rivalry. I give to them the disdain of weakness and undaunted confidence in their own strength. . . . I leave to them alone the power of making lasting friendships and of possessing companions, and to them exclusively I give all merry songs. . . .

"To lovers, I leave their imaginary world, the stars of the sky, the red roses by the wall, the snow of the hawthorn, the sweet strains of music, and everything else they may desire to tell each other of the lastingness and beauty of their love.

"To those who are no longer children, youths or lovers, I leave memory, the poems of Burns and Shakespeare, so that they may live the old days over freely and fully, and the knowledge of what a rare, rare world it is."

Gift tax in Quebec

As of January 1, 1972, the federal government stopped taxing gifts and started taxing capital gains. By the 1980s, only Quebec continued to impose a gift tax. The single rate of 20 percent was applied to all gifts made in Quebec after April 19, 1978, subject to deductions and exemptions allowed under provincial legislation. At this writing, the maximum tax exemption for a person receiving a gift was $5,000, and the total annual exemption on gifts made by an individual was $25,000.

What this means is that a person could give gifts of $5,000 each to five persons in each and every year without paying any gift tax on those gifts. The donor could give, say $2,500 each to ten persons without paying any tax. However, once a donor gives one person more than $5,000, or his donations in the year exceed $25,000, a gift tax is payable, levied only on the amount of the excess. For example, if the donor gives $6,000 to one person in the year, then only $1,000 of that is taxable.

In Quebec, certain gifts are completely exempt from gift tax:

(1) gifts made in contemplation of death and subject to succession duties;

(2) testamentary gifts;

(3) gifts to the Crown;

(4) gifts to municipalities;

(5) charitable gifts;

(6) small gifts ($100 or less to individual recipients a year, with no limit on the number of recipients);

(7) payments, such as maintenance, to a spouse living apart (moderate amounts are not considered as gifts);

(8) any gifts made to a spouse since April 19, 1978;

(9) renunciation by a beneficiary of an estate in favor of the spouse of the deceased when the latter died after April 18, 1978;

(10) a contribution to a spouse's Registered Retirement Savings Plan (R.R.S.P.); and, in certain cases, a gift to a trust is exempt if the beneficiary is the spouse.

The Quebec gift-tax legislation makes the donor responsible for the filing of an income tax return only if gift tax is payable or if it is "demanded" by the provincial government.

Succession duty in Quebec

Quebec is the only province that imposes succession duty, although some modifications to this tax have been proposed. Under Quebec legislation, if a donor gives a gift and dies within five years of making that gift, it is deemed that the value of that gift for succession-duty purposes (that is, a tax on succession of property to beneficiaries, those who receive something under a will) be added to the estate of the deceased donor.

As the Quebec Succession Duty Act now stands, the majority of estates are not taxable, so that if the gift is received on the donor's death, then no tax is paid. However, if the donor makes a gift before his death, he may pay a substantial tax. In this event, the beneficiary may deduct from his payable succession duties either gift taxes that have already been levied, or the succession duties still owing on the property, whichever is less.

In Quebec, a farmer can make a gift of property used in the operation of a farm or a gift of shares in a corporation which has a revenue mainly derived from agriculture. Under the Succession Duty Act, these gifts are tax free, as long as the value of the property or shares does not exceed $300,000.

Support payments as gifts

Since an absolute and irrevocable gift made by husband to wife (except a gift made by the creation of a settlement) is exempt from tax, so support payments made to a wife are also exempt from tax. We have said that, in Quebec, a donor can make a gift of up to $5,000 a year to any one person without paying a special tax. Therefore, a gift to a child of $5,000 or less will not be taxed, and this would apply equally to a gift made to a person's parents.

In a situation where husband and wife are legally separated and the husband is making support payments to the wife or children, then the husband—as well as being relieved from Quebec gift tax—may get relief on his income tax if, in making the payments, certain conditions are fulfilled. The conditions which would have to be met are: (1) the amount must be paid as the result of a decree, order, judgment or written agreement; (2) the amount must be paid for the support of the other spouse or children or of both spouse and children; (3) the payment must be periodic, that is, not a one-time or lump-sum payment. The same conditions apply to support of a divorcee. All support payments to a wife or an ex-wife are subject to income tax by the recipient.

Setting up a family trust

One definition of a trust is "a confidence reposed in another for the performance of a particular act or acts for the benefit of a beneficiary." In order to create a valid trust, three conditions must be fulfilled: (1) there must be clear and definite intention to create a trust; (2) what is being given must be clearly defined; (3) the object of the trust must be clearly defined. The subject matter of a trust may be land, money, or almost anything. The object, or purpose, must be defined very precisely to avoid uncertainty. As to the intention of a trust, it is enough that actions and words are such that anyone can clearly understand that the creation of a trust was intended.

Since gift tax in Quebec will be imposed on a trust where the amount of money given to the trust exceeds $5,000, the person who establishes a trust (a *settlor*) will begin the trust with $5,000 or less if he wishes to avoid gift tax. Every succeeding year the settlor would give $5,000 or a lesser amount to the trust, thus continuing to avoid gift tax.

The trust document would appoint a trustee, simply the person in whom the confidence is put, and would establish who the beneficiaries would be. The trust document would also establish how the proceeds of the trust are to be distributed. For example, the document might say: "The trustees shall invest and keep invested the trust fund and subject to the provisions here and after appearing shall accumulate and add to the capital of the trust fund the net annual income derived

What are you worth?

WHEN WAS the last time you sat down with a pencil, paper and your personal records to figure out, to the nearest dollar, what you are worth?

Most of us have a hazy idea of the value of our personal property—house, bank balance, automobile—but, according to estate planners, very few of us keep anything approaching an accurate record of our net financial position and even fewer keep that record up to date. This task should be considered essential.

There is, then, a hidden bonus when you decide to draw up a will: the first thing you will do is find out just what you've got to leave!

When they sit down with an estate specialist to draw up a personal balance sheet (assets minus liabilities), many middle-aged people find out with surprise and pleasure that they are better off than they thought.

Your estate is the total amount of your assets, less any debts.

There's your house and maybe a summer cottage (increasing in value year by year), all other property (including any antiques, stamp or coin collections), investments, pension funds, life insurance, cash on hand, accounts receivable (money owed to you).

If you should happen to be killed at work or in an automobile or aircraft accident, other sizable sums could accrue to your estate depending upon what insurance coverage you have.

A magazine poll showed that four out of every seven adults questioned had done absolutely nothing at all about planning their estates.

People never want to die intestate (that is, without making a will); it's just that death seems to come at an inconvenient time!

therefrom until the beneficiary attains the age of 18."

The trust document should also outline the powers that the trustee has in investing the money. These powers might, perhaps, restrict him to investment in gilt-edged securities, or government bonds only. If no restriction is listed, then the trustee is limited to the powers of investment found in the relevant trustee act. It may be unwise in properly managing an estate-in-trust for the trustee to be pinned down so tightly that he cannot adapt to changing conditions. If you don't trust his judgment, then don't appoint him as trustee. He may need power to mortgage or pledge all or part of a trust fund. He may have to borrow money from the trust fund for any good purpose at terms that he might feel are acceptable at the time. He might also need flexibility in altering payments under the trust, should unforeseen conditions arise.

The income-tax law relating to trusts is complicated, and a capital-gains tax might have to be paid on the gift to the trust. Because of the technical nature of a trust document, and because of gift and income taxes, it is plain common sense to consult both an accountant and a lawyer before attempting to enter into a trust.

Legal place of dwelling

When a will concerns land and the building on that land, the form of the will, as well as its intrinsic validity and effect, must be governed by the law of the place where the real estate is situated. This means that a bequest of real estate which might not be valid according to Canadian law could be valid according to the law of the country where the real estate is situated. It should always be remembered that a will concerning land abroad—even though the will is made by a person living in Canada—must dispose of the land according to the law of the place where the land is located.

As far as personal property is concerned, the law of all the provinces seems to say that a will made outside of the province is valid if its form complies with the law of the place where it was made. This is also true if the will was made

according to the law of the place where the testator had his domicile (generally, the place where the testator stayed with the intention of residing permanently) when it was made. That part of the will relating to personal estate is interpreted, and the personal estate is administered, according to the law of the place where the testator had his official domicile at the date of death, unless the testator indicates otherwise. Thus, if a foreigner dies while domiciled in Manitoba, his will—as far as personal property is concerned—must be administered according to the law of Manitoba, no matter where it was made. On the other hand, if you are domiciled abroad, the law of the foreign domicile governs the validity of the dispositions of your will at your death.

If a person domiciled in Quebec marries in Quebec without a settlement—so that the Quebec law of partnership of acquests (property acquired during marriage) applies—the effect is that he has executed a marriage settlement according to the law of Quebec. The result of this is that when he dies, whether domiciled in another province or not, he cannot dispose of his personal property in such a way as to interfere with his wife's rights under the Quebec law.

By the wills acts in all of the ten Canadian provinces, if a person changes his domicile after making his will, this change of domicile does not affect the validity of the will.

Donations to charities

You can give as much money as you like to any registered nonprofit charitable or educational institution without having to pay any gift tax. Your generosity might even result in your name being placed on the cornerstone of a library or on a hospital wing. Before you get carried away by thoughts of immortality, however, remember that even a promise to make a gift can have legal force in certain circumstances—for instance, in cases where the institution incurs certain obligations while relying on the promise of a gift.

The Quebec Succession Duty Act allows a bequest to charity to be made in your will without payment of duty. Also, under the Quebec law, there is no duty on legacies, gifts and subscriptions for religious, charitable or educational purposes.

Some difficulty has arisen over the years in defining exactly what a charitable organization is, and certain standards have been laid down. For example, the Quebec provincial government has set guidelines in its Taxation Act that are applicable under succession law. The provincial government also provides a list of organizations that qualify as worthwhile charities.

In general, where a gift or bequest helps to advance the ideas of religion or education, gives relief from poverty, or is for the public benefit, then—generally speaking—the bequest or gift is considered to be charitable. It would be wise, however, before leaving your money to that "Home for Retired Television Viewers" to check that the organization getting the bequest is truly charitable in the legal sense. For example, there was a case in Britain where a woman donated part of her estate to an antivivisection society. This organization opposes the dissection of animals for research purposes. The court ruled that since research work on animals was approved by the government, the gift to the society could not be considered as being in the public interest. Therefore, the antivivisection society was not considered a legal charity and succession duty had to be paid.

A gift to the Queen

Land, buildings, valuable paintings and other art objects, securities or hard cash given "to the Queen"—that is to "the Crown representing the public"—are exempt from gift tax. The gift can be made to Canada, to any province or municipality. In this way, some large and valuable private properties are saved from forced sale, and are transformed into public property of recreational, scenic and cultural importance.

Ten tips for a well-drawn will

WHEN WILLIAM SHAKESPEARE sat down to make his will, on March 25, 1616, he sharpened his quill and wrote:

"I gyve unto my wiefe, my second-best bed with its furniture . . . ."

You might be disposed to be more generous than the immortal bard, and your estate is probably more complex, but you must share with him the preliminary task of deciding exactly what your will should contain. Individual requirements naturally alter circumstances, but the following list will provide a general guide to the clauses of a well-drawn will:

(1) A revocation of all previous wills.

(2) Appointment of an executor, to act alone or in conjunction with a trust company.

(3) Disposal of goods, real estate, business, investments.

(4) Special bequests to friends, associates or charities.

(5) What to do with anything that's left.

(6) Naming of a guardian for your children in case you and your wife die while they are still legal infants.

(7) If trusts are set up providing income for children or others, can the executor (or trustee) dispose of any capital under any circumstances?

(8) Perhaps give the trustee the power to continue operating your business until the right time comes to sell.

(9) Can the trustee reinvest available funds, when required, in securities other than those designated by law as trustee securities?

(10) Proper "attestation" by witnesses confirming that the testator signed the will in their presence.

Last will and testament

Testamentary intent

Being of sound mind

Duress or undue influence

Widow's dower

Irrational or unreasonable

Holograph and notarial wills

A WILL is a document in which a testator (the person who has made a will) gives away property after his death that he owned during his lifetime. As the word implies, the "will" is a command—a formal and conscious instruction that must be carried out. Since the person who made the will cannot be there to explain the intention of the language of the document, the courts place great emphasis on the exactness of the wording. For example, the word "dependents" is too vague. The misspelling of a name may cost a dear friend his legacy. Making a will is a serious business.

Furthermore, the law can be complicated when it comes to interpreting the formalities of a will. In some cases, a will must conform to the law of the place where it was made, or with the law of the place where the testator was domiciled when it was made. At other times, the will must be made according to the law of the testator's place of domicile at the time of his death.

If the will is giving away real estate which is outside the testator's province or country of residence, then it must conform with the laws of the province or country where the real estate is situated. (This legal principle is valid in all provinces, except Quebec.)

In some cases, a will must be signed by the testator at the end of the document. The signing must be in the presence of at least two witnesses. They "attest" the will—that is, they confirm that it was signed properly in the presence of each other and of the testator. This does not involve the witnesses in any of the provisions of the will; they are merely acknowledging that they know the testator

and that they watched him sign the document. If the testator (testatrix if a woman) is physically incapable of signing the will, then another person can sign his own name in the presence of the testator (the witnesses being present as well), with that other person's signature being specially acknowledged by the testator as being valid.

The age when you are considered to be capable of making a valid will varies from province to province. Most provinces have special provisions for young soldiers on active service, as well as sailors at sea, to make valid wills. In general, the provinces also permit members of the Armed Forces to make wills with fewer formalities than are required of civilians.

In Alberta, a testator cannot make a will if he is under the age of 18, except if he is a minor who is a member of the Armed Forces, or a sailor at sea.

The law in British Columbia is similar to that of Alberta, except that a resident must be 19 to make a valid will. British Columbia also permits a testator to place his signature opposite to, at or after, the end of the will as long as it is apparent that the testator intended that what is written in the will is what he wanted done. Under British Columbia's laws, a military man in service or at sea can make a will signed by him or by someone in his presence as long as at least one other person is there to sign and attest to his intent.

Most provinces, except Newfoundland, will recognize an Armed Forces will even if it is not witnessed.

In Ontario, anyone 19 or older can make a will following the normal formalities, subject to the Armed Forces exemptions. Moreover, the province has special provisions for younger persons who are already married, as well as for those who are contemplating marriage and prepared to specify their intention, to make a legal will.

In Quebec, the testator must be 18 years of age. The testator has the choice of a notarial will, a will in the English form, or a holograph will that can be written and signed by the testator without witnessing signatures. A notarial will is made before either two notaries or one notary and two witnesses. The English form of will must be signed in the presence of two witnesses. In both instances, the witnesses must be at least 18, and they must not be related to the notary, or an employe of the notary. Moreover, in Quebec, the two witnesses must not be married to each other.

The Nova Scotia wills act follows the general pattern of other provinces, but the testator has to be 19, unless a soldier or seaman.

In New Brunswick, a will made by a minor is valid if he is married, or if he is a soldier or a seaman. But for others, the age is 19.

The law of Newfoundland allows any person of 17 to make a will, so long as it is done in the presence of two witnesses.

In the Yukon, a testator must be 21, unless he is a member of the Armed Forces or the R.C.M.P., or if he is a mariner on a sea voyage.

In all provinces, a wife may act as a witness to her husband's will—but she seldom does. In most provinces, she would forfeit any bequests made to her in the will. Ontario is an exception in this instance, because the bequest would be considered void if the court was satisfied that there was no undue influence or improper interference exercised upon the testator.

Testamentary intent

A will must disclose the *intention* of the testator as to how his property is to be disposed of. Even if a testator wrote the word "Will" at the top of a document, this does not guarantee that the document would be accepted as his last will and testament. The testamentary nature of a document that is executed in the presence of two witnesses, as the wills acts of most provinces insist, will probably not be questioned.

Testamentary intention comes into play in those provinces that allow handwritten, unwitnessed wills, as well as wills made by seamen and servicemen.

Let a lawyer handle it

In all the provinces of Canada, property left by a person who dies "without a will"—what the law refers to as "dying intestate"—or whose will is declared void or invalid by the courts, is distributed to his next of kin according to rigid legal regulations.

For example, a man in Ontario with a wife and two children might leave an estate with assets worth $78,000. The wife may be well-to-do in her own right, and the children married and struggling to get along. The man may leave a will bequeathing $25,000 to each child and the remainder to his wife. However, if his will had been drawn up wrongly or carelessly, the courts would declare it invalid and, under Ontario's Succession Law Reform Act, could grant the widow a preferential maximum amount of $75,000 when there are offspring surviving. The children could be left to split the remaining $3,000.

This kind of situation is more common than one might imagine and provides merely one of many good reasons why you should go to a lawyer to make sure your will is properly written and executed—that is, both properly signed and witnessed.

Certain words may have one meaning to you but quite another meaning in the law. For example, the word "children" may, in a testator's mind, include his grandchildren. But the law clearly states that "children" means just the testator's own children and excludes grandchildren. "Money" might mean stocks and bonds and mortgages and jewels to the testator because he considers these things as money (or its equivalent), yet the actual legal definition of money is considerably narrower. A lawyer is well aware of the correct words to use and the legal values attached to words by the courts. He will guide his client in choosing the correct words for his will.

The solicitor, for instance, might suggest that you add one simple paragraph that could save the estate a double set of succession duties. He might suggest some items that will allow for changes in the future—perhaps the birth of another child.

Cost is no reason to postpone the making of your will. Most legal tariffs (*See* Chapter 20, "How the lawyer is paid") provide for a modest fee, starting at approximately $50 for a simple will. Just remember that the financial penalty for leaving a will that isn't legal (or none at all) can add up to thousands.

Being of sound mind

It is felt that the state of a man's memory is the standard by which a testator's ability to make a will is judged. The law states that no person of "unsound mind" can make a will. But the obvious question is: at what point in law does the mind become "unsound"?

The law answers that the testator must understand the nature of what he is doing by his acts and the effects of those acts. This means that he must know the extent of the property which he is disposing of and he must fully understand to what

purposes he is trying to assign that property. No insane delusion should influence a testator to make bequests that he would not have made if his mind had been sound. Furthermore, the testator's memory must be such that when he is making his bequests, he understands his moral obligation and the effect of his decisions. A person may suffer from delusions, but may still make a valid will if the delusions do not affect the general faculties of his mind.

If a man gives instructions for the preparation of his will while he is of sound mind and if he becomes ill before he can sign it, it is only necessary that he realize when he is signing the document that he did give his solicitor instructions to prepare the will and that he now is accepting the document presented to him as the will which was prepared according to his instructions.

Being of "unsound mind" can arise from such causes as drunkenness (at the time of the making of the will) or senility, and also from actual mental illness.

If relatives can prove that a testator was of "unsound mind," the will can be declared invalid. However, the court may take a lot of convincing, especially if those relatives stand to gain by such a declaration.

Someone who is blind, deaf and mute or illiterate, has every right to make a will

The dangers of "do-it-yourself"

ALTHOUGH the simplest of handwritten, unwitnessed wills can be accepted by the courts in most of the provinces, it is a riskier procedure than Russian roulette. It is not as easy as it may seem to leave property to the person you wish to have it. Many cases could be quoted of estates sadly reduced by the ruinous legal costs incurred in untangling amateur testaments in the courts. Lord Charles Neaves, a Victorian lawyer with a taste for light-hearted verse, wrote this amusing thank-you for "do-it-yourself" wills:

Ye lawyers who live upon litigants'
fees,

And who need a good many to live at
your ease,

When a festive occasion your spirit
unbends,

You should never forget the Profession's
best friends;

So we'll send round the wine and bright
bumper fill,

To the jolly testator who makes his own
will.

as long as the document mentions his disability and shows that he understood and approved the content.

Duress or undue influence

A will can be declared invalid if it was made under duress, undue influence or fraud. (This has nothing to do with affection, gratitude or attachment to a person.) Duress or undue influence applies only when the testator is actually forced to make a will and that document expresses not his own wishes but those of the person who is forcing him to write the will with specific provisions. For instance, if a man was living with an overbearing sister and he made a will favoring his sister at his sister's insistence (perhaps to obtain peace and quiet for himself), then such a will might possibly be declared invalid on the grounds of undue influence. But if he left a fortune to a buxom bunny-girl at a nightclub for favors she may or may not have given, the will could be difficult to upset.

The widow's dower

Widow's dower is an old-fashioned term carrying over from the English law by which a wife, after her husband dies, is automatically left with a life interest in part or all of his property. As the term "life interest" implies, the property goes back to the husband's estate when the widow dies. In Canada, there are only two provinces where some form of dower remains in existence—Alberta and Manitoba. Elsewhere, dower acts have been abolished or repealed.

In Alberta, upon the death of any married person in that province, the surviving spouse has a life interest in "the homestead." "Homestead" is defined to mean: (1) land in a city, town or village consisting of not more than four adjoining lots in one block, and elsewhere a quarter section of land; in each case land on which the house occupied by the owner is situated; and (2) the personal property of the deceased that is declared in the Exemptions Act to be free from seizure under a writ of execution in his lifetime.

The dower act of Manitoba defines "homestead" in fairly similar terms to those used in Alberta. The Manitoba law entitles the widow to a life interest in the homestead. Where she has not already been left one-third of the estate, she is entitled to this in addition to the homestead. Under this law, a husband has similar rights.

In the two provinces with dower laws, anyone buying land from a man—even if that man is sole owner—must be sure to get the wife's signature on the deed of sale as well. Otherwise, on the death of the seller, the wife could claim her dower rights to the land and, for the rest of her life, could claim one-third of any rents or income from the land.

Where dower is law, the same right grants a man a life interest in all his deceased wife's real estate.

Remarriage of the widow

An outright gift to a wife made by a husband in his will gives the property to her absolutely. If she decides to remarry, the property cannot be taken away from her. Some husbands believe that their wives will need all the estate for as long as they remain widowed; but they feel that, should the wife remarry, the new husband should take care of her, and the bequeathed money should then go elsewhere. In order to do this, a man may state in his will that the estate is to be left to the wife for her lifetime, or until she should remarry.

Mandatory provisions

Only in Quebec does a testator still have the right to "cut off" family members from a will. However, even there, the surviving spouse has some specific rights. For example, under the provision of the Civil Code, the courts may allocate the family residence and household furniture to the surviving spouse. At the time of this writing, Quebec was considering a revision of the statutes to make them more consistent with the law elsewhere in the country.

In all other provinces, the law demands that the testator make dispositions in a will to satisfy certain legitimate claims which dependents might have against an estate. These claims are usually amounts that are no greater than what the dependents would receive if the testator had died "intestate"—that is, without leaving a will.

Under the Ontario Succession Law Reform Act, a judge can rule that a sum of money is to be set aside out of the estate to maintain the testator's dependents. (*See* Chapter 3, "Judges and courts.")

This statute is adhered to literally and its provisions are strictly observed, even though their application overrules a testa-

tor's right to do what he wishes with his property.

In provinces other than Ontario the authority for decisions in dependents' relief cases rests with the provincial superior courts.

In Ontario, the Succession Law Reform Act includes a number of different cases within its definition of a "dependent." The definition covers (1) a spouse (including a person whose marriage to the deceased was terminated or declared null); (2) a

Weird wills

HAVING THE FINAL WORD—and a will is literally the "last" word—gives some people an irresistible opportunity to "get even" with associates or relatives for old slights, either real or fancied. Others will show a macabre sense of humor, and more than a few will descend to petty spite and revenge.

The courts will usually disallow any humiliating or insulting bequests, or any conditions that are unduly restrictive, repellent or contrary to ordinary human dignity. Nevertheless, a will is a solemn document and a bequest will not be struck down just because it is unconventional, or even downright nutty.

By the same token, wills have been admitted to probate that were drawn up in the strangest ways. The following are actual Canadian cases:

• Disapproving his nephew's laziness, a man left $100,000 to the youth provided he spent it on wood which he then had to split and sell as firewood.

• A Toronto schoolteacher left her investments to "deserving convicts" in the penitentiary at Kingston. (The shares were worthless.)

• A Montrealer who died in 1933 chided his wife in his will for bobbing her hair and left a condition that she could not inherit until her hair was three feet long.

• Wills have been brought to the Probate Court written on table napkins, oyster shells, newspaper advertisements, a bedroom door, and a nurse's starched cuff. A Nova Scotia seaman wrote his underneath two postage stamps stuck on a letter to his fiancée.

• An Ontario hotelkeeper ordered that his funeral cortege stop at every one of 20 bars on its way to the cemetery. Drinks had to be paid for by his executor.

• Mike, a much-loved parrot in Victoria,

B.C., was left a fully furnished mansion and lifetime veterinarian care. A Chinese servant was paid to give Mike a drink of brandy every day.

• A bachelor from North Battleford ordered that a bottle of rye be given to each of his pallbearers, and that everyone who had driven out to his burial get a free tank of gas for the return trip.

• A long-suffering parson in Ontario left $3,000 to his daughter, on condition that she give up singing.

• A woman left her husband "just enough to buy a rope to hang himself." From the opposite corner, a husband left his wife "just enough for carfare to go someplace and drown herself."

• A North Carolina sailor plans to top all will stories. He has had his last will and testament tattooed on his back, in the presence of his lawyer. When he dies, his skin is to be removed, preserved, and unrolled before the startled eyes of the probate judge.

common-law spouse (if the couple had been cohabiting continuously for not less than five years, or in a relationship of some permanence where there is a natural child); (3) parents (including grandparents and a person who has shown the intention of treating the deceased as a child of the family, but not including a foster parent); (4) a child (born within or outside marriage, including a grandchild and a person to whom the deceased has shown the intention of treating the subject as a child of the family, but not including a foster child); and (5) a brother and sister. Only a dependent may seek support under the Succession Law Reform Act.

In deciding whether the testator has made at least the minimum provision for the future requirements of his or her dependents, the judge will determine what a reasonable standard would be. Then, if the testator has not provided this, the judge would in effect write such a standard into the will. The Ontario Succession Law Reform Act offers a number of guidelines: (1) the assets and means of the dependent; (2) the ability of the dependent to provide for his or her own support; (3) the age and physical and mental capacity of the dependent; (4) the measures available for the dependent to become financially independent, and the time and cost involved in this; (5) the proximity of the dependent's relationship with the testator and the duration of the relationship; and, (6) the contribution made by a dependent to the welfare of the deceased.

Irrational or unreasonable

A will is not the place for jokes, puns or put-ons; nor for insult or vengeance, no matter how these may be disguised. The courts will probably consider that if a will is absurd in itself, this is evidence of "lack of capacity" by the testator or testatrix. This point of view is taken because occasionally a man who apparently has all his mental faculties makes a very strange disposition of his property.

Charles Vance Millar, a Toronto bachelor lawyer and financier who died in 1926, left a will in which he bequeathed the bulk of his fortune to whichever Toronto woman gave birth to the largest number of children in the ten-year period following his death. Although other bizarre clauses in his will left jockey-club stock to clergymen and beer-company shares to civic figures opposed to liquor, it was the "Stork Derby" that made Millar's name notorious in Canada.

As you would expect from a highly experienced lawyer, the will was properly drawn in every detail and could not be overturned. Four women eventually tied with nine children each and shared $750,000. Another woman tried to top them with ten, but five of hers were illegitimate and the law sternly ruled that Millar had intended to recognize only children born in wedlock. There is little doubt that a will like Millar's would be ruled as contrary to the "public interest" in today's courts.

The holograph will

A will which is wholly written and signed by the testator himself is known as a holograph will. The term derives from the Greek *holos* (whole) and *graphe* (writing). Such a will has even been scratched in the paint of a car's dashboard by an accident victim trapped inside the vehicle.

A holograph will is valid in Alberta, Saskatchewan, Manitoba, Ontario, Quebec, New Brunswick and Newfoundland. In British Columbia and Nova Scotia, it is accepted in respect to movable property, but only under certain conditions. Prince Edward Island does not recognize a holograph will, unless it has been written by a member of the Armed Forces or by a mariner. In a contested case involving a holograph will, evidence may be demanded to prove that the signature on the document is genuine.

The notarial will

A notarial (or, as it is often called, an *authentic*) will is a form found only in Quebec. It is executed before two notaries or one notary and two witnesses. It does not require probate, or validation. It remains in the custody of the notary; any copy the notary issues is recognized as authentic.

Specimen of a simple will

A ready-made form like this can be bought for less than $2 from the stationer. But the drafting of wills is best left to lawyers.

This is the last Will and Testament of me,

_(A)_

John Doe, of the city of Toronto, Merchant,

hereby revoking all Wills, Testaments or Codicils by me at any time heretofore made.

I devise and bequeath all my Estate, real and personal, to my executors and trustees hereinafter named in trust for the purposes following:—

Firstly, to pay my just debts, funeral and Testamentary expenses, and thereafter in trust to dispose of and pay over or convey the same to the person or persons or corporations hereinafter named as follows:—

_(B)_

1. To convey to my wife, Jane, my farm, being Lot 10, Concession 6, Township of Peel, for her sole use and benefit. Or to pay to my wife, Jane, the income from my farm, being Lot 10, Concession 6, Township of Peel, during her lifetime, and upon her death to convey said Lot to my son, John jr., for his sole use and benefit.

2. To pay to my son, John jr., five hundred dollars; to my daughter, Mary, five hundred dollars; to my daughter, Kate, five hundred dollars; to my son, William, eight hundred dollars, to assist him in his education and support. Such sums to be advanced from time to time in the discretion of my executors, and any balance to be paid to them at the age of twenty-one.

3. To my wife, Jane, the use of my furniture and effects during her lifetime, and thereafter to my son, John jr.

4. To the Home for Incurable Children, Tor—

I nominate, constitute and appoint _(C)_ _William A. Smith, of Toronto, salesman; George Jones, of Toronto, merchant; and James Thomas, of Toronto, manufacturer,_

_____executors

and trustees of this my last Will, with full power and authority to sell and dispose of all my Estate where necessary, and execute any and all Documents requisite to carry out this my Will, and should one or more of my said Executors or Trustees wish to retire I authorize them to appoint a successor instead thereof.

In Witness whereof, I subscribed these presents as printed and written this

_(D)_ _fourth_ _____ day of _June_ _____ A.D. 19**53**

Signed, published and declared by the said Testator as _(E) his_ last Will and Testament in the presence of us both present at the same time, who in _his_ presence and in the presence of each other have hereunto set and subscribed our names as witness.

_(F)_ _John Doe_

Witness _(F)_ _C.M. Wilson_

Address _16 Maple Road, Toronto_

Witness _(F)_ _B. Weinber_

Address _4 E. Elm Avenue, Toronto_

The parties to a will

The testator

The beneficiary

Executor and trustee

The guardian

The witnesses

Safekeeping of wills

THE PEOPLE who actually sign the will are the testator and the two witnesses. In general, neither the witness nor the spouse of the witness can benefit from a will. In Ontario, however, a bequest to a witness or the spouse of a witness can be valid if the court is satisfied that no undue influence was exercised upon the testator by the witness.

An executor and trustee are normally aware that the will exists and have consented to act. But they are not parties to the will in the sense that they have to sign the document.

If a guardian is appointed in the will, he has to be consulted and has to have consented to act, but it is not necessary for him to sign either.

Beneficiaries may or may not be told that a will is being prepared, but they must never sign the will.

Your lawyer will not witness your will (if he did, he might not be able to collect his fee) but an employe in his office may sign it.

The testator
Originating in the ancient law handed down from Roman times, the term testator (*testatrix*, if female) describes the person making the will. It is his or her *testament*. Across Canada, there are a variety of age requirements and related exemptions for a testator. (*See* "Last will and testament" in this chapter.) The testator must be sane and fully understand his acts. Some provinces allow a married person who is a minor to sign a will.

Wives should make separate wills—without delay if they haven't done so—although wives usually outlive their husbands. Couples often draw up similar wills to be sure that joint property will pass to the persons they intend to have it. All of the inheritable assets disposed of in a will—personal property, real-estate income, etc—are referred to as "estate."

The beneficiary
A beneficiary is either a person or an institution that receives something under the will. It is important that the correct full name and address of a beneficiary be written into the will. If a testator were to name "Robert Smith" as beneficiary when he really meant "John Robert Smith," and there was a Robert Smith who was a relative or associate of the testator, then this Robert Smith would probably benefit instead of John R. Smith. This might happen even if John R. was usually known as "Robert" or "Bob."

If an incorrect name has been used to identify a beneficiary, and the name doesn't accurately apply to anyone else, some evidence will be admitted to verify the identity of the person whom the will was intended to benefit.

It is a good plan to refer to a beneficiary by a degree of relationship (if any) as well as by his own name. For example, "My uncle John Robert Smith" leaves little room for doubt.

The executor
The executor is the person appointed to ensure that the last will and testament of the deceased is properly carried out. The executor (*executrix*, if female) acts for the testator, making any claims on behalf of the estate or settling any debts of the estate. The executor derives his power from his appointment in the will, and he can refuse or resign the appointment.

Any person who is capable of executing a valid will is capable of acting as an executor—a trusted friend, your accountant, your lawyer. A trust company is another possible choice.

If you appoint an individual who lives fairly near you, then it will be easier (and cheaper) for him to appear when needed to sign papers or consult with others.

A minor can be appointed executor, but cannot act until he or she is of age. If you die when the executor is still a minor, the court will appoint someone to act as executor until your executor comes of age.

Persons who are mentally unsound are incapable of acting as executors. The court will probably also disqualify a person serving a long jail term. Persons who have attempted to defraud the beneficiaries, or who have become bankrupt, will not be allowed to remain as executors.

Except in extreme cases, anyone who is appointed by the testator will be allowed to be an executor. All provincial statutes provide for the compensation of the executor, who is entitled to charge between three and five percent of the value of the estate.

To my wife . . . my widow

CONSIDER LEAVING an unsentimental letter among your papers so that when you are no longer here, your life partner will still have the benefit of your cheerful guidance.

Sunday, April 30

Dear Jane:

A man does not always get advance news of his own death, and thus I thought it a good idea, this quiet Sunday afternoon, to write you a short letter about business details and similar things so that, when I'm gone, you should have very little trouble carrying on the plans we made.

Realizing that business has held little interest for you—you've been very well occupied bringing up our family—I've tried to arrange my affairs so that you will have an adequate steady income, enough to live on pleasantly anyway, with some provision made for the seemingly inevitable inflation.

You do know, of course, that the final schooling of the youngsters is taken care of through the educational trust fund—so they'll get through college all right.

My will is with our lawyers, Cameron, Fogg & Jones, and they will handle everything for you. I've made an arrangement so that you can get immediate cash if you need it. The house and everything in it goes automatically to you, so there's not the slightest need to rush about or worry about anything.

Don't be sentimental if you find the house too big later on—you could easily sell it and buy one of those nice condominium apartments in town, near your sister's. And there'd be something left over!

The business will be sold, but not until the time is ripe. There should be some useful amount from that, but remember that it pretty much turned on my personal participation and this will no doubt affect the price. For that reason, I went fairly heavily into insurance and there will be some largish sums coming in a lump to you as beneficiary.

They say that 75 percent of life insurance benefits are dissipated by the beneficiaries within seven years, so don't allow the big cheque to faze you! Put the proceeds on 90-day fixed deposit with Joe Cressy at the Commercial Bank until things settle down. Both Joe and Rod Cameron at the lawyer's office will be ready to discuss safe investments with you.

Well, that's all business, my dear . . . but there's one other bit of advice I want you to take to heart: don't forget to have some fun!

Yours,
John

An executor can only be appointed as the result of a signed and witnessed will. The appointment may be either *express*, that is, when an executor is actually named, or *constructive*, that is, when no one actually is named but it is obvious from the tone of the will that the testator intended a certain specific person to manage the affairs of his estate. For example, when someone who is not benefited by the will is directed to pay the debts of the testator, that instruction is sufficient to "constructively appoint" him as executor.

As a testator, you may ask someone else to appoint an executor. Two or more persons can, in fact, act as co-executors. An executor, however, cannot in turn assign the executorship to some other person. But if an executor dies and in his will he appoints an executor, his executor then becomes the executor of the original testator. Where there are co-executors and one dies, full executorship is always given to the surviving executor.

The executor has a multitude of duties, including the following:

(1) If the testator lived alone, the executor locks the house and makes sure he has all the keys.

(2) He obtains formal proof of the testator's death.

(3) He takes charge of all documents of title to real and personal property of the deceased.

(4) He makes a complete inventory and a statement of assets and liabilities.

(5) He investigates books of accounts and papers, collects valuables and places them in a safety deposit box.

(6) He notifies the bank, post office and other public institutions with which the deceased dealt that the death has occurred.

(7) He arranges to have the application filed for letters of probate, and obtains a certificate which establishes the validity of the will.

(8) He completes and files the succession-duty forms, paying any duty required, and obtains the releases from the beneficiaries for the real and personal property.

(9) He gets the information required by the insurance company to release the proceeds of policies payable on the death of the testator. He makes interim payments and adjusts any conflicting claims of the beneficiaries.

(10) If the deceased was in business, the executor considers if it is advisable to continue the operation of the business.

(11) He collects bills, accounts receivable, interest, dividends, etc.

(12) He advertises for creditors according to the legal requirements, obtaining proof of claims and disputing claims where necessary.

(13) He opens an executor's bank account and deposits any money received by the estate.

(14) He sets up and maintains a complete set of accounts, showing separately the capital and income of the estate. The executor keeps all vouchers for receipts and funds paid out and gets the accounts audited.

If all the beneficiaries are adults, then they can consent to the executor's accounts and agree with the executor on his remuneration. If they so desire—or if they are still minors—the executor has to pass his accounts before a Surrogate Court judge who settles any controversy, fixes the remuneration of the executor, and settles the terms of distribution to the various beneficiaries of any of the assets which still remain in the executor's hands.

Every executor must manage the estate with as much care as he would use in the management of his own affairs.

After determining the assets of the estate, it is the executor's duty to convert to cash within a reasonable time all the investments which require such conversion. Where real and personal property are blended and the estate is to be divided among numerous beneficiaries, it is assumed that the testator intended that these assets be sold to get cash. Power of sale may be spelled out by the terms of the will itself. If the executor fails to sell that specified property, he may be held responsible should the estate lose any money as a result. The testator, therefore, should consider giving his executor special (discretionary) power to retain particular investments.

The superior or supreme court of most provinces can compel an executor to account for his actions as executor. The court can also appoint an administrator if no executor is named; it can fix an executor's fee and it can prevent an executor from acting on behalf of the estate. The Trustee Act of Ontario allows the Supreme Court to remove a personal representative who the testator might have appointed for the same reason or reasons it may remove any other trustee. The court may appoint some other person or persons to act in the place of the executor or other person that it has removed. In deciding to remove a personal representative, the court follows the general principle that the welfare of the beneficiaries must come first.

The trustee

If a trust is set up in the will, perhaps to provide for children, careful consideration should be given to appointing a suitable trustee. He can be a relative or perhaps a friend with business or professional experience, but a trust company is often chosen because of its wide experience. The trustee, in effect, holds legal title to property for the benefit of another.

The trustee and the executor can be one and the same person, but this could lead to a conflict of interests.

While the executor represents *all* the beneficiaries or claimants under the will, the trustee is essentially concerned only with the interest of a single beneficiary or, at most, a designated group of them. Also, the trustee's job does not end until the period of the trust runs out—with young children, that could be a matter of several years.

If the will does not provide for a trustee, any share of an estate going to a minor is held in trust by the official guardian until the minor comes of age. The terms of the will may be written to allow a trustee much wider discretion in han-

Role of the guardian

WE THINK of a guardian only as being a person appointed to take the place of parents but, under most provincial laws, parents are joint guardians of the child. If one parent dies, the surviving parent becomes the guardian of any children who are still legally infants (age 18 or under in most provinces). He or she may have to serve jointly with a "testamentary guardian" appointed under the will.

Who should be appointed as legal guardian in case both parents die leaving dependent children? Preferably a family connection, or trusted friend of an age not greater than that of the parents themselves. A tie of blood or affection is indicated since guardians cannot be paid for performing this role.

The guardian literally takes the place of the parents. As the law says, he stands *in loco parentis*. He must ensure that his wards attend school as required by law, that they have moral and physical protec-tion—adequate food, clothing and shelter. He has custody and control of the ward, and must apply any income provided for the benefit of the ward under the direction of the courts.

If the will does not name a guardian, or if the testamentary guardian refuses to act (or cannot act) when the need arises, the court will appoint a guardian. The child is then known as a "ward of the Crown."

Lovers of the Gilbert and Sullivan operettas will remember the gay song of the Lord Chancellor in *Iolanthe*:

The constitutional guardian I
Of pretty young wards in Chancery,
All very agreeable girls and none
Is over the age of twenty-one.

And everyone who'd marry a ward
Must come to me for my accord,
And in my court I sit all day
Giving agreeable girls away.

dling investments than is allowed under the Trustee Act. For example, a trustee may be given the power to postpone the cashing of the testator's investments until a time the trustee considers favorable, or to reinvest in certain securities that, while sound, do not necessarily rate as "trustee investments." (*See* Chapter 8, "Anatomy of the stock market.")

A trustee must produce an account of his actions similar to the account made by the executor. The accounts are examined and filed in the office of the court which originally validated the will.

The guardian

When there are children to consider, a guardian should be appointed in the will to act in the place of a parent until they reach the age of majority. The father would normally appoint the mother (and *vice versa*), but it is also wise to name another guardian in case both parents should die together.

If no guardian is named, the province may appoint a relative or family friend, or an official in the Public Trustee office.

A divorced spouse, as the natural parent, would likely be the first choice.

A guardian is not entitled to a fee for his guardianship but may be allowed to charge a certain amount for handling funds spent on the minor's behalf. The Public Trust office has set scales to regulate these fees. Your lawyer can tell you whether, in your province, a person living in a different province (or country) can be appointed as a guardian.

The witnesses

Witnesses are not concerned with what is in the will and there is no reason why they should read a line of it. They act simply to confirm that they actually saw you signing the document. A blind man or woman cannot, therefore, be a witness to a will.

In Ontario, a testator must sign, or acknowledge his signature, in the presence of two or more witnesses. In Prince Edward Island, and in the English form of will in Quebec (as opposed to the notarial), the witnesses are also required to sign in the presence of each other.

Two witnesses are required in Alberta, British Columbia, Saskatchewan, Manitoba, Ontario and Nova Scotia. However, because of the wording of the statutes of these provinces, the witnesses must be in the same room and they must see the testator sign. This is all that is necessary from the witness to make the will valid. No particular form of wording for the witness' signature is required by statute. But there should be a paragraph indicating the presence of witnesses, which, for example, could be written in this fashion: "Signed by the testator in the presence of us both, present at the same time, who at his request and in his presence have put down our names as witnesses."

In all cases, it is necessary for at least one of the witnesses to "swear out an affidavit" (a signed oath in writing) that the will was actually signed by the testator. In order to find a witness, should it be necessary later, it is good practice to have the witness list his occupation and address along with his signature.

The initials of a witness are considered sufficient to constitute a "signature" but it is better to have the witness write his usual signature.

Whenever an executor, trustee or witness dies—or if the testator moves a considerable distance from where he lived when the will was originally made—the testator should re-examine his will to determine whether he should amend it or prepare a new one.

Safekeeping of wills

A will may be kept by you, your solicitor, the corporate trustee, or it may be filed with the appropriate court.

If you hold the will yourself, you should keep it in a safety deposit box and tell your executor and solicitor where it is.

A will deposited with the surrogate court is sealed and cannot be opened during the lifetime of the testator, except by the testator or by the order of a judge.

If a corporate trustee has been appointed, the will can be left with that corporation for safekeeping.

A will should not be kept at home in case an accident—fire, flood or some other disaster—destroys both the testator *and* his testament.

Changing your will

Altering a will

Adding new provisions

Revoking a will

Reviving a will

Effect of marriage or divorce

What you can't will

YOU CAN change or cancel your will at any time before death, and there can be good reasons for doing so. Certain acts, such as marriage, may revoke—that is, cancel—wills automatically. Although December-June romances or family feuds often provide writers of fiction with popular motives for rewriting wills, the reasons that apply in the realm of real life are much more practical. Tax law is constantly changing, the value of your assets may grow or shrink, the number of children (and grandchildren) may increase (or decrease) and some of them may develop special needs that you may want to consider when making your bequests. Your daughter may have married a millionaire and your Aunt Edith may have won the Irish Sweepstakes. You or the executor and trustee you chose some years ago may have moved, or it may appear that one or both may die before you. You might develop a new and deep interest in a religion or in a research philanthropy.

Your lawyer can explain to you the various ways of changing a will.

Alteration or excision

If the change is minor, it may be made simply by erasing or scratching out some words or phrases and adding new words, as required. Every single change must be signed in the nearest margin (initials will do) by the testator and the witnesses. If the alterations are not properly attested, or certified by those signatures, they will be disregarded in any legal action.

A question that has plagued the courts from time to time is what exactly is an alteration or "interliniation"—literally, writing "between the lines." In deciding

what particular words are to be regarded as an interliniation, the court will look at the whole will to try to make complete sense of it. If the words in doubt are obviously different from the original, then the court will probably consider them interliniations.

Where the will consists of a number of pages and the testator has properly signed the will on the last page, that is enough to make all the pages of the will valid. If it is proved that one of the pages of a lengthy will has been removed and a new page inserted—a page that has not been separately signed by the testator and witnesses—then the whole will could be ruled invalid. However, alterations or interliniations made before the will is signed by the testator are validly part of the will. If a beneficiary tries to rely upon the interliniations or alterations— and if they are not separately attested to—he must prove that these were made before the testator executed his will; that is, before it was signed and witnessed.

Incorporation of documents

Separate documents can become part of a will. The law states, "Where a testator in a duly executed will or *codicil* refers to an unattested but existing written paper (whether of a testamentary form or not), the paper so referred to becomes part of his will." This means that anyone disposing of property in a complex will could make that bequest dependent upon some previously written, or printed, document.

Adding new provisions

A separate paper that is a supplement or an addition to a will is called a *codicil*. It does not usually take the place of or totally eliminate the existing will. It has the effect, however, of making a new will which contains the same provisions as the old except for changes and new provisions contained in the codicil. The codicil is the normal method of adapting a will to changing circumstances. It is rather like adding a postscript to a letter.

When a codicil is added to a will, it usually reaffirms the provisions of any additions made previously. However, if the codicil refers specifically to the date on which a will was made, it has the effect of confirming the will and conversely not confirming any intervening codicils.

If a will has been canceled it can be made valid again by a codicil stating that the former will is once again in force.

A codicil, like a will, is signed by the testator and two witnesses. The introduction to the codicil should be precise. You could begin with something like, "This is a codicil to the last will and testament of me, John Smith, of the city of Belleville in the County of Hastings, Province of Ontario, which last will and testament bears the date of . . . " Following this, you would put in the new clauses. There can be literally dozens of codicils to a will, and sometimes lawyers and judges almost need a road map to trace a path through them.

Revoking a will

An existing will is usually effectively nullified or canceled either by the executing of a new will of later date, or by marriage or remarriage. (In Quebec, however, the marriage or remarriage of the testator does not nullify or cancel the will.) It can also be canceled by deliberate destruction of the will itself (by burning or tearing), or by a separate signed document. Lawyers can mean any of these acts when they speak of "revoking" the will. A testator cannot give the authority to revoke his will to another person.

If a person signed a contract with the testator in which the testator agreed not to revoke his will, such an agreement could not be enforced because the will is, by nature, revocable. However, if that contract had a bearing on something a testator put into his will—perhaps a promise to satisfy a debt after death—then the

person who was to have benefited under the revoked will would, through his contract, have a claim against the estate of the deceased for the amount he would otherwise have received.

If a testator was prevented from revoking his will by physical force, duress—such as a threat—or fraud, and this is a provable fact, the court might order that the executors hold the assets of the estate in trust for the persons who would have benefited if the duress had not been applied and the will had been revoked.

Since the purpose of a will is to dispose of the property of the deceased, it is logical that the will made last by the deceased should be the one that is presumed to be in force. Therefore, when a valid will is made, it should revoke other wills made prior to it. However, a new will does not automatically revoke prior wills; it does so only if it contains a clause expressly canceling former wills or if the terms of the former wills conflict with the latest will. All wills drawn up by legal firms include the necessary revocation clause.

A man may die having made two wills. In such a case both wills are considered valid if the terms of one do not conflict with the terms of the other. If the court finds a partial inconsistency, then the particular terms of the most recent will are in effect and the conflicting terms of the first will are disregarded. The general rule is that if a gift is clearly given in the will, then it won't be taken away unless the second will or a codicil clearly instructs otherwise; the intent of the deceased is the all-important factor.

The wills acts of most provinces provide that a will may be revoked not only by a subsequent new will but also by any written statement expressing an intention to revoke the will, as long as that statement is properly signed and witnessed. The intention to revoke must be clearly expressed. For instance, a letter that is witnessed and that directs someone to obtain the will and destroy it is sufficient to have the will revoked. The acts also state that a will may be destroyed by the testator, or by another person in the testator's presence and by his direction.

Just drawing a line through your signature so that the signature still can be read, and then adding the words "I hereby revoke this will," does not revoke the will. Even if the signature of the testator is so scratched out or covered over that it cannot be read, the will is not effectively revoked. The court demands proof that the person intended the will to be revoked. In a sense, the court weighs the *intent* of the contents of the whole will against the intent of the short statement or scratched-out signature, and finds the latter to be lacking in "weight" of intent.

How much destruction of the document is required? It is not necessary to completely destroy it, but it has to be torn or burned sufficiently that it could be said that the will no longer exists as it was, that it now is a different document from the one the testator signed. If certain portions of the will are cut out and the rest of the will remains the same, the chances are that only those portions of the will that were cut out will be revoked. This is because it appears that the testator's intentions were that the rest of the will is to remain valid. If the signature of the testator is not on the will, it is not valid at all.

If you want to revoke your will by destruction, you should take care to destroy all copies. In the course of time your newer will could be challenged in the courts, in which case a copy of the earlier will might be produced as evidence of what your intention was supposed to be.

As was stated earlier, the wills acts require that if the will is destroyed by someone other than the testator, it must be done in the testator's presence and by his direction. If someone, at the direction of the testator, should destroy the will—but not in the testator's presence—the testator could not afterward confirm, or "ratify," the act of destruction.

The destruction of a will by accident or error is not considered sufficient for revocation. Just as it is essential that the testator have the mental capacity to make a will, so he must fully understand what he is doing in revoking a will. A codicil must be revoked in the same way as a will, but separately. The revocation of a will doesn't automatically revoke the codicil.

What happens if a man dies and his will cannot be found? If it can be proved that he was the last person to have the will, it will be presumed that the document was destroyed and that the testator wanted to revoke the will. The strength of such a presumption depends upon the circumstances of the testator at his death. If it can be shown that he had lost his mental powers, then the question of his wish to cancel the will does not arise. In that case, the burden of proving that the will was destroyed with the intention to revoke while the testator was of sound mind rests on those who are making that claim.

Revocation of a will may be conditional, and if that condition is not fulfilled the revocation does not take effect. For instance, if a testator canceled his old will on the condition that his new will was valid, and if, for some reason, the new will was ruled invalid, then the old will would be considered valid. However, if a testator canceled his will intending to make a new will at some future date, but he died before making the new will, the old will would not be valid.

If the testator scratches out words in his will and inserts new words which are not themselves valid, it becomes what is called a "question of fact" whether or not the testator intended the obliterated words to be revoked only if the new words were to take effect. The court may try to determine the meaning of the obliterated words—sometimes even with the help of a magnifying glass. The courts lean toward letting a will stand as valid, for an intestacy (settling the estate of a person who dies without a will) is a clumsy and awkward affair.

Reviving a will

Even though a will has been revoked, it can be made valid again—in other words, "revived"—by the testator merely signing it again at a new date, with this new signature properly witnessed by two persons. Alternatively, a codicil expressing the intention to revive the will can be added to the document.

Every will re-executed, or revived by any codicil, is effective from the new date. Thus, bequests and trusteeship provisions made perhaps many years earlier would be made valid again. Before deciding on such a revival, the testator should review the entire will with his lawyer.

Effect of marriage or divorce

In all provinces, except Quebec, any will you might have made becomes invalid automatically upon registration of marriage (or remarriage) even if you should marry your main beneficiary. Therefore, one of the earliest acts in your new state of domestic bliss should be to make a new will. If you don't, and are killed by a champagne cork on your honeymoon, you are considered to have died "intestate"—without leaving a valid will—and your main beneficiary, your spouse, might be left with only a fraction of what you had wanted her to get—especially if you had children from a previous marriage.

The main idea of the law in this case is, of course, that the husband must make provision for his wife and for their lives together. The only exception to the automatic revocation occurs when the will is expressly stated to have been drawn up "in contemplation of marriage." However the law demands more than just the thought of marriage: the "contemplated" spouse must be specifically named.

The idea that a man and woman living together as man and wife—what is called common-law marriage—for a number of years is the same as their being married will not necessarily stand up in any legal action. After the testator's death, evidence may be given by a challenger that the couple was not married. But a common-law wife has often benefited under a will in which she was described by the testator simply as "my wife," for she could prove that she was indeed generally considered to be the man's wife. (The law rules on the basis of intent.)

A simple separation—that is, "living apart"—does not end a marriage; nor does it cancel the wife's right to inherit. A husband can, however, prevent his separated wife from inheriting by adding a standard clause to his will to the effect that the spouse cannot benefit under the will unless she is living with him at the time of death. By "living," the law assumes the full extent implied by a marital relationship and sets no minimum period of time.

A formal separation agreement, which is essentially a contract, will probably have provisions under which the parties give up their mutual inheritance rights.

A divorce, once final, totally ends any claim that the parties had on each other's estate through marriage. Of course there is nothing to prevent you from making a bequest in favor of a former marriage partner. Similarly, if a marriage has been annulled, any rights to a joint estate are ended on the date of the annulment.

The cost of professional management

MORE THAN 70 trust companies, with over 950 offices throughout Canada, offer complete executor and trustee services to the person about to draw up or change his will. They point out, with due emphasis, that their fees as executors are no higher than those normally allowed by the courts to the private executor.

As two estates are rarely alike, the fees charged by an executor vary according to the number and complexity of the assets. The following are general fee guidelines awarded by the courts to executors:

As executor—five percent of the first portion of the estate (usually about $250,000). In general, the percentage decreases as the assets increase in value.

As trustee (managing a continuing estate)—two-fifths of one percent per annum of the average market value of the assets. The percentage declines as the assets increase beyond a certain value.

Separate commissions would be required to retain agents if real estate was sold or leased, and all disbursements would be charged.

Simultaneous death

Until recently, the probability of a husband and wife dying at the same time was fairly slim. But jet-age transportation has increased the chances of simultaneous death. It is obvious that where there are no survivors of an accident, no one can prove who actually breathed last. The situation can have important bearing on the distribution of estates. In fact, in such a case, a testator's assets could sometimes go to people he has never met.

Throughout most of Canada, when it cannot be established by evidence as to who died last, the doctrine of *commorientes* comes into play. According to this doctrine, in the event of simultaneous death, the younger is assumed to have survived the older. If a husband had made a will leaving everything to his wife who is younger than he is, and they die simultaneously, then his estate passes, however briefly, to his wife. If she had not made a will of her own, her relatives would probably get the estate under the laws of "intestacy." (*See* "When there is no will" in this chapter.)

Under Quebec law, when two or more people who are entitled to inherit from each other and it is impossible to determine which ones survived the others, all are deemed to have died simultaneously. In this event, the succession devolves to those heirs who would be entitled to receive it in the place of the deceased.

To prepare for the possibility of "simultaneous death," lawyers advise that husband and wife both prepare wills and, furthermore, that a "survivorship clause" be inserted. This clause would state that no estate is to go to a wife unless she survives her husband by a given period of time, for example, 30 days. The wife would include a similar clause in her will. One benefit of this clause is obvious: there would only be one set of death duties.

Burial or otherwise

You can include a paragraph in your will ordering the disposal of your body by burial or by cremation but such requests may not be legally binding. (*See* Chapter 14, "When death occurs.") You may ask that your body or organs be made available for anatomical dissection at a medical school, but that clause will not be enforced if your relatives object. Because of possible delays in the will being read, you should make sure that close relatives or associates are aware of your wishes.

If you want any of your organs to be used in transplant surgery or research, separate arrangements should be made with a local hospital or university.

Funeral expenses, along with taxes and debts, will be charged against your estate before any beneficiary receives a penny. Make sure you take these expenses into account before you make your bequests.

What you can't will

A life insurance policy might be the biggest single asset of your estate. However, the benefits cannot be distributed in your will if you have already named a beneficiary in the policy itself. The same usually holds true for pensions and certain government savings bonds. If you had named your estate as beneficiary, only then could the proceeds of the policy, pension and bonds be added to the assets of the estate.

Other items which you cannot dispose of in your will include real estate owned jointly with some other party, a home in which you hold only a life tenancy, or an inheritance which you expect but have not yet received.

The conditional will

A conditional will can be drawn up to take effect upon condition that you die before a certain date. If you are still living on the day so designated, the condition has not been fulfilled and the will is invalid. Someone planning a hazardous journey might make a conditional will.

Date of execution

Your will is interpreted to be made from the date of execution (when it was signed and witnessed). However, the courts will presume that any property acquired by you after the date on the will is included in the will, unless a specific clause is appended which limits any bequests to only that property you owned at the time of the signing.

When there is no will

Appointment of administrator

Payment of debts

Distribution of the estate

Lineal descendants

Ascendant and collateral relatives

Out of wedlock

WHEN a person's death is certified, or "legally presumed"—such as when someone is lost at sea—a search is conducted for his last will and testament. If his family, his lawyer, business associates or religious adviser know nothing of a will, and if a search of the deceased's personal effects yields nothing, the man is assumed to have died intestate—that is, without a "testament." His worldly goods then are normally distributed through the courts, according to the statutes of the province or territory involved.

In the average case, once debts and taxes (if any) are paid, the testator's spouse and children get everything. If the deceased was not married, or if the spouse died earlier and there are no surviving children, the next of kin would inherit. If there are no kin, the government gets everything (except in Alberta, where such property is held in trust for the province's universities).

To guard against accidental loss of your will, you should tell your lawyer, your executor and, perhaps, some trusted member of your family where you keep it. Banks and trust companies offer safekeeping for valuable documents at a moderate fee, and will not permit unauthorized persons access to your papers. Special private safes hidden behind family portraits or behind bound copies of the Complete Dickens, can (and have been) "lost" for years when the secretive testator himself slips into the forgetfulness of old age.

Probably the best plan is to allow your lawyer to arrange for the safekeeping of all the important papers vital to the prompt and proper settlement of your affairs. These papers include not only your will but also insurance policies, contracts, partnership agreements, stocks and bonds, bank account statements and bankbooks, real estate deeds, mortgages, as well as any notes payable to you (or by you). You should also list your miscellaneous assets (noting any insurance that covers these), such as pleasure craft, cars, paintings, gold, jewelry and silverware. Give this list to your lawyer.

Appointment of administrator

If a person dies intestate, an administrator (or *administratrix*, if a woman) is appointed to take charge of his affairs. The duties are similar to those of an executor of a will. (*See* "The parties to a will" in this chapter.)

The court will normally choose the spouse or a close relative of the deceased as administrator. But if no relative seeks Letters of Administration (that is, offers to be administrator), then a trust company, the public trustee or even a creditor may be appointed.

An administrator, like an executor, cannot be appointed if he is mentally incompetent, if he is serving a long jail term or if he suffers some other disabling handicap. A minor cannot be appointed either.

Before the court allows a person who may have a lesser claim to become the administrator, a person or persons with greater claims must have refused the job.

Like the executor, the administrator collects all money that may be due the estate and pays all bills or duties owing. After receiving a formal notice from the receiver general that the government has no further claim, the administrator will then seek unanimous agreement among the beneficiaries on the distribution of the assets. If such agreement cannot be reached, he will sell all the property and distribute the proceeds as the law directs. The estate must pay the administrator's fee which will be set by the court.

Payment of debts

Again following the law that applies to an executor, the administrator of an intestacy (an estate for which no will was left) must pay any due bills out of the estate. When someone applies to become an administrator, he must furnish the court with a bond which serves as a guarantee that he will properly fulfill his duties. He is not released from this bond until he can prove that satisfactory advertisements have appeared in the newspapers asking any possible creditors of the deceased to send in their bills.

Under the Ontario Devolutions of Estates Act, if the deceased owned land, any of his debts can be charged against the land he owned. This might mean that the land would have to be sold or mortgaged to pay the debts. If the executor or administrator, after advertising for creditors, has sold the estate lands to satisfy any debts, the heir cannot then be sued by a creditor who subsequently appears on the scene. However, if the land passed into the hands of the beneficiary without a debt settlement having been made, then the heir is still liable to pay outstanding debts against the estate.

Distribution of the estate

The laws covering the disposal of the assets of a man who dies intestate, although varying in some detail among the provinces, all attempt to direct the bulk of the estate to the surviving spouse and to any children of the marriage. Hardship might sometimes be caused by the courts having to stick closely to the "letter of the law." The law is written to cover the "average case" and cannot possibly cover *all* possible circumstances. Thus, for example, a mentally retarded or physically handicapped child who would likely be the subject of special treatment in a will must, in a case of intestacy, be treated just like any other child.

In the provinces of Alberta and Saskatchewan, where a widow may exercise her right of *dower* over her husband's real estate, she would forfeit her over-riding rights in the intestacy (*See* "Last will and testament" in this chapter).

The laws of Alberta, British Columbia, Manitoba, Ontario, Saskatchewan and the Yukon regarding intestacy are quite similar and the following examples should illustrate the common position adequately.

If an Alberta man dies intestate, for example, leaving a widow only, she gets the entire estate. If there are widow and children, then the widow receives the entire estate if it is worth no more than $40,000. If the net value of the estate exceeds $40,000, the widow receives the first $40,000 plus any interest that has built up on that amount from the date of death until payment is made to her.

Of the amount over and above $40,000, if there is only one child, the widow gets one-half of anything above $40,000 and the child gets the other half.

If the "intestate" man dies leaving more than one child and a widow, the widow gets one-third of what remains over $40,000 and the other two-thirds is divided among the children.

These provisions apply equally to the widower.

If an intestate widower dies leaving a child, children or other lineal descendants, then all goes to the children or descendants. The children get shares *per capita* (Latin for "by heads")—that is, equal shares—and their representatives get shares *per stirpes* (from the Latin "by roots"—generally defined to mean "by family representation"). Simply, *per stirpes* describes the method of division of an estate where surviving descendants of the testator take the share to which an ancestor—or direct descendant—would have been entitled. If a deceased's own child were already dead, that child's children would inherit equal shares. (A $10,000 bequest to a son who died before the testator would be divided $2,500 to each of four grandchildren.)

If a single person dies intestate and his father, mother, brothers, sisters, nephews and nieces are alive, then all goes to the father and mother equally—or to one of them if only one is still living.

If only brothers, sisters, nephews and nieces survive, the brothers and sisters get *per capita* shares and the nephews and nieces are benefited *per stirpes*.

If a man dies intestate leaving brothers and sisters and grandfather and aunts, the estate all goes to the brothers and sisters.

If he dies leaving grandfather and grandmother, uncle or aunt, it goes equally to grandfather and grandmother.

If a testator dies leaving uncles and aunts, nephews and nieces, the entire estate would go to the nephews and nieces.

There is no line of inheritance among so-called collaterals—that is, "indirect relatives"—after brother's and sister's children.

In New Brunswick, when the intestate man has no children, the widow automatically gets all assets; in Newfoundland, Nova Scotia, Saskatchewan and Manitoba, the surviving spouse gets everything; in Prince Edward Island, the survivor gets only the first $8,000 plus half of the balance.

In New Brunswick, if an intestate dies leaving a widow and one child, one-half of the residue goes to the widow. If he leaves a widow and more than one child, one-third of the residue goes to his widow and the rest to his children.

In Quebec, if the intestate dies leaving children, the children get two-thirds and the wife gets one-third. If he dies childless, then one-third goes to his widow, one-third to his parent or parents, and one-third to his brothers and sisters or their children.

Under the Civil Code of Quebec, where there are children, a father or mother or both, or collateral relatives (up to nephews or nieces in the first degree), a surviving widow, in order to succeed to her husband's estate, must renounce her rights (by notarial deed) in any community of property or partnership of acquests which may have existed between them and any rights of survivorship under her marriage contract. If a wife dies intestate, her husband must first renounce his rights in the partnership of acquests or pay into the estate his share in any community of property which may have existed between him and his wife, or abandon all rights or advantages conferred by a marriage contract. On the other hand, a surviving spouse can choose to renounce her rights of intestacy. This means that she would get one-half of the community property, whereas she would only get one-third under her rights of intestacy.

In Quebec, relatives beyond the twelfth

"Faithful unto death"

How it can possibly matter after death is a good question—but it seems to go against the grain for some husbands to contemplate their widows remarrying, especially if there is a sizable estate involved. To prevent some other man from enjoying both the lady and the money, the husband can decree that the widow be cut off if she remarries, the funds then going to other beneficiaries.

Some wealthy old Romeos have been known to slyly make out their wills in this way if they are not entirely convinced of the undying love of their young wives.

If after the husband's death, a wife finds herself not mentioned in the will she can apply to the courts on behalf of herself and any children. Provincial laws differ, but she would be treated just as though the husband had left no will at all; that is, she could get all of the estate up to $40,000, and at least one-third of any excess.

It is important for a woman to remember that, except in Quebec, any will her husband made prior to the marriage is revoked automatically by the ceremony. Make sure he gets another down on paper, pronto.

Conundrum of Consanguinity

The tracing of degrees of relationship by bloodlines (*consanguinity*, from the Latin words for "together" and "blood") is less complicated than it may appear at first glance. If a man dies without leaving a will, the administrator appointed by the courts must examine the inheritance rights of his descendants. One guide is the "Table of Consanguinity," reproduced here in part, first published in the eighteenth century in Sir William Blackstone's *Commentaries on the Laws of England.* In the first column, the numeral 2 indicates that a man's *father* is in the second degree of blood relationship, his grandfather in the third degree, etc. The slanted lines show how the degree increases with each generation so that the *father* of an intestate is in the third degree of relationship to the intestate's *son,* and so on.

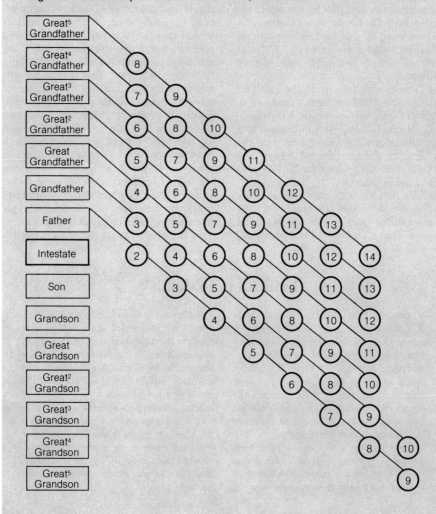

degree of consanguinity do not inherit. If the deceased leaves no relatives within that twelfth line, then the estate goes to the Crown.

It is interesting to note that you don't have to accept a legacy: an inheritance may be renounced by a notarial deed or judicial declaration. The unwanted legacy would "fall back" into the estate and be redistributed either according to a clause in the will covering rejected gifts or else according to the rules of intestacy.

Lineal descendants

Those descendants of the testator which are called *lineal*, descend directly from his bloodline—that is to say, his children, grandchildren, great-grandchildren, and so on, as far as it is possible to go. If there is no will and no widow, these descendants will inherit by law in priority over all other family connections. If there are several surviving children, they will share equally regardless of sex or age.

Ascendant and collateral relatives

Among your "next of kin," after the lineal, or direct, descendants come the *ascendant* (preceding) and *collateral* ("by the side") relatives. These include brothers and sisters, parents, grandparents, uncles and aunts, nieces and nephews, etc. If there is no lineal descendant, the collateral relative nearest in blood to the testator will get the entire estate; if several rank equally, they will share equally. It is possible that a distant cousin who never knew the testator could inherit everything.

In all provinces except Quebec, if a man dies intestate and no wife or children survive, his parents receive equal shares of his estate. If no parents survive, brothers and sisters share equally. If no brothers or sisters survive, the estate is shared equally among nephews and nieces. If none of these survive, any other relatives of equal degree share the estate equally.

In Quebec, if the deceased left no will and there is no surviving spouse or offspring, but there are surviving parents, brothers and sisters, and nephews and nieces in the first degree, his estate is divided into two equal portions. One half is shared among the surviving parents,

and the other half goes to his brothers, sisters, nephews and nieces. If there are no survivors, but other ascendants (grandfather and grandmother), the estate goes to them. Representation *per stirpes* is permitted as far down the line as brother's and sister's children—that is, as far as nephews and nieces.

Let us say that a person dies and his brother is dead but a sister is still living. The children of the deceased brother can represent their father, *per stirpes*, and share that portion of the estate that would have come to the brother had he still been alive. If no brothers or sisters are alive, however, then the children inherit in their own right.

To go one step further: If no brothers or sisters survived the intestate who has just died, or any of their children (nephews and nieces), the children of the intestate's nieces and nephews are not allowed to represent their parents and claim the estate; the law states that there will be no representation among collaterals after brother's and sister's children.

The "in-laws"

Relatives by marriage ("in-laws") who make up the *kith* of the well-known phrase "kith and kin," are not entitled to inherit in an intestacy.

Out of wedlock

In all provinces except Ontario and Quebec, illegitimate children are considered to be legitimate children of their mother for inheritance purposes. The law in Ontario makes no distinction between legitimate and illegitimate children. The law in Quebec provides that, when filiation is established, children born out of wedlock have the same rights and obligations as legitimate children, despite the circumstances of their birth, and they will share in the estate of their natural parents.

It can happen that a child will be considered illegitimate when the mother remarried after her husband had been officially, but erroneously, declared dead after a long absence. Whatever else may occur after the long-lost husband returns, that child would still inherit from its natural father in the case of intestacy.

How to challenge a will

IF SOME question arises as to the validity of a will or to the mental state of the testator, the will can be challenged in the surrogate or superior court. Notice must be given to all interested parties. If the challenge is opposed, the will is then said to be "contested."

If you are convinced that your rich elderly widowed aunt was "unduly influenced" into marrying a plumber half her age who came by her house to fix a leaky faucet, you should first have your lawyer investigate the circumstances. A classic situation arose in Toronto in 1969 when an 84-year-old millionairess married a 47-year-old man, immediately made a new will leaving everything to her husband, then passed away a little more than a month later. Her surviving relatives complained that she was senile at the time and that the suitor had brought undue influence to bear.

When the case was settled in mid-1972, "Mr. Lucky" (the judge used this name as the husband was permitted to remain anonymous) had paid off some of the wife's cousins (with a quarter-million) and had beaten off a raid by the taxmen who had sought $44,500. The estate had been given to him absolutely for his own use and, since 1968, such bequests to a surviving spouse have been exempt from taxation. "Mr. Lucky" indeed!

Where persons would inherit if the deceased had died intestate—but a will was left—these persons can legally require the executors or beneficiaries to produce (or "assert") the will for probate. If the will is produced in court, this gives the challengers an opportunity to contest its validity. If a will is not produced, the court may grant Letters of Administration as though

the property was in an intestacy. The court assumes, then, that the will was either invalid or was not written.

Such a ruling by the judge must contain the court's reasons for this action as well as the reasons why the persons seeking the action have done so. The ruling also calls upon those contesting the will to appear in court or to follow the rulings of the court order. Such orders (called "citations") may call upon a person to accept or refuse a grant of probate, to propound ("produce") a will, to bring in a grant for revocation, or to bring in accounts.

Another familiar device in probate is the *caveat* (Latin: "let him beware"), which is a signed formal notice, directed to the proper court, requesting that nothing be done in the estate of the deceased without notice to the parties concerned. A *caveat* is not a notice to an opponent, nor does it dispute the will. It only allows an interested person to be given notice of the proceedings. Delay caused by a *caveat* can only be temporary, but it allows a challenger to be sure that the estate will not be disposed of until he has had full opportunity to gather information and present any argument or evidence that could upset the will.

Grounds for contesting

Was the will properly signed by the testator and witnessed in accordance with the law? Was the mental capability of the testator such that he knew and fully understood what he was doing? Was he under "undue" influence—for example, had someone been trying to improve his or her own position by insinuations or lies about other beneficiaries? (It is not illegal, however, for someone to make a forceful attempt to gain a testator's affections.) Was he under duress—that is, was he threatened in any way to favor a particular person or persons?

The widow may ask the court to change the terms of a will's provisions regarding her, so that she can meet special circumstances (she may have need of a lump sum to clear some debt). A dependent may have a special financial (or other) problem unknown to the testator when the will was drawn up. A bequest may have unreasonable or repugnant conditions attached—such as a restriction on marrying, or perhaps a provision regarding religion. After years of service, a loyal housekeeper-companion may consider that a bequest does not amount to the sum she had been led to expect during the testator's life.

As a general rule, because the judge is trying to see that the last orders of a person concerning his lifetime possessions are carried out (in effect, the judge is speaking for the deceased owner who is unable to appear to explain his desires), it is difficult to challenge a will successfully even if it may appear that someone has been treated harshly. It is essential, therefore, to get legal advice before making such a challenge.

The surrogate court
In most provinces, judges of the surrogate court deal with the estates of deceased persons, granting *probate* (in other words, "certifying" that a will is authentic and valid), and appointing an administrator if a person leaves no will. Because of the work it does, the surrogate court is sometimes referred to as the probate court. It is in this court that the death certificate is filed.

The surrogate court is prepared to hear the arguments of dependents who seek to challenge the validity or the terms of a will, or seek a variation in the normal application of the laws which apply in an intestacy.

The witnesses to your will, if they are still living, will be asked by your executor to come to court to affirm that they saw you sign. Even if the witnesses are dead, or cannot be located, the court will prob-

Three "Xs" for ambiguity

An ambiguous will can give rise to a court battle between those who challenge its validity and those who oppose, or "contest," the challenge. Consider the document prepared by Mrs. Sheila Allan McEachern of Montreal. She drew up her handwritten, unwitnessed will in February 1971 and, some time before her death three years later, deleted part of a key passage.

Mrs. McEachern's will contained a number of bequests which revealed her special love of animals. By far her most generous gift was a million-dollar property, comprising five lots, which was left to the Montreal Urban Community (M.U.C.) for the creation of an animal park.

Unfortunately, the passage describing the gift had been partially struck out by three "Xs" in Mrs. McEachern's wavering handwriting. The deletions reduced the gift from five lots to two. According to Mrs. McEachern's heirs, who challenged the M.U.C. bequest in the courts, the "Xs" indicated that she intended to revoke her gift entirely. Moreover, the heirs claimed ownership of all five lots.

In contesting the challenge, the M.U.C. pointed out that Mrs. McEachern may have removed the reference to three of the lots because she knew that the city planned to expropriate them. Furthermore, the M.U.C. maintained that the bequest of the remaining two lots was still valid. To support its claim, the M.U.C. cited a clause added to the will by Mrs. McEachern which stated specifically that the two lots were to be given to the M.U.C.

After hearing both arguments, the judge ruled—unambiguously—in favor of the M.U.C.

Death in the river

FACTS

Mr. and Mrs. White had both made wills, each leaving all of their estate to the other if he or she survived the other; in the event that this did not happen, the estate was to go to named persons who were not the same in both wills. One summer's day, the Whites were alone in their automobile when it went out of control and plunged into a river adjoining the highway. Both occupants were drowned. To administer their estates, it was necessary for the court to determine who had died first.

ARGUMENT

The situation in law is that it is next to impossible that two persons can die at the exact, same moment. Accordingly, evidence was presented in an attempt to indicate which of the Whites had lived the longer. It was shown that less than half a cup of water was found in the lungs of Mrs. White and that nearly a quart of water had been taken from the lungs of Mr. White. There was also evidence that Mrs. White had received a blow on her forehead, presumably from the handle of a lawn mower which was in the car at the time of the accident. This wound probably had the result of stunning her and, as a consequence, she would be unable to hold her breath. In reflex action, when the automobile sank there would be a gulp of water into the lungs.

Other evidence was brought forward that the amount of fluid found in the lungs is not an accurate method of determining survivorship, and that evidence of struggle in the water on the part of Mr. White would probably have a tendency to shorten rather than to prolong life.

JUDGMENT

The court held that in determining which of two persons who were in a common accident died first, there was no presumption of survivorship based on sex, or age, or otherwise, and the question for the court was whether there was sufficient evidence from which it could make a finding. Surmise or speculation was not enough; there must be evidence sufficient to satisfy the conscience of the court. After reviewing the evidence, the judge ruled that Mrs. White died first. As a result, all of her estate went to her husband who was deemed to have survived her by a moment, and their joint estate was disposed of through his will.

Following this judgment, the Survivorship Act was passed. This provides that where two or more persons die at the same time—or in circumstances making it uncertain which of them survived the other or others—such deaths shall, for most purposes affecting the title to property, be presumed to have occurred in the order of seniority. Accordingly, the younger is deemed to have survived the older, if only by a moment. As a result of this law, it is no longer necessary to have a trial to determine by medical evidence who died first in a common disaster.*

* Based on an actual case (1936).

416

ably still recognize the will as valid, unless there is strong evidence presented to suggest that there may be something amiss. If the executor is dead or can no longer act as the testator has directed him to, the judge will appoint an administrator to carry out the provisions of your will. The absence of the witnesses or the executor does not invalidate the will.

As stated earlier, if there is no will the court will appoint an administrator to dispose of the estate under the appropriate provincial laws covering intestacy.

Under the Surrogate Court Act of Ontario, the court rules on all matters connected with granting or revoking probate of wills and letters of administration. Similar acts exist in other provinces.

The public trustee

The public trustee is a government official, usually someone in the provincial attorney general's department. He can act as executor, trustee or administrator of an estate which is being handled by—that is to say, under the guarantee of—the government. In British Columbia, Alberta and Ontario, he may be appointed by the courts to act in any matter where it appears that the Crown (that is, the government representing the public) has special interest. He can act together with other parties and sometimes will take over administration from an appointed executor who becomes ill or otherwise cannot carry out his responsibilities.

Strict impartiality and secrecy are the keynotes in all matters handled by the public trustee. He will charge for his services at about the same schedule of rates as do the banks and commercial trust companies.

Granting of probate

It is not strictly necessary to probate a will. But it is wise to have it done as probate is legal proof that a will is considered valid. It is necessary to obtain probate if the testator left company stock or real estate that has to be transferred to beneficiaries, or if money has to be released from bank accounts or insurance policies.

In the normal procedure for seeking probate, the executor files certain documents with the clerk of the surrogate court. These include an inventory of the estate, an application for probate, an affidavit of execution of the will (made by one of the witnesses at the time of executing the will), the original will and any other documents that may be required. As long as he is properly appointed under the will, all of the executor's acts on behalf of the estate will be authorized by the granting of probate.

If a person who was not appointed as the executor (even if that person is a son or daughter of the deceased) should decide to act as the executor—by entering the deceased's house, for example, and taking possession or otherwise disposing of property belonging to the estate—that person will more than likely be in serious legal trouble when probate is made. The headstrong intruder, known as an *executor de son tort*, can be sued by almost everybody connected with the estate, including any creditors of the deceased.

If the court decides that for any of the reasons previously discussed in this chapter a will is invalid, then probate will be denied and the estate will be distributed according to the laws of intestacy.

Debts of the estate

The order in which the assets of an estate are used to pay debts is as follows: (1) the general personal estate remaining after the specific bequests have been paid; (2) real estate which the will asks to be sold for payment of debts; (3) real estate which goes to the heirs because there were no separate instructions left about it; (4) real estate to be used to pay debts and then distributed under the will subject to those charges; (5) funds retained to pay general cash legacies; (6) real estate and personal property left to the heirs by specific instructions.

If there are no heirs

If there is no will—and no heirs can be found—an estate will go to the Crown. In actual practice, it will be converted into cash and turned over to the general funds of the province concerned. In Alberta, the province's universities benefit.

How to analyse your estate and plan your will

In a whole lifetime, many people never sit down to carefully asses "what they are worth." This is an essential exercise if you want to distribute your estate efficiently and properly in your will. At the same time, drawing up an analysis of your property—under the subheadings suggested on these pages—will provide you right now with an accurate assessment of your portion of the "things of this world."

CONFIDENTIAL

Date .... 19.....

Name: Mr. Mrs. Miss   Surname .... Given Names ....

Address: ....

.... Postal Code ....

Telephone: (business) .... (residence) ....   ☐ Married
Occupation: ....   ☐ Single
Birth Date .... Place ....   ☐ Divorced
Name of Spouse .... Née .... Given ....   ☐ Separated
Birth Date .... Place ....   ☐ Widowed

Children

	Name	Sex	Age	Marital Status	Dependents
1.					
2.					
3.					

Other Dependents

Name	Relationship

Have You a Will?   ☐ Yes   ☐ No   If "yes," where is it filed? ....

Has Spouse a Will?   ☐ Yes   ☐ No   If "yes," where is it filed? ....

Who is your —

Lawyer ....
Accountant ....
Broker ....
Life Underwriter ....
Bank ....

Where are your—

Credit Cards ....
Deposit Boxes ....
Deposit Box Keys ....
Life Policies ....
Stocks ....
Bonds ....
Other Valuables ....

ASSETS

Personal
☐ Personal and Household Effects .... $ _____
☐ Cars .... $ _____
☐ Boats .... $ _____

If Farmer
☐ Stock .... $ _____
☐ Machinery and Equipment .... $ _____
☐ Feed and Harvested Crops .... $ _____
Subtotal $ _____

Real Estate
☐ Residence .... $ _____
☐ Farm .... $ _____
☐ Summer Cottage .... $ _____
☐ Other Property .... $ _____
Subtotal $ _____

Cash and Bank Accounts
☐ Bank .... $ _____
☐ Trust Company .... $ _____
☐ Other .... $ _____
Subtotal $ _____

Investments
☐ Guaranteed (GIC, Deb, GTD) .... $ _____
☐ Tax Deferral (RRSP, RHOSP) .... $ _____
☐ Bonds .... $ _____
☐ Stocks .... $ _____
☐ Mortgages .... $ _____
☐ Business interests .... $ _____
Subtotal $ _____

Life Insurance/Retirement Planning
☐ Life Insurance .... $ _____
☐ R.R.I.F. .... $ _____
☐ Annuities .... $ _____
☐ Pensions .... $ _____
☐ C.P. Death Benefit .... $ _____
Subtotal $ _____

Miscellaneous Assets (Hobbies, Jewelry, Antiques, etc.)
.... $ _____
.... $ _____
Subtotal $ _____
TOTAL ASSETS $ _____

(CONTINUED)

HOW TO ANALYZE YOUR ESTATE AND PLAN YOUR WILL (CONTINUED)

Liabilities
- ☐ Loans—Bank .... $ _____
-        Mortgage .... $ _____
- ☐ Income Taxes.. $ _____
- ☐ Gift (Quebec) .... $ _____
- ☐ Capital Gains.. $ _____
- ☐ Succession Duty (Quebec) .... $ _____
- ☐ Leases .... $ _____
- ☐ Guarantees .... $ _____
- ☐ Contractual... $ _____

Subtotal $ _____

NET ESTATE $ _____

WILL PROVISIONS

Executor ....

Disposition:
1. Specific:
(a) Clothing, Jewelry and Personal Effects to: ....
....
(b) Automobile to: ....
(c) Household Goods and Furniture etc. to: ....
(d) Contents of Summer Home to: ....
(e) City Residence: ....
(f) Summer House: ....
(g) Other Disposition: ....

2. Legacies: ....
....

3. Special Trusts to be set up: ....
....

4. Income From Residue:
(a) To Be Paid To ....   For How Long? ....
(b) Are Trustees Empowered to Encroach on Capital?
Any Special Instructions: ....
(c) Other Special Provisions: ....

5. Final Distribution of Residue—if among Children, specify
age when they receive same: ....
....

Investment Powers
- ☐ Trustee Investments ....
- ☐ Canadian life insurance companies...
- ☐ Discretionary..

420

Additional Information

Should Will include clauses on the following?

Insurance Declaration ....

Succession Duty (Quebec) ....

Capital Gains ....

Minors ....

Stock participations ....

Power of Sale or Retention ....

Business ....

Borrow or Mortgage ....

Payment of proceeds of R.R.S.P. ....

Payment of proceeds of R.R.I.F. ....

Election by Executor ....

Illegitimate children exclusion ....

Co-Executor to Purchase Assets ....

Payment of other Retirement ....

Income ....

Gifts over ....

Guardian: To be consulted re care of infant children in the event of the death of both parents.

Name ....

Address ....

Relationship ....

Special Provisions (not covered above)

—Courtesy of Victoria and Grey Trust Company

You and

Your Family

10/Marriage and Divorce

The engagement

MOST PEOPLE in our society get married in a daze of happiness, with little idea of the deep legal consequences of their action. It's hardly the time to study the fine print and to ponder over "whereinases" and "heretofores." The "party of the first part" simply wants to take the "party of the second part" off on the honeymoon without delay and into the rosy future. Events can soon prove, however, that matrimony is a most serious matter in the eyes of the law. If things should go wrong, the couple will find that what was so easily entered into can be very difficult to get out of.

Under the Canadian constitution, the basic laws concerning marriage and divorce (descending from ancient church law) are held within the jurisdiction of the federal parliament. As a result, such matters as legal qualification for marriage and grounds for divorce are more or less uniform across the country. However, the actual marriage ceremonies, both church and civil, are provincial responsibilities, with many differences in the procedures to be followed. The provincial governments regulate other areas such as property rights within the marriage, separation and annulment—to name but a few. The Civil Code of Quebec creates a number of situations quite different from those found in the other provinces.

For every Canadian, though, the law's interest in his marital affairs begins with the same event: the marriage proposal.

"If you will marry me . . . "

The engagement of a man and a woman to marry is a legally binding contract with its own rights and obligations. It contains the mutual promise: "I will marry you if you will marry me"—and, like any promise, it is enforceable in the courts, provided certain legal conditions are met.

The promise must be clearly stated and not involve anything illegal or contrary to public policy. It has to meet two major requirements: "offer and acceptance" and "consideration."

A contract comes into existence the moment the person receiving an offer accepts it. In the case of an engagement contract, the offer or proposal, "Will you marry me?" and the acceptance, "Yes, I will" (or other such words—even "okay" will do), are all that is required, as long as the intention of marriage is clearly stated.

If the woman wants to think the offer over, she may do so. The offer does not have to be accepted immediately, unless a time limit was set by the man making the offer. The same would hold true, of course, if the woman did the proposing. The offer remains open for a reasonable time, or until it is withdrawn.

The doctrine of *consideration* is an ingredient of every valid contract. This means that "something of value" is given before any promise is legally binding. A simple promise to make an outright gift is not, for example, legally enforceable. If you want to commit yourself now to a future gift or obligation, you must make a "covenant under seal," in writing—signed, sealed and delivered. But as long as a promise is given in return for a promise, these formalities are not necessary. In other words, her promise to marry is given in consideration of his promise, and vice versa. That makes the deal binding.

Once the contract has been made, its terms—the promises given—continue to be binding until it is terminated. An engagement contract is automatically terminated by marriage; it can be legally broken by mutual consent, or by either party if the other party has not fulfilled the obligations of the engagement.

Although few people realize it, the law says that if a woman introduces a man to the public as her fiancé and he doesn't dispute it, he cannot deny at a later date that they are engaged.

When you can break it off

You have the right to break an engagement if your intended partner should break one of the agreed-upon conditions of the contract. For instance, if a woman lied when asked before the engagement if she had previous sexual experience, the man could, upon finding out that she was not a virgin, decide not to go through with the marriage. However, if he did not ask the question, she would be under no legal obligation to reveal that fact, and he would remain bound to the engagement. On the other hand, if one of the two discovers that the other is generally promiscuous, he or she can break the engagement without incurring penalty.

Numerous other things can take the legal bond off a marriage promise. One of the main conditions of an engagement is that the contract must have been made voluntarily, in complete free will. A promise to marry that was made under threat of violence, or while mentally impaired because of drugs or liquor, is not binding. Promises made in the small hours after a lively party should best be repeated in the cold sober light of morning to ensure their legal force.

If a married man should offer to marry another woman when he has divorced his wife—or after her death—that promise is regarded by the courts as immoral and will not be enforced.

Under general contract law, certain persons are not considered capable of entering into binding contracts. These include anyone who has not reached legal age—now set at 18–19, with some exceptions—and persons judged by law to be mentally incompetent.

Minors, or "infants" as the law terms them, can become engaged with parental consent. Although a minor can make a contract stick if he is prepared to keep his part of the bargain, he cannot be held to a promise of marriage made while he is a minor, even after he reaches majority. The same applies when a person is later judged to have been mentally incompetent at the time a contract was made.

Generally, under common law, a contract does not have to be in writing to be considered valid. According to the Statute of Frauds, however, an engagement to marry at a date more than one year in the future does require written support in order for it to be enforceable by court action. This evidence could take the form of a written promise of a *dowry* (money, goods or an estate that a woman brings to a marriage), or even a signed letter referring to the engagement. If a father promised to provide a dowry with his daughter's hand in marriage, this condition should be in writing.

The ring—a conditional gift

Although social custom expects an engaged man to give his fiancée a ring, the law does not require him to do so. The gift of an engagement ring, as well as engagement and wedding gifts from family and friends, are generally considered to be "conditional"—that is, given on condition that the marriage actually takes place.

If the wedding doesn't occur, these gifts should be returned to the people who gave them. But there are exceptions. For example, the courts have refused to order a gift returned when the person demanding its return broke the engagement without the consent of the other party. In Quebec, the law provides for a pre-nuptial contract which formally establishes the property rights of the parties.

The courts will not order the return of any gifts given in friendship and not conditional upon a marriage taking place. A courtroom tug-of-war over a fraternity pin would obviously be ridiculous.

Breach of promise

An engagement to be married is, as stated, a legal contract. Accordingly, a person can be taken to court for backing out of such a contract without good enough

427

reason. Legal action concerning such a breach of contract is popularly referred to as a "breach of promise" suit.

A judge obviously cannot order a man and a woman to stay in love, nor can he make them get married. Also, it is not his duty to penalize the person refusing to marry, or to soothe the feelings of the injured party. Rather, it is the role of the court to make sure the jilted person is repaid for any loss caused by the breaking of the contract by the other party.

If a girl, in the glow of her engagement, had spent her own money for furniture, a house or other goods, had left her job or had become pregnant, the courts would probably place a value on her losses and order the man to pay compensation. A man could also sue for breach of promise—if he could stand the leg-pulling of his buddies.

Breach-of-promise suits are becoming rarer in Canada and may disappear completely within a few years. They were abolished in England in 1970.

Parental consent

The law generally states that a person under a certain age cannot marry without parental consent. The legal age is 16 in Newfoundland, 18 in Alberta, Saskatchewan, Manitoba, Ontario, Quebec and

Quebecers must check their alliances

IF THE LADY is willing, and if the parties are in no way connected by bloodlines, the provincial law of Quebec still rules that they cannot, in some circumstances, be legally married.

For example, imagine a Montreal widower with a grown son meeting a Sherbrooke widow with a marriageable daughter. All four become friendly, go to hockey games together, and eventually both couples decide to marry. Naturally, they plan a double ceremony. But there's a catch. Unless the younger couple marries first, they will not be able to marry at all.

This surprising situation comes about because, under Articles 125 and 126 of the Civil Code (the formal written body of civil law adopted in Quebec in 1866), "alliances" resulting from a marriage can be legally dissolved only by death. (Of course, under *federal* law, a marriage in Quebec can also be dissolved by divorce.)

If the older couple in our example married first, their son and daughter (by the parents' previous marriages) would become "brother and sister" by marital alliance—and thus be barred from marrying each other.

The possible complications are endless. The law says that a woman cannot marry the former husband of her sister, even if that couple was divorced under federal law. If the sister should die, then the barrier to the marriage would be removed.

In an actual case, a Quebecer became enamored of his stepdaughter, following his divorce from the girl's mother. But because she would remain his "daughter" until death—in the strict sense of the law—they could not get a license to marry in the province. In another case, a divorcée fell in love with the nephew of her former husband, only to discover that the alliance provisions of the Civil Code prevented them from marrying.

In recent years, several applicants for civil marriage in Montreal have been turned down for reasons of alliance.

In the rest of Canada, where the civil law is based on English Common Law, this particular obstacle on the path to the altar is not recognized as valid. Thus, a Quebec couple unable to wed in their own province for reasons of alliance could be married elsewhere—but they could still be asked to show proof that they didn't travel simply to contract a marriage that would have been illegal in Quebec. A marriage thus performed, however, might not be recognized as valid under Quebec law simply because the parties got married elsewhere just to evade the law.

Prince Edward Island, and 19 in the other provinces and both territories. If the father is dead, or living apart from the mother and not helping support his children, the mother's written consent alone is acceptable. The consent of a court-appointed guardian is also acceptable. No consent is required if there is no guardian and both parents are dead, or if the parents are mentally ill or live in another province or cannot be found.

In most provinces, it is unlikely that healthy minors aged 16 or older will be refused legal permission to marry, even if both parents object. A county or district court judge has authority to dispense with the need for consent if it is unclear whose consent is required, or if the person whose consent is required unreasonably withholds it or is obviously not interested in the maintenance or well-being of the persons concerned. Finally, the office of the provincial secretary can authorize a license or special permit without parental consent when it considers it right and proper to do so.

In Quebec, marriage involving minors is prohibited if the parents withhold their consent. Under Quebec law, the court has no authority to dispense with the need for consent.

In some provinces persons younger than 16 may marry only if the girl involved is pregnant and if the marriage is necessary to prevent an illegitimate birth. In such a case, a doctor's certificate is required.

Violation of these requirements is a punishable offense. However, any such marriage remains valid if it was carried out in good faith, if the participants were not legally barred from getting married for some other reason and if they lived together afterward as man and wife.

Licenses and banns
Before a couple can marry, they must either obtain a license or have banns published in church. Banns, always used in the plural, are a proclamation read for several (often three consecutive) Sundays in the church where the marriage is to take place, giving the public an opportunity to object to the union.

Today, getting a license is the most common way of being granted permission to marry. The license is usually obtained by filling in an application form at city hall and paying a fee to a municipal clerk. The fee varies from $20 in Ontario, New Brunswick and Nova Scotia, to $10 elsewhere. In Quebec, there is no marriage license, as such. Instead, couples must fill out a questionnaire and present certain documentation. Once these documents are approved, a date is set for the marriage. A fee of $90 covers the entire procedure from the initial application to the final civil or religious ceremony.

In the territories licenses can be obtained from any person who has been authorized to issue them by the territorial commissioner, under section 28 of the Marriage Ordinance. The fee is $10 in the Yukon and Northwest Territories.

The application must carry with it an *affidavit* (a sworn statement in writing) indicating that there is no known legal barrier to the marriage. It must also provide certain personal information and state where the marriage will take place. The affidavit should be made by both parties, but it can be completed legally by one of them if he (or she) can present the birth certificate of the other. Quebec requires that the parties wait a minimum of 20 days from the completion of formalities before marrying. During this time, the license bureau publishes its own set of banns to determine if the couple are legally qualified to marry.

If the person issuing the license thinks any information in the affidavit might be false, he must not provide a license until it is cleared up to his satisfaction.

The custom of having banns published (or announced) in church is much less common than it once was. Although the details of the procedure vary from one church, or denomination, to another, as a minimum requirement the intention to marry must be announced during divine service at the church regularly attended. Proof that the banns have been published must then be obtained and given to the person performing the marriage.

The provincial secretary can issue a special permit authorizing a marriage.

Restrictions on licenses

You have to be resident in a province for a certain length of time before you can be legally married there. Residency requirements, waiting periods and expiry dates concerning licenses, as well as special permits and banns, vary from one province to another. Other restrictions refer to mental and physical conditions and any previous marriages.

It is an offense, for example, to issue a marriage license to anyone who is mentally incompetent, mentally ill or under the influence of alcohol or narcotics at the time.

Previous marriages have a definite bearing on how one can marry again. For instance, you cannot marry under the authority of banns if you have been divorced or have had a marriage annulled. The second time around, you have to get a license and you must file certified proof of the legal termination of the earlier marriage. If a previous marriage was dissolved or annulled outside of Canada, you must receive authorization from the provincial secretary before a marriage license will be issued.

The absent spouse

The "case of the missing spouse" has been a popular subject of mystery and romance stories for generations. In the courtroom it is subjected to a rigid procedure. You will be allowed to remarry if you can prove that your absent spouse has been away continuously for seven years; that you have not heard from, or of, him (or her), nor has any other person as far as you know; and that you have made reasonable attempts to locate him and have no reason to believe that he is alive.

The judge may decide to rule the missing spouse as legally dead and issue an order allowing the applicant to remarry under license, special permit or banns. However, the second marriage will be void if the missing spouse later turns up, although some provinces protect the status of any children in such instances.

Divorce on the specific grounds of *marriage breakdown* due to disappearance is a safer alternative. (*See* "The divorce" in this chapter.)

Disqualified for reason

There are two fundamental situations in which individuals are legally forbidden from marrying.

In the first, one or the other is already married and the previous marriage has not been terminated by death, divorce or annulment. Anyone who knowingly went ahead with a marriage under such conditions would be committing *bigamy*.

The second is when the parties are too closely related by either blood *(consanguinity)* or legal ties *(affinity)*. It does not matter whether the relationships are legitimate or illegitimate, or by whole or half blood *(whole blood* means relationship through both parents; *half blood*, through one parent only).

A man may not marry his grandmother, grandfather's wife, wife's grandmother; his aunt, uncle's wife (unless the uncle is dead), wife's aunt; his mother, stepmother, wife's mother; his daughter, wife's daughter, son's wife; his sister, his granddaughter, grandson's wife, wife's granddaughter; his niece, nephew's wife, wife's niece (unless the wife is dead) or his brother's wife (unless the brother is dead).

A woman may not marry her grandfather, grandmother's husband, husband's grandfather; her uncle, aunt's husband (unless the aunt is dead), husband's uncle; her father, stepfather, husband's father; her son, husband's son, daughter's husband; her brother, her grandson, granddaughter's husband, husband's grandson; her nephew , niece's husband, husband's nephew (unless the husband is dead) or husband's brother (unless the husband is dead).

Sexual intercourse between people who fall within the closest range of relationships amounts to the crime of *incest.* (*See* Chapter 19, "Offenses against authority.")

The question is often asked if a man may legally marry his first cousin. The answer is "yes." Two brothers may marry two sisters. And then there's the old chestnut about a man being unable to marry his widow's sister. Don't try to figure out any legal angle on that one—just work on the logic of the situation and you'll understand why it's correct.

The marriage

MARRIAGES are made in heaven, according to the poet Tennyson, but they are lived out on this planet within a framework of down-to-earth rights and obligations. The formal procedure of marriage is known as the *solemnization of marriage.* It can be either a religious or a civil ceremony.

The religious ceremony is performed by a properly ordained or appointed official of a permanently established religious body registered with the provincial government. The form of the ceremony differs from one sect to another and the words used in the solemn promises made by the parties to each other also vary. Seldom heard now is the complete Church of England text in which the bride is asked, in part . . . "Wilt thou obey him, and serve him, love, honor and keep him . . .?" Quebec's Civil Code demands that the couple promise each other "respect, fidelity, succor and assistance" and that each partner agree to supply the family with all necessities in proportion to their respective means.

However the details may differ, the ceremony must meet certain basic requirements: the two people being married must themselves be present, and the marriage must be witnessed by at least two other people. The parties must affirm that they are legally qualified to be married, and they must be formally pronounced husband and wife.

Priests of the Roman Catholic Church, and some of the Church of England (Anglican), will not marry a divorced person while the former spouse is still alive. A Roman Catholic in such a predicament would require special dispensation from the Vatican.

The civil ceremony is conducted by a county, district or provincial court judge (or magistrate) in his office or chambers. In Quebec, a quasi-judicial functionary, called a prothonotary, conducts the service. Some licensed laymen are also qualified to perform marriages, usually in isolated areas.

In Canada there is no proxy marriage—that is, a marriage in which one of the parties is represented by someone else due to his or her own inability to be at the wedding.

Under international law, in unusual circumstances, the captain of a ship at sea (or, presumably, the captain of a jetliner in flight over the ocean) has authority to perform a marriage.

Registering the marriage

Whether the ceremony is religious or civil in form, a "statement of marriage" must be filled out and signed by the couple, by the witnesses and by the presiding judge or clergyman. The latter must then send the document to the provincial registrar general within two days. He must also record the wedding in his own marriage register.

The officiating authority usually provides the couple with a written and signed certificate of the marriage.

The couple can also obtain a certificate of registration of the marriage at any time from the provincial registrar general for a small fee.

If you find out later that the person who conducted your marriage was not properly authorized to do so by law, it doesn't mean that you are single again. The marriage remains valid provided that the ceremony was carried out in good faith,

431

that it was intended to be in compliance with the law and that you have lived together as man and wife since then.

Provincial variations

Although the laws of marriage are basically similar in all the provinces, details differ. To find out what legislation applies in your province, check with the municipal authorities or a clergyman. Some of the more interesting variations:

Nova Scotia law requires both parents' written consent for the marriage of any person who is younger than 19 and not widowed.

New Brunswick imposes a waiting period of five days after a couple have obtained a license before their wedding can take place.

Civil marriage ceremonies have been legal in Quebec only since April 1, 1969. The fee is $90. Saskatchewan charges $25 for ceremonies conducted on weekdays from 9 A.M. to 5 P.M., and $35 on weekends and statutory holidays.

Alberta requires the prospective bride and groom to produce medical certificates proving that they do not suffer from a venereal disease.

In British Columbia, any person can object to a marriage license being issued. This is done by lodging a *caveat* (a "warning") with the office that issues the license. This action will postpone the issuance of the license until the objection is investigated.

Common-law bonds

Don't be misled by the term "common-law marriage." It is not a marriage at all, but merely a setup in which two people, who have not been married according to law, live together as though they were legally husband and wife. The term "companionate marriage" is also used; a religious person might call it "living in sin." Lawyers suggest the terms "informal union" or "cohabitation arrangement."

Under any name, this arrangement does not confer the legal protection accorded regular marriages. In recent decades, however, certain provinces have granted the arrangement some protections. For example, under Ontario's Family Law Reform Act, the woman can claim the right of support from her common-law spouse. Moreover, some provinces have enacted legal safeguards for the children of common-law parents. In Ontario, the distinction between legitimate and illegitimate children has been erased by the Children's Law Reform Act of 1977. The Civil Code of Quebec states that all children have the same rights and obligations, despite the circumstances of their birth, once filiation (the relationship between parents and children) has been established.

Some recognition is given the relationship by certain social assistance programs. There are numerous examples of people "living common-law" who have received welfare benefits and, under the workmen's compensation acts, benefits have been paid to a common-law spouse.

The marriage contract

Until fairly recent times, a wife was literally considered as part of the husband's property, with hardly anything resembling legal rights of her own. Upon marriage, all her possessions became the property of the husband. Furthermore, it was once customary for the father of the bride to pay a *dowry* to the groom—an inducement in the form of money, goods or estate for the husband to take over responsibility for the woman's upkeep. The present-day custom of the bride's father paying the costs of the wedding plus the reception is an echo of the dowry.

Today, marriage is looked upon more as a mutual contract, freely entered into by equal partners. Unquestionably, however, the law is more often interpreted to protect the wife, especially when children are involved.

It is perhaps more accurate to think of marriage as a ceremony that confers on the couple a new status with certain rights and obligations attached. For example, the duties of the new wife are not all the result of actual promises made to the husband; rather, they arise automatically because of her new legal status as "wife."

The social structure in general, and the institution of marriage in particular, are changing in Canada and throughout

Western society. It is impossible to list a hard-and-fast set of rights and duties for either husband or wife. However, the basic rights and duties are so firmly entrenched in our common law that legal action would be necessary to change them.

Duties of husband and wife

A husband has three primary legal obligations to his wife.

(1) He must grant her what is known as "exclusive consortium"—that is, live with her, consummate the marriage and grant her a reasonable amount of sexual love and companionship.

(2) He must support her and her children at a reasonable standard, according to his ability to do so. Basically, this covers food, clothing and shelter and does not legally extend to luxuries.

(3) He must not treat her cruelly. If she is beaten (or even threatened), a wife can charge her husband with assault. (In some provinces, the wife can also now sue the husband for torts—"criminal wrongs"—committed against her.)

A wife is similarly obligated to her husband. She must grant him exclusive consortium, she must not treat him cruelly and she must reside with him at the home chosen by him—as long as his choice is not unreasonable. In Quebec, the Civil Code provides that the spouses choose the family residence together.

Rights of the common-law spouse

IN THE PAST, there was little legal protection for common law spouses in Canada. The common-law spouse simply did not exist as far as the laws of intestacy were concerned. If a man died without making a will, the province, in effect, made one for him and under its conditions, the common-law spouse had no claim at all, unless she could prove a legitimate debt against the estate. If the legal wife was still alive, she would have priority to administer the estate, even if she had not lived with her husband for 20 years.

On the other hand, if the deceased left a will, the document would have to specify the common-law spouse as a beneficiary if she were to receive a penny. Even then, the legal wife (or her dependent children) might be able to upset any bequest to the common-law spouse.

Today, the legal position of the common-law spouse is improving. Under the Succession Law Reform Act in Ontario, for example, a common-law spouse can apply to the court for support after the death of the other spouse. According to the act, the couple must have lived together for a period of up to five years, or "in a relationship of some permanence" where they were the natural parents of a child.

The income tax laws do not allow a common-law spouse to deduct the normal marital exemption, and there are disadvantages under certain life insurance regulations. In Quebec, "community of property" or "partnership of acquests" cannot exist between an unmarried couple.

However, a more sympathetic hearing is granted common-law spouses by the Canada Pension and Quebec Pension Plan authorities. Under the Canada Pension Plan, a person may be deemed to be the surviving spouse of the contributor if neither party was married and the person was represented as the contributor's spouse for at least a year before death. In cases where the contributor was prohibited from marrying the surviving common-law spouse because of a previous marriage, the survivor will receive a pension, if he or she was represented as a spouse for a period of not less than three years before death.

Under the Quebec Pension Plan, a person is to be the surviving spouse if he or she had lived with the contributor for a number of years, had been represented as the contributor's spouse, and neither party was married. If either party was married, the number of years they are expected to have lived together is seven.

Upon marriage, the wife usually abandons her own family name and assumes her husband's. This time-honored practice is known as "the unity of legal personality." In Quebec, under the Civil Code, spouses retain their surnames and given names, and can exercise their civil rights under these names.

Some women, moreover, prefer to retain their maiden name along with their new name or to continue using their maiden name only. For example, the wife of former Prime Minister Joe Clark prefers to be known as Maureen McTeer.

If either party refuses to honor the obligation to live with the other, court action can follow. In British Columbia, Alberta, Saskatchewan, New Brunswick, and the Northwest Territories, a deserted husband or wife may sue in the Superior Court for a judgment ordering *restitution of conjugal rights.* ("Conjugal rights" means the normal rights of matrimony, including sexual privileges.) This step can be taken only after the deserted spouse has first written the other demanding his or her return and the deserter has refused to do so without good reason. If the deserter disregards the court order, the spouse can then apply for what is called a *judicial separation* without the normal two-year waiting period.

A wife is not usually considered a deserter if she leaves her husband's home because of his cruelty or because he did not grant her exclusive consortium. In such cases, in fact, the courts will generally rule that the husband is the deserter, even though it was the wife who left home.

In the traditional division of matrimonial obligations, it was the husband who went out to earn the daily bread and the wife who stayed at home to manage the household and care for the children. That pattern was shattered to a large extent in North America during World War II when women flocked to wartime jobs. About 58 percent of all Canadian women over 25 are now in the labor force.

If a wife goes out to work, can she lawfully expect her husband to perform a large share of her traditional activities? Should he have the right to veto her going out to work? And if the wife goes out to work, is the husband's duty to support her decreased according to her income? The courts are still struggling with these and similar questions arising from changing family life.

As far as children are concerned, husband and wife are at present considered by law to be jointly and equally responsible for their general upbringing, religious instruction and education, unless they have agreed differently or unless a court has ordered differently.

Ownership of property

There is not much temptation to marry the boss' daughter today—unless she happens to be pretty, and generous. A wife in nine of the ten provinces of Canada has full control over her possessions and property, none of which can be legally affected by her husband's private or business debts. She can also own property together or jointly with her husband. (The situation in the Province of Quebec is discussed separately later in this chapter.)

"Real property"—land and buildings—can be owned outright by either the husband or the wife; or owned jointly by husband and wife either by *joint tenancy* or by *tenancy in common.* (*See* Chapter 4, "Before you buy.") Under joint tenancy, the joint tenants own all the property equally. When one dies the property automatically passes to the survivor, regardless of whatever may be said about the property in the will. Many couples prefer to buy their family home in this way, particularly when both of them have contributed to the cost. The agreement of both joint tenants is required for resale of the property.

Under tenancy in common, a rare arrangement, each co-owner has a distinct, but not necessarily equal, share of ownership in the property and is free to deal with or sell that share without the agreement of the other. When a co-owner dies, his or her share does not automatically pass to the survivor, but is subject to the provisions of the will.

If the property was bought in part with the wife's money but was registered solely in the husband's name, the wife can apply to the courts for a declaration that her husband holds title to the property partially as a trustee for her. A husband can do the same thing in reverse.

A wife who is deserted by her husband has the exclusive right to occupy a home which the husband owns—until she leaves that home, or he provides other suitable living quarters for her, or the courts declare that her right has ended. If the husband tries to get around this right by selling the home "out from under her," she can still stay on and enforce the same right against the new owner.

Under Ontario's Family Law Reform Act, the husband of a deserting wife has the right to stay on in the family home even if it was owned by the wife.

Personal property

Husband and wife can choose to own all the family possessions either separately or jointly.

A familiar example of joint ownership is the joint bank account. The contract with the bank usually states that either spouse may deposit or withdraw any amount at any time. (*See* Chapter 7, "The role of the bank.") It also provides that if one dies, the account's balance automatically becomes the property of the other. The basic assumption in this kind of situation is that the two people own the contents of the joint account in equal shares. However, this can be legally changed if, for example, the wife as sole wage earner made all the deposits from her own funds.

Generally speaking, there is no need for a man and wife to determine individual ownership of shared personal property, as long as their marriage remains a happy one. A decision to separate can, however, set off a distressing scramble to gather in as many of the assets as possible. When a satisfactory division is impossible, either person can ask the courts to decide who gets what.

The court's decision would normally be based upon the established rules of property law, but there is room for discretion in individual cases. Personal items clearly bought by one of the parties, or given to one or the other, are usually easily awarded. Articles bought together for joint use are divided equally—for instance, if there was a boat and a car of equal value, one might be awarded the car, the other the

Sir Edward was in a hurry

EVERY LEGAL BOOK in English is dotted with references to the great Elizabethan jurist Sir Edward Coke, Speaker of the House of Commons (1593), Attorney-General (1594), then Chief Justice of the King's Bench. He was the rival of Francis Bacon and notorious for ordering the execution of Sir Walter Raleigh.

Coke opposed King James I's pretensions to absolute power and helped establish the position that the King could not make laws without the consent of Parliament.

The judge himself wasn't above taking the law into his own hands. His first wife having died, Sir Edward decided in 1598 to marry Lady Hatton, a granddaughter of Lord Burghley, chief adviser to Good Queen Bess. Not bothering with the routine pronouncement of banns in church or with obtaining a license, Coke arranged the ceremony in a private house, "according to the Book of Common Prayer," in the company of a few "great men."

The Archbishop of Canterbury, head of the Church of England, censured but did not excommunicate the couple and their attendants as the ecclesiastic law demanded. He granted them absolution for their "crime" because, according to a contemporary record, they were penitent and "the act seemingly had been done through ignorance of the law."

Sir Edward had acted hastily, and he would repent at leisure. The marriage turned out to be a very unhappy one.

boat. Compensatory recognition is given for the contribution made by the stay-at-home wife: by managing the household she has enabled the husband to go out and make the money to buy their possessions.

Court decisions settling ownership are seldom satisfactory to the people involved and a couple should put the problem in the hands of the court only as a last resort.

Husbands have been known to put an asset into the wife's name in order to place it beyond the reach of creditors. But this can backfire if the marriage goes on the rocks. Under the general rule that anything given to a wife as a gift cannot be automatically taken back, the husband may find that the asset is out of his reach as well, should his wife decide to keep it.

Right of dower
Until the late 1970s, a wife in Ontario enjoyed what was known as the right of dower. However, with the enactment of the Family Law Reform Act, the province repealed the Dower Act, and it abolished the right of dower starting from March 31, 1978. The legislation did not apply to the right of dower vested before this date.

Prior to the Family Law Reform Act, a widow had the right to continue living in her husband's "chief house", after his death, and to be maintained by his estate for that time. She was also entitled to possess for life one-third of all real estate fully owned by him when he died.

A man could apply for an order allowing him to sell or mortgage his land free of his wife's dower rights if they were living apart, if he did not know her whereabouts or if she was confined to a mental hospital. If the application was granted, the court could order money to be set aside for her benefit, covering the value of her dower rights.

A wife lost all dower rights upon divorce or if she left her husband to live with another man. However, she regained these rights if her husband took her back again to live with him.

Because of the possible existence of dower rights, it is important for anyone buying land in these provinces to make sure that the vendor's wife also signs the deed or mortgage, thereby ending her right of dower to that land. If the documents do not bear her signature, she could claim her dower right when her husband died—to the financial loss of the buyer.

Homestead rights
A wife in Alberta or Manitoba has a right in the family homestead (or farm). This is a form of dower right and includes both residence and land. Generally, a married man cannot sell or mortgage the "homestead," whether it is in the country or in the city, without his wife's consent or a court order.

Matrimonial property in Quebec
For persons married in Quebec before July 1, 1970, with no marriage contract, the regime of *community of property* applies. While husband and wife each keep control of any real estate owned before marriage or received after marriage by inheritance, almost all other possessions become their community property, unless they had agreed otherwise in a contract drawn up and signed before the wedding. Community property includes income from property, land acquired during marriage (except by succession) and moveable property owned by either husband or wife when they were married or acquired later. The husband controls the use of the community property, although it is owned equally by himself and his wife. Her consent is required for any sale or mortgaging of the immoveable property. It is also required for substantial gifts to other people.

The regime of *partnership of acquests* applies to people who have married after July 1, 1970 and who have no marriage contract.

The community of property, as well as partnership of acquests, ceases in certain situations. These include: when either spouse dies; if the couple obtains a judicial separation; if one party is absent under certain conditions; if the court grants the couple a "legal separation of property."

Upon gaining separation of property, a Quebec spouse can then dispose of it as he or she pleases.

Liability for debts

A century ago, a married woman could not legally enter into business contracts, and she could not be sued for any previous contract debts. When she married, her husband became responsible for her premarital debts.

Today, in all provinces, a married woman can contract debts up to the value of her own separate property; she can also be sued for them. A husband is no longer liable for his wife's premarital debts.

Throughout Canada, a husband and wife are not responsible for each other's debts, except those contracted while functioning as an agent for the other—such as under power of attorney, or by what is known as *implication*.

The wife is said to be acting as an agent by implication when, for instance, she does the normal family shopping or when she buys items for herself or others which rate as "necessaries." (It is difficult to define necessaries in any precise way.) The widely held idea that a husband can avoid responsibility for debts run up by his wife by publishing an advertisement in the personal column of the local newspaper is not legally sound. The court could rule this did not amount to "constructive notice." The husband holding the credit cards would be better advised to contact merchants directly.

"Agent of necessity"

If a husband deserts his wife or treats her with such cruelty that she is forced to leave him, she is considered to be his "agent of necessity." Unless she has agreed to maintain herself, this status allows her to pledge his credit to provide the necessities of life for herself and the children of their marriage for as long as he fails to do so. However, at the same time, she must also commit a reasonable amount of her own money or earning power as well. Her failure to contribute when able to do so might provide the husband with grounds for not paying her bills.

Creditors who take a man to court to collect for the debts of his wife under this provision may not succeed unless they can prove that she has really been deserted in the eyes of the law.

Although most people think otherwise,

Poets and marriage

Marriage, if one will face the truth, is an evil, but a necessary evil.
—Menander (343–292 B.C.)

Hasty marriage seldom proveth well.
—William Shakespeare (1564–1616)

Marriage is a noose.
—Miguel de Cervantes (1574–1616)

Marriage is a desperate thing.
—John Selden (1584–1654)

Deceive not thyself by over-expecting happiness in the married estate. Remember the nightingales which sing only some months in the spring, but commonly are silent when they have hatched their eggs.
—Thomas Fuller (1608–1661)

If marriages are made in heaven, they should be happier.
—Thomas Southerne (1660–1746)

All comedies are ended by a marriage.
—Lord Byron (1788–1824)

Marriage is . . . a field of battle, and not a bed of roses.
—R. L. Stevenson (1850–1894)

A good marriage is that in which each appoints the other guardian of his solitude.
—Rainer Maria Rilke (1875–1926)

Marriage is a damnably serious business, particularly around Boston.
—J. P. Marquand (1893–1960)

parents are generally not responsible for their children's debts. The exceptions are when a child becomes an "agent of necessity" or when the parent has specifically guaranteed some undertaking. Nor can minors be sued, except in contracts for the purchase of "necessaries of life." The storekeeper who allows a minor to take away a valuable item on the assumption that the parents will pay for it on their account may live to regret his trust.

Neither husband nor wife is liable for the other's wrongful acts against other people. Nor are they responsible for their children's wrongful acts, unless it can be proved that they were negligent for failing to provide proper supervision of their children's activities.

Lawsuits in the family

During the time when husband and wife were described in both legal and poetic terms as "one," they could not sue each other—because it was impossible that a person could sue himself. The situation is different today.

Each is now free to sue the other for breach of contract or to enforce his or her separate property rights. However, in many provinces, a husband still cannot sue his wife for any *tort* such as negligence, assault, battery or defamation. (*See* Chapter 18, "What is a tort?") A wife can only bring a civil lawsuit against her husband when "the protection and security of her own separate property" is threat-

ened. In such a case, she can bring any action against him that she could bring against a stranger. In Ontario, under the Married Women's Property Act, there is a special provision for settling land-title and land-possession disputes between husband and wife—for example, a wife could proceed to sue her husband for trespassing on land she owns separately.

Under the Canada Evidence Act, one spouse cannot normally be compelled to give evidence against the other in a criminal trial. Communication between husband and wife is privileged—that is, it cannot be used as evidence, or publicly broadcast. It is not, in legal terms, a breach of confidence to tell your spouse *anything*, however confidential or slanderous it may be. It may, of course, be a spectacular error of judgment.

Passing on the estate

Both spouses are free to bequeath their separate property in their wills as they see fit. Property that was owned as a joint tenant, however, passes automatically to the surviving joint tenant.

Court action to contest a will can only be taken by dependent relatives of the deceased person if no adequate provision was made in it for their future maintenance. They may apply to the probate court for a lump sum payment, periodic payments, or the transfer of certain assets into their names. (*See* Chapter 9, "Changing your will.")

The dilemma of the working wife

A STRESS IN MARRIAGE hardly known to our grandparents is that arising from the continued career of the wife—or of the mother, when the children grow up. The regulations under the codes of human rights in the provinces forbid any sex qualification in the advertising of jobs, and many women, looking for challenges and responsibilities beyond their household routines, are tempted to resume (or begin) careers in business or other fields.

There is no law that says a husband can forbid his wife to work at a job outside the home—and he has no right to any money she may make. But, if she no longer performs the woman's traditional home services, the question of equal responsibility for household expenses can arise.

The law does not seek to intrude in the living room, or in the bedroom, but in the last analysis, it will protect that well-tried human institution—the family.

The annulment

I F A MARRIAGE takes place that does not meet the requirements set out by the law, then it is not a marriage at all. It can be erased by the courts just as though it never happened. The process is referred to as *annulment*. Petitions for annulling a marriage can be presented in the superior court of every Canadian province; if granted, a *decree of nullity* will be issued. Then the parties are single and free from all ties to each other.

The provincial laws, in this instance, are similar almost to the point of being identical. Annulment has sometimes been called "the poor man's divorce."

There are many grounds for annulment and in all cases but one the marriage will be declared void *ab initio* ("from the beginning"), as if it had never taken place. However, when impotence—that is, inability to perform the complete sex act— is proved to the satisfaction of the court, the marriage is considered void only from the moment of the annulment order.

In addition to impotence, other grounds for annulment of marriage are bigamy (marriage to more than one partner), being under legal age or too closely related, and being mentally incompetent. A marriage can also be declared void if one of the persons was forced into it under threat of death or injury, or was genuinely mistaken about what was taking place, or if some major formality of the marriage process was not observed.

If a marriage is annulled, the man has a right to have the engagement ring returned. Similarly the persons who gave all other conditional gifts can expect to have them returned.

An annulment on all grounds except impotence can be requested not only by the man or woman involved, but also by any interested outside party. It is possible that a marriage can be annulled even after one of the parties has died.

The voluntary consummation of a marriage by sexual intercourse will generally prevent an annulment being granted, except in cases of bigamy or where the man and woman are too closely related.

Any children born in a marriage that is later annulled are considered legitimate as long as the man and woman married in good faith and were not aware of any legal obstacle. The custody of such children will be decided by the court. Jointly owned property can also be divided.

Among Roman Catholics

Annulment is still the only method recognized for ending a marriage within the Roman Catholic Church. The Pope can rule any marriage dissolved, but the Vatican uses the power sparingly.

In Quebec, where the majority of citizens are Roman Catholic, the number of annulment petitions decreased when civil divorce became possible in 1969. Until then, the courts were pressed into leniency by changing attitudes to the sanctity of marriage. The grounds for annulment, particularly those concerning relationship by ancestry and by legal affinity, were sometimes interpreted very liberally. Under the present divorce laws, Quebec now has the second highest annual number of divorces (19,193 in a recent year), just slightly behind Ontario (21,860).

The case of the bigamist

Bigamy is the crime of knowingly getting married while still legally wedded to another. (*See* Chapter 19, "Offenses against authority.") Some language experts might argue that the word should be *polygamy*—the offense (in Canada, at least) of having more than one spouse at the same time.

If the man who wooed and won you during your vacation should turn out to be legally married, you can seek an annulment and know your petition will succeed—because the second marriage has no legal standing. The bigamist too can apply for a decree of nullity. He could be sued by his spouse for damages and probably would be jailed for his crime.

If asked, the courts would, in effect, nullify the marriage contract because it was based on fraud. No contract made under *any* grounds that are false will be recognized in law.

It has been suggested that once a person is sure that his (or her) marriage is void, there is no need to "make a court case out of it." If you are the victim of a bigamist, your feelings are probably deeply hurt

and you would want to avoid public exposure. As the victim of a bigamist, you are as unmarried as any single person and have every right to contract a marriage with another person. However, you would be wise to discuss the situation thoroughly with a lawyer before you take any such action.

The lawyer will probably advise that you apply for a decree of annulment, officially stating the phony marriage to be void. This document can be invaluable, for instance, in clearing the title to property and, over the course of the years, may avoid headaches about inheritance.

Bigamists are not necessarily crooks. It does happen, for instance, that a girl makes a teen-age runaway marriage and is soon deserted. A number of years later, she falls in love and receives a proposal of marriage. Rather than risk losing her happiness, she doesn't tell the man about the previous incident. She may quite truthfully believe that the desertion and

The annulment that changed the world

THE MOST FAMOUS CASE of annulment of marriage was that of Henry VIII in his determined efforts to rid himself of his wife of 18 years, Catherine of Aragon, the widow of his brother Arthur.

Although Henry was warring with the spiritual power of Rome (that is, he did not acknowledge the supremacy of the Pope), it is likely he was genuinely concerned with Catherine's failure to produce a male heir to be the future monarch. Catherine did, however, produce Mary, Queen of England, 1553–1558.

Deciding he must have the vivacious Anne Boleyn, maid of honor to his sister, and in view of the fact that she refused to become his mistress, Henry applied to the Vatican for an annulment of his marriage to Catherine. When it was refused, he broke formally with the Roman Catholic Church—with results that had profound effect on the subsequent history of several nations (including our own).

The Pope (Clement VII) did not really have much freedom of choice. In 1527 the Hapsburgs had seized Rome and the Vatican was under the control of Charles V, the Emperor of the Holy Roman Empire. Charles was also King of Spain and he wasn't about to allow England's Henry to cast off his Aunt Catherine.

Henry married Anne secretly in January 1533 and their daughter, who would become Elizabeth I, was born the following September. But Anne, also, did not provide the desired male heir and, facing charges of adultery and incest, her marriage was annulled.

Henry's eye was now on Jane Seymour whom he married the same year. She did, at last, give the lusty Henry a son—the future King Edward VI, a sickly boy who mounted the throne at age 10 and died at 16. But the regents who ruled in his name ensured that the power of Rome in England was broken forever.

long separation was the same thing as a divorce, or that the ceremony she went through was not entirely legal. And she may honestly believe the first husband to be dead. It's only when he turns up—and bad pennies usually do turn up—that the issue of criminality arises. And, in the hypothetical case we have set up here, the woman might have a sound defense to any charge of bigamy. For example, having no knowledge of a spouse for seven years is an acceptable defense.

Couples have been happily "married" in an unintentional state of bigamy for many years, raising families and becoming pillars of the community. If unintentional bigamy is revealed (perhaps by learning after a span of years of the death of an earlier partner believed to have been dead), the couple can straighten the record by slipping quietly down to city hall and being "remarried" in a civil ceremony. On the other hand, if a missing spouse turns up, the court would probably grant the embarrassed partner a divorce on grounds of marriage breakdown.

Discretion of the court
The laws providing for annulment of marriage are based on common law (arising from customs and decisions in the courts rather than from legislation) which, in this area, is drawn from the earlier church, or canon, law. Thus, although the courts are seldom eager to grant annulments based on circumstances never before tested in the law, they have considerable leeway in making decisions in such cases.

A serious or important error or defect in the formalities of a wedding ceremony—either civil or religious—can be grounds for annulment. The judge would have to decide just how serious the defect was. Obviously, for example, a mistake about the identity of either the bride or groom would be sufficient. There are cases of recent immigrants with language difficulties going through a civil marriage ceremony under the impression that it was merely a formal betrothal, something that is routine in their homelands, or that it was some official procedure toward gaining Canadian citizenship.

The judge may have to rule in a particular case on the basis of the public interest. For example, if parents petitioned for the annulment of an underage daughter's marriage, the court may refuse the order if the girl is pregnant and the young couple want to stay together.

Even if it appears to fulfill all the requirements of the law, a marriage may be annulled if the court is convinced that the wedding took place because of some deceit or hoax practiced by either the bride or groom. Some places in the United States allow annulment, for instance, if financial promises made as an inducement to marriage turn out to be false. In Canada, such promises would not by themselves constitute grounds, nor would empty boasts about possessions, social status or career prospects.

Normally, if you find out after marriage that your spouse has a criminal record or one or more illegitimate children, you will not be able to use that as grounds for annulment. Do your detective work before you say "I do."

Any marriage between persons of the same sex is automatically void. So is any marriage where the parties deliberately make any false statements in the application for banns or a license.

For a petition for annulment to be considered on the grounds that there was a defect or mistake in the ceremony it must be brought out within a reasonable time after the wedding. The time varies from province to province.

The "shotgun wedding"
The essence of any contract—including a marriage contract—is the expressed free will of the participants. Anyone forced to marry under threat of death or injury has grounds to seek annulment.

The "shotgun wedding" beloved of Victorian novelists—when the seducer is forced at gunpoint to marry the girl he has wronged—falls into this category. So does the case of the woman who is told by a man that he will kill her if she does not marry him. The judge may have the difficult and delicate task of deciding whether the threat was genuine or merely an indication of the lover's desperation.

"For better, for worse"

FACTS

The plaintiff brought an action against the father, mother and brother of her husband for damages for false representations made to her before marriage as to the character and financial standing of her husband. She also charged them with entering into a fraudulent conspiracy to induce her to enter into the marriage contract. The wife said that the defendants had represented the husband to be a prosperous man who never drank intoxicating liquor, and who was of unblemished moral character and reputation. However, the facts, as alleged by the wife, were that the husband "was given passionately to intoxicating drink, and was of a very immoral character and was lewd and licentious, and had one or more illegitimate children." Moreover, he was a poor man.

ARGUMENT

For the wife, it was argued that the false representations on the part of the husband's family induced her to enter into the marriage. When the plaintiff discovered the falsity of the representations, she could not take steps to undo the marriage that she had contracted on her faith in them. It was a perfectly valid and binding marriage, as there had been no false representation by the husband. The wife had entered into the contract to improve her position, but did not improve her position; that was the result of the misrepresentation, and she argued that she should be compensated by damages.

For the defendants, it was alleged that the plaintiff had held to the contract for five years and had had the benefit of it.

There had been children. The plaintiff could not now try to disclaim the marriage contract.

JUDGMENT

The court ruled that, even if the wife had brought an action to void the marriage when she discovered the falsity of the representations that she alleged, she could not have succeeded. The law, observed the judge, makes no provision for the relief of a blind credulity, however it may have been produced. Fraudulent misrepresentations of one party as to birth, social position, fortune, good health and temperament cannot break the contract, nor even does the concealment of previous unchaste and immoral behavior in general.

After discussing the character and financial position of the husband, the court concluded that "the plaintiff and her friends allowed the marriage ceremony to be celebrated with great precipitation. Unless the husband has woefully changed for the worse in six years, I would have thought that a girl of ordinary discernment would have discovered, even in the very brief courtship which took place, that he was not a very safe person to whom to entrust her happiness, be the commendations of his father and mother ever so warm. She took her chances and must now, as far as this court is concerned, read into her contract the words 'for better, for worse; for richer, for poorer.' "*

* Based on an actual case (1889).

If either bride or groom was proved to have been under the influence of liquor or drugs at the wedding, and later claimed no knowledge of what she or he was doing, an annulment might be granted.

Impotence and repugnance

Enjoyment of a reasonable amount of sexual love with the spouse is legally guaranteed under the marriage contract. Impotence—the inability to perform the sex act completely—is usually sufficient grounds for annulment, because it means that the marriage cannot be consummated and, therefore, the contract is not fulfilled.

The impotence can be either physical or mental in origin. But it has to be detailed most exactly: to consummate the marriage there must be penetration of the vagina by the penis, and there must be an ejaculation of semen. Even the fathering of a child does not prove potency since a woman can conceive without there having been actual penetration.

Impotence must have existed when the marriage took place, and the person seeking the annulment must have been unaware of the condition at the time. Medical or psychiatric evidence of the disability is usually required by the courts.

Usually, a person presents the other's impotence as grounds for annulment. But a person can also claim his own impotence as a reason to seek annulment, especially if he was unaware of it before the marriage. Impotence occurring later in the marriage does not count as grounds for annulment; nor does sterility—the inability to father, or bear, children. (Some places in the United States do recognize sterility discovered after the marriage.)

The law recognizes that impotence can have its roots in both biological and mental causes. It is considered genuine, for example, if caused by a nervous disorder or an incurable hysterical condition, such as repugnance of the sex act. Repugnance—that is, finding the act acutely distasteful—will be accepted whether it involves sex in general or the marriage partner in particular. In other words, even though the person concerned can make love normally with other members of the opposite sex, he or she might find the marriage partner repugnant.

Refusal of sex relations

Willfully refusing to have sexual relations with the marriage partner is not grounds for annulment in Canada—although it has been a ground for divorce since the proclamation of the revised Divorce Act in 1968. Since the proclamation of this act, petitions for annulment because of impotence are becoming rare.

When the flesh is weak

ANNULMENT OF MARRIAGE will usually be declared if either the new husband or the wife cannot complete the normal act of sexual intercourse. Where the problem lies with the wife, it is sometimes referred to as *frigidity*. In an actual Canadian case, seven days after the wedding was considered ample time for impotence to be established.

It is obviously extraordinarily difficult to prove impotence, where it is not admitted. The condition can be caused by physical incapacity, by nervous apprehension and simply by a deep-rooted antipathy to the spouse as a sex partner. A man who is instantly potent in illicit circumstances can find out to his chagrin that he is flatly hopeless in the marriage bed.

If such a case should reach the courts, it must be proved by either medical or psychiatric evidence; but the respondent might refuse out of embarrassment to submit to any such examination. He (or she) would then run the risk of having his conduct construed as an admission of disability. A refusal to make love at all might also be construed as an admission of impotence.

The separation

IN MATRIMONIAL LAW, *separation* is defined as "the cessation of cohabitation of husband and wife by mutual agreement, or, in the case of *judicial separation*, under the decree of a court." It can perhaps be described as a half divorce; the parties are released from some of the legal commitments of marriage but are not free to marry anyone else.

Both kinds of separation—by private contract or through court action—are available in all provinces of Canada, except Ontario, where only the private separation agreement is available. Quebec permits the private agreement but will not enforce it through the courts.

The main practical difference is that the private agreement (like all contracts) must be entered into voluntarily by both of the parties, while the judicial separation decree can be awarded to only one of the parties in the absence of the other or even in the event of his or her opposition. There does not seem to be any particular reason behind the different position of Ontario in this matter; yet there is no apparent move afoot for this province to get into line.

The judicial separation is sometimes referred to as "a separation from bed and board." It has been particularly popular in Quebec where most residents are forbidden by their religion to get a complete divorce from the marriage ties.

Couples will separate when it is too difficult or expensive to get a divorce, when there are not sufficient grounds for divorce action or when some of the technical requirements for divorce have not yet been met. Separation may also be chosen if there is some hope for future reconciliation. The separation of a husband and wife ends when they start living together again on a permanent basis or when they get a divorce.

The mutual separation agreement

Exact statistics are impossible to obtain, but it is a fair estimate that about 40 percent of all Canadian marriages end in divorce. Couples who decide to separate may do so by verbal agreement. However, it is strongly recommended that they prepare a written agreement with the help of solicitors, carefully outlining the conditions of their separation.

The separation agreement falls under the general law of contracts. It is a matter for negotiation and must be made according to free will in order to be binding. Items often covered by separation agreements include:

(1) Support payments by one spouse to another.

(2) Custody, maintenance and access to children.

(3) Division of the matrimonial assets, such as property, stocks and bonds.

(4) Responsibility of the wife for her own debts.

(5) Release of any interest in the other's estate in the event of death.

(6) The wife's release of her right of dower (or some variant of this right) in any land owned then, or later acquired, by the husband.

In addition, the agreement usually provides that neither person will start court action against the other, except perhaps to later obtain a divorce or to enforce the agreement if the other is not living up to it. However, either person would still be allowed to go to family court about the welfare and needs of the children during custody proceedings. One partner could also take court action later to make the other person properly support and maintain the children if the other was not doing so as agreed.

Even though a wife may have signed away all claim to support from her husband, she may still go to court in an effort to get financial support if she is likely to become a welfare case without it. In the eyes of the law, the man is still her husband. This would be regarded as a case of the public good coming before private interest and would be decided within the discretion of the court.

If there is a valid separation agreement, neither party can charge the other with the matrimonial offense of *desertion*. This is discussed later in this chapter.

Separation agreements are only valid if they are made after the couple has actually decided to separate. An agreement calling for separation sometime in the future is considered to be against public policy and is, therefore, void. Similarly, an agreement to deliberately create legal grounds for a future divorce is also void.

Because the separated couple is still partly tied to the original marriage contract, and to many of its legal obligations and duties, both partners are, naturally enough, not allowed to remarry. Furthermore, they are not free to have a sexual affair with anyone else. However draconian this may appear in modern times, it must be clearly understood that were either to have such an affair, it would amount to *adultery* and, if it could be proved to the satisfaction of the courts, it would be grounds for divorce under federal divorce laws.

The judicial separation

A judicial separation, or "a separation from bed and board," can be granted by the courts in the form of a decree. It can be requested by one marriage partner even against the wishes of the other.

The recognized grounds for judicial separation are basically the same as those for divorce. They are fundamentally the same in the nine provinces that allow the procedure: adultery, rape, sodomy or bestiality (actual or attempted), cruelty or "grievous insult," desertion for two years or desertion coupled with failure to obey

The household tyrant

TODAY, WE IMAGINE that the stereotype of the brutal, possessive, and often drunken wife-beater—once the mainstay of popular novels and plays—has passed from the scene in our own enlightened times. Unfortunately, the frequent incidence of marital violence today provides no support for this belief. However, public awareness of the problem has increased legal protections for its victims.

Since 1968, physical cruelty has been ground for divorce everywhere in Canada. A spur-of-the-moment separation can arise from a sudden outbreak of maltreatment of the wife who becomes outraged by such a physical attack, especially when the action was unjustified.

No man has the "right" to strike his wife; she is most definitely not his "chattel." Psychologists are, however, quick to point out that the pressures and frustrations of a complex existence—particularly in crowded high-rise cities—can provoke an uncharacteristic physical outburst that may have little or nothing to do with regard or affection for the spouse.

Whatever the causes, the public was shocked by a 1980 study prepared for the Canadian Advisory Council on the Status of Women which estimated that one out of every ten women is battered by the man with whom she lives. Although the evidence of a wife, pro or con, is not normally accepted in court when the husband is in the dock, an exception is made in cases of assault when the wife is the victim. Generally speaking, allegations of marital cruelty have to be backed up with facts.

445

a judgment ordering *restitution of conjugal rights*. Several provinces also include mental illness.

The government of Ontario does not grant judicial separations. Ontario and Prince Edward Island do not order the restitution of conjugal rights.

Under a separation order, the marriage partners are released from the obligation of living together; yet the man, depending upon the terms of the separation, must usually contribute to the woman's financial support. Property is divided (including *community property* and *acquests* in Quebec) and neither party can be charged with desertion. As explained above, the separation decree does not allow either party to remarry.

The person who applies for a judicial separation must be a resident of the province in which he is petitioning, but he does not have to be domiciled there.

In Alberta and Saskatchewan, a judicial separation will not be granted if the person seeking the decree had *condoned*—that is, agreed to overlook—any of the matrimonial offenses complained of in the petition. Nor would it be granted if the petitioner had committed adultery which had not been condoned by the other spouse.

Everywhere in Canada, a petition will be thrown out of court if there has been *collusion*—that is, a secret agreement for a fraudulent purpose—in the preparation of the case. The grounds must be genuine in every detail, not trumped up by the parties. There must never be any effort to deceive a court.

Under the Civil Code of Quebec, excessive verbal violence is regarded as within the definition of cruelty that can justify the granting of a judicial separation. The degree of cruelty would be interpreted by the judge according to the normal lifestyle of the couple. For instance, it has been suggested that if a cabdriver swore continually at his wife, she wouldn't have much luck in seeking a separation decree; however, if a cabinet minister began to do so, the politician's wife might convince the court that this was cruelty on his part.

The Quebec courts will probably grant a separation decree to a wife who is either pushed out or locked out of the matrimonial home. And if she had brought a dowry into the marriage, it would have to be returned to her.

Desertion in marriage

There are at least a dozen definitions of desertion, but in matrimony it quite simply consists of one partner leaving the other without good enough reason and without the other consenting to the departure. The deserter is committing an offense with clearly defined penalties. A period of desertion can be used as grounds for judicial separation and, indeed, for a full divorce. It has become the most common of all matrimonial offenses, offering a dignified way out of an unhappy marriage with the minimum of publicity.

In all provinces, action for financial support of his wife and children can be taken against a deserting husband. When a woman deserts, her husband no longer has to support her. In Alberta and Manitoba, she loses homestead rights in her husband's property.

Two factors are essential for a spouse's absence to be labeled as desertion. There must be actual physical separation of the parties (they can't stay under the same roof unless they maintain separate households) and the one who has been deserted must want the deserter to return. This underlines the fact that living together is one of the terms of the marriage contract; if sexual and social companionship is refused (as by intentional absence), the contract is said to be willfully broken.

If a husband went away on a long—even unexplained—business trip, he would not be guilty of desertion. He may just be journeying afar to some other town (or province, or country) to look for a new job. While a man is serving a prison term, he cannot be guilty of desertion—although three years' imprisonment can be grounds for divorce under the terms of *marriage breakdown*.

Strange as it may seem, the validity of a desertion is not canceled if the couple should meet occasionally, even for the purpose of having sex. The court would take the attitude that such meetings might lead to a reconciliation and therefore should not carry any penalty. If the deserting party offers to return to the matrimonial home, it must be with the understanding that cohabitation will be resumed in the full sense.

Constructive desertion

There is also a reverse kind of desertion, known as *constructive desertion*. In this case, one of the parties feels compelled to leave because of an intolerable condition in the home, caused by the other. By a curious contradiction of language, in this instance the one left at home is considered to be the deserter.

Constructive desertion might be acknowledged by the court if the husband refused to provide a reasonable matrimonial home. Again, the judge would have to weigh the factors of life-style against the implications of what is to be considered "reasonable."

"Intolerable conditions" would not include playing the electric guitar or drums in the basement. A wife's laziness, or her habit of wearing her hair in curlers, would not rate either. Neurotic behavior will not satisfy the courts; nor will a wife's confession that she loves another man, or a husband's conviction for a crime (unless the crime involved is cruelty to the spouse.

On the other hand, leaving the matrimonial home would probably be condoned by the court if it was proved that either the husband or the wife made excessive or unnatural sexual demands. Wife beating or other cruelty (not necessarily physical), ungovernable temper and uncontrolled drinking are all likely grounds for constructive desertion, as are adultery and failure to provide a reasonable home and support.

Restitution of conjugal rights

Echoing an earlier era, an order for *restitution of conjugal rights* will be issued in the nine provinces (and in the territories) where decrees of judicial separation are granted. By this edict, the deserting wife or husband is ordered to return to the family home and resume full sexual and other responsibilities of the marriage contract.

The law can perform mighty feats but it cannot force a man to make love to a woman (or vice versa). The restitution order is mainly used as a technical device in cases of judicial separation. Even if the absentee does return home in response to the order, there's no compulsion for him or her to play the lover.

One of the grounds for judicial separation is two years' desertion except in Quebec, where there is no time period. This period may be shortened if the deserted party writes to the other, asking for a return to the marital bed. Assuming no reply or a refusal, the next step would be

---

Mrs., Miss or Ms.

FREQUENTLY, when a man meets a woman in a business or social situation, he finds it difficult to figure out whether she is single, married, or divorced. As the male title "Mr." does not reveal marital status, many women now take the same anonymity by using the new female title "Ms."

On marriage, a woman may take her husband's name and keep it forever, even if she is later legally separated or divorced from him, or if she is widowed.

Mrs. Patrick Campbell, the famous English actress who was a friend of Bernard Shaw, retained her husband's name even though he was killed at war early in her career and she later remarried.

It is custom that prevails, not law. A woman can marry in Canada and keep her own (or *maiden*) name, if she so chooses. Since April 1, 1981, a woman married in Quebec must retain her maiden name for legal purposes. A woman married before that date can choose to retain her husband's name or revert to her maiden name.

447

to apply for an order for restitution of conjugal rights. If this were ignored, the judge might consider it equal to two years' desertion.

Deciding that ordering its citizens to live together was somewhat out of place in these permissive times, England has abolished this kind of action.

The finances of separation

The general public thinks of alimony as payment to a divorcee. But, in law, *alimony* is financial support received by one spouse from the other—usually a wife from her husband—while they are separated, but still legally married. What the husband agrees to pay after a divorce is called *maintenance*.

The conditions surrounding the granting of alimony and maintenance are basically the same from province to province, with some differences concerning the support of children and court procedures. Fundamentally, a husband and father will always have to provide for his family as far as he is capable of doing so. And a woman doesn't have to file for a separation to obtain an order for alimony.

A wife can apply for alimony if her husband has committed adultery, deserted her or treated her with intentional cruelty. The cruelty must have been severe enough that it was likely to produce, or actually did produce, either physical illness or mental distress that would permanently affect her health. (Cruelty in marriage law is discussed in detail in the next section of this chapter.)

Alimony will not be granted to a wife if a husband has refused to live with her because of her adultery or cruelty. If alimony had previously been granted to such a wife, the husband could apply to have it suspended until her behavior proved whether she deserved it or not. (One must keep remembering that the separated couple is still "married" in the eyes of the law.)

The amount of alimony to be paid in any case is fixed at the court's discretion, based on the circumstances of the people involved. An average award in Ontario has been calculated at about one-third of the husband's take-home income. The wife's own earning capacity or wealth, if any, is also taken into account.

Having requested court action to seek alimony, a wife may also apply for interim, or temporary, alimony to tide her over until the trial, arguing that she cannot maintain herself and bring her action to court without it. The husband has a chance to argue against this claim. These temporary amounts are awarded to allow the wife to live "modestly" until the trial.

Support of minors

The age of children at which the parental obligation to support them ends varies from province to province. In general, the age limit is 16, or 16 to 18 if the child is attending school (except in Quebec, where there is no limit). In British Columbia, however, parents must provide support until the child is 19. In Newfoundland, parents are responsible until the child is 17, or as long as he or she is incapable of earning a living.

When a man deserts his wife or children without providing for their support, action can be taken against him immediately in the provincial family court. The court will almost certainly order the father to make regular payments. If he does not obey and has no good reason for his default, he can be sentenced to terms of three months in jail. If he cannot or will not pay, the family will be supported through the welfare system.

The payments for the support of the children will in most cases be calculated with the alimony for the deserted wife. They will be assessed according to the man's means, with notice being taken of any other funds that might be available for family support.

If conditions change after an order is made, the court will hold another hearing and cancel the order or alter it in any way it thinks necessary. A woman's subsequent adultery—not condoned by her husband—would prevent her from getting alimony, but payments to maintain the children of the marriage would continue. Support for the children of the marriage that are in her custody would continue even if the wife later obtained a divorce and remarried.

The divorce

| Grounds for divorce |
| Adultery, sodomy, sexual assault |
| Cruelty and homosexuality |
| Marriage breakdown |
| Illness, insanity |
| Procedure at the court |

I N THE CENTENNIAL YEAR of 1967, Canada's justice minister, a Roman Catholic bachelor from Montreal named Pierre Elliott Trudeau, introduced in the House of Commons the first thorough reform of Canada's divorce law since Confederation. It had been chewed over and attacked by the provinces, the churches and literally dozens of other organizations. It passed into law the following July as the Divorce Act, 1968.

During the mid-1970s, the Trudeau government proposed another major overhaul of divorce law, further loosening the "bonds of matrimony." The plans called for the introduction of what was labeled "no-fault divorce." Such a divorce would be granted to either husband or wife on the sole ground of *marriage breakdown*, without any need to prove either party guilty of anything. Both the Canadian Bar Association and the Law Reform Commission of Canada subsequently supported this proposal. By 1983, certain obstacles—chiefly the inequitable provincial matrimonial property-sharing laws—had been cleared away, and the federal government introduced legislation that would make no-fault divorce possible. There was also a hint that the period of separation before divorce would be reduced to one year.

The 1968 act had greatly broadened the recognized grounds for divorce and made divorce law uniform throughout Canada. It was a combination of the existing time-honored conditions, plus some concepts that in their time were considered almost revolutionary. Following 1968, divorces in Canada increased from 11,165 a year to 67,671. The 1981 national statistics revealed that there had been one divorce for every 2.8 marriages; in 1967, there was one divorce for every 14.9 marriages.

In plain language, divorce puts an end to marriage. Thus it is quite different from annulment or separation—both of which are described earlier in this chapter. All that remain of the marriage obligations and duties after a divorce are any conditions written into the decree by the courts, such as the payment of maintenance, division of property or rights concerning custody of any children.

Any person who is domiciled—that is, has his permanent residence—in Canada can start divorce proceedings in the superior court of any province where he or she has ordinarily resided for a period of one year immediately before presenting a "petition for divorce" to the court, and where he or she was actually residing for at least ten months of the preceding year. The person wanting the divorce is known as the *petitioner*. The other party becomes the *respondent* and any third person involved becomes the *corespondent*.

Although the 1968 legislation dramatically widened the grounds for getting a divorce, it was still slanted toward encouraging reconciliation of warring couples. If the marriage relationship is found to be hopelessly damaged, a *decree nisi*—a provisional order—will be made, to be followed by a *decree absolute*, usually after three months. *Nisi* is the Latin word for "unless." It implies a waiting period in case something happens to make the final severance either illegal or unnecessary (hopefully, the couple will reconsider before parting forever). Only after the waiting period is over and the decree absolute is granted are the parties free to marry again.

Although an unopposed divorce action is often basically straightforward, being conducted almost automatically by experienced clerks of the court, anyone who is contemplating divorce should seek legal advice at the outset. A divorce action is a civil suit like any other and is studded with pitfalls. Take magazine articles about "do-it-yourself divorce" with a grain of salt.

Grounds for divorce

Before the 1968 reform, the only grounds for divorce in Canada were adultery, unnatural sexual offenses and (in Nova Scotia only) cruelty. The Divorce Act recognized all three right across the country and added the new grounds of homosexuality, bigamy and permanent marriage breakdown.

Marriage breakdown can result from a spouse's imprisonment, addiction to alcohol or drugs, disappearance, nonconsummation of the marriage, separation or desertion.

Whatever ground is put forward, the petitioner must, at this writing, prove to a judge of the superior court that it exists with regard to the other person. In only one instance can the guilty party petition for a divorce: the deserter may seek legal freedom after an absence of five years. In the following sections, each of the grounds for divorce is discussed in detail.

Adultery

Adultery is voluntary sexual intercourse by a married person with someone of the opposite sex other than his or her spouse. It is the most basic offense against the traditional marriage contract and need only occur once for the wronged person to use it as a ground for divorce.

The decision to take action is, of course, up to the individual; you could always decide to overlook an isolated incident on the grounds that "one swallow doesn't make a summer." If you did overlook such an incident, however, and continued to live normally with the spouse, that transgression would not likely serve later as a ground for divorce.

In the strict view of the law, adultery does not require a complete sexual act.

The slightest degree of penetration of the vagina by the penis is sufficient. But petting, or fondling, even involving considerable intimacy, is not considered adultery in legal terms.

The petitioner in a divorce case involving adultery has at present the burden of proving that the respondent actually committed adultery with a third person, the corespondent. This can prove difficult for many reasons, one of them being that both the respondent and the corespondent can legally refuse to admit to the act of adultery by relying on the legal privilege to avoid self-incrimination. In the absence of absolute proof, the judge will accept what is called "a balance of probabilities" in divorce cases.

If the respondent and corespondent are cooperative and admit to adultery, the judge (if he believes the evidence to be truthful) will usually grant the divorce without the need for further evidence. However, he may also want confirmation of the admission—that is, some independent evidence supporting the testimony.

Eyewitness testimony to any adultery is rare. Canadian judges would frown upon such sensational evidence as photographs claiming to show an adulterous sex act in progress. Taken by stealth or surprise, such evidence would strongly suggest conspiracy and might bring a charge of breaking and entering.

You do not need to go to such dramatic extremes to prove adultery. Any of the following will serve as supporting evidence:

(1) Show that there is "undue familiarity" between the respondent and the corespondent, coupled with evidence that they were together in privacy for a long period, particularly at night.

(2) Show that the two people concerned have lived together in the same house or apartment and passed themselves off to their neighbors as husband and wife.

(3) Show that a respondent-wife has had a child if either her husband happens to be sterile or it appears that the husband could not have had intercourse with the wife during the time when the child might have been conceived.

The petitioner must make a serious attempt to find out the name of the person with whom the spouse is supposed to have committed adultery. Failure to establish the identity of the corespondent will not, however, eliminate chances of obtaining the divorce if the other circumstances warrant the grant.

A person who dies before a petition for divorce has been filed cannot be named as a corespondent, nor can a person who is merely described—the name being unknown to the petitioner.

Since adultery must be voluntary, a woman who is sexually assaulted has not committed adultery. But she will stand so accused if she is found to have visited a bawdy house, even as a client.

Sodomy, bestiality, sexual assault

Although a person convicted of sodomy, bestiality or sexual assault can be sued for divorce, the conviction will not necessarily be accepted as a ground for divorce unless the individual pleaded guilty at an earlier trial. Also, the offense has to be actually committed, rather than merely attempted.

Sodomy is anal intercourse by a man with any person, including his wife. If a wife consented to her husband practicing sodomy with her (without force or trickery) she cannot use the occurrence as a ground for divorce. A woman can be guilty of sodomy as well: by aiding and abetting it upon herself or upon some other woman.

Bestiality is an unnatural sexual act committed by a man or woman with an animal.

Buggery can be bestiality or sodomy.

Sexual assault has replaced *rape* as the name of the offense in the Canadian Criminal Code. A 1983 amendment to the Code abolished the offense as "rape" and substituted in its place "assault involving sexual intercourse." (A similar amendment was made to the Divorce Act.) The earlier legislation defined "rape" as a man's sexual intercourse with a woman, other than his wife, without her consent. According to the 1983 amendment, a person of either sex may commit sexual assault. Previously, the only time a man could "rape" his wife in the eyes of the law was when they were legally separated. This limitation has been removed by the 1983 amendment. Under the new provisions of the Criminal Code, either spouse may be guilty of sexually assaulting his or her partner at any time throughout their marriage.

The changing status of the divorcée

THE DIVORCEE REMAINED a scandalous figure until very recent times. Until 1925, the Canadian courts would grant a man a divorce if his wife committed adultery (that is, if she had sexual intercourse with anyone except him) but the wife could not get a divorce unless her husband's adultery was accompanied by any of the following: sodomy, bestiality, rape, incest or desertion for two years.

Things have obviously changed over the years, and even more revolutionary changes are in the wind. The Divorce Act of 1968 not only wiped out this double standard but made divorce available to either party on grounds of simple adultery (even one isolated transgression is enough) or through "marriage breakdown." The latter term encompasses a wide range of factors, including three years' separation by mutual consent, or five years' separation if there is no mutual consent. New laws may sweep away the "time factor."

The decision of King Edward VIII to abdicate his throne to marry Mrs. Wallis Warfield Simpson, a twice-divorced American woman, changed our view of the divorce. When the ex-King was dubbed Duke of Windsor, the ex-Mrs. Simpson became the Duchess. She was asked to Buckingham Palace for tea by her niece, Queen Elizabeth II. But 30 years later.

Cruelty

Before 1968, cruelty could be cited as a ground for divorce only in Nova Scotia; under the present law, it applies everywhere. Cruelty can be either mental or physical, but it must be severe enough to make it impossible for the couple to continue living together. Since cruelty covers a broad range, it is impossible to put forward an all-inclusive definition. At one end of the scale, repeated beatings are obviously cruel; at the other, irritations arising from the day-to-day normal friction between a man and a woman living together are not. To some, rock music is torture, but it's not necessarily cruel.

Judges will assess a case of alleged cruelty on the basis of its individual merits and are not likely to grant a decree lightly. The courts have been concerned that cruelty (especially alleged mental cruelty) not be used as a quick and easy gimmick for getting out of a marriage when other legal grounds are missing.

In most cases, the couple must be living apart as evidence that living together is impossible for them. Actual violence is not necessary, but there should be an element of fear or dire apprehension. In general, an accusation of physical cruelty must be backed up by confirmed facts—such as bruises or complaints made by the victim at the time of the act of cruelty or immediately afterward.

If the cruelty was provoked by, say, excessive nagging or bullying it would not justify divorce.

Cruelty would likely be found proved if there was "grossly insulting and intolerable conduct," such as a man forcing his wife into prostitution or making other excessive or revolting sexual demands upon her. The repeated excessive beating of children might be accepted as grounds; so, too, might refusal to maintain reasonable personal hygiene.

What could be described as severe cruelty is not accepted as a ground for divorce if the "victim" consented to it. The courts are alert to the possibility of masochism, the perverted enjoyment of pain. It has also been ruled that the cruelty does not have to be intentional on the part of the respondent. It is the effect of his conduct upon the other person that matters. It is usually required that there be witnesses to at least some of the acts of cruelty. In most cases of mental cruelty the evidence of a doctor is required.

Homosexuality

Although no longer a criminal offense between two consenting adults in private, *homosexuality* is still a matrimonial offense under the Divorce Act of 1968, and constitutes grounds for divorce.

The law allows a petition based on sodomy, bestiality, rape, or a homosexual act by *either* a husband or a wife. Thus a wife indulging in a lesbian relationship with another woman is guilty of a homosexual act and her husband could have the marriage terminated on that ground.

Bigamy is generally considered to encompass adultery, but under the law it is grounds for divorce whether the second marriage has been consummated by sexual intercourse, or not.

Marriage breakdown

Sir Alan Herbert (perhaps better known as humorist A.P. Herbert) once wrote a best seller called *Holy Deadlock*, about the indignity and perjury that then surrounded divorce in England. Later, as a member of the British parliament, he took a leading role in liberalizing the law. The reforms introduced 30 years later in Canada would no doubt have both delighted and astonished the British satirist. The most revolutionary part of the 1968 act in Canada was the section establishing *marriage breakdown* as a ground for divorce.

The act sets out six specific conditions, any one of which, if proved, will be accepted as permanent breakdown of the marriage. Apart from these conditions, the couple must be living apart, with no intention of resuming cohabitation.

Imprisonment is a basis for marriage breakdown if the respondent has been in jail for a total of three years during a five-year period dating back from when the divorce petition is filed, or for at least two years immediately before that date under a commuted sentence of death or of ten years' imprisonment. In the case of the ten-year sentence, all avenues of appeal must have been exhausted before divorce proceedings can be started.

Addiction to alcohol or a narcotic (including marijuana) is a basis for marriage breakdown. The respondent must have been grossly addicted for at least three years before a divorce petition can be filed and must not be expected to undergo rehabilitation within the near future. Medical evidence is required attesting both to the addiction itself and to the absence of reasonable hope for a cure.

Disappearance is a basis for marriage breakdown if a person has been absent for at least three years immediately before the petition is filed. The petitioner must have had no idea of the respondent's whereabouts during this period and have been unable to locate him (or her), in spite of strenuous efforts. Before "disappearance" was an acceptable ground for divorce, the spouse of a person "whereabouts unknown" was allowed to remarry after having that person declared legally dead; however, if the missing person turned up, the second marriage was made void. Now the returning wanderer finds himself divorced and this distressing problem has itself disappeared.

Nonconsummation is a basis for marriage breakdown if a person has refused to consummate his marriage (*i.e.*, perform the sex act completely) or has been unable to do so for any reason for at least one year. It should be noted that this ground for divorce—in contrast to the ground of *impotence* for annulment—allows for both inability and refusal to consummate the marriage.

Separation leads to marriage breakdown if the two persons concerned have mutually consented to live apart. One of the parties can file for divorce after they have lived apart continuously for at least three years and there is no chance of them ever living together again. No reason has to be given for the separation, although the testimony of a corespondent or other third party is usually required to verify the length of the separation period. This condition cannot be used by someone who has deserted the matrimonial home.

Desertion is a basis if the two people have been living apart continuously for at least five years immediately before filing of the petition. It should be remembered that in *desertion*, one of the parties has left without the consent of the other.

Separation is currently the most popular ground for divorce in Canada. When a couple decides to call it quits, they can part, wait for three years and then get a *decree nisi*; after that, a *decree absolute* is almost a certainty within the next three months. Since no reasons for the separation need be given, publicity as well as unsavory fact-finding are reduced.

In the case of the deserter—the guilty party, as it were—it is considered a matter of public policy that he or she should wait five years before being able to file for a divorce.

The three- and five-year periods required for separation and desertion under the Divorce Act must be continuous. However, they may be interrupted once for a 90-day period if the couple should decide to try living together again in a genuine attempt to reconcile their differences. Full cohabitation can be resumed in this period without affecting any later divorce action. At his discretion, a judge can refuse a decree based on separation or desertion if he feels it could be "unduly harsh or unjust to either spouse."

Illness and insanity

Long illness and protracted insanity are not themselves grounds for divorce in Canada but a person can gain a divorce due to either one of these conditions under the provision of marriage breakdown due to separation—if separation, in fact, existed.

It is possible, though, that the court might consider granting a divorce under these conditions to be "unduly harsh or unjust to either spouse." On the other hand, the judge would not want to lock anyone into a hopeless and tragic situation. As in so many cases where feelings are more involved than facts, the decision would largely depend on the circumstances.

Interference in marriage

Certain types of interference by an outside person can contribute materially to the breakup of a marriage and lead to divorce action. In some situations, the injured spouse can sue the third person for damages. Three types of conduct that fall into this category are enticement, criminal conversation and alienation of affections.

Enticement occurs when a husband or wife is lured away from his (or her) partner, thereby depriving that partner of the mate's *consortium*—that is, the normal marriage relationship. The deprived partner can sue the offender for damages under the tort of enticement. (*See* Chapter 18, "Seduction and enticement.")

The suit will not stand as grounds for divorce if the conduct in question did not actually result in separation of the spouses, if it was not the primary cause of a marriage breakdown or if the person charged was unaware that the enticed person was married.

Criminal conversation really involves action rather than talk; it is in fact an archaic term for committing adultery with someone's wife. Since adultery is a tort (a wrong) under common law, the husband may well be entitled to damages against his wife's lover.

It is interesting to note that a woman similarly wronged is not permitted the same recourse in some provinces.

A suit for damages resulting from criminal conversation remains a separate action in New Brunswick, Nova Scotia, Prince Edward Island, and Newfoundland. Criminal conversation does not exist as such in Quebec, though a husband can bring a suit for general damages against his wife's lover, charging a civil wrong. In British Columbia and Alberta, either a wife or a husband may bring an action for damages.

Alienation of affections, as the term implies, is the act of a third person in causing a married person to feel less love or affection for his or her spouse.

Although it is no longer recognized as the basis for a separate suit for damages, if someone can make a case for it in an action for criminal conversation or enticement, it will serve to increase the damages awarded to him.

Bars to divorce

The Divorce Act sets down certain circumstances in which the court will, or may, refuse to grant a divorce decree, despite the establishment of grounds for divorce. These circumstances are often referred to as "bars." Among the best known are the "three Cs"; collusion, connivance and condonation.

Collusion is an agreement, or conspiracy, involving the petitioner that is intended to deceive the court. It would cover any arrangement to either fabricate or suppress evidence. The judge has to dismiss the divorce petition if he finds that collusion exists.

What exactly is cruelty?

AS PUT FORWARD in some divorce courts, *cruelty* can cover everything from gross physical maltreatment to eating crackers in bed. Judges are, however, loath to accept cruelty as grounds for divorce without clear-cut evidence. They must be convinced that the actions complained of make continued cohabitation "intolerable."

A British Columbia husband was granted a divorce when he complained of his wife's cruelty. She had repeatedly taunted him with being a less vigorous lover than her previous boyfriends, and his health suffered under the continual strain of emulation.

An isolated punch-up might not be accepted as "cruelty." A Newfoundland wife was beaten by her husband but the judge decided she should bear with it under the terms of the marriage lines . . . for better or for worse. In general, a wife has to show that the husband's conduct is undermining her health, or putting her under fear that her health could be destroyed.

Clear examples of collusion would include: an agreement between the petitioner and the respondent that the latter will commit adultery in order to provide a ground for divorce; and an agreement that the respondent will not fight against the petition as well as he might.

Collusion does not normally apply to proper arrangements for separation, financial support, division of property, custody of children, and so on. But so many seemingly routine arrangements are "potentially collusive" that you would be wise to leave all such issues in the hands of a solicitor.

Lawyers acting in divorce cases are not only under a duty to the court to make sure that no collusive arrangements are made that they know of, but they must also inform the court of any potentially collusive deals they think might exist. If a judge suspects collusion, he can call in an official known as Her Majesty's Proctor, who will investigate and report to him. If the suspicion is confirmed, the judge will not grant the divorce.

Connivance occurs when one marriage partner encourages, aids or permits the other to perform an act that can then be used as a ground for divorce. Connivance sometimes arises in divorce petitions presented on grounds of adultery, unnatural sex offenses, bigamy or cruelty. For example, a wife who wishes to be free to marry someone else might arrange (or even pay) for her unwanted husband to spend a well-documented weekend with another woman.

If the presiding judge decides that connivance exists, he will dismiss the petition—unless he feels that the public interest would be better served by his granting the decree.

By definition, connivance occurs before the act it initiates. However, mere negligence, inattention, dullness of apprehension or indifference do not rate as connivance. The conniver's role must have been an active one. For instance, a husband is not guilty of connivance by watching for proof of suspected adultery between his wife and another man; nor is the wife if she accepts over and over again that her husband is only catching up with

correspondence when he takes his sexy secretary for weekends to some resort.

Condonation describes the circumstance where one marriage partner knows of but overlooks ("condones") some past misconduct of the other partner and acts in a manner that shows that the transgression has been forgiven. In other words, the court won't let you forgive an incident and then later decide to use it in a divorce petition.

If husband and wife resume their normal marital association following such an incident (including the resumption of sexual intercourse), the courts may consider that to be sufficient evidence of condonation. But not always. In Ontario, for example, it has been ruled that intercourse between husband and wife during a true attempt at reconciliation, which subsequently failed, is not conclusive evidence of forgiveness. It is considered, however, as *some* evidence of condonation and must be disclosed for consideration by the judge in the light of all surrounding circumstances.

The Divorce Act itself states that the continuation or resumption of cohabitation during any single period of up to 90 days in a genuine attempt at reconciliation does not constitute condonation.

Most judges would normally dismiss a petition for divorce if there was condonation. But they are permitted discretion to decide if the divorce would, after all, be in the best public interest.

The chance of reconciliation

Reform of Canadian divorce law attracts interest and controversy, because it seems always to make divorce much easier to obtain. However, in the 1968 revision, there were some provisions aimed at encouraging married couples to stay together that received little publicity.

When a divorce petition is presented on the ground of permanent marriage breakdown, the court must refuse the decree if there is hope that the couple may resume cohabitation within the reasonably foreseeable future. During *any* divorce hearing, the judge must ask the petitioner (and also the respondent, if present) if there is any chance of their reconciliation—unless, of course, the circumstances of the case make it clearly inappropriate to ask.

If the judge detects a possibility of the marriage being saved at any time during the hearing—and if the parties are willing to try—he will adjourn the proceedings to give the couple a chance to reconcile their differences. He may nominate a trained person to counsel them. If the attempted reconciliation doesn't succeed within two weeks, either party may ask that the hearing be resumed.

Except where obviously inappropriate, it is the duty of every lawyer representing a petitioner in a divorce case to point out the reconciliation provisions of the act. He must also discuss the possibility of reconciliation with his client and advise of any marriage counseling services known to him that might help to rescue the marriage. The lawyer has to sign a statement confirming that he has done these things.

"Undue harshness"

When a divorce petition is presented on grounds of permanent marriage breakdown because of three or five years' separation, the court must refuse the decree if its granting would be "unduly harsh or unjust" to either spouse, or if it might prevent reasonable maintenance arrangements being made for the persons concerned. A judge might make the divorce decree conditional upon steps being taken to remedy the potential injustice.

The court would refuse a decree under marriage breakdown if the decree would make it more difficult to ensure reasonable arrangements for the maintenance of any children of the marriage. This means, for instance, that a woman who is an invalid could be guaranteed support for herself and her children even if the sole reason for her receiving such maintenance was that it would be unjust to leave her stranded.

Serving the documents

If you decide to go ahead with your divorce, your lawyer will fill out the petition, including all particulars of your claim against the respondent. There is a stack of other papers, too. He will file these papers with, and have them approved by, the provincial superior court.

Before proceedings can begin, the petition must be "served upon"—that is, given to or brought to the notice of—the respondent, plus any corespondents. The "service" is performed by a sheriff's officer, or bailiff, who personally delivers copies of the petition. Normally, this is done within 60 days.

If the respondent or corespondents cannot be located, or are evading the "service," the court can authorize "substitutional service" of the documents. This is done either by serving them upon another person who is likely to bring them to the attention of the respondent, by advertising a notice of the proceedings or by sending them by registered mail.

Every effort must be made to avoid the possibility of someone being divorced without his or her knowledge.

The court hearing

In all of the provinces except Newfoundland, divorce petitions are heard by superior court judges who sit without a jury. British Columbia, Alberta, Ontario, Nova Scotia and Newfoundland relieve the load on their top courts by appointing county or district court judges to act temporarily, and this system is spreading. Divorce petitions from Newfoundland are heard by a trial division of the province's Supreme Court.

The respondent has two choices when served with a petition for divorce. He can simply do nothing about it altogether or he can go to court and fight it. The great majority of divorce cases in Canada, as elsewhere, are uncontested, the parties having already decided to part company. In most cases, also, the lawyers on each side have agreed on all, or most, of the items concerning property, maintenance and custody of children before the petition for divorce is served.

Even in the simplest of uncontested cases, however, it is rare for the divorce to clear the courts in less than six months. Apart from the heavy load of cases to be heard, the judiciary shows no inclination to turn our courts into a divorce mill. This attitude is unlikely to change, even if the politicians do vote for "divorce on demand." The courts are run by judges, not politicos.

Defended actions

When the respondent decides to contest the case brought against him, he must file an "answer" stating that intention within a set time after being served with the petition. The time allowed varies from eight to 60 days, depending upon the province where the petition is registered.

Divorce actions are opposed for various reasons: to deny having committed the alleged matrimonial offense; to deny the existence of a marriage breakdown; and to disagree with the petitioner's demands concerning financial settlement and custody of children. Should the respondent feel that he or she also has grounds for divorce, or feel entitled to support from the other, he (or she) might introduce a counterpetition. In this instance, the same judge will hear both petitions together.

Undefended actions

If the respondent decides not to contest the action, the petition will be treated as "uncontested" and the petitioner can proceed to the court hearing without involving the respondent further.

The judge will still demand proper evidence to show that grounds for divorce really do exist before granting any decree.

Role of the "private eye"

Once a familiar figure in divorce cases involving adultery is the private detective hired by the petitioner to help establish evidence of illegal sexual activity. He is seldom seen in Canadian courts today. His main task was to find evidence of misconduct in the past. If this failed, he would "shadow" the suspect in an attempt to catch the person in circumstances that support the charge of adultery.

Because the evidence of the "private eye" is sometimes suspect in the courts (after all, he is being paid to help his client win), investigators usually seek to involve other people in the operation—perhaps friends of the petitioner—who can then support any testimony in court. Most private detective agencies in Canada are entirely reputable—not at all like some of the absurd characters of television drama. They are supervised and licensed by

Divorce, Canadian-style

SINCE THE REFORM divorce law in 1968, the rate of divorce in Canada has quintupled. There are now 278 divorces per year for each 100,000 people.

Compared with earlier times when an uncontested divorce action might take a year to get before the courts, almost all are now tried within six months—in some cases in semirural counties, within four months. There is usually a three-month wait before the divorce is finalized (hopefully, the parties might decide to kiss and make up). Since the grounds for divorce were widened, about 95 percent of all actions are undefended. Most of the defended actions will eventually proceed without contest once disputes over custody of children or financial support are solved.

Women's magazines and newspaper columnists sometimes offer "do-it-yourself" kits to the intending divorcée, and it is certainly possible to gain an uncontested divorce without legal help. This is not recommended, however. There are few "average cases." Even the most straightforward cases can contain unforeseen problems and there is a daunting heap of official paperwork to be attended to with pinpoint accuracy. If rights are signed away in ignorance, they may be irrecoverable. One "divorce kit" was found to contain 20 errors.

The total cost of an uncomplicated, undefended divorce should range between $750 and $1000, according to a recent Montreal estimate. Not so much, perhaps, for a second fling at freedom.

government, and usually bonded—that is, held to their pledge of responsible conduct by having to deposit a sum of money with a government agency.

The detectives are adept at rounding up eyewitness evidence from motel clerks and chambermaids, waiters and cabdrivers as to the identity of couples seen in compromising circumstances.

Since reform of the divorce law made it easier to shed an unwanted mate in a reasonably dignified manner, the dramatics of the "private eye" have tended to fade from the scene.

The divorce decree
If the judge so rules, a *decree nisi* will be granted after the divorce hearing. This does not end the marriage; but states that it will end after a certain time period, unless some reason backed by solid evidence is given to the court why it should not. The *decree absolute* is granted at the end of the waiting period, depending on the outcome of any appeals that may have been made.

The usual time between the two decrees is three months. However, the court may shorten this time, or eliminate it altogether, if the judge feels that it would be in the public interest to do so, and if the people involved agree not to appeal. For instance, one of the parties may wish to remarry urgently to prevent a child from being born illegitimately.

During the normal waiting period, anyone may go to the court to explain why the decree should not be made absolute. The usual reasons given are that fraud or collusion were involved in obtaining the decree or that the couple have decided, at the last moment, not to part after all.

An appeal against the decree nisi can be made to the provincial appellate court. If that should fail, if it is on a point of law, the appeal may possibly be heard by the Supreme Court of Canada.

The court does not automatically grant the decree absolute: it must be applied for. If the petitioner fails to apply for it, the respondent may do so. This decree severs the last ties of the marriage, and the parties are completely free to remarry.

Corollary relief
Corollary (or "ancillary") relief under the Divorce Act refers to conditions made by the court concerning the maintenance, or financial support, of a spouse and children, as well as custody of and access to children. These conditions are similar to those in the case of judicial separation. The judge will base his decision on the financial strengths and needs of the persons involved.

All maintenance and custody orders granted under the Divorce Act are effective and enforceable throughout Canada. However, they can be varied or stopped afterward by the court that made them in light of any changing circumstances.

Maintenance of spouse
"Spouse" may be an awkward and confusing term to the layman, but it is used in this (and other) sections of this book when the reference is to either the husband or the wife.

Before the Divorce Act was revised in 1967, maintenance payments generally flowed from the man to the woman. Not any more. Equal pay and opportunity laws have wiped out the double standard. There are more wealthy women in North America than wealthy men: insurance policies and the stress of big-time business have seen to that.

After considering the financial circumstances of both parties, the court may order either of them to pay whatever lump sum, or periodic payments, it considers reasonable for the maintenance of the other. It may also order one spouse to pay interim alimony to the other while the divorce proceedings are still in progress.

Maintenance of children
The court will order the father—or the mother, in some cases—to pay whatever sums it deems reasonable for the maintenance of any eligible children. Temporary maintenance may also be ordered.

Children eligible for both maintenance and custody consideration are known as "children of the marriage." A "child of the marriage" is any child of the couple who is younger than 16 (18 in Quebec), or who is 16 or older but unable to provide for himself because of illness, disability or some other reason. Perhaps he is still at school. It doesn't matter if the child is the legitimate child of both of them, one of them, or neither, as long as the couple fills the role of parents to that child.

When a divorce petition is drawn up, certain information about the children of the marriage must be included. In Ontario, for example, a copy of the petition must be served on the Official Guardian of the province. He then makes an investigation concerning the children's custody, maintenance and education, and prepares a brief written certificate for the judge to consider. Either of the parties involved in the divorce action may challenge any statements in this report.

All provinces try to take care of the innocent victims of divorce. Since it is widely accepted that no amount of money compensates for the lack of a parent in the normal development of a child, the 1968 Divorce Act strongly emphasizes reconciliation. Divorce or no divorce, no one can easily dodge responsibilities to the children of the marriage.

Custody of the children

Awarding custody of children can be one of the most difficult aspects of a divorce case. Facts and emotions are tangled like spaghetti in a boiling pot. Judges maintain that it is the most wrenching of all decisions. All other considerations, including the interests of the parents, must yield to the welfare of the innocent children thrust into what is, for them, a personal tragedy they can barely understand.

The greater financial resources of one parent do not influence a custody decision to any extent, because the court can order the wealthy parent to make maintenance payments should it decide in the other parent's favor.

When a judge grants one parent exclusive custody of a child, he usually gives the other reasonable access, or visiting privileges. However, he might deny visiting privileges altogether if this might pose a threat of physical or mental harm to the child, or if the other parent has shown that he or she is not interested in the child's welfare and is not likely to make any beneficial contribution to the child's upbringing.

A custody or access order is never final. It is always open to review and can be varied in the light of changed attitudes and circumstances. The courts are aware that a person may have been a failure as a spouse but can still make an excellent parent.

Each custody situation is decided on its own merits, although certain patterns have emerged over the years. For example, custody of very young children is awarded to the mother on the theory that she plays a more direct and decisive role in early development. Older girls have also been more often awarded to the mother, while older boys have often been placed with the father.

Role of the divorcée

The ex-wife is seldom the "gay divorcée" made famous in Hollywood musicals. Perhaps she does have another man waiting eagerly in the wings—most times, she just vanishes into the shadows. Even if adequate maintenance is paid, there is no way to turn back the clock or to erase the memories of days that gleamed with "happily ever after."

The eighteenth-century writer Samuel Johnson was reported to have remarked about a gentleman, who had been very unhappy in marriage and yet had taken a second wife after the death of the first one, that he was demonstrating "the triumph of hope over experience."

If you are divorced and you want to marry again, you must file with the proper official at the marriage license bureau at city hall a certified copy of the decree absolute that you have been granted. If your first marriage was terminated (or annulled) outside Canada, you will need the authorization of the provincial secretary before you will get a marriage license.

After divorce, the wife assumes the status of spinster again, except for any ongoing responsibilities she may have under the terms of the decree. She can choose to keep her married name or go back to using her maiden name.

11/Youth and the Law

Children and parents 462

Children at school 474

Children at work 483

Children in trouble 491

Children and parents

WILLIAM SHAKESPEARE, sensitive to the fires of youth, once wrote that "Young blood doth not obey an old decree." And, later, in *Twelfth Night*, he gave us the thought that "Youth's a stuff will not endure." These comments together, echoing across a span of more than three and one-half centuries, perhaps provide a clearer insight to the problems of youth and the law than does much of the expert opinion that threatens to engulf us today.

While it is entirely normal for the middle-aged to consider that youth is "going to the dogs"—forgetting the time of their own immaturity—it is just as obvious that deep-seated social change is sweeping the country. It would be easy to prove that change is not always for the better. But change in itself is the continuing story of man, and it is only the startling swiftness of the contemporary wave that is truly unsettling. In many areas, this change has brought a sharp challenge to the "old decrees" of the traditional law.

More than two-thirds of the present population of Canada was born after the end of World War II—the nation's last great struggle for survival. Only from books, dated films and parental memory of the unquestioned concepts of personal discipline can these young people grasp the acceptance of established authority that ordered the lives of their elders. Happily, no major conflict has developed since their birth to demand a subjugation of self to national interest. More happily, there does not appear to be much risk of such a demand in the foreseeable future.

The superpowers now seem to be content to rattle the saber occasionally while satisfying the appetites of consumer materialism, and even the most die-hard traditionalist concerned about permissiveness must expect our youngsters to ape the world they see. On the home front—while the daily papers and television serials play up crime, violence and sexual excesses, and education theorists continue burying the image of the stern father figure—elders must expect the adolescent twigs to be bent to the prevailing winds of change.

Recent federal statistics show that persons in the 15–24 age group make up less than one-fifth of the population but they commit about half of all serious offenses. For offenders younger than 18, the national crime statistics showed a Canada-wide increase of 35 percent over three years. Over a ten-year span, the total number of cases had nearly quadrupled (from 31,424 in 1971 to 122,796 in 1981). It must be remembered that these figures do not include the many thousands of youngsters dealt with by police, schools or social agencies without a formal court appearance being registered. Theft, assault and immorality are responsible for most of the increases.

To maintain perspective, one should note that, in the census quoted, the age group mentioned numbered 4,658,695 in a total population of 24,343,181. It is still only a fraction of Canadian youth that falls foul of the law.

Change of direction

English common law treated children as the property of their fathers and this meant that a child really had no individual rights at all. Modern legislation has changed the status of children fundamentally. Generally, it is now the welfare of the child, or youth—rather than the rights of the father—that is of paramount consideration. Further change can be expected. In 1983, the Canadian Council on Children and Youth, with a staff of seven and an annual budget of $300,000, was pressing for the implementation of many of the 1979 recommendations of the Canadian Commission for the International Year of the Child. The Council was monitoring legislation to ensure that the constitutional rights of children and youth would receive the protections guaranteed by the Charter of Rights and Freedoms. It was also advocating the immediate proclamation of the Young Offenders Act, which was being introduced in stages following its passage by Ottawa in 1982.

The switch in thinking from punishment to correctional treatment has become routine in dealing with young people in trouble with the law—even if it is not universally supported by the general public. But more than 50 years have passed since our laws decreed that "every juvenile delinquent shall be treated, not as a criminal, but as a misdirected and misguided child, one needing aid, encouragement and assistance."

Recent legislation has continued to advance the rights of the young. The most important change has been the lowering of the age of *majority*, or legal independence, from 21 to 18. This radical move was given great leverage—even in reluctant provinces—by the setting of 18 as the voting age in federal elections. There has not been a complete sweep, however; a person must be 19, for example, to cast a vote in provincial elections in British Columbia. Several provinces are considering returning to an above-18 age level for purchase or consumption of alcoholic beverages: drink-related incidents zoomed when 18-year-olds (many of them still in high school) assumed official adult status. Ontario raised the age level from 18 to 19 in 1978.

The words "minor" and "infant" mean exactly the same thing in Canadian law, even if the public interprets them differently. Where the word "child" is used in this chapter it can also be taken to mean someone under the age of majority.

Being legally independent brings with it not only some attractive rights and freedoms but also a number of heavy responsibilities. These are detailed in the sections that follow.

Provincial responsibility

All of the laws relating to children—with the exception of those dealing with juvenile delinquency—fall within the jurisdiction of the provinces. The special courts for younger offenders, and the training schools and other institutions where correctional detention is provided, are provincially controlled and maintained.

With 11 jurisdictions (including the federal government) all passing laws, one might expect a great deal of diversity; however, there is actually a high degree of uniformity among the provinces in the field of child welfare. This is the result of two factors: first, all the English-speaking provinces share the British legal tradition; and, second, several provinces virtually copied pieces of legislation already on the statute books of other, older provinces.

The Children's Protection Act provides an example: first passed in Ontario in 1893, it was later adopted widely across Canada, with the name sometimes altered to the Child Welfare Act. Today, Ontario has 51 children's aid societies, while other provinces have children's aid societies or provincial social service departments performing the same functions. In Manitoba, the children's aid societies and the provincial facilities have been combined.

Legal capacity

A minor cannot bring a legal action in the courts without the assistance of some other person who will be responsible for the costs, and through whom the court may compel obedience to its orders. This person is called the *next friend* of the child. Although it is not necessary that a minor obtain the approval of the court for his choice, the "next friend" must file a formal acceptance of the responsibility.

The next friend can be any person who has reached the age of majority. He need not be the parent or even a relative of the child. The next friend cannot, however, be another minor, or a person who resides outside the jurisdiction of the court —for instance, in another province. A widow or an unmarried woman is eligible. The next friend must not have an interest in the case that is opposed to that of the minor—for instance, if the child's uncle was involved in a land dispute with the minor, a business associate of the uncle would probably not be accepted as the child's "next friend."

The next friend is not entitled to receive any pay for his services. He cannot withhold any money or property awarded to the minor but must deposit with the court any money recovered. The next friend cannot settle a claim out of court without the approval of the court itself.

Although a child cannot bring a legal suit against someone without assistance (except to collect wages owed to him, as discussed in "Children at work" later in this chapter), he can be sued in any court. Where the minor is the defendant, an application must be made to have a guardian *ad litem* appointed. (The term *ad litem* tells us that the guardian will act just as long as the court case does.)

If a lawsuit is begun and it is discovered at some time during the trial that the defendant is under legal age (the deciding date is when the summons starting the action is issued), or mentally incompetent, the case will be shelved until a guardian *ad litem* is appointed. If, however, this fact doesn't come out in time, whatever judgment the court hands down will be upheld unless there is some good reason why it should not. In deciding whether or not the judgment should be upheld, the court will consider such factors as whether the person who sued knew the defendant was a minor, whether the minor was adequately defended and whether the facts of the case demonstrated that the child was liable. The judgment would not be set aside simply because the defendant was a minor, or because he lost the case.

The official guardian
In addition to temporary guardians appointed by the courts, each province also has an official guardian who has a general power and duty to act for minors in certain situations.

The official guardian must act for a minor who is suing, or who is being sued, in connection with an interest he may have in an estate. Anyone bringing a case against a minor that affects the minor's rights to land or goods in his possession must give to the official guardian a copy of the writ of summons which sets out his claim. In such a case, the official guardian will decide whether or not to enter the action.

Rights of the unborn
Although it is entirely possible for a child to be born after a gestation of 190 days or less (average pregnancy lasts 280 days), the written law does not allow any specific rights for the unborn child. The child becomes an individual being as soon as it has completely left the mother's body alive—even though the umbilical cord is still attached. However, at this writing, it appeared that rights for the unborn might be established after cases arising from the abortion issue had been settled by the courts.

Under the Criminal Code, an effort is made to protect the unborn child by prohibiting certain acts directed at it. Except in strictly limited and regulated circumstances, anyone who attempts by any means to perform an abortion can face a maximum sentence of life imprisonment. This law applies also to any woman who attempts to perform an abortion on herself.

The only exception to this law is when the abortion is performed by doctors, as the statute directs. Any recognized hospital may elect an abortion committee and this committee may authorize an abortion if a majority of the members believe that the continuation of the pregnancy would be likely to endanger the woman's life or health. "Health," in this instance, includes "mental health," which opens a wide avenue of possible interpretations.

Any woman who is faced with the problem of an unwanted pregnancy is strongly advised to see her own doctor or any gynecologist or obstetrician, or to go to the outpatients' department of a hospital.

If her case does not fit the legal requirements for a therapeutic abortion, she could discuss the situation with someone in a branch of the Family Planning Association (in some provinces, it is called the Planned Parenthood Society). A woman risks her freedom, as well as her health, if she submits to an illegal abortion.

Not only is a pregnant woman forbidden to take part in an intentional act of abortion, it is also unlawful for a pregnant woman to neglect to obtain assistance in childbirth. If her child dies or is permanently injured because of neglect, a woman can be sent to prison for up to five years. (*See* Chapter 19, "Offenses against the person.")

Danger of drugs

An unborn child can suffer injury as a result of the negligence of others. Whether a child who has been deformed while in its mother's womb by reason of her taking a drug can recover damages later on against the manufacturer of the medicine is one point of law that has not yet been satisfactorily settled.

An unborn child can also be injured by other acts. If a pregnant woman is a passenger in an automobile involved in a crash, her unborn child might suffer injuries that will not show up until after it is born. If such a situation results in a civil suit for damages, it is impossible to predict what the court will do. Some judges have ruled in favor of the child, others against the child, depending on the degree of injury and the circumstances of the original accident. Of course, it must be proved that the prenatal injury caused the postnatal condition.

In such a case, the parent or a guardian would bring the suit on behalf of the child. The law is not clear-cut on whether a child can wait until it reaches majority in order to sue on its own behalf. As a rule, the courts prefer that legal action be taken as soon as possible after the offense has occurred; there are also deadlines for bringing a case to court. (*See* Chapter 3, "How a case is tried.")

The illegitimate child

It wasn't until this century that the law provided a way for an illegitimately born child to be made legitimate. Until recently, however, the legal status of an illegitimate child was negligible in many respects, particularly in property inheritance. If a parent died without leaving a will, for example, his property would pass to his legitimate children but not to any illegitimate children. If a father's will directed that some of his property go to "my children," the law interpreted this as excluding illegitimate children.

Today, in most provinces, illegitimate children enjoy the right of inheritance,

The illegitimacy rate

ALTHOUGH NATIONAL STATISTICS indicate that nearly 13 percent of all live births in Canada are illegitimate, no one really knows what the total is. The records list only those births in which the parents report themselves as being not married at the time of the registration of the birth.

The number of babies born out of wedlock in Canada has, however, moved upward sharply—despite the introduction of explicit sex education in the schools, the contraceptive pill, spermicide foams and other devices. In 1981, the number of illegitimate births was nearly ten times greater than it had been a decade earlier. During this period, illegitimate births in Ontario increased 14 times; in Quebec, 13 times; in Alberta, 12 times; and, in British Columbia, ten times.

The Northwest Territories has reported an illegitimacy rate of 33.6 percent of all live births. In the Yukon, it was 25.4 percent, and 17.9 percent in Saskatchewan.

Thirty-eight percent of all unwed mothers are younger than 20 and 77 percent are younger than 25.

unless they have been excluded from a will. For the purposes of inheritance, the distinction between legitimate and illegitimate children has been abolished.

If a child is born to a married woman, the law presumes that it is legitimate: the child is considered to be the legitimate offspring of the woman and her husband until the contrary is actually proved. If it is proved that the child resulted, in fact, from adultery between a married woman and a man not her husband, then the only way the child can become the legitimate child of the woman and her husband is through adoption.

A child born to an unmarried couple will become legitimate automatically from the date of its birth if the parents subsequently marry. When they marry, a new birth certificate will be issued.

There are at least two other situations in which a child's legitimacy can be questioned. A child might be conceived during a marriage but be born after the parents are divorced. The law regards such a child as legitimate. In the second situation, one spouse may honestly believe the other to be dead, remarry, and have a child. If the spouse believed to be dead turns up, the child is still considered to be legitimate even though the marriage will be invalid. Since the twice-married spouse could probably get a divorce from the long-lost partner on grounds of *marriage breakdown* (*See* Chapter 10, "The divorce"), the parties to the second "marriage" could then legalize their union.

Paternity suits

All of the provinces, plus the territories, have legislation enabling an unwed mother to bring a paternity suit—termed legally "affiliation proceedings"—against the alleged (*putative*) father of her child. The main object is to force him to contribute financially to the support of the child.

Proceedings are usually started by an application being made to a judge. In some provinces, only the unwed mother or the Children's Aid Society can make the application; in others, her parents can also apply.

The unwed mother or other applicant must prove to the court that there is a strong probability that the allegation is true. There must also be some other material evidence to back up the mother's claim—her unsupported word is not enough. For example, if the mother produces a maintenance agreement signed by the man she has named as the father, she would probably win her case. An admission by a man to a third person may be accepted as evidence of paternity. The "blood tests" made famous in fiction are not regarded as conclusive evidence in real-life paternity suits—they can only, in fact, prove that a man had *not* fathered a child.

Sometimes affiliation proceedings are begun before the child is actually born. If the pregnancy is terminated before the child is born, the father can be ordered to pay the mother's expenses up to that time.

Once a man is judged to be the father of a child born out of wedlock, the court declares him to be the father and issues an *affiliation order* against him. This orders him to pay maintenance for the child, as well as the mother's expenses in giving birth to the child. In setting the amount that the father must pay, the court considers how much will be required to maintain the child at a reasonable standard of living, as well as the financial means of the father.

The father must pay this maintenance until the child is 16 or, in some provinces, two or three years older. (The age limit depends on the child welfare act of the particular province.) However, the maintenance order may be changed from time to time as the circumstances of the child and the father change.

The court can enforce the order to the extent of sending a defaulting father to prison.

If the putative father dies before his child reaches the age limit specified in the provincial child welfare act, any estate he might leave would have to continue to honor the terms of the *affiliation order* issued against him.

Although the trend toward fuller equality between the sexes is good for some women, it is creating problems for others. For instance, the employed unmarried mother may find herself assessed by the court for a substantial part of the costs of supporting the child. If she happened to be wealthy, it is possible that the court would demand very little of the father.

On the other hand, if she was forced to give up her job in order to take care of the child, she could apply to the court to have the affiliation order revised upward.

In a case decided in Alberta, a woman who gave birth to the illegitimate child of X and later married Y was awarded maintenance only up to the time of her marriage.

The unmarried mother has first rights to the custody of her baby. However, the courts may award custody to the father or someone else if this seems to be in the best interests of the child.

The neglected child

All provinces have laws to protect children who are being neglected by their parents or guardians, or have been deserted. Usually titled either the Children's Protection Act or Child Welfare Act, these laws might easily be called "Oliver Twist Acts" for their purpose is to protect children from the kind of abuses that Charles Dickens's famous character encountered.

Social conditions have changed drasti-

The children's charter

OUT OF THE BRUTALIZING SHOCK of World War I came the ideal of the League of Nations. If a better, more humane society was to be built, a start had to be made with the children of the world. In 1924, the League adopted the Geneva Declaration of the Rights of the Child. In 1939, when World War II broke out, the declaration became just another "scrap of paper." When the United Nations took up the rebuilding job in 1945, humanists among the statesmen proposed that the Geneva Declaration be reconfirmed. In the stirring Universal Declaration of Human Rights (1948) the rights of children were implicitly included, but a special charter was still sought by those appalled by the deprivations of three-quarters of the world's youngsters.

For ten years, drafts of a children's charter were discussed and rewritten. In 1959, the General Assembly of the United Nations unanimously adopted the Declaration of the Rights of the Child.

Following a preamble which affirms to all children the fundamental human rights as promulgated by the U.N. in 1948—without regard to race, color, sex, religion or nationality—the declaration calls on mankind to grant children the following:

● Special protection and opportunities, by law and by other means, to develop physically, mentally, morally, spiritually and socially, in conditions of freedom and dignity.

● From birth, a name and nationality.

● Adequate nutrition, housing, medical and recreation services.

● Special care and education if handicapped.

● Love and understanding . . . in the care and under the responsibility of the parents, in an atmosphere of moral and material security.

● Compulsory, free education to enable the child to develop its abilities and judgment on a basis of equal opportunity.

● Priority in protection and relief in times of disaster.

● Protection against all forms of neglect, cruelty and exploitation, including employment before an appropriate minimum age.

● A childhood molded by ideals of tolerance, friendship among peoples, peace and universal brotherhood.

These aims, far from being achieved, are the guiding principles of the International Union of Child Welfare, of which the Canadian Save the Children Fund (CANSAVE) is the Canadian member. The United Nations Children's Fund (UNICEF) raises money worldwide to help bring the dream to reality.

cally since the cruel times of the orphan Oliver and his corrupt master Fagin. The child who needs protection today is more likely to be the child from a broken home. The law refers to any child who is not properly cared for as a "neglected child." A child committed to the custody of an institution such as a children's aid society is referred to as a *ward*.

A police officer or child-welfare worker, after he has obtained a warrant, can remove an apparently neglected child to a place of safety. The child may be kept there until he can be brought before a judge. Alternatively, the official can leave the child in the child's home and apply to a judge for an order requiring the person in charge of the child to bring him before the judge at a given time.

If an authorized welfare worker has reasonable cause to suspect that a child is neglected, he can get a search warrant, empowering him to enter any house and remove the child. A private citizen has no authority to rescue neglected children; he should report any suspicions to a children's aid society or to the police.

A judge must determine whether the child fits the legal standards of "neglected child." To do this, he has the power to summon any witnesses and have them testify under oath. He may also permit any other person to give evidence on behalf of the child. For example, in Ontario, if a judge decides that the "child in need of protection" is neglected, he can make one of the following orders, which is typical of what happens elsewhere in Canada:

(1) That the case be adjourned indefinitely and that the child be placed with, or returned to his parent or guardian, subject to supervision of a children's aid society;

(2) That the child be committed temporarily to the care and custody of the society for any length of time up to 12 months;

(3) That the child be committed for the rest of his childhood to the care and custody of the society.

In some provinces, legislation to protect children applies to persons up to 18 years old, while others set the maximum age at 16. A "child in need of protection" usually means any one of the following, in the age groups mentioned:

(1) An orphan not properly cared for.

(2) A child deserted by his parent or guardian either by death, abandonment or inability to care properly for him.

(3) A child whose guardian cannot care for him by reason of imprisonment, disease, mental disturbance or infirmity.

(4) A child living in an unfit or improper place.

(5) A child found begging, engaging in a street trade or loitering in public.

(6) A child who, with the consent or at the bidding of his guardian, commits an offense under a federal or provincial statute or a municipal bylaw.

(7) A child who is a delinquent due to lack of control by his guardian.

(8) A child who does not, or will not, attend school (in other words, is a *habitual truant*).

(9) A child whose parent or guardian refuses to provide medical or other necessary care.

(10) A child being neglected by his guardian to an extent that is, according to a psychiatrist, sufficient to endanger his emotional and mental development.

If a child is named as a "neglected child" and is placed permanently in the custody of a children's aid society, he remains there until he is 18, until he is adopted or until he is placed in the custody of some other legal guardian.

If a parent abandons or deserts his child, or allows the child to be brought up by another person or by a children's aid society, he runs the risk of being declared an unfit parent and thus losing his parental rights. Unless he can satisfy a judge that he has mended his ways and now is a fit person, having a genuine regard for the welfare of the child, he may lose his right to custody of the child.

Exploitation of children

In *Oliver Twist*, Fagin and the Artful Dodger organized orphaned or deserted children into gangs of pickpockets and housebreakers. Today, these villains would have to contend with the harsh penalties of the Criminal Code. It is a criminal offense to lead a child into criminal, immoral or other antisocial activities. Even leaving a young child unattended for an unreasonable time can bring a fine of up to $200 or imprisonment for a year.

No adult is permitted to cause or hire a young child to perform as an entertainer or to sell anything. Anyone employing a minor as an entertainer must obtain a license and will be under the watchful eye of the children's aid society.

Young girls hired as waitresses, hostesses, or even as dancers, have sometimes acted as prostitutes as well. Ontario will not permit a child younger than 16 to be in a place of public entertainment between 10 P.M. and 6 A.M. "unless provision has been made to ensure the health and proper treatment of the child."

In many provincial jurisdictions, it is forbidden for boys younger than 12 or girls younger than 16 to engage in any street trade. The special allowance for boys is meant to accommodate the traditional "paper boy" who is permitted to shout his wares until 9 P.M. (In Alberta, Ontario and Newfoundland, the law makes no distinction regarding the sex of the children.)

Any adult causing a child to beg in a public place can be fined or sentenced to prison. In Alberta, for example, an adult who exploits a child in this way can be fined $200 and/or sentenced to six months in prison.

Anyone who participates in adultery or other sexual immorality, drunkenness or any other vice in a home where there is a child younger than 18 can be imprisoned for two years. Any parent or guardian who encourages a girl in his charge to have illicit sexual relations with others, or to become a prostitute, can be imprisoned for up to 14 years (if the girl is younger than 14) or up to five years if the girl is 14 years old or more.

Persons have been prosecuted for leaving a child younger than ten exposed in such a way that its life was endangered. Depending on the circumstances, the charge could be criminal negligence or even attempted murder.

Every parent, foster parent or guardian is under a legal duty to provide the necessities of life for a child younger than 16; failure to do so can bring a prison term of up to two years.

The substitute home

Although the law attempts to protect the welfare of children, total protection seems unattainable given the nature of our society in general and the current erosion of the family unit in particular. Most problems affecting young people appear to stem from a breakdown of family life and of parental authority. However, society has not developed a structure, or a fresh approach, to replace the institution of the family.

Until something better comes along, the law is not prepared to set aside parental rights, except in extreme circumstances. It is generally agreed that however good and dedicated a children's institution might be, it is still inferior to all but the worst family environment. The *foster home* provides a popular substitute for the real thing.

A children's aid society may decide in the interests of the child to place its ward in a foster home. Foster parents should be friendly, sympathetic persons who take wards of the society into their homes and care for them on a temporary basis. They are paid for the maintenance of a child.

Foster parents should not be confused with adopting (or adoptive) parents. The child placed in a foster home is usually still in the custody of a children's aid society, and the society can demand that the child be returned at any time. The foster home can give a child family life and a depth of affection that is exceedingly difficult to provide in an institution. Foster parents, having grown to love a child put into their care, often eventually adopt the child.

Adoption procedure

All of our provinces and territories have legislation setting out the requirements for adoption. These laws are generally similar, with only minor variations from one province to the next. However, since the laws concerning the young are changing rapidly, those who would like to adopt should check the current position at their provincial welfare ministry, or with any branch of the local children's aid society.

Most provinces permit you to adopt only persons younger than 21 who have never been married. Others will allow you to adopt someone older than 21, provided you had raised the person.

To qualify as an adopting parent, an unmarried applicant must be older than 21. A husband and a wife may adopt a child provided that one of them is older than 21. This age requirement does not apply, however, if one of the spouses is a parent of the child.

The requirements are somewhat different in Ontario. An Ontario court may refuse an adoption application where either one or both of the applicants is younger than 18, or where the child is 18 or over, or is under 18 and has been married. The court may also refuse an adoption where the applicant is a widower or unmarried. However, if the court is satisfied there are special circumstances that justify adoption, it will permit this. Everywhere in Canada, the child's religion can be an important social consideration in the procedure leading to its adoption.

Each province insists that the consent of the child's parent or guardian be obtained. There are local variations. Some provinces (Alberta, for example) require only the consent of the child's guardian, whether or not he is a parent. If the child is a permanent ward of the Crown, the parent's consent is not required; the Children's Aid Society makes the decision. Ontario insists that the parent's consent be obtained, regardless of who has custody of the child.

An illegitimate child can be put up for adoption only with the written consent of the mother—which must be given seven days or more after the child is born. (If the child resides with and is maintained by the father, the father's consent is also necessary.) Either parent may withdraw consent within 21 days after it is given. And the court reserves the right to permit a parent to withdraw consent even after the 21 days have passed.

Most jurisdictions also require consent to an adoption by the director of a children's aid society; this is issued only after a set period during which the child has resided with the prospective parents under the scrutiny of the society. This waiting period is usually a year; in a few provinces, it is six months.

In most provinces, if a child is the age of 12 or older, you must also get his or her consent before adoption. In Alberta, the age is 14; in Ontario, 7. In Quebec, the minimum age is 10, although the court can override the refusal of a child to an adoption, if the minor is less than 14 years old.

The courts reserve the right to dispense with the consent of a parent or guardian. Perhaps the parent has abandoned, neglected; or has persistently ill-treated the child or otherwise failed to discharge his obligations as a parent. It might be that he cannot be found or is incapable of giving his consent. The parent might be withholding consent unreasonably, perhaps to spite the persons wishing to adopt the child. The court will overrule the parent's objections if it feels that the interests of the child will best be served by adoption.

To succeed in an adoption application then, the applicant must obtain all of the necessary consents—unless the court has ordered that they may be dispensed with. The court must be convinced that the applicant is a fit and proper person to be a parent, and that the adoption will serve the best interests of the child.

Once an adoption order is made, the adopted child becomes the child of the adopted parents just as if it had been born to those parents, and it ceases forever to be the child of its former parents. All the provinces will recognize and give effect to an adoption order made anywhere in Canada.

It is an offense for a parent to "sell" his child to another person. This would amount to slavery, outlawed in Canada in 1807. In Ontario, the penalty is a fine of up to $5,000 or imprisonment for up to three years, or both. The crime is not as rare as you might think. There is always a shortage of the most sought-after types of adoptable babies. The authorities must be notified within 30 days when a parent places a child with another person for adoption.

Parental rights and duties

The father is held legally responsible for the maintenance and education of his children, usually until they are 16 years old. Of course, public morals and social custom expect him to perform a much wider duty as a father. Despite all the feminist arguments of recent times, the law still places the major burden of support, education and protection on his shoulders. Modern legislation does, however, impose a duty on *both* parents to look after their children's welfare while they are living together.

All provinces have enacted laws protecting deserted wives and children. A wife may apply for an order of maintenance on the grounds that her husband has willfully neglected his duty of providing reasonably for her and the children. Such orders are made frequently in situations where a father—for any one of a multitude of reasons—has walked out on the mother and the children. If the father cannot, or does not, provide maintenance, the state welfare system will step into the breach.

The Divorce Act includes provisions by which either a woman or a man can apply for maintenance, and for support for the children. (*See* Chapter 10, "The divorce.")

The right to custody

Common law at one time upheld the paramount right of the father to the custody of his children, however tender their age might be. His rights prevailed over those of the mother and over the wishes of the children, even when he was not living with the mother. If he was, however, living with another woman, he was not permitted to bring his children into her company or even into the same house where the "scarlet" woman lived.

The court now has discretion to award custody to whichever parent it considers best fitted to the task of raising the children.

Although the judge must give paramount consideration to the welfare of the child, he may also consider the conduct, financial state and wishes of the parents.

In recent years, the courts have followed a policy which has come to be known as the "tender years" doctrine. According to this policy, if a child is very young it ought to be with its mother. This does not mean that the mother has an automatic right to the custody of a very young child, but rather that where the circumstances of the parents are roughly the same, the mother will be awarded custody.

Youth at the ballot box

IN THE FEDERAL ELECTION of 1972, for the first time, the voting age was lowered to 18. The major change resulting from the added votes by senior teenagers was a strong resurgence of the Progressive Conservative Party. To the political pundits, this change suggested that the graduates of the permissive society might be more conservative than their parents. Whatever the case may be, every Canadian citizen, 18 years or older, now may vote in a federal election if residing in Canada on the date of the issue of a writ ordering an election. If you turn 18 before the voting date, you are considered to have been 18 on the day of the issuance of the writ. Your name will be included on the election list drawn up by enumerators who are sent to register all eligible voters before the election.

Students absent from home because of full-time attendance at a recognized school or college during an academic term can vote by proxy—that is, they can name any other person on the list of electors for their home division to cast a vote for them. The person chosen as the proxy voter cannot represent more than one absent voter.

Unmarried students who have left home and are "on their own" should vote in the polling division in which they normally reside, and they should ensure they get on the list of electors for that division.

Where custody is awarded to the mother, the father will still be ordered to pay for the maintenance of the child. In some provinces, if he fails to obey without any justification, he can be sent to prison. If the father has custody, the mother can also be forced to pay maintenance, if she has the means to do so. Failure to obey may also result in the mother being sent to prison.

If the parents are separated or divorced, they can make a formal agreement as to who shall have custody of the children.

Frequently, the competing claims for custody are not between the mother and the father, but rather between a parent and another person who is not the natural parent of the child—for instance, where the mother has made a second marriage or where foster parents are involved. Here, generally, the courts will uphold the right of a true parent to the custody of his child over the right of persons who are not the parents, unless there are compelling reasons with regard to the welfare of the child.

The natural parents have a right to their own child. They can lose this claim only by neglecting or abandoning the child, or by conducting themselves so badly that the child would suffer in their custody.

In a Nova Scotia case, a mother had boarded out her child soon after its birth. When she came to visit him, the child ran away from her. She brought an action for custody but was refused. The court held that although she had the means to provide for the child and had never mistreated him, the child would suffer if he was forced to go with her.

Other grounds for refusing to grant custody to a parent would almost certainly include grossly immoral conduct, a history of mistreatment of the child, or drunkenness. The courts are reluctant to separate brothers and sisters, or to remove a child from a happy home in which he has been living for several years.

The courts will take into account the wishes of the child, if those wishes can be fairly ascertained.

The right to discipline

As the head of the household, the husband and father once held broad disciplinary powers over members of his family—his wife included. His duty of protection con-

Who would batter a baby?

THE ANSWER to that question seems to be: Just about anyone. Canadian statistics on child abuse are far from precise. But, the yearly total of child batterings in Canada could run as high as 12,000 cases a year. About one percent are fatal; 30 percent result in permanent injury.

Studies in the field so far have failed to pinpoint any particular type of person as a potential child batterer. Not only parents are involved—injuries are inflicted on helpless infants by older brothers and sisters, other relatives and babysitters. More women than men attack children; the average age of the guilty mother in proved cases is 26.

The baby batterers live in both rural and metropolitan areas; in both slums and high-class suburbs. They have I.Q.s varying from the low 70s to 130 and more. Neither excessive use of alcohol, nor divorce, appear to have any serious bearing on the problem. Perhaps ten percent of cases involve parents with actual mental disorders.

Under the child welfare laws in all provinces and territories, any suspected case of child abuse must be reported to the child protection authorities. These mandatory reporting provisions were instituted in response to the publicity arising from research on child abuse that appeared in the United States in the early 1960s. In 1982, Health and Welfare Canada set up the National Clearing House on Family Violence to gather and supply information on child abuse and other kinds of family violence.

ferred on him a matching right to maintain order and obedience by the use of whatever force or restraint seemed necessary. He could chastise his wife, though it seems to have been understood that he should use a stick no thicker than his thumb. And the children knew what a carpet slipper or a leather belt felt like. It was the era when literally everyone believed that to spare the rod was to spoil the child. And that era is not entirely past.

The right to punish a child physically is usually tied in with the right to have custody of the child. The right to chastise is usually raised these days only as a defense to a civil action for assault or in criminal proceedings. It is a right that is in part delegated by parents to school teachers, who often have contact with children for a longer period each day than do the parents.

Under the Criminal Code, which is applicable throughout Canada, every school teacher, parent, or person standing in the place of a parent, is justified in using force to discipline a pupil or child who is under his or her care. However, any punishment must not be excessive or prompted by evil motive; it must be reasonable in the circumstances. The age of the child must be taken into account. All too frequently, young children—even babies—are severely beaten by unbalanced parents, in the name of discipline. Those who commit such acts of violence are as criminally liable as if they had beaten up and injured any other member of society. (See Chapter 19, "Offenses against the person.")

Consent to marry

In general, any person younger than 18 must obtain the consent of his or her parents or guardian in order to marry, unless that parent or guardian is no longer interested in the maintenance or well-being of the child or has lost parental rights. In many provinces, if the parents refuse to consent, a young person wishing to marry may obtain the authorization of a judge. Generally, a girl younger than 16 is forbidden to marry unless she is pregnant or the mother of a child, or unless the court authorizes her marriage.

The child's property

Where the parents are living together, they are the joint guardians of their children. If they separate, they can make a written agreement concerning the custody of the children. However, this guardianship applies only to the custody, control and education of their children; it does not include the right to manage the property of the children. Guardianship of a child's property until he reaches official adulthood can be held only through a court order. This applies particularly where a child acquires property either through a will or through a gift from a living person.

The usual procedure is to appoint the child's parent or guardian as his *guardian of property*. A child can have two guardians: one in charge of his custody, control and education; another in charge of his property.

Frequently, the parent is charged with the custody and education of the child, while a trust company is appointed to manage the child's property. Whenever a person who is not the parent is appointed guardian of the child's property, the consent of the parent is necessary. This appears to be the case even when the parent has lost his right to the custody of the child. Furthermore, in most jurisdictions, the consent of the child is also required if he has reached a certain age. In Ontario, for example, if a child is older than 14, no appointment can be made without his consent.

The guardian of a child's property has authority only to manage the property; he must get special permission from a court to sell or otherwise dispose of the child's real property. For example, if a child inherited an apartment building, his guardian could manage it and collect the rents; however, he must hold the money for the use or benefit of the child.

If the guardian was managing the child's property badly or was suspected of taking part of the property or proceeds for himself, his guardianship could be terminated at a stroke and he would be ordered to account for his every action. Criminal proceedings would follow if there was evidence of theft.

Children at school

| Education is compulsory |
| The public school system |
| The separate school |
| The private school |
| Discipline at school |
| Going to university |

REPEATING the pattern of other societies largely established by immigrants, the law of Canada has taken a controlling and leveling interest in education. The emphasis is on the provision of schooling for all children potentially able to benefit, irrespective of their race, religion, social position or financial standing.

Constitutionally, the provinces are responsible for public education and the federal authority is concerned only with special groups and overriding national interests. At the base of the vast organizational pyramid is the district school board, which actually does the work of building and operating schools.

Canada has an international reputation regarding its concern for education, and its taxpayers have appeared willing, until lately, to absorb the ever-mounting cost of it. The total bill has recently been estimated at considerably more than $17 billion a year—which takes over 8 percent of Canada's Gross National Product to pay. How is this huge bill apportioned? The federal government pays less than 10 percent, the provinces 66 percent, the municipalities 18 percent, and the rest comes from fees and other sources. About 36 percent of the entire present population of Canada is actually receiving or dispensing education in some form or other. This includes the graduate scholar seeking a doctorate in the discipline of his choice, and the snowmobiler taking a course in the care and maintenance of his fun machine at the local community college.

The policy of the federal government in enforcing certain measures of bilingualism as the official languages of Canada (English and French) may well enrich the cultural fabric of the country. But it requires bilingual workers, especially in the civil service, to make it a reality. A working knowledge of both official languages is now considered a means to improve one's job prospects, and more and more parents are directing their children towards a bilingual education. By the 1982–83 school year, 60,000 students were enrolled in French-immersion programs in elementary and secondary schools across Canada, more than half of them in Ontario.

Of all children in the public school system (about six million), 60 percent go on to higher education at the scores of community colleges, vocational training institutions and universities empowered to grant degrees. These institutions are basically government supported. Only one-eighth of the universities' income, for example, comes from student fees.

Each province has a Schools Act, or the equivalent, which sets out its duty to provide education for all children between the ages of six and 16. The actual organization and executive administration may vary from province to province but the essential principles are the same. There is a department of education, in which the deputy minister is normally an educationist as well as a civil servant. Thus, although the minister will change with the fortunes of the political parties, there remains, hopefully, a measure of permanence in education policy.

The provinces set standards for the qualifications of teachers, appoint inspectors, issue approved lists of textbooks and courses, and control and regulate school building programs. Some of the provincial departments set year-end examinations at the matriculation level. In recent years, the provinces have provided massive funding to expand and improve local and regional education.

Federal participation in education has been keeping stride with the increasing concern to establish a general level of education and useful skills across the nation. No fewer than 60 federal governments departments and agencies now have educative programs of one kind or another. The federal treasury covers the cost of adult vocational training programs (most in the community colleges) and pays about half of the operating costs of all post-secondary education—a sum close to two billion dollars a year.

Under the terms of the Canada Student Loans Act, federal guarantees are given to the chartered banks to cover loans of up to $56.25 per week (to a maximum of $9,800 over 520 weeks) to full-time students who cannot meet university fees either out of their own pockets or with parental assistance. The loans are interest free until six months after the recipient ceases to be a full-time student. Some provinces have loan-rebate programs by which they reimburse the federal government on the student's behalf for part of the loan. The federal scheme applies throughout all of Canada except Quebec, which has its own plan.

The municipal or regional education boards—either appointed or elected—are responsible to the taxpayers (and to the provincial governments) for the provision of school buildings, staff, equipment, materials and any necessary transportation for the students in the area. These boards levy local taxes, which cover almost half of the total cost.

While "power to the people" has been the general trend in recent years, in the fundamental area of education, centralization has been the order of the day. The provinces have been removing power over schooling from local or village school boards and placing it in a series of large district or regional boards. In New Brunswick, 422 school districts were telescoped into 41, and Ontario's thousands of autonomous school boards were reduced to less than 200. Other provinces have done the same.

The school boards have the power to decide which school a child from a particular area of a city or rural area will attend. By law, the child must attend the school named as the one serving the area in which his parent or guardian is living. If the parents want to send their child to another school and the local board will not approve the change, the only choices open are for the parents to move into the area of the desired school or to arrange that someone in the desired area be appointed as the legal guardian of the child.

Education is compulsory

Parents or guardians have a legal duty to make sure their children attend school while between the ages of five or six and 16 (depending upon the province. There are certain exceptions. A child may be excused if he cannot attend school because of ill health or, temporarily in the case of a child 15 or older, if he has to work on the family farm or holds an employment certificate. (Children are excused from school only temporarily, and only to work on the family farm, in British Columbia and New Brunswick.) No child will be excused simply because the family needs support.

When a child achieves a certain level in high school (usually junior matriculation) before he reaches 16, he can drop out if he wishes.

A parent or guardian who refuses to send a child of compulsory school age to school is guilty of an offense that carries a fine of between $100 and $500, depending on the province. Instead of a fine, the parent or guardian may be ordered to post a bond (ranging between $200 and $1,000, according to provincial regulations), which will be forfeited if the child is not in class at school within five days. If a child is deemed to be a habitual truant—in other words, if he consistently ducks out of school—he can be committed to the custody of a children's aid society under provincial welfare acts.

It is also an offense to employ a child of compulsory school age during school hours, unless the child holds an employment certificate which was issued by the local school attendance officer—more commonly known as the *truant officer*. Where the child is going to engage in gainful employment outside of the home, the truant officer can issue a certificate only to those children who need the work in order to maintain themselves or to contribute to the maintenance of some person who is completely dependent upon them.

The school-leaving ages as laid down in the provincial statutes are as follows:

NEWFOUNDLAND 15, or completion of the school year in which the child reaches the age of 15.

PRINCE EDWARD ISLAND 16, unless the child has passed Grade 12.

NEW BRUNSWICK 16, unless the child has passed Grade 12.

NOVA SCOTIA 16.

QUEBEC 15; students may be absent for six weeks in any school year for home duties or to care for farm animals.

ONTARIO 16, unless the child has graduated from high school (Grade 12).

MANITOBA 16, with a provision that a child can leave at 15 on the recommendation of the school superintendent, his parents and the school attendance officer.

SASKATCHEWAN 16.

ALBERTA 16.

BRITISH COLUMBIA 15.

The age at which a child may leave school is calculated in different ways. In Quebec, Ontario, Nova Scotia and Newfoundland, the student must stay in school until he finishes the school year in which he, or she, reached the legal school-leaving age. In Alberta a child must remain only until the end of the June term of the year in which he, or she, turned 16. In Manitoba, the student may leave at any time after his 16th birthday.

The public school system

All provinces have the right to prescribe the curriculum for schools, the hours of attendance, the academic qualifications of teachers and the standards of conduct for students.

Each province provides free primary, or elementary (Grades 1–8), and secondary (Grades 9–12) education in its public school system to resident students. Some provinces offer more: one and even two years of pre-grade school in some cases; in others, the secondary-school period is extended to include Grade 13. There are also junior high schools that accept pupils after completion of Grade 6, as well as junior colleges in which the last two years of secondary (high) school and the first one or two years of college are offered. Vocational (technological) schools, for-

Taking the law into the little red schoolhouse

ON MARCH 1, 1844, one Israel Lewis issued an advertisement in Kingston, Ontario—then the capital of Canada—extolling his new book aimed at bringing knowledge of the law to the pioneer classroom. "What is more useful," he opined, "than give the community a full understanding of the Criminal Laws of the land, and the consequences of their being violated?" The volume is now a book collector's prize. The frontispiece is reproduced at the right.

Equally interesting, the learned Mr. Lewis was a black. He was perhaps the first of his race to publish a book in Canada.

A CLASS BOOK
for the use of
*Common Schools and Families,
in the United Canadas,*
entitled the
YOUTH'S GUARD AGAINST CRIME,
having embodied in it all the
CRIMINAL LAWS OF THE LAND,
Conveniently Abridged.

by Israel Lewis, C.M.

Kingston
Printed at The Atheneum Printing Office
1844

merly available only in major centers, are now more widespread. Many are "composites," offering courses leading either to university entrance or to the threshold of skilled trades. The choice of option courses is so wide that a student can get instruction for just about any occupation or skill; he may also study music and the other arts.

In Newfoundland and Quebec, the educational systems are different. Newfoundland has no fewer than four school systems—those organized by the Protestant churches (in the majority), the Roman Catholic, Pentecostal and Seventh-Day Adventist religious denominations. Apart from these general education systems, the College of Fisheries, Navigation and Engineering at St. John's, the College of Trade and Technology, and the Bay St. George Community College offer specialized training programs.

The education system of Quebec is diversified by religion and language. Within the ministry of education, there are two associate deputy ministers, one for the Roman Catholic sector and one for the Protestant sector.

In the early 1960s, Quebec faced the task of shifting a largely religion-centered education system into a secular style that would answer the needs of its modern youth. The former *collèges classiques,* as well as schools of nursing and many technical institutes, were drawn together in the school year 1967–68 to form community colleges, known as CEGEPs (*Collèges d'enseignement général et professionnel*). Providing both general education and professional instruction, these colleges offer three-year technical programs and two-year pre-university programs.

The proliferation of parish school boards in Quebec has been reduced to a network of 79 French and 24 English regional school boards. (Further changes to the Quebec school system, abolishing special schools and religious education, were announced in June 1983. The provincial government planned to implement the new educational system by 1985.)

Quebec's Bill 22 (1974) reduced access to the English school system for children whose mother tongue is not English. In 1977, Bill 101 tightened up controls even more. Under the provisions of the bill, only children of parents who had completed their elementary schooling in English in Quebec are eligible for English education. Other eligible categories include the children of parents who were residents of Quebec when the bill came into force and who had received their elementary education in English outside the province; and children already enrolled in English schools, as well as their younger siblings.

In 1974, the federal government inaugurated an industrial training program, which enables business and industrial establishments to train new employes, retrain experienced workers or upgrade their qualifications. Under cost-sharing agreements, the federal government reimburses companies that provide such training. The government also sponsors basic training for specific skills—for example, typing or bookkeeping for anyone who is interested—at vocational centers or community colleges. One community college advertises for members of the public to design their own courses, then commits itself to finding instructors for them. The federal Department of Employment and Immigration pays an allowance ranging from a minimum of $25 a week to a maximum of $135 per week to workers taking training courses.

The education of Indian and Inuit children, prisoners in penitentiaries, children in the Northwest Territories and of members of the armed forces on military bases is also handled by the federal authorities. The children usually follow the curriculum for the province where they live.

The separate school

Ontario, Alberta and Saskatchewan permit separate schools for certain religious minorities within their provincial public school systems. Although not bound by statute, Nova Scotia informally accepts that certain schools within its boundaries have traditionally been Roman Catholic. Ontario does not provide public financial support to separate secondary schools. Quebec provides a full-fledged minority school system for non-Roman Catholic children.

Separate schools should not be confused with private schools. In Alberta and Ontario, the institution of the separate school applies only to Roman Catholics: Jews or other ethnic or religious groups may establish private schools, which are not supported from tax moneys. In Saskatchewan, any minority religious group—whether Catholic, Anglican, or Jewish—can establish its own schools.

Separate schools differ from private schools in several ways, apart from financing. The separate school is a legislative creation and the private school is not. In a Protestant province, a Roman Catholic separate school cannot be considered as public since only Roman Catholics have the right to attend. On the other hand, it is not a private school since any Roman Catholic children who live within the school district have the right to attend.

Separate schools receive a level of government support, and taxpayers who declare themselves to be separate-school supporters have their school taxes channeled into the fund for separate schools.

To establish a separate school, a specified number of Roman Catholics (in Ontario, five heads of families) have to convene a public meeting at which a majority of the persons present, all being householders and Roman Catholics, elect trustees to represent their request. The number of trustees required—it ranges from six to 12—depends on the size of the total population in the district. In some jurisdictions, the trustees must themselves establish the school and find appropriate accommodation before they will receive government support for it. At the next municipal poll, persons who wish may declare themselves to be separate-school supporters; their taxes will be apportioned accordingly. Commercial corporations can also declare themselves as separate-school supporters; if they don't, the normal property taxes they pay are used for running the public schools.

Generally, all separate-school teachers must acquire the same qualifications as public school teachers in order to be certified. They must also conform to the same standards of proficiency and conduct that are set out by the provincial authorities for public school teachers. They also have the duties of public school teachers, including the maintenance of proper order and discipline in the classroom.

The teacher got rapped

WHEN LAWYER William Davis, Premier of Ontario, was minister of education in 1968, he offered this opinion to the Legislature: "The use of corporal punishment in any form is not appropriate in the schools of Ontario." But his government sidestepped any formal ban on the strap.

How should discipline be maintained in the blackboard jungle? These alternatives to the strap have been suggested: isolate misbehaving students with discretion; have agitated children move about; involve the parents; reward good behavior; provide more guidance training for teachers.

British Columbia went the whole way in 1973, abolishing corporal punishment in all provincial schools. And during his term of office, former N.D.P. Premier David Barrett really meant it. Principal Jerry Ruzicka, of the Crawford Bay High School, strapped two boys for fighting—after the parents had consented to the punishment. The school board ruled that the parents' wishes could not override the government edict, and reprimanded the principal.

A minor puzzle for future sociologists to ponder is that Canadian parents, who elect both governments and school trustees, can be flatly overruled by their servants in an issue at the core of the molding of their children. The doctrine of "spare the rod and spoil the child" can be traced back as far as *Proverbs* in the Old Testament: "He that spareth his rod hateth his son."

The private school

It is not compulsory for a child to attend either a public or a separate school supported by the government: the boy or girl may be accepted at one of Canada's many private schools. Every school—public or private—must conform to the standards of the provincial department of education. Some offer academic education up to the level of university entrance; others specialize in commercial courses.

Between three and four percent of Canadian children attend private schools, which receive no, or minimal, financial support from governments. In Quebec, private schools considered to be operating in the public interest are subsidized for 80 percent of the cost per pupil in the public school; other schools, eligible for grants, can receive subsidies reaching 60 percent.

Parents who pay to send their children to one of Canada's 800 private schools—more than half of which are in Quebec—still have to pay their share of the costs of educating everyone else's children. And the fees for the private institutions can be steep. For example, Toronto's famous Upper Canada College charges $5,550 a year for day students and $10,250 for boarders.

Almost all of the better-known private schools are operated as nonprofit educational trusts. Several of them are ancient institutions, by Canadian standards. Upper Canada College was founded in 1829; Bishop's College School, Lennoxville, Quebec, in 1836; Albert College, Belleville, Ontario, in 1857; and Bishop Strachan School for girls in Toronto in the Confederation year of 1867.

Not private, but restricted, are the special schools for handicapped persons. Canada has five schools for the blind, nine schools for the deaf, and a number of schools for the mentally retarded, run by the school boards. The Metropolitan Toronto School Board, for example, runs ten separate schools for the mentally retarded. Entry to these is arranged through the departments of education or health. Most are free but, if fees are charged, a government agency will usually cover the cost.

Education at home

It is not strictly compulsory for a child of school age to attend any school at all: in certain circumstances, teaching may be done at home, either by parents (if they happen to be qualified) or by a tutor. Correspondence courses are available from approved commercial schools and from the public school system for children in remote areas.

The responsibility is placed by law upon the parents or guardian to educate their children. If they choose to keep their child at home, an inspector from the provincial department of education has the right to check whether the child is receiving an education of a level roughly equal to what he or she would receive at the state-supported school in that residential area. If the inspector is not satisfied—and he could be hard to convince—he might order the child to attend the public (or separate) school, assuming, of course, that the child is normal and also that the school is not too far away.

Few parents today would choose to keep a normal child away from the outside world. In most cases, children are educated at home because they are physically or mentally handicapped in some way. Although schools for the handicapped are of high quality in Canada, they cannot be expected to meet the needs of every case.

Discipline at school

A child of school age must attend classes punctually and regularly; it is the responsibility of the school authorities to check that each child on their rolls does so.

Principals and teachers are empowered to maintain discipline and order at school and to enforce standards of hygiene for the general welfare of all. In effect, the law confers on them the rights of parental authority. The pupils are legally responsible to the teachers for their conduct while on school property.

There are two ways in which school authorities may enforce reasonable discipline: first, they may punish the student by detention, physical punishment, or expulsion; second, they may call in the police if necessary.

While on the property of the school, students are still subject to the laws of the land. Pupils who strike, threaten or abuse teachers or other pupils can be arrested and charged either as juvenile delinquents or, if older, under the provisions of the Criminal Code. While a teacher in most provinces still has the legal right to punish a student physically, the student has no right to strike the teacher—that would be assault.

The teacher (except in certain cases) may in the interest of correction use force toward a pupil who is under his care, as long as the force does not exceed what is reasonable under the circumstances. But what is reasonable? Although bruises on a child's body might seem to indicate that the force used was more than was justified, the force might still have been reasonable. The fact that the punishment caused pain does not make it unreasonable.

On the other hand, simply because there was no injury does not mean that the force was reasonable. In a case in Quebec, although the teacher who hit a student on the head caused no injury, a court of appeal ruled that the blow was unjustified.

The fact that an instrument such as a strap or a ruler is used to chastise a child does not necessarily mean that the force is unreasonable; but, if a pupil could prove that a teacher struck him deliberately because he "had it in for me," or that the punishment was too severe in relation to the misconduct, the teacher himself might be convicted of assault. The onus is on the child who complains to show that the punishment inflicted upon him was unreasonable. There is no duty upon the teacher to show that the punishment was justified.

In general, discipline by force is fading from the education scene. In Ontario, the Toronto Board of Education has abolished corporal punishment in its schools. It is also outlawed in British Columbia.

Provincial regulations usually state that children attending school must be neat and clean in their appearance. Until a few years ago, this rule was enforced strictly, and modified school "uniforms"

had to be worn in many school districts. The uniform was originally introduced as a democratic measure: where all pupils wore the same outfits, the poorer child was spared the subtle but sharp social pressures that can arise from juvenile, as well as adult, fashion trends.

In the turbulent sixties, the uniform was attacked as evidence of regimented conformity. At first, girls who came to school wearing jeans were sent home to change and boys with long hair were suspended from class until they got it cut. As parents permitted their sons' hair to get closer and closer to their collars and their daughters' skirts to gather dust in the closet, the stage was set for a confrontation between school officials and students. Eventually, the school authorities accepted the casual look of blue jeans and long hair. This nonchalant style prevailed in most Canadian classrooms throughout the 1970s. By the middle of the '80s, however, there were signs that the pendulum of fashion might be swinging back to a more conservative style among the young—at least within school precincts. At the time of this writing, a Montreal high school has been besieged with applicants, after it announced its intention to aim for higher academic standards and to return to a stricter dress code.

Going to university

A university education is not guaranteed in the Charter of Rights and Freedoms. The legal right to an education in Canada applies only to primary- and secondary-school levels, and then only until a child is 16 years old. Even if a student has excellent marks in high school and meets all the entrance requirements of a university, he may not be accepted. Many universities simply do not have the facilities to accommodate the numbers that apply for certain courses (such as law and medicine), even though the applicants have the required qualifications. However, the persistent applicant will usually be accepted somewhere—perhaps at a less well established university.

Canada has more than 60 degree-granting institutions, from Newfoundland's Memorial University to British Columbia's University of Victoria; however, several of this number confer degrees in theology only. A further 200 community colleges offer courses at or near university levels, but do not have degree-granting powers. Many of the French-language universities, which were run by Roman Catholic organizations, either religious or secular, now conform to the North American system of administration. The English-language universities, even those founded and still administered by various religious sects, are mainly nondenominational.

Except for the military colleges—at Kingston, Ontario, Saint-Jean, Quebec, and Victoria, British Columbia—and a few other institutions founded under federal charter, the universities of Canada are controlled under provincial legislation. Their charters vest authority in a board of governors which, in turn, appoints a president (or principal) as chief executive officer and "guiding light." He, in effect, is running a large organization with a plant worth many millions of dollars, and personnel (faculty and students) numbering several thousands. Seventeen universities have more than 10,000 full-time students: Alberta, British Columbia, Concordia, Guelph, Laval, McGill, McMaster, Manitoba, Montreal, Ottawa, Quebec, Queen's, Saskatchewan, Toronto, Waterloo, Western Ontario, and York. Most of the others range from between 1,000 and 5,000 students.

The board of governors is usually appointed by the provincial government from a pool of leading professionals, businessmen, clergymen and representatives of alumni associations. In recent years, the student body has been granted direct representation, sometimes including parity (equal voting power) with faculty members on some committees. At some universities, the committee that recommends promotions takes student evaluations of their professors into consideration. These moves may have helped defuse the campus unrest that marred higher education in the late 1960s.

The question of student rights at university is basically not a matter of special legislative action. Many undergraduates are already adults (at 18) and most are 21—the traditional age of majority—before they leave college. Students can expect to be treated by the law and its enforcement officers in exactly the same way as other Canadian adults.

Poverty is no bar to higher education

THE FEDERAL GOVERNMENT uses its taxation powers to enable qualified students to proceed to university or any other post-secondary institution when they plead that their financial resources are insufficient to cover tuition and living costs.

Through the system known since 1964 as the Canada Student Loans Plan, operated by the provinces (except Quebec) under the authority of the federal Department of the Secretary of State, interest-free loans of up to $56.25 per week may be granted for the length of the post-secondary course. The total loan permitted to any student during his entire educational career is $9,800.

To get a loan, once you can meet the entrance requirements of the post-second-

ary institution of your choice, you apply to your provincial education department.

If you succeed in your application, you will be given a "certificate of eligibility." When this has been endorsed by the university or college to prove your enrollment, any chartered bank, trust company, or credit union will advance the money to you, possibly in two installments. There will be no interest payable as long as you continue to provide proof of enrollment, and you will enjoy a six-month grace period afterward. Then you must begin to pay interest at the rate required under the legislation, and to start repaying the capital sum. Normally, you will be allowed a maximum of nine and one-half years to repay.

A sour note at the Academy

FACTS

The Academy of Music received an annual grant of $5,000 from the Province of Quebec under the terms of "An Act for the Encouragement of Music" so that a scholarship called the *Prix d'Europe* could be awarded. The judging was done by a special jury of five members appointed by the Academy who awarded the prize to the competitor who obtained the highest number of marks in an examination. One year, after the examination had been completed and the judges had handed their ballots to the secretary of the jury, and the number of marks allowed for each candidate had been added up, it was found that Bernard X. ranked first with 81.9 marks and Jules Y. second with 81.1 marks. But before the verdict was announced, one of the examiners expressed the opinion that Jules' marks should be increased so that he would get the scholarship because he deserved it. Another examiner agreed and increased his mark for Jules. Jules was publicly declared the winner of the scholarship with 82.1 points.

A few days after the examination, because of an unrelated inquiry, the president of the Academy then called a meeting of the members of the jury and of the officials of the Academy. The mistakes and errors in the allocation of the marks to Jules and Bernard were admitted by the jury. The review showed that Bernard really had scored 84.8 marks while Jules had only 76.9. Bernard was awarded the scholarship. Action was then taken on behalf of Jules against the Academy and the jury for a declaration that he had won the scholarship and claiming all the advantages deriving therefrom, and also $5,000 damages.

ARGUMENT

It was submitted on behalf of Bernard that he had obtained the highest number of marks in the examination, according to the method described in awarding marks in the statute authorizing the scholarship, after the initial errors and illegalities were ignored. On behalf of Jules, it was argued that once the jury had made its formal announcement that Jules had won, it did not have the authority or jurisdiction to reopen the matter.

JUDGMENT

The trial judge dismissed the action brought by Jules ruling that the scholarship was properly awarded to Bernard. The Quebec Court of Appeal reversed that verdict, holding that the jury had no power to revise its decision, and that the scholarship be given to Jules. The case was appealed by the Academy to the Supreme Court of Canada, which reversed the Quebec Court of Appeal, and upheld the trial judge. The Supreme Court decided that it was the right and duty of the Academy, acting for the legislature in the distribution of public moneys, to investigate the proceedings of the jury and, having found errors and illegalities, to award the scholarship to the competitor who had obtained "the highest number of marks according to the statute."*

* Based on an actual case (1932).

Children at work

MOST OF the laws dealing with children who have jobs—or who work under apprenticeship contracts—come from the provincial legislatures. Although these laws differ in details, their general principles are largely the same from one province to the next.

Except where expressly permitted under the various Schools Acts, no Canadian child younger than 16 years may work full time. In order to get regular work, a school-age child must have an employment certificate issued by the department of education. Under labor laws, many potentially dangerous jobs as well as those requiring strenuous physical effort are barred altogether to minors. Jobs that place youngsters in positions of moral danger are strictly supervised.

Despite the demand for young people to work in restaurants and clubs in the evening, the law forbids anyone younger than 17 to work between 11:00 P.M. and 6 A.M. The use of children in any paid entertainment—live or on film or television—is also controlled.

Most municipalities have bylaws forbidding minors from selling door-to-door, but the newspaper delivery boy is normally exempt for about two hours a day. Rural children may help out with harvesting and other chores on the family farm.

There are many more special regulations meant to protect the young person taking a job. There are many federal, provincial and municipal regulations that may also have a bearing on a particular case. Parents and employers concerned are advised to seek advice from the provincial departments of labor, from the nearest board of education or from the Children's Aid Society.

At times it may appear that the law is lagging somewhat behind the current youth scene. It is still an offense in Ontario, for instance, for any shopkeeper to supply cigarettes to a child younger than 18; if the retailer were caught, he could be fined between $2 and $50.

It is necessary, perhaps, to repeat once again that in the terminology of the law any person under the age of majority is an infant, or child. The editors continue to use "child" to describe the minor in this chapter, with an uneasy glance over the shoulder at the contemporary army of husky bearded young men of 17 to 20. It has been suggested that the lawmakers should apply the term "young person" to anyone between the ages of 12 and 18.

Right to wages

Any child who is employed is entitled to at least the provincial minimum wage, unless there is an exemption stated in the regulations or unless he is working under an apprenticeship contract (See "Learning a trade" later in this section). All labor standards and negotiated working conditions apply to him, despite his age.

If wages due to him are not paid, the child can usually sue in his own right; this is one of the rare occasions in which an infant can sue in his own name. Any jurisdiction that will not permit this will, as an alternative, allow the child's guardian to sue on his ward's behalf. A parent has no automatic right to sue for wages due to his child simply because he is the child's parent. He must first be appointed guardian *ad litem*—that is, for the duration of the legal action.

A parent has no right to the wages earned by his child, even when the child is

483

living with and being supported by the parent. Put another way, a Canadian parent has no right to hire out his children; a situation which, incidentally, is quite different in the United States.

An interesting question arises when a child enters an agreement to work for wages for his parent. Is the parent bound to pay the wages, or does he have an overriding common-law right to the labor of his children? If the child worked in the father's business the same as any other employe, a court would almost certainly rule that the father was bound to pay. In a precedent of 1857, a court ruled that a parent was indeed entitled to the labor of his child and that the child could not recover wages that would normally be due under a valid contract. However, despite the precedent set by this ruling, a court today would probably decide the issue on whether the work involved a commercial business or was a domestic chore.

Since World War II, the number of persons engaged in unpaid family work—mostly on farms or in small family businesses—has decreased sharply. In a recent census, these workers amounted to only six percent of the total labor force.

Contracts by minors

Although contracts are complex and full of conflicting conditions, the general rule in common law regarding contracts and children is that most contracts made by a child are either *void*, or they are *voidable* by the child. A void contract is one that, from the outset, was never a legal contract and cannot under any circumstances be enforced by either party. A voidable contract is an agreement that remains in force until the party who has the right to repudiate it, does so. Such a contract can be made binding on a minor later if he confirms it upon reaching his majority. (The laws of contract, ever present throughout our economic life, are discussed and detailed as they arise in several of the chapters of this book. *See* the Index, under "Contracts.")

The businessman is understandably cautious in concluding agreements or contracts with young persons, especial-ly time-payment contracts. Many young workers, still children in the eyes of the law, earn good wages and wield a significant purchasing power. They want to buy automobiles, musical instruments, expensive clothes—even houses. But a dealer, in many instances, could be "stuck" if he discovered too late that his customer was under contract age and that money owing was not recoverable at law.

Where one of the contracting parties is a child, the voidable contract created is binding on the other party unless it is repudiated, or canceled, by the child. The word "voidable" implies two situations with regard to children's contracts. Certain contracts are voidable in the sense that they are valid and binding upon a child unless he repudiates them before, or within a reasonable time after, he becomes an adult. Other contracts are voidable because they are not legally binding upon the young person unless he ratifies them when he reaches adulthood.

Contract for "necessaries"

Not all contracts made by a child are void or voidable. The child is obliged to pay for "necessaries" (or necessities) that have been supplied to him. "Necessaries" are not altogether confined to basic articles (like food and clothing), but can include goods and services that help maintain the particular person.

Although it may sound strange in an age that places so much stress on equality, the law recognizes different levels of "necessaries" for children of different economic backgrounds. One situation might call for an extensive wardrobe, another for jeans and a windbreaker.

It can be noted that if the "necessaries" clause did not exist, it would be the poorer children who would suffer: without the security of a contract that they could collect money due, shopkeepers would most likely not allow credit to young persons for food and clothing.

Necessaries for the minor's family are rated on the same basis as are necessaries for himself. It has been established, for instance, that a minor can be held responsible to pay on a contract for the burial of his wife or children.

In order to make the necessaries clause stick, it must be proved not only that the goods are suitable to the child's station in life, but also that they fit his actual requirements at the time of their delivery. If he already has enough of whatever goods he is ordering, then, even though the seller does not know this, the child cannot be forced to pay for the goods.

The basic question of law is whether, in the circumstances, the article can be called necessary. Food, clothing, lodging, medical services and routine education will normally be regarded as necessaries. Even an automobile can be considered a necessity, if it is not an expensive model and is needed by the child to get to and from work or school. A general rule of thumb is that a contract for necessaries will not be binding unless it is substantially for the benefit of the child.

Even though a contract for the supply of goods and services clearly fills legitimate requirements of a child, it will be void if it contains harsh or unfair terms, or if the price of the goods is exorbitant. For example, in an English precedent, a contract by which a child hired a car to transport his luggage was declared void because it stipulated that he should be absolutely liable for damage to the car whether caused by his neglect or not.

Even though a contract is found to be fair, if it is proved that the goods concerned are not necessaries, the contract is voidable and the child will not have to pay. If he had made a deposit, he could get his money back. If he had already taken delivery of the nonessential purchase, he could return it for a full refund. If the goods had been accidentally damaged in the meantime, or even lost, the retailer could probably do nothing but curse his bad luck.

Contracts of marriage (but not of promise to marry) and of apprenticeship are also binding upon a minor. However, in most provinces, a contract to supply goods to a child to enable him to carry on a business is voidable. A Saskatchewan court ruled, in the case of a single man, that a contract of life insurance could not be said to be a necessary requirement of a child and thus was voidable.

Void contracts

There is a group of similar contracts which the courts have held by their very nature to be harmful and unfair to minors, and thus void and unenforceable. Court cases over the years yield the following guidelines.

Contracts with penalty clauses in them will generally not be upheld by the courts. Under a penalty clause, the buyer must pay a certain amount of money on top of the contractual price if a certain event occurs (such as default). For example, where a contract made by a child for the purchase of an automobile contains provisions for the payment of interest, plus a penalty if those payments are not made, the contract is said to be void. Even if the car was considered "necessary," the conditions of the contract would invalidate it.

Other grounds for declaring children's contracts to be void include:

(1) Unreasonable agreements—such as where a child promises to repay his employer, out of wages, the value of any of the employer's property lost or damaged;

(2) Unfair deals in the sale of anything—for instance, if a child sold for $1 lands valued at $5,000;

(3) Loan agreements with unfair terms, for example, if a child borrowed money and assigned his wages to the lender to secure the loan.

The courts will go to considerable lengths to protect children from any bad bargains they might get themselves into. The following is a good example. A child who had been injured when he was struck by a car settled for $1,300 in damages. He signed a release under which he promised to accept the money as complete satisfaction of all his claims and not to bring any further action for damages. After he turned 21, he discovered that he required further treatment for his injuries and he took legal action.

The defendant argued that the contract was not void but only voidable and since the plaintiff could not return the $1,300 he could not cancel the contract. The court ruled that the young man could recover more damages though the agreement that he signed as a child was void because it was unfair to his best interests.

Voidable contracts

Let us now consider contracts that are voidable in the sense that they are binding upon a child unless he repudiates or cancels them during childhood, or within a reasonable time after he attains his majority. An obvious example would be a conditional-sales contract (time payment) made by a child for the purchase of an automobile.

Recruits for the 'oldest profession'

IN OUR TIMES, the sale of a girl into prostitution is unthinkable and the idea of children as young as the age of five working 12 hours a day in factories causes a shudder. But less than 100 years ago when William Thomas Stead, a blunt young newspaperman, joined London's *Pall Mall Gazette*, these were common facts of life in supposedly proper Victorian Britain.

In the summer of 1885, to try to force Parliament to raise the *age of consent* for girls from 13 to 16 and block the "white slave traffic" (selling young girls into brothels both in Britain and on the Continent), Stead wrote and published an article in the *Gazette* documenting the sale and purchase of girls between 13 and 15 (particularly a 13-year-old named Lizzie Armstrong). He pointed out that "the moment a child is 13 she is a woman in the eyes of the law with absolute right to dispose of her person to anyone who by force or fraud can bully or cajole her."

For 20 years, reformers (particularly Lord Shaftesbury, who is remembered by the statue of Eros at London's Piccadilly Circus) had tried to get similar laws passed to protect children, particularly young girls. In 1842, they had won a ban on the employment of children younger than 13 in the coal mines.

There were an estimated 30,000 children without homes or family ties in the streets of London alone. Prostitution offered an escape into a life of comparative ease for girls whose parents lived on the brink of direst poverty. Mothers sold their daughters for a few pounds (Stead actually bought Lizzie from her mother, to help prove his case). Young servant girls in Victorian households lived in virtual slavery, exposed to danger and temptation; an un-cooperative or complaining girl could be simply turned into the streets without a penny. About the time of Queen Victoria's Golden Jubilee, the port city of Liverpool had an estimated 9,000 prostitutes, 1,500 of whom were younger than 15, and 500 younger than 13.

Britain had several laws concerning prostitution at this time—not to protect the girls, but their clients. On the Continent, many countries had officially licensed brothels with an unofficial chain of procurers constantly bringing in recruits for training.

When Stead's article appeared, under the title, "The Maiden Tribute to Modern Babylon," he was accused of obscenity. W. H. Smith's, the national bookshop chain, refused to handle the *Gazette*. When he admitted buying Lizzie and sending her to Paris (actually, in care of the Salvation Army) he was charged with abduction and sentenced to three months' imprisonment—even though he had taken the Archbishop of Canterbury and the Roman Catholic Cardinal of London into his "plot" beforehand. He was permitted to practice his trade in prison, and thus his inflammatory articles continued to appear in the *Gazette*.

The Criminal Law Amendment Act, 1885, was passed within six weeks of the beginning of Stead's publicity campaign. Guardians or appointed social workers were given the right to search any premises (*i.e.*, brothels) for underage girls, and any youngster whose parents connived at immorality could be placed under official guardianship until the age of 21.

Stead's life ended tragically in the icy North Atlantic. He sailed on the maiden voyage of the *Titanic* in April 1912.

Provided that the terms of the contract are fair—for instance, that the rate of interest is reasonable—the contract will remain in force and be binding upon the child until or unless he exercises his right to cancel it out. He must make the monthly installment payments or the dealer can repossess the car. If the child repudiates the contract, his obligations cease. He must return the car and can recover at least a part of the money he has paid—what is left after the seller has recovered his expenses and any loss on the resale.

Similarly, where the child is the seller rather than the buyer of the goods, he may repudiate the contract by returning the money paid.

When a child who has entered into a contract reaches adulthood and the contract is still in force, he may become liable for obligations that could not have been enforced against him when he was a minor. If the contract is permanent or long-term, such as a time-payment sales contract, he must repudiate it within a reasonable time after coming of age or else he will be bound by it. If he does nothing about it, his opportunity passes; if he chooses to cancel the deal at that stage, the law will permit him to do so.

What amounts to "a reasonable time" depends, of course, upon the particular circumstances. In one recorded case, a landowner sold land, which he believed to be his own, while he was still a child. He had known that he was to inherit the land upon the death of another person and he had wrongly believed that person to be dead. Several years after he reached his majority, he did inherit the land and then sought to have his former and erroneous sale of the property nullified on the grounds of his infancy. The court ruled that he had not repudiated the contract soon enough.

Sometimes, contracts made as a child must be *ratified* after the person comes of age or else they will not be binding upon him. "Ratification" in this sense means an admission or confirmation by a person that he is bound by his contract. Merely failing to repudiate after attaining majority does not in itself amount to ratification.

An example of a contract that must be ratified after reaching adulthood is a simple debt incurred during minority. In general, where a child has borrowed money and given back a promissory note, he need not pay a cent after he attains his majority unless he ratifies the original promise. In effect, he must renew his obligation as an adult.

It is worth noting that an adult may cosign a note which guarantees payment if for any reason the minor should default. This is the normal practice with most substantial time-payment deals involving children.

Fraud by the child

A child will not be permitted to slip out of a contract on the grounds of his minority if he made some deliberately false statement which the other party to the contract took to be true. But for a court to rule that fraud occurred, it is not enough that a false statement was made; the speaker must have known that the statement was untrue when he made it. The following example should clarify the point. A young woman who knew that as a child she was incapable of making a legal transfer of land did so anyway. Later, she tried to repudiate the contract, but was refused by the court because she had known all along that she had no right to transfer the land.

A child who lies about his age and says that he has attained his majority (thus giving him the legal right to make a good contract) cannot later repudiate his contract on the ground of his minority. (This does not hold true in Quebec.) However, there are two important qualifications: first, the lie about age must actually have misled the person to whom it was made (thus, anyone who normally extends credit to minors may not be able to convince a court that he was defrauded); second, a child who merely allows another person to assume he is an adult, or does acts which only an adult can do, does not commit fraud (there must be some active misrepresentation on the part of the child.)

Where a child has made a contract by fraud, he can be made to send back the goods he has acquired. He is subject to the general principle that a person will not be allowed to benefit from his own wrongdoing.

Every child is responsible for any torts he commits—that is, any intentional or negligent acts that cause injury to others. When you consider this, together with the fact that a child is not generally responsible for his contracts, it raises the interesting question of what happens when a child breaches a void or voidable contract by committing a tort. (*See* Chapter 18, "What is a tort?")

This is not as abstract as it may sound, as the following actual case illustrates. A child bought an automobile under a conditional-sales contract and shortly afterward demolished it in a collision caused by his negligence. He then sought to repudiate the contract on the ground of his minority. The court held that the car dealer's action was not for negligence but really for the balance of the price of the car owed under the contract. Because the contract was voidable, all that the dealer could recover was the demolished car. This follows the old English doctrine that although a child is liable for a tort, he is not liable for a tort directly connected with a contract where the contract itself cannot be enforced.

Summary on contracts

The following should serve as a simplified guide through the thorny paths of contracts with children (infants):

(1) Generally speaking, all contracts of children (younger than 18–21) for the sale of land can be dissolved.

(2) The child may void (cancel) a contract while he is still a minor and for a reasonable time after reaching his majority, provided he has not done something after majority which might formally confirm the contract.

(3) The contract, until it is canceled by the child, is binding upon the other party.

(4) If the child "walks away from" the contract, he must give back anything he has obtained, but probably he need not do so immediately.

(5) The child cannot recover any payment he has made on the contract unless the other party did something (committed fraud, for example) that made the contract unenforceable.

(6) It is generally immaterial whether the infant has given the impression that he is an adult. He can exercise his right to cancel as a minor as long as he hasn't said, or deliberately led people to believe, that he has reached his majority.

(7) If the contract contains a penalty, or is otherwise to the disadvantage of the child, it is usually void, and the infant can recover any payments he has made.

Children and real estate

In the sense that we usually understand it, a child cannot hold title to real estate—land and buildings—but it can be held in trust for him and he can have the use of it. The legal ownership is normally held by an adult (parent or guardian) for the use and benefit of the child until the child attains his majority. Serious difficulties can arise if the child-owner (or his trustee) wants to sell the real estate before the owner attains the age of 18.

The problem is that a child can make a contract to purchase land, but he cannot take title of the land in his own name. When he reaches his majority, he can arrange for his trustee to transfer the legal title to him. Only when he receives title can he sell the real estate.

There is no law forbidding a child to acquire, hold or dispose of personal property—that is, anything moveable, such as automobiles, jewelry, stocks and bonds. As previously discussed, although a child may enter into contracts dealing with personal property, he will not necessarily be bound by them. Vendors might be sensibly leery of making big-money deals with minors.

If a parent transfers real estate or personal property into the name of his minor (or adult) child, the law presumes the transfer to be an outright gift and the parent will normally have no further right to it. If a parent transfers property to a child (stocks or bonds, perhaps) to avoid taxation, and later tries to recover the property or take income from it, he will discover that he has indeed given it away.

Sometimes a generous parent will make a gift of real or personal property to a child but later, getting into financial difficulties, will claim income from the property for himself. The courts would take the position that the parent had made an absolute gift and the onus would be on the parent to prove that an outright gift was not intended.

That wouldn't be easy.

The changing prospects of Canada's youth

I SEE no hope for the future of our people if they are dependent on the frivolous youth of today ... When I was a boy, we were taught to be discreet and respectful of elders, but the present youth are impatient of restraint. ... "

"The young people are eating us up ... The country is made for the rising generation; life is arranged for them; they are the destruction of society. People defer to them, bow down to them. Whenever they are present there is an end to everything else. ... "

These two quotations will sound familiar to most adults in Canada today. It is seldom that our magazines, newspapers or TV documentaries do not include some new anxious (or outraged) report from the rebellious kingdom of the young. But the opinions stated here were made by the Greek poet-philosopher Hesiod in the 8th century B.C., and by American novelist Henry James, writing in 1882.

It seems there has never been a time when youth everywhere was not "going to the dogs," and yet, somehow, those troublesome teenagers—generation after generation—grow up to be the adults who, in turn, see no hope for the spoiled brats of *their* times.

In the late sixties of long hair and campus riots, the federal government set up a "Committee on Youth" to study "the aspirations, attitudes and needs of youth." Some millions of dollars later, this group advocated several new programs to channel the supposedly frustrated energies and idealism of the "flower children" into creative endeavors that would culminate in radical change throughout society.

By the mid-seventies, however, most of the "new era" policies—the Company of Young Canadians, the Opportunities for Youth grants, foreign and home travel funding—had been quietly axed. The rumble of dissent from the "silent majority" over the use of taxes to support philosophies opposed to the "work ethic" had finally reached the ears of the political managers.

The youth of Canada was hard hit by the economic recession of the early 1980s. In 1983, young people accounted for about 50 percent of the regular clientele of the programs and services offered by the Canada Employment and Immigration Commission. Even university graduates and Ph.D. holders were unable to find employment in fields for which they had been trained. As industry stopped hiring young workers and began laying off those recently hired, some analysts worried that a whole generation might never take its proper place in the work force. A startling increase in the rate of crime, marital breakdown, mental illness and suicide was attributed to the anger and frustration experienced by many of the unemployed.

To alleviate the situation, the federal government budgeted $900 million in fiscal 1983 to create special programs to help the unemployed. The programs included job corps, outreach projects, specialized units for hard-to-employ youths, and training programs for those wishing to learn new trades. For students entering the work force for the first time, the government also expanded its summer internship programs and work-study pilot projects. The purpose of many of these programs was, in the words of Lloyd Axworthy, Minister of Employment and Immigration, designed to help young Canadians prepare "for a challenging future."

Inheritance by children

No minor can make a valid will, unless he is a member of the Canadian armed forces on active duty, a mariner at sea or, in some provinces, married. (*See* Chapter 9, "Last will and testament.")

Where property is given to a child, either through a will or by a gift from a living person, the child's guardian, appointed by a court, must receive and manage it until the child reaches his majority. Furthermore, the child can exercise no control over the guardian. He cannot, for example, order the guardian to sell the property; nor can he force the guardian to pass the property to certain persons if he should die. On the other hand, the guardian has no power either to sell or to dispose of the property without obtaining the consent of the court.

There is no restriction on gifts to minors by bequest. However, a minor has no power to give a valid receipt for a gift under a will. In other words, he cannot officially confirm to the deceased's executor that he has received the property. Because of this legal technicality, wills frequently contain provisions enabling the executor to accept a receipt made by the child's parent instead. If there is no such provision, the executor must either pay the gift into court to be held until the child reaches his majority (if the gift is money), or else set up a trust in which he holds the property for the sole benefit of the child until the child reaches his majority.

Learning a trade

The purpose of apprenticeship programs is to provide sound practical training in a trade. While working on the actual job, under the guidance of experienced men, the apprentice receives a wage considerably below that of a qualified tradesman. To avoid the possibility that a youngster might be exploited by an unscrupulous employer, provincial governments carefully oversee the provisions of all apprenticeship contracts.

To enter a contract of apprenticeship, a minor must be at least 16 years old. Apprenticeship only applies to trades designated by a provincial minister of labor, although employers and employes of any trade can ask the minister to have their trade added to the official list. (*See* Chapter 10, "Professions and trades.")

The apprentice, or his parent or guardian, should find out whether the trade union certified to bargain for the employes at the plant or business concerned will allow apprenticeships.

Before a youth enters an apprenticeship with an employer, the two parties must sign a written contract. If the apprentice is a minor, his parent or guardian must also sign. Where there is no parent or guardian, the contract must be signed by a judge of a county or district court. After the signing, the contract must then be approved by the provincial director of apprentices and it will then be registered with the appropriate provincial authority.

The apprenticeship contract must be for a period of at least two years. The exact length of time allotted for on-the-job training, as well as for instruction in a designated school or college, is carefully worked out for each trade and set down in the regulations. (*See* Chapter 12, "Within provincial powers.") The director of apprentices also sets the requirements for graduation to journeyman status in each trade, the hours of work, wages and other conditions.

A minor cannot be held responsible for a breach of his contract of employment. However, his employer is bound by the contract and cannot dismiss the apprentice unless he has good and sufficient cause. To do so, the employer must get the consent of the provincial director of apprentices.

There are apprenticeship programs for a great variety of trades in this country. The following is a short list of the most popular:

Construction trades—bricklaying, carpentry, masonry and electrician's work.

Painting and decorating.

Vehicle repair—including diesel- and gasoline-powered vehicles.

Plumbing, sheet-metal working and steam fitting.

Air conditioning and refrigeration.

Printing.

Children in trouble

IN A TIME of shifting values, it is the young person in society who appears to run afoul of the law more often. New concepts and new social habits often clash with old ones firmly established in the body of the law. The history of jurisprudence can be seen as a steady evolution, with the established laws adapting slowly to new ideas and customs arising from social change. It was in this way that our present laws were mainly fashioned, and the ongoing process can be witnessed in any Canadian courthouse today.

But the law is properly cautious about change. There are many variables and suggested solutions to be investigated, new principles to be tested, and side effects to be examined before we enthusiastically enter into the oft-proclaimed "new society." Nowhere is this caution more obvious than in the field of juvenile offenses, where even basic information is confused. For instance, it is impossible to know for certain whether more or fewer Canadian children are in trouble with the law now than was the case a generation ago. Why? Because the rules have been changed for reporting cases to the statisticians. For some years now, a large number of first offenders among minors, or those charged with less serious offenses, have not been brought to court at all, and consequently do not show up in the national figures of juvenile delinquency.

For statistical purposes, problem youth in Canada can be divided into two groups: young offenders between the ages of 12 and 18, and another group between 18 and 24. Recent annual statistics for the first group showed a national total of 93,635 convicted young offenders (of whom 36,728 were placed on probation).

At the same time, an estimated 60,000 offenders in the 18–24 age group had been admitted to prison. When these figures are placed against the total number of Canadians in all age groups quoted for that year (about 7,640,000), it will be seen that a relatively small proportion of Canadian youth (roughly one out of 50) is in any serious trouble with the law. While the figures given do not reflect all of those who actually see the inside of a police station, the percentage of lawless youth is lower than news stories would suggest.

Some might argue that the criminal element, even among children, is more stable than we care to admit. Despite the massive spending and concentration on behavioral studies and correctional alternatives, the percentage of youthful lawbreaking has not improved over the past century. To achieve a society without crime would perhaps require a completely fresh start—with a new generation in an innocent world. Regrettably, this tantalizing dream is far from realization.

Liable for negligence

Children, like adults, can be held responsible for actions that result in harm or injury to others (the law refers to these civil wrongs as *torts.—See* Chapter 18, "What is a tort?") But children, especially young children, are notoriously careless, or lacking in mature judgment, and the issues of intent and "taking due care" must always be studied.

If a child intentionally or negligently does something that causes injury, he will be held liable; but if the act is judged in the light of the child's age or development, it may be dismissed as sheer thoughtlessness, or waywardness, meriting a lecture or a warning rather than penalty or any award of damages. The following situation illustrates the point.

A child strolling on the shore of a lake throws a stone which hits and injures a scuba diver swimming beneath the surface. After his recovery, the diver sues the child for damages. Even if the child did not know that the diver was in that vicinity, the court would still have to decide whether or not the child was negligent for being so unaware. Suppose there were signs posted on the beach warning of the presence of scuba divers? Suppose the diver had stationed the regulation float on the surface with a diver's flag on it? Then the court might rule that the child was careless—that is, negligent. But is it reasonable to expect a child to take note of the warnings, or to understand the meaning of the diver's flag on the float?

It would probably be held that a reasonable adult, being aware that there might be divers in the vicinity, would not throw stones into the water. But is a child as reasonable? If the "child" was 17 years old, a judge might well find him guilty of negligence; but if the "child" was six years old, the judge might decide the act was accidental. Boys like to throw stones into lakes—nothing malicious about it.

Of course, anyone who knew the diver was there, and threw the stone with the intention of hitting him, would not only be liable for a tort, but also would be held criminally responsible for assault.

In legal theory, fault cannot be attributed to infants. Therefore, it is impossible to state flatly whether a child would be held guilty of intentionally injuring another's person or property. Where the child is not considered capable of having such an intention, general opinion holds that he is not liable. But there is some confusion in our law about whether a child's failure to understand the nature and consequences of his act, or to know that his action was wrong, should excuse him. In one case, a five-year-old boy who had slashed another child with a razor was found liable, even though he may not have realized how much damage the razor could do, or that it was wrong. In another case, a judge dismissed a claim against a little boy who

put out a playmate's eye while playing with bow and arrows. Although the boy aimed the arrow at his companion, it was ruled that he neither intended to hit him nor was he capable of negligence.

Understanding the consequences

The "standard of care" in negligence actions involving children is based on what one would expect of the "reasonable child," not the reasonable adult. How would the average child of the same age have acted? If a child is unable to understand the nature and consequences of his acts, the law considers him equally unable to be guilty of negligence. For example, if a toddler wanders into a busy street and a car, swerving to avoid him, collides with another car, the child would not be held liable. However, if a child engages in adult activities, such as driving a car, he is held to the same "standard of care" as is expected of an adult.

Although the victim of a child's act may not be able to pin the blame on the child, an adult who has not even breached the ordinary standard of care expected of him as an adult may still be liable if the victim should be a child. Consider this situation. The owner of property normally has no duty imposed upon him to protect trespassers from injury. Thus, if an adult trespasses on private property and is injured, he cannot normally hold the owner responsible. However, where the trespasser is a child who has no concept of private property and cannot recognize danger, the owner may very well have owed him "a duty" of protection. Suppose the landowner keeps a guard dog in an enclosure. If an adult enters the enclosure and is bitten by the dog, he probably would not be able to hold the owner liable; however, a child might see this dog as a big furry plaything and somehow get into the enclosure to pet it. If the child was attacked and injured, it is possible that the owner could be held responsible.

It is a dilemma. The courts know that a landowner cannot be expected to be concerned with the safety of intruders, yet they have to protect children who cannot comprehend danger. In grappling with this problem, the law has invented what is called the doctrine of *allurement*. Basically, it is a way of measuring the duty of protection: where a landowner or householder has something on his property that attracts children—such as a swimming pool—he must take special precautions to prevent child-trespassers from getting in. Otherwise he will be liable should an accident happen to any child that does get in.

In a well-known English case, a young boy went onto the property of a factory and started playing on a heap of furnace refuse. The slag caved in and the child was severely burned by hot embers beneath the outside layer. A court held that the owners were liable, even though the boy was a trespasser. What small boy could resist sliding down a slag heap? The judge classified it as an allurement.

Parents' liability

Parents are generally not liable for their children's torts; it is the child himself who is liable. However, suing a child is like trying to pump water from a dry well: the pump may work, but no water comes out—in other words, the child may be held liable, but he has no means to pay.

The law may attempt to remedy this either by holding the parents *vicariously* liable for their children, or by ruling that the parent was negligent in failing to exercise proper control and supervision over his child. "Vicarious" here means roughly the same as "substitute." Under some provincial laws, the owners of vehicles are liable for the negligence of persons, including children, who drive cars or trucks with the owners' knowledge and consent. On the other hand, the court might decide that the parent did not exercise the same degree of control and supervision over his child that a reasonable parent should have exercised in similar circumstances. Someone who was injured by a child might sucessfully sue for damages, not because of the act of the child but because of the lack of action of the parent. Thus, the injured scuba diver we talked of earlier might be able to collect damages from the parents of the child who had hit him with a stone.

In a case of theft or damage, the court would probably order *restitution*—that is,

order that the child restore anything he had taken, or replace anything he had damaged. This would involve parents in moral responsibility and, perhaps, legal obligation as well. Any adult, whether as the parent or guardian of the child or not, who instructs a child to commit a delinquency, or promotes or contributes to a delinquency, can be fined $500 or sent to prison for up to two years.

Criminal responsibility

Under the Canadian Constitution, criminal law in Canada falls within the exclusive jurisdiction of the federal authority. With a few exceptions, all criminal law and procedure is set out in the Criminal Code of Canada. Whether or not a young offender will be judged according to the letter of the Code depends on his age, the circumstances of the offense and the state of his mental development.

The Criminal Code states that no child younger than seven years may be convicted of an offense. It is presumed that a child younger than seven is incapable of forming the required intent to commit any crime (in Britain, the age is ten). To be excused, the child must have been younger than seven when the offense was committed; if he turns seven after the offense was committed but before he is tried, he is still excused.

The choice of seven years of age is arbitrary. But the victim of an offense cannot try to show, in law, that a child under seven actually did appreciate what he was doing and that he did it with intent. The important point is that a child under seven may not be convicted—even though it may be believed that a six-year old could deliberately commit an offense.

If a child offender is between the ages of seven and 14, the law still tends to presume him incapable of intent; but it allows this factor to be argued in court. The Criminal Code says that a seven- to 14-year-old child will be convicted of an offense only if he is considered capable of having known the nature and consequences of his conduct and of having understood that it was wrong.

Past rulings have yielded some guidelines for the courts to follow when trying to decide whether a child between seven and 14 is capable of committing an actual offense. The judge must generally try to make his own decision based on the facts before him. One rule of thumb is that the nearer a child is to seven years of age, the stronger the evidence must be to show that he had the required capacity. The judge may consider the child's family background, as well as the child's education to date, but he should try not to be influenced by the behavior or the attitude of the child (or even of his parent) in court.

A child who is 14 or older does not have the advantage of presumed incapacity to

The language gap

The federal government's Report on Youth stated there was "a widening discontinuity between young and old"—which is just bureaucratic jargon for the so-called "generation gap." A parent, schoolteacher, social worker, or law-enforcement officer seeking to help young people may have to negotiate a special kind of obstacle—a language gap—if they are to understand just what the problem is.

Only a fraction of youth employs the extremes of teenage argot (which is often obscene) and it may be that rebellious fraction which is in trouble at home, in school, or with the law. The following glossary provides a small sample of the rapidly changing language of youth.

airhead—A stupid person.
awesome—Amazing.
bad scene—Unpleasant experience.
ball—Have sexual intercourse.
blast—A good time.
blow your cool—Lose your temper.
bummer—Unpleasant situation.
busted—Arrested.
cop—To get drugs.
coke—Cocaine.
crash—To sleep.
downer—Depressant drug; barbiturate.
flake—An unreliable person.
fix—Injection of drug.
freak out—To lose touch with reality.
funky—"With it"; fashionable.
get it together—To clarify one's thoughts.
grass—Marijuana (also "weed").
grody—Grotesque.
hang in there—Continue, even if difficult.
hang loose—To be relaxed.
hang up—A problem.
hassle—An argument.
heavy, man—Very good.
horse—Heroin.
jive—To deceive.
john—Man who frequents prostitutes.
kinky—Unusual; "far out."

mickey mouse—Routine; simple.
mother—An insult ("You mother"!)
nerd—A stupid person.
pig—Policeman.
pop—To inject drug under the skin.
put-on—A pretense.
put-down—To humiliate.
psyched up—Excited; stimulated.
rap—Talk; a conversation.
rev up—To stir up.
ripped off—Robbed.
scuzzy—Dirty, filthy.
shades—Sunglasses.
shaft—To take advantage.
snow—Cocaine.
space cadet—A stupid person.
spaced out—Out of touch with daily life.
speeder—A user of amphetamines.
strung out—Worried, tired.
toke—A puff from a marijuana cigarette.
tracks—Marks on the skin from drug injections.
turn on—To interest, or excite.
up front—Truthful.
up tight—Anxious; tense.
upper—A stimulating drug.
vibes—Feelings and unspoken ideas.
wiped out—Extremely tired.

commit a crime, and may be treated the same as an adult offender. This means the law presumes that he understood the nature and consequences of his act and was capable of forming the intention to commit a crime. Until comparatively recently, a child could be sentenced to be hanged. This actually happened in Ontario in 1959 when a mature 14-year-old boy was accused of murdering a girl. He was judged to be "capable" and, after a trial in adult court, was sentenced to die. The sentence was commuted and the young man, in fact, served ten years' imprisonment.

In Canada today, children between 14 and 18 years are seldom tried as adult offenders but rather under the federal Juvenile Delinquents Act.

Juvenile delinquency

The federal parliament made the first move in 1894 to protect children from the full consequences of their crimes by passing legislation that segregated young offenders from older prisoners. It also granted a private trial for those younger than 16, in early recognition of the lifetime stigma of "a criminal record."

The separation of children from adults in criminal proceedings was formalized in the Juvenile Delinquents Act of 1908. The theory was that problem children were as much perhaps the victims of bad parental guidance or low mental ability as they were motivated by deliberate intent to break the law. When the act was redrafted in 1928, after a conference of experts and interested parties, this philosophy was paramount. Reform, not punishment, was to be society's approach to the lawbreaking child.

There was no doubt that this federal legislation invaded the jurisdictions of the provinces. Obviously, special courts, legal procedures, correctional techniques and reformatories (training schools) were needed if children were to be treated separately from adult offenders; yet all of these matters concerning children (quite apart from constitutional responsibility for civil law) were provincial matters. This problem was solved by the creation of a wholly new classification of offender, the *juvenile delinquent*, as well as the definition of a new kind of offense that cut across federal, provincial and even municipal lines of authority: *delinquency*.

The governing federal act defines a juvenile delinquent as "any child who violates any provision of the Criminal Code, or of any federal or provincial statute, or of any bylaw or ordinance of any municipality, or who is guilty of sexual immorality or any similar form of vice, or who is liable by reason of any other act to be committed to an industrial school or juvenile reformatory." Any of these violations by a child is considered a delinquency.

While this separate status worked effectively to shield children, in most cases, from the full force of the law, it did leave some difficulties in its wake. It meant that the single term, "juvenile delinquent," can include, for instance, the child who commits a serious offense—such as rape, murder or robbery—as well as the child who commits a relatively minor one—such as operating an automobile without a license or loitering in a public place.

When a child is charged with an offense, he is taken before a juvenile (or family, or social welfare) court. There, he is tried for juvenile delinquency, not for the specific offense of which he is accused. However, where the violation is listed as an indictable offense under the Criminal Code, or under some other federal statute such as the Narcotic Control Act, and the accused child is actually or apparently older than 14, the court has the right to order that the child be dealt with just as if he were an adult. The judge must not follow this course unless he believes that the welfare of the community and the best interests of the child demand it. If this decision is made, the child loses the protection of the Juvenile Delinquents Act and is tried in adult court.

While this may seem harsh, and contrary to the current philosophy behind the treatment of child lawbreakers, it is usually only invoked when the court considers that the interests of the child would be better served by confining him for a longer time than that permitted under the Juvenile Delinquents Act. The juvenile court has jurisdiction over a person only until he reaches the age of 21, at which time that court's power ceases. Where it is desirable to confine, or to continue to supervise, a young person beyond that time, only an adult court has the power to impose the longer sentence required.

How old is a juvenile?

The Juvenile Delinquents Act permits each province to set its own age at which an offender ceases to be considered a juvenile and comes to be judged under the adult court system. In the inevitable Canadian pattern, the cutoff age varies across the country, with the usual complaints of unfairness in many cases.

In Prince Edward Island, Nova Scotia, New Brunswick, Ontario, Saskatchewan, Alberta, the Yukon and the Northwest Territories, the young offender will be classed as a juvenile in this regard only until he turns 16. In Quebec and Manitoba, the age is 18, and, in British Columbia, it is 17.

It can easily be seen, therefore, that a young person can commit an offense in one province and be treated under the lenient procedures of the juvenile court, while the same offense committed a few yards away, but across the border of the next-door province, would put a child of the same age before the adult court.

Young Offenders Act

In the early 1970s, legislation was introduced to replace the Juvenile Delinquents Act with a new bill known as the Young Offenders Act. One of the main arguments put forward by the advocates of the new bill was that a young person before the courts did not always receive a fair trial. Under the Juvenile Delinquents Act, there was nothing specific to prevent the admission in a juvenile court of evidence that would be inadmissible in an adult court. The juvenile did not have the right to cross-examine witnesses.

The Young Offenders Act took more than ten years to draft and was finally given unanimous approval in the House of Commons in May 1982. The intention of the bill is to hold young offenders responsible for their criminal behavior and yet protect them from the often harsh atmosphere of the adult courts. Under the provisions of the new act, the young offender has the same rights as an adult, including the right to be represented by a lawyer and to appeal court decisions. The bill set the minimum age at which a young person could be charged with a criminal offense at 12 (previously it had been seven) and the maximum age at 18. At this writing, the new act was being introduced in stages.

Stealing by children

Theft is by far the most common juvenile offense in Canada. Considerably more than 27,000 cases reach the stage of formal court appearance each year. Another 32,254 cases are classified as "breaking and entering." Together, these two categories account for more than half of all youthful crime.

An adult convicted of theft of goods not exceeding $200 in value can be sentenced to as much as two years in prison, although a first offender usually gets a suspended sentence. A child who is a first offender, being tried for the same act but as a juvenile delinquent, will usually be placed on probation. Repeated acts may lead to treatment. The young person tempted by open displays in self-serve shops—or "dared" by companions in "chicken" games—should know that shopkeepers almost always lay theft charges when they catch someone shoplifting.

It is an offense under the Criminal Code to destroy or damage property, to render it useless, inoperative, or ineffective, or to interfere with any person in the lawful use, enjoyment or operation of his own property.

Vandalism

The dictionaries say that a *vandal* is a person who willfully or ignorantly destroys anything beautiful or venerable. The language of law widens the definition to include any mindless or vicious act of destruction—such as stoning school or church windows, breaking ornamental saplings, defacing signs and scratching automobile hoods, to name only a few of the offenses reported under this heading.

Vandalism appears to have an irresistible appeal to certain children and is the subject of study by psychologists. Some culprits appear to think they are "hitting back" at an authority that has punished or frustrated them; others (including children from middle-class and wealthy homes) appear to have no motive at all.

An adult can be imprisoned for up to five years for vandalism, but a child is usually treated more leniently. An adult vandal may be ordered to pay damages to the person whose property was harmed; a juvenile, or his parent, can be ordered to pay only the cost of having the property repaired or restored. The victim of the vandalism would have to take separate civil action if he sought anything more than that.

Young vandals sometimes do not realize the danger to life that can result from destructive actions, and the extreme bitterness and frustration an adult can feel as a result of wanton damage to his property. The enraged victim might just physically "hit back" more severely than a child would expect. A child who by smashing property caused actual danger to life could—in the extreme—find himself in adult court facing the prospect of imprisonment, possibly for life.

With vandals' attacks on school property having reached epidemic proportions, the punishment of persons who do willful damage to federal, provincial or municipal government property is much more severe than in previous years.

Drug offenses

After a decade of scare headlines, gloomy television documentaries and a federal fact-finding commission, the spotlight of public attention appears to be fading from the so-called youth drug scene. In late 1972, the federal minister of health announced that an older habit—drinking—was the No. 1 threat to youth.

To educate the young (as well as the public at large), Health and Welfare Canada launched its first five-year *Dialogue on Drinking* campaign in 1976 on television, in the newspapers, and through posters and booklets for community social workers. At this writing, the second five-year campaign, with a budget of more than a billion dollars, was under way. Its 1983 slogan, "Get active on overdrinking," was the message on television advertisements which featured well-known business figures and sportsmen who explained that they didn't drink on the job, nor did they need alcohol to enjoy their pastimes.

Impassioned appeals by numerous public figures failed to persuade the federal government to legalize the use of "soft drugs" like marijuana and hashish. Simple possession of soft drugs can still bring a jail sentence of up to seven years to all persons except those classed legally as juveniles.

Before you can be convicted of possession of prohibited drugs, it must be

The judgment of Solomon

SOLOMON, son of David and Bath-sheba, the third King of All Israel (970–931 B.C.), is remembered for his practical wisdom—and his love of beautiful women. He won his reputation as a judge by his decision in a family court case.

Two harlots who lived together had borne babies within a three-day span and one of the infants had been suffocated in bed. Each of them swore that she was the mother of the surviving child, and claimed custody.

The King ordered that a sword be brought into his court. "Divide the living child in two," he ordered, "and give half to one and half to the other."

One of the harlots agreed with this decision, but the other appealed to Solomon not to slay the child, but to give it instead to the other woman.

The King's strategy had worked. He figured that the real mother would deny herself rather than harm the child in any way. So he immediately awarded her the baby.

proved beyond a reasonable doubt that you actually had the drug in your possession. This may seem a simple matter: you either have it, or you don't. However, "possession" has a wide legal meaning. For the purposes of both the Narcotic Control Act and the Criminal Code, a person has anything in his possession if he:

(1) Has it in his personal possession—in short, on his person;

(2) *Knowingly* has it in the actual possession or custody of another person without that person's knowledge or consent;

(3) Has it in any place, whether or not that place belongs to or is occupied by him, for the use or benefit of himself or another person;

(4) Has it in the possession of another person with that person's knowledge and consent.

The key word is "knowingly." If you were caught with marijuana on your person and if you could prove that you honestly did not know what it was, or did not know that it was in your possession, you would not be convicted. The onus would be on the Crown to show that you did know. Suppose, for example, you were walking along the street and saw a small paper parcel. You picked it up to see what it was. Then a policeman stopped you and searched you, finding the parcel and discovering that it contained an illegal drug. As long as you could convince the court that you had merely picked up the parcel out of curiosity and by chance, you probably would not be convicted of possessing prohibited drugs.

If you were standing near a person who was about to be arrested and he slipped the evidence into your pocket unnoticed by you, you would probably be cleared—if the judge believed your story.

If the police raided your parents' house and found drugs concealed there, and if they sought to charge the parents with possession, they would have to prove that the parents *knew* the drugs were there. At the same time, the parents would need to be very plausible in explaining why it was there without their knowing it.

A much more serious offense than possession is *trafficking*, which, in terms of drugs, means to manufacture, sell, give, administer, transport, send, deliver or distribute—or to offer to do any of these things. Of course, this does not apply to a doctor, druggist or anyone else authorized to manufacture, give or deal in drugs. For anyone who is not authorized to do these things, the penalty can be as much as life imprisonment.

It is not only an offense to actually traffic but also to have drugs in your possession "for the purpose of trafficking." This means that you do not have to be caught actually transferring drugs to another person; it is enough for the prosecution to prove that you had them not for your own use, but for the purpose of selling or otherwise transferring them.

Growing opium poppy or marijuana carries a penalty of up to seven years' imprisonment.

Under the federal Food and Drugs Act, which controls the supply and use of such "restricted drugs" as L.S.D., mescaline and the amphetamines ("acid," "sunshine" and "speed" in street talk), the penalties are somewhat lighter. It is illegal to possess, sell or distribute these drugs without the appropriate authorization under the Act.

Privacy and penalty

The trials of children must take place in private, separate and apart from the trials of accused adult persons. Under the Juvenile Delinquents Act, no report of a child's delinquency may be published in the public press.

The child's parent or guardian must be notified of the hearing but is not forced to attend. Even if the parent does attend, he has no right to be heard, though the judge may, at his discretion, hear anything the parent may wish to say.

The penalties permitted under the act are clearly set out in Section 20. The judge has the following options.

(1) Suspend final decision.

(2) Adjourn the hearing or final decision of the case any number of times for any definite or indefinite period.

(3) Impose a fine not exceeding $25, which may be paid in periodic amounts or otherwise.

(4) Commit the child to the care or custody of a probation officer, or any other suitable person.

(5) Allow the child to remain in its home, with visits from a probation officer; the child has to report to the court or to the probation officer as often as may be required.

(6) Place the child in a suitable family home, such as a foster home, subject to the friendly supervision of a probation officer and the further order of the court.

(7) Impose upon the delinquent whatever conditions may seem advisable in relation to his delinquency.

(8) Commit the child to the charge of a children's aid society (or equivalent).

(9) Commit the child to an industrial (training) school which has been approved by the Lieutenant-governor in council.

No child who is being tried as a juvenile delinquent can be confined in any place where adults are imprisoned, unless he cannot be safely confined in any other place. If he is convicted of a delinquency, he cannot be sent to a penitentiary, jail or any other place where adults are held.

If the child is transferred to the jurisdiction of an adult court, however, he can be imprisoned in an adult jail, both during his trial and after his conviction. He cannot, however, be sentenced to a penitentiary unless he is at least 14 years old.

Once a child is judged to be a juvenile delinquent, he remains under the supervision of the court until he reaches the age of 21. The court can recall him at any time and make new orders affecting him. If the child had been committed to a training school, the court may decide to release him at any time upon the recommendation of the superintendent of the school. Similarly, some other order originally made (such as placing him on probation) may be taken back and the child committed to a training school.

The incorrigible child

If a parent or guardian decides, finally, that a child is beyond parental control, he should get in touch with the counselors at the juvenile court or with a children's aid society.

If no alternative can be found, the child will be considered incorrigible and sent for correctional treatment at a provincial training school.

The cult of youth worship

THE RENOWNED ANTHROPOLOGIST, Margaret Mead, once quipped that the middle class treated motherhood as a unique achievement. Other experts—usually Europeans—place the blame for much of North America's juvenile problems on the shoulders of overpermissive educators, judges and parents—or, more specifically, on those who both idealize and idolize youth. They call us "the youth-worshippers."

At first, our pioneer society was dominated by the autocratic father, then by the ambitious mother ("Momism"); now, they say, we are living in a filiarchy—a child-centered society. It is difficult to argue that youth and its myriad problems don't monopolize much of adult thinking and conversation. The sight of gray-haired mothers and fathers doggedly attempting the latest dances gives credence to the proposition.

Experts close to the troubled child suggest that teenagers are more embarrassed than pleased by their parents' efforts to stay young. Although they challenge the conventions of their elders, they may be deeply loyal to them underneath. Personalities are built in quest and learning—which is another way of saying "by trial and error." The parent should be the firm rock on which the child can build.

There's the well-known story of the 17-year-old who simply couldn't understand how Dad could be so dumb. By the time he was 22, he couldn't understand how Dad learned so much in five years.

At Factory

and Office

12/Workers, Bosses and Unions

Within provincial powers

Union rules and regulations

Strikes and lockouts

How labor won legality

ALTHOUGH the history of labor unionism in Canada goes back a surprisingly long way (at least to 1816), the growth of the movement has been closely linked with developments in other countries—primarily Britain and the United States. Although mainly international in form and character, it has still been up to the Canadian unions themselves to struggle separately for their existence; and they have been close to extinction on several occasions.

In the colonial period, the first trade unions were transplanted by immigrant British workers. Printers were organized in Quebec City in 1827. The Amalgamated Society of Engineers set up its first Canadian local in 1850. The British Society of Carpenters and Joiners got its start in Canada in 1860. For many years, even into modern times, immigrant Britons, raised in a more class-conscious environment, supplied a radical and highly individual leadership.

The early labor movement of the 1800s consisted of scattered locals (as branches are known) struggling in isolation. Small independent organizations were formed among the skilled handcraft workers of Canadian urban centers. These were the predecessors of today's large craft unions. There were the boot and shoe workers' "labor circles" in Lower Canada during the 1820s, as well as the tailors' "lodges." The Toronto Typographical Union boasts the longest continuous life of any union in Canada, tracing its origins back to 1844. (It is now part of the International Typographical Union.)

After the American Civil War, Canadian labor looked increasingly to the United States for its ideology, organization, policies, funds and affiliations. This association grew closer, paralleling the growing integration of the two great North American economies. Today about 80 percent of organized workers in Canada belong to so-called "international" unions. (An international union in this context is one with its headquarters and the great majority of its members in the United States.)

Seeking lawful recognition

By the beginning of the twentieth century, Canada's unions had grown to such size and strength that they were prepared to tackle the many legal barriers that stood in the path of their progress. To promote the type of legislation they wanted, locals banded together to form powerful lobbies—groups to pressure elected representatives. The first significant step in this direction was the formation of the Toronto Trades Assembly (T.T.A.) in 1871, representing 15 local unions—including sailmakers, iron molders and stonemasons. This group was instrumental in forming the Canadian Labor Union. Although the T.T.A. did not survive a serious depression in the late nineteenth century, it did instill in the minds of labor leaders the concept of an organization that would unite all Canada. This ideal has never been fully realized.

In 1886, the Trades and Labor Congress (T.L.C.) was founded following the establishment, earlier in the same year, of the American Federation of Labor (A.F.L.). The T.L.C. played a significant role in bringing about the first major piece of federal labor legislation passed in Canada: the Industrial Relations and Disputes Investigation Act, 1907. This act laid down the major principles that formed the basis both for the recognition of trade unions and for their participation in the industrial life of the country.

Lobbying became popular at that time and has continued as the main political weapon of unionism in Canada, rather than concentration of effort (as in the United Kingdom) to elect workers as members of parliament.

After a painful period of division, in which craft and industry-wide unions broke off into separate groups, reunion came in 1956 under the name of the Canadian Labor Congress (C.L.C.), representing nearly 58 percent of all trade unionists in Canada. Only the Quebec-based Confédération des Syndicats Nationaux— Confederation of National Trade Unions (C.N.T.U.)—with fewer than ten percent of Canada's organized workers, and a scattering of various unaffiliated bodies remain outside.

The Knights of Labor

In our prosaic times, it's hard to believe that for 40 years the Noble Order of the Knights of Labor was an important body on the Canadian labor scene. Its motto was, "An injury to one is the concern of all"; but its leaders regarded strikes as "a relic of barbarism." Started among Philadelphia tailors in 1869, the Knights organized everybody—skilled, unskilled, blue-collar, white-collar—into "trade assemblies." Only bankers, lawyers, gamblers, saloonkeepers and stockholders were barred. By 1890, there were 16,000 Canadian "Knights," formed into 257 assemblies. Membership in the United States once totaled 702,000.

Quebec was particularly open to the movement, but not until the Order had altered its ritual to suit Church tastes and its leaders had denounced socialism.

In the United States, the central organization of the Knights of Labor clashed with the swiftly developing American Federation of Labor and this dispute reached into Canada. For several years the Knights remained within the Trades and Labor Congress of Canada, even after the American Knights disbanded. However, the more powerful A.F.L. insisted on a purge and, in 1902, the T.L.C. expelled its remaining Knights. Some small trade assemblies lingered for another ten years, but eventually even they vanished.

Other unions that ran counter to the labor Establishment at various times included the Provincial Workmen's Association of Nova Scotia, the Western Federation of Miners, the One Big Union, and the Industrial Workers of the World —the I.W.W., widely known as the "Wobblies."

Aims of unionism

"United we stand, divided we fall"—the wise counsel of the slave Aesop in his *Fables*—has been the rallying cry of organized labor since the beginnings of the Industrial Revolution. By the end of the eighteenth century, more than 40 bills had been introduced in the British House of Commons to *prevent* workers from combining to press their demands on owners of the booming new factories. At the same time, decrees were issued in France prohibiting workers from organizing.

Employers feared that the workers were conspiring against them to the certain ruin of trade. In 1825 the right to organize was won in Britain—at least in theory; it was contested, sometimes violently, until mid-century. It wasn't until 1872 that the Canadian Parliament passed the Trade Unions Act and amended the criminal law to bring legal protection to organized groups of workers.

The primary purpose of unions is to organize workers into effective groups to conduct collective bargaining with the employer on such material matters as wages, hours of work and general conditions of labor. Some unions offer recreation and other benefits or facilities to their members, a tradition handed down from the "friendly societies" and guilds of earlier times.

In democratic countries, the union is free to pursue its aims toward improving the lot of the working man and to broaden its drive toward organizing the clerical white-collar class. In particular, it is permitted to use the weapon of the legal strike. On the other hand, in Communist and other one-party states where labor

Exile for union members!

This poster was circulated in England in the early nineteenth century, warning anyone joining "illegal societies or unions" that they were risking exile to the convict settlements. "Felony" was (and still is) the term used in Britain and the United States for a serious crime.

CAUTION.

WHEREAS it has been represented to us from several quarters, that mischievous and designing Persons have been for some time past, endeavouring to induce, and have induced, many Labourers in various Parishes in this County, to attend Meetings, and to enter into Illegal Societies or Unions, to which they bind themselves by unlawful oaths, administered secretly by Persons concealed, who artfully deceive the ignorant and unwary,—WE, the undersigned Justices think it our duty to give this PUBLIC NOTICE and CAUTION, that all Persons may know the danger they incur by entering into such Societies.

ANY PERSON who shall become a Member of such a Society, or take any Oath, or assent to any Test or Declaration not authorized by Law—

Any Person who shall administer, or be present at, or consenting to the administering or taking any Unlawful Oath, or who shall cause such Oath to be administered, although not actually present at the time—

Any Person who shall not reveal or discover any Illegal Oath which may have been administered, or any Illegal Act done or to be done—

Any Person who shall induce, or endeavour to persuade any other Person to become a Member of such Societies,

WILL BECOME

Guilty of Felony,

AND BE LIABLE TO BE

Transported for Seven Years.

ANY PERSON who shall be compelled to take such an Oath, unless he shall declare the same within four days, together with the whole of what he shall know touching the same, will be liable to the same Penalty.

Any Person who shall directly or indirectly maintain correspondence or intercourse with such Society, will be deemed Guilty of an Unlawful Combination and Confederacy, and on Conviction before one Justice, on the Oath of one Witness, be liable to a Penalty of TWENTY POUNDS, or to be committed to the Common Gaol or House of Correction, for THREE CALENDAR MONTHS ; or if proceeded against by Indictment, may be CONVICTED OF FELONY, and be TRANSPORTED FOR SEVEN YEARS.

Any Person who shall knowingly permit any Meeting of any such Society to be held in any House, Building, or other Place, shall for the first offence be liable to the Penalty of FIVE POUNDS ; and for every other offence committed after Conviction, be deemed Guilty of such Unlawful Combination and Confederacy, and on Conviction before one Justice, on the Oath of one Witness, be liable to a Penalty of TWENTY POUNDS, or to Committ-ment to the Common Gaol or House of Correction, FOR THREE CALENDAR MONTHS ; or if proceeded against by Indictment may be

CONVICTED OF FELONY,
And Transported for SEVEN YEARS.

| COUNTY OF DORSET, *Dorchester Division.* February 22d. 1834. | C. B. WOLLASTON, JAMES FRAMPTON, WILLIAM ENGLAND, THOS. DADE, JNO. MORTON COLSON, | HENRY FRAMPTON, RICHD. TUCKER STEWARD, WILLIAM R. CHURCHILL, AUGUSTUS FOSTER. |

leadership is virtually in the hands of the government, unions are not granted the right to strike or actively demonstrate.

Unions and politics

The Canadian trade union movement has pursued a different course from that of its British parent. Since the 1890s, the British movement has aimed at actual political power, in open alliance with the socialist Labor Party. It placed 29 members in the House of Commons in 1906, held the government reins briefly in 1924 and held power again in 1929. The Labor Party came fully to power immediately after World War II, introducing what has been called "the welfare state"—a social revolution by any terms. The party was defeated in 1951 but returned to govern between 1964 and 1970 and again between 1974 and 1979. Although the British Labor Party has remained largely working class in membership, it has grown more radical since the late 1970s: it now draws most of its political leaders from the professional middle class.

In Canada, the aims of organized labor have generally been of more materialistic concern: higher wages, shorter hours, better fringe benefits, union security. Since Confederation, labor has sought to influence government mainly by presenting briefs to the cabinet through the permanent Ottawa office of the Canadian Labor Congress (C.L.C.), and by lobbying provincial cabinets against certain measures. Steady success has been achieved by this method.

Efforts at direct political representation by Canadian unions have been made, notably through the Co-operative Commonwealth Federation (C.C.F.) and its successor, the New Democratic Party (N.D.P.). On the whole, union members in Canada have remained notably independent at the polling booth and the N.D.P. has never succeeded in sending a large number of members to Ottawa. On the provincial level, the N.D.P. has held power only in Saskatchewan, Manitoba and British Columbia, although it has been the "loyal opposition" in other provinces.

Nevertheless, organized labor has come a long way in Canada since the "father" of the movement, a printer named Daniel John O'Donoghue, proudly announced to Governor General Lord Dufferin: "Your Excellency, I represent the rag, tag and bobtail."

Legal status of unions

There was a time when Canadian workers banding together to try to enforce their demands were considered under the common law as conspirators and their unions or associations were ruled illegal. This had its origins in England, where the famed six "Tolpuddle martyrs" were transported as convicts to Australia in 1834 for forming a union local.

Employers argued that unions acted as a restraint on trade. Later, the main complaint was that unions were virtually monopolies and, just as any business that set out to monopolize an industry, they should be broken up. When the Toronto printers went on strike in 1872 for a nine-hour day, the employers had all 24 members of the union executive thrown into jail on conspiracy charges. By the late nineteenth century, however, the unions were legally accepted in all provinces.

A trade union (called a labor union in some provinces) can be an organization of the workers doing a variety of jobs in a single factory or it can represent all those performing similar work across the entire country. Sometimes, several unions will be represented within a single plant. The aircraft and broadcasting industries, where many skilled crafts are brought together, provide examples of this.

To speak and bargain legally for its members, a union must be able to prove that a majority of the workers want that union to represent them.

For a long time, labor leaders pushed for legislation that would have allowed unions to incorporate, just like any business. They have since changed their minds, fearing that incorporation might make it possible for the unions to be sued for breach of contract.

In many provinces, a union *can* be sued for damages in certain civil actions, and it can also bring suit.

Particularly since power has become more evenly divided between the major unions and company managements, the courts have wrestled with the problem of how the unions could, or should, be "brought to book" when they—or, more often, some of their members apparently acting as an independent group—break the contractual terms of a collective agreement. One such knotty legal problem arises in what is commonly known as the "wildcat" strike. (*See* "Strikes and lockouts" later in this chapter.)

Three types of union

There are three basic types of union:

(1) The so-called "company union" is organized solely among the workers of a particular company, or group of interlocking companies. It can be independent and even aggressive. On the other hand, if it can be shown that it is dominated or influenced by the employer, it will not be certified as the legal bargaining agent. Even the willingness of a sympathetic employer to post notices of union meetings on company bulletin boards can be the kiss of death.

Company unions still exist, with the same structure as regular unions, but are now fading from the labor scene. They are scorned by the union federations as being at best "creatures of capitalist paternalism."

Where there is a company union, the wages and conditions enjoyed are sometimes above what has been wrested from other companies by hard bargaining or even by costly strike. Thus, there is little reason for workers within a company union to seek outside representation, a fact of which employers are well aware.

(2) The craft union is sometimes referred to as "horizontal." Its members are all skilled in a certain trade and are scattered right across the country—the Painters and Decorators, or Bakers and Confectioners unions provide examples. Many of these unions were born in Canada; others were introduced by British immigrants. After 1866, most of these became affiliated with the American Federation of Labor and were grouped within the A.F. of L's fraternal associate in Canada, the Trades and Labor Congress. They have tended to be a comparatively conser-

vative force in organized labor, believing in "bread and butter unionism" and working mostly within traditional democratic channels.

(3) The great industrial unions recruit their members over an entire industry, regardless of the separate crafts represented, taking in skilled and unskilled workers alike. An early example of this type was the Nova Scotia Coal Miners Union (1879) which included not only miners but also wharf laborers, railwaymen and iron founders. Later, under the title of Provincial Workmen's Association, it also took in glassblowers, retail clerks, boot and shoe operators, and many other classifications. The quaintly named Knights of Labor were another example of an industrial, or "vertical," union.

The modern industrial giants (the United Steelworkers Union, for example, has more than 150,000 members) developed in Canada in the 1920s out of a distrust among some workers for the comparatively exclusive, highly skilled craft unions. The craft unions offered little welcome to the vast body of relatively unskilled laborers then being drawn into the new mass-production factories. Other examples of modern "verticals" are the Needle Trades Workers, the Auto Workers, the Mine, Mill and Smelter Workers. These unions, affiliated with the Congress of Industrial Organizations (C.I.O.) in the United States, became grouped under its parallel organization in this country, the Canadian Congress of Labor.

The A.F.L. and C.I.O. merged in the United States in 1955. This paved the way for the parallel marriage of the craft and industrial unions in Canada. In 1956, the T.L.C. and the C.C.L. formed the present ruling body, the Canadian Labor Congress. While 26.6 percent of the member unions of the C.L.C. are "internationals" affiliated with the A.F.L.-C.I.O., increasing stress is being laid on the autonomy of the Canadian units. The C.L.C. takes an active part in the International Confederation of Free Trade Unions, which is the worldwide body representing all organized workers outside the Communist bloc of countries.

508

The Communist challenge

During the Depression of the early 1930s, the Communist Party of Canada formed its own labor federation, the Workers' Unity League (W.U.L.). It was a direct rival of the Trades and Labor Congress of the time and of the All-Canadian Congress of Labor based in western Canada. There had been a persistent radical movement in the Canadian West ever since the days of the "Wobblies" and of the One Big Union involved in the tragic general strike at Winnipeg in 1919. This grassroots influence still persists, from time to time, helping to elect socialist governments at the provincial level.

The Communist revolutionary line attracted some fishermen and loggers in British Columbia, as well as longshoremen, seamen and some hard-rock miners, many of them then recent arrivals from central Europe. When a policy switch was made in Moscow in 1934, the W.U.L. was disbanded and its members were ordered to infiltrate the established Canadian federations. Here they proved to be good organizers, capturing the leadership and loyalty of several important affiliated unions. This was especially true during World War II while Russia was among the allied nations fighting Germany, Italy and Japan. Unions under Communist sway included the United Electrical Workers, International Woodworkers, Seamen's Union, United Fishermen, Textile and Chemical Workers and the United Automobile Workers.

The Communists tried, but without success, to swing the C.C.L. into outright political support of the Canadian Communist Party, known at the polls as the Labor Progressive Party. In 1945, when a Russian embassy employe, Igor Gouzenko, revealed that there was extensive Soviet spying in Canada, and when the Communists within the union movement persisted in pursuing hard-line aims opposed to the policy of the T.L.C. and C.C.L., both federations took punitive action. They moved, in due course, and with some reluctance, to expel the Communist-led affiliates and to purge known Communists from executive posts in other unions.

All together now: "Solidarity Forever!"

To sustain the faithful and build morale among waverers, most grassroots movements have enlisted the help of the inspirational song—and the trade union movement is no exception. It doesn't matter if the lyrics are a bit limp or if the tune is somewhat shaky. It's the volume and the fraternal spirit that's important.

When the Knights of Labor sallied forth against the railroad barons at the turn of the century, they sang (to the tune of the hymn *Hold the Fort*):

Storm the fort, ye Knights of Labor,
Battle for your cause;
Equal rights for every neighbor—
Down with tyrant laws!

If you pass a union hall today during a long strike you are likely to hear the strains of the ever-popular *Solidarity Forever!* (to the tune of *John Brown's Body*):

When the union's inspiration through
the worker's blood shall run,
There can be no power greater anywhere
beneath the sun.
Yet what force on earth is weaker than
the feeble strength of one?
But the union makes us strong.
(Chorus)
Solidarity forever!
For the union makes us strong.

It is we who plowed the prairies; built the
cities where they trade;
Dug the mines and built the workshops;
endless miles of railroad laid.
Now we stand, outcast and starving, 'mid
the wonders we have made;
But the union makes us strong.
Solidarity forever!

The laws of labor

WHEN YOU TAKE a job in Canada, or if you hire someone to work for you, most of the relationships or problems that may arise will be covered within areas of law and regulation. Through its unique interlocking of federal and provincial legislation, Canada probably protects its workers from exploitation as completely as any country in the world. And these laws and regulations are continually being revised.

The laws of labor fall into three main groups: the first is a loose collection handed down over the years called, archaically, the "law of master and servant"; the second contains the numerous federal and provincial laws that set safe and fair standards of employment; the third consists of the laws of collective bargaining. While all these laws differ in nature and purpose, they share the common principles of the law of contract: essentially, every employer-employe relationship is a contract of employment.

Considering the attention the mass media gives to trade-union news and views, it may come as a surprise to some to realize that less than 30 percent of Canada's more than 12 million workers are unionized. Thus, the law of master and servant must also recognize that a separate individual contract theoretically exists between every worker and his boss, though such a contract does not necessarily have to be written down and signed. Where a "closed shop" (*See* "Union rules and regulations" in this chapter) monopoly has not been granted to a union, an individual worker can negotiate his own terms—his success, of course, will probably depend on the value of his services to the employer. In theory, there could be as many employment contracts as there are workers, each with different terms.

Labor unions were organized because workers realized they could obtain a better contract if they negotiated as a group. Their action in withholding their labor (or threatening to withhold it), causing the employer financial loss, is enshrined as "the right to strike." This action gives the worker a strength roughly equaling the boss's economic power. Under the laws of collective bargaining, a contract is entered into between the union and the employer. This contract governs the relationship between the employer and every member of the group, whether there are a hundred or a thousand members.

However, the great majority of workers across the country are still without the collective strength of unions and thus could be largely at the mercy of any unscrupulous employer. To cover this lack, both federal and provincial governments have enacted a series of laws to ensure that workers everywhere get a fair deal, whether members of trade unions or not.

Employment standards
As the Industrial Revolution of the eighteenth century spread, companies realized that, as they grew larger, they acquired more bargaining power in the labor market. Some employers took advantage of their strength to demand longer working hours and to offer lower wages. The reaction was a fight for better working conditions. Reformers thought that the state should step in on the side of the worker to equalize his bargaining position. Legislation was passed in Britain and elsewhere providing for a minimum age for workers, maximum hours of

work, safer machinery on the job, as well as making the boss responsible when an employe was injured because of faulty equipment.

These laws are now universally accepted and approved in all Western countries.

In Canada, a variety of different statutes protect the many aspects of working conditions. Although each statute has its own title, collectively they have come to be known as the employment-standards laws. To keep pace with rapid developments in the modern world of work, these laws are being revised almost monthly; thus, the examples given in this chapter may be out of date by the time you read this book. If you are in any doubt, check with the department of labor in your province for the most recent revisions of the law. This is especially recommended for minimum-wage legislation.

Although the employment-standards laws regulate *all* employment contracts, it is usually only the worker hired on an individual basis who needs their protection. An employer cannot bargain a worker out of the terms granted by statute.

There is usually a minimum wage for each class of occupation, specified working conditions and a limit to the number of working hours in a day and week.

Mutual obligations

Where a worker does not belong to a union, the relationship between his boss and himself is governed by the law of master and servant. Although the wording used today is "employer and employe," the legal principle remains the same. The essential ingredient on the employer's side is his right to direct and control the work of the employe. On the other side, the employe is obliged to perform the work that the employer wants done and is entitled to payment for his labors.

The contract is held together by the mutual, satisfactory performance of these obligations. The employer has the power to dismiss, and the employe is entitled to quit. Each may do so if the other party clearly breaks the terms agreed upon. Naturally, the best employment contract from the legal point of view is

From Tolpuddle to Canada

TOLPUDDLE is a small village in Dorset, in southwestern England. You could drive through it in a minute and not realize that it is the major shrine of the worldwide trade union movement. Tolpuddle has a particular association with Canada, for it was in Canada that our story eventually came to a happy ending.

As the Industrial Revolution gathered pace, all "combinations" of workmen were banned in Britain, while employers were free to set any wage rates and hours of work they liked. While this seems astounding today, we must remember that Britain had just lost its American colonies to the "rabble" and the excesses of the French Revolution were fresh in the minds of the nation's leaders.

In 1834—a full generation later—repression was still the order of the day. When

six poorly paid farm laborers of Tolpuddle formed a branch (a "local") of the Grand National Consolidated Trades Union, they were arrested and charged under an obsolete law with "the administering of oaths by private persons." They were sentenced to be deported.

Although 100,000 people attended a protest rally in London, the "Tolpuddle martyrs" were put in irons and shipped to Australia. The protests continued, and two years later the government quashed the sentences. Two more years passed before enough money was raised by public subscription to bring the six back to Britain.

Shortly afterward, George Loveless and his family, with his brother James and two of the other "martyrs," emigrated to Upper Canada. They settled contentedly near the growing city of London, Ontario.

one that is in writing. Usually, however, it is only professionals (engineers, lawyers, and other specialists) entering managerial positions who have the luxury of seeing all the terms of the agreement set down on paper. If you are contemplating a top-flight post with a big corporation, you should consider getting legal assistance to make sure that your rights are protected.

Obviously, few employment contracts are put in writing. They can be described as "general hiring." The employer is only interested in hiring a good worker; the employe is only interested in what he has to do and how much he will be paid. But this does not mean that there are no legal obligations attached. Although you may move through a series of jobs without problems and be unaware of the presence of any laws, there are regulations that govern even the simple "general hiring" contract. They govern verbal agreements as well as written ones.

What the employer must do
The boss must pay you the wage or salary agreed upon, and he must itemize in writing all deductions from that wage. Minimum-wage regulations change fairly frequently and it is up to the employer to keep up and comply with them. If you have any doubts, you should check with the appropriate federal or provincial labor authority to ensure that the rate you have been offered is the minimum legal level. Where an employer did not specify an amount concerning wages—and he proves to be unwilling to comply with minimum-wage regulations—the law will force him to pay reasonable compensation for any work that has been done.

The law carefully protects the right of the worker to his wages. Even in the situation where the employer has gone bankrupt, the employe is given priority over most claims, for up to 90 days' wages or a total sum not exceeding $500. Each province provides the means for collecting unpaid wages.

The employer has the right to terminate the contract when he wants to, unless specified otherwise in the original agreement. But he must give the worker reasonable notice. How long is "reasonable notice"? Some provinces have legislation which sets out how much notice must be given. In Ontario, for example, an employer's obligation to give written notice varies from one week, if the period of employment is less than two years, to eight weeks' notice for employment that has lasted ten years or more. A boss need not give notice if he pays his worker an amount equal to what would have been earned during the notice period.

It is legal to hire someone for a definite term or task. Once that job is done, or the time elapsed, no notice is required.

Right to fire
The employer does not have to give advance notice to an employe he wishes to dismiss for "just cause." Certain conduct, detailed later in this chapter, justifies this immediate dismissal. For instance, the boss is entitled to trust his worker, and any misconduct that violates this trust can be sufficient cause for the sack—whether the conduct occurs on or off the job. Also, the employer has the right to direct the work being done for him, and any willful disobedience is justification for dismissal.

Malingering
An employe who is often away on sick leave—whether he is genuinely sick or not—or who becomes permanently disabled, may be discharged at any time without notice. The employment contract is terminated because the worker is incapable of fulfilling his part of the bargain. (He would presumably be taken care of under Workers' Compensation, or by a pension scheme.)

Wrongful dismissal
In most provinces, the employer's right to fire is an absolute right—that is, no law will force him to keep an employe if he doesn't want to. However, if a worker has been wrongfully dismissed, the law may order the employer to pay damages to that worker. The worker must be able to show that there was an existing employment contract and that he was not dismissed for any just cause. In other words, an employe who is not given adequate

notice of dismissal where there is no cause that is considered "proper," may claim damages. The damages would consist of wages for the period that would in the situation be considered "reasonable notice." (*See* Chapter 18, "The question of damages".)

In Quebec, under the provisions of the Labour Standards Act, an employe with more than five years of service may ask La Commission des Normes du Travail to investigate his complaint that his firing was without just and sufficient cause. The result of the investigation may be an order forcing the employer to reinstate the employe.

If you are still owed wages from before the date of your wrongful dismissal, you can bring the two claims in a single suit against your employer. However, the law treats these two situations differently.

While the amount awarded as unpaid wages cannot be changed by the court—it is based on the simple calculation of the hours of work time and the rate of pay—the damages given for wrongful dismissal must be established by the court. The amount of these damages could depend upon whether you had taken another job since your dismissal, or whether the court felt that you had a reasonable chance to take another job in the meantime but did not. You are always required under the laws of contract to act reasonably to lessen your loss.

Acting on behalf

Where an employe as part of his job orders work to be done or materials to be purchased for his boss, the employer must honor these orders or contracts. If a worker pays out of his own pocket any expenses for his employer, he is entitled to be paid back.

An employer may have undertaken to do a particular job—perhaps to install plumbing in an apartment building. If one of the plumbers who work for him does sloppy or negligent work, the employer is responsible to the apartment owner to correct the work and to pay for any damage resulting from the bad work.

The boss is responsible, together with his hired man, for any damage caused by

The way it used to be

QUESTION: Do you think it right to employ children of 12 years at all?

ANSWER: I think that at 12 years a child should be able to work.

Back in the Dark Ages? Wrong! This exchange took place between a royal commissioner investigating labor conditions in Canada in the 1880s and the president of the Hochelaga Cotton Manufacturing Company of Montreal.

Hochelaga was the largest textile concern in Quebec at the time. It employed 1,100—half of them women and about 200 children. Some of the children were as young as eight years. These little barefoot toilers worked from 6 A.M. to 6 P.M. (sometimes till 9 P.M.), earning 25 to 30 cents a day. They were recruited from rural areas; the company sent out agents to hire entire families.

Men were earning from 80 cents to $1 a day, and women about 75 cents. Most of them were on piecework, and fines for substandard work, or for lateness, were common. The commission was told that one girl earned $12.60 for two weeks' work and had $1 deducted for fines.

Hochelaga insisted that all employes sign an agreement to work on all public holidays, except Christmas and New Year's Day. Anyone who stayed away on a religious holiday was automatically fired, losing any wages earned but not yet paid. The company's motto was said to be: "When some work, all work." That included the youngest child on the roster.

The year that the last spike was driven for the Canadian Pacific Railway, these labor conditions were still relatively common in some industries.

the worker's carelessness on the job while the worker is doing a job called for by his employment.

From time to time, the courts have decided that the worker, though supposedly on the job, was in fact temporarily off the job. A truck driver who injures a pedestrian while on company deliveries involves his employer in a suit for damages. But where the driver takes the company truck off his fixed route to visit a friend, and injures a pedestrian on the way, he alone is held responsible. The injured party, in that case, can only claim damages against the driver and not against the company.

In another example, a company employing a bricklayer would be responsible for his negligence while on the job, but would not be responsible for any damage caused by the worker if he was doing something for a friend or a third party who had no contract with the employer.

What the employe must do

The employment contract is basically an exchange of labor for wages: the worker's obligations under it are just the opposite of those imposed on the boss. While it is the employer's duty to pay wages, it is the employe's obligation to arrive on the job on time and perform his work as directed until the end of the workday.

Just as a worker can sue for being fired wrongfully, a boss can sue an employe who quits when the agreement of employment has not been mutually satisfied. While this right exists in theory, employers rarely resort to it. However, under certain prearranged conditions, the wronged employer may apply for a court *injunction* (a court order by which someone must do or refrain from doing a specified act) to prevent the employe from working for a competing firm or from going into business for himself in direct competition. All injunctions have a time limit on them, and the courts would decide what would be reasonable under the circumstances of each case.

Just as the court will not force an employer to rehire a discharged worker (except in Quebec), neither will it force an unwilling worker to return to his job. The famous "Bette Davis case" of the late 1930s illustrates these principles. The fiery movie star signed an exclusive contract with Warner Brothers which contained a "noncompetition" clause. Later, she felt that the contract was one-sided, that it belittled her and prevented her from fully using her professional abilities. She went to Britain and began to make pictures there. When Warner Brothers brought a suit against her in an English court, the judge maintained that the law could not force Miss Davis to perform for the American film producer. But he did grant the Hollywood film company an injunction that prevented the showing of the British-made pictures which were already completed. The injunction also forbade Miss Davis from acting in any more films for anyone but Warner Brothers until her contract with them expired six years later. Such noncompetition clauses, whether in writing or implied, have to be "reasonable." They cannot prevent an employe from forever pursuing his trade anywhere. Canadian courts would probably disallow a noncompetition clause unless narrow geographical limits were set.

The boss's secrets

Trade secrets, patents and know-how, which have been developed by the employe as part of his job, belong to the employer. Any worker who leaves a job in order to make personal gain from the special skills learned at work can be prevented from revealing or using such information. However, the employer might find it hard to actually obtain such an injunction; the tradition of the employe starting up in business for himself is everywhere accepted, and even encouraged.

Moonlighting

The practice of taking a second job during off-hours—usually referred to as "moonlighting"—is not prohibited by common law, unless the "contract" controlling the worker's regular job expressly forbids the practice. However, if the second job results in the employe's not being able to do his first job properly, or in his being consistently late for work, he runs the risk of being fired—with just cause.

In the federal sphere

UNDER SECTIONS 91 and 92 of the Canadian constitution, authority to enact labor legislation is shared by the federal parliament and the provincial legislatures. Although the bulk of the power is held by the provinces, there are about 850,000 workers whose jobs, directly or indirectly, fall within the federal sphere. The countrywide spread and uniform character of federal employment gives Ottawa a special influence in setting national standards. For instance, when a typist in a federal office away from Ottawa gets a raise, all other typists doing similar work in that region are likely to push for equal treatment.

The Canada Department of Labor was established in 1900 to help prevent or to settle labor disputes, and to gather and publish information regarding labor. Later, it was called upon to administer the Fair Wages Policy protecting workers employed on federal projects, and other labor laws. In 1966, responsibility for all employment services was transferred to the Department of Manpower and Immigration. In 1977, the Canada Employment and Immigration Commission (C.E.I.C.) was established, amalgamating the Unemployment Insurance Commission and the programs of the former Department of Manpower and Immigration. A small department of employment and immigration remains to link the C.E.I.C. with the federal cabinet.

The Canadian constitution gives jurisdiction to the federal parliament over unemployment insurance, postal service, federal public servants, and navigation, shipping and ferries between provinces and to foreign countries. Industries or business undertakings of a national, in-terprovincial or international nature also fall under Ottawa's legislative control.

In addition, the federal government can regulate certain industries and activities wholly within a province which have been declared by parliament to be "for the general advantage of Canada or for the advantage of two or more of the provinces." Examples: uranium mines and grain elevators.

Federal legislation in the labor field, administered by the Department of Labor, the Public Service Commission and the Treasury Board, can be divided into two main categories. The first group of laws—known as the Canada Labor Code —applies to those persons anywhere in the country who work for industries or other organizations under federal control; the second category applies only to those who work directly for the federal government—that is, our 250,000 federal public servants.

The Canada Labor Code
Supplanting earlier legislation stretching back to the turn of the century, the Canada Labor Code in its present amended form came into force in 1972. The provisions of the three operative sections of the code apply to a wide range of employers, employes, trade unions and employe associations under federal jurisdiction in the following industries and services:

Works or undertakings connecting one province with another province (or another country), such as railways, bus operations, trucking, pipelines, ferries, tunnels, bridges, canals, and telephone, telegraph and cable systems;

All shipping outside provincial borders and all services connected with such shipping (examples: stevedoring and long-shoring);

Air transport, aircraft and airfields;

Television and radio;

Banks.

Most of the federally controlled Crown corporations, such as the Canadian Broadcasting Corporation, Air Canada and the St. Lawrence Seaway Authority (there are almost 50 Crown corporations—*See* Chapter 13, "The public corporation").

Special undertakings that have been named by parliament as of "general advantage" to Canada as a whole (examples: flour and seed-cleaning mills and certain mining operations for strategic ores).

The Canada Labor Code has three parts. (There once were five but Parts I and II were repealed and their provisions incorporated into other legislation.)

The code sets out fair employment practices, standards of employment (hours of work, minimum-wage rates, vacations), safety regulations and procedures for settling labor disputes.

Part III This section of the code sets standards for hours of work, wages and vacations and specifies nine statutory (paid) holidays. No absolute minimum age for employment is set but strict conditions are laid down for the employment of persons under 17 on federal jobs. For example, none may he hired if he or she is required to attend school under the laws of the province concerned. No one under 17 may be employed underground in a mine or be permitted to work anywhere between 11 P.M. and 6 A.M.

A minimum hourly wage rate of $3.50 is set for all workers over 17. The rate for workers under 17 is $3.25 an hour. The rate may be increased from time to time by order of the Governor General in Council (that is, in effect, by the incumbent minister of labor with the agreement of the cabinet). The wage rate for any worker under 17 is established under special regulations in each industry. The basic wage rate is set following study of the cost of living, and economic conditions generally, to protect the unskilled, unorganized worker. It is intended to serve as a "floor" above which trade unions or individuals may negotiate higher rates.

Supervisory and management personnel are excluded from these regulations, as are professionals, some salesmen, students and apprentices.

Severance pay must be given to a federal employe who has completed 12 months' service, unless he is fired for "just cause" (*See* "The laws of labor," in this chapter). He cannot be fired, suspended or laid off solely because his wages have been garnisheed by a creditor (*See* Chapter 7, "If you can't pay").

Part IV The legislation formerly known as the Canada Labor (Safety) Code is now incorporated in Part IV of the Canada Labor Code. It spells out provisions for ensuring the safety of federal workers. Special attention is paid to building construction methods and materials, boilers and other pressure vessels, escalators and elevators of all kinds and electrical, gas- and oil-burning equipment. The regulations for the fencing of dangerous equipment and the methods of storing dangerous liquids and explosives are included in this part of the code.

Every worker on a federal undertaking must take all reasonable precautions to ensure his own safety and the safety of his fellow workers. He must use any special safety devices and wear any safety clothing or equipment required on the job or supplied to him by his employer.

An appointed safety officer can insist that an employer supply statements respecting the conditions of work as they may affect the health or safety of any employe. The safety official is permitted to enter and inspect any "property, place or thing"; he may also question any worker in private. In a crisis situation he can shut down an operation until his safety directions are complied with.

The code has real teeth. Any employer or person in charge who deliberately violates the safety regulations or fails to obey directions from a safety officer can be fined or sent to jail for a year, or both.

Part V This is the biggest section of the Canada Labor Code—103 clauses—and it deals with industrial disputes.

This comprehensive trend-setting legislation applies to all workers connected with or involved in "the operation of any federal work, undertaking or business," to their employers and to any trade unions or employers' associations representing the parties. (It does not apply to the federal public service; their position is described later in this section.)

Every worker covered by the code is free, by law, to join the trade union of his choice, and every employer can likewise join any employers' association and participate in its lawful activities.

Division 2 of Part V is devoted to the powers and practices of the Canada Labor Relations Board (C.L.R.B.) for many years an important agency in the industrial world. The members of the C.L.R.B.—not more than 14 in total—are appointed by the governor general and report to parliament through the minister of labor. The board rules over the certification (and decertification) of trade unions as bargaining agents for all workers in the federal sphere. It investigates reports of unfair labor practices (such as an employer's refusal to hire someone because he is a union member or because he has taken part in a legal strike). It can hear and determine any application, complaint or dispute that is referred to it, and can compel witnesses to attend, to produce documents, and to give evidence under oath.

The C.L.R.B. will not certify any union as bargaining agent if it believes the union is "so dominated or influenced by" an employer that its fitness to speak in the true interest of the workers is impaired. Moreover, it will not certify a union if it thinks that the union has denied membership to any employe, or group of employes, because of some internal policy of the union regarding membership qualification.

Conciliation services

The federal department of labor has authority under Part V of the Canada Labor Code to provide conciliation services in industrial disputes—that is, to try to bring both sides to an agreement. Ottawa shies away from using the ultimate weapon, compulsory arbitration—which, in effect, forces a third person's decision on both sides—feeling that it is "an inappropriate way of proceeding in a democracy." The government may, however, intervene decisively if it considers the national interest is at stake.

Trade unions and employers are both required to bargain collectively in good faith. During the 1970s, the "good faith" system was under strain in the federal service. Exclusive of postal strikes, 84,130 man-days were lost in strikes during the 1974–75 fiscal year, compared with only 840 in the previous year.

The federal parliament has ultimate authority in labor matters in the Yukon and the Northwest Territories, but specific provision has been made for local government in those areas. The territorial councils govern property and civil rights. Thus, they are similar in the labor field to the provinces, except that their powers derive from a federal statute rather than from the Canadian constitution.

Working for the Queen

Parliament has over the years enacted separate laws covering all those who, in formal terms, are "employed by Her Majesty in right of Canada"—that is, the large and growing body (currently numbering about 250,000) directly employed by the federal government. These laborers, clerks, scientists, lawyers, diplomats and many other categories constitute the Public Service of Canada.

The Public Service Employment Act and its regulations control the hiring (by merit only) of employes wherever they work across the land. Conditions of employment are controlled by the Public Service Staff Relations Act, which came into force in the early 1970s. This legislation is matched in very few countries abroad. It gives public servants, already substantially protected as regards job security, the right to a system of collective bargaining by the trade union process and, under certain conditions, the right to strike. The joint committee of the House of Commons and Senate which recommended the legislation heard representatives of the workers and of other interested employe organizations, including the Canadian Labor Congress and the Confederation of National Trade Unions.

The act contains a number of unique provisions. For example, those lawyers, doctors, dentists and engineers—among other professionals—who work for the federal government are here included in "bargaining units" and are, therefore, the equivalent of trade unionists as defined in other labor legislation.

Unemployment insurance

Around the turn of the century, Switzerland, Belgium, France and then Britain, in that order, pioneered systems of insurance by which workers could contribute a fraction of their wage while working to provide them with some income if and when they became unemployed. The employers had to match their employes' contributions.

Though first proposed in 1919, Canada's national unemployment insurance scheme did not come into being until 1941. It was necessary for Ottawa to seek from Britain a special amendment to Section 91 of the British North America Act (now part of the Canadian constitution) to permit the federal government to enter this field. Originally, the Canadian plan covered only a handful of industries and occupations—manufacturing, mining, road and rail transportation—but other categories have been added. Now virtually all Canadian workers are covered.

The rates are constantly being revised but, by 1983, the maximum benefit rate was $231 a week. A special office, the Unemployment Insurance Commission, was set up to administer the scheme, which is now run by the Canada Employment and Immigration Commission.

When the national unemployment rate is 5.6 percent or less, the combined contributions (in effect, insurance premiums) of employers and employes finance the bulk of the plan. When unemployment goes over 5.6 percent, the federal government has to contribute tax money to balance the books.

Canada Employment Centres

As part of the original legislation of 1941, the Unemployment Insurance Commission was called upon to set up and maintain a nationwide job-finding agency, the forerunner of what we know today as the Canada Employment and Immigration Commission.

The Commission maintains ten regional offices across Canada and about 450 employment centres in large and small communities in each province and territory. This agency helps to find new openings for workers whose services are no longer required by their employers, and to find jobs for newcomers to the work force: recent school graduates, those who leave school before graduation and immigrants.

One of the stated aims of the Canada employment scheme is "to help workers adapt to economic and technological change by encouraging employers and workers to cooperatively preplan through the use of departmental training and mobility programs"—or, in less flowery language, to keep the employment machinery working smoothly.

The training mentioned, which is provided by the National Program, attempts to increase the skills of the unemployed or to teach them new technologies, either on the job or at post-secondary educational institutions such as community colleges. In 1983–84, about 279,000 people were to receive training through the National Program. Training is emphasized for careers which are in greatest demand by the Canadian economy. Accordingly, a multi-million dollar Skills Growth Fund provides capital and start-up operating funds to training institutions which provide programs in designated "national occupations." Special encouragement and financial incentives are offered to train women in nontraditional jobs and to provide career opportunities for the employment of the disadvantaged or the handicapped. The Canada Employment and Immigration Commission also has a mobility program to assist in the cost of relocation.

Federal public holidays

Nine public holidays with pay are provided under federal law: New Year's Day, Good Friday, Victoria Day, Canada Day, Labor Day, Thanksgiving, Remembrance Day, Christmas Day and Boxing Day.

518

Within provincial powers

Minimum-wage rates

How remuneration is paid

Hours of work and vacations

Notice and severance pay

Training of apprentices

Safety of the worker

IN REGARD to labor law, the provinces have greater powers than the federal government because the Constitution gives them exclusive authority to make laws regarding "property and civil rights in the province." Since the right to enter into contracts is regarded as a civil right and since labor laws control conditions of employment contracts, labor laws, therefore, concern civil rights.

To discuss only current provincial legislation in the field of industrial relations would require a book in itself, and these laws are constantly under revision. Space permits us to refer only briefly to the main areas of industrial relations and to outline general standards. To obtain the latest regulations applying to your trade or business, phone or write the Department of Labor in your province.

All the provinces have labor-standards legislation, and the variations that exist are only matters of degree. The laws deal with the basic conditions of the average employment contract, setting the rock-bottom terms. They assure the worker that he does not have to settle for less than the minimum specified. More sophisticated contracts are, of course, negotiated by the trade unions, or sometimes by the highly qualified individual employe.

The topics normally covered in these statutes are: minimum age for employment; minimum wages; wage payment and collection; equal pay regardless of sex; hours of work and vacations with pay; workmen's compensation; weekly rest days and public holidays; fair employment practices; and notice for termination of employment.

Procedures are established by the provinces for education in employer-employe relations and for enforcement of the regulations. Each province has a department of labor or manpower (the titles vary but the work is the same), headed by a minister of the Crown. These departments are charged with the administration of provincial labor laws. The labor-relations boards within these departments investigate complaints, hold hearings to determine whether violations have occurred, supply conciliation or mediation services and provide up-to-date statistical information on all matters of employment.

How old is old enough?

The provinces differ when it comes to determining how old a person must be before he or she is allowed to work. The laws vary according to the type of work, compulsory school-attendance laws and the hazards of the particular job. Since Canada sprang from a rural economy based on family farms, there is no minimum age established for agricultural workers.

Generally, children of up to 16 years old cannot be employed in factories, mines, shops or hotels. This age level is set to dovetail with the provincial minimum school-leaving age. However, the minister of labor has the power to grant a permit to someone below the minimum age where the parents have consented. (*See* Chapter 11, "Children at work.")

Minimum-wage rates

To insure an adequate standard of living, minimum-wage laws are in force everywhere, including the Yukon and the Northwest Territories. These acts authorize a minimum-wage board or other labor board to recommend or establish minimum rates of wages, usually after public hearings have been held. The rates are imposed under regulations issued by the appropriate labor board, or through decrees issued by the lieutenant-governor in council (that is, by a decision of the provincial cabinet). They are constantly being revised as the cost of living changes.

The eventual aim is to cover all areas of employment. However, in several provinces, the following categories were exempt: domestic servants, farm laborers, students, registered apprentices, certain types of salesmen, employes in fishing, and members of professions. The minimums set down apply to both sexes.

Some provinces have established special rates for specified jobs. Nova Scotia, for example, has established province-wide rates for logging, forest operations, road building and heavy construction, as well as for employes in beauty parlors. Saskatchewan has set a pay scale for truck drivers and for those working at well drilling, logging and lumbering.

British Columbia, Quebec, Saskatchewan, Manitoba, Ontario and Alberta rule that pay statements must be furnished to the individual worker. These statements specify the number of hours he is being paid for, the wage rate, details of deductions and net earnings. This information makes it possible for the employe to make sure he is being properly paid and that there are no hidden deductions or fines. It was once a common complaint that some employers held back part of the wage to pay for uniforms or tools, or else to fine a worker for being late. The worker was never sure why he was being "docked."

How remuneration is paid

Payment for regular work, except in the case of certain domestics and farmhands, is usually made by cheque, although some companies will make arrangements for cash to be picked up at a cashier's office. Payment by cheque is popular because it cuts out the fear of theft on payday for both employer and employe. It is illegal for a boss to pay his workers "in kind," that is by giving employes the products of the business instead of money.

Although all forms of compensation for services rendered—including commissions, bonuses and tips—are, in a sense, *wages*, this word is generally reserved to mean money paid at an hourly rate, or for

All the provinces set minimum employment standards

All the provinces control working conditions within their boundaries, excepting only those persons employed by the federal government or by its "business agents," the Crown corporations. The regulations are enforced under the authority of legislative acts which, as economic facts change, are frequently amended.

The standards for the work week vary from province to province. It will be noted (right) that Ontario sets a standard 48-hour week. But that does not mean that everybody must work 48 hours. In fact, following the federal lead, the 40-hour week has been widely adopted nationally.

EMPLOYMENT STANDARDS ACT

(d) defining "temporarily laid off", "termination of employment", and "employment for a definite term or task";

(e) prescribing what constitutes a period of employment; and

(f) exempting any activity, business, work, trade, occupation or profession, or any part thereof from the application of this Part. 1970, c. 45, s. 4, part.

PART II
HOURS OF WORK

7.—(1) Subject to subsection 2, the working hours of an employee shall not exceed eight in the day and forty-eight in the week.

(2) Subsection 1 does not apply to an employee whose work is supervisory or managerial in character, or of a character exempted by the regulations. 1968, c. 35, s. 7.

8.—(1) Subject to subsection 2, an employer may, with the approval of the Director, and upon such terms and conditions as the Director prescribes, adopt a working day in excess of eight hours, but the working hours of his employees shall not exceed forty-eight hours in a week.

(2) The maximum working hours of an employee in a day prescribed by section 7 is subject to any schedule in force under The Industrial [...]

piecework. The wage earner will get extra pay if he works more than the usual number of hours in the workday, but will receive no pay for hours not worked.

Employes who are paid a weekly, monthly and yearly rate are said to receive a *salary*. Generally, they are not penalized for short absences in the case of illness or for compassionate reasons—such as a death in the family—and the period of notice given before dismissal is longer than that given wage earners.

The salary earner often is working longer hours than the wage earner, and, unless he is covered by a collective agreement or a private contract stipulating the length of his workday, he will not necessarily receive overtime payments.

Legal hours of work

Most of the provinces have adopted the nine annual public ("statutory") holidays set out by the Canadian Labor Code for all workers employed within the federal sphere of authority. Manitoba, Quebec and Ontario do not include Remembrance Day. Some provinces have added particular holidays that have special meaning to their citizens. In Quebec, for instance, the patron saint, St. Jean Baptiste, is honored in a public holiday. Again following the federal policy, where Christmas, New Year's Day or July 1 fall on a Saturday or Sunday, the provinces grant employes a holiday with pay on the working day immediately before or after the particular public holiday.

Some provinces actually forbid work on specified holidays, except with special permission. For example, Quebec and Newfoundland require retail stores in all municipalities to be closed on public holidays, as well as on other days specified by legislation, by the lieutenant-governor in council or by the particular municipality.

In most provinces, these holidays differ from Sundays (when work is generally banned) in that employes are allowed to work under certain conditions: if they work, they must be given a day off at another time and be paid time and a half.

All the provinces except British Columbia and Prince Edward Island have copied the federal ruling that workers must be given at least 24 hours of rest in the week, on Sunday wherever possible. British Columbia sets the number of hours at 36, and Prince Edward Island has no legislation on the matter. The law usually provides for the minister of labor to alter the day of rest where sufficient reason can be shown.

Guaranteeing the weekly rest day and establishing the 40-hour work week were two of the earliest aims of social legislation in Canada. Where federal law applies, the eight-hour day and the 40-hour week are the standards recognized for workers. Within the provincial and territorial spheres, British Columbia, Saskatchewan, Manitoba, Nova Scotia and the Yukon have adopted a 40-hour week as the standard. The other provinces have varying standards. For example, Alberta limits the work week to 44 hours. Generally, all provinces recognize the eight-hour day. Overtime pay is calculated on the total number of hours worked in a week above the permitted maximum, not on the hours of work done in one day.

Annual vacations with pay

Generally, all workers are entitled by provincial law to an annual vacation with pay. There are exceptions, however: most professionals are excluded in British Columbia and Ontario. Farm workers are excluded in all provinces except Newfoundland and British Columbia. (Some farmers in Ontario, however, now receive paid vacations.) Domestic servants are exempted in all provinces except British Columbia, Saskatchewan, Ontario and Newfoundland. In Prince Edward Island, only employes who work 24 hours a week or less are excluded.

Normally, an employe has to have completed 12 consecutive months' work before he is entitled to a paid vacation. The length of vacation varies, according to the period of time worked, from one to two weeks—or more. Saskatchewan grants four weeks after ten years' service, while Ontario (like most other provinces) guarantees two weeks with pay after one year of service. Some provinces allow an employer to give pay instead of annual vacation. Where an employe has worked less than the required time to earn a full vacation, he is entitled in Alberta to a vacation on a proportionate basis. In British Columbia, Manitoba, Newfoundland, New Brunswick and Nova Scotia, he is entitled to pay covering the number of days of vacation he has earned for the period worked during the year.

In general, vacation pay is usually payable before the vacation commences. However, New Brunswick specifies that vacation pay be given on the next regular pay period after the end of the vacation pay year; in Manitoba, vacation pay is given on the date marking the anniversary of the person's employment; in Newfoundland, it is due within a week after the anniversary date; and in other provinces, it is due within a month after the anniversary date.

The rate of vacation pay ranges between two and four percent of the "total

The working woman

A RECENT COUNT showed there were 5,054,000 women and girls in the Canadian labor force—more than 40 percent of the total. Almost two-thirds of these were married. Fifty years ago, only one-tenth of all workers were female. Adult women re-entering the labor force make up the majority and they are concentrated in a few occupations. More than 60 percent are in clerical, sales and service jobs.

It is estimated that about 40 percent of working women are single, widowed or divorced. Ten percent are married, with their husbands earning below $10,000 a year. For 15 percent, the husband earns between $10,000 and $15,000, and for another 17 percent, the husband earns between $15,000 and $20,000. In other words, women in Canada work primarily for economic reasons. In fact, a recent study showed that 51 percent more two-spouse families would fall below the poverty line (set by Statistics Canada) without the wife's earnings. Approximately 46 percent of working mothers have at least one child under the age of three; 53 percent have children between three and five. Although day-care centres with trained staff exist to care for the children of mothers who work, there are not enough to fill present needs. Today, a total of 447,281 children between age 2 and 6 are not in day-care programs.

The campaign of "equal pay for equal work" is a story of slow and uneven progress. The earnings of working women remain about 60 percent of that of the employed male; this is partly because comparatively few women reach higher-paying appointments. It is also because clerical, sales and service jobs do not pay as much as typically male-oriented occupations such as construction and mining. Thirty-five percent of the nation's clerical workers are women, compared to 7 percent who are men. Only 4.2 percent are in management or administration, as compared to 8.6 percent men.

British Columbia made a start on improving working conditions for women more than 50 years ago with its Maternity Protection Act. A more recent advance was Ontario's Women's Equal Employment Opportunity Act of 1970 which prohibited even the classification (or advertising) of any job as a specifically "male" or "female" occupation. Under this legislation, a female applicant must be seriously considered for a job as a welder, bus driver or letter carrier. Ontario was the first province to pass such as law, and the act was later incorporated into other legislation.

Today, each province has a Human Rights Commission which guarantees there will be no discrimination in employment. If an employer—for example, a religious organization—feels it is necessary to hire a person of a specific sex, the onus is on the employer to apply to the Commission for an "exemption." In addition to banning discrimination by sex, Ontario was the first province to prohibit sexual harassment in its Human Rights Code of 1981.

pay" earned by the employe in the year for which the vacation is given. (In Quebec, for example, it is six percent after ten years' service.) These figures are becoming the national standard.

Notice and severance pay

Under the law of master and servant, which was discussed earlier in this chapter, an employe whose conduct sufficiently provokes his boss can be fired immediately. But what protection is there against being dismissed where your only "fault" is that you are caught in an economic slowdown? Laws in all the provinces (except New Brunswick and the two territories), as well as in industries regulated by the federal Labor Code, insist that an employe in such a case be given notice. The notice period varies among the different provincial laws from one week in Nova Scotia and Saskatchewan to eight weeks after ten years' service in Ontario. If you are in doubt about the minimum legal notice in your industry, ask the Department of Labor.

If an employe is paid the amount he would have earned in the notice period, he may be let go at once without notice.

Industries located in Ontario and Quebec, plus those regulated by the federal code, must also give advance notice to the minister of labor of any foreseeable group terminations or group layoffs. The reason for this is to allow the specialists in the labor agencies to prepare programs of job replacement for the workers who will be laid off.

The federal Labor Code makes severance pay compulsory after 12 months' consecutive service. (At this writing, British Columbia and Quebec have adopted severance pay legislation as well.) In practice, this means that if anyone on a federal payroll who has worked five consecutive years for the same employer is dismissed for any reason other than "just cause," his employer must give him two days' pay for each year of service up to a maximum of 40 days' pay. On the basis of a five-day week, this would mean a severance payment of two weeks' pay for an employe with ten years' service, six weeks' pay for an employe with 15 years'

service and eight weeks' pay—the maximum—for an employe with 20 or more years of service.

In favor of motherhood

Perhaps one of the most advanced and humane pieces of legislation in the field of labor standards is the maternity-leave law that has been enacted federally and provincially. All provinces provide for at least 12 to 18 weeks' maternity leave. The postnatal leave is compulsory. To be granted the six-week leave preceding, the expectant mother need only produce a medical certificate showing the expected date of confinement. The law in British Columbia and Quebec allows a longer period for postnatal recuperation, if it is recommended by a doctor.

In Ontario, the legislation only applies to employers with 25 or more employes, and only when the woman concerned has at least one year's service. The employer has the right to have the worker begin her leave at any time, if the duties of her position cannot reasonably be performed by a pregnant woman or if her performance is materially affected by the pregnancy. But she cannot be dismissed because of pregnancy or because she is taking her full leave. On her return, she must be reinstated without loss of seniority or accrued benefits. British Columbia and New Brunswick also protect the pregnant worker from dismissal.

While the otherwise-employed woman is out of circulation, she is not without income. Provided she is an "insured" employe, Unemployment Insurance will pay 60 percent of her average insurable earnings for the duration of her maternity leave. To qualify for this income, the woman must have worked ten or more weeks within a specified period before the expected date of the birth. The Unemployment Insurance Commission grants claims for a period of up to 15 weeks, although the average claim is usually slightly shorter than this period.

In certain industries

Seven provinces have enacted special statutes to regulate hours and conditions of work in certain specific industries—

including the fur and fishing trades, garment and furniture making, the construction industry, hairdressing and garages.

When representative groups of employers and employes in a particular trade or industry agree upon a schedule of hours of work and wages, the government will generally regard this schedule as applying across the entire trade or industry. Usually, the government will set up an advisory committee representing all sides to help enforce the schedule.

Under Quebec's Collective Agreement Decrees Act, some 52 decrees schedules apply as standards across the province, or else in specially designated areas. Manitoba's Construction Industry Wages Act sets down minimum rates of pay and hours of work for all building workers in the province.

Training of apprentices

On-the-job trade training and instruction in schools or community colleges are controlled in all provinces through apprenticeship regulations. Certificates of qualification are generally issued, if this documentation is requested.

In some provinces, legislation demands that certain classes of tradesmen (electricians, heating engineers, plumbers) hold a certificate of proficiency. (*See* Chapter 13, "Professions and trades.")

Safety of the worker

As technology creates evermore complicated machinery, new conditions arise that could endanger workmen. Thus, safety regulations—introduced as the Industrial Revolution gathered speed—are constantly being revised.

Provincial industrial-safety acts lay down strict rules to protect the health and safety of factory staff, not only in the operation of such equipment as pressure boilers, forges, cutting equipment and elevators, but also in sanitation, ventilation, heating and lighting.

Rigid safety standards must be met on high-rise building sites in the cities and special regulations apply to deep excavations and tunneling. If you plan to work with dangerous gases or chemicals, high water pressures, molten metals or power-ful electric currents, you should first get to know the safety code thoroughly. The familiar "hard hat" must be worn on construction sites; some road gangs are required to wear clothing of colors that are visible in all kinds of weather—or made of light-reflecting materials.

Industrial troubleshooters

Each province maintains a labor-relations agency—similar to the one on the federal level—which attempts to iron out problems between workers and bosses. Newspaper readers are accustomed to reports of the arrival of mediators on the scene when major industries are threatened with strikes or lockouts. The quiet, impartial chairmanship of this "middleman" from the labor-relations board can often bring opposing sides back into harmony after tempers have flared or dignity has been ruffled.

Fighting discrimination

Fair-employment laws that are in force across Canada prohibit discrimination in hiring, or in trade-union membership, because of race, color, religion or national origin. Seven provinces—British Columbia, Alberta, Saskatchewan, Manitoba, Ontario, New Brunswick and Newfoundland—also forbid discrimination in employment on the basis of age.

In these provinces, the law specifically forbids discrimination against persons who are between the ages of 40 and 65. Newfoundland also prohibits discrimination against any person "for political opinions."

All provincial human rights codes, as well as the Charter of Rights and Freedoms, ban discrimination on grounds of sex or marital status in the employment of women for work identical, or substantially identical, to that performed by males.

All provinces require equal pay for equal work for both sexes.

As publicity is directed more strongly at these problems, labor relations boards, human rights agencies and civil liberties groups everywhere in Canada are recommending new laws to fight discrimination.

Union rules and regulations

WHEN ORGANIZED LABOR won its fight for legal status, the unions acquired stern obligations. For example, the freedom of unions to choose their own members came to be limited, if not specifically by a law then by a clear declaration of legislative policy.

If you work in Canada, you have the right to join the union certified for your plant or operation, unless the union executive can produce a strong reason why you should be excluded. You can be refused membership on "reasonable grounds"—perhaps because of a previous record of failing to pay dues—but you can appeal that refusal to the officials of your provincial labor relations board.

Unions will sometimes stop accepting new members when a certain percentage of their membership is unemployed or when they anticipate serious unemployment. If a man could show that he lost a job because union membership was unreasonably withheld from him, he would have a case for a civil suit for damages against the union. Ontario, particularly, protects a worker from being dismissed in a "closed shop" if his membership has been denied or withdrawn by the union as a means of discipline.

Unions cannot refuse membership to anyone on grounds of race, color, religion or sex. There is some provision to protect the worker who refuses to join the union —even in a "closed shop"—but he will still have dues deducted from his pay.

Seeking certification

An employer is required by law to bargain "in good faith" with a union local that has been properly certified as bargaining agent for his employes. In every province, the law favors the formation of unions. The right to form a union, even in the face of company disapproval, has been guaranteed by the authorities for more than 40 years. To be certified, however, a union local must prove, with documented evidence, that it has been chosen by a majority of the workers concerned.

A non-union plant can become unionized either from the inside or from the outside. Workers inside a newly opened or expanding factory will sometimes form a committee and then approach a union to request organizing. In the more common case, the union will approach workers in a non-union plant. When a certain percentage of the work force has been signed up, the union can apply to the provincial labor relations board (L.R.B.) to have a vote taken for certification. In Ontario, 35 percent of the workers is sufficient for a prehearing vote. A 45-percent vote entitles the workers to a regular presentation vote.

A representative of the L.R.B. will get in touch with the company and the union. Perhaps a joint meeting will be held. The company might argue against unionization, possibly on the grounds that the business does not fall within the limits of the labor code (certain nonprofit operations are exempt, for instance). Normally, though, management will consent to the vote being taken and arrange for workers to have time off to cast ballots.

There is nothing to prevent the company from informing its workers of benefits that may come to them if they vote "no," but it cannot in any way intimidate or threaten them. For example, your boss is not allowed to hint that joining the union might cost you a promotion.

Where more than one union is seeking to represent the plant's workers, balloting could decide that issue as well.

If 51 percent or more of the voting workers vote for the union, the organizer will seek certitication of the new local as the legal bargaining agent. If there have been no irregularities in the election, certification will usually be granted by the L.R.B. as a matter of course. In Ontario, if 55 percent of the workers concerned had signed union cards, certification might be granted without a vote.

Decertification procedure

If a union can no longer claim to represent a majority of the workers in a plant, shop or industry, its certification will be withdrawn by the governing L.R.B. The union must be supported by the *free will* of the majority. Just as an employer is not permitted to threaten in any way to prevent union organization of his company, so too is the union forbidden in any way to threaten to maintain its certification.

A union can lose the right to act as bargaining agent for a worker group under the following circumstances: (1) if the union goes out of existence or changes its nature significantly; (2) if the employer closes his business for some reason, such as bankruptcy; (3) if the majority of workers want to switch to another union, or to no union at all; (4) if the L.R.B. finds the union guilty of irregular activity.

In Ontario, decertification is automatic if fraud was used in obtaining certification. In Quebec, an employer may request a labor commissioner to determine whether an association still exists or whether it still has majority support. In New Brunswick, the L.R.B. is allowed to conduct a vote at any time to determine if the majority still supports the union. British Columbia grants protection of certification for a ten-month period, but its L.R.B. can call for another vote.

Generally speaking, the certification of any union in Canada is protected for a fixed period during which no other union may raid. In the federal sphere, the period is one year. In British Columbia it is only six months but the province's L.R.B. has authority to vary the period.

Closed shop, open shop

Canadian labor law will generally permit a contract to contain a clause to the effect that every employe *must* be a member of the certified union. The term "closed shop" describes a plant covered by such an agreement. Granting this kind of a monopoly runs counter to the ideal of individual freedom of choice—but it is roughly similar, in effect, to the laws which insist that all persons seeking to practice law in Canada must be members of the provincial law societies.

In direct contrast, the "open shop" contract does not make union membership a requirement of employment even though a union has been certified as the bargaining agent for *all* employes. In such a situation, the union maintains a membership drive to sign up nonmembers.

The term "union shop" is applied to the situation in which the employer may hire any person who is not a member of the legally certified union, but that person must join the union within a certain period (usually a month). If the newcomer will not join, the boss must fire him.

The term "agency shop" is used in situations in which the worker will not be fired if he refuses to join the union but he must agree to pay his union dues just as though he *were* a regular member.

Another variety of union contract is termed the "preferential shop." The employer in this case must give preference to union members in his hiring policy.

Several provinces will not permit any clause in a labor contract that forces the employer to fire a man because he is a member of a union other than the certified union. However, in practical terms, this point is already covered by the fundamental custom honored throughout the labor movement that no man can be a member of two unions at once. Thus, if you belonged to a union other than the one certified by your company, you would have to choose between changing your union or changing your job.

First in, last out

One of the most important items in all union contracts is job security—to the limit that a supply-and-demand economy allows. The seniority clause, once a hard-fought issue, is commonly granted today. In this clause, the long-term employe asks that his loyalty to the company be recognized in legal terms and that he will not be replaced automatically as younger (and stronger) men become available. If layoffs come because of a work shortage, the seniority clause demands "first in, last out."

The long-service worker also considers it his right that he be given first chance to try out for any higher-paying job that may become available in his plant.

The "conscientious objector"

In an era of individualism, there are those people who object, by conscience, to being forced to do *anything*. Compulsory unionism falls within this territory, posing the delicate problem of how the courts can, while still permitting the closed, union or agency shop, also ensure a proper measure of individual freedom.

Britain has taken the lead in legislating against compulsory unionism. A worker who is told by his employer that he must join a union can appeal to what is called an industrial tribunal. If he is fired simply because he is not a union member he can recover compensation from the employer, the union or both; the same holds if he can prove that he was rejected for a job because a union did not want him employed.

This problem has been met in Canada with a section of the "Rand formula" (named for Ivan Rand, a judge of the Supreme Court of Canada, who headed a Royal Commission to study labor-law reform). Essentially a modification of the "agency shop" system, this legislation allows nonunion workers in an otherwise closed shop, as long as they pay all usual dues to the union or to a registered charity. It is not in force right across Canada—for instance, Saskatchewan holds strictly to compulsory membership.

Yellow dogs and sweethearts

ONE OF THE "FRINGE BENEFITS" of trade unionism is the colorful phraseology it has added to the language. Wherever English is spoken, people recognize the special meaning of words like "checkoff," "sit-down," "scab," "closed shop," "black" and "local." But some other terms may puzzle all except the most studious "brothers" of the labor movement.

Yellow-dog contract An agreement, usually secret, that an employer requires an employe to sign before hiring (or perhaps before promotion). It includes the condition that the worker must not join a union during the term of the contract.

Sweetheart contract An agreement by a union leader to accept a contract on behalf of his members containing poorer terms than might have been gained on the secret understanding that he receives a personal payoff from the company.

Father of the chapel No, he doesn't keep the family quiet in church. He is the shop steward, or leader, of the branch of a printing trade union where the "locals" are known as "chapels."

Have you ever heard of the "Molly Maguires" or the "Wobblies"? The former were members of a secret society of Irish-born coal miners a century ago. They resorted to violence in their campaign for higher wages and improved working conditions. They blew up trains and mines, and murdered several foremen and company executives. When the union was infiltrated by Pinkerton detectives, 24 leaders were convicted and 20 of them hanged.

The Wobblies were the members of the Industrial Workers of the World, the I.W.W. The initials suggested the nickname, but some said it stood for "I Won't Work." A fiery U.S.-born union that spread to Canada, it led some successful strikes but lost support when its leaders opposed war service in 1914 and then espoused communism after the Russian Revolution.

527

The dues checkoff

A vital item of security, from the union point of view, is the *checkoff* clause in the contract which requires the employer to deduct from each worker's pay cheque or wage envelope all fees charged by the union. This money is routed directly to the union's bank account. Most provinces authorize the checkoff. (A recent survey by the federal Department of Labor showed that about 93 percent of contracts studied contained a checkoff clause.) In Prince Edward Island, however, the checkoff is not permitted if union dues or levies are to be used for political purposes.

If there's a grievance

In the legal sense, a grievance can be defined as "an injury, injustice or wrong which provides grounds for complaint because it is unjust or oppressive." In terms of labor relations, the word has come to mean a complaint by the worker against some condition, event or circumstance of his employment. Quebec labor law defines a grievance as "any disagreement respecting the interpretation or application of a collective agreement."

The fact that a grievance can be examined quickly—and unemotionally—is regarded by many legal authorities as one of the greatest advances in labor law. If you have a grievance, take it to your shop steward or union business agent. If he considers the grievance to be genuine, the agent will meet with a management representative to discuss it. If it cannot be resolved at this level, it will rise step by step through both union and company ranks. If there is still no agreement, mediation can be sought under the labor relations acts.

No matter how serious the grievance, the law clearly states that the union may not call a strike, nor the company impose a lockout, during the term of the collective agreement—unless the contract specifically allows these moves. Such an action by either party would be, in legal terms, the same as any breach of contract under civil law.

If you are laid off

When there simply isn't enough work to keep a labor force profitably occupied, employers may resort to the *layoff*. This

---

"The Nine-Hour Pioneers"

YOU MAY NOT HAVE HEARD it sung to a folk guitar on the Top Forty lately, but—back in 1872—the verses at the right by Alec H. Wingfield, in *The Ontario Workman*, were sure to be recited in beery baritone at any gathering of members in the union halls.

In April of the same year, there was a mass rally at St. Catharines for the nine-hour workday. Toronto's carpenters, painters, iron and brass founders went on strike on May Day—labor's traditional day of action—and the Toronto Trades Assembly gave veiled hints of a possible general strike. In Hamilton, the printers went on strike on their own and they, too, won the nine-hour day. The Great Western and Grand Trunk railways knuckled under soon afterward.

Honor the men of Hamilton,
The Nine-Hour Pioneers;
Their memory will be kept green,
Throughout the coming years.

And every honest son of toil
That lives in freedom's light
Shall bless that glorious day in May
When might gave way to right.

Your cause was just, your motives pure,
Again, again, again,
You strove to smooth the path of toil
And help your fellowmen.

And Canada will bless your name
Through all the coming years,
And place upon the scroll of fame
The Nine-Hour Pioneers.

is a legally recognized method of temporary discharge or suspension from work. It can be caused by weather conditions on outdoor jobs, a lack of demand for the company's product, or by a shortage of raw materials or component parts.

Most collective bargaining agreements attempt to regulate the layoff. Some provincial labor laws require that large firms give a lengthy period of notice of intention to lay off a sizable number of workers. In Ontario, the period is one to eight weeks, depending on the length of service, if 50 workers are involved, and 16 weeks if the number exceeds 300. Most contracts state that, when a layoff is necessary, the workers are to be discharged in strict order of seniority. In some cases, the entire work force in a plant will work fewer hours each week, for a set limit of time, before layoffs are ordered.

Dismissal for cause

You can be dismissed from your job immediately without notice (or without pay to make up for notice) if you have been guilty of continued or serious misconduct. However, an employer firing without advance notice would probably have to justify his action, especially if you were working under a union contract and thought you didn't deserve the sack.

Almost all collective agreements attempt to regulate the ways in which a worker can be disciplined—warnings, suspensions and finally dismissal with a prescribed period of notice—and the provisions of any such contract have to be followed exactly. If there are no such terms in the contract, the boss does not have to state his reasons for firing you.

If you feel you have been unjustly dismissed, and you have no union to fight the issue, you should contact your provincial labor relations board. Even if you belong to a union and your union doesn't want to challenge the firing, the L.R.B. would, no doubt, at least listen to you.

It's important to remember that, whether or not all the obligations of the "servant" to the "master" are spelled out in the contract, you can be "fired on the spot" for unprovoked rudeness, dishonesty, drunkenness, disobedience of a reasonable order, for habitual negligence or destructiveness, and for other serious faults. In these circumstances, you must be fired immediately after the specific event. No matter what the reason, however, you must be paid for all wages earned up to the hour of the dismissal, including any accumulated vacation pay.

Incompetence, insolence, persistent unpunctuality or absence without leave are all grounds for justified dismissal. However, disobeying an "unreasonable" order would not be considered "just cause."

If a person is fired while a contract is in effect that sets a fixed term of employment—or a contract that runs until a certain job is completed—it is likely he would have a case for compensation, unless the boss could show that there was "just cause" for the sack. Negligent work would provide such grounds. Punching the boss in the nose would be an effective way for you to break the contract.

At the end of a fixed-term contract, the employe can be dropped from the payroll without notice.

In some cases, when it is suggested to an employe that he resign, he might be better off to demand to be fired. The difference here is that the man who resigns has, in the legal sense, left his job of his own free will and this could affect his eligibility for certain benefits.

When a person is fired and given payment instead of a period of notice, he must leave the job at once; he does not have the choice of working out the agreed period of notice.

Collective bargaining

Once a trade union has been certified as representing a definite group of workers, it will approach the employer to begin collective bargaining on wages and other terms of employment. The boss may take the initiative, but seldom does so. The employer is required by law to bargain "in good faith"—that is, he must make every effort to reach agreement with the union. The collective agreement, or contract, is the usual result of the negotiation. It becomes the basis of relationships between the employer and the union.

The collective bargaining procedure, as

far as Canada is concerned, is rooted in our acceptance of a convention of the International Labor Organization (I.L.O.) which states that the labor of a human being is not simply something to be bought and sold. In most countries enjoying the right to private ownership of property, free enterprise and free competition (or as near as we come to these freedoms in reality), collective bargaining is considered an instrument of social justice because it gives to the individual worker a collective strength which balances the economic power of the employer.

If the true needs and wants of the workers are met and satisfied in the fair give-and-take or bargaining, then—so the theory runs—there will be no need for the state to intervene.

While the process of collective bargaining is one of open give-and-take, the actual procedure is strictly controlled by legislation—much of it designed to protect the worker.

In most mass-production factories, the average worker is semiskilled and can usually be replaced without much diffi-

culty: in short, he is "expendable." Thus, without legal protection, most workmen could still be left with a "take it or leave it" choice.

The regulations normally provide for seven "ground rules" before the bargaining process can begin. These cover:
(1) Notice to begin bargaining;
(2) Time limits for negotiation;
(3) Announcement of representatives;
(4) When the bargaining process may be interrupted;
(5) If the parties are changed;
(6) Restrictions on employer's actions;
(7) Enforcement of the regulations.

Horse trading on terms
The union must put forward a set of demands for a new contract within the stated time limit. In Ontario, the deadline is 60 days from the certification of the union as bargaining agent. If the set date is not met, the union is open to a decertification challenge. In Saskatchewan, the labor relations board can order the parties to begin bargaining if it feels there are unnecessary delays.

In praise of older workers

"INTELLIGENCE, REFLECTION and judgment reside in old men and if there had been none of them, no states could exist at all." So wrote the Roman philosopher Cicero.

In recent times, however, the worship of youth has resulted in workers of mature years often being discarded on grounds of age alone, well before retirement age. Apart from its unfairness to the individual, this practice costs any country a wealth of experience in factory, shop and office.

Several provinces have taken legislative steps to block discrimination in employment on grounds of age. They recognize that health, mental and physical capacities, work attitudes and job performance are individual traits at any age, and that chronological age alone is no indicator of working ability. Merit and ability are the keys.

The worker between 40 and 65 must be granted equal opportunity to compete with the younger worker for a job on the basis of individual ability.

A typical statute requires that employers, in hiring and promoting, must apply equal standards to all persons, regardless of age. Such laws do not, of course, require companies to hire older workers; they do make it unlawful to refuse to hire persons between 40 and 65 solely on grounds of age.

Even if his locks are greying and his knees occasionally creak, the Canadian worker who dreads early retirement can confidently quote poet Robert Browning to a prospective boss:
Grow old along with me!
The best is yet to be,
The last of life, for which the first
*   was made.*

Collective bargaining is, in effect, the same as old-fashioned horse trading. Offers and counteroffers are put forward by the opposing sides on all or most of the clauses until a satisfactory compromise is reached. If there is a stalemate, with the opposing demands too far apart to make a workable compromise likely, the union committee will report back to the membership. It might ask for authorization to call a strike, at a favorable time, should no further progress seem possible.

There are, however, several methods of settlement to be tried before a legal strike, or lockout, can be called. The first is governmental mediation or conciliation.

Compulsory conciliation

Intervention by the government in industrial disputes, such as we know it today, developed from the Canadian Conciliation Act of 1900. This pioneer federal statute provided a method for voluntary conciliation. It allowed the minister of labor to send a representative to offer assistance in any situation where there was a potential or actual dispute. It was prompted by the public interest in maintaining employment and production.

It was the government's idea that a disinterested, yet knowledgeable, person might serve as an impartial chairman and provide a neutral meeting ground for the two sides in a dispute who were at loggerheads with each other. It was also felt that publication of the conciliator's recommendations would bring some public pressure to bear on the arguing parties— this still is the key to the conciliation process. The legal philosophy can be summed up in the belief that "private rights should cease when they become public wrongs."

W. L. Mackenzie King, later prime minister but then deputy minister of labor, introduced a plan in 1907 which proved to be the beginnings of compulsory conciliation. It was incorporated in the Industrial Relations and Disputes Investigation Act, previously mentioned. This plan prohibited any work stoppages and froze all terms and conditions while the dispute was "under investigation." Strikes or lockouts were not outlawed; they were suspended or postponed. During the "cooling-off" period thus imposed, reconsideration by both parties, common sense and public opinion often brought compromises and eventual agreement.

Conciliation and mediation legislation has been refined a great deal through the years. In the current federal and provincial statutes, the first move after an impasse is reached in collective bargaining is still to make use of the services of a conciliation officer (or commissioner) from the department of labor.

In British Columbia, the parties must bargain for ten days before they can call in a government conciliator; in Quebec, the parties may request a conciliator at anytime during the negotiations. However, the government anywhere may choose to step in and appoint a conciliator in a situation it considers explosive, or when the welfare of the public may be at stake. The Ontario act allows the disputing parties a second chance at conciliation under a different commissioner if the first fails.

In most jurisdictions, the conciliation officer must report to his minister within 14 days (in British Columbia it is ten days). He may recommend that a formal conciliation board be established. The board is allowed to summon witnesses, and to enter and inspect company premises. In Nova Scotia, a board will be appointed only if either party to the dispute asks for it. Several provinces reserve the right to impose the appointment of boards. British Columbia has a full-time independent Arbitration Board.

Machinery exists in all the provinces and territories for the appointment of an arbitrator at the request of the parties. The arbitrator's decision can be binding. In some provinces, the conciliation board can be converted into an arbitration board. If conciliation fails in certain public services (fire departments, hospitals, police), compulsory arbitration can follow. When all conciliation and mediation has failed and the prospect looms of a strike that could seriously harm the public, or national security, the various governments concerned can resort to legislation in order to keep the workers on the job pending arbitration.

531

Strikes and lockouts

The routine strike

Go-slow and work-to-rule

The sympathy strike

What is a lockout?

On the picket line

Use of the injunction

I T IS THE UNIONS' ARGUMENT that workers would be fundamentally powerless at the bargaining table if they did not have the weapons of the strike, the boycott and the picket. These can be seen as the "ace cards" to play against both the employer's right to refuse union demands and his ultimate denial of work by means of the lockout. Labor contends that without the right to strike, liberty as essentially understood in democratic countries would not exist. The majority of the people would not have any real freedom in their most important activity: work. They would have to accept any wage offered, as well as any abuse. Increasingly, the legislatures of the Western democracies have come to accept this argument.

While governments do have the power to bring a strike to an end, they will do so only when the public interest is being seriously threatened (as in a strike by schoolteachers or policemen)—or when public outcry is loud enough.

The routine strike
Labor legislation in the federal sphere, as well as in Newfoundland and New Brunswick, generally considers a strike to be a ceasing of work, or a refusal to work or to continue to work, by employes who have joined together for a common purpose. The other provinces use similar descriptions, some adding that the employes are trying to compel their employer "to agree to terms or conditions of employment." In a labor dispute, provided all the necessary steps through collective bargaining and conciliation (or, in British Columbia, mediation) have been taken, the strike— the ceasing of work—is a legal act. All statutes provide that the striker does not

lose his status as an employe during a legal strike.

In the routine strike, the union orders its members off the job and sets up a picket line, trying to choose a time likely to inconvenience the employer most. Arrangements often will be made for maintenance men to remain on the job where expensive or not easily replaceable machinery would suffer if left unattended.

Go-slow and work-to-rule
A union uses go-slow and work-to-rule techniques as means of forcing management to grant demands while stopping short of formal strike action. In the work-to-rule method, every regulation pertaining to the job is carried out with such thoroughness that less work actually gets done. As an illustration, under an old law which has never been repealed, a railwayman is required to walk in front of every locomotive, carrying a red warning flag. If this rule was followed today, normal service would be impossible.

Legislative attempts have been made by most provinces to curtail this type of direct action. In some statutes, the slowdown is simply considered as a strike. In Manitoba, for instance, the definition of "strike" now includes the refusal by an employe "to continue the . . . normal pattern of operation." Some Maritime provinces declare it an "unfair practice" for any union to "support, encourage or engage in any activity that is intended to restrict or limit production."

The sympathy strike
When a union is not directly involved in a dispute but wishes to express strong support for a union that is on strike, it may

call its members out "in sympathy." This action, of course, is not legal and the employer affected would most likely apply for an injunction against the union, and get it without difficulty.

Sympathy action is included within the legal definition of a strike in Nova Scotia, Manitoba, Alberta and British Columbia. In other provinces, the definition is broad enough to cover all organized stoppages. Saskatchewan, however, steers clear of defining either a strike or a lockout.

What is a lockout?
In a labor dispute where agreement seems unattainable, the employer may resort to the *lockout*—locking the door of the workplace against the employes, or perhaps only against a certain group of them. When a deadlock is reached in collective bargaining, the employer (or group of employers) can legally deny work in his plant to his workers. The lockout is the counter-balance to the workers' right to strike.

Most provincial legislation defines the lockout as "including the closing of a place of employment, a suspension of work, or a refusal by an employer to continue to employ a number of his employes, to agree to terms or conditions of employment."

Saskatchewan and Newfoundland both rule that it is an "unfair practice" for an employer to "threaten to shut down or move a plant or any part of a plant in the course of a labor dispute."

As with a strike, a lockout is forbidden by law until the parties have bargained unsuccessfully for a certain time and all possible conciliation or mediation procedures have been taken. In Alberta, if an employers' organization is concerned in the action, a secret ballot of the members will be held under the auspices of the Board of Industrial Relations, and 72 hours' notice of the lockout must be given to the workers.

A similar ballot is required in British Columbia.

Fines will be levied for any illegal lockout, ranging between $5,000 to $50,000 a day in Quebec to Alberta's maximum penalty of $1,000 a day for each worker locked out. In Quebec, the Labor Court can dissolve an employers' organization found guilty of imposing an illegal lockout. Any prohibition against lockouts, however, does not prevent an employer from dismissing a worker for cause.

"Public welfare is the supreme law"

Mr. Justice Georges Pelletier of the Superior Court of Quebec, in passing judgment in 1972 on unions and union officers found guilty of contempt of court for defying a court injunction, restated the cardinal principle of the law in stirring words.

"The law," he said, "has been trampled underfoot and has been openly disobeyed, in a concerted and premeditated manner. Such a situation is intolerable in a society which calls itself civilized. . . .

"When the law is ignored and the authority of the courts openly flouted in a society, there is reason to fear a situation which may degenerate, sooner or later, into anarchy.

"The welfare of the public is the supreme law. *Salus populi est suprema lex.*"

Great voices ring out over the years. The Greek orator and statesman Demosthenes put it this way: "The design and object of laws is to ascertain what is just, honorable and expedient; and, when that is discovered, it is proclaimed as a general ordinance, equal and impartial to all. This is the origin of law which all are under obligation to obey, especially because all law is the invention and gift of heaven, the resolution of wise men, the correction of every offense, and the general compact of the state." William Pitt, toward the close of his career, had said it all in but five words: "Where law ends, tyranny begins."

THE COURTS IN ACTION

When strikers defied the law

FACTS

Soon after the beginning of a strike that followed the inability of a plastics company and the trade union representing its workers to reach a collective agreement, the plaintiff company obtained an interim injunction restraining the union from "watching, besetting or picketing at or adjacent to the plaintiff's premises with more than a maximum of twelve pickets at the plant entrances, and from ordering, aiding, abetting, counseling, procuring or encouraging any other person to commit any of the acts enjoined." The news of the injunction was publicized through the newspapers and radio stations in the area where the plant was located.

A few days later, parading and demonstrating occurred, with a long human belt running along both edges of a five-foot sidewalk extending the length of the plaintiff's premises. The number of participants ranged from 200 to 300. The sheriff was called to read the injunction and he then affixed copies of it to two conspicuous places in the vicinity of the plaintiff's premises. At the height of the demonstrations, strikers carried placards protesting unfair labor laws and unfair labor injunctions, and stating that there was no room for "scabs" in the municipality. The attorney general for Ontario then began proceedings for an order committing several demonstrators to prison for defying the injunction.

ARGUMENT

The attorney general's case was based on the allegation of "watching, besetting, picketing and parading" in defiance of the court injunction, and he sought to invoke the inherent power of the court to punish summarily for the contempt of the court order. On behalf of the defendants, the lawyers advanced the argument that the signs and conduct of the participants in the demonstration were merely part of a campaign to promote changes in a branch of law which they considered, rightly or wrongly, to be unfair.

JUDGMENT

The court ruled that the means employed to attain a certain end must be as lawful and as justified as the end itself. The demonstrations were a direct and open challenge to the authority of the court, and the labor leaders concerned with them were determined that they be so. The court found that all of the demonstrators but one had acted in contempt of court.

In determining the appropriate sentence, the presiding judge said: "My role as a judge is to ensure continuity for the rule of law and to thereby aid in the preservation of freedom, not for some but for all citizens.

"No more serious challenge and defiance of the authority of the court could be found than one that resulted from an organized plan of a premeditated and willful course of conduct in which much publicity was deliberately sought."

Five of the picketers were sentenced to two months' imprisonment, and another to 15 days.*

*Based on an actual case (1966).

On the picket line

When a strike is called, the workers leave their jobs and set up a picket line. Members of a striking local, and their supporters, usually gather on the public sidewalk or roadway closest to the gates or doors to the plant to provide information about the cause or purpose of the strike, and to persuade all comers—such as delivery-men—not to enter and to stop doing business with the company.

In its duty to safeguard the freedom of all citizens, the law sets down rules on how the pickets may gather, how they may inform and how they may persuade. The strikers must obey the same laws that apply to any protesting group: they must not obstruct the public roadway, they must not commit libel in their "publishing" of information and they must not use any force whatever upon anyone who does not accept their "persuasion."

Although there is no generally adopted law specifically controlling picketing, the practice has acquired a definite status. In cases that have been tried in courts from coast to coast, the legality of peaceful picketing and persuasion seems to have been firmly established.

The Supreme Court of Canada, in a judgment in 1951, said that peaceful picketing was a "legitimate mode of waging the contest."

Any picketing in support of an illegal strike is itself illegal. Picketing—or any type of intimidation—is forbidden as a means to induce an employer to accept a union, or to persuade workers to sign cards for any union seeking certification.

Obstruction is unlawful

Elements of both civil and criminal law come into play when events on the picket line affect the safety or reputation of any person, or when they involve trespass or mischief on private property.

It is perfectly legal for a striker to try to persuade another worker (or anybody at all) not to enter the place being picketed; however, it is completely illegal to try to *prevent* him from doing so.

The courts must also keep in mind their over-all duty to see that the public interest is adequately protected.

Damage or sabotage

All provincial statutes penalize willful damage during a strike. Article 1053 of the Civil Code of Quebec states that every person who is capable of judging right from wrong is responsible for the damage caused by him to another person—or to another person's (or company's) property. Intimidation is equally prohibited to all sides in industrial disputes. In other words, "A threat to do an unlawful act is unlawful."

Under British Columbia's Trade Unions Act, an employer can be granted an injunction of four days' duration restraining a union from taking certain action when the threat of irreparable damage to property seems likely.

Use of the injunction

The injunction, in simplest terms, is a court order that forbids a certain act or acts from being performed. Granted for only a definite (and usually short) period of time, an injunction has all the force of law on a temporary basis. It is intended to prevent any further provocative action in a dispute until the issue can be decided through proper legal channels.

The order will be issued only when a judge who has the required authority is convinced that some wrong action is likely to occur. An injunction can stop someone either from beginning a certain action or from continuing it. It also can order that a situation be returned to the position at which it stood before the action was taken.

If an injunction is issued at the request of only one of the parties, and the opposing party is not present to contest it, it is called an *ex parte* injunction.

The penalty for failure to obey an injunction is usually a fine or a prison sentence for contempt of court. (*See* Chapter 3, "Decisions from the Bench.")

Injunctions have been granted where unions have attacked an employer's reputation and attempted to give the company's products a bad name. A statement of opinion (such as "unjust," "unfair") is acceptable, but deliberate falsehoods and libelous statements would probably result in an injunction.

13/Businesses and Professions

Going into business $\hspace{4cm}$ 538

Sole proprietorship $\hspace{4cm}$ 544

Partnerships $\hspace{5cm}$ 550

The private company $\hspace{4cm}$ 556

Going into business

ALMOST EVERY DAY Canadians are in touch with the world of business, and almost everyone has dreamed about going into business "on his own." The urge to be "your own boss" is strong in this free-enterprise society.

Some of us already own a business, or part of a business, either through a partnership or as a shareholder. Most work for businesses—from banks and shops to laundries and factories. As customers, we are always doing business at the supermarket, the drugstore, the barber shop, the gas station, the hardware or clothing store, or buying a ticket to the local movie house. The farmer drives to the general store at the nearest district center or sends away to a mail-order supplier. Even the trapper and oil driller in the far north are—like the Indian and Inuit—in touch with Hudson's Bay Company outlets.

The regulation and control of trade and commerce come within the wide scope of commercial law—a system of rules, customs and business practices descended from the *law merchant* of medieval times. (*See* Chapter 1, "The rise of English law.") The main source of commercial law in the Province of Quebec is the Civil Code, which has the same roots but which contains some variants to the practice of the other nine provinces. Commercial law is a category of private law—that is, the law that governs relations between private persons or groups of persons. In terms of the law, a company is a corporate entity, a legal "body," in the same way as a person is, so that it can sue and be sued.

Inasmuch as most business activities involve contracts, it is the law of contract which provides the basis for much of commercial law.

A business can be bought and sold and, if shares are available to the public, it may be vulnerable to a "takeover" by an individual investor or by another company. This can happen when a person or a corporation buys a sizable fraction of the target company's shares on the stock market. He will probably then make an offer to other shareholders for enough of their shares to give him 51 percent or more of the company's total voting stock. This will mean that he is in effective control of the company. Although elected directors determine the policies that the executives follow in running the business from day to day, the ultimate control naturally rests with the majority of the shareholders, those part owners of the business who elect the directors and can, therefore, turn them out of office as well.

While there is virtually no limit to the kinds of enterprises that can be set up, most businesses are organized in one of the following ways: as an individual ownership (sole proprietorship); as a partnership; or as a corporation (either private or public). There is also the cooperative form of business, owned and operated by its members or fellow employes on the "one man, one vote" system. Nonprofit companies and Crown corporations are other methods of conducting business in Canada.

Ethics of commerce
Ethics play a major role in the commercial community. Most businessmen are sensitive to their public "image" and normally conduct their affairs in keeping with standards of performance that the public expects of them. When the customer is not specifically protected by consum-

er law (*see* Chapter 6, "Guarantees and standards"), he will probably be safeguarded by the ethical behavior of the individual businessman or the established corporation. Quite apart from personal or company standards of conduct, responsibility and fair practice make sound business sense. A business can soon go bankrupt if the buying public becomes suspicious of the policy of that company or antagonized by attitudes of, perhaps, disregard for the public. Most larger businesses are now following the principle that "the customer is always right." The idea of *caveat emptor* ("let the buyer beware") is strictly limited in practice and because of common sense.

Business ethics frequently involve the elements of profit and competition. How far should one store go in trying to compete with another? How much profit is reasonable for a company? Is there a moral limit to the amount of profit? There are different answers that apply to different cases. It cannot be proclaimed, for instance, that ten percent is the moral profit margin for all products and all companies. A 20-percent profit, or higher, may be necessary in a certain year to pay off debts or to rebuild reserves after a year of deficits, or losses. Many other economic factors can affect profits: among them are research, expansion, retooling, and staff training and replacement.

The normal operation of the marketplace, based on the unwritten but powerful "laws" of supply and demand and conditioned by anti-monopoly legislation, usually keeps business profits at reasonable levels. In boom times, finance ministers may siphon off excessive profits by tax increases. Likewise, taxes may be reduced when business is slow and unemployment grows.

Government also holds the ultimate weapon of arbitrary price fixing. Although a matter of policy in communist countries, price fixing is used in the democracies only in times of deep national crisis, such as during a war. Sometimes prices will be frozen temporarily in an attempt to curb spiraling inflation; usually a matching "freeze" is imposed on wage increases as well.

Taking the plunge

Every year, several thousand Canadians decide to set up their own businesses. A sizable number are certain to fail, often for reasons that would have been obvious to them before they began if overoptimism had not clouded their judgment.

Most experienced businessmen agree that success or failure in a new undertaking depends more upon the personal abilities of those who manage its affairs than upon any other single factor. There must be expertise in each major area of the concern—management, planning, production—if the enterprise is to stand up to the sharp competition that exists in almost every avenue of business operation. In other words, you not only have to know exactly what you're doing, but you have to know how to do it better than your established competitor up the street.

Going into business for yourself rarely opens a magic door to wealth. Many small businesses struggle for years, with a lone proprietor or several partners working long hours for what amounts to meager wages. They would probably be better off as employes of more efficiently run companies. However, the financial return is not all that is involved; there can be advantages and deep satisfaction in going into business on your own. There is the inspiration and spur of being in sole control, of making money for yourself and not for others, and of having the opportunity to make the best use of your own talents, energy and resources.

The federal Department of Industry, Trade and Commerce and Regional Economic Expansion advises:

"Going into business for yourself is something which not only confers rewards and provides opportunities, but is also an undertaking which requires experience and capital. It may involve considerable financial risk. It is not a decision to be taken lightly. Carefully appraise your ability, personality and experience. Consult your local chamber of commerce, board of trade, better business bureau, bankers, trade suppliers, wholesalers, retail merchants association, etc., about the business you have in mind. Proceed on the basis of careful calculation and sound

539

advice, not on hunches or guesses. Weigh the evidence carefully before arriving at a decision. Then stick to it."

Know-how is essential

If you wish to open a retail shop, it is almost essential that you first work for a successful firm in the line you favor. You should stay with the firm for a period of years, working in as many departments as you can to broaden your general business know-how. There is really no substitute for actual workaday experience.

To further prepare yourself for your venture, you should consider enrolling in night classes in bookkeeping or business administration; such courses are probably offered at your local high school or community college. There are also several reputable correspondence schools operating in Canada, giving you the advantage of studying at home at times that suit your schedule best. The librarian in the reference room of your public library will probably be able to guide you to some books written in popular terms about your line of interest. Don't be shy about asking her—she is there to serve you.

There are obvious advantages in buying an already established business, if you have sufficient funds. You have the chance beforehand to watch the business in operation, and you can examine the account books to check on its profitability. The owner may be willing to help you master the inner problems of the trade. And, hopefully, you will be taking over a group of steady clients. If the owner wants to retire, and if he is confident of your ability, he may accept a modest down payment and then allow you to pay off the rest of the price from the profits.

In the classified pages of the telephone directory, you will find a handy list of your potential competition. Check them out by personal visits. The government will assist you in sizing up your chances. Statistics Canada can supply you with figures on regional and city population, manufacturing, retail trade and average income levels. Employment and Immigration Canada will discuss any labor needs you might have and advise you on standards you will have to meet if you take on employes. Economic development officers will provide you with important local information on rents and rates and show you land available for industry or other development. They will advise you of the federal, provincial and municipal laws and regulations that have a bearing on your project.

Under federal rule

The British North America Act (now part of the Canadian Constitution) established the division of powers between the federal and the provincial governments. In the area of commerce, it gave the federal authorities power over (1) public debt and property, (2) regulation of trade and commerce, (3) raising of money by any mode or system of taxation, (4) banking, (5) issuing of currency, (6) bankruptcy, (7) patents and (8) copyrights. It also ruled that any powers not specifically given to the provinces were considered to belong to the federal government.

If you wish, you may have your company incorporated under federal law rather than under the law of your own province. The main advantage is that a federally incorporated company can carry on business anywhere in Canada without obtaining special permission. Federal companies must obey provincial laws.

Federal laws regulate wages, working hours and conditions in certain trades and industries. (*See* Chapter 12, "In the federal sphere.") The federal Department of Consumer and Corporate Affairs acts as the national watchdog over corporate securities, combines, mergers and monopolies. The Restrictive Trade Practices Commission operates under powers from the federal Combines Investigation Act.

Federal income, corporation and sales taxes cover all regular businesses in Canada. The Department of National Revenue also collects a separate individual income tax on behalf of all provinces, except Quebec which levies its own. Federal excise tax is also charged on certain manufactured and wholesale goods.

Complete details on federal sales and excise taxes can be obtained from the Customs and Excise Division, Department of National Revenue, Ottawa.

Provincial jurisdiction

The majority of commercial transactions fall under provincial regulations. The federal power over the regulation of trade and commerce is mostly limited to transactions between provinces or between Canada and foreign countries. The provinces are responsible for direct taxation within the province for provincial purposes, the borrowing of money on the credit of the province and the establishment of provincial offices. They are also responsible for municipal institutions, the incorporation of companies with provincial objects—that is, intending to do business within the province only—and for the laws regulating labor and industry within the province.

Ontario and Quebec impose and collect their own corporation taxes. All other provinces have a corporation tax, but it is collected by the Department of National Revenue as part of the federal tax and is returned to the respective provinces.

In 1893, the British Parliament simplified and condensed much of the voluminous commercial law on sales contracts into a comprehensive statute called the Sale of Goods Act. All the common law provinces in Canada (*i.e.* all except Quebec) have adopted this act almost word-for-word. The 1893 act did not change the law, but simply clarified certain principles of commercial law that conflicted with each other. Where the Sale of Goods Act does not specifically cover a situation, common law—that is, laws derived from precedent, or former rulings—applies.

In Quebec, the Civil Code governs the business of selling. Although the general principles are similar to those of the other provinces, the differences are such that anyone planning to do business in Quebec should make separate inquiries to the De-

Funds for the small operator

THE FEDERAL GOVERNMENT, through the Department of Finance, has been guaranteeing loans for the small businessman since 1960. This money is available to a business operating as a sole proprietorship, patnership or incorporated limited liability company, provided its gross revenue does not exceed $1,500,000 in the year the application is made.

Under the terms of the Small Businesses Loans Act, firms in the following fields are eligible: communications, construction, manufacturing, retailing, service businesses, transportation and wholesaling. Loans are not available to those engaged in real estate, insurance or financial enterprises, or to any professional (such as a doctor or an accountant). Charitable or other non-profit bodies do not qualify. Loans are available for the purchase of land if it is necessary for the operation of a business.

Usually styled "business improvement loans," the funds are available on application to the chartered banks, and through certain credit unions, trust and loan companies which have been designated by the authorities as lenders under the act. The primary purposes of the loans are for the purchase, construction, improvement or renovation of business premises (up to 90 percent of cost), and for purchase and installation of equipment, either fixed or moveable (up to 80 percent of cost).

All small-business loans must be secured either by a chattel mortgage on any equipment purchased, or by a building mortgage on the premises concerned. Further security may be demanded, and a promissory note will be required from the borrower. No single operator or company can have more than $100,000 in outstanding loans at any one time, and the repayment period cannot exceed ten years.

The interest rate on these loans fluctuates and can be obtained from the branch nearest you of any chartered bank. Further details on the scheme are available from The Director, Guaranteed Loans Administration, Department of Finance, Ottawa, Ontario.

partment of Industry and Commerce, Quebec City. To give only one example: possession of goods is considered "nine-tenths of the law" in Quebec. A buyer does not actually own any purchased item until he has it in his possession. Thus, a shopkeeper could—in theory, at least—make a sale to you, promising later delivery of the goods. Then he could sell the same item to a second buyer. As long as the second customer actually got his hands on the goods concerned, he would enjoy legal ownership. (*See* Chapter 6, "The arts of selling.")

Registration of letters patent

If you have decided to form a corporation—more commonly known as a company—there are three methods by which you can seek incorporation. The grant of incorporation is actually permission from the authorities to create this new body which will have its own "personality," as well as its own rights and obligations.

Incorporation can take the form of a special act of either the federal parliament or a provincial legislature. This method is normally only used for certain major businesses—like railways and airlines, insurance or trust companies—and is outside the scope of this book.

The other methods are: by registration of a *memorandum and articles of association*, or by the issuance of *letters patent*. The term *patent*, meaning "open," has been used since the Middle Ages to describe a document issued by the Crown which gives some special right or privilege to a person.

In British Columbia, a company is incorporated by the delivery of a memorandum and articles of association, and the issuance of a certificate of incorporation.

The lure of the franchise

SINCE THE LATE 1960s, going into business by buying a franchise has become popular in Canada. There are few towns indeed that don't boast a bright and brassy hamburger or fried chicken drive-in doing business under nationally advertised names. The system extends to many "one line" businesses, including gas stations, doughnuts, car washes and auto mufflers.

It seems, at first glance, like the perfect set-up for the novice businessman. A company develops a successful product or service and, as it becomes a household word, the management offers (for a fee) to help set others up in the specialty, each operator becoming his own boss while paying a percentage of his revenue to the franchising company. Some franchisors assist with capital requirements and almost all supply staff training and advertising support.

A lot of the perils of "going it alone" are bridged by this current technique and many energetic newcomers have done very well with a franchise operation. However, some have had their fingers burned.

Experts suggest that the person eager to buy a franchise first obtain satisfactory answers to these questions:
- What sort of reputation does the franchisor enjoy in the business world? (Ask the Better Business Bureau, or your bank.)
- What do other holders of the same franchise have to say about their ventures? (Is the company fair to deal with once you're in?)
- If you are taking over an existing franchise, why did the other guy quit?
- Does the franchisor manufacture the product, or merely distribute it? (You could be left high and dry for goods to sell.)
- Are you being offered an exclusive territory? (Check the existing competition.)
- In estimating your costs of doing business under a franchise, have you allowed for a fair hourly wage rate for yourself?
- Finally, do you have clear right to sell the franchise? Would the company buy back any supplied equipment? What happens if you die suddenly—would your dependents be permitted to carry on?

In Alberta, Newfoundland and Nova Scotia, you can incorporate by delivering to a designated official a memorandum of association and articles of association (if desired). The official, in turn, issues a certificate of incorporation.

In Saskatchewan, Manitoba and Ontario, an incorporation may take place by the filing of articles of incorporation and the issuance of a certificate of incorporation. In Quebec, New Brunswick and Prince Edward Island, incorporation is by letters patent granting a charter of incorporation. Under the terms of the Canada Business Corporations Act, articles of association are used for companies incorporating federally.

If you seek federal incorporation, write to the Corporation Branch, Consumer and Corporate Affairs Canada, Place du Portage, Hull, Quebec, K1A 0C9. If you act within your province, write to the provincial secretary at your capital city (if you are in a letters-patent province) or to the registrar of companies (if registration is the accepted method). You will receive a copy of the applicable legislation with forms setting out all the detail you must supply.

While it is entirely possible for the new and inexperienced businessman to act on his own behalf in seeking incorporation, there are many reasons for recommending him to hire a solicitor to represent him and the company-to-be.

Municipal and provincial licensing

Most municipalities regulate businesses, trades and contractors that operate within their boundaries. Certain enterprises—restaurants and hairdressing parlors, for example—require special licenses because they must comply with the provisions of public health and other legislation. Other businesses may be restricted to certain designated districts.

Before they can open up, new businesses are normally required to pay what is sometimes called the "transient trader's deposit." This is one-half of the estimated first year's business tax on the property concerned. The "deposit" is basically meant to protect the already established traders against the newcomer who takes

a shop, conducts a number of "bargain sales," then departs without notice—and without paying his taxes. This payment is demanded the first year only.

Under provincial law, municipalities are permitted to require the licensing of trades operating in the municipality.

The requirements may vary by trade and by town. Qualifications accepted by provincial authorities for master electricians and plumbers are usually sufficient for the granting of a trading license anywhere in that province without further examination. (*See* "The licensed trades" in this chapter.)

It is the responsibility of the incoming contractor or tradesman to know and understand the licensing requirements of the municipality in which he seeks to do business. Information about these standards can be obtained from the city hall of the municipality concerned, or from the provincial department of labor.

In most provinces, a new retailer must obtain a provincial sales tax license. If he fails to do so, he could be charged a penalty on top of any uncollected tax.

The nonprofit corporation

Both federal and provincial legislation allow for the incorporation of associations or groups interested in patriotic, charitable, religious, scientific or athletic pursuits rather than in making a profit for private purposes. These include labor unions, chambers of commerce, and social and sports clubs permitted to serve liquor to members and their guests.

These groups and associations are classed as "non-trading corporations" or "corporations without share capital." The basic requirement is that they be operated without monetary gain to any person. The main benefit achieved by incorporation is that the members are not personally liable for any debts incurred.

The term "nonprofit" does not mean that these corporations cannot or do not make profits. Some are wealthy indeed. The difference is that they cannot distribute any profits to members or directors. Nonprofit corporations do not normally pay any income tax—but there are strict conditions to be met.

Sole proprietorship

A PERSON who carries on a business by himself, with or without employes, is called a sole proprietor. His type of organization can be called an individual enterprise, or individual ownership. It is the simplest way to set up a business, requiring no authority from any government or agency as long as the person maintains the business under his own name only. There is no special law regulating sole proprietorship. You simply extend your right as an individual to make contracts, and to buy and sell property, into the operation of a business.

Every year a large number of new businesses of this type, chiefly in the retail and service trades, are started by individuals who have decided to work for themselves. These persons are usually tradesmen and former employes who believe they can establish a successful operation because of their special skills and knowledge. Although a lot of these enterprises are doomed to fail within two or three years, many others will succeed.

If the proprietor's products or services are in demand and if he works hard to please his customers, he will stand a good chance of success. His chances will be better if he seeks and accepts advice from such experts as chartered accountants, bank managers and lawyers. A retired businessman who has been successful in the same line would probably enjoy the chance to steer a novice past or around the many pitfalls.

Here's a short list of the pros and cons of going into business as a sole proprietor:

ADVANTAGES. First there is that hard-to-define thrill of being your own boss. In a shop, for instance, you can decide exactly what stock you will carry, you can normally set your own prices and your own hours of work.

The growth of the business is entirely up to you, and you will reap all the profit you earn. The sole proprietor does, of course, pay income tax but he is not liable for the tax on profits at the same rate that corporations must pay.

The assets will be yours alone. If you are successful, you can sell the business to someone else and retire early. You can pass the thriving business over to a son or son-in-law without being accused of favoritism.

DISADVANTAGES. Perhaps the main drawback of this type of business is that the proprietor has what is called unlimited liability if his business should be forced into bankruptcy. The law would require that, if need be, all of his assets, both business and personal, be seized and sold to pay outstanding debts. These could include his home, his car, even some of his furniture. (*See* "If the business fails," later in this chapter.)

Unless the business starts to make a profit at the outset, its growth could be hampered by lack of capital. The sole proprietor cannot sell shares to the public to raise money; he must get along on his own capital, plus whatever he can borrow from his family or friends, or from a bank or loan company. And, no matter what the advertisements may seem to say, it's difficult to borrow any substantial sum without providing solid security to the lender.

Choosing a name
It is only under his own name that the sole proprietor can go into business without any formality. If he wishes to trade

under another name—such as "Superior Furniture Sales" or "Redfern Wreckers" —he must file an application with the registrar of companies in his province. He must do this even if all he wants is to add the words "and Co." to his name. The desired name will be refused if it is too similar to that of any other trading or professional concern registered anywhere in Canada.

In Quebec, anyone going into business as a sole proprietor under any name must register it in each judicial district where he intends to operate.

Freedom of action

Because he is his own boss, the sole proprietor makes all his own business decisions. He is the purchasing manager, the sales manager, the advertising manager and the administrator. He directs the course of the enterprise by the wisdom of his own judgment and decisions. Within the ability of the business to pay, he can set his own salary, or bonuses.

If the sole proprietor is not sufficiently expert in all the avenues of the chosen endeavor, he can hire a specialist as an employe or engage an independent business adviser as a consultant.

Freedom is never as total as one would like to think. Depending on the nature of his business, the sole proprietor must abide by certain government regulations. For example, if he is planning to operate a small family café—maybe just a hamburger joint—he must still obey all the public health laws, and that can run into real money. Also, if he is not careful, he can become a slave to his business, as there is no one with whom he can share the responsibility.

In many ways, however, the sole proprietorship is often more effective and enduring than a partnership, especially for the hard-working, self-sufficient type of person. Partnerships are frequently spoiled, or made ineffective, by disagreements or personality clashes that cannot be foreseen at the outset.

Check the competition

Before you rush into a sole proprietorship, consider that your small enterprise may well be facing competition from much larger and stronger concerns. Some of them are probably public companies or partnerships that can call on far greater financial resources when needed. Your competitors may have several specialists on staff, while you must rely on yourself. And, no matter how skilled you are, no man is an expert at everything. Ask yourself what you know about bookkeeping, marketing, customer relations and the host of other specialties that are a part of business today.

Consider this as a likely example: the bigger business up the street can probably make stock purchases at a "quantity discount" that may not be available to you. How will you leap that hurdle?

Manufacturers are not permitted by law in Canada to set the retail prices of the goods they make; they can only "suggest" a price. This brings up another angle: it means that retailers can lower prices whenever they want to. How long could you survive if your main competition slashed the prices of some of your staple items?

The woman in business

The single woman, or the widow, can enter business anywhere in Canada in exactly the same way as any man, and on equal footing. There are, however, some business restrictions on the married woman arising from the marital relationship. Where a sole proprietorship (or a partnership) is involved, the question of the separate property of the married woman must be closely studied.

As was pointed out earlier, the personal possessions of a sole proprietor can be seized by creditors to pay the debts of a business that has failed. Where the bankrupt proprietor was a married man, this would not include any property listed in his wife's name. Similarly, in most provinces, if a married woman failed in business, only her personal assets could be seized to pay debts or to fulfill contracts she had made.

The one-man corporation

The personal corporation, a limited company controlled by one man, has now

545

Are women really persons?

FACTS

In 1927, five women—Henrietta Muir Edwards, a vice-president for Alberta for the National Council of Women, Nellie L. McClung, and Louise C. McKinney, who for several years were members of the Legislative Assembly of Alberta, Emily F. Murphy, a police magistrate, and Irene Parlby who was also a member of the Legislative Assembly and its Executive Council—presented a petition to the federal government to ask the Supreme Court of Canada to consider the question,

"Does the word 'persons' in Section 24 of the British North America Act include female persons?" This is the section which authorizes the appointment of qualified "persons" to be members of the Canadian Senate. It was the opinion of the incumbent minister of justice that only males could be appointed members of the Senate, but he felt it would be an act of justice to the women of Canada to obtain the opinion of the Supreme Court in Ottawa.

ARGUMENT

On behalf of the minister of justice, it was said that when the British North America Act was passed (1867) women could not by law perform the duties of public office by a general rule of law, and that women were excluded by the law and practice of parliamentary institutes, both in England and in Canada, and indeed in the whole English-speaking world, from holding a place in a legislative or deliberating body, or from voting in the election of a member of such body. The word "persons," when used in a statute passed in 1867, must be deemed to exclude females.

Counsel on behalf of the five women who petitioned said that the word "persons" when standing alone would certainly include women and that the use of the word "persons" was obviously used in the B.N.A. Act in its more general significance, as including women as well as men.

JUDGMENT

The Supreme Court stated that it was in no way concerned with the desirability or undesirability of the presence of women in the Senate. It nevertheless came to the conclusion that "persons" as used did not include women. The verdict was based on broad lines, mainly arising from the common law disability of women to hold public office, and from the consideration of various cases which had been decided under different statutes as to the right to vote for a member of parliament.

At this time, the judicial committee of the British Privy Council was the final court of appeal for Canada, and the five indomitable women decided to appeal to Westminster. They won. The Privy Council reversed the decision of the Supreme Court of Canada, on the grounds that the B.N.A. Act in enacting a constitution for Canada should not be given a narrow and technical construction but a large and liberal interpretation. The British Privy Council held that the exclusion of women from all public offices was a relic of more barbarous days.*

*Based on a famous series of cases (1927–1929).

disappeared from the financial scene. It was a legal device used by the wealthy to avoid certain taxes. (It is legal to *avoid* taxes, but illegal to *evade* them.) The personal corporation has now been replaced by the private corporation—this entity obtains a lower effective tax rate only after dividends are paid. (*See* "The private company," in this chapter.)

The private corporation can carry on any kind of financial, commercial or industrial business.

The main advantage under the old system arose when a person transferred his assets to a personal corporation, taking shares of the corporation in return. Since a company is a legal entity, it does not cease with the death of any (or even the sole) shareholder. The shares of the corporation were always subject to succession duties and estate taxes, but the assets themselves could be freely sold or otherwise transferred. This could be a valuable consideration, especially in a situation involving inheritance by a minor. A trustee or guardian, given discretionary powers over a minor's inheritance, could continue the business of the deceased man until the child became an adult.

A second benefit could arise if the taxes in the province where the personal corporation was located were lower than those where the sole shareholder actually resides.

It should be kept in mind, however, that although the personal corporation has vanished a limited company can still be created to hold the investments of individuals. Also, the advantages noted above for the old personal corporation are still retained by such a limited company (now to be called a *private corporation)*. But its profits are taxed as being earned "in its own hands" (as are, say, Imperial Oil's). In addition, unless such profits are paid out to the shareholders as dividends, they will be taxed at the maximum federal corporate tax rate.

A reduced corporate tax rate is applicable only to active Canadian business income of private corporations, and to investment income of private corporations that is paid out to shareholders as dividends.

It is of general interest to point out that in an examination of tax returns, the Department of National Revenue normally restricts itself to the four years preceding the current tax year. However, if fraud is proved in any one year, then there is no limit to how far back the arm of the department can reach.

Copyrights and patents

Other examples of one-man operations are provided by the author, the playwright, the songwriter and the inventor. The creative work of these persons is protected by law, to some degree, by the copyright and patent legislation. Apart from outright fees, "free-lance" entrepreneurs (that is, persons whose employment is not regular or paid for on a regular salary basis) are sometimes paid by royalties. These terms can be explained as follows:

COPYRIGHT is the sole right to produce, reproduce, perform or publish any literary, dramatic, musical or artistic work, in any form. Copyrights are regulated under the Canadian Copyright Act.

Copyright (literally, "the right to copy") may be acquired in either unpublished or published works. Publishing means to make available for sale. In the case of an unpublished work, the author automatically has a Canadian copyright in it if he is at the time of making it: (1) a British subject; (2) a citizen of a country that is a member of the Berne Copyright Convention; (3) a citizen of the United States or any other country which has granted Canadians reciprocal rights. If the work has been published, copyright exists provided the publication occurred within "Her Majesty's Dominions" or within any of the countries that are mentioned in this paragraph.

The symbol © followed by the name of the owner of the copyright and the date of the first year of publication should be printed among the first four pages of any book. The usual place for the copyright notice is on the page following the title page of the book—see page 4 of this book as an example. This notice protects the author's copyright in the 74 countries, including Canada and the United States, that signed the Universal Copyright Convention of 1952. The Berne Convention, mentioned before, was an earlier copyright agreement, not ratified by the United States, among other countries. There are other copyright agreements among countries—each requires some specific wording to protect the work in those countries. The copyright of this book, for example, is held by the Reader's Digest Association (Canada) Ltd., and no one may reproduce any part of it in any way without the written permission of the company.

It is not ideas that are copyright, but the language by which the ideas are expressed, or explained. If the author created a work during the course of his employment in the field in which the work was done, copyright in the work would remain with the employer, unless there was an agreement to the contrary. But copyright in a novel would not, for example, belong to an engineering firm that employed the author as a public relations officer. The "author" of a photograph is the owner of the original negative—sometimes the photographer, other times his employer.

Copyright may be assigned to another person either wholly or partly, and for use anywhere or possibly only in a restricted territory. Such an assignment is not valid unless signed by the author or his agent.

To give public notice of copyright, you can register the work in question on a printed form available from the Copyright and Industrial Designs Office, Consumer and Corporate Affairs, Canada, 50 Victoria St., Place du Portage, Phase 1, Hull, Quebec, K1A 0C9.

A routine copyright in Canada exists until the death of the author and 50 years thereafter. If an author died leaving an unpublished book, his heirs could copyright it upon the date of its publication, and the copyright would then last for 50 years. (This occurred, for instance, after the discovery and publication of Boswell's *London Journal*. Boswell died in 1795; his *Journal* was published almost a century and a half later in 1950 and will remain in copyright until the year 2000.)

In the case of joint authorship, the term of copyright is for the life of the author who dies last, plus 50 years.

A PATENT is a document issued under the provisions of the federal Patent Act, granting a person exclusive rights in an invention which was; (1) not known or used by others before he invented it, (2) not described in any patent or in any publication in any country more than two years before presentation of the application or (3) not in public use or on sale in Canada for more than two years before the application.

The legal term "invention" is the process of contriving or devising and producing something not previously known or existing, by means of independent investigation and experiment. It can also be a new and useful improvement to some existing process, art or manufacture. Do not confuse the term "discovery" with invention: "discovery" describes the bringing to light, or making known, of something that already existed, even if unknown in human experience.

To obtain a patent, the inventor, or his representative, must apply to the commissioner of patents in Ottawa. The application must include technical specifications and performance claims in thorough detail, as required by the Patent Act. Inventors usually hire a lawyer specializing in patents to help them through these technicalities. About 21,000 patents are granted each year in Canada; however, only a small portion are for inventions created by residents of Canada. The majority originate in the U.S.A.

If your patent is granted, it will be registered and you will enjoy the exclusive right of making, using and selling the invention to the public for 17 years. Since a long period (for checking and study) can elapse between the time you apply for a patent and the time it is granted, you can obtain an interim license to cover the waiting period. Generally, all patents are issued within 12 months of the date of application.

If your application for a patent is rejected, you may appeal the decision to the Federal Court (formerly the Exchequer Court) within six months.

548

A foreign inventor who is granted a patent in another country is protected in Canada if that foreign country allows Canadians a similar privilege (reciprocal rights), and as long as the inventor makes certain that he files an application in Canada within 12 months.

As with copyright, a patent can be transferred, in whole or in part; but such a transfer must be in writing. A patent can also be bequeathed.

The *Patent Office Record*, published weekly, contains a brief description of all new patents granted, and gives useful information for the would-be inventor. Printed copies of all patents granted since January 1, 1948, are available for a small charge. The Patent Office maintains a library where all Canadian and a great many foreign patents can be studied. For instance, you could spend some rainy days checking all the British patents granted from 1617 to the present.

A ROYALTY in the broadest sense is the agreed fee which the seller or manufacturer of a product pays to the person who holds the patent or copyright. It is usually calculated at a specific rate for each article sold or produced. Royalties are also paid for lumber taken from forests and for ore and oil taken from the earth. A royalty—usually an agreed percentage of the retail price of the work—is normally paid by a publisher to his author or composer.

If a royalty is paid to an individual or company outside Canada, a 15-percent withholding tax must be deducted before the payment is made, and the deduction sent to the receiver general for Canada. This applies to Canadians living abroad as well. Royalties are taxable in the hands of those who receive them; they are also deductible as costs or expenses in the hands of those who pay them.

Where a Canadian subsidiary has the right to the use in Canada of property (such as patents, trademarks, trade names and technical know-how) owned by the parent company, licensing agreements can be established to compensate the parent company for use of this right. Such agreements must have a proper business basis—that is, the compensation must be based on the fair market value of this right. Otherwise, the federal government will designate that all, or a portion, of such payments are dividends—and thus not deductible from income for tax purposes.

Building a better mousetrap

IF YOU HAVE been tinkering in your basement workshop on an invention, or an improvement on some existing machine or process, you should consider protecting the commercial rights to your brainchild.

Ralph Waldo Emerson is credited with the remark that the world will "beat a path" to the door of the man who "makes a better mousetrap." However, we might also recall the story of the recluse who labored secretly for most of his life in a barricaded laboratory and recently gave the world his invention—the alarm clock.

There are, in fact, many things on which it's a waste of time to seek patent protection. They include, among other "inventions":

• An improvement to a known device that would be obvious to a person skilled in that particular subject.
• A device or material whose only difference to known devices is a mere change of size, shape or degree.
• A device which has either no use or some illicit use.
• A device that doesn't work.
• A mere idea, suggestion, method, principle or recipe.
• Designs.
• A new variety of garden plant.
• The discovery of a naturally occurring substance.
• A process that depends entirely on artistic skill and leads to an ornamental effect.

Partnerships

WHEN TWO OR MORE persons decide to combine their qualifications, skills, energies and resources and go into business together, they will often form a partnership. This form of organization is particularly suited to smaller service industries where several skills are required, and to groups of professionals, including lawyers, accountants and architects. In some provinces, there is no legal limit to the number of partners, although a large group may get unwieldy and difficult to manage efficiently. Husbands and wives may combine in business as partners.

Each partner may agree to invest the same sum of money in a new enterprise, or each may put up a different amount. One partner may supply money and another only services. Funds cannot be solicited from the public. The partners may each take the same share of profit, or the shares may be varied. Usually, all partners join in making policy and major business decisions.

The partnership is a relatively simple and inexpensive form of setting up a business organization. Essentially, it is created by persons who enter into a contract, written or verbal, that defines the contribution of each and outlines the manner in which the earnings are to be shared. It is similar to the sole proprietorship, except that it involves several co-owners rather than just one owner. It can be started merely on the strength of a handshake and, conversely, it can sometimes result in ending a lifelong friendship. The advantages and disadvantages of partnerships are discussed later in this section.

Nine of Canada's provinces have specific partnership acts. (The exception is Prince Edward Island, where partnerships are covered by general laws.) In Quebec, partnerships are governed by the Civil Code, which, in this regard, is similar in general application. Three kinds of partnership are generally recognized across Canada:

COMMERCIAL PARTNERSHIP Sometimes referred to as *general partnership*, the commercial partnership is by far the most common. It can be set up for all manner of trades, manufacturing and other commercial enterprises. A key point is that members of the partnership are "jointly and severally" responsible for any debts of the partnership. This means that creditors can sue any *one* of the partners, or *all* of them, to pay the total debt if the assets held within the partnership are insufficient to cover a financial crisis. In the case of bankruptcy, the personal possessions and holdings of all the partners can be seized and sold.

Any one partner in a commercial partnership can commit the partnership to a deal or an expenditure, even without the consent of his fellow members. In the eyes of the law, each partner is the *agent* of the other. If one partner commits fraud or steals the money of clients, then all partners are responsible, even if they had no idea what was going on. Thus, it is essential that partners be chosen with the greatest of care.

NONTRADING PARTNERSHIP This type of venture (also known as the *civil partnership*) usually involves the pooling of professional qualifications, or of resources of an investment nature. The partners may buy and sell shares, as well as other securities and property, or they may offer services to the public in law, accountancy, medicine, engineering, advertising and other specialties.

Although in most matters of government regulation, including taxation, the non-trading partnership is treated in the same way as the commercial partnership, there are some exceptions. In Quebec, the members are not held "jointly" and "severally" liable for any debts of the partnership. Each partner can be forced to cover only a pro rata share of the debt; he is not responsible for his partners' shares.

If a single member of a civil partnership makes a special deal in the name of the partnership without the agreement of his fellow members, then he is binding only himself by the contract unless it could be proved that the whole partnership benefited from his act.

LIMITED PARTNERSHIP This type of partnership may be formed in all provinces except Prince Edward Island. It consists of one or more *limited* partners and at least one *general* partner. A limited (or *special*) partner is personally liable to all creditors up to the amount of capital he has invested—but his liability ceases at that level. The general (or *commercial*) partner is treated as though he were a part of a commercial partnership and, as explained above, has unlimited liability.

The limited partner must not have anything to do with the management of the enterprise, nor can his name be used by the partnership. He can, of course, share in the profits in any way laid down in the partnership agreement.

The limited partnership might appeal to the investor who has full confidence in the general working partners and is content to risk his capital without having any legal say in the conduct of the business. He might have no resource to offer the partnership other than his investment capital. Regardless of how small his contribution might be, his participation in the partnership must, however, be disclosed in the registration procedure.

Registration of partnerships

All commercial partnerships formed for mining, manufacturing or trading must be registered, usually with either the registrar of companies or at the office of the provincial secretary. The same applies to any other kind of partnership that operates under a name that is different to the names of the existing partners. For example, Smith, Macdonald and Jones might form Robin Enterprises. However, the name would be refused if it too closely resembled the name of any concern previously registered in Canada.

In registering a partnership, you must make a declaration on an official form, giving the full names and addresses of all partners, the name under which business will be transacted, plus a confirmation that the partners who are thus named are, in fact, the only partners. All partners must sign the declaration.

The time allowed for registration, as well as some of the conditions imposed in the procedure, vary from province to province. For example, the rule in Nova Scotia is that the partnership declaration must be filed with the Nova Scotia registrar of companies before business is begun; an annual fee is to be paid; the names of all partners must be printed on the firm's letterhead and on all invoices.

Quebec allows 15 days for registration after the partnership has been formed.

With a limited partnership, a certificate must be sworn before a notary public and then filed before business can start. The certificate must be signed by all partners. It must contain the names of all *general* and *limited* members (identifying which is which) and state the amount of capital each limited partner has put in, plus other routine details.

Again, there are some individual provincial requirements. Newfoundland, for instance, insists that if the limited partnership is to operate in several districts, it must be registered with the registrar of deeds in each district concerned. Furthermore, the partnership certificate must be published for six consecutive weeks in the *Newfoundland Gazette* and in either of two other journals named by the minister of provincial affairs.

Formal agreement advisable

Although a partnership can be formed without any written agreement, it is in the best interests of all participants that a written contract be made with the guidance of a lawyer. Many profitable enterprises have been forced out of existence because of disputes that have developed among the partners.

A written agreement can help in avoiding these difficulties. In this way each partner knows exactly where he stands in his legal relationship with his fellows. It is much easier to reconcile conflicting viewpoints and obtain agreement on troublesome facts at the beginning of a venture than it is after operations have begun. Before the terms of the contract of partnership are drawn up, many issues should be discussed and clarified, thus cutting down the chance of later misunderstanding or resentment. A solid partnership agreement should contain most of the following items:

(1) Names of the partners and the rights and duties of each.

(2) Amount to be invested by each partner and procedure for valuing any non-cash assets invested.

(3) Procedure for sharing profits and losses.

(4) Periodic audit by a public accountant and preparation of financial statements.

(5) Methods for resolving disputes.

(6) Withdrawals allowed each partner.

(7) Provision for dissolution.

If the partnership is based on only a verbal agreement—or possibly just an understanding among friends—there are some basic rules within commercial law that will come into play should a dispute develop. For example, the law will insist that every partner has the right to participate equally in the decision-making of the firm. Clear and accurate account books must be kept and made available for inspection and copying by all partners, upon request.

Generally speaking, the assets and funds of a partnership can be used only in the interests of the partnership, and not for the personal purposes of any partner.

Rights and duties
The most important rights and duties of partners should be written into the partnership agreement. In the clauses of some

provincial partnership acts, these are listed as follows:

(1) All partners are entitled to share equally in the capital and profits of the business, and must contribute equally toward the losses.

(2) If a partner incurs expenses on behalf of the firm, he is given credit for the amount spent.

(3) Every partner may take part in management.

(4) As the agent of the partnership, each partner may sign orders and contracts on behalf of the firm.

(5) No partner is permitted to receive remuneration for any special services.

(6) A new partner cannot be accepted into the firm without the consent of all existing partners.

(7) Any difference arising in the ordinary business of the partnership may be decided by a majority of the partners, but no basic change may be made in the business without the consent of all.

Not a "legal entity"
The law does not regard a partnership either as a person or as a company for tax purposes. Each partner must include his share of the partnership profit on his individual income tax return. The partnership's net income—in other words, the profit remaining after deducting all charges, outlays and losses—is thus taxable to the partners individually in the year in which it is earned.

An important point is that each partner reports and pays tax on his or her share of the profits earned by the partnership during the year, rather than the amount which he or she has drawn out of the business during the year. Even if there had been no withdrawals at all, the entire net income of the partnership is taxable each year. This is similar to the treatment given a sole proprietorship.

Size of partnership
Common sense and the demands of business efficiency tend to keep down the number of people involved in a partnership. However, in some parts of Canada, the law imposes a limit. For example, 20 partners is the maximum number

allowed in a commercial partnership in Saskatchewan, Alberta, the Yukon and the Northwest Territories. (If more people are to become involved, an incorporated company must be formed.) Thirty-five is the limit in British Columbia. In Newfoundland, there can only be ten.

In the other provinces, no limit is placed by law on the number of partners.

Partnership profits

The profit earned by a partnership often consists of three distinct elements: (1) compensation for the personal services rendered by the partners; (2) interest from invested capital; and (3) compensation for risk taking. These elements should be analyzed carefully and a profit-taking plan set up before the partnership agreement is drawn up and signed.

Bear in mind that any salaries authorized for any or all of the partners are regarded as a preliminary division of profits, not as a business expense.

Liability for debt

It must be emphasized that each *general* partner is personally responsible for all the debts of the firm. A wealthy partner has more to lose by going into partnership than a person of only modest means. The well-to-do person may be the only partner financially able to pay off creditors from his personal funds if the partnership should founder on the financial rocks. And almost certainly, the wealthy partner would be the one the creditors would sue. This partner would, however, be legally entitled to reimbursement from the other partners, but only up to a certain deadline date imposed by either the federal or provincial statute of limitations, depending on the nature of the partnership.

When a new member joins an existing partnership, he or she may or may not become responsible for debts incurred by the firm before his or her admission. This is something that would be decided by all of the partners together.

When a partner withdraws or retires from membership, he or she must give adequate public notice of withdrawal. If the notice is insufficient, the partner may be held liable for debts incurred by the partnership after he or she has left. This

A lead from the executive suite

IF CANADIANS as a nation are really serious about protecting the environment, leadership must be given by the present generation of business executives. They must demonstrate more respect for, and conservation of, the natural blessings of our land. Our forests, for example.

Pulp and paper products give Canada its richest category of exports. Thirty-seven percent of the newspapers, magazines and books of the free world are printed on Canadian paper—and it takes 18 of our trees to make one tonne of newsprint. Although trees are a "renewable resource," experts estimate that the demand for our forest products will increase 30 percent by the year 2000.

A significant saving in living trees, and an obvious benefit to ecological balance, could be gained if all businesses began to use a proportion of recycled paper—paper reclaimed from the blizzard of waste.

Half of all municipal garbage is paper; it is relatively simple for dry, clean paper to be kept apart from other trash—especially in our shops and offices. Collections of waste paper for recycling are already being made by the civic authorities in many large Canadian cities. Boy Scouts and other volunteer groups interested in environmental protection are organizing pick-up services.

It's actually good business for all taxpayers to help build the demand for recycled paper: every tonne of waste paper being carted to our city incinerators costs us $18 just to get it there and another $14 to burn it!

notice must be placed in the provincial *Gazette*; publication in a general newspaper is not deemed as evidence unless it can be proved that the advertisement was actually seen by a person or company concerned in any subsequent claim. Even the *Gazette* announcement is not sufficient for clients who had been dealing with the partnership before the time of the retirement. These customers should receive a special notice of the partnership's change in personnel.

The retiring partner remains liable for partnership debts existing at the time of his withdrawal unless the creditors agree to release him. The creditors have the right to claim immediate payment of debts because, by the retirement of one of the partners, the old partnership no longer exists. However, this problem is usually solved by the remaining partners signing a covenant, or pact, in which they formally take over the obligations of the retiring man, and by their notifying any creditors of, and getting their consent to, the agreement.

The "silent partner"
The well-known label, "silent partner," usually refers to the *limited* (or special) partner, described under the heading "Limited partnership" earlier in this section. However, it can also describe the general partner whose name is not included in the name of the firm—for whatever reason.

The term silent, or "dormant," stems from the fact that this partner is not permitted to take any part in the management of the business, or can he let his name be used in the title of the firm. However, he is responsible for the debts of the partnership—up to the level of his original contribution of capital when the partnership was set up.

If the silent partner forgets his role and speaks up, the penalty is liability as a *general* partner.

There is still another variant: the *ostensible* partner. This title describes someone who lends his name and reputation to a partnership, but has no actual financial interest in it.

He can also work for and draw a salary

from the firm. However, if the firm fails, the ostensible partner will be liable for its debts just like any general partner would in such a situation.

When partners disagree
A majority of the partners can overrule a minority on run-of-the-mill business matters, but no change may be made in the nature of the partnership business without the agreement of all partners.

Sometimes, in a serious deadlock, the minority may insist that the particular decision did not concern an ordinary matter but vitally affected the nature of the business. In these circumstances, the dispute might have to be settled in the courts.

Death or retirement
A partnership is automatically dissolved by the death (or bankruptcy) of any member. To determine the amount owing to the estate (or, if there are debts, *by* the estate) of the deceased partner, it is usually necessary to close the books and prepare financial accounts. Thus, each partner would be credited with his share of the net income earned during that part of the accounting period—perhaps the fiscal year, depending on the policy of the partnership—ending with the date of dissolution. The partnership would then, in most cases, be reconstituted, or renewed. This occurs as part of the process known in law as *novation*.

A partner who retires may sell his or her interest to the remaining partners or, with the consent of the other partners, he or she may sell his or her interest to an outsider. If the retiring partner sells outside, the payment by the incoming partner goes directly to him or her. There is no change in the assets (what they own) or liabilities (what they owe) of the partnership. If the retiring partner sells his or her interest to the remaining partners, he or she may receive a greater or smaller amount than the balance of his or her capital account. The amount received will depend upon the present market value of partnership assets and also upon the goodwill developed during the life of the partnership.

Dissolution and liquidation

A partnership is *dissolved* when a new partner is added or when an old one withdraws. This does not mean that the business is discontinued—there might be no interruption at all. It simply indicates a change in the membership of the firm.

The process of breaking up and discontinuing a partnership business is called *liquidation*. When dissolution is followed by liquidation, the net assets of the partnership are shared by the partners, but not until all claims of creditors and liquidation fees have been paid. All the gains or losses that existed at the time of liquidation are allocated to the various partners. Normally, the profit-and-loss sharing arrangement in the partnership agreement will govern these allocations. Then the capital, or net assets, are calculated.

Where no fixed term of partnership was agreed upon, any partner may end the partnership by giving notice to the other partners. Where a partnership continues after a fixed term, then the same rights and duties continue to apply to the partners. On the application of one of the partners, a court may order that a partnership be dissolved if a partner is found to be of permanently unsound mind or incapable of performing his duties, or has been found guilty of conduct that would seriously affect the transaction of business by the partnership.

Distribution of assets

When a partnership is being liquidated, it may take quite a while to turn the assets into cash. The partners may not want to wait until this is done before receiving any money. In that case, a liquidator agreed to by the partners (or appointed by the court) will probably distribute the cash to the partners as it becomes available. Thus, cash can be distributed before the full extent of the monies available becomes known. The appointed liquidator must follow a certain procedure: first, pay all outside creditors; as each asset is sold, assume that no further amount will be gained on it, and allocate any loss to the partners in their profit-and-loss sharing ratio; assume that a partner is insolvent if his capital account is thrown into a deficit position, and charge whatever amount he is overdrawn to the other partners in the ratio of their share of the capital accounts prior to liquidation; finally, distribute the cash to each partner in accordance with each one's investment in the partnership.

Registering a partnership

ALL PROVINCES require partnerships and proprietorships to be registered, usually within a set time after founding. A special form is usually provided in which the fine print contains basic instructions.

The back of the form provides space for the names, addresses, signatures and status (*i.e.* as general or limited partners) of all members of the new firm. The form requires limited partners to list their contributions to the capital of the business.

The registration usually expires after five years, but it may be renewed—though the responsibility for renewal rests with the business concern, not the government.

The form warns that registration does not confer on the partnership or proprietorship any right to a name that it is not registered to use, or may it conduct any other business than that for which it was formed.

If the partnership is dissolved, another form must be filled in. Until the break-up of a partnership is registered, all the persons who signed the first form as partners remain liable for the firm's debts and decisions.

The dissolution form calls for particulars similar to those on the registration form—names and addresses of all partnership members or of the proprietorship. The fee for filing these forms is nominal.

The private company

THE LEGAL RIGHT of a group of individuals to form a private or public corporation (also called a joint-stock company) is one of the keystones of business in a free-enterprise society. The company assumes an identity separate from that of the individual owners, whose responsibility as shareholders for the company's debts is restricted to the amount of their investment in the company's stock. Any legal actions brought against the company do not involve the shareholders personally.

Without this legal protection, it is doubtful if the introduction of promising but risky business ideas and the expansion and continual renewal of established industry could ever have taken place at the level which has brought such tremendous economic progress and benefits to free-enterprise nations.

A company can be incorporated in Canada by the authorization of any provincial government or by the federal government, after formal application. Incorporation federally, under the Canada Business Corporations Act, is advisable for companies planning to trade or operate in more than one province.

The application forms ask for the following information: the names of the shareholders; the number of shares to be authorized and issued; the name of the company and its status (private or public), its objects or purpose, as well as a list of restrictions on the scope of the business the company will be operating. If all the legal requirements are satisfied, articles of association, letters patent or a certificate of registration will be issued to the company. This document will become the *charter* of the new corporation.

The interim directors then meet to prepare bylaws for the regulation of the company's affairs. These are presented for confirmation by the shareholders at their first meeting, which should be called as soon as possible after incorporation. At that meeting, the shareholders will elect a board of directors, who then take over control from the interim directors. An auditor (a chartered accountant) is appointed and a bank account opened in the company's name.

A certain style of share certificate is approved and a sample pasted into the firm's minute book. A copy of all company resolutions, signed by a director, will also go into that book. A register of shareholders and directors, a share ledger and a register for share transfers complete the basic administration records.

Professional guidance

Incorporating a business can be done without professional assistance. There are many books and brochures available that will tell you how to go about it—including a client information kit on various aspects of incorporation issued by the federal department of Consumer and Corporate Affairs. However, the theory is one thing and the actual practice is another.

It would be unwise for the novice to proceed with a business incorporation without specialist advice on such technical matters as authorized, issued and paid-up capital, the value of the shares to be issued, company objects and internal organization.

The smaller operator should consult a chartered accountant about the wisdom of incorporation from a business viewpoint. The accountant will explain how such a move could affect the taxation picture. He might advise his client to set up a *sole proprietorship*, or perhaps a *partnership*.

The lawyer in general practice and the chartered accountant usually have a lot of experience in company incorporation, particularly with small companies (90 percent of all Canadian companies are private and most of them small). Accountants are qualified to advise on all aspects of the formation of a company, but a solicitor should be called in to handle the actual incorporation.

In drawing up the official letters of incorporation, it is common for the lawyer's office staff to act as the incorporators. The reason is simple: the inconvenience of gathering the real promoters together at various times to sign the many forms involved. When the formation is complete, the lawyer's staff transfer their share allotments to the real holders and resign as directors. It may sound confusing, but it works well in practice.

Provincial governments spin a complex web of regulation around the operation of corporations. There are many statutory forms to be filled in and detailed annual reports to be filed. Some of these will seem bewildering to the untrained eye, but to the expert they are as clear as crystal—or so the experts stoutly maintain.

Power of directors
Although the shareholders do hold the decisive power—in that they can combine to wield a majority vote at a company's annual meeting—the business is in fact run from day to day by the elected directors or their executive appointees. Shareholders do not have the right to own any particular asset of the company. However, they are entitled to any dividends declared out of company profits, and to any funds realized after all creditors are paid from the sale of the company's assets should it go into liquidation. (*See* "If the business fails" in this chapter.) Of course, with the private company, the largest shareholders are usually also the directors.

Between annual meetings, the board of directors can appoint new directors to fill vacancies caused by death or resignation; these appointees serve at least until the next annual meeting. A company itself never dies; it has to be killed by formal action. The Hudson's Bay Company, for example, is still thriving after more than 300 years.

The president of a company must be a director; the vice-presidents and secretary treasurer are often directors, but not necessarily so. These persons (and other directors appointed to specific departments) are usually also salaried employes of the corporation. However, larger organizations often elect experienced men (or women) to the board from the outside to strengthen the expertise of the management; such appointees normally are paid a director's fee set by the board.

The director must at all times act in the best interests of the company and of the shareholders. Also, he must not use for his own financial advantage any information gained because of his appointment.

Points about privacy
The private corporation is mainly distinguished from the public corporation by the following factors:

(1) The right to transfer shares is restricted in some manner.

(2) The number of shareholders is generally limited to 50.

(3) The public may not be invited to buy shares.

(4) The financial statements are private documents.

The private company structure is mainly used for incorporating small and medium-sized business enterprises, where the number of investors is small and the need for capital is not massive. The vast majority of companies incorporated in Canada are private corporations. Many are wholly owned subsidiaries of other corporations, with each operating as a branch or department of the other enterprise but under a separate name. Companies which restrict, or limit, the transfer of their shares in some way are sometimes known as *close corporations*.

A private company can be converted

into a public company by obtaining *supplementary letters patent* from the same office where the original incorporation was granted. Such a move by a federally chartered company requires that a special bylaw be passed by the directors and then approved by a two-thirds majority of the shareholders. It is equally possible for a company to change from a public to a private status, after satisfying certain legal requirements.

Because the private company has no funds at stake in its operation that belong to the general public, the law gives it certain freedoms forbidden to public corporations. For instance, the treasury of a private company can lend money to a director to purchase shares held by another shareholder in the company. However, any such loan is subject to certain conditions set out in the Canada Business Corporations Act. Also, the financial statements made to the annual meeting do not have to disclose the sums paid to directors, as long as the shareholders have consented to this.

Share transfer restrictions

Although the federal and provincial acts state that the right to transfer shares of private companies must be restricted, they do not specify the type of restriction. It could take almost any form, although some are more common than others.

In practice, the almost universal restriction is that the board of directors must consent to any transfer. This gives the directors of a private company the right to approve or refuse a proposed member of the company—much as partners can determine whether they will admit a new person into their partnership.

Before you decide to invest in a private company, consider what would happen if, at a later date, you wanted to cash in your shares. Since the directors would have to agree to the transaction, and since those directors would most probably be drawn from among the larger shareholders, you, as a minority stockholder, might find that the majority shareholder is the only party interested in purchasing your holdings. Not only that, the board of directors is in

Writing a business letter

EVERYONE IN BUSINESS, from the sole proprietor of a corner grocery to the president of the large private or public corporation, should know how to write a competent and clear business letter. The telephone and telex communicate many day-to-day decisions but, in all deals with legal aspects, one side or the other is likely to require specific confirmation in writing. A verbal agreement—even a simple handshake—may be "as right as rain," but it is the signed piece of paper that stands up in court.

Every letter mutely says much about its sender. If you mail out a sloppy, badly written or poorly typed letter on low-quality stationery, you risk creating an instant "unbusinesslike" impression. This can prejudice a profitable deal even before you have made your pitch to a potential customer of your goods or services.

There are seven components to the typical efficient business letter: date, inside address, salutation, body, complimentary close, company name and signature. Each of these has earned its place by the exclusive job it does.

Without the inside address (full name of the addressee plus postal address in detail), the recipient is not clearly identified; similarly, the inclusion of the full name of the sending company (plus the title of the signing officer) identifies the "party of the second part."

The salutation in business letters—how to address the recipient—often causes confusion. It depends on how formal you wish to be. There are four common styles, ascending in formality: "Dear Mr. Jones," "My dear Mr. Jones," Dear Sir," and (very formal) "Sir." If the letter is addressed to a company, the salutation is, "Gentlemen."

a position to virtually set the price of your stock.

One of the main purposes behind restricting the transfer of shares is to enable the majority of the original shareholders to block the entry of well-financed outsiders who might well swallow them at a gulp when reports of the company's profits leak out.

Limit on shareholders

Until recently, the minimum number of shareholders allowed in private corporations was set by most provinces at three. New legislation, however, has reduced the requirement to one shareholder in British Columbia, Alberta, Ontario and Quebec. Although the maximum number is generally 50, there is no restriction on the number of employes who may be shareholders in a private company.

The limit of 50 shareholders represents the mathematical distinction between private and public companies. Although the figure is arbitrary, it provides a point at which the members of a company must decide between restricting their numbers (and their influence in the economic sphere) or converting the business into a public company.

Since it is illegal for a private company to invite the public to invest, the shares of private corporations are never quoted on the stock market.

Raising money privately

Barred from raising money by the public sale of shares, the directors of the private company first use the investment capital of the shareholders and then the funds provided by commercial operations. Sometimes, however, this is not enough if a large outlay of money—perhaps needed to purchase production machinery—is required, or if a large inventory of goods must be accumulated in advance of a selling season. In this situation, management must decide whether to ask the shareholders to contribute more of their own personal funds, or to turn to a chartered bank or other financial institution to borrow money.

One of the main uses of bank credit is to make loans to companies, partnerships or individuals for relatively short periods. (*See* Chapter 7, "When you borrow.")

Sellers will borrow from banks to help them carry their accounts and notes receivable, while buyers will resort to bank loans to pay the bills of insistent creditors, or possibly to take advantage of cash discounts. In the majority of loans to private companies, banks will insist that the loan be personally guaranteed by the controlling shareholder of the business. Although there is no shortage of other private lending corporations, Canadian businesses normally stick to the banks for financing. The major exception is when a company needs to borrow an amount for expensive capital items which would push the company's bank debt in excess of the credit limit set by the bank for that particular corporation.

Two other methods of financing that are open to the private company are through a federal or provincial government loan agency, or by the sale of equity (ownership) in the company. The first usually involves a considerable delay; the second is not popular because it involves sharing some of the control of the company with outsiders.

The costs of incorporation

The average fee charged by a province or the federal government for the incorporation of a private company is generally between $150 and $250. The fee is determined on the basis of a sliding scale according to the size of the authorized capital stock.

The lawyer's fee for handling an incorporation is usually between $400 and $500, plus approximately $50 for miscellaneous disbursements. It is not unusual, however, for the larger legal firms to charge more, depending on the amount of work involved. The more complex the corporate structure, the more legal work required and the higher the lawyer's fee.

While you are not required by law to hire a lawyer for incorporation, you are strongly advised to do so. If you are already organized and equipped to go into a business and all you need is incorporation, the cost of a lawyer to ensure that your organization is watertight is probably only a fraction of the outlay you are contemplating.

Don't skimp on this point.

Some tax advantages

There is a widespread notion that incorporation—"becoming a company"—confers a host of tax advantages on shareholders and directors, compared with the situation of a mere employe whose income tax is deducted from the wage envelope or salary cheque. There is always talk of "loopholes" and of 50-foot cruisers fueled on company expense accounts. If these tales were true, it wouldn't be saying much for the ability of our civil service, which includes accountants and financial experts who are as qualified, and as imaginative, as those hired by industry. In a matter as complex as corporate taxation, there are sure to be loopholes. But they are likely to be blocked by legislation as fast as they are discovered.

There are many different rules for taxing companies. Income tax, as it relates to individuals, is determined from a set of graduated rates, based on the individual's "ability to pay." The "top bracket" may be paying a tax rate of more than 60 percent, but these levels rarely apply in actual practice. In the separate schedule of income tax levied on the net profits of business corporations, the maximum rate normally runs between 41 and 46 percent depending on the type of industry. Some of those individuals who have incorporated as private corporations will pay only 21 percent on active business income, thus avoiding the highest tax brackets of the graduated rate structure.

This can be a valuable concession for the Canadian businessman, but it must be remembered that he will first have to pay the graduated rate on any salary he takes from his business and, secondly, he will have to pay personal tax on any dividends he is paid from the profits declared after corporation tax has been taken off. However, a dividend tax credit provides some relief. If he knowingly uses the funds of the company to cover private expenses, the law will consider it the equivalent of theft. Some prominent businessmen have been sent to prison for this offense.

To encourage the small and speculative business, the minister of revenue has allowed private companies a tax deduction to arrive at the 21 percent rate mentioned above. This applies only on the first $200,000 of annual profits, and the concession can be lost if the company fails to pay sufficient dividends or earns in excess of $200,000 a year.

When a business is incorporated, the company may employ the wives of shareholders and deduct their salaries as operating expense. This practice can produce an additional tax cut for a family, because the owner can divide salary payments between himself and his wife. This will usually obtain a lower combined tax rate than if the total salary was paid to himself. But even this is not as simple as it may sound.

The tax collectors look closely at such an arrangement, and may refuse the tax advantage to the husband if they feel that the wife does not actually perform a service to the corporation. They may ask if another person would have to be hired to do her company work if the wife was not on salary. If the answer is "yes," the wife's working situation will be described as being "at arm's length." And that's okay.

The tax inspectors will also look closely at any such incorporated ventures as the "gentleman's farm." Only the genuine "active business" will be entitled to any corporate tax advantages. Under the Income Tax Act, the definition of "active business" covers such activities as manufacturing, processing property for sale or lease, exploring or drilling for natural resources, mining, operating an oil or gas well, construction, logging, farming, fishing or transportation. The act also defines ventures not entitled to corporate-tax advantages. These "nonqualifying business" operations include the professional practices of accountants, dentists, lawyers, medical doctors, veterinarians or chiropractors, as well as enterprises that provide managerial, administrative, financial, maintenance or other similar services to one or more businesses connected to the same corporation. A personal-services business falls outside the definition of "nonqualifying business."

The public corporation

IT IS USUALLY the public corporation that conducts major undertakings in Canadian business—retailing, manufacturing, mining, forestry, construction, communications, financial and service industries. The laws that govern the private company are basically the same as those of the public corporation, except that in the latter there is an added emphasis on protection of the general public. The method of incorporation is the same.

The public corporation is distinguished from the private corporation principally by the fact that some of its shares are offered to the public for sale, and may be traded on one or more of Canada's stock exchanges. You can become a co-owner of any Canadian public corporation merely by paying the price asked for a block of shares. There are normally no restrictions on the sale of the shares and no limits on the number of shareholders. Under unusual circumstances, however, stock exchange authorities may halt trading in a particular stock.

Owners of a private company quite frequently will convert their business to a public corporation—it's called "going public"—either to obtain additional financing for a capital project or to obtain the best selling price for their business.

Public companies can raise money for expansion, or other purposes, by issuing to the public common (voting) shares or preferred shares, bonds, debentures or guaranteed-interest certificates. These are described in detail in Chapter 8.

The trading name

If you seek to do business under a name other than your own, the trading name you select must not already be in use by another company, nor may it be so close to another already registered name as to make confusion of the public possible.

A lot of midnight oil has been burned trying to think up an impressive or catchy business name, but there's little evidence to prove it is worth the effort. The Irving, Eaton, Steinberg and Woodward companies, for example, do not appear to have been handicapped by settling for the simple family name.

Under a federal order-in-council of 1909, you are not allowed to use words like "royal" or "imperial"—unless, of course, you happen to be directly connected with the Crown. In Newfoundland, you may not use the words "Canada," "Newfoundland" or "Labrador" in a company name without special consent. Alberta has restrictions on the use of words like "mortgage," "trust" and "loan." In Quebec your company must have a French name—or at least names in both French and English.

You can save considerable time and expense by checking the register of company names before you send in an application for registration or letters patent.

All public trading companies not formed by special acts of the federal parliament or provincial legislatures (or by royal charter) must have "Limited" ("Ltd.")—or the equivalent in French—as the last word of the company name. Quebec will also allow, as alternatives: "Company," "Corporation," or "Incorporated" ("Co.," "Corp.," or "Inc."). This tells the public that the liability of the owners of the business is limited to the amount of their investment.

If a company wants to change its name, it must produce evidence that this is the wish of two-thirds of its shareholders. An application is then made to the registration authority and, if approved, *supplementary letters patent* will be issued. Notice of the transaction will be published in the official *Gazette*. A change of name, once it has been authorized, has no effect on the rights and responsibilities of the company.

Frequently, a public corporation will transact business under one or more trade names, all of which are protected as registered trademarks. These names are adopted to direct public attention to a certain product in such a way that it cannot be confused with a competitor's product. The trade name is usually more relevant to the product than it is to the name of the corporation. Ski-Doo, a registered trade name of the Bombardier Company of Quebec, provides a well-known example.

Once a corporation has registered an original trade name (in connection with its products), it is entitled to the exclusive use of that name in Canada, and is protected against other companies or persons using it. The registration must be renewed every 15 years.

Shareholders' rights

The ownership of common stock in a public limited company carries the following collective rights:

(1) To participate in the voting to elect directors, thus having a voice in the management of the business.

(2) To share in profits by receiving dividends declared by the directors.

(3) To share in the distribution of assets if the company is liquidated.

Acting collectively, shareholders also appoint the company's auditors and accept or reject bylaws passed during the year by the directors. If an individual shareholder is at the same time a director, executive or employe of the company, that status must always be known to the other shareholders.

The majority must rule in final decisions taken by corporations. Thus, those holding more than half of the voting stock (even 50.1 percent) can elect or reject the directors who actually run the business.

A minority of shareholders could appeal to the courts against some decision of the majority only if the disputed decision or action was *ultra vires* (beyond the powers granted in the charter) or patently unfair to the minority.

If enough of the shareholders demand it, the minister concerned may have the affairs of a corporation investigated. The minister will decide what percentage is "sufficient" to have such an investigation made. While a company is governed principally by its own regulations, it is also bound by the overriding dictates of corporation law.

A shareholder in a public corporation is allowed to transfer (by sale or gift) all or any of his shares at any time. The new shareholder assumes all the rights of the old one as soon as the transaction is recorded in the share register kept at the head office of the company.

Every shareholder is entitled to a copy of the annual financial statement and of the auditor's report, but he does not have the right to inspect the company's books of accounts.

Other rights withheld from shareholders that are worth mentioning include the following:

(1) The ownership of shares does not give a person the right to intervene in the management of the company.

(2) The shareholder is not automatically entitled to transact business on the company's behalf.

(3) Present shareholders do not necessarily have a prior right over outsiders to subscribe in proportion to their present holdings for additional shares issued by the company.

(4) Generally speaking, the law does not permit a shareholder to borrow money from the public corporation of which he is part owner.

Approval of bylaws

The bylaws of a corporation—sometimes referred to as the *articles of association*—are the detailed operating rules for the company's day-to-day affairs. The power to originate bylaws lies in the hands of the directors; these bylaws must be confirmed by a majority of the shareholders, usually at the next annual meeting. By-laws fall into three main categories:

The first provides the general operating rules for carrying on the business of the company. These rules are found in the *bylaws of general application*, usually passed at the initial meeting of the shareholders. These bylaws deal with the number and qualifications of directors, their term of office, the required notice to be given for meetings of the board of directors, the categories of executive officers, and provisions for voting by proxy and for the declaration of dividends.

A second purpose of bylaws is to authorize a change in the incorporating document itself—such as a change in the name, objects, or authorized capital or the conversion from a public to a private company (or vice versa). A general meeting of the shareholders must confirm such bylaws by the majority (usually two-thirds) required under the relevant statute.

A third purpose of bylaws is to give the directors express authority from the shareholders to carry out specific transactions that are not covered under the general bylaws. For example, a special bylaw would be needed to approve some deal in which a director, or directors, had a personal interest.

A *bylaw* can be described as an expression of official company policy, a permanent rule binding the actions and decisions of the directors. By comparison, a *resolution* is a decision of the directors, passed to take care of the day-to-day operation of the company.

In provinces where companies are incorporated by registration (rather than by *letters patent*), a copy of the intended by-laws must be filed with the application. In fact, a model set of approved *articles* is supplied with the application form. Many companies simply adopt the set in its entirety.

If no different set of articles is supplied and approved, the registrar of companies will suggest that the directors adopt and approve the provisions in the model set as the legal rules for the internal operation of the new company.

The bylaws of a public corporation do

Working for the government

IN THE FIRST HALF of the 1970s, Ottawa expanded both the number of its employes and their incomes at dizzying speed. For example, between 1970 and 1975, the number of employes under the aegis of the Public Service Commission rose by 74,000. Some of the reasons for this growth were the new social programs introduced in this period, and the expansion of many traditional services, to accommodate the "baby boom" generation which was straining the existing resources of government services.

Austerity measures introduced in 1975 slowed the annual growth rate of the public service to less than one percent a year, compared to the six-percent growth in the preceding years. By 1978, the number of employes registered the first decrease since 1970, declining by 1.3 percent from 282,788 to 279,209 employes. By 1982, the number had fallen to 225,582—a 20-percent drop since 1977.

This total did not include the large staffs of Crown corporations such as the Canadian Broadcasting Corporation, Canada Mortgage and Housing, Canadian National Railways, Petro-Canada, Air Canada and Canada Post and many other government-controlled bodies. When all these employes on the federal payroll were lumped together, the total was 583,752 (1982).

In the seven years from 1976 to 1983, the federal public service payroll increased from $3.7 billion to $6.3 billion. In 1983, the average public service salary climbed from $15,944 in 1976 to $25,906 in 1983. Those classified as "executive, scientific and professional" staff averaged $40,806 in 1983.

not have to be made public knowledge, but they must be available for inspection (during business hours) by shareholders or creditors. Also, they must not contravene the laws of the land, the specific corporation law of the province, or the letters patent or registration certificate of the company.

Election of officers

The order of authority in a corporation descends as follows: shareholders, directors, executives (officers) and employes.

The shareholders alone have the right to elect the directors of a corporation and, conversely, to remove them from their position. Elections for the board of directors are held at the annual general meeting of the shareholders. Some provinces insist that there should be at least three directors. However, there has been a general trend to allow companies with only one director. This arrangement is permitted in British Columbia, Alberta, Saskatchewan, Quebec and Nova Scotia.

A shareholder has one vote for each share that he holds.

Any shareholder may offer himself as a candidate for election to the board of directors.

When there are more than six directors, they may, with the permission of the shareholders, elect an executive committee from among themselves. The decisions of the committee would be subject to review by the whole board. The Canada Business Corporations Act insists that an executive committee must consist of at least three members, two of whom must be present to form a quorum. Under the provisions of the act, however, a company with only one director may have an executive committee of only one person.

Voting by proxy

Sometimes it is difficult for shareholders to attend the annual general meeting of a corporation in which they hold an interest. Instead of losing out on the chance to cast their vote, they are able to vote by proxy—that is, by assigning their voting rights to another shareholder who will be present. This is done by signing a special printed proxy form in the name of the person to whom the rights are temporarily assigned. Such a person may be a director of the company or any other shareholder.

When there are two opposing groups of shareholders within a corporation, a contest may develop to gather "proxies" from shareholders who cannot attend to vote for themselves.

Each group solicits all the registered shareholders trying to persuade those nonattenders to assign their forms in such a way as to suit the purpose of the pressure group. When big companies and millions of dollars are involved, these "proxy fights" can become both dramatic and bitter confrontations.

Payment of dividends

The term "dividend" is generally understood to mean a distribution of cash by a company to its shareholders. Dividends represent one of the main reasons for investment in public corporations. The amount of cash involved is usually determined as a specific amount per share— for instance, a dividend of $1 per share. Thus, the total amount received by each shareholder is in proportion to the number of shares he owns.

Both the decision to declare a dividend, and how much to set it at are made by the directors, not the shareholders. Once the dividend is declared, it becomes a legal responsibility of the company and cannot be taken back, amended or revoked. There is no limit to the number of dividends that a company can declare.

A dividend need not be in cash. It can also be paid in the form of additional shares of a company's own share capital. This type of distribution is called the *stock dividend*. A shareholder who receives a stock dividend will possess an increased number of shares; however, his equity— that is, his amount of ownership—in the company will be no larger than before because every shareholder gets a proportionate number of new shares, too.

It is illegal for a company to pay dividends out of its operating capital.

If you have been intrigued by the rise or fall of the prices of certain shares on the stock market, one of the reasons for this fluctuation could be that the prices are reacting to a corresponding rise or fall in the dividend declared by the company concerned.

Generally, a 33⅓ percent tax credit is allowed to individual shareholders on dividends derived from Canadian-owned companies.

Profit-sharing plans

Profit-sharing plans are basically incentive arrangements under which a company's workers share in a prearranged percentage of the annual net profit. The percentage is decided by management.

Originating in France in 1842, the idea has not been widely introduced in North America except in cases where, for instance, unit or department managers have to be left without close supervision.

The workers' share of profit is paid by the corporation to a trustee appointed to act for the employes. Under a variation of this plan, the employe contributes to the company in order to share in the profits. Where such a plan is in force, the employes may make their contributions to the trustee, if the plan requires or allows it.

Under any approved profit-sharing plan, all amounts allocated must be paid to the employe not later than 90 days after the ending of his employment, his 71st birthday, his death or the date of termination of the plan.

The routine profit-sharing plan accepted by the federal authorities has the tax advantage that the employe does not pay tax on the profits allocated to him until he actually receives them.

Keeping books of account

All corporation legislation, both provincial and federal, requires corporations to keep *books of account*, from which the annual financial statements are drawn. These books must contain a record of all sums of money taken in or paid out by the company, all sales and purchases, all assets and liabilities, and any other transactions that affect the financial state of the company. Only the auditor, as representative of the shareholders, and the directors have the right to examine these books. If a shareholder suspects that something is wrong, he may ask the auditor to investigate; however, the auditor does not have to comply.

What time is it over there?

BUSINESS is international these days, with telephone and cable linking the trade centers of the world in a flash. Satellite space stations in permanent orbit are carrying some of this traffic, including special television broadcasts of major events. The day may not be far distant when telecommunication offers video-telephone service anywhere in the world.

The earth, however, still pursues its accustomed path around the sun and is likely to continue to do so for a while yet. Therefore it is useful to remember that when you are just leaving for a business luncheon, your colleague overseas may well be turning in to bed. The following chart gives you the time in other cities when it's midday in Ottawa.

At noon in Ottawa it's 2 A.M. tomorrow in Tokyo. Other handy comparisons:

City	Time	City	Time
Alèxandria	7.00 p.m.	London	6.00 p.m.
Amsterdam	6.00 p.m.	Madras	10.30 p.m.
Antwerp	6.00 p.m.	Madrid	6.00 p.m.
Athens	7.00 p.m.	Marseilles	6.00 p.m.
Bangkok	*12 midnight	Melbourne	*3.00 a.m.
Berlin	6.00 p.m.	Montreal	12 noon
Berne	6.00 p.m.	Moscow	8.00 p.m.
Bombay	10.30 p.m.	Munich	6.00 p.m.
Brussels	6.00 p.m.	Naples	6.00 p.m.
Buenos Aires	1.00 p.m.	New York	12 noon
Cairo	7.00 p.m.	Paris	6.00 p.m.
Calcutta	10.30 p.m.	Peking	*1.00 a.m.
Chicago	11.00 a.m.	Pretoria	7.00 p.m.
Colombo	10.30 p.m.	Rangoon	11.30 p.m.
Copenhagen	6.00 p.m.	Rio de Janeiro	2.00 p.m.
Dresden	6.00 p.m.	Rome	6.00 p.m.
Dublin	6.00 p.m.	Rotterdam	6.00 p.m.
Edinburgh	6.00 p.m.	San Francisco	9.00 a.m.
Florence	6.00 p.m.	Singapore	*12.30 a.m.
Gibraltar	6.00 p.m.	Stockholm	6.00 p.m.
Halifax	1.00 p.m.	Sydney	*3.00 a.m.
Hamburg	6.00 p.m.	Tokyo	*2.00 a.m.
Hobart	*3.00 a.m.	Vancouver	9.00 a.m.
Hong Kong	*1.00 a.m.	Vienna	6.00 p.m.
Istanbul	7.00 p.m.	Washington	12 noon
Lisbon	6.00 p.m.	Wellington	*5.00 a.m.
Liverpool	6.00 p.m.	Winnipeg	11.00 a.m.

*Denotes following day

The financial statements which are presented at each annual meeting of shareholders must contain a profit-and-loss statement for the year under review, a report on any surplus at the end of trading, a balance sheet of company assets and liabilities, and the report of the auditor.

Under the Canada Business Corporations Act, the penalties for improper financial disclosure are now generally fixed at a maximum of $5,000.

Annual returns required

Every corporation must make several annual reports to the governing federal or provincial authorities. These include a statement, signed by a director or appointed officer of the company, giving the following facts: (1) the name of the corporation; (2) the date and style of incorporation (by letters patent or registration); (3) the address of the head office; (4) the date and place of the last annual meeting; (5) the names and addresses of all directors.

A signed copy of the financial statements and of the auditor's report have to be filed with the government. The government also requires reports on what is called *insider trading* (when directors, officers and knowledgeable employes buy or sell shares of their own companies), changes of personnel on the board of directors (these to be sent to the government within 15 days of the change), returns on capital debt, and payments to nonresidents of Canada. Public corporations must also report any contemplated offer of securities to the public. The secretary of any incorporated company, who is usually an authority on the filing of reports, can tell you that even this list is far from complete.

The deadline for filing these returns is often June 1. However, there are many provincial variations in filing dates. Nova Scotia, for example, requires all provincial, federal and foreign corporations to file annual statements by January 31—these to include data up to December 31 of the previous year. In British Columbia, you can have until March 1 to file December 31 reports. However, all the provinces insist that companies file financial statements and auditor's report no later than seven days after these have been mailed to the shareholders.

Crown corporations

Successive governments have created what are called Crown corporations to conduct certain business in which, they believe, the public has a special interest. At the time of this writing, there were nearly 50, although not all of them were engaged in routine trading. They can be sorted into three categories: departmental, agency and proprietary. Well-known examples are the Canada Mortgage and Housing Corporation, the Canadian Broadcasting Corporation, Canadian National Railways, Air Canada, Canadian Arsenals Ltd., Crown Assets Disposal Corporation, Northern Canada Power Commission, Eldorado Nuclear Ltd., Cape Breton Development Corporation and the Royal Canadian Mint.

Crown corporations receive their charters as well as their operating capital under special acts passed by the federal parliament.

The federal government proposes to treat these corporations much like all other corporations, requiring some of them to act in a routine businesslike manner, without depending on future inflows of tax moneys. Several Crown corporations that compete with private industry now are subject to both federal and provincial income tax, and some pay provincial retail sales taxes, and gasoline and vehicle taxes.

It is well known, however, that these Crown corporations often find it difficult to increase their prices to economic levels because of the political pressure the public exerts on the government of the day.

The cultural corporations—including the Canada Council (which distributed $63.3 million in 1983–84), the National Arts Centre Corporation, the Science Council of Canada—were originally set up as Crown corporations but were later excluded from the strict controls and supervision which the Financial Administration Act exerts over Crown corporations. These, too, have felt the influence of political realities.

The cooperative idea

THE COOPERATIVE CONCEPT has long been vigorous in Canada and has played a prominent part in economic growth right across the country. Important cooperatives can be found in the production and marketing of grain, meat, fruit, dairy and fish products. The system extends to retail trading, insurance, housing, banking (the credit union) and also to the production of Inuit soapstone carvings.

In Canada, most cooperatives are incorporated like any other companies. The liability of a cooperative's members, like that of a public company or corporation, is restricted by the legislation under which it is incorporated. In all provinces, special legislation has been passed to govern cooperatives.

The writings of the American social reformer Robert Owen (1801–77) are widely regarded as the originating inspiration of the cooperative system. But examples of worker-operated businesses can be found in the late eighteenth century in France and Scandinavia. Cooperative marketing groups existed in Nova Scotia as early as 1765, and some took root temporarily in Quebec after the arrival of Loyalists from the American colonies. However, it was the famous "Rochdale experiment" that was mainly responsible for shaping the movement toward its present form.

In 1844, a group of 28 weavers in the textile town of Rochdale, England, formed themselves into a trading cooperative, and opened a grocery store in Toad Lane. Cutting out the middleman, they bought from the producers and sold directly to their members—themselves. Anyone wanting to buy their products had, of course, first to join the cooperative. They succeeded to the extent that they were able to move into the manufacturing business with their own footwear and weaving plants. Glowing reports spread quickly around the world.

Miners at Stellarton, Nova Scotia, opened a co-op store in 1861 and the Sydney Mines Cooperative Society was chartered two years later. Nine other stores were launched in Nova Scotia before 1900 but all disappeared.

The most important farmers' organization in Canada at the end of the nineteenth century was the Grange, with 31,000 members (of whom 26,000 were in Ontario). It was involved in many things on a co-op basis—from salt production to fire insurance.

Cooperative marketing by producers took hold in the western provinces as the prairie wheatlands were coming into full production.

The Co-operative Union of Canada and Le Conseil Canadien de la Coopération—national nonpartisan organizations that represent most Canadian cooperatives—lobby in Ottawa and with provincial lawmakers on issues of concern to their members.

How the co-op works

Like the corporation, the cooperative assembles its capital funds by selling shares to its members (shareholders); unlike the corporation, no matter how many shares a member may hold he has only one vote in management decisions. Like the corporation, the cooperative seeks to trade or operate profitably; however, at the end of the financial year, any profits (except for a small reserve) are paid to the members in proportion to their purchases during the period. Where the cooperative is engaged in manufacturing or processing—as with dairy farmers bringing milk to a cheese factory—the supplier-members share the profits at year's end in relation to the quantity of produce they have contributed.

Other distinctive features of cooperatives can be summarized as follows:

(1) Membership is open to all who may benefit from the services offered;

(2) Shares may not be transferred unless authorized by the directors;

(3) There is no voting by proxy;

(4) Capital for the company may be obtained by the sale of shares to the members or by securing from them promissory notes, payable on demand;

(5) Surplus funds are distributed to members, either in the form of interest on investment or by division of the surplus (profit).

The main disadvantage of the cooperative company—and it can be a severely limiting factor—lies, strangely enough, in its strict democratic structure. "One man, one vote" is a rewarding concept in theory but in business practice gives the informed and shrewd executive no more influence in making policy decisions than the inexperienced worker with little business acumen. In Canada, at any rate, cooperatives account for about 30 percent of all farm products marketed each year, but only about six percent of the country's retail business.

Marketing co-ops

Cooperation by producers and sellers involves the substitution of collective for individual action in order to enhance the profit position of the producers. Canada's largest and most successful cooperatives are those connected with farming in the western provinces—the Manitoba, Saskatchewan and Alberta wheat "pools," represented by their agency, Canadian Cooperative Wheat Producers Ltd.

All of the wheat, oats and barley grown on the prairies for interprovincial or foreign sale is bought, stored and shipped by the Canadian Wheat Board, which is a Crown corporation.

The co-op pioneers of Red Bay

SIR WILFRED GRENFELL, the medical missionary revered as the "saint of Labrador," devoted 50 years of his life to the welfare of the people of that harsh land. He plagued governments and philanthropists all over the world until he had established six hospitals, outlying nursing stations, orphanages, schools and craft centers. His hospital ship cruised the northern coasts each summer season. It's less widely known that this one-time English public schoolboy (Marlborough and Oxford) was also among Canada's pioneers of the cooperative movement.

When Grenfell was first sent to Labrador in 1892 by the Mission to Deep Sea Fishermen, he found the illiterate trappers and fishermen—mostly of mixed British and Inuit blood—in direst poverty and virtually in serfdom to the trading stores which took their catch and issued in payment colored tokens redeemable only at the same stores. Since credit was advanced before the seasonal hunts, the families were perpetually "in debt."

At the settlement of Red Bay, on the Strait of Belle Isle, Grenfell convinced the 17 families to first pay off their store debts (which took a year of privation), then to save some capital (a total of $85), and then to open their own store. Grenfell himself painted the sign: RED BAY CO-OPERATIVE STORE.

Grenfell wrote a score of books about his Canadian adventures and won many honors before his death in 1940. But he drew special satisfaction from the fact that all through the grinding Depression of the 1930s, the simple folk of Red Bay needed no handouts from the Newfoundland government. There were always victuals down at the co-op store.

The usual Canadian practice in producer's cooperatives is to pool the produce of members so that each one receives the average price of that particular grade of product marketed by the co-op during a specified period.

Each cooperative member manages his own farm in the way he chooses, and is under no compulsion to market his production through the co-op. The success of the co-op, however, obviously depends upon the maximum participation of its members.

Consumer co-ops

A consumer cooperative is a marketing organization—usually a retail store—owned and operated for the mutual benefit of the consumer-owners, who have voluntarily joined together for that purpose. It is an attempt to substitute joint, or cooperative effort for that of private enterprise, for the benefit of the consumer. The object is to buy directly from the manufacturer or producer, thus eliminating middlemen and lowering prices.

The success of consumer cooperatives has been meager in Canada; those in the United States have fared no better. In the United Kingdom, there has been a decline in recent years. In Africa, India and Southeast Asia, the movement has made progress since World War II, encouraged by government in the hope of developing self-reliance and training in democratic methods among a basically uneducated citizenry.

Canada is one of 72 nations of the International Co-operative Alliance (I.C.A.), founded in 1895. Its headquarters is in Geneva.

Insurance co-ops

An insurance cooperative is an organization of individuals or groups who associate to obtain the lowest possible price for insurance and the greatest amount of protection. This type of association is usually referred to under the general label of *service cooperative*.

Insurance cooperatives exist successfully in many areas of Canadian society, covering all types or risk, from life to boats. Usually they are made up for individuals or groups who share a common interest—such as farming, retailing or, perhaps, architecture. The joining together of these groups tends to produce cost savings for the members who are insured, through reduced premiums.

Fiscal co-ops (credit unions)

The object of a credit union (known in Quebec as a *caisse populaire*) is to make loans to members, with or without security, for "provident and productive purposes." The decision to make loans or refuse them lies with a credit committee that is elected at the annual meeting of members. The loans are granted (to members only) out of money received from the members as payment for shares or as deposits with the union.

Within a limited range, the credit union acts just like a bank. Deposits and withdrawals are made with a passbook. An added advantage is that deposits are insured for a minimum of $60,000. Loans at many of the larger credit unions are insured against death or disability. The insurance is paid for by the union from its central funds and the policies are held by a mutual company owned by the credit unions of Canada and the United States.

Every province has laws governing credit unions. Before a credit union can be incorporated in most provinces, it must have at least ten members. In Prince Edward Island, only seven members are required. In Ontario, credit unions must have no fewer than 20 members and, in Quebec, at least 12. The federal Cooperative Credit Associations Act controls interprovincial credit unions.

As in all cooperatives, no member of a credit union has more than one vote. The managing bodies are the board of directors, the credit committee and the supervisory committee.

The first credit union in Canada, established by journalist Alphonse Desjardins in Levis, Quebec, in 1900, still flourishes today. All the credit unions in Quebec combine within La Confédération des caisses populaires et d'économie Desjardins; elsewhere in Canada, the equivalent group is the Canadian Cooperative Credit Society.

Professions and trades

The regulated professions
The licensed trades

THE LICENSING of professions and trades in Canada, under the terms of the Canadian constitution, falls within the authority of the provincial governments. For the most part, the applicants are examined, and their qualifications checked out, by private bodies. The judgment of these organizations is accepted by the governments. The basic purpose of licensing is to protect the public from the incompetent practitioner, and to raise the standards of public service—whether the individual concerned is a psychiatrist or a plumber. The specialist in any trade or profession is normally able to produce written evidence that he is qualified for the specialized task he offers to do.

Occupational licensing is designed to ensure that a person has acquired certain education, training, experience, residence, citizenship or other qualifications to the satisfaction of a particular provincial or municipal authority, or of a trade union or professional association, before he is allowed to practice his occupation.

The regulated professions
Licensed professions in Canada are the following:

Accountants	Physiotherapists
Architects	Podiatrists
Dentists	Professional
Embalmers	engineers
Lawyers	Psychologists
Medical and dental	Registered
technicians	dieticians
Optometrists	Registered
Osteopaths	nurses
(and chiropractors)	Surveyors
Pharmacists	Teachers
Physicians	Therapists
and surgeons	Veterinarians

In Quebec *all* recognized professions are regulated under a professional code.

Accountancy
Accountancy in Canada is regulated by three organizations: the Canadian Institute of Chartered Accountants, the Certified General Accountants' Association of Canada and the Society of Management Accountants of Canada. For the most part, only chartered accountants are allowed to be auditors (an appointment that requires giving an opinion on financial statements) of any type of business. The members of the other two organizations usually work in industry or the civil service. Each accounting organization has a provincial body which helps regulate the profession in that province.

To become a chartered accountant (C.A.), you must first earn a university degree and then apply to the provincial institute for registration as a student. You will be required to complete a prescribed series of up to 45 credit courses (advanced standing will be given for equivalent university work completed before registration). Most students complete these credits at university extension night classes or at summer schools. After gaining practical experience by working for a firm of chartered accountants, you must pass the rigorous C.A. final examination which is the same across Canada.

The Certified General Accountants' Association and the Society of Management Accountants of Canada both require high-school graduation for admittance to their courses. Both organizations set out the number of course examinations that must be passed. It usually requires five years of study to complete these examinations.

The importance of the trained accountant to Canadian business cannot be overemphasized. It can be said that sophisticated management accounting has made possible the development, direction and control of the largest and most complex corporations.

Regardless of the technological foundation of big business, its growth would have been frozen if accounting had not solved certain problems in the vital area of administrative control.

Secondly, the principle of accountability of management took hold only due to the existence of a system of meaningful financial reporting.

Thirdly, accounting has provided the means for the independent audit which bridges the gap between management and shareholders in public limited companies.

Architecture

The professional body in the practice of architecture in Canada is the Royal Architectural Institute of Canada (R.A.I.C.), a federation of ten provincial associations of architects.

Each provincial legislature has delegated powers to its architects' association, or to a registration board, to establish rules and regulations governing professional conduct and to examine the qualifications of applicants for registration as architects. Only those persons who have met the standards set by the examining body may call themselves architects; anyone representing himself as such without registration and membership in the provincial association may be prosecuted.

The architect is the person most responsible for the quality of our surroundings. He is the only man specifically trained to provide advisory planning, design, coordination, production, supervisory and consulting services in building construction. Almost all major construction is carried out under the direction of an architect. In order to qualify for studying architecture, you must at least have completed the matriculation requirements for entrance to a university.

There are ten schools of architecture in Canada. After completing your degree course, you must spend a period (from two to three years) working under the direction of an architect, in order to become eligible to be registered by the provincial association. It is possible to become a registered architect without a university education. This can be done by entering an architect's office as a junior with matriculation standing and some training in architectural drafting. This route involves evening courses and home study, and takes from ten to 12 years.

Dentistry

The Canadian Dental Association has regulated the practice of dentistry since 1902. It is a federation of provincial associations which has power to establish rules and regulations governing professional conduct and qualification for membership. The oldest dental association was founded in Ontario in 1867.

There are ten schools of dentistry on university campuses in Canada, with two in Ontario and three in Quebec. It usually requires five years of study to earn a Doctorate of Dental Surgery (D.D.S.). A dentist becomes registered to practice when he passes the final year's examination.

The undergraduate dentist gets practical experience between his third and fifth year. At facilities provided at each dental school, he can practice on those of the general public who wish to have dental work done for a much lower fee than would be charged by a graduate dentist.

A dentist is responsible for the health of his patient's teeth and mouth. Most dentists set up their own practice; some operate in partnership with one or more other dentists.

A small number of dentists work for industry or government.

Engineering

The first course of study in engineering in Canada began in 1854 at King's College, the forerunner of the University of New Brunswick.

McGill University and the University of Toronto soon followed, calling their courses "practical science."

Engineering is now described as the science of designing objects or structures for use. Begun as a military practice, it is now divided into many branches, including civil, mining, mechanical, chemical, electrical, metallurgical and industrial engineering.

Within the broad scope of any one of these branches, the engineer may further confine himself to research or development, design, construction, production, operation, sales or management.

The practice of professional engineering is controlled in Canada by the Canadian Council of Professional Engineers, which represents the separate associations in each province. The provincial associations are responsible for granting licenses.

Only a small proportion of engineers do not have a university degree. Those who don't are required to have had extensive practical experience in order to be granted qualification after passing written examinations set by the profession.

There are 28 professional engineering schools in Canada empowered to grant degrees. The curriculum usually involves four years of study. After graduation, the engineer must acquire at least two years of supervised experience before he can become eligible for registration as a professional engineer.

Education

More than eight percent of Canada's Gross National Product is spent on education. About 36 percent of all Canadians are either receiving or providing education. In short, education can be considered a major "industry."

The profession of teaching in Canada is regulated by the provincial teachers' associations. These combine to form the Canadian Teachers' Federation. The provincial associations obtain their powers from acts of the provincial legislatures, as education is a right reserved to the provinces under the Canadian Constitution.

The provinces, through their departments of education, set over-all policy—both cultural and financial—and they provide research, inspectors and directors of school programs, teacher training, textbook selection, correspondence courses and adult training.

The federal government, through Employment and Immigration Canada, assumes financial responsibility for retraining adult workers, and it pays about half of the operating costs of all postsecondary education.

While Ontario's association is divided between primary-school teachers (usually grades one to eight) and secondary-school teachers (grades nine to 13), other provincial associations make no such distinction. You must have an education de-

gree (four years of university after high school or, in Quebec, three years after C.E.G.E.P.) to be a certified primary- or secondary-school teacher.

If your aim was to teach at a university, you would first take a bachelor's degree (preferably with honors) in your chosen major subject, and then work for a master's degree. Most top professors at major universities hold doctorates (Ph. D.), the highest qualification obtainable.

Law

The legal profession in Canada is controlled by the provincial law societies and by the Canadian Bar Association. The societies obtain their powers for regulation of members' conduct and qualification requirements by acts of the respective provincial legislatures. Only members of the associations are permitted to practice law. (*See* Chapter 20, "Choosing the profession.")

Membership in a provincial Bar restricts a lawyer to practicing law in that province alone. He must meet the standards, become a member and pay fees to another provincial Bar before he can practice in another province.

A member of any provincial Bar, however, may appear before the Supreme Court or any other federal court.

Medicine

The first moves to govern the practice of medicine in Canada came in Quebec in 1788 when the handful of doctors with European qualifications complained to the governor that the community was suffering "from inexperienced and illiterate men practicing the art of physic and surgery." Ontario and Nova Scotia followed the Quebec lead.

The first properly organized Canadian medical school was begun in 1823 by four Scottish doctors in Montreal, with the General Hospital (opened the previous year) providing clinical training. This school eventually became the medical faculty of McGill University, with the power to grant the M.D. degree. Canada now has 16 medical schools.

Possession of a degree in medicine will not in itself qualify you to practice in

Canada. The right to license doctors is retained by each of the provinces; however, under the Canada Medical Act, any graduate accepted by the Dominion Medical Council is permitted to register for practice in any province.

The provincial colleges of physicians and surgeons are all members of the Canadian Medical Association, which speaks for the entire profession in Canada. It also publishes the highly acclaimed C.M.A. *Journal.*

The provincial colleges are chartered by acts of the legislatures and only their members will be licensed to practice medicine.

If you feel called to medicine, you must be prepared to become, in effect, a student for life. The introduction of new methods and new theories never ends. If successful, you will join the most highly paid group of Canadian professional men. But the life you will lead will be one of stress and tension.

The first step in becoming a doctor is to qualify academically for one of Canada's medical schools. All of them accept women, although women represent fewer than

Careers at home

THE COTTAGE INDUSTRIES of Europe and the East are as old as commerce itself. There has, however, been a distinct revival in advanced societies over the past generation as more and more women are freed from time-consuming domestic chores by appliances, and inspired by the concept that marriage and family don't necessarily mean the end of outside profitable activity. Women all over Canada are going back to school (at community colleges and high school night classes) to perfect old skills or learn new ones. In the United States, more than one million women are reported to be operating successful businesses at home.

When trained secretaries marry, they don't forget how to type and many of them fit several hours of typing into their everyday activities. Much of the manuscript of this book was typed by such a person, with two toddlers running interference. But it is the rapid growth of boutiques and other specialty shops that has brought glamour and profit into many home careers. They provide a ready and continuing market for quality items of individual design—from handmade jewelry to pottery.

Sizable fortunes have grown from ideas developed at home by women with time to spare. The remarkable person known as Grandma Moses once made needlework pictures and turned to paint (at 78) only when arthritis stiffened her fingers. She sold her simple country scenes for $3 each as a backup to her homemade jams and jellies. Her paintings have since sold for as much as $20,000.

The well-known black cosmetics tycoon Rose Morgan once gave shampoos and sets in her family's bathroom in Chicago. Once married to boxer Joe Louis, she now lists Diahann Carroll, Lena Horne, Ella Fitzgerald and Mahalia Jackson as clients at her many beauty parlors.

Evelyn Wood, whose name has become synonymous with speed reading, saw her highly marketable system take off into profitability after she was 50 and had raised a family. She first took an interest in problem readers at home because of her husband's work as a bishop of the Mormon church. Prime Minister Indira Gandhi of India is a pupil.

Perhaps less exotic but still successful are home businesses based on apron-making, beading, belts, body massage, candy-making, costume rental, dance classes, doll-dressing, dried flowers, felt novelties, gift-wrapping, herb-packaging, illustrating, jam-making, jewelry, knitting, macramé, magazine sales, mail-order selling, party favors, photography, pottery, rug-hooking, scarf-making, sign-painting, speech-writing, stenography, ties for men, toys, translating, tutoring, upholstering, weaving and wig-making.

five percent of all practicing doctors in Canada.

For approximately seven years, your time will be divided between premedical, medical and internship studies. If you want to specialize in some branch of medicine, this could require a further five years of study.

Nursing

The professional body in the practice of nursing is the Canadian Nurses Association, a federation of the separate provincial and territorial nursing associations. These associations have power delegated by the government to establish rules governing professional conduct and qualification for membership.

High-school graduation is usually required before you can enter a nursing school. Some schools in British Columbia, Nova Scotia and Newfoundland are affiliated with large hospitals, while others have access to clinical areas in hospitals, nursing homes and public health facilities. In Quebec, nursing training is handled by the community colleges (the CEGEP system). There are similar training arrangements in Ontario and Saskatchewan. In other provinces, training is handled by a variety of institutions—technical institutes, community colleges and hospitals. A number of Canadian universities offer degree courses in nursing science as well.

When you have successfully completed a diploma course after two to three years of nursing school, you become a registered nurse (R.N.). The training program always includes clinical practice in hospitals or other health agencies.

The university programs in nursing involve four years of study, including the basic sciences and humanities, with a major in nursing. The programs combine theory with practice in a variety of settings in the community, including hospital and public health agencies. Students are awarded a bachelor of science degree (B.Sc.) upon successful completion of the program, and are eligible to write the registration examination administered by the provincial registered nurses association (college of nurses). In Ontario, the association is known as the Ontario College of Nursing. Graduate nurses with B.N. or B.Sc.N. degrees, like graduates of diploma courses, are prepared for bedside nursing. To assume supervising and administrative responsibilities, nurses must have masters' degrees, which usually require another two years of study.

Pharmacy

The pharmacist is best known to the public as the druggist at the local drugstore. He is the qualified professional who prepares the medicine ordered by the patient's doctor (he is usually the only one around who can read the prescription!). Pharmacists are also employed by corporations engaged in the manufacture of drugs or related products, as well as by hospitals and government agencies involved in chemical research.

There are eight faculties of pharmacy at the larger universities in Canada, two of them offering programs taught in French.

The main entrance requirement is secondary-school graduation with a high standing. The program of study lasts between four and five years, including courses in chemistry, physics, mathematics and botany.

The skills of the pharmacist are in great demand, and the graduate (B.Sc.Phm., B.Pharm. or other variations, depending on the province) often has a wide choice of job opportunities right across the country.

The Canadian Pharmaceutical Association (established 1907) is a federation of the provincial associations, each of which has power to establish rules governing professional conduct and qualification for membership in its province.

Religion

The profession of theology has many different roots in this country, where every man is by law free to worship according to the dictates of his own conscience. All religions are on an equal footing; Catholics, Protestants, Jews and those of other religious denominations (there are at least 70 sects) enjoy complete liberty of thought.

The larger religions have long established their own theological colleges, where students can earn the divinity degrees, Bachelor of Divinity (B.D.) and Doctor of Divinity (D.D.). There are numerous bible-study schools as well, some of them interdenominational.

High-school graduation is the normal requirement for acceptance into the theological colleges, but this is not always strictly demanded. The most important "requirement" of a student planning to become a priest, minister or rabbi is felt to be the desire to help his fellowman and to serve God.

Veterinary science

When you think of a vet, you probably think of the man you take your pup to when it's sick. If you live on a farm, he's the man who checks your cows, horses and pigs, and helps keep them all healthy. These men represent some important branches of veterinary science, but there are many others. Canada has about 4,500 practicing veterinarians.

Some qualified veterinarians (D.V.M., M.V.Sc. or D.V.Sc.) study animals and animal diseases as they relate to diseases in human beings. And their work has resulted in many important advances in human medicine. The "management group" of veterinarians works in government, drafting laws and regulations covering animals and animal diseases. Still others supervise research laboratories in government and industry.

There are veterinary colleges in Quebec, Ontario and Saskatchewan. One of the best known in the world is the Ontario Veterinary College, which was founded in

How to put your best foot forward

MANY ACCOUNTANTS, architects, engineers and lawyers hold down appointments in the business world or in the higher echelons of the public service where their special skills and talents are highly regarded. It's a world of change, however, and the executive who finds himself "blocked in," overworked or underpaid, will begin to think of making a move. Perhaps he'll answer a Careers advertisement where his inquiry will be held "in strictest confidence," or maybe he'll be netted by one of the "head hunters" (professional placement consultants) and be offered to a list of potential employers.

If the right opening doesn't soon occur—and this is the average case—then the applicant must go looking for it. He must, in hard fact, sell himself at the best price he can get. Career counselors offer this advice:

● Stay in your present post until suited elsewhere: don't quit first, or you'll be dealing from weakness.

● Examine the product (yourself) with beady buyer's eyes so that you can answer any question without hesitation.

● Get to know the market throroughly, just like any good salesman must.

● Learn *how* to sell yourself. You must be able to show a new employer how he can make a good profit from hiring you.

● Assuming you are married, make your wife an "accessory before the fact." Many bosses want to be sure that a potential executive is happy at home.

You will certainly be asked why you want to leave your present job. Don't exaggerate or prevaricate. Patently honest answers: "I want more money"; "I am bored"; and "I just feel like a change after five years"—these can score higher with potential employers than phony sentiments about fulfilling one's destiny, etc.

A final word. Don't ruin your chance by being unrealistic about salary. There may be a high, middle and low rate for the job you want, but there *is* a rate. If your demands are modest, and you succeed at the task, only a very short-sighted employer will be slow with the raises. It will be in his interests to pay you as much as he can afford—or else he knows you'll get the wanderlust again.

Toronto in 1862 and moved to Guelph in 1922. Now an integral part of the University of Guelph, it offers a four-year degree course after two years of previous university training.

In Quebec, veterinary studies center at St. Hyacinthe, where, through affiliation with the University of Montreal, the degree of doctor of veterinary medicine can be earned. Courses leading to a master's degree are also available.

The profession is supervised everywhere under provincial legislation, but the Canadian Veterinary Medical Association, with headquarters in Ottawa, voices the collective views and policies of the independent provincial associations.

The licensed trades
Air-conditioning and
  refrigeration mechanics
Alignment and brakes mechanics
Auto body repairs
Barbers
Compressor engineers
Electricians
Fuel and electrical
  transmission mechanics
Hairdressers
Hoisting engineers
Hoisting engineers (steam)
Motor vehicle mechanics
Motorcycle mechanics
Plumbers
Provisional stationary engineers
Refrigeration operators
Stationary engineers
Sheet-metal workers
Steam fitters
System mechanics
Truck trailer repairs
Water-supply repairs
Welders

If you wish to obtain detailed information on any of the above trades, write to the department of labor in the province where you live.

Each trade and occupation has its own entrance requirements and its own classifications.

A sample schedule
Although terms and requirements vary to some extent from province to prov-

ince, the following description of entry requirements to the electrical trade in Ontario can serve as a general example. There are two branches:

The first, Branch I, is the trade of the construction and maintenance electrician. He lays out, assembles, installs, repairs and maintains electrical fixtures, control equipment and wiring systems of alarm, communication, light, heat or power installations in buildings.

The second, Branch II, is the trade of domestic and rural electrician. He does all the work required of an electrician in the construction, erection, repair, remodeling or alteration of houses, multiple dwellings of six or fewer units, and farm buildings.

Ontario electricians learn their trade through a formal apprenticeship program established by the Ministry of Colleges and Universities. It consists of full-time day classes at a college of applied arts and technology—or of classes recognized as the equivalent by the director of the Skills Development Division—as well as practical on-the-job instruction provided by the employer.

You have to be at least 16 years old and have to have completed at least grade ten in order to enter an apprenticeship program. If you have finished grade 12, your training period is reduced. The periods of training—in class and on the job—necessary for the Certificate of Apprenticeship in either branch are as follows:

	Branch I	Branch II
With Grade 10	5 periods of 1800 hours	4 periods of 1800 hours
With Grade 12	5 periods of 1600 hours	4 periods of 1600 hours

During the training period, your wages will be calculated as a progressive percentage of the rate paid to the *journeyman* electrician. The journeyman is the next level of proficiency above the apprentice status recognized by the law. When you have finished the course, you are required to write an examination. You need at least a 60-percent standing on the examination to get your certificate.

Farming and fishing

The business of farming

The business of fishing

FARMING AND FISHING are two of the founding industries of Canada. Although they no longer dominate the national economy, they are still very important elements of the country's commerce. In some areas, they remain paramount. Collectively, they add up to big business—over $15 billion annually. More than that, they are indispensable in providing food to the ever-swelling urban populations.

At the dawn of this century, there was close to a balance between the numbers of people living in urban and rural areas; today, more than three-quarters of all Canadians live in cities, towns or villages of more than 1,000 population—yet the total output of farm produce has increased more than three times. The average Canadian farmer produces enough food annually for 55 people; a great deal of this is, of course, exported.

Familiar products are Alberta's beef, British Columbia's fish and fruit, Manitoba's grains, New Brunswick's potatoes and pigs, Newfoundland's cod, Nova Scotia's lobsters, Ontario's cheese and meat, Prince Edward Island's potatoes, Quebec's milk products and Saskatchewan's cereals. With many thousands of miles of coastline facing three great oceans and with about half of the world's supply of fresh water, Canada has the largest fishing grounds on the globe. Our northern climate has blessed us with the best food fish known: salmon, cod, halibut, herring, mackerel, whitefish and perch.

As the nineteenth century advanced and more of Canada's food products entered the markets of the world, laws were introduced to regulate and control primary production. The British North America Act (now part of the Canadian Constitution) split the authority over farming between the two major levels of government. Section 95 states:

"In each province, the legislature may make laws in relation to agriculture in the province . . . and it is hereby declared that the Parliament of Canada may from time to time make laws in relation to agriculture in all or any of the provinces. . . . Any law of the legislature of a province relative to agriculture . . . shall have effect only as it is not repugnant to any act of the Parliament of Canada."

Despite this, the federal authorities were hesitant at first to interfere with the free play of the unwritten laws of supply and demand. Grain and other supplies were controlled during World War I, and a price-stabilization program was introduced in 1929. But when a federal marketing act was passed in 1934, the Supreme Court declared it *ultra vires* ("beyond the powers") of the parliament.

During the worldwide Depression of the '30s, several of the provincial legislatures—led by British Columbia—passed laws controlling production and marketing of produce within provincial boundaries. Encouragement was given to the many cooperatives then springing up—such as the wheat pools that were to become so important on the prairies and the fishermen's co-ops of the Maritimes. In many cases, regulations made it compulsory for all producers to sell through the marketing boards.

At the start of World War II, Parliament moved boldly once again, this time guaranteeing a certain level of payment to farmers in the form of the Agricultural Cooperative Marketing Act. Under the umbrella of the War Measures Act (1914), the federal authority stepped in to control the marketing of just about all primary products. The Prices Support Act of 1944 guaranteed the stabilization of returns to producers through the techniques of automatic purchase and set basic prices, announced beforehand and adjusted seasonally.

It was hoped that cash surpluses built up in prosperous years would balance out deficiency payments made from general

577

tax revenues in poor trading seasons. This has become the fiscal reasoning behind all state marketing legislation, and now is widely applied.

As the primary producing countries recovered from the wounds of war, surpluses soon replaced shortages. When more food was being harvested than could be sold, the government storage elevators and freezers were soon jammed to bursting. Skating arenas on the prairies were pressed into service to store unwanted grain, bought at guaranteed prices with tax dollars. The government was forced to enact quotas, decreeing just how much each producer was permitted to bring in.

From the sowing to the selling, almost all of Canada's primary produce which goes to the market now stands within the direction and protection of the state.

The business of farming

Most of the 300,000 farms in Canada still are owned and operated as family units. In business terms, the great majority are operated either as sole proprietorships or as partnerships of a father and one or more of his sons. Few small family farms are incorporated simply because of the cost involved and the lack of any immediate tax advantage. Everywhere, however, the family farm is declining, giving way to larger, more efficient units.

The larger farms, especially those in the prairie provinces and in parts of southwestern Ontario, are usually incorporated. This allows them to operate in the manner of the modern businesses they are. The larger profits made from their streamlined, scientific operations are subject to lower tax rates because of incorporation.

The laws of the *seigneury*

UNDER the semifeudal land-holding system entrenched in New France by the orders of Cardinal Richelieu, the *seigneur* was judge and jury, and master of all he surveyed—although his rights were curbed in several areas. His tenant farmers (the *habitants*) had legal obligations to him, and the *seigneur* in turn had obligations both to them and to the French Crown.

When Dr. Robert Giffard was granted the *seigneury* of Beauport, a few miles above Quebec City, in 1634, he assumed the obligation of cultivating the estate and of settling immigrant peasant farmers on the land. True to his word, he established five French families on the property in his first season. Before his death at 80, Giffard had brought out nearly 50 families and his *seigneury* was the most heavily populated place in the entire land we know today as Canada. Giffard ranks as Canada's first successful farmer.

The *seigneur* worked hard alongside his tenants. ("They are their own horses," noted a Jesuit priest.) The law stated that the *seigneur* had to erect a mill and the

habitants had to pay a small fee to use it.

The tenant had a notarized deed establishing his right to his plot of land but he had to pay his *seigneur* an annual rental—usually a small sum in cash plus a quantity of produce—known as the *cens et rentes*. If the tenant sold his land rights, he paid the *seigneur* one-twelfth of the price.

The average *seigneury*, near to the few settlements, would consist of about 8 kilometres of river frontage, with the depth running vaguely back into the forest hinterland. About 3.2 million hectares were granted in all, a quarter of that being held by the Roman Catholic Church. The tenant farms usually had a frontage of about 300 metres and a depth of perhaps 3,000 metres. With all the houses and barns placed near the riverbanks—the only highway in summer or winter—the impression was created of a continuous ribbon village.

The tenant farmers had to provide without pay three or four days' labor (the *corvée*), either cultivating the *seigneur's* fields or in building or repairing the roads and bridges on the estate.

The sale or purchase of a farm—even the takeover by a son from his father—is much more easily made if the farm is incorporated. If it is incorporated, only a transfer of shares is involved. Farming operations are usually chartered as private corporations under provincial company legislation.

The larger farms normally have ready access to low-cost, long-term financing. Chartered banks make loans based on the credit rating of each individual farmer. They also make provincially guaranteed low-interest loans when approval is received from the provincial government.

The federal government, in the shape of the Farm Credit Corporation, lends money directly to farmers to purchase machinery or property, or even to carry them over a poor crop season.

Groups of farmers (syndicates) which combine to purchase such necessities as new machinery or buildings can get special loans to cover up to 80 percent of the cost, to a maximum of $100,000. Interest rates are lower than in normal money circles, and the group can take up to 15 years to repay.

Since pioneering a veterinarian service in 1869, the federal department of agriculture has been handed more than 40 Acts of Parliament to administer. Twelve different branches have evolved: food production and inspection, research, communications, personnel administration, marketing and economics, finance and administration, farm income services, regional development, legal services, audit and evaluation, prairie-farm rehabilitation administration, and a special advisory group on grains. Special programs are introduced as specific problems arise (for example, widespread hail damage), then discontinued as the market returns to normal. Under the Agricultural Stabilization Act, support prices for nine commodities are calculated annually. When the market returns for that commodity fall below the calculated support price, a deficiency payment is made to producers. For the market years 1974–1976, deficiency payments were made to beef producers, but none have been made since that time.

Few urban Canadians realize the value of Canada's oilseeds—even the plants themselves sound unfamiliar: sunflower, flax, rape and soybean. But the seeds of the plants are crushed to release important oils for human, livestock and industrial use. In a recent year, 518,000 hectares were sown to flax.

Other federal agricultural regulatory and research bodies include the Canadian Dairy Commission (paying a subsidy to all producers of milk), the Canadian Grain Commission, the Agricultural Stabilization Board, the Agricultural Products Board, the Canadian Livestock Feed Board, plus those agencies that enforce regulations under the Meat Inspection Act, the Animal Disease and Protection Act, the Humane Slaughter of Food Animals Act and the Plant Quarantine Act. Federal legislation sets grading standards for meat, poultry, vegetables and fruit.

The business of fishing

In total, more than 150 species of fish and shellfish are harvested by Canada's commercial fishermen. While the main grounds are off the northeast and northwest coasts, the Great Lakes and other fishing lakes offer an inland area of 274,500 square kilometres. The total volume of fish caught annually is approximately 1.3 million tonnes, worth over $580 million to the nation's 80,000 fishermen. Export value of fish-related products was $1.6 billion in a recent year.

Surplus meat production and sharply increased competition in the fish harvest from low-income, high-technology countries (like Japan and Korea) caused a reduction of more than 12 percent in Canada's fish export trade in one recent season (1973–1974). The 1974 gross volume of fish landed was the smallest since 1960. To maintain fishermen's incomes in the current slump, the federal government is giving financial assistance to help meet cold storage and inventory costs. In recent years, Canada's competitive advantage in world markets has improved dramatically. This change has been attributed to the extension of Canada's jurisdiction over a 370-kilometre belt of ocean ("the 200-mile limit") around the nation's coastlines, and the federal government's quality enhancement program to upgrade handling and storage facilities and to develop better quality fish. Today, Canada is the biggest supplier in the world, exporting $1.5 billion worth of fish a year.

Fishing is big business in six of Canada's provinces. In British Columbia, salmon is at the top of the money list, accounting for $108 million of the annual total of $141 million. On the Atlantic coast, Nova Scotia leads with an annual catch worth $257 million; then comes Newfoundland with $175 million; New Brunswick, with $66 million; Quebec, with $50 million; and Prince Edward Island, with $36 million.

Most commercial fishing is done under sole proprietorships: occasionally fishermen form partnerships. It is usually the fish processor who forms an incorporated company. Wholesaling and distribution of fish and fish products are handled by other companies. One Atlantic-based company controls 60 to 80 percent of both domestic and export distribution.

In total, there are 30,000 firms engaged in the fishing business, more than two-thirds of them on or near the Atlantic coast. Another 1,100 companies process fish into a wide range of secondary products, from pet food to fertilizer. Canadians, however, are not eager fish eaters, and 80 percent of the output is exported, mostly to the United States.

Authority over the industry was given to the federal government at Confederation, and the first Fisheries Act was passed in 1868. The Act brought together all "provincial" laws that existed then. Later, some provinces contested the federal authority, especially over freshwater fishing. Several appeals were made to the British Privy Council, the final court of appeal at that time. Today, Ottawa and the provinces share control and responsibilities in some areas.

The federal Department of Fisheries and Oceans retains power over all fishing—both ocean and freshwater—in the Atlantic provinces. In the central provinces of Ontario, Manitoba, Saskatchewan and Alberta, the provincial governments have effectual control. In

Quebec and British Columbia, authority is divided.

Wherever the levers of power are situated, there is close cooperation between all the administrative bodies. All subscribe to the common goal not only of managing the resource by curbing over-exploitation and the pollution of waters, but also of attempting to provide the fisherman with a steady income. The product is closely inspected at freezers and caneries to insure that high standards of quality and cleanliness are maintained. Inspectors have the authority to condemn establishments and to confiscate fish products that do not meet the standards.

The Fisheries Prices Support Board was created by federal law in 1947, with the power to recommend support payments to fishermen when wholesale prices drop below certain minimums. The board can also buy and sell fish and fish products.

Other federal legislation provides insurance schemes for fishing boats and gear lost or damaged in storms, as well as credit arrangements for capital expenditure, repair or maintenance. Outright cash grants of up to 25 percent of the cost of a new vessel, or the conversion or modification of an old one, are made through the Fishing Vessel Assistance Plan. Bait is provided to fishermen from federal depots, especially along the coast of Newfoundland and Labrador.

Some provinces maintain separate loan agencies. For example, Nova Scotia's Fisheries Loan Board, established in the early 1930s, has advanced nearly $100 million to that province's fishermen to build fishing vessels and to buy engines.

Since 1957, coverage under the Unemployment Insurance Act has been available to commercial fishermen.

Marketing is controlled by the Freshwater Fish Marketing Corporation and the Canadian Saltfish Corporation. The purpose of these corporations is to establish higher and more stable prices.

Fisheries and Oceans Canada has regional institutes which conduct biological research, fisheries management and ocean science at St. Andrews, New Brunswick; St. John's, Newfoundland; Ste. Anne de Bellevue, Quebec; Winnipeg,

Manitoba; and Nanaimo, British Columbia. The staff of 883 includes 203 scientists.

In international waters

Canada participates in the deliberations and decisions of no fewer than ten international commissions and councils, embracing all aspects of "the fishery" (the all-embracing term referring to the business of fish) from whitefish to whales.

In 1977, 13 nations ratified the Northwest Atlantic Fisheries Organization (N.A.F.O.)—"Northwest" describes the Grand Banks and other waters off Canada's East coast as they are seen from Europe. The commission has agreed on such conservation methods as the establishment of minimum mesh sizes for trawl nets, closed seasons in certain areas and overall seasonal catch limits.

The conservation measures on the Fraser River of the International Pacific Salmon Fisheries Commission have met with some success in reviving the runs of two species of salmon—the sockeye, and the pink. Although the Commission

has done a good job for these species, the resource is still far from being used to its maximum potential.

While seeking some measure of international accord, Canada moved on its own in 1964 to exclude the fishermen of all other countries from a 19-kilometre zone off all her coasts. This zone was extended to 370 kilometres in 1977. Some exceptions are made for countries that signed bilateral fishing agreements with Canada: Bulgaria, Cuba, the Common Market nations, the Faeroe Islands, East Germany, Japan, Norway, Poland, Portugal, Rumania, Spain, and the U.S.S.R. The huge Gulf of St. Lawrence has been totally closed to foreign fishermen, except for the French whose traditional presence in the area was formalized in a separate agreement in 1976.

Fishing rights on the Great Lakes are shared with the United States under the Great Lakes Fishery Convention. Both countries act jointly in biology and behavior research. They have been particularly active in the eradication of the sea lamprey which attacks lake trout.

Who will own the fish farms of the future?

IN QUANTITATIVE TERMS, there is no shortage of food in the world—but a lot of it happens to be in places where it's not needed. And a lot of what we do grow doesn't suit the needs and tastes of the hungry; you can't pass laws to say that rice-eaters have to switch to oatmeal. But just about everybody is partial to a nice piece of fish. And no less than 71 percent of the earth's surface is water. Starting out with this proposition, fish scientists are hopeful that such maritime nations as Canada will soon turn in earnest to the farming of the seas.

Mola mola, a common Pacific coast fish, produces about 300 million eggs during its lifetime. If its predators were controlled, and its natural food supply augmented, how many extra nutritious meals could be supplied by this species alone? The teeming cod, haddock and pollock that first

brought Europeans to the Canadian shore could, the enthusiasts believe, swarm in greater numbers than ever before if we could learn to prevent the vast natural wastage. We already know how to grow some plants on barren areas of the seabed merely by providing artificial lighting.

Sir Alistair Hardy, an eminent British zoologist once predicted that seabed tractors would be developed to "till" the ocean floor much as the prairies are worked today. One thing is certain: before fish-farming could be developed on a major scale, the maritime nations must get together to decide peacefully who owns the vast silent mountains and prairies of the seabed. On January 1, 1977, Canada extended its fisheries jurisdiction over a 370-kilometre strip of ocean ("the 200-mile limit") off the nation's coastlines.

If the business fails

EDERAL STATISTICS reveal that business failures are on the rise. There were more than 10,000 in 1982, almost double the number that had occurred just three years previously. These businesses left behind unpaid debts totaling more than $2 billion. Most of the bankruptcies and insolvencies involve small firms that do not have the volume to go into debt too far, but the occasional crash of a major corporation boosts the loss figure dramatically. For example, in British Columbia, the number of bankruptcies grew from 687 in 1979 to 1,042 in 1982—a 52-percent increase. The total liabilities for these firms, however, grew from $84.4 million to $413.8 million in the same period—a 320-percent rise.

What is the difference between an *insolvency* and a *bankruptcy*? Not much, when you look at the average case. Generally speaking, a company (or an individual person) is considered insolvent when total debts exceed total assets and it is impossible to meet financial obligations of at least $1,000. The company (or person) reaches the status of bankrupt once a *receiving order* is issued under the terms of the Bankruptcy Act. One situation usually follows the other.

Although provincially incorporated companies may be wound up—or closed down, if you prefer—under provincial laws for a variety of reasons, when they become insolvent they are governed by federal law. The federal statutes concerned are the Winding-up Act and the Bankruptcy Act. The latter act, passed in 1949 and amended in 1966, is the legislation we are concerned with in this section. The provinces have no authority in the area of bankruptcy.

Applying equally across the country, the Bankruptcy Act sets government machinery in motion to realize (turn into

cash) any remaining assets of the bankrupt person or business and to distribute that cash fairly among the creditors. This act protects creditors from the unscrupulous operator who might try to salt away income or assets and then claim bankruptcy. It also protects the debtor, to a large extent, allowing him to get rid of his obligations eventually so that, if he has the will and the ability, he can try again. In other words, the act gives him a second chance. His business career is not necessarily extinguished by one failure or mistake, which might, after all, have been caused mostly by bad luck. Many a small company has gone under simply because another company did not make good on promises—for instance, a six-month delay in the delivery of bathtubs could force a contracting plumber into insolvency.

When a businessman realizes that he is insolvent, he must not engage in any further trading. Furthermore, he must not pay off any creditor at the expense of the others.

If bankruptcy should threaten, don't panic. Don't try to raise extra money at ridiculous rates of interest. Take your records and proposals to a chartered accountant, or seek an interview with one of the people or companies or government officials licensed by the authorities as a *trustee in bankruptcy*. They will save you from bankruptcy, if they can.

Common causes of failure

A common cause of business failure is weak management—a lack of determination in insisting upon tests or standards of profitability in every area of a company's operations. Another error management makes is that of mixing up priorities—for instance, paying more attention to growth in size and not enough to comparative growth in profits. It is not at all certain that all increases in sales dollars, or sales volume, will automatically increase profits.

At the outset, you must have enough capital to launch your enterprise and keep it afloat until it can begin to generate profit. Novice businessmen often overburden themselves with bills for such nonsalable things as alluring shop fittings or decor, or commit themselves to credit purchases of production machinery or merchandise beyond their real ability to finance. You may be able to swim for a while on the strength of bank or finance company loans, but how will you pay them back?

It is natural for the new businessman to be optimistic (he wouldn't start on his own if he wasn't) but it is sheer foolishness for him to assume that trade will roll in quickly enough to provide sufficient profit to pay off loans. Early profits are seldom as large as the new proprietor hopes. It takes time to become known.

Some people simply spend their way into insolvency. The simplest way to do this is to grant yourself a salary larger than the business can afford. In effect, you are paying yourself with your own capital. All salaries and expenses should be held down to a minimum until the business is well established and patents profitable.

Another common cause of failure is not keeping up the *books of account*, the company records that every corporation must maintain by law. It is a wise company that prepares a monthly profit-and-loss statement at least. There are other pitfalls you should watch out for:

(1) Don't expand too early into other branches. Until the business has substantial reserves, one branch failure can bring down the whole company structure.

(2) Beware of the dishonest worker. Keep track of any cash in the till or in the office. Never permit employes to borrow from the cash drawer. Check for noncompany use of vehicles and telephones (especially long-distance calls).

(3) Guard against petty theft. Check the goods on shop shelves frequently against invoices and sales records. Valuable raw materials and equipment in a factory or service industry should also be watched closely.

(4) Don't be tempted to cut the prices of your goods or services to levels that do

The all-conquering computer

BACK IN THE MIDDLE of the nineteenth century an English inventor named Charles Babbage designed what he called an analytical engine. This is the dubious ancestor of the humming electronic computers which are increasingly taking over all humdrum and repetitive clerical work.

Today's computer with its terminals, central processor, spinning tape drives, disc files, and high-speed printer is capable of lightning-fast and infinitely complex operations. For instance, it can perform millions of additions of ten-digit numbers in seconds. Instantaneously, it can give a salesclerk a private printed answer to a coded query about the current state of a customer's account. Most of the bills you receive today are issued by computer.

Of course, the computer doesn't think. It merely performs certain functions to the orders provided by a technician (the *programmer*). With virtually limitless data available on magnetic discs and tapes for instant referral, plus all the capability of the most sophisticated calculating machine, the computer has become an indispensable tool of modern business.

Before a computer is given a job to do, an expert known as a systems analyst works out a sequence of steps that will solve the problem. This plan of operation depends, however, upon the logic of the program. If the program is well conceived, the computer will do the job expected of it—if the program is "garbage" then the work done by the computer will also be garbage.

not allow you a reasonable profit. You may get a rush of customers but it should be obvious that, in the long run, you won't have enough revenue to cover your wholesale costs plus your operating expenses. Later, if you reverse your sales policy, your customers may desert you, thinking that you are raising prices.

Meeting the creditors

When you admit your insolvency, the usual procedure is that you call a meeting of creditors. There, you explain your financial situation to them, and ask their approval for the reorganization of operations. Such a reorganization, it is hoped, will produce the best possible recovery for the creditors and investors and,

should more favorable circumstances develop, make it possible for you to make a comeback. This procedure is sometimes called a *proposal* and sometimes referred to as *voluntary composition*, or a *scheme of arrangement*.

The creditors of an insolvent company quite often find it more advantageous to work out a reorganization of the finances and operations of a corporation than to force its liquidation. Proposals for producing recovery could include a drastic reduction in the operating costs of the business, salary cuts to senior company officers, the closing of unprofitable branches, the elimination of unsuccessful lines of goods and the temporary suspension of interest payments on loans.

Inside the debtors' prison

IT IS a widely held belief that no Canadian can be sent to prison for not paying his debts in these enlightened days. But, as it is with most generalities, this is a belief that is only partly true.

For one example, any person who has a court judgment against him for debt and who actually has the means to pay that debt but does not or will not, can find himself reconsidering the entire matter as he sits on the cot of a jail cell.

Similarly, it is best to know that you cannot avoid responsibility for repaying a debt just because the person to whom you owe the money fails to or forgets to ask you for repayment (or is, perhaps, too shy or diffident to ask or mention the unhappy fact to you). There is an old legal maxim that the debtor must seek out the creditor. Your obligation to pay your bills can be stated in another way: it is part of a contract between you and the person to whom you owe the money, a contract into which you entered voluntarily.

It's only about a century or so since debtors were put into special debtors' prisons until they could square their accounts with their creditors. It was not uncommon for these unfortunates to spend several years in jail—sometimes accompanied by their entire families—in cramped and wretched quarters.

There is an imperishable record of this system as it existed in England of the nineteenth century in the classic novels of the great Charles Dickens.

The novelist's father John (the original Micawber) was tossed into London's Marshalsea prison for debt, and his ten-year-old son Charles was put to work for two years in a boot-polish factory. The son's bitter experiences were later recounted graphically in *David Copperfield* (1849).

It was in the sentimental novel *Little Dorrit* (1855) that Dickens drew his most detailed picture of the Marshalsea. Dorrit was born in the debtors' prison and when aged 14 was producing fine needlework to earn money for food for herself and her destitute father. After the family was finally set free through a lucky inheritance, Dorrit went back to the prison to be married in the chapel.

Dickens had little good to say for the law. He satirized the courts savagely in *Bleak House* (1852), and had his unforgettable Mr. Bumble tell us (in *Oliver Twist*) that "the law is a ass, a idiot."

Faced with the prospect of heavy loss in a bankruptcy, the creditors would probably go along with any reasonable plan that offered them some chance of recouping their money. But it would have to be a most realistic proposal before they would risk losing a dollar beyond what they would get if the insolvency proceeded immediately into a bankruptcy. In such cases, the character and determination of the individual debtor could be decisive factors.

A copy of the proposal must be filed with a licensed trustee in bankruptcy, who will make sure that it meets the standards set out in the Bankruptcy Act, and that it is fair to all parties. If the proposal is approved by creditors holding 75 percent of the claims, as well as by the court, it will be binding on all the creditors.

Trustee and receiver

If the creditors refuse to accept the proposals of the debtor, then a receiving order is issued under which all his assets are held for the general benefit of the creditors. The trustee advises the debtor of his duties and, in turn, files the assignment with the official receiver. This official, an officer of the court, sets a date for a meeting of the creditors at which the affairs of the bankrupt will be considered. Advertisements asking creditors to come forward are placed in the Canada *Gazette* and in local newspapers.

The creditors and the trustee decide how best to turn the assets into cash. The trustee, who has become the legal holder of the bankrupt's assets, carries out the sale and then distributes the cash among the creditors according to their standing, as set out in the legislation.

If the trustee discovers that a fraudulent claim has been put forward, he can have that creditor charged with a punishable offense.

If the creditors agree, the trustee can continue to operate the business himself.

The law demands that the bankrupt debtor assist the trustee as best he can, giving the official any information he may require in carrying out his duties. The trustee also has the authority to de-clare void any gifts or other transfers of property that the debtor might have made in the period preceding the bankruptcy.

The "act of bankruptcy"

A business concern is bankrupt only when formally declared so by the courts. The court may, at the request of a creditor or creditors, or even the debtor himself, declare bankrupt any business which is shown to have committed an "act of bankruptcy."

It is an act of bankruptcy if:

(1) A debtor makes an assignment of his assets—that is, if he transfers the property of the business to be held in trust, or for the benefit of a creditor.

(2) A debtor makes a fraudulent conveyance, gift or transfer of property.

(3) A debtor gives undue preference to one or more creditors.

(4) A debtor is unable to meet payments—on bills, loans or mortgages—as they become due.

(5) A debtor has left Canada or gone into hiding.

A full-time fisherman or farmer cannot be declared bankrupt, nor can any person whose annual income is below $2,500.

Discharge from bankruptcy

At any time after three months from the formal declaration of a bankruptcy, assuming that the administration work involved has been cleared up, the trustee may apply to the court or have the bankrupt debtor discharged from bankruptcy. The creditors in the case must be advised so that they can attend the hearing to object, if they so choose.

In olden days, the man who failed to pay his debts had his workbench (*banco)* broken up, which effectively prevented him from resuming his trade.

This custom provides the origin of our term "bankrupt" (the Latin word *rumpere* means "to break"). Today, if the application for discharge for bankruptcy is granted (and in most cases, it is), the debtor's business slate is wiped clean, and his right to sign legal documents is restored. He can launch a new enterprise, incorporate it and seek new investment funds from the public.

14/Your Social Security

The community responsibility

THE STRUGGLE for survival is the oldest of man's instincts—and the strongest. Although to suggest that the average citizen must struggle every day to survive sounds farfetched in the context of our modern civilization, he still struggles to make his existence as secure as possible. Thus, while his cave-dwelling forebears worked simply to stay alive from day to day, modern man works to guarantee that he will be alive the next day and the day after.

There are, of course, different levels of "survival." In most countries, though, simple survival—food, shelter and other basic necessities—is now taken for granted. The citizens can work to make the continuation of their well-being as secure as possible.

One of the first steps man took toward civilization was to form community groups. The great ideas that have characterized advancing societies—division of labor, sharing and joint effort—were spawned in these communities. So, too, was the idea of social security. There are two sides to this ideal: (1) the individual must be guaranteed the freedom and opportunity to seek his own goals, to look after himself and his family; (2) the community must be prepared to acknowledge the general responsibility of society for the basic well-being of those unable to fend for themselves.

The concepts of community and respect for the dignity of the individual are central to the whole idea. Only through cooperative planning and action will all people be able to realize their potential and contribute creatively to the society in which they live.

All social-security legislation at all levels in Canada is based on these beliefs. There is a clear desire to share the national wealth and productivity so that no Canadian will be penalized because of his age, state of health, place of birth, province or residence.

The wide range of governmental social programs is backed up by numerous private and community social services, operated by a centralized executive in practically every city and town.

Happily, it can be said that no Canadian—and that includes Indians and Inuit—need suffer from deprivation or lack of understanding advice and practical assistance. It may well be, however, that some isolated people are still not fully aware of the social services available to them, or perhaps do not choose to take advantage of them. The right of the individual to choose *not* to be helped has also to be respected, in the last analysis.

Because of the division of lawmaking authority decreed at the time of Confederation, Canadian social-security policies have been developed by both the federal and provincial governments—often on a joint basis. At the federal level are programs of youth and family allowances, the Canada Pension Plan, old-age security and guaranteed income supplement, unemployment insurance, war veterans' allowances, disability and dependents' pensions and assistance plans for Indians and Inuit.

Joint federal-provincial programs include hospital and medical-care schemes, housing assistance, the Canada Assistance Plan, and vocational training, rehabilitation, and financial assistance to the aged, blind and disabled. Programs offered by the provinces include workers' compensation for injury, a variety of medical plans, day-care centers, and support services for special groups.

All these programs and services are outlined in this chapter. So are the major matters a family must deal with when a death occurs.

Helping everyone everywhere
The idea of a cradle-to-grave social security has given rise to a wide variety of special services from drug-addiction

588

clinics, anti-cigarette campaigns and prisoner-rehabilitation programs to the provision of ambulances, hospital ships and planes making mercy flights to and from Arctic and wilderness regions.

The mercy flight is an especially dramatic example of this new social security: the service is provided to anyone in a remote area who needs urgent medical treatment not immediately available.

Canadian forces to the rescue

THROUGH 32 TENSE DAYS of November and December of 1972, millions in Canada, the United States and abroad became caught up in a chilling drama as the planes and personnel of the Search and Rescue service of the Canadian Forces looked desperately for a twin-engined Beechcraft aircraft missing with four aboard, somewhere in the tundra wastes of the Northwest Territories. The eventual sensational denouement turned a bright spotlight on the most spectacular of Canada's social-welfare services.

The Search and Rescue (S.A.R.) branch was set up by the Royal Canadian Air force immediately after World War II. It provides a 24-hour "find 'em and bring 'em out" service for lost flyers, children, hunters, climbers, and sick or injured persons in remote areas. Marine units aid sinking ships or pleasure boats in distress. The total zone of operations measures nearly sixteen million square kilometres.

In a recent year, the S.A.R. had 2,900 alerts, and from these arose 33 major searches. Thirty-one concerned missing civil aircraft, mostly in the far north, of which 28 were found. Nearly 9,000 hours of flying time was logged and the cost to the taxpayer was approximately $10 million. In that particular year, eight members of the C.F. lost their lives while playing the Good Samaritan.

The 1972 drama began on November 8 when a German immigrant bush pilot known as Marten Hartwell (real name: Leopold Herrmann) took off from Cambridge Bay, Victoria Island, with two Inuit patients and an English-born nurse, Judy Hill. The destination was Yellowknife, capital of the Northwest Territories: the weather was threatening. Hartwell's plane dropped out of radio contact about 113 kilometres out of Cambridge Bay.

When the plane was overdue at Yellowknife, a routine call went into the rescue coordination center at the C.F. Namao base, near Edmonton. The plane was equipped with wheels, not skis, and it could have made a normal landing at only Coppermine or Contwoyto Lake. These bases were checked. The Beechcraft was carrying a battery-operated emergency locator transmitter (known as a E.L.T.) which would put out a guiding beep for search planes.

For nearly three weeks, as hope grew dimmer for the missing quartet, the S.A.R. planes, manned by voluntary spotters, combed the bleak, snowy landscape without luck. A hundred leads were examined fruitlessly. The probable crash areas had been plotted and more than 208,400 square kilometres had been searched.

The search was regretfully canceled after 19 days, then reactivated in response to emotional publicity. Ten days later, a pilot on a routine flight from Yellowknife to Inuvik, on the Mackenzie Delta, picked up an E.L.T. signal from somewhere to the south of Great Bear Lake, many kilometres to the west of Hartwell's planned course. The S.A.R. planes flocked to that area and, on December 9, spotted the bearded pilot waving a distress flare near his wrecked plane which was partly concealed by trees. Parachutists were dropped and a helicopter sped to the site with supplies.

Only Hartwell was alive. To survive, he had eaten portions of the bodies of two of his passengers. The sensational confession of cannibalism ensured headlines around the world. No charges were preferred against the pilot.

Sometimes a doctor-and-nurse team will be flown in; or the patient may be flown out—sometimes directly to the hospital. For example, a helicopter service operates directly to the roof of Sick Children's Hospital in Toronto. This high-rise heliport serves other nearby hospitals. A deep-sea diver suffering "the bends" was flown from Georgian Bay to the roof of Sick Children's and taken via tunnel to Toronto General Hospital's decompression chamber.

Mercy planes also rush human organs from city to city for transplant operations. A typical example involved a man killed in an auto accident in Edmonton: within a matter of hours, his kidneys had been removed and were being transplanted in two separate operations in Toronto and Vancouver.

The Search and Rescue Units of the Canadian Forces are famous for their operations across the country and in the waters of the oceans beyond. There are bases in Halifax, Trenton (Ontario), Edmonton and Victoria. When requested by the Coast Guard, R.C.M.P., provincial police or airport personnel, they send out planes, helicopters, ground forces or whatever else is necessary to locate missing aircraft and vessels.

The rocky road to G.A.I.

By the mid-1970s it appeared that the headlong advance of the Canadian social-security system had been checked. In late 1975, the federal government announced that a decade of unprecedented expansion of social services had ended: "From now on, the thrust of government will be away from big-spending programs and move toward intervention and regulation to improve life." One of the immediate casualties appeared to be the social scientists' dream of a guaranteed annual income (G.A.I.).

Supporters of G.A.I. hoped it would encompass and replace most, if not all, of the existing network of social-welfare plans and programs. Economists would decide on the amount of money an individual or a family needed to maintain an acceptable standard of living—considering cost-of-living fluctuations. Any pay-

ment needed to bring an individual's income up to the established level would come to him as a right—without the "stigma of welfare"—from general taxation revenues.

Critics point to the abuses that have come to light within the unemployment-insurance and welfare programs, and to the extra expense the G.A.I. would mean to the average taxpayer.

There is, however, considerable disagreement about whether a guaranteed-income plan would cost that much more than the existing variety of support and welfare programs now operating at the federal and provincial levels. There is, too, widespread agreement that the danger of fostering a class of "willingly unemployed employables" must be studied with great care.

While G.A.I. itself appears stalled, piecemeal progress has been made toward the central aim of the planners. They point with satisfaction at the guaranteed annual income supplement for the elderly and their dependents, and to increases in other benefits to allow for the rising cost of living.

The meaning of poverty

In recent years, there has evolved a changing attitude toward poverty and a new assessment of what it means to be poor.

A federal White Paper, "Income Security for Canadians," prepared by the Department of National Health and Welfare in 1970, quoted the outmoded concept of poverty as meaning that one was so poor that he was "unable to maintain life and working capacity." It went on to say that poverty, today, meant more than just lack of income: "It means also a lack of opportunities—for good health, for education, for meaningful employment and for recreation. It means a depressing environment, a sense of failure, and a feeling of alienation from society."

More specifically, Statistics Canada in the late 1970's defined the conditions of poverty as existing "when more than 58.5 percent of family income is required to provide the minimum necessities of food, shelter and clothing."

Health services

ALL LEVELS of government are involved in the provision and supervision of tax-supported health services. Constitutionally, health is a provincial concern; however, the provincial governments delegate much of their authority to the municipalities. The federal government has jurisdiction over health matters that are of national importance—such as standards of quality and purity of foods—and provides support funds for the provincial health plans and hospital facilities. It also provides certain direct medical-treatment services through the Department of National Health and Welfare. Medical treatment and hospitalization of armed forces personnel and war veterans are provided by the various departments of National Defense and Veterans' Affairs.

A comprehensive occupational health program is provided for employes of the federal government whether stationed inside or outside of the country. This includes health counseling, surveillance of working conditions, medical examinations and emergency treatment, plus other advisory services. Provincial and municipal government workers are taken care of in a similar way. Many industrial plants and other large businesses also provide certain medical services for their own workers, often including a resident staff nurse.

Coordination of health services at all levels is carried out at the Federal-Provincial Meetings of Health Ministers and by regular meetings of the federal deputy ministers of health. In a continuous process of improving and safeguarding the welfare of the general public, legislators have the health laws under almost continuous revision. This is particularly so in the field of food and drugs. (*See* Chapter 6, "Safeguards when shopping.")

Quarantine and immigration

The Health Services Branch of the Department of National Health and Welfare has quarantine officers available to inspect all vessels, airplanes and other carriers arriving from other countries, as well as their crews and passengers. It is their job to detect and prevent the entry of smallpox, plague, cholera, typhus, yellow fever and all forms of relapsing fever. Major seaports and international airports have quarantine stations.

The branch also checks that the national standards of hygiene are being maintained on all vehicles used in interprovincial transport, on all Canadian ships and aircraft, as well as on all federal property—including ports and terminals.

All persons applying for immigration to Canada are examined by the department's medical officers. The Health Services Branch also provides treatment for immigrants in an emergency until they have enrolled in the medical-care plan of the province they settle in—for instance, if they fall ill on the way to Canada, or while they are looking for a job.

The branch advises the Department of Transport on the physical and mental health of flying personnel employed in civil aviation. Branch doctors review the results of medical examinations, help with flying safety programs and assist in investigating air accidents.

Indian health

Apart from being entitled to the medical care and hospital insurance benefits provided by the province in which they live, Canada's 323,782 Indians receive assistance directly from the Department of National Health and Welfare.

The Health Services Branch conducts a complete public health program, providing Indians with dental care for children, immunization, school health services, health education, pre- and post-natal clinics and well-baby clinics. It also provides funds for adult education, family planning, venereal disease prevention and for campaigns against alcoholism and drug abuse.

The role of the federal government has, however, been changing as Indian bands increasingly take over their own affairs. Both Indians and Inuit are becoming community health representatives and family health aids, giving health instruction and making home visits.

Indians and Inuit now generally use the same hospitals and services as everyone else. Separate hospitals established for their benefit in the past are now being phased out. Only 14 hospitals still remain in operation; however, other forms of health care include 89 nursery stations, 123 health centers, 181 health stations and 12 outpatient clinics. Situated in a remote area, a typical nursing station is a combined emergency treatment and public health unit, with from two to four beds and basic equipment.

Inuit health

Both the Yukon Territory and the Northwest Territories have tax-supported hospital insurance programs. The Northwest Territories has a medical-care insurance program, and a similar one is being planned for the Yukon. Most employed persons in the Yukon are at present insured under private medical plans provided by their employers—usually big companies; any Inuit not so covered is taken care of by the Department of National Health and Welfare.

The federal department functions as a health department for the two territories, which contain the great majority of Canada's Inuit population of 25,390. The services include a public health program and the transportation of patients from isolat-

ed communities to major medical centers. Most Inuit now live in permanent housing within reach of stores, schools and the department's medical facilities.

Several universities provide medical personnel and students who serve on a rotational basis in remote areas under government contract.

Veterans' services

Canada provides comprehensive medical, dental and artificial limb service to its veterans of the two World Wars and the Korean War. The Department of Veterans' Affairs also provides the same services to members of the present Canadian Forces, the Royal Canadian Mounted Police and to the wards of other governments or departments of the federal government upon request.

The federal government maintains one active-treatment hospital and two home-care units across Canada for veterans, and the National Defense Medical Care Centre in Ottawa for chronic patients requiring special treatment. In addition, there are numerous community hospitals which set aside some of their beds for veterans on a priority basis.

Veterans' welfare officers stationed at regional headquarters work closely with other social security agencies in assisting ex-servicemen and their dependents with problems arising from physical disabilities or the deteriorations of advancing age.

Provincial health services

The provinces bear the primary responsibility for preventing disease and improving community health standards. Their authority covers preventive services, hospitals of several kinds, treatment of tuberculosis, mental illness and other diseases, as well as care and rehabilitation of the chronically ill and disabled. Legislation dealing with these aspects of public health is proposed by the provincial health departments and other official agencies, backed by voluntary health organizations, the medical profession, and teaching and research institutions.

Organization, financing and administration varies from province to province,

592

but the services provided to the public are basically the same across the country. No Canadian (or alien, for that matter) will ever be refused needed medical care in any emergency, irrespective of his ability to pay. Emergency ambulance service (by air, if necessary) is ready to move at your telephone call.

Some provinces, such as Saskatchewan, offer phone-in services, providing the latest medical knowledge to doctors. Any physician who phones in will be given information covering emergency situations (*i.e.*, coronary care, suicide threats, child problems).

Some programs, including hospital and medical-care insurance and the control of tuberculosis, cancer and alcoholism, are occasionally administered by separate public agencies responsible to the provincial minister of health. There are also voluntary organizations that provide specialized services with government support.

At the local level

While provincial health departments devise and control overall health programs, they delegate the responsibility for putting them into effect to city health departments and health units wherever possible. In some places—for example, in remote communities in the north—the province will provide direct service itself.

The community health services are mostly administered by city, district or regional boards of health. You can usually find them cataloged under "Health" in the government listings of your telephone directory. The basic staff of a local health unit, or city health department, usually consists of a full-time medical officer of health (known as the M.O.H.), a number of public health nurses and a public health inspector.

Local health programs deal with the following: the prevention and control of infectious diseases using vaccines and prophylactics; improving maternal, child and dental health; registering vital statistics; health education and counseling; and sanitation. Larger metropolitan health departments also have special services for mental health, home care, as well as for care and rehabilitation of the chronically ill and handicapped.

In most provinces, there are family-planning clinics; and health-screening programs exist to detect chronic conditions. City health departments also work with provincial agencies in accident prevention, and in pollution control.

Hospitals and clinics

Canadians receive direct medical care at home, in doctors' offices, in clinics and at hospitals where they are treated as either outpatients or inpatients.

Hospitals, our major medical institutions, are classified by type of support as public, private or federal, as well as by type of service provided: general, special (orthopedic, maternity, etc.), and for mental illness or tuberculosis. Together, they offer the public more than 172,000 beds. Ten hospitals cater exclusively to children.

Federal hospitals are operated for native peoples in areas where provincial or community facilities are not available, and there are separate hospitals for veterans and members currently serving in the armed forces. Provincial governments operate most of the mental and tuberculosis hospitals and clinics, and provide specialized treatment for other conditions such as venereal disease, alcoholism and drug addiction. They also run a small number of general hospitals. Most of the latter—the best known of all hospitals for the general public—are run under provincial licenses by religious and secular organizations, and by municipalities.

There are numerous private hospitals, most of them small compared to the public ones; these can provide either specialized forms of treatment or general health care. Some private hospitals are famous for especially intricate surgery. And one private hospital in Toronto offers a multilingual medical staff to serve patients from various ethnic groups.

Hospital services are provided on either an inpatient or outpatient basis. A patient will usually remain in hospital when his condition warrants the close attention of doctors and nurses. Included among the outpatients would be those sent to the emergency department—perhaps after a street or domestic accident—or to one of the many specialty clinics for a pre-admission checkup or follow-up treatment, or to the family-practice clinic for a routine medical examination.

The specialty clinics cover a wide range including obstetrics, mental health, speech therapy, podiatry, physiotherapy, ophthalmology, cardiology, neurology, and renal and gastro-intestinal conditions. These clinics usually handle cases referred to them by general practitioners and largely serve public patients.

The family-practice clinic has assumed more importance recently, especially in the larger cities. Staffed by a hospital's own doctors and nurses, it provides the same services as general practitioners do in private practice. Its purpose is to make basic health and medical services more readily available to the public, emphasizing preventive medicine in particular.

There is also a growing trend toward group practice by physicians in private clinics. In some towns, in fact, the solo general practitioner is all but extinct. Most of the private clinics have four to eight doctors, but some have as many as 40 or 50 working together.

The clinics vary in the skills offered. Some consist of only general family practitioners (the G.P.'s), while others consist exclusively of specialists—some offer both. These doctors are paid on a regular fee-for-service basis partly or totally through the medical insurance plans. The payment pattern varies across the country, mainly in relation to whether membership in the medical-insurance plan is optional or compulsory for the residents. In Quebec, for instance, the doctor bills the provincial plan for all permanent residents; in British Columbia the doctor bills only for persons enrolled in the plan.

Both the hospital and private clinics offer the big advantage of shared talents and facilities. The cooperating doctors can fill in for each other for holidays and arrange to take turns being on call.

Another form of group practice, the group health center, has been in operation for many years but has not achieved great popularity with the medical profession. These general-practice clinics tend to be established by rural groups or trade unions, with the doctors working on a salaried basis. The centers are funded by the government on a *per capita* basis: this amount is the average per capita cost of that province's medical-care program adjusted within a special formula, multiplied by the number of people served by the center.

First aid from the aristocrats

CERTAINLY THE OLDEST in origin—and one of the most valuable—of the voluntary organizations providing humanitarian services in Canada is the St. John Ambulance Association. It can trace its aristocratic beginnings back to the Crusaders of 600 A.D. Its motto is *Pro utilitate hominum* ("For the service of mankind").

Known particularly for its first-aid services at large public gatherings, the Most Venerable Order of the Hospital of St. John of Jerusalem (to give its full title) began operations in Canada in 1883.

Since the days of Queen Victoria, the ruling monarch has always assumed the post of Sovereign Head of the British Order, and a member of the royal family holds the title of Grand Prior. The Prior of Canada is traditionally the incumbent governor general. The fieldwork of the order is supported financially, in part, by a remarkable system of granting sonorous honors and titles—including "knights" (or "dames")—created by the governor general with three taps of a sword on the shoulder of the kneeling applicant at Rideau Hall. There are six grades of members in the order; the Rt. Hon. Vincent Massey (governor general 1952–59) held the highest rank, that of Bailiff Grand Cross.

The public health nurse

Among the many health professionals working in the community, the public health nurse is often the best known. She is involved particularly in preventive medicine. Working with city health departments, local health units, hospitals and boards of education, she is an important link between these agencies and the home, carrying the message of the need for good health to the families, as well as carrying the families' needs back to the agencies.

In the schools, she helps supervise child health programs, assisting with medical examinations, hearing and vision testing, immunization and tuberculin testing. With other health agencies, she helps rehabilitate the sick, injured, handicapped and the chronically ill. She is also involved in pre-natal and baby-care programs, mental health counseling and general health care of persons who reside in children's boarding homes and nursing homes.

All provinces have established intensive home care programs under either direct hospital or voluntary service sponsorship, aimed at relieving the strain on hospital beds (which cost somewhere between $200 and $450 a day to maintain), keeping people out of chronic-care institutions, and allowing some people to be treated at home instead of in hospital. These programs provide nursing, physiotherapy and other professional skills to care for the aged, disabled, chronically ill or convalescent patient; they also provide certain homemaker services where required.

Red Cross services

Among the many voluntary health and welfare agencies in Canada, the Red Cross is the largest and best known. It is also one of the oldest, dating back to 1896 when it was founded as the Canadian branch of the British National Society for Aid to the Sick and Wounded; it became the Canadian Red Cross Society in 1909.

Its programs include a nationwide blood-transfusion service, hospitals and nursing stations in isolated areas, home nursing, homemaking, transportation and sickroom supply services. It also runs extensive youth programs helping needy children both in Canada and elsewhere. Dedicated to the alleviation of human suffering, the Red Cross will always offer you help if you are sick or in an accident, or will put you in touch with the agency best able to assist you.

The blood-transfusion service which calls continually for donations of blood from the public is perhaps the Red Cross's best known work. In its rare-blood "library," it keeps on file the names of those people with uncommon blood types who can be called upon when blood of their type is needed in emergencies.

In the area of general public welfare, the Red Cross offers instruction in family nutrition and homemaking skills; provides home nursing service; and supplies clothing and layettes to the needy. It maintains large and varied programs for needy children, providing money for specialist heart surgery, artificial limbs and adaptive appliances, dental care and speech therapy. It also funds kindergartens devoted to the instruction of deaf children.

Overseas, the Canadian branch joins other members of the Red Cross organization in running and funding disaster relief and other humanitarian projects. Clothing, food and medical aid are provided, and a special service is organized to help reunite families separated by war or other emergencies. In war, all combatants normally permit the Red Cross to police the humane treatment of prisoners of war.

The Red Cross Youth (membership: 2.1 million) is Canada's largest youth organization, providing a steady source of graduates for the senior Red Cross. It carries out its own selfless program of improving the health and safety practices of youth, promoting volunteer involvement in the community and developing humanitarian concerns in young people with an understanding of the international Red Cross movement.

Other important voluntary organizations include the venerable St. John Ambulance Association and the Victorian Order of Nurses.

Health insurance

Hospital insurance

Medical-care insurance

Provincial variations

Low earnings subsidized

Private supplementary plans

Complaints about service

MEDICARE seems already to be so much a part of the Canadian scene that it is almost taken for granted. But in fact, the first provincial public hospital insurance scheme began only in 1947, and the first province-wide public medical-care plan in 1962; in each case, Saskatchewan took the lead. Much earlier, following both British and American experience, municipal tax-supported plans providing physicians' services had been established in some western towns and villages, and Newfoundland operated a cottage hospital system.

Private plans came first. More than a century ago, groups from fraternal lodges, large industrial plants, farm communities and the public in general banded together to hire doctors on a salary (or per capita fee) basis to provide medical service for their dues-paying members. Trade unions and cooperatives developed similar schemes. Many of these plans could not survive the Depression years prior to World War II and, when prosperity returned, the commercial insurance companies moved into the field with a wide variety of premium-based medical-care plans. The medical profession itself sponsored nonprofit agencies, offering service contracts to the public at moderate cost.

The federal government had been discussing ways to provide universal health protection as early as 1928. During World War II, the problem was again looked into, this time on the basis of shared federal-provincial initiative and financial responsibility. This approach led to the passage, in 1957, of the Hospital Insurance and Diagnosis Services Act, a milestone in federal-provincial legislation.

The following year, federal grants began to flow to the provinces, expanding existing provincial hospital insurance plans and permitting new ones to develop. Only five provinces were involved at the beginning. By 1961, the other five, plus the two territories, had joined, providing a comprehensive hospital service for an estimated 99 percent of Canadians. All provinces accept landed immigrants into their plans. All immigrants other than landed immigrants are considered individually according to their immigration status, or whether they come from another province or another country.

The second arm of medicare—making the professional services of the nation's doctors available to the entire populace—developed more slowly. By the mid-1960s, 11.5 million Canadians were enrolled in various plans, public and private. Only four provinces—Ontario, Alberta, Saskatchewan and British Columbia—had province-wide plans in actual operation. After lengthy study, a Royal Commission on Health Services recommended in 1965 that another federal-provincial deal be struck, allowing a comprehensive country-wide medical plan to be implemented.

In 1968, with the passing of the federal Medical Care Act, the dream of total nationwide hospital and medical-care insurance became a reality. The cost? In 1981–82, the price of hospital insurance met by the federal and provincial governments soared to over $10 billion, causing the provinces to talk about bringing in "user fees." At this writing, Alberta was proposing to add a user fee of $25 for hospital beds. In New Brunswick, the proposal was to add a surcharge for diagnostic and outpatient clinics.

Hospital insurance

All provinces and the territories have hospital insurance programs providing complete and comprehensive coverage for all residents—not excluding temporary visitors or aliens in an emergency. Although most patients are admitted to hospital at the request of doctors, no one in genuine need of hospital care will be refused. Residents are issued a numbered card verifying their insured status. In an average case, they will make no cash payments at the hospital; an uninsured person will be charged for care, depending on ability to pay and other factors.

Provincial authorities run the hospitals: however, to qualify for the substantial financial aid from federal funds, they must provide at least public-ward accommodation in an approved hospital, meals, nursing service, diagnostic procedures, drugs as required, operating rooms, case rooms and anesthetic facilities, as well as the use of radiotherapy and physiotherapy if available. They must also provide certain outpatient services.

The provinces may provide any other services that they choose above the stipulated minimum, and are free to finance their portion of the cost as they like. The administrative and financial arrangements, true to the Canadian tradition, vary widely from province to province.

Under provincial laws, administration of hospital insurance plans is handled by either the departments of health, internal ministries of health or government-appointed commissions. Ontario combines hospital and practitioner care in the same administration. Money comes from general revenue and special sales taxes, from payroll deductions and premiums paid by individuals. A Nova Scotian contributes to his province's plan through a special sales tax. In Ontario, the public pays a premium, with certain exceptions such as the elderly, the disabled, and those on limited incomes. In British Columbia and Alberta, you pay authorized charges.

The federal government pays 50 percent of the total national costs, according to a complicated formula that allows a larger percentage to the "have not" provinces and rather less to others. Under this formula, Ontario is refunded only 41 percent of its hospital-operating budget.

The provinces pick up the full tab for operating their tuberculosis hospitals, their sanatoriums, hospitals or institutions for the mentally ill, their nursing homes and homes for the aged.

Although federal funds are not generally available for the construction of hospitals, money can be provided under the Health Resources Program for the building and equipping of teaching hospitals, medical schools and nursing-training facilities. The reasoning here is that such projects fall within Ottawa's constitutional responsibility for the health and welfare of the nation as a whole.

Medical-care insurance

All provinces and the territories have medical-care insurance programs under which their residents have all but a fraction of their basic doctor's bills paid. Insurance payments usually cover 100 percent according to the agreement arranged between the provincial government and the provincial medical association. In some provinces, however, physicians are permitted to charge an extra amount.

The provinces run their own plans, with federal financial assistance meeting about one-half of the net operating costs —that is, costs remaining after expenses have been deducted. The federal contribution is conditional upon the plan's meeting minimum statutory requirements.

Each provincial plan must first provide for all the facilities and equipment required for doctors to provide proper medical service, with no dollar limit or exclusion. This applies also to the treatment of patients in mental and tuberculosis hospitals, as well as to preventive services provided by public health agencies. The plans must be universally available to all eligible residents on equal terms and conditions in spite of previous health, age, nonmembership in a group, lack of income or other considerations.

The plans must provide portability—in other words, a person living in one province must still be entitled to the benefits of its insurance program while he is temporarily away from that province or while he is moving to another province. Some plans provide basic coverage anywhere in the world.

The plans must be run on a nonprofit basis by public authorities who are financially responsible to the provincial governments; however, this condition does not prevent provinces from turning over certain administrative functions to private nongovernment agencies.

The provinces themselves decide how to finance their part of the cost and whether membership by their residents will be voluntary or compulsory. When premiums are charged, the plans also provide for the subsidization of low-income families. Ontario is currently providing totally free health protection to over 1.6 million residents (including welfare re-cipients and old-age pensioners) and partially assisting another 86,000.

In the financial year ended March 31, 1975, federal taxes provided a total contribution to provincial hospital and medical-care insurance plans of more than $2.5 billion. While this sum seems huge enough, the total national health bill is, of course, many times greater. The 1982–83 Ontario provincial health bill alone reached $6.6 billion.

Provincial variations

Apart from meeting the minimum requirements of services and facilities demanded by the federal health authorities as a condition of federal financial participation, the provincial plans also offer a considerable range of "extras." To find

The Oath of Hippocrates

EACH YEAR as newly qualified doctors are admitted into practice, medicine continues to pay its respects to the memory of the physician Hippocrates, who died in Greece about 375 years before the birth of Christ. The "father of medicine" gathered a group of students about him on the Aegean island of Kos, and most of the large number of medical writings that ensued were attributed to Hippocrates himself.

He was the first to lift medicine to a scientific level, away from the superstition and dark ignorance of his times. He was also deeply concerned with the ethics of the profession. The Hippocratic Oath is still administered in many countries to graduating doctors: "You do solemnly swear, each man by whatever he holds most sacred, that you will be loyal to the profession of medicine and just and generous to its members; that you will lead your life and practice your art in uprightness and honor; that into whatsoever house you shall enter, it shall be for the good of the sick to the utmost of your power, you holding yourself aloof from wrong, from corruption, from the tempting of others to vice; that you will exercise your art solely for the cure of your patients and will give no drug, perform no operation, for a criminal purpose even if solicited, far less suggest it; that whatsoever you shall see or hear of the lives of men which is not fitting to be spoken, you will keep inviolably secret. These things do you swear."

The Oath is part of the *Hippocratic Collection*, and this vast work contains many treatises on the practice of medicine.

In his segment on surgery, his modern approach is remarkable. For example: "The nails [of the doctor performing the operation] neither to exceed nor come short of the finger tips. Practice using the finger ends. Practice all the operations with each hand and with both together, your object being to attain ability, grace, speed, painlessness, elegance and readiness."

Hippocrates extracted more than 400 drugs from plants, and at least 200 of them are still used. His philosophy was almost as renowned. In his *Aphorisms*, Hippocrates concluded: "Life is short, and art is long; the occasion fleeting; experience fallacious and judgment difficult." The passage of 2,000 years hasn't caused us to change a single syllable.

out about these, ask your doctor, or get in touch with your local health unit or the provincial department of health.

For example, Ontario's combined plan for hospital and practitioner benefits offer to every resident not only the care and treatment medically required in a standard (public) ward, but also:

(1) A broad range of outpatient services at hospitals and medically prescribed physiotherapy in approved private centers.

(2) Essential ambulance service (the insured person is required to pay a small portion of the cost of each trip).

(3) Medically necessary physicians' service—including specialists' care—at home, as well as in a doctor's office or in hospital.

(4) Specified dental surgery performed in hospital (100 percent of the fee set by the Ontario Health Insurance dental schedule of benefits).

(5) Eye examinations by an optometrist to determine the need for glasses ($10 per person).

(6) Chiropractic, osteopathic and chiropody (podiatry) services (up to $100, plus up to $25 for radiographic examinations, per person per year).

(7) Extended health care—in nursing homes and homes for the aged—is provided for people who have been insured in Ontario for one year or more, and who require continued nursing service and regular medical supervision. Patients pay a nominal daily fee, plus additional charges beyond standard ward levels.

(8) Home care: upon request by a physician, an insured person can receive special health services in the home.

(9) Insured physicians' and practitioners' services received outside Ontario covered to the same extent they would be paid for in Ontario.

Some provincial plans cover dentistry for children. For example, since 1964, Nova Scotia has provided free preventive dental care for all children under the age of 16. In Manitoba, 44,000 children under the age of 14 were being provided this service in the early 1980s.

On the other hand, the following list of exclusions from the Ontario scheme should give you a general idea of what most health insurance plans won't cover:

(1) Hospital visits solely for the administration of drugs.

(2) Dental care in hospital which is normally provided in the dentist's office.

(3) Eyeglasses or special appliances.

(4) The services of a private nurse.

(5) Drugs, vaccines, biological serum, extracts of their synthetic substitutes (except when provided in hospital); drugs taken home from the hospital.

(6) Transportation charges, other than approved ambulance service (even in an emergency, the insured person is required to pay a small charge).

(7) Medical examinations required for job applications, continuance of employment, life insurance, schools, camps or recreation.

The provinces operate their medicare schemes under different financial setups. In Newfoundland, Nova Scotia, Prince Edward Island, New Brunswick, Saskatchewan and the Northwest Territories, medicare payments are drawn from general revenues. There are premiums to pay in Manitoba, Ontario, Alberta and British Columbia. In Quebec, fees are paid partially from general taxation revenues and partially from an extra deduction from earnings, which is supplemented by a contribution from employers.

Low earnings subsidized

The percentage of medicare costs charged in the form of premiums varies among the five provinces that impose them. They are low in Saskatchewan and Manitoba, for lower-income families, but are relatively high in Ontario, Alberta and British Columbia—where average incomes are somewhat higher. In all five provinces, these premiums can be reduced by subsidies (or totally remitted) for families and individuals who had little or no taxable income in the preceding year. In addition, all those on welfare have their premiums paid for them.

Under the federal Canada Assistance Plan (*See* "The welfare system," later in this chapter), the federal government authorities share the costs which the provincial governments incur to provide drugs, dental care, prosthetic and other health services to people in need. This cost-sharing arrangement is necessary because these services are not covered under the universal health-care programs of the provinces, nor are they funded under the federal government's Established Programs Financial Act.

Private supplementary plans

Before Canada's medical and hospital insurance programs were established, insurance companies and other private agencies provided a high level of sickness and accident protection, at least for those who could afford the premiums. Most of these programs were phased out as the public plans went into operation during the 1960s. However, some private plans continued and still function to assist or supplement the public schemes.

In Saskatchewan, for example, two nonprofit private agencies continue to transfer claims and payments between physicians and the public insurance administration. A private insurance agency in Nova Scotia continues (on a nonprofit basis) to do for the province such work as enrolling, checking the eligibility of claimants and the payment of claims.

Private plans are still available, concentrating on specific services not yet available under the provincial public schemes. Such plans might cover the cost of prescribed drugs, private-duty nursing care and the services of paramedical personnel. Another kind of plan covers the additional costs of semiprivate accommodation in hospital.

Sick-leave provisions

A degree of health insurance coverage is written into some trade union contracts, general employment agreements, as well as civil service and private sector contracts with individual executives. Commonly called *sick leave*, this clause in the contract guarantees the employe his full normal rate of pay for an agreed number of days of absence through sickness or accident in every year.

The allowance is sometimes figured as a day's paid sick leave for each month worked, although it may be extended to cover as many as 90 days in a year for someone in a senior position. Some employers demand a doctor's verification of the fact that the employe was truly unable to work.

A number of major industrial corporations maintain their own limited medical service, free to their work force; a few provide convalescent care, either free or at rock-bottom cost.

Complaints about service

If you feel that you have not been treated as you deserve, either by a doctor or therapist or by any hospital staff (either as an inpatient or outpatient), there are several avenues of complaint open to you.

The medical association in your province (or the local members of the Canadian Medical Association in the territories) maintains a special committee to look into complaints by the public.

Although there is almost certain to be a black sheep in every flock, Canadian physicians and surgeons voluntarily bind themselves to observe a strict code of ethics, embodied in the Hippocratic Oath (drafted by Hippocrates, the Greek "father of medicine," *c.* 400 B.C.). Licensing is handled by the provincial medical associations; on finding a doctor guilty in a serious matter, an association may strip him of his right to practice.

Doctors can be sued in the courts like anyone else; alleged professional negligence (as with lawyers) is referred to as *malpractice.* Prey to mistakes like other human beings, doctors take out insurance policies which give some protection against the huge claims that can arise when the value of a human life is assessed.

If you want to complain about something in the hospital, you could begin by talking to the medical director—usually a senior member of the local medical profession; then, depending on developments, you could approach the secretary of the board of governors of the hospital; or, finally, the provincial minister of health. Bureaucracy can be baffling, but if you stick to the facts (as you see them) and present them politely, you should get satisfaction eventually.

Accidents at work

MISHAPS occurring on the job take a tragic toll of human life. In a recent year in Canada, 866 people were killed, 564,494 received disabling injuries and some 640,000 more were hurt in minor accidents during working hours. The yearly cost of on-the-job accidents to Canadian business is estimated at $2.1 billion. The law tackles this problem on two fronts: it strives to make work safer by setting and enforcing standards, and it provides financial compensation and support for the injured and their dependents.

Almost all work categories are represented in the accident statistics but serious accidents are much more frequent in mining, manufacturing, construction and transportation. A breakdown of fatal accidents would include falls or slips from bridges, trestles, catwalks, platforms, ramps and vehicles; involvement in collisions, derailments, wrecks, fires and explosions; being struck by moving or falling objects; and from electrocution, gassing and overexertion. The most dangerous jobs are those done by the tunneler, stevedore, building wrecker, miner, construction worker, logger, diamond driller, scrapyard worker and welder.

The safest jobs, on the other hand, are those of the teacher, accountant, lawyer and other white-collar workers. Included in the safest category is, of all things, gunpowder and dynamite manufacturing: this work is so hazardous that safety regulations are rigorously enforced. This example provides the key to reducing job accidents: the introduction and maintenance of safe working conditions.

Although there is an obvious legislative role here, experts in the field believe that creating a greater safety awareness in the individual—both the boss and the worker—is perhaps as important in cutting down accident statistics as is the enforcement of strict regulations. An accident doesn't just happen, they maintain, it is caused—by some earlier failure to establish proper safeguards or failure to insist upon thorough safety training.

Departments of both federal and provincial governments are working toward instilling this awareness and installing these safety measures. Their allies include such organizations as the Canada Safety Council, the Ontario Industrial Accident Prevention Association, the Mines Accident Prevention Association, the Transportation Safety Association of Ontario, the Electrical Utilities Safety Association of Ontario, the Forest Products Accident Prevention Association, the Farm Safety Association Inc., and the provincial workers' compensation boards.

Safety legislation
Under the Canadian Constitution, labor law is basically the responsibility of the provinces. Each province has passed a body of statutes in the field, including laws concerning job safety. In 1968, the federal government entered the scene by formulating a national Labor Code.

The federal code is primarily aimed at ensuring safe working conditions in industries and undertakings that fall under federal jurisdiction; however it is also intended to spur the provinces in order to strengthen the cause of job safety in the nation as a whole. The code sets down an industrial safety program: it outlines the general obligations of employer and employe; it recommends that task forces be set up in which representatives from government, industry and labor would make and administer safety regulations; and it advocates research into the causes and prevention of accidents, and safety-education programs.

For a long time, the provinces have had a wide range of factory, or industrial, acts to protect the health and safety of workers. Employers are required by law to post copies of some of these regulations where workers can see them. If you are not familiar with the safety regulations at your place of work, your union representative should be able to provide you with exact information; you can also check the statutes themselves in the reference room of any large public library.

The provincial safety regulations cover sanitation, heating, lighting, ventilation, the use of any dangerous machinery, the construction, installation and operation of such equipment as boilers and all other pressure vessels, elevators and electrical installations; construction and excavation work; and the use of gas and oil-burning equipment.

What is an accident?

The word "accident" derives from the Latin word meaning "to fall upon" or "to happen." In legal usage an accident is defined as "a fortuitous circumstance, event or happening, without any human agency . . . under which the circumstance is unusual or unexpected by the person to whom it happens."

The workers' compensation acts of all provinces provide for workers to be compensated for injuries received "through accident" in the course of their employment. Thus, all injuries would seem to be covered, except those that are self-inflicted. A traveling salesman would be covered on his rounds, and an airline stewardess while serving cocktails aloft.

On the other hand, although you may "accidentally" pick up an influenza virus, the resulting sickness is not counted as a work accident.

Compensation would be paid, however, for any illness resulting from an occupational hazard—poisoning from handling chemicals, for example.

If an accident occurs

If you are involved in an accident at work, you should immediately seek first aid (if practical), and then notify your employer and your provincial Workers' Compensation Board (W.C.B.). If the injury is serious, arrange with your employer for medical attention and ask that a full report be made to the compensation board.

Your employer is required by law to cooperate in these functions. Depending on the circumstances, he will arrange for an ambulance or other transportation to a doctor's office, a hospital or your home. Within a time specified by the province, the employer must notify the W.C.B. of any accident that disables a worker or requires medical aid. In Saskatchewan and Ontario, for example, the report must be made within three days of the occurrence of the accident. In Manitoba, the report may be prepared within a period of 30 days. Alberta and Quebec require immediate notification of an accident.

The Workers' Compensation Board

Since 1949, all provinces have provided compensation to any worker who is injured on the job or disabled by disease as a result of the work he is involved in—such as lead poisoning from handling paints. These laws (generally known under the label of "Workers' Compensation") also provide for the support of widows and children of workers who die from industrial accidents or disease.

This type of legislation first appeared in Britain in 1906. Before that time, the only way a worker could get compensation for injuries was to take his employer to court, and it was difficult for him to prove that it was the boss (and not perhaps another worker) who was to blame. Normal delay in the courts, plus the expense of the court action itself, added to the worker's problem. There was a great deal of bitterness and hardship. British labor leaders and enlightened employers gave the world a lead toward easing this bitterness by devising a system of insurance against work hazards under which the employers would pay the premiums and the employes would get the benefits; in return, all workers covered by the plans would

The case of the injured foreman

FACTS

The defendant company carried on extensive farm operations, growing potatoes in New Brunswick. It engaged the plaintiff to take charge, as boss or foreman, of one of its farms. He had general supervision and management of the farming operations with authority to hire and fire help, arrange for the repair of equipment and to purchase spare parts and tools. He had under him a regular crew of about a dozen men, and at certain seasons a total crew of 150 or more. He was employed all year, receiving a regular monthly wage and the use of a house on the farm. One day, the plaintiff was helping one of the hired hands to split wood on a block. Each man faced the other and struck blows alternately. The ax being used by the hired hand flew off its handle on a down stroke and struck the foreman in the eye. The foreman sued the farm owner, a limited company, for damages.

ARGUMENT

Counsel for the foreman argued that a master was obliged to take reasonable care to see that his servants, jointly engaged with him in carrying on his work, should not suffer injury, either by his personal negligence or through his failure properly to superintend or to control the undertaking. It was further stated that an employer was bound to carry on his business so as not to expose his workmen to unreasonable risks. A breach of this duty causing personal injury gave the servant a right of action against the master for damages.

The employer company submitted that it should not be held responsible for providing safe equipment and tools because it was the foreman's responsibility to look after them. Similarly, it was argued that the defendant should not be responsible for any alleged failure to provide a safe and proper method for splitting wood as it was the foreman himself who had permitted the method used.

JUDGMENT

The court decided that at the time of the accident there was nothing in the experience of the hired hand or in the feel of the ax, to indicate that the tool was not in good working condition. If examination of the ax would have disclosed otherwise, it was the duty of the foreman to have made that examination. Any breach of duty in this regard was his own.

A similar conclusion applied to the alleged failure of the employer to provide a safe and proper method of splitting wood. On the day in question, the foreman had assigned the hired hand to his task and given directions to the man. The court observed that the foreman said that the method employed was that used on the farm, over which operations he had full management and control. It would be inconsistent if the foreman could recover damages against his employer on the grounds of an unsafe and improper method of work which he himself had permitted and, in this particular case, dictated.

Accordingly, it was found by the court that the foreman could not succeed in his suit, and judgment was entered for the defendant company.*

*Based on an actual case (1957).

renounce the right to sue their bosses for damages if injured.

Ontario pioneered the system in Canada. Sir William Meredith, a former chief justice of the province, made a three-year study of existing plans, and then recommended (in 1914) a plan which contained the basic principles under which the Ontario Workers' Compensation Board operates today. Similar legislation followed in all other provinces, the variations dealing more with different levels of com-

pensation and death benefits than with principles.

Under workers' compensation, you will be paid almost automatically for injury on the job. The question of negligence will not arise—either your own or your employer's—unless there was some willfully reckless act involved (and even in that case, payment would be made for serious injury).

All employers in one industry are responsible on a compulsory collective

Your credit card for accidents

No one can tell when an accident will happen—at work, on the highway or at home. Luckily, in Canada, the health programs of all provinces and territories provide immediate hospitalization and medical care where necessary.

As a member of your provincial scheme, the head of the household will be issued with a numbered identification card. It is a wise precaution to carry your health insurance card at all times; if you should be injured and unconscious, it will quickly provide the attending doctor, or the hospital authorities, with necessary data.

The card illustrated below is issued to all members of the Ontario Health Insurance Plan. It entitles the bearer to the full range of medical services provided, including payment of 90 percent of doctor's bills. Surgery, X-ray and follow-up physiotherapy are all covered. All provinces issue similar cards.

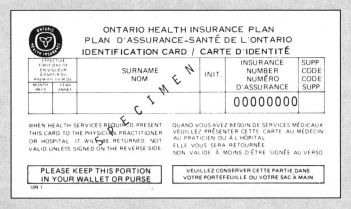

Under all plans, when a dependent child reaches the age of 21, marries, or becomes self-supporting, he ceases at the end of that month to be covered under the parent's insurance. Application is to be made immediately for separate enrollment, and an individual identity card will be issued. If the former dependent has married, he should notify the Health Insurance Office, within 30 days, giving the bride's maiden name, the date of the marriage, and the present address of the couple.

basis for workers who are injured or become ill as a result of their work. They contribute to a central fund at a rate based upon the accident rate among their industrial or trade group. Recently, the median payment in an industrial province was set at $3 for every $100 of wages paid. Each group is liable for the costs of all accidents happening within the group. The workers pay nothing.

The provincial laws governing compensation for job injury are administered by the Workers' Compensation Board. The regulations cover a wide range of jobs, but the following are generally excluded: domestic servants and casual workers; employes of financial and certain professional businesses; employes of nonprofit religious or charitable organizations; and workers in photographic studios, barber shops and beauty parlors. Farm workers can now opt to be included in British Columbia, Alberta, Saskatchewan, Manitoba, Prince Edward Island and Newfoundland. In Ontario, coverage for farm workers is compulsory. Usually, the regulations set down a minimum number of employes in order to qualify, but just about any group can be brought into the plan if the employers apply for coverage.

At the national level, federal employes are covered by a separate plan which pays benefits according to the scale of the province in which they are employed. Merchant seamen are also covered.

Scale of benefits

In total, compensation payments to workers, or to their dependents, plus medical-aid payments, run to well over a billion dollars a year. The levels of compensation vary from one province to another, but the base rate of 75 percent of gross earnings, up to a certain ceiling (currently $25,000 in Ontario) is accepted everywhere, except in Quebec where the rate is 90 percent of net earnings. However, these rates may eventually change.

All necessary medical services are provided, with no expense or time limits attached. Widows and dependent children receive various lump-sum benefits and monthly pension payments. In Ontario, for example, a widow currently receives

$564 a month as long as she does not remarry; if she does remarry, she gets a lump-sum payment equal to two years' pension (the rights of dependent widowers are now being recognized). A dependent child is entitled to $157 a month up to the age of 16. However, this can be continued if the child remains at school or is an invalid. The children each receive $176 a month if they are the sole dependents or if their mother later dies while they are still classed as her dependents. Other dependents, apart from spouses or children, may receive compensation of up to $564 a month.

Normally, the total pension paid the dependents of a worker killed on the job will not exceed the average amount that the man was earning around the time of his death. Dependents of a totally disabled employe are entitled to death benefits, regardless of the cause of death.

Although you cannot appeal a decision of a workers' compensation board to any other body, the board itself contains a review structure. If you have a complaint, take it to the review board, or have a trade union official, a lawyer or any other responsible person present it for you.

Getting back to work

An important service provided by workers' compensation boards is the rehabilitation program aimed at getting disabled workers back into useful employment. The best of these programs provide, apart from physical rehabilitation, vocational and social counseling, selective job placement with the former (or perhaps a new) employer, as well as psychological testing to determine the retraining possibilities of each individual. Some boards also run industrial workshops. These are used for testing a worker's practical skills and for conditioning him again for work after a long period of recuperation.

If it is not possible for an individual to return to work after an accident, the board may sponsor retraining at a community college, at a trade institution operated by the province or by a board of education, or at an approved private training school. The board would pay living allowances during such training.

Unemployment insurance

Who is covered?

How payments are made

Rate of benefits

The "major" and the "minor"

Sickness and maternity benefits

How to appeal

CANADA was comparatively late among the nations to introduce a national unemployment insurance scheme. This was partially due to the long predominance of agriculture in our economy. The distribution of a small population across a vast tract of land, and the seasonal nature of work dictated by the harsh climate, posed organizational and financial problems to the planners. Furthermore, a constitutional amendment was required before the federal government could enter the provincial field of labor law.

The first benefit cheques were made out to Canadian unemployed workers in February 1942. There were then two million workers in the scheme. Nowadays, the program is compulsory and virtually universal, covering a work force of 12,185,000, and "unemployment benefits" represent one of the pillars in our social-security structure. It is familiarly known as "pogey."

Since its revisions in 1971 and 1976, the program operated by Unemployment Insurance (U.I.) ranks as one of the most comprehensive in the world. Its basic purpose is to provide income to workers laid off from their jobs. Basically, the program operates as follows: when working, the employe pays into the fund a weekly contribution from his wages; this is added to by the employer and is further subsidized from general federal taxation revenues. If he loses his job—or even, in some cases, if he quits—the worker draws on the fund until he returns to work. A worker on strike or involved in a lockout cannot normally draw pogey.

The benefits you receive if unemployed are based upon your previous income;

they are not as much as you made while employed, in order to encourage you to look for work. However, they are meant to be high enough to allow you and your family to maintain an adequate standard of living. How high is high enough? Employers of unskilled labor are quick to point out their difficulty in finding workers willing to accept the federal minimum hourly wage (currently $3.50 and hour) when as much as $231 a week is paid to the unemployed in U.I. benefits.

Who is covered?

Most jobs in Canada today fall into the category known as *insurable employment* under the terms of the Unemployment Insurance Act. In fact, all jobs are insurable unless specifically labeled otherwise. Whether you are required to contribute to the plan, and therefore qualify for its benefits, can depend upon a variety of factors including your age, how much you make and the kind of work you do.

You are not covered by the U.I. plan, for example, if you are older than 65, or are considered self-employed or earn below the minimum weekly insurable wage. (If you are self-employed, you could be eligible if you were engaged in such businesses as taxi driving or hairdressing, but you would have to be working a certain number of hours and meet certain other conditions.) There is no coverage if you are a clergyman or a member of a religious order that required you to take a vow of poverty, or are helping in a national disaster.

You will not be covered for any work for which you do not receive actual cash payment, or for any exchange or barter of work or services, or for casual work for someone which is not directly related to that person's trade or business. For example, you would not pay a U.I. contribution on the $25 you made raking leaves on an autumn Saturday. You are excluded if you work for your spouse, or for anyone who claims you as a dependent. In addition, both husband and wife are excluded if employed by a corporation in which, either separately or together, they control more than 40 percent of its issued voting shares.

You will not be insured if you happen to be an exchange teacher paid by an employer outside Canada. However, if you work for the Canadian government abroad or for an international organization based in Canada, you may be covered if special arrangements have been made with U.I.

The contribution system

The individual's U.I. premium is worked out as a percentage of his *insurable earnings*. The percentage rate is revised annually in relation to the anticipated demands that will be made on the fund during the following year. As this was written, the employer's premium was 1.4 times the amount contributed by his or her workers. The government makes sure there is always enough money available to cover the benefit payments demanded, transferring funds from consolidated taxation revenue as required. Despite its title, U.I. could not run on straight insurance principles; for instance, the total contributions from the fishing industry in 1982 were about $9 million, but payments in the same year were more than $110 million.

Your *insurable earnings* consist of the total value of what you receive as payment for work that is classed as insurable employment. In addition to your regular salary or wage, insurable earnings include bonuses, tips, retroactive pay increases, any sharing of profits, overtime settlements or awards, plus those items that may be included in any final payment of wages such as a lump-sum vacation payment, sick-leave credits or separation payments, as well as the estimated value of free room or board, or any other

such considerations you may be receiving as part of your job.

Insurable earnings do not include workmen's compensation payments, payments under a supplemental unemployment-benefit plan that has been approved by U.I., noncash payments for work done, stock-option benefits, pension payments, death benefits, director's fees or any remuneration paid after you have left a job and have received the normal final payment of wages and vacation pay.

Not all of your gross earnings are assessed for U.I. premiums. The cutoff point for 1983, for example, was $385 a week.

You are permitted to deduct your unemployment-insurance premiums for income-tax purposes. This also means that any benefits received under the program now are counted as taxable income and are subject to deduction at source.

Who is qualified?

To qualify for U.I. benefits, you must first have worked for at least 10 to 12 weeks in a job classified as insurable employment—that is, one that required your boss to deduct U.I. premiums from your pay. The exact number of weeks you will need is determined by the unemployment rate in the area where you live. The higher the unemployment rate in your region the fewer weeks you will need. (The minimum number of weeks is set at ten.) The total number of weeks that you have worked in the previous 52 weeks or since the start of your last *benefit period* (whichever adds up to the shorter time) is known as your *qualifying period*. The number of weeks of insurable employment that you have in this period has a direct bearing on how long you will be eligible to receive benefits. The longest any individual can receive payments is 50 weeks.

If you have worked for at least 10 to 14 "insured" weeks and then lose or leave your job, you qualify for benefits. However, the law requires you to satisfy certain additional conditions in order to establish and maintain your right to benefits. You must be actually available for work, be willing to accept any suitable work you are offered and be making every effort on your own part to find work. In other words, you are expected to spend your regular working hours looking for a job, not just sitting at home waiting for a job to be found for you.

A worker who is dismissed from a job, for cause, or quits, or refuses suitable employment without just cause, will be disqualified from certain benefits; he will also not receive payments during the first two weeks (known as the "waiting period").

In 1976, the former Unemployment Insurance Commission and the Department of Manpower and Immigration Commission merged to form the Canada Employment and Immigration. As a result of this merger, unemployed workers can apply for U.I. benefits and employment services at the same time and in the same place— the Canada Employment Centre (C.E.C.).

How to apply

Claim forms are available at any Canada Employment Centre and at the post of-

fice. You must be scrupulously accurate in filling out a claim form; if you are found guilty of making false statements or misrepresentations to the U.I. you will be prosecuted.

If you are filing a claim because you are out of work, you will require a *record of employment* from your former employer. You will receive this certificate no matter what the conditions of your leaving a job, as long as you were paying the premiums while working in the first place. It contains information vital to your claim: the date of your last day on the job, the number of insured weeks you worked, your insurable weekly earnings, and the total of any final lump-sum settlement of vacation or sick-pay credits or other separation payments that you may have received in addition to your last week's wages when you left. The separation payments are particularly important. Your benefit period will not start until this money has been used up at the rate of your regular weekly earnings. For example, if you earned $100 a week at your job

Trapping the U.I. cheats

Any Croesus who is paying out $8.5 billion a year is sure to attract cheats, and the Canadian Employment and Immigration Commission (which paid out this sum for unemployment insurance in 1982) certainly attracts its share. After its great expansion in 1971, U.I. became one of Canada's biggest "businesses," spending about $700 million in 1982 in administration costs alone.

The number of outright cheaters is thought to be about three percent of all claimants—but this is just a loose estimate. Even at that rate, though, the U.I. has through the years been swindled of about $300 million. Since there is a large element of faith involved—a claim is likely to be paid, lacking any evidence to the contrary—the temptation to "get some of the government's money" is irresistible to some people.

The U.I. has its own police—they are called "investigation and control officers"—who do their best to monitor the scheme. Among the cases they have uncovered is that of the electrician who, while earning as much as $165 a week, collected $3,575 from the U.I. A Halifax woman whose husband had taken a job after filing a claim continued to forge his signature to the fortnightly benefit forms, and collect the cash. Another woman who was a long-term claimant ran a profitable nursing home . . . her husband was a policeman.

In its 1976 reorganization, U.I. strengthened its policing activities. It checks more thoroughly the reasons that unemployed claimants give for not accepting jobs offered to them. But the stipulation in the regulations that the work offered must be "suitable" creates a loophole that the cheat could drive a truck through.

and received a final separation settlement of $300, the start of your U.I. benefits would be delayed for three weeks.

If there is no such lump-sum settlement, your benefit period starts on the Sunday of the week in which you left your job, provided you applied for benefit within one week after your last day at work. Otherwise, your claim starts from the Sunday of the week in which you actually do apply.

How payments are made

You will receive payments by mail, usually every two weeks; however, before the commission sends out each cheque, you must first fill out and return a special report form mailed to you in advance by the U.I. In this way, the commission keeps track of your employment status and determines how much benefit you are actually entitled to at any given time.

The main questions on the claim form ask: if you have worked during the one- or two-week period it covers; if you have made any money; and if you were actually "ready, able and willing" to take suitable work. You must indicate how much money you received or will receive for any work you do during each of the weeks you are reporting on. Any amount that is greater than 25 percent of your gross weekly benefit from the commission will be deducted from the amount of your benefit for that period. This means that if you made $50 during a benefit period and your benefit is pegged at $100, you will only receive $75 from the U.I.

You will normally receive your first payment during the fifth week of your claim period, and only after the U.I. has received the report form covering your third week of unemployment. The first two weeks of your claim represent, therefore, a waiting period for which you do not receive benefits.

Rate of benefits

As discussed previously, the rate paid by U.I. is based on the level of previous wages. You will—at rates prevailing when this was written—receive 60 percent of the average weekly insured amount you earned during your qualifying period,

up to a maximum of $231 a week in 1983 (60 percent of $385).

The minimum and maximum insurable earnings are reviewed each year. In 1983, workers could insure up to $385 a week and had to earn a minimum of $77 a week (or work 15 hours) to be insurable.

Benefits are paid within a phased program which contains two basic periods, initial benefit and extended benefit. These periods are assigned differently to what are classified as major and minor attachment claimants.

The "major" and the "minor"

Upon applying for unemployment insurance, you will be classed as either a *major attachment claimant* or a *minor attachment claimant*, depending on the number of insured weeks you have worked. You become a minor attachment claimant if you have worked 10 to 19 insured weeks, and a major attachment claimant if you have worked for at least 20 insured weeks. A "major" is entitled to more weeks of benefits than a "minor." He is also eligible for benefits on wider grounds. These terms ("major" and "minor") are now being phased out.

If you have worked less than 20 insured weeks, you are eligible for benefits when your earnings are interrupted, whether this is due to your being fired, quitting or being a nonparticipant in a labor dispute. You would not be eligible, though, if you were not working because of pregnancy, illness, accident or through being placed in quarantine.

When the Unemployment Insurance Commission and the Department of Manpower and Immigration merged in 1976, the changes in unemployment insurance benefits were as follows: (1) The length of insured employment required to qualify for benefits was increased to 12 weeks from eight weeks; (2) Weeks during which benefits may be drawn were related more directly to weeks worked, and regional benefits were related more closely to regional unemployment; (3) Severance pay no longer affected an individual's eligibility for benefits.

Amendments to the law also permitted the payment of pogey to beneficiaries when they take part in such activities as selective employment or training programs.

Under what is known as the "one-for-one" rule, 10 to 14 insured weeks is required to qualify in the initial phase. One benefit week is then paid for each insured week to a maximum of 25 weeks. For example, a man who loses his job and has 17 insured weeks will be entitled to receive 17 weeks of benefits.

In the extended phase, a "one-for-two" rule has been implemented. Entitlement is based on one benefit week for every two insured weeks over 25 insured weeks to a maximum of 13 benefit weeks.

There is also a regional extended benefit phase, calculated on the basis of an entitlement of two weeks for each .05 percent increment to the regional unemployment rate when the regional rate is over 4 percent, to a maximum of 20 benefit weeks.

Sickness benefit

Before 1972, the unemployment insurance program included only minimal provision against sickness. Now, as long as you have worked 20 insured weeks, you are eligible for 15 weeks of payments if your earnings are interrupted by sickness, quarantine or injury not covered by workers' compensation (*See* "Accidents at work" in this chapter).

In all cases, the two-week waiting period must be observed. After the waiting period, you receive normal unemployment benefits; however, any other group sick leave or sickness-insurance benefits you may receive from your employer or union are deducted from your U.I. payments.

Maternity benefit

A special maternity benefit of 15 weeks' unemployment insurance is available to women whose earnings are interrupted by pregnancy. As with the sickness benefit, you must have completed 20 weeks of insured employment in order to qualify.

A woman claiming under this provision could begin her claim as early as ten weeks before her confinement or as late as the week following the baby's delivery. She could also receive additional benefits if unemployed at the end of this period, as

Getting back into harness

NO BENEFITS are paid by the Canada Employment and Immigration Commission for the first two weeks you are out of work. Like the "$100 deductible" clause in automobile insurance policies, this waiting period disposes of thousands of small claims that would otherwise be made by those who quickly find a new job, or are taken back by the same employer. The cost of U.I. claims—estimated for 1982 at $8.5 billion—would be much higher if these short-term claims had to be met.

The Canada Employment and Immigration Commission will assist the long-term claimant—the person who appears to be having difficulty locating a suitable job—to find employment. (The claims form allows the individual to apply for U.I. and employment at the same time.) The emphasis is, frankly, on trying to get the claimant off the benefit rolls and back on his own feet in the job market.

Apart from its functions as a job-finding agency, the Canada Employment and Immigration Commission has a training program aimed at increasing the skills of the unemployed and teaching them new techniques if necessary (*See* Chapter 12, "In the federal sphere"). This program is available to all U.I. claimants as well as to the general public. Furthermore, the department's mobility programs give financial assistance to the worker who must relocate for his new job. The C.E.I.C. has ten regional offices across Canada and approximately 450 Canada Employment Centres in communities of every size in all provinces and territories.

long as she was physically capable of work and willing to accept any suitable job offered to her.

Retirement benefit

There is a special three-week severance benefit for 65-year-olds. To be eligible, you must have worked at least 20 insured weeks and be aged 65. The basic aim of this benefit is to provide the person with some ready cash before the regular pension payments start to arrive.

How to appeal

Any claimant or former employer of a claimant not satisfied with a decision has the right to appeal.

IF YOU ARE A CLAIMANT An agent of the U.I. may make any of several decisions about a claimant's right to benefit. For example, he may decide that claimants have received overpayments, that they should stop receiving benefits for some reason, or that they should be disqualified from receiving future benefits.

If you should receive a notice giving a decision with which you do not agree, you should write or go immediately to your U.I. district office with any information which you believe might affect or even reverse this decision. If the agent who is handling your claim does not reverse his decision, or alter it to your satisfaction, or if you still feel that the decision is wrong or unfair, then you may make use of the appeal procedure provided.

IF YOU ARE AN EMPLOYER You have a right to appeal any decision of the U.I. to pay benefits to one of your former workers if you believe that he or she is not entitled, or that a disqualification should be imposed. Normally, you will express your views on a person's entitlement by indicating the reason for separation on the record of employment. If you check "layoff, shortage of work," "illness or injury," "retired," "pregnancy," or "return to school," then it will be assumed that you have no objections to whatever decision is made. However, if you check "other (explain)," "quit" or "labor dispute," it will be assumed that you are recommending a disqualification. In this case, the U.I. will automatically notify you of any decision to allow such a claim without disqualification.

The claimant must file an appeal to the Board of Referees within 30 days (these referees are not U.I. employes). Follow this procedure: Write, stating your wish to appeal the decision to a Board of Referees. Give the date of the U.I. letter advising you of their decision. Give the reasons why you are making the appeal. State whether you wish the appeal to be heard in English or French. Remember to include your social insurance number.

When the district office receives your letter, a clerk will prepare a formal submission to the Board of Referees for you, and mail you a copy. It will contain all the facts and the reasons for your appeal. Any other information you may have provided will be included. If you feel the submission is incomplete or incorrect, tell the C.E.C. immediately what is wrong.

The claimant will be advised when the Board of Referees will hear the appeal, at least three days before the date of the hearing. Appeals are normally heard within 30 days. You have the right to attend or to be represented at the hearing of your appeal. When a decision is reached by the board on your appeal, a copy will be mailed to you.

The employer who feels that a disqualification should have been imposed on a former worker and wishes to formally appeal the U.I. decision to pay benefits must forward his appeal within 30 days, or within a further period which may be allowed in a particular case. You have the right to attend the hearing or to delegate someone to appear on your behalf.

Under certain circumstances, if either party is not satisfied with the decision of the Board of Referees, the matter can be appealed automatically to a higher level, the Umpire, who is a judge of the Federal Court of Canada. For example, you can appeal to the Umpire when certain principles of natural justice have not been recognized by the Board of Referees, or when the decision of fact was made in a perverse or capricious manner or without regard for the material before the Board. Beyond these special circumstances, there is no appeal before the Umpire.

The pension network

| Old-age security pension |
| Guaranteed income supplement |
| Canada Pension Plan |
| If you are disabled |
| Family allowances |
| Payments to war veterans |

THE CONTINUED SUCCESS of the Canadian pension network—acclaimed as one of the world's most generous—is based upon the ability and willingness of the majority to work productively, and also upon the stability of the total economic environment. The federal government's 1970 White Paper on "Income Security for Canadians" pointed out that unless the system gives individuals who are physically capable of working the opportunity to use their initiative, the national wealth essential to provide income security will not be generated and the country will lack the means to assist those who do not, for many reasons, fully or even partly earn enough to provide themselves with basic necessities.

More than half a century ago, the federal government decided to take the responsibility of interfering with the natural flow of economics by passing laws that would ensure an adequate income for all. Obviously, achievement of what could be called an adequate income was impossible for a significant fraction of the population—one has only to think of the deserted mother struggling to raise children decently, or of the blind or otherwise handicapped.

The steady expansion of compulsory pensions, both contributory and tax supported, administered by government has made it possible for more people to achieve that level. A "pension" was originally restricted to mean a plan, public or private, to provide income for an individual after his retirement from employment; now the term seems to cover almost any steady income received under social security legislation.

Beginning with the joint federal-provincial Old Age Pension Program in 1927, Canadians now enjoy old-age security pensions, guaranteed income supplements, the Canada Pension Plan, family allowances, and pensions exclusively for war veterans and the physically handicapped. These can be combined in various ways for an individual or a family, depending on qualification and need. Less than one-half of the total work force is enrolled in private retirement plans, usually operating on insurance principles; in most of these, the employer contributes significantly in the hope of attracting and retaining stable and satisfied labor. Governments encourage private plans by allowing tax exemptions on the contributions. In general, the individual who plans ahead for himself is unlikely to become a drain on public finances.

Old-age security pension

The old-age security pension is adjusted quarterly in accordance with the cost-of-living index and was $256.67 in July 1983. This full amount is payable to anyone age 65 or over who has resided in Canada for 40 years since the age of 18. Anyone who has resided at least ten years in Canada but less than 40 years qualifies for a partial pension. For example, if you have resided here for one year less than 40 years, your pension is calculated at the rate of one-fortieth of the full pension for each year of such residence.

You must be a Canadian citizen or a legal resident of Canada on the day preceding approval of your application or, if you are no longer residing in Canada, to have been a citizen on the day preceding the day you ceased to reside in Canada.

In order to allow for the progressive implementation of the 40-year residence requirement for the full pension, if you were 25 years of age or over and resided or had resided in Canada or possessed a valid immigration visa on July 1, 1977 when the requirement came into force, you may still qualify for a full pension. In this case you must have resided in Canada for the ten years immediately prior to the approval of your application. Any absences in the 10-year period may be offset if you had been present in Canada prior to those ten years after reaching the age of 18 for a total period equal to at least three times the length of the absences. In this instance, however, you must also reside in Canada for at least one year immediately prior to the date on which your application for a pension is approved.

Certain types of absences from Canada are not counted against you. Chief among these are absences while working abroad for the Canadian government, for a Canadian firm or an international agency, as a member of the Canadian Forces or as a missionary.

You can apply for your old-age pension through the regional office of the Department of National Health and Welfare in your provincial capital. The office in Edmonton handles the Yukon and the Northwest Territories, as well as residents of Alberta. Applications should be made six months before your 65th birthday, and proof of age and your Social Insurance number must be included.

You can receive your pension while living outside of Canada, but only after your have satisfied the conditions for getting it in the first place and, furthermore, have lived in Canada for at least 20 years after your 18th birthday. If you have not, you can receive the pension for only six months while you are away from Canada; after that period, it will be suspended until you return.

At the beginning of 1983, more than 2,400,000 Canadians 65 and older were receiving old-age security cheques.

Guaranteed income supplement

One and a quarter million of those persons receiving old-age security pensions are also getting the *guaranteed income supplement*. Introduced in 1967, the supplement provides additional income for old-age pensioners who have little or no other income beyond the pension itself. It is administrated by the federal Department of National Health and Welfare, under an amendment to the Old Age Security Act.

The amount of the supplement you get depends on the amount of income you have over and above the old-age pension, adjusted to the cost-of-living index. The maximum payment in July 1983 was $256.68 a month for a single pensioner. Together with the full Old Age Security pension of $256.67, this payment provided what can almost be called a guaranteed income of $514.35 a month for single Canadians who were aged 65 and up. The maximum total for a married couple who are both pensioners was $910.68 a month.

When you begin receiving the old-age pension, you will automatically be sent an application form for the supplement. You will receive one again at the beginning of each calendar year afterward. The reason for this is to give you a chance to reassess your financial situation, based upon the income you received in the previous year.

For the single pensioner, the maximum amount of the supplement is reduced by $1 a month for every $2 a month he makes over and above the old-age pension. For married couples, the supplement is reduced in a somewhat different manner to achieve the same basic result. The types of income considered are the same ones used for calculating income tax. In other words, it is your taxable income that is checked for any reduction in your supplement.

If you leave Canada while receiving the supplement, you continue to receive it for six months after the month of your departure. At that time, it will be cut off until your return to Canada.

Some provinces add to senior citizens' incomes through supplementary plans. For example, an Ontario couple, both of whom qualify, will get a minimum of $13,395.36 per year.

Canada Pension Plan

Unlike the old-age pension, the Canada Pension is based on give and take: you can only receive it if you have worked and paid contributions toward it. But it is a compulsory plan, covering most types of employment—including self-employment. Accordingly, it is almost universal in its coverage of wage earners. You can receive both the old-age pension and the Canada pension at the same time.

The Canada Pension Plan (the C.P.P.) operates in all provinces, except in Quebec where the almost-identical Quebec Pension Plan is in effect. The two plans are closely coordinated to function virtually as one. This means that you can move back and forth between Quebec and other parts of Canada (and go abroad) and suffer no change in your pension coverage. The C.P.P. provides six benefits:

(1) A monthly retirement pension.

(2) A monthly disability pension.

(3) Monthly benefits for your dependent children if you are disabled.

(4) A lump-sum payment into your estate when you die.

(5) A monthly pension to your spouse, when you die.

(6) Monthly benefits for your children when you die.

Common-law marriages are recognized under the plan, and equal benefits are paid to male and female contributors.

You receive your full Canada Pension at 65, whether you actually retire or not, and irrespective of how much you may continue to earn. You should apply for your C.P.P. three months before you are due to receive it.

The amount of your pension depends on how many years after the age of 18 you worked in a job covered by the plan, plus how much you earned. However, for a year to be counted under the plan, you have to make a certain minimum called the year's basic exemption (Y.B.E.), which was $1,800 in 1983 and is adjusted annually in accordance with the cost of living.

Benefits under the plan are portable—that is, you carry them from one job to another. They also remain if you leave the country for any period of time or work some years in employment not covered by the plan.

Benefit amounts do not remain fixed at the same levels but can be altered annually in line with changes in the cost-of-living index.

C.P.P. contributions have been deducted since 1966. Because the Canada Pension Plan provides for a minimum of ten years over which earnings have to be averaged, full retirement pensions did not start to be paid until January 1976. If you are enrolled in any other form of old-age or retirement pension plan, it will not be

How to get the old-age pension

At age 65, all persons who have resided in Canada at least for the prior ten years (certain temporary absences are accepted) are eligible to receive the old-age security pension. You do not have to be a citizen of Canada to qualify.

To get your monthly cheque you fill out a form and mail it to the Regional Director of Old-Age Security in the capital city of your province. A document proving your age should be submitted (it will be returned to you).

A birth or baptismal certificate is best for establishing your age; but any of the following will be considered: family Bible entries; marriage, communion or confirmation certificates; passport or citizenship certificate; insurance or annuity records; school registers and diplomas; voters' rolls and jury lists; military honors or records (paybooks); medical or other pension records; newspaper clippings: membership certificates in lodges, clubs or associations. If anyone has difficulty in obtaining proof of age, the regional office will provide assistance.

affected by the Canada Pension Plan; on the other hand, you still have to contribute to the C.P.P.

Only wage earners covered

Certain types of work are not covered by the Canada Pension Plan. Generally, these are the same as those that exclude you from coverage under unemployment insurance. You are not eligible, for example, if you work for your father or mother or for anyone else who supports you but who does not pay you cash wages. Nor are you covered if your work is on a casual basis that is not for the direct purpose of your employer's business.

You are also excluded if you are an exchange teacher from another country or a member of a religious order that required you to take a vow of perpetual poverty.

You are not covered when employed as a migratory worker in occupations like farming, fishing, trapping, hunting, and logging, when you work less than 25 days a year for the same employer or earn less than $250 from the same employer.

How C.P.P. contributions are paid

The amount you pay into the Canada Pension Plan is based only upon your earnings from employment. You cannot contribute on the basis of any other kind of income—such as investments, annuities or other pension plans.

Not all of your earnings will necessarily be assessed for C.P.P. contributions. For 1983, the cutoff point was $18,500 a year. Any money you earned above this amount, called the year's maximum pensionable earnings (Y.M.P.E.), would not have been assessed for contributions. The Y.M.P.E., like the Y.B.E., is adjusted annually to reflect the cost of living. The same immunity from assessment would apply to the first $1,800 (*that is*, the Y.B.E.) earned whether as an employe or on a self-employed basis.

If you are an employe, your yearly contribution consists of 1.8 percent of what you earn between the Y.B.E. and the Y.M.P.E. ($1,800 and $18,500 in 1983). It is taken off your pay in regular installments by your employer who, in turn, is

required to pay an equal amount into the fund on your behalf; he forwards the total amount to the Department of National Revenue.

If you are self-employed, you send your C.P.P. contribution directly to the government when you pay your income tax—usually in quarterly installments. Like the employe, your earnings between the Y.B.E. and the Y.M.P.E. are assessed but, unlike him, you are required to pay both halves of the contribution, totaling 3.6 percent of your earnings.

If you are contributing to the plan, you are entitled to know what amount of your earnings was used for calculating your pension contribution for any given year. If by chance a mistake has been made, you can easily have it corrected, but only if you make your inquiry within four years of the year in question—at which point the statute of limitations closes the door to further negotiation. For example, your 1983 contribution will automatically be presumed correct—whether or not it actually is—after 1987. Contributions are allowable deductions for income-tax purposes. At the receiving end of the plan, benefits count as taxable income.

When you retire

Your retirement pension under the Canada Pension Plan (C.P.P.) is calculated as 25 percent of the average of your annual pensionable earnings, either from the original starting date of the plan, January 1, 1966, or from your 18th birthday if it comes after that date.

To provide you with a simplified but basically correct example, suppose you retired on January 1, 1983, having earned at least the Y.M.P.E. each year. Your pensionable earnings would be adjusted to 1983 dollar values totalled and divided by the number of months in your contributory period (that is, 192 months). The result would be $16,567 and you would receive 25 percent of that amount or $4,141.75, which works out to $345.15 a month. (The actual calculation process is somewhat more sophisticated.)

There are two things that you, as an average wage earner, should note: first, because you will probably earn more in later years, your lower earlier earnings will be adjusted upward by a special formula so that the final value of your earnings will be somewhat increased; second, the years over which your earnings are averaged are not just the years you actually contributed to the pension plan, but all the years you could have been contributing to it.

The C.P.P. also recognizes that you may have years during your contributory period when you earn little or no money. You may, for example, return to school or take an extended holiday. Whatever the reason, the upshot might be that you contributed for only 14 out of a possible 16 years and your pension would be smaller as a result.

To compensate for this, a procedure has been set up to disregard certain periods of low income or no earnings, thus reducing the losses that would otherwise occur.

The C.P.P. also makes special provisions to disregard periods when a contributor drops out of the work force to raise children.

The maximum C.P.P. pension for an individual in 1983 was $345.15; this is adjusted each year in accordance with the consumer price index.

If you are disabled

To receive a disability pension under C.P.P. you must have undergone some physical or mental impairment that can be classed as both severe and prolonged. It must be severe enough that you are "incapable of regularly pursuing any substantially gainful occupation," and that your incapacity is "likely to be long continued and of indefinite duration, or likely to result in death."

Medical evidence of your disability is obviously necessary for you to back up your claim to this type of pension. This requires, at the least, a report from your family doctor; perhaps additional medical examination will be called for by the pension board.

The Canada Pension Plan pays for any extra medical costs, as well as for rehabilitation treatment that it may ask you to take. If you refuse to undergo additional medical examination or to follow suggested rehabilitation measures, the pension board may refuse to pay you a disability pension.

The amount of your disability pension (as of 1983) is $78.60 a month, plus 75 percent of the current value of your monthly retirement pension (calculated over a minimum of ten years' contributions). Even if you are below retirement age, you will be paid the pension just as if you had become eligible for it at the time payment of the disability pension was to begin. (The maximum disability pension payable in 1983 was $337.46.) You do not contribute to the pension plan while receiving a disability pension.

In addition to being disabled within the meaning set down by the legislation, you must also have contributed to the plan for a certain length of time in order to receive a pension. From February 1976 to January 1981, you would have been granted a pension if you had similarly contributed for five years in the previous ten-year period. After February 1981, the qualifying period was progressively increased to ten years' worth of contributions, five years having to be within the previous ten-year period.

A disability pension starts four months after the disability occurs. You receive it until you recover, reach 65, or die—whichever happens first. At age 65, your disability pension is automatically replaced by a retirement pension. If you die while receiving a disability pension, your widow and children can receive survivors' benefits, described later in this chapter.

While you are receiving a C.P.P. disability pension, you can also receive benefits on behalf of your dependent children. You may claim a benefit for a child on the following conditions: the child must be yours by natural birth or adoption or at least be in your custody or control; he must also be unmarried, under 18, or between 18 and 25 and attending school full time; and he must not be disabled himself, under the terms of the legislation, if between 18 and 25.

Child benefits can start at the same time as the disability pension itself. In 1983, they amounted to $78.60 monthly for each child.

The benefit for a child younger than 18 is paid to the person having custody and control of him, usually the person receiving the pension. A child older than 18 is paid the benefit directly.

Benefits cease when a child no longer qualifies as a dependent, dies or is legally adopted by someone else, or when the disability pension itself stops.

C.P.P. benefits for survivors

If you die after having contributed to the Canada Pension Plan for a required number of years, there are several types of benefits available to your survivors. It does not matter if you were still working and contributing at your death or if you were already retired and receiving a pension.

The possible benefits include a lump-sum death benefit payable to your estate, a monthly survivor's pension and a monthly orphan's benefit.

The basic requirement for any of these payments is that you must have contributed to the plan for either ten years or at least one-third of the total calendar years you could have contributed had you lived, whichever is the shorter period of time. You must have contributed for at least three years in order to qualify under the second alternative.

Death benefit

Assuming that you meet the qualifications, a lump sum equal to six times your

The case of the self-employed

THE COMPULSORY Canada Pension Plan (or Quebec Pension Plan) provides a retirement income on top of the old-age pension for just about every working person in Canada, whatever his (or her) occupation. The self-employed person must personally contribute 3.6 percent of his earnings (if he makes more than $18,500 a year) along with the wage-earner who has his contribution deducted at source by the employer. But what exactly are "self-employed earnings"?

The law says they are the total of the profits from businesses, less any business losses. If you are in a partnership, then only your share of the profits and losses for the year are taken into account. It doesn't matter if the business is carried on inside or outside Canada.

Self-employed earnings do not include income from dividends, bonds or other securities, unless that income forms part of the revenue of a business and is included in computing profits or losses. Also excluded are profits or losses from businesses in which more than half of the gross revenue comes from the rental of lands or buildings; an exception to this would be the motel or rooming house where services are supplied as well as accommodation.

When you are assessing your contributions to C.P.P., charitable donations or medical expenses, and personal exemptions as allowed under the Income Tax Act, you cannot be used to reduce the total of self-employed earnings.

If you estimate that your annual contribution to C.P.P. will be only $40 or less, you can pay it retroactively in a lump sum; if contributions will exceed $40, then equal quarterly payments must be made on March 31, June 30, September 30 and December 31.

The self-employed person is required to file (by April 30) a return of his earnings for the year ended the previous December 31. He must keep books of account and record sufficiently detailed so that accurate computation of earnings can be made. Failure to keep proper books, or the making of "false or deceptive" returns to the Department of National Revenue (which administers the C.P.P.) is an offense.

You are permitted to deduct your C.P.P. contributions when totaling your earnings for income tax purposes.

monthly pension will go to your estate at your death. If you are not receiving a retirement pension at your death, one is calculated as if you had become eligible at that time. The maximum death benefit in 1983 was $1,850. This is in line with the ruling that this benefit cannot be more than ten percent of the maximum earning being assessed for contributions in the year in which the death occurs. The present limit on earnings is $18,500.

Survivor's pension

A surviving spouse receives a monthly pension based upon age and circumstances. How it is determined depends on whether the survivor is younger or older than 65 at the contributor's death. If the survivor is older than 65, the pension will be 60 percent of the current value of the contributor's monthly retirement pension; this value will be calculated even if the contributor was not eligible to receive a pension at the time of death. If the survivor is younger than 65, he or she can get as much as $78.50 plus 37.5 percent of the contributor's pension.

The survivor gets the full amount if he or she is between 45 and 65 years of age. The survivor also qualifies if he or she is younger than 45 and caring for dependent or disabled children, or if he or she is disabled. If the survivor has no dependent or disabled children and is not disabled, he or she will receive a reduced pension if between 35 and 45, but none if younger than 35. A widow or widower younger than 35 with no children and no personal disability is not eligible for a survivor's pension until the age of 65, unless he or she also becomes disabled in the meantime.

Under certain conditions, a full pension may later be reduced. Consider, for example, a 40-year-old widow who was originally granted a full pension because she was caring for dependent or disabled children, or was disabled herself. If her children leave her care or if she ceases to be disabled while she is still younger than 45, her pension will be reduced by ten percent for each year she is under 45.

Any pension awarded to a person younger than 65 is recalculated when that person reaches 65; he or she then receives a new pension at the 60-percent rate.

A man or woman receiving a survivor's pension may actually have contributed to the Canada Pension Plan and, as a result, may be eligible for his or her own retirement or disability pension. If so, that person is allowed to receive both pensions, according to a specified procedure. However, the total of the two cannot be more than the maximum allowed under the regulations—$345.15 monthly when this was written.

In 1975, widowers became eligible for a pension under the same terms and conditions as widows. Formerly called the "widow's pension", it is now known as the "survivor's pension", because it applies to both sexes.

Orphan's benefits

The unmarried dependent children of a deceased contributor to the Canada Pension Plan are entitled to the same benefits as described above for the dependent children of a disabled contributor.

The disabled widower

Formerly, a disabled widower was entitled to a special pension if he was substantially dependent upon his wife at the time of her death. Today, the widower is covered under the terms of the "survivor's pension."

The Pension Appeals Board

Either as a contributor or a beneficiary under the Canada Pension Plan, you can appeal any decision the board makes concerning you.

Employers and employes disputing matters concerning coverage and contributions first send their complaint to the Minister of National Revenue; if not satisfied with the decision, they proceed to the Pension Appeals Board which is part of the Department of National Health and Welfare. The decision of this board is final.

The self-employed person would appeal assessment of his pensionable earnings in the same way as he would appeal his income tax. If his dispute was over benefits, he could take it through three levels of appeal: the first appeal is to the Minister of National Health and Welfare; the second to a review committee; and the third to the Pension Appeals Board. Appeal board decisions are final.

Family allowances

The Department of National Health and Welfare contributed nearly two and a quarter billion dollars in 1982 to the financing of income-support programs aimed at providing "equal opportunity for all Canadian children." These programs exist in all provinces. Nationally, nearly 7 million children are involved.

The federal Family Allowance Act provides for monthly support payments to an average of $28.52 for all dependent children under 18 resident in Canada with at least one parent who is a citizen (or landed immigrant) living in Canada. Quebec and Alberta adjust payments on a sliding scale to the ages of the children involved, and to the number of children in a family. Family allowances can also be paid for children who are living outside Canada. Applicants are not required to undergo a means test.

Family allowance payments are made by monthly cheque, usually payable to the mother, but they can be made out to any person who maintains the child.

The family allowance may be suspended for all or part of the year if the child is considered to be self-supporting—that is, if the child earns a taxable income in that year. As well, the family allowance will not be payable in respect to a married child, unless neither the child nor the spouse has a taxable income, and the child is not claimed as a dependent for income tax purposes.

All family allowances are taxable to the person who claims the child as a dependent.

If the child is cared for by a government agency, or approved private institution, a special monthly allowance is paid. This payment is usually made to the institution but, in special circumstances, it may be paid to the child's foster parents.

The family allowance is adjusted every January in accordance with the 12-month average of the consumer price index.

The child tax-credit program

To provide increased financial assistance to low- and middle-income families with children, the federal government introduced the refundable child tax credit in 1979. The same parent who receives the family allowance benefit, usually the mother, is eligible to claim the child tax credit. The net incomes of both parents in a given taxation year are added together for purposes of determining the amount of the child tax credit payable in the following year.

For the 1982 taxation year, the child tax-credit program provided up to $343 in 1983 for each child whose eligibility for family allowances existed in January 1983. The benefit was available in full to families with annual incomes of up to $26,330. Above that amount, the child tax credit was reduced by $5 for every $100 of family income.

The credit is claimed when the family allowance recipient files an income tax return. The child tax credit is entirely independent of the child tax exemption which is also claimed through the income tax system.

Payments to war veterans

More than two decades after the last involvement in active service (the Korean War, 1950–53), Canada' war veterans still receive a variety of benefits in recognition of their services to this country. Principal benefits include medical treatment for those eligible, financial assistance in the purchase of land and houses, veterans' insurance, as well as disability and dependents' pensions and allowances. Servicemen and merchant seamen taken prisoner by the enemy in Europe or Asia (a total of about 6,000) qualify for extra benefits. Special education funds are also available for the dependents of those who gave their lives.

Veterans' pensions

Canada's program of paying compensation for disability and death arising from military service began in 1916 during World War I. From that time, pensions have been granted to veterans or their dependents in cases of death, disability or aggravation of a pre-enlistment disability resulting from military service.

The amount of a disability pension varies with the degree of disability, and the cash levels are reviewed annually. Total disability, at this writing, brought a pension of $1,015.16 a month, with an additional $253.79 a month if married, plus $131.97 for the first child, $96.46 for the second child and $76.14 for each additional child. There is also an additional "exceptional incapacity allowance" of between $179.14 and $537.40 a month that can be paid to persons living entirely off their pensions.

Pensions are paid to the survivor and children of a deceased veteran if the injury or disease that caused his death was directly connected with military service. At the time of this writing, the survivor's pension was $761.37 a month, plus $263.94 for one child, an extra $192.88 for the second child, and $152.27 for each additional child. There are also smaller pensions for dependent parents, brothers and sisters.

A disability pensioner receives free medical treatment for the pensioned condition whenever required, whether he is living inside or outside of Canada. The free treatment includes any artificial devices that may help to minimize the handicap.

Disability pensions are not taxable, and awarded without regard to other income; the rates apply equally to male and female pensioners. They are increased if the condition of the disability worsens, regardless of age. Conversely, they are decreased if it improves, but only up to

Concern for the white cane

COMMUNITY CONCERN for the support and education of the blind in Canada is more than a century old. The first special school was opened in Montreal in 1861, and was followed by institutions in Halifax, Brantford (Ontario), Vancouver and Westmount (Quebec). Today, special schools still exist throughout Canada, but their enrollment figures are steadily decreasing as more and more young people are being integrated into the regular school system.

Financial support was at first provided under old-age pension legislation, then under the Blind Persons Act, 1951. The federal treasury reimburses the provinces for 75 percent of allowances paid to blind persons; in recent national statistics, the annual federal expenditure under this heading totaled over $4 million. Allowances were being paid to nearly 5,500 persons in an average month.

The total number of blind in Canada is almost 40,000, the large majority of whom lost their sight as adults. More than half of all blind persons are older than 65. Contrary to popular belief, accidents stand only in ninth place as a cause of blindness; the two main causes are macular degeneration (sight loss due to aging) and diabetes.

The outstanding champion of the blind in Canada for 50 years was Lt. Col. E. A. Baker, M.C., of Ontario, a founder and onetime managing director of the Canadian National Institute for the Blind. As a lieutenant in the Canadian Engineers in World War I, Baker lost the sight of both eyes in enemy action in 1915. After training at Britain's far-famed St. Dunstan's Hostel for Blinded Soldiers, he returned to Canada to enter government service.

Under his drive, the C.N.I.B. grew from a small Braille library to a large multi-million-dollar operation with training facilities, rehabilitation workshops, an extensive library of Braille and "talking" books, and residences for the elderly blind. The institute now has more than 40 offices throughout Canada and is supported by all levels of government, the United Way, community services, private and corporate donations and the more than 5,000 volunteers across Canada who contribute their time and effort.

the age of 55. At that age, a disabled person's pension will no longer be reduced as long as he has had it for at least three years.

If you served in wartime in the armed forces of Canada, or of any British Commonwealth or Allied country, and now are suffering from residual effects of that service, you should get in touch with the nearest branch of the Royal Canadian Legion or the Army, Navy and Air Force Veterans in Canada. You could also send a report of your service to the Minister of Veterans' Affairs in Ottawa.

War veterans' allowances

There is a system of support-income allowances for war veterans and their families. It covers veterans not only of the Canadian Forces but also of other Commonwealth and Allied forces, provided they meet certain Canadian residence requirements. The granting of the allowances depends upon war service, ability to work and existing income.

Actual wartime service is the first major requirement for obtaining these allowances. A Canadian becomes eligible as a veteran under the War Veterans' Allowance Act if he served in any theater of actual war; if he served without territorial limitation in both World Wars and was honorably discharged from the last enlistment in each; if he served at least 365 days in the United Kingdom during World War I before November 12, 1918; if he served in the United Nations forces in Korea; or if he is receiving a wartime disability pension.

The allowances are aimed basically at boosting low-income levels in later years, but they also serve to compensate for the difficulties of disability without regard to age. They may be awarded to male veterans at age 60 and female veterans or widows at age 55, or to either at an earlier age if they are unable to work because of a physical or mental disability or are no longer capable of fully maintaining themselves due to combined disability and other economic handicaps.

The monthly allowance for single veterans and widows (or widowers) was, at this writing, $537.46, and for married veterans, $896.13. These rates may be increased by subsidy payments—for example, to help meet rent and other basic charges. The basic allowance for each orphan is $316.24 per month (less family allowances paid for that orphan).

These allowances are awarded only in cases that meet certain financial conditions. There is a ceiling on permitted annual income, which counts the allowance total in with income from other sources. The income ceiling for a single person is $537.46 a month; for a married person, $896.13; for each orphan, $316.24. If either the person receiving an allowance or his spouse is blind, the income ceiling is increased. Casual earnings up to $2,700 a year for a single person and $3,900 for a veteran with dependents are excepted.

If you are receiving a war veterans' allowance and decide to move to another country, you will continue to receive the allowance outside of Canada.

More than 90,800 persons are receiving allowances under this program at an annual (1982) cost to the taxpayer of more than $347 million.

Veterans of Commonwealth or Allied Forces may also obtain allowances if they meet certain requirements. Similarly, those Canadians who served with British or Allied Forces in World War I may also receive allowances.

Civilian war allowances

More than 4,300 civilians who served in close support of the Canadian Forces are eligible for the same allowances which are available to war veterans. To receive a civilian war allowance, the individual must meet certain conditions relating to the length and area of war service.

Among the eligible civilian groups who assisted the Canadian war effort in World War II are: fire fighters; overseas welfare workers; Canadian trans-Atlantic air crews; and the Newfoundland Overseas Forestry Unit.

Other eligible civilians include Canadian merchant seamen of either war; foreigners who served in Canadian merchant ships in either war; and those who served in voluntary-aid detachments in World War I.

621

The welfare system

Canada Assistance Plan

Provincial and municipal welfare

Caring for the elderly

Caring for children

IN AN ERA of deepening concern for one's fellowman, there is increasing pressure upon both the state and the individual to furnish assistance—in the form of what is generally known as welfare—to those who appear in need of special help not otherwise provided by the social insurance system.

Although most welfare programs operate under provincial legislation, responsibility is sometimes shared with the municipalities. The federal government is also deeply involved, providing welfare funds to the provinces, through the Canada Assistance Plan. In addition, there is an impressive array of voluntary agencies in all fields of welfare, often working closely with government agencies.

The federal government's current outlay on health and welfare represents 30 percent of its total expenditure. In 1982–83, payments under the Canada Assistance Plan to the provinces and territories totalled $3.2 billion.

In Ottawa, as in the provincial capitals, the function of the welfare system is continually under study. Modifying the system is necessary just to keep up with changing social needs and conditions. Some forms of assistance appear to need strengthening, such as those providing income to people who cannot work—the aged, the blind, and the disabled.

In the 1980's, however, the major problem faced by the welfare system is the poor economic situation with its high rate of unemployment and poor job prospects. Many individuals who would have enjoyed full-time employment in better times are on the social assistance rolls. The problem is particularly acute among young, single people with little or no job experience. In re-

sponse to this situation, the provinces have put into place new programs to help people on social assistance improve their employability.

Canada Assistance Plan

The major portion of the federal financial contribution to welfare is channeled through the Canada Assistance Plan (the C.A.P.). Through C.A.P., the federal government reimburses the provinces and territories for 50 percent of the costs involved in providing social assistance and welfare services to persons in need.

The plan seeks to encourage the provision of adequate levels of assistance and institutional care to the needy, and to develop and extend welfare services which lessen, remove or prevent poverty, child neglect and dependence on public social assistance.

Under C.A.P., the federal government shares the costs to the provinces of providing food, shelter, clothing, fuel and other basic requirements to persons in need. Welfare services supported by the plan include rehabilitation (including assessment, referral, counseling and job placement), community development, homemaking, day care and other services aimed at helping people remain self-supporting.

C.P.A. provides funding toward the cost of caring for the needy in homes for the aged, nursing homes, child-care facilities, and hostels for battered women and children. Since 1977, the cost of long-term adult residential care has been covered by Federal-Provincial Fiscal Arrangements and the Established Programs Finance Act (E.P.F.)

Certain health-care costs for drugs, dental care and other services, which are covered neither by the provincial health-care programs nor by the E.P.F. are shared under C.A.P.

Provincial and municipal welfare

All the provinces and territories administer programs of social assistance and a wide range of welfare services. The cost of these programs and services is shared by three levels of government: the federal authorities, the provinces, and the municipalities. (Only Nova Scotia, Ontario and Manitoba actually involve their municipalities in the administration of welfare programs.)

In Ontario, the province assumes 80 percent of the cost of general welfare assistance and the municipality, 20 percent. The total payments are then shared federally on a 50 percent basis through C.A.P. This translates into a ratio of 50 percent from federal funds, and 30 and 20 percent from provincial and municipal sources respectively.

In other provinces, where there is no municipal involvement, the federal government shares 50 percent of the provincial social assistance costs.

Under C.A.P., the provinces have agreed to provide social assistance to people in need without imposing any time period for residence in the province, and to establish appeal procedures for those who are dissatisfied with decisions relating to the social assistance they have received.

All persons who are in need for whatever reason may request social assistance from the provinces (or territories) or the municipalities. Each province administers its own test to identify those who are truly needy. The test compares an individual's income and resources with his or her basic requirements. Social assistance is provided when income and resources are insufficient to meet fundamental needs. The most likely recipients are one-parent or large low-income families, the disabled, the aged, and the unemployed.

Caring for the elderly

There are homes for the aged and the infirm in all provinces, operated under provincial or municipal auspices, or voluntary administration. Some provinces operate their own facilities while also contributing funds to homes established and run by municipalities, church groups and service clubs.

Homes run by voluntary organizations must meet strict government standards concerning construction, operation and facilities, and usually must be licensed. Provincial inspectors check that the standards are met.

Through C.A.P., the federal government shares in the provincial costs for the care of needy people in such recognized welfare institutions as nursing homes and homes for the aged. Since 1977, the major portion of federal funding for long-term adult residential care has been covered under the Established Programs Financial Act.

Caring for children

Since 1893 when the Children's Protection Act became law in Ontario, child-welfare programs have been a notable feature of the Canadian social structure. All provinces provide child protection and care, services for unmarried parents and adoption services.

These programs are provided either by provincial agencies directly or by local children's aid societies operating under charter (See Chapter 11, "Children and parents"). The major portion of the provincial costs relating to child welfare is shared with the federal government through the Established Programs Financial Act. These expenditures include maintenance costs of children in foster homes or in other residential facilities, as well as adoption and protective services.

Child-welfare agencies are run by the provincial governments in Newfoundland, Prince Edward Island, New Brunswick, Saskatchewan, Alberta and British Columbia and, in Quebec, by the social services centers.

In Nova Scotia, Ontario and Manitoba, the children's aid societies carry the principal load.

The nongovernmental agencies receive substantial provincial grants, as well as support from municipalities, private citizens, community chests and united charity drives.

The child-welfare agencies will investigate cases of alleged child neglect and bring them to the attention of the courts. In a case of proven neglect, a court will either order that the child be returned to his parents under supervision, or make him a ward of the province or of a Children's Aid society. Depending on the circumstances, such a child may be placed in a foster boarding home, adoption home or some other selected institution. Between 15,000 and 16,000 adoptions are arranged in Canada every year.

The range of services provided by child-welfare agencies for unmarried parents includes care in homes for unmarried mothers, health care, counseling, legal assistance to arrange for child-support payments from the father, child-welfare and day-care services.

Day-care centers where working mothers can leave their children in skilled hands are becoming common in cities and towns. As yet, there is no universal support for day-care centers. The provinces, however, will subsidize some facilities. C.P.A. will share provincial costs for needy children in these particular centers.

The voluntary agencies

People helping people ... that is the shining common denominator in all the impressive work done by a vast array of nongovernmental social welfare organizations. There are national, provincial, regional, county and municipal agencies. If you should wish to avail yourself of any of their services, you should telephone or write the society named, or drop in at your nearest United Community Service, United Way, Community Chest or Red Feather office.

The Canadian Council on Social Development moves on the national level to improve social policies in general. Other organizations work in specialized health and welfare areas. These include the Canada Safety Council, the Arthritis Society, Canadian Association for the Mentally Retarded, Canadian Cancer Society, Canadian Cystic Fibrosis Foundation, Canada Diabetes Association, Canadian Hearing Society, Canadian Heart Foundation, Canadian Med-Alert Foundation Inc., Canadian Mental Health Association, Canadian National Institute for the Blind, Canadian Paraplegic Association, Canadian Red Cross Society, Canadian Rehabilitation Council for the Disabled, Canadian Lung Association, Health League of Canada, Multiple Sclerosis Society of Canada, Muscular Dystrophy Association of Canada, National Cancer Institute of Canada, St. John Ambulance, Victorian Order of Nurses for Canada and The War Amputations of Canada.

Money that enables these associations to perform their important work comes from government grants, national and local charity drives and private donations. Many of them have unpaid volunteers working alongside professionals.

At the local level in every province are many other organizations that take on welfare projects. This group includes the service clubs—Lions, Kiwanis, Kinsmen, Rotary—fraternal orders, church groups and B'nai Brith; youth organizations such as the Scouts and Guides; I.O.D.E., Y.W. and Y.M.C.A., and Y.W. and Y.M.H.A.; the Junior League, the Chamber of Commerce, and the Jaycees.

The voluntary agencies undertake to establish and operate a wide range of welfare services including: homemaker and day care; information and referral; legal aid; neighborhood development and self-help programs; residential care for children, youth and the aged; vocational counseling, training and placement; family planning; and casework in support of other services.

If you have the time and energy to spare you can be sure of a worthwhile job to do at one of the welfare agencies.

Appealing a welfare decision

To permit welfare applicants or recipients to appeal decisions that have gone against them, provincial review boards have been established. To arrange for a hearing, write to the department of social services in the capital city of your province. Departmental names vary across the country; any public library or post office will advise you.

When death occurs

The death certificate

Disposal of the body

Donation of organs

The cost of dying

A DEATH in the family will bring you into contact with a whole range of provincial laws, many of which you have perhaps never heard of. If the death is sudden, you can be forced into quick decisions at a time when your emotions are unsettled. Mistakes, easily made during a time of grief and loss, can be costly and hard to correct. It is wise before the event for everyone to understand the basic requirements of the law; it is definitely not "in bad taste" to discuss these questions frankly with your family, or with trusted friends. Obtaining the advice of the family lawyer is a wise move.

The death certificate

When a death occurs, a death certificate must be obtained from a doctor (registered medical practitioner), coroner or medical examiner. As the law requires, one of these professionals must examine the deceased and pronounce him or her legally dead. On the certificate the doctor will put down the time, place and cause of death. Several copies will be needed to arrange such matters as the reading of the will and the payment of social security benefits, life insurance and benefits under public or private pension schemes.

The *cause of death* will be particularly important for life insurance purposes; thus, it is crucial that it is accurately and clearly stated on the certificate, so that payments are not delayed unnecessarily.

In most cases, the family physician or other attending doctor will make out the death certificate. However, in some circumstances, the law may require that it be done by either a coroner or a medical examiner. The latter may be called upon when someone dies suddenly or unexpectedly, or following pregnancy, or when there is possible medical malpractice, foul play or suicide involved, or

when death occurs in an institution such as a hospital, nursing home or jail.

If the coroner is not satisfied as to the cause of death, he (or the medical examiner) may order an *autopsy*, or perhaps an *inquest*. He does not require the permission of the next of kin to order an autopsy. Except in Quebec, the death certificate must be deposited at the registry office.

Disposal of the body

A body may be buried or cremated (burned), or it may be donated in whole or in part for medical research or organ transplant. Universities conducting medical research want only complete normal bodies (for dissection). They can use only a certain number of these and may refuse some; transportation will have to be paid. The best way to assist medical research is to permit an autopsy.

No legal time limits are set for burial, beyond the requirements of public health laws; Protestants and Roman Catholics usually wait three days after death before interment, but Orthodox Jews are buried within 24 hours of death. A body cannot be cremated until approval has been given by a coroner or medical examiner, and there must be a 48-hour waiting period.

Although cemeteries and crematoriums are operated by municipalities, church parishes, private organizations and commercial companies, they are all subject to provincial control. The laws vary in detail across the country; all of them, however, lay down basic requirements of operation as set by zoning, public health and environment authorities.

If you wish to be buried, it is both a practical and considerate idea to buy a plot before you die, saving your family the problem of having to do so in a rush.

You cannot be buried on your own land without special permission.

625

Compensation for the victim

IF A DEATH has occurred as the direct result of a criminal act, the victim's dependents can be optimistic of being awarded compensation under comparatively new laws adopted widely in Canada, as in most Western countries. If nonfatal injuries are sustained, the victim himself will likely be compensated. At this writing, all provinces, with the exception of Prince Edward Island, had enacted legislation similar to Ontario's Compensation for Victims of Crime Act.

The legislation was prompted by the failure of the state to ensure the safety of its citizens, and by the sense of sympathy and responsibility felt in a humane society.

The Ontario law, passed in 1971, replaced and consolidated earlier legislation which first allowed compensation only if the victim was killed or injured while assisting a law officer, then was amended to cover any occurrence of death or injury due to crime. In this typical law, compensation is possible if you are the victim of a violent crime, such as murder, rape or assault, or if you suffer through poisoning, arson and criminal negligence. You are also covered if you are attempting to help the police arrest an offender. Death or injury from motoring offenses is not included.

An application for compensation must be made to the Criminal Injuries Compensation Board (the names of the provincial authorities vary a little) within a year of the occurrence; this time limit might be extended in certain circumstances. Compensation may be awarded for expenses resulting from death or injury; financial loss as a result of being partially or completely disabled; pain and suffering; the support of a child born as a result of rape; any other financial losses or expenses (by you or your dependents) considered reasonable by the board.

Compensation payments in Ontario during a recent two-year period totaled over $5,000,000. Individual payments averaged $2,217.58. The Ontario board can award up to a maximum of $175,000 for all applicants in respect of any one occurrence; for a single victim, the maximum is a lump sum of $15,000, or monthly payments of $500. Under certain conditions, an applicant can receive both a lump sum and periodic payments, subject to annual review. Assault causing bodily harm is the most frequent offense involved in compensation cases, and about half of all money awarded goes to requite pain and suffering of the victims.

One of the higher awards granted in Ontario was to a 23-year-old university student who was stabbed. He was awarded $7,500 for pain and suffering, as well as $1,183 for expenses and loss of earnings (from a part-time job). The expenses included $515 for tuition fees the university would not refund for the time the victim was absent from classes while recovering. The man who committed this crime was set free on probation for psychiatric treatment and, two months later, was sent to jail for robbing a bank.

One of the lower awards went to a middle-aged man who was caught in the midst of a fight between youths on a streetcar. He got $131.60 for a sprained neck.

A 76-year-old woman who suffered a broken hip when she was knocked down by hustling crowds at the Toronto National Exhibition grounds was awarded $839. The Ontario board ruled that the "assault was so violent, brutal and careless as to amount to criminal negligence."

The board may make an order for compensation, whether the offender was prosecuted or convicted or not. Since many of the offenders concerned are in jail, or are listed as "whereabouts unknown," it is not considered feasible to track them down to recover the sums granted to their victims. In recent years, the Ontario Treasury has been able to regain the money granted in compensation in only a few of the many hundreds of cases dealt with.

Donation of organs
Requests made by a person in his will, or otherwise, concerning the nature of his funeral or burial are usually honored but are not legally binding upon his executor or his family. On the other hand, stipulations about donation of bodily organs for research or transplant operations usually are binding. Institutions, however, seldom contest the objections of survivors in court. If you want to leave your body or certain organs to medical science, you should get the agreement of your family now, to avoid any controversy later.

Even if you have made no provision for such a donation, your family has the right to do so on your behalf.

The cost of dying
A funeral and burial can cost hundreds—even thousands—of dollars; however, it doesn't have to. Burial expenses take precedence over all other debts against the deceased's estate; however, government and private pension plans cushion the financial shock. (*See* "The pension network" in this chapter.)

The law requires that the body be placed in a casket or other suitable container. This can be made of almost any material—it doesn't have to be of oak, with silver or brass handles. The introduction of lawn cemeteries (without upright gravestones) has reduced costs considerably; the nineteenth-century-style funeral with black carriages and huge floral wreaths is no longer necessary to show proper respect for the dead.

Embalming (treating the body to protect it from decay) is not required by law, except in special circumstances—for instance, when a body is being shipped some distance.

Discuss all funeral and burial charges in detail with the prospective undertaker before you commission him to handle things for you. Don't accept the first suggestion he makes just because you think it wrong to talk about money "at a time like this." Don't hesitate to try another firm if you are not entirely satisfied.

More and more, cremation is replacing burial in Canada as in all civilized countries, mostly among the Protestant sects.

It costs on average about half the price of burial. Incidentally, in the modern crematorium, there is no flame and no smoke. Only a white mineral ash remains (about 5 pounds) which can be put, if you wish, in an urn and taken home, or left in the *columbarium* usually attached to the crematorium chapel.

In most long-established funeral homes, you will always be served with dignity and discretion; and you will not be pressured into spending more than you can afford. The funeral director will probably take care of many of the minor legal problems. He is skilled in helping solicitously in emotional situations.

You can prearrange your own funeral with an undertaker and prepay it. The money must be put in a trust account where it will earn compound interest.

In each province, there is a Registrar of the Provincial Licensing Board for Funeral Directors. You can telephone or write to him for impartial detailed information about any arrangements.

Memorial societies
In recent years, a movement has developed for foster funeral observances that will be simple, spiritual, dignified and—above all—inexpensive. These objectives led to the founding of memorial societies throughout North America. At this writing, there were about 25 societies in Canada—from coast to coast. Membership costs $10 for an adult and $5 for people of limited means.

The societies provide each member with an opportunity—after calm consideration and while free from emotional strain—to record his wishes as to disposal of his body. He can also choose between a funeral and a memorial service (if he desires either) and leave instructions on the appointment of a funeral director, a minister and executors. Each society has an office where this information is kept on file. Besides, the society makes arrangements with an undertaker to fulfill the member's wishes.

For further information you can write to The Memorial Society Association of Canada, Box 96, Station "A", Weston, Ont., M9N 3M6.

You and

Your Leisure

15/Traveling and Transportation

Rights of the traveler

As BEFITS THE PEOPLE who inhabit the world's second largest country (the largest by far is, of course, the Soviet Union), Canadians are wide-ranging travelers. In 1982, one and a half million Canadians traveled abroad, spending about $1.8 billion. In St. Mark's Square in Venice, around London's Leicester Square, along Leningrad's Nevsky Prospect, by the canals of Amsterdam, or on the Champs-Elysées in Paris, the couple who sink thankfully into the café chairs next to yours are likely from Taber or Timmins, Terrebonne or Tignish.

On every journey—by plane, ship, train, automobile or bus—and in every hotel and restaurant along the way, the law is your silent companion, attempting to protect you from physical harm, from loss of property and from smooth operators who might try to sell you fragments of Noah's Ark. Of course, in foreign lands you are governed by foreign laws (and they can be very different from our own—don't try driving on the right-hand side of the road in Britain) but your Canadian citizenship is a powerful talisman. Showing your Canadian passport can help you out of minor difficulties that result from your ignorance of strange regulations. Foreign airlines and shipping companies offering to serve the Canadian public must abide by Canadian law, both in the methods of their operation and in the standards of their performance.

Canadian travel facts are hard to pin down due to the presence of "the world's longest undefended border." Although the United States is, strictly speaking, a foreign country, it is not thought of as such by the majority of Canadians. More than 33 million border crossings were recorded in 1982 and Canadians spent an estimated $3 billion south of the border. When the term "abroad" is used in this chapter, it refers to the rest of the world, excluding the United States.

In 1982, Canada welcomed almost two million visitors from abroad. But most years, even more Canadians travel abroad—a fact that concerns the Canadian Government Office of Tourism (more correctly known as Tourism Canada). With tourism officers affiliated with embassies or consulates in London, Paris, Frankfurt, The Hague, Mexico City, Tokyo and Sydney—as well as a total of 14 in the United States—Tourism Canada sends out about two million items of travel information each year. The marketing branch of Tourism Canada is responsible for the development and the actual marketing of "travel product"; planning and research, both strategic and operational, are the responsibility of the corporate affairs branch. Tourism Canada's services are available to the general public.

The carriers' contract
The law steps in as soon as you make your first move toward going on a trip. When you buy a ticket for bus, train, ship or plane travel, you automatically enter into a contract with the carrier involved. Those companies that offer to carry passengers (or to transport any class of goods) are known as *common carriers*. For example, Canadian Pacific is a common carrier, though a distinctly uncommon company. Such corporations may not pick and choose their customers and are, in fact, treated similarly in Canadian law to publicly owned utilities. Their rates and fares, liabilities and responsi-

bilities are all scrutinized by various authorized agencies and boards, of which the main body is the Canadian Transport Commission. This large (17-member) board regulates all interprovincial and international transportation in Canada by rail, air and water. Constitutionally, interprovincial and international highway transportation is also under the control of the federal government; however, in 1954, Ottawa passed this authority on to the various provincial highway transport boards.

While the carriers have an explicit and extensive responsibility for their passengers' safety (and for the safety of all baggage), they are permitted to limit their liability to a certain extent. These limiting conditions are usually set out in posters at terminals or in the schedules issued by the companies. The key points must be brought to your attention before you start your trip; you will probably find a summary of the conditions printed on your ticket.

It is important to read any conditions printed on your ticket so that you clearly understand what your rights would be in the event of a traffic accident or some other mishap. It is unclear whether you can demand a magnifying glass to read the fine print.

Carriers must take every reasonable precaution to transport their passengers safely. If you were injured on the deck of an ocean liner, the shipping company would have to prove that its safety measures were sufficient to meet all reasonable conditions; otherwise, you might well succeed with a claim for damages.

A carrier will also be held responsible for the safety of a passenger's baggage, unless it can prove that the passenger took complete personal charge of the baggage and that any loss or damage was due directly to the passenger's own negligence. When the baggage is handled by the carrier, it is the company's duty to have it readily available for pickup; if the passenger fails to collect it within a reasonable time, the company is then obliged to store it safely in its baggage room. The law of *bailment* then applies (*See* "Goods in transit" in this chapter).

Passenger carriers bear particularly heavy safety responsibilities, especially the airlines that hold so many lives at risk on every flight. Selection and training of employes and maintenance of equipment are given high priority. Every facet of the operation comes under the scrutiny of national and international government experts. A company cannot evade liability for equipment failure by claiming that it had relied on the reputation or promises of the manufacturer. It has a prior contract to honor: to transport people or cargo to a certain destination safely.

Passenger carriers must also make sure they provide safe facilities for boarding and leaving a plane, train, vehicle or boat. The platform, ramp or stairs should be in such a condition that a passenger taking reasonable care will be able to make his entry or exit without injury.

Getting a passport

If you are a Canadian citizen, you must have a valid passport for travel anywhere outside of this country, except to the United States, Mexico, and some Caribbean countries. It is the best identification you can have, so you might as well take it along even if you travel south of the border. It is issued by the Department of External Affairs and its purpose is to inform all foreign governments that you are a Canadian citizen.

To get a passport, you can pick up an application form at passport offices, most post offices and travel agencies. Upon completing the form, you mail it, along with other documents required, to the Passport Office in Ottawa or take it in person to one of the 18 regional offices. Normally, it takes two weeks from receipt for an application to be processed—so leave yourself enough time before your planned departure.

If you apply directly to Ottawa, mail your application to:

The Passport Office
Department of External Affairs
Ottawa, Canada   K1A 0G3

The regional offices, where you can apply in person and can get a passport in three working days—provided you can meet all the requirements for getting a passport—are located in large cities in all provinces except Prince Edward Island. Check your telephone directory for the nearest passport office. Following are the addresses of the offices in the major cities in Canada.

Royal Trust Tower
Suite 1012
Toronto Dominion Centre
Toronto, Ontario   M5K 1K2

Guy Favreau Complex
200 Dorchester West
West Tower, Suite 215
Montreal, Quebec   H2Z 1X4

800 W. Pender Street
Suite 610
Vancouver, B.C.   V6C 2V6

10117 Jasper Avenue
Suite 500
Edmonton, Alberta   T5J 1W8

391 York Avenue
Suite 308
Winnipeg, Manitoba   R3C 0P6

Barrington Tower
Suite 1210
Scotia Square
Halifax, Nova Scotia
B3J 1P3

If you live abroad, apply to the Canadian diplomatic mission (embassy or High Commissioner's office), or the consular or trade office in the country of your residence.

A passport is valid for five years—and it cannot be renewed. When it expires, you have to apply for a new one. This entails making a new application and supplying all the material, such as photographs and birth certificate, once again. And it takes just as long each time to process your application.

Passports are issued only to Canadian citizens (*See* Chapter 2, "How to become a citizen"). A man and his wife require individual passports. The names of children younger than 16 who are Canadian citizens may be included in the passport of either parent, but not in the passports of both. However, a child younger than 16 may apply for a separate passport by completing a special form.

A passport must never be altered in any way by the holder. A woman who has married can have her passport amended or obtain a new one.

Along with the completed application form, you have to supply two unmounted photographs of yourself. Both prints must be made from the same negative and should measure 50 x 70 millimetres with an extra 13-millimetre blank strip at the bottom for your signature. The photograph, taken not more than a year previously, must show a full front view of your head and shoulders (without a hat), taken against a plain, light background. Slot machine photographs or those subject to fading or sensitive to heat are not acceptable. You must sign each photograph in the signature strip. As some ballpoint pens will not write well on a photograph, use an ordinary fountain or felt pen.

You need a *guarantor* who must certify on the back of both photographs that it is a true photograph of you—and he must sign that statement. Any one of the following people can be a guarantor, provided he (or she) is a Canadian citizen and has known you for at least two years: mayor, magistrate or provincial judge, police officer (R.C.M.P., provincial or municipal), postmaster, minister of religion, lawyer, notary public, doctor, dentist, school principal or university professor, manager of a bank, trust company or credit union, professional accountant (including any accountant who is a member of any of the following recognized professional accountant organizations: C.A., C.P.A., R.I.A., C.G.A. and A.P.A.) and professional engineer. If you don't know anyone who would qualify within the above group, you can submit what is called a *declaration in lieu of guarantor*—sworn before a commissioner for oaths, notary public or justice of the peace—in which you guarantee that the photo is one of yourself.

Another important document you need

is proof of your Canadian citizenship. If you were born in Canada, you must send your birth certificate issued by the provincial vital statistics authorities or a certificate of proof of Canadian citizenship issued by the Registrar of Canadian Citizenship in Ottawa or the nearest federal citizenship court. A certificate of birth or of baptism issued by religious or other authorities is also acceptable from Quebec residents, as long as it states the date and place of your birth.

Persons not born in Canada must submit one of the following documents: certificate of Canadian citizenship; certificate of naturalization; certificate of registration of Canadian birth abroad, issued by the Registrar of Canadian Citizenship; or certificate of retention of Canadian citizenship. These documents may be obtained from the nearest federal citizenship court office or from the Registrar of Canadian Citizenship.

If you say or write something that is false or misleading in an effort to get a passport, whether for yourself or for someone else, you are committing an indictable offense, punishable by two years' imprisonment.

When you send in your application, enclose a certified cheque, bank draft, or a bank express or postal money order for $21 payable to the Receiver General for Canada. A special businessman's passport costs $23; it has an extra 24 pages.

Loss of passport

If you have lost your passport or if it has been stolen, report the fact immediately to the closest issuing passport office and the police. You must make out an official declaration and send it to the Passport Office. It must include your name and address, passport number and date of issue (if known), the approximate date and the circumstances of the loss, the date the loss was reported to the local police, as well as a report on your attempts to recover it. If you lose your passport when traveling, you can apply for a new one at the Canadian embassy or consular office—or, if there is none, the nearest British consular office will assist you. The circumstances of the loss will be investigated thoroughly—there is a booming black market for "lost" Canadian passports.

If you need a visa

Besides needing valid passports, Canadians may also need visas or tourist cards for short visits (up to three months) to some foreign countries. Allow sufficient time before your departure for your application to be processed by the appropriate embassy or consulate. Some countries may also require that your passport be valid for a minimum period of time. If the country you are visiting enforces exit controls, necessitating special papers or procedures before you are permitted to leave, you should register with the nearest Cana-

Have you had your shots?

EXPERIENCED travelers keep their "medical certificate" up-to-date, and close at hand with their passport, rather than in their luggage. Wise travelers also take note of the vaccination requirements of the countries on their itinerary. This information is available from travel agents or from the Medical Services Branch of the Department of National Health and Welfare.

Some countries require proof of immunization against cholera and yellow fever. You may also be advised to obtain protection against other diseases, such as typhoid, tetanus, polio and hepatitis. Malaria—potentially fatal—is endemic to most areas of the world. A treatment of protective drugs against malaria must be started prior to departure.

If you have recently had some serious illness, or have some continuing medical problem, you should carry a separate certificate from your physician. The telephone number of your doctor should be carried on your person.

dian diplomatic or consular post upon arrival and at departure.

Since visa regulations can be changed without notice, you would be wise to check first with the consulate or embassy of the country you want to visit or with your travel agent.

Canadian citizens, or British subjects who are permanent residents of Canada, require neither passports nor visas for visits to the United States.

Canadians do not require visas for visits to most Commonwealth countries; however, before you take off for Australia or New Zealand, you should check with the local representatives of these countries, or with a travel agency or international transportation company.

Got enough money?

Besides your passport, and visa (if required), you must be able to satisfy authorities abroad that you have enough money for your planned stay, that you hold return or onward transportation tickets and that you are in good health.

Most countries will not permit nonresidents to accept a job during their stay unless they have applied for and been granted work permits before entry.

There are several ways in which you can keep your money safe while abroad (See Chapter 7, "The role of the bank"): for the average tourist, the well known traveler's cheques are the best bet.

Dual nationality

Canadian citizens who were born abroad, or whose parents were born abroad or who were nationals of a foreign country, are warned that if they visit the country of their birth or descent, they may be considered by that government to be nationals of the country in question, even though by our law they are Canadian citizens. A Canadian woman married to an alien may be regarded as having automatically acquired his nationality on marriage. If these nationality problems affect you in any way, remember that when you are within the jurisdiction of such a country, you are subject to its laws and may not be exempt from certain obligations, including compulsory military service. The Ca-

nadian government may not be able to protect you. You can obtain more detailed information about dual nationality from any Court of Canadian Citizenship or by writing to the Registrar of Canadian Citizenship, Department of the Secretary of State, Ottawa, K1A 0M5.

Registration abroad

If you remain in a foreign country for a lengthy period, or take up residence there, you should register at the nearest Canadian diplomatic or consular post. If there is none, you may register with the nearest British representative. If you do not register, you might run into difficulty or delay in getting assistance and protection in an emergency. This applies particularly to areas with tense or unstable political conditions, or where natural disasters can occur.

Medical requirements

Canada has adopted the standards of the World Health Organization for travelers. An international vaccination certificate will be issued to you by the Medical Services Branch of the Department of National Health and Welfare. In accordance with the requirements of the certificate, a public health official or any qualified doctor will vaccinate you against cholera, tetanus, or other diseases. Yellow fever vaccinations are given at designated yellow fever vaccination centers accredited by the Department of National Health and Welfare. These are located in major cities across the country and on Canadian Forces bases. Your certificate must be stamped and dated by the public health authorities; the dates are important because the vaccines have a limited "life"— for instance, a yellow fever vaccination is good for ten years, and a cholera shot only for six months.

Generally speaking, cholera and yellow fever vaccinations are required only of persons who will be traveling in those parts of the world where these diseases are not fully under control. No health documents are needed for Canadians traveling in the United States.

However, medical requirements for travel abroad can and do change abrupt-

The airline ticket: read the fine print

The laws of travel reach back into dimmest antiquity—to the days of the Phoenician galleys that once plied the Mediterranean, and no doubt beyond them. It might seem a giant step from the trireme to the jumbo jet, but some of the legal questions raised between the carrier and his passenger are the same today as at the dawn of recorded history.

It's a fair bet that the average air traveler today picks up his ticket, stuffs it in his pocket, and boards his plane without much further thought or worry. Someone else "up there," he figures, is fretting about his safety—and what can he do about it, anyway? It's not all that simple.

That ticket is, in effect, a contract between you and the carrier and, like all contracts, it has conditions attached to it. When you accept the ticket, you are accepting those conditions. Here are the contract conditions, for example, which apply to every ticket issued by Air Canada:

Issued by Air Canada **NOTICE** Sold Subject to Tariff Regulations

If the passenger's journey involves an ultimate destination or stop in a country other than the country of departure the Warsaw Convention may be applicable and the Convention governs and in most cases limits the liability of carriers for death or personal injury and in respect of loss of or damage to baggage. See also notice headed "Advice to International Passengers on Limitation of Liability".

CONDITIONS OF CONTRACT

1. As used in this contract "ticket" means this passenger ticket and baggage check, of which these conditions and the notices form part, "carriage" is equivalent to "transportation", "carrier" means all air carriers that carry or undertake to carry the passenger or his baggage hereunder or perform any other service incidental to such air carriage."WARSAW CONVENTION" means the Convention for the Unification of Certain Rules Relating to International Carriage by Air signed at Warsaw 12th October 1929, or that Convention as amended at The Hague, 28th September 1955, whichever may be applicable.

2. Carriage hereunder is subject to the rules and limitations relating to liability established by the Warsaw Convention unless such carriage is not "international carriage" as defined by that Convention.

3. To the extent not in conflict with the foregoing carriage and other services performed by each carrier are subject to (i) provisions contained in this ticket, (ii) applicable tariffs, (iii) carrier's conditions of carriage and related regulations which are made part hereof (and are available on application at the offices of carrier), except in transportation between a place in the United States or Canada and any place outside thereof to which tariffs in force in those countries apply.

4. Carrier's name may be abbreviated in the ticket, the full name and its abbreviation being set forth in carrier's tariffs, conditions of carriage, regulations or timetables; carrier's address shall be the airport of departure shown opposite the first abbreviation of carrier's name in the ticket; the agreed stopping places are those places set forth in this ticket or as shown in carrier's timetables as scheduled stopping places on the passenger's route; carriage to be performed hereunder by several successive carriers is regarded as a single operation.

5. An air carrier issuing a ticket for carriage over the lines of another air carrier does so only as its agent.

6. Any exclusion or limitation of liability of carrier shall apply to and be for the benefit of agents, servants and representatives of carrier and any person whose aircraft is used by carrier for carriage and its agents, servants and representatives.

7. Checked baggage will be delivered to bearer of the baggage check. In case of damage to baggage moving in international transportation complaint must be made in writing to carrier forthwith after discovery of damage and, at the latest, within 7 days from receipt, in case of delay, complaint must be made within 21 days from date the baggage was delivered. See tariffs or conditions of carriage regarding non-international transportation.

8. This ticket is good for carriage for one year from date of issue, except as otherwise provided in this ticket, in carrier's tariffs, conditions of carriage, or related regulations. The fare for carriage hereunder is subject to change prior to commencement of carriage. Carrier may refuse transportation if the applicable fare has not been paid.

9. Carrier undertakes to use its best efforts to carry the passenger and baggage with reasonable dispatch. Times shown in timetable or elsewhere are not guaranteed and form no part of this contract. Carrier may without notice substitute alternate carriers or aircraft, and may alter or omit stopping places shown on the ticket in case of necessity. Schedules are subject to change without notice. Carrier assumes no responsibility for making connections.

10. Passenger shall comply with Government travel requirements, present exit, entry and other required documents and arrive at airport by time fixed by carrier or, if no time is fixed, early enough to complete departure procedures.

11. No agent, servant or representative of carrier has authority to alter, modify or waive any provision of this contract.

CARRIER RESERVES THE RIGHT TO REFUSE CARRIAGE TO ANY PERSON WHO HAS ACQUIRED A TICKET IN VIOLATION OF APPLICABLE LAW OR CARRIER'S TARIFFS, RULES OR REGULATIONS.

The Warsaw Convention rules

Air Canada offers the following explanation (and warning) that an international agreement known as the Warsaw Convention can limit the amount of indemnity that airlines can be required to pay in the case of death or injury, or in the loss of passenger baggage.

ADVICE TO INTERNATIONAL PASSENGERS ON LIMITATION OF LIABILITY

Passengers on a journey involving an ultimate destination or a stop in a country other than the country of origin are advised that the provisions of a treaty known as the Warsaw Convention may be applicable to the entire journey, including any portion entirely within the country of origin or destination. For such passengers on a journey to, from, or with an agreed stopping place in the United States of America, the Convention and special contracts of carriage embodied in applicable tariffs provide that the liability of certain carriers, parties to such special contracts, for death of or personal injury to passengers is limited in most cases to proven damages not to exceed U.S. $75,000 per passenger, and that this liability up to such limit shall not depend on negligence on the part of the carrier.

For such passengers travelling by a carrier not a party to such special contracts or on a journey not to, from, or having an agreed stopping place in the United States of America, liability of the carrier for death or personal injury to passengers is limited in most cases to approximately U.S. $10,000 or U.S. $20,000.

The names of carriers, parties to such special contracts, are available at all ticket offices of such carriers and may be examined on request.

Additional protection can usually be obtained by purchasing insurance from a private company. Such insurance is not affected by any limitation of the carrier's liability under the Warsaw Convention or such special contracts of carriage. For further information please consult your airline or insurance company representative.

NOTE: The limit of liability of U.S. $75,000 above is inclusive of legal fees and costs except that in case of a claim brought in a state where provision is made for separate award of legal fees and costs, the limit shall be the sum of U.S. $58,000 exclusive of legal fees and costs.

---

ly. Typhoid and tetanus inoculations might suddenly be required. Travel agents are kept informed by government health authorities and can usually advise you accurately. For complete peace of mind, contact the public health unit nearest your home. If the rules change while you are abroad, you might have to submit to an inoculation at the airport upon your return to Canada.

When you fly

Air travel within Canada is governed more by the everyday domestic law than by any special air-travel legislation. The technical side of civil aviation is governed by the Federal Aeronautics Act and the National Transportation Act. For the price of the ticket, the airline contracts to carry you (and your baggage) safely to your destination. If the company fails to reasonably fulfill this contract, you may be able to take civil action against it, depending on the terms of the contract.

There are several separate technical definitions of "carriage by air"; in this section, we are discussing only the carrying of passengers by Canadian *common carriers*. Since the contracts offered by foreign-based airlines can vary in many ways from the Canadian model, you should study the conditions summarized on the ticket issued by the airline.

Despite the wording of the conditions printed on your ticket, Canadian airlines are never completely free of liability. As a condition of licensing, the Canadian Transport Commission insists that the airlines hold insurance policies which guarantee a minimum coverage in the case of passenger injury, and for damage or loss of baggage.

If the head of a family dies in the crash of a scheduled Canadian airliner in Canada, his dependents can naturally claim according to whatever flight or personal insurance the victim held. In Ontario, under the Family Law Reform Act, the family would be able to take separate action against the airline. The family would have to show that the dead man, had he lived, would have been able to sue and recover damages from the airline on grounds of negligence or other causes. The courts

would probably rule that the family was entitled to that payment.

Foreign airlines usually pay compensation for death or injury on the basis of standards set out under various international treaties, including the Warsaw Convention. These levels of payment may be considerably less than the expectations of most Canadian travelers.

If the plane involved in an accident is not a normal commercial carrier (let us say that it is a privately owned and privately piloted plane), there is nothing to prevent the plane's operator from making any deal he wants with the passenger, even to the extent of freeing himself from all liability.

The liability of a Canadian airline during a domestic flight would not apply in the case of injury or illness due to the passenger's old age or mental or physical condition. The company would have to establish the condition of such a passenger in advance, and make it clear when they accept the passenger that they will not be responsible for anything resulting from his condition.

For overseas flights or trips into the United States, the various conditions under which a Canadian airline would be held liable are printed on the ticket. These are subject to change in accordance with international air-travel conventions. If a Canadian commercial aircraft was involved in an accident abroad, its liability would, however, be much the same as it would be within Canada.

The ocean voyage

Shipping companies have moved agressively into the "holiday package" business with all-inclusive cruises in both the economy and luxury price ranges. Mostly sailing tropical routes, they offer thousands of Canadians each year a welcome breakaway from winter weather. Oceangoing freighters are still the most important means of moving manufactured goods and raw materials to the international marketplace.

On both kinds of ships—cruising and cargo carrying—there are legal responsibilities which affect passengers and their belongings, commercial goods and materials, as well as binding the shipping companies themselves.

As a cruise ship passenger (or as a passenger on a freighter), you have the right to expect what you have paid for; clean livable quarters, meals as advertised, departure on schedule, port stops as announced and end-of-journey arrival on schedule—conditions permitting. Provided no major mishap or unusual weather conditions (a hurricane or a typhoon) occur, it is the shipping company's responsibility to live up to its contract. Unless the company could prove that the circumstances causing failure had been beyond its control—for instance, if the ship was late because it was caught in a storm—you could consider a suit for breach of contract if the delay had caused you loss.

All passengers must be prepared to be careful with baggage and valuables kept in their staterooms or cabins. The companies usually limit their liability for the loss or damage of personal baggage. This liability varies: a survey of major cruise lines shows a range of $150–$280 US. Unless the stewards formally announce that they will be policing the area, you should keep your door locked.

Any gold or silver, diamonds or other precious stones, money or securities, or any other valuable items you may be carrying, should be deposited under seal with the ship's purser. You can get your tiara out in time for the gala dinner.

The shipping line is not responsible for the loss or theft of personal property left in the dining room or other public areas.

In reading the mass of conditions printed on your ticket, you might get the impression that the shipping company is absolving itself from just about all liability. However, the company's employes and agents cannot be exempted from negligence, and you could bring such a charge against them. If such a situation arises, you should always sue both employe and company, for the company is responsible for the acts of its agents.

Going by rail

In 1977, Via Rail Canada took over responsibility for inter-city passenger train service from C.N. and C.P. rail. Via Rail, an autonomous Crown corporation, reports to the Minister of Transport.

When a passenger enters a train, the law implies a contract on the part of the railway company to carry him to any station on the line for which he holds a proper ticket. This also holds good if the passenger pays in cash to the conductor.

The conductor is entitled to demand to see your ticket. If you cannot produce it, you must buy one on the spot or be put off at the next stop. Saying that you have lost your ticket is not acceptable.

You can buy a ticket with any of the major credit cards, with cash or, with proper identification, by cheque.

The conductor's right to remove a non-paying or disorderly passenger is not absolute; it must be exercised reasonably. To put a drunken passenger off, for example, the conductor must use no more force than is necessary and should choose a safe place at a scheduled stop.

The times of departure and arrival of trains as published in the timetable cannot be considered as part of the carrier's contract.

A ticket for a continuous journey between two points entitles you to transportation for the entire distance and the railway must give a refund for any unused portion of a ticket. You are not entitled to stopovers unless you get your ticket extended by the conductor or at a railway station.

Unless seats are numbered and you have bought a ticket for a numbered seat, you have no right to expect any particular seat in a railway coach or club car. A "reserved seat ticket" guarantees you a seat, for Via Rail sells only as many tickets as there are seats; but it does not guarantee a specific seat. In Europe's first-class trains, you can reserve exactly the seat you want, much like choosing a seat at the theater.

You cannot "reserve" a seat by placing your hat, handbag or a newspaper on it— even for two minutes when you go to the washroom. If a seat which has not been reserved and allotted to you by the conductor is vacant for any reason, another passenger has every right to take it.

The rail company must provide all reasonable protection to its passengers at stations so that they can get on and off the train in safety.

On the other hand, the railway company is entitled to assume that all passengers will act with reasonable prudence and care.

A railway is responsible as a common carrier for a passenger's baggage in the car with him: however, if it is lost (or stolen) due to the negligence or default of the passenger, the railway is not liable. The company is both the *bailee* and carrier of the goods.

Any baggage you check with the railway must be delivered to the platform at your destination. The liability of the railway company does not end until you pick it up or you have had a reasonable time to pick it up.

If any goods remain unclaimed for three months in possession of the company, the company will advertise in the provincial *Gazette*, and in any other newspapers considered necessary. Failing to get any response, it may sell the baggage by public auction.

Any profits from such sale, above the carriage and storage charges, go to the federal treasury.

You may not carry gunpowder, dynamite, nitroglycerine or any other goods of a dangerous or explosive nature on a train.

If you travel on trains when abroad, any claim you may have for injury or damage will be judged under the statutes of the country in which the accident took place.

The bus trip

Touring by bus ("coach," if you like) is an economical and, in these days, comfortable method of travel, both on this continent and abroad. Canadians by the thousands daily go to work or school or on shopping trips by a reliable public bus service.

The operations of public or chartered buses in Canada are normally under the control of provincial and municipal transport boards, or commissions, which issue licenses and set standards aimed at ensuring the safety and efficient transportation of passengers.

The driver can refuse admission if his vehicle is full (standing passengers must not number more than one-third of those seated). He can also turn away persons he believes to be drunk or "high" on drugs, who are overly noisy or disorderly, or who are using profane or obscene language.

Some regulations forbid passengers to converse with the driver while the bus is in motion.

Buses and other public vehicles must be constructed to guarantee easy and safe entry and exit for passengers. Long-distance buses are usually equipped with overhead hand-baggage racks which have to be approved for safety. Before starting the journey, the driver must inspect these racks to make sure luggage is stored securely and is not liable to fall and injure anyone.

Timetables are particularly important in city-to-city travel where the public does not have a wide (or any) choice of carrier. Every licensed bus line must file a timetable with the provincial department of transport, showing scheduled departure and arrival as well as the number of daily trips over each route. The bus line must make every effort to stick to the times listed in its schedule.

If scheduled service is interrupted for more than 24 hours, the bus line must notify the public through newspaper advertisements and signs posted at regular stopping places.

If a bus breaks down during a trip, the company must arrange immediately to pick up the stranded passengers and carry them to their destinations.

All public transportation lines must hold insurance policies covering every vehicle and the policies must be obtained from a company that is licensed under the Insurance Act. The minimum coverage varies across the provinces providing for at least $35,000 in the case of injury to, or death of, any passenger, as well as coverage of $1,000 for damage to property of all passengers. The subject of travel insurance is more fully explained in "Trouble while traveling" in this chapter.

Package tours and cruises

Charter flights

Special youth fares

Fares for pensioners

Baggage allowances

Transportation of animals

Taking a taxicab

A s THE AUTUMN leaves flutter down, the travel sections of Canadian newspapers fill with advertisements offering ways to escape oncoming winter. Favorite retreats for Canadian sun lovers include Florida, Mexico, Hawaii, the Caribbean Islands and the Mediterranean coasts. More recently, jet transportation has brought remote destinations such as Australia and New Zealand, where the Christmas holiday is in high summer, within the reach of well-heeled vacationers.

The summer vacation season sees Canadians surge in another direction: mostly to Europe, many of them drawn (perhaps unconsciously) back to the towns and green valleys that were the original homes of their forefathers. Londoners and Parisians, for example, have just about thrown in the towel and good-naturedly handed over their cities to the tourist throngs during the months of July and August.

Until the jet engine shrank the oceans, international travel was mostly for the well-to-do, or it was indulged in by retired couples dipping cautiously into a lifetime's savings. The big jets became ravenous for passengers and the inclusive charter holiday was born; more than half of today's transatlantic air traffic is by charter. The passenger liners, the proud queens of travel, were within a few short years broken up or remodeled as cruise ships offering package tours in every combination of ship 'n' shore recreation.

Although the increased involvement by the general public in foreign legal systems might have been expected to create a bulging casebook, there have been surprisingly few serious problems. This re-flects the careful staff work and organization of the major international tour operators.

The package tour

Sophisticates who have sometimes seen more guidebooks than great sights tend to dismiss the highly organized, prepaid tour as being strictly for squares. But the guided tour has an honorable history; in an earlier century, the wealthy and titled families of England gave their sons that final polish by sending them on "the grand tour" of Europe, accompanied by experienced and knowledgeable companions (in effect they were paid guides) both as mentors and chaperons. Today, the package tour provides a somewhat similar way for the inexperienced traveler to see "all the sights" without risking the snarls and delays so easily caused by ignorance of local regulations and customs.

Taking an organized tour has many other advantages. For one thing, you know before you start just how much your trip is going to cost and you can pay for everything—even including your tips, if you like—before you leave home. The tour officials will solve all problems of immigration and customs checks, of money changing, airport–hotel transfers, hotel check-ins, restaurant reservations and dozens of other arrangements that tourists traveling alone must struggle with individually.

You can easily run afoul of strange regulations and local laws when you don't speak or read a word of the language. Some police authorities insist on surrender of your passport at the hotel desk. And do you know in which country your wife will be forbidden to wear shorts in the streets?

Hotels and booking agencies abroad now depend for much of their income on group tours and will usually bend over backward to ensure that "the tour people" have no complaints. The individual traveler, on the other hand, may find he has second choice. A lot can depend, in some countries, on how low a price the agency has negotiated in its package deal. If an individual turns up willing to pay a higher dollar, the group leader could discover that he is suddenly one room-with-bath short.

The savings made possible by guaranteed-capacity bookings, which the tour operators can offer to hotels and nightclubs, airlines, shipping companies and rent-a-car firms, have brought the price of package tours within reach of the average Canadian. One famous package deal offers jet travel to London, several nights of hotel accommodation (with breakfast) and a fistful of theater tickets for hit shows, all for about the regular price of the plane seats alone.

The all-inclusive cruise

The "all-in" cruise soared into popularity as shipping companies fought back against the jumbo jets. The oceangoing package tour provides, in effect, a floating luxury hotel that migrates from northern ports to sunny and smooth tropical waters. The total cost is known in advance (to the cent, if you drink only coffee or soda pop), and this can include nominated onshore sight-seeing.

Some ships are first class only, making round-the-world cruises at fabulous prices. One line offered a 1984 world cruise from Los Angeles to Southampton, with stops at exotic ports of call on the way, in 69 days. The luxury liners are rare today, and becoming rarer. Even Britain's *Queen Elizabeth II* has been redesigned to carry less-demanding middle-income Canadian and American patrons on economical cruises to the Caribbean and Europe.

Italian, Greek and Scandinavian shipyards are humming with construction of sleek ships of moderate size designed spe-cifically for package cruising. They cheerfully sacrifice the quiet leather lounges of yesteryear for chrome and vinyls, and *haute cuisine* seems to be giving way to the glorified hamburger.

The operators of both jet package tours and all-in cruises are regulated by the civil and commercial law of the countries in which they are incorporated or registered. But the Canadian planning a cruise on a Greek ship in the Aegean Sea does not have to bone up on Greek law. The Canadian agent of the shipping company will generally be held responsible under Canadian law for safe and reasonable performance of the contract created by your purchase of the ticket.

More than that, the air and ocean carriers of all countries going after international business must conform to the equipment and safety standards set out by the multinational regulatory organizations, like I.C.A.O. (the International Civil Aviation Organization, with headquarters in Montreal). Article 44 of the I.C.A.O. convention, for example, particularly emphasizes safety in international air navigation and dedicates the organization to "meet the needs of the peoples of the world for safe, regular, efficient and economical air transport."

Charter flights

The I.T.C. (inclusive tour charter) is travel's big business today. The Danes and the British are granted the pioneer's palm. They were the first in the field to send sunstarved holidaymakers to Spain and other countries around the Mediterranean. Canada now has many charter companies. Wardair of Edmonton is our biggest charter airline.

It's quite impossible in a book like this to quote fixed charter air fares—there are dozens of combinations, so shop around. As a sample, in the fall of 1983, Air Canada was offering return flights to Britain for as low as $498 (plus tax of $12.50). To get in on that bargain, you had to book at least 21 days in advance and put down a $100 non-refundable deposit; you had to pay the rest of the ticket price 21 days before departure. If you had to cancel, you would be hit with a $100 cancellation charge—a forfeiture of your deposit. You can, however, insure against those charges for a modest premium, provided you have a valid reason for canceling. At that fare, you had to stay abroad for between seven days and six months.

For several years, the charter scene was chaotic as only club or "affinity" groups could be carried at the special low rates. Prospective passengers were supposed to be genuine members of social clubs or associations for at least six months. But the rule could not be adequately policed and legislation did not exist to effectively screen out inexperienced or unscrupulous operators. Some went bankrupt, failing to pay equipment owners for contracted flights, leaving travelers stranded in foreign countries, or still at home base without the trips they had paid for. The Canadian Transport Commission (C.T.C.) stepped into the picture and ruled that Canadians did not have to belong to so-called affinity groups to fly to Europe on round-trip charters. Soon, the *advance booking charter* system (generally described above) was in operation. But the

situation is still fluid. Ten people could be flying the Atlantic in the same plane with each of them paying a different ticket price!

Special youth fares

Canada's major airlines, as well as most others in the northern hemisphere, offer reduced fares to those aged from 12 to 21 years. Other special plans are sometimes offered to families traveling together. Canada's CP Air flies infants under two years free on domestic flights, and charges children between two and 11 years two-thirds of the adult economy fare. In a family group, CP Air will also give a 17-percent discount on one of the two normal adult fares. On international flights, CP Air carries infants for 10 percent of adult fare. It is advisable, however, to check rates locally before you draw up any final plans.

A typical airline offer within North America is a reduction of 50 percent for youths who travel on a standby basis. If you are younger than 22, you can choose a flight, head for the airport, check in, and

Sending souvenirs home

THE AMOUNT OF LUGGAGE carried free for participants in a package tour or cruise is usually restricted (32 kilograms per item for nearly all air travel). While these limits are generous enough to cover all normal clothing and toiletry needs, they don't permit the addition of bulky or weighty purchases made abroad. What to do about the gifts you want to send home to family and friends from foreign climes?

One answer is to take advantage of the privilege of sending packages home by mail—duty free—as your tour progresses. In almost every port or city abroad you will find reputable stores willing to relieve you of all chores, usually for only the cost of the postage and the insurance.

The law permits the free entry of gifts of a value not exceeding $25 Canadian. You can send as many as you like, but not more

than one package a day to any one recipient. Each package must be clearly marked, *Unsolicited gift, valued under $25.*

If the gift was found to be of a value greater than $25, it would be subject to duty and taxes on the excess value.

Unsolicited gifts cannot consist of tobacco in any form, alcohol or advertising matter. Nor, of course, can they include any items generally prohibited from entry to Canada, such as plants, vegetables, fruits and meats.

If you want to send Uncle Albert an Egyptian camel saddle for his den, that's okay; but don't send an African violet to Aunt Edith. Applications for permission to import plants, or similar organic items that might carry diseases or pests, must be sought from the Department of Agriculture, Ottawa.

have your name put on the standby list. When all full-fare passengers have been boarded, any spare seats are allocated to the standbys on a first-come first-served basis. Reservation clerks will usually advise by telephone about which flights are most likely to have space available. There are generally no standby offers at peak travel times; late-night flights offer the best chances.

To qualify for this scheme, a birth certificate, passport or other official document must be produced as evidence of age. Students can obtain an International Student Identity Card or International Scholar Card through student unions and from the Canadian Federation of Student Services. (The regional offices of the Federation's travel arm, the Canadian Universities Travel Services Ltd., are listed in telephone directories under "Travel CUTS.") In addition to these cards, some countries require other proof of a student's status, such as a letter from the school, college or student union. Non-students and working youths up to the age of 26 can obtain a Federation of International Youth Travel Organization (F.I.Y.T.O.) Card, from the Canadian Hostelling Association. All these cards can provide savings on transportation, accommodations and other costs.

Canadian students 23 or younger can fly across the Atlantic on a "registration space-available basis" at close to half the regular summer fares. In actual practice, there is no difference between these and normal bookings, except that the seat can not be confirmed until 7 days before departure; on the return flight, the same condition applies.

The return flights are often "open-ended" within a one-year period. This means that the student may book a seat on any return flight the airline makes within one year—provided, of course, that space is available at the time the booking is confirmed. This booking can be made from any city in which the airline has an office.

University student unions sometimes make their own special arrangements for cut-price round-trip international flights, either through travel agencies or directly with airline companies. Many sight-seeing coach lines will also offer a lower rate to young people who have the required identification.

Hoteliers make a point of warning that they reserve the right to refuse rooms to those "whose appearance or behavior is contrary to the standards established by management." It might be noted, too, that in England you can be prevented from boarding a bus, or be thrown off it, if you are "likely to offend" other passengers, or if your clothes look (to the conductor or driver) as though they might make the seats dirty.

Fares for pensioners

Canada's senior citizens (65 and older) qualify for reduced air fares for domestic flights on both of the national networks, Air Canada and CP Air and on other airlines. Reduced-fare plans also exist in some cities on the subway and bus systems.

Baggage allowances

Airlines will provide free transportation of enough baggage to hold the personal belongings you will require for just about any conceivable trip.

On North American flights, you will be limited to two items of checked luggage of which the largest must not exceed 158 centimetres in total length, width and height. Hand luggage carried to your seat will be limited to one bag you can put under your seat without causing inconvenience or possible injury to fellow passengers.

On overseas flights, your free baggage allowance will be limited to two checked items, weighing no more than 32 kilograms each, with the largest not more than 153 centimetres long. Those traveling at reduced fares are also allowed two checked items of luggage. Baggage in excess of these limits will be carried at the company's discretion at charges in proportion to the distance involved. If the aircraft is loaded to capacity, the company might offer to put the extra baggage on the next available flight, charging you according to its weight.

For both domestic and international flights, certain restrictions are placed on the type of baggage accepted. Liquids, for example, are not permitted; if a bottle of wine breaks in your checked luggage, the airline will not be responsible for any damage it causes. Also excluded from checked luggage are matches, cigarette lighters and other flammable items.

Despite the antihijacking procedures in force, airlines will still carry firearms, ammunition and explosives under certain conditions which you can check at any airline office. Of course, nothing even remotely resembling a weapon can be carried on your person or in your hand luggage without special permission. You could be in a real jam if a search before boarding a plane turned up anything suspicious. And, please, no wisecracks about hijacking—even an attempt at a mild joke could swiftly land you in trouble.

Airlines will not compensate for loss or damage to currency, jewelry, silverware, negotiable papers, securities or business documents carried in a passenger's checked baggage, with or without the airline's knowledge. Most of these restrictions also apply to personal baggage on trains and buses as well.

Ground transportation
Canadian airlines are not responsible for the transportation of any passenger or his baggage to or from any airport. This service is provided by independent companies or taxi operators who are usually bound by the terms of municipal or provincial licenses.

In Europe, the situation is different. Many airlines provide their own bus service to and from central pickup points. To avoid congestion at the airport check-in counters, passenger baggage is accepted at central depots in several major cities (London and Paris, for example). If this service is used, the airlines are responsible for the safety of the passengers and their luggage from that point on.

Transportation of animals
If you plan to take your pet on any vehicle provided by public transportation, be warned that the company has the right of refusal. It is too risky just to show up at a departure point with an animal in

your arms or on a leash, protesting that your Doberman Fritz is as gentle as a lamb. Check ahead of travel time.

If animals are accepted, the carriage conditions usually require that they be held in a secure carrying case (for cats or small dogs) or in a solid crate (for larger animals).

Many people have found it convenient to leave pets at boarding kennels. Licensed by municipal authorities, kennels provide specialized facilities. The law regards the kennel operator as having an express or implied contract to take reasonable care of any animal entrusted to his keeping.

Taking a taxicab
Cabbies are often colorful characters and they sometimes serve as knowledgeable guides. They are usually excellent drivers—their income depends upon this. Their liability (and that of the companies they work for) is restricted to injury or damage arising from their negligence. When a passenger traveling in a taxicab is injured in an accident, he cannot collect damages from the hire company if the other party involved in the accident was to blame.

The cab owner will be liable for injuries suffered by a passenger only if it can be proved that the accident was caused by the defective condition of the vehicle or by negligence on the part of the taxicab driver.

The cabbie who transports a passenger and his luggage is, in legal terms, a *bailee for reward*.

As a bailee, his duty to the passenger to safeguard luggage extends only to using that standard of care which the average careful person would exercise in looking after his own property.

Municipalities have power to enact by-laws for the licensing and operation of taxis for hire, and for setting the fares to be charged for passengers and their baggage. Other regulations can require the companies to carry liability insurance against personal injury or property damage.

Usually, the local police commission handles all taxi licensing.

645

Trouble while traveling

THE WORST SELDOM HAPPENS, but even a moderate mishap can seem a major one when you are surrounded by strangers—however solicitous they may be. When you encounter trouble overseas, language difficulties compound your worries.

Phrase books aren't much help if, for instance, someone has stolen your rented car and all your baggage from the side street of a small Spanish town. Nor do they solve everything if you need a doctor in Italy. Even in the United States you can innocently run afoul of the law—and remember that everywhere you go, ignorance of the law is no excuse.

Intelligent planning can increase your chances of trouble-free travel and give you instant friends-in-court if your luck turns sour. To avoid organizational problems—such as double-booking (of plane seats) and underbooking (of hotel rooms) —use a travel agent who is a member of the Alliance of Canadian Travel Associations (A.C.T.A.) or of the American Society of Travel Agents and is listed as an official agent by the International Air Transport Association and by shipping and railroad companies.

Some of the smooth-talking agents might offer you a package tour at a tempting discount. However, when you reach the resort, you could find your hotel to be a verminous hovel or only half-built. Worse still, your return tickets may not be honored by the airline because the tour operator has skipped out without paying the carrier. Every season, complaints along these lines appear in the letters-to-the-editor columns of newspapers, and are lodged with consumer-protection agencies at provincial and federal level.

The well-established and reputable travel agent will ensure that you get just what you have paid for—allowing for a bit of exaggeration in the lyrical brochures. Any resort or hotel that would risk the displeasure of the highly organized travel-agent business would be foolish indeed. Thus, if something serious occurred and you became embroiled innocently with the law, you could expect your agency to go to bat for you on the local scene. If you are traveling in a tour group, your guide will be there to assist you; he can instantly enlist local legal help should that be necessary.

If you are in deep trouble and you are traveling independently, do what you would do at home—call the police. There is no reason to assume that they will be anything but helpful and the chances are they are more accustomed to wandering Anglophones than you may expect.

Embassies and consulates

If you're in difficulties in a foreign country, head for the nearest Canadian diplomatic office. Canada has diplomatic or consular offices in more than 90 countries. If there is no Canadian representative within reasonable distance, you can contact any official British representative or, perhaps, the United States consul.

As the wheels often turn slowly for visitors abroad, give your Canadian embassy, legation or consulate as much time as possible to straighten out your problem. No matter what notions you might have about "one phone call to the right person," these government officials are seldom able to provide instant solutions.

The Canadian diplomatic and consular offices are prepared to help out in cases of illness, accident, death, arrest or other emergency. In extreme cases, they can arrange for your transportation home. However, you would be legally obligated to repay the government for plane tickets or any other expenses incurred on your behalf. Government representatives cannot pay fines, bail fees, hospital or burial expenses, but they can assist you in the transfer of funds from Canada to cover such costs.

Before receiving financial aid from any Canadian office abroad, you will have to show that you are unable to get help from anyone else. Any requests for aid are carefully examined. A cable will be sent to the Department of External Affairs in Ottawa and that department must approve any financial assistance.

If you have been arrested abroad, the Canadian diplomatic office will send someone to give you advice and to explore ways of straightening out your problem.

A copy of *Canadian Representatives Abroad* could be a useful addition to your luggage. It can be ordered from the Canadian Government Publishing Centre, Supply and Services Canada, Ottawa, Ontario, K1A 0S9. Your local library may also keep a copy. The Department of External Affairs also distributes a free

Where to seek assistance

THE Department of External Affairs warns Canadians traveling abroad that the possession or smuggling of illegal drugs and narcotics brings severe penalties (including the death sentence) in some foreign countries. More than 100 Canadians were languishing in foreign jails on drug-related offenses in late 1982.

On the whole, the Canadians who travel abroad appear to be a law-abiding lot, but traffic violations and assault charges (often associated with drunkenness) wreck more than a few vacations. If you should run afoul of the law—even if you admit your guilt—you should immediately get in touch with the nearest Canadian diplomatic mission. There are High Commissioners in most Commonwealth countries, and embassies or consulates just about everywhere else (including eight resident embassies in Communist countries).

In Great Britain, the High Commissioner's Office is in the Sir John A. Macdonald Building at 38 Grosvenor Street, London. A consulate is maintained in Ashley House, 195 George Street W., Glasgow, Scotland.

Following are addresses of our embassies in the countries which are most visited by Canadian tourists:
Austria: Dr. Karl Lueger-Ring 10, Vienna A-1010.

Belgium: rue de Loxum 6, Brussels 1000.
Brazil: Avenida das Naçoes, Number 16, Setor das Embaixadas Sul, Brasilia, D.F.
Denmark: Kr. Bernikowsgade 1, 1105, Copenhagen K.
Finland: Pohjois Esplanadi 25B, Helsinki.
France: 35 avenue Montaigne, Paris 75008.
Germany: Michaelsplatz, 5300 Bonn 2.
Greece: 4 Ioannou Ghennadiou St., Athens 140.
Ireland: 65 St. Stephens Green, Dublin 2.
Israel: 220 Hayarkon, Tel Aviv.
Italy: Via Zara, 30, Rome.
Japan: 3-38 Akasaka 7-chome, Minato-ku, Tokyo 107.
Mexico: Calle Schiller 529, colonia Polanco, 11580 Mexico, D.F.
Netherlands: 7 Sophialaan, The Hague.
Norway: Oscar's Gate 20, Oslo 3.
Portugal: Rua Rosa Araujo 2, 6th Floor, Lisbon 2.
Spain: Edificio Goya, Calle Nunez de Balboa 35, Madrid.
Sweden: Tegelbacken 4, 7th Floor, S-10323, Stockholm 16.
Switzerland: 88 Kirchenfeldstrasse, 3005 Berne.
United States: 1746 Massachusetts Avenue N.W., Washington, D.C. 20036.
Yugoslavia: Proleterskih Brigada 69, 11000 Belgrade.

booklet of information for Canadians traveling abroad, called *Bon Voyage*. It is available at passport offices, major airports and travel agencies.

Travelers' Aid
Although most social-service agencies will attempt to advise or assist you, the Travelers' Aid Society exists specifically to help travelers in trouble. Not only does it provide special services and information, it also promotes measures to improve conditions for the traveling public. Inquiry booths may be found at major railroad stations, bus terminals and airports in most North American cities. Although "Travelers' Aid" is a general name to remember, the labels can vary. For instance, in some cities this help is provided under the auspices of the Y.M.C.A. or Y.W.C.A. In Toronto, for example, Travelers' Aid can be reached from locations or special telephones at Union Station, at the downtown bus depot, and at Toronto International Airport.

Travelers' Aid will help with such problems as illness, loss of money or travel tickets, or finding a suitable hotel. It may provide financial assistance, usually on a loan basis, for overnight lodging.

Voluntary workers will meet certain travelers—such as elderly, ill and handicapped individuals traveling alone—and take them to connecting services.

There is a network of Travelers' Aid societies and similar organizations in Canada and the United States, which are affiliated with similar organizations in some countries abroad. The "aid" is generally free, although for some services the societies charge fees. Usually, people who can afford to do so offer contributions.

Safeguarding your money
Experienced travelers simply never carry "a wad" of cash with them. Pickpockets have it too easy at crowded rail stations and airports when the tourist pats his hip pocket to assure himself that his wallet is still there. And the hotel thief knows every likely spot in a room where you might hide money.

The traveler is a prime target because he usually doesn't have the time to stay in the town to pursue any prosecution the local police might launch.

If you are heading abroad, it is a good idea to carry a small amount of foreign currency for immediate expenses on arrival. Some countries limit the importation of currency; a bank or travel agency can advise you on this point.

Travelers' cheques are the safest way to carry money when you're on the move. The cheques issued by the major agencies (American Express, Thos. Cook, etc.) and the chartered banks are accepted practically everywhere abroad and your money is always refunded on any unsigned cheques that are lost or stolen.

Credit cards issued by major North American companies are honored by hotels, airlines, car-rental agencies, as well as by many restaurants and shops, in most of the major cities and resorts of the world (outside the Communist bloc). In fact, a traveler can actually make a trip around the world armed only with his folder of credit cards and some change.

Menace of the hijacker
The hijacking of passenger planes has brought back the day of the highwayman with the added terror of political anarchy. The 1976 Air France hijacking to Entebbe, Uganda, followed by the Israeli rescue, caused headlines around the world.

Canada has no specific law governing the illegal seizure of an aircraft. Action can be taken, of course, under the provisions of the Criminal Code against kidnapping, committing a mischief, assault and other crimes against the public.

Attempts have been made to define international law on hijacking: examples are the Tokyo Convention on Offenses and Certain Other Acts Committed on Board Aircraft (1963), and The Hague Diplomatic Conference on Unlawful Seizure of Aircraft (1970).

Under these treaties, when a hijacking occurs, the countries concerned must make every reasonable effort to help the pilot regain command of his aircraft, assist the crew and passengers to continue their journey as quickly as possible, and to return the plane and its cargo to its owners without delay. Political terrorists have shown that there are no real teeth in these treaties—in fact, some countries appear to condone these seizures.

Travel risks insurance

While your familiar life insurance policy takes care of long-term protection for you and your family (*See* Chapter 8, "Insurance at home"), travel insurance is designed for the short term. You should consider getting under the cover of its more detailed protection before you leave on any extended journey.

If you're traveling by car in Canada or the United States, your routine automobile policy will probably answer all your needs. These policies usually protect you as long as your car is being operated, stored or parked anywhere in either country, or on any ship operating within the territorial waters of North America. If you're planning to ship your vehicle and drive it in any other part of the world, you should read the terms of the policy carefully to see whether you would still be covered.

Travel insurance is available from most insurance or travel agents; you can even pick up applications from booths at most major airports. The formalities take only a few minutes, and there are no medical examinations or other qualifying tests.

One large company, for example, offers three degrees of protection. *Plan A* insures you for travel by scheduled airlines and covers you for injuries or death suffered while getting on or off, or riding as a passenger in a plane. It also covers you while you are on the airport premises and while you are a passenger on airport buses or other transportation provided by the airlines.

Plan B covers you against accidents at all times during your travels, including travel on any common carrier—plane, train, bus or ship. Besides providing all of the coverage in Plan A, it protects you as a passenger in any private or public vehicle (including taxis) operated on land, water or in the air. You are covered while getting in or out of a passenger car, while driving it or riding in it as a passenger, and if you are hit by a motor vehicle on a public street or highway.

Plan C is a total vacation "package," combining the coverage of Plans A and B with hospital medical insurance and insurance for baggage and personal effects.

In case you are the adventurous type, you should note that parachute jumps are excluded from these plans, except when made for emergency reasons from a plane covered by the policy. Mountaineering, bodily contact sports and professional sports are also excluded from coverage under these plans. Other plans are specifically designed to cover you for accidents and heavy medical expenses in a foreign country, stolen money, baggage or personal effects lost or damaged,

Closing in on the skyjacker

TRYING TO DEFUSE the threat of a skyjacker, special security agents are in training at the Royal Canadian Mounted Police center at Regina. These officers are stationed at our airports with full powers to search passengers, baggage and cargo and to forbid persons who resist a search to board any aircraft.

Authority to establish these "airport police" was included in an amendment to the Aeronautics Act, passed by parliament in 1973. It provides that any person who refuses to obey the orders of the security officers can be fined up to $5,000, or sentenced to a year in jail, or both. Notices must be posted prominently at all airports warning that searches may be made. The agents can force open any locked baggage or cargo. They can also order a person already on board a plane to disembark.

The government also assumed the power to require the owners or operators of any aircraft to establish and maintain security measures.

skiing mishaps or the unavoidable cancellation of a trip after you had made nonrefundable payments.

Full coverage under these types of travel plans pays up to $350,000 in benefits for accidental loss of life, limb or eyesight. Double the amount ("double indemnity") will be paid in the case of an accident while you are a passenger on a scheduled bus, train, ship or aircraft. The plans also pay medical and hospital expenses over and above those covered by any government health plan. The insurance company will not insure against suicide, attempted suicide, war injuries and injuries from abuse of medication, drugs or alcohol.

If there's no insurance

Even if no insurance is carried, a death while traveling does not necessarily leave the traveler's family without support. In Ontario, for example, the Family Law Reform Act permits dependents to sue and recover damages whenever negligence (a lack of reasonable care) or default (if the terms of the contract are not fulfilled) play a part in the fatality. Under the act, the person or company responsible must answer to the family, which, in effect, represents the breadwinner's claim. The family of the victim can take court action to recover damages, provided the suit is started within 12 months after the victim's death.

Damages are usually awarded according to the circumstances in which the family has been left as a result of the fatal accident. How the money is distributed among the family is decided by the court. In estimating damages, the court would ignore any life- or accident-insurance payments to the victim's family. Funeral expenses can be awarded, and additional sums should the body have to be shipped to a distant point.

It is important to note that unless the victim would have been able to recover damages, if he had lived, the survivors also have no hope of doing so. Also, these provisions apply only to dependants and the immediate family.

Another fact to note in your travel diary is that your provincial medicare plan will continue to protect you if you have an accident or take sick while traveling. Assuming that your contributions are up to date, the plan will usually provide the normal scale of benefits at any acceptable hospital around the world. (*See* Chapter 14, "Health insurance.") You can also get a refund—on production of receipts—for medical services (including ambulance charges) you paid for in cash that would have been covered if you had been at home. But remember, you will get only the scale effective in your own province, which is often a great deal less than, say, the princely fee demanded by a specialist on Harley Street in London, England.

Canadian travelers are strongly advised to acquire accident and hospitalization insurance—as well as dental insurance—before leaving home.

Life on the ocean wave

THE TRAVELER going to sea for the first time may be nervous—even if his cruise brochure spells out all the details. Men have gone to sea for thousands of years and have created a whole fabric of salty legend and tradition—even a special language of the sea. (Which side is *port?*) Nobody wants to be tongue-tied when the bar crowd talks of speed in knots.

If you're booked on a one-class "love boat", the lore of the sea may not intrude too much upon your holiday. Some modern sailors never appear on open deck. Dress etiquette is relaxed and bikinis are seen in lounges. If your liner is divided into classes, the "uppers" will change for dinner, though the black tie and tuxedo are losing ground. Dress is informal the first or last night aboard. Ties and jackets are generally worn at all indoor social activities.

Hotels and motels

The Innkeepers Act

Rights and obligations

Checking in

American and European plans

Is your automobile safe?

If you don't pay the bill

THE CONCEPT of the inn is buried in the sands of time . . . and quite literally buried in the sands of Mesopotamia and the Middle East. It was thousands of years old when Joseph and Mary were turned away in Bethlehem and joined the animals in the stable. The modern word, *hôtel*, was adopted from Bourbon France and came to be used in English about the middle of the eighteenth century. The *motel* seems to have been born with the Chrysler Airflow and the superhighway in the late 1930s.

With this lineage, and considering the basic role it has played as temporary bed and board for just about everybody at some time or another, it is perhaps not surprising that the hotel and its guests are governed by law as complicated as anything in the legal record.

While it may seem a routine matter to check in at some downtown hotel and follow the bellboy to your room, you are really moving through a legal maze. Here are some of the legal questions that could arise: What is a hotel? When is a guest not a guest? Can you stay as long as you like? If you fall over a mop in the hall, who is to blame? Can your friend of the opposite sex visit you in your room? Can the proprietor enter your room uninvited? Is the hotel responsible for thefts from your luggage?

These and other issues are discussed below.

The Innkeepers Act

The responsibility of the hotelier for your person and your goods has been developed through centuries of case law. As each judicial decision—first in England and later in Canada—provided an answer

to a new problem, the legal file grew thicker. Many European hotels have still not quite bridged the gap between the horse and the automobile in their innkeeping rules and regulations.

The "law of innkeepers," as the law of hotelkeeping is commonly called, is a subdivision of the law of *bailment;* the position of the hotelier is thus similar in many ways to that of the *common carrier*.

Bailment involves one person's goods being put into the possession of another person. The person who takes possession, the *bailee*, only exercises physical control over the goods until the owner wants them back; he never owns the goods. If the bailee refuses to return the goods when the owner asks for them back, he could be sued for *conversion*. Not falling within the general offense of theft in the Criminal Code (because the goods came lawfully into the possessor's hands), conversion involves using someone else's property as though it were your own, and withholding it from the owner.

In a hotel, the goods (your baggage) are handled at the *bailor's* risk (you, as guest, are the bailor) and both the risk and title of the goods remain with you. The *bailee* (the hotelier) must, however, take reasonable care while the goods are in his possession. If he cannot return your baggage, or returns it damaged due to dishonesty of some member of his staff or his own negligence, he will generally be held fully liable.

Government legislation over the years has given the innkeeper in Canada a considerable measure of protection against being held totally liable for his guests' property. All provinces have passed some kind of innkeepers act (the titles vary

651

somewhat) that restricts, and in some cases removes, the liability of the hotel in the event of a guest's property being lost or damaged. The most a hotel can be held responsible for ranges from $40 in Ontario to $200 in Newfoundland. For this to stand, however, the section of the innkeepers act that sets out the limited liability must be posted in bedrooms and all public rooms. However, there is no escape from full liability when the hotel is proved to have been negligent.

Arising from specific legislation and from relevant court decisions, the legal definition of an "inn" can be seen to include a hotel, motel, tavern, public house or other place of lodging and refreshment. The test is whether the proprietor is offering to cater to the traveling public generally. It doesn't matter if he puts out a sign or not. Thus, a tourist lodge would fall within the category, but a boarding-house would not.

The legal guest was defined in a court action in 1907:

"A guest is one who resorts to and is received at an inn for the purpose of obtaining the accommodation which it purports to afford. He comes for a more or less temporary stay without any bargain for time, remains without one, and may go when he pleases, paying only for the actual entertainment received. If the relationship of innkeeper and guest is once established, the presumption is that it continues until a change of that relationship is shown. The relationship of innkeeper and guest commences when the person presents himself as a guest and is accepted."

To be considered a guest requires what the law calls "a positive act"—such as checking in, or eating a meal in the hotel dining room. That means that the person who goes into a hotel to use the washroom or the telephone, or who merely sits in the lobby reading a newspaper while he waits for someone, is not a guest.

Only registered guests are permitted to stay overnight; the hotelier would be within his rights to call the police to eject any unregistered guest whom he felt to be undesirable. On the other hand, any person who offered to pay the going rate could not be unreasonably refused accommodation if there was a bed available.

Innkeepers' rights and obligations

The hotelier is obliged to provide livable accommodation and lodging at advertised rates (which must be posted in every room). Once the innkeeper has accepted someone as a guest, he may not deprive that person of normal privileges or evict him without being able to prove he had cause to do so. Under human rights codes, there must not be any discrimination against a guest on the basis of color, race or religion.

According to the law, the innkeeper is not permitted to select his guests. But he does have the right to refuse those not sober or orderly, those unable to pay his charges or those whose filthy condition would offend other guests.

He may legally eject any guest who is objectionable by commonly accepted standards, obnoxious because of intoxication or who is soliciting business from other guests. The grounds for refusal could be that these people would injure the business or would place the innkeeper or his guests in a hazardous or uncomfortable situation.

This means also that a guest who becomes seriously ill, or contracts a contagious disease, can be asked to leave.

The hotel is not obligated to provide a particular room the guest might want. All the law requires is that it provide reasonable and proper accommodation. The hotel or motel has the right to rent any room it chooses to a guest, and the guest can be asked to move to another room after registration.

Hoteliers have a duty to protect their guests. They can be held responsible for personal injuries suffered by guests (and even visiting friends) if it can be proved the injuries resulted from any failure to exercise due care on the part of the establishment.

Many modern hotels and motels have swimming pools for their guests' pleasure, which may give the manager the added responsibility of having a qualified lifeguard on duty whenever the pool is open. The water must be tested regularly, for bacteria or for the presence of too much chlorine.

Damaged fixtures—such as diving boards or ladders—must be fixed immediately or warning signs posted until repairs can be made.

It is the innkeeper's responsibility to regularly check his furniture and furnishings for wear and tear. Injuries suffered by a guest, from a bed collapsing or a broken chair or bar stool, could lead to a successful legal action for damages.

A guest who can prove he was treated improperly, harassed or annoyed without reason, can sue a hotel for failure to live up to its obligations.

Guests' rights and obligations

As a guest you are obliged to keep the rented quarters in the same livable condition as you found them. This doesn't mean you have to make the bed or clean the bathroom, but you would be responsible for any unusual damage you might cause within your room or in any other part of the premises—dining room, bar, coffee shop or pool.

You will also be required to conform to any house rules regarding excessive noise, particularly late at night. The innkeeper would be within his rights to call the police to deal with a noisy room party after midnight.

If the owner suspects that one of his rooms is being used for gambling, or for any other illegal activity (including prostitution), he has every right to investigate the situation and, if he thinks it necessary, inform the police about it.

Unless a departure date has been agreed upon by both parties in advance, the guest is within his rights to stay as long as he likes, provided that he is able to pay his bills and that he is not mistreating the space he is renting or behaving unreasonably anywhere on the premises. Repeated drunken scenes in the bar would release the innkeeper from any obligation to a guest.

In the case of a lengthy stay, you should consider, after a week or ten days, settling your account up to that time and giving the establishment at least a general idea of how long you may wish to remain. There are two reasons for this. First, by paying a good part of your bill, you would reassure the management that you were not likely to skip without paying. Second, larger hotels book many business conventions in advance and keeping a room indefinitely often causes a problem.

While you are not obliged by law to do any of these things, it is the courteous

---

Check before you check in

IF A SOJOURN in a strange hotel—in Canada, the United States or abroad—will be an important part of your next trip, you may avoid a spoiled vacation by checking out the hotel's amenities and services in advance. This is especially true if you are signing up for all the details about the package tour that locks you into a particular establishment.

Persist in asking the booking agent just what kind of room you'll get. If it's a resort hotel, rooms near the pool or bars are likely to be noisy—if you want peace at night, ask for space on the upper floors. Will you have your own bathroom, or must you walk down the hallway to share one?

There's no reason to doubt the basic statements in the hotel's brochure—most civilized countries have laws against false advertising—but you must expect "puffery" and learn to "read between the lines" of the official publicity. "Overlooking the bay" can turn out to be on a hill five miles from the shore. "On the water" or "at the edge of the sparkling sea" doesn't necessarily mean that there will be a beach for the kids. A "suite" can be two poky rooms or the equivalent of a small house (in some big-city hotels abroad, suites are served by their own butlers).

thing to do and would maintain the good-will of the management.

Persons who are not guests, and have not been invited by registered guests, remain on the premises as a privilege only. The hotelkeeper, in effect, puts up with the presence of these persons; however, he has the right to revoke the privilege at any time.

If a registered guest has invited you to visit him at his hotel you are considered as an *invitee* and are welcome within reasonable hours as long as you do not behave objectionably.

In general, if you are a casual caller and if the innkeeper asks you to leave the premises, you must go; if you refuse, you can be considered as a trespasser.

Checking in
Every innkeeper must keep a complete registry, or record book, of his guests. When you check in, he will hand you either a registration form or the guest register. You are required to write down your name and home address, and signature.

In some provinces, anyone found guilty of giving a false name or address on a hotel register can be fined (maximum

$200), or sent to jail for three months if he does not pay the fine.

If the hotel or motel owner knowingly admits anyone using a false name or address, he too is committing an offense that can carry a jail term.

If a hotel fails to post notices in each room stating the exact charge for that room, the owner is liable to a fine.

"American" or "European"
Room charges are calculated on the basis of room rental only, or room-plus-meals.

The great majority of hotels and motels in Canada and the United States are run on what is known here as the *European Plan*—that is, the room rental charge only.

The *American Plan*, seldom found these days, charges a set daily rate for the room plus all meals. In a lot of resort areas in North America and the Caribbean, the *Modified American Plan* is used: the daily rate includes room, breakfast and one other meal (either lunch or dinner).

The *Continental Plan* is followed throughout most of Europe. This provides room and a breakfast of rolls and coffee. The *British Continental Plan* is more commonly known as "Bed and Breakfast."

Packing within legal limits

INTERNATIONAL airline regulations permit the free carriage in the cargo compartment of two checked bags not exceeding a total weight of 64 kilograms. Excess baggage is charged by the piece, according to distance. You are allowed to carry on to the plane without charge a topcoat, umbrella, reading materials, camera or binoculars, infant's feeding package, and a small bag that can be stowed under the seat.

Tourists going abroad for lengthy holidays often worry that they cannot pack enough clothing, footwear, toilet gear and so on within those legal limits. Airline public relations people and independent travel writers agree that, with the develop-

ment of light washable clothing, it's a cinch.

The day of personalized all-leather luggage is past. Buy the mundane, lightweight plastic cases you see everywhere (maybe adding a distinctive stripe of colored tape to help you recognize your bags in the pile-ups at the airport) and try a trial pack some days before your scheduled takeoff. A man's two-piece suit weighs about 1.5 kilograms (wool) and 1 kilogram (synthetic), a pair of heavyweight slacks 500 grams, a pair of shoes 1.25 kilograms, pajamas 300 grams, handkerchiefs are about 28 grams each. A woman's suit weighs about 1 kilogram, a dress 500 grams, a pair of lightweight shoes 500 grams, and panty-hose about 30 grams.

The variation stems from the fact that the hearty British breakfast may include juice or fruit, porridge, eggs and bacon or sausages, toast and tea or coffee.

Because residential hotels must keep a kitchen in regular operation, the American Plan, where offered, is usually the best bargain in town. However, it's not much use to the tourist who ranges out on all-day excursion trips.

Safekeeping of valuables

Because of his heavy liability for loss of a guest's goods, the innkeeper is entitled to insist that anything of great value be deposited, in a sealed container, in the hotel or motel safe. Otherwise, he will not accept responsibility for its safekeeping.

The innkeeper is expected to be able to provide this service. If the hotel is unable, or refuses, to provide safe storage when you ask for it, it is automatically liable for any theft that might occur.

Traveling salesmen often use a hotel room or suite to display their merchandise. The innkeeper cannot be held responsible for any loss or damage that occurs to the salesman's goods while the space is being used as a showroom. The guest automatically takes that responsibility.

Is your automobile safe?

Some sections of the "law of the innkeeper" still echo the leisurely days of Mr. Pickwick and Sam Weller. The "ostler" who took care of their horses and carriages has been replaced by the car jockey in the parking lot. But the law still insists that the operators of hotels and motels guarantee the safety of your vehicle when you place it in their care. Their liability can only be limited, not evaded, by the posting of notices. (*See* Chapter 5, "Using a car on holiday.")

As long as the proprietor offers to receive his guest's car on his premises, his establishment will be responsible for any damage it suffers, other than that caused by another car driven by someone not in his employ. The parking lot does not even have to be part of the hotel's own grounds.

The regulations concerning goods left in your parked car on a hotel lot are different than those concerning luggage or goods left in your room. As owner or driver of the car, you normally would hold the car keys and would be expected to lock your vehicle. The hotel or motel could not then be held responsible for theft or damage of anything not considered part of the car's equipment. This means that luggage, commercial goods or anything else of a business or personal nature—even a canoe carried atop your car—would be excluded. Such items of car equipment as slipcovers, floor mats, a car radio or tape deck and seat belts would be covered.

To stay in the clear, the innkeeper must be able to prove that neither he nor any of his staff were guilty of negligence when a guest's car was robbed.

These innkeeping regulations do not apply to the same extent to casual guests who are present only to attend a wedding reception, dance or business convention meeting. In such cases, the innkeeper puts on the hat of a caterer or dance-hall operator, assuming only the lesser obligations attached to such business.

If you don't pay the bill

Failure to pay your bill or other charges when they are due will normally result in the seizure of your luggage and your eviction from the hotel, and subsequent legal action by the innkeeper to get his money.

If you feel the charges are inaccurate or unfair you can, of course, dispute them with the manager. However, if he stands firm, you must pay the stated amount, leaving any other action to the courts.

You can also be locked out of your room in a hotel if you have not paid bills that are due. The hotelier's right to seize and hold your luggage can be viewed as a *lien*, a security which he holds until you pay. He is given this lien on your goods as a compensating factor for his having to safeguard them. However, he has no right to seize or hold you, or any clothes you are wearing.

The hotel is entitled to seize luggage or goods even though it turns out they were stolen and are not really the guest's belongings at all. As long as the hotelkeeper does not know they were stolen, he has the legal right to hold them. He must also place a value on the luggage or goods seized and not hold anything that would be greatly in excess of the amount of money owed.

In some provinces, the guest is given as much as three months' grace to settle the bill. If he doesn't settle, the innkeeper can sell any seized luggage or goods at public auction, giving one week's notice of the sale through an advertisement in a local newspaper. Proceeds from the sale are used to pay the amount due, plus the costs of advertising and of the sale itself. Anything leftover must go to the guest provided he has asked for it in writing.

The guest can contest seizure of his luggage or other goods in court if he feels the innkeeper didn't have legal grounds for taking action in the first place.

There is another possibility open to the delinquent guest: to pay the bill for the first week of his stay, leaving the hotel to collect the rest of the debt by other means—that is, through the courts. However, this move can be blocked by a court order sought by the innkeeper. The court would probably grant the order, demanding total and immediate payment, if the unpaid bill was massive.

The youth hostel

Seeing the world is a big part of twentieth-century living, and many young Canadians take advantage of the worldwide network of youth hostels along the way. In Canada, the legal responsibilities of the hostel operator are no different from those of any other innkeeper, except that the member-guests have generally agreed in advance to conditions that limit or cancel out the hotelier's liability.

The Canadian Hostelling Association (C.H.A.) is among more than 60 national hostel associations affiliated with the International Youth Hostel Federation (I.Y.H.F.). The C.H.A. is open to all: a junior membership costs $9 a year (up to age 17) and the senior, $15. Families with children under age 18 can buy a year's membership for $30. A three-year senior card costs $40, while a life membership is $90. Groups of 3 to 15 individuals (over

the age of 14) traveling with a leader can buy a single card for $25 a year.

Although the emphasis is naturally on youth, the hostel network is usually open to people of all ages and backgrounds, for groups, families or individuals. In Canada, a bed costs from $3 to $9 a night, depending on local circumstances. Most beds overseas cost $7 to $10 per person a night.

All youth hostels accepted by the I.Y.H.F. contain separate sleeping quarters for men and women and many have a common kitchen where travelers can cook their own meals. Blankets, pillows, cooking utensils and cleaning equipment are usually provided and guests are often expected to help out around the hostel during their stay.

In the larger hostels, there are usually "houseparents" who live there permanently, and who provide cooked meals as well as hot showers.

The hosteler in North America or Europe will be required to show a membership card bearing photograph and signature. Other regulations usually forbid smoking in the sleeping areas or bringing liquor into the hostel.

The hosteler must be at least 14 years old to travel alone.

Most hostels impose length-of-stay limits during peak travel periods. Some may also impose a maximum age limit. In Bavaria, for example, you have to be younger than 27. Generally speaking, those younger than 30 may be given first call on available space. Hikers and cyclists are given space before those with cars. You are usually only allowed to stay three days.

Any hosteler who shows a lack of consideration for other guests may have his membership card withdrawn.

Late-night arrivals at a hostel are often refused entry after the curfew hour.

When you sign your application to become a member of the Canadian Hostelling Association, you are also agreeing to a clause that frees the C.H.A. and any of its agents from responsibility in any claims resulting from delay, injury (including death), as well as loss or damage to your belongings.

Restaurant regulations

PERHAPS THE BEST WAY to keep a clear view of the law as it applies to the patron of a café or restaurant is to remember that you are on private property (just as in any shop), and that the proprietor is entitled to set the conditions under which he will serve you. Provisions of the provincial human rights codes prevent him, of course, from discriminating against anyone on the basis of race, religion, sex or color. On the other hand, he is not forced to give reasons for refusing to serve a customer or for asking one to leave his premises.

If he wants to restrict his business to selling food and drink only to those men who are wearing ties and jackets and to women wearing dresses or blouses and skirts, that's his affair. If he wants to cater only to men, then he may find that his province does not permit sex discrimination in certain public places.

Should you feel that you have been improperly treated, or turned away for no good reason, you can complain to the municipal authorities who have issued the business permit. If the premises are licensed to serve beer, wines or spirits, your complaint could be sent to the provincial licensing body; support accusations with statements from witnesses, if possible. Liquor licenses are usually renewed annually and you may appear before the licensing commission to argue against a permit being renewed for a certain restaurant. Since the loss of his liquor license would, in most cases, put the operator out of business, this threat is a strong deterrent to mistreatment of patrons.

If you are told the price of a food dish or beverage, or if the menu or *carte des vins* lists the price, you cannot be charged more than that amount, unless the alteration has been explained to you before you are served. Any cover charge (a charge made by a restaurant for allowing you to sit at one of its tables) must be clearly advertised. These rules apply to any restaurant open to the public in Canada and the United States, and generally hold good abroad as well.

Wherever food is prepared or handled, the federal Food and Drugs Act and the provincial public health acts stand guard to protect the consumer. (*See* Chapter 6, "Safeguards when shopping.") Every municipality must have a board of health, or at least a health unit, which appoints food inspectors. Although there is a basic set of regulations applying to all food outlets, there may be additional rules in some municipalities. If there is conflict between public health regulations and municipal bylaws, the provincial authority will apply.

Any establishment serving food must provide washroom and toilet facilities, at least one for men and one for women. In some municipalities, the number of rest rooms required might increase according to the size of the establishment.

The maximum number of persons permitted to occupy any café or restaurant at any one time is usually fixed by the local fire marshal. Fire exits must be clearly marked, and the exit route kept clear.

If you are offered a table by the kitchen door, or too close to the music, you do not have to take it. But unless you have a confirmed reservation for a specific table, you do not have the right to demand any table that happens to be unoccupied. The proprietor or his *maître d'hôtel* might simply prefer to keep a specific table empty: of course, for a "consideration," the *maître d'* might suddenly decide you may have it after all.

A la carte and soup to nuts

Depending on the class of business, the restaurant will offer you food by placing a notice on the wall that lists the bill of fare ("Sandwich and coffee"; "Fish & Chips") or by handing you a menu that contains a wider choice. In Europe, the menu is often framed behind glass and hung outside the restaurant. Most menus are split between *table d'hôte* (or *prix fixe*), and *à la carte*.

To head off possible disputes with cashiers, you should understand that *table d'hôte* means that the price listed against the main dish covers the whole meal, which is usually three or four courses; *à la carte* means that the price quoted covers only that one item. Since the *à la carte* items will probably have to be individually prepared, they will generally take longer and cost more. Even with this information, things can still be a bit chancy; sometimes an *à la carte* dish (a steak, for example) will come heavily supported by French fried potatoes and salad at no extra charge.

Just because a dish is listed on the menu doesn't mean that the restaurant has to provide it. The kitchen may be out of it by the time you place your order.

You will have an easier time in a quality restaurant if you make a mental note of the unwritten laws of rank among the staff. The *maître d'*, or captain, who seats you will probably be wearing a dark jacket and black bow tie. He may take your order, but more likely he will call a waiter to take it. The waiter will probably be wearing a hip-length white coat, but these days it may be some other color. The busboy, usually a young trainee who fills your water glass and removes used plates, will probably be wearing a short jacket similar to that worn by the bellhop in the lobby of your hotel. The important-looking man with a chain around his neck or waist who offers you a wine list will be the wine waiter or steward, more properly called the *sommelier*.

You may get faster service at the local lunch counter if you snap your fingers, but best not try it abroad. A discrete cough might work, but it's better to be patient until you catch the waiter's eye. Too many Canadians and Americans are in a hurry to eat, to the delight and profit of the manufacturers of stomach tablets.

The laws of hygiene

Wherever food is sold, the buying public is protected by what lawyers call "implied warranties." This means that, in accordance with public health regulations, the restaurant has taken all steps to make sure that the food is pure and that the surroundings in which it is served are sanitary. If the regulations are not met, the customer can claim damages for the breach of warranty. (*See* Chapter 6, "Guarantees and standards.")

The regulations controlling all types of food-service operations are enforced by your local board of health, or health unit. If you have a complaint which a restaurant operator refuses to satisfy, you should contact a public health officer at city hall.

The provincial health laws protect you at two levels. First, they demand certain standards of construction, operation and upkeep of any premises where food is manufactured, processed or handled. This applies to processing and manufacturing plants, warehouses, supermarkets, corner stores, restaurants and hotel dining rooms. Second, in the restaurant or café itself, the regulations call for strict inspection by public health officers. These inspectors look for food impurities, unsanitary equipment, cracked, chipped or dirty plates, cups and glasses, and dirty spoons, knives and forks. They also look for cockroaches and other vermin sometimes found where food is stored or served. Cleanliness of staff is checked: fingernails must be clean and long hair must be kept in such a way that it does not come into contact with food.

The restaurant must dispose of all garbage, either by burning it (if permitted) or placing it in tightly covered cans or pails which the restaurant must have removed at least twice a week.

The dissatisfied diner

If you have good reason to be dissatisfied with anything concerning the food or service, don't hesitate to express your complaint politely to the person in charge of the establishment. Contrary to popular opinion, a concerned restaurateur would sooner receive a genuine complaint than lose a long-time customer. He and his staff can make mistakes, like anybody else; he will probably try to correct the matter and thank you for bringing it to his attention.

In offering food to the public, the proprietor guarantees that it is what he says it is and that it is in every way suitable for consumption by the dining public. If you show him that your porterhouse steak is cooked through when you ordered it "rare," he will probably offer to get you another one to your liking. If you have ordered sole from the menu and you are served flounder, he could be guilty of false representation, or at least an error that calls for adjustment.

If the proprietor refused to satisfy you, and if you felt the issue was important enough, you could discuss with a lawyer the possibility of bringing a civil action in the courts for damages. On a question of unsanitary conditions or of food unfit to eat, the nearest public health office is open to you.

Standards of service are difficult to categorize. What is "impertinent" to one diner is merely "casual" to another. Some customers don't mind waitresses who chew gum, but others do. Cleanliness of staff is, however, enforceable by law; smoking while handling food—even taking the occasional puff and leaving a cigarette going in an ashtray at some distance while cooking or serving—is forbidden.

If you found the service intolerably slow or offensive or the food inedible, you could leave your meal uneaten and quit the premises, refusing to pay your bill. Explain your view to the proprietor or the cashier, and give him your name and address. This gives him the opportunity of bringing a suit against you for his money, if he so decides. If you don't give your name and address, he would be within his rights to hold you and summon the police. Unless the situation is drastic, you are better off to simply grumble quietly,

Detectives in the dining room

IF THE FRENCH seem at times to lay down the law rather arrogantly in matters of the kitchen and the table, humble tourists may take some comfort in the knowledge that the greatest chefs and maître d's in the world themselves tremble before the autocratic judgments of a small band of anonymous secret agents. Armed with nothing more dangerous than a knife and fork— and an acute and practiced glance—these detectives of the dining room can make a millionaire out of one struggling restaurateur while consigning another to frustration and failure.

These "James Bonds of the table" are the senior inspectors employed by the Services de Tourisme du Pneu Michelin to judge the standards of French restaurants and decide on the allocation of "stars" in the famed red-covered *Guide Michelin*. In true cloak-and-dagger style, they are known by numbers, not names; this applies to all members of the staff of the tire company's highly respected 1,000-page guidebook which not only lists the best places to eat but tells you how to get there, and much more besides. The professionals are backed up by the company's own traveling salesmen and enthusiastic volunteers from the food-conscious public.

Utmost secrecy is preserved as each yearly edition nears publication, and all over France restaurant owners await the star ratings with bated breath. These are the "Academy Awards" of France. Thousands of dining rooms—from the most elegant Parisian establishments to some simple rural inns—are listed, but only the best.

TRAVELING AND TRANSPORTATION

giving the proprietor the chance to correct things. That way, you won't ruin your evening.

To tip or not to tip

Although no law exists anywhere that says you are obliged to leave a tip for service, tipping is often the accepted thing to do. Self-appointed arbiters say that between ten and 15 percent of the total amount of the bill is customary—though higher tips are sometimes recommended in exceptional circumstances.

When setting pay scales for employes in the service industries, some proprietors may take tipping into consideration and pay lower rates than they would if tips were not involved. Thus, it is argued that if you don't tip, you are, in effect, being unfair to the individual who is serving you—be it a waitress, waiter, barman or cabdriver. Of course, this does not excuse any employer from underpaying.

There's no reason, however, why social justice—fair play if you prefer—should be overlooked. You probably should tip when you feel that the service given has been a notch above what was required. The tip should be considered a reward for extra effort—even a smile is still worth something in this mechanized age.

In Europe, South America and much of Asia, it has become the custom for restaurants and nightclubs to add a percentage to your bill for service; this practice is not often followed in Canada unless the customer agrees to it in advance. This question often comes up in situations involving service to groups—such as banquets, wedding receptions and similar social functions. If a tip is added to the bill without your knowledge or agreement, you can simply refuse to pay it.

If your chair collapses

Hoteliers and restaurateurs sometimes think that the public has a law book in its pocket. Why is it, they ask, that the simplest accident—something that could be immediately dismissed at home—becomes a possible ground for legal action when people are "out on the town"?

It is true, however, that as soon as a restaurant invites you onto the premises for its own gain, it assumes a high level of responsibility for your safety. If you tripped over a torn rug and fell, you could probably sue and recover damages for any injuries you suffered. The proprietor has a legal obligation to make sure that torn rugs, as well as faulty chairs and loose table legs, are repaired immediately so that his customers are reasonably guarded against danger.

If the waiter tips a plate of hot soup down your back, or in your lap, you have an "open and shut" case of negligence. At the very least, you could collect for your dry-cleaning bill.

A restaurant normally holds an insurance policy covering all these hazards; thus, you may find yourself involved in lengthy discussion with the insurance company before a claim is settled. Don't be put off by any haggling. It might be the insurance company's strategy to stall and delay long enough for you to become fed up with the whole thing and either walk away from it entirely, or settle for less than your original claim.

The vanishing overcoat

In most Canadian restaurants today, you will see a notice near the coatrack reading: "The management will not be responsible for lost or stolen articles." Not necessarily so. According to the law, and in spite of any warning signs, the restaurant is generally responsible for the safekeeping of your goods on its premises. That's why larger restaurants, nightclubs and hotels maintain cloakrooms where you can check your things.

Of course, if you had neglected to check your coat in the cloakroom provided and it was stolen while you were dancing, your chances of holding the nightclub responsible would be small.

The court would normally view the proved loss of a customer's personal belongings from a restaurant's premises as a case of negligence, or lack of ordinary care, on the part of the proprietor.

In its defense, the restaurant would have to prove that the loss or theft had been due to causes other than lack of ordinary care. It's one of the hazards of the business.

Laws about liquor

THE SALE OF ALCOHOLIC BEVERAGES is regulated and strictly controlled by the provincial or territorial governments. You cannot import your own and all bottles of wines and spirits must be purchased "under seal" from government outlets.

When it comes to drinking, although you will find that the basic laws are similar across the country, there are literally hundreds of minor variations.

With ten provinces, two territories and many municipalities issuing their own regulations, the traveler trying to trace the exact letter of the local liquor laws faces an uphill task. The best place for the visitor to start is the provincial retail liquor store, where the regulations will be posted. The annual price lists available there usually include an abstract of the key legal points. A postcard or phone call to the liquor control board of your province will get you all the regulations by mail.

Restrictions in our drinking laws strike some visitors from abroad as curious, ridiculous and even laughable. They don't really reflect our country's modern lifestyle. They are, instead, reminders of the horror of wide-open boozing that seized respectable folk in our not-so-distant pioneer past. In the 1840s, for example, there were 147 distilleries and 96 breweries going full blast in Upper Canada alone (the population at that time numbered just half a million). Whiskey and rum were supplied free from an open barrel in many retail stores—as a bonus to customers.

Today, the legal hours of drinking across Canada are set in various patterns, beginning some time between 10 A.M. and noon. The traveler seems expected to know the difference between a public house, tavern, beverage room, lounge, licensed dining room, licensed restaurant and other establishments where liquor may be served. Men and women can drink beer together in some places but not in others. Certain districts (West Toronto, Ontario, is one) are totally "dry." Others prohibit licensed establishments from serving spirits, although beer and wine are permitted.

Canada Temperance Act

Although total prohibition of public sale and serving of liquor was tried briefly (in New Brunswick) in 1855, impassioned lobbying for more than half a century by "teetotalers"—as the nondrinking abolitionists were called—failed to persuade the federal government to impose national prohibition. (It was, however, temporarily imposed as a special conservation measure across the country during the later years of World War I and continued in some provinces for a period afterward.) The disastrous experiment in the United States, under the 18th Amendment, was repealed in 1933 after more than 14 years of bootlegging and gang violence.

Pre-Confederation Canada had turned to the system of *local option*, permitting municipalities to prohibit the manufacture or sale of all intoxicating liquors within their boundaries, on the strength of a majority decision of the voting population.

In 1878, exercising its power under the British North America Act to legislate for "the peace, order and good government" of the nation as a whole, the federal government passed the Canada Temperance Act. Also known as the Scott Act (after its chief advocate, Secretary of State Sir Richard Scott), this law applied the local-option idea to the whole country, allowing any city, county or smaller subdivision to go "dry" if so voted by a majority of the qualified voters in the community.

High-level argument soon developed as to whether the federal authority was overstepping its bounds and a succession of cases were taken by the provinces to the British Privy Council (then Canada's highest court of appeal). Finally, it was established that the sale of liquor lay within provincial power while the federal government would control imports, exports and manufacture.

After World War I, the abolitionist organizations (of which the Women's Christian Temperance Union is a notable survivor) fought to retain the special wartime prohibition policy. However, by the end of the 1920s all the provinces, with the exception of Prince Edward Island, had adopted policies permitting sale of liquor under government control. (Prince Edward Island continued its prohibition policy until 1948.)

It isn't difficult to discover the reason for the provinces' keen interest in the question. Recent annual statistics show that revenue extracted by the provinces and territories from the liquor trade was almost two billion dollars. This includes the sums collected as license fees from premises that serve spirits, wine or beer to the public. The federal government also fares well; its revenue in a recent year from liquor excise taxes, import duties and license fees was more than $914 million.

Powers of the commissioners

The federal Importation of Intoxicating Liquors Act (1928) delegated authority to the provinces to control and regulate the importing and sale of liquor. Each province, in turn, passed a liquor control act which established a provincial liquor control board.

The duties of the provincial liquor control board commissioners (the titles vary in some provinces) include purchasing, importing, exporting, storing and selling liquor through retail outlets, as well as controlling the possession, sale, transportation, delivery and use of alcohol by private individuals.

The provincial liquor control boards decide which cities, towns and villages will have government liquor stores, and which brands will be sold.

The boards set the days and hours the liquor stores will be open and are responsible for making and distributing price lists for all brands they carry. They set the terms and conditions of licenses or permits, and they sometimes set limits on the quantities that can be bought within certain periods of time.

The commissioners establish operating standards for licensed outlets and appoint inspectors to check that all board regulations, as well as public health requirements, are being observed by the operators. Acting as both judge and jury, the commissioners can impose fines, suspend licenses and even throw an offender in jail.

The penalty for selling liquor without a license, for instance, is a fine that ranges up to $10,000, imprisonment for up to one year, or both.

The provinces have power to ban the manufacture of liquor within their borders if it is found that production facilities and working conditions are not up to acceptable standards.

Retail outlets are operated independently by commercial wine makers and breweries, and other independent outlets are licensed and supervised. Everywhere, minors are prohibited from buying or consuming liquor.

Liquor may be purchased from duty-free outlets located at certain international airports and Canada–U.S. border points. These outlets are operated under the supervision of the federal Department of National Revenue and their goods are available only to travelers leaving Canada. Nor can the travelers bring back to Canada liquor thus bought without paying duty. They can, of course, bring in liquor bought in duty-free shops in other countries—in limited quantity.

In the bottle store

At one time, in some provinces, you had to fill out order forms for spirit and wine purchases and get them stamped by the cashier before you could be served. The trend is now toward self-service stores which give the customer a chance to browse around and compare labels.

If you notice that the seal is broken on a bottle you are buying, you should refuse it and call the management's attention to the broken seal. Not all liquor board staff are connoisseurs: if the attendant gives your bottle of vintage bordeaux a kindly shake, you can ask for another bottle.

Beer stores, retail wine outlets and provincial liquor stores in some provinces can accept telephone orders for home delivery for a charge. You can have spirits delivered to your home only if you pay in advance. Delivery can be made to the purchaser only at his residence, or to anyone 18 years or older who lives there. On delivery, a receipt for the bottles must be signed.

Drinking at home

It is generally accepted in Canada that the state has no place in the nation's bedrooms. However, the government is still interested in any drinking that goes on in your home. Liquor for private use may be stored or consumed only in the home of the purchaser, or in the home of someone who received the liquor as a gift from the purchaser.

How strong is that liquor?

DURING WORLD WAR II, when vast supplies of alcohol were required for war purposes—such as explosives, synthetic rubber, pharmaceuticals and paints—the federal government virtually commandeered all distilleries. The production of spirits for drinking was cut to a maximum of 70 percent of the output in the base year (1941–42).

A clause in the Wartime Alcoholic Beverages Order in the dark year of 1942 prohibited the sale of spirits stronger than 70 percent proof. Although that edict has long since been repealed, almost all spirits (whiskey, gin, rum, etc.) are still sold in Canada today at the same strength. But what is *proof*?

This system of measuring the alcoholic strength of liquors can be confusing to the layman, but the essential point to remember is that if a bottle of rum was 100 proof, the contents would be 57 percent straight alcohol and 42.9 percent water. Thus, a normal bottle of rum or other spirits bought over the counter at your provincial liquor control board store, at 70 proof, actually contains only about 40 percent alcohol by volume.

To determine proof in Canadian terms, multiply the percentage of alcohol by 1.752.

The system of classification in the United States is slightly different; to determine U.S. proof you multiply the percentage of alcohol by two.

Percentage of Alcohol by volume	Canadian (or British) proof
100 (pure alcohol)	175.2
90	157.7
80	140
70	122.7
60	105
57.1	100
50	87.6
40	70.1
30	52.6
20	35
10	17.5
0 (water)	0

A home, in this reference, means a person's actual living quarters. It doesn't matter whether it is a house, apartment, boardinghouse, hotel or motel room, tent or trailer, or a boat, as long as the individual is occupying the facilities for dwelling, either on a temporary or permanent basis. If a boat is involved, it must be a cabin cruiser or at least be equipped with some sleeping accommodation. Land considered to be part of any of the dwelling area would be included.

You can transport bottles of liquor to your home by any legal means but you must not break the seals or open them on the way. However, the law allows you to take an opened bottle from one residence to another, as from your home to your summer cottage.

You may bring liquor home from another province for your own use. You may also bring in a limited amount from abroad, as long as you declare it and have it stamped by customs.

Drinking in public

Some day it might be possible for the Canadian adult to simply order a drink anywhere at any time he feels like one, as long as he can afford to pay for it. But that day is not yet here. What you can have, where and at what time it must be consumed, all these are subject to provincial control.

All the regulations can seem like hurdles on an obstacle course to the visitor. Ontario, for example, licenses the following establishments: dining lounges for the sale of liquor where food is available; dining rooms for the sale of beer and wine where food is available; lounges for the sale of liquor; public houses for the sale of beer in premises where men only are admitted; public houses for the sale of beer only; clubs for the sale of liquor with or without meals; clubs for the sale of beer and wine with meals, and beer without meals. Little wonder the stranger is sometimes confused.

Drinking in a hotel is restricted to licensed public rooms and to a registered guest's private room or suite.

Licensed premises are not allowed to sell or serve any type of beverage other than those their licenses allow them to sell; furthermore, they must not allow any alcoholic beverage to be taken from their premises. If you are in a "pub" (public house or tavern) in Ontario and you ask for a glass of sherry, the provincial regulations say you can't have it—it's beer or nothing.

Every licensed establishment is obliged by law to provide customers with price lists or to have signs clearly indicating what drinks are available, the amount and type of spirits in each type of drink and the prices being asked for each.

Lounges and public houses must have a service bar, with or without stools or chairs for the customers, as well as an area that is equipped with tables and chairs.

All drinks must be handled at the bar in such a way that customers have a clear view of the preparation. And, at one time in Ontario, for example, no kind of partition or other obstruction preventing full view of the room by any one customer was allowed in a dining room, lounge or public house.

Customers have the right to insist that all liquor that goes into their drink be poured from the original bottle and that each drink containing spirits should measure 28.4 millilitres. When any nonalcoholic "mix" is added to a drink, it must be done in full view of the customer.

Establishments licensed for wine may sell it by the bottle, half bottle, carafe or glass. If he is selling by the carafe or glass, the proprietor must be prepared to answer correctly, to the best of his knowledge, if a customer wants to know the brand name, type or country origin of the wine.

Hours of sale

Legal drinking hours vary from province to province, from city to city, and according to the type of license held. Public houses for beer only—called *brasseries* in Quebec—often open earlier than bars selling spirits and beer. To drink legally on Sundays, Christmas Day and Good Friday, customers are sometimes obliged to order a "normal meal"—though this could be as little as a hot dog.

Public houses must be cleared of customers, and of all signs of service and drinking within 45 minutes after closing time. In dining rooms, lounges (bars), or clubs, customers may linger, but drinking must have stopped within 45 minutes after closing time.

In private clubs, liquor, beer or wine can be sold during legal drinking hours only to members. Of course, they in turn can treat their guests. Every club must keep a guest register.

No liquor flows while the polls are open on federal election days in Canada. Most provinces forbid liquor sales on provincial election days.

Special occasion permits

Liquor control boards will normally issue special permits to allow liquor to be sold at social functions not being held for profit (charitable functions excepted).

Application for such a "banquet permit" should be filed with the board about ten days before the function—though sometimes more time is required. After it

has issued a permit, the board retains the right to cancel it if it finds that circumstances have been misrepresented.

After the function, the permit holder may have to make a written report to the liquor board stating the amount of liquor purchased and the amount left over (if any); the board may ask that any extra bottles be returned. The fees for special permits vary according to the amount of liquor being ordered or the type of function, but are generally reasonable.

Entertainment while you drink

"Blue" laws once forbade singing or music of any kind in drinking establishments in most of Canada—with the notable exception of the taverns of Quebec. Now, licensed establishments everywhere offer entertainment, usually between 9 P.M. and closing time, although some offer attractions during the early evening cocktail hours. During the entertainment periods, the price of drinks is usually increased because an added entertainment tax has to be met.

Getting the drunk home safely

ONE WINTER EVENING in 1968, a regular patron of a hotel beverage room near St. Catharines, Ontario, who had already consumed more beer than he could cope with, was refused further service and put out the door. There was no violence.

It had, apparently, happened before and the customer's "tendency to drink to excess" was known to both the owner of the "pub" and his waiters. That night, however, the man was struck by a car and severely injured.

When the case came before the courts, the injured man was awarded a total of $38,870 in damages against the driver of the car and the tavern company. The tavern appealed and the issue reached the Supreme Court of Canada. What degree of responsibility did the hotel have for a customer after he had left the premises?

The Supreme Court ruled that the tavern

was liable for damages and that it must pay $19,435. Ordinarily, the judgment said, it would be difficult to impose liability on a hotel for later events if it had merely supplied beer to the customer—although supplying liquor to a person already drunk was, of course, a separate offense under liquor control legislation. In this particular case, however, the hotel was aware of the patron's condition when it turned him out into the street, and there was a probable risk of injury to an unsteady person from the traffic on the busy highway in front of the premises.

It was not unreasonable, the court ruled, to expect the hotel to take care that the patron—whom it had "invited" onto the premises—was not exposed to danger because of his intoxication. At the least, the staff could have summoned the man a taxicab, or called the police.

Some liquor control boards once acted as moral censors of entertainment (such as striptease acts) booked into pubs and bars. Today they restrict themselves to checking the credentials of the booking agent and confirming that the establishment has been granted permission to present entertainment. Approval also must be obtained before an establishment can offer space for dancing; where approved, the dance area must occupy not less than one-fifth of the total floor space.

Gambling devices are not permitted, nor is card playing for money. (A quiet game of cribbage to see who pays the bar bill might go unnoticed.) Shuffleboard and sometimes darts are allowed and are particularly popular pastimes in the public houses.

Problem of intoxication

It is an offense to appear in drunken condition in a public place.

Proprietors of bars and pubs can be subject to severe penalties if they serve liquor to anyone who is under the influence of alcohol. If a drunken customer left the bar and later injured himself or someone else, committed suicide or suffered accidental death as a result of his condition, the licensee could find himself facing serious legal action. He could be sued by the customer if he lived, by his relatives if he died accidentally or by his own hand, or by others who might have been injured as a result of the man's intoxication.

This explains why the barman or the manager has the right to refuse you that extra drink.

Since a bar, pub or restaurant is private property, the owner, or his agent, can ask you to leave. Unless you can convince the management that you are sober and prepared to act reasonably, considering the safety and comfort of other clients, the owner has the right to have you removed from the premises—with reasonable force, if necessary.

A police officer can arrest without warrant any person believed to be committing an offense against the liquor laws.

The intoxicated driver is one of the major menaces to our society, and both police and the courts are attempting to reduce the number of fatal and near-fatal accidents resulting from this callous disregard of the public safety.

Search and seizure

Depending on the province, if a police officer has reasonable grounds to believe that liquor is being carried illegally in an automobile, he doesn't need a warrant to search the vehicle and any of its occupants. The officer would require a warrant, however, if he wanted to search any residence, building or any other place where he suspected liquor was being kept illegally. The warrant would also allow him to search anyone found in those places.

A search warrant is granted by a judge (or justice of the peace) once he has accepted a sworn statement that there are reasonable grounds for believing that liquor is being kept illegally or kept for unlawful purposes in a particular residence, building or place. The warrant entitles the police to break open any door, window, lock, fastener, floor, wall, ceiling, compartment, plumbing fixture, box, or anything else blocking the way. The policeman making the search can seize and take away with him any liquor, as well as any book, paper or other item he reasonably believes could be regarded as evidence in the case; this could include any vehicle in which the alleged illegal liquor was found.

When liquor has been seized, those involved can apply within 30 days for return of the goods. The court would have to decide whether the goods might be needed as evidence in any action concerned with the seizure. They could be held for as long as three months, by which time the court would have either made a conviction for illegal possession or dismissed the case. If there was a conviction, the seized liquor would be forfeited to the Crown.

Where a vehicle (car or boat) had been part of the goods confiscated and a person had been convicted on a charge of illegal possession of liquor, the judge could order the vehicle to be forfeited to the Crown.

Going through Customs

MOST CANADIANS agree that their jobs or industries should be protected against unfair competition from abroad; yet it is usually the same people who grumble about paying customs duty when they bring back bargain items from abroad. There's something curiously tempting about trying to evade the clutches of the officers of the Customs and Excise division of the federal Department of National Revenue—it can make petty criminals of citizens otherwise described as pillars of society. Perhaps this temptation carries the echo of a more reckless past when smuggling was something of a game for some of our seafaring ancestors.

The customs officers you will encounter when you come back into Canada will not be playing games, however. They know that they aren't going to win popularity contests by insisting that you open your bags, poking into your packages and delving through your dirty laundry. But they are performing a valid and valuable professional function (for one thing, customs duties provide the federal treasury with more than three billion dollars a year) and they are responsible for protecting the public from moral or physical harm (for example, in seizing weapons and dangerous drugs).

On returning from abroad, you can help both yourself and the customs officers by making out your declaration in advance and keeping handy the receipts for all your purchases.

The dates on the receipts can help prove the length of time you were away (an important factor in allowances) and the amounts prove the true value of your purchases.

Although customs and excise legislation—which covers the entire range of items imported into Canada in business transactions—is so detailed that it can make the layman's head spin, the essential point to remember is that when you return to Canada from a foreign country, you must account for ("declare") *everything* you have bought—or been given—while you were away. The government is not really interested in the tube of toothpaste you bought in Tallahassee—such small items for your normal personal use are forgiven—but it *is* interested in the bottle of perfume you bought in Paris. Don't fret. There are generous allowances that are described in the sections that follow.

The complete schedule attached to the Customs Tariff Act, which lists more than one thousand duty-free and duty-chargeable goods, is available from bookstores that carry government publications or from the Canadian Government Publishing Centre, Supply and Services Canada, Ottawa K1A 0S5. Condensed versions of the list, containing the main items of consumer interest, are usually available from travel agents, at railway and shipping offices and at post offices.

Anything to declare?

Customs officers are found at all international airports, seaports, international bridges, and at all main highway and railway border points between Canada and the United States.

However and wherever you enter Canada, you are required to "go through customs," as the saying goes. You will be asked politely whether you have "anything to declare." Even if you answer no, you must, if the officer asks, open your luggage for his inspection. If he orders a search of the clothes you're wearing, you are obliged by law to cooperate.

Although customs inspection for travelers is on a 24-hour basis, there are restrictions on entry of commercial shipments. No goods for commercial use can be brought into Canada in any vehicle or on any person between sunset and sunrise on any day, nor on any Sunday or statutory holiday, except under a written permit from a government revenue collector. (*See* Chapter 16, "Private planes and gliders.")

Border crossings to and from the United States give customs by far the greatest proportion of their work. If you enter Canada by automobile, your first duty is to report to the nearest customs office. Until you have been checked through, you must not remove any article from your car, luggage or person.

People arriving by plane or ship are automatically channeled into the customs department.

Don't overlook the fact that the customs officer will naturally be interested in all items of foreign manufacture, even if you bought them at home before you left on your trip. This may well apply to your camera, tape recorder or portable TV set. It is advisable to declare such things when you are leaving Canada, supplying the serial numbers if possible. Otherwise, you might be charged duty on these items when you return.

The duty on imported goods—above your duty-free allowance—will be calculated on the basis of their fair market value and can vary according to where the goods were purchased. In calculating the market value, you should not include any taxes on the goods that you had to pay in the country where you made your purchases.

Tariffs are worked out on five levels: British (or Commonwealth) preferential, most-favored nation, interim tariff rate for Great Britain, general preferential and general. Generally speaking, you can assume that, after duty is paid, the item you have lugged back from the depths of Africa may cost you just about the same

as (or perhaps more than) if you had bought it through a mail-order catalog at home.

The "beneficial" duty rate

The regulations also allow what is called a "beneficial" tariff rate to Canadian citizens. This applies when you have been outside Canada for at least 48 hours and are returning with goods valued over the limit of your exemption. Under the beneficial tariff scheme, you will be charged 25 percent, up to a maximum of $300. Beyond that, regular rates will be charged. Tobacco products and alcoholic beverages are not covered by the beneficial tariff.

Incidentally, if the quantity of liquor you want to bring in is more than the duty-free allowance, you must get permission from the provincial liquor control board. If the board approves, you will receive a permit allowing you to bring the liquor in; however, you will have to pay the going provincial rates of duty and tax. As long as you are prepared to pay the duty on tobacco, you can bring in as much as you like.

Any goods on which you are claiming duty-free exemption, or the beneficial tariff, must be for your personal or household use only. They may be souvenirs or gifts, but not things bought on behalf of others or for sale or for any use in business.

Claiming your exemptions

Often, families arriving at a customs office become confused by the forms they must fill out and thus lose out on the exemptions they are entitled to. Take your time; study the forms carefully so that you don't shortchange yourself or misrepresent any situation. Don't be afraid to ask a customs officer's help; getting it straight the first time makes his job that much easier in the long run.

Children who can read and write, and understand the regulations, are entitled to fill out their own customs forms. Parents and guardians can complete and sign forms for younger children if the goods are for the children. Tobacco cannot be claimed by anyone under age 16: liquor cannot be claimed by anyone who does not meet the minimum age requirements of the province or territory where he or she lives.

Note carefully that the $100 quarterly and $300 annual exemptions are considered as personal and cannot be combined with someone else's exemption to cover any particular purchase you have made abroad. Nor can your exemption be transferred to someone else.

When you have been out of the country for 24 hours or more, you can make a simple verbal declaration to customs officers and be allowed to import, duty and tax free, any article or combination of articles valued at not more than $20. This does not apply to cigars, cigarettes, loose tobacco or liquor.

If you have been out of the country 48 hours or more, think twice before you make the $20 verbal declaration, because it would cancel out your privilege, on the same trip, of making a written declaration to the value of $100.

The $100 declaration can be made once in each of the following periods: Jan. 1–Mar. 31; April 1–June 30; July 1–Sept. 30; and Oct. 1–Dec. 31. Within each period, you can bring in up to 50 cigars, 200 cigarettes, 0.9 kilograms of pipe or cigarette tobacco and up to 1.1 litres of liquor or wine free of duty.

If beer is substituted for liquor or wine, your limit will be 24 cans or bottles (336 millilitres each).

Under both the $20 verbal claim and the $100 written declaration, all of the articles involved must be either carried by hand, or contained in your luggage, for quick inspection by a customs officer. Remember you must declare items purchased in Canadian or foreign duty-free stores.

Canadians who have been abroad for at least seven days are given a further exemption: they may import, duty and tax free, articles valued up to a total of $300. But they may do this only once a year. It's important to note that this $300 exemption can be used even though you may have claimed $100 exemptions on previous quarterly trips. You may not, however, combine the $300 and $100 duty-free allowances on the same trip. Thus, as you may have already figured out, it is possible to bring into Canada duty-free goods to the value of $700 every year, by making five separate trips.

Remember that the seven-day period for the $300 exemption begins the day after your departure; however, it includes the day of your return, regardless of the hour. If you want to take advantage of the $300 exemption, all foreign purchases from continental North America must accompany you in hand or checked luggage. According to customs law, continental North America includes Panama, Costa Rica, Nicaragua, El Salvador, Guatemala, Honduras, British Honduras, Mexico, the United States, and the French islands of St-Pierre and Miquelon in the Gulf of St. Lawrence. Not included are the islands of the Bahamas, Bermuda, the West Indies and Hawaii.

If you buy something in a country outside continental North America you may have it shipped home to your home. You must declare it on your return and, if it has not been sent by mail, you must make arrangements to have it cleared through customs on its arrival and forwarded to you later.

Postal packages that follow you home will be held at customs for free no more than 35 days. Goods shipped through other channels can start to run up storage charges within 10 days after notice of their arrival has been sent to the intended receiver. Unclaimed postal packages will be "returned to sender"; other unclaimed goods will be disposed of at the public auctions which customs holds about every three months. No matter what the circumstances, liquor, cigars, cigarettes or other tobacco products cannot be declared as "goods to follow."

Powers of the customs official

Customs officers and anyone else employed in the collection of customs duties and taxes (including sheriffs and justices of the peace) can, on the basis of reasonable suspicion, examine any package they think might contain illegal or smuggled goods.

They can board or enter any boat or

vehicle and delay it while carrying out a thorough search. If any illegal goods are found, the officers can seize and hold the boat or vehicle, and everything on or in it.

Any officer, having sworn before a justice of the peace that he has reason to suspect there are illegal goods in any building or place—open or enclosed—can be granted a warrant to enter those premises to carry out a search. If the place is locked, he must first explain his purpose to the occupant and ask permission to enter. If he is turned down, he has the right to enter by force. He is entitled to break down any doors or open any containers in carrying out his search.

Any customs officer who has seized a boat, vehicle, property or goods suspected of being illegal can call for whatever lawful aid and assistance is needed to make sure the seized items will remain secure while he continues his investigation. He has the power to arrest, without a warrant, anyone actually found in the act of committing an indictable offense against customs laws and regulations, or even merely suspected of doing so.

The powers of search are as wide as democratic law can reasonably allow them to be. They cover anyone on board any boat in any Canadian port, aboard any boat or vehicle entering Canada by land or inland water routes, or anyone who has entered from a foreign country by any means of transportation, including air travel.

If an officer has reasonable cause to suspect someone of concealing goods on his person that are either subject to duty or on the list of prohibited items, he can have that person "frisked" and, in extreme cases, stripped and searched. Before this can happen, however, the person being searched may ask of the officer to be taken before a police magistrate, justice of the peace or the chief officer of

Behind the Iron Curtain

RELATIONS BETWEEN Communist countries and the West have warmed up considerably since the days of the "Cold War," and travel behind the Iron Curtain has become less complicated. Nevertheless, the Department of External Affairs advises Canadians traveling to the Soviet Union to check whether the visas they receive from the Soviet Embassy or consulate permit them to visit each town and city on their itinerary and to make stopovers in Moscow. And hotel reservations should be confirmed before arrival in the Soviet Union.

Canadians residing in or visiting a Communist country for an extended period are advised—in their own interest—to register with the nearest Canadian (or British), diplomatic or consular office, and to notify the same office on departure. If a personal call is not possible, then supply the following information by mail: Name, Canadian address, current address and telephone number, passport number and date of issue, details of itinerary.

The addresses to which Canadian travelers in Communist countries should report are as follows:

Bulgaria: British Embassy, Boulevard Marshal Tolbukhin 65–67, Sofia.

China: Canadian Embassy, NO. 10, San Li Tun Road, Chao Yang District, Peking.

Czechoslovakia: Canadian Embassy, Mickiweiczova 6, Prague.

Hungary: Canadian Embassy, Budakeszi, u. 55/d P. 8, Budapest 1021.

Poland: Canadian Embassy, Ulica Matejki 1/5, Warsaw 00-481.

Rumania: Canadian Embassy, 36 Nicolae Iorga, 71118 Bucharest.

Russia (U.S.S.R.): Canadian Embassy, 23 Starokonyushenny Pereulok, Moscow.

Vietnam: British Embassy, 16 Pho Ly Thuong Kiet, Hanoi.

Yugoslavia: Canadian Embassy, Proleterskih Brigada 69, 11000 Belgrade.

There are no resident Canadian or British missions in Albania, Kampuchea (Cambodia), Taiwan or North Korea.

customs at the location in question. (A female is used to search women.)

The customs officer is protected to a great extent by federal law in carrying out duties which sometimes cause people to feel their civil and human rights are being violated. Some staff members may have what is called a *writ of assistance*, meaning that while serving as members of Canada Customs and in any customs case being considered by a court, they cannot be sued by anyone involved in that case. Once the case has been settled, however, the traveler involved may sue for damages if he feels that an employe of the department acted improperly.

If you should find yourself in this situation, there are certain rules you must follow. First, you must send the officer concerned written notice of what you intend to do and then wait at least a month before taking any further action. Within the month's waiting period, the officer is entitled to plead his case before a judge, explaining his actions and, perhaps, offering an apology.

If the judge decided the customs employe was technically guilty but had acted in good faith and for good reasons, he would probably award you only token damages—perhaps one dollar or less. You would not be entitled to any legal costs nor would you be permitted to appeal to any other courts. (Of course, there's always the Ombudsman!)

The customs officer is also protected in cases where the search has failed to uncover any smuggled or banned merchandise. As long as he could satisfy a judge that he had good reason to *suspect* illegal goods were being hidden, you would not be able to sue him.

Cars, planes and boats

To protect the Canadian automobile industry, steep rates of duty and taxes are levied on foreign cars (in this instance, "foreign" includes U.S.-manufactured) being brought into Canada; this applies to automobiles and all other kinds of motor vehicles. Just about every country places strict controls on the entry of all motor vehicles inside its borders (*See* Chapter 5, "Using a car on holiday").

The regulations are particularly rigid about used cars, so readily available at comparatively low prices just south of the border. Any vehicle of other than current-year manufacture is considered to be a used or secondhand model; as such, you will not be allowed to bring it into Canada—even if you're willing to pay the duty and taxes. However, "vintage" cars and vehicles at least 15 years old can be imported.

There are certain exceptions. An immigrant settler is permitted to import a used car for his personal use, provided he owned the vehicle before coming to Canada and it meets federal and provincial safety and emission standards. Provincial sales tax may have to be paid. Exceptions also are made for representatives of foreign governments who use their vehicles for official or personal reasons. A Canadian citizen who receives an automobile as a gift can bring it into the country after certifying that no money changed hands. If, while traveling outside Canada, your car should be damaged beyond repair, you are permitted to bring back a car of equal replacement value, provided you have an insurance company statement or police report proving the extent of damage. Keep receipts for any new auto parts you have to buy on trips to the United States; they may be subject to duty and taxes.

Similar regulations apply to all types of used or secondhand aircraft. Again there are exceptions, for instance in the case of aircraft used in international commercial traffic or brought in by nonresidents for temporary use under a special permit issued by the Department of National Revenue.

Canadians are permitted to import pleasure boats, new or used, on payment of the duty assessed. Non-Canadians must obtain permits from customs at their port of entry.

Importation of firearms

Certain types of firearms are admitted into Canada only with special permission and under strictly controlled circumstances (*See* Chapter 17, "Guns and guides"). These include pistols, revolvers, semi-automatic weapons or firearms that can be fired when folded or telescoped to less than 66 centimetres in length. Other firearms are totally prohibited. Fully automatic weapons and sawed-off riffles or shotguns with barrels of less than 46 centimetres in length or less than 66 centimetres in overall length, are not admitted into Canada.

Standard shotguns and rifles, as well as longbows, spear guns and any other firearms measuring more than 66 centimetres in length, for sporting use only, may be imported; they must be declared at customs and are dutiable like any other purchase.

Due to the prevalence of air piracy and other in-flight crime, the airlines take special precautions—such as checking hand luggage and "frisking" with a metal detector before allowing passengers to board. If you wish to bring onto a plane with you anything even faintly resembling a weapon—even in the luggage that you have checked—volunteer the information to airline and customs personnel when you are checking in.

An antique gun will be admitted free of duty if you have proof it was manufactured more than 100 years ago. Two thousand safety cartridges are also admitted free of duty.

Plants and pets

In trying to protect Canada's farm and forest industries from the introduction of destructive pests and diseases, Canada Customs strictly controls the importing of soil, seeds, plants, meat, fruits, vegetables, pets, animals, and unprocessed animal and plant products. Hundreds of items are flatly prohibited to the returning tourist; for some, entry is restricted severely. If you want to import some item in this field, contact in advance either the Plant Health Division or the Animal Health Division at the Department of Agriculture, Ottawa. Along with an application form, you will receive the current regulations and the procedure that you will have to follow. Under the Convention on International Trade in Endangered Species, specially designated plants and animals, as well as their products (such as

skins and mounted trophies), are not permitted to be brought into Canada without a Canadian import permit and an export permit from the country of origin. For further information, contact the Canadian Wildlife Service of the Department of the Environment.

The returning tourist, or an over-the-border shopper, must keep in mind that *every* plant, plant product, animal or animal product must be declared at customs and presented for inspection. This would include your souvenir orange tree from Florida and that cute little pup that adopted you in California.

All pets are inspected on entry. If you are bringing in a cat or dog, you must be able to produce a health certificate from a veterinarian, particularly to prove that the cat or dog has had an antirabies vaccination within the previous 36 months for the United States, and 12 months for other countries in which rabies exists. Otherwise, your cat or dog will be held in quarantine for at least a month. If you want to take your cat or dog into the United States, you must have vaccination certificates for it.

Some countries, such as Britain, Australia, and certain Caribbean nations, are rabies-free. Domestic cats and dogs can be imported into Canada from these countries without proof of rabies vaccination and without quarantine. But they must be shipped directly to Canada and you must provide a certificate from the government of that country certifying that rabies has not existed for at least six months before the departure of your pet.

Sending gifts home

While you are abroad, you can send any number of gifts (but not advertising matter, tobacco or liquor) to friends in Canada free of duty, provided the value of each gift is not more than $25 in Canadian funds.

Gifts valued at more than $25 are subject to customs duty. Only one package, per person, per day is permitted under this arrangement.

To help clear the item through customs, you should write on the package: "Unsolicited gift. Value: under $25."

Customs exemptions at a glance

Admittedly, customs regulations can be confusing to the occasional traveler but even bureaucrats are human. The Customs and Excise division of the Department of National Revenue provides this simplified chart in an attempt to boil the requirements down to the essentials. Everyone—even the babe in arms—is entitled to exemptions, provided the goods claimed are for the personal use of the claimant; don't try to tell customs that your toddler needs that new electric razor. Parents or guardians may sign declaration forms for children.

IF	YOU CAN	YOU CAN'T
AFTER 48 HOURS' ABSENCE		
If you claim no other exemption or the special tariff rate. / If goods are carried in hand or checked baggage.	WITH A VERBAL DECLARATION ... claim duty-free entry of articles to a total value of $20.00 upon your return from each trip abroad.	... include tobacco products or alcoholic beverages.
If goods are carried in hand or checked baggage.	WITH A WRITTEN DECLARATION ... claim one duty-free entry of articles up to a value of $100.00 once in each calendar quarter.	... combine this with any other exemption.
AFTER SEVEN DAYS' ABSENCE*		
If goods are acquired inside continental North America and they are carried in hand or checked baggage. (Continental North America includes the islands of St-Pierre and Miquelon, Panama and the mainland north of Panama.) / If goods are acquired OUTSIDE continental North America they may be shipped or mailed separately if they are declared at your first port of arrival.	WITH A WRITTEN DECLARATION ... claim one duty-free entry of articles up to a value of $300.00 once in each calendar year.	... combine this with any other exemption. / ... ship goods separately when purchased in continental North America.

*In calculating the seven days, do not count the day of departure from Canada

Penalties are severe

It is illegal to bring goods into Canada without clearing them through an official customs office. It is also against the law to slip through a customs checkpoint without reporting or to remove goods while they are awaiting official inspection or before all duties have been paid.

Stiff penalties can be imposed under the Customs Act for violations of the law. All goods involved will be seized and forfeited, and every person involved in an offense can be fined an amount equal to the value of the goods.

If the value of the goods is under $200, additional fines of $50 to $200 could be imposed by a court following conviction. The court could also impose prison terms of from 30 days to a year in addition to the fines.

If the value of the goods on which duty should have been paid amounted to $200 or more, those involved would be guilty of a more serious offense and liable, on conviction, to a fine of between $200 and $1,000, or to a prison term of from one to four years, or both.

If you unload goods from a car or boat before a proper declaration is made, or if you fail to make a report, fail to produce the goods, or tell lies when questioned, you could be fined $400 for each separate offense. Your boat or car will be held until the fine is paid. If payment is not made within 30 days, the boat or car can be sold to cover the fine and any expenses involved.

Any forgery, counterfeiting or falsification of any customs document is an indictable offense—that is, punishable by at least two years' imprisonment—and all goods involved will be forfeited.

Drivers of cars or boats who refuse to stop at the border for customs inspection or refuse to assist a customs officer in carrying out his duties, could be fined from $50 to $1,000, sent to jail for up to one year, or both.

If you obstruct or resist any authorized customs search of your person, or help someone else to obstruct and resist, you will be fined $100. If you deny having unlawful goods anywhere on your person when, in fact, you do, or do not produce

them when the Canadian customs official asks whether you have anything to declare, the goods will be seized and you will be fined a sum equal to three times the value of the goods.

Persons caught smuggling while carrying weapons would not only have their goods seized but also could be sentenced to ten years' imprisonment.

Any animal, vehicle or goods of any kind brought into Canada on a tax-exempt basis by any traveler must not be sold in Canada without the duty being paid. If the duty wasn't paid and the sale was discovered, the goods would be immediately seized and forfeited.

Retrieving seized goods

Anyone who wants to claim goods seized by customs must file a claim with the clerk of the Federal Court. On the claim form he must state his name, address and occupation. This must be accompanied by an *affidavit* (a sworn statement in writing signed by the claimant) setting out the reason for his claim to the seized goods. The claimant must also post a bond, which serves as a pledge to back up the validity of his claim.

To avoid the possibility of the seized goods being sold by customs at public auction, a claim should be made within 30 days.

The claimant—the owner of the goods, or anyone who had the goods in his possession at the time of seizure, or anyone who had made a payment or deposit on the goods while they were being held at customs—should write to the Collector of customs at the nearest port of entry, advising that a claim is being entered for the goods.

Unless the claimant starts proceedings for retrieval within the time limit, he could lose his chance to recover the seized goods.

Where any vessel, vehicle or any other kind of goods has been seized and is likely to be forfeited, any person who claims an interest as an owner, mortgagee or lien holder though he is not involved with the offense can, within 60 days after the seizure, write to a judge for an order on which he can declare such an interest. He would have to satisfy the judge that he was in no way connected with the offense. Such an interest, if legally established, would also be considered in the disposal of funds should the seized goods already have been sold at a public auction.

The commercial importer

It is against the law for anyone to possess, hide, buy, sell or trade goods known to have been smuggled into Canada, whether or not they are dutiable. Any such goods, if they are found, will be seized and forfeited.

If a licensed importer falsely describes or appraises incoming goods, the shipment is liable to forfeiture.

Anyone importing commercial goods to Canada must provide customs with an invoice showing the place and date of purchase, the name of the firm or person that sold him the goods and a full description of the merchandise, including quantities and cost price.

On an official *bill of entry* form, the importer must repeat the above information, adding the name of the country in which the goods were grown, produced or manufactured. The invoice and bill of entry are required even when the goods involved are not subject to duty. Any duty charged must be paid at time of entry; the customs officer then issues a permit allowing the goods to be shipped further into Canada.

Until the customs officer is satisfied that the bill of entry and the invoice are in order and the duty has been paid, he has the right, after waiting a reasonable time, to order that the shipment be sent to a customs warehouse and kept there at the risk and cost of the owner. If these problems are not solved within 30 days, the goods can be sold and the funds used to pay duties and charges.

If there is any money left over, it will go to the owner.

No bill of entry will be accepted without a supporting invoice, signed by the purchaser as being accurate, and delivered to customs. This certification on the part of the owner must be written on the invoice or bill of entry, or attached to it, and must be witnessed by another person.

When you take valuables out

Canadians leaving the country with valuable equipment, or foreign-made goods previously bought in Canada—such as jewelry, watches, cameras, binoculars, firearms, sporting equipment, typewriters, boats, motors and trailers—should declare them and have them identified by customs on the way out of Canada.

The items are listed on a special card, with identifying serial numbers. You carry the card with you and show it to customs on your return.

The identification card can also be used for articles previously purchased abroad and declared, and for which any necessary duty has already been paid. Without this card, you might have trouble proving certain articles were taken out of Canada with you and you could be held liable for tax and duty.

Visitors to Canada who bring valuables for personal use while traveling in Canada should declare them with Canada Customs on entry.

Although no law demands it, they may find that this practice will save a lot of time and trouble at border crossings on their return journey.

The visitor's privileges

Visitors to Canada do not have to pay duty on personal effects such as sports equipment, radios and cameras, and wearing apparel that they bring with them for their own use during their stay.

Travelers from abroad are also allowed to bring in the following items duty free: 50 cigars and 200 cigarettes and up to .9 kilograms per person of manufactured tobacco; 1.1 litres of spirits or wines, or 24 cans or bottles (336 millilitres each) of beer.

With the exception of alcohol, advertising matter and tobacco products, anything that Canada Customs will permit you to import may be brought in duty free as a gift—to a maximum value of $25 for each gift.

A visitor is also allowed to bring in two days' supply of food duty free (as long as the food meets public health regulations), as well as a full tank of gasoline in his automobile.

Goods in transit

WHEN GOODS ARE TRANSPORTED in the normal way from mine or mill to factory, from factory to shop, and from shop to customer, a series of contracts are formed between the shipper (the *bailor* or *consignor*) and the carrier (the *bailee*, or temporary holder) until the goods are accepted by the buyer or receiver (the *consignee*).

The document that represents the contract for carrying the goods is called the *bill of lading*. Prepared in triplicate, it describes in detail the goods to be carried and it gives the destination and any route instructions. The main conditions of the contract are usually printed on the back of the form. One copy becomes the shipping order and the others, when signed by the carrier's agent, act as the receipts for the goods. When the buyer receives the goods, he signs the two copies, keeping one as his own receipt and giving one back to the carrier. If property is shipped by sea or air, the bill of lading can require as many as 10 copies. An *order* bill of lading requires that the goods be delivered only to the actual person named as consignee or receiver; the carrier must not hand over the goods until the receiver produces the top copy—that is, the original—of the bill of lading. More common is the *straight* bill of lading, allowing the carrier to deliver the goods to anyone at the consignee's address. The person who receives the goods must sign a receipt.

If the conditions of the contract are being properly observed, the carrier is responsible for safe delivery of undamaged goods except in circumstances beyond his control, such as labor strikes, acts of war and "acts of God" (earthquakes and the like).

Why does the law saddle the carrier with this heavy liability? Because while he is holding someone's property he is considered to be in total charge of it. He could, if he was a thief, accept a cargo for Saskatoon, then head with it to Sarnia and sell it there for his own profit.

The common carrier

There are basically two kinds of carriers: private and common. These terms have nothing to do with their social status. The *private carrier* has a restricted trade, in that he offers a specialized vehicle (perhaps for carrying ready-mix concrete or frozen TV dinners); the *common carrier* will move anything that his vehicle can hold (goods or people), thus providing service for virtually all who request it.

Apart from his duty to safeguard passengers on his vehicle (described earlier in this chapter), the common carrier is widely responsible for the safety of the property turned over to him for shipment. He could be likened to an *insurer*. His responsibility begins as soon as goods are delivered to him. If the owner, the consignee, retains the goods for any reason, thus preventing the carrier from completing the duties of his contract, safety of the goods will then be the responsibility of the owner.

If the carrier fails to deliver the goods, he must be prepared to show why he was unable to do so, or he must show there was some term in his contract with the shipper that relieved him of his responsibility. Otherwise, he could be liable for damages on the grounds of negligence.

Most common carriers using air, water or rail transport are licensed by the Canadian Transport Commission. Truckers come under provincial jurisdiction. Generally speaking, any member of the public has the right to call upon a common carrier to receive and carry goods. The carrier's liability to deliver your property safely to its destination may be limited to some extent but he cannot evade his responsibility by writing some one-sided limitations into the contract.

Although C.O.D. shipments (shipments for which the recipient pays "cash on delivery") are marked "at owner's risk," the carrier must still take care of the goods for the owner. If the shipper could prove that any loss, damage or injury was due solely to carelessness, the carrier would be held liable.

The private carrier

More formally called a *private carrier for reward or value*, the private carrier does not undertake generally to carry goods for the public. Although he does not have to bear the responsibilities of an *insurer* against loss or damage to the goods he is carrying (as the *common carrier* does), the private carrier does have the responsibility of taking reasonable care of the goods and is responsible should they be damaged due to his negligence.

A private carrier is considered a *bailee for hire* and must, in the case of a mishap, show that the damage occurred despite his having used the same amount of care and diligence a reasonably careful man would have taken with his own property.

The carrier's liability

The amount of the common carrier's financial liability for any loss, damage or injury of goods will be assessed according to the value of the goods and the place of shipment. Unless limited by some special agreement with the shipper, or by some notice, condition or declaration which he might lawfully make or give to the shipper, the carrier must generally assume full responsibility and take on all the risks of carrying and safely delivering the goods he has been hired to transport.

The carrier must have insurance for the goods he carries of from $1,000 to $20,000 for each vehicle, depending on the amount of goods carried.

Railway liability for noncarload shipments is limited to $50 for 45 kilograms or less, and $1.10 per kilogram over 45 kilograms and truckers' liability often to $4.41 per kilogram. If there is a higher value declared on the bill of lading, you can take out a short-term insurance policy for the higher value; often the transportation company will assume the liability if you pay a premium over the normal freight charges.

Generally there is no limited liability on shipments by air and water within Canada or on carload lots by rail.

Right of refusal

The carrier cannot be forced to transport articles of extraordinary value. If you have such an article, you should reveal its nature and value to the carrier. It will then be his duty to suggest a special agreement—possibly full-risk coverage at a premium higher than ordinary rates.

Any person shipping explosives or dangerous goods without previous, full written disclosure to the carrier of their nature, thus giving him the chance to refuse the job, must pay the carrier if any loss, damage or injury results from the dangerous goods being carried.

Although the common carrier must always be ready to provide the transport service he offers to the public, the law does not force him to carry for every person who demands his services. If you were not satisfied with the carrier's reason for refusing you, you could complain to the Canadian Transport Commission or your provincial licensing-authority.

On the high seas

Shipping companies must provide a seaworthy ship, a proper crew, equipment, supplies and fit-and-safe storage space for the goods you entrust to them.

After delivery of the goods to the docks, the shipper should get his signed copy of the *bill of lading* from the ship's officers. In effect, this copy is the shipper's receipt—covering every item in the shipment. It also serves as a warranty that the goods will be transported in safety (subject to the conditions listed on the document—the "fine print").

677

When the goods are unloaded, the receiver (the *consignee*) should make a close inspection to check for loss or damage. Written notice of any damage must be given the carrier within three days; otherwise the law allows the carrier to assume the unloading was a complete and satisfactory delivery. If the receiver and carrier made a joint inspection, written notice of damage would be unnecessary as the carrier would obviously be aware of the loss or damage.

Any legal action against the carrier must be taken within a year following delivery, or one year after the promised delivery date.

A charge of damage due to unseaworthiness will not be supported in court unless it can be proved there was lack of proper seamanlike care and effort throughout the voyage.

According to the terms of the Carriage of Goods by Water Act, a shipping company is not liable for loss or damage resulting from any breakdown in the navigation or management of the vessel—such as a fault in the steering mechanism that causes the ship to run aground. Neither would it be responsible for loss or damage caused by a fire unless it could be proved that the crew was negligent. The generally accepted "acts of God," war, strikes or riots and civil disturbances are listed as valid loopholes.

Unless the shipper had specifically described and evaluated his goods in the bill of lading, the carrier would not be liable for more than $500 in the event of loss or damage.

The shipper must advise the carrier in advance about any flammable, explosive, or otherwise dangerous goods in his shipment. If he failed to do so, the ship's officers could, upon discovery of such

When you move house

IF YOU TAKE A JOB in another city, or decide to move to a different climate or milieu, you will have the choice of hiring a mover or of doing the job yourself.

Calling in a professional mover is, of course, the simplest, safest—and costliest—way. All members of the Canadian Association of Movers will provide an estimate of cost; remember that it will be an estimate, and not a guaranteed final figure. Ask about possible extra costs. These could include packing boxes and unpacking in your new home.

You might want to arrange extra insurance coverage for your furniture and other goods during transit. Unless you make some such arrangement, the moving company's liability for loss or damage is limited to $1.32 a kilogram for each item or package. You will be required to sign a paper acknowledging that some of your things were marred or scratched before the move began. You should examine everything carefully on arrival to see if any additional damage has been done.

Unless you have made credit arrangements, you will be expected to pay on the nail when the furniture is unloaded. If you wish to pay by personal cheque, make sure, in advance, that the mover accepts such an arrangement. If the mover can't get into your new home on the set date, he will charge you extra for storage.

You'll spend a lot less if you hire a truck or trailer for a do-it-yourself move—but, of course, the labor and total financial responsibility will be yours, too. If you have some friendly workmates or a grown family to help out, you should manage.

The truck-rental dealers now offer a wide range of vehicles and services. You can pick up a truck in one city and hand it back in another on the other side of the continent. You can insure both the truck and its contents from damage due to accident. If the hired truck should break down, a telephone call will bring you road service from the nearest dealer.

A seven-metre rented truck will move all the furniture in an eight-room house.

items, throw the goods overboard, or unload them at the nearest port. The shipper would have no recourse for damages in such a case. In fact, he would be held responsible for any damage or expense that resulted, directly or indirectly, from his shipment.

In the warehouse

When you store any goods in a warehouse (or even send them out to be repaired), your transaction will be regulated by the law of *bailment*. It is another division of the law of contracts.

A contract of bailment is created when you (the *bailor*) entrust some of your property temporarily to another party (the *bailee*). This contract exists both if you store some furniture in a warehouse or if you lend your garden tools to the neighbor. In either case, you are not transferring any title of ownership (nor any of the rights that go with ownership) and have the right to get your goods back whenever you want them.

As in any contract, your agreement with the warehousing company can be made subject to any special conditions that you both agree to. In general terms, the bailee (in this instance, the warehouse) is not automatically classed as an *insurer*, but is expected only to act with reasonable care and caution in the custody of your goods. It could be said that his responsibility is conditioned almost as much by his good reputation and professional integrity as by the letter of the law.

All you can actually demand is that the warehouseman give you a receipt and that he handle your goods with the same care that he would give his own belongings. You would be able to claim from him for any damage caused by negligence or by delivery of your goods to the wrong person. In most other cases, your chances would be slim. If you want to be covered against all risks, you can always purchase insurance; the warehouseman himself may offer you a low-cost policy.

The warehouseman is obliged to provide a building in which your goods will be reasonably safe and secure from weather and other normal hazards. However, he is not liable for loss arising from any accident that was not his fault. If a packing case full of your wife's clothes became mildewed and deteriorated, he would not be liable unless a special arrangement had been made beforehand for the air-conditioned storage of such materials. Large warehouses maintain some areas at a humidity and temperature especially suited for goods that are known to be vulnerable.

Every warehouseman has a *lien*, a right on goods deposited with him for storage. A lien is basically a charge or claim on some property for the satisfaction of a debt. This means that if his storage charges or other bills are not met, he has the right to hold and, if need be, eventually sell the stored items.

His lawful charges can include any money he has advanced, interest, insurance, transportation, labor, weighing, crating, and the cost of any advertisements announcing the forthcoming sale of the goods.

Apart from his normal civil right to sue for payments owing to him lawfully, a warehouseman may sell at public auction any goods upon which he has a lien. At any time before the goods are sold, any person claiming an interest in the goods may pay the warehouseman the amount necessary to satisfy the lien.

If you should happen to lose your warehouse receipt, you can apply to the courts for an order giving you possession of you property. The judge would require satisfactory proof of the loss (or accidental destruction) of the receipt, and would probably require you to post a bond to guarantee the warehouseman against any further liability, cost or expense.

Warehouse receipts, like pawnbrokers' tickets, can be bought and sold. The bailor who originally put the goods into storage can assign his receipt to another person by name and that person can then claim the stored goods.

If a carrier, through no fault of his own, is unable to deliver your goods, he is within his rights to have them stored at reasonable rates either in his company's own warehouse or, after sending you written notice, in someone else's warehouse—in both cases, at your expense.

16/The Fun Machines

Owning a boat 689

Guides to navigation 692

Private planes 696

The "house on wheels"

THE "HOUSE ON WHEELS" is almost as old as history. Modern accommodation—whether self-propelled or towed—descends from the caravans mentioned many times in the Bible. (The British still use the term "caravan" for what we call a house trailer.)

In Canada, holiday vehicles include motor homes (as opposed to mobile homes), camper pickups, travel trailers and tent trailers. All are called recreational vehicles or RVs by the Canadian Recreational Vehicle Association. To the insurance industry, however, recreational vehicles are "motorized vehicles used for recreation" but not classed as motor vehicles. It's a difference to keep in mind when talking insurance.

Motor homes

A motor home, according to the insurance industry and most provincial licensing authorities, is a large, self-contained, self-propelled motor vehicle used for luxury camping. A mobile home is a large trailer which can become a semipermanent house. A house trailer is a smaller unit towed by another vehicle and most often used on trips.

Motor homes, despite their often massive size and weight, are treated like all other passenger vehicles in most regulations. Registration fees are usually based on weight or wheelbase, and no special driver's license is required. Some provinces set limits on weight and size. Depending on parking regulations, you can park a motor home on the street overnight and sleep in it.

A camper pickup is a modest version of the motor home—a self-contained living unit that fastens to the box of a pickup truck. After your holiday the truck reverts to its normal role. No special license is required.

Trailers

The many types of trailers for camping and hauling include enclosed and tandem-axle models. The most common use is for pulling boats; other special trailers carry horses, cars and snowmobiles.

It is dangerous to try to pull too big or too heavy a trailer with too small a vehicle. Your vehicle's maker should be able to tell you how much it can pull safely. Ontario sets a basic length limit of 21 metres for combinations, such as an auto plus trailer. Most car makers offer special equipment which makes a vehicle better suited to pulling. The equipment is best installed at the factory.

About 10–15 percent of a trailer's weight should rest on the hitch. However, it should not pull down the rear of your car. Unbalanced loading will make a trailer unstable and cause undue wear of tires and other parts.

Hitching up

All trailers must be registered and must display license plates. In most provinces trailers must have reflectors and taillights, and often stoplights and turn signals as well. A separate braking system is usually mandatory for trailers over a certain weight. Most provinces require two hitching systems, usually a ball-and-socket arrangement and a chain; if one fails the other must hold. You may need special mirrors on the towing vehicle.

You should not pull a trailer without checking your insurance. Your policy may have to be altered and there may be an additional premium. Most provinces forbid riding in any type of trailer while it is being towed. It is an offense to pull more than one trailer at a time.

When renting a trailer make sure that the dealer has taken care of all safety and licensing regulations and that you will be fully insured.

When you're towing

If you've never towed a trailer, demand a demonstration; then practice in a quiet area before entering heavy traffic.

Always remember that the car-trailer combination is longer and heavier than what you're used to. With it you need more time both to build up speed and to slow down or stop. When turning you must swing wider, always signaling well in advance and watching other vehicles carefully. Don't swerve suddenly or the trailer may sway out of control.

When you have to back up remember that you must turn the steering wheel left to go right, and right to go left. Some drivers turn a little then straighten out repeatedly as they move. Don't turn the wheel too far or hold it turned too long; the trailer may jackknife.

Station wagons

The station wagon, with its big capacity and space for sleeping bags, can make a holiday "house on wheels." Children love to ride in the deck area where they have room to spread out and play. For the protection of the children, however, check the provincial regulations relating to seat belts and car seats. Safety counselors warn that in a crash anything loose in a vehicle continues to travel at the speed the vehicle was going. Don't think you would be able to catch a baby in a 100 km/h frontal collision. A 14-kilogram infant hurtles forward with an effective weight of almost one tonne.

A wooden playpen can still be hazardous even if it is anchored and the posts and railings are heavily padded: nylon rope nets, anchored in place, provide some security, but seat belts are best.

Never leave children in the back of a wagon if the tailgate window is open. Your exhaust, containing deadly, odorless carbon monoxide, can enter when you lift your foot from the accelerator. Infants in bassinettes have died from carbon monoxide poisoning while the parents in the front seat were unaware of any danger.

Beware of fire

Camper bodies are built of aluminum or heavy plastic, and makers limit the use of flammable material inside. However, there is a serious smoke hazard during a fire among furnishings or clothing. A fire can quickly become fatal in a fully occupied vehicle. Sensible trailer families carry small, easy-to-operate fire extinguishers, some prohibit smoking indoors.

Taking delivery of your RV

IF YOU BUY a holiday vehicle it should be conditioned and serviced by the dealer before delivery. Check the papers. Where applicable, the dealer should:

- Check doors and locks,
- check moldings and caulking,
- check that windows are watertight,
- test electrical fixtures and outlets,
- check the water system,
- check the sewage system,
- check the gas system,
- check and properly adjust the stove, refrigerator, oven, water heater, heating system and gas lamp,
- check the running gear, brakes, wheel bearings, wheel lugs and tire pressure,
- touch up scuffs and scratches,
- clean the interior and exterior,
- explain how all parts and accessories work.

You may need new fender-mounted rear-vision mirrors to see traffic on both sides of your trailer. Mirrors should be as near the driver as possible.

Your merry snowmobile

CANADA INVENTED THE SNOWMOBILE and as the lively little machine roared to popularity, drivers ventured out onto the thin ice of strange lakes and rivers, down highways and along railway tracks. There were drownings, there were collisions with motor vehicles and trains, and the snowmobile's engine roar brought charges of noise pollution.

Ontario's Motorized Snow Vehicles Act, passed in 1968 and later revised, the first comprehensive snowmobile legislation, was followed by similar legislation elsewhere. Quebec's Regulation 7 covered all aspects of snowmobiling including the operation of clubs. Lawmakers had to recognize that although the snowmobile may be a fun machine in southern Canada, it is a utility vehicle in the North.

A snowmobile is called a recreational vehicle by the insurance industry, although the same term is used by the camper and trailer industry to refer to its products.

Regulations

Snowmobiles, usually called MSVs, must be registered with a provincial or territorial licensing authority. License plates or painted numbers must be kept visible. In some provinces, for any reasonable cause, a registration permit can be suspended by the authorities.

In most provinces a person must be 18 years old, or 16 with the permission of a parent or guardian, to register a snowmobile. A special driver's license is required, unless the machine remains on the owner's property.

Trail permits are required in some provinces. Contact your snowmobile club or association for more details.

Many provinces bar snowmobiles from the roadways or shoulders of highways, except to cross, unless the road is closed to ordinary traffic for the winter or because of a storm. Before crossing a highway on a snowmobile you must stop and yield the right-of-way to all traffic. You must cross at approximately 90 degrees to the direction of the roadway. Snowmobiles are barred from all major highways.

Liability insurance is compulsory in some provinces.

Criminal Code offenses

Driving offenses covered in the Criminal Code apply to snowmobiles. You can be charged with impaired driving, dangerous driving, failing to remain at the scene of an accident, or criminal negligence. You can be ordered to take a breathalyzer test on suspicion of impaired driving.

Federal standards

The Canada Motor Vehicle Safety Regulations include these requirements for the MSV: a white headlight, a red taillight and a red stop light; reflectors on the rear and sides; handgrips for passengers; shielding over the transmission and fan; controls to stop the engine if the driver's hand is moved from the steering position; brakes that will stop the snowmobile in 12 metres at 30 km/h, and will lock the tracks.

If an accident occurs

If you are involved in a snowmobile accident the procedure is generally the same as it is after a traffic accident.

If the accident results in property damage apparently over $100, or any bodily injury, the driver must: remain at the scene, help the injured, warn approaching drivers, and notify police. This information must be given to police and to anybody sustaining loss or injury: name and address of the driver, name and address of the registered owner of the MSV, name of his or her insurance company, and the registration number of the vehicle.

On private property
Just as farmers once resented the intrusion of the horseless carriage, many landowners today resent the MSV.

You must not drive a snowmobile on private property without the landowner's permission; if you find yourself on private property marked or unmarked, you must leave when asked to do so. In some provinces, trespassing with your MSV can bring you a fine of up to $500.

It is illegal, however, for a landowner to turn a fierce dog on an intruder, or to place traps, hidden wires or other hazards where a snowmobile driver might run into them. Many country landowners are, of course, MSV enthusiasts themselves and respond generously to polite requests from obviously reasonable people.

In public parks
Snowmobile trails are open in many provincial and national parks, adding up to hundreds of kilometres of beautiful riding. Drivers are asked to keep to the trails to avoid damaging trees or shrubs covered with snow. Drivers are also asked to show consideration for wildlife. Some drivers have chased wild animals until they dropped dead of exhaustion.

All-terrain vehicles
Canadians have invented various specialized vehicles, some amphibious, for traveling over muskeg, swamp, broken country, snow and ice. Many have extra-fat balloon tires such as those found on the dune buggy—another specialized vehicle built on a small-car chassis to run on sand dunes. Although Canada has relatively few dune areas, the buggies are popular with young people.

All these vehicles must conform to the standards and laws governing ordinary motor vehicles if driven along the verges of approved highways. All MSV drivers and passengers must wear the government approved helmet.

Snowmobiler's Code of Ethics

SNOWMOBILE clubs and manufacturers are acutely aware of their public relations problems. They publicize the Snowmobiler's Code of Ethics and encourage compliance with it. Snowmobilers are urged to join a club and learn the proper use of their machines. The code reads:

I will be a good sportsman. I recognize that people judge all snowmobile owners by my actions. I will use my influence with others to promote sportsmanlike conduct.

I will not litter trails or camping areas. I will not pollute streams or lakes.

I will not damage living trees, shrubs, or other natural features.

I will respect other people's property and rights.

I will lend a helping hand when I see someone in distress.

I will make myself and my vehicle available to assist search and rescue parties.

I will not interfere with or harass hikers, skiers, snowshoers, ice fishermen or other winter sportsmen. I will respect their rights to enjoy our recreational facilities.

I will know and obey all federal, provincial and local rules regulating the operation of snowmobiles in areas where I use my vehicle.

I will not harass wildlife and will avoid areas posted for the protection or feeding of wildlife.

I will come to a complete stop before crossing any street or highway.

I will not jump a snowbank without first finding out what's on the other side.

I will remain on snowmobile trails and obey all private property signs.

The frightened passenger

FACTS

On an evening's group snowmobile jaunt, John White was riding as a passenger astride the backseat of a machine driven by William Black. The weather was clear and cold. About half an hour past midnight on the night in question, the party of four on three snowmobiles was proceeding in single file on a private logging road through the bush. The machine on which White was a passenger was in the lead, followed by a snowmobile driven by Thomas Green. The road was approximately five metres wide with snowbanks on each side and ruts in the center which were made by the wheels of trucks.

Because of the bumpiness of the road—and possibly because of the speed at which they were traveling—White felt insecure on the seat and became frightened, but he did not indicate his fears to the driver, Black. While going around a curve, White thought that the machine was going to tip and, to protect himself from the expected fall, he put up his hands, letting go of the handle grips. Inadvertently, he lost his balance and fell off the machine. Immediately after falling, White was struck by the snowmobile driven by Green following behind. White sued for damages against both Black and Green.

ARGUMENT

For the plaintiff, it was argued that both Black and Green were negligent. It was alleged that Black was driving too fast and Green was following too closely behind.

For the defendant Black it was stated that people frequently fall off snowmobiles. This was, in fact, part of the very nature of the sport. The hazard of falling off into the snow and the sensation of risk were part of the thrill of the sport.

JUDGMENT

The judge stated that anyone volunteering to ride as a passenger on a snowmobile assumes that his driver will not be negligent, in the sense that he will act with the care expected from a reasonable, prudent driver. The court in this case could find no negligence on the part of Black. It was quite clear that there was nothing to indicate to Black that his passenger was in particular danger or particular apprehension of falling off. The action against Black was dismissed.

The judge found, however, that Green was driving too close to the machine in front of him, considering the condition of the road, the snowbanks which restricted the maneuverability, the ruts, and the speed at which they were traveling. He found that the defendant Green was negligent.

The judge further found that the plaintiff White was also guilty of contributory negligence in having failed to tell his own driver that he felt insecure and unsafe so that steps could have been taken that might have prevented his falling off.

The judge assessed the degrees of negligence, 75 percent against Green and 25 percent against White; accordingly, he allowed the plaintiff White to recover 75 percent of the damages he had claimed.*

*Based on an actual case (1971).

Motorcycles and bicycles

GOTTLIEB DAIMLER, a German, first attached an internal combustion engine to a two-wheeled vehicle in 1885, just 22 years after Etienne Lenoir of France operated the first internal combustion automobile. Soon after 1900, motorcycles were reliable enough for sport and then for cheap transportation. They were widely used by dispatch riders in both world wars.

Today motorcycles are used mainly by police and for sport—and it's a dangerous sport. The motorcycle's swift acceleration and maneuverability require skilled control, and its lack of protection makes it hazardous. Some authorities insist that running lights be used both by day and night to make the vehicle more noticeable on the road.

Registration and licenses

Motorcycles are classed as motor vehicles. They must be registered and display license plates. More and more provinces require motorcyclists to have special driver's licenses for which they must pass a driving test and a written examination: if you wish to drive a car and a motorcycle you have to pass tests for both.

Compulsory equipment

Most provinces set standards for motorcycle equipment, requiring adequate lighting, brakes on both wheels, and mufflers. Some bikers admire bizarre equipment and some of this is controlled; for example, handlebars must generally be no more than 38 centimetres above the highest part of the seat. Copies of the regulations are available from provincial and territorial transport licensing authorities and motoring clubs.

All provinces require that drivers and passengers wear helmets in case of collision. Helmets must bear the seal of the Canadian Standards Association or other approved certifying body. A passenger must sit astride a seat which is fastened securely behind the operator, and must be provided with separate footrests.

Scooters and trail bikes

Also classed as motor vehicles are scooters and trail bikes. Both are popular with young people—scooters for cheap, handy travel around town, trail bikes for sports riding in the country. The moped (motor-assisted bicycle), long popular in Europe, is becoming established with Canadian commuters since the rise in gasoline prices in the mid-70s. Its top legal speed is 50 km/h. Passengers are not permitted.

Parents who permit children to operate trail bikes should warn them to stay off public roads until they are old enough for motorcycle driver's licenses. Trail bikes operated on public roads must have the same safety equipment as motorcycles; they are a poor safety bet on highways—especially in winter. All these types of vehicles are banned from freeways.

Take care with bicycles

A person riding a pedal bicycle on the road has the same rights and duties as a motorist and must obey all rules of the road and traffic laws. *A cyclist should:*
—keep as far to the right as possible,
—keep at least one hand on the handlebars,
—sit only on the seat of the bicycle.
A cyclist should not:
—ride on the sidewalk,
—ride abreast of another bicycle,

—carry a passenger unless the bicycle is specially equipped,

—ride on a highway where signs forbid it, or ride on a road if a usable bicycle path is provided,

—hitch a ride on another vehicle.

Registration of bicycles is usually left to municipalities, which have become more rigorous than they were a decade ago in prosecuting cyclists who break traffic regulations. Progressive school administrations arrange for policemen or interested organizations to conduct safe-riding classes. District rallies offer skill contests and prizes.

Reducing bicycle accidents

To reduce bicycle accidents it is necessary to know how they happen. The Canadian Automobile Association, as part of its traffic fatality research program, studied accidents involving injury or death to bicyclists in more than 100 municipalities. The research showed that more than 83 percent of the victims were in the 5–19 age group.

Other findings:

—Collisions with motor vehicles accounted for more than 95 percent of the accidents;

—More than 80 percent of the accidents occurred in fine weather;

—Thursday was the most dangerous day, and between 3 and 6 P.M. the most dangerous time.

Three careless maneuvers by cyclists led to one-third of the accidents: failure to yield the right-of-way when entering a road, failure to obey traffic signs, and making improper left turns. More than one-third of the accidents occurred when motorists failed to leave enough room when overtaking or passing cyclists.

Gasoline economy has started a Canadian bike boom and sales of adult bicycles are now nearly one million each year. At least 12 million Canadians own adult bicycles.

Only study of the rules of the road and the development of "traffic sense" can avoid increased fatal bicycle accidents.

Guard your machine

Unlocked motorcycles and bicycles are easily stolen and, once stolen, hard to trace. Even municipalities that register bicycles have no common index system. A machine can be stolen in one town and registered the next day in another town with little chance of detection.

When you are a pedestrian

WHEN YOU PARK your car or motorbike, you are, like other pedestrians, vulnerable to speeding vehicles. But you can protect yourself by walking safely: since 1960 pedestrian deaths in Canada have decreased by 33 percent while all other traffic deaths have increased by 27 percent. After extensive study of accidents, the Canadian Automobile Association offers these rules for pedestrians:

• Look carefully in all directions before crossing a road; continue to take short, quick glances as you cross.

• Never step into a road from between parked cars.

• Cross only at intersections, preferably on a green light or a "walk" signal.

• After getting off a bus, wait until it has gone before attempting to cross the road unless you are protected by a green traffic signal or a police officer.

Traffic accidents involving pedestrians are usually more serious in the country than in heavily populated areas.

If you are a rural pedestrian the C.A.A. advises you to walk on the left, facing oncoming traffic, unless footpaths are provided. Make sure you know the speed of an oncoming car before you cross a highway. Wear light-colored clothing at night and carry a flashlight. Step off the road if cars are going to pass each other near you: the drivers may be momentarily blinded by headlight glare and not see you.

Owning a boat

ALL PLEASURE BOATS in Canadian waters are subject to the Small Vessels Regulations of the Canada Shipping Act. There are special rules for the Great Lakes, and the International Regulations for Preventing Collisions at Sea must be observed where applicable.

Other regulations cover noise from outboard engines, danger to swimmers, water-skiing without due care, and the erosion of banks in narrow waterways by the wash from passing boats. They also permit the imposition of speed limits or the prohibition of boats from some waters. To protect the environment, certain rivers and bays are closed to all boats. Individuals, municipal governments and private or public bodies can apply to provincial governments to have these regulations extended to various waters.

Before you buy
Buying a boat is usually trickier than buying a car because the average buyer is unfamiliar with boats.

Most reputable boat builders and dealers offer warranties on new boats and sometimes used ones. In the average private sale, however, you get the craft "as is." Consumer and Corporate Affairs Canada suggests that you get an expert's opinion on a used boat or engine. Insist on a trial run, preferably when the water is rough enough to provide a real test.

Small Vessels Regulations
When a landlubber finally gets a pleasure boat he may launch himself on a sea of troubles. The Small Vessels Regulations can guide him into calmer waters. Among other things the regulations deal with licensing, safety and lifesaving equipment, horsepower and load capacities, fire protection, lights, for signaling and maneuvering, steering rules, and how to measure register tonnage. (Register tonnage is a vessel's internal carrying capacity.)

You can buy a copy of the Small Vessels Regulations from bookstores that carry

Maximum capacity plates for small craft.

Applications for these plates are obtainable from any customs house or from the Department of Transport, Ottawa. Fill in all particulars, including the measurements asked for, and send the form, in the envelope provided, to Ottawa, with a money order for $1 payable to the Receiver General for Canada. A plate will be sent to you.

government publications. You can also order it from: *Canadian Government Publishing Centre, Supply and Services Canada, Ottawa   K1A 0S9*

The *Safe Boating Guide*, published yearly by the federal Department of Transport, summarizes information in the Small Vessels Regulations, adds boating tips and data on hovercraft, and illustrates navigation markers and correct lighting. It is available free from: *Department of Transport, Public Affairs Branch, Tower C, Place de Ville, Ottawa K1A 0N7* or from any customs house, Department of Transport office, marina and boating association.

Licensing and registration

Whether a boat is licensed or registered often depends on its size. Every pleasure craft up to 20 register tons with an engine of 7.5 kW or more must be licensed. All larger vessels must be registered. A license is obtainable free from the nearest office of Revenue Canada, Customs and Excise. It is mainly for identification, like a motor vehicle's license plate. Registration (which involves a fee) establishes a vessel's nationality.

Power and loading limits

Putting too big an engine on too small a boat can make the craft unsafe. For fishing in quiet waters a 6- or 7.5-kW outboard is probably adequate on a 5.5-metre boat. On a big lake, or if you have far to go, you may need a 19- or 30-kW engine. To water-ski, even with a child, you need at least a 15-kW engine. A 2-kW engine will push a canoe along satisfactorily, but remember that operating a canoe under power is a job for the experienced.

Dealers will recommend a safe engine for your boat.

Every pleasure boat up to 5 metres long with an engine of 7.5 kW or more must carry a silver and blue plate issued by the Department of Transport stating the maximum recommended engine power and load. If the plate isn't attached by the manufacturer you can apply for one through any customs house or the Department of Transport in Ottawa.

Loading limits depend on the boat, distribution of passengers, equipment carried and weather.

The federal government issues this table as a rough guide:

Length of Boat	Number of Persons	Maximum Weight Load
3 m	2	185 kg
3.7 m	3	260 kg
4 m	4	335 kg
5 m	5	440 kg

Lifesaving equipment

Compulsory lifesaving equipment for most boats includes at least one approved life jacket, one flotation device or lifesaving cushion per person, plus paddles or oars, and a bailer or manual pump. Big vessels require fire extinguishers, anchors, lights and distress signals.

Life jackets must have been approved by Transport Canada. It's a good idea to test them yourself. Wade into chest-deep water, then bend your knees; the jacket should support you. If tied correctly it will tend to keep your mouth and nose above water.

When children develop confidence in a jacket they will not fight to "climb out" of the water in an emergency—an act which tends to nullify the jacket's buoyancy. Children can drown even wearing a jacket. Mark all life jackets with both "dayglow" and "retro-reflective" tape.

Kapok jackets should be replaced if they become torn, if water has soaked the kapok or if the fibers have become matted. Unicellular-foam jackets are more durable but careless treatment, overexposure to sunlight and heat shorten their life.

If you have to swim with a life jacket use a side stroke, or backstroke.

Fire prevention

Every vessel except a canoe, rowboat or outboard up to 5.5 metres, must carry one or more Class BI or BII fire extinguishers, depending on the length of the vessel.

Inboard engines in pleasure craft must have a pan or other device to keep gasoline from dripping into the bilges. Engines which are below deck or enclosed must have flame arresters, and the enclosed space around an engine must be ventilated. Gas tanks and lines must be installed and maintained to prevent leaks or spills. A funnel must be used during filling and passengers must be ashore.

Any square flag and ball combination will serve as a distress signal. Wave a flashlight in a circle at night.

Searchlights

It is unlawful to direct a searchlight or spotlight on another boat so as to dazzle the operator. Searchlights should be used to spot a buoy or mooring, to assist in docking, or to identify an object in the water. Full night vision takes about 20 minutes to develop: the wheelhouse is kept dark, instruments are illuminated with dim red light, and running lights are arranged so they don't shine in the eyes or illuminate the forward deck.

Insurance

A standard homeowner's policy with a liability provision usually covers the operation of boats up to eight metres long, those with engines up to 12 kW, and boats with inboard-outboard engines up to 38 kW. Other boats must have specific liability insurance. Most policies give limited coverage for damage (up to about $500). If damage to the boat is not mentioned in an existing policy, have it insured specifically. Check with your insurance agent.

DOs and DON'Ts for safe boating

YOUR PLEASURE boat could cost you heartache and financial hardship if used carelessly or without due regard for the rights of others. The Criminal Code provides for fines, or even imprisonment for such offenses. The federal Department of Transport suggests that operators be guided by this list of DOs and DON'Ts:

Do

Learn the "rules of the road" for boating and practice them.

Keep bilges free from gasoline, oil, etc., and properly ventilated.

Check battery and its ventilation.

Respect your boat and know its limitations.

Carry proper fire-extinguishing and life-saving equipment.

Carry red flares in a watertight container when operating at night.

Carry an anchor and a good length of sound cable, rope or chain.

Join a yacht or boat club if possible, and know the regulations.

Assist any boat in distress.

Give fishermen, sailboats, rowboats and canoes a wide berth.

Slow down when making sharp turns or when passing dredges or waters where divers may be working.

Head for the closest safe anchorage or landing when a storm threatens; avoid the temptation to "buck it."

Don't

Mix liquor and boating.

Use a leaky or poorly built boat.

Carry outdated charts.

Cruise fast enough to create a dangerous swell when near other boats.

Leave a steering wheel or tiller unattended especially when under way in harbors or narrow channels.

Blow your horn or use your spotlight unnecessarily.

Stand or change seats in a small boat, particularly when the boat is full.

Operate near swimmers.

Wait until last minute to signify your intentions of obeying the Rules of the Road.

Hold impromptu races with other craft, since smaller boats are endangered by the wash.

Attempt to swim ashore if your boat is swamped.

Overload your boat.

Throw your garbage overboard.

Be a show-off.

Guides to navigation

Rules afloat

Canal regulations

Anchoring

Offenses afloat

Riding on air

In serious trouble

WATERWAYS have traffic rules just as roads do and failure to observe the rules causes accidents. There are universally recognized signals for passing, for example, and requirements for lights at night. In general, power boats must keep out of the way of sailboats, rowboats and canoes, although every operator must maintain a proper lookout and take every precaution required by due care. An exception to the "power gives way to sail" tradition occurs when an unpowered boat is overtaking a motorboat. Under these circumstances, right-of-way always belongs to the craft being overtaken.

Rules afloat
Check the weather before casting off on anything more than the briefest trip. If the sky is threatening, don't go.

If you are caught in bad weather keep your bow headed at an angle into the waves; make sure everyone has a life jacket on and is sitting still. Stay near shore.

The federal weather office provides regional marine weather reports several times daily. They are supplemented by district and local radio forecasts.

Keep to your right (*starboard*) in narrow channels and when approaching another vessel. Give way to any craft approaching in your "danger zone"—an arc on your right-hand side from dead ahead to an angle of 112.5 degrees.

Vessels leaving docks or landing stages have no right-of-way until they are clear of traffic in nearby waterways.

Fishing boats have the right-of-way when being used for fishing, but their operators may not fish in traffic channels or obstruct normal navigation.

Get reliable charts
The federal Department of Fisheries and Oceans publishes charts, sailing directions and tide tables for all navigable waters of Canada. Lists of available charts are free on request. Order these from: *Hydrographic Chart Distribution Office, Department of Fisheries and Oceans, 1675 Russel Road, P.O. Box 8080, Ottawa K1G 3H6*

Canal regulations
Any vessel licensed or registered under the Canada Shipping Act can use these canals: Canso and St. Peters in Nova Scotia; Saint-Ours, Chambly, Sainte-Anne-de-Bellevue and Carillon in Quebec; Rideau, Trent and Murray in Ontario.

Craft of less than six metres are not permitted to use the St. Lawrence locks.

The navigation seasons vary from one federal canal to another. In general, the canals are open from mid-May to mid-October. Locks schedules are usually from 8:30 A.M. to 8:30 P.M. in the summer, and from 8:30 A.M. to 4:30 P.M. in the spring and the autumn. The St. Lawrence locks between Montreal and Toronto charge pleasure craft $5 each.

All traveled waterways are marked with buoys—the sailor's road signs. The complete system of buoys is described in *Canadian Aids to Navigation System* available from: *Aids and Waterways, Canadian Coast Guard, Tower A, Place de Ville, Ottawa K1A 0N7*

Anchoring
Any Canadian may take a boat on any navigable body of water but, in most provinces, an owner whose land touches the water (a *riparian* owner) has certain

rights over the shoreline. (*See* Chapter 4, "Closing the deal.") To anchor without permission at a private shore can be the same as trespassing. You may anchor anywhere in an emergency—to make repairs, for example, or to ride out bad weather—but normally you must embark and disembark from your own dock, a public dock or a place where a public road gives access to the water's edge.

Offenses afloat

It is an offense to operate a boat or hovercraft or to use water skis or a surfboard in a manner dangerous to navigation, life or limb. Specifically forbidden are: operating a vessel while impaired, towing a water-skier after dark or without another person watching, and failing to stop after an accident.

Charges can be laid against a reckless operator by "laying an information"—making a sworn statement before a magistrate (judge) or a justice of the peace.

Pump-out stations

Most provinces prohibit pleasure boats from discharging sewage and garbage into the water. All vessels with toilets must have holding tanks that can be pumped out at shore facilities, usually at marinas or boat clubs. Boats are subject to random inspection; an approval sticker is issued after a satisfactory check.

Riding on air

Small hovercraft (ACVs—air-cushion vehicles) used as pleasure boats over land or water are subject to the usual Collision Regulations ("rules of the road"), but all boat operators are warned that ACVs do not maneuver as do conventional boats.

Below the "hump speed" at which it rises out of the water (about 7 knots for the average two-seater) the ACV operates like a boat, but it creates a big wash and can be difficult to handle. Above its hump speed, the ACV is susceptible to winds; the direction it's pointing may not be the direction it's traveling. Transport Canada advises operators to watch wind direction and velocity closely, and to cruise above the hump speed near boats and swimmers to reduce wash and provide controllability—and to stay below 20 knots within 45 metres of shore.

In serious trouble

The Coast Guard and the Department of National Defence maintain search and rescue centers at Halifax, Nova Scotia; Trenton, Ontario; and Victoria, British Columbia. The Coast Guard also operates two rescue sub-centers in St. John's, Newfoundland; and Quebec City.

The Department of Transport recommends six ways in which pleasure boat operators can help search-and-rescue work and reduce false alarms.

Waterway whistles

THE FOLLOWING whistle codes are recognized by the federal Department of Transport:

On the Great Lakes:

ONE BLAST—"Altering course to starboard."

TWO BLASTS—"Altering course to port."

FIVE OR MORE BLASTS—"Signal not understood" or "Emergency or danger signal."

Every power-driven vessel receiving one of these signals from another power vessel must promptly respond to the signal with the same signal, or sound the danger signal.

On waters other than the Great Lakes:

ONE BLAST—"Altering course to starboard."

TWO BLASTS—"Altering course to port."

THREE BLASTS—"My engines are going astern."

FIVE OR MORE BLASTS—"Signal not understood" or "Emergency or danger signal."

Exemption: a vessel not more than 8 metres long is not required to sound the maneuvering signals, but if it does not do so, it must be shifted in such a way as to prevent collision or misunderstanding.

Aids to navigation

In 1983, the Canadian Coast Guard introduced a new buoyage system for Canadian waters. The principal features and uses of Lateral, Bifurcation, Fairway and two types of Special buoys are illustrated below. Those which should be on the left side when proceeding upstream are on the left side of the page; those which should be on the right are on the right side of the page. Other navigation aids include lighthouses, fog signals, and radio beacons. Proceeding upstream means traveling into a harbor, up a river, to a headwater, or with the flood tide; arbitrarily, it also means traveling north off the Pacific coast and south off the Atlantic coast. Further information about navigation aids is contained in *Canadian Aids to Navigation System,* a publication available from all Canadian Coast Guard offices.

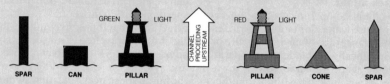

Lateral buoys

Port hand buoys are green and flat-topped, with green lights or reflective material and odd numbers if any.

Starboard hand buoys are red and pointed, with red lights or reflective material and even numbers if any.

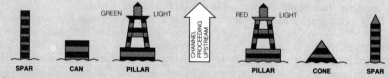

Bifurcation buoys

Bifurcation buoys where the preferred channel is on the right are green and red horizontally striped with green on top.

Bifurcation buoys where the preferred channel is on the left are red and green horizontally striped with red on top.

Fairway buoys

Fairway buoys are red and white vertically striped with white lights or reflective material.

Vessels can pass on either side of this type of buoy.

Special buoys

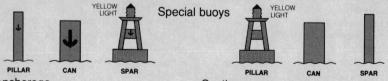

Anchorage

Anchorage buoys are used to mark the perimeter of designated anchorage areas. Before anchoring in these areas, the boat operator should consult the navigation charts for such details as water depths.

Cautionary

Cautionary buoys are used to mark such dangers as underwater pipelines, as well as areas where no through channel exists. Both anchorage and cautionary buoys are yellow. Anchorage buoys have black markings.

1. A boat club should appoint a safety officer for the day or week; all arrivals and departures should be reported to this individual.

2. If you plan to go on a cruise, give your safety officer an itinerary with estimated times of departure and arrival.

3. If you do not belong to a club give your itinerary to a friend or relative; leave arrangements for him to contact one of the search-and-rescue centers if you haven't reported in by a certain time.

4. If you change plans inform your club or the person who has your itinerary.

5. Carry up-to-date charts and an accurate compass at all times.

6. Carry the international distress signal. This is a square flag, or something resembling one, and a ball or ball-shaped object. Flag and ball are hoisted together.

A two-way radiotelephone (often called a ship-to-shore radio) will reach help in an emergency. The Department of Transport has stations on the coasts and the Great Lakes which monitor the international distress and calling frequencies of 2182 kHz and 156.8 MHz during the navigation season.

Some steering and sailing rules

In a narrow channel a power-driven vessel of less than 20 metres or a sailing vessel must not hamper the safe passage of a vessel which can navigate only within such a channel.

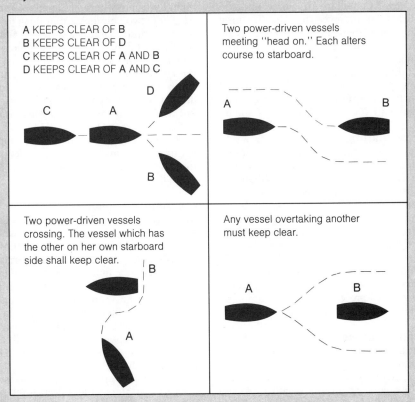

A KEEPS CLEAR OF B
B KEEPS CLEAR OF D
C KEEPS CLEAR OF A AND B
D KEEPS CLEAR OF A AND C

Two power-driven vessels meeting "head on." Each alters course to starboard.

Two power-driven vessels crossing. The vessel which has the other on her own starboard side shall keep clear.

Any vessel overtaking another must keep clear.

Private planes

Air regulations and orders

Weather forecasts

Charts available

Customs clearance

Protection of wildlife

Rescue services

FLYING CLUBS started in Montreal, Toronto and Winnipeg in the mid-1920s when the Department of National Defense offered two light aircraft to any nonprofit group that would train pilots. A bonus of $100 was offered for every flier who qualified; within a year, membership in the clubs soared to 5,000.

During World War II civilian clubs played a major role in training pilots for the Royal Canadian Air Force and the British Commonwealth Air Training Plan. Today there are 48 private flying clubs, affiliated with the Royal Canadian Flying Clubs Association.

Gliding—properly called soaring—is also popular. There are 46 clubs affiliated with the Soaring Association of Canada and about 1,700 licensed pilots in Canada.

Air regulations and orders

All pleasure fliers in Canada must comply with the *Air Regulations* and *Air Navigation Orders* issued by the Canadian Air Transportation Administration of the Department of Transport. These publications are available from the department or from: *Canadian Government Publishing Centre, Supply and Services Canada, Ottawa   K1A 0S9*

Pilots are expected to check the current *Notices to Airmen* for the latest revisions. The *Notices* are available free at major airports and at flight services stations.

Weather forecasts

Information on weather services of importance to airmen is contained in a pamphlet, *Aviation Weather Services*. Copies are available at airport weather offices, regional offices of the Atmospheric Environment Service of Environment Canada, or from: *Atmospheric Environment Service, 4905 Dufferin Street, Downsview, Ont.   M3H 5T4*

Across the country, urgent warnings of hazardous weather conditions are broadcast for airplanes in flight.

Charts available

Navigation information available for pilots includes charts for visual or instrument flying anywhere in Canada; *Canada Air Pilot* (two volumes: "Winnipeg to the Atlantic" and "Winnipeg to the Pacific"); the Visual Flight Rules chart supplement and northern supplement which list all known airports and airfields in Canada south and north of 60 degrees; and the annual *Water Aerodrome Supplement*. All are available from: *Canada Map Office, 615 Booth Street, Ottawa   K1A 0E9*

The flying charts and the VFR supplements are also available from bookstores that carry government publications, and some flying clubs.

Customs clearance

Anybody flying a private plane into Canada should choose a port of entry which has customs clearance and must notify customs at the intended airport of arrival. The notice—by mail, telephone or telegraph—must give the expected landing time and the number of passengers aboard. If the flier makes a forced landing, or is diverted to another airport, he or she must report as soon as possible to the nearest collector of customs, or to the Royal Canadian Mounted Police.

Customs clearance is free for pleasure aircraft operators unless a customs officer must make a special trip to the airport.

Protection of wildlife

All pilots flying in Canada—especially in the Prairies—are warned to comply with game laws in areas that provide migratory-bird havens. Planes landing on lakes where birds feed, or flying low over nesting areas, can cause serious disturbances, particularly to geese. Penalties can include confiscation of the aircraft.

Rescue services

The Search and Rescue Service of the Canadian Forces is on call 24 hours a day to aid disabled planes. For safety, pilots must file flight plans for trips 40 kilometres beyond the departure point. Plans can be filed with any air-traffic-control unit through a flight services station or an airport manager's office.

Maps for the air tourist

The Canadian Air Transportation Administration of the federal Department of Transport provides information for the air tourist and the private pilot. Air-facilities maps are published by aviation councils in British Columbia and Alberta, and by the surveys and mapping agency of Saskatchewan's Supply and Services Department. A portion of the Alberta air-facilities map for daytime use is shown here with Calgary International Airport prominently displayed. The black circles mark minor airports in southwest Alberta, and the lines through the circles indicate landing patterns.

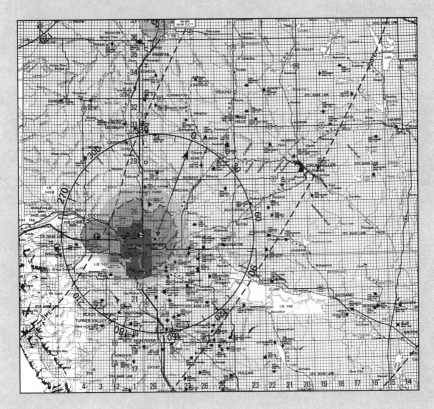

17/The Sporting Scene

The compleat angler   727

Where and what to fish   733

Playing field perils   742

The armchair sportsman   745

Protection of wildlife

Unwritten laws of hunting

The protected species

Success of the sanctuaries

Migratory Birds Convention

Canadian Wildlife Service

Cruelty to animals

ACROSS ITS 9,922,330 square kilometres, meagerly sprinkled with pockets of population, Canada offers one of the greatest game ranges in the world. To fly across our continental spread at night, seeing the small bracelets of lights tossed against the vast expanses of blackness, brings home to the traveler just how much of the country remains in a near-primeval state. Only about 11 percent of the land is permanently occupied.

Almost all of the 50 tribes of Indians, which barely left a mark on this huge land, lived by the hunt. And it was wildlife—principally the beaver with its warm and glossy coat—that first lured adventurers from Europe on to the eastern Canadian shore. The Indians brought beaver, moose meat, ducks and fish to the newcomers in quantities that made men from the narrow fields of Europe stir with the deeper hunger of avarice.

The *voyageur*, and then the pioneer, pushed into a country teeming with game. Bears, deer, cougars, lynx, wolves, wild sheep, bison, caribou, seals and musk-oxen in the higher latitudes, wildfowl that darkened the skies, salmon and sturgeon, sparkling trout and lurking pike—all these fell to the early hunter and kept larder and icehouse well stocked.

When guns were loaded at the muzzle and men hunted almost exclusively for their own table or to trade with others, little effect on the abundance of wildlife could be seen. Even as the twentieth century opened, commercial hunters, working within the area that is now the City of Toronto, could be sure of getting between 100 and 150 ducks a day. With one shot from his fowling piece, a sharpshooter by the name of William Logan once brought down 48 ducks. He got 50 cents each for mallards but could get only 30 cents for mergansers, the fish-eating duck that offers a dinner too gamy for most palates.

The first game laws

The idea of preventing uncontrolled destruction of game came slowly, and then more to farm the resource than to protect it. An isolated early game law, to protect grouse, is recorded in Nova Scotia in 1794. Ontario (then Upper Canada) made a faltering start 25 years later. But a century had to pass before worried sportsmen and naturalists prodded the legislators into significant conservation action.

The federal government passed the Northwest Game Act in 1906 and two years later established the Dominion Commission of Conservation to "advise on the conservation of natural resources, including wildlife . . . ." Its investigations and proposals prompted a growing public interest in wildlife preservation. Its direct successor is the present-day Canadian Wildlife Service, a branch of the federal Department of the Environment.

Federal-provincial collaboration

Although control over hunting, fishing and other sporting activities was placed constitutionally within provincial powers, the federal government was authorized to act in interprovincial and international areas, where wild animals and birds still give scant respect to human boundaries. The Migratory Birds Convention with the United States, signed in 1916, was an early triumph for the conservationists, protecting the great duck and geese flocks along their entire yearly journeys between the Arctic and the Gulf of Mexico.

With the federal development of national parks (Banff was the first such area, and it was set aside in 1887), protected game ranges were marked off. The provinces followed with the creation of provincial parks, which greatly increased wilderness sanctuary for animals—although some controlled hunting is permitted in these parks. There are also a few private game refuges.

Federal and provincial wildlife officials now meet annually to study new problems and coordinate regulatory action. The Royal Canadian Mounted Police plays a key role in the enforcement of some game laws, and most provinces have special staffs of wardens and field officers to enforce provincial regulations.

The angler or hunter eager to enter the Canadian hinterland with rod or gun must first familiarize himself with the latest regulations covering the area of his choice. The law as quoted in this chapter is generally similar across the country, but variations definitely exist. Depending on resource-management decisions, there are closed seasons in certain districts and open seasons in others. Normally, hunting and fishing for certain species is limited to periods between specified dates. Licenses are usually required by the visiting hunter and fisherman, and the regulations on what hunting or fishing equipment can be used, as well as limits on the amounts of game killed or fish caught, are strictly enforced.

To avoid trouble, and perhaps a ruined holiday, always obtain copies of the current regulations from provincial authorities, tourist information offices, hunting lodges or sporting goods shops. They are usually not published until shortly before the season opens. Ignorance of the law is no excuse, even in the densest bush. Fines are stiff—the maximum is $1,000—and the penalty can include the seizure of cars, boats and aircraft.

Definition of hunting

In Europe, hunting is defined as "the taking of wild animals by the aid of hounds that hunt by nose." This describes the ancient sport of hunting from horseback, begun in the Middle Ages and still popular today in the stylized form of fox hunting. Until the nineteenth century, all hunting in Europe was strictly reserved by law for the ruling classes.

In North America, the term "hunting" describes more broadly the field sport of shooting small or large game. (There is, however, some fox hunting in the European style; Canada has a few permanent packs of foxhounds.)

Canadian lawmakers have attempted, in several statutes, to define hunting more exactly. Here, for example, is the definition as given in the federal Migratory Birds Regulations:

"Hunt means chase, pursue, worry, follow after or on the trail of, wait for, or attempt in any manner to capture, kill, injure or harass a migratory bird, whether or not the migratory bird is captured, killed or injured."

Unwritten laws of hunting

In addition to the many restrictions set out in legislation, the worldwide fraternity of hunters obeys certain unwritten laws. The honor code of the hunter may be hard to define, but it can be summed up in the adage that the true sportsman does not shoot the sitting duck.

In practical terms, it is advisable to wear conspicuous clothes in the field or forest—even when it is not demanded by regulation. All too often the inexperienced and excited hunter will shoot at any movement where he is expecting game to be. The hunter must always be sure of his target.

When shooting, the wise hunter avoids targets that are set against a background of water or any flat, hard surface.

Guns should be carried with safety locks on, and hunters should never walk in single file. Care must be taken to pass, not carry, guns over obstacles such as fences. Set, or spring, guns and automatics are banned. Guns must not be fired across highways. When you have finished shooting, you should unload, if not dismantle, your gun.

Ammunition should be stored separately from the guns and beyond the reach of young children. Only shells and bullets of the proper size and weight for the weapon being used should be fired.

The universal distress signal of hunters is three rapid shots—fired in the air—answerable by a single shot.

Horseplay or practical joking have no place in the hunting field, and any hunter who drinks liquor before shooting can expect to be ostracized.

The responsible hunter or angler willingly observes regulations applying to forests and rivers, and also respects farm crops and the rights of property owners.

The protected species

In all of Canada's 29 national parks hunting is prohibited; this means total protection for all game in the parks. In the provincial parks, there are regulations regarding permitted hunting seasons, license requirements and bag, or daily, limits; these provide considerable protection for the species popular with hunters. Prince Edward Island alone, smallest of the provinces, has 38 designated parks. Quebec has set aside as parkland eight percent of the province, an area of more than 100,000 square kilometres.

The great buffalo hunt

UNTIL HUNTED to near-extinction, the North American bison—the shaggy buffalo of the western plains—was, in terms of numbers, size and distribution, the largest game species ever known to man. A bull in his prime might stand 1.8 metres tall at the shoulder and weigh up to 900 kilograms. Before the arrival of the European with his firearms, they roamed in vast herds from Mexico to the Northwest Territories, and from the Rockies to the Great Lakes.

To the western Indian, the buffalo was a general store on the hoof. The body provided fresh and dried meat and the makings of pemmican; the bone marrow was stored in bladders and the tongues smoked to eat as a delicacy. The hide, treated in various fashions, gave tepee covers, clothing, bedding, shields and ropes—even winding-sheets for the dead. The sinews made fastenings, bowstrings and webs for snowshoes. The curved horns were carved into spoons and drinking vessels, and the hair plaited into belts and ornaments. Even the dung was prized for fuel on the treeless prairie.

The first white man to describe an Indian buffalo hunt on the Canadian plains was an H.B.C. employe, Henry Kelsey, who traveled by foot during 1690–91 from Hudson Bay to within sight of the Rockies in modern Alberta. His journal states:

Ye Indians going a hunting Kill'd great store of Buffilo. Now ye manner of their hunting this Beast on ye Barren ground is when they see a great parcel of them together they surround them with men wch done they gather themselves together into a smaller Compass Keeping ye Beast still in ye middle & so shooting ym till they break out at some place or other . . . .

While the Indians killed only for tribal needs, the buffalo teemed. Numbers were estimated at 40 million beasts in the eighteenth century; herds in the 1860s were still reported stretching two miles wide and twenty-five miles long. Early trains were forced to a halt by the dense masses moving across the tracks.

In the half-century beginning around 1840, Indian, *Métis* and European hide-hunters, armed first with muskets and then with repeating rifles, began slaughtering the herds in earnest. In one day, Sioux hunters took 1,400 buffalo tongues which they traded for rotgut whisky. Between 1870 and 1875, perhaps 15 million beasts were killed on the southern plains, most of the carcasses left to rot in the summer heat.

Within another decade, the thunder of the herds was stilled forever, and Indian bands, once so superbly fit and warlike, were reduced to pathetic want and even starvation.

Strict regulations are in force on game preserves and in fish sanctuaries, ranging from total prohibition to set limits on game killed and fish caught in defined seasons. For instance, as part of its wildlife management policy, Ontario permits a limited moose hunt for residents and allocates only ten percent of the harvest to tourist outfitters.

Apart from designated locations, animals in open areas are protected by the often strict regulations issued under the broad terms of the provincial fish and game acts.

In Ontario, such game animals as the black bear, deer and moose may only be hunted under authority of a license and under detailed terms and conditions which are set out in the regulations. The limit for black bear, deer and moose is one per license. It is forbidden to hunt caribou, deer or moose when they are swimming.

There is a prohibition against hunting pheasant with a rifle; and the nest or eggs of any game bird may not be taken or destroyed, except with the written authority of the minister.

Fur-bearing animals are also protected, except that farmers may, without a license, hunt or trap fur-bearing animals on their land during the open season. (This does not apply to caribou, deer, elk, or moose.)

No live game (including wolves) may be kept in captivity longer than ten days, except under the authority of a special license. This does not apply to zoos or to animals used for scientific or educational purposes in a public institution.

Perhaps the most publicized bird protected by the Canadian Wildlife Service under the terms of the Migratory Birds Convention is the tallest North American bird, the whooping crane. Acutely endangered, the species now numbers 83 in the wild, up from only 20 in 1941. The Canadian Wildlife Service has banded together to help increase that number through strict protection and an innovative breeding program. In the spring, scientists collect one egg from each clutch of two produced by breeding whoopers in their marshy nesting grounds in Wood

Buffalo National Park in the Northwest Territories. The eggs are placed in the nests of the closely related greater sandhill cranes, which act as foster parents to the young whoopers, increasing their chances of survival. But the whooping crane's future is still uncertain.

Success of the sanctuaries

Apart from the national and provincial parks, each province also maintains wildlife sanctuaries, game preserves and fish sanctuaries to provide protection and regeneration. The Canadian Wildlife Service maintains 92 bird sanctuaries and 42 national wildlife areas. Ontario itself has more than 200 fish sanctuaries. These range in size from an entire lake to a portion of a stream.

Some sanctuaries are of private origin—the most famous being the Jack Miner bird refuge and banding station at Kingsville, Ontario. Established in 1904, it was later incorporated by parliament. Over the decades, it has banded tens of thousands of birds.

Hunting in sanctuaries is not necessarily prohibited, but you do have to get a special permit.

The sanctuaries and parks have helped notch some notable victories for the game laws—as well as for human compassion. Many threatened species have, under protection and management, fought back. They provide better hunting today than was available 50 years ago. The great auk, the passenger pigeon and the Labrador duck have vanished, but the bison (or buffalo), musk-ox, caribou, elk, polar bear and arctic fox are thriving again. Even the trumpeter swan, once endangered, is now being bred in captivity.

Moose, deer, grouse, muskrat and beaver are considered more plentiful today than in Indian times. The most recent federal statistics show a decline in the number of wild pelts, probably due to a falling demand in the fur market. However, the number of commercial pelts has increased during the same period.

Migratory Birds Convention

The Canadian Parliament passed the Migratory Birds Convention Act in 1917,

703

putting into effect the terms of the Migratory Birds Convention which had been negotiated with the United States the previous year. The provincial fish and game laws generally confirm the provisions of the convention and often include extra protection for certain birds of more local interest that were not mentioned in the federal legislation. The federal law was amended in 1970 and revised regulations are usually issued each season.

The convention protects three groups of birds: migratory game birds (like ducks, geese and pigeons); migratory insect-eating birds (like chickadees, orioles, warblers and woodpeckers); and, migratory nongame birds (like gulls, herons and terns).

It is an offense at any time of the year to hunt, capture or kill migratory insect-eating birds or migratory nongame birds. Subject to certain conditions of the license, season and zone, it is legal to hunt migratory game birds.

The hunter must get a federal game-bird permit (available at post offices for $3.50), as well as a provincial or territorial hunting permit. Special concessions exist for northern Indians and Inuit.

You are not allowed to destroy or molest nests or eggs of migratory birds, or even have them in your possession, unless you have been granted a special permit.

Migratory game birds—mainly ducks and geese—may be hunted legally only during the day from a half hour before sunrise until noon, and only during the season specified.

You may not hunt them within 400 metres of a baited area. Nor may you use live birds and recorded birdcalls as decoys. Accepted hunting methods are outlined in the regulations: except in the Northwest Territories, rifles are prohibited; the only weapons permitted are the bow and arrow or shotgun not larger than 10 gauge.

Birds cannot be hunted from aircraft, sailboats, powerboats or other motorized vehicles. However, you may use a boat for retrieving, and for hunting as long as it isn't in motion. You are allowed to hunt with only one shotgun at a time; any others must be kept unloaded and cased.

If migratory birds are causing damage to crops or property, they may be scared away with any noise-making equipment other than firearms. Firearms may be used to scare off birds, but only under the authority of a special permit issued by the chief game officer of a province. In some regions (Alberta, for example), compensation can be claimed for damage done to crops by wildlife.

A taxidermist must hold a permit to be entitled to have a migratory bird in his possession for the purpose of stuffing and mounting it. Before he can accept specimens for mounting, he must obtain the name and address of the owner as well as the date and place the bird was obtained. The taxidermist must keep exact records and allow a game officer to inspect them at any reasonable time.

Pollution is not dealt with specifically under the Migratory Birds Convention Act, although it is the subject of numerous other federal and provincial statutes. (*See* Chapter 6, "The consumer watchdogs.") The regulations under the Act, however, prohibit the deposit of oil, oil waste or any other substances harmful to migratory birds in any waters or bird-frequented areas.

Canadian Wildlife Service

The Canadian Wildlife Service administers the Migratory Birds Convention Act, the Canada Wildlife Act, and the Game Export Act. It conducts wildlife and environmental management in the Northwest Territories, Yukon and the national parks.

In the field of research, the Wildlife Service cooperates with the provinces, and also conducts its own studies. Investigations into the present state of the caribou of the barren grounds are under way. Studies are also being made in wolf-caribou relationships and on the grizzly bear, the elk and the mountain sheep. From this research, new or revised provincial hunting regulations will emerge.

The habitat management and research sciences sections of the Wildlife Service have conducted wetland inventories across Canada. In conjunction with the provinces, the Wildlife Service is developing a new program for wetlands protection and waterfowl. In cooperation with a private sporting foundation called Ducks Unlimited, marshy land is being acquired or improved to increase feeding grounds and refuge areas for waterfowl. Although some 3,000,000 ducks are shot every season in Canada, the level of harvest does not appear to have had an impact on the overall size of the duck population. Toxic pesticides and industrial wastes, however, still remain a hazard to wildlife, particularly to birds and fish.

Ornithologists are concerned with the recent phenomenon of birds endangering human life at large airports. Birds feeding on grassy areas tend to rise in alarm as planes either take off or land. Literally hundreds of birds can be sucked into the fan blades of a jet turbine, clogging the engines and causing the plane to crash. The Wildlife Service has had these areas sprayed, eliminating earthworms and insects, and killing weeds and bushes used for nesting. And garbage dumps have been relocated in some cities.

The pathology section of the Canadian Wildlife Service has pioneered some important developments in the prevention of animal disease. Bison have been vaccinated against anthrax, and particular attention has been paid to diseases attacking the sled dog in northern communities where this animal is of great importance. After studying outbreaks of hepatitis, distemper and rabies, regulations were drafted for immunization; this was an immediate success in protecting wildlife of the eastern Arctic and northern Quebec.

Cruelty to animals

Under the Criminal Code of Canada, it is a crime to deliberately cause unnecessary pain, suffering or injury to an animal or bird. If an animal is found to have been caused pain or suffering because some

The immortal birdman

ALTHOUGH HE DIED during World War II, the name of Jack Miner, Canada's famous birdman, still carries a unique magic around the world whenever conservationists gather. When he was 38, after winning a reputation as a crack game-bird hunter, he switched from destruction to protection, founding the Jack Miner Bird Sanctuary at his home in Kingsville, on the marshy northern shore of Lake Erie.

The American-born Miner had no formal education (he was still illiterate at 30) but he enjoyed a natural gift of insight about wildlife habits and management. In his first attempt at conservation in 1904, he marked seven Canada geese with wing clips and freed them. He thought he had failed because for three years no birds returned to his ponds. But the fourth season, 11 geese showed up and, in the years thereafter, they were followed by literally millions of ducks and geese.

Miner's pioneer bird-banding work, supported by private donations, traced the 9,000-kilometre yearly journey of the flocks between the sub-Arctic swamps and the Mississippi Delta, and led to the passing of the Migratory Birds Convention Act under which Canada and the United States coordinate efforts to protect feathered wildlife.

Miner was further stamped on the public mind by his habit of including short, pithy Biblical quotations on his bird tags. He began lecturing to help raise money for his sanctuary, filling auditoriums as large as New York's Carnegie Hall. He would often start his homely talks by asking the audience to join in a hymn. His "Minerisms" became widely quoted; a favorite one offered the Canada goose as a model to mankind:

They conduct themselves with dignity, never fight unless it's absolutely necessary to protect their family—and then their wrath is terrible. The gander takes only one mate in a lifetime, and I've never known one to make application for divorce.

person failed to exercise reasonable care or supervision of it, this, in the absence of contrary evidence, is considered sufficient proof that the pain or suffering was caused willfully. The punishment for a conviction in such an instance is a maximum fine of $500, six months' imprisonment, or both. If convicted a second time, an offender may be prohibited by the court from owning an animal for a period of up to two years.

In all provinces, the Canadian Society for the Prevention of Cruelty to Animals (C.S.P.C.A.) is backed up by legislation in its work. ("Animal" as used in this sense includes domestic fowl and pet birds.)

The most common cruelty is neglect of pet cats and dogs or animals usually kept in stables. The society's inspectors have authority to enter any building, on the strength of a warrant issued by a justice of the peace, to see whether there is any animal inside in distress. To get the warrant, the inspector must swear that he has reasonable grounds for believing that distress exists. If the inspector sees a suffering animal, no warrant is required.

"Distress" is generally defined in the provincial statutes as "the state of being in need of proper care, sick, in pain or suffering, or being abused, or subject to undue or unnecessary hardship, privation or neglect."

The C.S.P.C.A. inspector may order food, care and treatment for any distressed animal, and he also may order the owner to have the animal examined by a veterinarian at the owner's expense.

If the owner refuses to comply, the society may take possession of the animal and provide it with food, care or treatment. This will also be done at the expense of the owner. Should the owner refuse to pay these costs, the society has the authority to sell the animal and pay the bills from the proceeds.

The society also maintains facilities where unwanted pets will be destroyed humanely and without charge.

The regulations under the Migratory Birds Convention Act also legislate against cruelty. For instance, if you cripple or injure a migratory bird, you must immediately make all reasonable efforts to retrieve the bird and kill it.

The provincial fish and game laws contain a general prohibition against keeping wild animals in captivity, except under special regulations. In Ontario, for example, if you want to keep a wolf or other wild animal captive for more than ten days, you must obtain a special license and obey regulations concerning the physical measurements of the cage, and you are required to feed the beast every 12 hours.

Is the wolf an outlaw?

THE GRAY or timber wolf, *Canis lupus*, prowls the forests and thinly settled areas of Canada, never failing to set men's teeth on edge with his eerie, mournful howl. Outdoorsmen debate whether the healthy wolf, unprovoked, will attack man. In any case, there are no records of wolves killing humans in North America, and in areas where they are hunted or trapped, wolves are very wary of man.

Provincial, territorial, county and township governments in Canada have paid bounties to wolf killers (many municipalities and townships still do). The creatures have been shot from low-flying planes and poisoned with strychnine baits. It's certain that the wolf claims many caribou, elk, moose and deer—but all these species are also on the increase in Canada today.

The wolf has his champions, too. They point out that he plays a vital part in the cycle of life—or, if you prefer, the ecosystem. The leavings from his sometimes-excessive kills, for example, help to feed a host of lesser wildlife—such as fox, fisher and marten. The wolf packs run down the weaker and older members of game herds, thus culling the stock.

Where and what to hunt

Licenses required

Open seasons

Bag limits

Minimum age of hunters

T HE GOVERNMENTS of the provinces have control over wildlife within their borders, except for the jurisdiction of the federal government over migratory birds and over all wildlife in the national parks. The majority of our hunting regulations are therefore issued under provincial legislation.

These regulations cover the requirement of licenses and the collection of fees. They also establish compulsory safety programs. Hunting methods and permitted types of firearms are specified, and the use of aircraft, snares and traps is strictly controlled. In some areas, licensed guides must be hired.

The regulations dictate the seasons in which animals, birds or fish may be hunted, or caught, as well as the numbers of each type that may be taken per day, and per hunting or fishing trip. They also cover the conditions under which game and fish may be sold, propagated—that is, increased in number, as in fish hatcheries—or exported. Minimum age restrictions of hunters are also set out.

Since the hunting regulations are frequently changed, the prospective hunter must take steps to acquaint himself with the current law. The information given here was accurate for the season when this chapter was revised so it should be taken as a general guide only.

Licenses required

Licenses are required to hunt in Canada, with few exceptions. A provincial license is required for hunting migratory birds. (Only a federal license is needed in the territories.) Licenses for provincial residents are less expensive than those for nonresidents; if the nonresident is not a Canadian citizen, the licenses are even more expensive. Resident senior citizens get licenses free, or at nominal cost.

Indians and Inuit are allowed to hunt without a license for migratory birds, as well as certain protected species, for food and clothing. They must have a special permit, however, for hunting in migratory-bird sanctuaries. In general, there is a right reserved to them to hunt for food on unoccupied Crown land, unless the game in question has been declared to be in danger of becoming extinct.

THE NORTHWEST TERRITORIES Residents in the territories require licenses to hunt. Nonresidents also require licenses, and, if any game is killed, trophy fees must be paid before an export permit is issued. The fee for the license depends on the species—for example, $5 for each woodland caribou killed. The Northwest Territories restricts nonresident license holders to specific zones and also insists that a licensed guide accompany them. Export permits are required. Non-native residents and nonresidents require a license to hunt seals. Export permits for seals must be obtained from the federal fisheries department. Write for detailed information to: *Chief, Field Services, Department of Renewable Resources, Government of the Northwest Territories, Yellowknife, N.W.T., X1A 2L9.*

THE YUKON Hunting restrictions and licenses are similar to those in the Northwest Territories. Further information available from: *Director, Wildlife and Parks Services, Department of Renewable Resources, Government of the Yukon, Box 2703, Whitehorse, Yukon, Y1A 2C6.*

BRITISH COLUMBIA Hunters must obtain a separate "species license" for big game before they set out. B.C. residents pay on the following scale: black bear, $8; caribou, $20; cougar, $20; mountain sheep, $50; grizzly bear, $70. Nonresidents pay approximately six times as much in each category (*e.g.*, $300 for mountain sheep).

707

Residents and nonresidents require permits to export game. Further information from: *Fish and Wildlife Branch, Ministry of Environment, Parliament Buildings, Victoria, B.C., V8V 1X4.*

ALBERTA Special licenses are available to Alberta residents only for hunting nontrophy mountain sheep, Camp Wainwright deer, mountain goat, and nontrophy antelope in designated areas. A wildlife certificate and resource development stamp are also required in addition to the usual licenses. Archery enthusiasts require a bow-hunting license. The nonresident requires an export permit to take out trophy sheep, grizzly bear, cougar and other species. Write: *Fish and Wildlife Division, Department of Energy and Natural Resources, Main Floor, North Tower, Petroleum Plaza, 9945 108th Street, Edmonton, Alta., T5K 2G6.*

SASKATCHEWAN There are three classes of licenses in Saskatchewan (as in most provinces): provincial resident, Canadian

Signals of distress

BEFORE YOU SET OUT on a hunt—or on any journey—into or across the Canadian forest, or any thinly settled area, make sure that your travel plans are lodged with a government or administrative agency, or with a responsible person.

The following signals are understood internationally and, properly given, would greatly increase chances of rescue.

Smoke works anytime, but is particularly effective on a calm day. If materials are available, build three signal fires in a triangle, or in line along a stream. They can be built on a raft on a nearby lake, close enough to reach quickly and ignite, if an aircraft is heard. Build a small tepee of sticks, with shaved kindling in the center, and thatch the outside with green boughs or moss. If you are near a crashed plane, burning rubber and oil will make a thick black smoke.

At night, a strong light (a flashlight, or even candlelight) inside a tent shows up like a Japanese lantern. A single evergreen tree can be prepared as a torch, ready for instant lighting. Any mirror, or piece of polished metal, with a pinhole in the center, can be aimed to flash a signal to an aircraft from the ground.

There is a ground-to-air sign language you can use to seek help. Make each figure at least 12 metres long, using branches in the snow, peeled logs, stones, strips of sod, or parachute cloth, arranged for maximum contrast with the surroundings.

Require doctor; serious injuries	—
Require medical supplies	=
Unable to proceed	X
Require food and water	F
Require firearms and ammunition	⋙
Require map and compass	□
Require signal lamp with battery, and radio	– –
Indicate direction to proceed	K
Am proceeding in this direction	→
Will attempt takeoff	I >
Aircraft seriously damaged	L⌐
Probably safe to land here	△
Require fuel and oil	L
All well	LL
No	N
Yes	Y
Not understood	JL

resident, and nonresident. In special zones, there is a lottery among residents to determine who will receive one of the restricted number of licenses. Nonresident moose hunters receive an allotted number of licenses on a "first come, first served" basis. Contact: *Wildlife Branch, Department of Parks and Renewable Resources, 3211 Albert Street, Regina, Sask., S4S 5W6.*

MANITOBA Both residents and nonresidents must have a wildlife certificate in order to get a hunting license in Manitoba. This is not required, however, for farmers hunting game birds in season on their farms. Senior citizens resident in the province can get game-bird licenses free. For information write: *Public Information Services, Dept. of National Resources, 1495 St. James Street, Winnipeg, Manitoba R3H 0W9*

ONTARIO Residents and nonresidents require licenses to hunt deer, moose, black bear or small game. Those applying for their first license must pass a hunting examination. Nonresidents must register with a tourist outfitter to hunt moose. Export-permit fees are required for moose, deer and bear. Certain southern townships require a special license to hunt pheasants and rabbits. All hunters must be 16 or older. Write: *Wildlife Branch, Ministry of Natural Resources, Whitney Block, Queen's Park, Toronto, Ont., M7A 1W3.*

QUEBEC Residents of Quebec must have a hunter's certificate before being issued a license. Nonresidents must provide documented evidence of expertise with firearms. Licenses are issued for specific animals only; they also prohibit certain firearms. The license fee includes a compulsory premium for accident and liability insurance. Contact: *Ministère du Loisir, de la Chasse et de la Pêche, Direction des communications, C.P. 22 000, Québec, Qué., G1K 7X2.*

MARITIME PROVINCES The resident and nonresident classification of licenses also prevails in the Maritimes. Nova Scotia issues licenses for game according to open seasons. Write: *Department of Lands and Forests, P.O. Box 516, Kentville, N.S., B4N 3X3.*

PRINCE EDWARD ISLAND issues what are called shipping coupons, and no game may be taken from the province by either residents or nonresidents without one. You need a regular hunting license as well. Information from: *Fish and Wildlife Division, Department of Community and Cultural Affairs, Box 2000, Charlottetown, P.E.I., C1A 7N8.*

NEW BRUNSWICK has five types of license; each one allows a certain age group to hunt certain species. To find out more about these provisions, write: *Fish and Wildlife Branch, Dept. of Natural Resources, P.O. Box 6000, Fredericton, N.B., E3B 5H1.*

NEWFOUNDLAND License fees are required in Newfoundland for both residents and nonresidents to hunt caribou, moose, bear, ruffed and spruce grouse, ptarmigan and rabbit. Caribou and moose licenses are issued on a quota basis. Successful big-game hunters are required to turn in their license within seven days after their kill and, if unsuccessful, within seven days after the license expires. Information from: *Wildlife Division, Department of Culture, Recreation and Youth, Building 810, Pleasantville, St. John's, Nfld., A1A 1P9.*

Open seasons and bag limits

Hunting seasons and game-possession limits—that is, how many you can have in your possession in one hunting foray—vary not only from province to province but often within a province from zone to zone. Changes are made in the regulations nearly every year, based on the latest information about various species.

Game animals and wildfowl are widespread in Canada. Forested and sparsely settled areas contain moose, deer, bear and dozens of smaller animals. The western and mountain zones provide elk, antelope, bighorn and Dall's sheep, mountain goats, grizzly bears, lynx and cougars. Caribou are hunted in Newfoundland and in the territories.

Wildfowl abound, with the world's greatest flocks of migratory game birds, and several kinds of grouse and partridge.

The following is a summary of open seasons and daily bag limits of most of the

Open season and bag limits

British Columbia is divided into eight hunting regions; these are further subdivided into over 200 "management units." Seasons may apply only to certain parts within units, and not all animals are available in all regions.

Species	Open Season	Bag Limit	Possession
Mule deer	Sept. 1–Dec. 18	2	
Deer	Sept. 1–Dec. 18	2	
Moose	Aug. 15–Nov. 20	1	
Elk	Aug. 15–Nov. 15	1	
Mountain goat	Aug. 1–Nov. 30	1	
Caribou	Aug. 15–Oct. 23	1	
Mountain sheep	Aug. 1–Oct. 31	1	
Grizzly bear	Sept. 1–Nov. 20/Apr. 1–June 15	1	
Black bear	Sept. 1–Dec. 31/Apr. 1–June 30	2	
Cougar	Apr. 1–Mar. 31	2	
Wolf	Apr. 1–Mar. 31	3	
Coyote	Apr. 1–Mar. 31	no limit	
Raccoon	Apr. 1–Mar. 31	no limit	
Skunk	Apr. 1–Mar. 31	no limit	
Bobcat	Nov. 1–Mar. 31	5	
Fox	Apr. 1–Mar. 31	no limit	
Wolverine	Sept. 15–Feb. 29	1	
Lynx	Oct. 15–Feb. 29	1	
Grouse	Aug. 27–Dec. 31	10	30
Ptarmigan	Aug. 15–Feb. 29	10	30
Pheasant	Oct. 8–Nov. 15	3	9
Partridge	Sept. 10–Dec. 8	8	24
Quail	Oct. 8–Nov. 22	10	30

Migratory Game Birds

Species	Open Season	Bag Limit	Possession
Ducks	Sept. 1–Jan. 22	8	16
Geese	Sept. 1–Jan. 22	5	10
Snipe	Sept. 1–Jan. 22	10	20

Alberta is divided into eight zones for game birds and 16 zones for big game. Each zone is divided into management units with different seasons and bag limits for each sex of a species. For big game, there are additional extended seasons and closed seasons for some of the zones. Black bear, wolf and fox may be killed without a license on private land by residents who have a right of access. The same regulations apply to the porcupine, rabbit, skunk, raccoon and woodchuck.

Species	Open Season	Bag Limit	Possession
Deer	Sept. 1–Dec. 3	1	
Moose	Sept. 1–Dec. 3	1	
Elk	Sept. 1–Dec. 3	1	

ALBERTA (CONTINUED)

Species	Open Season	Bag Limit	Possession
Sheep (trophy)	Aug. 24–Oct. 29	1	
Sheep (nontrophy)	Sept. 5–Oct. 29	1	
Black bear	Sept. 1–Dec. 3	1	
Grizzly bear	Apr. 2–May 19/Sept. 14–Dec. 3	1	
Pheasants	Oct. 12–Nov. 30	3	9
Grouse	Sept. 1–Dec. 10	10	20
Ptarmigan	Sept. 1–Dec. 10	5	20

Migratory Game Birds

Species	Open Season	Bag Limit	Possession
Ducks	Sept. 1–Dec. 31	8	16
Geese	Sept. 1–Dec. 31	5	10
Snipe	Sept. 1–Dec. 31	10	20

Saskatchewan is divided into 37 game management zones each with its own season and bag limit for particular species. Sometimes special seasons for antelope, barren-ground caribou, elk and pheasant are opened for residents only. On Sundays, hunting is illegal in this province.

Species	Open Season	Bag Limit	Possession
Deer (white-tailed)	Nov. 7–Dec. 3	1 (2 in a 2-deer zone)	
Moose	Sept. 5–Dec. 3	1	
Woodland caribou	Sept. 12–Dec. 3	1	
Barren-ground caribou	Nov. 1–Feb. 25	2	
Bear	Aug. 29–Oct. 22	2	
Elk	Sept. 19–Dec.10	1	

Migratory Game Birds

Species	Open Season	Bag Limit	Possession
Ducks	Sept. 1–Dec. 10	8	16
Geese	Sept. 1–Dec. 10	5	10
Snipe and coots	Sept. 1–Dec. 10	10	20

Manitoba has 38 game-hunting areas and four migratory-bird zones. Three-quarters of the province is wooded, providing excellent cover for moose, black bear and deer.

Species	Open Season	Bag Limit	Possession
Moose	Sept. 1–Dec. 17	1	
Woodland caribou	Sept. 1–Feb. 18	1	
Elk	Aug. 22–Feb. 4	1	
Black bear	Aug. 22–Nov. 19	2	
Ruffed grouse	Sept. 1–Dec. 17	4	8
Sharp-tailed grouse	Sept. 1–Dec. 17	4	8
Partridge	Sept. 16–Nov. 12	4	8
Ptarmigan	Sept. 1–Feb. 18	10	30
Ducks	Sept. 1–Nov. 20	8	16

(CONTINUED)

711

MANITOBA (CONTINUED)

Migratory Game Birds

Geese	Sept. 1–Nov. 20	8	16
Coots	Sept. 1–Nov. 20	8	16
Snipe and rail	Sept. 1–Nov. 20	10	20
Sandhill crane	Sept. 1–Oct. 2	5	10

Ontario is divided into wildlife management units with different open seasons and hunting restrictions on big and small game. These are shown on free provincial hunting maps, along with a summary of the current year's regulations. Seasons may vary according to the residency status of the hunter.

Species	Open Season	Bag Limit	Possession
Black bear	Sept. 1–Nov.30/Apr. 15–June 15	1	
Moose	Sept. 17–Dec. 15	1	
Deer	Oct. 1–Dec. 15	1	
(bow and arrow only)	Oct. 17–Dec. 11	1	
Raccoon	Oct. 15–Dec. 31		
Fox (most of Ontario)	no closed season		
Rabbit and hare	Sept. 1–June 15	6	
Squirrel	Sept. 24–Dec. 15	5–10	
Wolf, coyote	no closed season		
Pheasants	Sept. 24–Dec. 15	3	
Partridge	Sept. 24–Dec. 15	8	16
Grouse	Sept. 11–Jan. 15	5	15

Migratory Game Birds

Ducks	Sept. 11–Dec. 18	6	12
Snipe, coots, rails	Sept. 11–Dec. 18	10	20
Geese	Sept. 11–Dec. 18	5	10
Woodcock	Sept. 11–Dec. 18	8	16

Quebec boasts about 120 million hectares of game-bearing country. This area is divided into zones, each of which is likely to have its own seasons and bag limits. Big game is abundant: in one 15-day season, 4,330 bull moose were taken, some weighing as much as 680 kilograms.

Species	Open Season	Bag Limit	Possession
Caribou	Aug. 25–Sept. 30	1	
Deer	Oct. 29–Nov. 13	1	
Moose	Sept. 10–Oct. 23	1	
Black bear	Aug. 25–Nov. 6	1	
Hare	Aug. 25–March 1		
Fox	Oct. 22–March 1		
Raccoon, Porcupine	No restrictions		
Grouse	Sept. 30–Dec. 31	5	15
Partridge	Sept. 17–Nov. 15	5	15
Ptarmigan	Sept. 17–March 1	10	30

QUEBEC (CONTINUED)

Migratory Game Birds

Ducks	Sept. 1–Dec. 26	6	12
Geese	Sept. 1–Dec. 26	5	15
Woodcock	Sept. 1–Dec. 26	8	16

New Brunswick's black bear is now so plentiful that the government has opened a season for hunting in the spring in addition to the usual autumn season; a bear license is required. Woodcocks are a great attraction near streams and swamps. The season dates for hunting deer and other game differ with each provincial zone.

Species	Open Season	Bag Limit	Possession
Deer	Oct. 24–Nov. 19	1	
Moose (residents only)	Sept. 22–Sept. 24	1	
Bear	Apr. 18–June 25 Oct. 1–Nov. 12	2 (of either sex)	
Rabbit	Oct. 1–Feb. 29	no limit	
Fox, raccoon, skunk	Oct. 1–Feb. 29	no limit	
Porcupine	Oct. 1–Feb. 29	no limit	

Migratory Game Birds

	Open Season	Bag Limit	Possession
Ducks, geese and snipe			
Zone 1	Oct. 18–Jan. 8	(ducks) 6	12
Zone 2	Oct. 1–Dec. 18	(geese) 5	10
Zone 3	Oct. 1–Dec. 18	(snipe) 10	20
Woodcock: Zone 1	Sept. 27–Nov. 20	8	16
Zone 2	Sept. 20–Nov. 20		
Zone 3	Sept. 27–Nov. 20		

Nova Scotia reports that Virginia (white-tailed) deer provide exciting hunting—about 40,000 are taken annually. Canada geese fly across Nova Scotia on their annual migratory route, and some winter over. These fowl provide excellent hunting as well. A county system of zoning is in force for some species.

Species	Open Season	Bag Limit	Possession
Deer	Oct. 28–Dec. 3	1	
Bear	Oct. 28–Dec. 3	no limit	
Beaver	Nov. 1–Jan. 15	2–20	
Mink, otter, muskrat	Nov. 1–Jan. 15	no limit	
Fox	Nov. 1–Feb. 28	no limit	
Raccoon	Nov. 1–Feb. 28	no limit	
Bobcat	Nov. 1–Feb. 28	no limit	
Pheasants and Hungarian partridge in counties of Annapolis, Kings, Hants and Lunenberg	Nov. 1–Dec. 15	2 cockbirds	
Remainder of province	Oct. 1–Dec. 15	2 cockbirds	
Ruffed grouse	Oct. 1–Dec. 15	5	10
Hungarian partridge	Oct. 1–Dec. 15	5	10

(CONTINUED)

NOVA SCOTIA (CONTINUED)

Migratory Game Birds

Ducks and geese, depending on counties	Oct. 1–Jan. 15	Ducks 6 Geese 5	12 10
Snipe	Oct. 1–Nov. 30	10	20
Woodcock	Oct. 1–Nov. 30	8	16

Prince Edward Island (only 225 kilometres long) has no big game, but upland game birds provide good sport. No Sunday hunting here.

Species	Open Season	Bag Limit	Possession
Fox	Nov. 1–Jan. 15	no limit	
Snowshoe hare	Nov. 1–Feb. 28	5	
Raccoon	Oct. 15–Jan. 15		
Ruffed grouse	Oct. 4–Dec. 11	3	6
Partridge	Oct. 11–Nov. 13	3	6

Migratory Game Birds

Ducks	Oct. 3–Dec. 10	6	12
	(not more than 4 black ducks and 1 wood duck)		
Geese	Oct. 3–Dec. 10	5	10
Snipe	Oct. 3–Dec. 10	10	20
Woodcock	Oct. 3–Dec. 10	8	16

Newfoundland and Labrador were first stocked with moose in 1904; now, hunters bag approximately 5,000 every year. Licenses for big-game hunting are still limited, however, and you must use a licensed guide. Special seasons for nonresidents apply in some zones, including on the Avalon Peninsula.

Species	Open Season	Bag Limit
Caribou (either sex)	Sept. 10–Oct. 29	1
Moose (male only)	Sept. 10–Nov. 12	1
Bear	Sept. 10–Nov. 12	1
Rabbit	Oct. 1–Dec. 31	no limit
Ptarmigan	Sept. 19–Dec. 31	50
Ruffed grouse	Sept. 19–Dec. 31	25
Spruce grouse	Sept. 19–Dec. 31	25

Migratory Game Birds

Ducks (other than eider):		
Newfoundland	Sept. 4–Dec. 18	6
Labrador	Sept. 1–Dec. 21	6
Eiders:		
Newfoundland	Nov. 22–March 10	12
Labrador	Sept. 1–March 10	15
Geese and snipe	Sept. 4–Dec. 18	5 (geese)
Newfoundland		10 (snipe)
Labrador	Sept. 1–Dec. 21	5 (geese) 10 (snipe)

The Yukon provides wilderness that will daunt even the most experienced hunter. A big-game and game-bird license costs the visiting Canadian $75 (the alien pays $150). Both barren-ground and mountain caribou can be hunted and the huge grizzly bear awaits those with nerves of steel. A grizzly trophy will cost you $500–$750.

Species	Open Season	Bag Limit
Bear	Apr. 15–June 15/Aug. 1–Oct. 31	1
Moose (antlered)	Aug. 1–Oct. 31	1
Moose (antlerless)	Sept. 10–Sept. 20	1
Caribou	Aug. 1–Oct. 31	1
Mountain goat	Aug. 1–Oct. 31	1
Mountain sheep	Aug. 1–Oct. 31	1
Spruce and ruffed grouse	Sept. 1–Nov. 30	10
Ptarmigan	Sept. 1–Jan. 31	10
Blue & sharp-tailed grouse	Sept. 1–Nov. 30	5 each

Migratory Game Birds

Species	Open Season	Bag Limit
Ducks	Sept. 1–Oct. 31	25
Geese	Sept. 1–Oct. 31	15
Rails and coots	Sept. 1–Oct. 31	25
Snipe	Sept. 1–Oct. 31	10

The Northwest Territories, for big-game hunting, are divided into 10 wildlife management units, which are further subdivided into zones. Hunting is restricted to particular species—for example, caribou and moose—in certain seasons and, in some cases, to residents only. A safari to this hunting ground requires careful planning and involves considerable expense.

Species	Open Season	Bag Limit
Musk-ox	Oct. 1–March 31	1 (male only)
Polar bear	Oct. 1–May 31	1 (adult without cubs)
Black bear	Aug. 15–June 30	1 (adult without cubs)
Grizzly bear	Aug. 15–Oct. 31	1 (adult without cubs)
Moose	Sept. 1–Jan. 31	1
Dall's sheep	July 15–Oct. 31	1 male (¾ curl or greater)
Mountain goat	July 15–Oct. 31	1
Barren-ground caribou	Aug. 15–April 30	2
Woodland caribou	July 15–Jan. 31	1
Wolf	July 15–Nov. 15	no limit

Migratory Game Birds

Species	Open Season	Bag Limit
Ducks	Sept. 1–Dec. 10	25
Geese	Sept. 1–Dec. 10	15
Rails and coots	Sept. 1–Dec. 10	25
Snipe	Sept. 1–Dec. 10	10

commonly sought game in the provinces and territories. Although accurate at the time of writing, the editors emphasize that these lists should be used only as a general rule of thumb.

Minimum age for hunters

The legal age for hunters in Canada varies slightly from province to province. The general minimum age is 16, but this can depend on the requirements of license examinations, safety training and experienced hunter accompaniment.

Licenses in New Brunswick are issued in four classes according to age and purpose. A Class 1 or Class 3 license is issued to residents or nonresidents older than 18 to hunt deer, rabbit, partridge, migratory game birds, porcupine and crow. Class 2 and Class 4 licenses covering the same species (except deer) are issued to those older than 16. To obtain a bear license, you must be at least 18. A minor's license can be issued to those aged 14 and 15 for the same species as in the Class 4 license; to be eligible for this, the applicant must have passed an approved firearms-safety course.

In Newfoundland, applicants must be 16 to qualify for a small-game license—or to carry a firearm in the woods; applicants for a big-game license must be 18.

In Quebec, hunting is forbidden for those under 16, unless accompanied by a license-holder who is at least 21.

Residents and nonresidents who want to hunt in Ontario must be at least 16 years old before being eligible for a license; however, 15-year-old residents may apply if they have written consent from parents or guardians.

In Manitoba, hunting is prohibited for those under 12 years of age. Persons younger than 19 and all new hunters are required to pass a hunter safety course before they can receive a permit.

Those younger than 14 are prohibited from hunting big game or birds in Alberta. Those age 14 and 15 must have a license and be accompanied by a parent or by a person 18 or older who is authorized in writing by the parent.

In British Columbia, those younger than 19 can obtain a junior hunting license for big game. Children under ten years of age are not permitted to hunt or carry any firearms.

In the Yukon, no person younger than 14 may obtain a big-game license and those younger than 16 must be accompanied by a license holder who is 19 or older. The 14- to 16-year old hunter must also have a firearms permit issued by the R.C.M.P.

The grizzly: high-country menace

THE UNDISPUTED KING of Canadian game animals is *Ursus horribilis*, the grizzly bear, roaming the cordilleran region of Alberta and British Columbia. Standing up to two metres tall, weighing up to 400 kilograms, the carnivorous grizzly can move faster than man and has knife-like teeth and razor-sharp claws.

In the national parks, all hunting is prohibited by law (except in Point Pelee where duck hunting is still allowed) and in magnificent wildernesses like Banff, Jasper, Waterton Lakes, Glacier, Yoho and Mount Revelstoke parks, the grizzly flourishes unmolested. It is only when he discovers the easy pickings of garbage that he comes into conflict with man.

City folks who have never spent a single night under the stars drive into the national parks and, ignoring or missing warnings, stretch out in bedrolls in the center of the grizzly kingdom.

Should the grizzly be eliminated from the national parks that were set aside so that future generations may enjoy our wildlife heritage in its unfettered state? If not, must we accept that a number of innocent humans may die under those terrible claws? The law has no answer to conundrums such as this.

Guns and guides

REVOLVERS, pistols and fully automatic firearms are banned from the Canadian hunting scene. Other weapons are restricted by provincial legislation, according to the class of license, the game hunted and the game zone or wildlife area involved. By "firearm" the law also means the longbow and the crossbow, as well as the air-powered or pellet gun.

Semiautomatic or repeating shotguns must be plugged in such a way that they will not hold more than three cartridges in the chamber and magazine.

Most provincial game laws have a similar clause to that in force in Ontario which rules that it is illegal for an unlicensed person to be carrying a rifle greater than .22 caliber or a shotgun using shot larger than No. 2 in any area that is open for deer or moose hunting.

In the following brief survey of hunt-armament rules, examples from the Northwest Territories, British Columbia, Manitoba and New Brunswick are used to give a cross section of the regulations that hunters in Canada may be required to observe. Moreover, the Criminal Code has a number of strict regulations regarding the possession of firearms and requires owners to have a firearms possession certificate.

When hunting big game in the Northwest Territories, you are not permitted to use rimfire ammunition or ammunition of less than .23 caliber. The wildlife officers want the animals killed outright, not merely wounded. Nonexpanding or steel-jacketed bullets, and tracer bullets are prohibited. Although seals may be hunted with any type or caliber of rifle, semiautomatic rifles are considered unsafe. For waterfowl, shotguns must be 10 gauge or smaller.

British Columbia restricts the use of firearms in wildlife management areas. These restrictions range from permitting only certain shell sizes to totally forbidding guns. The use of tracer (having a chemical that leaves a trail of smoke or fire) and explosive bullets and shells is prohibited. In hunting all big game you are not allowed to use rimfire cartridges. You may use a rifle for hunting all game birds except pheasant, partridge, quail and migratory game birds. You may use only a shotgun for hunting deer, black bear, cougar, wolf, small game and game birds. When hunting deer, black bear, cougar and wolf, you must use a shotgun that is at least 20 gauge or larger.

In Manitoba, you may not use a rifle or shotgun loaded with ball cartridge when hunting waterfowl and sandhill cranes. Nor may you use a shotgun larger than 10 gauge for bird hunting. For big game, you may not use a rifle that requires a rimfire cartridge.

In New Brunswick, silencers on guns are strictly prohibited. Hunting moose, deer or bear with a rifle designed to fire a rimfire shell or cartridge is also prohibited. During January and February, you may hunt migratory game birds only with shot no larger than No. 2 in a shotgun. Those holding a Class 2 or Class 4, or a minor's hunting license are not permitted to use rifles of more than .23 caliber or shotguns with cartridges loading ball or slug. Holders of Class 1 and Class 3 licenses may use such guns only during the deer season.

The firearms regulations under the Migratory Birds Convention Act are applied throughout Canada. Migratory game birds may be hunted only with a bow and arrow, or a shotgun no larger than 10 gauge. It is illegal to use live birds or recorded birdcalls as decoys.

If you are carrying more than one shotgun, the extras must be kept not only empty but also disassembled or cased. It is generally forbidden to use rifles or shotguns that are loaded with a single bullet. An exception on this last point is made for the licensed hunter who is a resident of the Northwest Territories and is not required to hold a migratory bird permit. He may hunt migratory game, with a rifle of not greater than .22 caliber or with a shotgun that is loaded with a single bullet.

The general reasoning behind this rule is that often a single bullet is not enough to kill the game, and the wounded animal has time to escape before the average hunter can reload his gun. Game laws reflect the belief that animals should be killed outright, not left wounded and in pain—probably to die eventually.

Everywhere in Canada, hunting without "due care and attention" is an offense. The careless discharge of firearms, without consideration of other persons or property, can bring a fine of $1,000 or more, or a jail term—and sometimes both a fine and imprisonment.

Shooting from vehicles

Hunting from an aircraft or transporting a loaded gun in an aircraft, whether it is in motion or not, is prohibited. The same prohibition extends generally to all vehicles, and to powerboats while they are in motion. A gun is considered loaded if it has a cartridge in the firing chamber or the magazine.

The federal Migratory Birds Regulations impose additional restrictions relating to the use of aircraft and boats.

The law states that a hunter may use a powerboat for retrieval of a migratory game bird, but may not hunt from a powerboat. Presumably, this is meant to discourage hunters from firing from too great a range.

The popularity of the snowmobile as a mode of travel has brought it into the

scope of the law (*See* Chapter 16, "The merry snowmobile"). It is considered a motorized vehicle; thus, hunting from snowmobiles is prohibited. You are also committing an offense if you use your snowmobile to chase, molest, injure or kill any wildlife.

The development of snow vehicles into powerful and fast machines has given the hunter a new advantage over the deer or moose floundering in deep snow. This has led, in some provinces, to a designated trail system. For example, during the hunting season in Saskatchewan's zones 26 and 27, snow vehicles may be operated only on numbered highways or on trails marked by colored plastic ribbons. Hunters may leave the trails to retrieve a kill, but must do so in the most direct manner possible. Trail maps are supplied to all holders of a moose-hunting license for the zone.

In Manitoba, hunting from any vehicle is prohibited. In some areas, snowmobiles and other vehicles may be used to retrieve a big-game animal that has been killed. Vehicles are restricted to roads and designated trails in other areas.

Bow and arrow regulations

Hunting in the Robin Hood style is increasingly popular among hunters in Canada, and all provincial game laws now contain specific bow and arrow rules. There are even some exclusive archery seasons. Manitoba normally allows for a short archery season for deer from late August to early September. Nova Scotia has an archery season, October 28 to December 8 in the Chignecto Game Sanctuary and a special province-wide archery season for deer during the first week of October. The bow and arrow is a method of hunting migratory game birds which is legally permitted everywhere in Canada.

In Newfoundland, hunting big game with a bow and arrow is permitted in all areas under regular licenses. Bows must have a minimum of 20.5 kilograms pull at fulldraw and arrows must be tipped with metal and of not less than 22 millimetres width.

New Brunswick permits a special three-week deer season for archers before the regular deer hunting season. Bows must have a 20-kilogram pull and arrows must be broad-heads.

Archery is permitted in Quebec for hunting small game and also such big game as deer, bear, moose and caribou as long as the bow has at least an 18-kilogram pull and the arrows used have at least 22-millimetre steel arrowheads.

Since the bow is classified as a firearm, the hunting archers of Ontario must conform to the gun regulations of the Game and Fish Act. Bows must have draw weights of at least 18 kilograms for hunting deer and at least 22 kilograms for moose and black bear. There are special "archery only" seasons for deer and moose in some areas. A regular deer license and special archery tag are required.

In Manitoba game-hunting Area 34A, the longbow is the only permitted method of hunting big game. There is also a special deer-archery season, and a regular deer-hunting license is required. If a hunter is not successful during the archery season, he may also use his license during the firearm season. Bows must have at least an 18-kilogram pull at a 71-centimetre draw.

Saskatchewan also has an archery season for deer hunting during which the clothing-requirement law, which normally insists that bright orange be worn, is relaxed to allow camouflaged clothing.

Although crossbows are prohibited in Alberta, an archery license allows you to use the bow and arrow to hunt big game during the open season. In three wildlife management districts only the bow and arrow are permitted for big game. Bows must have a pull of 18 kilograms at a 71-centimetre draw and be capable of propelling an arrow 137 metres. Arrows must be at least 61 centimetres in length and may not have barbed points.

Bow and arrow may be used in British Columbia for hunting all big and small game, but exploding arrows are banned. Bows must have a pull greater than 18 kilograms at full draw and the shaft must have an arrowhead of 2.2 centimetres or greater at the widest point.

Bow hunters in the Yukon and the Northwest Territories are subject to the same hunting regulations as those using firearms. The Northwest Territories stipulate that the draw weight of the bow must be at least 20 kilograms at a 700-millimetre draw, and arrows must be at least 25 millimetres at the widest point or have a three-bladed embarbed head.

Mandatory use of guides
The sheer size of the Canadian game range and the sparsely settled nature of the forested northlands make guides a necessity for strangers, and a sensible precaution for all. In addition, the assistance of a guide (who is often a local resident) will tend to increase your chances of trophy success.

In some areas, you must have a licensed guide to go hunting; this applies mostly to big-game hunting by nonresidents.

In Newfoundland and Labrador, nonresidents must be accompanied by at least one licensed guide for every two hunters.

Nonresidents must also employ licensed guides in New Brunswick. In Quebec, hunting north of the 52nd parallel is prohibited for nonresidents except when accompanied by a licensed outfitter.

Ontario imposes mandatory guiding in a 2:1 ratio for nonresident deer and moose hunters in the Rainy River District. Guides must have a valid guide's license.

Nonresidents hunting in Alberta must be accompanied by either a guide or a resident when hunting big game. In certain designated big-game zones, it is mandatory for all nonresident hunters to have guides.

In British Columbia, nonresidents must be accompanied by a licensed guide (or a resident of the immediate family with a special permit) while hunting all big game. Game-bird hunters do not require guides.

Nonresident hunters in the Northwest Territories must hire licensed outfitters; both nonresidents and residents must use them for hunting polar bear. Those hunting seals must have Inuit guides and crewmen. Game-bird hunters, however, are exempt from the mandatory guide law.

719

In the Yukon, nonresidents from other countries hunting big game must also use licensed guides. Nonresident Canadians may be accompanied by a resident holding a special guiding license. The hunting territory is divided into guiding areas with one outfitter in each area. If you are interested in going on a hunt, which usually lasts 14 days, you should book a year in advance.

Traps and poisons

Poisons are strictly prohibited in the taking of game animals or birds. Under the Criminal Code, it is also an offense to poison an animal or bird, wild by nature, that is being kept in captivity. Such an offense is punishable on summary conviction.

Traps and snares are generally prohibited to sport hunters, although they may be used for certain species in designated seasons. Big game (except bear, under a special license) may not be trapped.

Those who trap for a living are regulated by a special license under different provincial regulations. Trapline areas are set out in the license and the trapper has exclusive rights to the area described in his license. Quotas are set for the different fur-bearing animals which the trapper must not exceed. When his license runs out, the trapper must make a statement of returns stating the number of pelts obtained of each species and a report on what happened to them.

A variety of licenses are required for those connected in other ways with trapping. These include: a fur-dealer's license, a tanner's license, export licenses, and fur-farming licenses.

The trapping of fur-bearing animals is totally restricted to licensed residents, and it is unlawful to touch or interfere with any set trap unless authorized by law or the owner to do so. The common fur-bearing animals are beaver, fisher, lynx, otter, marten, muskrat, wolverine, weasel and mink.

Forest-travel permits

The preservation of timberlands both as a wildlife habitat and a harvestable resource is of great concern to conservationists and governments. Fifteen percent or more of Canada's export income comes from wood products. As an aid in preventing loss of forest, as well as animal and human life, there are laws restricting both forest travel and the setting of fires

The professional guide

THE RELATIONSHIP of the professional guide to his hunting or fishing party is unique; he is at once both the laborer and the leader. Responsibility for planning the day's sport in a safe and successful way is his; and yet he is also the servant, taking care of the party's chores. News of an expert and pleasing guide travels fast by word-of-mouth among outdoorsmen who can afford the service, and such guides are usually booked up for several seasons ahead.

The guide can be hired on a personal basis, or he may be supplied by a hunting outfitter or a vacation resort operator. He may provide all boats, motors and other equipment, and basic food supplies. Every guide should carry a compass, small ax, hunting knife, waterproof matches and a first-aid kit.

The best guides are truly versatile men. Apart from the ability to locate game, they must have an instant and detailed knowledge of all the relevant laws concerning game, conservation and fire, the current forest-travel regulations and boat safety codes. Their camp-craft knowledge must be extensive as they will be making and breaking camp, cooking and cleaning, possibly instructing novices in canoe and weapon technique. As important as any of these, they must lead with a persuasive friendliness that can be acquired only by experience.

in designated areas. Figures gathered by the Canadian Forestry Service of Environment Canada over a ten-year period show that an average of about two million hectares of forest are lost to fire every year. Humans are blamed for 70 percent of the average 9,000 forest fires in Canada each year.

Areas where timberland is predominant are designated as "fire districts"; within these, there are certain areas that are labeled "restricted fire zones" and "restricted travel zones." Travel in a restricted travel zone during the fire season is prohibited, except under authority of a forest-travel permit issued by a fire warden. These restrictions do not apply, however, to travel on public roads or within cities, towns and villages, supervised campgrounds or on adjacent waters.

A forest-travel permit may be limited in duration and may contain certain conditions that the issuing officer thinks necessary under the ruling local circumstances. It would normally expire with the fire season, but it may be canceled or suspended at any time.

Smoking is prohibited while walking in these forests where travel is restricted.

A person who enters the forest without a permit when one is required for forest travel is guilty of an offense punishable by either fine or imprisonment. Furthermore, he may be held responsible for expenses incurred in controlling or extinguishing any fire caused by his neglect.

Campfire regulations

In designated "fire districts," there are strict regulations regarding campfires during the fire season. Permits are not needed for outdoor fires if you want to cook something or warm yourself but they are required for such other purposes as to burn refuse. These permits are issued under conditions similar to forest-travel permits. They expire at the end of the fire season but may be canceled at any time. Regardless of permits, a fire warden can order you to put out a fire, or can extinguish it himself, in the interest of forest protection.

In "restricted fire zones," if you want to start a fire for cooking or for obtaining warmth, you must use a portable stove or charcoal burner. In ordinary zones, the cooking fire must be either on bare rock or bare mineral soil. An area at least three feet wide around the fire must be either bare rock or cleared to bare mineral soil. You must take all reasonable steps to keep the fire under control and make sure that a responsible person tends it at all times. Before leaving the site, make sure that the cooking fire has been completely extinguished.

Outdoor incinerators must be of a type that can contain the fire, and none of the parts may be flammable. They must be situated at least five metres from the forest, on either bare rock or bare mineral soil with a cleared area 1.5 metres wide surrounding them.

The regulations reflect the vital importance of the forest industries to Canada's total economy. Wood products from commercial tree species make up 15 percent of all commodity exports.

Respecting private property

Every year, more and more farmers and other persons owning lands suitable for hunting put up notices forbidding hunters to come on their land. This situation is aggravated by the few ignorant or careless hunters who spoil the sport for the majority.

When lands have been "posted" by the owner, hunters must not enter the property, nor may they deface notices that have been posted. (*See* Chapter 18, "Our conditional rights.") Even without posted notices, groups of more than 12 hunters must have a landowner's permission to go on his property to hunt, whether the land is fenced in or not.

If a landowner asks you to leave his property, you must do so immediately.

A landowner does not have to prove damage to sue an intentional trespasser; but if no significant damage has been done, he will be awarded only a nominal sum. An intentional trespasser can, however, be held responsible for all damage caused by his presence on the land. To be guilty of trespassing, a hunter need not actually set foot upon a property but need only fire a bullet that reaches the land.

As well as charging a person with trespassing, a landowner may obtain a court order which prevents continued acts of trespass.

Much can be done to improve the public image of the hunter and to ensure the future of hunting as a recreation. Whether land is posted or not, and regardless of the size of the party, it is a common courtesy to ask a farmer's permission to hunt on his land. And why not share your game with him?

Farm outbuildings and equipment (as well as utility poles and road signs) should never be used for target practice. Great care should be taken to avoid shooting near farm animals. Fences should be climbed with care and all gates closed.

The private hunting club

Hunting clubs take a variety of forms. Some own land of their own and perhaps breed game birds and animals to be hunted within the confines of their land. Some lease land or hunt by permission. Most private clubs are for members only; others welcome paying guests, and supply guides as well as all equipment.

The Province of Quebec is particularly noted for its hunting clubs. Large tracts are leased by outfitters or sportsmen's associations which, in turn, may license or permit hunting within the designated territory. Hunting within these areas is still subject to the Wildlife Conservation Act of the province, but success is practically assured.

Under a special license, a game-bird hunting preserve may be operated to provide for controlled hunting. Regulations govern the size of the preserve and the species to be hunted.

Daily records must be kept by the owner of a preserve, including the names of the hunters and total of their kill.

Crossing the border

The Canadian who travels to a province other than his own to hunt or fish must, of course, adhere to the laws of that province; in addition, he should check to see if he is subject as a nonresident to additional license requirements and, possibly, mandatory use of a guide.

The many thousands of American sportsmen who travel to Canada are faced with considerably greater restrictions. They do not require passports to enter the country (as most other aliens do) but should carry some document that establishes their citizenship or residence. Those holding alien registration cards should bring them, if only to facilitate their reentry on the way home.

A car licensed in the United States can be driven in Canada without any duty or fee for 12 months, and a home-state operator's license is acceptable. There is no extra fee for trailers, but a returnable deposit may be asked; truck-type campers are sometimes charged.

Before leaving home, all drivers should obtain from their insurance agents the Canadian nonresident interprovincial insurance card.

All hunting and angling equipment, plus 2,000 safety cartridges, can be brought into Canada duty free, but all firearms must be declared with Canada Customs.

It is also advisable that the American visitor make lists of all portable items—such as radios and outboard motors—complete with registration numbers, where possible, so that one list can be deposited with customs on entry and exit from Canada. The same applies to Canadian hunters or campers entering the United States.

Hunting dogs are permitted entry from the United States provided they have a certificate proving immunization against rabies within the previous 36 months.

The American hunter must pay a larger license fee and may find himself asked for certain fees when exporting his game. Ontario, for instance, demands export permit fees of $25 for a moose and $20 for a black bear.

A federal license is needed to possess rifles or shotguns in Canada. Firearms should be declared at Customs in full detail by the incoming hunter to facilitate clearing on return. Revolvers, pistols and fully automatic firearms are prohibited unless required for a marksmanship competition; in such a case, Customs may grant temporary permission.

722

Safety in the field

WITH FIREARMS in use, a hunting accident can be a serious and even tragic event. Canadian game laws attempt to promote the maximum of safety in the field but, in the last analysis, security is largely dependent on the skill and common sense of the individual hunter.

If an accident should occur, remember the distress signal in the field: three shots, fired in the air at a few seconds interval. If you hear such a distress signal, answer it by a single shot.

The legal consequences of a hunting accident can be surprisingly complex. For instance, any rescuer who undertakes to lend assistance comes under a legal duty to do so if his omission to do so would be dangerous to life.

The person who causes the accident may be charged under the Criminal Code. Charges could include criminal negligence causing death, criminal negligence causing bodily harm, or manslaughter. These offenses can bring long terms of imprisonment.

In addition, charges could be laid under provincial laws. "Hunting carelessly" (without "due care and attention") provides an example.

An accident-insurance premium is included in the hunting license fee charged by the Province of Quebec; it covers both personal accident compensation and legal liability for accident in that province up to a limit of $10,000. There is no payoff under the policy, however, if the accident occurs as a result of breaking the hunting laws of the province. This insurance coverage is in addition to any other liability policy that may be held by the license holder.

Mandatory safety training

A knowledge of hunting safety is demanded from anyone who applies for a hunting license in Canada. A current or recent license will serve as proof of previous hunting experience. When you apply for a license, you will generally receive a summary of hunting regulations which also contain safety precautions. Some provinces, in addition, have established tests to measure the firearms and first aid knowledge of the applicant—especially the teenage applicant.

In Ontario, applicants born after December 31, 1954 must complete a course in hunting safety before applying to take a hunting examination. After passing the test, they will receive a certificate that must be shown to the issuer of licenses.

In Quebec, a resident must have a hunting certificate before he can get a license. This is given upon passing the examination at the end of a course in firearms safety. Nonresidents must have a similar document certifying that they are proficient in handling firearms for hunting.

In Manitoba, residents must first obtain a wildlife certificate to be eligible for a hunting license. This is given to those who have previously held a hunting license or who have graduated from the Manitoba hunter and firearm safety-training course. An equivalent course in another province or country will suffice. Hunters younger than 19 must hold a certificate, regardless of the hunting license they have.

All hunters who are residents of British Columbia and have never held a hunting license, are required to produce a certificate showing that they have successfully completed a conservation and outdoor-education program, or other qualification, before a hunting or firearms license is issued to them.

Special clothing requirements

Hunters should always wear conspicuous clothes and be absolutely sure of their target before they shoot. Farmers' wives have been peppered with shot while they hung their washing on the clothesline. Brother has shot brother in mistake, and valuable cows are often mistaken for deer or moose. To minimize accidents, some provinces add high-visibility clothing requirements to their hunting laws.

The following provides a typical sample of the regulations:

British Columbia recommends that hunters wear a bright orange vest or other outer article when hunting big game and upland game birds.

In Saskatchewan, all big-game hunters and their companions must wear a complete outer suit of scarlet, white, bright yellow or orange or any combination of these colors. Caps must be any of these colors, except white. An exception is granted to deer hunters using a bow and arrow during the archery season, who may wear camouflaged clothing.

Alberta insists that big-game hunters and hunters of upland game birds be clothed in a long-sleeved coat, or other long-sleeved outergarment, and a head-dress of scarlet or bright-orange material. Those hunting with bow and arrow in certain designated areas are exempted from these requirements.

Big-game hunters in Manitoba must wear a white or orange outer suit that extends below the knees, plus an orange head covering.

The "Ten Commandments" of hunter safety

NO AGE is too early to begin to learn the rudiments of safe handling of guns. The future hunter, like most children, is usually fascinated by firearms from the time he first visits a toy shop. The uncomplicated, fearsome power of the gun is grasped by even the immature mind. Some young people learn control over reflexes as early as age eight; some never do.

Complete control over the emotions is an absolute requirement for those who wish to shoot. No child should be permitted to fire a single live shell until he (or she) has mastered and can demonstrate all the fundamentals of safety and routine firearms technique.

Governments and hunting clubs combine in proclaiming the following rules as the "Ten Commandments" of safety in the hunting field:

- Treat every gun as if it were a loaded gun.
- Be certain of your target before you squeeze the trigger.
- Never point your gun at anything you do not want to kill.
- Carry your gun so that the muzzle is always under control.
- Always unload your gun when carried into camp, or when not in use.
- Ensure that the barrel and the bolt action are free of obstruction.
- Unattended guns should always be unloaded.
- Never climb a fence or jump a ditch with a loaded gun.
- Don't shoot at hard or flat objects, or the surface of water.
- Don't drink any alcohol before or during a hunt.

If an accident should occur, you'll be glad if your party has a first-aid kit. Such a kit should contain: rolls of 2.5-centimetre and 5-centimetre wide gauze bandage; sterile gauze dressings, 7.5 centimetres square; absorbent cotton; adhesive tape; adhesive bandages; tube of antiseptic ointment; aromatic spirits of ammonia; tube of burn ointment; bottle of headache tablets. The St. John Ambulance Society offers instruction in first aid which could easily save a life some day in the remote bush.

Powers of wardens

To enforce the hunting, fishing and forest laws, game wardens, conservation officers and fire wardens are given wide-ranging powers.

A provincial conservation officer can get a warrant to hold you, or to enter and search premises, cars, boats or aircraft. He doesn't need a warrant if he has reasonable grounds to believe an offense has been committed against wildlife regulations. He has authority to open and inspect any trunk, box or parcel. He may use force if necessary and may arrest without a warrant.

Information on the number and species of game or fish taken must be given to an officer on request. If he suspects that you have taken game or fish unlawfully, he may seize the game and any property used in breaking the law. If you are convicted, whatever was seized goes to the Crown. You could lose your guns, tackle, car or boat.

Similar powers are given to wardens under the Migratory Birds Convention Act. This authority is extended to provincial game and fishery officers and game-management officers of the territories. They have the right to seize game and any property, vehicle or aircraft used in violation of the law, if they have reasonable grounds for believing a violation has taken place.

It is an offense to assault, interfere with or provide false information to a game warden or officer.

The game census

One method of assuring the continued existence of good hunting is for all hunters to cooperate when a game officer requests information. The officer has the authority to demand an accurate report on your hunting.

Information may be required when you are issued a license, and you may be given documents to complete and return when your hunting trip is over.

The Canadian Wildlife Service of the federal Department of the Environment mails survey questionnaires to a sampling of people buying permits. About half are usually returned. These are analyzed and provide data that is used to make bag limits and open seasons as generous as possible and yet assure an adequate breeding population.

The number of hunters, their ages, sex and the area of hunting terrain reveal where concentrated hunting is taking place and whether or not hunters as a group are increasing. The time when permits are purchased helps establish when and where peak periods of hunting occur. The relation between the home address of the hunter and the place where he bought a permit reveals hunter movements and provides information on the numbers of nonresident hunters.

The number of birds taken, their species and sex enables bag limits to be adjusted in the various hunting zones. The date of the kill plays a role in determining open seasons.

Use of hunting dogs

The use of dogs is generally permitted in hunting small game and birds, although the hunter is cautioned to investigate the licensing requirements of local municipal law. Prince Edward Island, New Brunswick, Nova Scotia and Ontario allow raccoon hunting at night with a dog, provided a special permit is obtained.

Although hunting big game with dogs is generally prohibited in Canada, there are some exceptions.

In British Columbia, a leashed dog may be used to hunt deer, elk and moose. Dogs may also be used to hunt other big game, but not mountain sheep, mountain goats or caribou.

In the Northwest Territories, hunters must use dog teams to hunt polar bear.

Ontario allows the use of dogs to drive deer or moose in certain wildlife management units.

Dogs must not be permitted to molest or disturb any wild game bird during the months of April, May, June or July. And they must not run free in moose or deer country during the closed season.

Quite apart from any hunting restriction, municipal or township bylaws usually require that all dogs six months or older be licensed. Working dogs on farms are often exempt.

The owner of a dog that has caused damage or injury is generally liable when it can be proved that his negligence was a contributing factor. The owner, or keeper, is presumed by the law to be aware of any vicious tendencies that his dog may have. When a normally quiet and obedient dog bites someone, it might be forgiven; this has given rise to the saying, "Every dog is entitled to one bite," a modern twist to a Biblical quotation. However, if the dog bites twice, he will likely be ordered destroyed.

Farmers who see a dog attack their livestock (cattle, sheep or poultry) are entitled to shoot it, or to order an employe to do so.

Dogs found running loose in settled communities will usually be picked up by the official dogcatcher. They are normally held at a public dog pound for a week or so in case owners claim them. If not, they are given away to new owners or painlessly killed.

Seldom on Sunday

With but a few exceptions, hunting in Canada is prohibited on Sundays. You should also note that on any "day," hunting in the period from a half hour after sunset to a half hour before sunrise—the official period of night—is prohibited. The main exception is Quebec, where Sunday shooting is not only legal but highly popular. British Columbia and the Northwest Territories permit it, too.

In Ontario, it is illegal to hunt on Sunday south of the French and Mattawa rivers, except in a few counties and townships. Longbow hunting is permitted seven days a week, in season.

A limited amount of Sunday hunting is allowed in Alberta. It is restricted to certain areas of Big Game Zone 1 (in northern Alberta), and to parts of Big Game Zones 5 and 6 in central Alberta. In these areas, big game and upland birds, but not migratory birds, may be hunted on Sunday.

Getting to know your gun

A RECENT GALLUP POLL showed that a majority of Canadians are in favor of stricter gun control. At present, anyone wishing to buy a gun must be at least 16 years old and must apply to the police to obtain a Firearms Acquisition Certificate. While guns are plentiful in Canadian homes, instruction in gun care and handling often lags behind. It is advisable that all sporting guns displayed in the home be kept locked into a cabinet or rack. For that single gun in the garage or attic, a simple trigger lock can be bought cheaply. In the automobile, keep your gun in the locked trunk, or install one of the thiefproof dashboard mounts that are available at sporting goods stores.

Many accidents are caused by ignorance, as well as by negligence. Become thoroughly familiar with your gun, examining and working the loading mechanism, the trigger pull, the safety catch, before you take to the field and before you load it for the first time. Learn the proper names of the parts of the gun, and check their condition for rust or wear.

Every sporting gun is built to do a specific job. Know the range, power and other capabilities of your armament, and always use only the recommended ammunition. Examine each shotgun shell before you load the gun.

A membership in a trapshooting or skeet club provides invaluable training in gun handling, as well as sharpening the aim. These are sports for women as well as men. For example, a Canadian woman, Susan Nattrass, has won a number of world titles in trapshooting.

Cleanliness is vital. Barrels must be scrupulously clean and the action very lightly oiled. If you have dropped your gun, ensure that the barrel has not become blocked by mud or snow—an obstruction can cause the barrel to burst when next the weapon is fired.

The compleat angler

WITH LITERALLY THOUSANDS of rivers and lakes in easy reach, angling in Canada offers tremendous scope to all fishermen, from the clumsiest rookie to the "compleat angler" made famous by England's Izaak Walton in the seventeenth century. The sportsman free to travel by plane and car can find game fishing somewhere in Canada the year round.

One thing has definitely changed, however: the fisherman of modern times is faced with regulations and restrictions that would have seemed incredible to our own pioneers of the nineteenth century. Because control over game is basically a provincial matter, Canada has no fewer than 12 sets of regulations, all of which can be changed each spring. It is a price we must pay for population growth, the spread of leisure and the advance of transportation technology.

In the legal sense, angling means taking or attempting to take fish by means of a hook and line, including casting or trolling. Canada offers perhaps the world's widest range of game fish: there are salmon and trout in the Atlantic provinces; bass, pike, pickerel and muskellunge in central areas; trout and salmon on the Pacific coast; and swordfish and bluefin tuna in the ocean off Nova Scotia. This list ignores the multitude of panfish—such as rock bass, sunfish, bullheads, catfish, crappies, perch—that abound in most shallow or weedy waters to the delight of holidaying children.

Under the multiplicity of provincial game laws, angling generally is restricted by season, species, bag limits and license requirements. Tackle and bait are regulated, while fishing with explosives or guns is strictly forbidden. Spearguns may be used, but require a special license in some areas.

Every province sets aside areas where fishing is prohibited entirely. In some places nonresidents must be accompanied by a resident or guide. Fishermen, like hunters, must cooperate with conservation officers when questioned.

Provincial licenses are not valid in national parks, which have their own regulations regarding seasons and limits.

Angling, unlike hunting, can be enjoyed 24 hours a day, where permitted.

Apart from angling law, the fisherman must obey numerous regulations governing the vessel he uses in the water. (*See* Chapter 16, "Owning a boat.") Safety laws regulate the licensing of boats, the number of passengers in a boat and the provision of paddles, running lights and life jackets.

Liquor laws apply afloat as ashore. Sections of the Criminal Code make it an offense to operate a vessel while your ability is impaired or to operate a vessel in a manner that is dangerous to navigation, life or limb.

Tackle and lures
Torches or other artificial lights are prohibited in fishing, as are guns and all explosives.

Only one fishing line is permitted—except when fishing through ice. The line must be baited so as to include not more than four hooks (a gang of three barbs counts as one hook).

Unbaited hooks, except those on artificial lures, are prohibited.

Spears, spearguns, and bows and arrows are permitted only in certain areas and under special licenses. Snagging or jigging is illegal in freshwater fishing, and night lines are generally prohibited. You are usually allowed to use gaffs (spearheaded hooks) to land fish; however, in New Brunswick and the territories they are prohibited. Spring gaffs are prohibited everywhere.

On certain rivers, only fly fishing is permitted by provincial authorities.

Dip net regulations

Generally speaking, dip nets may be used only for catching coarse fish—such as smelt—but there are exceptions.

In Manitoba, whitefish may be taken with dip nets from September 7 to November 30 in specified waters.

In certain areas of Ontario, a resident may take herring and whitefish by dip net in October, November and December. The dip net, if angular, may not measure more than 183 centimetres in any of its dimensions; if circular, it may not exceed 183 centimetres in diameter.

Smelt may be taken by dip net in most of Ontario in March, April and May. A seine (a net with sinkers at the bottom and floats at the top) may be used under authority of a special license.

Quebec permits the use of a dip net to take smelt or whitefish in designated waters during specified seasons. The nets must not exceed 1.3 metres in length or diameter and the mesh must not exceed 2.5 centimetres when fully extended.

Spear and bow fishing

Generally speaking, Canadian fishing laws prohibit the use of spears or bows for game fish. British Columbia, for example, does not permit their use to take salmon, trout or other game fish, with the exception of burbot in some areas.

Spears are prohibited in Alberta, except to underwater divers who may use them under the authority of a special license. The spear must be tethered to a speargun (or to the diver) by a line no longer than five metres—and the line must be strong enough to withstand the thrust of the firing device. While spearfishing, a person must display a scuba diver's flag and must fish within a 30-metre radius of the flag.

Saskatchewan allows divers to spearfish with a regular angling license. Spearfishing is prohibited within 300 metres of a recognized swimming area.

Manitoba permits spearfishing for certain species, depending on whether a person is snorkelling or diving, and only rubber-band-propelled or hand-propelled spears may be used. Bow fishing for carp and suckers is permitted from May 15 to September 30. A fish arrow must be used and the line must be at least 23 kilograms test—i.e., be able to withstand 23 kilograms of pull.

Spearguns are prohibited in Ontario, but hand spears and bows may be used to take coarse fish in some counties during the spring. A spearfishing and bow fishing license costs $5.

Quebec residents require a spearfishing license which costs $5.25 (for nonresidents, $15.50). Special insurance coverage offered with game licenses in Quebec does not cover underwater spearfishing. The sport is restricted to certain waters and the bag—or daily—limit is generally the same as for angling in these waters. From December 1 to March 31 in Quebec's York River estuary, smelt may be taken through the ice or in open water with a spear or smelt harpoon. Residents do not need a license for this sport.

Ice fishing

Ice fishing brings to mind a picture of huts, each with its glowing stovepipe, standing in lines on frozen lakes—a scene that never fails to fascinate the winter visitor from softer climes.

While there are only a few areas in Canada where the sport is prohibited, the patient ice fisherman is still subject to restrictions of season, bag limits and tackle. Seasons and closed areas vary in each province and if you are thinking of adding your hut to the parade, you should check the provincial regulations.

Two and sometimes three lines are permitted in ice fishing. If "tip-ups" (a balanced device to hold the line) are allowed, someone must stay with them at all times.

Quebec permits smelt to be taken through the ice by means of a fish spear or smelt harpoon.

In Alberta, ice fishing is prohibited in waters that are frequented by trout, grayling or mountain whitefish. Any line not held by hand must have a marker attached to it. The marker must have the fisherman's license number on it and must extend 60 centimetres above the ice or snow. Holes cut in the ice must be marked to prevent accidents.

Quebec requires the owner's name and address to be marked on the outside of his hut. If the hut belongs to an outfitter who hires out more than one, a serial number must be marked on each.

On Ontario lakes where ice fishing is common, all huts must be registered with the local district office.

A date is set, by which all huts must be gone from the lakes (usually March 31). This is done to avoid water pollution and boat hazards, as well as to prevent the nuisance of unsightly wreckage being washed ashore.

You should note that it takes *five centimetres* of clear blue ice to support a man, *eight centimetres* for a group in single file, and about *20 centimetres* for a vehicle. If you are unfamiliar with the lake, stick to the route marked by the veterans. Currents and springs can create strips and pockets of dangerously thin ice.

Modern science has come to the assistance of the ice fisherman. Before you start sawing the required hole, an elec-

How old is that fish?

A fish's length usually indicates its age unless the fish is very large or old. A 154-year-old lake sturgeon measuring 206 centimetres and weighing over 94 kilograms is the oldest recorded Canadian freshwater fish. The biggest is a 629-kilogram white sturgeon but its age and that of an unofficially reported 816-kilogram white sturgeon are unknown.

The muskellunge is Canada's next biggest species; the largest on record measured 164 centimetres and weighed almost 32 kilograms although a 183-centimetre 57-kilogram specimen has been reported. Lake trout can top 45 kilograms and northern pike 18 kilograms.

This chart, giving length in inches, indicates the average year by year growth of popular freshwater fish.

YEARS	1	2	3	4	5	6	7	8
Brook trout	9.5	14.6	18.4	33	–	–	–	–
Brown trout	10.8	20.3	28	35.5	44.5	50.8	56	–
Lake trout	13.3	20.3	25.4	35.5	42	48.3	56	63.5
Rainbow trout	10.2	19.7	33	43.2	53.3	61	76.2	–
Muskellunge	20.3	38	53.3	66	76.2	83.8	94	104
Pike	14	31.8	43.2	50.8	58.4	66	73.7	81.3
Walleye	14	25.4	33	38	43.2	48.3	50.8	56
Largemouth bass	12.7	23	28	33	38	42	45.7	48.3
Smallmouth bass	10.2	17.8	25.4	30.5	35.6	39.4	40	40.6

Names commonly given to fish vary across the country. A muskellunge may be called a maskinonge or a muskie. A walleye may be known as a pickerel or a doré. The Kamloops trout of the west is the rainbow trout of the east, and British Columbia's coastal steelhead trout becomes a rainbow when it moves upriver to spawn. Brook and speckled trout are the same, as are lake and gray trout: a hybrid from these species is called a splake, or wendigo.

tronic sonar device is available to check the depths for you—and even to indicate the presence of fish.

Saltwater fishing

The federal Department of Fisheries and Oceans controls tidal and saltwater fishing grounds. The governing legislation is the Fisheries Act of Canada. Seasons, bag limits and size limits are set for game fish (particularly salmon) in tidal waters, but everyone has the right to dangle a hook in the open sea.

Fishery department officers have extensive powers of investigation when they believe, on reasonable grounds, that someone has violated the law.

In addition to the Fisheries Act, the federal parliament has passed several other laws controlling commercial saltwater fishing. (*See* Chapter 13, "The business of fishing.")

Baitfish restrictions

Nothing harms the game fish population of any water more than the introduction of coarse fish that do not normally inhabit those waters. Therefore, the use of baitfish is strictly regulated by law. They are either prohibited or are permissible only under specified conditions.

The lamprey must not be used as a baitfish at any stage of its development.

In British Columbia, fish are not allowed for bait anywhere. Only crustaceans, mollusks or roe are permitted to be used as bait.

In Alberta, you are not allowed to use any live fish for bait.

Saskatchewan permits only commercially preserved minnows or frozen smelt for bait.

Manitoba allows dead baitfish to be used wherever angling is allowed, but live baitfish may be used only in certain designated areas.

Ontario prohibits the use of live baitfish in certain waters, and forbids the release of baitfish into waters other than those from which they were originally taken. From April 1 to October 14, no angler may have in his possession more than 50 live baitfish.

Quebec prohibits the use of some 23 species of fish as bait and has extensive rules covering the use of the baitfish permitted.

In Prince Edward Island, minnow and smelt may be used as bait for trout, but smelt may not be used after June 15.

Angling licenses required

The provinces are divided in their requirements that residents take out angling licenses, but all of them insist that nonresidents do so. Ontario offers an exemption to Quebec residents in the border area along the Ottawa River.

The current year's licensing regulations can be obtained by writing to the following provincial authorities. Usually, maps and a short summary of fish and game laws will be sent to you. The information given here should be regarded as a general guideline only.

For the resident

Residents of Newfoundland must have a license to fish for salmon in inland waters. A resident salmon license costs $10 a season. Write *Wildlife Division, Department of Culture, Recreation and Youth, Building 810, Pleasantville, St. John's, Newfoundland A1A 1P9.*

A resident fishing license in Nova Scotia costs $4 and may be obtained from the *Department of Lands and Forests, P.O. Box 698, Halifax, Nova Scotia B3J 2T9,* and from authorized vendors throughout the province.

Residents of New Brunswick can get a free license to fish for all species, except salmon. Residents aged 16–65 pay $15 for a seasonal salmon license ($7.50 if over 65). Depending on the river, a resident rod license ($15) is required for Crown reserve waters. *Fish and Wildlife Branch, Department of Natural Resources, P.O. Box 6000, Fredericton, New Brunswick E3B 5H1.*

Prince Edward Island residents require angling licenses ($4.25) to go after the brown, speckled and rainbow trout that lurk in the winding sleepy streams of that province. *Fish and Wildlife Division, Department of Community and Cultural Affairs, Box 2000, Charlottetown, Prince Edward Island C1A 7N8.*

A Quebec resident may fish in certain places without a license, but generally all residents older than 18 must pay $5.25 for angling privileges; residents older than 65 pay only $2.50. Residents younger than 18 may fish without a license if accompanied by a license holder. *Ministère du Loisir, de la Chasse et de la Pêche, Direction des communications, C.P. 22 000, Québec, Qué., G1K 7X2.*

Ontario residents require licenses only to take smelt for personal use by seine net, to take baitfish by seine net in certain waters, or to take coarse fish by dip net for personal use in specified waters and periods. These licenses cost $1.25, $1.25 and $2.50 respectively. *Ministry of Natural Resources, Whitney Block, Queen's Park, Toronto, Ontario M7A 1W3.*

In Manitoba, all Canadian residents between 16 and 65 require a license to angle, spearfish, or bow fish ($5). Residents under 16 may fish without a license, but they must obey the regulations. *Travel Manitoba, 101 Legislative Building, Winnipeg, Manitoba R3C 0V8.*

Residents 16 to 65 require an angling license ($5) in Saskatchewan. The license is valid for all waters with the exception of Prince Albert National Park. Residents 15 and younger do not require a license but are still bound by the game laws. Residents over 65 years of age are entitled to free angling licenses. *Tourism Saskatchewan, 3211 Albert Street, Regina, Saskatchewan S4S 5W6.*

Alberta requires residents between the ages of 16 and 65 to have angling licenses costing $5. If they want to spearfish, that will cost $3. A trophy lake license costs an additional $5. Write to *Department of Energy and Natural Resources, Main Floor, North Tower, Petroleum Plaza, 9945 108th Street, Edmonton, Alberta T5K 2G6.*

Residents of British Columbia who are 16 or older require a license costing $10 (only $1 if over 65). A $3 surcharge is added to the cost of a basic angling license to support the Habitat Conservation Fund which preserves fish and wildlife habitats in the province. Also, those intending to fish for steelhead trout have to pay an extra license fee of $6. *Ministry of the Environment, Fish and Wildlife Branch, Parliament Buildings, Victoria, British Columbia V8V 1X5.*

All Canadians, 16 and older, must buy a resident angling license ($5) to fish in the Northwest Territories. This holds true for the Yukon as well. *Department of Fisheries and Oceans, Yellowknife, Northwest Territories,* or *Wildlife and Parks Services, Department of Renewable Resources, Government of Yukon, Box 2703, Whitehorse, Yukon Y1A 2C6.*

Fishing licenses are required in national parks. They may be purchased ($4)

Angling, exclusive and otherwise

ASSOCIATIONS for the improvement of fishing and hunting were founded long before Confederation, and these private bodies have had much to say in the shaping of fish and game laws by successive governments at all levels of authority.

They have advocated and supported research into fish-spawning habits, growth patterns, predation, and have assisted in stocking and conservation programs. Long before the current concern over water pollution, the clubs and societies were pressuring government agencies to clear commercial effluents and raw sewage from the lakes and rivers.

In the 1860s, the Prince of Wales Fishing Club in Montreal was so exclusive that it would admit only eight members. Canada today has many hundreds of private trout and bass ponds where owners invite friends to cast a fly for hungry lunkers. Some private fishing clubs maintain their own well-stocked waters for members and guests. Those fishing in private waters still must obey all regulations that apply to public waters in that province or region.

inside the parks and used at different national parks during the season. Fish caught by persons younger than 16 are included in the catch of the accompanying license holder. Youngsters 16 or younger may, however, purchase a permit and go for their own limit.

For the nonresident

Unless exempted by age (younger than 16), all nonresidents require angling licenses. This term applies to Canadians visiting from other provinces—unless the host province specifically welcomes visitors—as well as to aliens. After deciding in which province he intends to fish, the traveler should write for current license and other information to the relevant address given in the previous section.

While angling, the person must have his license with him and must produce it at the request of a conservation officer. The license is nontransferable.

NEWFOUNDLAND Nonresident licenses for trout cost $10; and for salmon, $40 for the season. To fish for salmon, a nonresident must be accompanied by a licensed guide, except when 500 metres either upstream or downstream from bridges on highways crossing designated streams.

NOVA SCOTIA The angling license costs $15. When fishing in places frequented by game, nonresidents must be accompanied by a resident 21 or older or by a licensed guide.

NEW BRUNSWICK Licenses are required for angling in all waters open to nonresident fishing. Season licenses for salmon, trout, pickerel, bass and any other fish cost $100. A seven-day license for the fish listed above costs $50. A season license for everything except salmon can be purchased for $30; a seven-day license costs $20, while a three-day license costs $15. Nonresidents can purchase a three-day angling license for salmon for $25.

PRINCE EDWARD ISLAND A license for angling may be purchased from authorized vendors in the province. Nonresidents must pay $10.60 for a trout-angling license or $10 for a two-week family trout license. A salmon license costs $5.

QUEBEC Nonresidents must purchase one of four different types of license.

There is a season license for all species; this costs $15.50. A salmon fishing license costs $25.50 for nonresidents and is valid for certain rivers during the season when salmon ascend these streams from the sea for breeding.

ONTARIO There are six types of nonresident angling license. A yearly license for Canadian residents costs $6, while nonresidents of Canada must pay $15 for a season license or $8 for a four-day license. A special angling license for an organized camp costs a minimum of $10 for adults. A special camp rate of $2 a person is available for groups of at least five children younger than 17 if accompanied by an adult; the adult will have to buy the routine angling license. Nonresidents younger than 17 do not need angling licenses when accompanied by family members who do have licenses.

MANITOBA Licenses ($20) are required for nonresidents 16 and older. A special three-day license for Division 1 waters costs $8.

SASKATCHEWAN Nonresident Canadians 16 and older may purchase a season license for $5. A one-day angling license costs $2 for Canadians. Other nonresidents may pay $15 for a season's license.

ALBERTA Nonresident Canadians must purchase a $5 season license. Nonresident aliens may purchase either a season license for $12 or a three-day license for $5.

BRITISH COLUMBIA Visiting Canadians from other provinces may purchase a license for all species (except steelhead trout) for $12 (aliens must pay $20, plus a $3 surcharge to support the Habitat Conservation Fund.) To include steelhead, the license costs an extra $15 for all nonresidents. There are also six-day licenses for nonresidents of Canada at $10, plus a $1 surcharge.

THE NORTHWEST TERRITORIES If you are a nonresident Canadian 16 or older, you must purchase a season license for $5. Aliens are charged $15.

THE YUKON Nonresident Canadians pay $5 for an angling license. Nonresident aliens can purchase a season license for $20, a five-day license for $10, or a one-day license for $5.

Where and what to fish

In the lakes

Sale and export

Species

Bag limits

Open seasons

Possession limits

ALMOST ANYWHERE in Canada the angler may find that his catch bears a tag or a fin clip. This tells him that his fish was probably raised in a hatchery and released in wild waters after having the identifying mark attached. Sportsmen are asked to forward tags, or details of the clips, to the game authorities in the province involved.

All information about the length, weight and condition of the fish, where and when caught, is most welcome. This cooperation allows scientists to check on the movement, growth, abundance and survival of species. This, in turn, affects the regulations that are revised each spring under the fish-and-game laws.

No live fish (or spawn) may be moved from one body of water to another without the consent of the authorities. This applies also to waters on private property. Whether inhabited by wild or stocked fish, private lakes or ponds still come within the scope of all regulations establishing angling seasons and bag limits.

As already stated, the provincial as well as federal fishing regulations can (and usually do) change in some particulars each season. Therefore it is not possible to provide hard-and-fast detailed information in book form; nevertheless, the information listed on the following pages can serve as a useful general guide.

You will notice that the lists of the provincial requirements refer to regions, zones and divisions. Each province catalogs its rules in its own style, providing maps marked with numbered (or lettered) geographical zones. These maps can be obtained by writing to the provincial conservation or tourist offices; the addresses appear earlier in this chapter.

In the lakes

More than 600 lakes are fished commercially within Canada's borders, producing large catches of whitefish, pickerel, perch and other salable species. In these waters—and in thousands of smaller lakes— the angler can find fine sport also. The fighting bass and wily trout are star attractions. The mighty muskellunge (up to 22 kilograms) will test any expert.

In Alberta, Saskatchewan, Manitoba and Ontario, the provincial authorities control all lake—as well as river—fishing; in British Columbia and Quebec, control is shared with the federal government. In the Maritimes and in the territories, all fishing, in both fresh and salt water, is under federal regulation.

The holiday fisherman is warned against setting out in small boats on wide waters. (*See* Chapter 16, "Owning a boat.")

Sale and export

It is illegal for game fish to be sold or bartered in Canada, except under a special license which is not available to the angler. It is also an offense to hire someone to catch game fish for you.

As much fish as the possession limit allows may be taken across provincial boundaries, or exported. However, if fish are cut into fillets at the angling site, this must be done in such a way that wardens or customs officers can identify the species, as well as the number taken.

To ease this problem, a piece of skin large enough for identification can be left attached. In the Northwest Territories, all the skin must be left on fillets.

If you freeze your catch into a solid block of ice, you could have a long wait at a border point while it thaws.

733

Species, limits and seasons

British Columbia's rainbow trout (known also as both the steelhead and Kamloops) is this province's most elite and exciting game fish, although the lordly coho salmon has his loyal devotees. The Kootenay and Okanagan lakes, the Kamloops, Skeena and Chilcotin districts and the rivers of Vancouver Island all provide great rainbow angling. Other trout include the brown, cutthroat lake, brook and the Dolly Varden (the last three are really chars).

For the purpose of sportfishing in nontidal waters, British Columbia is divided into eight regions. Closed seasons vary for each region and also for species within each region.

Limits of daily catch and possession (how many fish in hand at any time) for most species are constant throughout the province but the limit on trout varies according to the region. In general, only one steelhead longer than 50 centimetres may be taken each day.

Area	Species	Bag Limit	Possession
Region 1	Trout	8	16
Region 2	Trout	8	16
Region 3	Trout	8	16
Region 4	Trout	8	16
Region 5	Trout	8	16
Region 6	Trout	5	10
Region 7	Trout & grayling	5	10
Region 8	Trout	8	16
Province–wide	Steelhead trout	10 per year	
Province–wide	Kokanee	8–25	16–50
Province–wide	Whitefish	25	50
Province–wide	Bass, pike, walleye	8	16
Province–wide	Sturgeon (by angling)	1	2
Province–wide	Salmon (over 50 centimetres)	2	4
Province–wide	Chinook and coho salmon	8	16

Alberta offers deep, glacial mountain lakes that don't thaw until May, the waters of the North and South Saskatchewan river systems, and the Peace, Red Deer and the tumultuous Smoky rivers. Rainbow and Dolly Varden, walleye (pickerel or doré), northern pike, and coho salmon in Cold Lake, all provide exciting sport. All licensed anglers may fish in any natural lake or stream not closed by regulation. There are also impoundments—like Tyrell Lake, south of Lethbridge—where stocking from hatcheries has produced fine fishing. In the north, the following have been designated as "trophy" lakes: May, Seibert, Gods, Andrew, Gardiner, Namur and Winefred. The bag limit in these lakes ranges from two to five pike and five walleye, and the possession limit is the same.

Species	Bag Limit	Possession
Trout	2–10	4–20
Lake whitefish	10	20
Pike	10	10

(CONTINUED)

ALBERTA (CONTINUED)

Species	Bag Limit	Possession
Pickerel	5	10
Lake trout	5	5
Perch	30	30

Saskatchewan's map of its northern territory should show enough at a quick glance to convince you that the province's lakes are indeed "countless." North of Prince Albert National Park, they are thrown across the Precambrian wilderness like a shower of diamonds. Major rivers—the Saskatchewan, Athabasca, Churchill, Qu'Appelle—carry the province's water toward distant oceans.

Charter planes fly fishermen into the far north where lodges and guides await. Lac la Ronge offers huge pike and walleye; Lakes Wollaston and Cree offer grayling; and Waterbury, Black and Tazin lakes are known for lake trout. More southerly waters produce brook, rainbow and some brown trout.

The open season for southern zones in Saskatchewan is from the first Saturday in May to April 15; the opening date in northern zones is two or three weeks later. The possession limit is twice the one-day allowance. If fish are filleted, two fillets are counted as equaling one fish.

There is a daily limit of eight fish, or 15.8 kilograms weight of fish, whichever is the lesser. The bag may consist of a combination of the following:

Species	Bag Limit	Species	Bag Limit
Pike	8	Rainbow trout	5
Pickerel	8	Splake (Wendigo)	5
Sauger	8	Brown trout	5
Goldeye	8	Kokanee salmon	5
Whitefish	8	Coho salmon	5
Grayling	8	Bass	5
Lake trout	5	Sturgeon	1
Brook trout	5	Perch	unrestricted

(If, however, the bag is wholly of one species, the limit is the figure shown.)

Manitoba's name gives the clue to this province's fishing potential: it comes from the words *Minne* ("water" in Assiniboine Indian dialect) and *Toba* ("prairie" in Sioux). "Prairie water" it certainly is, with about 40,000 lakes and seven major rivers spread across its 650,087 square kilometres. Its capital, Winnipeg, crowns the junction of the Red and Assiniboine rivers.

The game fish mostly occur in the northern reaches, where the Churchill, Nelson, Hayes and Seal river systems drain lake waters into Hudson Bay. Trains penetrate the muskeg to Churchill and Lynn Lake but tourist offices will probably suggest charter flights organized by the lodges and outfitters during the brief summer. The experts' choices for angling in northern Manitoba include Gunisao Lake for walleye, Nueltin Lake for arctic grayling and huge lake trout, and Sickle Lake for pike.

In southern Manitoba, Whiteshell and Nopiming provincial parks are noted for walleye, channel catfish and smallmouth bass. The Winnipeg River system

(CONTINUED)

MANITOBA (CONTINUED)

provides excellent angling for pike and bass. Reed Lake yields large pike and lake trout, while Falcon Lake is a popular choice for walleye and bass. Trophy trout lie in the icy waters of Athapapuskow Lake, which once held the world trout record. Most deep lakes north of Winnipeg abound in whitefish (*Coregonidae*) which can tip the scales to nine kilograms.

The waters of Manitoba are divided into two sections, each with a different season for angling.

Waters	Open Season
Southern Manitoba	One week prior to Victoria Day weekend to March 31
Northern Manitoba	Victoria Day weekend to May 1

Note: Special restrictions apply to certain species, and on some lakes and streams within the above areas.

Limits, all waters

Species	Bag limit
Stocked brook trout, brown trout, rainbow trout and splake or any combination of these	6
Mooneye and goldeye or any combination of these	10
Smallmouth bass	8
Walleye and sauger or any combination of these (only one fish may exceed 60 cm)	8
Pike only one fish may exceed 90 cm	8
Lake trout only one fish may exceed 75 cm	3
Muskellunge	1
Lake sturgeon	1
Whitefish	25
Channel catfish	8
Arctic char	8
Arctic grayling only one fish may exceed 40 cm	5
All other species	no limit

N.B.: Some of these species have special limits on some lakes.

The province of Ontario holds or borders on about 25 percent of the entire world's supply of fresh water and a large portion of it teems with game fish. It has been estimated that it would take 500 years just to cast a rod into each one of Ontario's fishing lakes.

Bass, both the largemouth variety (which is found in the southeastern part of the province) and the smallmouth variety (found in the Great Lakes and towards the northwest), are keenly sought, while the solitary giant "muskies"

(CONTINUED)

ONTARIO (CONTINUED)

(muskellunge, or maskinonge) range from Lake of the Woods on the western boundary clear across to the St. Lawrence River in the east. Trophy fish range upwards from 14 kilograms.

Georgian Bay, the Kawarthas, the Rideau Lakes, Algonquin Park, and Lake Nipigon with its vast hinterland, all these regions can provide up to the bag limits for the angler.

The fish and game legislation divides Ontario into 29 fishing zones, and the map that will be supplied, on request, by the provincial Ministry of Natural Resources is essential for the newcomer to orient himself. Game fish may be caught in various seasons according to zone, and it is essential that the would-be fisherman study current regulations.

Possession of game fish is restricted to one day's legal limit. Minimum-size restrictions are imposed on a small number of species as follows; Muskellunge from Lake St. Clair must be a minimum of 76 centimetres in length; from Divisions 8 and 11, a minimum of 91 centimetres; from all other waters, 71 centimetres. Bass from Division 10 must be 30 centimetres in length; no restrictions are imposed in other waters. In Division 10, pickerel must be at least 35 centimetres long. Sturgeon from Divisions 21 and 22 must be 114 centimetres in length.

The bag limits given here are approximates, as the limit varies according to the division you are fishing in:

Species	Bag Limit
Lake trout (includes splake)	2–3
Brook trout	7
Rainbow trout	5
Brown trout	5
Atlantic salmon	1
Sauger	6
Bass (largemouth or smallmouth)	6
Muskellunge	1–2
Pickerel	6
Pike	6
Sturgeon	1
Whitefish	25

Most of Quebec's 1,356,791 square kilometres is unoccupied—a vast silent wilderness stretching from Labrador to the Ottawa River and from Hudson Bay and Hudson Strait to the American border. This virtual empire offers one of the world's best environments for exciting game fishing.

Trout, salmon and muskellunge, bass, pike and pickerel (doré)—the province of Quebec offers anglers all of these species, plus some local specialties. There is the fighting ouananiche—the miniature landlocked (or sebago) salmon—which is found along the upper Saguenay River and in Lac Saint-Jean. There is also the arctic char, both the landlocked (Quebec red trout) and sea-run varieties.

The fishing laws of Quebec set angling seasons that vary by species and from

(CONTINUED)

zone to zone. The following list is a general guide to the regulations for fishing in waters other than those in provincial parks, game reserves, wildlife sanctuaries or designated salmon rivers.

Area	Species	Open Season	Bag Limit
Most zones	Smallmouth bass	June 17–Mar. 31	10
Most zones	Largemouth bass	June 17–Mar. 31	10
Everywhere	Muskellunge	June 17–Mar. 31	2
Zones AG	Pike	May 13–Mar. 31	6
Zones C(2)DF	Pike	May 20–Mar. 31	10
Zones BHJ	Pike	May 20–Mar. 31	6
Zones KL	Pike	May 20–Apr. 15	6
Zones L(2)M	Pike	June 3–Apr. 15	10
Zones AG	Walleye	May 13–Mar. 31	6
Zones BJH	Walleye	May 20–Mar. 31	6
Zone F	Walleye	May 27–Mar. 31	10
Zones L(2)MN	Walleye	June 3–April 15	10
Most zones	Sturgeon	June 15–May 14	2
Zones A(2)BG	Speckled trout	Apr. 22–Sept. 25	10
Zones DF	Speckled trout	Apr. 22–Sept. 11	20
Zones JK	Speckled trout	Apr. 22–Sept. 18	10
Zone N	Arctic char	June 3–Sept. 11	5

N.B.: Seasons and bag limits for parks, salmon rivers and sanctuaries are available on application to the provincial authorities.

New Brunswick's major attraction is the Atlantic salmon, *Salmo salar*, the king of the species. Rivers like the Miramichi, Dungarvon and Restigouche are known to anglers the world over. Much of the best water is under private lease to fishing clubs, commercial outfitters or wealthy individuals who take great care not to deplete the stock.

Fishing regulations are complicated—varying by the river, or even part of a river—and are strictly enforced to conserve the valuable resource. Brown, brook and lake trout, plus the smallmouth bass are also plentiful.

Species	Open Season	Bag Limit	Size Limit
Spring salmon	Apr. 15–May 14	2	none
Trout	Apr. 15–Sept. 30	15	none
Landlocked salmon (*Ouananiche*)	Apr. 15–Sept. 30	5	35 cm
Black bass	Apr. 15–June 30	3	not less than 30 cm
Pickerel, perch	no closed season	none	none

Nova Scotia's rainbow, brown and speckled (brook) trout shimmer in about 100 fishing rivers throughout the province, and the salmon is the sovereign of the Medway and Margaree rivers.

Fishing regulations establish open seasons which vary across this compact province according to the zone.

From the harbors of Wedgeport, Shelburne, Liverpool and Yarmouth, the

(CONTINUED)

NOVA SCOTIA (CONTINUED)

Bluenose skippers have led some of the world's most famous anglers in search of the bluefin tuna (443 kilograms is a record catch with rod and reel). The tuna season runs through August and September.

Species	Open Season	Bag Limit
Trout	Apr. 1–Sept. 30	10 of 1 species or 10 in total
Striped bass	Apr. 15–Oct. 31	5
Atlantic salmon	May 25–Sept. 30; or	3
	June 15–Oct. 15 (depending on areas)	

Prince Edward Island's freshwater area is less than one square kilometre and almost all rivers and lakes are tidal. The fish population still draws the angler however. This small sandy isle (just 0.1 percent of the Canadian landmass) provides some salmon, a lot of rainbow and brook trout and plenty of striped bass and white perch.

Off the southern shore of Prince Edward Island, in the racing waters of Northumberland Strait, there are lobsters to match the best in the world. The Gulf of St. Lawrence provides all the mackerel, haddock and halibut that you can pull into your boat.

The game-fish seasons are extended here, enabling anglers to combine fishing with family vacations.

Species	Open Season	Bag Limit
Brook trout	Apr. 15–Sept. 30	20
Rainbow trout	Apr. 15–Sept. 30	5
Atlantic salmon	May 15–Oct. 31	1 per day

Newfoundland is the oldest, and newest, part of Canada, where history is all but written in fish. The province welcomes anglers to its island streams—Humber, Exploits, Gander—and to the great rivers of Labrador, Churchill, Naskaupi, Paradise, Eagle and St. Lewis. The interior highlands are dotted with lakes, most of which still lack highway access.

Atlantic salmon run in from the ocean and the smaller landlocked variety (*ouananiche*) can be found in the lakes and chains of connected ponds. The trout family is represented by the rainbow, brown and brook species. Labrador offers trophy fish just about everywhere, with arctic char, northern pike and salmon on the coastal stretches.

The game laws allow bigger bag limits in Newfoundland, rewarding the mainland angler for the length and expense of his safari. The possession is set at twice the limit of one day's bag.

Species	Open Season	Bag Limit
Salmon (Newfoundland)	June 20–Aug. 31	2
Trout (other than rainbow) in license areas	Jan. 15–Sept. 15	24, or 4.5 kg fish
Lake trout	Jan. 15–Sept. 15	4

(CONTINUED)

NEWFOUNDLAND (CONTINUED)

Species	Open Season	Bag Limit
Rainbow trout	June 1–Sept. 15	24, or 4.5 kg fish
Pike	Jan. 15–Sept. 15	24
Arctic char	Jan. 15–Sept. 15	4

Yukon proudly lists an 8.6-kilogram steelhead (rainbow) trout as the record for this fighting species in its cold rivers and lakes. Salmon surge up the 3,200 kilometre Yukon River into its tributaries—such as the Teslin and Pelly and the aptly named Big Salmon. Lake trout and whitefish abound, with grayling and char, within easy reach of the Alaska Highway where it passes through the southern part of the Yukon.

As a territory (not a province), the Yukon is under federal authority; but regional laws are made in the territorial executive council. Seasons are short so far north, and frost can be expected in any month.

Bag limits for certain fish are given below. Grayling, salmon and trout must be at least 20 centimetres in length.

Species	Bag Limit	Species	Bag Limit
Northern pike	5	Kokanee salmon	5
Arctic grayling	5	Rainbow (steelhead) trout	5
Lake trout, cutthroat trout	5	Arctic char	2
Dolly Varden	5	Chinook, coho, sockeye salmon	5 in all

The Northwest Territories, reaching up to touch the North Pole, run 3,400 kilometres from north to south and 3,280 kilometres from east to west. This area represents a third of Canada, yet it is peopled by fewer than 50,000—Inuit, Indians and Europeans.

The angler who wants to challenge the huge rivers and innumerable lakes of this muskeg wilderness should plan on taking a float plane out of Yellowknife, the regional capital on Great Slave Lake.

Great Bear Lake—with an expanse larger than either Lake Winnipeg or Lake Erie—produces 2.5-kilogram grayling, and lake trout up to 11 kilograms are not uncommon.

The fishing regulations do not enforce any closed seasons, but they impose a possession limit of five for the following species:

Species	Bag Limit	Species	Bag Limit
Lake trout	3	Pike	5
Grayling	5	Arctic char	4
Pickerel	5		

National parks in Canada permit sport fishing (unlike hunting) under regulations stemming from the federal National Parks Act. The parks are under the jurisdiction of the Minister of the Environment in Ottawa, and are administered by Parks Canada. A season permit costs $4 and can be used in different national parks.

(CONTINUED)

NATIONAL PARKS (CONTINUED)

The closed seasons vary from one park to another and also between regions. Up-to-date angling guides are available from the federal authority or regional offices. An up-to-date sampling follows:

National Park	Open Seasons
Kootenay, Yoho, Glacier, Mt. Revelstoke	July 1–Oct. 31 or Victoria Day*–Labor Day
Banff	July 1–Oct. 31 Victoria Day*–Labor Day
Jasper	July 1–Oct. 31 Victoria Day*–Labor Day Aug. 1–Oct. 1
Waterton Lakes	July 1–Oct. 31 Victoria Day*–Labor Day Aug. 1–Oct. 1
Wood Buffalo	Victoria Day*–Oct. 15
Prince Albert and Riding Mountain	May 15–Sept. 30
Georgian Bay Islands and Point Pelee	July 1–Sept. 30 second Saturday of June– second Sunday of Sept.
Fundy	Victoria Day*–Sept. 15 Salmon: Victoria Day*–Oct. 15
Prince Edward Island and Terra Nova	Victoria Day*–Sept. 15
Cape Breton Highlands	April 15–Sept. 30

*Victoria Day falls on the Monday closest to May 24.

Limits of catch and possession in the National Parks

Species	Limit
Bass	5
Pike and muskellunge	5
Salmon (Kokanee)	5
Atlantic salmon, ouananiche	2
Arctic char	10
Walleye	8
Rainbow, brook, cutthroat, speckled, lake trout, splake	10
Whitefish	10
All species in aggregate (except perch)	10

Playing field perils

Trading players

Injuries to players

Injuries to spectators

Is the stadium liable?

THE LEGAL HAZARDS of athletics fall into two main groups: the contractual problems of professional athletes; and actions arising from injuries which are common to both professional and amateur athletes—and occasionally are suffered by spectators.

Disputes and legal actions arising from the contract obligations undertaken by professional athletes—mostly in ice hockey, baseball, football and boxing—usually involve the wording and validity of option and reserve clauses, guaranteed payment clauses and similar conditions.

The vigorous expansion of professional hockey and baseball in the early '70s—particularly the establishment of the now-defunct World Hockey Association in competition with the National Hockey League—brought these questions into sharp focus.

Unless a player is an outstanding performer, there will not likely be a lot to tempt him to break his present contract; on the contrary, he will probably be glad of its protection. But when the boot (or the skate) is on the other foot, the star player sometimes works determinedly to find a way to free himself from his legally binding commitments. Several lawyers in Canada and the United States now specialize in contracts for athletes. Their task is made somewhat easier by the fact that the courts find it just about impossible to compel specific performance of a personal service contract.

Trading players

Where a team organization purchases the services of a player on an exclusive basis, it has the right to sell those services—perhaps to another team in another city. This is known as *trading* a player; it's a kind of barter as an exchange of players is often involved. These conditions are usu-

ally fully spelled out in the contract that each professional player accepts. The conditions of trading clauses can vary widely, mostly depending on the leverage that the individual player has.

The philosophical, rather than legal, question tends to arise as to whether a human can be "owned" at all. Such ownership would be tantamount to slavery, outlawed (under British law) since 1807. The athletic contract is more of a formal agreement for the exchange of money for services over a period of time. The U.S. Commissioner of Baseball, a nonlegal figure, attempts to exercise an overriding power in the interests of the game.

Newspaper coverage of some of the more famous player-management contract disputes seldom dwells upon the investment and financial overheads of the owner (which is sometimes a public corporation with thousands of shareholders) or the support and training of the player in question as he developed his skills. Nor do the newspapers dwell upon the responsibilities of the owner to the rest of his club's signed players whose prospects can suffer if the few stars among them were permitted to desert to the biggest purse. If there were completely open bidding for professionals, the richest club would probably quickly "own" the best players.

Yet, there is another angle worth considering. Sometimes, a young player will be offered a chance to get into a major league club system. He might still be under age, but his parents eagerly sign the forms that will make their "Johnny" rich and famous. As he gains experience, however, Johnny may decide that his contract is far from attractive.

Injuries to players

Many sports involve body contact and therefore tend to be dangerous. Even ta-

742

The spectator was clobbered

FACTS

During a game at Maple Leaf Gardens against the Chicago Black Hawks, Gaye Stewart, a Toronto Maple Leaf player, became involved in a scuffle over a hockey stick that he mistakenly believed to be his own. During the melee, which occurred close to the boards separating the ice from the spectator seats, a female fan was struck by Stewart's stick. When the referee saw the struggle, he stopped the play and imposed a minor penalty upon Stewart. The female spectator subsequently sued the Maple Leaf Gardens, Stewart and the Chicago Black Hawks player.

ARGUMENT

On behalf of the spectator, it was alleged that, notwithstanding she was a holder of a season's ticket, she could not be held to have "assumed the risk of injuries resulting directly from negligence or improper conduct on the part of the player." Such a player could not properly say that she assumed a risk created by his own wrongdoing.

On behalf of the Maple Leaf Gardens and Stewart, it was alleged that an occupant of a rail seat must realize that there is danger of the puck going over the boards, or even that there may be danger resulting from body checking, in which case she would have a reasonable opportunity to protect herself against such dangers. (The spectator was watching the play and something occurred that was not part of the play but a separate incident, and she had no chance to protect herself.)

JUDGMENT

The court held that the action must fail against the Maple Leaf Gardens and the Chicago Black Hawks player but should succeed against Stewart. The Maple Leaf Gardens action was framed on the basis of breach of duty in respect of the safety of the premises, but it was ruled that no case had been made out on those grounds. There was no evidence that a spectator had ever before been injured in this way, nor did the evidence show any failure on the part of the company, or its employes, to take reasonable care of the premises to make them reasonably safe for its spectators.

The case against the two players was based upon the allegation that the injuries were due to an assault or negligence on their part during an illegal struggle. The court found that Stewart had attacked the Chicago Black Hawks player in an effort to get possession of his stick without making any effort to discover (as he could easily have done) whose stick it was. He knew that the spectators were gathered behind him and that those in the front row were only a short distance away. There was a reckless disregard for their safety, and the spectator's injuries resulted directly from his negligence or improper conduct.

The judge ruled, however, that there was no fault to be found with the Chicago Black Hawks player. He was not the aggressor at any stage of the struggle and it appeared he did nothing more than to try to retain possession of his own property.*

*Based on an actual case (1949).

ble tennis players collide at the net. The helmets and pads of the gridiron giants are not proof against injury.

Major team organizations carry heavy insurance to protect their players financially; however, the amateur athlete must look to his routine family policies for coverage (*See* Chapter 8, "Insurance at home"). Some amateur clubs arrange special "match" coverage against injury at minor cost.

Injuries arising from contact during the normal course of play are usually part of the risk the athletes take by playing the game.

If injury were to develop out of an unusual accident with a competitor—something excessively rough or deliberate—it is ranked outside the class of "risk of the game" injury, and a court action for damages could develop. Since 1975, in an attempt to curb "goon" hockey, Ontario has brought assault charges against offending players.

When two competing players are involved, the argument of consent is generally put forward as a defense, the argument being that players voluntarily assume and consent to the risk of injury. It would be ludicrous, so they say, for a boxer to sue his opponent or to bring an assault charge for injuries suffered in a prize fight. However, in other sports, although players are said to run the risk of injury and minor assaults, they are not pugilists. The question arises: what is the legal difference between a lively skirmish in the course of a game and an assault?

In assault cases—perhaps concerning two high-sticking hockey players—self-defense is another answer to the charge, but self-defense is permissible only to the extent that it is required to defend oneself.

Every case in the sporting field must of necessity be judged on the basis of its particular facts. The question was troubling our courts as this was being written.

Injuries to spectators
Injuries to spectators generally fall into three categories: those caused by another fan or fans; those caused by a player; and those caused by a physical object that is directly or indirectly part of the game—such as a lacrosse ball, baseball, puck, or perhaps shattered rinkside glass.

When the injury is caused by another spectator—if, say, a fistfight breaks out in the bleachers—the issue may be settled in the courts, depending on the facts. There also might be a separate criminal charge laid against the aggressor (*See* Chapter 19, "Offenses against the person").

Injuries caused in a fight with a player fall into the same general category as regards settling the issue; an offending player could be sued or could be charged with a crime. (*See* Chapter 18, "The accidental tort.") Most professional athletes are under strict instructions not to respond physically to provocation from partisan fans. They can, of course, sue if they are attacked either during or after a game.

If a spectator was injured by a player deliberately throwing a baseball bat into the crowd, the spectator would probably win a suit for damages.

On the other hand, if a spectator was injured by a foul ball, or a flying puck, it is extremely unlikely that an action for damages would succeed in the courts. Such risks are part of those particular sports and the law assumes that the spectator accepted that risk in coming to the game.

Is the stadium liable?
Often, an admission ticket to a ball park, stadium or arena has a clause printed on it that exempts the management from liability for accidents. The wording, usually in very small type on the back of the ticket, says something to the effect that the management "shall be free from liability for loss, damage or injury suffered by the holder."

This raises an involved question of contract law, but it is not likely that such a clause would stand up in court as providing blanket exemption.

If negligence on the part of the management could be proved, the clause could conceivably count for nothing and the management would be held responsible for any injury suffered by the unfortunate sports fan.

The armchair sportsman

GAMBLING has been a sidelight of the sporting scene ever since the time when a lady's favors rode on the lances of the knights in the medieval jousts. It has even been suggested that some men would bet on two flies crawling up a wall—and probably fight over the result. Today, the yearly expenditure in Canada on gambling of all types is estimated at several billions of dollars.

Gaming and betting—the legal labels for gambling—are quite different and both are permitted by federal legislation, under strict conditions. However, betting is strictly illegal when it takes the form of a business operation conducted for private gain.

In Canada, most betting is on horse racing (including races held outside Canada), on ice hockey and football matches. Gambling on prize fights has dwindled with the decline of that sport. On a different plane is the gambling in provincial and other licensed lotteries, bingo games and raffles.

Under the Criminal Code of Canada, a "game" means a game of chance, or mixed chance and skill; "gaming equipment" is defined as anything that is, or may be, used for playing these games or for betting.

The common gaming house

Anyone who operates a *common gaming house*—that is, runs a gambling business—may be sentenced to imprisonment for two years if convicted. A person who is found without lawful excuse in such a house, or the owner of a house who permits it to be used as a common gaming house, can be fined $500 or sent to prison for six months—or both.

Under the Criminal Code, if evidence is introduced that a police officer who was authorized to enter a particular house was prevented from doing so, it is proof (in the absence of contrary evidence) that the establishment was a common gaming house. This provision makes it worthless for professional gamblers to set up elaborate security barriers. Evidence that a house contained gaming equipment is usually proof enough that the place was used as a common gaming house and that the persons found in the house were gambling.

Police may enter such a house and take into custody the keeper of the house and the people they find in the house; they may seize any equipment they find, except the telephones.

Under the gaming sections of the Code, genuine social clubs are allowed to conduct gambling games as long as no part of the proceeds is retained by the club, except a small fee for the privilege of playing—the maximum fee recently was 50 cents a day per person. These fees are set by the provincial authority that has issued the license to the club. Also, gaming is permitted to charitable or religious bodies that charge a fee for playing and who use the proceeds for "good works."

These regulations on gaming do not apply to bets, or records of bets, made through the agency of an authorized pari-mutuel system.

The private wager

Bets (wagers) between persons not engaged in the business of betting are completely legal. You can have a bet on the Grey Cup with your neighbor, or bet someone $5 that you can stop smoking.

You can also organize an office pool on the Stanley Cup—but among not more than ten persons!

If you do win a bet, however, the courts will not help you to collect your winnings. In civil law, actions to recover any money allegedly won on a bet will not be heard. Wagers are not made illegal by this law; they are simply unenforceable.

A wager has been defined in legal terms as the staking of something of value upon the result of an uncertain fact or event. One party must win and the other lose, and it follows that a wager must be between two persons, or two groups.

If two competitors put up money on a winner-take-all basis in some game of chance, the winner is not entitled to recover the prize money in court. The money is classified as a wager, or stake, put up by the people involved. On the other hand, if more than two competitors put up a prize for the winner of an event—such as in a lottery, or a raffle—the court would help the winner to recover the prize money; when more than two competitors contribute, the law no longer considers it a wager.

Betting on the horses

The gambling provisions of the Criminal Code do not apply to bets made through a pari-mutuel system at a racecourse during a race meeting. However, some other regulations must be respected; for example, federal and provincial authorities must approve the schedule of future race meetings.

The operation of the betting system is supervised by a federally appointed official. The person, club or association conducting the races must pay to the Receiver General for Canada a percentage—not more than one percent—of the total amount of bets made. The percentage deductible by the race club management of the total amount bet is set out in a schedule based on the amount wagered per race in the previous year (recently, it ranged between 9.5 and 12 percent).

The Rules of Racing

THE PROVINCES control horse racing in all its forms, usually through a special Racing Commission that has power to "govern, direct, control and regulate" the sport. However, betting at the tracks is supervised by the federal Department of Agriculture, under provisions of the Criminal Code. Thus the various commissions work closely with the federal authorities in the setting of racing dates, standards of accommodation and other matters.

The "Rules of Racing" for both galloping and trotting horses are published periodically, and can be amended without notice by the commissions. The basic regulations for thoroughbreds are much the same across the country, and in the United States. The main purpose of the close supervision is to assure the spectator public and the competing owners that:

• Every owner and trainer seeking to enter a horse in competition is a person of good character and of financial responsibility.

• Every horse appearing in a race is the animal he is represented to be on the program, is carrying the correct weight, and wearing the true colors of the owner.

• Every race will represent a true competitive effort by every horse and rider.

• No rider will commit any act that would unfairly tend to make the race anything but a fair test.

• Every horse is physically fit to race.

• No forbidden medication has been administered to a competing animal.

Officials of the Racing Commissions and employes of the commissions are not permitted to drink alcoholic beverages while on duty. Announcements by the commissions are normally published in the *Daily Racing Form*. As with the laws of the land, ignorance of the Rules of Racing will not be accepted as an excuse for any violation.

If the official appointed by the government is not satisfied with the manner in which the regulations are being obeyed, he can order the betting be stopped. The government has authority to issue regulations concerning the standard of equipment, buildings and services provided at the racecourse for the proper supervision and operation of a pari-mutuel system.

The "one-arm bandits"

Slot machines are, legally speaking, games of chance. Thus, any premises in which they were installed would be a *common gaming house*.

A slot machine is an automatic amusement device used "for any purpose other than vending merchandise or services"— that is, for gambling. (In cases where a device offers merchandise or services, or discharges slugs or tokens, it is a slot machine if the result of its operation is a matter of chance). Canada does not have a Las Vegas with its hundreds of "one-arm bandits." When the federal gaming legislation was last amended, the slot machine was generally replaced by the pinball machine. This device is not illegal as long as there is no payoff for a winning combination.

The bingo halls

Bingo is considered a *game* in the eyes of the law. Accordingly, the provisions of the Criminal Code on the keeping of a common gaming house, being found in a gaming house, or allowing one's premises to be used as a gaming house, apply to the game of bingo.

This doesn't mean, however, that your weekly bingo session at the church or Legion hall is going to be raided by the vice squad.

Exemptions from the code allow bingo to be played if certain conditions are met. One condition is that the building in which the game is played is used by an incorporated *bona fide* social club. The courts insist that not only must the club have been incorporated, but it also must still be in existence. Another condition is that none of the proceeds may be paid either directly or indirectly to the keeper of the house.

A fee may be charged for playing— usually a small sum per card—but this must be authorized under the license issued by the attorney general of the province concerned.

Raffles and lotteries

By definition, lotteries are prohibited by the Criminal Code. (The raffle is a form of lottery.) Anyone who sets up a lottery scheme, conducts one or participates in one, is committing an offense. Property that has been won in an illegal lottery is forfeited to the Crown. However, once again, wide exemptions are permitted from the law.

The government of Canada, the governments of the provinces, and even individual municipalities may conduct or license lotteries. In the late 1960s, the City of Montreal launched its own lottery across Canada; since then, several provincial and regional lotteries have gained wide popularity. A temporary Olympic lottery (with several million-dollar prizes) was conducted to help defray the enormous costs of the 1976 Games.

Charitable and religious organizations, after obtaining a license, may conduct lotteries—as long as there is no relationship to a dice game, three-card monte, a punchboard or a coin table. The proceeds from the lottery (or raffle) must be used for a charitable or religious purpose. Art galleries and sporting bodies, among other nonprofit organizations, are turning to this method of raising funds.

If a lottery is conducted at a bazaar, it requires a license. The amount of the prize awarded must not exceed $100, and the price of each unit of chance (perhaps a ticket or a guess) must not exceed 50 cents.

Premiums distributed by lot as rewards to promote thrift by making deposits in a chartered savings bank are legal.

Agricultural fairs and exhibitions—like Toronto's Canadian National Exhibition or Vancouver's Pacific National Exhibition—require a license to dispose of goods by lottery on the fairgrounds. You can't try your luck with dice and three-card monte on the Midway, but you can have a flutter at bingo.

You, Crime

and the Law

18/The Tort—A Personal Matter

Defamation of character

The accidental tort

The question of damages

What is a tort?

WITHIN THE SPECIAL LANGUAGE of the law, no term is more difficult to explain than the *tort*. In the dusty pages of large legal tomes you will find ponderous paragraphs explaining that the tort is, well, just about impossible to explain with any certainty. The average citizen is often quite unfamiliar with the word. Yet there is no element of the great body of the law that more often touches the lives of us all. Therefore, we must now join the ranks of those who have struggled to explain how an old Latin word for "twisted" or "wrung" became, by the sixteenth century, a "breach of duty" and then, in more modern times, a civil (or private) wrong committed against the individual.

It is indeed a curiosity that just about everyone knows—or thinks he knows—what a crime is. But if you should ask what a tort is, few people could provide an answer. Yet you are far more likely to be the victim of a tort than of a crime—and you are also much more likely to commit a tort than you are to commit a crime. Perhaps one reason for the confusion lies in the fact that torts are so common, so universal, that they seem to be almost a normal, if unwelcome, part of life itself. Any automobile accident, for example, will almost invariably result in damage to property, and would, therefore, be classified under the law of torts. Any nuisance that amounts to a violation of your personal rights (*i.e.*, a shrieking stereo at 2 A.M. when reasonable people are sleeping) is a tort.

Generally speaking, just about any violation of your private rights not grave enough to be considered a crime is a tort. A tort is committed against you when your person, your property or your character is harmed by the negligent or willful act of another. If you are the injured party, you have the right under provincial law to sue the other party for damages. The guilty party is known in law as the *tort feasor* (the "maker" of the tort).

In a crime—which is an offense against the Crown, *i.e.*, the general public (*See* Chapter 19)—the question of *intent* is all-important. On the other hand, in those torts where damage is caused through negligence, the question of intent is immaterial. If a child breaks your picture window with a baseball, you could sue for negligence—even though the child was too young to be legally capable of committing a crime. If someone's car skids uncontrollably on an icy patch and knocks down your fancy stone wall, you can sue for enough money to get it rebuilt.

The basic question to be decided by the courts in an action for tort is: who should bear the cost of the damage or loss?—the victim, the feasor (the person who committed the tort), the group that may be involved (perhaps all those who would be able to have the loss spread over their future insurance premiums) or the general public (the taxpayers who would provide the funds for any government compensation)?

The decision to make a court case out of a tort is entirely yours. It is a private matter between you and the person who has harmed you. But remember, the cost is yours, too. The police and the whole apparatus of law enforcement will not swing into action unless a crime has also been committed; as explained later in this chapter, a tort and a crime are sometimes committed in the same incident.

Is suit the answer?

Some people always seem willing—indeed, even eager—to jump headlong into a legal action for a minor tort which has been committed against them. Sometimes they see it as a question of principle; money may have nothing to do with the matter. Generally, unless you have money to throw away, you shouldn't bother taking such a case to court. These nominal-damage actions take up a lot of valuable court time, they seldom teach a lesson and they often intensify situations that should have been cooled off and forgotten from the beginning.

Of course, where there is substantial injury to your property, person or reputation and a reasonable settlement is not offered, you should sue for *compensatory*—and perhaps for *exemplary* or *punitive*—damages (*See* Chapter 3, "Decisions from the Bench").

Sometimes, a lawsuit is not the answer simply because it will cost more than the action is worth. You may be better off financially if you simmer down and write off the incident to experience. In other cases, suing might do more harm by creating hostilities. For instance, if an employe were to sue an employer for a nominal amount, it's not hard to see that he could suffer indirect hardships as a result.

In other circumstances a lawsuit is not the answer simply because the law with all its technicalities and complexities just will not produce the effect you intend by taking the matter to court. These are all factors on which your lawyer would be able to advise you.

Consult your lawyer

While it is quite possible for one citizen to sue another without even speaking to a lawyer, the editors offer one word of advice: don't! If a tort has been committed against you and you are thinking of taking the matter to court, you should consult a lawyer as soon as possible.

Some things that in your life may be a most serious and unusual set of circumstances, the lawyer is probably accustomed to seeing and handling frequently. After listening to your tale of woe, your lawyer may abruptly suggest that you drop the case. Don't forget that emotions can often make a mountain out of a molehill. However, if you proceed with the case, the lawyer will be able to advise you to do certain things that you would probably never have considered on your own—for instance, to keep a diary of the pain and suffering resulting from, say, injuries in an automobile accident.

The experienced lawyer can advise, on an educated guess, whether or not your lawsuit will be successful if taken to court and what damages you might expect if you win. The lawyer should also be prepared to tell you, on request, what fee will be charged for representing you.

Once "retained" by you (*See* Chapter 20, "How the lawyer is paid"), the lawyer will then take over all the procedural problems of handling the case. He or she will formally initiate the suit, with careful regard for the time limits set by law, and conduct the case in court on your behalf.

Suits within the family

The law guards your personal rights with such jealousy that if you have been harmed by somebody, you can sue that person, no matter who—even the Queen (with her delegated permission). There are, however, certain limitations to suits within your own family.

A married woman can sue her husband for a tort against her personal property but generally not for tort against her person or reputation. (Prince Edward Island and Ontario are two provinces where this restriction has been abolished.) If a man hit his wife with his automobile, she could sue him if her bracelet were broken but would not be allowed to recover damages for a broken arm. In some provinces, a husband cannot sue his wife for a tort at all. This stems from when the law considered husband and wife to be literally one person. (Quebec has no restrictions regarding suits between spouses.)

One spouse can lay certain criminal charges against the other and can bring action for breach of contract—but not for tort. The only exception concerns the personal property of the wife. As the old law still has it: how can "one person" sue himself or seek damages against himself?

If a wife was hit and hurt by her husband's car, she would be able to collect the insurance that anyone else would be entitled to collect if the husband had been driving negligently—but only if the accident took place in another country.

When a wife seeks to sue her husband for an assault, the circumstances of the marriage are usually such that she is no longer living with him. Instead of suing her husband in a tort, the wife would probably apply either for support under the Deserted Wives and Children's Maintenance Act or for a divorce and maintenance under the Divorce Act. (*See* Chapter 10, "The divorce.")

There are other ways in which actions between family members are limited. In Canada, a son most probably could not sue his father for allowing him to be born illegitimately or physically handicapped. On the other hand, he could sue his father for assault or for neglect. If he were to do so as a minor, he would need another adult to act for him as his *next friend*. The "next friend" can be virtually any person who has reached the age of majority, and who will undertake to pay the costs of the case in the event that the "infant" plaintiff should lose (*See* Chapter 11, "Children and parents").

Although tempers can rise as high inside families as outside them, most lawyers warn that an intrafamily court action presents extra difficulties for all concerned and is best avoided if at all possible. A fight between strangers can be forgotten when the dust settles, but one between family members can cause bitternesses that seem to last forever.

Torts by children

Although any child, even one who is mentally retarded, can be sued for causing harm or damage, it would normally be a complete waste of time because the child usually has no money or property of his own at the time with which to pay damages. He is what is called *judgment proof*. And in most provinces the law does not insist that the parent pay for damage caused by his child (parents will normally do so out of moral obligation).

However, the situation can be different

If you are sued . . .

THERE IS an old saying that the man who takes a case to the courts needs nine things: A good deal of money, a good deal of patience, a good cause, a good lawyer, good counsel, good evidence, a good jury, a good judge and—*good luck*.

If you should find yourself cast as the defendant in a suit under the law of torts, don't ignore the summons you receive, no matter how upset or angry it may make you. Take the summons to your lawyer immediately, or seek advice from the nearest Legal Aid office. If you don't turn up in court as demanded, it's likely that the plaintiff will win by default.

Be totally honest with your lawyer. If you did commit the act of which you are accused, admit it. Provide your counsel with all the relevant unbiased detail you can remember. There may well be legal ways in which he can minimize—or even eliminate—the costs to you.

Take your lawyer's advice, if he advocates an out-of-court settlement, even if you are convinced you are "in the right."

You won't be alone if you come to think that the law is not always perfect. The Emperor Napoleon, whose Civil Code (in amended versions) governs civil law in modern France, Quebec, Louisiana and elsewhere, once stated that "lawsuits are an absolute leprosy, a social cancer." As the old proverb has it, "Law suits consume time, money, rest, and friends."

Even the saints cautioned us about going to the courts. The Apostle Paul chided the Corinthians: "There is a fault among you, because you go to law one with another . . . . Do you not know that the saints shall judge the world?"

if the parent, guardian or custodian of a child is "joined" in the action to the feasor-child as a codefendant for not controlling the child properly, or with enough care.

The tort of negligence is determined by the test of reasonableness. What would a reasonably prudent person have done in these circumstances? In the case of a child or a minor, the test would be what it would be reasonable to expect a child or minor at that age to do.

The age of the child is a critical factor in assessing the parent's responsibility. A younger child would normally be supervised more closely by his parents than an older child would be. A 16-year-old boy who was driving his automobile without due care and attention would be held responsible for the tort of negligence, but his parents could hardly be blamed for allowing him to drive if he had a driver's license. However, if parents allowed a 12-year-old boy to drive and an accident occurred because of the boy's negligence, then the parents might well be held liable.

A tort can be a crime

The rules we live by in Canada say, basically, that we have the right to do almost anything we desire—up to a limit; that limit is reached when we extend our liberty to the point of interfering with the freedom of others. (*See* Chapter 2, "The two faces of freedom.") Our civil laws allow plenty of room to seek relief and compensation for most breaches of those rules. A severe violation of the rules, however, may be more than a tort—it may be a crime. An individual action may, in fact, be both a tort and a crime.

It should be remembered that the prime purpose of the law of torts is not to punish the offender but to compensate the victim. Punishment belongs to the realm of criminal law.

Although you have the liberty to drive an automobile, that liberty is limited by the provincial highway traffic acts and by the negligence laws. You must drive by the rules of the road and must keep a constant lookout to make sure that you do no damage to innocent pedestrians or other drivers who are also following the rules of the road. If you should carelessly ram another car and dent its fender, you have committed a tort ("injury to property") and the owner of the other vehicle can sue you under civil law. But you have not committed a crime. If, however, a breathalyzer test showed that you had been driving while impaired by alcohol, then you could be charged by the police with an offense, in addition to the fact that you could be sued for the tort of negligence.

In another illustration, we can say that *assault and battery* is a tort. If someone threatens to hit you, you can sue him for assault. If he makes good his threat and does hit you, you can sue him for battery.

In these cases, the state steps into the situation. Since a man who goes around attacking his neighbors is a threat to society in general, the penalty must be more than just paying compensation. His action is classed as a crime. Perhaps such a menace should temporarily be deprived of his physical freedom by being sent to prison? Perhaps this severe treatment will make him think twice and will serve as a deterrent to other potentially dangerous people? Perhaps a fine, or a period on probation will be discipline enough? The judge will decide (*See* Chapter 3, "Decisions from the Bench").

Persons with privilege

In the greater public interest, to allow certain classes of people to speak their minds freely without the threat of being sued for the torts of *libel* or *slander* (*See* "Defamation of character" later in this chapter), they are permitted what is known as *privilege*. They can without worry make statements or accusations that could normally carry risk for defamation of character. Anyone publishing an accurate report of those statements is also protected.

There are two levels of privilege: *absolute* and *qualified*. Then there is a gray area where the courts will try to permit as much privilege as possible to certain persons, under certain circumstances.

The members of the federal parliament and of all provincial legislatures, municipal councils, most government-appointed tribunals or commissions and other judicial bodies, enjoy absolute privilege while within the walls of the chamber of debate or deliberation. This protection also covers all members of the judiciary, court staff, prosecutors, lawyers and witnesses while they are actually engaged in the hearing of a case within the courtroom. Both our legislators and our judges must be free to speak without fear or hindrance when engaged in the high duties of serving the public as a whole.

In heated political debates, you will sometimes hear someone being challenged to repeat a statement "outside the House." This is, in effect, an invitation to make the same charge at a place where one is not covered by privilege, thus risking being sued for defamation. Politicians of integrity, aware of the harm that can be done by widely reported critical statements made under privilege, are extremely cautious. They recognize that, unless the person attacked is in fact a member of a privileged body, there is no way that the charge may be answered with the same force. However barbed politicians may get in their verbal fencing, they are required by custom to conceal the hook behind a cloak of courtesies.

In some countries, the privilege of having private communications—and of choosing not to disclose them even on demand in court—has been extended to the doctor and patients, the clergy and its parishioners, the lawyer and clients, the news media and their contacts.

In Quebec the protection is extended to priests and to all professionals who receive confidential information in the exercise of their profession.

Elsewhere in Canada this privilege is permitted only between the solicitor and client. Its purpose is to allow the lawyer to prepare a case properly without being subjected to examination, and also to allow the client the freedom to talk openly to the legal adviser. Without this type of privilege, it would be difficult, if not impossible, for anyone—whether innocent or guilty—to be defended adequately in a court of law.

Although privilege is limited in Canada, there is an understanding among lawyers and Crown attorneys that doctors and other professionals will not be pushed into violating confidences which were entrusted to them, unless it is absolutely necessary for the sake of justice being done in a particular situation (*See* "Defamation of character" in this chapter).

Quebec's law of delicts

In this chapter, discussion has centered on the law of torts as it applies in the English-speaking provinces. Torts lurk everywhere in different guises and it would be endlessly confusing to add details in each paragraph about the differences in the law of Quebec in this field.

The equivalent Quebec law is set out in six main sections of the Civil Code where torts are known as *delicts* (literally, offenses against the law). It can be said that there are more broad similarities between torts and delicts than there are detailed differences.

This means that, in Quebec, whether you are thinking about your responsibility to compensate others, or about your own right to recover damages, you can be guided generally by most of the items set out in this chapter. Your lawyer (the *avocat*) will guide you precisely.

Being surrounded by states and provinces that live by the English Common Law, the Quebec courts have been influenced by this closeness through many generations with the result that it is not possible to get precise answers on the law of delicts from the Civil Code alone: the trend of decisions in the courts has to be watched carefully. In fact, the articles in the Code are themselves more a set of guiding principles than a catalog of detailed rules.

Article 1053 of the Civil Code says, "Every person capable of discerning right from wrong is responsible for the damage caused by fault to another, whether by positive act [meaning intentionally], imprudence, neglect, or want of skill..." In this general principle, the requirement of "fault" is central. In Quebec then, you can expect to be liable for both intentional and negligent actions that cause damage to others; the Common Law fails as yet to provide such a firm principle.

The standard of care required of a person is stated everywhere in nearly identical terms. In Quebec, as in other provinces, liabilities are stricter for owners (or custodians) of animals, dangerous premises or noxious substances. There are also the same general excuses for those who are unable to understand what they are doing. And Quebec courts are as hesitant as those of the Common Law provinces to grant punitive damages, or damages for purely mental distress and suffering.

Yet the Civil Code does contain some differences in detail. For one thing, Quebec law places great emphasis on the role of the family, and the liability of parents for the actions of their young children is generally greater than elsewhere in Canada. On the other hand, because the Civil Code expressly makes "fault" a necessary ingredient of delict, strict liability in the matter of insuring others against certain kinds of heavy risks has not been enforced as readily as it has in the Common Law provinces.

The ordeal of Maud Allan

DURING World War I, the Canadian exotic dancer Maud Allan was cast as the central figure in one of the strangest and most sensational libel cases ever heard. In the early 1960s, the sex scandals involving British cabinet ministers Profumo, Lambton and Jellicoe had caused an uproar, but these affairs were minor when compared with what came to be known as the "Case of the Black Book." Before it ended, the names of many prominent British figures, including a former prime minister, were besmirched.

By early 1918, a tense Britain had suffered grievous losses in men and material and the German Army was still attacking in France. An independent member of parliament named Noel Pemberton Billing attracted wide attention when he published in his weekly newspaper a report that a member of the German royal family possessed a "black book" listing the names of no fewer than 47,000 British men and women in high positions who were alleged to indulge in sexual perversions. The German Secret Service had compiled the list during several years of research for possible use in political blackmail.

Shortly afterward, it was announced that two private performances of Oscar Wilde's play *Salome* were to be given, featuring Maud Allan's version of the "dance of the seven veils."

Public performances had been forbidden by the censor. Wilde had spent two years in jail on vice charges.

Billing's paper now published a brief item headed, "The Cult of the Clitoris," in which he suggested that the names of those who went to see *Salome* would no doubt also be found in the infamous Black Book. The title of the item and the context carried the unmistakable innuendo that Maud Allan was a lesbian. Jointly with the owner of the sponsoring theatrical society, she brought suit against Billing in London's Old Bailey.

Billing conducted his own case. He first brought out that the dancer's brother had been executed in the United States for a double rape-murder. He established that she had danced near-nude in Germany. Wilde was attacked as "the greatest force for evil in Europe." Billing claimed that the presiding judge himself was listed in the Black Book (which was not produced in evidence—if indeed it ever existed).

The hearing was interrupted continuously by yells and applause from the public gallery, and the judge was hissed as he attempted to control the freewheeling M.P. When the jury cleared Billing of any liability, he was cheered to the echo by the packed courtroom and by the large crowd waiting outside in the street. In the uproar, no one seemed to notice, or care, that the Canadian dancer was, by implication, left with her public reputation ruined.

The intentional tort

IN THE LAW it is known as *mens rea*—the "guilty mind." In everyday terms, *mens rea* can be expressed as wrongful purpose, or intention to injure or damage. Intent is not only a vital element in most crimes but also an important element in a wide range of torts—including assault and battery, defamation, trespass, fraud, false imprisonment, malicious prosecution, seduction and conversion. It is sometimes present in the lesser tort of nuisance. These items will be taken up separately as this chapter proceeds.

It has already been pointed out that a tort can be committed whether the person at fault intended any harm or not, even if the act complained of was entirely accidental. This is common in cases involving the tort of negligence. (The accidental tort is discussed in a later section.)

It should be kept in mind that the law of torts, which can be traced back to Biblical times, is not basically aimed at punishing the wrongdoer, but at compensating the person who has suffered in some way. However, where *intention* is proved in a tort, the court may, in some narrowly defined circumstances, award a substantial sum of money as punitive damages. From this point of view, it has the effect of a fine in a criminal case.

Cases occur where it would not be just, or even possible, to assess compensatory damages purely on the basis of the actual loss or damage suffered by the victim. A successful civil action for malicious prosecution provides a good example. Consider the possibility that someone who hates you lays a false criminal charge against you at the police station and is able to persuade the authorities to bring you to trial. There is no shred of honest evidence against you, and you are acquitted. During the hearing, it is plainly revealed that your accuser had trumped up the charges out of sheer personal hostility. This would probably provide you with grounds to launch a civil suit for damages.

People do read and talk about court cases involving their friends, acquaintances and business colleagues and, as the old saying goes, "mud sticks." You have obviously suffered—but how much, in terms of money? To compensate you for the injury done to your reputation as well as for your mental suffering, the judge might award you a substantial sum on top of the value of any actual financial loss you might be able to prove to have suffered as a consequence of being falsely and maliciously accused. With this judgment, he would also be punishing the other party for what is known as *abuse of process* (deliberate misuse of the courts).

In another example, if you should commit the tort of nuisance by disturbing your neighbor at night, you could be ordered to compensate him up to the point of the court's evaluation of the neighbor's "injuries." But if you did the same thing deliberately, and if your neighbor could prove that malice was involved, then you could end up paying a much larger sum as damages. This extra amount should not be considered as punitive, but rather as *aggravated*, damages. The judicial reasoning here is that in a case of downright malice, the hurt to the plaintiff's dignity and pride is greater and the episode much more worrying.

Assault on the person

Our law guarantees you the right to freedom from both threats of assault and actual physical attack of all kinds. Except for everyday passing contact with other humans, your person is sacrosanct. But, if you are threatened or attacked, the law of torts offers you a legal substitute to the recourse of shouting or hitting back.

The legal distinction between the terms *assault* and *battery*—often linked or merged in court cases—is this: "assault" describes the open threat of violence (brandishing your fist under someone's nose) while "battery" involves the threat being put into action. The latter requires physical contact, but not necessarily as explicit as a punch in the nose—having your lapels grabbed might be enough. If someone spat in your face, that would be an insult; but it would also, technically, be battery—and you could sue.

The law recognizes that you can be harmed in a mental as well as a physical way by someone who threatens violence as well as by someone who actually resorts to it. Of course, you must be able to prove that the threat would cause fright or anxiety to a reasonable person. A few angry shouts from a distance would not constitute an assault.

If the actual actions of assault and battery were threatening or harmful enough, a policeman might intervene and lay the criminal charge of *assault*. (*See* Chapter 19, "Offenses against the person"). Accordingly, serious cases of assault are seldom heard in the civil courts.

Retribution is out
The rise of law in the Western world is part of a long historical process in which impartial adjudication in the courts slowly supplanted the jungle laws of retribution and personal vengeance (*See* Chapter 1, "From earliest times"). It is through the law of torts that you are provided with a civilized method of settling scores with the violent bully without having to resort to *his* tactics, and of being compensated by the wrongdoer for his actions without having to twist his arm. The impartial hands of justice do the work for you.

The veneer of civilization is still seemingly thin. Vendettas (vengeful blood feuds) are still being reported from member countries of the United Nations.

Newspaper readers everywhere follow with grim fascination the periodic rounds of retaliatory gang killings in New York's underworld. And in Montreal, a man fired from his job returned with a gun and killed three executives in reprisal.

While it is understandable that a man will instinctively bridle under insult, or want to hit back in self-defense, it is worth remembering that the courts offer a better alternative. The popularity of "vigilante" movies where the hero takes the law into his own hands and guns down the villains may be a sign of society's ills, but it remains a fact that we have come a long way from the concepts of "an eye for an eye" justice. You must not respond to verbal insult with physical action and, if you are acting in self-defense, you are permitted to use only *reasonable force*— but no more than is reasonable.

Injury in horseplay
People get injured every day while just fooling around, or due to practical jokes that misfire. Horseplay may or may not involve the participation of the so-called victim as well as the tort feasor, the perpetrator. Generally speaking, if the victim is a consenting party in the situation, he is considered to have contributed to the damage he suffered.

Under the Negligence Act of Ontario, for example, responsibility for paying for damages suffered in these and similar cases of contributory negligence is based on the amount of fault attributed to the plaintiff and to the defendant. If two people were involved equally in a game and one of the parties was injured so that his damages totaled $10,000, the court would probably award the plaintiff $5,000. Although the defendant would claim that the plaintiff contributed to his negligence, the court might maintain that the defendant has been equally negligent.

Not so long ago, the slightest fault on the part of the plaintiff ruined any chance he might have had for a successful action against the tort feasor, even if the court realized that the tort feasor was responsible for most of the damage. The plaintiff was said to be "the author of his own misfortune," and that was that. The principle of *comparative negligence* was introduced in an Ontario statute of 1924. The courts do not set any percentages for assessing damages under this law, leaving that to the judges and juries dealing with individual cases.

Stealing a kiss

It may seem the most innocent thing in the world for a young man in the spring to steal a kiss from his pretty neighbor. If she is flattered, willing or even apathetic, then no tort is committed. However, if she takes exception to his conduct, she might reply with a suit for assault.

Was the kiss too long, disturbing, too bruising? If so—and if it was unwelcome—then the kiss could even be considered a crime. The Criminal Code includes this type of behavior under the label of assault. This is an indictable offense and if the young man was found guilty, he could be sentenced to imprisonment for five years. At one time (until 1972) he could even be whipped!

Any kind of bodily touch can be counted as assault, if the object of the touch does not permit it. The admiring "pinch" of a Latin Don Juan can result in a "pinch" by the cop on the beat. But it is not illegal to touch someone in a respectful way—to draw his or her attention to something—and normal jostling in a bus queue or crowded shop has to be accepted.

False imprisonment

The tort of false imprisonment applies to any unjustified interference with your right to total freedom of movement. Such an act might involve your being detained against your wishes in a restaurant (*See* Chapter 15, "Restaurant regulations") or someone deliberately blocking your path. The element of intent is necessary for such actions to be considered torts. A court may take the view that someone was subjected to restraint even if no physical force of any kind was used; the simple command to remain, if forcefully given or carrying a veiled threat, would be sufficient. (*See* Chapter 3, "When the law is broken.")

The classic illustration of false imprisonment is the action of an over-zealous store detective in making a citizen's arrest of a shopper whom he wrongly accuses of shoplifting (*See* Chapter 6, "In the supermarket"). A civil suit against the detective would probably succeed unless he could convince the court that the crime had indeed been committed but that he

The unanswerable argument

JUDGE GERALD SPARROW, a British barrister who once presided over the International Court in Bangkok, recounts among his memoirs a singular case in which a Chinese merchant sued for slander because it had been alleged he was incapable of making physical love to a young woman. Where men of other races would probably have gone to great lengths to avoid any publicity on the question, the wealthy Mr. Swee Ho was fearful of "losing face" with family and associates.

Mr. Pu Lin, a business rival, had stated sneeringly at a party that Mr. Swee's new "wife," the beautiful Li Bua, was merely a decoration to indicate how rich her patron was—Swee Ho could no longer "please the ladies."

Swee Ho, his manhood challenged, stated categorically that Li Bua was in every sense his concubine. Every rich and successful Chinese in those times had one—or several—"social wives," usually introduced to the household by the true wife. Swee Ho brought suit for slander in the British consular court.

The plaintiff won his case, and substantial damages, without a word of evidence being taken. His lawyer put the blushing Li Bua in the witness box. She had long gold-painted fingernails and she was unmistakably pregnant.

had arrested the wrong person with reasonable cause. This is the only sound defense to a charge of false imprisonment (and to one of false arrest) brought against a citizen. If you should ever feel required to make a citizen's arrest, make sure of your ground. Did you actually see an offense being committed? Are you sure of the identity of the offender? Thieves will sometimes set a trap for shopkeepers, or car owners. Pretending to steal but actually taking nothing, they will deliberately invite arrest. If you detain them while you call the police, they would possibly have grounds to sue you for damages.

These restrictions are imposed by law to restrain hasty or vigilante-type action but they would be overly frustrating to police and other peace officers. These officers, whether on duty or off, are permitted to arrest without warrant when they have "reasonable grounds" to believe that someone has committed a crime or is about to commit one (*See* Chapter 3, "The policeman's lot"). Even if the arrested person is totally innocent, there are no grounds for a damages action as long as the constable can point to "reasonable grounds." Perhaps the policeman was convinced that the person apprehended was a wanted criminal with a record of violence. Perhaps the officer saw someone climbing through a factory window at midnight and did not believe that the prisoner was a locked-out boss. The possibilities are endless.

The great majority of innocent citizens who meet with such an unsettling experience are glad, on later reflection, to have had first-hand evidence of the willingness and promptness of the police to act in the protection of society—even if they might "blow it" once in a while.

Recent bail-reform legislation places extra responsibility on the arresting police officer, on the officer in charge at the station and on the justice of the peace to allow an arrested person as much freedom as would seem prudent within the overall necessity of justice being done.

The burden of proof
In the prosecution of almost all criminal charges, the onus is on the Crown to prove beyond reasonable doubt that the accused in fact committed the alleged offense. In an action for tort, however, the onus is on the accuser to prove the case against the accused.

As long as the defendant can show innocence, or even that his or her testimony is slightly more believable than that of the plaintiff, the defendant should win.

It has been stated that some harmful actions often contain the ingredients of both torts and crimes, which means that in such cases the injured party must choose between laying criminal charges or civil charges. There can also be confusion in some breach-of-contract cases about whether to bring action within the law of torts or the law of contracts. (*See* Chapter 6, "Safeguards when shopping.") Many lawyers will advise a plaintiff, where there is a choice, to proceed under torts because, if successful, the damages he is awarded are likely to be higher.

After the state has tried, found guilty and sentenced a wrongdoer, his victim might launch a separate civil action arising from that crime. An example is provided by the reckless or dangerous driver who has ended his zigzag course by demolishing your front porch. The police will certainly charge him with a criminal offense for having endangered the public at large. However, it would be up to you, as a private citizen, to seek monetary compensation for the damage to your property by taking civil action. Of course, if the guilty driver carried adequate diversified insurance, you probably would not actually have to go to court to get your money. (*See* Chapter 8, "Insurance at home.") Nevertheless, the fact that you would almost certainly succeed in an action for tort in the circumstances described, effectively reduces the possibility of any hang-up over the insurance payoff.

It must be noted, however, that the reckless driver's conviction on the criminal count would not necessarily be accepted in civil court as proof of responsibility in your tort action. It would only be allowed as evidence if the driver had either pleaded guilty to the criminal charge or admitted his guilt at some stage during the proceedings.

Trespassing prohibited!

Invitees and licensees

Keeping a fierce dog

Trespass by children

Invasion of privacy

Interference with your affairs

Creating and abating nuisance

TRESPASS, the unauthorized entry onto another person's land, is perhaps the most ancient of all torts, having an unbroken descent from the writs of twelfth-century England, which are the forerunners of civil law as we know it in this field.

Many of the other torts we are discussing in this chapter developed or branched off from trespass to property: trespass to the person, for example, which we know under its modern name of *assault;* and trespass to goods, the most common forms of which we call theft, or *conversion. (See* Chapter 15, "Goods in transit.") There is now also protection against the space-age trespass of wiretapping, electronic surveillance, and controls regulate the computer storage of personal data.

The right to private property is jealously guarded in all countries that have legal systems deriving from English Common Law *(See* Chapter 2, "Our conditional rights"). Yet there seem to be many widely held misconceptions about trespassing. For one, trespass is a criminal offense by night but not by day. TRESPASSERS WILL BE PROSECUTED therefore has limited meaning.

For the most part, the Crown will not prosecute anyone for merely walking across your lawn or yard; it is normally up to you, as the landowner, to bring a civil action against the uninvited stroller. Before you would get anything more than nominal ("token") damages you would, however, have to show the court convincing evidence that your property had been damaged by the intruder.

On the other hand, the simple act of entering private property (land, house or apartment) without actual or implied permission is definitely trespassing. The tort itself does not depend on whether you do any damage. You can commit the tort by wandering from public lands onto unfenced or unmarked private property without even being aware that you are trespassing. In such a case, if you left when asked or when you became aware you were on another's land, having caused no damage, you would be safe from suit. In the wide open spaces of Canada, it is not generally considered wrong to go hiking or hunting on either Crown or private land unless there are notices (NO TRESPASSING, NO HUNTING) or unless the property is fenced or otherwise marked off.

Tenants or lessees are sometimes unsure about whether they have the same rights as an owner to order trespassers off the property they have rented (or to have them put off if they are unwilling to go). Since trespass is basically a tort against possession, it follows that the tenant has every right to sue. The owner can also sue in certain circumstances—for instance, if a trespasser caused some permanent damage to the land (perhaps by cutting down a tree?). This right to legal action remains with the owner because when the tenancy or lease expires, the possession of the land reverts to him and he is entitled to get it back undamaged.

Another interesting aspect of trespass to property concerns the airspace above the private land. Who owns that? You or the Crown? It is a question that has not yet been completely settled to everyone's satisfaction. The erection of a business sign that overhangs the property next door, or wires strung across the neighbor's property without the neighbor's consent, have been labeled trespass. However, the flight of an airplane over your land at a reasonable height is permitted, subject to the aeronautical regulations of the region. If the pilot dropped something harmful onto your land, or if the noise or vibration of his engines caused some kind of damage—such as stopping your hens from laying—you could sue for trespass (you might have to call on your hens to testify!). In the latter case, you might be better off to charge the pilot with committing a nuisance. (Nuisances are discussed later in this section.)

If your neighbor extended his basement or wine cellar under your land, that would be trespass as well.

Invitees and licensees

Anyone who owns a home or leases property where he or she is granted the right of quiet enjoyment over that property has the right to invite anyone he or she wishes onto that property (these are *invitees*), or to order off anyone not wanted on the property. However, this right is limited by certain statutes, as there are some persons who are permitted to enter private property uninvited. The law classifies these people as *licensees*. For example, the policeman who has reasonable grounds to believe that a crime is being committed may enter your property without invitation. The people who deliver milk and newspapers do not commit trespass when they call; they are licensees by custom or by the fact that they have previously been allowed on your property (*See* Chapter 4, "Closing the deal").

Any person who is not invited and who has no "license" to enter is committing the tort of trespass. You do not necessarily even have to walk upon the land itself to commit the tort: it is enough to send your dog onto it, to shoot your firearm over it or to place something on the land (such as a truckload of gravel). The owner of the property or the tenant has the right to exclude trespassing persons, or any of their possessions, using whatever reasonable force is necessary. Some provinces have backed up the owner's rights with legislation. For example, under Ontario's Trespass to Property Act, any person tres-passing within an enclosed area (a fenced or marked-off property) after being given notice by the owner to leave is subject to a fine of up to $1,000. (This represents one of the few cases where the Crown takes action against trespassing.)

Keeping a fierce dog

As a landowner, you have certain duties toward anyone who comes onto your property, including the trespasser. You cannot, for example, turn a fierce dog on him. If a dog that was known to have a tendency to attack or bite people injured a person who trespassed, the intruder would probably have grounds for a civil suit for damages.

If an animal kept on your property was by nature wild—a lion or a wolf, for example—then you, as the owner of that animal, would be held completely responsible should anyone be injured by it. The law practically makes the owner of wild animals an insurer of any person who might be attacked by them. Animals which are normally tame—cattle, dogs, cats, and even camels—although they may, in fact, be vicious, are likely to be given a second chance if they are generally docile. Lawyers say flippantly that, "every dog is entitled to one bite." This would probably not hold good if a tooth-marked trespasser could convince the magistrate that your dog had tried to bite him (or someone else) previously.

If you have a fierce dog or a boa constrictor—or any other animal that could be considered dangerous—on your property, you are expected to provide warning to the innocent wayfarer. Most people are familiar with the sign BEWARE OF THE DOG. While such a sign serves its purpose as a warning (except to a blind or very near-sighted person) it also eliminates any chance you might otherwise have had of convincing a judge later that your dog was normally tame and thus "entitled to one bite."

If you are annoyed by trespassers and are considering buying a guard dog, first check your provincial and municipal regulations. In some urban communities, the dog that bites is picked up by the local dogcatcher and disposed of without much ceremony. In rural areas, the law allows a farmer to shoot any dog that attacks his livestock. Usually, a municipality which licenses dogs will pay compensation to the owner of any injured livestock and will then make a claim against the owner of the dog.

If an animal trespasses and causes damage, even when following the ordinary instincts of its kind, then the owner of that animal may be held responsible. In a case where a horse bit and kicked another horse through a wire fence, the defendant owner was found liable, even though there was no proof that the horse had a vicious temper. The liability arose because "some portion of the offending horse's body must have been over the boundary"—it was trespassing, at least in part.

Anyone who approached too close to a chained or fenced-in dog and was bitten by the dog would have to admit personal blame.

However, this would depend on the circumstances; the proviso might not apply to, for instance, a small child.

Hidden traps

In your efforts to protect your property from trespassers, don't set any traps that could injure someone, certainly not any guns with trip wires, secretly electrified fences or concealed pits. If anyone were to be injured by such a hidden trap, you would be liable in civil law under the tort of *occupier's liability.*

If, however, a trespasser intent upon burglary was injured in such a hidden trap, he could not sue for damages—as long as the trap represented a "reasonable force" necessary to deter the activities of would-be burglars.

Different degrees of responsibility are placed on the occupier for different classes of people who enter his private property. The most protected person is the invitee—you must take care of him as much as is reasonably possible. Almost as protected as the invitee is the licensee—you must warn him of any unusual dangers (such as an unsanded icy walk). The third-class citizen is the trespasser—including the burglar entering your home

in the middle of the night. Although the law offers scant protection for the burglar even in the event of the roof falling in on him (*See* Chapter 19, "Offenses against property"), a simple trespasser in your home without evil intentions might receive some compensation if he were injured, but this would depend entirely upon the circumstances.

Don't put barbed wire, spikes or broken glass on your fences without checking the local building code first. Such devices are often prohibited under municipal bylaws; and, even if they are allowed, these "defensive weapons" must be easily visible from outside your property.

Trespass by children

Children can be found guilty of the tort of trespass, just like any adult. If a child is old enough to understand that he is doing something wrong—there is no statutory "age of reason"—the court might even award some nominal damages against him. Children younger than six who trespass and cause damage can cost their parents a lot of money as well as worry; the court might decide, because of the child's tender age, to shift the blame onto the parents, who should have been watching him more diligently. The parents would be held responsible under the tort of negligence.

Every householder, businessman and farmer should be aware of the terms "allurement" and "attractive nuisance." These terms refer to anything that is likely to entice young children—such as an open cellar, or a piece of interesting machinery like an electric fan, a crane or a grain combine (*See* Chapter 11, "Children in trouble"). The law, recognizing the adventurous streak in normal youngsters, places a general duty on adults to protect them from hazards that would not normally be regarded as dangerous. Swimming pools normally have to be fenced in. There should be warning signs, and perhaps even a guard who watches over potentially harmful machinery.

You could be held liable for injury to a child trespasser, even if you were on holiday a thousand miles away at the time. The wise occupier will make sure that accident liability insurance is adequate and that premiums are always paid up. However, if a mishap does occur and the distraught parents are going to sue you "for all you've got," consult your lawyer. He may be able to get the parents to agree to an out-of-court settlement, or advise you on a valid defense.

Invasion of privacy

Privacy is a right that Canadians cherish and strive to protect; however, it is difficult to define in legal terms. Although Canadian law is still a mixture of a little legislation and considerable precedent, there is doubtless a growing protection against trespass on the privacy of the individual. British Columbia has had a Privacy Act since 1968. Both Common Law and the Civil Code followed in Quebec favor the principle that a person has some right to seclusion and to the privacy of his name, his likeness and his personal past—even if these rights are not yet widely set down in the written law (as they are in several American states). Also acknowl-

The adulterous Queen

GEORGE IV reigned as monarch for only ten years but earned a reputation as a profligate. Perhaps his most outrageous act was to bring action against his wife, Queen Caroline, for adultery.

As Prince of Wales, George was handsome, cultured and charming. He was chased ardently by women, chaste and otherwise. In 1785, when he was 23, he secretly married Maria Fitzherbert who had already had two husbands. This did not offer the promise of a legal heir to the British throne. So the prospective king formally married his German cousin, Caroline of Brunswick.

Caroline was a cheerful, coarse, lusty creature who never washed until it was practically forced upon her. George actually sent his current mistress to meet his legal bride when she arrived by ship at Greenwich. The regal couple lived together for about two weeks.

Caroline was a woman of normal (if greedy) appetites and desires and when she was more or less banished to a house at Blackheath she was not without callers. In 1806, the vengeful George—enjoying several mistresses himself—put the Chief Justice of England to the task of investigating the morals of his wife.

Adultery against a prince was high treason and the penalty was death. Caroline was not permitted to speak in her own defense. She was snubbed in public and her 15-year-old daughter was taken away from her for "re-education." In vengeful mood, she went to Europe, where she danced topless in Geneva and had an affair with Napoleon's brother-in-law. Her liaison with her majordomo Bartolomeo Bergami was the scandal of Europe.

When "Prinny" became King in 1820, one of his first acts was to order his government to rid him of his Queen. Caroline immediately set sail for England to claim her crown; the King threatened to abdicate unless the politicians did something about it. Caroline was charged specifically with adultery with Bergami, a person of "low station." The liberal Lord Brougham undertook the defense of the Queen.

The sensational case went before the House of Lords. The evidence included sworn testimony of how Caroline and Bergami had entered each other's bedrooms. She had entertained him in her bath. But the more the evidence piled up, the more the public seemed to support the Queen.

Eventually, after 49 days of debate, the bill to impeach the Queen was dropped, to the fury of George IV. Caroline was the rightful Queen of Britain and the colonies overseas—including Canada—though even Lord Brougham admitted privately that she was a strumpet.

The constitutional crisis ended abruptly when Caroline died within a year, at the age of 53.

edged is the individual's right to his self-respect and dignity. (*See* Chapter 2, "The two faces of freedom.")

A breach of privacy could take the form of an unauthorized search of your home or your person, the tapping of your telephone, prying into your mail, or possibly the use of your photograph without your permission for advertising purposes, or its publication in an embarrassing or humiliating context. The following are two well-known cases, the first from a common-law province and the other involving a breach of Article 1053 of Quebec's Civil Code.

In Alberta, a surgeon performed an autopsy on a woman with the permission of a funeral home but without authorization from the widower. The doctor was found guilty of committing a tort because he had interfered with the widower's right to the "custody and control of the remains of his deceased wife."

The Quebec case also involves a doctor—but as the plaintiff this time. The Canadian Broadcasting Corporation was the defendant. The doctor wrote a letter to the producer of a television program, criticizing the show. He enclosed his name and address, and an article he had clipped from a newspaper which also criticized the program. The CBC then televised the newspaper article and the plaintiff's letter on a later program, adding its own comments and suggesting that the viewers write or telephone the doctor. A tremendous volume of mail and phone calls resulted.

The doctor complained that his privacy had been invaded and that the announce-

The pride of the amateur

IN CANADA, as elsewhere in North America, the cult of the amateur is not generally encouraged. Rather it is the paid performer—in hockey, football, golf, boxing, tennis—who is widely admired. The salaries of the "stars" are the subject of as much press attention as their athletic prowess. In the United Kingdom and in much of Europe and Asia, this is not so much the case and the amateur sportsman goes to great lengths to avoid any taint of professionalism. For example, in horse-race programs in Britain and France today, the amateur rider (never "jockey") is described as "Mister" or "*Monsieur*" while surname only suffices for the professional. It's not so long ago at cricket matches that the "players" (professionals) and the "gentlemen" (amateurs) used separate locker rooms.

On the golf course abroad, the professionals stick pretty much to the giving of lessons and selling clubs and balls. British amateur champion Cyril Tolley was so incensed when he found a cartoon of himself in a chocolate advertisement that he sued Fry's, the giant British candy concern. Under a drawing of the champion, complete with his regulation tweed plus fours, the ad carried this verse:

The caddy to Tolley said, "Oh sir!
Good shot, sir, that ball, see it go, sir!
My word, how it flies,
Like a packet of Fry's.
They're handy, they're good
and priced low, sir!"

To make things worse, there was a bar of chocolate sticking out of the golfer's pocket. Tolley was outraged. Although no one had exclusive right to his name or likeness, he claimed that his associates might think he had accepted money for permitting the ad to appear. That would make him a professional, by gad!

Believe it or not, this 1930 case went all the way to the Judicial Committee of the House of Lords, where Tolley won a resounding victory at the final hole. In total, 12 lawyers and eight different judges were involved.

The costs were enormous, and Fry's had to pay them.

ments on the program caused damage to his reputation and brought him great humiliation. The CBC was found guilty and ordered to pay damages of $3,000.

If you feel you have been the victim of a deliberate invasion of your privacy, tell the facts to an experienced lawyer. Even if he does not consider that you have a good case for action under the law as it stands, he can probably suggest some way that will most likely lessen the chances of a repeat offense. A stern "lawyer's letter" can sometimes be effective.

Interference with your affairs

Is interference—the act of hindering or meddling in the affairs of others—a tort? In many instances, it can amount to that. Interference with someone's business, domestic relations, expectancies, or contracts, may provide the ingredients for the torts of nuisance, enticement, criminal conversation, alienation of affection, and defamation of character, all of which are discussed later in this chapter.

Placing obscene or harassing telephone calls falls into the category of interference with a person's (the recipient's) peace of mind.

It is a tort to interfere with a contract between two other parties, by enticing or inducing one of them to break the contract. This was laid down in a case in England, in 1853. His Lordship Mr. Justice Crompton ruled that someone who lured a servant away from his master, thus depriving the master of service for which he and the servant had contracted, was committing a wrongful act.

What is the situation if two or more persons plan together to interfere with a private contract? They can be indicted for the crime of conspiracy. The Canadian Criminal Code stipulates that if two or more persons conspire to do something unlawful, or to achieve something lawful but in an illegal way, they are committing an indictable offense, punishable by two years' imprisonment. If the victim suffered actual damage, he or she could sue the conspirators.

Unfair competition in business may be considered in the realm of interference. When two or more persons agree to cause a third party to suffer damage by price fixing or intimidation, molestation or other illegalities, they are liable to be prosecuted under the federal Combines Investigation Act. (*See* Chapter 6, "Safeguards when shopping.") Although such a conspiracy is an offense against federal law which applies equally throughout Canada, it has been held in some cases that a civil suit for damages based on the losses caused by such a combine, or conspiracy, cannot be launched. This is because Canada's Constitution gives the provinces jurisdiction over property and civil rights, and the federal parliament cannot legislate in this field (*See* Chapter 1, "Under Canadian writ"). This is an odd situation, since it means that there may be criminal liability but no civil liability for conspiring to increase one's business by unfair competition.

A case heard in Quebec in 1959 provides an interesting example of an actionable interference. The plaintiff was the proprietor of a restaurant in Montreal and was active in supporting the religious sect known as Jehovah's Witnesses. The defendant was Maurice Duplessis, the premier of the province. The police had broken up some meetings of the Jehovah's Witnesses and had arrested some members of the sect. The plaintiff had posted bonds to secure the release on bail of many of the arrested persons. There was evidence that Premier Duplessis had ordered the chairman of the *Société des alcools du Québec* (Quebec Liquor Commission) to cancel the restaurateur's liquor license. The license was revoked and the plaintiff suffered heavy financial loss as a result.

At the end of a long trial, the Supreme Court of Canada made the premier pay damages to the restaurateur to make up for the loss he had suffered as a result of losing his liquor license. The case is an encouraging illustration of the principle that all people, even leaders of the country, must answer equally before the law.

Creating and abating nuisance

When a harried mother scolds her child, "Don't be a nuisance," she is giving him sound legal advice as well. In the law of

767

Enjoyment of clear water

FACTS

At the town of Espanola, 35 miles upstream from the mouth of the Spanish River, which empties into the North Channel of Lake Huron, a kraft paper mill was discharging industrial wastes that caused the river water to give off foul odors. The smell was prevalent down to the mouth of the river and could be detected ten miles out in the channel. The water had a bad taste even after being boiled, and was unfit for cooking or other common household uses. One witness said that the water could not be used for washing because when heated the vapours given off were unbearably offensive.

The effluent was a fibrous material from wood that had gone through a chemical digesting process of the mill. On an average day, approximately five tonnes of chemically impregnated fiber was discharged into the river.

There was evidence to show that the pollution of the water so affected fish that they had been driven out of the Spanish River, killed or prevented from spawning.

Several tourist-camp operators on the Spanish River entered a lawsuit against the paper company, seeking damages and an injunction to prohibit the pollution of the river.

ARGUMENT

The plaintiffs submitted that, as owners of lands along the Spanish River below the mill, they had a right to the flow of water in its natural state free from pollution, and as members of the public they had a public right to fish in navigable waters. The defendant argued, on the other hand, that if the deposit of industrial wastes from the kraft paper mill did amount to a nuisance in law, it was a public nuisance on Crown property and, consequently, the plaintiffs did not have a cause for bringing a civil action against the company.

JUDGMENT

The court awarded damages to the plaintiffs to compensate them for the interference in the enjoyment of their property rights. The court also granted an injunction restraining the company from depositing "foreign substances or matter in the Spanish River which alter the character or quality of the water." The operation of the judgment was suspended for six months to give the company an opportunity to provide other means of disposal of the effluent.

The matter did not end there, however. The company could not find an effective method to lessen the pollution it was causing. As it could not comply with the injunction, it appeared the company would have to close down, causing considerable hardship in an area of the province where there were few job opportunities. The Ontario government thereupon passed a special act dissolving the injunction and instructed the Research Council of Ontario to endeavor to develop methods that would abate or lessen the pollution of the waters of the Spanish River by the company.

At a time when there was little concern with the protection of the environment, jobs were held to be more important than pollution.*

*Based on an actual case (1948).

torts, *nuisance* is an "actionable wrong." This means that you can sue for damages if someone commits a nuisance against you, or your property. If the nuisance continues, you can apply for an *injunction* (a court order) to have it stopped; if it is not obeyed, the nuisance feasor will be charged with contempt of court. (*See* Chapter 3, "Decisions from the Bench.")

The law of nuisance is extremely complicated; it dates back to medieval times. Nuisances usually involve noise, vibration, smells, smoke and all kinds of pollution. But the list is getting longer as more and more people pack into closely settled urban areas. While nuisances may not involve physical trespass, they do involve some interference with your guaranteed right to "quiet enjoyment" of your own property. Legally, nuisances are classed as either public (common) or private.

A public nuisance is a crime. But if it causes some particular and special loss or damage to a person beyond the annoyance and inconvenience suffered by the public, the public nuisance becomes a tort and the person affected can sue for damages. He might well get an injunction against repetition of the nuisance as well. Persons or companies who pollute the atmosphere, soil or water, may well find themselves guilty of a tort and a crime. People who are subjected to this kind of annoyance should check with lawyers or police to see whether there are provincial penal laws or municipal bylaws which enlarge the category of public nuisances.

The tort of private nuisance is defined as unlawful interference with the use and enjoyment of a person's land. The annoyances which the tort covers are essentially the same as in a public nuisance—noise, smells, poisonous gases. If you do not own or occupy land, you may not get protection under law.

If a couple moves in next door to you and begins to play amplified rock music nonstop that rattles the dishes in your cupboards, the law of torts comes to your rescue. Cases that are not clearly defined are always arising where the real issue concerns what is unreasonable conduct when one considers the general necessity for peace and quiet.

It is not the law that in carrying on our own trade and pursuing our own interests we must, at our peril, avoid any annoyance or loss to our neighbors. A variety of circumstances have to be considered in deciding what is an actionable nuisance.

A key precedent in the law of nuisance was set by British Justice Lord Watson: "No proprietor has absolute right to create noises upon his own land, because any right which the law gives him is qualified by the condition that it must not be exercised to the nuisance of his neighbors, or of the public. If he violates that condition, he commits a legal wrong and if he does so intentionally he is guilty of a malicious wrong in its strict and legal sense."

It is obvious that a noise or even a strong odor that might be termed an "actionable wrong"—that is, one against which you can take legal action—in the suburbs would have to be tolerated in an industrial zone. The courts must balance the nuisance to an individual with the necessity that the business of life in our complex society must go on. Should a plant employing 500 men be closed because its unavoidable odors are a nuisance to a few nearby householders?

The courts have maintained that the degree of nuisance must be such as to cause some suffering and some serious interference with another's comfort and enjoyment of life. In one case, an injunction was refused where a plaintiff objected to a hospital nearby because of his fear of infection and his objection to seeing human suffering through the windows. On the other hand, in an English case, an injunction was granted against the use of the next-door property for the purposes of prostitution.

The law gives you the right to *abate* (or put an end to) a nuisance, without having to go to court about it. For instance, if the boughs of your neighbor's maple tree overhang your land and you feel they create a nuisance or a danger, you have the right to lop them off. But you do not have the right to trespass on to your neighbor's land to do so unless you advise of your intention in advance and get consent. And, you could be liable for damages if your pruning killed the tree.

Seduction and enticement

The finances of seduction

Luring the spouse away

Alienation of affection

Criminal conversation

U NTIL RECENTLY, the law of torts, as it related to the private lives of men and women, still contained some echoes of those bygone days when the daughter of the house was rated by her value as a housemaid, and the wife was regarded, basically, as one of the husband's chattels.

It was the case, for example, that if a wife were injured through someone's negligence, perhaps requiring her to enter hospital, the husband could sue the guilty party for depriving him of his wife's services. In blunt terms, he had been deprived of her labor in caring for the home and family, and of the comfort and gratification of *consortium*. However, if it was the husband who had been injured, the wife did not have the right to sue on the same grounds.

Today, the wife, as well as the husband, has the right to bring a legal action for loss of consortium in most provinces of Canada.

Consortium, in marriage, can be defined broadly as the legal right of one spouse to the company, companionship, sexual gratification and services of the other. It is, if you like, the necessary *consideration* of the marriage contract. "Consideration" used as a term in a contract refers to the substance of the mutual agreement—that is, the services (or goods) being given or exchanged as promised.

The finances of seduction

Although enforcing the laws of morality—many of them hangovers from a different era—may be declining as a duty for the state, it remains a crime in Canada for a man 18 or older to seduce an unmarried female of 16 years or more but less than 18. Not only that, the seducer can be sued for damages by the girl's father.

A law dictionary defines "seduction"

as the "act of man enticing woman to have unlawful sexual intercourse with him by means of persuasion, solicitation, promises, bribes or other means, without employment of force." Where does the girl's father enter the picture? It is not because of outraged dignity. Harking back to the time when the female was considered as property and as the provider of valuable services in the house, the father can sue for the theoretical reduction in the value of his servant's productivity. (If she has had sexual relations, the law considers it likely that she will become pregnant and eventually be confined, thus being unable to work as effectively in her father's house. It does not have to be proved that she did, in fact, become pregnant.)

As head of the household, the father would, in fact, be able to sue just as readily if it were indeed a housemaid, or any unmarried female under his protection, who was seduced. Formerly, it was necessary that "loss of service" had to be proved. The mother of the girl concerned could not bring the action because the daughter was not her "property." The following case illustrates the point.

In 1918, the Supreme Court of Ontario threw out an action for seduction because the action was brought by the mother of the seduced daughter, and the girl had been seduced while her father was still alive. It might have been possible, the court ruled, for the father to sue the seducer; but it was impossible for the mother because she could not show a loss of service of the daughter. Today, the Family Law Reform Act of Ontario states that no legal action can be brought by a parent for "the enticement, harboring, seduction or loss of services of his or her child," or for any damages resulting from these circumstances.

In Saskatchewan and Alberta, the seduction laws still provide that any unmarried female who has been seduced may herself charge her seducer in the same manner as for any other tort. And she—not her father—is entitled to any damages that may be awarded by the court. However, such charges are rare in the permissive society of today.

Luring the spouse away

The way the law sees it, all's not fair in love or war. Either the husband or the wife can bring an action for the tort of *enticement* against any man or woman who deprives him (or her) of consortium by luring the spouse away. Unless the plaintiff wants the wandering spouse to return, it is likely that a divorce action will be stated at the same time. (*See* Chapter 10, "The divorce.")

To make the charge stick, thus entitling the plaintiff to damages, it must be proved that the defendant actively encouraged the spouse to leave bed and board—but the act does not have to be of a sexual nature. There are provincial variations.

The Domestic Relations Act of Alberta stipulates: "A person who, without lawful excuse, knowingly and willfully persuades or procures a woman to leave her husband against the latter's will, whereby the husband is deprived of the society and comfort of the wife, shall be liable to an action for damages by the husband . . . . A husband shall also have the right of action for damages against any person who, without lawful excuse, knowingly receives, harbors and detains his wife against his [the husband's] will."

The Ontario Court of Appeal ruled some years ago that a married woman had the right to sue another woman for deliberately enticing her husband to cease "cohabiting and consorting," thus depriving her of her husband's society and services. The Bench decided that, in the face of social change, it was impossible to maintain that a married woman did

When Winston went to court

IN AN ALMOST FORGOTTEN episode of his career, Sir Winston Churchill was the key figure in a libel suit brought on his behalf by the Crown. He had been accused, as a cabinet minister, of falsifying an official report on the naval battle of Jutland in 1916 when, although suffering loss, the Royal Navy drove the German battle fleet off the high seas.

Churchill was said to have reported that the Royal Navy had, in fact, been defeated; the motive was supposed to be that when this news was flashed, the prices of British securities would tumble on the world's stock exchanges, allowing a group of named Jewish financiers to snap them up cheaply. Churchill's reward was said to be a houseful of fine furniture, valued at £40,000.

The allegations were presented by Lord Alfred Douglas, a strange star-crossed member of the illustrious Scottish clan, in a journal called *Plain English* and later at a public meeting in London.

The whole affair may have had its roots in Douglas's anti-Semitism. A false report of a crushing British naval defeat had indeed been planted in the New York press by German interests but, by this time (following the failure of his Dardanelles campaign), Churchill was not connected in any way with the Admiralty.

As the attorney-general stated in court, on Churchill's behalf, there was no plot, no phony communiqué, no stock market raid and no present of fine furniture. In the box, Churchill personally branded the statements "from beginning to end, a monstrous and malicious invention."

Douglas was found guilty of criminal libel, and was sent to prison for six months. There, curiously enough, he remade his reputation by writing a book of poems, *In Excelsis*.

not enjoy the "status of equality" with her husband as far as the right of consortium was concerned. Although this decision was made in an enticement suit it does not appear to have been followed in other provinces.

Under the law of torts in the United States, if a woman alienates the affections of a husband, induces him to separate from, or not to return to, his wife or has sexual intercourse with him, the wife in question may sue the other woman for having been deprived of her legally protected marital interests.

Alienation of affection

In a legal action for the tort of enticement, the successful plaintiff may win higher damages if he (or she) can also prove *alienation of affection* of the spouse. To "alienate" in this sense means to "transfer." It is tantamount to the theft of the conjugal love and companionship that is an essential part of every marriage contract.

Any damages awarded by the court would not be *exemplary* or *punitive* but would attempt to compensate for the actual "value" of the wife to the husband and for the injury to his feelings, honor and family life. Proof of adultery is not necessary to win such a suit.

Although the laws of some American states permit suits strictly for the alienation of affection, the laws of Canada do not. It is possible, however, for a husband while proving a case of *criminal conversation* to produce evidence of a wrong having been committed which is proof of the conduct of enticement, resulting in adultery. In cases such as this, the loss of affection could be considered in assessing damages.

In an interesting case in England, a woman was sued by her son-in-law for what amounted to alienation of the affection of the woman's daughter. The daughter had left her husband, returning to the home of her mother. In his suit, the young man charged that his mother-in-law had wrongfully enticed his wife to leave him.

The Bench ruled that while an action for enticement could be brought against

a wife's lover, it could not be brought against her mother. Justice Lord Denning ruled that a man's wife's parents become his parents when he marries, and that family matters of the sort represented by the man's case are outside of the realm of law. Even if such an action could be brought to court, it would be an adequate defense for the mother-in-law to show that she acted, to the best of her knowledge, for the good of her daughter. To win his case, the husband would have to prove that his mother-in-law had acted maliciously against him.

Criminal conversation

One of the most misleading of legal terms, *criminal conversation,* is neither a crime nor conversation. It is the act of debauching or seducing another man's wife. One authority describes it as "the defilement of the marriage bed." Proof of adultery is necessary. It is, basically, a trespass on the husband's rights to the exclusive sexual enjoyment of his wife; the husband has the right to sue for damages, which he often couples with a divorce action.

Once again there is a double standard— the wife does not have a matching right under some provincial laws. In 1954, for example, the chief justice of the Ontario Supreme Court specifically ruled that a wife had no right to launch a suit for criminal conversation against a woman with whom her husband had been committing adultery.

Although legal action for criminal conversation has long since been abolished in England, it can still be brought in Newfoundland, New Brunswick, Nova Scotia and Prince Edward Island. In nine provinces, it is a matrimonial offense and can be used as grounds for divorce. Although the offense doesn't exist as such in Quebec, the act of adultery that it refers to is an acceptable ground for divorce.

Alberta gave its Supreme Court the power to hear actions for criminal conversation under the terms of the English law as it stood prior to its abolition. The Domestic Relations Act, now in effect in that province, gives a husband the right to sue for damages against anyone who commits adultery with his wife.

Defamation of character

ANYONE who attacks the reputation of another person is taking considerable risk. Miguel de Cervantes' famous hero Don Quixote tells us, "A good name is better than riches," and our law upholds the idea that a good name is at least the equivalent. The law protects the individual (and his property) from untruthful and harmful public criticism and will allow damages in proven cases. This kind of attack is known as the tort of *defamation.*

Defamation does not have to be intentional or malicious; nor do you always have to prove that you actually suffered any injury or loss. In some circumstances, you can be defamed without having been specifically named. You can be defamed by word of mouth, in a newspaper or book, or in a drawing or painting.

To be a defamation, the injurious statement must be *published;* this means that it must be somehow conveyed to a person other than the victim. Even one other person is sufficient. The third person need only become aware of the statement without being directly informed.

Any statements that expose one to hatred, ridicule or contempt, or cause one to be shunned or avoided can be labeled defamatory. Such statements have a tendency to injure an individual in his office, profession or trade. In another general definition, they "cause the loss of esteem among one's fellows."

To determine whether a statement is defamatory, the courts will look at its natural and ordinary meaning. The test is not what a professor of English might *know* a remark means but what the average reasonable person might *think* it means. If it is not defamatory in such a way, then the courts will want an explanation of the special meaning—if any—in which it is understood by the person to whom it was published. Generally, it is a point of law and for the judge to say whether or not the words have a defamatory meaning. However, it is for the jury to say whether in the context in which they were published the words do in fact bear that meaning and, if they do, what damages should be awarded.

If the defamatory statement was in any permanent form, it is referred to as *libel.* If the attack was only spoken, it is *slander.* Both terms have been in use since the sixteenth century.

Libel and slander

Libel is defamation by means of writing, printing or publishing in a permanent form, including radio or television broadcasts (which are usually scripted and taped) and movies (where the sound track is printed on the film).

The perfect defense against an action for libel is to show that the defamatory statement is true and that it was made without malice. Freedom of speech would be an empty phrase indeed if we were prevented by law from speaking the truth about anything. Other defenses are that although the statement was written, it wasn't published and thus, there was no defamation; or that the words used were incapable of a defamatory meaning; or that the publication was *privileged.* (*See* "What is a tort?" in this chapter.)

In all provinces, defamatory words that appear in a newspaper or a broadcast are deemed to be "published" and thus to constitute libel. The term *broadcast* refers to any form of electronic communication including radio, television, telegraph, radiotelephone, the wireless transmission of writing, signs, signals, pictures and sounds of all kinds, by means of Hertzian waves (or other means of transmission) intended to be received by the public either directly or through the medium of relay stations. The term *newspaper* refers to any journal containing public news, intelligence or occurrences, as well as remarks or observations on such information, printed and published periodically or in parts or numbers at intervals not exceeding 31 days between the publication of any two such papers, parts or numbers. Also included are those giveaway papers containing only, or mostly, advertisements.

If you consider that you have been libeled—and if your lawyer advises a court action—you can sue not only the writer of the offending article but possibly also the newspaper that published it, its editor and printer and, theoretically, even the paper boy who delivered it. Each of these persons contributed to the publishing of the libel.

Defamatory libel may also be a crime when malice is present, if the malice is such that it could theoretically provoke violence (a breach of the peace). (*See* Chapter 19, "Offenses against the person.")

Slander is a defamatory statement published by means of spoken words or gestures. It is a tort, not a crime, and is not actionable without proof of special damage; however, in four types of slander, the words are said to be actionable *per se* ("by themselves"). These four types of statement are:

(1) When a crime punishable by imprisonment is falsely said to have been committed.

(2) When one publishes the story that another person has a contagious or infectious disease.

(3) When one imputes incompetency in the business or profession of another.

(4) When one casts slurs on the sexual habits of a woman.

In the simplest terms, you cannot go around saying that Mr. XYZ, the lawyer, is a shyster, or that Miss ABC, the spinster, takes her exercise horizontally. It is not required for the plaintiffs to prove any special damage resulting from the utterance of such words. In Newfoundland, "imputations of unchastity," or allegations of adultery or other immorality, are actionable without proof of damage. In the other provinces, different terms are used and there are different requirements for evidence.

An accusation of lesbianism has been held as an "imputation of unchastity."

In an action for slander stemming from words calculated to disparage a person in any office, profession, calling, trade or business, it is not necessary for the plaintiff to prove actual damage. The law takes it for granted that any such attack harms the plaintiff's ability to make his living.

If you are ever threatened with a libel or slander action, consider making an immediate apology. You could earn acquittal, or at least hope to reduce damages, by making or offering a written apology to the plaintiff for any alleged libel or slander before the other party started the action. If you didn't apologize until after the action was begun, there is still some hope for your defense if you can show that you apologized as soon as you had the opportunity to do so. In the event that only one person heard the defamatory remark, the apology should be made directly to that person, preferably in the presence of the plaintiff (or prospective plaintiff).

When a newspaper makes a significant error, it will usually publish a statement in a subsequent issue explaining the error and offering an apology to anyone who may have been libeled through the error. Although this apology does not wipe out the libel, if court action ensues it would probably be accepted as indicating humble regret and thus could serve as a defense to the action or reduce the damages. If an out-of-court settlement is reached (as often happens in defamation cases), the sincere apology would probably serve the same purpose.

Who can be libeled?

For a libel case to stand, there must be no doubt about the identity of the person who has been defamed. Also, the person allegedly defamed must sue on his own behalf. Thus, an action for libel or slander cannot be brought to court on behalf of a deceased person.

There is no problem of identity, of course, if the plaintiff has actually been named in the defamatory statement. The question of identity becomes a bit tricky in the case of a gossip columnist who writes about "a certain millionaire who likes fast cars and faster women." If it is likely that any reasonably well informed person in that city would be able to figure out the millionaire's identity, that gentleman could probably sue.

A large group or class of people cannot institute action for libel or slander. The attack would be too generalized, and torts are by their nature personal. If offensive words spoken or printed were directed at a particular racial or religious group, the police might act to forestall a breach of the peace; alternatively, the group might press charges under human-rights laws or under amendments to the Criminal Code which make it an offense to deliberately stir up hatred and contempt of an identifiable group. (*See* Chapter 2, "Our conditional rights.")

Don't leap for the courtroom merely because someone has made a derogatory

Speaking ill of the dead

UNDER ENGLISH COMMON LAW, a suit for either libel or slander of a deceased person will have no chance of success, except in the rare case that the offended survivors can prove the libel to be so defamatory that it brings serious "injury" or contempt upon them. Even then, the malice expressed must be such as to provoke a likely breach of the peace.

Generally speaking, defamation is a tort—a personal civil wrong—and the right of action dies with the individual who is defamed. Although Roman law—from which the Civil Code of Quebec is derived—allowed for punishment for an insult to the dead, the development of democratic principles brought the doctrine that "the living stand upon their own feet" and cannot be damaged financially by attacks on their ancestors. There is, however, one way around this legal obstacle and, in 1927, this route was taken by the two surviving sons of the British Prime Minister William Ewart Gladstone.

Prime Minister Gladstone, a man of stern religious principles, had a particular interest in rehabilitating London's prostitutes in the Victorian era and was seen talking with them at night. He was known to visit their rooms. He was alleged to be the lover of actress Lillie Langtry, and oth-

er women. Such slanderous remarks circulated widely during his lifetime but he had been dead 30 years when Captain Peter Wright, in a book of essays, made a passing reference to Gladstone's alleged hypocrisy. The Liberal prime minister, he wrote, had spoken in public "the language of highest and strictest principle" but in private he was known to "pursue and possess every sort of woman."

The outraged sons—one of them now a viscount—could not sue Wright but they proceeded to deliberately libel him so thoroughly that he would have no alternative but to sue them. In that way, they planned, the whole story would be aired and their famous father's name cleared.

The case lasted five days. Almost all of those intimately concerned with the events were dead and the Gladstones' lawyers ripped Wright's case to shreds. Rumor and conjecture—the journalist's tools—were there aplenty but, after three decades, provable facts were scarce indeed. Lillie Langtry, then 74, cabled from France that she had never given "her favors" to Gladstone.

Captain Wright lost his case against the Gladstones and had to meet their legal costs of £5,000. In this roundabout way, he paid heavily for speaking ill of the dead.

remark about you. To have any hope of succeeding with a suit for defamation, you must be able to show that your character has really been besmirched in the eyes of sensible level-headed people. You are expected to be mature enough to be able to turn your back on a certain amount of abuse, especially if uttered during a heated argument.

When a letter is libelous

Even if the defamatory statements are made in a private letter marked "personal" they can be libelous if the letter is read by a third party, someone who is not the object of the remarks. An executive's secretary can become the "third party" when taking dictation for a letter; the recipient's secretary will also fill the bill if that person is normally instructed to open and read all the boss's mail.

If this same letter were handwritten and delivered directly to the recipient, there would be no "publication" and therefore no opportunity for legal action. If the defamed party shows the letter to a third party, he or she is publishing the letter and thus would have no recourse to the courts.

Action on innuendo

Clever or scheming writers and orators, in publishing an attack on someone, can quite easily choose words that, while not defamatory in themselves, conceal defamation in a second meaning that is quite obvious to the average reader or listener. This kind of sly, oblique expression is known as *innuendo* and can be the basis for suits of libel or slander—although arguing such a case in court presents many difficulties.

As an illustration of innuendo in its legal context, consider the following. A story is published in a local newspaper reporting that a large deficit has been discovered in the cash reserves of a finance company and that the police are investigating. So far, the statement is clear and could not be the cause of complaint. But then, in a subsequent or nearby paragraph, it is stated that Mr. PQR, the manager of the company, is understood to be visiting Monte Carlo. The

average reader would be inclined to tie the two statements together, and would probably conclude that the peripatetic finance company manager had made off with the money. Assuming that his innocence is provable, the manager could probably sue the newspaper for libel by implication, or by innuendo.

A somewhat similar situation can arise when an author or playwright—even quite accidentally—uses the name of a real person as a character in his fiction. Of course, if the character concerned is tall and handsome and saves the girl from a fate worse than death, the reader who bears the same name is not likely to sue (he will buy ten copies to send to his friends). But if the reader's name is used for the villain of the piece, and if he can show that reasonable people believed the story was really a true account of his own villainy, then he could probably successfully sue for damages. It may help but it will not always give protection if the publisher routinely inserts a statement at the beginning of the book declaring that all the characters are fictional and that any resemblance to living persons is purely coincidental.

It is worth noting that no one holds an automatic *copyright* (*See* Chapter 13, "Sole proprietorship") in his facial likeness or name, unless he has registered either or both under commercial law as either a trademark or trading name.

Publication of photographs

However much you may dislike or despise some newspaper or magazine, you cannot sue the publishers for the simple acts of taking or publishing your photograph. Of course, if a photographer harassed you, or invaded your privacy, or if the photograph was published in a context that contained an injurious innuendo, the situation would be quite different. Mrs. Aristotle Onassis, the former wife of U.S. President John F. Kennedy, successfully sued a photographer who made a business of dogging her to take photographs which he sold to magazines the world over.

In Manitoba, a man's picture was used for the purposes of advertisement in two

Winnipeg newspapers. The pictures appeared in a form which seemed to be a testimonial spoken by the plaintiff of the benefits he had derived from the use of a patent medicine sold and advertised by the defendant. The advertisement stated that he had suffered from dizzy spells, constipation and indigestion but, after using the product for a short time, all of his ailments were relieved.

As a result of the unauthorized publication, the plaintiff claimed that he had received a great number of inquiries regarding his health and that his fiancée's father forbade the marriage until he had cleared things up. He won his case when the court decided that he had been effectively defamed. The advertisement, according to the court, was humiliating and tended to subject the plaintiff to ridicule.

The Libel and Slander Act of Ontario specifies that any reference to "words" in the act is meant to include pictures, visual images, gestures and other methods of "signifying meaning". Thus, any picture included in any newspaper, or included in any broadcast, can provide the basis for an action for libel in that province.

In heat of passion

Sometimes the defendant in a libel or slander action will admit the defamatory nature of his statements but argue that he was responding angrily, or in the heat of passion, to provocation by the plaintiff. The defense lawyer would probably point out that normal social life would be impossible, especially in crowded cities, if we were all too sensitive in the ordinary ups and downs of routine existence.

The courts usually rule that such evidence denying the existence of harmful intent (or malice) may be considered by the jury only in relation to the amount of damages that it thinks should be awarded—in short, whether an amount for punitive damages should be added to the amount for compensatory damages.

There is a minority view that the humiliation or mental suffering of the plaintiff

What price defamation?

THE LAW protects an individual who has been falsely and publicly maligned. If the courts find that the attacker has committed defamation, the victim can seek to recover thousands of dollars in damages for injury to name and reputation.

In 1975, Gerry Snyder, a former Montreal city councillor and a member of the organizing committee for the Olympic Games, found himself falsely described in an article published on March 13 in the Montreal *Gazette*. The article was based on information given at a Quebec police commission hearing held the previous day. Although the *Gazette* did not mention Snyder by name, it identified the target of police investigation as a public official, with an impressive record of civic achievement, who was connected with the Mafia.

Shortly after the *Gazette* story appeared, Snyder came forward to identify himself with the article, and sent a notice, through his attorneys, to the newspaper, forcing it publish a retraction. In a subsequent libel action, Snyder maintained that reasonably informed readers would assume that he was the man referred to by the *Gazette*. He pointed out that the story was misleading, and that its publication had injured his public career. Snyder asked for damages totalling $735,000.

Snyder's case was tried in February 1978. A six-person jury found that the Montreal *Gazette* had published a false story, and that Snyder was an honest, dedicated public official.

At the end of the trial, the jury ruled that Snyder had been unjustly defamed and that he had the right to vindicate his name. It recommended a figure of $135,000 for "moral damages." The verdict was confirmed by a Superior Court, but it was later reduced to a tenth of the recommended amount by a Court of Appeal.

is increased by the fact that the defendant intended to hurt the person. According to this view, then, proof of the defendant's good faith could be also considered in reduction of compensatory damages.

What is fair comment?

On reading a newspaper article that contains a sharp, even personal, attack on a politician or some actor or author, you might wonder at times why the person concerned doesn't sue for libel. The reason is that persons in public life are, in a sense, offering themselves for comment. Just as they soak up praise for their work, so they must swallow criticism. Although such critiques can be highly uncomplimentary, as long as they are based on the honest opinion of the writer—and not on personal spite—the law does not consider them defamatory. In the interests of freedom of speech, such statements are protected under qualified privilege. (*See* "What is a tort?" in this chapter.)

Critical opinion in the press on matters of public interest is regarded as *fair comment*. However, the comment given must be honestly believed to be true; not inspired by any malicious motive, nor irrelevant. Whether the matter complained of is a comment or a statement of fact is a question of law and thus for the judge to decide. If it is a comment, whether it is fair or not is a question of fact for the jury to decide. The plea of fair comment is a defense in an action for libel, but the burden of proof is upon the defendant who is offering that plea. If it is a false statement, the jury has to decide whether it caused any real damage to the plaintiff.

If the defendant in a libel suit offers a defense based partly on fair comment and partly on justification (that the statements made were true), he or she will not automatically lose if every allegation of fact cannot be proved; the defense may stand if his or her expression of opinion is accepted as fair comment. It is notoriously difficult to prove truth in every facet of a given statement. Philosopher Alfred North Whitehead put it this way: "There are no whole truths; all truths are half-truths. It is trying to treat them as whole truths that plays the devil."

In one well-known case, a drama critic was sued by a playwright for referring in his article to the "hash up of ingredients which have been used *ad nauseam* until one rises in protestation against the loving, confiding, fatuous husband with a naughty wife and her double existence." The plaintiff sued for libel, based on an innuendo that the play was of an immoral character. The critic admitted during the trial that the play did not actually contain any adulterous scenes.

The plaintiff won his case on the grounds that the article was an inaccurate description of his play and therefore the defendant was not entitled to a defense of fair comment. The writer had gone beyond the limits of criticism into the realm of false statement, and therefore beyond the limits of fair comment. Even the casual reader of theatrical or movie criticism today will have doubts about the strength of this precedent in our courts.

Giving your frank opinion

Have you ever been asked to give your frank opinion about someone, either verbally or in writing? Most employers have been asked to provide a reference for former employes. Bankers, clergymen and justices of the peace are always being asked for to give character and other assessments. By giving a frank opinion, which may be uncomplimentary to the person named (it might even cost him a good job), can you be sued for libel or slander?

The answer is no—as long as you give the opinion in good faith, believing it to represent the truth about the person concerned: at least, the truth as it had been revealed to you in your association with the person.

In the event that you make some misstatement of fact, or cannot prove all your points to be true, the law grants you *qualified privilege*. This protects you in much the same way as the right to fair comment protects the drama critic or the political correspondent who is reporting on events in Ottawa. The lawyer enjoys the same privilege with his clients. Without this protection, nobody would utter anything except praise.

The accidental tort

ALTHOUGH WE READILY ADMIT that "accidents will happen," when we are personally injured or our property is damaged we look to see both who is to blame and how much we can recover. At that point we discover the tort of *negligence*, perhaps the commonest form of legal trouble. In layman's language, negligence is simply carelessness.

In perhaps half of the chapters of this book, negligence will be seen as the yeast of litigation. It crops up in cases involving automobiles and traveling, as well as accidents in the home, while shopping or at work and play. It is difficult to think of areas of our lives where we are free of the risks of negligent damage. At the society wedding between the young surgeon and the banker's daughter, if the chauffeur slammed the door of the limousine breaking the bridegroom's fingers, who pays?

For a long time, negligence was a component part of many specific torts. But finally it was recognized that there was a general principle underlying the law of torts: in all the varied circumstances of life, whoever caused damage to others should be responsible for his fault. Negligence, so to speak, became a respectable tort, in itself, easing the task of providing uniform and reliable justice across the wide spectrum of human error. In a famous definition, *negligence* is stated as the failure to carry out the duty of care we owe to each other, including responsibility for any injury resulting from that failure. To fulfill this duty, you must take reasonable pains not to commit acts—and, in the reverse, not to fail to perform acts—that a reasonable person should have foreseen as likely to harm another person, his family or his property.

You don't, generally, have any legal obligation to act to protect others, but if you have taken some part in creating a potentially perilous situation, then you are duty bound to try to make the situation safe. It is important to remember, though, that parents and guardians have a legal responsibility to act to protect their children. The Criminal Code stipulates, for instance, that anyone who unlawfully abandons or exposes a child who is under the age of ten, so that his or her life and health are endangered, is guilty of an indictable offense and is liable to imprisonment for two years.

Normally, we are obliged to do what a reasonable and prudent person (such as, say, a member of the jury?) would have done in those circumstances. But a doctor, an engineer, or anyone else representing himself as a specialist, is expected to maintain a higher standard of care in his line of work. More is demanded of the surgeon in the operating room than of the butcher at his block; the taxi driver should drive better than the novice motorist. Although the ordinary citizen who does his best to help an injured party in an auto accident can be sued for negligence if his or her intervention further harms the victim, that person will not be expected to apply a doctor's skills.

Just as we accept that a lack of care, or attention, causes accidents (excepting "acts of God" or sheer bad luck), we can also grasp that insisting upon total care—in effect, ensuring the safety of everyone we deal with—would result in all of us being afraid to get out of bed in the morning in case we bumped into someone on the stairs. As usual, there is a compromise in which we don't compel everyone to be

779

paragons of prudence but rely on the law to ensure, as far as it can, that victims of carelessness are compensated for their suffering by the award of damages.

Fault and causation

The Old Testament lists some penalties that were exacted in the ancient Hebrew kingdoms when one citizen suffered from the negligence of another. Direct linkage between the injurer and the injured, without any consideration given to the reasons for the action of the injurer, is termed *strict liability;* we still see it today in, for example, our workers' compensation acts. The boss is counted to be responsible, no matter what.

When the courts began to consider that the negligent person may not have been entirely to blame for what had or had not been done—perhaps it wasn't wholly the shopkeeper's fault that the new floor collapsed, injuring some customers—the idea of *causation* entered the law of torts. Assuming a case involving blameworthy behavior in which some person was at fault—for instance, careless disregard for the safety of others—one school of thought argued that punishment through punitive damages would act as a deterrent on other careless (negligent) people. Other judges argued that only naturally careful or attentive persons would be deterred—the others would carry on just as before. This same argument might be made about no-fault automobile accident insurance: the good driver will be paying by his insurance premiums to cover the apparently ineradicable carelessness (or lower standard of skill) of the poor driver.

Although liability for negligence in most actions is still gauged by fault, the law is in the process of change. We lean even more heavily on insurance companies and government programs to protect us from our own negligence.

But there are times when the law, in attempting to apportion fault or blame, enters a maze as tricky as the one Cardinal Wolsey built at Hampton Court to puzzle King Henry VIII—and which now puzzles a million modern-day tourists. Each turn leads only into another alley and yet another turn. Similarly, one careless human action can lead to another, and it may be a subsequent but inevitable reaction that causes the actual injury.

Through the problem, however, runs the principle of what is called *the unbroken chain.* A budding rally driver screeches around a suburban street corner, scaring the wits out of a church deacon in his sedan who then swerves into the path of an oncoming truck; the truck driver turns his wheel quickly, colliding with a milk van which, in turn, careens across your lawn and demolishes your sundial. Who is at fault? Who pays to fix the sundial (not to mention the milk van's bumper)? Answer: probably the hot-rodder as there appears to be an unbroken chain of events between his initial negligence and the shattered sundial.

The chain of causation will be severed if too much time elapses between the original negligent act and its consequences, or if another negligent action is committed by someone who forms a later link in the chain of actions. If a firebug used gasoline to burn down a building, the owner probably couldn't sue the service station attendant from whom he bought the fuel (or the oil company). But the packers of a canned food may be responsible if a consumer falls ill after eating their product even though it was bought months after it was manufactured; the law considers that the chain in this and similar cases does stretch back unbroken to the source.

Taking reasonable care

It is the responsibility of each individual to take *reasonable care* to avoid acts, or omissions, if the consequences could reasonably be foreseen as likely to cause damage to another person or his property. The emphasis is obviously on the word "reasonable." Although the word defies a neat definition, it can be generally understood to mean the degree of care which is reasonable under the circumstances of the particular situation.

The accepted standard is the foresight and caution usually shown by the average prudent person—the man on the street or the woman sitting next to you on the bus. The exception to this rule, as stated, is the defendant in a negligence action who belongs to a class that claims special skills: the doctor, the dentist, the druggist, and other professionals.

The burden of proof in demonstrating negligence in court rests on the shoulders of the plaintiff, the injured party. Generally, there must be evidence presented of the direct negligence of the defendant, except where the maximum *res ipsa loquitur* (Latin for "the thing speaks for itself") applies. This maxim applies whenever a physical object does something it would not normally do. An example of a case involving *res ipsa loquitur* occurred when a barrel of flour rolled out of the open doorway of an upper floor of a warehouse and fell on a person who was walking by in the street below. Although the actual act of negligence was not brought out in evidence (often, it cannot be proved), it was clear that this barrel of flour must have come loose due to negligence on the part of someone in the defendant's warehouse. The falling barrel spoke for itself.

When the fault is shared

As in the case of so many other incidents involving human error, the whole truth about an accident can seldom be told in black and white. Public sympathy always goes out to the child struck down in the street. But we all know that children have a tendency to dart thoughtlessly into the road when they are playing stickball and other games. Can we wholly blame the motorist—who may have a spotless 20-year driving record—if he or she runs down and kills that youngster? The motorist is heartsick about the accident and swears that the child ran into the vehicle's path, which may be true.

For many years, our courts accepted as a valid defense in negligence cases of this kind that the plaintiff-victim was "the author of his or her own misfortune" (at least in part) and the defendant could not be held liable. This was the doctrine known as *contributory negligence*. It was a valid defense even if the defendant was mostly to blame, and admitted it.

Common fallacies about accidents

UNLESS HELD BACK by seat belts (or kiddie safety seats) the occupants of an automobile in collision continue to travel in the same direction and at the same speed that the car was going. The back-seat passenger can fly right over the top of the front seat. If you are in a car that is hit on the side, you will not be thrown in the opposite direction; you will, in fact, fly *toward* the impact. How come? Because the car is knocked away from under you.

Although it's a common phrase, you never really "see an accident coming" in time to do anything about it. You may avoid an incident by quick response to danger, but the accident that gets you is usually all over before your shocked mind has registered that it is happening. Studies indicate that the average auto accident is set up and completed within three seconds, or less. Allow a wider safety margin in your driving.

Drivers naturally fear the head-on collision most, but more than half of all accidents involve only one vehicle. They occur when cars skid on ice or wet asphalt, run off the road, hit power poles, trees or "safety" fences. The rear and side of the vehicle is smashed just as often as the front. Even when two cars are involved, one of them is usually hit in the side.

The idea that a big solid engine up front provides a safety buffer is hard to eradicate. In a collision with a solid object at speeds greater that 40 kilometres per hour, that quarter-tonne of engine metal actually flies backward toward you—as you continue forward by momentum. Your "cushion" acts like an army tank.

If you think that you can protect a child by grabbing him at the last minute before an accident—forget it! At 100 km/h in a head-on collision, little 25-kilogram Freddie exerts enormous force; in effect, he will weigh the equivalent of a tonne.

As the courts strove to provide a more equitable justice, the doctrine of *the last clear chance* was introduced. Briefly, this meant that even if the plaintiff contributed in some way to the accident that caused the injury, the responsibility for the tort was put on the person who had had the last opportunity to avoid creating the injury. Thus, to continue the previous illustration, even if the young ballplayer did dart into the path of the car, the driver still possibly had that last chance to brake or swerve. This line of reasoning began to falter as lawyers and judges struggled with the apportionment of fault and blame—already discussed in this section. The weakness of the doctrine was that it again provided an all-or-nothing decision, taking the law back close to the primitive doctrine of strict liability.

The modern answer has been the introduction of *comparative negligence.* Practically identical in all provinces, the laws of comparative negligence require judge or jury to assess the degree of responsibility of each of the parties to the action and to consider those "percentages" when making any award of damages. If it is not possible to establish different degrees of fault, then the parties are held equally liable.

The recent automobile seat-belt laws, requiring us to "buckle up, or else," provide a new slant on comparative negligence. Following pioneer legislation in Britain and Australia, Canadian authorities are accepting that the person who refuses (or forgets) to use the safety belts now installed in cars contributes to injuries he or she may receive in an accident on the highway.

The negligent motorist

By far the greatest number of tort cases in the courts today is based on the negligence of drivers of motor vehicles. To drive without due care and attention (that is, negligently) is an offense in all provinces. The tort of negligence occurs when that careless driver injures someone or damages property. The main types of automobile tort are briefly noted here; you will find a wider treatment of the subject in Chapter 5, "On the road."

A negligent motorist is liable to the person he harms. His liability will be decided on the basis of his obedience to the rules of the road, as laid down in the highway traffic acts and by the courts. There is space here for only one illustration: When one driver attempts to pass another car heading in the same direction on a two-lane road, the driver about to overtake must ensure it is safe to do so. The driver should check to make sure that no hill or hollow is blocking the view of the road ahead; that there are no intersections immediately ahead; and that there is no indication from the car ahead that it is about to make a left-hand turn.

Once the overtaker makes the move to enter the passing lane, and once the initial moves are completed, it is then up to the driver in the first car to ensure that he or she does not interfere with the passing driver by crossing over the center line of the road, by suddenly speeding up, or obstructing in any other way. If the driver in the first car does any of these things, that person is driving negligently and will probably be liable for the tort of negligence if there is any damage.

If the weather is foggy, snowy, rainy or icy, all drivers are expected to use extra caution, and to adjust the speed and operation of their vehicles to meet the conditions of the road. If you travel at the maximum speed limit in stormy weather, you would seem to be asking for trouble and, should you be involved in an accident, this might be the factor that would convict you as a negligent motorist.

Responsibility of the pedestrian

The law of negligence does not apply to the motorist alone. It is the responsibility of the pedestrian to act in the manner least likely to cause an accident. For instance, if you walk on an unlit roadway in dark clothing without keeping a sharp lookout and are hit by an automobile, a court might rule that the accident was your own fault. If the car had improper lighting, or if the driver was impaired or traveling at an excessive speed, then the court might decide that there was a contribution of negligence by the driver. Any damages awarded would then be assessed with regard to the percentages of negligence on the part of you and the driver.

The ruling of comparative negligence would also apply if a pedestrian were to run out from between parked cars into the path of an oncoming automobile, or were to jaywalk or otherwise disturb the normal flow of traffic.

Although the pedestrian must exercise reasonable care, the courts will at times lean backward to find the motorist—who generally has adequate insurance coverage—liable for the accident. It may not be good law but it seems to make good sense socially.

Young hitchhikers often seem willing to tempt fate as they crowd the road verges thumbing rides. Nearly every motorist during the Canadian winter has at some time swerved violently after suddenly seeing parka-clad figures on the very edge of the paved road. Most provinces prohibit hitchhiking on superhighways, and some municipalities try to control it—in the interests of the thumbers themselves (*See* Chapter 5, "On the Road"). Nevertheless, if a hitchhiker,

or any pedestrian, was struck by a motor vehicle traveling along that roadway, then the driver might still be found at fault and liable for negligence. Of course, if the pedestrian had committed some act contributing to the accident that could also be classed as negligent, the blame would probably have to be shared.

Protection of visitors

Earlier in this chapter (*See* "Trespassing prohibited!"), it was explained that there is a duty of care on an occupier of property to make sure that any invitees or licensees do not injure themselves by any hidden traps on the property. This duty also covers trespassers to a certain extent.

Because of the occupier's liability for visitors on his or her property, the property owner or occupier is wise to invest in liability insurance. If your daughter gets married at home and you hold the reception in a marquee on the lawn, a tort might result if wind blew the tent down on top of the guests. You, as the host, would have breached your duty of reasonable care and would be liable for any

In trouble, down Mexico way

THE CANADIAN, like his American cousin, takes abroad the image of the rich big-spender—however false that may be in fact. If he finds himself involved in a civil suit in a foreign country, he might seek in vain the kind of impartial justice that he leaves at home.

Ask Bill Maddix of Sudbury, Ontario. He was driving toward Saltillo, Mexico, when there was a collision with a truck full of watermelons. The truck banged into the side of the Maddix automobile at an intersection, as photographs confirmed.

Maddix and his wife were taken to hospital to have their cuts stitched, and then found themselves accused by police of ramming the truck. In surprise and anger, fearing an unfair award of damages, Maddix went temporarily to Canada rather than face an immediate trial before the

local magistrate. He left his (Mexican-born) wife and three children south of the border, with his damaged car.

The big mistake that Maddix made was not to read the signs at the U.S.-Mexico border which warn that regular American and Canadian automobile insurance does not hold good in Mexico. You are advised to take out a special policy at the border (maximum cost, about $5 U.S. a day). Canadian consuls say that many visitors don't bother to buy it. Yet the chances of the "wealthy" visitor being "to blame" are high, irrespective of the circumstances.

The Mexican police have authority to throw into jail anyone involved in an accident unless there is valid (i.e., Mexican) insurance.

Moral: You should be aware of and obey the laws of the country you visit.

injury that might occur to anyone at the reception.

If the tent fell down due to some defect in its construction that you had no way of knowing about, or if the wind which blew the tent down was unusually strong, you probably would not be held responsible for damages. The great American jurist Oliver Wendell Holmes once commented on a similar point of law: "The blind man is not required to see at his peril."

The injured worker

If you are involved in an accident at your place of employment, what you do about it will largely depend on whether your occupation is covered under the workers' compensation act in your province (*See* Chapter 8, "Accidents at work"). Most jobs are covered, except those in agriculture, domestic service or the professions. If you are covered, then you will be compensated for injury, regardless of the question of negligence. If you are not covered by worker's compensation, you might find that you are covered under a private plan in force in your business. Outside of these schemes, you should probably seek legal advice to find out whom you should sue. It could be your employer, the owner or occupier of the property or building, another employe or possibly your employer and another employe together.

If one worker is injured by another, an action for damages can be brought against the employer, provided the accident occurred during the course of the job. In this situation, contrary to the normal application of the law of torts, wives and husbands can commit and sue for accidental torts against each other when they are acting as employes of another person. This point is illustrated in the following case involving a husband and wife who were managing a hotel. The husband left a trapdoor open, and his wife fell through it and injured herself. The court ruled that the husband had been negligent. Although the wife was not able to sue her husband directly for the tort, it was held that her husband's employer was vicariously liable for the tort, and the boss was ordered to pay damages. (*See* Chapter 12, "The laws of labor"). On the other hand, if the husband himself was the employer, the wife could not have sued him for damages.

Hurt while shopping

You are protected against the negligence of others while shopping—even while just window-shopping—through the doctrine of *occupier's liability* (*See* Chapter 6, "In the supermarket"). When you enter shopping premises you do so, in effect, on the invitation of the proprietor of the business; you are an *invitee*, with the high-

Too much muscle in the muscle-car?

THERE IS no public highway in Canada where you are permitted to drive at speeds exceeding 100 kilometres an hour. Why then are automobile manufacturers allowed to produce and advertise cars capable of 185 km/h and more? Does the argument about the safety factor of their swift acceleration really hold good in the face of Canada's more than half-million traffic accidents yearly?

This question was taken up by a coroner's jury when considering the death of an 18-year-old boy during a drag race. (Drag racing is illegal on the highway and can be very dangerous anywhere.)

The Crown attorney urged the jury to recommend the imposition of horsepower limits on the "muscle cars" used in the drag contests.

The jury contented itself with a recommendation that special conditions be attached to operators' licenses granted to drivers between the ages of 16 and 21 who were using high-powered automobiles on the public highway.

The Crown wins some, and loses some.

est claim to "reasonable care" on the part of the owner or occupier of the premises.

The proprietor must ensure that his premises are safe to enter and to move about in. Floors must be swept, and spills mopped up as soon as reasonably possible after they occur. A guardrail or adequate notice must warn you of any unusual hazard. But the supermarket might not be liable if you hurt yourself by running into a glass door: such equipment is common in supermarkets, and *you* are expected to take "reasonable care" also.

In one case, a shopper picked up a bottle of soda pop in a supermarket and the bottle, having a hidden defect, exploded, causing her injury. If the bottle had already been purchased and then had exploded, she would have had a right to sue under the law of contract, on the ground of injury caused by a defective product. Since she had not yet purchased the bottle, the only "agreement" between herself and the management was that she had been invited to enter the store and pick out merchandise. However, that invitation gave her grounds to sue under the tort of occupier's liability and she was able to collect damages from the occupier of the supermarket premises.

Liability for accidents that occur on the open plaza surrounding many shopping centers is more complicated. If you are injured on the commonly shared parking lot, because of some dangerous conditions existing there, who is responsible? Should you sue the shop you intended to visit, all the stores in the shopping center together or the owner of the property?

Since the accident occurred on the common property, the landlord would most likely be responsible, being the owner and occupier and in charge of general maintenance of that area. The same holds true for an accident that occurs on the common property surrounding an apartment building or in the commonly used hallways or lobby.

On the sporting field

In the law of torts, there is a defense known as *volenti non fit injuria*, which translates colloquially as, "there is no legal claim by those who consent to take the risk." This expression has a special application to all sports. If you join a game of hockey, you must expect some rough play and, if you are hurt during the course of the game, you cannot sue for damages (*See* Chapter 17, "Playing field perils"). No one can enforce a right he has voluntarily waived or abandoned.

The ruling usually applies to spectators also. If you attend hockey games, you are accepting to a certain extent the normal risks associated with that activity. For instance, if during the game a puck is deflected off the ice into the crowd and hits a spectator, the principle of consent would apply. Everybody knows pucks sometimes come over the boards.

There can be exceptions to this rule, however. In one little-known case, a fight broke out among the players on the ice. One of them flicked the puck into the crowd and it struck a spectator on the head. It was held in court that *volenti* did not apply because, although the fan had taken the chance of watching a game with the knowledge that it might result in the puck causing some injury, he had not "consented" to watch a fight—which is not considered part of the game—nor to the risk of a puck leaving the ice while such a fight was in progress. The spectator won his case.

To curb the spread of "goon" hockey, when the sport is marred by vicious attacks not excusable as outbreaks of hot temper under stress, Ontario authorities have ordered police to bring assault charges against offending players.

If a person acts in some way that injures another person while trying to save that person from impending danger, or out of a legal or moral duty, he does not "consent" to accept liability for his action. Even if the spectator should know beforehand of the possibility of danger—say, that a racing car might jump the track— that basic knowledge does not make him responsible to save himself; the car driver, the track owners or management would still have to compensate the spectator for any injuries he suffered should an accident occur. For the spectator to be responsible, he would have had to agree specifically to run that risk.

The question of damages

How damages are measured

Compensation for loss of income

Settling out of court

Plaintiff and defendant

If you sue the Queen

What do you stand to gain?

IF YOU HAVE BEEN HARMED by another in your business or profession, in your property or in your reputation, you can look to the law for redress. Whether the harm was intentional or accidental there is a good chance that you will be awarded adequate financial compensation, if you can offer reasonable proof of the injury. But before you leap into court, consider this advice from leading lawyers:

(1) The law of torts is seldom, if ever, simple; discuss the whole situation with a lawyer experienced in civil suits.

(2) The courts can't be worried about your hurt pride; don't sue at all unless you have been really injured. If you lose, it could be very expensive.

(3) Remain open to a private settlement. Most cases are settled out of court, saving time and money—and maybe heartache—for all concerned. There is often a delay of a year or more before a civil action can be heard.

(4) If you have been injured by a child or teenager, by a thief or mugger, by a bankrupt or by a welfare recipient, there's little point in suing—even if you are sure to win. These persons usually have no assets that could be used to pay any damages you would be awarded. They are, in legal terms, *judgment-proof*.

It sometimes seems that the law of torts has a special monopoly on legal jargon—those microscopically exact terms that often have meanings quite different to what the same words convey to the ordinary citizen. For instance, the two words that crop up so often in this chapter, "damage" and "damages," have entirely different meanings. One is definitely not the plural of the other. Damage is another

word for the injury or loss you may suffer, while damages is the money the court awards in compensation. An "injury" in tort does not necessarily mean a physical injury. And we have shown earlier that a person can be legally negligent in the most accidental of happenings.

It is often said that an arbitrary dollar value cannot be placed on pain and suffering or the loss of a loved one in an accident; yet this does not prevent the plaintiff's lawyer from asking for a very definite sum. The court has a set of guidelines to help it assess those damages. The court can, in effect, arbitrate the value of the most intangible damage.

The basic principle of awarding damages is to allow the injured party to recover what he lost (insofar as money can do it) due to the injury. Chances of recovery in negligence cases are far better today than they were a generation ago because of the great expansion that has occurred in the purchase of liability insurance. All motor-vehicle operators, and most home-owners, now carry at least a minimum of this coverage (*See* Chapter 10, "Insurance at home"). Remember, however, that even if the defendant is insured against every misfortune, as the plaintiff you will still have to convince the judge or jury that he or she was legally responsible.

The damage done in any particular tort, or breach of contract, must be recovered once and for all at the same time. For example, let's say you were in an auto accident in which your neck was badly jarred. Less than one year later, you brought a tort action asking for compensation for your pain and suffering up to the date of that action. If your case is over and complications then set in, you could not bring another action to recover for the additional pain and suffering. You must estimate how long the suffering is going to continue before you go to court; any and all damages you feel entitled to for past, present and future suffering will be assessed entirely at that time.

If you haven't been able to recover goods or papers wrongly held by another, you may ask the court to issue an order of *replevin* in your favor. This order in effect authorizes the sheriff to seize the goods on your behalf if the other party still refuses to hand them over.

How damages are measured

The general principle that our courts use to assess damages is to compensate, or repay, the injured party for the loss suffered owing to the breach of a contract or to a tort. If, for example, the side of your new car was crushed as a result of someone's negligence, then the negligent party could be forced to pay the cost of all repairs to put the automobile back into its original shape and condition. Other expense may result due to the temporary loss of your car while it is at the garage. It would be the responsibility of the tort *feasor* (*See* "What is a tort" in this chapter) to compensate you for any necessary or reasonable taxi fares or car-hire charges you incurred due to the fact that your own car was not available.

As a rule, any harm done must be proved; however, there are a few exceptions (*See* "Defamation of character" in this chapter).

The injured party is expected to try to minimize its losses. In other words, don't think you can "make money" out of damages. The plaintiff could not expect full reimbursement for a hired chauffeur-driven limousine during the time that his or her own economy car was being repaired. If the injured party was physically hurt, it would have to be shown that the medical bills being added to the claim were actually for treatment of injuries.

Your lawyer will decide on the amount of your claim with great care because the damages awarded may be limited to the amount that is claimed. The lawyer also knows that if the claim is too high, a jury

might swing its sympathy away from you. The decision reached by the jury on damages will not be altered or quashed by the judge or by a court of appeal unless the final consensus is that "reasonable persons" could not possibly have awarded that amount. The judge might decide, for instance, that the jury has obviously been under some misconception about the case in making its decision.

Before the action actually gets into court, the papers known as the *pleadings* (*See* Chapter 3, " How a case is tried") are passed back and forth between the solicitors representing the plaintiff and the defendant. The pleadings state the basic cause of action, the main items of evidence and the amount of the claim. The plaintiff's lawyer will usually limit his claim to an amount only slightly above what he expects to receive, since his client may be ordered to pay the costs of the action (*See* Chapter 3, "Decisions from the Bench") if he claims for an excessive amount. It is a matter of delicate judgment. If you claim in the pleadings that there are damages of $7,000 and a jury awards $10,000 in damages, the actual damages paid will be limited to $7,000. You would only be able to get more than that if the pleadings were amended prior to the jury decision.

The test by which the amount of damages is ascertained by the jury is called the *measure of damages*. Sometimes, although a plaintiff may have a legal point in claiming damages, the jury will decide that there was actually little real injury, and will award only nominal damages (a trifling amount) in acknowledgment of the invasion of right. Punitive (or exemplary) damages are occasionally awarded, serving not only to compensate the victim but also to punish the offender. Although not common, this kind of award does occur in libel or slander actions and in suits for malicious nuisance.

Following British precedents, the Canadian courts do not take inflation into account when awarding damages, even though an injury may be expected to persist into the future.

The most common type awarded is *compensatory damages*. This award is meant to repay the victim for any loss suffered due to the injury, as well as to compensate for physical and emotional suffering.

Compensation for loss of income

Although it may sound scandalous in our egalitarian society, the fact remains that it is cheaper to injure or kill a poor person in an accident than a rich one.

The courts assess damages in negligence cases under two headings: *general damages*, covering very real but abstract matters such as pain and suffering and shortened life expectancy; and *special damages*, including such tangible injuries as lost wages or other earnings and reduced future earning capacity.

In the case of death, in an action brought under Section 60 of the Family Law Reform Act of Ontario, the victim's family will normally claim a lump sum representing the amount of earnings that would have come to the family if the wage earner had lived out his or her full quota of working years to retirement. In the case of a corporation executive who could have been earning $50,000 a year or more and was still in his forties at the time, this could add up to an extremely large sum of money. The family of a skilled laborer in an industrial plant could claim under this heading only the going rate for the type of work he had been doing though his "promotion possibilities" might be taken into consideration in computing a claim.

If you are the defendant in such a suit, you (or your insurance company) will have to pay the full loss-of-income amount even if it could be proved in court that the accident victim had a bad heart and thus would possibly not have lived until normal age for retirement from the job. The law takes things as they are, not as they may turn out to be.

Where the accident is not fatal and the loss of income is only temporary—perhaps during hospital treatment or convalescence—this loss will be determined on the basis of the plaintiff's current earning rate, possibly averaged over the previous twelve months.

When dog eats dog

ONE OF THE OLDEST JOKES in journalism is that it's not worth printing when dog bites man, but when man bites dog, that's news! The law provided a new twist to this cliché when two New Yorkers named Wiley and Slater took a dogfight to court.

In a dog-bites-dog encounter, Mr. Wiley's pet was killed and he sued Mr. Slater for the value of the animal. He claimed that Slater had been negligent in not controlling his dog. Wiley won a judgment in the lower courts, but Slater appealed to the state Supreme Court.

The judge reversed the verdict, adding that the owner of the dead dog would be entitled to its skin, although some might say it should go to the victor. The judge noted: "The branch of the law applicable to direct conflicts ... between dog and dog is entirely new to me. I am constrained to admit total ignorance of the *code duello* among dogs, or what constitutes a just cause of offense and justifies a resort to arms, rather than to teeth, for redress; whether jealousy is a just cause for war, or what different ... kinds of insults or slight, or what violation of the rules of etiquette, entitle the injured or offended beast to insist upon prompt and appropriate satisfaction.

"It is not claimed upon either side that the struggle was not in all respects doglike and fair. Indeed, I was not before aware that it was claimed that any law, human or divine, common or statute, undertook to regulate and control these matters, but supposed that this was one of the few privileges which this class of animals still retained ... to settle and avenge, in their own way, all individual wrongs and insults, without regard to what Blackstone or any other jurist might write, speak or think."

If the plaintiff is left with a physical or mental handicap that will reduce his money-making ability below his normal average level, this will probably have the effect of increasing the amount of damages awarded.

Settling out of court

The majority of damage claims are settled out of court today to avoid having a case tied up in litigation, or legal dispute, for what could be years. There are many other good reasons for avoiding unnecessary court action. They include the expense of legal and court costs; the ordeal for the victim in having to relive tragic circumstances; and the uncertainty of receiving payment. Sometimes a bird in the hand resulting from an out-of-court settlement can be worth much more than two birds in the bush. The defendant may be willing to pay now while his or her liability insurance will cover for the loss, but—who knows?—the same person might be bankrupt in a year's time.

In most cases settled out of court, the amount offered by the defendant is about the same as what the jury would probably award in court. If the settlement offered is unreasonably low, however, the matter will normally be advanced into court. Of course, the case itself might be weak or there might be some other strong reason for settling out of court.

There are some instances where an action must be brought to court. For instance, if a minor (younger than 18 years) is involved, a judge must make an order for the protection of the "infant." This is so even if an out-of-court settlement has, in fact, been reached.

The advantage of arbitration

Disputes over damages in commercial suits are often resolved by one or more arbitrators, as provided for under the terms of a contract.

There are several advantages to arbitration. For one thing, it is usually much less expensive than court action. The greatest advantage, however, is that the persons chosen as arbitrators are normally specialists who may be more suited than judges to understand and deal with diffi-cult or technical situations. Arbitration is much faster than court action, and this can be of great importance when compensation is needed urgently or when a matter must be decided quickly in order for work to progress.

An agreement to refer a dispute to arbitration is called a *submission;* if any legal proceedings are set in motion in violation of the submission the defendant can apply to the court to have them stopped. The decision of an arbitrator (or an arbitration board) is called an *award.* This decision can be appealed, but usually only on grounds that a mistake had been made in law or jurisdiction. A valid award can be enforced by legal processes.

When you are the plaintiff

If you have been physically injured or harmed in your property or your character—either by the negligence or by an intentional act of another—and if you sue for damages, you will be called the *plaintiff* if your case goes to court. A lawyer should be consulted as soon as possible. He or she will instruct you to do certain things in preparation for your claim.

Remember that it is almost always the responsibility of the plaintiff to prove that actual damage has been inflicted. This is not always simple. For example, pain is a very hard thing to prove. Your lawyer will advise you to keep a diary describing on which day what degree of pain was suffered, what medicine you took to ease the pain, whether you saw a doctor on that date, any equipment given to you—perhaps a special collar—any physiotherapy you underwent, what work you missed, and so on. In cases where no such diary is kept, a person who has suffered for six months may look back and only be able to tell the jury, "I had pain off and on and I took aspirins and other pills and, yes, I did see a doctor on several occasions."

Although such a statement might inspire a jury's sympathy, it is ineffective when compared to testimony consisting of a detailed written account of pain suffered day after day. The diary would also contain any corroborative items that you could gather. For example, if you had been in an automobile accident and had noted statements made by the driver responsible, or by eyewitnesses, you could include those as evidence.

It is also important for the plaintiff to get an assessment of property damage from an expert. If your automobile is damaged, you must get estimates of the cost for repairing the damage from a qualified mechanic. The same reasoning applies to other situations. If you have been hurt bodily, it is necessary to have any injuries taken care of immediately and to have the injury assessed by a qualified doctor.

It has been mentioned earlier that the plaintiff must try to mitigate, or lessen, his losses. Let's say you have been injured physically and the injury will worsen (thus creating a greater loss) unless you take certain action—perhaps by submitting to a remedial operation. If you unreasonably refused to have that operation, you could have trouble in claiming for the increase of damage caused by your not having had the operation. Any expense incurred in having the operation—or in taking other steps to lessen your loss—could legitimately be added to the total of your claim.

When you are the defendant

If you have committed a tort, or expect to be sued for having committed a tort (unless it is only a minor matter that will be settled in the small claims court), you should consult a lawyer as soon as possible. There are almost always two sides to a case, and you owe it to yourself to make sure that everything that can be said in your defense is brought out. Biblical scholars will remind you that even God did not pass judgment on Adam without giving him a chance to speak in his own defense.

Even if you are the defendant in the case, you may have suffered damage as did the plaintiff and some of the fault may lie with the so-called injured party. Depending on the circumstances, you may have to make a counterclaim against the plaintiff in order to recover for your injuries.

Your lawyer will most probably suggest you write a detailed statement of exactly what happened. He or she will then investigate to see if it is possible to have the injuries lessened in any way and attempt a settlement out of court. If he is successful, he will be saving you the amount of the court costs which are usually levied against the defendant.

In civil actions, there are several *pleadings* (documents relating to the suit) which must be passed between the parties. Although there are time limits for these pleadings the court may extend most of these limits at its discretion. However, there are some limits which cannot be extended, as well as some instances in which they will not be extended. When a writ is issued and served, for instance, the defendant generally has between 10 and 20 days to *enter an appearance* (*See* Chapter 3, "How a case is tried"). If the defendant does not appear, the plaintiff can apply for an immediate judgment and have the matter set down for trial to assess the damages. The defendant may be able to have this time extended, and to have set aside the judgment made in his absence but this is more costly than responding properly in the first place.

If you sue the Queen

It is quite possible to sue the Queen (in effect, the government) for damages resulting from torts committed by government employes. Although there are laws that protect people in authority (police and other agents of the Crown) from being sued for certain acts which they believe to be proper, the ordinary citizen can sue the Crown for torts committed by these agents. For example, if a member of the armed forces is at fault in a traffic accident and the government owns the vehicle he was driving, an action can be brought against the Crown.

It is important in such cases to consult a lawyer immediately since the time limits on suits against the Crown cannot be extended and there are certain notices that must be served.

What do you stand to gain?

Going to court is an expensive proposition and, even if you are awarded damages, you still have to collect them. Some people, as we have mentioned, are considered *judgment-proof* (they have no money—or none that you can touch). Thus, although you may win your case, you may end up having lost disastrously when you add up all the bills.

The costs of going to court are threefold. First, there are the court expenses: paying to have a writ issued and to have an *examination for discovery* made prior to trial, as well as numerous other court costs. These costs, published in a schedule of court fees, vary according to the court in which the case is being heard; the higher the court, the higher the charges.

The second cost is your lawyer's bill (*See* Chapter 20, "How the lawyer is paid"). Published fee schedules will give you a pretty firm idea of basic charges. These fees must be paid win, lose or draw.

The third cost should be considered carefully before any legal action is begun. This is the sum the losing party will probably have to pay to the winning party, on top of any damages awarded. This sum is the other person's legal costs. The court often orders the losing party to pay the winner's legal costs as part of the judgment. In deciding whether to award costs, the court will sometimes compare the size of the award the jury has granted to the plaintiff as opposed to the amount that was claimed. For example, if a plaintiff claims $100,000 in damages and receives only $20,000, he or she may not be awarded costs—in other words, costs of the action will have to be paid by the plaintiff. If half of the claim or better is awarded, then the plaintiff will often be awarded full costs.

There is a complex formula for assessing legal costs; it is based on the fee schedule published by the controlling bar association. The main point for the nonprofessional to grasp is that the costs awarded by the court seldom, if ever, satisfy the total amount of the lawyer's bill.

If you win your suit, what do you stand to gain in financial terms? Perhaps no more than you have already lost. The damages (if you get them) will probably merely compensate you for losses you have already paid for. Even if you are awarded your legal costs against the defendant, you will probably still have some costly bills to pay.

What is a leg worth?

CALIFORNIA ATTORNEY Melvin M. Belli is widely regarded as one of the world's foremost pleaders of personal injury suits. His clients have received damages of several hundred thousand dollars on occasion, when the hard-and-fast evidence was wispy indeed.

A well-known illustration of the potent Belli technique was provided when he argued the case of a young mother of three children who had lost a leg in a streetcar accident. He asked for $100,000 damages.

The defending lawyer protested that this was astronomical; it could be invested to produce a sizable income without ever touching the capital which could then be willed, after 40 years, to the woman's children. The children would not have suffered, yet they would be comparatively well-to-do. The advances in artificial limbs, he went on, meant that a wearer could now dance, swim, drive an automobile, play bridge, and so on. The city would provide the victim with such a limb, free.

Belli had said little during all this. But he kept moving a large parcel from place to place on the counsel table. When it was his time to address the jury, he slowly unwrapped his parcel. It was an artificial limb, complete with all the straps, metal plates and hinged foot.

He presented the device to the jurors and asked them to compare it with their own limbs. The attractive one-legged victim sat in full view in the courtroom.

The jury was out for only 30 minutes. When it returned, Belli's client had her hundred grand.

19/The Crime — Society at Bay

Offenses against the person 810

Offenses against property 818

Trial and sentence 824

Threat to the community

O F ALL THE SUBJECTS in this book, *crime* is certainly the most familiar. Through more than 100 years of detective novels, 55 years of radio shows and 30 years of television melodramas, just about everyone has become well aware of the violent or venal side of human nature. Since the days of the Victorian "penny dreadfuls," the newspapers have never spared us the gory or salacious details. True, the communications media give a highly glamorized impression of this basically sick and vicious half-world, but the level of public interest and vicarious involvement is obvious.

Paralleling the popular fascination with the sensational side of wrongdoing is the serious study of the causes of crime and the methods used to deter or "cure" offenders. These efforts persist, but no breakthrough seems yet in sight. At one time, poverty was thought to be the main cause of crime, but offenses everywhere have increased since the introduction of the welfare state. The theory that repeated crime has its roots in emotional or mental incapacity now has its advocates among medical criminologists.

Many attempts have been made to define "crime." It is said to be the intentional violation of a law designed to protect society or the state, or an offense against the public at large. While a tort (*See* Chapter 18, "What is a tort?") is a civil wrong committed against an individual, a crime is a more serious matter, causing harm or posing a threat to the whole community, or to some section of it.

The individual who has been injured by a civil wrong can choose either to bring an action for damages against the person who has injured him or to let the matter drop. However, if the wrongdoing is classed as a crime (all crimes are known in Canada as *offenses*), then it is the Crown acting in the public interest that will prosecute the offender and try to punish him as the law requires.

Crimes range from treason and murder, to sexual assault and robbery, continuing through the gamut of human frailty to such relatively minor offenses as begging in a public place or disturbing the peace during a college sit-in. The penalties set by the law include imprisonment and fines. (The death penalty no longer exists under the Criminal Code, but it can be imposed, in cases of treason, under the National Defence Act.) Conviction for a criminal offense is itself a considerable punishment since those "with a record" find themselves excluded from many career opportunities and subject to the general disapproval of law-abiding citizens. (Any offense under the Criminal Code that results in a prison sentence is entered on the offender's record.)

In the sections that follow, in an attempt to simplify a complex subject and to avoid repetition, the most common crimes have been grouped under generalized headings: offenses against authority; offenses against the person; and offenses against property. But these distinctions are not necessarily exclusive. Many crimes—such as incest, conspiracy, assault, fraud—can fall into different classifications depending on the surrounding circumstances. And, as law reform proceeds, the federal parliament has started to initiate changes. For example, new and tighter gun-control legislation was introduced in 1976 as part of a crackdown on violent crime. In 1982, parliament amended the sections of the Criminal Code relating to sexual offenses and other crimes against the person. To try to speed up the wheels of justice, the law has also been changed to allow county, or district, and provincial courts (not just superior courts) to try such crimes as manslaughter, death due to criminal negligence, sexual assault, and bribery of a peace officer. If not frustrated by a proliferation of appeals, this move may in the course of time do more to promote the cause of justice than many other more widely heralded reforms.

The Canadian Criminal Code

Under the Constitution Act 1867 (formerly the British North America Act), criminal law is placed within the authority of the federal parliament, thus providing uniform criminal law across the entire country. The law is written in the 772 sections of the Canadian Criminal Code, which was first adopted in 1893 (*See* Chapter 1, "Under Canadian writ").

The original author of the Criminal Code was an English jurist, Sir James Stephen. In 1878, his *Draft Criminal Code* was introduced into the British Parliament, where it was promptly rejected. (To this day, the British have not codified—that is, drawn together in a single unified statute—their criminal law.) In 1893, Stephen's code was adopted with minor changes by the Canadian Parliament. Between 1952 and 1953, the code was thoroughly revised, and it has been changed from time to time since then.

In 1984, the federal government introduced a 306-page bill that outlined sweeping changes to criminal law. The bill, for example, proposed tougher sentences for violent criminals while allowing crime victims to seek restitution. Under the new legislation, the courts could impose stiff prison terms for drunken driving, and seize money and assets gained by criminal activity. The bill enlarged the meaning of obscenity and pornography to embrace anything that degradingly exploits crime, horror, violence, as well as sex.

The Canadian Criminal Code is much admired by nations plagued by higher levels of crime or citizen unrest than Canada has to deal with. First, it gathers in one book the bulk of the criminal law. Other legislation dealing with criminal law includes the Official Secrets Act, the Narcotic Control Act, the Juvenile Delinquents Act (to be repealed and replaced by the Young Offenders Act in 1985), the Canada Evidence Act, the Combines Investigation Act and the Charter of Rights and Freedoms—and most of these Acts are being gathered into the same volume.

The code is most specific and definite in its terms. No action or conduct is a crime unless it is expressly stated to be a crime in the Criminal Code or other criminal legislation. You cannot be convicted for some act that a court finds morally wrong or offensive unless it is expressly made an offense in the code. On the other hand, defenses for criminal acts are not restricted to those set down in the code; you can offer any defense that is a defense under the broad range of common law.

A particularly commendable feature of the code is that it is written in reasonably simple language, with most technical terms carefully defined. A strenuous effort was made by Sir James Stephen, as well as by later revisers, to make the code easily understood by the average person.

While the Criminal Code itself could serve as a model of clarity, it must be emphasized that criminal law as a whole is one of the most complex fields of justice. It is one thing to be able to generally understand the written law, but quite another to be able to put it to use in the courtroom. The practice of criminal law is so complicated, and the penalties potentially so severe, that no layman accused of a crime should ever consider trying to conduct his own defense. If no money or credit is available, Legal Aid can almost certainly be arranged.

Two types of offenses

As part of the effort to make the criminal law as concise as possible, certain technical distinctions have been abolished from the Criminal Code. For instance, the classification of crimes into *felonies* and *misdemeanors* has been dropped and all crimes now are referred to as *offenses*.

One distinction remains: all offenses are either *summary-conviction offenses* or *indictable offenses*. These categories relate not so much to the offenses themselves, but to the mode of trial. A person accused of a summary-conviction offense (a minor violation of some kind) will appear before a magistrate (or provincial judge) and the hearing will normally proceed swiftly and without much formality.

Crimes of greater magnitude—such as sexual assault, riot or robbery—are classed as indictable offenses. If a person is believed guilty of a serious wrongdoing, the accusation and the evidence on which it is based may be presented to a *grand jury*. This is called "preferring an indictment." If the grand jury decides that there is sufficient valid evidence to back up the accusation, it will confirm the indictment, or formal charge, and the accused will be sent to trial. If the grand jury decides that the evidence doesn't stand up, the accusation papers will be endorsed with the words "no bill" and the accused will be discharged.

The grand-jury system has never been used in Alberta and Saskatchewan and has been abolished in British Columbia, Manitoba, New Brunswick and Quebec. In those provinces in which it is not used, legal action against a person accused of an indictable offense is begun with an indictment, or charge, in writing.

The guilty mind

Generally, to be guilty of a crime you must have intended to commit it. The Crown attorney prosecuting the case must prove the existence of "a guilty mind" (lawyers use the Latin term *mens rea*). Although there are two major exceptions to this (*See* "Strict liability" later in this section), most offenses require proof that the accused is guilty of the act itself and that he intended to commit it.

The two elements must occur together. A person cannot be convicted of an offense if he did a forbidden act without intending to do it. For example, if a man coming home late at night after having had a "few too many" at the local tavern mistakenly enters a nearby house instead of his own, he cannot be convicted of illegal entry. Certainly he has committed an act forbidden by law, but the circumstances clearly indicate that it was not his intention to commit a criminal offense.

Similarly, "a guilty mind" not accompanied by a criminal act is not evidence of an offense. A person cannot be convicted of a crime because he admits that he would like to shoot his mother-in-law or raid the vaults of the Bank of Canada. The crime of *conspiracy* provides the exception. Where two or more persons conspire (plot) to commit an illegal act, they are guilty of conspiracy even though they did not go beyond the planning stage.

Without *intent* to serve as the decisive factor, it would be impossible to distinguish accidents and innocent acts from criminal behavior. Consider the following:

A man weary of caring for his chronically ill wife calmly decides to kill her. Instead of administering the prescription pill, he substitutes a deadly poisonous tablet. She swallows it and dies.

Another man caring for his chronically ill wife is just as weary of the burden. By an honest mistake, he gives her a deadly poisonous tablet instead of her prescription pill, and she dies.

Without a doubt the man in the first example is guilty of murder; however, the man in the second is not. In this illustration, guilt is decided on the basis of the husbands' intentions. The first man intended to kill his wife; the second did not. Of course, the evidence presented at the trial would have to make the intent clear "beyond a reasonable doubt."

This concept of *criminal intent* is at the root of our criminal law. It is necessary not only to prove that an accused person did a criminal act but also to show that he knew the act was unlawful and that he intended to do it. The accused cannot, of course, simply maintain that he was not aware that a given act was unlawful—one of the best-known legal clichés is that "ignorance of the law is no excuse." The Crown seldom has to present actual proof of the intention either; it is presumed until the acused proves otherwise that we all foresee the "natural consequences" of our actions.

Understanding the consequences

If a person does not have the mental capacity to conceive or commit a criminal offense, or if he is incapable of understanding the nature and consequences of his act, he may be excused from *criminal liability*.

There is in law what is called an "irrebuttable presumption" that a child is incapable of forming the intent to commit a crime. Under the Young Offenders Act, passed by the federal parliament in 1982 and destined to come into force in 1985, the age of criminal responsibility is raised from seven to 12. The law considers that, below this age, a child is too young to know right from wrong. The "irrebuttable presumption" holds good even if the child actually did the deed and didn't merely contribute to it—for example, if the child was seen throwing a baby into a river, or setting fire to a forest in summer.

The new Act states that a "young person"—that is, a person who is 12 years or more but under 18 years of age—is still presumed to be incapable of forming the intent to commit a crime. The Act sets up youth courts, separate from the adult

The scientific detectives

NOBODY IS PERFECT and, they say, there is no such thing as the perfect crime. The cleverest and coolest murderer always leaves some evidence of his deed—but the clue may be invisible to the ordinary eye. That's where the white-coated detectives of the forensic science laboratory step in.

Now collected universally from persons charged with offenses, fingerprints have been an accepted method of identification in law enforcement since 1901. The odds against any fingertip producing an identical print with that of another finger are literally billions to one.

Bullet and firearm identification is also now routine. The grooves in the barrel of guns vary in number, width and direction of twist and, since 1911, microscopic examination of a spent bullet has been enough to tie it to the weapon from which it was fired. Later developments made it possible to identify cartridge cases found at the scene of the crime.

The problems brought to the crime laboratory today sometimes make these familiar procedures seem like child's play. For example, at the Ontario Centre of Forensic Sciences—an agency of the provincial solicitor general's department—experts can often work out from a flake of paint not only the color of an automobile but its make and year. From a few specks of dried blood, they can narrow the number of people it could have come from to as few as one in a hundred thousand.

The centre's main work is to identify and compare materials to provide information to the police, the courts and other investigating agencies. The documents division examines handwriting and forgeries; the biological division examines hair, body fluids, fibers and plant materials. Other divisions handle poisons and firearms.

In one celebrated case, where three persons in a family were attacked with an ax (two of them succumbed), a young couple were accused of the crime. They swore that bloodstains on their clothing had come solely from their efforts to aid the survivor. But laboratory tests proved that the stains on the man's clothing were caused by blood of three different types, and by two types on the woman's.

In another case, experts identified blood that had been spilled on a wooden floor in an isolated cabin nine years earlier. This corroborated other evidence put forward, and the murderer was convicted even though the body was never found.

Forensic medicine has become so important in aiding the police to nail the guilty that all doctors study this branch during their qualifying years. The subjects include evidence of age and identity, rape or abortion, death by drowning, poisoning or other causes.

court system, where judges can decide on the offenses that may have been committed by individuals in this age group.

Under the new Act, anyone older than 17 is presumed to have the mental capacity to intend the outcome of his actions and the onus is on him, if accused of an offense, to prove that he did not. If charged with an indictable offense, anyone above 17 can be tried in adult court.

The defense of insanity

No one can be judged guilty of a crime if it can be proved that he (or she) was not of sound mind at the time the offense was committed. Medical science recognizes several degrees of insanity and the courts attempt to weigh the degree of illness against the gravity of the crime. Developments in psychiatry have enormously complicated this field.

The Criminal Code offers the following guidance:

"A person is insane when he is in a state of natural imbecility or has disease of the mind to an extent that renders him incapable of appreciating the nature and quality of an act or omission, or of knowing that an act or omission is wrong.

"A person who has specific delusions, but is in other respects sane, shall not be acquitted on the ground of insanity unless the delusions caused him to believe in the existence of a state of things that, if it existed, would have justified or excused his act or omission.

"Everyone shall, until the contrary is proved, be presumed to be and to have been sane."

The Criminal Code also states that if a person is insane when the time arrives for his trial, he cannot be brought to judgment even if he was sane at the time the offense was committed. He will be placed in a mental institution until deemed sane and able to stand trial. If he never recovers his sanity, he will be confined to the institution for life.

Pleas of insanity were more frequent in murder trials when the death penalty was being carried out. With the suspension of capital punishment, a plea of insanity could result in a longer term of confinement in a mental hospital than a convicted murderer would be likely to serve in a penitentiary. Generally speaking, the defense of insanity is virtually obsolete since the death penalty can no longer be imposed under the Criminal Code. Where the circumstances permit a choice, the defending lawyer will opt for a definite term in prison for his client rather than an indefinite period in a mental institution. The lawyer knows that if found guilty, his mentally ill client will probably be sent to a treatment center anyway.

When drunk or drugged

Sometimes the newspapers will carry a story of someone who admits having committed a crime but argues that he was so drunk he didn't know what he was doing. Drunkenness can never be an excuse for criminal conduct (the drunken driver is treated severely by the law) but it can be raised as evidence of the accused person's temporary incapacity to form *criminal intent*.

If the accused person can establish that he was incapable of appreciating the nature and consequences of his act, he might be acquitted of an offense where criminal intent is an essential element but convicted of a lesser offense where specific intent is not a necessary ingredient of the offense. In these circumstances, a charge of murder might be reduced to one of manslaughter.

The true drunkard or the confirmed drug addict is seldom involved in serious crime. He has given up the struggle and his mind is so befuddled that he is at least partially insane—and is so regarded in enlightened countries.

Defense of automatism

A rare defense, and extremely difficult to establish, is the plea of *automatism*. This term is used to describe a state of mind in which a person is not conscious of what he is doing—in effect, he responds automatically. It is also known as "involuntary conduct." The best illustration of this is provided by the sleepwalker who may do something without being conscious of his act. In another case, someone may claim that he "blacked out" and does not remember doing some act.

The following case came before the Supreme Court of Canada on appeal in 1964:

In the course of a fight, the accused was knocked down and struck his head on the sidewalk. He regained his feet, pulled out a knife and stabbed his victim to death. Later he claimed to have "blacked out" and that he had had no control over his actions. The evidence of a number of witnesses as to his dazed state and the evidence of a psychiatrist who believed that such a blackout was possible in the circumstances raised a reasonable doubt in the mind of the jury that he did not intend his act, and he was acquitted. The acquittal was upheld by the Supreme Court.

Crimes of passion

A crime committed in the heat of passion brought on by sudden provocation will probably be regarded in a different light from one committed with cool calculation, or premeditation. The law would ask whether the provocation was sufficient to truly inflame "an ordinary man". Without that "man-in-the-street" test, a hotheaded person might be excused for acts that would bring a conviction to a more evenly tempered person. We must all conquer our dangerous impulses or be prepared to pay the price if another is injured by our giving vent to them.

A so-called "crime of passion" may occur when a husband discovers his wife making love with another man and, in a fit of rage, kills either or both of them. He might be acquitted on a charge of murder and convicted of the lesser offense of manslaughter if he caused death in the heat of passion brought about by sudden provocation. The word "sudden" is very important in this context. If the husband,

The meaning of guilt

IN THE LAW as revealed to Moses and described in the Old Testament, it is stated that "The innocent and the just you shall not put to death, nor shall you acquit the guilty." But in the 3,200 years that have passed since then, lawmakers and philosophers have struggled without success to agree on a definition of guilt.

The dictionaries, confessing the word has no known root, say it means, "a failure of duty; a delinquency, offense, crime or sin." In the complexities of the human mind, what is guilt to one man may seem justice to another. The written law—and especially the Criminal Code—tries to throw a light by setting out in detail the actions that, if committed, will bring official punishment. It also makes plain, however, that the *intention* of the accused is a vital element. Thus, the law usually must try to establish the existence of an abstraction—the so-called "guilty mind."

Few would deny that the operation of this doctrine has set free many a guilty party. But most would agree that every accused person must be given the benefit of any doubt that may exist. They echo the conclusion of Sir John Fortescue, chief justice of the King's Bench in fifteenth-century England. "One would rather," he said, "that 20 guilty persons should escape the punishment of death, than one innocent person should be executed."

The jury system illustrates our uneasiness at permitting any one man to decide the guilt of another in any serious wrongdoing. The novelist G. K. Chesterton put it this way: "Our civilization has decided, and very justly decided, that determining the guilt or innocence of men is a thing too important to be trusted to trained men. It wishes for light upon that awful matter, it asks men who know no more law than I know, but who can feel the things that I felt in the jurybox. When it wants a library catalogued, or the solar system discovered, or any trifle of that kind, it uses up its specialists. But when it wishes anything done which is really serious, it collects 12 of the ordinary men standing round. The same thing was done, if I remember right, by the Founder of Christianity."

after discovering his wife in bed with his neighbor, goes for a walk to think things over and then resolves to kill one or both of them, he will not be able to claim that the homicide was the result of sudden provocation. A jury would almost certainly consider that there had been time for his passion to cool and would find him guilty of murder.

There is no tradition in Canada (sometimes reputed as existing in Europe) that allows a wronged husband to attack his wife's lover to avenge his honor. The Canadian Lothario who was punched on the nose could bring an action for assault. (*See* Chapter 18, "The intentional tort.") The sober Canadian remedy for infidelity lies in divorce.

The defense of sudden provocation is not restricted to outraged husbands (or wives). Whether the act or insult preceding a murder is considered sufficiently provocative to constitute a defense will depend on the facts of each case. The following case illustrates the doctrine in operation:

During a street brawl, a man was running toward the combatants when a woman cried out, "You won't murder the man, will you?" He replied, "What's that to you,

you bitch!" The woman then struck him in the face with a heavy object, causing a severe injury. The man turned and chased her and fatally stabbed her in the back. He was charged with murder, but this was reduced to manslaughter when the jury decided that he had acted in the heat of passion caused by sudden provocation.

Acting in self-defense

There are well-known circumstances when the killing of another is legally justified. The soldier defending his country in war or revolution, or the policeman attempting to prevent the escape of a dangerous criminal when other measures have failed, provide only two of several possible examples. There is also the situation where the citizen is acting to defend himself, or those in his care or protection, against a violent attack or threat.

To succeed with a plea of *justifiable homicide* on the grounds of self-defense, it is necessary for the accused to show that his life (or the lives of those in his care) was in actual danger at the time he did the killing. If you are awakened at night by a strange sound and you surprise a burglar, you are not allowed to simply blast him with your shotgun or crush his

The example of Daniel M'Naghten

IN 1843, Edward Drummond, private secretary to British Prime Minister Sir Robert Peel, was shot dead in his office by a deranged man, Daniel M'Naghten. The assassin's intended victim was Sir Robert himself, the founder of the London police force.

At the ensuing murder trial—to the consternation of traditionalists—M'Naghten was found not guilty on grounds of insanity.

A furious debate followed in the House of Lords, resulting in the Law Lords (the Lord Chancellor and those peers who had held high judicial appointments) being asked to define insanity from the point of view of law. They did so, as follows:

• The accused is regarded as sane until the contrary is proved.
• The accused must produce evidence that he was insane at the time of the offense.
• The accused must convince the court that he did not know the nature of his act, or that he was doing wrong.
• If the accused is found to have been insane at the time of the offense, then a verdict of "not guilty on the grounds of insanity" is returned and he is detained in a mental institution for an indefinite period.

Commonly known as M'Naghten's rules, these conditions have been applied ever since with little change wherever there is an inheritance of British law.

skull with a heavy ashtray. That would be murder, pure and simple. But if the burglar flourished a gun at you or swung at you with a tire iron—that would be a different story.

You are permitted to protect yourself and your property with no more force than is necessary under the circumstances. You must endeavor to use civilized means, even if the other party is acting like a barbarian. Of course you are not really expected to wait so long that your assailant shoots you first!

A mistake of fact

An accused person may be acquitted on a criminal charge if he produces evidence proving (within "reasonable doubt") that he simply made a mistake. While ignorance of the law is never a defense to a criminal charge, ignorance of fact may be. "I didn't know the gun was loaded" is an example of this type of defense.

If you grab a familiar-looking overcoat from the rack at the restaurant and find out later that it is not your own, you haven't committed theft (assuming you take it back). That would be a "mistake of fact"—and mistake of fact rules out any *intent*.

Strict liability

Under the Criminal Code, certain acts are forbidden absolutely, and the person who commits them will be judged guilty, whether there was intention or not. For example, it is a criminal offense for a male to have sexual intercourse with a girl who is younger than 14. It doesn't matter whether he was under the impression that the girl was older than 13, or whether she consented, encouraged or even solicited the act. The offender could be sentenced to life imprisonment; until quite recently, he could also be whipped.

There are also some offenses under other federal or provincial legislation that do not require the prosecutor to establish that the accused was aware he was committing a crime (thus raising the question of intent). For instance, it is possible to commit an offense simply by failing to exercise reasonable care and attention (*See* Chapter 18, "The accidental tort").

The burden of proof

One of the brightest jewels of our legacy of English law is the doctrine that a man is innocent until he is proved guilty. What this means, in practical terms, is that a person accused of a crime does not have to prove that he is innocent; the burden (or "onus") is almost always on the Crown to prove that he is guilty beyond a reasonable doubt. This is what is known as the *burden of proof*.

At times, the Crown in a criminal case will put forward evidence that, unless contradicted, would prove the guilt of the accused. The accused then has the opportunity to counter with evidence that would serve to either discount the incriminating evidence or suggest that he is innocent of the crime.

The accused person does not need to prove that he did not commit the offense, but only that there is a reasonable probability that he did not. He is always entitled to the benefit of the doubt.

The doctrine of *reasonable doubt* is virtually impossible to define, simply because what is and what is not "reasonable" is always open to question. Normally, "reasonable" relates to the attitudes or reactions of the ordinary, law-abiding, tax-paying citizen—Mr. Average Man, if you like. No charge has to be proved "beyond the shadow of a doubt." On the other hand, there must be strongly conclusive evidence that the accused is guilty. Satisfying this high standard of proof has sometimes caused the general public to complain bitterly that too many people are acquitted of crimes on "technicalities" or that they escape punishment through "loopholes."

In seeking a conviction, the prosecution must show that the accused is being proceeded against in total conformity with all the law. If a person is charged with possession of stolen goods, for example, it is not enough for the Crown to prove that he had goods alleged to be stolen in his possession, and then to assume, or take for granted, that the goods are the ones that were stolen and that the accused knew they were stolen. Each element of the charge must be proved. (*See* Chapter 3, "How a case is tried.")

801

Offenses against authority

An act of treason

The Official Secrets Act

Piracy and hijacking

Offensive weapons

Disorderly conduct

Bribery of officials

EVEN A QUICK GLANCE at Canadian history will show you that this country has known its share of bloody events—with several invasions from south of the border and more than one armed revolt from within. In this century, however, the domestic scene has remained comparatively serene, with only moderate clashes arising mostly from labor tensions and frustrations. The only seemingly significant threat to established authority appeared to come from separatist extremists in Quebec and this was crushed by firm federal action in October 1970. Thus, speaking of "crimes against the state" has an unaccustomed ring in Canada, evoking thoughts of harsh military or totalitarian dictatorships in unemancipated lands.

It is the fact, however, that offenses committed against authority still rank among the gravest crimes in Canada. Any organization or any individual acting against public order and the welfare of the nation—as exemplified by the Crown and by our elected and appointed officialdom—can expect a stern and unrelenting justice. The proclamation of the War Measures Act in 1970 graphically illustrates the truth of this (*See* Chapter 2, "When rights are suspended"). *Treason* remains the most serious of all offenses against authority, with *sedition* and *riot* ranking not far behind.

Crime is such an all-embracing term—running the gamut of human fallibility and weakness—that many of its aspects have already been discussed to some degree in earlier chapters, where they rose naturally in the course of examining the interplay of the law and our everyday lives. In this chapter, we explore the ma-

jor categories and classes of crime as they are more completely set out in the Criminal Code and other legislation.

An act of treason
Under the Criminal Code, life imprisonment is the penalty for a Canadian who is convicted of treason, whether he (or she) commits the crime inside or outside our national borders. Any attempt, however unsuccessful, to overthrow the federal—or any provincial—government by violence carries the penalty of life imprisonment. Even conspiring (that is, "planning" by two or more persons) to commit such an act can draw this sentence. Under the National Defence Act, the death penalty may be imposed in rare cases involving treasonable activity.

The following acts amount to treason:
(1) Killing, attempting to kill or causing bodily harm to the Queen;
(2) Taking part in a war against Canada;
(3) Assisting an enemy at war with Canada;
(4) Attempting to overthrow by force the government of Canada or of a province;
(5) Passing to a foreign agent military or scientific information prejudicial to the safety and defense of Canada.

Under our system of constitutional monarchy, all citizens owe allegiance to the monarch (at present, Queen Elizabeth II) whether they are living in Canada or not. (*See* Chapter 2, "How to become a Canadian citizen.") The Canadian citizen who has been living in the United States for years is still officially a subject of Her Majesty.

If an alien becomes a permanent resident of Canada, he also owes allegiance to the Queen. The principle is that all those who claim the Queen's protection owe her their allegiance in return. It is understood that in this sense the Sovereign stands "in right of" Canada—that is, represents all citizens of Canada through the cabinet; thus, when we speak of "the Crown," we are really referring to the people of Canada as a whole.

Anyone convicted of passing classified secrets to a foreign state against which Canada is at war may be sentenced to life imprisonment; for the same action committed in peacetime, the maximum penalty is 14 years' imprisonment.

Advocating revolution

The offense of *sedition* is committed by any person who teaches, advocates, or publishes any writing that proposes the violent overthrow of a government in Canada. The penalty for sedition is 14 years' imprisonment (*See* Chapter 2, "When rights are suspended").

The Criminal Code formally sets out the several actions that constitute sedition: speaking words that express a seditious intention; publishing such words; or entering into an agreement with another person to carry out a seditious intention.

When the charge is one of speaking seditious words, the circumstances in which they were spoken, as well as the time and place, are of some importance. Two drunks breathing revolution in a bar aren't much of a threat to the nation. With publications, the effect of the publishing is of no importance; the only evidence necessary for a conviction is the intention revealed in the words.

No one will be found guilty of sedition merely for criticizing an administration, no matter how sharp or excessive the statements. There must be an intention to incite persons to overthrow a government by violence.

The Official Secrets Act

If James Bond had worked for Canada, he would have been enforcing the Official Secrets Act, Canada's law dealing with espionage, or "spying." The Official Secrets Act can deprive an alleged spy of some rights he would enjoy under the Criminal Code. For example, if a person is accused of an offense under this act and the Crown makes proof of certain facts, there will be a presumption that the accused is guilty of the offense without the Crown having to prove that the accused intended to commit the offense. The accused, however, can rebut this presumption by presenting contrary evidence.

If you were found without reasonable excuse in or near a military establishment, a place where munitions are kept or made, or a place where secret research is done, or if you made or communicated to a foreign agent any sketch, plan, model or notes used in such places, you could be sentenced to 14 years in prison. The main point is the purpose, or intent, of the person concerned. You could be convicted of passing secret information to a foreign agent even if such facts were not harmful to Canada's interests—provided that you intended to cause harm.

If a person is caught obtaining or communicating secret information, he is presumed to have intended to use it against the best interests of Canada—until he proves the contrary.

Since Confederation in 1867, Canada's experience with spies has been limited. German agents were landed on the Atlantic coast during both world wars but they failed in their missions. When the cipher clerk Igor Gouzenko defected from the Russian Embassy in Ottawa in 1945, he revealed that the Soviet Union had been actively spying on Canada since 1924; the Russians' greatest coup was the gathering of significant information concerning the top-secret atomic bomb.

Piracy and hijacking

A person commits *piracy* if he steals a Canadian ship or if he steals, throws overboard, damages or destroys part of a ship or its cargo. The penalty for piracy can be life imprisonment.

The charge of piracy can be laid by the Crown against anyone who commits piracy on a Canadian ship, whether within Canadian territorial waters or anywhere else on the globe. If the pirate is a subject of a nation at war with Canada at the time, his act would not be piracy but an "act of hostility."

803

The *hijacking* of aircraft reached epidemic proportions throughout the world in 1972, and a number of incidents involved Canadian aircraft. In response, extensive additions were made to the Criminal Code that year.

Anyone who, by force or threat or by any other form of intimidation, seizes control of an aircraft—that is, hijacks it—with the intention of confining or imprisoning any person against his will, or of transporting any person against his will to any place other than the next place the plane is scheduled to land, is liable to imprisonment for life. The hijacker is also guilty of the offense if he intends to hold for ransom any person on board the aircraft or if he causes the plane to deviate from its flight plan.

Other special "aircraft offenses" were created in 1972. Anyone on board a plane in flight who commits an assault likely to

Fateful verdict: the tragedy of Louis Riel

THE MOST FAMOUS, and most controversial, criminal trial in Canadian history is undoubtedly that of Louis David Riel, self-styled President of the Republic of Manitoba, indubitable leader of the *Métis* people of the plains, one-time inmate of mental asylums at Longue Pointe and Beauport in Quebec.

In 1869, after the purchase of the vast Northwest by the Dominion of Canada, the Montreal-educated Riel took a lead in blocking the path of government survey teams who were sent out to organize the 6.4 million square kilometres of territory. Stupidly, no attempt had been made to win over the *Métis*, a few thousand French-speaking descendants of Indian women and European fathers who lived along the Red River. Subsequently, Riel with a motley group of followers seized Fort Garry, forerunner of modern Winnipeg, and formed a provisional government.

The small number of English-speaking settlers and traders would not acknowledge Riel's "authority" and, early in 1870, he had a party of them arrested. One man, Thomas Scott, was executed by firing squad at Riel's command. With the approach of troops from the east, the "republic" collapsed and Riel fled to the United States.

In 1873, although a fugitive with a price on his head, Riel was elected to the House of Commons as M.P. for Provencher. Two years later, he was formally expelled and, in effect, banished for five years. For a time, he slipped into madness and was smuggled back to Quebec for treatment, entering the St. Jean-de-Dieu asylum under the name of Louis R. David.

Riel was teaching at a Jesuit school at Sun River, Montana (he had taken American citizenship), when he was invited back to Canada by *Métis* groups who were again in conflict with the federal government over land rights. This confrontation boiled over into what the history books call the Riel (or Northwest) Rebellion of 1885. Again, Riel established an illegal provisional government and tried—with some success—to bring the western Indians into insurrection. At Frog Lake, the Crees massacred nine persons, including two priests.

After fighting bravely, but hopelessly, against superior forces, the *Métis* cause was lost, and Riel was brought to trial for treason in Regina in July 1885.

When Riel's three lawyers tried to plead that their client was not responsible for his actions because of insanity, he indignantly rejected the move. The six-man all-white jury found him guilty, recommending mercy. But there was only one sentence permitted the judge—death by hanging.

Petitions from several countries asked Prime Minister Sir John A. Macdonald to save Riel. Even Queen Victoria let it be known that she was for clemency. But, although execution was set back three times, Riel finally mounted the scaffold in the Regina jailyard at dawn on November 16. He died bravely, just past his 41st birthday.

endanger the safety of the aircraft, or who causes damage that makes the plane incapable of flight, or that is likely to endanger its safety, may be sentenced to life imprisonment.

Anyone who places, or is responsible for the placing, on board an aircraft anything that is likely to damage the aircraft, or anyone who interferes with any navigational equipment so as to endanger the plane and its passengers, is guilty of an indictable offense. Again, the maximum punishment is life imprisonment.

Another item in the new legislation forbids anyone to take an "offensive weapon" aboard an aircraft without the consent of the operator or the owner. Any passenger who breaks this law can be sentenced to 14 years' imprisonment. An offensive weapon does not only mean a gun.

All Canadians who travel frequently by air have become accustomed to airport inspection of their persons and their baggage before boarding their planes. Special metal detectors are often used by security personnel.

Offensive weapons
Anything that is designed to be used as a weapon, as well as anything that a person uses or intends to use as a weapon, is classified as an *offensive weapon* under the law. Naturally, this includes all types of firearms; but it can also include a butcher knife, a shovel—or even a broken beer glass.

Several weapons are completely banned in Canada; examples include gun silencers (even though they are not weapons in themselves), the "stun gun," unregistered fully automatic weapons, sawed-off shotguns with barrels less than 46 centimetres long or a total length of less than 60 centimetres, switchblade knives and certain weapons associated with the martial arts. Anyone found with a weapon of this description in his possession can be sent to prison for up to five years. In addition, the Criminal Code sets restrictions on the possession of several other weapons: hand guns, semi-automatic centre-fire weapons with barrels less than 47 centimetres long and firearms which

can be folded up or telescoped to less than 66 centimetres in length.

Anyone who wants to keep a restricted weapon must register it and obtain a permit from the police. A permit will be issued only for such purposes as target practice—usually under the auspices of a shooting club—or the protection of life or property where such protection is shown to be required (*See* Chapter 17, "Guns and guides").

Anyone in possession of a restricted weapon without a permit is liable to imprisonment for five years.

When this chapter was under revision, plans were afoot to require licenses for *all* firearms—much to the consternation of the hunting fraternity. It is estimated that there are at least ten million rifles and shotguns in Canada.

Unlawful assembly
As the offense of *unlawful assembly* occurs mostly during the exercise—or attempted exercise—of the basic freedom of assembly and association, it has been discussed at some length in the chapter devoted to civil rights and liberties (*See* Chapter 2, "When rights are suspended"). It is worth noting, however, how the Criminal Code distinguishes an unlawful assembly from a lawful one. When three or more persons gather together with the intention of carrying out a common purpose, they are an assembly, or association. An unlawful assembly occurs if they assemble, or conduct themselves when assembled, in such a way as to cause persons in the neighborhood of the assembly to fear, on reasonable grounds, that the group will: (1) disturb the peace tumultuously; or (2) by that assembly needlessly and without reasonable cause provoke other persons to thus disturb the peace.

There does not need to be a breach of the peace. It is sufficient if there is a reasonable likelihood of a breach of the peace occurring. The hour of the day and the language of those assembled are matters that would be considered. It is no crime to assemble; the offense does not occur until a group begins to disturb the peace "tumultuously," or shows obvious intentions of doing so. And this involves much more than just the usual noisy theatricals of demonstrations.

If the meeting gets out of hand—or if the police consider that it has gone too far (for instance, if the crowd is breaking up park benches)—what was an unlawful assembly becomes, in official terminology, a *riot*. The maximum penalty for participating in a riot is two years' imprisonment. If the violence escalates and the "Riot Act" is read (this is an official proclamation warning a crowd to disperse), the penalties escalate as well. Anyone who has not dispersed within 30 minutes after the Riot Act is read can be sentenced to life imprisonment.

Disorderly conduct

A number of separate offenses against public order are grouped together within the term *disorderly conduct*. These include *causing a disturbance*, and *indecent acts*.

The Criminal Code rules that anyone not in a dwelling house who commits any one of the following acts is guilty of causing a disturbance:
(1) Fighting, screaming, shouting, swearing, singing or using insulting or obscene language;
(2) Being drunk, or impeding or molesting other persons;
(3) Openly exposing or showing an indecent exhibition in a public place;
(4) Loitering in a public place and in any way obstructing persons who are there;
(5) Disturbing the peace and quiet by discharging firearms, or by other disorderly conduct in a public place.

A public place includes any place to which the public has access either by right or by invitation. The definition is wide enough to include not only a street or a tavern but also private property frequented by members of the public without objection from the owner.

In British Columbia in 1970, an ingenious attempt was made to convince a judge that a public place had become a private place. A group of university students occupied parts of the university library during a demonstration. Upon being charged with causing a distur-

bance, they put forward the defense that they had converted the library into their residence, thereby making it a dwelling house. The defense was rejected and the students were convicted.

It is not necessary for the Crown to prove that anybody was actually disturbed by the "disturbance." The offense exists if there is a reasonable likelihood that someone might be disturbed.

The charge must set out the details of the offense most carefully. A person charged with causing a disturbance by fighting cannot be convicted of causing a disturbance by swearing. In one case, a man was acquitted of causing a disturbance by swearing when he proved that the words he used were obscene but were not "swearing." The court held that "swearing" was the employment of an oath in a manner contemptuous or irreverent of God.

Indecent acts

Anyone who willfully commits an indecent act in a public place in the presence of one or more persons is guilty of a summary-conviction offense. A man who urinated in the street when no one was in sight was acquitted on a charge of committing an indecent act; had there been others present, he would have been guilty even though he did not perhaps intend to insult or offend anyone.

In another case, it was ruled that a private place would be a public place if the indecent act was likely to be seen by a number of casual observers. For example, a woman sunbathing in the nude on the roof of her house was convicted because it was proved that the roof was visible from the windows of neighboring houses.

If an indecent act was done in a private place, the prosecution must prove that the person concerned intended to insult or offend others. A person who was seen to pass by a window of his house in the nude on the way from his shower to his bedroom would not be guilty if he did not intend to insult or offend anyone. However, a person who paraded in the nude in front of a window for the supposed enjoyment of passersby or to fulfill his own exhibitionistic desires would be guilty of an indecent act.

Since the amendment of the Criminal Code in 1969, in keeping with the government's decision that the state has no business in the nation's bedrooms, acts of homosexuality and fellatio between consenting adults in private are no longer illegal. However, any such activity in a public place is considered *gross indecency*.

Bigamy

The state claims an interest in protecting the institutions of marriage and family. Under the Criminal Code, anyone who

The forger was a genius

FORGERY has always attracted creative talents that, properly developed in the "straight" world, would have brought prosperity and maybe fortune to their owners. If easy money has been the main motive for forgery, there have also been those cases where the forger appears to have collected a bonus in pleasure at outwitting so-called specialists. When these cases appear in the courts, public opinion seems to lean toward clemency. Everybody likes to see the expert with egg on his face.

The curious career of Henricus Anthonius van Meegeren (known as "Hans"), a delicate dapper little Amsterdam artist, provides perhaps the perfect illustration of all these points. During World War II, he produced a series of oils in the style of the seventeenth-century Dutch painters Vermeer and De Hooch. They were accepted, after rigorous examination, as genuine "old masters" and Van Meegeren amassed a fortune of about $3 million.

It is obvious that the forger was an artist of great talent. He had so immersed himself in the technique and style of his idol Jan Vermeer that his own works—for which there was little demand—began step by step over a considerable period, to resemble the master's own paintings so closely that even dealers were fooled. Van Meegeren was in his 50s when the Germans occupied he Netherlands and the Nazi warlords began to gather up large collections, either by theft or purchase.

Van Meegeren now slipped across the line into forgery. He purchased old used canvasses and obtained the same paints and brushes that Vermeer had used 300 years earlier. New "Vermeers" now began to surface, each one carefully documented. The bemedalled Hermann Göring, second only to Adolf Hitler in power, bought *Christ and the Adultress*, attributed to Vermeer, paying a fabulous price. Other paintings were bought very quietly by several museums and art galleries.

It was the Göring picture that broke the case. It was traced by American investigators to Van Meegeren after the German defeat and he was accused of selling his nation's art treasures to the enemy. Now, the forger's pride was stung. No, he insisted, it was not a Vermeer—it was a Van Meegeren! He had painted the picture, and others like it, signing the names of Vermeer and De Hooch.

The owners of the fake "Vermeers" now rose with red faces to insist that their experts could not have been fooled. Van Meegeren must be lying, simply trying to build a name for himself through the publicity. So the authorities asked the little man with the toothbrush moustache to paint a new "Vermeer" to order. It was virtually indistinguishable from the master's work. Even the judges hid their grins.

Van Meegeren achieved the seemingly impossible feat of duplicating the work of Vermeer, regarded as the most perfect technician among all the Dutch masters.

Instead of drawing a life sentence as a traitor, Van Meegeren was handed a one-year term in prison. He died there in 1947, at the age of 58. He could be laughing still: Van Meegerens, bearing his own or other signatures, now change hands at prices that truly reflect the forger's genius.

807

goes through a marriage ceremony knowing that he, or his partner, is already married commits the offense of bigamy. The convicted offender can be sentenced to five years in prison. Certain aspects of *bigamy* have already been discussed (*See* Chapter 10, "The annulment").

Any Canadian citizen who left the country and became involved in a bigamous marriage in another country would be just as guilty.

The offense requires a guilty mind—meaning that knowledge and intent are required. If the accused believed that his spouse was dead or that his first marriage was invalid, and if he could show this belief to be honest and reasonable, he would not be convicted of bigamy. If the spouse had been continuously absent for seven years immediately preceding the second ceremony, and if there had been no evidence that he (or she) was still alive, then the first spouse would be presumed to be dead and no offense would have occurred.

If a person charged with bigamy offers the defense that the first marriage was dissolved, the onus is on him to prove that the dissolution actually took place and that it is recognized under Canadian law.

Incest

A subject of taboo even in primitive societies, incest is strictly forbidden under Canadian law—but, it must be added, the federal Law Reform Commission proposed in 1976 that incest (along with indecency, obscenity, and abortion) be re-evaluated "in the light of present social attitudes." The current penalty for incest is up to 14 years' imprisonment.

Incest is sexual intercourse between two persons who are so closely related by blood that they are forbidden to marry. (*See* Chapter 10, "The engagement.") It applies equally to men and women. The code states that "everyone commits incest who, knowing that another person is by blood relationship his or her parent, child, brother, sister, grandparent or grandchild, as the case may be, has sexual intercourse with that person." Brother and sister, in this regard, include half-brother and half-sister.

There is sound medical logic to this law. Incest can result in genetic weaknesses being compounded. The law also seeks to protect particularly girls and boys who may be vulnerable in some family situations.

Where a woman or girl is convicted of incest and the court is satisfied that she committed the offense only because she was under "restraint, duress or fear of the person with whom she had the intercourse," the court is not required to impose any punishment.

Perjury

The criminal offense of *perjury* is committed when a witness in a judicial proceeding gives false evidence, orally or by affidavit (a sworn statement in writing signed by the witness), knowing it to be false and intending that it mislead the court. It makes no difference if the court was actually misled or not. A witness who gives false evidence but believes it to be true has not committed perjury.

A "judicial proceeding" includes not only a hearing in a court of justice, but also proceedings before a parliamentary body or committee, before a justice of the peace, magistrate or coroner, before an arbitrator or before any person, or group of persons, authorized by law to make an inquiry and take evidence under oath.

If a person accused of murder was convicted on the basis of false evidence, the perjurer could be sentenced to life imprisonment.

Obstructing justice

You can be convicted of *obstructing justice* by committing any number of separate but related offenses. It is an offense, for example, for a bondsman (that is, a person who has provided bail for another) to accept a fee or any other compensation from the person who is being bailed out, or from anyone else. Similarly, it is an offense to offer to indemnify the bondsman—that is, offer to compensate him should he lose his bond money. If Mr. X posted bail of $1,000 to secure Mr. Y's release from custody pending his trial, and Y paid X a fee for doing so, both would be guilty of obstructing justice.

You are also committing an offense to obstruct justice if you dissuade a witness from giving evidence by threats, bribes or other corrupt means, or if you influence a juror by threats, bribes or other corrupt means.

Similarly, both the witness and the juror are committing crimes if they either accept or seek a bribe. These offenses, or criminal actions to obstruct justice, were once known as *embracery*—a term still used in the United States.

Bribery of officials

The payment of money, or any valuable goods, to a judge or any holder of public office, for the purpose of influencing his behavior and of inducing him to act contrary to the known rules of honesty and integrity, is a serious offense under the Criminal Code. It is an equally serious offense for the public official to accept such a bribe. The maximum penalty for offering or accepting a bribe is 14 years' imprisonment.

Counterfeiting

Under the Canadian Constitution the federal authority alone has power to issue coinage and paper money (also postage and excise stamps); this is one area where the initiative of private enterprise is strictly discouraged.

It is unlawful to make, to have in one's possession or to pass off as genuine any false coins or paper money intended to resemble lawful money. The term lawful money includes not only money issued by the federal government of Canada but also the official money of any other country. The maximum sentence is 14 years' imprisonment.

It is also an offense to have counterfeit slugs or tokens, or anything else similarly intended for use in coin-operated machines—including coins from foreign countries. The crime exists as soon as the intent of using the tokens or foreign coins to defraud is determined.

It is still a crime to clip gold or silver coins in the hope of building up your own hoard of precious metal. Of course, the first trick would be to find some gold or silver coins in circulation. All our usual coinage today is *token* coinage—that is, it represents a certain value but the value does not normally exist in the coin itself (*See* Chapter 7, "All about money").

It is technically a crime to deface a coin that is lawful money in Canada—*i.e*, to mark or mar its surface. But don't think that Grandfather is a criminal because he has a gold sovereign or eagle dangling from his watch chain!

Forgery

A maximum sentence of 14 years in the penitentiary also faces anyone convicted of *forgery*. This is the offense of "making a false document" with the intention that it be used—or acted upon as genuine—to someone's advantage or disadvantage. This includes altering a genuine document in some material way or adding false information—such as a phony date. It also includes cutting out or obliterating any important part of a document.

As far as the law is concerned, "a document" is any paper or parchment containing writing or printing: books, magazines, letters, account books, cheques, wills or the prospectus of a company. It is the *making* of the false document with the intention that it be used or acted upon that is the crime. Bear in mind that the crime still stands even if the document is not, in fact, acted upon.

Watching and besetting

For a long time, the charge of *watching and besetting* was directed at strikers to prevent them from picketing their employer's premises (*See* Chapter 12, "Strikes and lockouts"). This application of the offense was ended by an amendment to the Criminal Code in 1953.

Watching and besetting is a summary-conviction offense, meaning that it is a relatively minor violation of the law. (*See* "Threat to the community" earlier in this chapter.) It applies to anyone who intimidates another by following him (or her) from place to place, or by persistently watching the dwelling or business premises where the victim happens to be. The crime occurs when the follower intends to annoy or harass, or to influence the victim in some course of legal activity.

Offenses against the person

Murder

Manslaughter

Infanticide and abortion

Criminal negligence

Assault

Sexual assault

THE MACABRE FASCINATION of murder—the ultimate offense one person can commit against another—has troubled man since Cain slew Abel. The famous Elizabethan playwright John Webster wrote, "Other sins only speak: murder shrieks out." Our newspaper headlines and television bulletins bear witness to that pronouncement to the present day.

The unjustified taking of a human life stands next to treason as the most serious crime in Canada and the sentence decreed by law is the minimum of life imprisonment. However, a person who has been sentenced to life can be eligible for parole after 25 years, and not before, in the case of first-degree murder, and after ten years, in the case of second-degree murder.

A person commits *homicide* when he causes the death of another human being. Depending on the circumstances of the act, homicide is classified as either culpable or not culpable—that is, legally blameworthy or legally excused. We have given examples of how a killing may be justified. (*See* "Threat to the community" in this chapter.) *Culpable homicide* is murder, manslaughter or infanticide.

A person commits culpable homicide when he causes the death of another human being: (1) by means of an unlawful act; (2) by criminal negligence; (3) by willfully frightening a human being, in the case of a child or a sick person; (4) by causing a human being, through threats or fear of violence, or through deception, to do anything that causes his death. No one can be convicted of culpable homicide unless the death of the victim occurs within a year and a day.

Murder

A culpable homicide is classified as *murder* if the person who causes the death of a human means to cause his death, or means to cause him bodily harm that he knows is likely to cause his death. Murder is more difficult to define than perhaps we make it appear in this summary; each case has to be evaluated individually.

The intention of the accused is always of prime importance to the court. Did he actually intend to kill or did he intend merely to cause bodily harm—but went too far? The classical premeditated murder beloved of the whodunit fan, where the murderer decides to kill someone and plans everything in advance, requires little comment. However, criminologists believe that few murders occur this way. Most convicted murderers, they say, did not plan to kill in advance and many did not even plan to cause their victims any really serious bodily harm. The following murder case is typical of many:

During a drunken brawl on a bitterly cold night, the accused knocked his opponent down, kicked him in the head, gagged him with a belt and stripped him of his overcoat. He left him unconscious, but alive. Unknown to the accused, his opponent had suffered a fractured skull which, together with the effects of alcohol and exposure, caused his death. The accused was convicted of murder. He had not intended to kill his victim but only to "teach him a good lesson." However, he had caused bodily harm which he knew could possibly result in death.

Murder during other offenses

A person is guilty of murder if he kills someone while committing, or attempt-

The rights of a murderer

FACTS

In her lifetime, Mary Ellen Black was the wife of William Black. They owned a house in British Columbia as joint tenants. On the death of one joint tenant, the law provides that ownership of a house so held passes automatically to the surviving joint tenant.

Probate of Mrs. Black's will was granted to her husband. On the following day, William Black was arrested and charged with the murder of his wife and, a few months later, he was convicted of the crime.

The plaintiff in the case was Mrs. Black's sister who sued on behalf of herself and the other next of kin, claiming ownership of the house, notwithstanding the rule of law that the title to it would vest in William Black as the surviving joint tenant.

ARGUMENT

Counsel for the next of kin put forward the proposition that it was contrary to public policy that Black should be able to hold the property as his own because of the death of his wife at his own hand.

Counsel for Black agreed that no one should gain a right by his own wrong, but submitted that if he already had a right he should not lose it because of any wrong done by him in connection with it.

JUDGMENT

The court took the position that it could not take away from the husband the title to the property which he had already acquired, but that it was open to the court to prevent him from acquiring property in an unauthorized or unlawful way (that is, by an act of murder). Accordingly, it was held that, under the circumstances, the usual rule of survivorship applied and the full interest in the property accrued to the husband who was the survivor. However, the court also held that it must be deemed that the survivor—in this case, the murderer—held his wife's one-half share in the property, being the interest she would have enjoyed, had he permitted her to live, in trust for the benefit of her next of kin on the basis that it was contrary to public policy that a man should be allowed to claim a benefit resulting from his own crime.*

*Based on an actual case (1967).

811

ing to commit, certain other criminal offenses—as long as it is established that he meant to cause his victim bodily harm. Anyone who uses a weapon to commit one of these offenses is automatically guilty of murder if he kills someone. The offenses named in the Criminal Code are treason, sabotage, piracy, escape from prison or lawful custody, resisting lawful arrest, sexual assault, indecent assault, forcible abduction, robbery, burglary and arson.

This Victorian case is often quoted as an illustration of unintentional murder during the commission of another crime:

A girl on her way to church was waylaid by a man who wrapped her head in a shawl to muffle her cries and then dragged her into the woods to rape her. She died of suffocation before he had reached his chosen spot. He was convicted of murder and executed. It was plain that the man did not intend to kill; indeed, his object was frustrated by her death. Nor can it be said that he intended to cause her any bodily injury. Yet he did cause her bodily injury that resulted in death, and he was expected to know that such injury might result in death.

One of the most difficult aspects of the law of homicide arises when two or more persons are robbing someone and one of the thugs kills the victim. Are all of the robbers guilty of murder?

They would probably all be convicted of murder if they all knew that one of them was carrying an offensive weapon at the time of the robbery. (*See* "Offenses against authority" in this chapter.)

If the thieves were not armed, the Crown would probably have to prove that the person or persons involved—who were merely robbing—formed an intention in common with the actual killer to carry out an unlawful act and, furthermore, to assist each other. The Crown would also have to prove that all the participants knew, or ought to have known, that the death of a human being would be a probable consequence.

First- and second-degree murder

In July 1976, the House of Commons voted by a margin of only six votes to abolish the death penalty. Prior to this (since 1961), murder had been classified as either *capital* or *non-capital* (a capital offense is one punishable by death). In Canada, murder was a "capital offense" if the victim was a police officer or a prison employe acting in the course of his duties. But from 1962 on, *all* death sentences had been commuted by the cabinet in apparent defiance of the spirit of the law.

The 1976 law does not alter the fact that capital punishment is retained for exceptionally serious military crimes. Under the National Defence Act, death may be the penalty imposed on those who act traitorously—that is, against the vital interests of Canada. Traitorous crimes include desertion and spying.

Manslaughter

Someone who causes the death of another without intending to do so may be convicted of *manslaughter*. The borderline between murder and manslaughter is difficult to define and each case is classified on its own facts. Generally, where there is doubt about whether the homicide is murder or manslaughter, the accused is entitled to the benefit of the doubt and is charged with the lesser crime. Life imprisonment is the maximum sentence for manslaughter, but it is rarely imposed.

A *culpable homicide* that would otherwise be murder may be labeled manslaughter if it was committed in the heat of passion caused by sudden provocation. If a woman in a flash of anger shoves her husband and he falls backward, striking his head on the table edge, and dies from the injury, the wife would most likely be found guilty of manslaughter.

Infanticide

A mother commits *infanticide* if she intentionally, by some act or omission, causes the death of her newborn child while she is mentally disturbed as an after-effect of childbirth. The maximum punishment for this offense is imprisonment for five years.

The abortion controversy

Because a child is not recognized by the law as existing until it is born (*See* Chapter 11, "Children and parents"), the intentional premature termination of a pregnancy—known as *abortion*—cannot be classed as murder (although many Canadians obviously do so regard it). According to the law, a qualified doctor may perform an abortion on a woman only when the life of the mother is endangered, or her health is likely to be impaired by the continued pregnancy. Anyone else—including the pregnant woman herself—who carries out an abortion is liable to imprisonment for life. The soaring number of legal abortions seems to indicate that the "impairment" requirement is being fairly freely interpreted.

For those who take the view that human life exists from the moment of conception, abortion becomes a form of mercy killing if the woman's life is genuinely endangered, and a form of murder if it is not. Advocates of "abortion on

Injustice: the trial of Jesus

WHEN HE WAS Chief Justice of Ontario, James C. McRuer set himself the task of examining the trial of Jesus Christ in A.D. 30 with the cool, analytical detachment of the modern jurist. His verdict? That even by the legal standards and procedure of the day, the finding of guilt and the imposition of the death penalty were a mockery and a total miscarriage of justice.

Justice McRuer began by accepting as fact the recital of events as given in the four Gospels of the New Testament. Although there are distinct differences in the testimony, he decided they were to be regarded "just as those to be found in the evidence of honest witnesses."

Arrested in the dark, late on a Thursday evening on the Mount of Olives, Jesus was beaten and interrogated illegally in private before being brought before the Sanhedrin early the next day. This court, appointed by the high priest of Jerusalem, Caiaphas, could hear only charges against religious laws (blasphemy, heresy or sorcery); it could not order the death penalty—that power remained in the hands of the Roman Governor Pontius Pilate.

The Sadducees who dominated the Sanhedrin regarded Jesus as a dangerous radical who had gained a large following by pretending to be the Son of God. Their efforts to trap Jesus into confessions of sorcery or blasphemy failed dismally. Then Caiaphas asked, "Are you the Son of God?" The answer came back from the bound prisoner, "You say that I am."

(There are three versions of this passage in the Gospels.) This was enough for the priests to take Jesus to Pilate, and ask for the death penalty.

Justice McRuer points out that no evidence of insult to God had been proved. The legal safeguards against hasty decisions in capital cases had been brushed aside, probably because no action would be possible against Jesus on the following (Sabbath) day.

Leaving the blasphemy charge aside, the priests played on Pilate's fears by saying that, since Jesus claimed to be a king, he was guilty of treason against the state (*i.e.*, against the Roman Empire). When Pilate asked Christ if he was indeed a king, Jesus answered that his kingdom was "not of this world." Pilate announced, "I find no crime in this man."

This was, McRuer notes, a clear acquittal, under the law. But the priests and their followers—the political leaders of Jerusalem—protested loudly, and, after an attempt to "pass the buck" to Herod Antipas, the Governor of Galilee (who happened to be in Jerusalem for the imminent Passover feast), the vacillating Pilate eventually permitted Jesus to be whipped and crucified.

In all the annals of legal history, wrote jurist McRuer, it would be difficult to find another case in which a prisoner who had been declared not guilty by a court of competent jurisdiction was delivered to the executioner by the same judge who had acquitted him.

demand" respond with arguments based on scientific assessments of when life "really begins," the rights of the individual woman and theories that the world has enough (or too many) people as it is.

Mercy killing

Euthanasia (mercy killing) is the subject of much controversy. But as far as the Criminal Code is concerned, it is culpable homicide—that is, murder.

The tragic circumstances of such a homicide usually arise when someone—often a much-loved spouse or relative—is suffering from a fatal disease and is in great and prolonged pain.

A person is not allowed to consent to having death inflicted upon him; thus, consent—even in writing—does not relieve from criminal responsibility the person who kills for reasons of mercy.

In Canadian criminal law, the motive of a person who commits homicide—or any other offense for that matter—is not a factor in determining guilt or innocence; what matters is the *intention*. If you intend to cause death and do cause death, then you are guilty of murder; it is of no consequence that you may have been motivated by kindness or pity.

Suicide

It is no longer a criminal offense in Canada to commit, or attempt to commit, suicide.

However, it is a criminal offense, punishable by imprisonment for up to 14 years, to encourage or assist anyone to commit suicide.

Kidnapping and abduction

Life imprisonment is the maximum punishment for kidnapping. This offense involves taking victims away against their will with the intent of confining or imprisoning them, transporting them out of Canada, holding them for ransom or forcing them to work against their will. The basic intent of the crime is to deprive the kidnapped person of freedom.

There have been a number of famous kidnapping cases in Canada. For example, the wife of Mel Lastman, the millionaire mayor of North York, a Toronto

suburb, was the victim of kidnappers. In 1970, James Cross, a minor British diplomat, was kidnapped by Quebec terrorists with political motives.

Only young people, below a certain age, can be victims of *abduction*. On the surface, the offense is hard to distinguish from kidnapping; but differences do exist. First of all, the intention of the abductor is different; secondly, the consent of the victim to the abduction is irrelevant (in kidnapping, the act must be done against the victim's will); thirdly, the offense need not involve confinement or detention.

The law stipulates that anyone who unlawfully takes or entices away a person under 16 out of the possession of a parent or guardian is guilty of an indictable offense and is liable to imprisonment for five years.

The law also states that a parent or guardian who takes or conceals a person under 14, in contravention of custody provisions, with the intention of depriving another parent or guardian of possession of that child, is guilty of an offense and could be liable to imprisonment for ten years.

Similarly, it is an offense to abduct a person under 14, where no custody order has been made. (It is, however, a defense to claim that the abduction was necessary to protect the child from danger.)

Generally, the punishment for abduction varies from five to ten years depending on the circumstances of the crime.

Criminal negligence

Any person who displays a wanton or reckless disregard for the life or safety of other persons commits the offense of *criminal negligence*.

Criminal negligence requires something more than civil negligence (*See* Chapter 18, "The accidental tort"). It is necessary for the prosecution to establish not only that the accused's conduct fell below that expected of a reasonably responsible person but also that he was aware of the probability that his conduct might cause injury or death to another. The driver of an automobile whose attention was distracted for a moment by a passing blonde and who ran down a pedestrian would not be guilty of criminal negligence. He was certainly negligent, but it could not be said that he showed a "wanton or reckless disregard." But a person who drove down a busy street at high speed, narrowly missing other cars, and then ran down a pedestrian would be guilty of criminal negligence.

It is his "reckless disregard"—that is, his disregard for the probable consequences of his behavior—that makes it a crime. The test in criminal negligence is not what the average person might or might not do; it is whether the accused himself appreciated, or should have appreciated, the danger involved in his conduct. The "guilty mind" (*mens rea*) is an essential ingredient.

Another illustration is provided by the following case:

The accused was in a moving automobile drinking beer from a bottle. He threw the empty bottle out of the window. A person nearby was injured by flying glass. The accused was convicted of criminal negligence, because his action showed wanton indifference and unconcern.

If your criminal negligence causes someone's death, you can be sentenced to life imprisonment. You can be guilty of criminal negligence even if no one is actually injured.

Assault

When people clash, when a few punches are thrown or kicks delivered, it is difficult to determine exactly at what point a "trespass to the person," that is, *assault and battery* under civil law (*See* Chapter 18, "The intentional tort"), becomes the offense of *assault* under the Criminal Code. It usually depends on the severity of the case.

Generally speaking, anything that involves *wounding*—in other words, intentionally causing bodily harm—is a crime and not merely a tort; the victim could sue the attacker for damages in a parallel or subsequent civil action.

It is important to remember that criminal law does not attempt to compensate the victim of a crime but only to punish the offender.

There are three classes of assault: ordinary assault, assault with a weapon or

One crime, one conviction

UNTIL 1975, a person could be convicted of two or more offenses for the same criminal act. For example, there could be convictions for both robbery and assault causing bodily harm, even though the underlying act of violence (the use of firearms) was the same for both offenses. In 1975, the Supreme Court of Canada ruled against such multiple convictions. The Court held that a person could be convicted of only one offense (usually the more serious one) arising out of a single criminal act. In 1983, the Ontario Court of Appeal restated this principle when it heard an appeal brought by two convicted robbers, David Allison and Donald Dinel.

Two years earlier, Allison and Dinel had held up a jewellery store in London, Ontario. During the course of the robbery, Allison fired his gun, wounding the proprietor. Without taking anything, the two fled the premises. They were soon arrested and charged on four counts: wounding; robbery; using a firearm while committing an indictable offense; and possessing a prohibited weapon.

The Ontario Court of Appeal decided that the wounding of the victim and the use of violence in the robbery attempt were part of the same act. It held that the two counts infringed the rule against multiple convictions. The accused were found guilty of the more serious offense—robbery. Applying the same principle to the other counts, the Court dismissed possession of a prohibited weapon, but retained the graver charge— the use of a firearm while committing an indictable offense.

Hanged for treason

ALTHOUGH FAR REMOVED from the cockpit of Europe with its cloak-and-dagger and firing-squad traditions, Canada has known treason trials that ended with citizens swinging in the wind on the gallows tree for aiding their country's enemies. One of the earliest of these took place in Ancaster, southwest of Toronto, during the War of 1812.

The lower peninsula of Upper Canada had been settled originally by Loyalist families after the American War of Independence, but these had been followed by many land-hungry Americans whose loyalty to the far-off George III was dubious, to say the least.

Of the 75,000 residents of Upper Canada, perhaps two-thirds were comparatively recent arrivals from the United States. Some of these immigrants were actually officers in the compulsory Upper Canada Militia when the Americans attacked the Niagara Peninsula in 1812. After the Canadian victory at Queenston Heights, a proclamation ordered that the recent arrivals must either appear before loyalty boards at Niagara, York (Toronto) or Kingston, or be "considered as enemy aliens and become liable to be treated ... as a spy."

Joseph Willcocks, an Irish-born member of the Upper Canada Legislative Assembly, defected to the enemy in 1813 and recruited a mounted force of 70 known as the Canadian Volunteers. They harassed the border areas, acting as (to borrow a later term) a "fifth column" for the invaders. American troops penetrated briefly to Moraviantown, near today's London. As the fortunes of war favored one side, then the other, a minor civil war seemed to be threatening in Upper Canada.

In the early months of 1814, the British commander, Lt.-Gen. Gordon Drummond, using the wide powers of martial law, ordered the rounding-up of about 100 suspected traitors in the area of what is now southwestern Ontario.

Nineteen of these were held in custody for trial before the Court of King's Bench at Ancaster, at that time a thriving little town situated on the escarpment above Burlington Bay.

The charge was high treason, the gravest charge that could be laid under the law. The trial began before a jury on May 23, 1814 in the former Union Hotel, which had been used as a military hospital. Indictments had been issued not only against the prisoners, but also against another 50 men not yet apprehended.

The first man to be tried, Luther McNeal, was quickly acquitted. Three others—Robert Loundsberry, Jesse Holly and Robert Troup—were also found not guilty. The fifteen others—Jacob Overholtzer, Aaron Stevens, Garrett Neill, John Johnston, Samuel and Stephen Hartwell, Dayton Lindsey, George Peacock, Isaiah Brink, Benjamin Simmons, Adam Crysler, Isaac Petit, Cornelius Howey, John Dunham and Noah Hopkins—were convicted and sentenced to death.

Pleas for clemency poured into the government at York and these probably helped to win reprieves for seven of the men; but eight of them—Stevens, Lindsey, Peacock, Brink, Simmons, Crysler, Dunham and Hopkins—were hanged by the sheriff at Burlington on July 20, 1814. The Hamilton cemetery today occupies the site of the gallows.

Three of those saved from the noose—Neill, Overholtzer and Petit—died of fever the next spring while still languishing in Kingston jail awaiting word from England as to their fate. Stephen Hartwell escaped from custody and was never heard of again. The three others were finally banished for life from Upper Canada (and from all other British possessions).

The courts did not forget those against whom indictments had been issued but who had eluded capture. Slowly the mills of justice ground, until 30 of them were officially branded outlaws.

causing bodily harm, and aggravated assault, which occurs when one person wounds, maims, disfigures or endangers the life of another. An assault that causes no bodily harm, or only slight bodily harm, is an ordinary assault. Such an assault would bring a charge of aggravated assault, however, if the victim was a peace officer engaged in his duties, or any person aiding such an officer.

A person who assaults another with the idea of robbing him could be guilty of any of the three classes of assault, depending on the circumstances.

The argument of provocation is never a defense to a charge of assault, although it may result in a lighter sentence being given. Self-defense is justification for an assault, provided that the force used is no more than is reasonably necessary. A person who was spat upon would not be justified in seriously injuring his attacker.

The police may use force in carrying out their duties, provided the force used is reasonable in the circumstances. In some jurisdictions, school teachers may also use force in disciplining a child (*See* Chapter 11, "Children at school"). The following case occurred in Saskatchewan.

An accused school teacher testified that some boys shouted names at him as they were leaving the school on a Friday. On the following Monday, he slapped the boys' faces. He was charged with assault but was later acquitted. The force used was considered reasonable and did not become unreasonable because of three days' delay.

Ordinary assault is punishable on summary conviction, and the penalty can be a $500 fine or a six-month term in jail, or both. Assault with a weapon or causing bodily harm carries a penalty of up to ten years' imprisonment. Aggravated assault is punishable by a sentence of up to 14 years.

Sexual assault

The offense of rape was stricken from the Criminal Code by a new law that came into force in January 1983. Under the provisions of this law, which was passed by parliament in October 1982, sexual offenses, including rape, became assault offenses. It was generally felt that the change of terms would emphasize the violent aspect of the crime and de-emphasize the sexist attitudes about the offense.

The new law creates new categories of assault offenses in the Code—sexual assault and aggravated sexual assault. In case of sexual assault, the penalty is up to ten years in prison. Aggravated sexual assault, in which a weapon has been used to threaten the victim, carries a maximum sentence of life imprisonment. Sexual assaults in which the victim has been maimed, carry the same sentence.

The new law provides equal protection for both male and female against sexual assault. (Under previous laws, only women were seen as victims, although men could be indecently assaulted.) The 1982 amendments permit either spouse to bring a charge of sexual assault or, if the attack included a beating, aggravated sexual assault. Before the amendments, common-law wives had this legal recourse, but not married women.

Formerly, the law required that there should be some definite *corroboration* of the evidence presented by the woman, as a prerequisite for the conviction of the accused. Corroboration was some evidence, apart from the victim's own account of the incident, that would confirm her version of the story and implicate the accused. The new law abolishes the need for independent evidence—for example, bloodstains or torn clothing. Moreover, in court, the judge may no longer instruct the jurors that it would be unsafe to find the accused guilty in the absence of corroboration.

In the past, a rape victim who failed to complain to the first person encountered after the attack could be discredited as a witness. Under the new provisions, it is no longer relevant that this is not done at the first occasion.

Except in special cases, no evidence can be cited by the accused about the victim's sexual conduct with others. Similarly, any information about sexual reputation, advanced to discredit or support the credibility of the victim, is inadmissible, except in precise cases listed in the Criminal Code.

Offenses against property

| Theft and embezzlement |
| Robbery |
| Breaking and entering |
| Fraud and false pretenses |
| Extortion |
| Malicious damage to property |

AMONG THE HUNDREDS of crimes listed in the Criminal Code of Canada, *theft* in its many forms is by far the most prevalent. Slightly more than 110,000 adults are charged with theft every year; and only an estimated ten to 25 percent of reported thefts are solved.

Offenses against property loom large in the eyes of the average law-abiding citizen because it is here that one is most likely to encounter the criminal element of society. While the daring payroll holdup is featured in the headlines, it is the petty burglary that causes most anger and unhappiness to the average citizen. There are few frustrations to match the discovery that someone has entered your home by stealth and made off with your prized property or hard-earned cash savings, even down to the piggy banks of your tearful children. The merchant would suggest that *shoplifting*—which is simply theft in a shop—is an even greater curse (*See* Chapter 9, "In the supermarket"); to compensate for his losses, which can add up to as much as five percent of his total sales, the shopkeeper must raise his prices—thus making the honest customer bear the cost of the crime.

Only those without property profess to despise it. The Charter of Rights and Freedoms mentions the right of the individual not to be deprived of the enjoyment of property. We do not chop off the right hand of the apprehended thief (a traditional Islamic punishment), nor do we brand him to warn the general citizenry (as was done in early Quebec). However, *breaking and entering* a dwelling in modern-day Canada still carries severe penalties. For instance, if the act endangers life in any way, the maximum penalty of life

imprisonment could theoretically be imposed. Even wearing a disguise (such as a stocking mask) with intent to commit an indictable offense can bring ten years' imprisonment. The theft of a single package of cigarettes (or of anything worth less than $200) can bring a maximum of two years in jail.

There is considerable confusion in the public mind over the different terms used in classifying theft—or *stealing*, as it is often called. This is compounded by the fact that elements of theft can also fall within the law of torts (*See* Chapter 18, "Trespassing prohibited!"). The crimes of theft, robbery, breaking and entering, embezzlement, extortion ("blackmail") and obtaining goods by trick or under false pretenses—all involve the illegal taking away of the property belonging to other people, and they are examined separately in the paragraphs below. Later in this section, we will discuss other offenses against property.

Theft and embezzlement

The crime of *theft* is committed when a person fraudulently and without "color of right" converts to his own use anything belonging to someone else with intent to deprive that person (or corporation, or association) either temporarily or permanently of the property. "Color of right" means a legal justification or excuse; thus, if a person takes something he knows does not belong to him but which he believes he has a genuine right to take, he will not be convicted of theft, as long as the court considers that his belief is reasonable.

A tow-truck driver towed Mr. Q's automobile away from a private parking lot where it was parked without the permission of the owner of the lot. When Mr. Q demanded the return of his car, the accused refused until Q paid the towing and storage costs. The tow-truck driver was then accused of theft, but acquitted. Although he had no right to withhold the car, he had acted upon a belief that he did have such a right, and that belief was considered reasonable by the court.

There is no longer a separate crime of *embezzlement;* the offense, a form of conversion, now is dealt with under the general classification of theft. The term embezzlement refers to the fraudulent taking of the goods of another by someone who has the right to possess, but not own, them. If a clerk goes into his employer's vault and steals money, he has committed theft; but if the clerk re-ceives money—that he has authority to receive—from a customer in payment of a debt and then pockets it, he has committed embezzlement.

For the purposes of punishment, the crime of theft is divided into two classes: theft of goods exceeding $200 in value, and theft of goods valued at less than $200. In the first category, the maximum penalty is ten years' imprisonment; the maximum penalty in the second is two years in prison. The alternative sentences of probation, suspended sentence or a fine are frequently imposed, especially for the first offender (*See* Chapter 3, "Decisions from the Bench").

Robbery

When theft is accompanied by violence, the crime of *robbery* is committed. Al-

The white-collar thief

THE ONLY CLEAR DIFFERENCE between so-called "white-collar crime" and any other kind is that it always involves a violation of trust. The bank robber who wears a collar and tie and a suit is not a "white-collar criminal" in the jargon of the law. The label would, however, fit the bank accountant who lifts a bundle of bills from the vault and doctors the books to cover the theft.

Law-enforcement officials say that white-collar crime is increasing in a generally more permissive society, and sociologists fear that a growing distrust at all levels will lower social morale and encourage the disintegration of our society. They include in the category not only the cashier stealing from the till, but the theft and sale of the employer's trade secrets and know-how, the padding of expense accounts, falsification of time cards or work sheets, theft of merchandise by insiders with the manipulation of inventories, the acceptance of kickbacks and bribes. Sabotage by vengeful employes is also noted.

In Canada, white-collar crime in total is estimated to involve as much as one to two billion dollars a year—admittedly, just a guesstimate. Many such crimes do not result in court actions even if the theft is discovered as companies often prefer to accept restitution of stolen funds, when available, and avoid the publicity that surrounds the prosecution of employes.

The white-collar criminal is often the least suspected, most respected person in the office or store. A spinster bookkeeper once stole nearly $3 million, using only her fountain pen—a much greater haul than from many widely publicized crimes. A major insurance company once published a profile of the "average" white-collar thief: Age 35, married, two children, homeowner, three years in present job, has been stealing for eight months.

The general public—including the thieves and their families—eventually pay the bill for white-collar crime. Embezzlers have wrecked thousands of businesses, throwing people out of work and onto welfare rolls. Companies step up their theft-insurance coverage and, as losses mount, the insurance firms increase their premiums. To meet this extra burden, the businessmen hike their prices to the public.

though the term is widely used, there is no such thing in law as "armed robbery." In fact, possession of a weapon by the crook is itself immaterial.

Robbery can be committed in a number of ways; the one essential ingredient is that it must be accompanied by violence, or the threat of violence, either to person or to property.

Obviously, the man who brandishes a gun, or knife, as he steals is committing robbery—and he is risking life imprisonment. A person can be convicted of robbery even if the "weapon" he waves at his victim is only a toy gun, or even if he is completely unarmed.

A man who walks into a bank and announces that he has a weapon, or has dynamite strapped to his body, and then demands money from a teller is guilty of robbery, or attempted robbery if his mission fails. If the man walked into the bank unarmed and simply demanded money, he might not, however, be guilty of robbery, since there would be no threat of violence; but he would be guilty of theft, or attempted theft.

Breaking and entering

The words "breaking" and "entering" have special meanings in the Criminal Code. A person can be convicted of *breaking and entering* even though he neither broke anything nor entered any premises. The word "break" in law has a broader meaning than actually breaking a lock or a window; it refers to opening anything that is used to close or cover an internal or external opening.

A person "enters" as soon as any part of his body, or any part of an instrument that he is using, is within any place (or vehicle) that he is entering. This would cover, for example, the insertion of a fishing rod through a hole in a shop window in the hope of hooking an expensive wristwatch from a display.

The expression "break and enter" also includes entering a place by a threat or trick, or entering with the assistance of someone inside. It also means entering a place without lawful justification or excuse ("color of right") through a permanent or temporary opening. If you walked

in through the open rear door of a shop and stole something, you could be convicted of breaking and entering.

For it to be a crime, the act of breaking and entering must be accompanied by the commission of an indictable offense (such as theft) within, or by the intent to commit such an offense. The following example illustrates this.

A motorist comes upon a highway accident in which several persons have been seriously injured. He goes to a farmhouse nearby to seek assistance. Finding no one at home, he kicks the door in, enters and uses the telephone to call the police and an ambulance. He then returns to the scene of the accident. Although he committed the physical act of breaking and entering, he would not be convicted of any offense since he neither committed, nor intended to commit, an indictable offense within.

Breaking into a place other than a residence with intent to commit a crime is punishable by 14 years' imprisonment, but breaking into a dwelling carries the maximum sentence, life imprisonment. This distinction is another reminder that under our inheritance of English common law, a man's home is indeed his castle. The stiffer penalty would also deter the burglar from committing a crime which carries with it a high risk of personal injury.

Illegal possession

The offense of *being in possession* applies not just to stolen goods but to all property obtained by the commission of any indictable offense.

"Possession" is not restricted to personal possession; the property concerned can be in someone else's possession or in some place for the use and benefit of the offender, or any person other than the one who has the legal right to it.

Before a person can be convicted of possession, it is necessary to prove that the property in question was obtained illegally and that the accused person was aware of that fact. In most cases, someone who is convicted of this offense not only is aware that the goods were illegally obtained but had also instigated or encouraged the crime in the first place. Such an operator is known in the underworld as a *fence*. He prompts the crime by assuring the would-be thief or robber that he has a market for "hot" (*i.e.*, stolen) property of certain desirable types.

If someone approaches you in a bar, or at a football game, and offers to sell you an expensive diamond ring, don't buy. The property might not have been stolen but, if it was, you could have trouble convincing a magistrate that you didn't know that diamond rings are usually sold in jewelers' shops.

Fraud and false pretenses

Deliberate deception, or lies, to induce another person to do something—or to abstain from doing something—is the offense of *fraud*. This offense brings us face to face with the "con artist" who will, for a price, sell you the Lion's Gate Bridge, the Crown jewels or an infallible system for beating the odds a the racetrack.

The offense of fraud covers a wide variety of illegal activity. It is difficult to distinguish fraud from *false pretense*. A false pretense is a false representation of fact, either by word or deed, and the person making it knows it to be false.

It becomes a crime once some specific thing is actually *obtained*. The offense is known formally as "obtaining by false pretenses."

Getting goods (or cash) by writing cheques on accounts that either do not exist or have insufficient funds is "obtaining by false pretenses," if the person knows that the cheques he is writing will "bounce." Similarly, using a credit card

Bank robbery at Benito

BANK ROBBERY brings to mind the depredations of Jesse James, John Dillinger, Clyde Barrow and Bonnie Mae Parker, all of them vicious criminals who, unfortunately, have been romanticized by the movie scriptwriter. It is Canada's gain that we haven't added a name to that world-famous rogues' gallery, although the lure of money lying at the teller's wicket "for the taking" still tempts a regular quota of the desperate every year.

There was a day, though, in the frontier settlement of Benito, Manitoba, when we came close to adding a legendary figure to the robbers' roster. It was in the first decade of this century, when the eastern banks were spreading quickly—if not feverishly—through the prairie provinces. The bank concerned was a branch of the Bank of Toronto (now, the Toronto-Dominion); the bandit was known as "Wad" and he was flourishing not a six-shooter but a double-bitted ax.

Wad was an unsuccessful homesteader who had turned to booze, making his own moonshine in a remote cabin. He was mostly known for his ambition to become Canada's official hangman. He would appear in the dusty main street of Benito and try to enlist the aid of the citizenry to petition Sir Wilfrid Laurier on his behalf. He asked that the prime minister be told that Wad had "plenty of nerve and would enjoy hanging anyone who should be hanged."

At high noon one day a young teller fresh from the effete East looked up from his cash drawer in the bank to behold Wad brandishing his ax and incoherently demanding money. He was dressed solely in tattered coveralls, tied at the top with binder twine. He was very drunk.

The elements of drama were at hand. But the Canadian "Wild West" wasn't quite that wild. Helped by a passing farmer, the bank manager eased Wad away from the counter and frog-marched him down to the livery stable where he was tossed into a box stall to sleep it off.

The following day, a group of Benito's leading citizens privately advised the shaken would-be bank bandit that he should leave town, and not come back. And he never did.

that belongs to somebody else to obtain goods or services is an offense.

With the general offense of fraud, it is not necessary that something be actually obtained by the deception. For example, you are committing *criminal fraud* if you make a gift of something you own specifically to defeat your creditors. If you felt that the loan company was about to seize your color television set because you hadn't kept up repayments on your loan and you transferred the ownership to your wife, you would be guilty of defrauding the loan company. Similarly, if you deliberately destroyed or concealed insured property to collect the insurance, you would be guilty of defrauding the insurance company.

Fraud in business

There are probably as many ways to commit fraud as there are devious minds. It is not fraud or false pretenses, however, for the salesman to "puff" a product. Only some hermit from a mountaintop cave would take "gigantic clearance sale" and "unbelievable values" as being strictly true to label; the average intelligent person is expected to discount the exaggerated prose. But deliberately deceptive advertising is indeed a crime, with penalties of up to $25,000 or more in fines (*See* Chapter 6, "Guarantees and standards").

True fraud would consist of falsifying account books so that a business appeared to be more prosperous than it really was in order to get others to invest in it or, possibly, to obtain a loan. The crime would not exist, however, unless someone actually acted upon the deception. It is also fraud to publish a false prospectus, or description of a company's business, to induce others to invest in a company (*See* Chapter 8, "Anatomy of the stock exchange").

The fraudulent manipulation of the stock market, by practices such as "wash trading" (that is, fictitious buying or selling of securities) is a criminal offense. Both the provincial securities commissions and the stock-exchange authorities maintain a vigilant watch for such practices, not only because of their concern that the law be obeyed but also because

of the danger that public confidence in the market would be eroded.

The butcher who puts his thumb on the scales while weighing your steak is cheating you—and that's a type of fraud, too.

Extortion

The ancient crime of extortion—more commonly called *blackmail*—usually involves a demand for money in exchange for a promise not to reveal some damaging information. The classic case is where a man receives a threat that his wife will be told of an infidelity unless he pays a certain amount of money. It is no defense for the blackmailer to say that the information he threatened to reveal is true. The victim in these circumstances is strongly advised to go immediately to the police; there's at least a chance the wife will forgive and forget—but little chance that an extortionist will be satisfied with one payment.

It is extortion to threaten to report a crime to the police unless the criminal pays up. It is not extortion to threaten to begin civil proceedings against a person who owes a legitimate debt. But there is no "reasonable justification or excuse" for threatening someone with violence in order to collect a debt.

Malicious damage to property

The intentional destruction or damaging of property is known, curiously, as *mischief*. But there is nothing lighthearted about the punishment provided under the Criminal Code: 14 years' imprisonment, and a life sentence if the damage done puts anyone's life in danger.

Where private property is concerned, the owner may also bring a civil action for damages (*See* Chapter 18, "The intentional tort").

Vandalism and arson are perhaps the most common examples of malicious damage. Vandalism has already been discussed (*See* Chapter 11, "Children in trouble").

Arson is the deliberate setting of a fire with intent to destroy any of the following types of property:
(1) A building or structure, whether completed or not;

(2) A crop, whether standing or cut down;

(3) Military or public stores, or munitions of war;

(4) A mine;

(5) A stack of vegetable produce, or of mineral or vegetable fuel;

(6) Timber or materials placed in a shipyard for building, repairing or fitting out a ship;

(7) A vessel, vehicle or aircraft, whether completed or not;

(8) A well of combustible substance;

(9) Any wood, forest, or natural growth, or any lumber, timber, log, float, boom, dam or slide.

The penalty on conviction for any of these counts of malicious damage can be 14 years' imprisonment; it can be life imprisonment if there was any danger caused to life.

Setting a fire by negligence, or allowing a fire to burn after discovering it, may also be an offense in certain circumstances. If you violate a law in force to prevent fires by causing a fire (such as making a campfire in a fire zone—where lighting a fire is strictly prohibited), you are committing an offense and may be sentenced on conviction to five years in prison. (*See* Chapter 17, "Guns and guides.")

Once in a while, someone decides to "accidentally" burn down his shop or residence to collect the fire insurance. If detected, he will be charged with arson. Furthermore, once it is established that he holds fire insurance on the gutted building and might stand to gain by the fire, if there is evidence that he caused the fire himself, the onus might be put on him to prove that he did not cause the blaze with intent to defraud.

You are certainly allowed to burn your house to the ground provided that you have any permission that is required under municipal bylaws, that there is no danger of injury to anyone and, of course, that you have previously canceled your fire insurance policy.

Mass murder in the sky

IN THE AUTUMN of 1949, a thin dapper Quebec jeweler earned the dubious distinction of inventing a new means of murder. In order to get rid of his wife, he had a time bomb manufactured and placed aboard a scheduled airliner. The wife was duly blown to bits—with 22 others.

Joseph Albert Guay, a spoiled child with delusions of grandeur—he was always just about to "make a million"—had married a co-worker at a Canadian Arsenals war plant. They lived in the St. Sauveur district of Quebec City where Guay in 1945 opened a small jewelry and watch-repair store.

He had a series of suspicious thefts and fires at his shop, and his dreams of financial success never materialized. About this time, using an assumed name, he began an affair with a 17-year-old waitress whom he wooed openly at her home three nights a week. They lived together as husband-and-wife for a short time, but she threatened to leave him when Mme Guay discovered the liaison.

Guay appeared to be reunited with his wife Rita, but he now was secretly planning the most fiendish murder. His crippled watch-repairer, Généreux Ruest, put together a compact but powerful time bomb, and Ruest's sister, Marguerite Pitre, placed it aboard a plane about to leave for Baie Comeau.

Before Rita Guay went aboard that plane on a family visit, Albert took out an extra $10,000 insurance policy on her life at the airport desk, with himself as beneficiary. The plane disintegrated somewhat prematurely above Sault-au-Cochon, 40 miles from Quebec.

Ten days later Mme Pitre confessed to her part in the plot. All three conspirators were found guilty of murder and hanged. Guay had one last request—that he be buried beside his beloved wife.

Trial and sentence

THE PERSON accused of a crime in Canada may be tried in any one of several courts depending on the gravity and type of the offense; and by any one of several procedures. The choice of procedure will depend partially on the accused person's (or his lawyer's) individual preference and partially on the seriousness of the crime.

Every person charged with an *indictable offense* (except some specific matters such as theft under $200) is entitled to a trial by jury—that is, by a panel of impartial ordinary citizens. Every convicted person has the right of appeal to a higher court if he is not satisfied with the verdict—of course, the Crown prosecutor has the same privilege.

In nine of our provinces, offenses that carry the penalty of life imprisonment *must* be tried before a judge and jury in a superior, or provincial supreme, court. The exception is Alberta where a judge sitting alone may try any case with the consent of the accused. Just about all other crimes can be heard by a county, or district, court judge alone; even offenses as serious as manslaughter and sexual assault can now be heard by magistrates, or provincial judges—as magistrates are sometimes called. (*See* Chapter 3, "Judges and courts.")

The sentences laid down in the Criminal Code by our federal lawmakers are clear and stern, but they are seldom imposed to the limit (*See* Chapter 3, "Decisions from the Bench"). These are, of course, maximum sentences, and it was always intended that the punishment should fit the specific crime—and not merely the category. When a term of imprisonment is imposed, the offender is immediately taken to prison to start serving it—unless he appeals and is granted bail until the appeal is heard. After a certain time, the National Parole Board will routinely enter the picture to review his case and may decide to return the convict to the community by granting him parole (*See* Chapter 3, "The penal system"). Thus, the term of life imprisonment—the least that must by law be imposed on a man found guilty of committing first-degree murder—may, through reductions for good behavior and parole, turn out to be 25 years.

Charged with a crime

The initial step in the prosecution of anyone accused of having committed a criminal offense is the commencement of proceedings by a peace officer (or a private citizen) to bring the accused before a court so that he may be tried. Someone may have been caught "red-handed" (*i.e.,* actually committing the crime) or he may have been implicated by evidence accumulated by detectives or constables (the "clues" of the crime novels) and apprehended later.

The methods by which a person is brought to the Bar of Justice are described fully elsewhere (*See* Chapter 3, "The policeman's lot"). The gravity of the offense, as well as the behavior and reputation of the accused, play a large part in determining the course taken. Essentially, a person can be arrested—that is, physically seized—either with or without a warrant, or the individual can be left at large and ordered to appear in court by means of a *summons* or a *notice of appearance.*

Particularly in the more serious areas

of criminal activity, the police exercise wide powers of arrest. A peace officer may, of course, arrest anyone whom he finds actually committing an offense; he may also arrest anyone whom he believes has committed or is about to commit an indictable offense. These powers were not cut back by the Bail Reform Act of 1970, as was popularly supposed. Rather, an extra duty was imposed upon the police not to arrest without a warrant (which is issued by a justice of the peace, or magistrate) except in the graver offenses, unless they had reasonable grounds for believing that by not carrying through an arrest, the public might be endangered or the suspect might not appear for trial.

If you are ever arrested, with or without a warrant, you are entitled to a bail hearing. If you are not granted bail, however, you can be legally held in custody pending trial. You are entitled to know the nature of the offense with which you are being charged, and the Charter of Rights and Freedoms guarantees you "the right to retain and instruct counsel without delay and to be informed of that right." Most of the provinces have some form of legal assistance for those without the financial resources to fully finance their own defense (*See* Chapter 20, "How the lawyer is paid").

Process of trial

We have already sketched the general trial procedure followed in Canadian courts (*See* Chapter 3, "How a case is tried"), and pointed out that there can be quite wide variations across the provincial and territorial systems. Under the terms of the uniform Criminal Code, however, there is an established routine to be followed, according to the classification of the offense. All crimes are classified under the code as being either *summary-conviction offenses* or *indictable offenses*. You have already been introduced to these terms (*See* "Threat to the community" in this chapter) and you are probably aware that summary-conviction offenses are the minor ones, while indictable offenses include everything of a more serious nature.

All summary-conviction offenses are tried only by magistrates or provincial judges, who sit on the lower rungs of the judicial ladder. Many indictable offenses can also be tried by summary procedure, with the decision lying in the hands of the Crown attorney. For example, theft involving less than $200 is an indictable offense, but it will always be tried before a magistrate.

Let's follow a typical case in each classification. A person charged with a summary-conviction offense (say, *causing a disturbance*) will be brought before a magistrate. The charge will be read to him and he will be called upon to enter a *plea*. If he pleads *guilty*, sentence will be imposed, probably immediately, and the trial will end. If a plea of *not guilty* is entered, the accused will either be tried immediately, or ordered to appear in court at a later date—that is, he has been "remanded."

If the accused is charged with a crime that can be labeled either an indictable *or* a summary-conviction offense, the trial will begin with the reading of the charge. Next, the Crown attorney will be asked whether he wants to proceed by indictment or by summary procedure. If the Crown elects to proceed summarily, the trial will be conducted in the same way as outlined above. Appeals from summary convictions are made to a higher level court.

Certain offenses may be tried by indictment only and these must be heard before a "Superior Court of criminal jurisdiction." This is, in effect, the supreme court in each province, although the actual names of the courts vary widely (in Quebec, it is the Superior Court and, in Manitoba, the Court of Queen's Bench). Such offenses are usually the most serious—for example, treason, murder and hijacking. These offenses, furthermore, must be tried by judge and jury—except, as previously stated, in Alberta.

Where a specific court is not laid down in the regulations, the accused has the right to *elect* ("choose") his mode of trial. This choice consists of being tried by a magistrate (provincial judge), by a judge without a jury or by a judge with a jury in the indictable procedure.

825

All persons charged with indictable offenses are first brought before a magistrate for a preliminary hearing or inquiry. The purpose of the hearing is to find out if there is sufficient evidence to warrant putting the accused on trial. The Crown presents its evidence and the accused has a right to cross-examine witnesses. After the evidence is heard, the magistrate will then either commit the accused to trial, or discharge him.

In those provinces that retain the *grand jury*, the next step is for a *bill of indictment* to be placed before it. The members of the grand jury will hear in secrecy the evidence against the accused and return either a "true bill" or "no bill." If "no bill" is returned, the accused will be discharged; if a "true bill" is returned, he will be ordered to stand trial. (*See* Chapter 2, "The duties of the citizen.")

It is only when the actual criminal trial begins that the accused will be called upon to plead. If he pleads guilty, then the court may proceed to sentence him. An accused person who refuses to plead will have a plea of not guilty entered on his behalf.

Surveillance in the street

MOST OFFENDERS are not dangerous, or vicious, or violent—and they should not be in prison." The man whom we are quoting was the man most responsible for the operation of the Canadian parole system, George Street (now a judge). In an interview in 1973, replying to criticism that prisoners were being mollycoddled in the penitentiaries and released too soon, Street said that he believed Canada was keeping far too many people behind bars (the figure at that time was about 20,000 in an average month) and that he hoped for the population of our prisons to decrease to half within ten years.

Judge Street believes that criminals are made, not born, and that sending them to jail is one of the best ways of turning them into professional criminals. Half of all crimes are committed by persons who already have three or more convictions.

Street argued that a man who, say, commits breaking and entering should not be imprisoned, unless he is too dangerous to be "outside." Upon conviction, he should be sent to a detention home that would allow him to go out every day to work or to school. Whenever possible, prisoners who are not dangerous should be kept in society under strict supervision and required to work at whatever jobs are available. The supervision should be adequate and the greater the risk involved, the stricter the supervision should be. If prisoners are working, they could be required to make restitution or pay fines rather than being kept in prison at a cost of about $35,000 a year per person.

While Street was on the parole board, a prisoner wrote to him and offered to have an electronic "bug" stitched into his skin so that the police could trace him. The prisoner also suggested that, if the police would tap his telephone, it would be virtually impossible for him to commit a crime without being detected.

This is a rather radical proposal but Street feels that, if a high-risk prisoner wants this type of electronic surveillance to serve his sentence outside prison, he should be allowed to have it.

While this idea might offend some civil rights advocates who are concerned about an individual's right to privacy, Street says, "I am more concerned with the protection and welfare of 25 million Canadians than I am with the exaggerated rights of a handful of criminals. I do not agree with the dogooder's theory that every vulture is a maladjusted nightingale." In other words, if prisoners are dangerous, vicious or violent, they should be kept under control for as long as necessary to protect the public and they should not be released into society until it is safe to do so, or until they can be strictly and adequately supervised.

The trial will then proceed with each side calling witnesses, and the other side cross-examining them. When all the evidence has been presented, each side may address the judge or the jury. The accused may offer as a defense that he did not do the deed at all, that he did it but was justified in doing it, or that he is excused by law from criminal liability for doing it—for instance, because of his age or, perhaps, mental incompetence.

Duress and self-defense

The defenses of insanity, drunkenness and "ignorance of fact" (discussed earlier in this chapter) may be used by someone who has committed a criminal act but had no criminal intent.

The defenses of *duress* and *self-defense* are different in that the accused admits doing and knowing that he was doing a forbidden act, and may even admit having intended to do it; however, he pleads special circumstances to excuse himself from criminal liability.

Neither duress nor self-defense is always a complete defense. A person who can prove that he was forced by threats to do a criminal act will not be excused if the act done is any one of the following: treason, murder or attempted murder, sexual assault, sexual assault with a weapon, or aggravated sexual assault, forcible abduction, robbery, piracy, causing bodily harm or arson. Thus, the defense strategy of Patty Hearst, the American multimillionaire's daughter who claimed she was forced by threat to help in the robbery of a bank, would not stand up in Canadian courts. You cannot endanger another person's life in order to save your own.

Self-defense will be accepted as justifying an act that would otherwise be criminal, provided the force used is reasonable in the circumstances. (*See* Chapter 18, "Trespassing prohibited!").

Sometimes, a plea that the accused did not do the deed will not be a defense at all. It is not necessary to have actually committed some particular act to be convicted of some criminal offenses. For example, a person who encourages, assists or agrees with other persons to commit an offense (say, fraud) may be guilty of that offense or of a related offense (such as *conspiracy*).

Aiding and abetting

Guilt may descend on a person who has not actually committed a criminal act himself. A person is considered to be a party to an offense not only if he himself does the deed but also if he does, or omits to do, something for the purpose of aiding someone else to commit an offense. Although the person who assists another to commit an offense is commonly referred to as an "accomplice," the label is not used in the criminal law.

To be convicted of *aiding and abetting*, it is not necessary that the person so accused be present during the commission of the offense or that he participate directly. All that is necessary is for the accused to have known that the *principal*—the person who did the deed—intended to commit an offense and to have done some act, or omitted to do some act, in order to assist him. Thus, if you supplied weapons to some person who intended to commit robbery or provided someone with a house and telephone so that he could carry on an illegal betting shop while knowing these persons' intentions, you would be considered as guilty of the offense as the principal.

A member of the public who merely stands by watching a criminal act being committed has not committed the offense of aiding and abetting—although his sense of civic responsibility should prompt him to at least telephone for the police or, perhaps, jot down a license-plate number. A person will not be convicted if he was duped into committing a crime; the person who duped him will be guilty of the crime as if *he* had committed it.

Counseling a crime

The Criminal Code stipulates that anyone who counsels, procures or incites another person to commit an offense is himself guilty of the offense, and subject to the same punishment as the actual doer.

"Counseling" means inducing, encouraging or instructing another to commit an offense. "Procuring" means hiring, ordering or requesting another person to commit a crime. If X hires Y to murder Z, then X is guilty of murder just as clearly as Y.

"Procuring" is also widely used to describe the crime of arranging to supply a woman for the purposes of prostitution. The procurer (a "madam" if female; a "pimp" if male) can draw ten years' imprisonment.

Accessory after the fact

Anyone who knows that a person has committed a crime and who receives, comforts or assists him in any way to enable that person's escape, is himself committing an offense.

To convict a person of this offense, known as being an *accessory after the fact*, it is necessary to establish three conditions: (1) There must have been a criminal offense committed by the person harbored or assisted; (2) The alleged accessory must have been aware that the person he harbored or assisted had committed the offense; (3) He must have been harboring, or assisting, the principal offender for the purpose of concealing the crime or of preventing his being caught by the authorities.

No married person whose spouse is a party to an offense can be convicted of being an accessory for harboring or assisting the spouse.

Conspiracy

A criminal *conspiracy* is an agreement between two or more persons to do an unlawful act, or to do a lawful act by unlawful means. In a conspiracy, there must be a common design and a common consent to do something with a criminal or illegal purpose.

It is not necessary that the conspirators actually carry out their plan; it is enough for the Crown to prove that their plan had an illegal intent and that they had agreed to do an unlawful act.

The attempt that fails

Sometimes a person who intends to commit a crime is prevented from doing so by some circumstance beyond his control. In this event, the individual could not be convicted of the crime if he did not do it, but he might be convicted of an *attempt* to commit the crime.

A person who intends to commit a crime and does something for the purpose of carrying out his intention is guilty of an attempt, whether he could have achieved his purpose or not. For example, a person who shoots a corpse, believing it to have been a living person and intending to kill that living person, is guilty of attempted murder.

While a street dance was going on in Calgary during Stampede Week, a man was caught trying to pick a pocket. At the trial, his defense was that he could not be convicted of attempting to steal money because the victim had no money in the pocket. The accused was convicted of attempted theft. The offense itself was not altered by the fact that the victim's pockets were empty.

The question of whether a person can be convicted of attempting to do something that is impossible to complete is thorny enough, but thornier still is the question of when the attempt can be said to have begun.

It is not an offense for one individual to plan a criminal act or to prepare to carry it out. Thinking evil is not a crime. A person who plans alone to rob the Bank of Canada is not guilty of anything. Nor is he guilty of attempted robbery just because he acquires a gun to use in the crime. His actions after that point cannot be so clearly classified. No rule could possibly be formulated to determine in all cases where preparation ends and an attempt begins. The following case illustrates the dilemma of the courts:

Mr. X, the owner of a jewelry store, insured some valuable gems, concealed them, and then reported to the police that he had been robbed. He later admitted that he did it to collect the insurance. He was charged and convicted of an attempt to obtain by false pretenses, although the crime had been detected by the police before he was able to make a claim on the insurance company. The jeweler appealed his sentence and the conviction was quashed. The court held that the act of concealing the jewels and complaining to the police was not the same thing as an attempt to obtain by false pretenses.

The penalties of crime

The competing theories of sentencing can be reduced to three words: retribution, deterrence and reformation. In sentencing a convicted criminal, the presiding judge tries to balance these conflicting theories, even though the task may seem virtually impossible (*See* Chapter 3, "Decisions from the Bench"). It does not greatly help or comfort the judge to realize that none of the three theories has proved to be a complete answer in either protecting the public or reducing crime. Of the tens of thousands of Canadians convicted of indictable offenses every year, the majority are "repeaters."

The gravest of all penalties that can be imposed under the Criminal Code is life imprisonment. Capital punishment for murder has been abolished in Canada. Under the provisions of the National Defence Act, however, it remains as the penalty for treason in rare cases.

The Criminal Code provides five terms of maximum imprisonment that can be imposed for various indictable offenses: Life (with the possibility of release after a certain minimum period in jail), 14 years, ten years, five years and two years. A court imposes the maximum penalty only when it also hands down the minimum sentence. For example, a person convicted of dealing in narcotics may receive the maximum penalty of life imprisonment, as well as the minimum of seven years. This means the sentence has to be at least

Concubine—or wife?

IN HIS DECADE as Justice of the Territorial Court of the Northwest, Judge John H. Sissons often faced judicial problems that his colleagues in the south would never meet in a full career on the Bench. The only judge in an area of almost 3,250,000 square kilometres—from the Mackenzie Delta to Baffin Island—Sissons became famous (notorious, according to some) for his determination to defend native customs, even when they ran counter to the white man's law.

When a young Inuit named Noah was killed accidentally at Cape Dyer on Baffin Island, he left $25,000 under an insurance policy provided by his employer. The beneficiaries were his wife Igah and their infant daughter, Joan.

Noah and Igah had been married on Broughton Island without benefit of church (although they were recorded as Christians) and the federal administrator of the area moved formally to have the estate divided among Noah's three brothers and two sisters. Officially, the marriage had not been valid.

The application came before Judge Sissons at Frobisher Bay. The administrator explained that Igah was a concubine, not a wife. By custom among the Inuit, a concubine could be shared with other men and thus the "marriage" was not binding.

The judge insisted on flying south to Broughton Island in Hudson Bay to check for himself into the official concept of the traditional tribal union.

At a special hearing, Sissons probed into marriage customs until he became convinced that Noah and Igah had been truly married, according to the native custom, the contract being approved by the girl's father. He decided also that the stories of Inuit women being supplied as gifts to honored guests visiting the settlements were just highly colored travelers' tales.

The estate was awarded to the wife and child. Judge Sissons wrote: "It may be that, in spite of our conceits, customs other than our own may be generally accepted or condoned in other societies, and may even be more moral."

Sissons earned his own title, in Inuktituk. They called him *Ekoktoegee*, "The one who listens."

seven years, although the period of imprisonment may, in fact, be shorter.

In deciding how long a term of imprisonment to impose, a judge will probably consider some or all of the following factors:

(1) The degree of premeditation involved;

(2) The circumstances surrounding the commission of the crime;

(3) The gravity of the crime;

(4) The attitude of the offender after the crime was committed;

(5) The previous criminal record of the offender;

(6) The age, character and personality of the offender, as well as the circumstances of his life;

(7) Any recommendations contained in any pre-sentence or probation officer's reports.

Where an offender is sentenced for more than one crime, he may be ordered to serve his sentences either *concurrently* or *consecutively*, at the discretion of the judge. The concurrent sentence is served at the same time as another sentence previously imposed on the offender; the consecutive sentence begins only after any existing sentence is completely served. The general practice is to impose concurrent terms where the offenses were committed close together, or were part of one criminal action.

Sentences of up to two years are served in a provincial jail (or reformatory) while a longer sentence is served in a federal penitentiary. In Newfoundland, all sentences are served in a provincial jail.

The maximum punishment for a summary-conviction offense is six months' imprisonment and a fine of $500.

When a crime carries a penalty of up to five years' imprisonment, a judge has the option of imposing a fine in addition to or instead of imprisonment. There is no limit to the amount of the fine, but it is presumed that it will be reasonable in the circumstances.

Where a crime carries a penalty of more than five years' imprisonment, a fine may be levied in addition to, but not instead of, the prison term.

Failure to pay any fine levied in the time provided may result in the imposition of a prison term.

When a "repeater" (the legal term is *recidivist*) has been convicted of yet another indictable offense, the Crown prosecutor may then ask the court to label that individual a *dangerous offender* and to impose a sentence of *preventive deten-*

The man who caught Mimile

FRENCH DETECTIVE Charles Chenevier could have been the real-life model for Georges Simenon's renowned fictional character, Inspector Maigret.

His three-year duel in the 1950s with France's Public Enemy No. 1, a bank robber and murderer named Emile Buisson, reads exactly like one of Simenon's most exciting novels. Known to the Sûreté as Mimile, Buisson was wanted for more than 80 robberies and at least ten murders.

Police were frustrated by the uncanny ability of the Buisson gang to evade the roadblocks which were thrown up immediately after each robbery.

With infinite patience, Chenevier maneuvered his man into a pre-arranged hideout, an inn on the outskirts of Paris. Since the detective was well known personally to the bandit, he could never appear. One June day (the French detective set the time to an exact minute) he had Buisson arrested while he was eating on the terrace of the inn.

There was no struggle. In fact, when Chenevier strolled on the terrace a minute later, he sat down and ordered a full luncheon at the table while the handcuffed prisoner waited.

Knowing that Mimile had an early date with Mme Guillotine, he even bought him a final glass of cognac.

tion instead of any other sentence. Anyone so sentenced could, theoretically, spend the remainder of his life behind prison bars.

A dangerous offender is defined as a person who has been convicted of the following offenses: (1) a serious personal injury offense involving the use or the attempted use of violence against another person; (2) conduct endangering or likely to endanger the life or safety of another person; (3) inflicting or likely to inflict severe psychological damage upon another person; or (4) persistent aggressive behavior indicating that the person's future actions are unlikely to be inhibited by normal standards of behavioral restraint. The sentence requires the approval of the provincial attorney general.

A person who has been convicted of sex offenses may also be sentenced to preventive detention as a dangerous offender if "... his conduct in any sexual matter ... has shown a failure to control his sexual impulses and a likelihood of his causing injury, pain or other evil to other persons through failure in the future to control his sexual impulses."

After conviction, persons classified as dangerous offenders could be imprisoned for an indeterminate period. However, the National Parole Board reviews all such sentences after three years, and then every two years thereafter, to decide whether parole should be granted and, if so, on what conditions.

Civil disabilities
Under the Canadian Criminal Code, there is, with one exception, no civil disability that can be imposed on a convicted criminal. The exception is that holders of offices under the Crown or public servants automatically lose their office or job if they commit treason or any other indictable offense carrying a penalty of imprisonment for more than five years. A person thus convicted cannot sit as a member of parliament or of a provincial legislature, nor can he vote, until after the sentence has been served or he has been granted a pardon.

One of the most forbidding aspects of crime in the past has been the fact that the ex-con is dogged by a criminal record for the rest of his life. He may be barred from service in the armed forces and refused employment in many civil jobs.

However, the Criminal Records Act attempts to reduce this hardship. Now, a person who has not committed any offenses for five years after having served a sentence may apply to the National Parole Board to have his record sealed. Also, a judge is now empowered to record a discharge, rather than a conviction, in certain criminal cases when he is convinced such a move is not contrary to the public interest. Such an offender, even though found guilty, would not earn a criminal record.

Suspended sentence
A person who has been convicted of a criminal offense may be given what is called a suspended sentence and be placed on *probation* (*See* Chapter 3, "Decisions from the Bench"). It is important to note that it is the sentencing—or the act of passing sentence—that is suspended and not the sentence itself. A judge or magistrate cannot pass a sentence and then suspend it. If the convicted person breaks any of the conditions or terms imposed in the *probation order* issued by the court, he is guilty of the offense of *breach of probation*. He will usually then be returned to the court and the suspension of sentencing will be lifted—that is, he will begin paying the penalty originally imposed on him, plus any extra penalties for any further offenses committed.

A probation order will automatically contain the conditions that the accused shall keep the peace and be of good behavior and shall appear before the court when required to do so. No probation order can be made for a period longer than three years.

Among other things, a probation order may contain a condition that the offender make *restitution*—by, for instance, returning any money or goods acquired by criminal activity.

Restitution can be ordered only as a condition of probation; the court has no authority to order restitution separately from probation.

20/You and Your Lawyer

The lawyer in society

L AWYERS PLAY a part in our society similar to that of doctors. They counsel, guide and defend clients much as M.D.s do their patients. Among legal ranks, there exists every kind of specialist, and a large body of family lawyers, who are much like the G.P.s of medicine. As our mode of living, our business structure and our government apparatus become more complex, we turn more and more to these highly trained individuals.

There is this one essential difference between the lawyer and the doctor: the doctor must place the health and welfare of the patient above all other considerations; the lawyer has an overriding duty to truth and justice. A lawyer is an "officer of the court" first, and a professional gun-for-hire second. However, once you are accepted as a client—whether you require a will drawn up, or defense against a murder charge—the lawyer will maintain a total discretion about your affairs. He will do his utmost to serve you and forward your interests under the law. A lawyer who does less could be in trouble with his or her colleagues. The Bar associations—the associations of lawyers of each province—maintain strict discipline.

There were no lawyers in Canada during the French-regime tenure, or among the first English settlers in North America, but as the society in the New World became more tightly tied by regulations and red tape the legal profession rose to its task. The lawyer now contributes heavily to the well-being and smooth functioning of the community. He or she does this by applying the rules under which we live to our disputes and problems in an attempt to resolve them in orderly manner.

However much it runs against the Perry Mason television "image," the modern lawyer will feel more successful if you can be kept *out* of court. Lawyers follow the sensible advice of an earlier jurist, "Honest Abe" Lincoln: "Discourage litigation. Persuade your neighbors to compromise whenever you can."

Canada's pioneer lawyers were generally self-taught, their practice consisting mainly of land transactions, line-fence disputes, domestic problems and courtroom actions. A few well-to-do families sent their sons to the Inns of Court in London and they came back to introduce English custom and tradition. The most influential lawyers were the courtroom pleaders whose fame and fortune depended on their success at winning cases.

Gradually, as society changed from rural to urban, lawyers became active in commercial and industrial transactions. Through the expertise of the lawyer, many of our modern financial and commercial organizations were set on solid bases, then developed and refined. Some civil and corporation lawyers began to gain the fame and wealth which formerly only the courtroom lawyers had.

Today, lawyers are found within all major financial institutions—such as insurance, trust and banking houses—and among the executives of commercial and industrial concerns. They are equally present in government administration, at the headquarters of the big trade unions, and as advisers in professional sport and entertainment enterprises.

To the average Canadian, the lawyer is most visible when helping with difficult personal or domestic problems or as a counselor in relatively simple business affairs. It is the lawyer's duty to tell you what law applies in your particular situation, and to serve you by applying it. A large number of citizens never enter a courtroom, all their lives, and may meet a lawyer only twice: when they buy a house or condominium apartment, and when they draw up a will.

Beyond reasonable doubt

Lawyers play an important role in the control of crime and in the administration of justice. It is their duty to defend you if you have been charged with an offense, and to obtain for you the fullest protection the law allows. It is their responsibility to see that you are not convicted unless you are proved guilty beyond all reasonable doubt—for, under Canadian law, you are innocent until proved guilty. (It may surprise many people that in most of Europe and Asia, a person charged by the police is considered guilty until proved innocent.)

Your lawyer is responsible for making sure that you are never improperly charged with an offense. And, if you are found guilty, it is his duty to see that the penalty imposed is as light as possible and, obviously, no heavier than that set by law. In your defense, the lawyer must raise every issue, advance every argument and ask every question—however distasteful—which he or she thinks will help your cause.

The increasing complexity, regulation and urbanization of Canadian life seem certain to inflate the demand for legal services of all kinds. As this happens, not only governmental, financial, commercial and industrial organizations will require more lawyers, but the family man will find himself, however reluctantly, calling in a legal adviser to help solve problems that his grandfather could possibly have settled in a chat over the garden fence.

A lingering distrust

When the Persian king Cambyses, son of Cyrus the Great, found out that his chief justice had been taking bribes, he had him flayed and used his skin to upholster the Seat of Judgment. Then he appointed the son of the executed man as chief justice, warning him to remember "in which way his seat was cushioned." The suspicion of dishonesty in judges and lawyers can be traced back to the earliest writings, and it still lingers faintly today. In England, four lord chancellors have been accused in parliament of various degrees of bribery and corruption, and two were convicted. The most famous case was that of Francis Bacon, Lord Verulam, in the seventeenth century; the most recent was that of Lord Westbury in 1865. The Canadian Bar and Bench is not without stain; we still find stories in the news about lawyers who are disbarred, and even prosecuted, mostly for misusing their clients' money.

Lawyers are just as human as the rest of us. There will always be, in an imperfect world, some dishonest lawyers and some bad judges. But in actual fact there are very few untrustworthy lawyers and even fewer bad judges in Canada today. Quite apart from the quality of man now attracted to the law—and the sifting process that occurs through the long years of higher education—the provincial law societies, the Canadian Bar Association, as well as the provincial and federal departments of justice, all combine to oversee the work of the profession.

Nevertheless, bad news travels faster and farther than good, and many people still distrust lawyers and are reluctant to seek legal advice. Some of these people feel that lawyers are a greedy group, trying to exploit them.

Actually, the lawyer is often a real friend in need and, in many cases, can even save you money. Many of the problems which a lawyer is called upon to solve could have been avoided altogether if legal advice had been sought sooner. Whatever cynics may say, you should be confident that the lawyer is a highly trained, ethical and responsible person who is there to serve you and the community in which both of you live.

Heritage of Osgoode Hall

The name of Osgoode Hall is deeply rooted in the history of Canadian law, and its influence extends far beyond Toronto and Ontario. Half the chief justices of the Supreme Court of Canada have been members of its alumni. The late Chief Justice, the Rt. Hon. Bora Laskin, was a graduate of Osgoode Hall. The questions settled in its courts still blaze the legal trail for the rest of Canada. The building itself has been described as the most important "ancient monument" in Ontario. It is the home of the Law Society of Upper Canada, and the seat of the Supreme Court of Ontario.

The Hall itself is an imposing stone-pillared building in downtown Toronto, immediately beside Nathan Phillips Square. The Law Society of Upper Canada purchased the land in 1828 from the attorney general of Upper Canada, John Beverley Robinson, for $2,500, and erected its permanent home there. It was named Osgoode Hall after the first chief justice of Upper Canada, William Osgoode, an Oxford-trained lawyer who sat in Toronto (then called York), 1792–94. Osgoode later served as chief justice of Lower Canada (Quebec) for seven years.

In 1874, the Law Society sold to the province that part of the Hall which contained the courts of the provincial government. This unique transaction resulted in the two bodies owning rooms and halls above and below those owned by the other, there being no straight split as is normal in the sale of part of a building.

The Law Society of Upper Canada, from its handsome home at Osgoode Hall, has controlled the practice of law in Ontario since its beginning. In 1857, an act of the legislature gave complete control of the profession to the society; two years earlier the society had set up its first law school. For a full century, all those seeking to practice law in Ontario had to attend Osgoode Hall to study its prescribed course. Today, Osgoode Hall no longer contains a law school, having granted its name and prestige to a new law school at York University in northern Toronto. The new facility is known as the Osgoode Hall Law School of York University. Every graduate lawyer who wishes to practice in Ontario must still go to Osgoode to attend the Bar admission course run by the Law Society of Upper Canada.

The heritage of Osgoode remains, symbolizing the coming of British justice, the cream of a thousand years of civilization, to Canada. In the pioneer years, that heritage spread from the Osgoode Law School throughout the developing nation. With the opening of the West, many Osgoode graduates moved to the prairies and be-

The lawyer's "Bible"

Established by "an Act of the Parliament of Upper Canada passed in the 37th year of the reign of his late Majesty George III" (1797), the Law Society of Upper Canada is the oldest law society in the Commonwealth. Its Canons of Legal Ethics (the *Professional Conduct Handbook*) are virtually the same as those regulating the profession in all ten Canadian provinces. A sample page from the regulations is shown here.

© Law Society of Upper Canada

PROFESSIONAL CONDUCT HANDBOOK

Ruling 9

DISBARRED PERSONS

Employment by solicitors

No member of The Law Society of Upper Canada shall retain, occupy office space with, use the services of or employ in any capacity having to do with the practice of law any person who in Ontario, or elsewhere, has been disbarred and struck off the Rolls, or has been suspended, or has been involved in disciplinary action and has been permitted to resign as a result thereof, and who has not yet been readmitted.

PROFESSIONAL CONDUCT HANDBOOK

Ruling 28

SPLITTING FEES

With conveyancers, notaries public, students, clerks and others

Any arrangement whereby solicitors directly or indirectly share, split or divide fees with conveyancers, notaries public, students, clerks or other persons who bring or refer business to the solicitor's office is improper and constitutes professional misconduct.

came prominent citizens. Some became premiers and senators. Many leading lawyers and judges all across Canada today are graduates of Osgoode and, as such, play major roles in shaping both the present laws and the future lawyers of Canada. The portrait gallery at Osgoode includes many famous faces of the past.

Another feature of Osgoode Hall, almost as famous as its legal heritage, is its fence—an elegant scroll of iron set on a long low brick wall, built in 1868 for the sum of $12,242. Anyone who wants to pass through the wall into the front courtyard of the Hall must negotiate the celebrated Cow Gates—built to keep out the roaming cows of another era. Many a portly lawyer has struggled to squeeze his paunch through the 45-centimetre space. The Law Society has stoutly resisted all efforts to remove the famous fence.

The Establishment figure
Although they may not be entirely content with their image, most lawyers are definitely "members of the Establishment." They serve in charitable, service and cultural organizations and are particularly active in politics at all levels.

As a group, lawyers are generally considered to be part of the conservative element in society, although many new students entering the law schools are more radically oriented than their predecessors. Most of these will, in the long run, join large established firms and become pillars of the community themselves. Law is irrevocably based on the experience and decisions of the past. Change comes about cautiously when it must be applied evenly across the widely varied mass of a democratic nation. However, lawyers are activists within their own sphere, particularly in the area of law reform. They are continually pressing legislators for changes to bring the statutes into line with the modern needs of society. Lawyers have been prominent in moves to abolish capital punishment and to ease the requirements of bail for arrested persons. They actively support Legal Aid programs, plans offering free legal advice to the poor. (*See* "How the lawyer is paid" in this chapter.)

Even the young lawyer who yearns to break the conservative mold must retain a high degree of objectivity in order to advise clients properly. He or she must advise on what the law is, not what the law should perhaps be; and must help to resolve a present crisis, not some hypothetical question of the future.

New role in Justicare
In several of the larger Canadian cities today, young reform-minded lawyers have opened neighborhood legal offices in vacant stores in an effort to bring inexpensive or free legal services to people in poor circumstances. Some of these citizens, for various reasons, may not care to present themselves at regular lawyers' offices or "chambers"—the very idea of "legal chambers" may scare them. Lack of education, even lack of presentable clothes, prevents some applicants from going to downtown legal offices for help. Others may not qualify for the official Legal Aid programs and therefore seek out the "storefront lawyers."

Often these storefront lawyers are still undergraduates supported and advised by their professors. To gain the confidence of their clients, they adopt the dress of the areas where they work, and try to minimize legal jargon and bureaucratic routine. By helping low-income groups, young lawyers acquire practical schooling in dealing with human problems that they might miss in formal training. Social workers are often associated with this work to offer follow-up assistance.

The problems brought to the storefront lawyer may be basically minor, but they can be major worries to the persons concerned. The bulk of the business at the "law shop" is divided between landlord-tenant problems and domestic matters. Once in a Toronto center, when a law student won a tenancy case for an 85-year-old woman, she "paid" him with a homemade cake and cigarettes.

The federal government currently shares with the provincial governments up to 90 percent of the cost of provincial Legal Aid plans for persons charged with criminal offenses, but some lawyers believe that certain people are still without coverage when they need advice. They point to the means-test provisions of the plans which require an interview with a welfare worker to prove inability to pay—to which some low-income groups object. On the other hand, Legal Aid costs have been increasing, as has the number of people eligible for Legal Aid. In a time of fiscal restraints, a freeze or cutback in Legal Aid services seems likely.

Reformers suggest that the total application of Justicare—free legal advice for everyone—would require a new subject in law schools: clinical practice. Unless the young lawyer is taught special skills in interviewing and negotiating, the law may still have trouble in breaking the poverty barrier.

The advocate as politician

Thomas Jefferson once observed that the legal profession was the nursery of the legislature. This has certainly been true of Canada, perhaps even more so today than it was in the eighteenth century.

Lawyers form the largest occupation group in Canadian politics; ten of the first 15 prime ministers of Canada were trained in law. Of 38 provincial premiers in a recent 20-year span, 16 were lawyers. Lawyers have dominated the federal cabinet since Confederation—almost 50 percent of its ministers have been lawyers.

Why are there so many lawyers in government? One reason is that many of them are able to carry on their practices part-time in their home towns while they are members of parliament, assuring them not only of security for the future but also of a financial addition to their salaries as M.P.s. The fact that they have been members of a federal or provincial government adds dignity and luster to their practice, an unspoken "advertisement" that can be profitable when they resume steady practice.

The professional skills of lawyers also suit them to politics. They have developed talents for mediation and conciliation as well as for using words. Their special education and position in society creates in them a natural interest in politics and political activities, for they are dealing every day with the laws that the governing bodies pass. As the purpose of their work is to interpret and apply these laws, it is understandable that they would want to take a hand in their creation.

Politics is "the art of the possible"—that is to say, it is based on compromise. Therefore, a certain skill in avoiding being pinned down to concrete proposals has to be cultivated. The blunt "straight-from-the-shoulder" politician is seldom reelected, and almost never given a cabinet position.

The lawyer under fire

IN THE WORLD'S LITERATURE, the lawyer seldom cuts a sympathetic figure. His duty to follow fact and form does not often appeal to soaring imaginations. Chaucer, Shakespeare, Voltaire and Dickens all took potshots at the bewigged attorney.

Why may not that be the skull of a lawyer? Where be his quiddities now, his quillets, his cases, his tenures and his tricks?
—from *Hamlet*

The first thing we do, let's kill all the lawyers.
—from *King Henry VI*

'Tis like the breath of an unfee'd lawyer; you gave me nothing for 't.
—from *King Lear*

Shakespeare was not the only poet to put the lawyer down. John Keats said this: "I think we may class the lawyer in the natural history of monsters."

Dr. Samuel Johnson adjusted the balance with his remark recorded by the faithful Boswell: "Lawyers know life practically; a bookish man should always have them to converse with."

Choosing the profession

IF YOU are thinking about a career in law, one of the toughest hurdles to overcome is gaining admission to a law school. A few years ago, almost all qualified applicants across Canada were admitted. Now, because of increased interest in the profession, law schools are being flooded with applications of which only a small percentage can be accepted. In an average year before World War II, about 1,000 law students were enrolled; now the figure is slightly more than 9,000.

Why has law become so popular? Some young men and women are attracted by the high incomes that can be made: only doctors and dentists rank higher in national statistics of average income. To most, however, money is a secondary consideration. The growing concern with civil rights, poverty and the environment attracts students with high ideals.

The many fields open to the law graduate are also attractive. If he or she decides to practice, there is the choice of joining a large, medium or small firm, or of working independently. The graduate may choose to specialize in some particular subject, such as real estate, corporate, commercial or criminal law, civil litigation, or a variety of these. If practice is not an objective, then he or she can go into business; many corporations are eager to hire law graduates, and these men generally do well, judging by the number who are currently company presidents and in other executive positions.

Some use law as a springboard to a career in government, either as politicians, public servants or as diplomats. Scholarly persons may be adding law to whatever other knowledge or training they may already have acquired. A law degree, from any viewpoint, is a fine investment.

Once you have decided to study law, check the academic requirements of the various law schools. Every province except Prince Edward Island and Newfoundland has at least one. Most require a B.A. or B.Sc. degree, although some will accept students who have completed only two years in a degree course.

In Ontario, there are six law schools: the Osgoode Law School at York University, the University of Toronto, Queen's University, the University of Western Ontario, the University of Windsor and the University of Ottawa. In the Atlantic provinces, there are law schools at Dalhousie University in Halifax, at the University of Moncton, and at the University of New Brunswick in Fredericton. In western Canada, you could apply either to the University of Manitoba, the University of Saskatchewan, the University of Alberta, the University of Calgary, the University of Victoria, or the University of British Columbia. All these are "common law provinces" because their law is based on the Common Law of England. (*See* Chapter 1, "The rise of English law.")

Upon graduation from a common law university in Canada, you may practice in any province other than Quebec, provided you meet the requirements of the provincial Bar association.

If you want to practice in Quebec, the lone "civil law province," you will have to attend one of the civil law universities. They are: the University of Laval in Quebec City, the University of Montreal, McGill University and the University of Quebec in Montreal, the University of Sherbrooke, and the University of Ottawa

(Civil Law section). You can take both civil and common law degrees at McGill—as well as at the University of Ottawa—although it requires one extra year of study beyond the normal three-year period. All qualified lawyers in Canada may practice in all federal courts, including the Supreme Court of Canada.

The law school years

Although the earliest influences on Canadian legal education came from England and France, later developments have tended to follow, with some variations, the American pattern of full-time university law schools. Law became a second university degree, the professional qualification generally being added to a broad humanities preparation in the arts or, in lesser number, the sciences. When Osgoode Hall Law School moved to York University in 1966, the era of legal education being entirely controlled and operated by the Bar itself ended in Canada.

Until 1819, applicants were admitted into the Law Society of Upper Canada without any kind of examination. Beginning that year, students had to pass a test which consisted of a written translation of one of Cicero's *Orations*. Up until 1855, the student merely had to show aptitude to read and write and that five years had been spent in the service of a lawyer. That year, the Law Society of Upper Canada set up its first school at Osgoode Hall. After that, all students hoping to be admitted to the society had to attend the school and meet its requirements before being allowed to practice. Today, six generations later, all law graduates in Ontario must still attend the law society's school for six months before being admitted to the Ontario Bar.

Generally across Canada, students must spend three years at a university law school. The courses taught include contracts, torts, constitutional law, procedure, property, wills and trusts, communal and criminal law and such recent subjects as urban and poverty law.

LL.B., LL.M., D.Jur., LL.D.

When you enter your lawyer's office you will probably see his framed diploma on the wall of the waiting room. It is there to assure you that the lawyer is qualified to sell you legal advice. The counselor will, in all probability, list some of the following initials after his or her name: LL.B., LL.M., D.Jur., LL.D.

LL.B. is the abbreviation of the Latin form of bachelor of laws, the first degree in law (*Legum* = "laws"; the "B" originally stood for *Baccalaurens*). Usually, this degree requires three years of study beyond the arts or science degree course.

LL.M. represents master of laws, requiring a further year's work at the postgraduate level. This degree now is being offered by at least five law faculties. A master's degree is a necessity for anyone planning to teach law at university.

D.Jur. is a further distinction: doctor of laws (*Jur.* for jurisprudence). At least one Canadian graduate school also offers the degree of D.C.L. (doctor of civil law). LL.D. (doctor of laws) is an honorary degree granted to persons for distinction in many different fields of endeavor.

Some practicing members of the Bar, now middle-aged or older, have none of the degrees mentioned here, although they generally do have recognized degrees in other branches of study. They were admitted to the Bar under an earlier code of regulations.

In Quebec, the notary holds a special place in the legal life of the community. A notary is specially trained in civil law, and holds a law degree. Like a lawyer, he or she is a commissioner for oaths, before whom *affidavits* (signed written statements) are "sworn." He practices outside the courts, drawing up wills and other documents, settling estates and performing other work normally done by lawyers in the other nine provinces.

In the other nine provinces, the notary public is appointed by the incumbent lieutenant-governor to handle civil matters. He is usually already a lawyer.

A taste of experience

The amount of practical experience you acquire during your law school years depends entirely on you. Some schools organize student-operated legal services which provide free aid and advice to people who are referred to them by the provincial Legal Aid service, or by court officials. Work on this service is voluntary, but will provide the student with an opportunity to practice legal skills as they are acquired.

During summer months, jobs are often available in law firms and in government legal departments. Such experience enables you to see for yourself what these firms do and how they do it, and also whether this is the type of law you would like to pursue after graduation.

Law schools hold what they call "moot court" competitions, and stage mock trials for the student who wishes to develop skills as a courtroom lawyer.

Admission to the Bar

What people refer to as the "Bar" was originally the wooden rail at which prisoners stood when they were being charged and sentenced. Since the sixteenth century, it has come to mean "court." To practice law in Canada, you must be admitted to the Bar of the province where you intend to work. (The word is given the capital letter "B" to avoid unfortunate comparisons.)

Each provincial Bar association has different rules for admission, but they all require that the law graduate who has applied complete an apprenticeship period of "articling." (Ontario, for example, demands a year.) This means that following graduation (you can sometimes serve

part of the period during the last two years of study), you must work in an established law office getting some practical experience to balance and enrich your academic knowledge. Upon completing the term, or sometimes during it, you may have to write a set of examinations. In some provinces, you have to attend a law-society school for additional instruction before writing the examinations.

Upon completion of this additional training, candidates are then "called" to the provincial Bar as qualified lawyers, entitled to practice law in that province and in the courts of federal jurisdiction as well. In Quebec, only *avocats* are members of the Quebec Bar Association.

As an individual honor, some provinces will admit a distinguished person to the Bar without requiring articling or writing any Bar admission examinations. This could be done, for example, for a professor who has taught for a certain length of time in one of the law schools of the province. In that case, it is assumed that the entrant has the necessary qualifications; also, it is unlikely he or she would actually ever practice law. The federal minister of justice is always "admitted."

The law societies

Each province has a law society, incorporated by the legislature, whose responsibility it is to set the standards in the profession for admission, training, practice and discipline. Anyone wanting to

Studying for the Bar

THE YOUNG MAN OR WOMAN who enters the study of law—on average, it requires seven years following high-school graduation—does not lack for inspiration during the long struggle for admission to the provincial Bar association (*i.e.*, permission to practice).

Liberal statesman Edmund Burke, once a law student himself, wrote of the law that it was "one of the first and noblest of human sciences; it does more to quicken and

invigorate the understanding than all the other kinds of learning put together...."

Burke's political opposite, Lord Bolingbroke, agreed on this score. The lawyer, he said, "must pry into the secret recesses of the human heart, and become well acquainted with the whole moral world."

When asked to advise a student going in for law, the British Lord Chancellor, the Earl of Eldon, replied: "Live like a hermit and work like a horse."

practice in a province must join the association in that province, and must comply with its rules and regulations.

The first law society was formed at Niagara-on-the-Lake in 1797, when that village was the capital of what is now Ontario. Ten lawyers met in Wilson's Hotel and formed the Law Society of Upper Canada. Their action was recognized and confirmed by a special statute of the legislature. The society was duly incorporated in 1822 and, six years later, erected its permanent home, Osgoode Hall, in Toronto. The Law Society of Newfoundland dates from 1834. Then, in order, follow New Brunswick (1846), Quebec (1849), Nova Scotia (1850), British Columbia (1869), Prince Edward Island (1876), Manitoba (1877), and Alberta and Saskatchewan (1907).

If you wish to practice law in the Northwest Territories, you must be accepted into the territorial law society. To qualify, you must be a member of a provincial Bar association. The society requires that you pass an examination and pay an admission fee. Before practicing in the Northwest Territories, law graduates from other parts of Canada must also pass the Alberta Bar admission course and article for 12 months.

In the Yukon Territory, most lawyers belong to the territorial Bar association and law society. Any qualified lawyer who is a member of a provincial Bar association may be admitted to practice after paying a $400 fee and after advertising in the Yukon *Gazette* that he or she intends to enroll as a lawyer. Any graduate of a Canadian common law university may practice in the Yukon after serving a 12-month articling period and paying the fee.

Ideals and ethics

Each provincial Bar association maintains a code of ethics and conduct for each member lawyer to follow. Regulations cover many aspects of practice—such as how to keep account books, how to set up a special fund to hold money belonging to clients, and whether interest may be collected on that fund. Detailed rules govern the lawyer's conduct with clients and certain practices *must* be followed on pain of penalty—such as suspension and even expulsion from the Bar.

All law societies in Canada strictly regulate advertising by their members. Lawyers may place notices in the press advertising their practices and giving their addresses, but they are not permitted to include personal photographs in the announcements. In some provinces, lawyers may advertise fees for certain routine legal services.

Normally, a lawyer will not permit attributive quoting by name in a press interview if there is any possibility that it might be interpreted as self-advertisement. A lawyer must also be wary of self-promotion when appearing on television, or when writing books or magazine articles. Even the words a lawyer uses on the letterhead of his office can be criticized.

If a lawyer breaks any of the rules and regulations of the law society, or acts in "an unprofessional manner," he or she will be investigated by the society. If the executive members of the society (usually called "Benchers") feel the situation is serious enough, they will hold a hearing at which the accused lawyer, or someone in representation, may present an explanation, or defense. If the "Benchers" find the counselor guilty, there will be either suspension for a period, or disbarment—that is, expulsion from the Bar. This means that the lawyer is not allowed to practice law until either the period of suspension has expired or he or she is reinstated.

Canadian Bar Association

It is not compulsory for lawyers to join the country-wide Canadian Bar Association (C.B.A.). About 30,000 of the more than 40,000 Canadian lawyers are members. The C.B.A. was formed March 31, 1914, and was incorporated in 1921 by a special act of the federal parliament.

The objects of the association are: (1) to advance the science of jurisprudence; (2) to promote the administration of justice and uniformity of legislation throughout Canada as far as is possible while still preserving the basic system of law in respective provinces; (3) to uphold the honor of the legal profession and encourage harmonious relations and cooperation among law societies of the provinces; (4) to encourage a high standard of legal education, training and ethics; and (5) to promote cordial relationships among the members of the Canadian Bar.

The association provides a continuing forum where lawyers of the various provinces can discuss their problems and compare their provincial laws in an effort to update and reform them. It allows the profession to speak with a single voice.

The question of law reform is always before the Law Reform Commission of Canada, which was established as a permanent body in 1970. The commission, which reports to the federal parliament through the minister of justice, seeks to remove "anachronisms and anomalies" from the law in both common law and civil law provinces. Particularly, it tries to develop "new approaches" to the law, responsive to the changing needs of society.

The liberalizing recommendations of the Law Reform Commission have not, however, met with wide public interest or approval, either from parliament or the profession. A former Ontario ombudsman (and a former federal minister of justice), Arthur Maloney, has stated that a public poll on capital punishment would probably draw an 85-percent vote for the restoration of hanging.

A typical advertisement by a legal partnership

Lawyers are generally not permitted to solicit for clients, but they can publish "cards" and list themselves in a country-wide legal directory.

Howard, Mackie

Barristers and Solicitors

Suite 700-801-7th Ave. S.W., CALGARY, Alta. T2P 3S4
Telephone (403) 232-9500   TWX 610-821-7348
Telecopier (403) 266-1395   Cable Howsyth
Telex 03-822851

W.A. Howard, Q.C.	J.A. N. Mackie, Q.C.	T. J. Hopwood, Q.C.
P. T. Kueber, Q.C.	D. H. Mitchell	W. W. Stanford
E. F. McRory	M. J. O'Brien Kelly	R. G. Powers
G. C. Hawco	H. D. Williamson	G. E. Anderson
F. R. Foran	A. D. Nielsen	J. P. Petch*
R. A. Reaburn	P. T. McCarthy	D. F. Mackie
J. W. Surbey	S. P. Sibold	D. W. Ross*
F. W. T. Somerville	D. A. Follett	D. J. Pettie
M. J. Hill*	B. E. Roberts*	J. E. Fletcher
M. A. Smith	J. L. Ircandia	B. A. Yaworski
I. Ash	M. D. Sharpe	N. E. Hall
W. L. Hess	M. S. Paperny	J. E. Tyrrell
D. R. Wright	C. A. Fee	J. Poetker
J. D. Vallis	S. W. Wilson	L. Leuschner
M. B. Cohen	A. J. Tonken	F. P. Cahill
E. J. Barichello		

Counsel: E. M. Bredin, Q.C.   M. H. Patterson, Q.C.

*Professional Corporation

— from *Canada Legal Directory*, by permission

Hanging out the shingle

IN THIS and the following sections are outlined the options available to a newly qualified member of the Bar. It should be remembered that not all lawyers practice law—perhaps only half do, in the way that the public understands.

When the new lawyer does decide to offer the public legal skills, he or she figuratively comes under the protection of Honest St. Ives, the thirteenth-century patron saint of lawyers, and "hangs out the shingle." The shingle in question was, in pioneer America, actually a cedar shingle painted white with the practitioner's name on it. The shingle was hung on hooks outside a house to announce the ever-available services of lawyer or doctor. It exists in another form today in the lists of partners' names that hang in the entry halls of law offices.

The law graduate can decide to join a law firm in one of the major cities; a smaller firm in, say, a county town; or he can plunge in on his own.

Most large law firms are situated in the major cities and consist of between 20 and 70 lawyers, divided into various departments. If you want to specialize in one particular aspect of the law, you should try to join that specific department in a larger firm. This applies particularly if you are interested in corporation or tax law, for large firms usually have the clients who require these services.

There are both advantages and disadvantages to joining a large firm. There is the feeling that fame and fortune might be easier to find in a larger firm. When a rich corporation says, "We want the best," they think automatically of the legal talent that inhabits the quiet book-lined and air-conditioned offices in the city sky-scrapers. Some of the glory might even rub off on the most junior counsel.

Money is no problem in the "department store" offices; the pay is superior and working conditions range from excellent to fabulous. On the other hand, there are usually a great number of people ahead of you on the promotion list, all striving to become partners.

Options for the individual

Smaller law firms offer the advantage of being more or less your own boss, and you are thus freer to engage in community affairs. Smaller cities may also offer a more attractive way of life and a better atmosphere in which to raise a family. Remember that two prime ministers, John Macdonald and John Diefenbaker, were with law firms in small cities—Macdonald in Picton, Ontario, and Diefenbaker in Prince Albert, Saskatchewan.

The brave lawyer who decides to "go it alone" will have to borrow money from a bank or other institution—unless he has a sponsor or is wealthy. Setting up a practice is expensive; books, furniture, typewriters, forms and documents must be purchased, and rent and salaries paid. The first years of a new practice can be slow, and the revenue that comes in is seldom enough to cover expenses.

Perhaps the biggest single handicap of the one-lawyer operation is that you do not have the constantly available advice and assistance of an older, experienced lawyer. Once you become established, however, you do have the satisfaction of working for yourself. This may seem a mixed blessing when you consider there is no one around to relieve you for vacations, family crises, or if you are sick.

844

Speaking for the State

Another alternative is to join a government department, either provincial or federal. These provide a number of jobs of wide variety, many of them offering salaries on a par with industry and most of them guaranteeing a high level of security.

If you wish to concentrate on courtroom work, which is generally labeled "litigation," you should apply to a firm that does a great deal of litigation, or to your provincial attorney general's department or the federal Department of Justice. These two departments handle the prosecution of all criminal charges. They also bring a wide variety of civil suits—for instance, if someone was dumping garbage on the road and no neighbor sued him, the government could itself lay a charge.

If you are particularly interested in criminal law, it would be profitable to become associated with the attorney general's office for a year or more in order to gain experience in the prosecuting of a criminal case; then you would be well armed if you decided to switch to the other side—the side of the defense.

There are also jobs at the municipal level open to lawyers, as most cities of any size require a city solicitor to handle the inevitable pile of legal work. Large public utilities, such as hydroelectric, gas and telephone companies, can offer well-paid posts, often leading to executive appointments.

Barristers and solicitors

In Canada, we think of our legal adviser as, simply, the lawyer (in Quebec, *l'avocat*), but he or she is really both a barrister and a solicitor. The counterpart in the United States is referred to as an attorney-at-law and often addressed as "Counselor."

In Britain, and especially in England, there is a sharp distinction between barristers and solicitors, both in the work they do and in the societies to which they belong.

Barristers take their training in, and belong to, one of the Inns of Court in London. They spend most of their time as

"I solemnly swear . . . "

BEFORE BEING "called to the Bar"—that is, being authorized to practice in the courts—the graduate lawyer must swear the Oath of Allegiance to Queen Elizabeth II and also the following special oaths:

Barristers' Oath:

You are called to the Degree of Barrister-at-law to protect and defend the rights and interest of such of your fellow-citizens as may employ you. You shall conduct all cases faithfully and to the best of your ability. You shall neglect no man's interest nor seek to destroy any man's property. You shall not be guilty of champerty or maintenance. You shall not refuse causes of complaint reasonably founded, nor shall you promote suits upon frivolous pretenses. You shall not pervert the law to favor or prejudice any man, but in all things shall conduct yourself truly and with integrity. In fine, the Queen's interest and your fellow-citizens' you shall uphold and maintain according to the constitution and law of this Province. All this you swear to observe and perform to the best of your knowledge and ability. So help you God.

Solicitors' Oath:

You also do sincerely promise and swear that you will truly and honestly conduct yourself in the practice of a solicitor of the Supreme Court of this province, according to the best of your knowledge and ability. So help you God.

While these are the oaths administered in Ontario, they are virtually the same in all provinces.

advocates in the higher courts where they are the only "men of law" allowed to appear. They also give advice and draft documents concerning suits in the lower courts. Traditionally, they are expected to be above mere money matters. They do not have clients, as such, but are hired by solicitors.

Once the actual courtroom phase is over, the barrister's work is done. The famous murder trials at London's Old Bailey are conducted by barristers, some of whom are brilliant orators capable of drawing a full house when they plead a case.

The solicitor in England, whose work is mainly outside the courtroom, drafts documents and advises on a wide range of legal matters. He is the legal adviser to whom the client speaks. Although the solicitor has the right to appear in the lower courts, this is not his main function. Some never enter a courtroom after their student days.

Canadian lawyers may appear in courts at all levels and may concern themselves with any aspect of law they please. There is one exception to this rule: the Quebec notary usually cannot appear in court.

The Q.C.: "taking silk"

A Canadian lawyer who has been practicing for a certain period (usually 10 years) is eligible to be appointed a Queen's Counsel—or King's Counsel when there's a king on the throne—and to put the initials Q.C. (or K.C.) after his or her name. All the provincial governments appoint Q.C.s, usually at New Year's. The federal government also appoints a limited number. In some provinces, as many as one-third of all registered lawyers are Q.C.s.

In England, only barristers are eligible to be appointed Queen's Counselors and the distinction is keenly sought. With the appointment comes the right to wear a silk robe in court; it is for this reason that the appointment is often referred to as "taking silk." English Q.C.s are sometimes called "leaders" since, after their appointment, they cannot appear in court without a junior in attendance. Judges in Great Britain come only from the ranks of barristers.

Canadian Q.C.s will also wear the silk robe in court, but the main privilege of the appointment is that the Q.C. is permitted to argue his case in a section of the courtroom closer to the judge ("within the Bar"); Q.C.s have the right to be heard first. Canadian Queen's Counselors do not have to take a junior into court with them.

Going on the Bench

To many lawyers, and in the eyes of the general public, the crowning point of a successful career in law is becoming a judge—referred to in legal terms as being appointed to "the Bench." Judges hold positions of high honor in the Canadian community and are respected, if not always admired, by their fellow citizens. Most Canadians feel that our system of judges being appointed "for life" (actually, they must retire at 70 or 75, depending on the court in which they serve) is superior to the American tradition under which most judges in the lower courts are elected for a term of office in political campaigns.

The appointment of judges is both a federal and provincial responsibility. The federal government appoints justices of the Supreme Court of Canada, of the Federal Court of Canada, of the Supreme (or Superior) Courts of the provinces, and the judges of the County (or District) Courts of the provinces. The provinces designate the judges (or magistrates) of the Provincial (or Magistrate's) Courts. (*See* Chapter 3, "Judges and courts.")

Although his decisions can be reviewed by the courts of appeal, the judge holds a unique power in our society. Any newly appointed magistrate (now often referred to as provincial judge) can order a cabinet minister—even the prime minister—into jail if he has been found guilty of a charge carrying that punishment. If the judge finds that his court has not been respected, he can impose instant penalties for contempt of court; these penalties can include fines, jail, or both. The judge holds a commission to act in the name of the Queen and, unless overruled by another judge higher up the legal ladder, his word is literally the law. Judges in the superior courts can be removed from office only by the governor general with the approval of both houses of parliament.

The appointment of federal judges is the right of the federal minister of justice. As of the late 1960s, all names being considered for an appointment are submitted to the Canadian Bar Association whose national committee on the judiciary checks each person's qualifications and abilities. Names are also submitted to the provincial law societies to check whether the candidate happens to be under investigation for any reason. The qualifications for the job have never been spelled out publicly, other than that judges must be persons "of integrity and merit."

Judges' salaries

Judges are paid well to lift them above any monetary temptations. The justices of the Supreme Court of Canada—there are nine—receive salaries of $98,100 a year, with the chief justice getting $8,500 more. The judges of the provincial supreme courts are paid $89,000, while the chief justice of each province receives $92,100; county or district court judges get $78,700, with an extra $7,300 added for the chief judge of a county (or district) court.

All judges paid by the federal government get an extra $1,000 in incidental expenses, plus any traveling expenses they may incur. A judge who uses his or her own car gets a fuel allowance. There are generous pension benefits payable from retirement to the judge and, upon death, to his or her dependents.

The salaries paid to provincial court judges (or magistrates) vary from province to province. Ontario pays its chief provincial judge $73,000 a year, while other judges receive either $65,700 or $66,925.

Despite the fact that these salaries may seem high when compared to the national average wage, some lawyers are reluctant to accept appointments to judgeships because they make still more money in private practice.

Elevated to the Bench

NAPOLEON once exhorted his troops by saying that every soldier carried in his knapsack the baton of a marshal of France. Similarly, a humble young lawyer, plowing through dusty land titles, domestic squabbles and petty thievery, carries in a briefcase a blank Judge's Commission.

Appointment as a judge in Canada is gained through a process never made public in detail (basically it is merit and reputation), but being "His or Her Honor" isn't a sinecure. About 360 B.C. the Greek philosopher Plato laid down this formula:

"The judge should not be young; he should have learned to know evil, not from his own soul, but from long observance of the nature of evil in others: knowledge should be his guide, not personal experience."

More than 2,000 years later, a down-to-earth American jurist added this warning:

"A judge is almost of necessity surrounded by people who keep telling him what a wonderful fellow he is. And if he once begins to believe it, he is a lost soul."

Judges have never lacked for critics eager to point out that they suffer from most, if not all, of the defects of ordinary mortals. Thomas Jefferson wrote to a friend, "Our judges are as honest as other men, and not more so. They have with others the same passions for party, for power and the privilege of their corps." Oliver Wendell Holmes (himself a Justice of the U.S. Supreme Court) said, "Judges are apt to be naive, simple-minded men, and they need something of Mephistopheles."

How do you judge a judge? English essayist Thomas Fuller said that the "private affections" of the good judge should be "swallowed up in the common cause as rivers lose their names in the ocean."

When you need a lawyer

IT HAS often been said that the man who acts as his own lawyer has a fool for a client. There is, however, no law that says you must be represented by legal counsel in court. We still read in the papers once in a while of some person "conducting his own case" in court. There are those who probably enjoy the idea of an ordinary citizen bravely cutting his way through "all that legal red tape." There's a touch of David and Goliath about it all—especially if David wins his case. But, in reality, it rarely happens that way.

The complexity of the law and the confusion of court procedure make it virtually impossible for the layman to present and argue his case effectively. He will waste the time of the court and all its officers, thus delaying the attack on the ever-mounting backlog of cases waiting to be heard. And so, for the individual's own sake and in the interest of justice being done, the court will try to get legal assistance for the unrepresented person.

Government-supported Legal Aid programs are available to almost all who meet the requirements, and neighborhood legal agencies supplement the service. Some provinces provide what is called a "duty counsel" who is available to assist and advise those who appear in court without their own lawyer.

Since there is obviously a difference between what you *should* do and what you *must* do in the matter of being represented by a lawyer, the use of such words as "essential" in the following paragraphs must be regarded only as the opinion of the editors. The editors advise the reader to arm himself with professional advice in all legal disputes, especially if the other party to any deal or action has legal counsel. If the cost factor should make you waver about consulting a lawyer, consider that a small outlay now might save a lot of expense and trouble later. Lawyers take their cases into court only after all negotiation has failed—about 90 percent of all actions are settled out of court.

How to find a lawyer

If no one in your family or business circle knows a lawyer, you could ask for a recommendation from your religious adviser, your doctor, your bank manager, your union secretary, or from anyone you know who is in business. An accountant is usually in touch with local lawyers. You can consult the classified telephone directory under *Lawyers*, beginning with the one whose office is near your home. The provincial law society will provide a list of its members in your area.

If you need a lawyer with special skills—if, for instance, you have been charged with a crime—you could inquire from any social welfare agency about the names of those members of the Bar who appear most often as defense lawyers in criminal trials. If you approach any lawyer, a sense of duty would demand that he or she advise you to find other counsel if his or her own legal skills were inappropriate to your needs.

When you want to sue

If you are considering bringing a civil action against someone (except in the small claims court), you should contact a lawyer. Even though you may feel you have a watertight case, the lawyer may tell you differently. Perhaps you are acting in haste, or out of anger or hurt feelings. Lawyers are experienced in the ways of the court and can save you the time, trouble and expense of fighting a hopeless court battle.

The lawyer is familiar with all the ritual and procedure, with all the documents and forms, and with all the regulations—such as the expiration of time limits—that may apply to your case. He or she will explore the possibilities of settling out of court and advise on what is a reasonable amount to settle for.

If charged with a crime

In all criminal cases, you have a lot to lose; if convicted, you stand to be immediately fined or imprisoned, and you will acquire a criminal record—a lasting handicap in our society. A lawyer is essential to giving you the best chance of acquittal. In the United States, while it is not legally required that you be represented by an attorney in all criminal trials, the Supreme Court has recently stated that it will overturn all convictions resulting from trials in which a defendant did not have a lawyer. Most American judges will not permit a person to be unrepresented.

It is imperative that you see a lawyer long before you go into court on a criminal offense; your lawyer will need every advantage, including time, in the attempt to keep you from being wrongly convicted. This applies also to any preliminary hearing. The lawyer will argue that you be set free on your own recognizance or that, if bail is required, it be an amount you can meet.

Perhaps you haven't really committed a crime at all. Your lawyer will tell you that in some circumstances a crime does not count as a crime. When the act was committed by someone described as "legally incompetent"—perhaps temporarily insane, or under unbearable provocation or pressure—it is not considered a crime. In another circumstance, if a man is accused of sex relations with a girl younger than 16, this is the crime of sexual assault (formerly called "statutory rape"). But it will not be considered a crime if, for example, a mature 15-year-old girl can be proved to be more to blame than the accused man. She could, in fact, be in business as a prostitute.

It might reassure you to know that a crime has to be an *intentional* violation of the law: a pure accident is not a crime—even if it should have a fatal result.

In strictest confidence

ANYTHING you tell your lawyer when consulting him professionally must be kept in strictest confidence. Under the Code of Ethics, he or she is bound not to disclose any information about your past, your personal relationships or your business. Your lawyer can break this secrecy only if you authorize so, or if the law requires it.

This duty extends to the lawyer not even disclosing that you have either consulted or retained him (or her) to act for you. The overall secrecy continues indefinitely—it does not end with the completion of the trial, or even if you and the lawyer part company over some difference of opinion.

The lawyer is under stricture not to talk in any detail about your affairs ("indiscreet conversations") even with his wife and family, and must not gossip publicly about you, even if your name is not mentioned. He is warned about "shop talk" with other lawyers. Of course, this does not cover matters of public knowledge.

The bond of confidence covers the entire staff of the lawyer's office. Unless you expressly forbid it, your lawyer may discuss your case with partners and, where necessary (such as in typing and filing), with a secretary. It is the lawyer's responsibility, though, to take "reasonable care" that *they* don't blab.

If the law requires your lawyer to break this secrecy (maybe to prevent a crime), special care must be taken to disclose only that information demanded.

Deeds, documents, divorces

Any important business contract, especially an agreement to purchase a house, should be looked over by a lawyer, so that the hazards and responsibilities involved can be pointed out in the particular agreement. Remember, for instance, that an "offer" becomes a "deal" as soon as the seller accepts it.

Without a lawyer's assistance in "searching title" to your new residence before you purchase, you can never be sure that the proposed seller really owned the land or that it is not subject to a hidden mortgage which you would have to pay off. (*See* Chapter 4, "Closing the deal.") Also, most laymen do not know how to draft any of the essential documents involved in the purchase of property. When you are the seller, the lawyer will protect your financial interest, arrange to close the deal properly, and also arrange for the receipt of all monies.

A lawyer is a necessity if you wish to make or change your will. (*See* Chapter 9, "Last will and testament.") He or she will advise you about taxes and other problems that may result from the planned distribution of your assets. You will be advised of sensible—perhaps profitable—alternatives. Lawyers are familiar with the standard wording used in all wills, so that at your death there will be no doubt about exactly what you meant. Your lawyer will make sure that your will is properly signed and witnessed.

A lot has been written on the do-it-yourself divorce. (*See* Chapter 10, "The divorce.") Whether or not a lawyer is necessary in a divorce action depends on the complications. A lawyer is usually essential if the divorce is going to be opposed by the other spouse—that is, "contested"—which is likely to happen if there is any dispute about alimony, custody of any children or the division of property. If the spouse who is asked for a divorce agrees, and no claim is made for custody, alimony or the division of property, then a lawyer may not be necessary.

Anyone facing divorce should note that there are forms to be filled in and filed, and also that you still must prove to the judge that you are entitled to a divorce—that the reasons you are giving for divorce are indeed true.

For the most part, a lawyer will be able to take all these problems off your shoulders at a time of extreme stress, and to ensure that your divorce decree is not hindered by any errors.

The lawyer's obligation

A lawyer represents to a client the possession of adequate skill, knowledge and education to conduct properly everything he or she undertakes. Lawyers are more than mere citizens in this regard: they are officers of the courts, their clients' advocates, and members of an ancient and honorable profession. Lawyers have a duty to the government to uphold its integrity and its laws, a duty to the courts, a duty to clients, and a duty to self.

In duty to you, the client, the lawyer should act for you only. Once having acted for you, he or she cannot act against you in the same matter or in any other related matter. When he or she accepts the payment by which you hire counsel, your lawyer must disclose to you any previous relations with the other parties and any interest or connection with the controversy that might influence your decision to retain this counselor. A lawyer cannot represent conflicting interests.

It is your lawyer's duty to obtain full knowledge of your case before advising you and then to give you an honest opinion of how your case stands in relation to the law as well as the probable results of any upcoming or proposed court action. A lawyer must also try to avoid going to court if your action can be settled outside the court in a satisfactory way. Every fair and honorable method must be used to obtain for you any and every remedy and defense which the law provides.

Your lawyer must always work within the bounds of the law and must follow the code of ethics set down by the Bar association. He or she is not permitted to profit in any way from confidential information received from you in the course of the case. A lawyer cannot acquire by purchase or otherwise (unless the law expressly allows it) any interest in the goods or property involved in the court case

The lawyer who dared

FACTS

The Irish-born journalist, Thomas D'Arcy McGee, was a Father of Confederation. He strongly opposed the efforts of the Fenians, a revolutionary secret society trying to advance Irish independence by fomenting disloyalty among Irish immigrants. This earned him the hatred of the Fenians and he was murdered by one of them in Sparks Street, Ottawa, outside his lodgings.

The Canadian people were outraged by the crime. Patrick James Whelan, a young Fenian, was arrested and charged with the murder. Immediately, he was "tried and found guilty" on the front pages of every newspaper. It seemed next to impossible for him to obtain a fair trial. Lawyers who were approached to defend Whelan were threatened.

When it appeared that no counsel would risk the intense unpopularity of defending Whelan, the Treasurer of the Law Society of Upper Canada—that is, the head of the legal profession in Ontario—John Hilliard Cameron, Q.C., stepped forward. He was also the grand master of the Orange Order (the accused was a Roman Catholic). The case came before Chief Justice Richards in 1868.

ARGUMENT

In his address to the jury, J. H. Cameron said: "A great crime has been committed, a noble name blotted from the roll of the living, the name of a great man who had set a grand example by his wise and patriotic counsels. The country has showed its gratitude to him by its stern demand for atonement for the crime, and has by the almost unanimous shout of its press and people pronounced the prisoner at the Bar guilty. There has been a shout ringing through . . . the land, proclaiming that the prisoner must be found guilty, before anything whatever has been adduced in evidence against him . . .

"It had been said, and well said, in language that admits of no doubt, that it is impossible for any man to secure a clear defense unless those who are to act in his defense are permitted to pursue their course without cajolement or coercion, and it would ill become those who are the leaders of the Bar if they were to allow themselves to swerve from the high duties of their profession under intimidating influences exerted either through the angry frowns of power, or through the less definite rage, and perhaps madness, of the people.

"What would have been the result if one upon whom people are pleased to look as a leader of the Bar of Upper Canada had thought it proper to refuse his advocacy? Had he thus withheld his services, he would have proved himself unworthy of the position which he held, and a craven to the profession to which he belonged."

JUDGMENT

The accused was convicted and hanged. However, the action of Cameron in coming forward to defend this intensely hated prisoner at great personal risk represents a proud moment for the Canadian legal profession.

851

being conducted—for example, he or she could not invest in land under dispute in the case. These restrictions apply to all people who work in a lawyer's office.

Your lawyer must deposit any money received on your behalf in a special trust fund and immediately report receipt of such money to you (*See* Chapter 9, "Giving your money away"). He or she must not mix personal money with trust money unless you expressly instruct your lawyer to do so.

Lawyers are not obliged to take on as a client everyone who knocks on their doors. They can refuse to act for you. But should you be accepted as a client, your lawyer must serve you faithfully. When the layman sees a lawyer fighting hard in court to defend a known criminal, he often wonders: "How can he do it? He must know the guy is guilty!" But it is our tradition that the accused be given *every* chance to prove a "reasonable doubt,"

and, regardless of the lawyer's own personal opinion as to the guilt of the accused, it is his or her duty to present every available defense.

Even after you have hired a lawyer and he has accepted you as a client, he can withdraw in the following circumstances: (1) If you refuse to advance sufficient money for conducting the action. (2) If the lawyer cannot obtain instructions from you, or if you are not capable of instructing the lawyer. (3) If you instruct the lawyer to take some steps which he or she knows to be dishonorable, if your claim is fraudulent or fictitious or if, after accepting the retainer, a conflict of interest arises which forces the lawyer to withdraw.

If you feel that your lawyer is not fulfilling his or her duty to you, you are entitled to leave that person and go to another, although you will still have to pay what you owe the first lawyer. You may also

A cartoonist looks at legal jargon

If a "hereto" costs $1.50, how much for a "party of the first part"?

THE WIZARD OF ID   by Brant parker and Johnny hart

By permission of John Hart and Field Enterprises, Inc.

complain formally to the provincial Bar association, if you feel your lawyer's conduct is illegal, improper or unethical.

The client's obligation

In any relationship between two people there are certain duties and obligations that each party has to the other. So it is with you and your lawyer. Your lawyer's obligations have already been listed, but there are certain things *you*, the client, must do before a good working relationship can be established.

You must be completely frank and open with your lawyer. You must tell everything that has anything to do with your problem. Trivial though you might consider some detail to be, let your lawyer be the judge of its importance—that's one of the reasons you hired legal counsel. It is impossible for a lawyer to do the job without full knowledge of the case, and it may be embarrassing to counsel (and you) at a later stage if a fact that you failed to tell is discovered.

You should make up your mind at the start that you are going to follow advice. Don't forget that when you went to the lawyer's office, you had a problem which you could not solve yourself. If you fail to follow advice, you are wasting not only your own time and money but also your lawyer's. You may also injure your situation further and make a simple problem more complicated.

If you feel the advice given you is wrong, it is best to end your relationship with your lawyer right there. It is your right and your decision to take.

Do not waste your lawyer's time. Time is what counts, and what he or she will bill you for. If a lawyer spends an hour running around for you over some minor matter, you must be billed for that hour. Don't take up time with needless telephone calls or visits. If you are late for your appointment, he or she will usually bill you for this time wasted, because lawyers (unlike doctors) work to a fixed time schedule and do not have a waiting room full of people they can substitute.

If you are careless with your lawyer's time, you embarrass your counsel when he or she sends in accounts. Little may have been accomplished, but hours have been spent, at your request, and you must be charged for them.

If you cannot understand what your lawyer is doing or some papers he or she has prepared, ask for an explanation in everyday terms. Documents are written primarily for the courts and consist of a special jargon not readily understandable to the layperson. No lawyer should expect a client to understand legal language, nor should you, the client, feel embarrassed in asking for a translation.

You may not need a lawyer

Plenty of situations will arise in a normal lifetime when professional advice is needed but when a lawyer is not essential because there are other kinds of experts available who can serve you. For example, accountants assist with taxation and bookkeeping problems; provincial and federal government agencies deal with old-age pensions, unemployment and other social security difficulties.

Your local post office can be a mine of general information and assistance in almost any area affected by government regulations, from where to get a dog license to lodging objections to taxes. The reference rooms of public libraries can supply authoritative advice in up-to-date books and pamphlets. Statistics Canada offices will provide you with printed material on regulations on a wide variety of subjects. Newspaper offices will usually advise on the best channels for reaching officialdom. Every province (except Prince Edward Island) has an ombudsman to handle complaints against provincial or municipal governments.

If you are suing, or being sued, for a sum of money that would send the case to the small claims court (sometimes called division court, or magistrate's court—*see* Chapter 3, "Judges and courts") a lawyer is not necessary. These courts handle claims of up to $1,000 (in Quebec, $800). There is a minimum of formality, and the court officers are accustomed to helping people who are acting on their own behalf. The routine is quite simple.

Finally, in deciding whether you need a lawyer, let common sense be your guide.

The lawyer as a specialist

| The family lawyer |
| The trial lawyer |
| The corporation lawyer |
| The patent lawyer |
| The tax lawyer |
| The labor lawyer |

THE SHEER bulk of this book should serve as convincing evidence of the endless complexity of the law—yet this volume does not pretend to do more than sketch a broad outline. Consider that the statute law of Ontario alone requires volumes containing well over 10,000 pages—and this is the record of the laws passed by that single provincial legislature over the years. It excludes the vast bulk of the common law and the veritable ocean of print that records the federal, other provincial and municipal laws.

As the graduate earns a degree and is called to the Bar in the dual role of barrister and solicitor, the lawyer gets a thorough grounding in general principle and practice. But no lawyer would claim to be entirely master over the whole body of Canadian law. It would be an impossible achievement, even for Oliver Goldsmith's village oracle of whom they said, ". . . and still the wonder grew, that one small head could carry all he knew."

Increasingly, the lawyer has been forced to specialize, first by dividing law intellectually into its two main categories of *substantive* and *procedural,* then further subdividing these categories into *public* and *private.* Substantive law is concerned with the rights and duties we each possess. Procedural law consists of the rules for enforcement and protection of those rights and duties. Public law directs and controls the interaction between the various governments, governmental agencies, and the individual. Private law governs relationships between individuals or between groups of persons.

Within these general areas, prompted by personal interest or career opportunity, many lawyers single out a defined field for their major activity. If successful, they soon become known as specialists and begin to get cases referred to them from other lawyers. You may find, for instance, that a lawyer of your choice will courteously but firmly refuse to act for you in, say, a divorce action. However, that lawyer will undoubtedly refer you to another lawyer who is an expert in that field. It must be added that there are still plenty of sturdy souls around who will cheerfully tackle anything.

Canadian lawyers can specialize in one of at least a dozen fields: family law, litigation, administrative, real estate, corporation, taxation, bankruptcy, patents and copyrights, labor relations, constitutional, military and international law. New categories—space law, poverty, environment—are now demanding their own specialists. In the following paragraphs we can briefly discuss only the half-dozen major lawyer categories, but the reader will find the subject of legal specialization developed in the separate chapters of this book devoted to each field.

The family lawyer

The similarity between lawyer and doctor in Canada is greatest when we consider the role of the so-called family lawyer. That familiar trustworthy figure of the television serial and small-town novel—counselor and conscience to generations from the time of law-school days to comfortable white-thatched retirement as the town sage. This authority on grass-roots law can be found in almost every town, or sizable village, across the country. To the great majority of Canadians, the family lawyer is the only lawyer they know or ever will know.

Apart from legal expertise, discretion, compassion and public spirit, the family lawyer sometimes knits whole communities together. He or she is often a leader of the local Establishment, promoter of good causes, and *confidant* to hundreds in all kinds of emergencies. With the local clergy the lawyer is the rock to which people in trouble will turn and cling, solver of problems.

The family lawyer advises clients on the sale and purchase of land, on the drawing of mortgages, leases, wills and business contracts, divorce and separation proceedings, and a hundred other problems that can arise in everyday life. He or she will appear in the local and regional courts but will most often call in a litigation specialist when any cases go to the higher courts.

The longer your relationship with a lawyer lasts, the better he or she will know you, your family and your affairs. Through the years, a mutual confidence will grow so that problems can be discussed in a relaxed and thorough manner that leads frequently to settlement. The family lawyer tries to keep you and your family out of trouble and out of the courts. If you do get into trouble, he or she will try to get you out of it in the most painless and least expensive manner.

The relationship between you and your lawyer is a fiduciary one—that is, a relationship of trust and confidence—for a lawyer must never let personal interests conflict with those of a client. It is understood in the client relationship that all partners or employes of the lawyer are bound by these same rules of conduct.

The most important obligation your lawyer accepts when you retain counsel (other than to act only in your best interests), is to keep secret all information received from you. You should be able to place unrestricted confidence in your lawyer, secure in the knowledge that anything you say is confidential. This confidence is referred to as "privilege"—and the privilege is yours, not the lawyer's. This means that if you wish your lawyer to disclose any information then he or she may, but must otherwise keep silent.

This privilege applies to face-to-face consultations, telephone conversations, correspondence and any information your lawyer may obtain as a result of any research or investigation done on your

Taking the law to the people

IN A CONVERTED WAREHOUSE among the dilapidated rooming houses of the Parkdale district of Toronto, a "poverty law" experiment has attracted national attention. The front-runner (est. 1971) among Canadian "storefront" legal clinics, the Parkdale center is staffed by students from the Osgoode Hall Law School of York University, under the supervision of lawyers.

Believing that Toronto's disadvantaged citizens needed legal advice in civil matters not covered by the provincial Legal Aid system, the founders successfully sought federal and private grants to take the law to the people without charge. Working among people said to be suspicious of lawyers and courts, the students adopted an informal "neighborhood image." As they won the confidence of their "clients," they gained experience difficult to get in the classroom.

From the record of its first few years, the Parkdale clinic handles mostly domestic troubles, welfare and landlord-tenant difficulties. Sometimes, disturbed people will drop in and it may take several visits before the problem can be defined legally. At one time, the clinic found itself acting for a rooming house proprietor who claimed he couldn't afford a regular lawyer.

There's an old adage that "in a thousand pounds of law there's not an ounce of love." The concerned students of the Parkdale center—some of them now fully fledged lawyers—are trying to prove that's just not true.

behalf. Your lawyer must keep all information secret and must not reveal it—even in court—unless you give consent.

Therefore, you should not hesitate to divulge everything pertaining to your problem to your lawyer—no matter how "personal" it might be or seem to be. You may put complete trust and confidence in your lawyer and his or her firm.

The trial lawyer

In Canada, *all* lawyers are qualified to appear in court, although many do not do so by choice. Those who do appear sometimes find themselves falling into one of two groups: those who do criminal work only and those who do nothing but civil litigation—such as motor vehicle accident suits. Many mix both fields.

If you are in serious trouble, your family lawyer will often send you to a trial lawyer who, because of his experience in court, will be more alert to the fine points of a case and to the subtleties of presenting evidence. Skill in cross-examination as well as precise and persuasive performance before a jury can be decisive.

A recent book suggests that "lawyers should not be picked on the basis of their personal charm. They should be pulled off the rack with the same objectivity with which a big-game hunter selects a rifle."

When you hire a trial lawyer you should think ahead to the eventual contest in the courtroom. Your case will be heard by a judge who must come to a decision based only upon the facts presented to him. If there is a jury, the judge is there to guide and to instruct the jury in the law—but the jury will have the ultimate responsibility of deciding the facts.

The judge hearing your case must at all times remain independent and impartial; and never enter the dispute. Your lawyer is also obliged to act with frankness and fairness, maintain toward the judge a courteous and respectful attitude, and must make sure that you, the client, conduct yourself in a similar manner.

Neither you nor your lawyer must ever try to privately influence, directly or indirectly, the judge or the jury members. The advocate must not let your personal feelings and prejudices influence reason.

Whatever your ill-feelings may be toward the other party, it must not influence your lawyer in his or her conduct toward the lawyer for the opposing party. Your lawyer must, however, be dutiful to you with firmness, and without fear of public unpopularity or disapproval of the court.

In court, every issue must be raised, every argument put forward, and every question asked that your lawyer thinks may help your case. A lawyer must not mislead the court, or make accusations against the other party or witnesses without good reason. Your lawyer must not support or tell a lie; must not say you are innocent if he or she *knows* you are guilty, nor may your lawyer put you in the witness box to tell lies. However, with skill, a lawyer can urge that the other side has not proved its case.

Our trial procedure is, in a sense, based on the medieval joust, or duel. Legal experts refer to it as an "adversary proceeding." It is designed to provide a fair contest in which the adversaries, presumably evenly matched, flail away at each other, using all their sharpest weapons and every tactic in the book. The judge knows all the rules and is, in effect, the referee in the contest.

The antagonists must fight within the traditional rules which declare certain evidence to be inadmissible (for instance, a wife cannot be forced to testify against her husband). Each antagonist brings forward witnesses, who may be sharply questioned. From this "duel," we hope truth and justice will emerge.

The corporation lawyer

The corporation lawyer generally works in the legal department of a large commercial company, and like any employe, receives a salary and is entitled to all company benefits.

The corporation seldom keeps a general counsel on staff, but hires specialists in fields of law that are important to management. The corporation lawyer may never appear in court; this will depend on the kind of company represented. If the lawyer works for, say, a transportation firm, he or she will no doubt appear in court more often than if the firm represented is an investment corporation. Truck drivers will likely be involved in more accidents requiring court appearances than stock-brokers.

A lawyer may decide to join a particular legal firm during the final years at law school, or after being admitted to the Bar, or, perhaps, after several years in practice, will have acquired an expertise in some particular field that is of great value to a certain company. If executive judgment can match legal ability, then, earning power is virtually unlimited.

Lawyers who work as partners in large law firms and who deal only in corporate law are often referred to as corporate lawyers. They specialize in the setting up, financing, and other aspects of organizing and running a corporation.

The patent lawyer

Patent law is a precise area of specialization. The patent lawyer advises clients if their inventions are patentable. Any invention can be patented (*i.e.*, protected for a set period for the inventor's profit) if it has not been known or used by others in Canada before its invention by the applicant. This is established by the rule that the invention must not have been described in any publication anywhere in the world for more than two years prior to the application. The degree of newness is determined by the commissioner of patents. Canada is a member of many international patent and trademark pacts.

Patent law is a highly scientific and technical field and the average lawyer, with his liberal arts or business training, tends to steer clear of it. Of those who do become patent lawyers, many hold science or engineering degrees.

The granting of patents is a federal concern, and most of the firms that handle such work are located in Ottawa where they are in great demand. It usually takes about two and a half years for a patent to be granted. About 23,000 applications for patents are made each year, and about 21,000 are granted.

The tax lawyer

Taxation statutes, for the most part, might as well be written in some ancient, indecipherable language as far as the layperson is concerned. Quite apart from their complexity, they contain many technical terms and phrases understood only by experts. It is a field in which change is so constant that the editors decided against attempting a chapter on tax law. Much of what could be stated as this chapter is written might be obsolete by the time the book left the printer and thus would possibly be more misleading than useful.

Every "revision" of the Income Tax Act increases the need not only for tax accountants but also for tax lawyers. Many of these specialists are involved with corporation law which, to the average citizen, is complicated in the extreme.

Many tax lawyers are active in the field of estate planning. In Quebec, it is their specialty to help arrange estates in such a way that succession duties and gift taxes are kept to a minimum. The almost continuous change and the numbing complexity of taxation law and regulations ensure that these experts will remain busy and prosperous.

In recent years, hundreds of mainstreet offices have opened across Canada, offering to fill in the average man's personal income tax forms for a modest fee. Their commercial success is perhaps the best evidence of the inability of our bureaucracy to formulate a clear and simple tax form.

The labor lawyer

Of the more recent additions to the specialist ranks, one of the most interesting is the labor lawyer. He is an independent who works, on retainer or fee basis, for a trade union or for a corporation in its dealings with a union. He is not a member of the union which he represents.

He may be called upon to argue cases before workers' compensation and labor relations boards and other government agencies. If a brief on trade union interests is to be presented to a parliamentary committee, the labor lawyer may be asked to draft it. He is almost certain to check any new collective bargaining agreement before it is accepted, and he is likely to be found sitting at the bargaining table for key sessions.

How the lawyer is paid

THE CANON OF ETHICS of the Canadian Bar Association states that a lawyer is entitled to "reasonable compensation for his services, but he should avoid charges which either overestimate or undervalue the services rendered. Where possible, he should adhere to the established tariff. The client's ability to pay cannot justify a charge in excess of the value of the services, although his poverty may require a lesser charge or even none at all."

The subject of this "reasonable compensation" paid to lawyers for their services and knowledge is a difficult and delicate aspect of the profession's relationship with the public.

Many people feel that lawyers overcharge. Therefore they are reluctant to discuss their affairs and problems with a lawyer for fear of receiving a large bill. As a result they often suffer from the illegal acts of others, or fail to protect their own rights. While this fear is understandable, it is largely unreasonable today. Certainly, "padding" a bill is not entirely unheard of in our times. But the basic reasons for the public's worry lie more in its general ignorance of how a lawyer actually works, and of the labor and hours that are spent in trying to bring a client's affairs to a satisfactory conclusion.

The amount of time and effort a lawyer puts in on a particular problem or case is seldom obvious to the client. Few can understand how the lawyer can claim to have spent so much expensive time and yet produce such a seemingly small amount of paperwork; or, on the other hand, why he thinks it necessary to produce so much paperwork for what turns out to be such a short trial.

The layperson does not realize the amount of research and knowledge required to produce that short trial, or to prepare an airtight document, and may come to the hurried conclusion that the lawyer is deliberately padding the bill for services rendered.

The same feeling of suspicion can arise when a lawyer is concerned about protecting his client from some wrong which the client fails to see or understand. To the client, this concern of the lawyer appears to be nothing more than a means of increasing the bill. It may not be until sometime later (if at all) that the client realizes that the lawyer was actually doing a real service.

Although it has been said before that a lawyer's time is money, clients still get upset when they realize that the lawyer is billing them even for their telephone conversations, and for the letters written concerning the case. Yet a lawyer has to charge for time spent discussing a problem, whether the meeting is over the phone or face-to-face.

You should remember that the advice you get from a lawyer is based on knowledge acquired only after long years of study and practice. And since it is this knowledge which the lawyer sells, you must be billed for each item upon which time has been spent.

The fee guideline

Canadian lawyers generally do not work within a set schedule of fees, but are guided by a general pattern of charges established both by the Bar association of the city or district in which the lawyer practices, and by the provincial Bar association.

These fee schedules, which might be described as "suggested prices," are available to the public on request from the Bar associations and law societies.

The provincial associations or Legal Aid commissions set down billing rates for routine lawyer services paid for under Legal Aid systems. The county or district association generally suggests a fee for non-courtroom matters, such as wills and codicils (*See* Chapter 9, "Changing your will"), real estate transactions, drawing up separation agreements, and so on. These fees are guidelines only, and it is left to each individual lawyer to decide how to follow them.

Few lawyers charge less than the suggested fee; many charge more. Larger fees are usually charged by those who believe that their reputation and knowledge justify the higher fee. Perhaps they consider that the particular case is more complicated, and therefore more time-consuming, than was contemplated by the fee structure. If you retain one of the better-known and more experienced lawyers in your area, you must expect to pay more than if you go to someone who has just hung out his shingle. The better-known lawyer will most likely have clients clamoring for his time and expertise, and therefore can justify the higher fee for his services.

The fees set by the provincial Bar associations are usually followed to the letter when costs are levied: when, for example, after the trial, the judge awards costs to the successful party. The lawyer for the winning party will then prepare a bill according to the fee schedule and will proceed to have it certified as proper ("taxed," as it is called) by an officer of the court. The amount "taxed" is the amount payable by the losing party to the winning party to cover the costs of the court case. These costs do not, however, cover the entire amount that the successful party will have to pay his or her lawyer, as most lawyers charge more than the scheduled fee for courtroom work (*See* Chapter 3, "Decisions from the Bench").

Lawyers usually keep track of the time they and their associates spend on your problems, but the hourly rates vary from lawyer to lawyer. If your business or case is to be handled on an hourly basis, ask your lawyer for the rate. This will give you a rough idea of how much the procedure will cost. It will be only a rough idea, because it is often difficult for a busy lawyer to estimate the exact time needed to spend on an individual matter. This is one reason lawyers are often hesitant to give an advance estimate of their fees.

Signing the retainer

When you first go to a lawyer, especially if you are to be involved in a court action, the lawyer will often request that you sign a paper authorizing him or her to proceed with the action and to take all steps necessary to bring the matter to the best possible conclusion. By signing the paper, you are hiring, or "retaining," the lawyer to act for you, or on your behalf. The document you sign is called the retainer.

The term "retainer" actually has a number of meanings: (1) the act of authorizing or employing a solicitor or counsel; (2) the document which serves as evidence of such employment; (3) a set fee given to obtain the services of a solicitor or counsel; (4) a deposit to be held on account for the payment of future fees and expenditures.

The retainer mentioned last is the most common type. This money is held by the lawyer as security for the fee—in effect, a down payment—and it is taken into account in the final billing. It can also be recovered from the other side if costs are awarded by the court in a successful action.

The retainer mentioned third is regarded as an outright gift. It is separate from the lawyer's fee and is not included in the final bill. Before a lawyer can regard money paid in advance as a gift, he or she must fully explain the meaning of that kind of retainer to you. As the payment of a retainer is wholly voluntary, a promise to pay a retainer cannot be enforced. A lawyer who receives money on your behalf is not entitled to keep any of that money to cover a sum which you had promised to pay as a retainer. The money must be specifically given as a retainer to the lawyer.

Retainers are ended by the death, insanity or bankruptcy of either the client or the lawyer. Since your lawyer acts with your authority, he or she has to pay any expense which may be incurred after your death or other disability, even if the knowledge of this cost had not been previously foreseen.

Unless you have specifically agreed otherwise, your lawyer cannot demand a fee until the end of the lawsuit. If you end the retainer—for instance, if you fire your lawyer—before the end of the suit, your lawyer can then immediately ask for the fee and sue you, the client, if the payment is not forthcoming.

Since it is the client, and not the lawyer, who is in charge of the action, the client can fire a lawyer and carry on with the case as he or she sees fit. The client cannot, however, fire a lawyer and carry on with the case if the sole purpose in doing so is to avoid paying the lawyer's fee. If the judge decided that this was the client's intention, he or she would order full payment of the lawyer's fee.

A formal retainer is not necessary to establish a solicitor-client relationship. It is generally advisable, however, so as to provide clear evidence of the relationship and of your lawyer's authority to proceed on your behalf.

What lawyers charge

IT IS IMPOSSIBLE to provide an accurate "price list" of the cost of legal services in Canada—there are just too many variables. Apart from the complexities of cases and the multitude of circumstances, costs vary depending on the part of the country you are in. Rents for legal offices in downtown Toronto, for example, are rather higher than those in such smaller centres as Truro, Thompson or Teslin. The vastly experienced Queen's Counsel has an obvious right to charge more than the newly qualified lawyer.

In conformity with general guidelines laid down by the Canadian Bar Association, the many county, district (and even city-wide) associations of lawyers have drawn up their own schedules of fees, covering cases and transactions of "average complexity." These do not bind the individual lawyer. They do not include disbursements of any kind, and seldom include time charges incurred for conference or the preparation and filing of statutory documents.

The following "average" charges have been based on the 1982 suggested fee schedule of the County of York Law Association (which includes Toronto):

REAL ESTATE. Purchase or sale of a residential property (from search of title to completion): $500 for the first $50,000 of the sale price, plus ¼ to ½ of 1 percent of the next $50,000 to $200,000. On any excess over $200,000, an additional fee may be charged.

MORTGAGE. Preparation of first mortgage, the same percentage rate as above (if a prior mortgage has to be paid off, the fee may increase). When a lawyer arranges the mortgage and the purchase, the charge is more than this amount, but not twice as much.

WILLS, LEASES. Preparation of simple wills and codicils, $75. Drawing up a non-commercial lease, $125; reviewing a non-commercial lease for the lessee, $75.

AGREEMENTS, etc. Adoption papers, $500; power of attorney, $75; assignment or release documents, $50; short letter, $10; oaths, including affidavits, $45; Income tax returns, $75.

BUSINESS. Purchase and sale of a business: where no trustee is appointed, 2 percent on the first $50,000, plus 1 percent on excess over $50,000, up to $100,000. On excess over $100,000, additional fees may be charged. Where a trustee is appointed, 3 percent on the first $50,000, plus 2 percent on excess over $50,000, up to $100,000. On excess over $100,000, additional fees may be charged.

Hiring the specialist

The hourly charge that the lawyer will make is only one of the factors to be considered when you retain counsel. If you have a difficult problem involving a certain area of law—for instance, income tax, estate planning, business organization—you are usually better off to go to a lawyer who specializes in that particular field, rather than to a general or family lawyer.

Although the specialist will no doubt charge more than the family lawyer, he or she will probably be able to solve your problem in a shorter time being well versed in the subject. In the end, the fee will often be the same as—or perhaps less than—that of a lawyer with no expertise in that field of practice.

The size of the fee in each case will depend upon the nature or difficulty of the legal problems. Some lawyers, particularly specialists, are reluctant to discuss fees with clients, because so often it is almost impossible for them to assess all the problems in advance. They may see the likelihood of many hours of research ahead. Experience with similar cases may warn them of possible complications.

Nevertheless, you should try to reach some understanding with your lawyer about how you are going to be charged and approximately how much the final account is likely to be. This precaution can lessen the chance of some breathtaking shocks later on.

Sharing the proceeds

Most Canadian lawyers are allowed to make a contingency-fee arrangement—that is, a fee determined as a percentage of the total amount recovered in an action. Under this system, the percentage (often about 20 percent) is set before the case is begun. If the lawyer is successful, he or she will receive the share of the money awarded, plus out-of-pocket expenses. If the action is unsuccessful, the lawyer will receive expenses and costs and little, if any, other payment. (In New Brunswick, an unsuccessful lawyer is not paid expenses.)

The higher the award, the greater the lawyer's fee—and it is for this reason that

most Canadian provinces, following the British rather than the American view, once frowned on the practice.

Today, contingency fees are prohibited only in the provinces of Ontario and Newfoundland. In Saskatchewan, contingency-fee arrangements are only permitted in personal injury claims arising from automobile accidents. New Brunswick permits contingency fees if the client cannot pay, or if it is foreseen that the client will be unable to pay.

It is felt by some that the lawyer taking an action on a contingency basis really becomes a partner of the client and ceases to be an independent adviser. Opponents of this kind of fee believe that this is not in the best interests of the courts, or of the public.

Contingency fees may also tend to encourage legal action, leading to what is often called "ambulance chasing." Bar associations stand ready to move strongly against any member engaged in clearly unethical behavior.

Anyone not involved in a suit is prohibited from contributing funds to finance the legal action with the understanding that he or she will share in any proceeds or property won in a successful case. The ancient term "champerty" is applied to such illegal contracts.

Although contingency-fee arrangements are permitted in all cases in Alberta, they must be filed in writing with the clerk of the court to make them binding. In New Brunswick, such arrangements must be approved by the Registrar of the Court of Queen's Bench.

In Manitoba, contingency-fee arrangements are permissible but are closely supervised by the courts. Each arrangement or contract must be presented to a judge of the Queen's Bench for approval. The judge determines whether the proposed arrangement is fair to the client.

Those Canadian lawyers prohibited from charging contingency fees can, however, work for a fee based on results—that is, compensation based on the value of the services rendered and the benefits received by the client. While this may sound like practically the same thing, the fee is actually determined *after* the services are performed, unlike the contingency fee which is fixed and agreed to before anything is done.

How to get Legal Aid

If you cannot afford to hire a lawyer, you need not despair. All provinces maintain a Legal Aid service which will provide you with free, or partly free, legal aid. Each province guarantees a lawyer to everyone who cannot afford to pay without depriving self or dependents of the reasonable necessities of life or sacrificing any small capital assets he or she might have saved.

Modest capital assets may disqualify you from Legal Aid, although help may still be given on a "pay later" basis, either fully or partially, depending on the amount of the assets. Only in Quebec and Prince Edward Island are Legal Aid clients not expected to make any financial contribution. Manitoba requires a small flat-rate user fee, which is often waived in cases of financial hardship. Elsewhere, the Legal Aid client, depending on his circumstances, may be required to contribute. In Ontario, for example, all applicants for Legal Aid are given what amounts to a "needs test" (that is, their ability to pay is examined) by a government social worker. Assets such as a mortgaged house often rule out free assistance. Even so, in a recent financial year, Ontario taxpayers had to meet a bill of over $46 million for their provincial legal aid plan.

In many provincial courts (except in the provinces of Nova Scotia, Prince Edward Island and Saskatchewan), both family and criminal, there is a lawyer called a "duty counsel," to whom you can speak before appearing in court. This counselor is there to assist you to understand your rights and to help if you do not have your own lawyer. If you are eligible for Legal Aid, this lawyer will provide assistance in helping you fill out the application form.

Depending on the province, you may have the right to choose your own lawyer. In Ontario, Quebec, New Brunswick, Manitoba and the Yukon, you may pick a lawyer from those on the Legal Aid list. In Prince Edward Island, Nova Scotia, Saskatchewan, Alberta and the Northwest Territories, a lawyer will usually be assigned to you. Newfoundland and British Columbia will allow you to select a lawyer if you so request.

To find out whether you qualify for Legal Aid, you should contact the nearest Legal Aid Society and explain first of all why you need a lawyer and, secondly, your financial situation. If you do not qualify for Legal Aid and you happen to live near a university with a law school, you might be able to get help from a student law clinic. These services are often partially funded by the provincial Legal Aid plan or the provincial law society. Even if the students cannot appear for you in court, they inform you of your rights and the law covering your problem.

A list of the addresses of all Legal Aid offices in Canada is printed at the end of this book.

Out-of-pocket costs

When a lawyer sends out a final bill, he or she will charge you for all the out-of-pocket expenses, commonly called "disbursements," that have been incurred. For example, if you are buying a house, you will have to pay your lawyer for the cost of searching the title to your house, the cost of registering your deed, including any other expenses incurred—such as long-distance phone calls and even postage stamps.

In a court matter, expenses include the cost of issuing a writ and having it served, and all other costs involved in bringing the action to trial.

The disbursements will be listed separately in the account sent to you by your lawyer, and are naturally in addition to the fee.

If the bill isn't paid

If you refuse to pay your lawyer's bill, he or she has various remedies open. You may be sued for recovery of fees, charges and disbursements. If the suit is successful, then you will be stuck with another set of costs, as the court will hold you responsible for the lawyer's cost in collecting the account.

The lawyer may also keep property of yours that he or she may have in possession until the debt is paid. However, if there is a third party with a legitimate interest in the possessions held by the lawyer, the lawyer must relinquish them to this third party. Otherwise, he or she is entitled to hold them until the bill is paid in full.

If your lawyer recovers personal property for you under a judgment, he may ask the court to hold the property as security for his unpaid fee. The lawyer's claim on this property covers only the cost of the proceedings concerned, not unpaid fees relating to other matters. If money in a settlement has been paid to the court for transfer to the client, the lawyer who has not been paid may ask the court not to pay the client until he, the lawyer, has been notified.

A lawyer may also have his or her bills "taxed" by the court. When the lawyer is "taxing" bills, he or she is, in effect, asking the court to declare that the charges to the client are perfectly proper in view of the results achieved and the difficulty involved.

Once the bill has been approved, the lawyer may proceed to issue a writ against the lands and goods of the client by which he or she has the right to instruct the sheriff of the county to seize possessions of the nonpaying client. Fur-thermore, the lawyer has the right to garnishee, or seize, the client's wages for nonpayment of a legal account. (*See* Chapter 7, "If you can't pay.")

If you receive a bill from your lawyer that, for whatever reason, you feel is too high, you can apply to the provincial law society to have it reviewed; you may also apply to have the bill "taxed" (that is, checked) at the local courthouse. (In Quebec, if you feel your account is unreasonable, you must take it to the trustee of the Quebec Bar Association rather than to the courts.) The rules applying to this procedure vary from province to province, but usually the lawyer concerned must be given notice of your intention to "tax" so that he has the chance of defending his charges. You will probably have to pay a modest fee to have your bill looked into and evaluated, and for notice to be sent to your lawyer.

To avoid any of these unhappy situations, ask your lawyer (when you first talk to him) for the approximate cost of handling your problem, and the likely total of any disbursements he will be required to make on your behalf. Then, if you feel that the fee is going to be higher than you can afford, you can either try to work out an arrangement for a deposit and time payment, or look for other alternatives. In other words, check the depth of the river before you dive in.

When the bill was padded

BACK IN THE SEVENTEENTH CENTURY, Francis Bacon said, "As for lawyer's fees, I must leave it to the conscience and merit of the lawyer." In the nineteenth century, Abraham Lincoln, when paid $25 for a legal fee, sent back $10, chiding his client for being far too generous with his money.

In Canada today, anyone who believes his lawyer's bill is padded can take it to the courts for checking (it's called "taxing"). On occasion, this has paid off spectacularly. In 1972, the taxing office of the On-tario Supreme Court reduced one bill from $24,000 to $4,000.

The case in question concerned the negotiation of a separation agreement between a woman and her wealthy husband. The court official stated that lawyers are not entitled to share in the wealth of a client, but could charge only a reasonable fee for services rendered.

In other words, lawyers can't charge "what the traffic will bear." This is made clear in the Canadian Bar Association's Canon of Ethics.

Canada's lawyer leaders

Ten of Canada's 15 prime ministers have been lawyers. Here they are:

John A. Macdonald (1815–1891)

Articled as a law student at 15, Macdonald practiced in Kingston, Ont., and willingly acted for the defense in unpopular cases. Turning to politics, he eventually became the leading exponent of Confederation and Canada's first prime minister. A Conservative, he served in 1867–1873 and 1878–1891.

John Abbott (1821–1893)

A graduate of McGill University, where he was later dean of law, Abbott was an authority on commercial law and was closely involved with the CPR during its construction. He served 14 years as a member of Parliament and became Conservative prime minister in 1891 while a senator. He resigned in 1892 due to illness.

John Thompson (1844–1894)

A former Nova Scotia attorney general, premier and supreme court judge, Thompson became federal justice minister in 1885. He revised and codified Canada's criminal law and was named Conservative prime minister in 1892. His sudden death cut short a promising career.

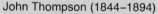

Wilfrid Laurier (1841–1919)

A graduate of McGill University, Laurier practiced law in Montreal and Arthabaska, Que., before becoming a member of Parliament in 1874. He was a stirring orator in the cause of tolerance and understanding, and was Liberal prime minister from 1896 to 1911.

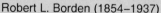

Robert L. Borden (1854–1937)

Turning to law after six years as a school teacher, Borden practiced in Halifax and became president of the Barristers' Society of Nova Scotia. Conservative prime minister from 1911 to 1920, he insisted on a distinct role for Canadian forces during World War I.

Arthur Meighen (1874–1960)

After teaching school in his native Ontario, and practicing law in Portage la Prairie, Man., Meighen entered Parliament in 1908 and became solicitor general in 1913. He served as Conservative prime minister in 1920–21 and again for 89 days at the time of the 1926 constitutional crisis.

R. B. Bennett (1870–1947)

After teaching school and practicing law in his native New Brunswick, Bennett moved to Calgary in 1897 and became a successful corporation lawyer. Conservative prime minister from 1930 to 1935, he struggled to guide Canada through the great Depression. Later, he became a viscount.

Louis St. Laurent (1882–1973)

A successful corporation lawyer, St. Laurent had also taught law and headed the Quebec Bar and the Canadian Bar Association. He became Liberal justice minister and attorney general in 1941 and was prime minister from 1948 to 1957, helping make the Supreme Court Canada's court of final appeal.

John Diefenbaker (1895–1979)

Born in Ontario, Diefenbaker moved to Saskatchewan in 1903 and became a brilliant defense lawyer following army service in World War I. Conservative prime minister from 1957 to 1963, he introduced the Bill of Rights and in 1958 led his party to the biggest majority in Canadian political history.

Pierre Trudeau (b.1919)

A graduate of the University of Montreal, Trudeau specialized in labor and civil liberties cases as a practicing lawyer, and also taught law. First elected to Parliament as a Liberal in 1965, he became justice minister and attorney general in 1967 and prime minister the following year. Trudeau remained in power for 16 years, except for a 9-month interval in 1979–80, when the Conservatives formed a minority government.

865

Where to apply for Legal Aid

In every province and territory of Canada, the advice or active assistance of a qualified lawyer is available to all who can demonstrate a genuine need. If an applicant can't afford the minimum scale of fees, the lawyer's bill will be paid through state-aided funds. Under most of the provincial Legal Aid plans, he will be required to disclose details of his financial standing; once a request is approved, the legal action will be carried forward without charges as far as our system of law provides—even to the Supreme Court of Canada.

Anyone who may have need of this assistance can write to the relevant provincial office, as set out below:

ALBERTA

Suite 401, Melton Building
10310 Jasper Avenue
Edmonton, Alberta   T5J 2W4

BRITISH COLUMBIA

Legal Services Society
Box 12120
555 West Hastings Street
Vancouver
British Columbia   V6B 4N6

MANITOBA

Legal Aid Society of Manitoba
325 Portage Avenue
Winnipeg, Manitoba   R3B 2B9

NEW BRUNSWICK

Legal Aid New Brunswick
Box 666
Fredericton, New Brunswick   E3B 5B4

NEWFOUNDLAND

Newfoundland Legal Aid Commission
21 Church Hill
St. John's, Newfoundland   A1C 3Z8

NOVA SCOTIA

Nova Scotia Legal Aid Commission
5212 Sackville Street
Suite 301
Halifax, Nova Scotia   B3J 1K6

ONTARIO

Ontario Legal Aid Plan
145 King Street West
Suite 1000
Toronto, Ontario   M5H 3L7

PRINCE EDWARD ISLAND

Public Defender
42 Water Street
Box 2200
Charlottetown
Prince Edward Island   C1A 8B9

QUEBEC

Commission des services juridiques
(Legal Services Commission)
2 Complexe Desjardins
Tour de l'Est, Bureau 1404
Montréal, Québec   H5B 1B3

SASKATCHEWAN

Saskatchewan Legal Aid Commission
311 21st Street East
Saskatoon, Saskatchewan   S7K 0C1

NORTHWEST TERRITORIES

Legal Services Board of the
   Northwest Territories
Box 1320
Yellowknife
Northwest Territories   X1A 2L9

YUKON

Legal Aid
Department of Justice
Box 2703
Whitehorse, Yukon   Y1A 2C6

An A.B.C. of Canadian law

Abandonment: permanently giving up property or a right.

Abate: reduce or remove; to abate a nuisance is to remove or destroy the thing that causes it.

Abduction: taking away a person by force or persuasion, usually a wife, child or ward.

Abet: aid in the commission of a crime; incite or encourage someone to crime.

Ab initio: Latin—"from the beginning"; if a marriage was unlawful *ab initio*, it never had any validity.

Abortion: removal or expulsion of a human fetus from the womb before it is capable of sustaining independent life.

Abrogate: to annul, repeal or cancel; a former rule or custom can be abrogated.

Abscond: to leave the jurisdiction of a court in order to avoid legal action or process; a debtor who conceals himself from his creditors is absconding.

Absentee: in Quebec, a person domiciled in the province who has disappeared.

Abstract of title: condensed history of the title to a unit of land, recording conveyances, transfers, liabilities, covenants or liens against the property.

Acceleration clause: a clause in a contract whereby when one installment is not paid on its due date, the remaining installments become due immediately.

Accession: legal acquisition by an owner of something added to his property; coming into possession of a right or office.

Accessory: a person who contributes or aids in the commission of a crime.

Accomplice: someone who takes part in the commission of a crime, either as a principal or as an accessory.

Accusation: a formal charge against a person to the effect that he has committed a punishable offense, laid before a court or magistrate having jurisdiction to inquire into the alleged crime.

Accused: a person charged with a crime; the defendant.

Acquit: to set free by verdict or other legal process; to release from a criminal charge.

Act: a law or statute; an exercise of power.

Acte: a document or solemn written deed in French law.

Action: a legal process or suit, taken to enforce or protect a right, to redress or prevent a wrong; a civil lawsuit is termed an action. In French commercial law, a share in a corporation.

Actionable: furnishing legal grounds for an action; one speaks of an actionable tort.

Act of God: an unforeseeable accident due to natural causes beyond human control, which could not have been avoided by foresight; an earthquake, for example.

Ad curiam vocare: Latin— "to summon to court."

Ad damnum: Latin—"to the damage"; technical term for that part of a writ which states the damages demanded by a plaintiff.

Ademption: the withdrawal of a legacy by the testator of a will; equivalent to a revocation.

Adjournment: postponing or suspending the sitting of a court or other session, temporarily or indefinitely.

Adjournment sine die: an adjournment "without a day" set for another meeting; an indefinite postponement.

Adjudicataire: a purchaser at a sheriff's sale (Quebec).

Adjure: to put under oath; to bind a person under some penalty; entreat solemnly.

Admiralty law: the law of the sea.

Admissible: relevant and proper to be introduced in court as evidence or testimony; allowable as judicial proof.

Adult: one who has attained the age of majority (from 18 to 21 years, depending on provincial law); only adults have full competence to enter into contracts or undertake a legal action on their own behalf.

Adultery: voluntary sexual love between a married person and someone who is not that person's husband or wife; adultery is not a crime in Canada but is a matrimonial offense and grounds for divorce.

Adversary proceeding: part of the basic system of trial in which each side presents its version of the facts and the law for impartial consideration before judge and/or jury.

Advisory opinion: given by a judge or a court on a legal question submitted by a government official, a legislative body or any interested party.

Advocate: anyone who defends or pleads the cause of another person, especially before a tribunal or court; a lawyer (in Quebec: *avocat*).

Affiant: the person who swears out an affidavit.

Affidavit: a voluntary, sworn and signed statement made upon oath before an officer authorized to receive and administer oaths.

Agarder: to sentence, award, or determine (Quebec).

Age of consent: the age at which one is legally competent to give consent, especially to marriage or sexual intercourse.

Alias: Latin—"otherwise"; an assumed name.

Alibi: Latin—"elsewhere"; the defense put forward by an accused that he was "elsewhere" when the crime was committed.

Alienable: transferable; those (rights) that can be transferred to another.

Alienation of affection: the deprivation of the love and affection normally received by a husband or wife in a marital relationship; often caused by the actions of a third party.

Alimony: sustenance or support of a wife (or husband) by the divorced husband (or wife); also paid during a legal separation; the payment usually ceases on remarriage of the supported person.

All and singular: "all without exception"; term used in the writing of wills.

Allegation: a charge or assertion; an accusation in a trial.

Amendment: an alteration, modification or change of motion before a meeting, or of a law already passed or being discussed in a legislature; the correction of an error or defect in any process or proceeding at law.

Amicus curiae: Latin— "friend of the court"; usually a lawyer who provides information for the assistance of the court; a person who, although he has no right to appear in a suit, is allowed to introduce evidence or arguments to protect his interests.

Amnesty: a general pardon granted by a government to persons guilty of an offense (often a political offense).

Amortization: the payment of a debt (particularly a mortgage) by means of periodic payments.

Anarchy: lawlessness, political disorder or nonrecognition of authority; a state in which

there is neither law nor supreme power.

Annuity: a yearly fixed amount of money—granted, bequeathed or contracted for —payable for life or for a specified period; one entitled to receive an annuity is called an annuitant.

Annulment: the act of making something legally void retroactively; when something is annulled, it is as though it never existed.

Antedate: to date a document at a point before the writing.

Antenuptial settlement (or contract): an agreement made before marriage in which the property rights of either or both marriage partners are set out or determined.

Appeal: the legal process of asking a higher court to review a decision of a lower court; basis of an appeal is usually either that injustice was done or that an error was committed at law.

Appearance: the act of coming into court or into the record of a proceeding (in person or represented by a lawyer) by a party to a lawsuit.

Appearance notice: in Canadian bail law, a notice issued by a peace officer to a person not yet formally charged with an offense, requiring him to appear in court at a specific time.

Appellant: the party in a court action who is responsible for taking an appeal against the decision to a higher court.

Appellate court: a court that has the power to review judgments given in lower courts; the Supreme Court of Canada is the highest appellate court.

Appraise: to estimate the value of any property; to set a price upon a house or land.

Appreciation (in value): used in property law to describe an increase in value not the result of added buildings or improvements.

Apprehension: arrest, seizure or taking into custody of a person to answer a criminal charge.

Appropriation: the setting aside of money for a specific purpose.

A priori: Latin—"from what is before"; used to describe an argument that proceeds from cause to effect, or from an assumption to its logical conclusion.

Arbitrate: to settle a dispute by referring it to a neutral person or persons whose decision the contestants have agreed to accept; the process itself is called arbitration.

Arraign: to bring a prisoner into court to answer a charge made against him.

Arrest: to stop, take, apprehend and hold a person by legal authority.

Arson: the act of willfully and maliciously setting fire to another person's house, automobile, woods, etc.; also setting fire to one's own property with the intention of defrauding an insurance company.

Assault: an intentional threat, attempt or application of force to another person which might cause injury.

Assessment: valuation of real estate for taxation purpose; the estimation of damages by a jury in a civil action; the person who makes assessments is known as an assessor.

Assets: the funds and property of a person, a corporation or an estate; the worth of a person's property as contrasted to his debts or liabilities.

Assign: to transfer goods, money, property or rights usually by deed; the recipient is the assignee; the person who makes the assignment is the assignor.

Assizes: sessions or sittings of certain criminal courts.

Assured: in general, the individual in whose favor an insurance policy is issued.

Asylum: as in "political asylum"—refuge that may be given by one state to a fugitive from another; an institution for the care of the mentally ill.

At law: according to law; as the law states or rules.

At sight: in law, indicating that a bill of exchange is payable when seen; three days' grace are usually allowed.

Attachment: taking or seizing persons or property into the custody of the law by a summons or writ; a writ of attachment may be issued before a case has been tried.

Attainder: the loss of all civil rights as a result of being convicted of treason or certain other major felonies.

Attestation: the act of bearing witness to the execution of a document, confirmed by the signature of the witness.

Attested copy: a certified copy of a document; can normally be used as the legal equivalent of the original.

Attorney: one who is appointed or authorized to act in the place of another person; in United States usage, a lawyer. The federal Minister of Justice is Attorney General for the Queen in Canada.

Attractive nuisance: any machine, apparatus or condition that is potentially dangerous to young children and may attract them onto the owner's property; if they are injured, the owner may be held responsible.

Autopsy: dissection of a body to ascertain cause of death; same as post mortem.

Autrefois acquit and autrefois convict: (from French) a defense to a criminal prosecution in which the accused pleads that he has already been acquitted or convicted of that very crime at a former time.

Averment: an offer to prove or justify a plea in court; an allegation of fact.

Bad faith: implying fraud or intention to deceive; refusal to fulfill a contract from questionable motives.

Bail: security in cash or in promise given to procure the release from custody of a person under arrest and to assure that he will appear when required. To leave goods in trust with another party; the person to whom property is entrusted is termed the bailee and the person who entrusts the goods is called the bailor.

Bailiff: a court officer who engages in serving and executing writs, summonses and other legal documents; in court he keeps order, seats witnesses and guards the jury.

Bankrupt: a person or company that cannot pay due debts and has been adjudged bankrupt by the court.

Bar: originally a railing across the courtroom separating the judges and jury from the public; all the members of the legal profession must be formally "admitted to the Bar."

Barratry: frequently provoking suits and quarrels; any intentional and unlawful act by the master or crew of a ship, whereby the owners sustain injury.

Bastard: an illegitimate child.

Battery: assailing with blows; the unlawful use of force by one person upon another; in the term "assault and battery," battery is the actual use of force.

Beneficiary: the recipient under a will or trust deed; the person to whom the proceeds of an insurance policy are payable.

Bequest: a gift of property in a will; the term is often used synonymously with legacy.

Bestiality: sexual intercourse by either man or woman with any animal.

Betroth: to promise to marry or give in marriage.

Bigamy: willfully contracting a second marriage when the first marriage has never been dissolved through annulment or divorce, or ended by death.

Bill: the draft of a proposed law submitted to parliament for enactment (sometimes the statute itself); any formal declaration, statement in law or petition; a commercial paper detailing the value of goods or services bought or sold; a negotiable instrument.

Bill of exchange: a negotiable instrument, such as the cheque, promissory note or draft; formally, "an unconditional order in writing, addressed by one person to another, signed by the person giving it, requiring the person to whom it is addressed to pay on demand or at a fixed or determinable future time a certain sum in money to, or to the order of, a specified person or to bearer."

Bill of rights: a formal declaration of the fundamental freedoms and rights of individuals; the Canadian Bill of Rights was enacted in 1960, and the Charter of Rights and Freedoms, the first part of the Canadian Constitution, in 1982; the U.S. Bill of Rights is made up of the first ten amendments to the American Constitution.

Blackmail: any payment enforced by intimidation, particularly by threatened attack on a person's reputation.

Blank endorsement: the writing by the endorser of his name, and nothing else, on a bill of exchange or other negotiable instrument.

Bona fide: Latin—"in good faith"; genuine, without any element of dishonesty or fraud.

Bond: evidence of a debt; a written promise to pay another a certain sum of money at a specified time; an interest-bearing certificate of debt issued by a corporation or government; an obligation to do or to abstain from doing a certain act; as applied to Customs, to place dutiable goods in a bonded warehouse, in which case the property becomes "bonded goods," releasable on payment of tariff duties.

Bootlegging: illegal manufacture, possession, transportation and sale of liquor.

Breach: the breaking of a law or contract; a violation or infringement.

Breach of the peace: causing a disturbance; violent or disorderly behavior.

Breach of promise: breaking a promise which may constitute a breach of contract; breach of promise to marry can be grounds of a suit for damages.

Breaking and entering: entering "a place" (house, office, etc.) with intent to commit an offense; it is not essential that force be used in "breaking."

Bribery: offering, giving, soliciting or receiving something of value in an attempt to influence the action of a person in a position of trust—for instance, a public official.

Brief: a summary of a client's case drawn up by a lawyer for use in the conduct of a court action; any condensed statement or summary.

Burden of proof: the necessity or duty to prove a disputed fact as required by the laws of evidence.

Burglary: breaking and entering of premises with intent to commit a crime.

Calendar: a schedule of the cases to be tried or heard in a court; a "calendar day" has 24 hours.

Calumny: slander; false and malicious misrepresentation; detraction.

Canon law: rules and doctrines adopted by church authorities; law of the Roman Catholic Church as published in the *Codex juris canonici.*

Carnal knowledge: sexual intercourse; usually refers to illegal intercourse between a man and a female who is under 16.

Case: an action or suit at law.

Causing a disturbance: a summary conviction offense

which is committed by disturbing other persons; by fighting, screaming, shouting, swearing, singing or being drunk in or near a public place.

C.A.V.: abbreviation for "curia advisari vult"; Latin—"the court will consider."

Caveat: Latin—"let him beware"; a means by which one qualifies or points out a condition in a statement. Also a notice given by a party that he will produce a formal objection to an act, proceeding or document, especially an attack on the validity of an alleged will.

Caveat emptor: Latin—"let the buyer beware"; the buyer has some responsibility to examine the goods he has purchased for defects.

Certification (of a union): the official recognition of a union giving it the right to represent a specific bargaining unit in collective bargaining with employers.

Certiorari: a writ from a higher court to a lower court, directing that a certified record of a named case be sent up for review; usually issued on a complaint by someone that he had not received justice in the lower court.

Champerty: sharing in the proceeds of litigation; usually arises when an outside party agrees to bear the expense of a lawsuit in consideration of receiving a share of the damages.

Chattel: an item of personal property; any kind of property except real estate.

Chattel mortgage: a mortgage on personal property; conditional transfer of ownership as security for a debt or obligation which leaves the goods, the chattel, in the possession of the debtor.

Choses in action: items of property of no intrinsic value, such as debts, mortgages, insurance policies, bills of exchange, not in actual possession but recoverable by a suit at law.

Circuit court: a court whose jurisdiction extends over several districts, counties or territories. The sessions of such courts are usually held alternately in each separate area of the jurisdiction.

Circumstantial evidence: the facts and circumstances providing reasonable grounds for inferring the existence of other connected facts; indirect evidence.

Citation: a formal reference to published judgments, statutes or legal authorities, quoted to establish or support a legal argument.

Citizen's arrest: an arrest which may be made by anyone without warrant in circumstances (among others) where the suspect is found committing an indictable offense.

Civil action: a lawsuit that deals with private, or civil, rights and obligations.

Civil Code: the Civil Code of the Province of Quebec, which in 2,715 Articles lays down civil and commercial law.

Civil law: that part of the law which deals with the exposition and enforcement of civil rights and obligations, as distinguished from criminal law.

Class action: a lawsuit on behalf of a group of persons who are similarly situated or have suffered a similar wrong; also, a representative action.

Clemency: mercy, leniency.

Codicil: an addition or postscript to a will that alters or explains the original document.

Codification: the recording and collection of the laws of a province or country into written form.

Coexecutor: a person named in a will to perform the duties of an executor in cooperation with another.

Cohabitation: living together as husband and wife; often used in reference to persons not married.

Collateral relations: relations who descend from one

common ancestor, not from one another, *e.g.,* brothers, cousins.

Collusion: a secret agreement or understanding, usually in the course of fraud or deceit; trickery; underhand scheming.

Combines: groups of companies or persons acting together illegally for the purpose of price fixing or restraining free competition.

Commercial law: the wide-ranging body of law governing all commerce, trade and merchandising.

Commit: to perpetrate or perform, as in "commit a crime"; to give in charge; entrust.

Common law: the great bulk of the law which is not written in statutes but based on custom and court decisions of the past; especially, the ancient unwritten law of England as inherited by Canada, among many other countries.

Common-law marriage: an agreement between a man and a woman to live together as husband and wife without a formal marriage ceremony of any kind.

Community of acquests: in Quebec, property acquired by married couples which remains separate to each partner as long as they remain married.

Community property: property belonging jointly to husband and wife.

Comparative negligence: occurring in a civil lawsuit, when the negligence (or fault) of the plaintiff as well as that of the defendant is taken into account in assessing damages.

Compensation: payment for services; recompense for loss or damage; indemnification; in the Civil Code, the automatic extinguishing of mutual debts.

Complaint: a statement of grievance or injury made to a court; the record (declaration) setting forth the plain-tiff's action; an accusation or charge; the person who lays a complaint is called the complainant.

Concealment: the withholding, or hiding of something that the law requires one to reveal.

Conclusive evidence: evidence so strong and convincing that it establishes the point in question beyond reasonable doubt; incontrovertible proof.

Concurrent: running together or in conjunction; as in two prison sentences being served concurrently, or simultaneously.

Conditional sale: a contract where the title to the goods concerned will not pass to the purchaser until a certain condition is fulfilled; in a purchase by installments, the condition would be full payment.

Condonation: the action of a husband or wife in forgiving a transgression by the resumption of cohabitation; the pardoning or remission of an offense.

Confession: acknowledging guilt, fault, weakness; voluntary admission before a proper authority of the truth of a statement of charge.

Confidential communication: private discussions such as between husband and wife, or lawyer and client, which cannot be required to be divulged in court.

Confiscate: to appropriate private property for the use of the public; to take away someone's property as a penalty, without compensation.

Conjugal: matrimonial; the relationship of husband and wife; conjugal rights cover the enjoyment by the married couple of each other's company, comfort and society.

Connivance: secret or indirect consent to another's wrongful or criminal act; shutting one's eyes to something; tacit encouragement by not condemning; a voluntary blindness.

Consanguinity: blood relationship; the relationship by descent from a common ancestry, as distinguished from affinity or relationship by marriage.

Consecutive sentences: sentences which are imposed on a criminal so as to run one immediately after another.

Consortium: the right of a husband or wife to the care, affection and company of the other partner in the marriage relationship; same as conjugal rights.

Conspiracy: an agreement between two or more persons to do something criminal, illegal or antisocial; a union or combination for some such end or purpose.

Consummate: to perfect; to complete a marriage by sexual intercourse.

Contempt of court: disobedience of the orders and authority of the court; disregard or disrespect for the dignity of the court; punishable by sentence of imprisonment.

Continuance: adjournment of the proceedings in a case from one day to another.

Contraband: illegal or prohibited possession; goods that by law or treaty may not be imported or exported.

Contract: a legally enforceable agreement by two or more competent parties to do some legal act for good consideration.

Contributory negligence: usually refers to an act or omission of the plaintiff to an action by which he is found partially responsible for his own misfortune.

Conversion: illegal appropriation to one's own use of the property of another; wrongful keeping, disposal or use of property originally received in a legal way.

Convey: to transfer property from one person to another; the deed or instrument under seal by which property is transferred is called a conveyance.

Conviction: declaration of guilt after trial.

Copyright: the author's exclusive right of ownership of a literary, artistic or musical property for a term of years (usually his lifetime and 50 years thereafter); an intangible but assignable right granted by statute for the exclusive multiplying (or copying) of the work.

Corespondent: in divorce, a person charged with having committed adultery with the respondent husband or wife.

Corollary relief: an award in a divorce action involving matters incidental to the divorce, such as alimony, custody of children.

Coroner: county or municipal medical officer whose main duty today is the investigation of the cause of deaths that occur in accident or through violence and with some suspicion attached.

Corpus delicti: Latin—"the body of the crime"; generally referring to the body of the victim in a murder.

Corroborate: to support or confirm; to strengthen; to give credibility to evidence by furnishing further evidence.

Costs: a successful party in a civil action may get reimbursement of reasonable costs he had incurred; at the discretion of the judge, these include lawyer's fees on established scale; the loser normally pays such costs; a successful defendant in a criminal case is expected to pay the costs of his defense.

Counterclaim: a claim presented by a defendant to reduce or oppose the plaintiff's claim; if the plaintiff's claim failed, judgment could be given on the counterclaim as if it were a separate action.

Court: ancient term deriving from the courtyard of the king or his barons where justice was meted out; the judge and courtroom officials taken together.

Court-martial: a judicial body made up of military officers for the trial of military offenses; or for the administration of martial law.

Court of last resort: popular reference to a final court, from which there is no appeal; the Supreme Court of Canada.

c.r.: in Quebec, *conseil de la Reine* (or *du Roi*); same as Queen's (or King's) Counsel.

Crime: the breach of a law designed to protect society; violation of the terms of the Canadian Criminal Code; an offense against the Crown, or state.

Criminal: a person who has been legally convicted of a crime.

Cross action: when in defense to an action the defendant claims a sum for the plaintiff.

Cross-examination: the strict questioning of a witness in a court case on behalf of an opposing party; process designed to test the accuracy and credibility of testimony given by a witness or to bring out facts not already stated.

Crown: the monarchy, the sovereign power; in Canadian law, usually synonymous with the state as representing "the sovereign power of the people."

Crown attorney: a lawyer employed by the government to present and argue the case for the prosecution.

Curfew: originally "cover fire"; an edict issued by the proper authorities demanding that all persons, or one class of persons (often juveniles), keep off the streets between stated hours.

Curtesy: the ancient right by which a man is entitled in some circumstances to enjoy his widow's estate, or part of it, during his lifetime; similar to the widow's dower.

Custody: the detention of a person by legal means; safekeeping; guardianship; the person who has custody is called a custodian.

Damages: the sum of money claimed or awarded in compensation for injury to person, property or rights through the negligence, default or unlawful act of another, or through breach of contract.

Dangerous offender: a person who has been convicted of a serious personal-injury offense involving the use of violence against another person, and who constitutes a threat to the life, safety, or physical or mental well-being of another person; an offender who has committed a sex crime, and who has failed to control his sexual impulses and is likely to cause injury to another person in the future through his failure to control these impulses.

Days of grace: the three days' additional time allowed after the stated due date for payment of notes and bills, except those payable on demand.

Debauch: to corrupt; deprave; to make lewd; with a woman, to seduce.

Decedent: one whose estate is being administered; a deceased person (mostly United States usage).

Deceit: a trick, stratagem or false statement deliberately intended to mislead another; deception; fraud.

Decree: a sentence or order of a court determining the rights of the parties to an action; *e.g.,* a divorce decree.

Decree absolute: the final judgment declaring a divorce to be absolute; as a general rule can only be obtained a minimum of three months after the decree nisi.

Decree nisi: a judgment ordering a divorce which is provisional until such time as a decree absolute is obtained.

Decree of nullity: in relation to marriage, a judgment of the court pronouncing a marriage to be null and of no effect—as if the marriage had never been entered into. This is not to be confused with divorce or separation.

Deed: a written document signed and sealed, evidencing a contract; the conveyance of real estate; deed of gift, deed of separation, etc.

Defalcation: the fraudulent misappropriation of money in one's charge.

Defamation: an intentional injury to one's reputation by either libel or slander; the offense of deliberately injuring a person's character with false statements.

Default: failure or omission to fulfill a legal duty or requirement; culpable neglect; a misdeed.

Defendant: a person who is sued or one who is accused of an offense: the party defending or denying a claim.

Defense: the opposing or denial in court of a claim or of the truth of an accusation of the prosecution; the defendant's pleading; the total actions taken by defendant and his legal counsel.

Defraud: to trick or swindle or cheat, thereby depriving someone of money, property or rights.

Delict: in Quebec civil law, any wrong or injury; violation of public or private obligation.

Delinquent: an underage person convicted of a "delinquency" (any offense before a juvenile court is a "delinquency"); a person who fails to perform some duty; an account or a debt unpaid.

Demeanor: bearing of a witness; attitude; manner of composing oneself toward others.

Demurrer: a statement by a party to a legal action that, even if the facts stated by the other party are true, they do not add up to an enforceable claim; any objection taken to evidence that is considered insufficient to sustain the issue or to make out the case.

Dependent: a person who derives support or maintenance from another; one who relies upon another for the necessities of life.

Deponent: one who makes a deposition under oath; person supplying written testimony in a lawsuit.

Deport: to send a person back to his country of origin (or previous residence) and forbid his reentry.

Desertion: the willful abandonment of an obligation or duty; especially a duty to a person with legal right of support; desertion by a spouse for three years is ground for divorce in Canada.

Devise: transfer of real estate by a last will and testament.

Disability: legal disqualification or incapacity to act; temporary or permanent physical disability from illness or injury.

Disbar: the expulsion of a lawyer from the Bar; retraction of the lawyer's right to practice.

Discharge: to cancel, annul, revoke, or refuse to confirm a court order; to free from prison or from restraint of injunction; to release a bankrupt from the obligation of his debts; to dismiss a jury, or any person from a duty or position.

Discovery: a time-saving legal process by which each party to a suit must disclose to the other such material as books, letters and other factual documents intended as evidence.

Discrimination: any failure to treat individuals equally; under the Charter of Rights and Freedoms, discrimination based on race, national or ethnic origin, color, religion, sex, age, mental or physical disability is illegal.

Disinherit: to cut an heir off from coming into possession of any property or right that would normally become his.

Dismissal: an order or judgment ending a case without further consideration; a discharge; disposal of an action; a dismissal "without prejudice" permits a plaintiff to bring another suit based on the same

general cause; the termination by an employer of an employe's services before the expiry of the term agreed upon by both parties.

Disorderly conduct: generally, a disturbance of the peace, or a threat to disturb the peace.

Dissolution: the dissolving of a company or a partnership; the cancellation of a contract; the ending of a marriage by divorce.

Distrain: seizure of goods to satisfy rent due; an execution for the satisfaction of any debt for which judgment has been obtained.

Disturbing the peace: disorderly, violent or threatening conduct; an interruption of peace, quiet and tranquillity of the community; to deprive others of peaceful enjoyment or possession of their homes or lands.

Divorce: legal dissolution of a marriage; the legal document involved is called the divorce decree.

Docket: list of cases to be tried before a court at a sitting; also known as the court calendar; any brief list or abstract.

Domicile: permanent place of dwelling; domicile "of origin" is that of a person's father at the time of the person's birth; domicile "by choice" is that chosen by a person as his permanent home.

Donatio mortis causa: a gift made by someone expecting to die.

Dot: in French usage—the money or goods a woman brings to her husband at marriage; dowry.

Double indemnity: a provision in a life insurance policy by which double the face value is to be paid in the event of the accidental death of the insured.

Double jeopardy: a term for the safeguard against being tried again on a charge on which one has already been convicted or acquitted.

Dower: the interest in a deceased husband's real estate that the law grants to the widow for life. In Canada, dower has virtually ceased to exist.

Droit: in French law—a legal right; the law; justice.

Dual nationality: while it is possible for a Canadian to have dual nationality or citizenship, he or she must opt for Canadian citizenship by his or her 28th birthday or thereafter lose the privilege.

Due process of law: the rights or principles of justice gained over the centuries which limit any government's power to deprive a person of his fundamental freedoms (civil rights); guaranteed under the Charter of Rights and Freedoms.

Durance: imprisonment; usually expressed poetically as "in durance vile" (Robert Burns).

Duress: illegal compulsion; making a person do or say something against his will; harsh treatment; under constraint or threat.

Easement: a privilege allowed by the owner of land to the owner of adjoining property, such as a right of passage; a liberty, privilege or advantage without profit obtained by deed, will or legal custom.

Edict: an ordinance or proclamation having the force of law; once issued by the Sovereign to his subjects.

Elopement: the act of a girl who runs away from her home to get married without her parents' consent; the act of a couple who leave secretly to marry.

Emancipate: to set free from some control or restraint; to make a minor free of parental control.

Embargo: a prohibiting order; the suspension of certain rights; an order by a government restraining merchant vessels from leaving or entering its ports.

Embezzlement: the appropriation by an individual of someone else's money or property while occupying a position of trust; to divert the property of another person to one's own use.

Emblements: the profits to be derived from land that is already sown or planted; the term also carries the right of a tenant to carry away after his tenancy has ended the products of the land resulting from his own labor.

Embracery: the crime of attempting to illegally influence a jury by promises, gifts or entertainment.

Eminent domain: the sovereign power of the Crown to take private property for public use as for airports, highways, hospitals, schools, etc.

Encumbrance: a claim or lien attached to real estate—such as a mortgage.

Endorsement: writing your name, with or without instructions, on the back of a cheque or other commercial or financial document.

Endowment: the provision of a permanent income by gift or bequest, usually to a college, society or charity; type of life insurance which is payable when the insured reaches a given age.

Enjoin: to direct or prohibit some act by injunction issued by a court.

Entrapment: inducing a person to commit a crime he had not contemplated so that he can be prosecuted; to ensnare; to catch by trickery.

Equity: the administration of law, according to the spirit rather than the letter of the law; justice based on the concepts of natural reason, ethics and fairness independent of any codified body of law; also, the net value of property in excess of the value of all encumbrances attaching to the property.

Escalator clause: sometimes found in leases and supply and labor contracts which are subject to, or affected by, rises in the cost of living.

Escheat: reversion of property to the Crown when no legal heir or other qualified claimant can be found.

Estate: the extent of interest which a person has in property, personal or real; "personal estate" covers money and goods; "real estate" includes land, buildings and related rights; also refers to the real estate itself.

Estoppel: a restriction which prevents a person from denying or from admitting something, because of former actions or behavior made by him which indicated the contrary of that which he now wishes to state or deny; it can apply to a person's conduct as well as to his oral or written statements.

Eviction: turning out a person (a tenant) from property he had occupied; dispossession by process of law or by virtue of superior title.

Evidence: testimony, documents, objects or any other materials which are put forward at a judicial hearing to establish the fact or point at issue; the laws of evidence generally define that which is admissible in court.

Examination for discovery: an oral examination of the plaintiff by the defendant to determine the precise nature of the plaintiff's case and to help establish a defense.

Executor: person named in a will to carry out its provisions; a woman so named is called an executrix.

Execution: carrying out court judgments, especially enforcing any legislative or judicial order or decree; due performance of all formalities.

Exemplary: suitable to serve as a deterrent; *i.e.*, exemplary damages given in a lawsuit.

Exhibit: any document or object produced in court and identified in evidence.

874

Exonerate: to free from an accusation; to discharge; to relieve from blame or obligation.

Ex parte: Latin—"from (or in) the interest of one party only"; an *ex parte* order may be granted at the request of one party to a court action without prior notification to the other side involved.

Expert witness: usually a specialist on a particular subject qualified beyond the normal range of a layman, whose factual testimony and opinions are taken in evidence.

Expropriate: the taking over of private land by some level of government for the public good; an action under the power of "eminent domain."

Extortion: the action of extracting anything, especially money, from a person by force or by undue exercise of authority or power.

Extradite: to give up a fugitive to the government within whose jurisdiction an alleged crime was committed.

Extraterritoriality: (from Latin) "outside the territory"; usually refers to laws which have effect outside the territorial jurisdiction in which they were passed.

Factum: Latin—"deed"; a legal argument set out in written form to be presented to a court, usually to a court of appeal.

False arrest: unlawful physical restraint or detention.

False pretenses: intentional misrepresentation of facts made to cheat or defraud another.

False witness: a person who deliberately offers inaccurate "witness," or evidence; the report, or evidence, itself.

Feasance: the doing or performing of an act; the person who does the act is the "feasor"; also: malfeasance, meaning wrongdoing.

Fee simple: outright ownership of real estate; often stated as "fee simple absolute."

Felony: former term for serious crime, now known as an "offense."

Fiat: a court order authorizing certain proceedings.

Fieri facias: Latin—"cause (it) to be done"; a court document authorizing a sheriff to seize and sell goods to recover the amount of a judgment; usually written "fi fa."

Fine: a financial penalty imposed by the courts on a convicted person, association or corporation.

For cause: reasons which the law accepts as justified.

Foreclosure: the seizing of property to secure repayment of a loan, or payment of an overdue debt; the legal proceeding by which a mortgagee takes over possession of a mortgaged property.

Forensic medicine: any medical knowledge applied to the purposes of the law; also called "medical jurisprudence."

Forgery: the act of making a false document with intent to present it as authentic; the counterfeiting of another person's signature; materially altering any writing with fraudulent intent.

Fornication: voluntary sexual intercourse between unmarried persons.

Foster parent: one who performs the duties of a parent to the child of another.

Frame-up: conspiracy to incriminate someone with false evidence.

Franchise: a freedom, especially the citizen's right to vote; any special privilege or right granted by the government; permission granted by a company to sell its products or services under a contract.

Fraud: trickery, misrepresentation of fact made with the purpose of inducing another person to act on false representation; criminal deception.

Friend of the court: a person who has no actual right to appear in a case but is permitted to introduce evidence or advice; usually an expert in a field relevant to the hearing; the phrase is often seen in Latin: *amicus curiae.*

Frivolous: in legal use, evidence or argument not bearing on the case, possibly introduced for reasons of delay.

Garnishment: a court order notifying a person that property in his possession belonging to another party is attached, pending settlement of claims; a court order to an employer of a debtor to pay a portion of the debtor's wages to a creditor; also garnishee.

German: in law, "whole" or "full"; a full brother is a brother-german, as opposed to a half-brother; germane: in close relationship.

Gift inter vivos: (from Latin) a gift "between the living"; the free transfer of ownership to another person.

Gifts mortis causa: (from Latin) a gift made in expectation of imminent death and received by the heirs after the donor has passed away.

Goods and chattels: personal property (*i.e.,* furniture, tools, automobiles) as distinguished from real property (land and buildings).

Grace period: usually 30–31 days after a due date for payment of a major obligation, such as an insurance premium.

Grand jury: a jury called to hear accusations of the commission of crimes; to hear evidence produced by the Crown and to issue indictments where it is believed that a crime has been committed.

Grievance: in labor law, an injustice or wrong, serving as ground for complaint.

Gross indecency: any marked departure from the decent conduct expected of the average citizen that is not specifically covered elsewhere in the Criminal Code.

Grounds for divorce: in Canada includes cases where the

spouse has committed adultery, has been found guilty of illegal sexual acts, has gone through a form of marriage with another person, has committed mental cruelty of such a kind as to render continued cohabitation impossible; continuous separation, usually over a period of three years, is also a ground for divorce.

Grub stake: in mining law, a contract under which a prospector is provided with provisions, tools and other supplies in exchange for a share in any claims staked.

Guarantee: an undertaking to be responsible for another person's discharge of his obligations; a pledge by a manufacturer as to quality or serviceability of his product (correctly, "warranty").

Guardian: someone legally appointed to care for the person or property of an individual not competent to act for himself.

Guardian ad litem: a person appointed by the court to represent in a specific hearing or case someone considered incompetent because of age or mental incapacity.

Habeas corpus: Latin— "you have the body"; the name of a writ designed to compel the bringing of a person before a court or judge.

Habentes homines: Latin— "wealthy men"; used in formal legal talk.

Hearing: the presentation of evidence or argument before the court at any stage of proceeding.

Hearsay: evidence of facts not from the personal knowledge of a witness, but from what the witness has been told by others; not firsthand.

Hereditament: any property that can be inherited; anything that in the absence of a will descends to the heir in an intestacy.

High-grading: in mining, stealing valuable ores.

Hijacking: originally stealing from a vessel or vehicle in transit, now mainly seizing aircraft in flight.

Holograph will: a will and testament entirely written and signed by the testator in his own hand without witnesses.

Homestead: a house or dwelling; more particularly in Canada a farm occupied by the owner and his family; "homestead rights" in the western provinces generally refer to joint ownership by husband and wife.

Homicide: the killing of any human being by another; our law provides for both justifiable and culpable homicide.

Homosexual: a person who prefers sexual relations with persons of the same sex; homosexual acts in private between consenting adults are not illegal in Canada.

Hung jury: a jury that is irreconcilably divided and thus is unable to agree on a verdict.

Hypothec: Quebec legal term for "mortgage."

Hypothecate: to mortgage or pledge property as security, while retaining possession of the property.

Illegal: not authorized by law; contrary to law.

Illegitimate child: a child whose parents were not married at the time of his or her birth; a bastard; in most provinces, such a child becomes officially legitimate if its parents subsequently marry.

Illicit: forbidden by law; prohibited.

Immeubles: in French law, "immovables" such as land and buildings.

Immunity: exemption from duty or penalty; a privilege.

Impeach: to charge a public official before a special tribunal with misconduct in office; to discredit a witness.

Impertinent: in law, refers to any pleading or evidence irrelevant to the issue before the court.

Implied warranty: refers to a warranty required by law or custom which is not stipulated in a contract; usually applies in the case of a sale or lease.

Impotence: inability from mental or physical causes of the male or female to perform normal sexual intercourse; grounds for annulment of marriage in Canada.

Imprisonment: placing and holding a person in confinement; loss of personal liberty as a penalty for crime.

Incest: sexual intercourse between a man and a woman so closely related that marriage between them is prohibited; also, an offense committed by anyone who knows that another person is by blood relationship his or her parent, child, brother, sister, grandparent, grandchild, as the case may be, and yet has sexual intercourse with that person.

Incite: to arouse; instigate; to urge another to commit a crime.

Incompetent: one who does not have the legal fitness to perform a certain act; an unskilled person.

Incriminate: to charge with a crime; to expose to an accusation; an incriminating admission is one that tends to establish guilt.

Indecent: morally offensive or unseemly; grossly vulgar; lewd; not fit to be seen or heard.

Indecent exposure: showing the private parts of the body in a lewd or obscene manner.

Indenture: a deed or contract, to which two or more persons are parties.

Indictment: a formal written charge of a serious crime, requiring a formal trial.

Infant: a person younger than adult age (which varies between 18 and 21 years, depending on the province); also known as a minor.

Infanticide: the murder of an infant by its mother soon after its birth.

In flagrante delicto: Latin—"while the crime is blazing"; in the very act of committing a crime; "red-handed."

Information: an accusation presented under oath by a complainant.

Infraction: a breach of law; an infringement of an obligation or contract.

Infringement: a trespass upon a right, privilege or regulation, particularly referring to copyrights, patents and trademarks.

Ingratitude: in French law, ingratitude is sufficient legal cause for revoking a gift.

Iniquitous: grossly unjust; wicked; contrary to law.

Injunction: a court order to do or not to do a specific act.

Injuria non excusat injuriam: Latin—"one wrong does not justify another."

In loco parentis: Latin—"in the place of a parent"; a person who assumes parental obligations toward a child who is not his own.

Innocence: in law, the absence of guilt; also the state of virginity in a woman.

Innocent trespasser: one who enters another's land illegally but unintentionally.

In pari delicto: Latin—"in equal fault"; equal in guilt.

Inquest: investigation by a coroner of the cause or manner of death of anyone who had died from other than natural causes.

Insane: suffering from mental alienation or derangement; unsound in mind; mad. Legal insanity is defined at length in the Criminal Code.

Instrument: a formal document with legal effect, such as a contract, a will or a lease.

Intent: state of mind in which an act is performed; resolve; determination.

Interdiction: restriction of civil rights by a court order, placing a person's affairs in the hands of a guardian or administrator for reasons of insanity, imbecility, habitual drunkenness, addiction to narcotics or prodigality.

International law: that body of law, usually set out in treaties, which states feel themselves bound to observe in their international relations; also known as public international law.

Inter vivos: Latin—"between the living"; from one living person to another (as with a gift).

Intestate: a person who dies without making a valid will and testament.

Intimidation: illegal coercion; duress, putting someone in fear.

Invalid: of no binding force; without authority.

Irrevocable: cannot be revoked or recalled.

Jactitation: a boasting or assertion that is challenged by someone who is harmed thereby; false claim to be married to a particular person.

Jaywalking: crossing a street intersection diagonally; or crossing any street between intersections or crosswalks.

Jeopardy: hazard; peril; the danger of punishment which a person faces when placed on trial.

Joint, joint and several: types of legal liability binding two or more persons collectively and individually; if a promissory note, signed by several makers, is worded "we jointly and severally promise to pay," the holder could in the appropriate circumstances, sue all makers together as a group or each separately for the total amount of the debt; if worded "we jointly promise to pay," the makers could be sued only jointly, or as a group.

Judgment: a judicial decision; the official sentence of a court.

Judgment debtor: a person against whom a court order has been issued demanding payment of a debt.

Judicial: pertaining to the administration of justice; belonging to the office or status of a judge.

Judicial review: review by a court of a decision of an administrative body or inferior court.

Judiciary: the judges of the courts considered as a body.

Jurisdiction: the extent of a court's authority; the right or authority by which courts and judicial officers interpret and administer the law.

Jurisprudence: the philosophy or science of law; knowledge or skill in law; also, the law as set out in previous judicial decisions.

Jurist: an expert student of the law; usually applied to those who write on legal subjects.

Jury: a body of men and women (usually 12) selected and sworn in in court to determine questions of fact in any civil or criminal proceeding; an individual member of a jury is a *juror.*

Justice: exercise of authority or power in maintenance of right; the administration of law; title of judge of the Superior (Supreme) and Appellate Courts.

Justice of the Peace: an experienced citizen appointed to try minor infractions; two such citizens sitting together can try summary conviction offenses and take preliminary hearings; a justice of the peace can authorize arrest, and issue search warrants and summonses.

Justifiable homicide: the legally excusable taking of life, as in war, rebellion, or in self-defense when attacked or threatened.

Keeping the peace: an order from the Bench requiring a person to be of good behavior and to dissuade others from breaching the peace; if not obeyed, a punishment usually follows.

Kidnapping: seizure, detention and confinement of a person by force or fraud; the unlawful carrying off of a person usually for the purpose of obtaining ransom.

Kiting: slang term describing the fraudulent manipulating of cheques near the end of an accounting period in order to cover a cash shortage.

Kleptomania: a symptom of mental disorder manifesting in an irresistible impulse to steal.

Labor Code: consolidation of statutes relating to labor; the Canada Labor Code lays down minimum standards for wages, hours and other working conditions for all federal workers.

Laches: undue delay in asserting a legal right or privilege.

Landlord: the owner (also "lessor") of a property who leases it for a period at a stated rental to another person called the "tenant" or "lessee."

Larceny: theft; stealing, the taking away of property with the intention of depriving the rightful owner.

Last clear chance: the person who has the last obvious opportunity to avoid injuring another may be liable for damages if he does not do so.

Last resort: final venue for appeal; the "court of last resort" is the Supreme Court of Canada.

Law merchant: customs and commercial usages formerly adhered to in foreign trade; ratified by various court decisions, it finally became part of common law.

Leading question: a question to a witness designed to suggest or produce the reply desired by the questioner.

Lease: a legal agreement by which the lessor grants to the lessee the possession and use of property for a stated period and for an agreed periodic payment called rent.

Legacy: a gift of personal property transmitted by a will; bequest; inheritance.

Legal Aid society: an organization supported by public funds that offers free advice and representation in court to persons who cannot afford legal counsel.

Legal tender: currency that a creditor is obliged by law to accept in settlement of a money debt; in Canada, any Bank of Canada notes, or Canadian coins as follows: pennies for debts up to 25¢; nickels up to $5, dimes or larger up to $10.

Legislation: officially enacted and authorized law or laws.

Legitimate: in accordance with the law; authorized or sanctioned by law; being born in wedlock.

Lesbian: a woman who indulges in sexual activities with other women.

Lèse-majesté: French—any offense against the Sovereign; sometimes, an attack upon a person's dignity.

Lessee: *see* Tenant.

Lessor: *see* Landlord.

Lethal: deadly or fatal, as in a "lethal weapon."

Letter of indemnity: a written agreement to guarantee another against loss or damage with respect to some event or act.

Letters of administration: a document issued by a Probate Court authorizing a specified person to administer the estate of someone who has died without drawing up a will.

Letters Patent: documents issued by the Crown, addressed to "whom they may concern" and published in the *Official Gazette* ("patent" means "open for general inspection"). Letters patent confer specific rights on an individual or a corporation.

Levy: to impose a tax or fine; also the tax itself.

Lex: Latin—"law," used with many other terms to denote a particular branch of law.

Liability: responsibility by an individual or an organization either for damages resulting from a negligent act, or for an obligation, or the payment of a debt.

Libel: a statement in printed form that injures another's reputation; a form of defamation, expressed in writing, printing or other recorded representation.

License: permission to perform some act or engage in some business; the document that grants such permission; also, abuse of freedom and disregard of law or propriety.

Licensee: a person granted a license to perform some act of business; a person who enters another's premises with the owner's permission but without invitation.

Lie detector: a machine that records emotional disturbance on a graph; the polygraph; evidence based on readings from this machine is not admissible in Canadian courts.

Lien: a legal claim upon real or personal property for the satisfaction of a debt.

Life estate: an estate held by a person for the duration of his life, or the life of some other person or persons.

Limitation of actions: provincial laws stipulate varying periods in which certain legal actions must be commenced.

Lineal: in a direct line, as from father to son.

Litigation: a lawsuit; the process of carrying on a judicial contest.

Lobbying: lawful solicitation of legislators to consider certain aspects in connection with the passage of a particular act affecting the lobbyist's interests.

Machination: contriving a scheme for some shady, or illegal, purpose.

Magistrate: a judge of a court of limited jurisdiction; in some provinces, magistrates are known as "provincial judges."

Maim: to injure seriously; to wound with permanent injury; to cripple.

Majority: legal adulthood; the age when full civil and personal rights can be exercised.

Maker: one who frames, draws up or makes, as in "the maker" of a promissory note.

Mala fides: Latin—"bad faith."

Malfeasance: mostly used to describe misconduct by an official, or someone in a position of trust.

Malice: an intentional violation of the law to the injury or detriment of another; the wrongful act itself; "malice aforethought" is the premeditated intention to do something to injure another; in libel law, malice usually involves evil intent arising from hatred or spite.

Malicious prosecution: a civil or criminal action begun with the intention of injuring the defendant, without cause to believe the charges are true or possible of being sustained at law.

Malpractice: any professional misconduct; any evil, immoral or negligent conduct in the performance of professional or fiduciary duties.

Mandamus: Latin—"we command"; a writ of mandamus is an order issued by high courts to lower courts or public officials, directing them to do or not to do something that is within the scope of their powers.

Mandate: a judicial command, order or direction to obey an order of the court; a contract by which one person acts for another.

Manslaughter: the unlawful killing of a person without malice, premeditation, or intention.

Mantrap: any potentially harmful device set as a defense against a burglar or trespasser; prohibited under Canadian law.

Maritime law: the system of laws of commercial navigation on the seas, harbors and coastal waters.

Marriage settlement: a contract signed by the prospective spouses conveying, or "settling," certain property that must follow a prescribed line of ownership and succession.

Martial law: temporary rule by military forces when civil law and order either do not exist or have broken down.

Master and servant: the parties to a contract of service; the formally stated relationship between employer and employe.

Matricide: the murder of one's mother; one who has killed his (or her) mother.

Maturity date: the date on which a bill of exchange or other negotiable instrument falls due and payable.

Mechanic's lien: an artisan's (craftsman's) right to enforce payment for his supplies and services, mainly in the construction industry, by making a legal claim on the land and its buildings.

Mens legis: Latin—"the mind of the law"; the purpose, spirit, or intention of a law.

Mens rea: Latin—"the guilty mind"; wrongful purpose; criminal intent.

Mental cruelty: conduct on the part of a spouse which can endanger the mental or physical health of the other spouse so as to render continuance of marital relation intolerable.

Mineral rights: a proprietary interest in the minerals in land; the right to take ores, or to receive a royalty from the miner.

Minor: a person below the age of full legal competence (18–21 years) when all civil rights may be legally exercised; an infant or child in the eyes of the law.

Miscegenation: mixture of races; marriage between persons of different races.

Mischief: malicious damage to property.

Misdemeanor: wrongdoing of a lesser degree; similar to a summary-conviction offense.

Misrepresentation: words or actions that mislead the party to whom they are made; a statement deliberately not in accordance with fact.

Mistrial: a trial ending without a judgment because of legal error or because of unacceptable conduct by a party to the trial; declaration following a jury's inability to agree.

Monogamy: the only legal state of marriage in Canada, consisting of two parties; being married to one person at a time.

Moral turpitude: behavior contrary to the accepted rules of propriety; immorality or depravity.

Mortgage: a legal document given by one person (the mortgagor) to another (the mortgagee) which conveys an interest in the property as security for a debt; a lien upon land, or other property.

Motion: an application to a court for an order or rule directing or permitting some act to be done.

Motive: that which moves or induces a person to act in a certain way.

Mulct: to impose a fine or financial forfeit; also any such fine.

Murder: the killing of one person by another with malice aforethought; a form of culpable homicide along with manslaughter or infanticide.

Mutiny: rebellion by armed forces against their commanders, or by seamen against their captain; to refuse to obey lawful orders.

Naturalization: the process of admitting an alien to citizenship; granting the same rights and privileges as enjoyed by a native.

Navigable waters: any waters which afford a channel for commerce; a navigable river is one that can allow the passage of craft.

Negligence: failure to exercise the standard of care that would be expected of a reasonable and prudent person; if a prudent man would act in certain circumstances, then failure to act could be considered negligence.

Nephew: legally, only children of brothers and sisters are "nephews" or "nieces."

Next friend: a guardian or tutor given to an infant for the purposes of bringing or defending an action at law involving the latter.

Next of kin: person or persons most closely related by blood.

No-fault insurance: a system of insurance in which the insuring company is obliged to pay damages suffered by its insured, regardless of who could be held legally responsible for the accident.

Nolle prosequi: Latin—"will not prosecute further"; an entry by the plaintiff in a civil case, or the Crown attorney in a criminal case, that he will not proceed any further in a suit or action.

Nolo contendere: Latin—"I will not contest it"; a plea by a defendant with the same effect as a plea of guilty.

Nominal: "in name only"; inconsiderable or trivial; "nominal damages" are merely a token amount acknowledging violation of a legal right, but without any real damage to the plaintiff.

Non compos mentis: Latin —"not of sound mind"; mentally incapable; insane.

Nonjuridical day: a day on which the court does not sit and on which certain acts may not be legally done; usually refers to Sundays and holidays. A cheque is valid even if made on a nonjuridical day.

Nonsuit: termination of a lawsuit without any judgment; a judgment against a plaintiff because he cannot prove his case or does not proceed to a trial; withdrawal of an action at law by the parties concerned.

Notary public: a public officer (usually a lawyer) empow-

ered to administer oaths, to witness signatures or to certify documents; in Quebec, *M. le notaire,* or "the notary," fulfills a role similar to that of the solicitor in the English-speaking provinces.

Nullity: an act or proceeding that is regarded as having not taken place; of no legal effect.

Nuncupative will: an oral will made by a person in a terminal illness before witnesses, sometimes later put in writing.

Oath: a form of attestation by which a person confirms that he is bound in conscience to do or state something faithfully and truthfully.

Oath of allegiance: a solemn statement confirming loyalty to the Queen and obedience to the laws of Canada; required of immigrants before the granting of citizenship.

Obiter dictum: a general opinion expressed by a judge that is incidental, not essential, to the main issue of the case.

Objection: calling the judge's attention to a statement or argument by counsel that one of the parties in a lawsuit considers improper or illegal.

Obscene: offensive to the senses or the mind; lewd, repulsive or indecent; considered (by some) to corrupt or deprave the morals of society.

Occupier's liability: responsibility of the owner or possessor of property for accidents occurring thereon to third parties.

Offense: a violation of the law; in Canada, synonymous with "crime."

Offensive weapon: anything capable of being used to cause (or threaten to cause) physical injury.

Official receiver: a person appointed to act as an officer of the court in performing duties in cases of bankruptcy.

Ombudsman: an official appointed to investigate complaints against the administrative branch of government.

Omission: neglect or failure to perform some act required by law or by private obligation.

Opinion: a formal considered statement by a lawyer or judge; an expression of the reasons and principles upon which a decision has been based.

Ordinance: a law or statute; a rule by authority; usually, a municipal bylaw.

Orphan: a person (usually a minor) who has lost both parents.

Ouster la mer: French—"beyond the sea"; used as an excuse for someone not appearing in court when summoned.

Overt act: an open act, with intention and design; often with an implication of criminal behavior.

Oyer and terminer: the traditional instruction of judges at the beginning of assizes to "hear and determine" all cases.

Panderer: one who solicits for prostitutes; a pimp.

Pardon: to release a convicted person from punishment for his crime; an act of grace, blotting out guilt.

Parol evidence: evidence based on verbal testimony.

Parole: conditional release of a prisoner; if the conditions are not observed, the convict can be returned to prison to serve the rest of his sentence.

Parricide: the crime of killing a close relative, usually one's father; a person who has been convicted of that crime.

Patent: an official certificate or license granting the exclusive right to make, use and sell an invention for a period of 17 years; an open letter ("letters patent") from the Crown or other authority granting some right or privilege.

Patent pending: the period of time after the application for a patent but before its issuance.

Pederasty: sodomy; anal intercourse between males, particularly between an adult male and a young boy.

Peeping Tom: prowler who makes a habit of peering in dwelling windows hoping to see women undressed.

Penal: inflicting a penalty or punishment; refers to any system of imprisonment.

Penalty: the punishment set by law for breaches of the peace or for the commission of some offense; a sum of money ("fine") to be forfeited as a punishment.

Penalty clause: a section of a contract specifying an amount to be paid by a defaulting party in case of nonfulfillment.

Pendente lite: Latin—"pending or during suit"; that is, while a case is in progress.

Penetration: in criminal law (mostly cases of sexual assault), the insertion of the penis in a woman's sexual organs to the slightest extent.

Peppercorn: a purely nominal rent (perhaps $1 a year) or payment—for instance, of damages in a civil lawsuit.

Per curiam: Latin—"by the court"; by the whole court, or the chief justice on behalf of the court, rather than by any one judge.

Perjury: making a false statement under oath; the willful giving of false testimony by a witness in a judicial proceeding.

Perverse verdict: a decision by a jury that goes against the established law as stated by the presiding judge.

Petition: a written request to a court, asking for the exercise of judicial powers in any of many ways.

Pilferage: theft or stealing; particularly petty theft of goods—in small quantity and often of small value.

Pimp: one who procures participants for illegal sexual activities; a panderer; one who lives off the earnings of prostitutes.

Piracy: hijacking or robbery on the ocean.

Plaintiff: the complaining party who institutes a lawsuit

against another, known as the defendant.

Plea: the answer of the defendant to a charge made against him; a defense; any "pleading" (formal statements) in court.

Pleadings: the positions taken by the parties to an action as expressed in writings that form part of the court record.

Polygamy: the crime of having more than one wife or husband at the same time; formally, "a plurality of spouses."

Pornography: from the Greek—"the writing of harlots"; the expression of obscene or lewd matters in art or literature.

Postdate: to date a document (including a cheque) at a point in time subsequent to the date of writing.

Posthumous child: a child born after the death of its father.

Post mortem: Latin—"after death"; a medical examination of a body made after death to determine the cause of death; autopsy.

Postnuptial settlement: an agreement made after marriage to settle property on a wife or children; possibly made by a father on his newly married daughter.

Power of attorney: a legal document granting authority for one person to act as another's representative.

Precedent: a judicial decision that serves as an authoritative guide for making decisions in similar cases; a rule or model.

Preempt: to appropriate beforehand; in property law, to obtain possession of public land by occupation.

Preliminary hearing: the hearing before a judge or magistrate to determine whether or not there is sufficient evidence to require the indictment of the accused.

Premeditation: deliberate planning of an act beforehand, and the determination to do it.

Prescription: the rights a person may acquire over another person's property by unrestricted use for a length of time.

Presumption: an inference drawn from probable reasoning in the absence of certainty; an inference based on legal history or precedent.

Pretext: a stated motive designed to conceal the real reason for a statement or act; false appearance.

Prima facie: Latin—"at first view"; a fact assumed at law to be true in the absence of evidence to the contrary.

Primogeniture: the state of being the first-born child among several children of the same parents; the right (where permitted) of the eldest son to inherit the property or title of a parent, to the exclusion of all other children.

Privacy: the right to be let alone, free from public scrutiny, curiosity, and publicity, as far as the law allows.

Privity: any juridical relationship between two parties.

Probate: a legal certificate acknowledging the validity of the will of a deceased person; the process by which a will is proved.

Probation: a judicial decision to permit a person convicted of an offense to go free under supervision in the hope that he will lead a law-abiding life thereafter. He must obey certain conditions set out by the court in his probation order or else he will be returned to prison.

Process: the course of proceedings in a case, civil or criminal, from beginning to end; a series of actions and occurrences by which a result or effect is produced; a particular method of manufacture.

Profit à prendre: French—"the right a person may have to enter upon another's land to take profit from the land or its produce."

Prohibition: an edict or decree that forbids or debars; a writ from a high court to stop proceedings in some action that is beyond the lower court's jurisdiction.

Promise to appear: under Canadian bail law, a promise given by an accused after arrest that he will appear in court at a fixed time.

Proper lookout: the duty of motorists to exercise watchfulness, prudence and caution for other road users.

Prosecute: to proceed against a person in a criminal action.

Prosecutor: the Crown attorney who conducts criminal proceedings on behalf of the Crown, or the public.

Prostitution: the selling of sexual gratification; whoring; lewdness for gain.

Proviso: a statement in a contract or law, limiting, modifying or rendering conditional some element in the affair; a conditional clause.

Prudence: precaution, attentiveness; good judgment; a degree of care required by law in certain dealings with others.

Public mischief: intentionally misleading a police officer to carry out an investigation by accusing another person of having committed an offense, usually to divert suspicion from oneself.

Puisne judge: (from Latin) *post-natus*, meaning "born later"; refers to junior judge in a court.

Punitive damages: extra damages awarded to a plaintiff in a civil lawsuit because of the special character of the wrong done, or to punish and make an example of the defendant to deter others.

Q.C.: abbreviation of "Queen's Counsel," a distinction granted to experienced lawyers in Canada during the reign of a queen; same as c.r. (*conseil de la Reine*).

Quash: to annul; set aside; or make void.

Quid pro quo: Latin—"something for something"; mutual concessions made by the parties to a transaction.

Quittance: release from an obligation.

Racketeer: one who lives by crime; a member of an organized gang of lawbreakers; especially one who blackmails by intimidation.

Ransom: sum of money demanded by kidnappers for the release of a person held in captivity.

Rape: sexual intercourse with a woman by a man without her consent and usually by force or deception. The term has been stricken from the Criminal Code and replaced by "sexual assault."

Rapine: a term for openly taking by force another's personal property.

Ratify: to approve or confirm; to make legal.

Re: Latin—"in the matter of"; in legal use, the meaning is usually "in the case of . . . "

Reasonable doubt: in criminal law, a degree of doubt raised in the mind of the judge or jury as to the guilt of the accused which requires a finding of not guilty; this must be a real doubt, not fanciful or illusory.

Rebut: to refute or oppose; to put forward evidence that denies the truth of an accusation.

Receiver: a person appointed by the court in a bankruptcy to care for property pending its final disposition.

Receiving order: a court order proclaiming a debtor to be bankrupt and placing his property in the care of a trustee for the distribution to the creditors.

Recidivist: an incorrigible criminal; a "repeater."

Reciprocal wills: wills made by two persons (usually husband and wife) in which they make matching provisions in favor of each other.

Recision of contract: the canceling of a contract, often through the intervention of judicial authority.

Recognizance: an agreement entered into before a magistrate by which an accused person is released "on his own recognizance," without bail, on his undertaking to keep the peace or obey any other court instruction.

Rectum rogare: Latin—"to ask for right"; to petition a judge for justice, or fair play.

Reformatory: typical name used to describe a provincial prison for young offenders where sentences of up to two years are served.

Registry office system: a land-titles system where all deeds pertaining to specific properties are registered at the registry office for a district in order to form a public record of all rights affecting immovables situated within such registration division.

Rehabilitate: to reestablish a delinquent person to former capacity, status or privilege; to restore to reputation.

Relevant: connected with the subject at hand; legally pertinent.

Relict: the survivor (of either sex) of a married couple.

Remand: a court order sending a prisoner back into custody while further evidence is sought.

Remedy: legal redress; to right a wrong; to rectify.

Remission: reduction of a sentence by reason of good behavior; release from a debt or payment.

Renunciation: the surrendering or disclaiming of a right or privilege.

Repeal: the canceling of a previous law; to revoke or rescind; to withdraw any resolution or privilege.

Replevin: action to regain possession of property taken or detained; especially chattels seized by landlords for nonpayment of rent.

Reply: the answer by a plaintiff to the plea, or defense, of the defendant in a civil action.

Res: Latin—"a thing"; in modern law refers mostly to any object, or subject matter, that is the basis of a civil action, including "objects" (like rights) that cannot be normally defined as "property."

Residence and domicile: "residence" refers to the place of abode, whether it is temporary or permanent; "domicile" means that place where a person has his principal establishment and where his paramount interests and affections lie.

Residue: any portion of an estate that remains after all charges, debts and bequests have been satisfied.

Res ipsa loquitur: Latin— "the thing speaks for itself"; in civil law, it refers, for example, to the presumption that the defendant was guilty of negligence because the thing that caused the damage was under his exclusive control at the time.

Resisting arrest: assaulting a police officer or any other person with intent to resist or prevent the lawful arrest or detention of oneself or of another person.

Res judicata: Latin—"a matter decided"; point of law previously decided in respect to the parties involved.

Respondent: the party called upon to answer in any legal proceeding; the defendant, especially in a divorce suit; the party who contends against an appeal.

Restitution: restoration or return of something to the original owner; restoring a person to a previous position, honor or status.

Restrictive covenant: a clause in a deed which restricts the use of land by subsequent purchasers; a clause in a contract of employment which forbids an employe from practicing his trade in a certain area for a definite amount of time

after the termination of the contract.

Retainer: essentially, in the hiring of a lawyer or other professional counselor, the fee that the client agrees to pay (or an advance on it); the right of an executor or administrator to retain from the assets of an estate enough to pay a debt due to himself before other debts of equal standing.

Reverse: to set aside or revoke a judgment or decree.

Rider: an addition to a contract, an insurance policy or the finding of a coroner's jury; an additional clause to a document.

Right-of-way: the right of passage, established by usage or by contract, over another person's land; the right of the operator of one vehicle or vessel to move in front of another.

Riparian rights: the rights of a property owner whose land borders on a river, relating to the use of water for fishing, boating and household or commercial use.

Robbery: theft, or attempted theft, while armed with an offensive weapon, or with an imitation weapon (a toy gun).

Sabbath laws: regulations usually forbidding trading on Sunday; the Lord's Day Act.

Sabotage: malicious damaging of property by workers to interfere with industrial production; any wanton destruction.

Sacerdotal: pertaining to priests and the priesthood.

Sadism: sexual perversion in which pleasure is found in inflicting pain.

Sanctuary: a place that provides shelter or protection for a fugitive from arrest and punishment; churches once offered sanctuary but only embassies do so today.

Search warrant: a legal document authorizing an officer to search premises for persons or property allegedly concealed there.

Security: something given as a pledge to assure the fulfillment of an obligation or the payment of a debt; stocks and bonds.

Sedition: speech or writing inciting to rebellion; action against public order short of open rebellion.

Seduction: tempting, bribing or inciting a woman to consent to sexual intercourse; if a man is the victim the woman is known as a "seductress."

Seizure: an act done under the authority of the court which puts property at the disposal of the sheriff or bailiff.

Self-defense: defending oneself or one's family with force from assault or threat, or one's property from theft or destruction: a justifiable violent act in the face of imminent danger.

Senility: feebleness of body and mind due to old age; decay of the faculties amounting to incompetence to enter into a contract, or to execute a will.

Sentence: lawful penalty imposed by a judge on a person convicted by due process in a criminal prosecution; to condemn to punishment.

Separation: a legally recognized parting by a married couple; the agreed cessation of cohabitation; used mainly by those who do not believe in divorce.

Separation agreement: in a separation by mutual agreement (not through the courts) a separation agreement is usually drawn up by legal counsel by providing for support of the wife and any children and for the distribution of property.

Sequestration: the placing of a thing in dispute, usually as a result of a court order, into the hands of a third party, who is obliged to restore the property to the person to whom it is subsequently awarded.

Service of process: notification of an impending action by personal or constructive service (by hand delivery, or through the mails).

Servient land: that land which is subject to an easement of servitude; *e.g.*, the land over which a right-of-way exists.

Servitude: in real estate, an easement; a charge on a person's property for the benefit of another (such as a right-of-way).

Severance pay: a sum of money which is added to a person's salary pursuant to a law or agreement upon termination of employment.

Sheriff: the representative of the Crown in the county, charged with certain duties in the courts and the execution of court orders; dates from pre-Norman times in England.

Shoplifting: stealing from a shop, or store during business hours; not distinguished at law from ordinary theft.

Shyster: generally, a lawyer engaged in sharp practice; any professional who conducts his business in a tricky manner.

Sine die: Latin—"without a day"; used to indicate the indefinite postponement or adjournment of a trial or a meeting.

Slander: a verbal statement that harms another's reputation; words of a false, malicious or defamatory nature.

Sodomy: anal sexual intercourse between males, or between man and woman.

Soliciting: both men and women can be charged with soliciting—the offense of approaching the public offering to sell sexual favors.

Solicitor general: the federal cabinet minister who is responsible for law enforcement and prisons. He also reports to cabinet for the National Parole Board.

Sovereign: currently Elizabeth II, Queen of Canada, in whose name all laws are passed and all justice dispensed.

Specific performance: the actual carrying out of a contract; the courts may enforce the performance of a legal

agreement rather than allow a contracting party to pay damages for breach of contract.

Squatter: someone who settles on land without permission or legal title; an unauthorized occupant.

Stale-dated cheque: a cheque which has not been presented for payment within a reasonable time of the date of its making (usually six months) and can be refused by the bank.

Stare decisis: Latin—"to abide by decided matters"; the following of legal principles established in previous court decisions on similar cases.

Statute: a law passed by any legislative body; the written will and command of the government.

Statute of Frauds: a law requiring that several classes of contracts must be in writing, signed by the party to be charged, or his agent.

Statute of Limitations: a law passed by each province which limits the period within which action may be brought to collect a debt, enforce a contract or sue for damages; the periods vary widely and should be checked in your province.

Statutory declaration: a written statement in which declaration is made under oath in verification of circumstances of facts.

Stay: a suspension of court proceedings or of the execution of a judgment.

Stipulation: an agreement between the parties to a legal action; a condition of a contract.

Stumpage: payment to the owner of land for the right to cut and remove trees from the property.

Subdivide: to redraw land into smaller lots for sale for housing; to create a subdivision.

Sub judice: Latin—"under judicial consideration"; presently before a court and thus not a subject of public debate.

Sublease: a subordinate lease made by a lessee for property already under lease to him; the term of a sublease can be no longer than that for which the lessee holds it.

Subpoena: Latin—"under a penalty"; a writ of summons demanding that a certain person appear in court to give testimony or to produce a document.

Substantive law: that body of law which determines the actual legal rights in force in any jurisdiction; to be distinguished from procedural law.

Sue: to institute legal proceedings in a civil suit.

Sui juris: Latin—"of one's own right"; legally competent to manage one's own affairs.

Suit: a civil action in which a plaintiff seeks the redress of a wrong; litigation; a petition.

Summary: immediate; without ceremony; a summary proceeding is one in which a minor crime is dealt with by a magistrate or judge quickly and without a jury.

Summing up: a recapitulation of main points of evidence at a criminal trial before a jury.

Summons: a court writ (order) to notify some specified person to appear in court to take part in an action that has been launched.

Supplementary letters patent: letters patent issued by the Crown which confirm changes in a corporation's structure; *e.g.*, the creation of new shares in a corporation requires supplementary letters patent.

Supreme Court: each province has a Superior Court called the Supreme Court in some cases; the Supreme Court of Canada is an appellate court with final judicial authority.

Surrogate Court: often called Probate Court; where wills are examined for authenticity, and the distribution of property in an intestacy is supervised.

Survivorship clause: a clause in an agreement whereby the survivor succeeds to certain property or rights.

Suspended sentence: an order by a judge that a sentence to be imposed on a guilty party need not be served provided that the accused complies with certain conditions usually determined by the probation officer.

Tenancy: the holding or occupancy of lands or buildings by any kind of right or title; especially, the temporary occupancy of a house or apartment under a lease.

Tenancy at will: a tenancy in which the occupation can be put to an end at any time either by the will of the landlord or of the tenant.

Tenant: a person who, in return for a consideration, has temporary occupation and use of another person's land or building, under a lease or other rental agreement.

Term: the period of time during which a court holds a session; a separate expression carrying meaning in a statute or contract; the length of time a tenant may occupy premises under a lease; a type of life insurance with no cashable value. A period of time allowed for payment or performance of an obligation.

Testament: the "last will" of a person, ordering the disposition of his estate after his death.

Testamentary intent: an expression of a person's intention to dispose of his property in a certain way at death, which has not been consecrated to the form of a will.

Testator: a man who dies leaving a last will and testament; the feminine style is "testatrix."

Testify: to give evidence or testimony under oath before a court or a tribunal.

Theft: the crime commonly known as stealing; the fraudulent taking away of the property of another; if a weapon is used, the crime becomes robbery.

Ticket-of-leave: official permission for a convict to leave prison before serving the full term of the sentence; parole.

Title: the right to exclusive ownership and possession of property; legal evidence (by deed) of the right of ownership; the official name and designation of a legal (or other) document.

Tort: any private or civil wrong or injury caused by any act or omission; a violation or neglect of duty for which the injured party may sue for damages or compensation in a civil suit.

Tort feasor: the person guilty of a tort; a wrongdoer.

Traduce: to malign or slander; to expose to disgrace; to deliberately misrepresent one person to another.

Trafficking: in relation to narcotics; manufacturing, selling, giving, administering, transporting, sending, delivering, distributing or offering to do any of the above.

Treason: betrayal of loyalty to the Sovereign, as in an attempt to overthrow the legal government.

Trespass: any unlawful act, such as unauthorized entry of another person's land, either intentionally or unintentionally; to intrude upon, encroach.

Trial: a judicial examination and determination, according to the law of the land, of the guilt, innocence or rights of parties to a civil or criminal action.

Tribunal: technically, the raised bench set aside for judges; any court of law, or a body examining or adjudicating a matter of public interest.

True bill: the endorsement by a grand jury that the indictment as presented, is sustained by the evidence.

Trust: an estate vested in a trustee for the benefit of another; the trustee cares for the property so vested and usually pays income to a beneficiary provided for in the trust; disposition of the principal is also usually arranged for; the confidence placed in a trustee that he will apply the property for the benefit of the beneficiary.

Trustee: one who accepts the obligations of a trust; the person (or corporation) administering a trust.

Trustee in bankruptcy: the official in whom the estate of the bankrupt rests and whose job it is to conduct the bankruptcy and pay the creditors their proper dividend.

Turpitude: usually "moral turpitude"—meaning behavior that is contrary to justice, honesty or morality.

Ullage: in commercial law, the amount by which a barrel or bottle falls short of being full; also, drainings left in used wine or spirit casks.

Ultra vires: Latin—"beyond the powers"; used in reference to acts or contracts beyond the jurisdiction of a court, or government, or beyond the power stated in the charter of a corporation.

Under protest: a term that qualifies an action taken under conditions deemed to be illegal or improper.

Undue influence: the improper use of any power or threat so that consent is not voluntary.

Unlawful assembly: the meeting together of three or more persons with intent to disturb the peace; if the "disturbance" becomes "tumultuous," the "assembly" becomes a "riot."

Unnatural offenses: "crimes against nature"—sodomy, buggery, bestiality, etc.

Unsatisfied judgment fund: a fund established by some provinces to meet the claims against uninsured motorists who are held liable for automobile accidents.

Unwritten law: the great bulk of the Common Law, inherited from England, formed from the decisions of judges, as contrasted with that written in statutes; the romantic (and quite incorrect) legend that a husband who deliberately kills his wife's lover is not guilty of murder.

Usufruct: the right of temporary enjoyment of the advantages of another's property without damaging or altering it in any substantial way.

Usurpation: unlawful seizure or occupation of another's property, privilege or power.

Usury: once, the charging of any interest on money; now, the charging of an exorbitant rate of interest.

Utter: to put into circulation; usually, to try to pass counterfeit money or forged securities.

Vacate: to set aside; to make void in law; to rescind or cancel a judgment or entry; to surrender possession by removal.

Vagrancy: with no visible means of support; without a fixed home or employment; vagabondage.

Valid: having legal strength and force; binding, sufficient and effective to be upheld by the courts.

Vandalism: ruthless, mindless destruction or spoiling of any useful or beautiful property.

Variance: the discrepancy between statements or legal documents; any divergent or inconstant factor.

Venir facias: Latin—"that you cause to come"; a court order to the sheriff of a county directing him to summon a jury.

Venue: where a crime was committed or the cause of an action arose; where a trial must be held.

Verdict: from the Latin *veredictum*, a true saying; the final decision by a jury or judge on the case before a court; the judgment.

Vest: to confer ownership on a person; to give a fixed right of present or future enjoyment, or possession.

Vested interest: a fixed right to the present or future enjoyment of property which cannot be arbitrarily disturbed; a complete right, not depending on any future event.

Vexatious suit: malicious legal proceeding instituted without probable cause.

Vicarious liability: liability of one person through the act of another, as where the master is liable for the negligence of his servant.

Vice: depravity; indulgence in wicked or immoral pursuits; moral fault.

Virgin: a woman (or man) who has not had sexual intercourse.

Virtue: the observance of accepted moral standards; personal excellence; especially chastity in woman.

Voidable contract: an agreement that may be declared void, at the option of one or both of the parties.

Voir dire: French—"to speak the truth"; a trial within a trial to determine the admissibility of certain evidence, usually a confession.

Waiver: the voluntary release of a right, claim or debt; an agreement to abandon or relinquish, or to refrain from enforcement at law.

Ward: a minor (infant) placed in the charge, or under the protection, of a guardian, or a court of law.

Warrant: a court writ giving legal authority, as for arresting a person or searching premises; a written authority to make payment of money; a guarantee of good title and undisturbed possession of an estate.

Warranty: a promise of quality or serviceability made with respect to goods which are the subject of a contract of sale; an assurance by the vendor that property is as it is represented or promised to be; a term of a contract that is so essential that failure to observe it would result in nullification of the contract.

Will: an instrument by which a person disposes of his property after death; to bequeath, or devise.

Willful: intending the result; deliberate; not accidental.

Without prejudice: a term that protects the legal rights of the speaker; when inscribed on correspondence usually renders such written matter confidential and unusable as evidence in a court action, except with the permission of the writer.

Without recourse: an endorsement of a negotiable instrument (such as a draft) by which the endorser merely passes it on, accepting no personal liability for its payment to subsequent holders.

Witness: a beholder or spectator; a person who gives evidence in court under oath, either orally or by affidavit; a person who signs his name to a document written by another in order to testify to the authenticity of the maker's signature.

Writ: used very widely in the law to describe many forms of written orders that are issued by the court or by officers of the court.

Wrongdoer: an individual who commits any injury, injustice or crime; generally, a tort feasor.

Yellow dog contract: a labor contract by which the employer requires the worker to promise, as a condition, that he will not join a union.

Zealous witness: one testifying in a court who shows a marked partiality for the side that has called him.

Canadian Bill of Rights

An Act for the Recognition and Protection of Human Rights and Fundamental Freedoms
8-9 Elizabeth II, c. 44 (Canada) *[Assented to 10th August 1960]*

The Parliament of Canada affirming that the Canadian Nation is founded upon principles that acknowledge the supremacy of God, the dignity and worth of the human person and the position of the family in a society of free men and free institutions;

Affirming also that men and institutions remain free only when freedom is founded upon respect for moral and spiritual values and the rule of law;

And being desirous of enshrining these principles and the human rights and fundamental freedoms derived from them, in a Bill of Rights which shall reflect the respect of Parliament for its constitutional authority and which shall ensure the protection of these rights and freedoms in Canada:

Therefore Her Majesty, by and with the advice and consent of the Senate and House of Commons of Canada, enacts as follows:

PART I

BILL OF RIGHTS

1. It is hereby recognized and declared that in Canada there have existed and shall continue to exist without discrimination by reason of race, national origin, colour, religion or sex, the following human rights and fundamental freedoms, namely,

  (a) the right of the individual to life, liberty, security of the person and enjoyment of property, and the right not to be deprived thereof except by due process of law;
  (b) the right of the individual to equality before the law and the protection of the law;
  (c) freedom of religion;
  (d) freedom of speech;
  (e) freedom of assembly and association; and
  (f) freedom of the press.

2. Every law of Canada shall, unless it is expressly declared by an Act of the Parliament of Canada that it shall operate notwithstanding the *Canadian Bill of Rights*, be so construed and applied as not to abrogate, abridge or infringe or to authorize the abrogation, abridgment or infringement of any of the rights or freedoms herein recognized and declared, and in particular, no law of Canada shall be construed or applied so as to

  (a) authorize or effect the arbitrary detention, imprisonment or exile of any person;
  (b) impose or authorize the imposition of cruel and unusual treatment or punishment;
  (c) deprive a person who has been arrested or detained
      (i) of the right to be informed promptly of the reason for his arrest or detention,
      (ii) of the right to retain and instruct counsel without delay, or
      (iii) of the remedy by way of *habeas corpus* for the determination of the validity of his detention and for his release if the detention is not lawful;
  (d) authorize a court, tribunal, commission, board or other authority to compel a person to give evidence if he is denied counsel, protection against self-crimination or other constitutional safeguards;
  (e) deprive a person of the right to a fair hearing in accordance with the principles of fundamental justice for the determination of his rights and obligations;
  (f) deprive a person charged with a criminal offence of the right to be presumed innocent until proved guilty according to law in a fair and public hearing by an independent and impartial tribunal, or of the right to reasonable bail without just cause; or
  (g) deprive a person of the right to the assistance of an interpreter in any proceedings in which he is involved or in which he is a party or a witness, before a court, commission, board or other tribunal, if he does not understand or speak the language in which such proceedings are conducted.

3. The Minister of Justice shall, in accordance with such regulations as may be prescribed by the Governor in Council, examine every proposed regulation submitted in draft form to the Clerk of the Privy Council pursuant to the *Regulations Act* and every Bill introduced in or presented to the House of Commons, in order to ascertain whether any of the provisions thereof are inconsistent with the purposes and provisions of this Part and he shall report any such inconsistency to the House of Commons at the first convenient opportunity.

4. The provisions of this Part shall be known as the *Canadian Bill of Rights*.

PART II

5. (1) Nothing in Part I shall be construed to abrogate or abridge any human right or fundamental freedom not enumerated therein that may have existed in Canada at the commencement of this Act.

(2) The expression "law of Canada" in Part I means an Act of the Parliament of Canada enacted before or after the coming into force of this Act, any order, rule or regulation thereunder, and any law in force in Canada or in any part of Canada at the commencement of this Act that is subject to be repealed, abolished or altered by the Parliament of Canada.

(3) The provisions of Part I shall be construed as extending only to matters coming within the legislative authority of the Parliament of Canada.

The Canadian Constitution

Patriation resolution

The request from the Canadian Parliament sent to the Queen in December, 1981:
 THAT, WHEREAS in the past certain amendments to the Constitution of Canada have been made by the Parliament of the United Kingdom at the request and with the consent of Canada;
 AND WHEREAS it is in accord with the status of Canada as an independent state that Canadians be able to amend their Constitution in Canada in all respects;
 AND WHEREAS it is also desirable to provide in the Constitution of Canada for the recognition of certain fundamental rights and freedoms and to make other amendments to that Constitution;
 A respectful address be presented to Her Majesty the Queen in the following words:
To the Queen's Most Excellent Majesty:
Most Gracious Sovereign:
We, Your Majesty's loyal subjects, the House of Commons of Canada in Parliament assembled, respectfully approach Your Majesty, requesting that you may graciously be pleased to cause to be laid before the Parliament of the United Kingdom a measure containing the recitals and clauses hereinafter set forth:

SCHEDULE A

An act to give effect to a request by the Senate and House of Commons of Canada
Whereas Canada has requested and consented to the enactment of an Act of the Parliament of the United Kingdom to give effect to the provisions hereinafter set forth and the Senate and the House of Commons of Canada in Parliament assembled have submitted an address to Her Majesty requesting that Her Majesty may graciously be pleased to cause a bill to be laid before the Parliament of the United Kingdom for that purpose;
 Be it therefore enacted by the Queen's Most Excellent Majesty, by and with the advice and consent of the Lords Spiritual and Temporal, and Commons, in this present Parliament assembled, and by the authority of the same, as follows:
 1. The Constitution Act, 1982 set out in Schedule B to this Act is hereby enacted for and shall have the force of law in Canada and shall come into force as provided in that Act.
 2. No Act of the Parliament of the United Kingdom passed after the Constitution Act, 1982 comes into force shall extend to Canada as part of its law.
 3. So far as it is not contained in Schedule B, the French version of this Act is set out in Schedule A to this Act and has the same authority in Canada as the English version thereof.
 4. This act may be cited as the Canada Act 1982.

SCHEDULE B

Constitution Act, 1982

PART I

Canadian Charter of Rights and Freedoms
 Whereas Canada is founded upon principles that recognize the supremacy of God and the rule of law:

Guarantee of Rights and Freedoms
 1. The Canadian Charter of Rights and Freedoms guarantees the rights and freedoms set out in it subject only to such reasonable limits prescribed by law as can be demonstrably justified in a free and democratic society.

Fundamental Freedoms
 2. Everyone has the following fundamental freedoms:
 (a) freedom of conscience and religion;
 (b) freedom of thought, belief, opinion and expression, including freedom of the press and other media of communication;
 (c) freedom of peaceful assembly; and
 (d) freedom of association.

Democratic Rights
 3. Every Citizen of Canada has the right to vote in an election of members of the House of Commons or of a legislative assembly and to be qualified for membership therein.

4. (1) No House of Commons and no legislative assembly shall continue for longer than five years from the date fixed for the return of the writs at a general election of its members.

(2) In time of real or apprehended war, invasion or insurrection, a House of Commons may be continued by Parliament and a legislative assembly may be continued by the legislature beyond five years if such continuation is not opposed by the votes of more than one-third of the members of the House of Commons or the legislative assembly, as the case may be.

5. There shall be a sitting of Parliament and of each legislature at least once every 12 months.

Mobility Rights

6. (1) Every citizen of Canada has the right to enter, remain in and leave Canada.

(2) Every citizen of Canada and every person who has the status of a permanent resident of Canada has the right

(a) to move to and take up residence in any province; and

(b) to pursue the gaining of a livelihood in any province.

(3) The rights specified in Subsection (2) are subject to

(a) any laws or practices of general application in force in a province other than those that discriminate among persons primarily on the basis of province of present or previous residence; and

(b) any laws providing for reasonable residency requirements as a qualification for the receipt of publicly provided social services.

(4) Subsections (2) and (3) do not preclude any law, program or activity that has as its object the amelioration in a province of conditions of individuals in that province who are socially or economically disadvantaged if the rate of employment in that province is below the rate of employment in Canada.

Legal Rights

7. Everyone has the right to life, liberty and security of the person and the right not to be deprived thereof except in accordance with the principles of fundamental justice.

8. Everyone has the right to be secure against unreasonable search or seizure.

9. Everyone has the right not to be arbitrarily detained or imprisoned.

10. Everyone has the right on arrest or detention

(a) to be informed promptly of the reasons therefor;

(b) to retain and instruct counsel without delay and to be informed of that right; and

(c) to have the validity of the detention determined by way of *habeas corpus* and to be released if the detention is not lawful.

11. Any person charged with an offence has the right

(a) to be informed without unreasonable delay of the specific offence;

(b) to be tried within a reasonable time;

(c) not to be compelled to be a witness in proceedings against that person in respect of the offence;

(d) to be presumed innocent until proven guilty according to law in a fair and public hearing by an independent and impartial tribunal;

(e) not to be denied reasonable bail without just cause;

(f) except in the case of an offence under military law tried before a military tribunal, to the benefit of trial by jury where the maximum punishment for the offence is imprisonment for five years or a more severe punishment;

(g) not to be found guilty on account of any act or omission unless, at the time of the act or omission, it constituted an offence under Canadian or international law or was criminal according to the general principles of law recognized by the community of nations;

(h) if finally acquitted of the offence, not to be tried for it again and, if finally found guilty and punished for the offence, not to be tried or punished for it again; and

(i) if found guilty of the offence and if the punishment for the offence has been varied between the time of commission and the time of sentencing, to the benefit of the lesser punishment.

12. Everyone has the right not to be subjected to any cruel and unusual treatment or punishment.

13. A witness who testifies in any proceedings has the right not to have any incriminating evidence so given used to incriminate that witness in any other proceedings, except in a prosecution for perjury or for the giving of contradictory evidence.

14. A party or witness in any proceedings who does not understand or speak the language in which the proceedings are conducted or who is deaf has the right to the assistance of an interpreter.

Equality Rights

15. (1) Every individual is equal before and under the law and has the right to the equal protection and equal benefit of the law without discrimination and, in particular, without discrimination based on race, national or ethnic origin, colour, religion, sex, age or mental or physical disability.

(2) Subsection (1) does not preclude any law, program or activity that has as its object the amelioration of conditions of disadvantaged individuals or groups including those that are disadvantaged because of race, national or ethnic origin, colour, religion, sex, age or mental or physical disability.

Official Languages of Canada

16. (1) English and French are the official languages of Canada and have equality of status and equal rights and privileges as to their use in all institutions of the Parliament and Government of Canada.

(2) English and French are the official languages of New Brunswick and have equality of status and equal rights and privileges as to their use in all institutions of the legislature and government of New Brunswick.

(3) Nothing in this Charter limits the authority of Parliament or a legislature to advance the equality of status or use of English and French.

17. (1) Everyone has the right to use English or French in any debates and other proceedings of Parliament.

(2) Everyone has the right to use English or French in any debates and other proceedings of the legislature of New Brunswick.

18. (1) The statutes, records and journals of Parliament shall be printed and published in English and French and both language versions are equally authoritative.

(2) The statutes, records and journals of the legislature of New Brunswick shall be printed and published in English and French and both language versions are equally authoritative.

19. (1) Either English or French may be used by any person in, or in any pleading in or process issuing from, any court established by Parliament.

(2) Either English or French may be used by any person in, or in any pleading in or process issuing from, any court of New Brunswick.

20. (1) Any member of the public in Canada has the right to communicate with, and to receive available services from, any head or central office of an institution of the Parliament or Government of Canada in English or French, and has the same right with respect to any other office of any such institution where

(a) there is a significant demand for communications with and services from that office in such language; or

(b) due to the nature of the office, it is reasonable that communications with and services from that office be available in both English and French.

(2) Any member of the public in New Brunswick has the right to communicate with, and to receive available services from, any office of an institution of the legislature or government of New Brunswick in English or French.

21. Nothing in sections 16 to 20 abrogates or derogates from any right, privilege or obligation with respect to the English and French languages, or either of them, that exists or is continued by virtue of any other provision of the Constitution of Canada.

22. Nothing in sections 16 to 20 abrogates or derogates from any legal or customary right or privilege acquired or enjoyed either before or after the coming into force of this Charter with respect to any language that is not English or French.

Minority Language Educational Rights

23. (1) Citizens of Canada

(a) whose first language learned and still understood is that of the English or French linguistic minority population of the province in which they reside, or

(b) who have received their primary school instruction in Canada in English or French and reside in a province where the language in which they received that instruction is the language of the English or French linguistic minority population of the province,

have the right to have their children receive primary and secondary school instruction in that language in that province.

(2) Citizens of Canada of whom any child has received or is receiving primary or secondary school instruction in English or French in Canada, have the right to have all their children receive primary and secondary school instruction in the same language.

(3) The right of citizens of Canada under subsections (1) and (2) to have their children

receive primary and secondary school instruction in the language of the English or French linguistic minority population of a province

(a) applies wherever in the province the number of children of citizens who have such a right is sufficient to warrant the provision to them out of public funds of minority language instruction; and

(b) includes, where the number of those children so warrants, the right to have them receive that instruction in minority language educational facilities provided out of public funds.

Enforcement

24. (1) Anyone whose rights or freedoms, as guaranteed by this Charter, have been infringed or denied may apply to a court of competent jurisdiction to obtain such remedy as the court considers appropriate and just in the circumstances.

(2) Where, in proceedings under subsection (1), a court concludes that evidence was obtained in a manner that infringed or denied any rights or freedoms guaranteed by this Charter, the evidence shall be excluded if it is established that, having regard to all the circumstances, the admission of it in the proceedings would bring the administration of justice into disrepute.

General

25. The guarantee in this Charter of certain rights and freedoms shall not be construed so as to abrogate or derogate from any aboriginal, treaty or other rights or freedoms that pertain to the aboriginal peoples of Canada including

(a) any rights or freedoms that have been recognized by the Royal Proclamation of October 7, 1763; and

(b) any rights or freedoms that may be acquired by the aboriginal peoples of Canada by way of land claims settlement.

26. The guarantee in this Charter of certain rights and freedoms shall not be construed as denying the existence of any other rights or freedoms that exist in Canada.

27. This Charter shall be interpreted in a manner consistent with the preservation and enhancement of the multicultural heritage of Canadians.

28. Notwithstanding anything in this Charter, the rights and freedoms referred to in it are guaranteed equally to male and female persons.

29. Nothing in this Charter abrogates or derogates from any rights or privileges guaranteed by or under the Constitution of Canada in respect of denominational, separate or dissentient schools.

30. A reference in this Charter to a province or to the legislative assembly or legislature of a province shall be deemed to include a reference to the Yukon Territory and to the Northwest Territories, or to the appropriate legislative authority thereof, as the case may be.

31. Nothing in this Charter extends the legislative powers of any body or authority.

Application of Charter

32. (1) This Charter applies

(a) to the Parliament and government of Canada in respect of all matters within the authority of Parliament including all matters relating to the Yukon Territory and Northwest Territories; and

(b) to the legislature and government of each province in respect of all matters within the authority of the legislature of each province.

(2) Notwithstanding subsection (1), section 15 shall not have effect until three years after this section comes into force.

33. (1) Parliament or the legislature of a province may expressly declare in an Act of Parliament or of the legislature, as the case may be, that the Act or a provision thereof shall operate notwithstanding a provision included in section 2 or sections 7 to 15 of this Charter.

(2) An Act or a provision of an Act in respect of which a declaration made under this section is in effect shall have such operation as it would have but for the provision of this Charter referred to in the declaration.

(3) A declaration made under subsection (1) shall cease to have effect five years after it comes into force or on such earlier date as may be specified in the declaration.

(4) Parliament or a legislature of a province may re-enact a declaration made under subsection (1).

(5) subsection (3) applies in respect of a re-enactment made under subsection (4).

Citation

34. This part may be cited as the *Canadian Charter of Rights and Freedoms.*

PART II

Rights of the Aboriginal Peoples

35. (1) The existing aboriginal and treaty rights of the aboriginal peoples of Canada are hereby recognized and affirmed.

(2) In this Act, "aboriginal peoples of Canada" includes the Indian, Inuit and Metis peoples of Canada.

PART III

Equalization and Regional Disparities

36. (1) Without altering the legislative authority of Parliament or of the provincial legislatures, or the rights of any of them with respect to the exercise of their legislative authority, Parliament and the legislatures, together with the government of Canada and the provincial governments, are committed to

(a) promoting equal opportunities for the well-being of Canadians;

(b) furthering economic development to reduce disparity in opportunities; and

(c) providing essential public services of reasonable quality to all Canadians.

(2) Parliament and the government of Canada are committed to the principle of making equalization payments to ensure that provincial governments have sufficient revenues to provide reasonably comparable levels of public services at reasonably comparable levels of taxation.

PART IV

Constitutional Conference

37. (1) A constitutional conference composed of the Prime Minister of Canada and the first ministers of the provinces shall be convened by the Prime Minister of Canada within one year after this part comes into force.

(2) The conference convened under subsection (1) shall have included in its agenda an item respecting constitutional matters that directly affect the aboriginal peoples of Canada, including the identification and definition of the rights of those peoples to be included in the Constitution of Canada, and the Prime Minister of Canada shall invite representatives of those peoples to participate in the discussions on that item.

(3) The Prime Minister of Canada shall invite elected representatives of the governments of the Yukon Territory and the Northwest Territories to participate in the discussions on any item on the agenda of the conference convened under subsection (1) that, in the opinion of the Prime Minister, directly affects the Yukon Territory and the Northwest Territories.

PART V

Procedure for Amending Constitution of Canada

38. (1) An amendment to the Constitution of Canada may be made by proclamation issued by the Governor General under the Great Seal of Canada where so authorized by

(a) resolutions of the Senate and House of Commons; and

(b) resolutions of the legislative assemblies of at least two-thirds of the provinces that have, in the aggregate, according to the then latest general census, at least 50 per cent of the population of all the provinces.

(2) An amendment made under subsection (1) that derogates from the legislative powers, the proprietary rights or any other rights or privileges of the legislature or government of a province shall require a resolution supported by a majority of the members of each of the Senate, the House of Commons and the legislative assemblies required under subsection (1).

(3) An amendment referred to in subsection (2) shall not have effect in a province the legislative assembly of which has expressed its dissent thereto by resolution supported by a majority of its members prior to the issue of the proclamation to which the amendment relates unless that legislative assembly, subsequently, by resolution supported by a majority of its members, revokes its dissent and authorizes the amendment.

(4) A resolution of dissent made for the purposes of subsection (3) may be revoked at any time before or after the issue of the proclamation to which it relates.

39. (1) A proclamation shall not be issued under subsection 38(1) before the expiration of one year from the adoption of the resolution initiating the amendment procedure thereunder,

unless the legislative assembly of each province has previously adopted a resolution of assent or dissent.

(2) A proclamation shall not be issued under subsection 38(1) after the expiration of three years from the adoption of the resolution initiating the amendment procedure thereunder.

40. Where an amendment is made under subsection 38(1) that transfers provincial legislative powers relating to education or other cultural matters from provincial legislatures to Parliament, Canada shall provide reasonable compensation to any province to which the amendment does not apply.

41. An amendment to the Constitution of Canada in relation to the following matters may be made by proclamation issued by the Governor General under the Great Seal of Canada only where authorized by resolutions of the Senate and House of Commons and of the legislative assembly of each province:

(a) the office of the Queen, the Governor General and the Lieutenant Governor of a province;

(b) the right of a province to a number of members in the House of Commons not less than the number of Senators by which the province is entitled to be represented at the time this Part comes into force;

(c) subject to section 43, the use of the English or the French language;

(d) the composition of the Supreme Court of Canada; and

(e) an amendment to this Part.

42. (1) An amendment to the Constitution of Canada in relation to the following matters may be made only in accordance with subsection 38(1):

(a) the principle of proportionate representation of the provinces in the House of Commons prescribed by the Constitution of Canada;

(b) the powers of the Senate and the method of selecting Senators;

(c) the number of members by which a province is entitled to be represented in the Senate and the residence qualifications of Senators;

(d) subject to paragraph 41(d), the Supreme Court of Canada;

(e) the extension of existing provinces into the territories; and

(f) notwithstanding any other law or practice, the establishment of new provinces.

(2) subsections 38(2) to (4) do not apply in respect of amendments in relation to matters referred to in subsection (1).

43. An amendment to the Constitution of Canada in relation to any provision that applies to one or more, but not all, provinces, including

(a) any alteration of boundaries between provinces, and

(b) any amendment to any provision that relates to the use of the English or the French language within a province,

may be made by proclamation issued by the Governor General under the Great Seal of Canada only where so authorized by resolutions of the Senate and House of Commons and of the legislative assembly of each province to which the amendment applies.

44. Subject to sections 41 and 42, Parliament may exclusively make laws amending the Constitution of Canada in relation to the executive government of Canada or the Senate and House of Commons.

45. Subject to section 41, the legislature of each province may exclusively make laws amending the constitution of the province.

46. (1) The procedures for amendment under sections 38, 41, 42 and 43 may be initiated either by the Senate or the House of Commons or by the legislative assembly of a province.

(2) A resolution of assent made for the purpose of this part may be revoked at any time before the issue of a proclamation authorized by it.

47. (1) An amendment to the Constitution of Canada made by proclamation under sections 38, 41, 42 or 43 may be made without a resolution of the Senate authorizing the issue of the proclamation if, within one hundred and eighty days after the adoption by the House of Commons of a resolution authorizing its issue, the Senate has not adopted such a resolution and if, at any time after the expiration of that period, the House of Commons again adopts the resolution.

(2) Any period when Parliament is prorogued or dissolved shall not be counted in computing the one hundred and eighty day period referred to in subsection (1).

48. The Queen's Privy Council for Canada shall advise the Governor General to issue a proclamation under this Part forthwith on the adoption of the resolutions required for an amendment made by proclamation under this Part.

49. A constitutional conference composed of the Prime Minister of Canada and the first ministers of the provinces shall be convened by the Prime Minister of Canada within fifteen years after this part comes into force to review the provisions of this part.

PART VI

Amendment to the Constitution Act, 1867

50. *The Constitution Act, 1867* (formerly named the *British North America Act, 1867*) is amended by adding thereto, immediately after section 92 thereof, the following heading and section:

Non-Renewable Natural Resources, Forestry Resources and Electrical Energy.

92A. (1) In each province, the legislature may exclusively make laws in relation to
(a) exploration for non-renewable natural resources in the province;
(b) development, conservation and management of non-renewable natural resources and forestry resources in the province, including laws in relation to the rate of primary production therefrom; and
(c) development, conservation and management of sites and facilities in the province for the generation and production of electrical energy.

(2) In each province, the legislature may make laws in relation to the export from the province to another part of Canada of the primary production from non-renewable natural resources and forestry resources in the province and the production from facilities in the province for the generation of electrical energy, but such laws may not authorize or provide for discrimination in prices or in supplies exported to another part of Canada.

(3) Nothing in subsection (2) derogates from the authority of Parliament to enact laws in relation to the matters referred to in that subsection and, where such a law of Parliament and a law of a province conflict, the law of Parliament prevails to the extent of the conflict.

(4) In each province, the Legislature may make laws in relation to the raising of money by any mode or system of taxation in respect of
(a) non-renewable natural resources and forestry resources in the province and the primary production therefrom, and
(b) sites and facilities in the province for the generation of electrical energy and the production therefrom,
whether or not such production is exported in whole or in part from the province, but such laws may not authorize or provide for taxation that differentiates between production exported to another part of Canada and production not exported from the province.

(5) The expression "primary production" has the meaning assigned by the Sixth Schedule.

(6) Nothing in subsections (1) to (5) derogates from any powers or rights that a legislature or government of a province had immediately before the coming into force of this section.

51. The said Act is further amended by adding thereto the following schedule:

THE SIXTH SCHEDULE

Primary Production from Non-Renewable Natural Resources and Forestry Resources.

1 For the purposes of section 92(a) of this Act,
(a) production from a non-renewable natural resource is primary production therefrom if
i) it is in the form in which it exists upon its recovery or severance from its natural state, or
ii) it is a product resulting from processing or refining the resource, and is not a manufactured product or a product resulting from refining crude oil, refining upgraded heavy crude oil, refining gases or liquids derived from coal or refining a synthetic equivalent of crude oil; and
(b) production from a forestry resource is primary production therefrom if it consists of sawlogs, poles, lumber, wood chips, sawdust or any other primary wood product, or wood pulp, and is not a product manufactured from wood.

PART VII

General

52. (1) The Constitution of Canada is the supreme law of Canada, and any law that is inconsistent with the provisions of the Constitution is, to the extent of the inconsistency, of no force or effect.

(2) The Constitution of Canada includes
(a) the Canada Act 1982, including this Act;

894

(b) the Acts and orders referred to in schedule I; and

(c) any amendment to any act or order referred to in paragraph (a) or (b).

(3) Amendments to the Constitution of Canada shall be made only in accordance with the authority contained in the Constitution of Canada.

53. (1) The enactments referred to in Column I of the schedule are hereby repealed or amended to the extent indicated in Column II thereof and, unless repealed, shall continue as law in Canada under the names set out in Column III thereof.

(2) Every enactment, except the Canada Act 1982, that refers to an enactment referred to in the schedule by the name in Column I thereof is hereby amended by substituting for that name the corresponding name in Column III thereof, and any British North America Act not referred to in the schedule may be cited as the *Constitution Act* followed by the year and number, if any, of its enactment.

54. Part IV is repealed on the day that is one year after this Part comes into force and this section may be repealed and this Act renumbered, consequentially upon the repeal of Part IV and this section, by proclamation issued by the Governor General under the Great Seal of Canada.

55. A French version of the portions of the Constitution of Canada referred to in the schedule shall be prepared by the Minister of Justice of Canada as expeditiously as possible and, when any portion thereof sufficient to warrant action being taken has been so prepared, it shall be put forward for enactment by proclamation issued by the Governor General under the Great Seal of Canada pursuant to the procedure then applicable to an amendment of the same provisions of the Constitution of Canada.

56. Where any portion of the Constitution of Canada has been or is enacted in English and French or where a French version of any portion of the Constitution is enacted pursuant to section 55, the English and French versions of that portion of the Constitution are equally authoritative.

57. The English and French versions of this Act are equally authoritative.

58. Subject to section 59, this Act shall come into force on a day to be fixed by proclamation issued by the Queen or the Governor General under the Great Seal of Canada.

59. (1) Paragraph 23(1)(a) shall come into force in respect of Quebec on a day to be fixed by proclamation issued by the Queen or the Governor General under the Great Seal of Canada.

(2) A proclamation under subsection (1) shall be issued only where authorized by the legislative assembly or government of Quebec.

(3) This section may be repealed on the day paragraph 23(1)(a) comes into force in respect of Quebec and this Act amended and renumbered, consequentially upon the repeal of this section, by proclamation issued by the Queen or the Governor General under the Great Seal of Canada.

60. This Act may be cited as the *Constitution Act, 1982,* and the Constitution Acts 1867 to 1975 (No. 2) and this Act may be cited together as the Constitution Acts, 1867 to 1982.

In an ever-changing society, the law cannot stand still

AFTER DIPPING INTO THIS BOOK, you will have seen how much the law surrounds us. You will realize how useful it is to know something about the law. It is useful in telling you what you may do safely, when you are on the edge of trouble, and what you can count on in a pinch in your dealings with other people.

But you may well have concluded that the law is a pretty difficult matter to keep track of. You have, perhaps, even wondered whether it is worthwhile trying at all to think about its complexities in all your actions. You may be getting like the centipede who began to wonder how he managed to move all his hundred legs at once—he has been paralyzed ever since!

You can look at the law in two quite different ways. First, you can think of it as a series of ambushes into which you can blunder. If you let your mind run on this track, you can become fearful of dealings with other people, because something may go wrong. As a result, you may feel like drawing back into your own shells, like turtles, and begin to long for the security of the cradle or the tomb. You are likely to think how comforting it would be to have somebody to tell you, not only what you are forbidden to do but also what you must do, so that you can escape making decisions and incurring risks. If you think too much along this line, you are inviting a dictatorship where what is not forbidden is compulsory. When too many people in a society become afraid to exercise their freedom, they are certain to lose it.

The second way of looking at the law encourages you to take the risks of freedom. You should look at the law as primarily a protector of your freedom, which it can only be if, at the same time, it provides ambushes for wrongdoers. The law always works both ways. It tells you what you will be protected in doing with a minimum of risk; it tells you what protection you can have against the thoughtless or hostile actions of others.

In this way, the law minimizes the risk of using your talents and trying out your powers. But it cannot abolish all the risks of freedom. Freedom is an adventure in which you can guess wrong as well as right. If you guess correctly, you win—and you will demand to get and keep the winnings. If you guess wrong, you must expect to take the responsibility for your bad guess. Don't be too ready to blame the law for the fix you are in! Much of the hostility to the law comes from people who blame the law rather than blaming themselves for their miscalculations. Often, the law has nothing at all to do with their misfortunes.

On the other hand, the law has had a great deal to do with the general good fortune of us all in Canada. You get upset about the rise of violence and crime, and rightly so: a few untrustworthy and violent people can spread terror through a community. Even so, their number is still small—one among some many thousands of the population. How fortunate we Canadians are that we can trust nearly everybody a long way without fear that the trust will be misplaced!

Common sense should tell you to think of the law as a friend rather than an enemy. You should not worry too much about your inevitable ignorance of many of its rules. Of course, you do need to know more about the law than would have been required 75 years ago. To make it genuinely understandable, it needs to be simplified. Unfortunately, however, it has been getting more difficult to understand because the complexities it has to deal with have been getting more involved. Compare the income tax forms of 1925 with those of today!

In trying to clarify and simplify the law, more systematic efforts are being made. Most of the provinces have appointed permanent law-reform commissions; the federal government took the same step in 1971.

At recent meetings of Bar associations, lawyers have been saying some sharp things about the duty of lawyers to improve the service the legal profession gives, and about the need to make the law and the administration of justice more intelligible to the public. The support given by lawyers and provincial law societies to Legal Aid is symptomatic of the same concern. They know they must act to counter the suspicion that the law is just a lucrative playground for the legal profession.

Many judges are known to feel that all is not entirely well. But since judges have sworn solemn oaths to apply the law, as it is, without fear or favor, they can scarcely be expected to act as radical law reformers in the courts. If sweeping action is to be taken, it must be taken by legislatures which have the power to change the law.

Simplifying the wording of parts of the law for better public understanding without changing its effect at all is one thing; ensuring that the law is kept up-to-date is an entirely different and much more difficult proposition. First, laws found by experience to be inadequate or unjust have to be improved. Progress on this front is being made all the time, as the annual volumes of statutes with their clarifications and amendments show. Second, technical developments and economic and social changes are always producing new situations, and new abuses. Often there is no law at all for these new situations, or only an old law that does not fit the need.

The snowmobile provides a recent and relatively easy illustration of this problem. What was mostly at stake here was physical safety. The general law of negligence, the obligation to use reasonable care, applied, of course, to snowmobiles as well as to other machinery. But it was soon found out that the snowmobile was a particularly dangerous machine in the hands of careless drivers, and specific supplementary precautions were needed. In a relatively short time, special legislation for snowmobiles was enacted in many provinces.

The computer provides another more complex illustration, particularly regarding what it does in storing and distributing information drawn from credit records. The whole question of confidentiality of records is now at stake. There should be firm laws protecting personal privacy, but what such laws should cover is sharply contentious. The uncertainty delays action.

These considerations will serve to underline a warning given earlier in this book. Some of the laws outlined will inevitably be out-of-date, and changed, even by the time this revised edition is published. And, if not by that time, then sometime soon. In an ever-changing society, the law cannot stand still.

To keep the law up-to-date in any of these senses, the legislatures need help. This is the function of the law-reform commissions which have been set up to advise the politicians on technical aspects and to propose forms of words that will have the desired effect in making the law what we want it to be.

But what do Canadians really want of their law? This is where the serious troubles of the law-reform commissions begin. For example, one chairman of the federal commission believed he must first consult the people about their needs and requirements, and then tailor the law to those requirements. But only a mere trickle of replies resulted from the questionnaires that had been sent out to the public. Does this reaction mean that most of the people in Canada are happy with the law as it is? Or does it mean that they simply can't be bothered answering?

Those members of the public who did respond often disagreed with each other. The chairman was reported as saying that "50 percent of the people I talk to say we are putting too many people in jail, another 50 percent say we are not putting enough offenders in jail."

In a Western democracy, how do you make the law better, clearer and more responsive to social change if the people don't agree? Jurists are well aware that the law must keep in close touch with the community's sense of right. One thing is certain: desirable change will take a long time coming unless, in many matters, the law-reform commissioners are willing to give a lead from their own deeper knowledge instead of waiting to follow a lead from the general public.

High-minded reformers are often disappointed and frustrated by the seeming obstinacy of the community about accepting ambitious legislative or social advances. The law must obviously be set at a level that the bulk of the people find tolerable. Man's reach, however, should always exceed his grasp, and we must continue to reach for the stars. As the law reaches for improvement it must take care not to reach beyond what the common sense of ordinary folk can follow.

Essentially, we must all become more civilized. If we fail to do so, as a nation, there's not much that either legislators or the law can do for us.

– J.A.C.

INDEX

Page numbers in **bold type** refer to general discussions of subjects.

906

Acknowledgments

The editors wish to thank the large number of persons, legal firms, law societies, provincial and federal agencies, and other organizations, whose expert contributions helped in the preparation of this Third Edition of *You and the Law,* as with previous editions. For his contributions of the Introduction and the Afterword, the editors especially wish to thank

James Alexander Corry, LL.B., LL.M., B.C.L.
retired professor of law and former Principal of Queen's University
Companion of the Order of Canada
Fellow of the Royal Society of Canada

Neither Dr. Corry nor any of the following distinguished contributors is responsible for any error that may have eluded the exhaustive research and checking procedures employed by the editors.

Lonsdale Requirement Limited

A. W. Bellstedt, LL.B.
Mary J. Blenkhorne, B.A.
G. Roderick Cameron, B.Com.
Jack W. Chong, LL.B.
A. Gus Comello, B.A., B.Ed.
Isidore Cooperman, M.S.W.
Kenneth J. M. Coull, LL.B.
Ross M. Durant, C.L.U.
Bertram R. Garrett, LL.B.
A. McLean Haig, O.B.E.
Stanley G. Helleur
His Honor Judge Hugh S. Honsberger
John D. Honsberger, Q.C., LL.B.
Elizabeth Kuglin, LL.B.
Laura Legge, Q.C., LL.B.
Douglas V. Lintula, B.Arch.
G. Edward Lloyd, LL.B.

John McCormick, LL.B.
W. Lorne McDougall, B.Com.
P. H. Megginson, LL.B.
William Mellalieu
George K. Murray, LL.B.
Sidney I. F. Murray, LL.B.
James F. O'Brien, LL.B.
John D. O'Flynn, Q.C., LL.B.
Edward G. Paul
His Honor Judge John A. Pringle
Benjamin A. Ring, LL.B.
William G. Sirman, LL.B.
Kenneth G. Smith, M.A.
Kerry J. Soden, B.A., C.A.
Lyle A. Sullivan, LL.B.
Peter D. Ticktin, LL.B.
Camillo A. Tofano, B.A.

Editor: A. R. Byers (Revision)
Designer: Diane Mitrofanow
Researchers: Wadad Bashour (Chief); Michèle McLaughlin
Text Preparation: F. R. Legge
Picture Researcher: Michelle Turbide
Coordinator: Susan Wong
Production: Bruce Hoskins

Contributing Legal Advisers: Messrs. Lavery, O'Brien, Montreal
Contributing Researchers: Morri Mostow, Karen Raymer-Simon
Contributing Proofreaders: Luc Granger, Billy Wisse